Fundamentals of
Sensory Perception

Fundamentals of
Sensory Perception

Avi Chaudhuri

OXFORD
UNIVERSITY PRESS

8 Sampson Mews, Suite 204, Don Mills, Ontario M3C 0H5
www.oupcanada.com

Oxford University Press is a department of the University of Oxford.
It furthers the University's objective of excellence in research, scholarship,
and education by publishing worldwide in

Oxford   New York

Auckland   Cape Town   Dar es Salaam   Hong Kong   Karachi
Kuala Lumpur   Madrid   Melbourne   Mexico City   Nairobi
New Delhi   Shanghai   Taipei   Toronto

With offices in

Argentina   Austria   Brazil   Chile   Czech Republic   France   Greece
Guatemala   Hungary   Italy   Japan   Poland   Portugal   Singapore
South Korea   Switzerland   Thailand   Turkey   Ukraine   Vietnam

Oxford is a trade mark of Oxford University Press
in the UK and in certain other countries

Published in Canada
by Oxford University Press

Library and Archives Canada Cataloguing in Publication

Chaudhuri, Avi
Fundamentals of sensory perception / Avi Chaudhuri.

Includes bibliographical references and index.
ISBN 978-0-19-543375-3

1. Senses and sensation—Textbooks. 2. Perception—Textbooks. I. Title.

QP431.C53 2010   612.8   C2010-903816-9

Cover image: Kaleidoscope of butterfly wings © Charles Krebs/Getty Images

This book is printed on permanent (acid-free) paper ∞
which contains a minimum of 10% post-consumer waste

Printed and bound in the United States of America.

1 2 3 4 — 14 13 12 11

Brief Contents

Contents

1 Principles of Perceptual Measurement

2 Biological Foundations of Sensory Perception

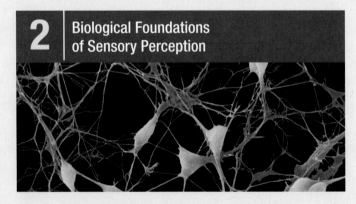

3 The Somatosensory System: Touch, Feeling, and Pain

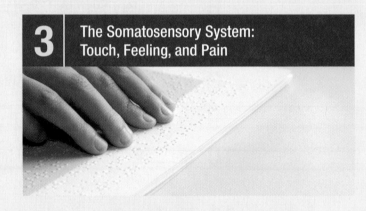

4 | The Chemosensory Systems: Taste and Smell

5 | The Auditory System: Sound and the Ear

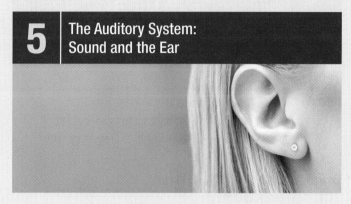

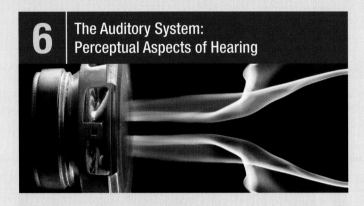
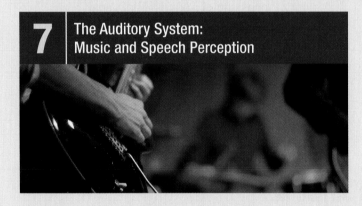
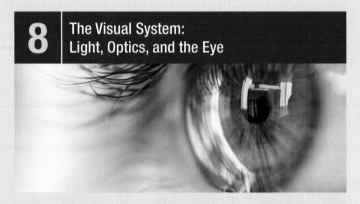

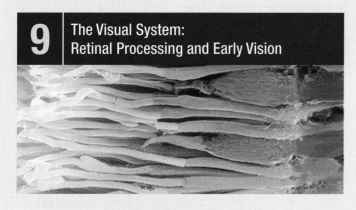
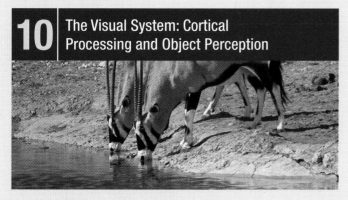
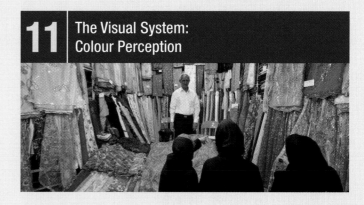

12 | The Visual System: Depth Perception and Stereopsis

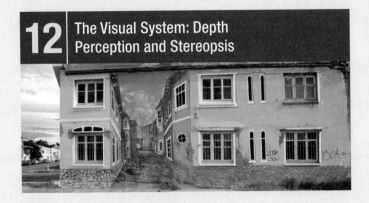

13 | The Visual System: Motion Perception, Eye Movements, and Action

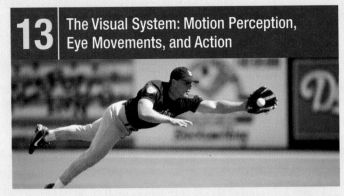

Advanced Sections

Investigation Boxes

INVESTIGATION

Methodology Boxes

METHODOLOGY

Preface

From the Publisher

We are constantly engaged in sensory perception. Physical stimuli are transformed into signals in our nervous system that are used by the brain to create our fundamental understanding and experience of the world. Gaining a deeper understanding of perceptual experience is both fascinating and exciting: everyday experiences of sound, sight, smell, taste, and touch are revealed to be processes of astonishing complexity.

Despite the intrinsic fascination and excitement of the subject, designing an academic course on sensory perception is not an easy task. On the one hand, instructors and authors must avoid overwhelming students with the considerable amount of research that exists on the subject. On the other hand, we have to avoid oversimplifying the material so that students can fully appreciate the various phenomena that make perception possible. The whole package must fit within an academic term and be designed in a way that facilitates teaching and learning.

Fundamentals of Sensory Perception uses an approach to the material that will serve instructors and students well. It gives students a comprehensive, engaging, and clear introduction to the study of sensory perception, ensuring that they fully understand the scientific principles and the phenomena at the basis of perception and the physical world. Additionally, the book includes several innovative features that further enhance engagement with the material:

- **Unique, accessible organization.** Beginning chapters explore touch and the chemical senses before moving on to auditory systems and vision. This structure allows students to gradually build their knowledge about sensation and perception prior to tackling more complex and challenging concepts.
- **Extensive figures and illustrations.** With 366 figures, 25 tables, and over 100 photos, *Fundamentals of Sensory Perception* provides the most brilliant art program currently available. Each figure and illustration has been carefully selected to ensure it best represents crucial subject matter.
- **Balanced coverage of classic and contemporary material.** The most current research, references, and examples have been infused with classic content to give students the perfect mix of historical perspective and cutting-edge information.
- **Accessible, attention-holding writing style.** Careful attention has been paid to ensure the language and tone throughout *Fundamentals of Sensory Perception* are suitable for all students in perception studies.

PEDAGOGY

Fundamentals of Sensory Perception uses a pedagogical approach that helps students better understand core information and see how it applies to research and the real world.

Methodology **boxes** appear throughout the book and profile topics related to perceptual research, demonstrating to students how the information they are learning can be applied. These include topics such as "Reducing Salt Content in Foods" (Chapter 4), "Music Therapy and Well-being" (Chapter 7), and "Visual Biological Motion" (Chapter 13).

Investigation **boxes** offer suggested experiments and hands-on demonstrations that students can perform to observe phenomena described in the book. Demonstrations and experiments include "Cognitive Factors That Influence Perception" (Chapter 1), "Studying the Cocktail Party Effect" (Chapter 6), and "Exploring Musical Notes and Timbre" (Chapter 7).

Portrait **sidebars** highlight key figures from the history of perceptual research whose contributions are described in the book.

Advanced Sections **listing** appears at the front of the book, indicating the book's more challenging sections so that students and instructors can plan their engagement with the material efficiently.

SideNote **boxes** provide additional, sometimes humorous, material on a topic discussed in the book and challenge students to extend and apply the information they are learning.

CONTEMPORARY DESIGN

An increasingly digital, quickly changing world of communication calls for a design that evolves and adapts. We have striven for a look that is contemporary yet clean, a design that reflects the vibrancy and excitement of sensory perception today without sacrificing content or authoritativeness. The use of colour and innovative design elements are a necessary acknowledgment to the changes wrought by new media and how readers expect information to be packaged and presented. At the same time we remain well aware that this is indeed a printed book, with both the limitations and the very real and enduring strengths that are a product of the print's long history as the pre-eminent method of codifying and transmitting knowledge.

AIDS TO STUDENT LEARNING

A textbook must fulfill a double duty: while meeting instructors' expectations for accuracy, currency, and comprehensiveness, it must also speak to the needs and interests of today's students, providing them with an accessible introduction to a body of knowledge. To that end, numerous features that promote student learning have been incorporated throughout the book. They include the following:

- *Chapter Outlines* allow students and instructors to see how the material within a chapter is cohesive.

- *Chapter Objectives* provide a concise overview of the key concepts to be covered.

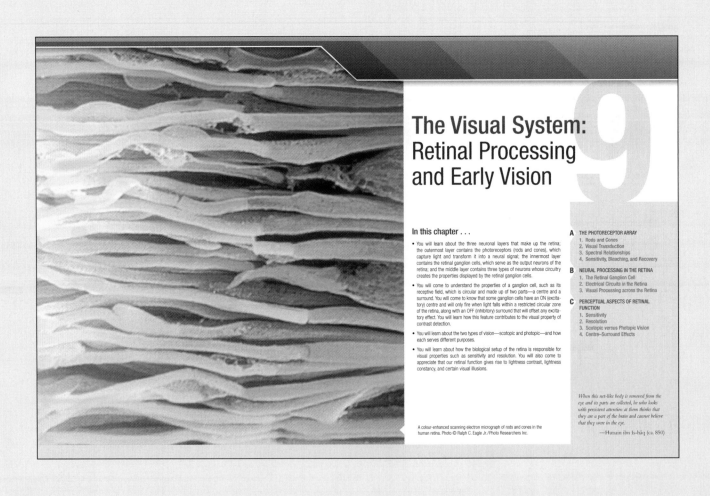

The Visual System: Retinal Processing and Early Vision

9

In this chapter . . .

- You will learn about the three neuronal layers that make up the retina; the outermost layer contains the photoreceptors (rods and cones), which capture light and transform it into a neural signal; the innermost layer contains the retinal ganglion cells, which serve as the output neurons of the retina; and the middle layer contains three types of neurons whose circuitry creates the properties displayed by the retinal ganglion cells.

- You will come to understand the properties of a ganglion cell, such as its receptive field, which is circular and made up of two parts—a centre and a surround. You will come to know that some ganglion cells have an ON (excitatory) centre and will only fire when light falls within a restricted circular zone of the retina, along with an OFF (inhibitory) surround that will offset any excitatory effect. You will learn how this feature contributes to the visual property of contrast detection.

- You will learn about the two types of vision—scotopic and photopic—and how each serves different purposes.

- You will learn about how the biological setup of the retina is responsible for visual properties such as sensitivity and resolution. You will also come to appreciate that our retinal function gives rise to lightness contrast, lightness constancy, and certain visual illusions.

A THE PHOTORECEPTOR ARRAY
1. Rods and Cones
2. Visual Transduction
3. Spectral Relationships
4. Sensitivity, Bleaching, and Recovery

B NEURAL PROCESSING IN THE RETINA
1. The Retinal Ganglion Cell
2. Electrical Circuits in the Retina
3. Visual Processing across the Retina

C PERCEPTUAL ASPECTS OF RETINAL FUNCTION
1. Sensitivity
2. Resolution
3. Scotopic versus Photopic Vision
4. Centre–Surround Effects

When this net-like body is removed from the eye and its parts are collected, he who looks with persistent attention at them thinks that they are a part of the brain and cannot believe that they were in the eye.

—Hunain ibn Is-hâq (ca. 850)

A colour-enhanced scanning electron micrograph of rods and cones in the human retina. Photo © Ralph C. Eagle Jr. / Photo Researchers Inc.

Chapter Summaries ensure a thorough understanding of key concepts and aid in reviewing for tests and exams.

Key Terms listed with page references at the end of each chapter also provide an excellent revision tool for tests and exams.

Recall Questions are organized by increasing level of difficulty and ensure students can fully understand and apply the concepts presented in the chapter.

Further Readings point students toward relevant resources, giving them an excellent starting point for further research.

A Glossary located at the end of the book for easy reference defines important terms which have been highlighted in **bold** throughout the textbook.

Chapter 11   The Visual System: Colour Perception   397

Summary

1. The notion that colour perception is associated with the spectral nature of light was demonstrated by Newton in the seventeenth century through his famous prism experiment. The differential refraction of light as a function of wavelength creates a continuous band that appears as a rainbow of colours, leading to Newton's conclusion that colour is associated with light rather than being an intrinsic property of objects. Newton created a colour circle to represent the seven spectral colours contained in sunlight, which in turn provided a simple geometric way to predict intermediate colours that arise from the mixture of any two coloured lights. A pair of colours that produces white when mixed together is referred to as being *complementary*. Because sunlight is made up of all of the spectral colours mixed together, the end result of that mixture produces a point in the middle of the colour circle—white.

2. An object can absorb, scatter, or reflect light. Objects that display a large amount of specular reflection are glossy in nature, whereas those that display little reflection at the surface take on a matte appearance. A second type, known as *body reflection*, influences the perceived colour of an object. Objects that reflect all wavelengths equally will take on a whitish appearance; those that reflect very little light will appear grey or black. A precise description of the nature of body reflection is given by an object's *reflectance spectrum*. The actual perceived colour of an object is determined by this parameter in conjunction with the spectrum of the incident light, which together generates the *colour signal* of the object.

3. A physical description of light is given by its emission spectrum—that is, energy content at each wavelength across the visible range. The perceptual parameter that corresponds to wavelength is known as *hue* and can be represented in a circular manner where the distance around the circle corresponds to changing hue sensations. The flatter the emission spectrum, the more the signal encompasses neighbouring wavelengths, leading to changes in perceived vividness, or *saturation*. Saturation is represented in a radial manner in colour space, where the centre occupies a neutral colour, and the edges represent the most

saturated hues. The emission spectra of two sources can have similar profiles but different levels of energy content. Hue and saturation remain unaffected in this case, but each stimulus produces a different perceived *value* (brightness or lightness). Value is represented along the vertical dimension in colour space.

4. Additive colour mixing of three primaries (red, green, and blue-violet) in varying amounts can produce virtually all of the other perceptible colours. Young postulated that there were three separate light-capturing elements in the eye whose ability to detect light coincided with the primary colours. Any pair of lights or surfaces that are perceptually identical but physically different are called *metamers*. Metamers can be produced by any trio of primaries, and in fact, there can be a very large number of metamers. Von Helmholtz resurrected Young's postulate

---

398   Fundamentals of Sensory Perception

6. All behavioural data in colour vision cannot be accounted for by trichromatic theory alone, and many phenomena (e.g., colour afterimages and the subjective appearance of colour) are better explained by Hering's theory of colour opponency. According to this theory, two pairs of colours (red/green and blue/yellow) are never simultaneously processed but instead represent opponent colour mechanisms. Psychophysical research in the 1950s (chromatic cancellation) and neurobiological studies on monkeys in the 1960s that found LGN neurons with R/G, G/R, Y/B, or B/Y receptive fields firmly established the colour-opponent theory. The neural output of colour-opponent cells correlates well with the perceptual impressions of the primary hues; for example, the perception of *red* is largely the result of activity in R/G neurons, the perception of *yellow* in Y/B neurons, etc. Both the trichromatic and opponent process theory are correct but at different levels of visual processing, leading to the *dual process* theory.

7. Colour opponency in the retina is generated by selective input of cone signals upon a ganglion cell. An R/G colour-opponent cell receives input from a central group of L cones in an excitatory manner and a peripheral group of M cones in an inhibitory manner. The receptive field of an R/G neuron shows centre–surround colour opponency (i.e., red centre, green surround). A similar selective nature of

cone inputs is responsible for generating the other subtypes of colour-opponent cells. The retinal output can be parsed into two channels—a chromatic output (composed of signals from the four colour-opponent subtypes) and an achromatic output responsible for encoding luminance information (composed of signals from the two light-opponent subtypes—ON/OFF, OFF/ON). The chromatic output of the retina arrives at the four upper (parvocellular) layers of the LGN and the achromatic output at the two lower (magnocellular) layers.

8. Wavelength discrimination studies have shown that humans with normal colour vision have an excellent ability to perceive changes in hue for much of the visible spectrum (less than a 2 nm change in

Key Terms

Abney effect, 395
achromatic channel, 385
adaptation, 383
aperture condition, 394
Bezold-Brücke effect, 395
bistratified ganglion cell, 387
body reflection, 361
brightness/lightness, 367
chromatic channel, 385
chromaticity, 356
colour afterimage, 371
colour circle, 358
colour constancy, 394
colour contrast, 393
colour signal, 362
colour space, 365
colour vision, 356

colour-opponent
complementary
contingent aftere
deuteranopia, 37
dichromatic, 378
double-opponen
389
dual process theo
emission spectru
hue, 366
isoluminance, 38
luminance, 385
metamer, 370
midget ganglion
monochromatic,
monochromatic
neutral colour, 3

Chapter 11   The Visual System: Colour Perception   399

Recall Questions

1. What is the order of colours that appeared in Newton's prism experiment? Why was this experiment so important in the history of science? What are complementary colours, and what do they produce when mixed together?

2. What is the difference between *specular* and *body* reflection? How does the reflectance spectrum of an object help to determine its colour? What is the colour signal of an object, and how is it derived?

3. How is *hue* represented in colour space? What is the difference in physical spectra between two stimuli that differ in terms of saturation? How are saturation and value represented in colour space?

4. What are metamers, and how did they influence the development of our ideas on colour vision? How did the results of colour matching experiments give rise to the idea of trichromacy?

5. How does the Hering theory of colour opponency differ from the Young–Helmholtz theory of trichromacy? What are the different pieces of evidence that support each theory?

6. What is the principle of univariance, and why is it important for understanding colour vision? Why is scotopic vision colour-blind? What are the names of the different types of colour deficiency, and how do they arise? What is the argument that trichromacy represents the best evolutionary solution for human vision?

7. What were the two key advances that led to a resurgence of the opponent colour theory? What are the different subtypes of colour-opponent neurons? What is the evidence to support the notion that perceptual impressions of colour are generated from the neural output of colour opponent neurons?

8. How do colour-opponent neurons arise in the retina from the three cone subtypes? What are the different types of neurons that make up the chromatic and achromatic channels?

9. How can a hue discrimination experiment be conducted, and what are the general findings for humans? What are the ideal colour contrast conditions in terms of foreground versus background colours? What is *colour constancy*, and why is it important?

10. What are some examples of non-spectral colours? How is subtractive colour mixing different from additive mixing?

11. How does the opponent theory account for colour afterimages, and why does the trichromatic theory fail in this regard? Why are colour-opponent neurons unable to signal isoluminant colour contrast? How do double-opponent neurons resolve this problem?

12. How can colour constancy be explained? What is the McCollough aftereffect, and how can it be explained by known mechanisms of visual cortex function?

Further Reading

• Backhaus, W. G. K., Kleigl, R., & Werner, J. S. (1998). *Color vision: Perspectives from different disciplines*. Berlin, Germany: de Gruyter.

• Ebner, M. (2007). *Color constancy*. Chichester, UK: Wiley.

• Gegenfurtner, K. R. (2000). *Color vision: From genes to perception*. Cambridge, UK: Cambridge University Press.

• Hurvich, L. M. (1981). *Color vision*. Sunderland, MA: Sinauer Associates.

• Kuehni, R. G., & Schwarz, A. (2008). *Color ordered: A survey of color systems from antiquity to the present*. New York, NY: Oxford University Press.

• Livingstone, M. S. (2002). *Vision and art: The biology of seeing*. New York, NY: Harry N. Abrams.

• Lynch, D. K., & Livingston, W. (2001). *Color and light in nature*. Cambridge, UK: Cambridge University Press.

• Thompson, E. (1995). *Colour vision: A study in cognitive science and the philosophy of perception*. London, UK: Routledge Press.

• Waldman, G. (2002). *Introduction to light: The physics of light, vision, and color*. Mineola, NY: Dover Publications.

• Wandell, B. A. (1995). *Foundations of vision*. Sunderland, MA: Sinauer Associates.

INSTRUCTOR AND STUDENT SUPPLEMENTS ACCOMPANYING THE TEXT

Today's textbook is no longer a volume that stands on its own—it is but the central element of a complete learning and teaching package. *Fundamentals of Sensory Perception* is no exception. The book is supported by an outstanding array of ancillary materials for both students and instructors, all available on the companion website:

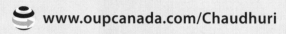 **www.oupcanada.com/Chaudhuri**

For the instructor

An **Instructor's Manual** includes chapter summaries, learning objectives, lecture suggestions, and lists of activities, exercises, and further readings. The instructor's manual also includes suggested course syllabi.

A **Test Generator** offers a comprehensive set of multiple choice, true/false, short-answer, and essay questions, with suggested answers, for every chapter.

PowerPoint® Slides annotated by Avi Chaudhuri summarizing key points from each chapter and incorporating figures and tables from the book as well as an image bank are available to adopters of *Fundamentals of Sensory Perception*.

Instructors should contact their Oxford University Press sales representative for details on these supplements and for login and password information.

For the student

The Student Study Guide includes study questions, links to further readings and websites, timelines, chapter outlines, and learning objectives. Go to www.oupcanada.com/Chaudhuri and follow the links!

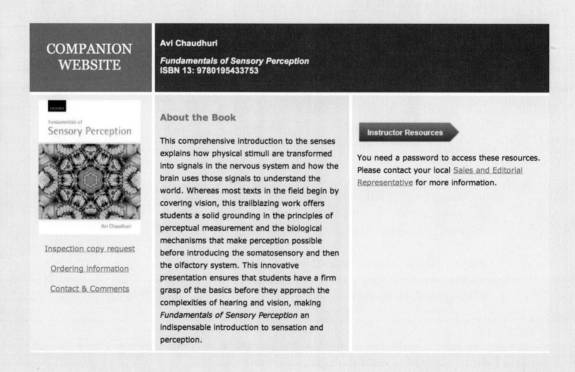

COMPANION WEBSITE

Avi Chaudhuri

Fundamentals of Sensory Perception
ISBN 13: 9780195433753

Inspection copy request

Ordering information

Contact & Comments

About the Book

This comprehensive introduction to the senses explains how physical stimuli are transformed into signals in the nervous system and how the brain uses those signals to understand the world. Whereas most texts in the field begin by covering vision, this trailblazing work offers students a solid grounding in the principles of perceptual measurement and the biological mechanisms that make perception possible before introducing the somatosensory and then the olfactory system. This innovative presentation ensures that students have a firm grasp of the basics before they approach the complexities of hearing and vision, making *Fundamentals of Sensory Perception* an indispensable introduction to sensation and perception.

Instructor Resources

You need a password to access these resources. Please contact your local Sales and Editorial Representative for more information.

From the Author

This book has been a labour of love, and a long one at that. The idea arose in the mid-1990s for a textbook on sensory perception that had a blend of core concepts and yet presented advanced material in a way that was different from existing books. Just about every college in Canada and the United States offers degree or diploma programs in psychology, and one of the usual requirements is a course in perceptual psychology. Most of the students enrolled in this program are oriented toward the arts and have had little exposure to scientific principles or processes. This led to the belief that a significant need existed for a book that would be sensitive to this aspect of the students' background and yet serve the purpose of clearly explaining the biological mechanisms underlying perceptual phenomena.

Most existing sensory perception textbooks begin with basic concepts, such as perceptual measurement, and then proceed immediately to cover visual function. *Vision* is one of the most difficult topics in perception, and from my own teaching experience, it is usually a burden on many students to begin a course with the complexities of visual function and then progress to the other perceptual systems. As a result, I have placed the chapters on touch and the chemical senses at the beginning of this book, followed by the auditory and visual systems.

This arrangement has several advantages. First, it follows the sequence (to a first-order approximation) of the evolution of sensory systems. Second, some of the basic principles of sensory function—receptive fields, transduction mechanisms, stimulus coding, etc.—are more difficult to grasp with the visual system, and therefore prior coverage of these principles better prepares the student for the later chapters. For example, the concept of receptive fields is especially difficult to convey when first approached by way of vision, whereas it can be more easily explained from the perspective of tactile stimulation. Similarly, the concept and application of Fourier analysis is far easier to grasp when first applied to auditory function. And lastly, it seems logical to begin with the *near* senses and then proceed to the *distant* senses.

In addition to this unique overall layout, each chapter provides core information that I believe most instructors feel students need to acquire after completing a course in sensory perception. And yet, there are many programs in which more advanced aspects of this topic are taught. One of the joys that all instructors experience is encountering that small subset of the student population who wish to go beyond the core material. This book attempts to serve these students and instructors by incorporating advanced material in each chapter, as delineated in the list of advanced sections at the outset of the text.

Another feature of this book is the provision of a rather comprehensive treatment of each sensory system, starting with a discussion on the nature of a stimulus itself before proceeding to the biological and perceptual aspects of that system. For example, the interaction of light with objects (e.g., reflection, absorption, scattering, etc.) is an important topic that serves as a foundation for how light interacts with the eye. Similarly, to truly understand music perception, it is essential to intertwine the physics of music with the corresponding perceptual experiences. Accompanying these discussions is the historical development of ideas that have been instrumental to our current understanding of sensory systems.

I often find that students take a keen interest in sidebars—especially portraits, figures, and side notes. Therefore, this textbook includes small portraits of some of the great scientists in perceptual research whose contributions are described in the text. Another function of the sidebar is the inclusion of interesting ideas, anecdotes, and pertinent information that would break up the flow if contained in the main body of the text. These notes are incorporated in a sequential manner with numerical references. Together, I hope these components will add considerable information, humour, and historical insight as well as invoke academic curiosity and subject clarification to make for an interesting read.

Finally, as a course instructor, I often wish that all science textbooks had sections that were labelled for ease of reference and communicating reading requirements to the students. This is a small technical detail but one which I believe is very helpful to instructors. Accordingly, I have lettered and numbered the major sections and subsections of this book.

It is undeniably true that publishing a textbook relies on the contributions of many individuals who have considerable impact on the final outcome. I had the good fortune of working with a first-rate publisher and an extremely talented staff of editors, formatters, and graphic artists. Amanda Maurice was an absolute joy to have collaborated with in the editorial preparation of these chapters. I have certainly cherished her offbeat humour and persistent patience with the crotchety ways of a stubborn writer. I am also grateful to Peter Chambers, whose efforts and attention to detail are unfortunately hidden, but present throughout this book. I truly appreciate the work of Steven Hall and his team for their sterling job on the text's presentation and format. And I also thank Jacqueline Mason, who put it all together and whose warmth and friendship made this whole project work from the very outset.

In addition to my graduate students, whose discourses have prompted many of the important questions embedded in this text, I would also like to thank a number of my colleagues who helped to ensure that I was on the right track by reviewing chapters that were well within their domain of expertise. In this regard, I especially wish to thank Albert Bregman, Daniel Levitin, and Ronald Melzack at McGill University. I also gratefully acknowledge the contributions of the following reviewers, whose thoughtful comments and suggestions have helped to shape this text: Nicole Anderson (Grant MacEwan University), Deborah Giaschi (University of British Columbia), Laurence R. Harris (York University), Debbie M. Kelly (University of Saskatchewan), Stephen G. Lomber (University of Western Ontario), Gautam Ullal (McMaster University), and Daniel Voyer (University of New Brunswick).

And finally, this labour of love thing—it begins somewhere and is most definitely shaped by environment, community, and upbringing. My father, Amala Charan Chaudhuri, a retired chemistry professor, instilled in me a compelling appreciation for the beauty of science and the joy of research. My mother, Purnima Chaudhuri, who was a college physics instructor, showed by sheer example what can be achieved through hard work, uncompromising tenacity, and the dogged will to succeed. Had she survived to see this book published, I believe that in the midst of her joy she would have asked me when I shall start my next book. My sons, Sanjay and Arjun, would often—and sometimes nervously—ask when I would be completing this project, to which I had to constantly come up with creative answers. They were always understanding and supportive and were also real troopers in happily (*ahem*) volunteering to provide eye movement image sequences for the *VOR* and *saccade* examples in Figures 13.23 and 13.24. And finally, the fact that I am even at the point of writing this preface is entirely due to the unwavering support, unmitigated confidence, and uncommon compassion that my wife, Shoma, has shown from the very outset—and to whom I dedicate this book with joyful love.

For Shoma
(at last!)

Principles of Perceptual Measurement

In this chapter . . .

- You will discover the main controversies that arose in studies to determine the relationship between physical stimuli and the sensations they evoke within us. You will also learn how to describe and give examples of the human ability to estimate sensations.

- You will examine famous classical psychophysicists, such as Gustav Fechner and Ernst Weber, and the experimental methods they designed to study sensory perception. You will become familiar with *psychometric function* and how it can be affected by both sensory and nonsensory parameters.

- You will become familiar with the *difference threshold*, which determines how much extra stimulus is needed in order to *just* notice a change. You will also become familiar with *Weber's law*, which states that the difference threshold does not remain constant as the stimulus increases in intensity; and Fechner's law, which was found to be flawed but transformed the field of sensory science and remains influential to this day.

- You will learn about Stanley S. Stevens, who began the era of modern psychophysics. You will also learn about the method of *magnitude estimation*, which led to the development of the power law.

- You will study the difference between *prothetic* and *metathetic* stimuli and how they are assessed. Finally, you will become familiar with differences in human sensitivity to stimuli and how researchers use techniques to compare those differences in terms of z-scores.

Most of us would be able to correctly identify the colour red or green or blue. But does that mean we are all experiencing an identical psychological event, or could it be that each of us experiences something slightly different? Photo: Trout55/iStockphoto.com

True science investigates and brings to human perception such truths and such knowledge as the people of a given time and society consider most important.

— Leo Tolstoy

We are constantly being bombarded by energy from the physical world, whether it is in the form of visual, auditory, tactile, or chemosensory stimulation. These stimuli are very real and can be measured. The intensity of light reflected by an object, for example, can be exactly determined with a device called a *radiometer*. This device will specify the intensity in a set of units for which it has been calibrated. In general, all physical stimuli that we are capable of perceiving can be specified in real terms that give us a value according to some dimension of its physical reality.

But what about the psychological events that evoke within us an appreciation of that physical **stimulus**? Can the resulting perceptual experience also be measured? That depends on who is doing the measuring. If it happens to be anyone other than the perceiver, the answer of course is *no*. Perception is a very private experience, and since it cannot be exposed to anyone else, it cannot be directly measured by anyone else either. Consider the following. Most of us would be able to correctly identify the colour of a stoplight. But does that mean we are all experiencing an identical psychological event, or could it be that each of us experiences something slightly different but that we have all been taught to call it *red* since childhood? We may never know the answer to this.

If an outsider is not capable of measuring our own perceptions, then are we? Are we capable of determining, say, the psychological intensity of a sound that is experienced in our mind, giving it a value, and comparing its perceived intensity with a different sound or a different type of sensation altogether? Remarkably, the answer is *yes*. And it turns out that we are actually quite good at it even though perceptions do not reside in the very real world of physics (Stevens, 1986). And therein lies a rather thorny problem. Many psychologists have asserted that even making the attempt at measuring a perceptual event is fruitless because it is not a measurable thing and therefore can never be verified (Heidelberger & Klohr, 2004).

To say that this issue has generated some lively debate in the past would be an understatement. This is largely because of the opposite view held by some experimental psychologists that the perceived intensity of sensations can indeed be reliably estimated by the perceiver. Furthermore, the information so obtained is generally consistent across individuals, and therefore the data can be scientifically validated (Gescheider, 1997). We will return to this debate and explore the issues on both sides later in this chapter. But first, it is necessary to learn something about the experimental approaches to studying sensory processes, the kinds of problems to which they can be applied, and the information they reveal about the operation of the brain. What will follow is a set of core concepts that will surface throughout this book as we examine each of the sensory systems in detail.

A. Scientific Basis of Perceptual Measurement

The most obvious question to begin with is "Why take a scientific approach to this problem?" That is, what do we hope to gain by developing and applying a set of rigorous experimental procedures to the study of perception? The reason most psychologists would first offer is that it satisfies an intellectual curiosity. Perception is such a mysterious and almost magical phenomenon that a first step toward learning anything about it is to establish a quantifiable relationship between the two variables in this process—the physical stimulus and the resulting perceptual impression (SideNote 1.1). Since it is impossible to open up the mind and observe the process of perception, one advantage of knowing this relationship is that it may offer clues about the nature of the brain, the way it processes information, and, ultimately, how the biological operations within it lead to sensation and perception.

Quantitative relationships and their benefits

There are several additional advantages to understanding the mathematical relationship between the physical and perceptual worlds. One is that it provides an estimate of the perceptual quality of a stimulus in numerical terms and thus allows comparisons with other stimuli. Say for example that a new perfume has just been developed and the company wishes to test its aromatic acceptance by the public before spending millions of dollars on its promotion. By applying a set of experimental procedures, which we will soon learn, it is possible to obtain a numerical index of its impact on the sense of smell and then use this to provide a meaningful comparison with the perceptual impression made by other perfumes. Such data

SideNote | **1.1**

Although the terms *sensation* and *perception* are often used interchangeably, it is important to establish the distinction between them at the outset. Sensory processes capture information from the physical world and transform them into biological signals that are interpreted by the brain. In so doing, the brain creates a perceptual representation in our mind that allows us to appreciate the physical world. Thus, *perception* represents a single unified awareness of a stimulus that in turn arises from the *sensation* produced by our sensory systems.

can predict the likely social acceptability of the new product and therefore can be used by the company's executives to make important commercial decisions (Lodge, 1981).

Quantitative relationships also have the advantage that they allow comparisons among individuals and even species. The later chapters of this book will cover many details about our limits and capacities in processing information from the physical world, how they vary with age, and, where appropriate, how they compare with other animals. The factors that are used in such comparisons are always mathematical descriptors of the system in question. An extension of this idea is the comparison among the different sensory modalities—a so-called *cross-modal comparison*—to see if any similarities exist among them (Luce, 1990). For example, if we perceive warmth on the skin in some definable way to the temperature of the object, then how does this relationship compare to the way in which we perceive the loudness of sound as a function of its physical intensity? Before we explore such sophisticated issues, we need to address a basic question.

Is there a general relationship between physical stimulus and perception?

This is one of the fundamental questions of perceptual psychology and one to which much effort has been directed over the last 150 years. The early experimentalists who approached this problem were motivated in finding a general formula that could describe all sensory systems. What might such a formula look like—or, rather, what kind of a **function** could relate the physical intensity of a stimulus to its perceived magnitude? We know from everyday experience that this will be an increasing function. That is, as the physical intensity of the stimulus increases, so will our perception of it. But that could happen in a number of ways, as shown in Figure 1.1.

The simplest is a linear function. For any given increase in physical intensity, there is a certain increment in the perceived intensity. The proportion between the two remains constant across the whole range. In other words, the slope remains constant. This is not the case for the other two possibilities shown in Figure 1.1. In an exponential relationship, the perceived sensation intensity changes very slowly at low values of physical intensity. But after a certain point, the function takes off such that even small changes in stimulus intensity produce a dramatic increase in perception. In an exponential function, therefore, the slope itself progressively increases with physical intensity. The opposite is true of a logarithmic function where the slope is very large at the beginning such that perceived intensities can change dramatically with small changes in stimulus intensity. However, this effect diminishes and the function tails off at higher stimulus intensities. A logarithmic function therefore displays a decreasing slope over its entire range. According to this mathematical description, a sensory system would no longer be additionally responsive to further increments in stimulus intensity beyond a certain point.

There are two general approaches to obtaining the precise relationship between physical events and perceptual experience. The first is to simply ask human subjects to rate the perceived intensity of a certain stimulus, say the loudness of a sound, at various physical intensities (Gescheider, 1984). It would then be possible to plot the two sets of values and determine which of the general functions shown in Figure 1.1 best describes the transformation of a physical input—in this case, sound—into a perceptual event. We will look at the information revealed by this kind of approach later

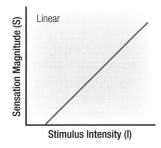
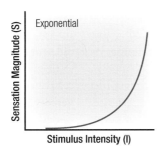
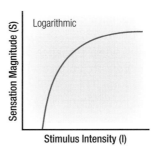

Figure 1.1

Three possible functions that may relate the physical intensity of a stimulus (I) to the perceived intensity of sensation (S).

Gustav Theodor Fechner
(1801–1887)
© INTERFOTO/Alamy

in this chapter. The second approach is a bit more convoluted because it requires a measure of the smallest change in stimulus input that causes a just discriminable change in sensation. To understand how this can reveal anything important, we have to examine the ideas first proposed by the experimental psychologists of the 19th century. They had understood that a mathematical relationship between physical and perceptual qualities could be established by obtaining two basic characteristics or descriptors of that function—the starting point and the slope.

B. Classical Psychophysics

Looking again at Figure 1.1, we see that all three functions do not begin at the origin but are displaced somewhat to the right. This is because we are unable to detect very low levels of stimulus intensity. Although a stimulus is physically present, the biological elements that are involved in capturing the stimulus and transforming it into a sensory experience do not normally function well if the physical intensity is too low (Engen, 1971). Rather, the intensity has to reach a certain minimum level, the so-called **absolute threshold**, before it is registered by the brain as a sensory event. Stimulus intensities below this point are called **subthreshold** and will not produce detectable sensation. So the first item that has to be determined is the absolute threshold, which would then tell us the point from which to begin plotting our function.

We would next want to know what happens beyond this point in the so-called **suprathreshold** region where sensation takes place. For this, we will have to determine how the slope changes as a function of physical intensity. Furthermore, the slope would have to be determined not just for one suprathreshold point but also for several others in order to see how it is changing. One possible way to obtain this information is by knowing just how small a change in stimulus intensity is required to produce a discriminable change in sensation. This so-called **difference threshold** can be used to estimate how the slope changes at suprathreshold levels. And once we know this, we can determine which function best describes the transformation of physical stimuli in the real world into psychological events that we experience as perception.

We have just described the general outline of a scientific approach that had been formulated by the German physicist Gustav Fechner in 1860. Fechner wanted to determine the relationship between mind and body and set out to establish not only a guiding principle but also a set of experimental methods that were to be used in this new field called **psychophysics**. He believed that there existed a general relationship between physical and perceptual qualities, that it was similar for all types of sensations, and that it could be obtained by knowing the stimulus energy at which the output can just be detected or discriminated—that is, the absolute threshold and the difference threshold (Heidelberger & Klohr, 2004). Fechner was not just interested in knowing these thresholds because they would reveal something about the operational sensitivity of sensory systems but because he believed that they represented fundamental parameters in the grand formula of perception.

1. PSYCHOPHYSICAL METHODS

It is possible to apply any one of three general methods that were developed by Fechner to obtain absolute and difference thresholds (Gescheider, 1997). The simplest of these is the **Method of Adjustment** where a human subject is told to simply adjust the physical intensity of a stimulus until it is barely detectable. The initial intensity would be set either above or below threshold, and the subject would accordingly change the value until the stimulus is just perceptible or when the sensation just disappears. Although this procedure is very fast and actively engages the subject in the psychophysical experiment, the **Method of Limits** is preferable if speed is not an issue because this technique provides more reliable estimates. Here, the subject is presented with a stimulus whose intensity is chosen from an ascending or descending series. If an ascending series is used, the intensity of the stimulus is initially set at a subthreshold value and increased by a fixed amount in successive trials until the subject reports that it is perceived. Alternatively, if a descending series is used, a suprathreshold intensity value is gradually reduced until the percept disappears. The transition points from several such ascending and descending series provide a reasonable estimate of the threshold.

Both the Method of Limits and the Method of Adjustment allow the subject to have an idea of what the next stimulus will be like compared to the last one. This predictability in stimulus presentation makes both of these methods less accurate. A more suitable procedure is the **Method of Constant Stimuli** where the intensity values are randomly chosen from a preset range and presented to the subject. Neither the experimenter nor the subject usually knows the value of the next stimulus to be presented. The subject merely replies whether or not a sensation occurred and a frequency chart is established based on the responses collected from many presentations at each intensity.

As an example, let us consider an experiment on the visual system where we will attempt to obtain the absolute threshold for detecting light using the Method of Constant Stimuli. Such experiments are typically conducted with a sophisticated optical setup. However, we will simplify the experiment so that the stimulus will be under computer control and presented on a monitor. The subject will view the stimulus from a fixed distance and after each trial will indicate a response to the computer. This is a typical setup for most modern psychophysical experiments on vision (SideNote 1.2). After each stimulus presentation, the subject hits either a *YES* or a *NO* button to indicate whether a sensation occurred, that is, whether light was detected or not. For any given trial, the stimulus intensity will be randomly chosen by the computer from a predefined set of values. The lowest intensity value must be one that is never detected, whereas the highest value should always be detected. In this way, the threshold intensity will be located somewhere within this range (SideNote 1.3). At the end of the experiment, each intensity will have been presented an equal number of times, and a summary of the frequency of *YES* responses to each stimulus intensity will be provided by the computer.

2.   ABSOLUTE THRESHOLD

Before looking at the data that such an experiment might generate, let us consider what the response profile would look like based simply on intuition. One likely possibility is shown in Figure 1.2 where the response curve looks like what is called a **step function**. All intensities below a certain point would be too weak

to produce detectable sensation, and so our subject should consistently respond *NO* when asked if something is visible. However, once we reach an intensity that is sufficient to trigger sensation, the subject should then consistently respond *YES*. The transition between these two response levels can then be defined as the absolute threshold. The subject is presumed to behave like an **ideal detector** in such a scenario—that is, all subthreshold intensities fail to produce a detectable sensory event, whereas all suprathreshold ones consistently produce a positive sensation. Furthermore, the subject is absolutely perfect in being able to distinguish between these two conditions.

Humans are not ideal detectors

In reality, however, our responses are quite different. As Figure 1.3 (page 8) shows, the response curve that would emerge from an actual experiment would look more like an S-shaped function or **ogive**. Although we reliably detect very high intensities and always fail to detect very low ones, it appears that the intervening intensity levels cause some uncertainty as to whether or not a sensory event occurred. According to Figure 1.3, it is clear that as the intensity increases, there is a progressive increase in the likelihood that it will be detected. This so-called **psychometric function** provides a typical profile of how our sensory systems respond as a function of physical intensity (Falmagne, 2002). And as such, it is clear that

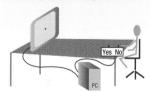

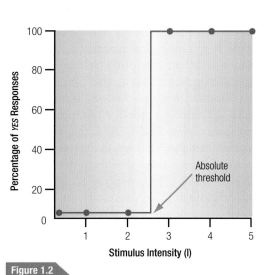

Figure 1.2

The expected response profile in an absolute threshold experiment looks like a step function. All stimulus intensities up to a certain point will fail to produce sensation, whereas all intensities beyond that point will always do so. The absolute threshold is the intensity at which this transition occurs.

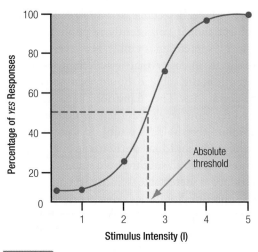

Figure 1.3

The actual response profile (psychometric function) that is obtained in an absolute threshold experiment. The absolute threshold is usually taken as the intensity at which the stimulus was detected on 50% of the trials.

SideNote | 1.4

Cognitive factors can arise from noise in the decision-making process. For example, a subject may actually perceive the stimulus but opt to respond *NO* due to reduced confidence. Alternatively, a subject may not actually have perceived the stimulus but chose to respond *YES* due to eagerness. Cognitive factors are extremely important in psychophysical experiments and will be discussed later in Section C.4.

SideNote | 1.5

Let us assume that the sensation produced by a stimulus has a normal probability distribution due to the effects of noise. The detection probability of a signal is given by the cumulative probabilities—that is, the area under the distribution—up to that point. The ogive psychometric function results from the cumulative probabilities determined in this manner at progressively greater values of sensation magnitude. The 0.5 (or 50%) level in the ogive corresponds to the mean of the distribution, which is why it is used to estimate the threshold.

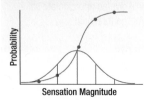

we do not behave as ideal detectors, leading to the natural question of why this is so.

Under most circumstances, our sensory systems have to deal with several sources of uncertainty (Marks, 1974). These factors become especially critical at very low physical intensities where detection thresholds typically arise. One such source is the stimulus itself. There is usually some variability in the intensity of a stimulus simply because no physical device can provide perfect delivery at a specified intensity, especially when it is very low. This stimulus is then captured by a sensory system that adds further noise to the signal. It is a biological fact that our nervous system is inherently noisy, which becomes especially problematic at the limits of sensory function where the noise interferes with signal detection to produce instances of misperception. And finally, once this somewhat variable stimulus has been delivered and then captured by our noisy sensory system, we still have to make a judgment as to whether it was perceived. That judgment can be influenced by a number of physical, emotional, and cognitive factors (SideNote 1.4). While the magnitude of these would certainly vary among different people, these factors can also vary with time within an individual subject. Together, these different sources of variability—from stimulus to subject—make our sensory systems behave quite differently from an ideal detector.

Conventional approaches to threshold estimation

Given that we are not ideal detectors, then which intensity value do we take from Figure 1.3 to represent the absolute threshold? Because there is a gradual increment in stimulus detectability with increasing physical intensity, there actually is no well-defined point that can serve as the threshold. We therefore have to adopt an arbitrary response level that can be used to obtain the threshold (Engen, 1971). By convention, psychophysicists have used the 50% response level for that purpose (SideNote 1.5). Therefore, the physical intensity that produces this response is taken to be the absolute threshold. An experimenter can certainly use a different criterion so long as it is made clear which response level that is. For example, it is possible to use the 60% *YES* value as the definition of threshold sensation. In that case, the stimulus intensity that produces this would be taken as the absolute threshold of detection. What this means is that in reality there is no *all-or-none* condition for stimulus detection. Rather, our thresholds can fluctuate a little, and therefore the notion of a threshold now becomes defined in a more statistical manner.

Since Fechner's time, there has been much effort at determining absolute threshold values for different sensory systems under different conditions (Gescheider, 1997; Stevens, 1986). These results have shown that we are indeed extremely sensitive creatures, and under some conditions, the laws of physics often impose the limits to detection. Here are some examples of how well we do.

Touch—a dimpling of the skin by as little as 10^{-5} cm is sufficient to be detected.

Smell—under optimal conditions, the absorption of only 40 molecules by detectors in the nose is sufficient to produce a detectable smell.

Hearing—detection threshold is so small that it represents movement of the eardrum by only 10^{-10} cm. This is smaller than the diameter of a hydrogen molecule.

Vision—the eye can be exposed to as little as 54–148 photons to produce a detectable sensation of light. If losses in transmission through the eye are considered, it turns out that this represents the absorption of a single photon in about 5 to 14 detector cells of the retina.

These figures attest to the remarkable biological construction of our sensory systems.

3. DIFFERENCE THRESHOLD

As noted before, one of Fechner's central goals was to understand the relationship between the physical and mental worlds—in other words, the way in which stimuli of different physical intensities produce different amounts of sensation, or sensory magnitude. The absolute threshold gives only one point in that profile, that is, the starting point for any of the possible relationships that are shown in Figure 1.1. But this is obviously not enough to determine what the rest of the function would look like. For this, Fechner needed to have an idea of what the slope of the function was at suprathreshold levels and how that slope changed with increasing intensity (Engen, 1971; Manning & Rosenstock, 1967). If the slope remains constant, then the relationship between sensory magnitude and stimulus intensity is described by a linear function. However, if the slope is either increasing or decreasing, then the function becomes either an exponential or a logarithmic one, respectively.

A clue as to which of these possible functions correctly describes the transformation of physical to mental events came to Fechner from a series of experiments on difference thresholds that were carried out by a contemporary German physiologist named Ernst Weber. Weber had been interested in determining the gradations of sensory experience at suprathreshold levels (Weber, 1996). The question now was no longer whether or not a stimulus was perceived but rather how much it needed to change in order to produce a detectable change in sensation. The difference in physical intensity that was required to accomplish this became known as the *difference threshold*. Weber worked mainly with the discrimination of object weights, carrying out a series of careful experiments on the smallest detectable change for a series of different starting weights.

A difference threshold experiment on the visual system

Let us illustrate the principles that Weber developed using discrimination of light intensities as an example. We can set up a psychophysical experiment as before but now ask the subject to examine two stimuli—a reference light, whose intensity is always kept constant, and a target light, whose intensity is either lower or higher than that of the reference. The subject must compare the two and indicate whether the target light is *brighter* or *dimmer*. No other choices are allowed.

We can adopt Fechner's Method of Constant Stimuli again to perform this experiment. A computer will randomly choose the intensity level of the target light from a range and display that stimulus along with the fixed reference stimulus. The subject's task is to compare the two stimuli, make a decision, and hit one of two buttons to register the response. This sequence is repeated many times until a sufficient number of trials (say 50) have been accumulated for each intensity point. We can then calculate the proportion (or percentage) of trials in which the subject judged the target light to be brighter. Of course, we could just as well examine the proportion judged to be dimmer. Either way, the idea is to look at the data and see how much of a change in physical intensity was required for a detectable change in sensation. Since we gave the subject an equal number of brighter and dimmer intensities, one possibility is that all truly *dimmer* intensities were judged correctly as were all truly *brighter* intensities. In this case, the subjects theoretically behaved like an ideal detector because they never failed in distinguishing true differences in stimulus intensities.

However, similar to what we saw earlier for detection judgments, it turns out that we do not behave as ideal detectors when it comes to difference judgments either. The psychometric function in Figure 1.4 (page 10) shows a plot of percentage *brighter* responses against target light intensity. Again, as in Figure 1.3, performance data displays an ogive rather than a step function, indicating that certain intensities generated mixed responses. The intensity that produced 50% *brighter* responses (point a on the x-axis) can be taken as the point of perceptual equivalence. In other words, at this intensity our subject could not decide whether the target light was brighter or dimmer, and it was therefore perceptually equivalent to the reference light.

Our task now is to use this data to determine the difference threshold—that is, that extra bit of physical intensity that needs to be added to or subtracted from the target light intensity at this perceptual equivalence point in order for there to be a **just noticeable difference (JND)** in sensation. This amount will in turn depend on exactly what level of noticeable difference we want as our criterion. By convention, most psychophysicists use

Ernst Heinrich Weber (1795–1878)
© INTERFOTO/Alamy

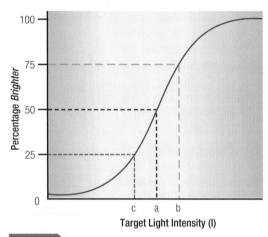

Figure 1.4

A typical psychometric function that is obtained in a difference threshold experiment where the subject has to judge two stimuli and determine whether the target was brighter or dimmer than the reference. The 25% and 75% *brighter* response levels are generally used as the points for a just noticeable difference (JND) in sensation decrement and increment, respectively.

the 75% *brighter* response level as the measure for a noticeable increment in the stimulus (Gescheider, 1997). Thus, when the target light intensity is raised to point b in Figure 1.4, we will achieve this result, and the difference between the two intensities (b *minus* a) is taken as the difference threshold (ΔI). In other words, ΔI represents the extra bit of physical intensity that we would need to add in order to make a stimulus just noticeably brighter. Exactly the same logic can be used if we want to determine the difference threshold for a reduction in sensation, except now we use the 25% *brighter* response level (which corresponds to 75% *dimmer* judgments). The target light intensity now needs to be lowered to point c, and the difference between the two intensities (a *minus* c) is also a difference threshold (ΔI). These two measures of difference threshold are usually distinguished by the terms *increment threshold* and *decrement threshold*, respectively, and are often averaged to provide a composite value.

4. WEBER'S LAW

In the last experiment, brightness comparisons were made to a reference light that was fixed at a particular intensity. What happens if we now change the reference light to a higher level and redo the experiment to find a new difference threshold? Does the difference threshold value (ΔI) still remain the same or will it

become different? This was precisely the question that Weber addressed in his experiments with weights, and in so doing, he discovered a fundamental relationship that has come to bear his name (Weber, 1996).

Multiple discrimination threshold experiments

Let us return to the difference threshold experiment with lights. Figure 1.5 shows the psychometric functions that we would likely obtain if we conducted this experiment three times by setting the reference light at progressively higher intensities each time. The psychometric functions are correspondingly displaced to the right and become somewhat flatter. For each psychometric function, we can now determine the difference threshold. To keep it simple, we will restrict this analysis to just the increment threshold.

As before, we would first determine the target light intensities that are perceptually equivalent in brightness to the reference light for all three cases (a_1, a_2, a_3) and then find the intensities producing 75% *brighter* responses (b_1, b_2, b_3). Looking closely at Figure 1.5, we can see that the increment threshold for the first psychometric function (b_1 *minus* a_1) will be less than that of the second function, which in turn will be less than that of the third. In other words, the greater the intensity level at which we have to make a JND judgment, the greater the difference threshold (ΔI) needed to attain that JND. The difference threshold is therefore not constant but actually increases in a linear fashion with stimulus intensity. This is what Weber discovered, and the equation describing this relationship is known as **Weber's law**:

$$\Delta I = k \cdot I$$

Implications of Weber's law

We know from everyday experience that if a small number of items is incremented by just one, it is more likely that we will notice that difference than if the same addition is made to a much larger set. Weber noticed that if one lit candle was added to 60 others, then that addition would be sufficient to cause a JND in brightness perception. However, if there were 120 burning candles, then adding just one more was no longer sufficient to cause a detectable change in sensation. Thus, the requirement for a JND is that the incremental (or decremental) amount be scaled to the stimulus intensity.

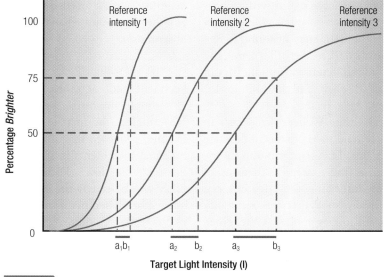

Figure 1.5

Psychometric functions from difference threshold experiments in which the reference light is set at progressively higher intensities. The lowest reference intensity (left curve) produces a small difference threshold, whereas the highest reference intensity (right curve) produces a much larger threshold. The bar lengths below the x-axis show the relative size of the difference thresholds for the three psychometric functions.

The difference threshold (ΔI) is therefore not a constant value but some proportion (k) of the stimulus intensity (I). This proportion (k) is also known as **Weber's fraction**.

Once the Weber fraction is known, the difference threshold can be easily calculated from Weber's law for any given intensity value. But what is the value of k? This must be experimentally determined. The preferred way to do so is to determine the difference threshold at a number of different intensities, as we did in the experiment above. The difference thresholds can then be plotted against the different values of intensity to reveal a straight line (SideNote 1.6). The slope of this linear function is the Weber fraction (k). For the brightness experiment we just performed, we would have found the value of k from the slope to be about 0.08. Thus, an 8% increase (or decrease) in light intensity is sufficient to produce a JND and allow us to detect that change in perceived brightness.

Weber fractions for different sensory systems

We could have conducted a similar difference threshold experiment in any of the other sensory systems, such as taste, touch, hearing, etc., to determine their respective Weber fractions. This has indeed been done by psychophysicists since Weber's time, and some of the results are shown in Table 1.1. Notice that there is

no universal Weber fraction that applies to all sensory systems. Rather, there is considerable variation such that certain sensory processes are very sensitive to change, whereas others are

Table 1.1

Weber Fractions for Different Sensory Systems

Sensory Dimension	Weber Fraction (k)
Touch (heaviness)	0.02
Touch (vibration)	0.04
Taste	0.2
Smell	0.07
Loudness	0.3
Pitch	0.003
Brightness	0.08

Note. Small values of k imply greater sensitivity in detecting changes of intensity. Adapted from "Psychophysics: I. Discrimination and Detection," by J. Engen, 1971, in *Woodworth & Schlossberg's Experimental Psychology*, Eds. J. W. Kling and L. A. Riggs, New York, NY: Holt, Rinehart & Winston; "On the Exponents in Stevens' Power Law and the Constant in Ekman's Law," by R. Teghtsoonian, 1971, *Psychological Review, 78*, pp. 71–80; "Differential Sensitivity for Smell," by W. S. Cain, 1977, *Science, 195*, pp. 796–798; "Psychological Dimensions and Perceptual Analysis of Taste," by D. H. McBurney, 1978, in *Handbook of Perception*, Eds. E. C. Carterette and M. P. Friedman, New York, NY: Academic Press.

SideNote | **1.6**

A straight line is produced if we make a plot of the difference threshold (ΔI) that was obtained at each of the three intensity (I) levels. This is the graphical form of Weber's law and has been found to hold true for all sensory systems within a broad range of intensities. The Weber fraction (k) is taken from the slope of this line.

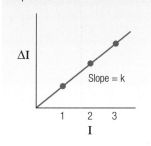

not. Among the most acute of our sensory parameters is the detection of pitch where just a 0.3% change in the frequency of sound is sufficient to cause a JND. On the other hand, the perception of sound intensity (loudness) can require up to a 30% change in the stimulus for that difference to be detected.

In general, the Weber fractions in Table 1.1 are accurate predictors of difference thresholds for a broad range of stimulus intensities. However, at the extreme situations of very high or low intensities, the value of k can change dramatically, such that the generality of Weber's law no longer applies (Gescheider, 1984). This is true of all sensory dimensions. Although the applicability of Weber's law is limited to a certain range of intensities, it nevertheless remains one of most useful equations in perceptual psychology.

5.   FECHNER'S LAW

We remarked earlier that one of Fechner's central goals was to obtain the relationship between sensory magnitude and stimulus intensity. We are now ready to complete that story. Fechner knew that to uncover the relationship between those two parameters, it was necessary to know the way in which that function changed at progressively greater suprathreshold values (Fechner & Lowrie, 2008). As we have already seen, Weber's law asserts that higher levels of suprathreshold intensity require a correspondingly greater change in intensity (ΔI) to produce a change in sensation (ΔS) that is just distinguishable (JND). But Fechner knew nothing about the actual magnitude of ΔS needed to produce a JND or whether that value changed at different levels of sensation.

Fechner's assumption

Fechner could not resolve this problem because it is simply impossible to measure sensations. Nevertheless, he made a bold assumption. Fechner proposed that all JNDs were produced by equal increments in sensation regardless of the operating level (Fechner, 1860/1966). In other words, exactly the same value of ΔS was needed at all sensory magnitudes because the JND is a standard unit of change that represents a psychological constant. Fechner was also well aware of Weber's results and the implications they had for his quest to determine the relationship that he sought. Figure 1.6 (left side) shows how Fechner's assumption can be integrated with Weber's law. As shown, higher intensity levels require a greater change in the physical stimulus (ΔI) to produce identical changes in sensation (ΔS). In all of these cases, a JND event is presumed to occur through identical changes in sensation (Fechner's assumption) that are brought about by progressively greater changes in stimulus intensity (Weber's law).

Deriving the stimulus–sensation relationship

Only one of the three possible functions that we explored in Figure 1.1, relating intensity and sensation, can account for this. Figure 1.6 (right side) shows that the stimulus–sensation relationship must necessarily follow a logarithmic function. The intensity values from the difference threshold experiment in Figure 1.5 are shown here on the x-axis. The progressively

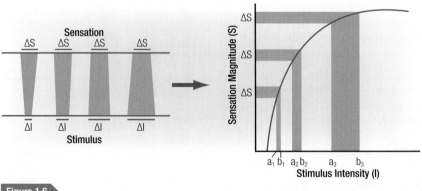

Figure 1.6

The integration of Weber's law and Fechner's assumption implies that with increasing stimulus intensities, the difference threshold (ΔI) progressively increases but continues to be mapped onto a constant change in sensation (ΔS) to produce JNDs (left). Only the logarithmic function allows this condition to hold true (right). Fechner therefore concluded that the relationship between stimulus intensity and sensation is a logarithmic function.

greater change in ΔI that was revealed in that experiment can now be related to Fechner's assumption of ΔS being constant at all levels for a JND. Fechner could reach only one conclusion—the logarithmic function is the only one that will allow for ΔI to increase according to Weber's law but still retain the same values of ΔS. Neither the linear nor exponential functions will permit this.

What we have just seen is a tour de force of experimentation and insight. In the absence of any direct means to study sensation, Fechner was still able to derive a fundamental relationship between sensation magnitude and stimulus intensity. As a tribute to his work, that relationship is now called **Fechner's law** and is formally specified as

$$S = k \cdot \log (I)$$

where the constant k is related to, but not identical to, the constant in Weber's law. Fechner's law asserts that at low intensity levels, the magnitude of our sensations can change quite rapidly with small changes in stimulus intensity, whereas we become much less sensitive at higher intensities. Indeed, at the very highest intensities, our perception of a stimulus should not change appreciably, regardless of how much intensity is added.

These results were soon generalized across the entire domain of perception such that the relationship between all physical events and conscious experience was taken to be largely logarithmic in nature. This eventually turned out to be a flawed conjecture, and indeed the logarithmic function itself later became replaced by somewhat different functions as descriptors of the stimulus–sensation relationship. Nevertheless, the psychophysicists of the 19th century continued to have a profound influence on perceptual psychology, even to this day, in both theory and practice (SideNote 1.7).

C. Modern Psychophysics

The field of psychophysics flourished during Fechner and Weber's time. On the one hand, there was the sheer elegance by which the logarithmic relationship was established, and on the other, there was the persuasive simplicity of Fechner's assumption that JNDs represent fundamental and immutable units of sensory change. Fechner's law thus became the cornerstone of perceptual psychology, and

many psychophysicists simply became preoccupied with the logarithmic function as the master descriptor of mental processes. Nothing else was acceptable.

And yet, there were many opponents as well, some of who became quite influential in their criticism of Fechnerian psychophysics (SideNote 1.8). The main objection was not against the logarithmic relationship *per se* but against the very notion that sensations can be described by mathematical functions at all. One of the most scornful critics was William James, who believed that it was simply futile to put numbers on sensations (Richardson, 2007). Nothing about the empirical process, he argued, can allow any quantitative estimate of such private experiences as sensation, and therefore any psychophysical law is fundamentally meaningless. In a classic rebuke, James wrote how terrible it would be if Fechner should "saddle our Science forever with his patient whimsies, and, in a world so full of more nutritious objects of attention, compel all future students to plough through the difficulties, not only of his own works, but of the still drier ones written in his refutation."

Fechner's supporters believed that the stimulus–sensation problem had been solved, whereas his critics believed that the problem could never be solved. Both intransigent attitudes in their own way produced a general decline of interest in the measurement of sensation that lasted until the 1930s, when a Harvard psychologist named Stanley S. Stevens began his psychophysical work. Stevens boldly rejected the assertion that sensation cannot be measured. However, his approach was completely different from the German psychophysicists of the 19th century. Rather than determine psychophysical laws through indirect procedures, Stevens proposed a set of direct methods for studying sensation. And thus began the era of *modern psychophysics*—an entirely new approach that would galvanize the field and produce dramatic insights into sensory processing by the 1950s, revealing psychophysical relationships that in some cases did not even slightly resemble logarithmic functions.

1. MAGNITUDE ESTIMATION AND THE POWER LAW

Whereas Fechner believed that sensations could only be measured indirectly through difference thresholds, Stevens believed that an

exact relationship between stimulus and sensation could be directly obtained (Krueger, 1989). Stevens was instrumental in establishing a set of procedures that are collectively known as **scaling**. Rather than taking the Fechnerian approach of comparing stimuli and judging their differences, Stevens simply asked his subjects to provide a direct rating of the sensation that they experienced. This technique came to be known as **magnitude estimation**.

Experimental design and outcomes

The subject is first presented with a standard stimulus, which is known as the *modulus*, and told that it represents a certain value, say 10. If for example the experiment required loudness estimation, the subject would first experience the modulus and then provide a relative numerical rating for other tones of varying intensity that are randomly presented (Stevens,

Table **1.2**

Power Law Exponents for Different Sensory Systems

Sensory Dimension	Power Law Exponent
Touch	
Steady pressure (palm)	1.1
Vibration (250 Hz)	0.6
Temperature (cold)	1.0
Temperature (warmth)	1.6
Electric shock (fingers)	3.5
Taste	
Sweet	1.3
Salt	1.4
Bitter	0.8
Smell	
Coffee	0.55
Hearing	
Loudness	0.67
Vision	
Brightness (extended target)	0.33
Brightness (point source)	0.5
Estimated length (line)	1.0
Estimated area (square)	0.7

Note. The exponent values can be different for different aspects of sensation within a particular system. Adapted from "On the Psychophysical Law," by S. S. Stevens, 1957, *Psychological Review, 64*, pp. 153–181.

1966). The numerical estimate represents the subject's judgment of the sensation triggered by that particular stimulus. In one variation of this method, first suggested to Stevens by his wife, Geraldine, subjects are not presented with a modulus to constrain their judgments. Rather, they are free to develop their own modulus and assign numbers in proportion to the sensation magnitude that they experience (SideNote 1.9).

A remarkable outcome of these experiments was the consistency with which subjects produced their ratings and the similarity in the trends observed among different individuals. The actual numbers obtained were different across subjects because they were free to choose their own scale. But when the numbers were equated by taking into account subject variability, it turned out that there was considerable agreement among different people with regard to their sensory ratings for any given type of stimulus.

The magnitude estimation experiments were a direct challenge to William James' doctrine that sensations simply cannot be measured. Stevens showed that they indeed can and that the data fit very nicely into mathematical functions that were consistent with a **power law**. The general form of the power law is the following:

$$S = k \cdot I^b$$

where S is the sensation experienced by the subject, I is the physical intensity of the stimulus, k is a so-called *scaling constant* that takes into account the units used to represent the stimulus intensity, and b is the exponent (or power) value. According to this relationship, sensation is related to intensity raised to a certain power. But what is the value of that power or exponent? It turned out that there was no one general exponent value that served all of the senses. Rather, different sensory experiences are related to stimulus intensity by a particular exponent (Stevens, 1957). Table 1.2 provides some examples of power law exponents that were derived from experiments on the various senses. As this table shows, there is no uniformity in the exponent values. Furthermore, for any given sense (taste is a good example), the actual exponent value depends on the particular aspect of that sensory dimension, for example, taste sensations generated by salt, bitter, etc.

Power law exponents

Although sensation magnitude is related to stimulus intensity by the power law, the precise nature of that relationship is very much governed by the exponent. Table 1.2 shows that for some sensory dimensions, the exponent is less than 1.0, whereas for others it is greater. Figure 1.7 shows a graph of the two extreme cases from Table 1.2—brightness for extended targets (0.33) and electric shock (3.5). The brightness curve shows what is generally described as a negatively accelerating function. Brightness perception grows rapidly at first with increasing light intensity, though further increments will gradually reduce the rate at which perceived brightness increases. In a similar manner, loudness perception is related to sound intensity by a negatively accelerating function. But its exponent value of 0.67 (see Table 1.2) means that this relationship would show a somewhat steeper rise with intensity (Stevens, 1966). Nevertheless, the power law relationship for loudness perception is such that perception does not keep up with intensity. Indeed, to double loudness requires nearly a threefold increase in sound intensity, whereas for brightness it requires nearly an eightfold increase in light intensity.

The power law relationship predicts quite different perceptual increments for certain sensory parameters where the exponent is greater than 1.0. For example, as seen in Figure 1.7, the sensation of electric shock rises slowly at first but then takes off dramatically with further increases in electric current. Certain other touch parameters, along with a few taste sensations, also display a similar exponential relationship. But what about the case where the exponent value is equal to 1.0, as with the visual impression of line length? This is shown by the dashed line in Figure 1.7. In such cases, there is an exact perceptual relationship with intensity such that our mental impression changes exactly in step with changes in the stimulus.

Implications of the power law

Neuroscientists and perceptual psychologists have postulated the origins of the power function and the reasons why there can be such large differences in the exponent value. Stevens suggested that the power law reflects the operation of sensory systems at their lowest levels—that is, at the interface where the

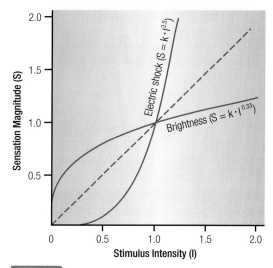

Figure 1.7

Power law functions for two extreme cases of perception. Brightness perception has an exponent value of 0.33 and appears as a negatively accelerating function. The perception of electric shock, with an exponent value of 3.5, rises dramatically with small increments of intensity.

physical stimulus becomes converted into a biological signal (Stevens, 1962). According to this idea, the neural output of sensory systems must follow a power law relationship with the incoming stimulus. The exponent in this case is determined by the nature of the transformation at this site.

While there has been general support for this notion from biological experiments (SideNote 1.10), there has also been a fair amount of criticism levelled at this so–called **sensory transducer theory**. British psychologist E. Christopher Poulton suggested that psychophysical magnitude functions are not only related to low-level transformation processes but also to those at the highest levels of the mind where judgments are made on mental impressions (Poulton, 1968). According to Poulton, differences in the power law exponent may be caused by variability in a number of different experimental situations that in turn affect human judgment. Although this issue is still not completely resolved, there has been much discussion on the implications of the power law and the factors that affect the exponent value. Scaling experiments, which became an integral part of modern psychophysics, not only changed our understanding of how stimuli from the physical world map onto our inner world of perception but also introduced new ways of thinking about sensory processes.

SideNote | **1.10**

In one remarkable experiment by Borg, Diamant, Ström, and Zotterman in 1967, physiological recordings were made from the nerve that carries taste information to the brain in a patient having ear surgery under local anesthesia. The patient was asked to make magnitude estimations on several substances that were applied to the tongue at different concentrations. The results showed that neural signals in the taste nerve and the subjective judgments of the patient were both related to concentration (intensity) by a power function with a similar exponent.

2. PSYCHOPHYSICAL SCALING

The importance of magnitude estimation as a psychophysical technique stems from the fact that humans are remarkably good at being able to match numbers to what we perceive. As a result, several different scaling techniques have been developed to analyze our sensory and perceptual functions in a quantitative manner (SideNote 1.11). With the advent of these techniques, psychologists soon became interested in measuring different aspects of sensory function, not only within that particular domain but also in relation to other sensory dimensions (Baird & Noma, 1978). The technique of **intramodal matching**, for example, produced new insights into how sensitive a particular sensory system is to diverse kinds of stimulation. As we will see in later chapters, much of that effort was applied in vision and hearing to examine how perceived brightness was affected by different colours of lights or how perceived loudness changed for different tones.

Cross-modal experiments

Stevens developed a rather unusual procedure called **cross-modality matching** where subjects were asked to compare stimuli from one sensory modality to those of another (e.g., loudness vs. brightness, electric shock vs. vibration, etc.) (Stevens, 1966). What makes this procedure unusual is that comparisons are required not within a single sensory dimension, where the task is easier, but rather with two entirely different sensory experiences, where the task is to make a judgment of equal sensory magnitude. However, it turns out that we are also quite good at these kinds of comparisons (Luce, 1990).

Figure 1.8 shows the collective results of 10 different experiments where subjects were asked to adjust sound level until it matched the perceived intensity of a stimulus from another sensory domain. The resulting *equal sensation functions* show different slopes depending upon the power function for the sensory parameter that was being compared. In fact, the actual slope of these functions turned out to be very close to the predicted slope based on the power law exponents for loudness and the particular sensory parameter to which it was being matched. Thus, electric shock (which has a large exponent value) shows a steep relationship for cross-modal matching with loudness, implying that small changes in electric current require large changes in sound setting for a judgment of equality. The opposite is true for cross-modal matches with brightness (which has a small exponent value). These results not only validated the power law but also showed the utility of psychophysical scaling procedures in comparing sensory function across different systems.

Prothetic and metathetic sensations

The sensory experiences that allow scaling such as those described above have a direct underlying relationship to the physical intensity of the stimulus. Perceptual qualities such

SideNote | 1.11

Psychophysical scaling procedures can be classified into three general types. In *confusion scaling*, subjects determine whether one sensation is greater or less than another. Fechner used this kind of indirect discriminative judgment in his experiments. The technique of *partition scaling* requires subjects to make direct judgments of differences in sensory magnitude by placing the stimuli into a limited number of categories. Only the *ratio scaling* procedures, such as magnitude estimation, produce measurements that can be placed on a numerical scale.

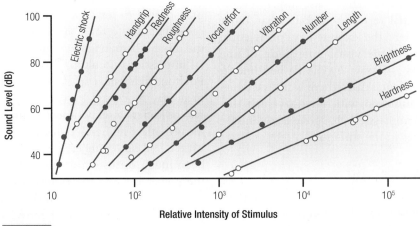

Figure 1.8

Cross-modal matching between loudness and 10 other sensory stimuli. The slope of each *equal sensation function* is determined by comparing exponent values from the power functions of loudness and the particular stimulus. Adapted from "Matching Functions between Loudness and Ten Other Continua," by S. S. Stevens, 1966, *Perception and Psychophysics, 1*, pp. 5–8.

as brightness or loudness, for example, can be associated with a numerical value of physical intensity. Sensory experiences where subjects can make a judgment of "how much" are termed **prothetic**. However, there exists a different class of sensory experience that cannot be directly linked to stimulus intensity. Colour perception is a good example, where there is no quantitative difference between, say, the hues of red or green. They produce two entirely different kinds of perception, which though linked to the wavelength of light, cannot be scaled to wavelength in a meaningful way. Increasing the wavelength of light does not add to the magnitude of the sensory experience but rather changes it entirely. Such perceptual qualities are called **metathetic**.

It turns out that prothetic processes generally obey the power law, but metathetic processes do not (Gescheider, 1997). The reason for this is likely due to the way the two kinds of sensory dimensions are processed by the brain. Prothetic perceptions are believed to rely on additive processes such that changes in stimulus intensity produce either an increase or decrease in the activity of the associated sensory neurons. The collective behaviour of this system is such that it follows the power law. Metathetic perceptions, on the other hand, show a change in quality, and this in turn is associated with the substitution of one kind of neural excitation by another. Therefore, in the absence of an additive process, there is little scope for relating metathetic experiences with the stimulus in a quantitative manner because there is no exact relationship between sensory impression and variation in the stimulus (Manning, 1979).

Multi-dimensional scaling

Psychologists have had to devise some clever techniques to analyze metathetic percepts. In general, these techniques rely on the notion of similarity or dissimilarity (Borg & Groenen, 2005). Consider colour perception as an example. Subjects can be presented with three colours at a time and asked to judge which pair is the most similar—a procedure called the *method of triads*. After enough data has been collected with a sufficient number of colours, it is possible to represent the information by way of a similarity map where those colours that are perceived to be similar occupy nearby positions, and those that are dissimilar are placed farther apart. Thus, psychological

similarity is now represented by physical distance in a spatial map. This technique, which is known as **multi-dimensional scaling**, allows an investigator to peer into the underlying attributes or qualities of the stimulus that produce similar or dissimilar perceptual experiences. Multi-dimensional scaling is now well established as the tool of choice for pairwise evaluations of entities in such diverse fields as genetics, linguistics, social sciences, and psychology (Baird & Noma, 1978; Schiffman, Reynolds, & Young, 1981).

3. SCALING OF NONSENSORY VARIABLES

Our keen judgmental abilities are not just restricted to the primary senses but extend to some rather complex aspects of human perception. The general principles of intramodal and cross-modality matching may also be applied to nonsensory variables within the fields of sociology, political science, and esthetics. The same procedures that were used to scale loudness and brightness, for example, can also be applied to questions such as the value of art, the importance of certain occupations, the seriousness of crimes, etc. In other words, a set of scaling methods can be employed in what some have called *social psychophysics* to establish measures of subjective magnitude in the areas of esthetic preference or social/political opinion (Lodge, 1981).

Discrimination scaling versus ratio scaling

The original work in this area actually began with Fechner and was later refined by Louis Thurstone in the 1920s (SideNote 1.12). The basic logic of Fechner's sensory psychophysics was used by Thurstone to study social issues such as preferences for nationalities and the seriousness of crimes (SideNote 1.13). Thurstone made the assumption that dispersions in judgment represented a standard distance in subjective impression (Thurstone, 1959). His use of a nonsensory JND-like parameter produced functions that retained the same mathematical quality as those seen in classical sensory psychophysics. Both Thurstone and Fechner thus made a fundamental assumption that each increment in discrimination, measured as a JND, produces equivalent increases in subjective impression—in other words, the variability in psychological units is constant along a linear psychological continuum. This kind

SideNote | **1.12**

Fechner himself worked for some time on problems of esthetics and how to apply techniques from sensory psychophysics to matters of social opinion. In one experiment, he obtained esthetic judgments for two versions of Hans Holbein's *Madonna*. There was quite a bit of controversy at the time as to which had actually been painted by Holbein.

SideNote | **1.13**

"Instead of asking students to decide which of two weights seemed to be the heavier, it was more interesting to ask, for example, which of two nationalities they would generally prefer to associate with, or which they would prefer to have their sister marry, or which of two offenses seemed to them to be the more serious" (Thurstone, 1959).

of psychophysics became generally known as **discrimination scaling** or *confusion scaling* (Torgerson, 1958).

The alternative view that had led to psychophysical power functions was based on the notion that equal units of discrimination along the stimulus continuum did not represent equal distances but rather equal ratios along the subjective continuum. The so-called **ratio scaling** procedures that were developed as a result, including Stevens' magnitude estimation technique, soon found their way into studies of social consensus as well (Ekman & Sjöbert, 1965). Among the more colourful examples in this category are studies on the political importance of Swedish monarchs, the prestige of certain occupations, the factors contributing to social status, the esthetic value of art and music, the perceptions of national power, and the judged seriousness of certain crimes (Chang & Chiou, 2007; Ekman, 1962; Vrij, 2000).

The above examples show how ratio scaling can be used to assess nonsensory variables. In a classic study, Thorsten Sellin and Marvin E. Wolfgang showed that there is a general consensus across society on the perceived seriousness of a variety of criminal offences (Sellin & Wolfgang, 1978). Using magnitude estimation procedures, they showed that the theft of progressively greater sums of money was accompanied by growth in the judged seriousness. While this is hardly surprising, it turned out that the power function for judged seriousness grew with the amount stolen by an exponent value of only 0.17. Thus, approximately 60 times as much money needs to be stolen in order to be perceived as being twice as serious by most people. Similarly, Sellin and Wolfgang found that the judged seriousness of crime is related to jail time prescribed by the Pennsylvania Penal Code by a power function with an exponent value of 0.7. These examples illustrate how important societal issues can be addressed by psychophysical scaling techniques that were originally developed to study sensory processes.

Ekman's law

As with sensory stimuli, discrimination scaling of nonsensory parameters produced logarithmic functions, whereas ratio scaling procedures consistently yielded power functions. Göesta Ekman at the University of Stockholm provided a theoretical account for this difference (Ekman & Sjöbert, 1965). Ekman proposed that detectable changes in sensation (JND), rather than being constant at all levels as proposed by Fechner, were actually related to sensation in a linear manner. In other words, the relationship between changes in sensation that are just detectable at a particular sensation level (or magnitude) is exactly analogous to Weber's law and can be stated as follows:

$$\Delta S = k \cdot S$$

This relationship was actually proposed as early as 1874 by Franz Brentano. By that time, however, the Fechnerian way of thinking so dominated perceptual psychology that Brentano's idea was largely ignored and remained without influence until Ekman restored the validity of this principle in the 1950s. As a result, the relationship is now known as **Ekman's law**.

Fechner's missed opportunity

The implications of Ekman's law are quite profound. The notion that the JND is not constant at all levels of sensation marks a dramatic departure from the Fechnerian way of thinking. If we strictly adhere to Fechner's postulate that the JND remains constant along the sensory continuum, then, as we saw earlier, logarithmic functions relating stimulus to sensation are the natural consequence, given the existence of Weber's law. If, however, Fechner had applied the idea behind Weber's law to the sensory continuum as well and adopted the view that the JND was not constant but rather a constant ratio of the sensory level, then he would have derived the psychophysical power function. In other words, if both Weber's law and Ekman's law are applied, then the mathematical outcome necessarily becomes Stevens' power law (SideNote 1.14).

But is Ekman's law valid? It has been argued that since the proportionality rule is generally true for the physical sciences and since it also applies in perceptual science by way of Weber's law, it is reasonable to assume that a similar relationship would hold true for the sensory continuum. Several empirical studies have provided support for this view. For example, Robert Teghtsoonian showed that the proportionality rule appeared to be the same for several different sensory experiences (Teghtsoonian, 1971). In other words, the value of k in Ekman's law, which was found to be 0.03, does not change with the nature of the sensory experience. This means

SideNote | **1.14**

If Fechner had changed his view and adopted Brentano's suggestion that the JND was related to sensation level in a manner similar to Weber's law, then Fechner would actually have been the first to derive the power law function in sensory science, which is now widely accepted.

that for all types of sensation, the size of the JND expressed in subjective units is approximately 3% of the actual sensation magnitude at any level.

4. SIGNAL DETECTION THEORY

To close this chapter, we return to the idea that the threshold represents a fundamental boundary between stimulus intensities that do not evoke sensation and those that do. We discussed earlier in Section B.2 that there is no such entity as a clear-cut, all-or-none absolute threshold. Rather, there is always some variability due to internal and external **noise** so that the threshold in turn depends on the likelihood that the **signal** exceeds this noise to produce a detectable sensory event. This means that the same stimulus may be detected on some occasions and not on others. The idea that emerged from classical psychophysics is that the threshold itself can vary over time. Modern psychophysicists have sought to identify the sources of this variability and develop new theoretical foundations that take into account nonsensory factors that can affect signal detection. As we will later discover, these developments have revised our thinking about the threshold concept itself.

A major advance in this field was made in the 1950s by Wilson P. Tanner and John A. Swets who proposed the use of statistical decision theory to understand how humans behave in a detection situation (Green & Swets, 1989). This new model, called **signal detection theory (SDT)**, uses statistical concepts that take into account cognitive factors that may influence a subject's decision-making process. Thus, there is not only a signal to be detected, which in turn relies on the inherent sensitivity of the sensory system, but also the decision by the subject as to whether a signal worthy of a positive response indeed existed.

Basic foundations of signal detection theory

In SDT, sensation magnitudes evoked by noise (N) and signal + noise (S + N) are represented as separate distributions. A major source of noise is the baseline firing of nerve cells that produces spontaneous activity in sensory pathways. Because of the random nature of this activity, a probability plot of sensation magnitudes evoked by internal noise alone will appear in the form of a normal distribution, as shown in Figure 1.9. This random fluctuation

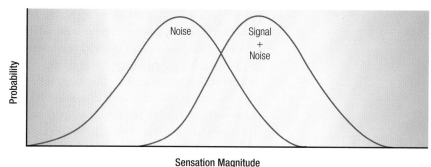

Figure 1.9

Background noise varies randomly over time and therefore appears in the form of a normal distribution. When a weak stimulus is present, the sensory magnitudes produced by it are added to noise and therefore result in a distribution that is shifted to the right.

implies that sensory events triggered by noise alone will vary with time. In an absolute threshold experiment, the subject is asked to detect a weak stimulus against this random background activity. Since the stimulus must be detected by the same *noisy* nervous system, a probability plot of sensation magnitude evoked by the stimulus will also show a normal distribution because the signal must be added to the noise distribution. Because of this additivity, the combined signal + noise distribution must always lie to the right of the noise distribution alone, as shown in Figure 1.9.

The random variation in background noise poses an interesting problem. When the stimulus to be detected is quite weak, the two distributions will have considerable overlap, as is the case in Figure 1.9. Therefore, there may be some instances where the noise itself may be so high that it could be mistaken for the signal, whereas in others the noise may be so weak that the signal is mistaken for noise (Swets, 1996). On each trial, the subject must therefore make a decision whether the evoked sensation was due to a signal added to the noise or to the noise alone. Clearly there are two different processes at work here, and the subject must make a distinction between the effects of one versus the other. But how can we parse the effects of noise versus signal + noise at the behavioural level in a detection situation? In other words, how can we measure the relative effects of signal and noise through psychophysical methods?

Measuring the effects of signal and noise

In early psychophysics experiments, a stimulus of some intensity, however weak, was always present in each trial. The assumption was that the subject would provide a response based solely on whether the signal produced a detectable sensation. In terms of the SDT scheme, only the signal + noise parameter was being tested, and psychometric functions therefore reflected the cumulative effects of that distribution (e.g., see SideNote 1.5 on page 8). The way to test the effects of noise alone in a detection experiment is to randomly give the subject a number of trials in which no stimulus is present. All instances of a YES response in such trials can then be assumed to be the effects of noise alone because no signal was present. In other words, some internal process within the subject either produced a sensation that coincided with the trial and therefore led to a positive response or, alternatively, an erroneous judgment was made in the belief that a sensory event had occurred. Either way, "no stimulus" trials allow researchers to get a handle on the pervasive effects of noise, regardless of its source, in that particular detection experiment.

The possible outcomes in such a study are shown in Table 1.3. If a trial did not contain a stimulus, then the two possible responses of the subject can be categorized as follows. A NO response is termed as a **correct rejection** and implies that at that moment in time, the noise level was not intense enough for the subject to judge that a detectable sensory event had occurred. A YES response on the other hand implies just the opposite and is termed a **false**

alarm. The subject indicated that a signal was present when in fact the sensation was only produced by noise. If however a signal was actually present in the trial, then the effects of signal + noise in that event may be sufficient for the subject to respond YES, which is termed a **hit**. The alternative possibility is that the subject responds NO, in which case it is termed a **miss** because the subject failed to detect the signal. Thus, there are only four possible outcomes in an SDT experiment with two being attributed to the effects of the noise component and the other two to the effects of signal + noise (Wickens, 2001).

Criterion effects—general properties

If false alarms are the product of noise, and hits are the result of the combined effects of signal and noise, then which point along the x-axis in Figure 1.9 can these effects be attributed to? In other words, how much sensation must take place before the relative effects of noise and signal + noise yield a false alarm or a hit, respectively? One of the basic assumptions of SDT is that each subject establishes a set point or **criterion (β)** in a given detection experiment. That is, a certain value of sensory magnitude is chosen as a cut-off point that in turn governs the response. If on a particular trial the evoked sensation is greater than this value, the response will be YES. If it fails to reach that level, the subject will respond NO. The mental process that underlies either decision can in turn be triggered by noise or signal + noise. That is, on each trial the evoked sensation can be attributed to either of the two distributions, and the subject must make a judgment as to which one is correct (Green & Swets, 1966).

The way that the criterion interacts with the noise and signal + noise distributions is shown in Figure 1.10. For clarity, the two distributions are vertically offset in this figure. Let us assume that the subject has adopted a certain criterion value, as shown by the vertical line in this figure. If the sensory magnitude exceeds the criterion, then the subject will always respond YES. However, this decision may be either a hit (stimulus was actually present) or a false alarm (stimulus was absent). The area under the noise distribution to the right of the criterion stipulates the probability of false alarms that will be seen in this experiment from noise trials alone (SideNote 1.15). Similarly, the area under the signal + noise

Table **1.3**

Parameters Involved in the Design and Execution of an SDT Experiment

Signal	Distribution	Response	
		NO	YES
Absent	Noise	Correct rejection	False alarm
Present	Signal + Noise	Miss	Hit

Note. In an SDT experiment, the subject must answer either YES or NO as to whether a detectable or discriminable stimulus was perceived in a given trial. However, the trial may or may not contain a stimulus. If the stimulus is absent, then the relative effects of noise are being assessed, and the two possible answers are termed *false alarm* and *correct rejection*. If a stimulus is present in the trial, then the effects of the signal + noise distribution are being assessed, and the two possible answers are termed *hit* and *miss*.

SideNote | **1.15**

The likelihood that a YES response will be determined by noise alone is given by the cumulative probabilities of all the points on the noise distribution that lie to the right of the criterion. In mathematical terms, this amounts to determining the area under this portion of the noise distribution.

distribution to the right of the criterion gives the probability of hits that will be observed in trials that contained the stimulus. As we can see in Figure 1.10, the number of hits will be far greater than false alarms in this particular situation, given the nature of the two distributions and the criterion value that was adopted by the subject.

Criterion effects—expectation

Is it possible for the subject to adopt a different criterion value? Let us consider what would happen if we conducted two experiments, one in which we told the subject that a stimulus will only be present on 30% of the trials and a second experiment in which we told the subject that the stimulus will be present on 70% of the trials. In the first experiment, the subject will not expect a stimulus on the majority of trials and therefore will likely adopt a conservative criterion. In other words, the criterion value will shift to the right of the one shown in Figure 1.10, implying that the subject will only choose to respond YES when the evoked sensory magnitude is quite large. In the second experiment, a more liberal criterion will be adopted, reflecting the higher probability of stimulus appearance. The criterion will now move to the left of the one shown in Figure 1.10. Compared to the first experiment, much lower sensory magnitudes will now be sufficient to elicit a YES response because the subject will expect more trials to contain a stimulus. Thus, depending on an inherent expectation of stimulus appearance, the subject will be either more or perhaps less inclined to give a positive answer on each trial, even though none of the other parameters in the experiment have changed.

Both situations will affect the hit and false alarm rates. As we shift the criterion more and more to the right (i.e., reduced expectation), there will be fewer instances of false alarms as well as hits. This is shown by the data in Table 1.4 where a stimulus appearance probability of 30%, and the accompanying rightward (conservative) criterion shift, results in rates of 0.09 and 0.36 for false alarms and hits, respectively (SideNote 1.16). When the subject is notified that stimulus appearance probability will be set at 70%, the accompanying leftward (liberal) criterion shift results in higher rates of false alarms and hits—0.64 and 0.91, respectively. The bottom line is that the criterion level adopted by the subject is changeable

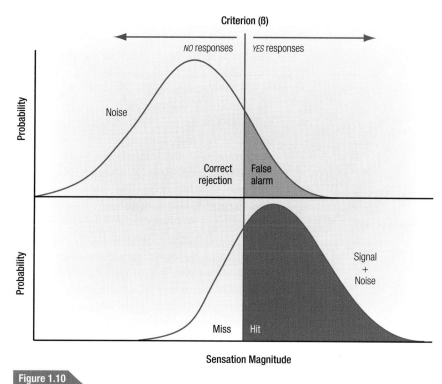

Figure 1.10

The criterion level (β) established by each subject determines the sensation magnitude that must occur for a YES response. The interaction of β with the two distributions determines the relative proportion of each of the four possible outcomes in an SDT experiment. The noise and signal + noise distributions are shown at different vertical levels for clarity.

and simply defines the sensory magnitude that will be required under the circumstances for a YES response. For any given pair of noise and signal + noise distributions, the criterion value will in turn specify the rates of hits and false alarms (Wickens, 2001).

Table 1.4

The Effects of Expectation on Detection Performance in an SDT Experiment

Stimulus Likelihood	False Alarm	Hit
30%	0.09	0.36
70%	0.64	0.91

Note. If the subject is aware that the likelihood of stimulus appearance is low, she will adopt a conservative criterion that will in turn produce low hit and false alarm rates. The opposite happens if the subject has a high expectation of stimulus appearance because she will then adopt a liberal criterion.

SideNote | **1.16**

We need not show the rates for correct rejection since it is simply 1 *minus* the false alarm rate. Similarly, the miss rate need not be shown since it is always 1 *minus* the hit rate.

The ROC curve

In a typical detection experiment, several hundred trials are given that fall either in the noise (stimulus absent) category or in the signal + noise (stimulus present) category. The actual proportion of trials in each category is set in advance and communicated to the subject. As we have just seen, the subject establishes a criterion based on this information, which in turn will impact performance. A convenient way of illustrating those effects is by way of a **receiver operating characteristic (ROC)** curve (Egan, 1975; Green & Swets, 1966). An example of an ROC curve that takes into account our results is shown in Figure 1.11. So far, we have been interested in two outcomes—false alarms and hits—that tell us how much the noise and signal + noise distributions contribute to detection performance. An ROC curve plots the probabilities of these two factors with false alarms represented on the x-axis and hits on the y-axis. Each point on an ROC curve is therefore specified by the subject's criterion since that determines the relative values of hits and false alarms in an experiment.

The two experimental situations discussed on the previous page produced different criterion levels because of different stimulus expectations. The resulting hit and false alarm rates from Table 1.4 are shown in the ROC curve of Figure 1.11. The experiment with the higher stimulus appearance probability (70%) produced a liberal criterion, which on an ROC plot appears as a point toward the upper end of the curve. Had the stimulus appearance probability been set even higher, then this point too would have edged farther up the ROC curve in response to the adoption of an even more liberal criterion. In contrast, the experiment with the lower stimulus appearance probability (30%) produced a more conservative criterion, which on the ROC curve shows up as a point toward the lower end. If we had chosen an even lower stimulus appearance probability, then this point would have edged farther down the ROC curve. All intermediate values of stimulus appearance would have produced hit and false alarm rates that map onto the ROC curve between the two that have been outlined. The important feature of an ROC curve is that it illustrates the effects of different criterion levels in a detection experiment. As the criterion shifts from low to high, the probabilities of hits and false alarms will change and when plotted in relation to each other will produce the ROC curve.

Criterion effects—motivation

In addition to stimulus expectation, there are other factors that can affect a subject's criterion and therefore also influence the detection of weak stimuli. An especially powerful factor is motivation (Swets, 1996). Consider a situation where a subject is paid to participate in a stimulus detection experiment in which there are neither penalties for wrong answers (i.e., false alarms) nor rewards for correct ones (i.e., hits). The experimenter is entirely at the mercy of the subject, hoping that the subject will give a conscientious effort despite being guaranteed a certain amount of money for merely participating. Let us make this experiment a little more interesting. As in all SDT experiments, we give a certain number of trials that will contain a very weak stimulus (i.e., signal + noise trials) and others that will not (i.e., noise-only trials). But now we will tell the subject that payment is contingent upon performance in both sets of trials. That is, every time there is a correct response to a signal + noise trial (hit), the subject will be rewarded. However, there will be a penalty if an incorrect response is given in a noise trial (false alarm). This way we will ensure that the subject will not arbitrarily respond

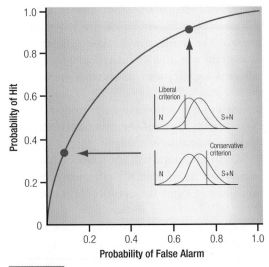

Figure 1.11

The receiver operating characteristic (ROC) curve plots the relative effects of hits vs. false alarms for a signal of fixed intensity. Changes in criterion produce hit and false alarm rates that fall on different points of the ROC curve. A liberal criterion appears toward the left end of the noise and signal + noise distributions (see inset), which in turn produces relatively high hit and false alarm rates. A conservative criterion produces the opposite result and maps onto the bottom end of the ROC curve.

YES throughout the experiment because of the false alarm penalty or similarly respond NO throughout because then rewards will not accumulate. In short, we will now have a highly motivated subject who will try very hard to distinguish the signal from noise trials (Lu & Dosher, 2008).

It turns out that the way we set up the rewards and penalties will influence the subject's criterion in the same way that we found for stimulus expectancies. Table 1.5 shows two possible payoff conditions that may be used. If the subject is told in advance that each hit will be worth 50¢ and each false alarm will incur a penalty of 10¢, then we will create a greater tendency for YES votes because the disparity in reward vs. penalty will assure a greater payoff in the long run. In other words, the subject will adopt a liberal criterion. If however we reverse the payment conditions and impose a penalty for false alarms that is much greater than the reward for hits, then the subject will tend to be very cautious and take fewer risks. The subject now adopts a conservative criterion. If we take the hit and false alarm rates from these two situations and plot them on an ROC curve, we will find a situation analogous to that seen in Figure 1.11. The first payoff condition will place the criterion value more toward the left side of the noise/signal + noise distributions and therefore will produce hit and false alarm rates that will plot toward the upper end of the ROC curve. The second payoff condition will produce a criterion more toward the right side of the two distributions, and this will yield a point on the lower end of the ROC curve. If we employed other payoff conditions, then the reward/penalty ratio would produce appropriate points elsewhere on the ROC curve. In effect, we find that motivational states induced by different payoff conditions produce criterion shifts that are similar to those we saw on the previous page for stimulus expectancies.

The problem with thresholds

The two factors that we have considered thus far—stimulus expectancy and motivation—have nothing to do with the signal itself (SideNote 1.17). In the experiments considered above, the signal strength was kept constant throughout, and the only parameter that changed was the nonsensory factors. And yet, we have shown that these factors can produce considerable **response bias** that in turn affects the probability of signal detection. These results call into question the very existence of thresholds that supposedly demarcate the onset of detectable sensations because clearly such boundaries are susceptible to the effects of nonsensory variables (King-Smith, 2005).

In classical psychophysics, the physical intensity of a stimulus that produced YES responses 50% of the time was taken as the absolute threshold of detection. Given what we now know about the hit rate being susceptible to criterion effects, the actual intensity value producing 50% YES responses should therefore also vary. In other words, the psychometric functions themselves should change with the subject's criterion, and therefore no single all-encompassing threshold value can be derived (SideNote 1.18). Given that detection performance relies so heavily on the effects of nonsensory factors, the very concept of an immutable absolute threshold has become meaningless.

Signal intensity and detection sensitivity

According to SDT, there is a certain inherent sensitivity that applies to the operation of sensory systems. Human performance in detection experiments is governed by that sensitivity as well as various nonsensory factors. If the detectability of sensory events is

Table **1.5**

Payoff Conditions for Two Different SDT Experiments

Signal	Payment Conditions for a *YES* Response	
	Experiment 1	Experiment 2
Absent (false alarm)	−10¢	−50¢
Present (hit)	50¢	10¢
	Liberal criterion	Conservative criterion

Note. In the first experiment, hits are rewarded at a far greater level than the penalty for false alarms, leading to the adoption of a liberal criterion. In the second experiment, the penalty for false alarms is far greater than the reward for hits, leading to the adoption of a conservative criterion.

SideNote | **1.17**

An often-used example can serve to distinguish the relative effects of expectancy and motivation. A person who is in charge of observing a radarscope to detect enemy aircraft is highly motivated to ensure that a true signal does not go undetected because the cost for that failure is too high. Thus, we have an individual who will likely adopt a liberal criterion based on this factor alone. However, the likelihood of a signal actually appearing is quite small since enemy aircraft usually do not pop up too often. Therefore the criterion will tend to shift toward more conservative levels that will reduce the likelihood of a hit. Nevertheless, given the importance of signal detection (and the penalty for a miss), the probability for a hit is kept high and must be accompanied by a relatively high false alarm rate as well.

SideNote | **1.18**

Early psychophysicists were aware that biasing factors were present in their absolute and difference threshold experiments and that these factors could influence their data. One way to reduce bias was to use highly trained subjects who could be relied upon to make accurate detection judgments. Another technique was the use of so-called *catch trials*, in which no stimulus was present. The false alarm rate taken from these trials was then used to scale the data from stimulus-containing trials.

susceptible to higher-level mental functions that influence our judgments, then how is it possible to gather insight into detection sensitivity that is uncontaminated by such factors? To answer this, we have to take a closer look at the noise and the signal + noise distributions in relation to each other.

Thus far we have said very little about the stimulus itself and have vaguely referred to it as a weak signal that is added to noise and whose detectability is assessed by way of a simple "YES–NO" experiment. The signal + noise distribution that we have become familiar with is actually a reflection of two different parameters—signal intensity and detection sensitivity. To understand this, let us consider three different stimuli, each one being of a progressively greater intensity. The signal + noise distribution of each stimulus progressively shifts farther away from the noise distribution, which does not change because the underlying effects (e.g., random noise in the nervous system) are not disturbed. This is shown in Figure 1.12 where the separation between the two distributions is quite small in

the top panel (weak stimulus) and very large in the bottom one (strong stimulus). A measure of the separation between the two distributions is taken at their peaks and is denoted as **d'** (pronounced *d-prime*) (Swets, 1996).

The three pairs of distributions in Figure 1.12 can be interpreted another way. Let us assume that the signal is now kept constant and instead three different individuals are being tested, each one having a different inherent sensitivity to the stimulus. The more sensitive a person is to this particular stimulus, the greater the sensation evoked by that stimulus. Since the signal + noise distribution is a probability plot of sensory magnitudes, a highly sensitive individual will have a distribution shifted farther to the right and away from the noise distribution, as shown in the bottom panel of Figure 1.12. In other words, the same stimulus will generate greater sensory magnitudes in a more sensitive person and therefore produce a more rightward shifted signal + noise distribution. In this context, a large d' value is taken to represent an individual with a high detection sensitivity. The less sensitive the subject is to

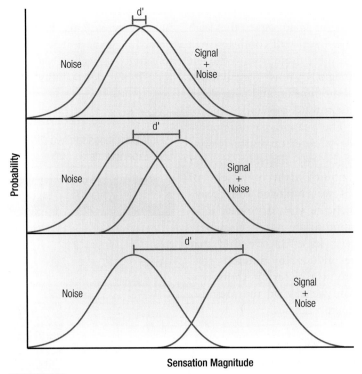

Figure 1.12

The relative positions of the noise and signal + noise distributions are determined by signal intensity and detection sensitivity. The signal + noise distribution is progressively shifted to the right and away from the noise distribution as signal strength increases. A similar effect is seen if the signal is kept constant but the detector becomes more sensitive. The relative separation of the two distributions is taken at their peaks and denoted as d'.

INVESTIGATION

Cognitive Factors That Influence Perception

We see cognitive factors at play all the time in our ability to perceive stimuli. In fact, two people can be in the same place experiencing the same stimuli yet perceive different things. For example, say you are driving with a friend and a dog runs out in the middle of the road. You as the driver are more likely to see the dog first and react accordingly. Why? (See SideNote 1.17 for some hints.)

the stimulus, the closer the two distributions will be with respect to each other, and accordingly d' will be smaller (Wickens, 2001).

Sensitivity and d'

The importance of d' is that it provides a numerical estimate of a person's sensitivity and therefore allows comparisons among different individuals. Unlike threshold values that can change with criterion levels, it has been shown that d' remains relatively robust and is unaffected by nonsensory factors. In other words, d' as a measure of sensitivity simply stipulates the relative separation of the noise and the signal + noise distributions. The different criterion

levels can operate independently upon these distributions to produce different experimental outcomes of hit and false alarm rates. This idea is illustrated in Figure 1.13 where four different pairs of noise/signal + noise distributions are shown, each with a different d' value ranging from 0.5 to 3.0 (SideNote 1.19). The accompanying ROC curves show the expected detection performance if we apply a continuously variable criterion to each of these sets of distributions.

As an example, let us consider the two extreme cases. If d' = 3.0, then the large separation of noise and signal + noise distributions will ensure that the hit rate far exceeds the

SideNote | **1.19**

By convention, d' is expressed as standard deviation units of the noise distribution. Thus, d' values of 0.5, 1.0, 3.0, etc., represent respective factors of standard deviation (or z-score).

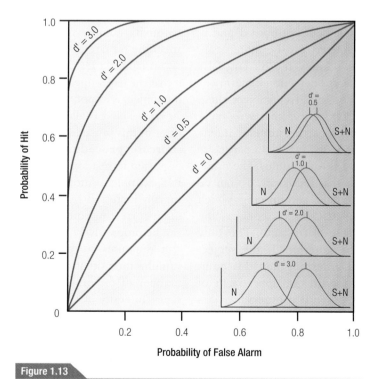

Figure 1.13

A family of ROC curves that are generated by different values of d'. The greater the sensitivity to a particular stimulus, the greater the separation of the noise and the signal + noise distributions. A large d' value produces an ROC curve that is bowed toward the upper left. As the two distributions get closer (smaller d' values), and eventually overlap, the ROC curve flattens out and becomes a straight line.

false alarm rate for moderate to liberal criterion levels (i.e., rightward criterion placement). The ROC curve will bow upward to reflect a far greater proportion of hits in comparison to false alarms. If however the two distributions are very close together (e.g., d' = 0.5), then there will be a greater similarity in hit and false alarm rates because of the closeness of the two distributions. This situation will produce a weakly bowed ROC curve. Thus, as the noise/signal + noise distributions approach each other, the ROC curves will progressively flatten out. The limit is reached when the two distributions overlap each other (i.e., d' = 0) and produce a straight line. In this case, either there is no signal or the subject is simply incapable of detecting the stimulus. In either event, detection performance will be random, and there will be equal probabilities of hits and false alarms regardless of the criterion.

Procedural aspects

SDT has become highly popular among perceptual psychologists because it provides both an estimate of the relative sensitivities of different individuals to a particular stimulus and a measure of how nonsensory factors may influence the judgments of various subjects in its detection. The purpose in any SDT experiment therefore is to obtain values of both d' and ß. Both of these parameters can be quite easily determined once we know the hit and false alarm rates from a signal detection experiment (McNicol, 2004). For any given subject, there will be only one ROC curve that will apply in that experiment since the stimulus intensity is fixed and the individual has a particular inherent sensitivity to that stimulus. The numerical descriptor of that sensitivity, d', can be obtained by graphically determining which one of a family of ROC curves contains the subject's hit and false alarm rates. The only variable now is the criterion. If the subject employed a liberal criterion, then this point would be located toward the upper right of that particular ROC curve. If a conservative criterion was employed, then this point would be

toward the lower left. We can obtain a measure of the criterion used by the subject because all possible points will map onto a single ROC curve that in turn will be governed by that person's detection sensitivity.

SDT provides insight not only into the intrinsic sensitivity of the sensory system but also into the motives, expectancies, and other human psychological factors that influence the decision-making process (Macmillan & Creelman, 2004). However, there may be situations where a sensitivity measure is required without the influence of such nonsensory factors. In such cases, the use of forced choice procedures allows rapid estimation of only the sensitivity parameter. In the **two-alternative forced choice (2AFC)** procedure, two presentations are made on each trial. The subject is told that one of the presentations will contain the signal and the other will not. The task is to indicate which presentation contained the signal. The impact of criterion effects is minimized because the subject knows that one of the two presentations will definitely contain a stimulus. The only experimental outcome to consider then is the hit rate, which can fluctuate between 0.5 (random guessing) to 1.0 (perfect performance). The proportion of correct responses can then be used as a measure of sensitivity because nonsensory factors do not affect the hit rate in this situation.

A valuable feature of the 2AFC procedure is that the experimenter knows whether or not the subject is responding correctly in a particular trial. This has allowed more elaborate versions of this procedure to be developed. In the **staircase procedure**, the stimulus level can be varied in relation to the subject's responses. For example, stimulus intensity may be continually increased as long as the subject is making incorrect responses. Similarly, the intensity can be progressively decreased when only correct responses are given. This alternation in stimulus intensity is continued until a specified number of response reversals take place. The signal intensity at this point can be used as a measure of sensitivity.

Summary

1. There is a rich history of scientific research on sensory perception, beginning with the German psychophysicists of the 19th century. Their goal was to arrive at a quantitative relationship between stimulus intensities and sensation magnitudes. Knowing the quantitative relationship has several advantages, though it is difficult to obtain directly because of our inability to measure sensation. The approach taken by the German scientists was to first obtain two parameters—the starting point and the slope of the function. This information could then be used to reveal the nature of the mathematical relationship between stimulus and sensation.

2. Fechner developed several psychophysical techniques to determine the absolute threshold (which represents the starting point of the stimulus–sensation relationship) and the difference threshold (which provides insight into how the slope of the stimulus–sensation function changes at suprathreshold levels). The Method of Constant Stimuli provides the most accurate data, whereas the Method of Adjustment is the easiest to conduct and produces the fastest results. Psychophysical experiments with these techniques have shown that humans do not behave as ideal detectors but instead show a gradual progression of responsiveness when increasing some physical parameter related to the stimulus.

3. Weber was interested in the gradation of sensory experience by studying how the difference threshold itself varied with the stimulus level. He found that the difference threshold is not constant but actually increases linearly with stimulus intensity (known as *Weber's law*). To derive the stimulus–sensation relationship, Fechner made the assumption that a detectable change in sensation (ΔS) caused by the difference threshold (ΔI) remained constant at all levels of sensory magnitude. This insight, in conjunction with Weber's law, led Fechner to postulate that sensation magnitude is related to stimulus intensity by way of a logarithmic function (known as *Fechner's law*).

4. The era of modern psychophysics began with Stevens who believed that sensory magnitudes could be directly determined through quantitative methods. His technique of magnitude estimation led him to establish the *power law*, which states that sensory magnitude is related to stimulus intensity raised to an exponent value that is generally less than 1.0, though some sensory experiences (e.g., electric shock) have an exponent greater than 1.0.

5. Psychophysical techniques can be used to determine quantitative relationships within the same sensory system (intramodal matching) or across sensory systems (cross-modality matching). Whereas techniques such as magnitude estimation can be used to assess sensations that have a direct relationship to the stimulus (prothetic sensations), a different set of techniques such as *multi-dimensional scaling* must be used to assess those sensations that are entirely altered when a stimulus parameter is changed (metathetic sensations).

6. The same psychophysical principles and techniques used to understand sensory perception can also be used to assess various nonsensory questions in the domains of economics, marketing, sociology, and politics. A power law function is derived in all cases where the exponent value provides insight into the underlying relationship between the variables being probed.

7. Signal detection theory (SDT) is based on statistical concepts that examine the possible relationships between the stimulus (signal) and the underlying noise. The probability distributions of the signal and signal + noise profiles provide the basis for estimating the behaviour of individuals in terms of their criterion level, expectation, and motivation in a psychophysical setting. The way in which noise and signal + noise can affect detection performance is given by the *receiver operating characteristic* (ROC) curve. SDT experiments have shown that there is no exact threshold value for any sensory parameter but rather the threshold is something that is affected by other nonsensory parameters. Consequently, a more reliable parameter is d', which provides a more robust numerical estimate of a person's sensitivity that is unaffected by nonsensory factors.

Key Terms

Recall Questions

1. What are the three principal advantages of obtaining a mathematical relationship between stimulus intensity and the resulting sensation magnitude?

2. What are the parameters that prevent human subjects from behaving as ideal detectors?

3. What is the difference between the *absolute threshold* and the *difference threshold*? Why did Weber have to undertake multiple experiments on the difference threshold to derive the law that bears his name?

4. What was the fundamental problem in Fechner's assumption on the constancy of the JND at all sensory magnitudes? Could Fechner have derived his law without this assumption?

5. How did modern psychophysics depart from classical psychophysics in terms of both its methodology and its core underlying principle?

6. What is the fundamental difference between a prothetic and a metathetic sensation? Provide some examples other than the ones discussed in this chapter.

7. What would Weber's law have to look like for the stimulus–sensation function to have an exponential profile?

8. How does Ekman's law differ from the assumption of JND constancy made by Fechner? Is it possible to verify Ekman's law with absolute certainty?

9. What are the key departures in the *signal detection theory* model from the concept of an all-or-none threshold? What are the different variables that can affect the threshold? What is the advantage of using d' as a measure of sensitivity?

Further Reading

- Borg, I., & Groenen, P. (2005). *Modern multidimensional scaling: Theory and applications*. New York, NY: Springer.

- Gescheider, G. A. (1997). *Psychophysics: The fundamentals*. Hillsdale, NJ: Lawrence Erlbaum.

- Green, D. M., & Swets, J. A. (1989). *Signal detection theory and psychophysics*. New York, NY: Peninsula Publishing.

- Heidelberger, M., & Klohr, C. (2004). *Nature from within: Gustav Theodor Fechner and his psychophysical worldview*. Pittsburgh, PA: University of Pittsburgh Press.

- Marks, L. E. (1974). *Sensory processes: The new psychophysics*. New York, NY: Academic Press.

- McNicol, D. (2004). *A primer of signal detection theory*. Hillsdale, NJ: Lawrence Erlbaum.

- Richardson, R. D. (2007). *William James: In the maelstrom of American Modernism*. New York, NY: Mariner Books.

- Stevens, S. S. (1986). *Psychophysic: Introduction to its perceptual, neural, and social prospects*. New Brunswick, NJ: Transaction Publishers.

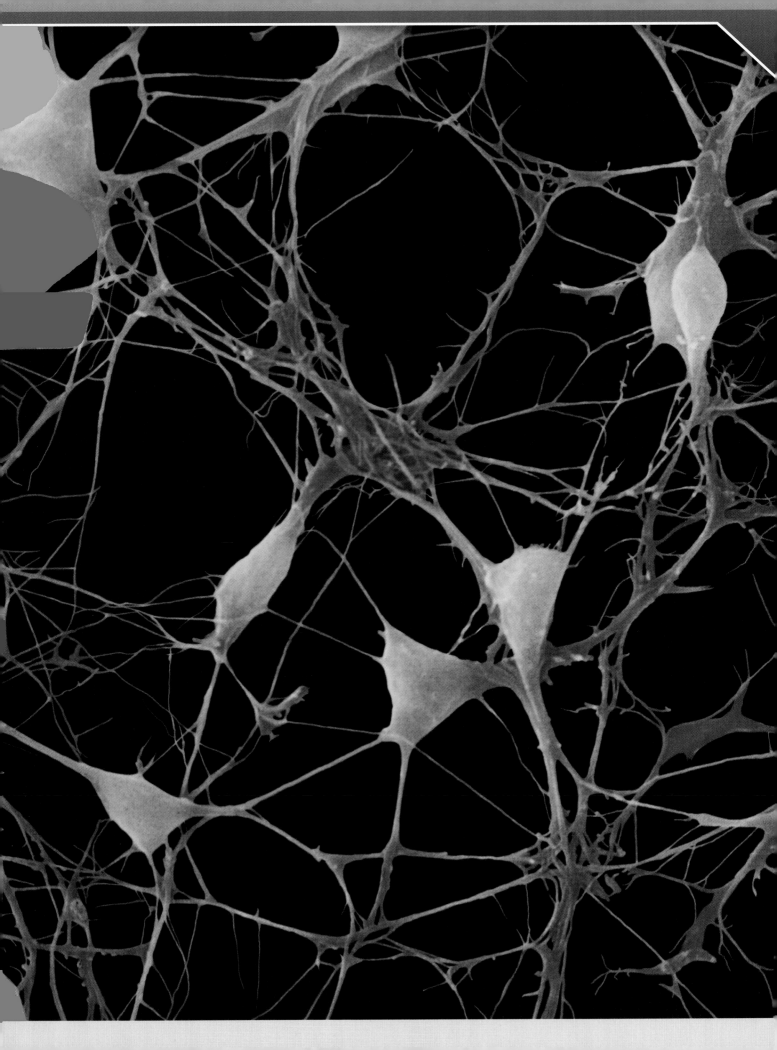

Biological Foundations of Sensory Perception

2

In this chapter . . .

- You will learn about the early work that went into exploring the organization of the nervous system, from Franz Joseph Gall and the study of phrenology to electrical stimulation of animal brains and the study of clinical cases. You will discover that the brain usually operates through two or more parallel pathways that process and transmit different aspects of sensory function.

- You will explore the different divisions of the nervous system, from gross differences such as the division between the central nervous system and the peripheral nervous system to smaller anatomical ones that were used as architectural criteria to help researchers demarcate over 50 discrete regions of the cerebral cortex.

- You will discover that there are many different types of cells, but you will learn about the neuron in particular and how this type of cell is responsible for all of the brain's operations, leading to perceptual awareness. You will come to understand both the structural details of neurons as well as various aspects of their function. You will study how neurons utilize ions such as Na^+ and K^+ to create a membrane potential, and how the changing nature of that membrane potential is responsible for all aspects of neurological function, from moving muscles to thinking.

- You will learn how neurons communicate with each other through a hierarchical series of brain structures. In particular, the notion that neurons operate as a local decision-making unit will be reinforced through the concept of excitatory and inhibitory transmission by way of specialized chemicals that migrate across the synapse from one neuron to another.

- You will become familiar with the different technologies used to study brain functioning such as single-unit recordings, EEG, fMRI, and PET.

A scanning electron micrograph of cortical neurons.
Photo: PHOTOTAKE Inc./Alamy

A ORGANIZATION OF THE NERVOUS SYSTEM
1. Functional Specialization—History
2. Functional Specialization—Modern Views
3. The Central Nervous System
4. General Principles of Sensory Processing

B BRAIN FUNCTION AT THE CELLULAR LEVEL
1. Brain Cells—Neurons
2. Brain Cells—Glia
3. Electrical Activity in Neurons
4. Signal Transmission between Neurons
5. General Principles of Sensory Coding

C TECHNIQUES FOR STUDYING BRAIN FUNCTION
1. Electrophysiology
2. Functional Brain Imaging

You, your joys and your sorrows, your memories and your ambitions, your sense of personal identity and free will, are in fact no more than the behaviour of a vast assembly of nerve cells.

—Francis Crick

SideNote 2.1

Two alternative views on the role of the brain from the early Greeks:

> And of course, the brain is not responsible for any of the sensations at all. The correct view is that the seat and source of sensation is the region of the heart.
>
> Aristotle

> Men ought to know that from nothing else but the brain come joys, delights, laughter and sports, and sorrows, griefs, despondency, and lamentations.
>
> Hippocrates

SideNote 2.2

Phenomenology is a 20th-century philosophical movement that was dedicated to descriptions of events and experiences without any reference to theory or basis in experimentation. Founded by German philosopher Edmund Husserl, phenomenology attempted to use pure description in deciphering the mind. French existentialist Jean-Paul Sartre pursued this notion and applied it to the study of consciousness.

Franz Joseph Gall (1758–1828)
© The Print Collector/Alamy

The quotation above from one of the greatest biologists of the 20th century serves as a powerful reminder that some of the most awe-inspiring facets of human existence occur within three pounds of jelly-like matter that we carry inside our head. All functions of the mind, sensory perception included, take place in the brain. To pursue an understanding of perception, we must therefore know something about the brain itself—how it is organized, what elements act as its building blocks, how sensory signals are transmitted, and what tricks the brain uses to encode and decode sensory information. Our current understanding of brain function is far from complete, although we have come a long way since the Greek philosophers who debated whether the brain was responsible for perceptual function at all (SideNote 2.1). Indeed, there is still so much left to learn about the brain that our accumulated knowledge thus far is trivial compared to what remains to be uncovered. This human aspiration has spawned the exciting field of neuroscience, which embraces research that spans from molecules to behaviour, to further advance our understanding of brain function.

In the chapters that follow, we will cover each of the sensory domains from two perspectives—the neural mechanisms that are involved in mediating that particular sensory process and the behavioural phenomena that are produced as a result. A discussion of any sensory process in the absence of a neural or brain-based foundation would be rather unsatisfying since it would deprive us of a mechanistic account and provide nothing more than a phenomenological treatment (SideNote 2.2). A discussion of sensory perception must therefore be woven with the known biological mechanisms that are involved. The fundamentals of brain function will be covered in this chapter to set the stage for that discussion throughout this book.

A. Organization of the Nervous System

The brain is responsible for a large range of functions, from the simplest motor acts that we routinely execute to the ethereal thing that we experience as consciousness. There has been considerable debate in recent history on how the human brain is organized to carry out those functions. Two dominant themes have emerged in the course of this debate over the past 150 years. One of the earliest views of brain organization came from 18th-century Austrian physician Franz Joseph Gall, who proposed that all mental functions can be precisely localized to certain parts of the brain (Zeki, 1993). And thus began the first of many contentious interchanges among his contemporaries between two fundamentally different ideas—that the brain is a heterogeneous collection of functionally specialized structures (or areas) and the opposing view of the brain as a homogeneous organ in which the various functions of the mind are diffuse and synergistic.

1. FUNCTIONAL SPECIALIZATION—HISTORY

Gall proposed that the human brain was divided into precise anatomical modules, each of them responsible for different mental functions. These functions varied from the most basic perceptions to the highest levels of human behaviour: for example, generosity, spirituality, and self-esteem. Nearly three dozen such faculties were postulated by Gall to occupy certain defined locations on the surface of the brain, as shown in Figure 2.1. The actual locations were largely identified through inference after carefully studying friends and associates and correlating their behavioural characteristics to the external features of the skull. Gall believed that bumps and depressions on the skull were related to the underlying brain matter. If an individual was blessed with a large measure of a certain faculty or attribute, then that part of the brain was believed to be well developed, and this in turn produced a bump on the skull. Thus, a new field called **phrenology** was born in which behavioural characteristics could be assessed by external landmarks on the skull.

Although phrenology could not survive even the most elementary levels of scientific rigour, Gall was nevertheless successful in stimulating much thinking and experimentation on the question of functional specialization in the brain. These efforts came in two forms—brain **lesion studies** in animals followed by behavioural analysis and the study of clinical cases in humans who suffered some form of brain damage (Finger, 1994). One of Gall's earliest critics was French physiologist Pierre Flourens, who performed localized brain lesions in rabbits and pigeons. Although Flourens was able to disrupt certain motor functions, he was unable to find deficits in more elaborate forms

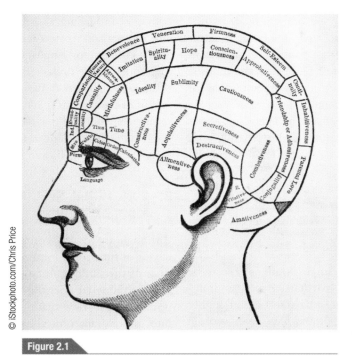

© iStockphoto.com/Chris Price

Figure 2.1

The phrenological map showing locations on the surface of the brain where certain human faculties and emotions were thought to reside.

of behaviour. He concluded that there was no localization of function and that injury to any one part of the brain affects all higher functions equally rather than selectively. This idea became quite popular at the time because of prevailing philosophical trends that viewed the mind as something so special that its functions could not simply be broken down and processed by discrete biological modules.

Clinical and experimental studies in the 19th century

The doctrine of functional specialization began to take shape again by the middle of the 19th century, largely as the result of several very convincing clinical studies on human patients. French neurologist Pierre Paul Broca became interested in a patient who had lost the ability to speak, a condition known as **aphasia** (Kandel, Schwartz, & Jessell, 2000). The patient, who became known in the hospital as *Tan*, because that was all he could utter, was able to understand language and even had normal motor function of the mouth and tongue. However, he could not speak grammatically or even express ideas in writing. After Tan's death in 1861, Broca discovered a lesion in the frontal part of the brain that was only present in the left cerebral hemisphere. Similar postmortem findings from other aphasic patients led Broca to proclaim that this discrete part of the brain,

now known as *Broca's area*, is responsible for the production of speech (SideNote 2.3).

The idea that speech production can be localized to a distinct part of the brain, and even then to only one of the hemispheres, came as a jolt to brain scientists in the 19th century. As convincing as Broca's studies were, his findings still failed to convince many contemporary scientists who continued to support the view of a functionally unitary brain (SideNote 2.4). However, soon after Broca published his results in 1861, other clinical and experimental findings that provided further evidence for functional localization quickly followed (Grodzinsky & Santi, 2008). It was shown, for example, that electrical stimulation of certain discrete regions in one cerebral hemisphere of dogs produced limb movements on the opposite side and that very precise movements could be localized to distinct parts of the brain. German neurologist Carl Wernicke also showed that a lesion in the posterior part of the left hemisphere, now known as *Wernicke's area*, produced a different kind of aphasia in which the ability to understand speech was impaired, but the ability to speak remained unaffected (Kandel et al., 2000).

Wernicke came up with a theory that sought to compromise the two opposing views by taking into account the accumulated evidence on functional specialization and blending

SideNote 2.3

One of the most famous principles in neuroscience was expressed by Broca in 1864: "Nous parlons avec l'hémisphere gauche!" ("We speak with the left hemisphere!").

Pierre Paul Broca (1824–1880)
© INTERFOTO/Alamy

SideNote 2.4

Broca's critics argued that the frontal part of the monkey brain shows many similarities to that of humans, and yet monkeys are incapable of a language faculty. Clinical examples were also cited. In one case, in a fit of rage, a man dealt such a severe blow to his wife's head that a significant part of her frontal brain was damaged, and yet she was able to hurl one last verbal insult at him before dying (Zeki, 1993).

it with the idea that mental functions are homogeneously distributed across the brain. He proposed that simple sensory and motor functions are localized to discrete brain areas but that the interaction of these modules is responsible for producing more complex aspects of perception, action, and behaviour. Language serves as an excellent example of this scheme, with one area (Broca's) responsible for the articulation of speech sounds and another (Wernicke's) responsible for speech comprehension. As we shall see later, our current view of brain function is very similar to Wernicke's theory.

The remarkable case of Phineas Gage

The idea that no single brain area can be responsible for a particular mental function, especially those characteristic of higher forms of behaviour, should have been rejected in 1848, after a strange accident in Vermont. The foreman of a railway construction crew, Phineas Gage, was preparing a rail bed with a tapered crowbar-like tool (Macmillan, 2002). While tamping down the blasting powder with this tool, Gage accidentally sparked an explosion. The iron rod flew out of his hand, entered just under his left cheekbone, and took out his left eye on its way through the brain and out the top of his skull. Remarkably, Gage was not killed, and after a brief loss of consciousness, he actually got up and spoke. His physical recovery was nearly complete after several months, upon which he was ready to return to work. However, a profound change had taken place in Gage's personality. He had been transformed from a diligent, good-humoured, and well-liked individual to a lazy, profane, ill-mannered liar. He eventually lost his family and friends and died 12 years later in an epileptic fit.

The case of Phineas Gage was widely used at the time to argue against functional localization. Because Gage was mentally functional despite having a large chunk of his brain destroyed, his case was taken not only as evidence against localization but also against the connection of Broca's area with aphasia, since much of the damage was to the frontal lobe. However, the severe personality changes that Gage experienced were not widely known, and his physician's attempts to argue the case for brain localization of social behaviour were soundly rejected. It was not until the recent application of modern scientific tools that the precise nature of Gage's injuries could be determined (SideNote 2.5). An autopsy on Gage's preserved skull, combined with computer modelling, showed that the tamping rod had actually spared regions of the frontal lobe necessary for language and instead damaged much of the underbelly of the frontal lobe (Damasio et al., 1994). We now know that this region of the brain is indeed critical for human social behaviour and that damage to it produces personality changes similar to those that affected Gage (Squire, Berg, Bloom, & du Lac, 2008).

2. FUNCTIONAL SPECIALIZATION— MODERN VIEWS

Although there was compelling evidence in favour of functional localization by the beginning of the 20th century, there still remained a few influential scientists who simply could not accept the view that the brain was divided into discrete anatomical and functional areas. Such dissenting views, however, did not persist due to rapid developments in technology for studying the brain. Advances in **histology** produced a better understanding of brain structure at the microscopic level. Neuroanatomists began to look at the human brain in terms of anatomical divisions defined largely on the basis of differences in fine structure and organization at the cellular level. Further progress came from refinements in electrical recording and stimulation techniques that brought about many new insights into how individual parts of the brain were engaged in different kinds of sensory, and even cognitive, operations.

Localization of functions in the human brain

The first definitive studies in functional localization were conducted by Canadian neurosurgeon Wilder Penfield in the 1950s. Penfield used electrodes to stimulate the brains of patients undergoing surgery for relief of epileptic seizures (Penfield, 1958). In most cases, these patients were operated on under local anesthesia only and therefore remained awake throughout the surgery. It turns out that brain tissue itself does not generate any feelings of sensation or pain when it is physically manipulated or damaged. Penfield stimulated the brain directly by passing small amounts of electrical current through electrodes and observed the effects, often through verbal responses from the patients. Through a series of landmark studies, Penfield confirmed many of the localization features of the human brain, including the distinctive language capabilities of Broca's and Wernicke's areas.

SideNote | **2.5**

Computer modelling of autopsy results on Phineas Gage's skull revealed the trajectory of the tamping iron.

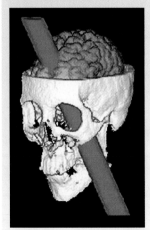

From H. Damasio, T. Grabowski, R. Frank, A.M. Galaburda & A.R. Damasio (1994). "The return of Phineas Gage: clues about the brain from a famous patient." *Science*, 264, 1102–1105. Dornsife Neuroscience Imaging Center and Brain and Creativity Institute, University of Southern California.

Current approaches to the study of brain localization rely on the use of sophisticated instruments that can actually image the living brain in action. In much the same way that X-rays provide a snapshot of the underlying anatomy, these instruments are able to provide pictures of discrete anatomical sites in the brain that are active during a particular sensory, motor, or cognitive task (Friston, 2002). We will return to how these machines work in Section C and discuss some of the remarkable advances that have been made through their use. The bottom line is that the brain is indeed functionally subdivided into areas, regions, or modules that are specialized for certain types of function. This does not mean that each mental function is exclusively localized to one particular brain area or that there is no distribution of processing to include other brain areas. Much effort is currently under way to fully understand how the brain is organized to carry out various functions—a field of inquiry that has come to be known as **functional anatomy**.

Parallel processing

Despite all of the evidence that clearly pointed to functional localization, there is still the nagging problem of why it was not so apparent in earlier studies and why the opposite view of homogeneity persisted for so long. The reason is due to one of the fundamental organizational principles of the brain—**parallelism**. A large number of mental functions are simultaneously processed along two or more pathways, each having their own set of dedicated anatomical modules (Bear, Connors, & Paradiso, 2006; Kandel et al., 2000). Thus, damage to one pathway, while sparing the other, may produce only marginal effects on behaviour. Furthermore, the surviving pathways almost invariably take over some of the functions that the other pathway served, making behavioural deficits even less noticeable and obscuring the evidence for functional localization.

Parallel processing pathways are especially prominent in the visual, auditory, and **somatosensory** systems (Mountcastle, 1998). The transformation of physical input into neural signals in these systems can occur through different types of receptors, with each having its own transmission pathway to the brain. Thus, the very notion of parallelism as a basic feature of brain organization arises at the earliest points in sensory processing. Once information reaches the cerebral cortex, it can travel along multiple cortical pathways, reaching different sites, with each making its own contribution to decoding and interpreting the signals. Damage to any one of the functional modules at the higher end of this chain will impair function to a certain extent, depending on the precise nature of its contribution, but it will not lead to total and unrecoverable sensory loss. Brain organization based on modularity and parallelism produces a division of labour and allows different aspects of a complex stimulus to be processed separately.

Brain lateralization

Another reason why it was difficult to observe functional deficits in many of the early lesion studies is that the brain allocates many functions across two cerebral hemispheres. As we have already seen, there are certain notable exceptions—language comprehension and speech production among them—where one hemisphere dominates. Nevertheless, the broad distribution of many mental functions across the two hemispheres means that a localized injury to one of them will be of limited consequence because the same site in the opposite hemisphere may still be active and remain functional.

The fact that cerebral function is the product of two separate hemispheres has fascinated anatomists, clinicians, and philosophers for several centuries. Sixteenth-century descriptions of the brain by anatomist Andreas Vesalius (Figure 2.2) stimulated much later thinking on how different aspects of our very

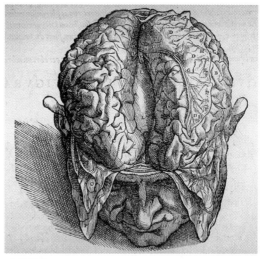

Image from the History of Medicine (NLM)

Figure 2.2

Anterior view of the two cerebral hemispheres, as illustrated by Andreas Vesalius in *De humani corporis fabrica libri septem* (1543).

being are coordinated by the two halves of the brain (Kinsbourne, 1978). We have come to know that despite their similarities, there are certain differences in the functionality of the two hemispheres (Christman, 1997). To begin with, in most individuals, the left hemisphere is actually larger; it is also specialized for handedness along with speech. Even higher-level functions, such as mood and emotion, are thought to have different degrees of representation in the two halves of the brain (Springer & Deutsch, 1998). This kind of representational or functional difference between the two hemispheres is known as cerebral or hemispheric **lateralization**. New techniques in brain mapping along with standard psychophysical methods are now being applied to further understand how each hemisphere is specialized for different functions. Of particular interest are questions on how cerebral functions are coordinated between the two halves, the role that handedness plays in hemispheric specialization, and how gender can affect differences in lateralization (Witelson, 1976).

3. THE CENTRAL NERVOUS SYSTEM

We now turn to the actual details of how the brain is anatomically organized and the roles played by some of the brain structures in processing sensory function. All sensory processes take place in the nervous system, which itself is broken down into two major divisions—the **central nervous system (CNS)** and the **peripheral nervous system**. The CNS is composed of the brain and spinal cord and can be subdivided into a number of components, which are discussed in the remainder of this section.

Cerebrum

Together, the two cerebral hemispheres make up the largest component of the brain. The **cerebrum** is broadly divided into four anatomical regions, or lobes, that are named after the overlying bones of the skull. The occipital lobe is located at the very back of the head; the temporal lobe, along the sides (behind the temples); the parietal lobe, along the top middle portion; and the frontal lobe, at the front (behind the forehead). Each of the lobes is involved in carrying out a certain set of sensory and cognitive functions, a partial list of which is given in Table 2.1.

If we dissected the cerebrum, we would find certain regions to be either white or grey (Kandel et al., 2000; Purves, 2007). The so-called *white matter* forms much of the bulk within the cerebral interior and is composed of fibres that interconnect various brain areas. The *grey matter*, on the other hand, is the actual collection of cells responsible for processing sensory, motor, and cognitive functions. There are large tracts of grey matter within the interior portions of each cerebral hemisphere. These include the so-called *hippocampal formation*, *amygdala*, and *basal ganglia*. We will not discuss these structures in detail, but it is worth noting that they serve important functions in memory, emotion, and the control of movement. The largest amount of grey matter, however, is found within a 2 mm thin band of tissue that makes up the surface of the brain. It is here in the **cerebral cortex** that we will focus much of our attention in later chapters when we discuss the various sensory functions.

Cerebral cortex

When discussing the different functions of the lobes, as in Table 2.1, we are really referring to the operations that take place within the cerebral cortex in the associated parts of the brain. It is in the cortex that sensory inputs are biologically processed to ultimately produce the experience of perception. All sensory

Table **2.1**

A Partial List of Functions Attributed to Each of the Brain's Four Lobes

Lobe	Function
Frontal	Emotional response
	Expressive language
	Word associations
	Motor planning
	Judgments about future activities
	Social behaviour
Parietal	Touch perception
	Higher-order sensory areas
	Visual attention
	Integration of multiple senses
	Processing of spatial relationships
Temporal	Auditory perception
	Memory acquisition
	Processing of complex visual information
	Speech comprehension
	Emotional behaviour
Occipital	Visual perception

inputs first arrive into a primary cortical area. For example, the *primary visual cortex* located in the occipital lobe is the first cortical recipient of visual input, whereas the *primary auditory cortex* located in the temporal lobe similarly receives auditory input (Squire et al., 2008). From there, sensory signals are transmitted to higher-order areas that surround the primary areas. In this way, the sensory stimulus is processed in a sequentially more sophisticated way at later cortical sites.

Human evolution placed an increasing requirement on the brain for a greater processing capacity, a demand that could only be met by increasing its size. Although this occurred to a certain extent, ultimately it became difficult for the cranium to accommodate the increasing brain volume (SideNote 2.6). The solution to this problem

was for the cerebral cortex to become progressively more convoluted, or folded, so that the total surface area could increase within a relatively constant brain (and hence cranial) volume. This allowed the human brain, through its expanding cortex, to assume more complex sensory and cognitive functions.

The convolutions of the cerebral cortex form a very distinctive feature and stand out when the human brain is examined, as can be seen in Figure 2.3 (left side). Each groove (or **sulcus**) is accompanied by elevated regions on either side (also known as a **gyrus**). A number of sulci are especially prominent, not only because of their depth but also because they separate major divisions of the brain such as the cortical lobes. These include the lunate sulcus, the central sulcus, and the sylvian fissure (Figure 2.4, left side).

SideNote | **2.6**

Because of the relatively fixed size of the birth canal, the cranium could not simply keep expanding to keep up with the growing brain.

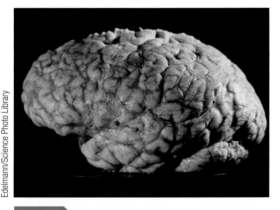
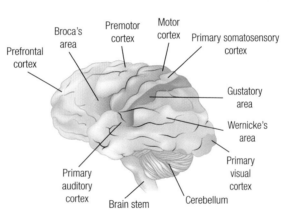

Edelmann/Science Photo Library

Figure 2.3

The cerebral cortex of the human brain is highly convoluted. The cortex itself is subdivided into modules that are functionally specialized (right).

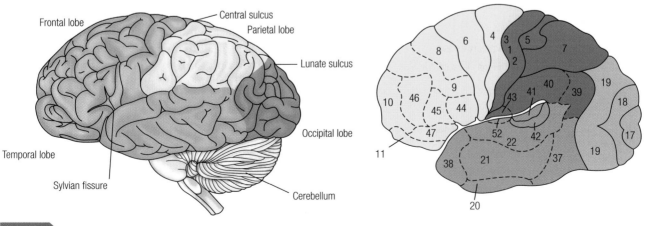

Figure 2.4

The human brain can be broadly divided into four lobes, with certain major grooves (sulci) serving as their borders (left). In 1909, Korbinian Brodmann proposed that the thin band of brain tissue known as the *cerebral cortex* can be further divided, using histological criteria, into 52 areas that are anatomically distinguishable (right).

A further division of the cerebral cortex can be considered on grounds of microscopic appearance. The cortex is not entirely homogeneous and therefore will not appear throughout its entirety to be identical in terms of structural criteria such as thickness, composition, and cellular distribution. The regional difference in cellular architecture, or **cytoarchitectonics**, led German neurologist Korbinian Brodmann to undertake a systematic examination of the entire human cortex in the early 1900s. He found that discrete areas of the cortex had a common cytoarchitectonic appearance that could be distinguished from neighbouring regions. Brodmann found a total of 52 such distinctive areas, now commonly referred to as Brodmann's areas (Figure 2.4, right) (Brodmann & Garey, 2005). Although these divisions were made on the basis of anatomical criteria, Brodmann suggested that each was functionally distinct as well. Table 2.2 contains a partial list of functions associated with various Brodmann areas.

Subcortical structures

A subcortical structure is composed of a collection of brain cells that reside below the cerebral cortex. In general, such formations are given the generic title **nucleus**, though

Table **2.2**

The Location of Sensory and Motor Areas within Brodmann's Classification Scheme

Sensory/Motor Modality	Brodmann's Area
Vision	
Primary cortex	17
Higher-level centres	18, 19, 20, 21, 37
Audition	
Primary cortex	41
Higher-level centres	22, 42
Touch	
Primary cortex	1, 2, 3
Higher-level centres	5, 7
Motor	
Primary cortex	4
Higher-level centres	6, 8
Speech	
Broca's area	44, 45
Wernicke's area	22

individual structures have very precise and elaborate names. An important subcortical structure in the transmission of sensory function is the thalamus. This large, paired structure has extensive connections with the cortex and is composed of a set of anatomically distinct nuclei, each serving different functions in the transmission of sensory and motor information to and from the cortex. Visual, auditory, and touch signals travel through the thalamus on the way to the cortex (Bear et al., 2006; Squire et al., 2008). Each of these sensory modalities projects to a particular thalamic nucleus, which in turn projects to a particular region of the cerebral cortex. (Figure 2.3, right side, shows some of the sensory cortical areas.)

Brain stem

The brain stem is a collective term given to three distinct areas that lie just below the brain and extend down to junction with the spinal cord (Kandel et al., 2000). The three brain stem areas, whose locations are shown in Figure 2.5, are referred to as the *midbrain*, *pons*, and *medulla*. A number of sensory and motor functions are associated with the brain stem, including signal transmission into and out of these structures through the so-called **cranial nerves**. Somatosensory information from the face, head, and neck, as well as auditory and taste signals, enter the brain through cranial nerves that are attached to the brain stem. The brain stem also contains networks of fibre pathways that carry sensory and motor signals to and from the brain.

Cerebellum

The cerebellum is a large, foliated structure that wraps around the brain stem (see Figure 2.5). A striking feature of the cerebellum is its high cellular density. In fact, it contains nearly one-half of all brain cells even though it accounts for only a 10th of the brain's volume. The cerebellum is highly connected with most parts of the brain. Its function is to coordinate and fine-tune motor signals. The cerebellum is not directly involved in sensory perception, although its various motor functions can have an indirect effect on sensory processing.

Spinal cord

The spinal cord is the lowermost component of the CNS, emerging from the base of the skull and extending along the vertebral column. The primary function of the spinal cord is to

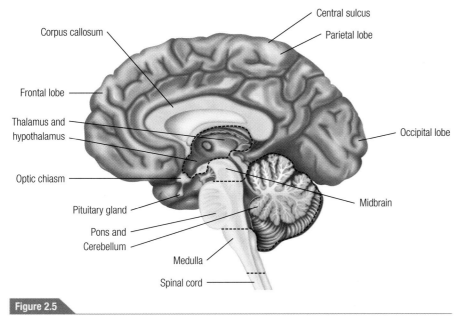

Corpus callosum

Central sulcus

Parietal lobe

Frontal lobe

Thalamus and
hypothalamus

Occipital lobe

Optic chiasm

Pituitary gland

Midbrain

Pons and
Cerebellum

Medulla

Spinal cord

Figure 2.5

A medial view of the right cerebral hemisphere showing its major structures and landmarks.

transmit sensory and motor information to and from the brain. Sensory signals from the skin, joints, and muscles of the trunk and limbs enter the spinal cord at segmented junctions. The signals are then transmitted to the brain through fibre tracts that span the entire length of the spinal cord. Similarly, motor signals from the brain are transmitted by a different set of fibre tracts within the spinal cord and emerge through spinal nerves to reach the muscles. A total of 31 pairs of spinal nerves are responsible for carrying both sensory and motor signals to and from the spinal cord and innervating the entire body below the neck. Although the spinal cord itself is a component of the central nervous system, the spinal nerves are considered to be part of the peripheral nervous system.

4. GENERAL PRINCIPLES OF SENSORY PROCESSING

We conclude this section on brain organization with some of the key principles that govern the operation of the nervous system. All sensory systems have common features in terms of how their inputs are processed. For example, sensory systems are generally responsible for extracting information on **modality**, location, intensity, and duration. The key difference, though, is that different sensory stimuli generate different perceptual experiences within us. As evident from our discussion above on functional specialization, the reason for the perceptual dissimilarity lies in the fact that different pathways are

activated by each sensory modality, which in turn stimulates a different set of brain structures.

Sensory coding and modality representation

We are sensitive to different forms of energy that are available to us from our physical environment. Five major sensory modalities have evolved in humans that are capable of capturing the energy present in mechanical (touch), chemical (taste and smell), sound (auditory), and light (visual) stimuli. As early as 1826, German physiologist Johannes Müller proposed the idea that sensory signals from each of the modalities are transmitted by a specific set of nerve fibres. According to his *law of specific nerve energies*, different nerve fibres are dedicated to each sensory modality, and each in turn makes specific connections within the nervous system so that, ultimately, different centres in the brain are stimulated. As we have seen, the cerebral cortex is indeed parsed into major functional divisions that are responsible for processing the different sensory modalities. The separate perceptions we experience from each sensory modality are therefore the product of stimulation in certain dedicated parts of our physical brain. We *see* light only when certain parts of our brain become stimulated, *hear* sound only when other parts become stimulated, and so on (SideNote 2.7).

Multiple pathways, parallelism, and hierarchies

Sensory systems transmit signals through several anatomically distinct pathways. This

SideNote | **2.7**

What would happen if we could somehow reroute the nerve fibres that carry sensory signals to another part of the brain? For example, if visual fibres could somehow be connected to the auditory cortex, and auditory fibres, to the visual cortex, would we *hear* light or *see* sound?

multiplicity is evident not only in signal transmission from the sensory organ to the brain but also within the brain itself (Averbeck & Lee, 2004). The visual system, for example, has two dominant pathways that carry different aspects of visual information from the eyes to the brain. Multiple pathways are also found in the somatosensory, auditory, and motor systems.

As noted earlier, the multiple pathways within a given sensory system are parallel. This means that there are distinct fibre tracts that arise from functionally different receptors, which in turn are sensitive to different features of the stimulus. In general, at lower levels of the nervous system, parallel pathways function independently so that there is little mixing of signals from one pathway to the other. However, at higher levels within the cortex, signals from multiple pathways must be integrated so that a coherent perception is produced, one that encompasses all aspects of the sensory stimulus (Rousselet, Thorpe, & Fabre-Thorpe, 2004).

The different levels that we speak of within the nervous system arise because of a fundamental hierarchy in the brain's organizational structure. The receptor and associated fibres represent the lowest level, followed by relay structures in the thalamus, and thereafter by a sequence of specialized modules in the cerebral cortex. Parallel pathways arising from the receptor level are an important feature of this hierarchical scheme, allowing individual components at progressively higher cortical levels to maintain the functional identity that arose from earlier levels.

Topographic organization

The brain compartments that process sensory information have an orderly, or topographic, representation of the structure from which sensory signals originate. Consider the cortical representation (or map) of touch and related sensations from the entire body surface. This map is located on a gyrus just behind the central sulcus (see Figure 2.3). Here, the body parts are not represented in a haphazard manner but rather in a strict topographic fashion so that sensations arising from adjacent parts of the body will in turn stimulate adjacent parts of the cortex (Gattass et al., 2005; Kaas, 2005). This does not mean that all body parts will enjoy an equal representation. The brain allocates larger amounts of cortical tissue to certain parts of the body that have greater sensitivity to touch (e.g., lips, fingertips) than

others (e.g., back, legs, trunk). We will explore this so-called *somatotopic map* in greater detail in the next chapter.

Contralateral representation and control

One of the distinctive and puzzling features of brain organization is that of contralateral representation (Kinsbourne, 1978). Most of the sensory pathways are set up so that their fibres project to the opposite (or contralateral) side of the brain. This means that sensations arising on the right side of the body are processed by the left cerebral hemisphere, and vice versa. A similar crossover occurs in the motor system so that the signals that control muscles on a particular side arise from the motor cortex of the opposite hemisphere. The sensory and motor pathways cross over in the brain stem or spinal cord. The contralateral nature of central nervous system organization remains unexplained, though a number of interesting theories have been proposed (SideNote 2.8).

B. Brain Function at the Cellular Level

From our discussion above, we have come to know that the various functions of the nervous system are carried out by parallel systems that unite different brain structures. Thus far, we have spoken only of the brain in organizational terms that involved structures, systems, and connections. However, all of the brain's functions are ultimately coordinated by individual nerve cells, or *neurons* (SideNote 2.9). All complex aspects of human behaviour, perception included, are the result of concerted action and interaction among an incredibly large number of neurons. A further remarkable fact is that all neurons essentially display a similar set of properties (Shepherd, 1998). And yet a large collection of neurons—through a precise set of connections—are able to produce a diverse set of sensory, perceptual, and cognitive experiences.

The idea that neurons are the central functional unit of the nervous system was born in the late 1800s. However, it was not an easy birth. The cell theory—that all tissues and organs are made up of discrete cells—seemed not to apply to the brain because of its strange appearance where large, complex cell-like structures appeared to be embedded within a tangled matrix of fibres. Throughout the 19th

Camillo Golgi (1843–1926)
© INTERFOTO/Alamy

century, there was rapid progress in visualizing this fine structure of the brain, largely through advances in techniques for preparing and staining brain tissue for microscopic analysis (SideNote 2.10) (De Carlos & Borrell, 2007). The most important of these was a silver-based stain developed in Italy by Camillo Golgi. These developments, however, also led to the emergence of two opposite views about brain structure. Golgi was among those who believed that nerve cells were contained within a sort of reticular structure, one in which neurons somehow interacted with large networks of fibres that were independent entities, separate from the neurons themselves. The opposite view was that all fibres in the brain arise from neurons and therefore are an integral part of their structure and function within the nervous system.

In one of the more ironic twists in the history of science, it was the use of the Golgi stain itself by Spanish scientist Santiago Ramón y Cajal that was decisive in rejecting the reticular theory (Lopez-Munoz, Boya, & Alamo, 2006). Cajal had improved the Golgi stain, which was somewhat capricious and unreliable, and used it to show that the brain was really composed of an intricate network of discrete cells (Kruger & Otis, 2007). Furthermore, the diffuse fibres that had caused nearly a century of confusion were definitively shown to be associated with neurons. The unification of nerve fibres and nerve cells into a single anatomical unit gave birth to one of the major principles of modern biology—the **neuron doctrine**. Golgi's and Cajal's differing opinions boiled over into a memorable confrontation in Stockholm when they both went to receive the Nobel Prize in 1906 (SideNote 2.11) (Shepherd, 1991).

1. BRAIN CELLS—NEURONS

The wide acceptance of the neuron doctrine by the beginning of the 20th century was largely due to the efforts of Cajal and many other gifted scientists who by then had already compiled an impressive amount of information on the fine structure of the nervous system (Agnati et al., 2007). Although these anatomists had noted the presence of a large variety of neurons within different brain structures, it turned out that all neurons were basically similar in terms of their structural logic. We now regard a typical neuron as having four identifiable segments, as shown in Figure 2.6.

The components of a neuron

The cell body or soma is the metabolic centre of the neuron. It contains the nucleus and most of the cellular machinery for producing energy as well as the biochemical components necessary to keep the cell functional. The soma gives rise to two processes—the axon and the dendrites. A neuron usually has many dendrites that branch out in different directions. These processes are responsible for receiving inputs from other neurons and channelling that information to the soma. In contrast, all neurons have only a single axon that is responsible for carrying information away from the soma to other neurons. The axon is a very thin, tubular structure that in some cases can transmit information over very large distances. The axon ends into a set of terminals at its contact site with other neurons. Thus, information flow in all neurons takes place in a consistent manner, arising in the dendrites followed by transmission to the soma and then out through the axon to the next set of neurons.

Santiago Ramón y Cajal
(1852–1934)
© INTERFOTO/Alamy

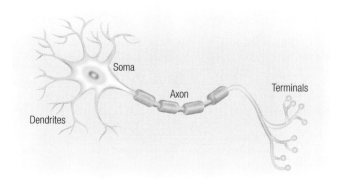

Figure 2.6

The main structural features of a neuron.

Cajal's laws

The unidirectional nature of information flow in neurons was first proposed by Cajal and is called the *law of dynamic polarization*. This principle has been found to apply to all neurons, regardless of the brain structure to which they belong. Thus, even though the physical appearance of neurons can vary quite a bit, information flow always occurs in a predictable direction. A second important idea proposed by Cajal is the *law of connectional specificity*. Here, Cajal used his exceptional histological skills to show that each neuron is a separate entity and that there is no physical continuity between one neuron and the next (Peters, 2007). Furthermore, the connections between neurons occur at specialized contact points in an extremely precise manner. Although at close inspection the brain appears to be a random meshwork of cells and processes, it is in reality a very precise and highly structured network of interconnected neurons. Despite wide variations in structure and layout, all neurons follow Cajal's laws.

Neuronal diversity

There is considerable variability in the physical appearance of neurons, as shown in Figure 2.7. It has been estimated that there are literally thousands of different types of neurons. The primary feature that distinguishes one neuron from another is the number and layout of the dendritic processes (Levitan & Kaczmarek, 1997). Some neurons, such as Purkinje cells in the cerebellum, have a large complex dendritic field, whereas others, such as the bipolar receptor neuron, have much simpler dendritic fields. In fact, **bipolar neurons** actually have a single dendrite, which may then arborize. Most types of cortical neurons, however, generally have multiple dendrites that emerge from the cell body. These are known as **multipolar neurons**.

Functional classification

A general feature of sensory processing among all animal species is that they receive sensory inputs, process that information, and generate a motor output when necessary (Squire et al., 2008). Neurons can be functionally classified into three major groups that reflect this organization. Sensory (afferent) neurons are triggered by stimuli of one form or another from the physical environment and transmit this information to the brain. There, a second general class of neurons, called **interneurons**, process the signals locally within a particular module or transmit the information to other

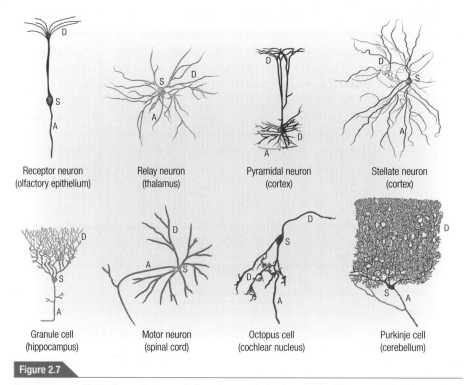

Receptor neuron (olfactory epithelium)   Relay neuron (thalamus)   Pyramidal neuron (cortex)   Stellate neuron (cortex)

Granule cell (hippocampus)   Motor neuron (spinal cord)   Octopus cell (cochlear nucleus)   Purkinje cell (cerebellum)

Figure 2.7

Neurons can be highly diverse in terms of size, shape, and structure. Each of these examples shows a true neuron in that it has a cell body or soma (S), a set of dendrites (D), and a single axon (A). In most cases, the distinguishing feature of each of these neurons arises from the number and layout of the dendritic processes.

brain sites. And finally, motor (efferent) neurons carry signals to the various muscles in the body so that a coordinated motor action can be taken in response to the sensory stimulus. Of these three classes, the interneurons make up the largest number and essentially account for all of the neuronal processing that occurs in the cerebral cortex.

2. BRAIN CELLS—GLIA

Glial cells, also called neuroglia, represent the other major cell type found in the brain (Kandel et al., 2000; Squire et al., 2008). Although glial cells outnumber neurons by 10–50 times, they receive far less attention largely because they are not directly involved in signal processing. Nevertheless, they serve important functions in the central and peripheral nervous systems. One type of glial cell provides structural support for neurons, whereas a second type is responsible for providing insulation to axons. The insulating material, known as **myelin**, gives axons the ability to conduct signals efficiently over large distances.

Glial cells provide support to neurons

A type of glial cell known as an **astrocyte** provides much of the brain's structural support and firmness. These cells are the most numerous among glia. They have an irregular appearance with many processes that can often extend for some distance (Figure 2.8A). Astrocytes act as a sort of glue that holds neurons together within a structural matrix. Astrocytes also play important roles in maintaining an adequate microenvironment for neurons by ensuring that electrolyte balance is maintained and that toxic substances are quickly removed. And finally, astrocytes make contact with small blood vessels, or capillaries, in the brain where they help to form a tight seal that is known as the *blood–brain barrier* (Figure 2.8B). This barrier serves a protective function by preventing toxic substances that may be circulating in the blood from easily entering the brain.

Glial cells provide insulation to neurons

The insulating material in the central nervous system is provided by glial cells known as **oligodendrocytes** (Figure 2.8C). These cells form a myelin sheath by wrapping their cell membranes around an axon several times in a spiral fashion to form a concentric layer. In peripheral nerves, a different type of glial cell, known as the **Schwann cell**, is responsible for producing the myelin sheath (Figure 2.8D). In all cases, the axon is the only neuronal structure that becomes myelinated. Myelination allows efficient conduction of neuronal signals over large distances. This may include transmission within the brain among different cortical areas or to the opposite cerebral hemisphere. In the peripheral nervous system, signal transmission over large distances can include muscle targets located at the extremities of the human body.

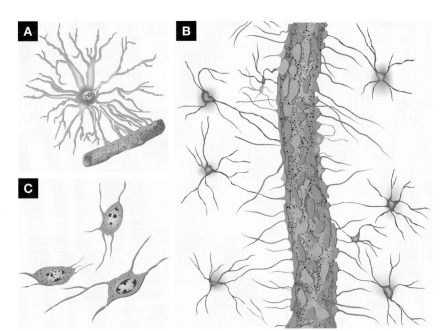

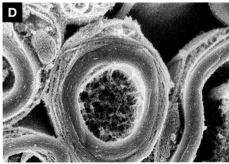

Figure 2.8

A. Schematic diagram of an astrocyte with its profusely branching processes. B. Many astrocytes interact with blood vessels to form a tight seal. This creates the so-called *blood–brain barrier*. C. Schematic diagram of an oligodendrocyte that myelinates axons in the CNS. D. Cross-section of an axon from a peripheral nerve showing its myelin sheath formed by a Schwann cell.

Photo D: DR DAVID FURNESS, KEELE UNIVERSITY/SCIENCE PHOTO LIBRARY

3. ELECTRICAL ACTIVITY IN NEURONS

So far, we have said nothing about the nature of the signals that the nervous system uses to process sensory information. In particular, we now need to know how sensory signals arise at the receptors in the first place and how those signals are propagated along neurons to reach the next site. These are the very core issues of neural function, to which we now turn for a closer examination.

One of the early triumphs of neuroscience research in the 20th century was discovering the exact details of signal processing by neurons. It became clear by the 1940s that information flow within the nervous system occurs through electrical and chemical signals (Purves, 2007). The electrical component in neurons is similar in principle to what we find in our homes, where charged electrons are rapidly conducted through a metal wire. The key difference is that the wires in the nervous system are biological elements, such as axons and dendrites, and the charged particles are ions rather than free electrons. To understand how biological electricity works, we need to first discuss some fundamental properties of neurons. It turns out though that the entire basis for electrical signalling in the brain begins with a feature that all cells in our body have in common—the membrane potential.

The membrane potential

The cell is a veritable storehouse of chemicals, from complex acids and proteins right down to simple charged atoms, or ions. Among the many ion species present within the cell, there are two that are of special importance—potassium (K^+) and sodium (Na^+). These two ions exert considerable influence on the electrical state of neurons (Kandel et al., 2000). We will return to these in a moment.

The story really begins with the more complex chemicals, such as organic acids and proteins, which are an integral part of the chemical machinery of a cell. Organic chemicals are largely negatively charged (**anions**) and only found inside the cells. Because of this concentration difference between the interior and exterior compartments, there is a strong tendency for the organic anions to leave the cell through simple **diffusion**. However, the cell membrane is impermeable to these large anions, and therefore the diffusion process cannot be completed, resulting in a buildup of negative charges on the inside of the cell membrane, as shown in Figure 2.9. This in turn attracts positive charges (**cations**) in the fluid surrounding the neuron (also known as *extracellular fluid*). The separation of positive and negative charges leads to a potential difference, or voltage, across the membrane. Although the actual voltage can vary among neurons, it is usually in the range of 55–85 millivolts (mV) and referred to as the resting **membrane potential** (Bear et al., 2006; Squire et al., 2008). This potential difference is specified as being *inside negative* by convention—that is, the inside of the cell is negative compared to the outside.

Next, we introduce K^+ (potassium) ions into the picture and impose two specific conditions. First, we place all of the K^+ inside the cell, and second, we actually allow these ions to move across the cell membrane. Just as with the organic anions, the concentration gradient will produce an immediate tendency for K^+ to diffuse out of the cell. Because these small ions are permitted to flow across the membrane, some will actually move to the extracellular compartment where they will cause a further buildup of positive charges. After a while, the movement of K^+ out of the cell becomes less favourable because the accumulation of positive charges will electrically repel these ions, and they will be drawn back into the cell. This process will also be favoured by the presence of the organic anions, which create an attractive negative environment inside the cell for the positively charged K^+ ions. Eventually an equilibrium point will be reached where the outward diffusive force will be balanced by the inward electrical force on K^+. The concentration values for K^+ at this equilibrium condition are such that most of the ions actually end up inside the cell (see Figure 2.9).

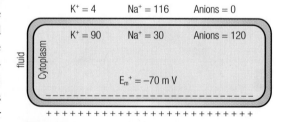

Figure 2.9

A model neuron showing the distribution of the major ions that contribute to electrical signalling. The fluid inside the neuron contains greater numbers of K^+ and organic anions compared to the exterior (extracellular) fluid. However, there are many more Na^+ ions outside the cell than inside.

And finally, we introduce Na⁺ (sodium) ions to this model neuron such that most of them are placed outside of the cell. Two forces will now act on these Na⁺ ions to drive them into the cell. The diffusive force will favour the movement of Na⁺ into the cell, given its far higher concentration in the extracellular fluid. Similarly, the potential difference across the membrane, with the inside being negative, will attract the positively charged Na⁺ ions into the cell as well. However, there is one important difference in this scenario. The cell membrane is only weakly permeable to Na⁺. As a result, very few of these ions will penetrate the membrane and gain entry into the cell, despite the combined diffusive and electrical forces that act on them, leaving the vast majority of Na⁺ ions in the extracellular fluid.

We have thus created a situation where there is an unequal distribution of ions on the inside and outside of the cell. The K⁺ ions are in a state of equilibrium, free to move inside and outside the cell, but they are retained largely within the cell because of the forces acting on them. The Na⁺ ions, on the other hand, have a strong preference to flow down the diffusive and electrical gradients and enter the cell but are prevented from doing so by the cell membrane. It turns out though that the cell membrane is not totally impermeable to Na⁺, and therefore a few of these ions will eventually gain entry into the cell. The question then is "How is the Na⁺ gradient shown in Figure 2.9 maintained over the long term and why does it not break down as more and more of these ions slowly get into the cell?"

Ion channels and membrane pumps

The flow of ions does not occur randomly over the cell surface but rather through selective channels that permit only a certain type of ion to move across the membrane. The channels are large protein structures that are embedded within the membrane and contain a pore through which the ion can flow into or out of the cell. The potassium channel shown in Figure 2.10 allows K⁺ ions to move freely across the membrane in either direction with little hindrance. The sodium channel, on the other hand, is much more restrictive and prevents a large influx of Na⁺ ions into the cell that would naturally occur given the forces acting on them. This is a critical feature of the sodium channel because it allows the cell to maintain a stable membrane potential. If Na⁺

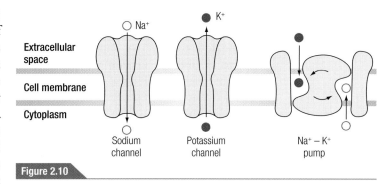

Figure 2.10

Ion channels in the cell membrane allow the passage of Na⁺ and K⁺ ions. The potassium channel is generally quite permeable, whereas the sodium channel is not. However, if a Na⁺ ion leaks into the cell then a K⁺ ion must leave. This effect is reversed by the sodium–potassium pump.

ions were allowed to flow freely into the cell, then the charge separation across the membrane would be altered, leading to a destabilization of the resting potential.

The sodium channel, however, is not absolutely impermeable and, as we noted before, actually allows a few Na⁺ ions to enter the cell. Each time a Na⁺ ion enters the cell, a K⁺ ion automatically leaves in order to maintain an overall charge balance. If this were permitted to continue, then we would have exactly the situation we want to prevent—a breakdown of the ionic difference between the inside and outside of the cell, which would in turn affect the resting potential. To prevent this, another protein structure within the membrane kicks in and actually grabs some Na⁺ ions and moves them out of the cell. This is the so-called **sodium–potassium pump**, and it works by actively ejecting Na⁺ ions out of the cell and bringing K⁺ ions back into the cell. Consequently, the ionic balance shown in Figure 2.9 is maintained and the resting membrane potential remains unaffected.

The action potential

The resting membrane potential is the result of a number of factors—the accumulation of organic anions inside the cell, the concentration gradient of specific ions across the membrane, the relative permeability of the cell membrane to these ions, and the action of the sodium–potassium pump to correct any deviations in the ionic balance should they occur. So far we have said nothing that is unique about neurons, and indeed, all of these descriptions fully apply to other cells in our body as well.

The unique feature of neurons and other excitable cells such as muscle is that the

SideNote | **2.12**

The sodium channel is said to be voltage-gated. At the resting membrane potential, it allows very few Na⁺ ions to go through. However, as the voltage changes with increased depolarization, the channel opens up. This dependence of permeability on voltage is not unique to this ion channel alone.

permeability of the cell membrane to specific ions can be momentarily altered. Let us consider the following. If we somehow allowed Na^+ ions to enter the neuron, then the membrane potential would very quickly change. Specifically, the entry of positively charged Na^+ ions into the neuron would alter the charge makeup across the membrane, making the inside a little bit more positive (or less negative) than before. When the membrane potential becomes more positive, the neuron is said to be **depolarized**. The greater the inward Na^+ flux, the more the neuron will be depolarized. The increasingly positive environment inside the neuron will in turn cause K^+ to leave in equal numbers. Recall that the cell membrane is quite permeable to K^+, and therefore this ion can relocate freely depending on the local forces. The outward K^+ flux will have the effect of *repolarizing* the neuron and returning its membrane potential to the baseline value. The impact on the membrane potential due to influx and efflux of the two ions is shown in Figure 2.11A.

The changeable permeability of Na^+ ions across the cell membrane to produce depolarization is one of the special properties of neurons. The other is the remarkable sequence of events that takes place once a sufficient amount of depolarization has occurred. Figure 2.11B shows this sequence in schematic form. If a sufficient amount of depolarization occurs so that membrane potential reaches a threshold value, then the sodium channels open completely, and the cell membrane becomes highly permeable to Na^+ ions (SideNote

SideNote | **2.13**

Although K⁺ can freely cross the membrane, the presence of voltage-gated potassium channels, which open at the peak of the action potential, help to eject K⁺ ions out of the neuron quickly. Otherwise, the falling phase of the action potential would be much longer if it simply depended on the diffusive exit of K⁺ ions.

2.12). Given that the cell membrane no longer acts as a barrier, Na^+ ions are free to enter the cell. This in turn produces even more depolarization, so much so that the membrane potential actually becomes positive and can reach a value of +30 mV.

We now have the makings of an **action potential** (Figure 2.11C). We somehow depolarized the neuron just enough to cause an explosive process of sodium channel openings that in turn led to a sudden upward shift in the membrane potential. At the peak of the action potential, the sodium channels return to their native state and prevent any further movement of Na^+ ions into the cell. This is accompanied by a sudden opening of potassium channels that allow K^+ ions to rapidly leave the neuron (SideNote 2.13). The repolarization that results from this efflux accounts for the falling phase of the action potential. In some cases, the K^+ efflux can be excessive and therefore produces a momentary **hyperpolarization**.

The process that we have just described happens to be a fundamental property of neurons, something that distinguishes it from other cells, and which forms the entire basis for neuronal signalling. Action potentials are the very means by which neurons communicate with each other. They are brief in duration, lasting for approximately one millisecond. They are singular events and cannot be modified. In other words, there is no such thing as a bigger, longer, or stronger action potential. They are all-or-none in nature. An action potential will only occur when the

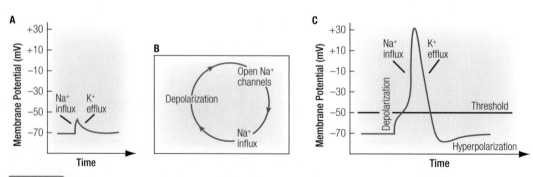

Figure 2.11

The sequence of events that leads to an action potential. A. Neurons are excitable cells and can change their membrane potential from the resting (baseline) value due to Na⁺ influx into the cell. This is followed by K⁺ efflux to return the potential back to baseline. B. If depolarization (or excitation) is large enough to reach a threshold value, the neuron enters a regenerative cycle where K⁺ efflux cannot keep up with the explosive sequential opening of sodium channels. C. The result is an action potential—a spike in the membrane potential where a brief moment of intense depolarization is quickly followed by repolarization due to K⁺ efflux. In some cases, a momentary hyperpolarization can occur at the end of the action potential due to excess K⁺ efflux.

METHODOLOGY

Electrical Activity in Neurons and the Voltage Clamp Method

Much of our understanding concerning the function of neurons comes from the pioneering work of Nobel Prize winners Alan Hodgkin and Andrew Huxley in the late 1930s to the 1950s. Hodgkin and Huxley applied an electrophysiology technique known as the *voltage clamp* on the giant axons of squid. Because an action potential is a combination of Na^+ ion conductance and K^+ ion conductance, which is constantly changing over time and conductance, the voltage clamp method holds the voltage constant to see how the Na^+ and K^+ conductances change over time. A squid's giant axon was placed in a saline solution, with an electrode in the axon and another reference electrode in the saline solution. These two voltages were compared, and if any difference was detected, a feedback mechanism adjusted the voltage in the squid axon by sending a current, if needed. These adjustments were recorded and analyzed, and they indicated the opening and closing of ion channels. By changing the voltage of the reference electrode from -65 mV to zero, Hodgkin and Huxley could examine how the axon responded in order to match the new voltage. They found that the current of the squid axon first went negative, then positive, and then settled down to zero. By selectively blocking Na^+ ions or K^+ ions, it was determined that the Na^+ ions cause the negative current change (and are therefore fast acting) and that the K^+ ions caused the positive current change (and are therefore slower acting).

membrane potential has reached threshold. Otherwise, there will be no action potential at all. And perhaps the most important feature is that an action potential is self-generating as it proceeds down an axon. Once created, it will propagate down the fibre without decaying until it reaches the axon terminal.

Signal generation and propagation

Now that we have discussed the basic properties of action potentials, we still need to understand how they are generated in the first place. In other words, what events trigger the initial sodium influx to cause the membrane potential to reach threshold, upon which an action potential is generated? There are two ways in which this can happen.

The first pertains to the very beginnings of signal generation by sensory systems. All sensory processing begins with specialized receptor neurons that transform the energy in a physical stimulus into a neural signal, a process that is known as sensory **transduction**. In future chapters, we will come to know much more about the specific receptors that serve the various sensory modalities such as touch, taste, vision, etc. In general terms though, the transduction process can create a depolarizing signal, or **receptor potential**, that is similar in nature to the one shown in Figure 2.11A. Sodium channels open up whenever sensory receptor neurons are stimulated. The sensory stimulus may cause enough membrane depolarization to reach threshold, in which case an action potential is generated, as shown in Figure 2.12 (left). If so, then the first of a series of action potentials will ultimately reach the brain to produce a perceptual experience.

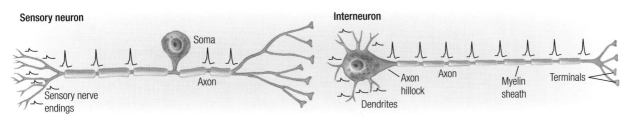

Figure 2.12

Receptor potentials are generated in sensory neurons as a result of the transduction process, which in turn can produce action potentials that are propagated to the next neuron. An action potential in one neuron may produce a depolarizing signal in the next. If this depolarization is intense enough, then action potentials are produced here as well and sent to the next neuron in the chain.

SideNote | **2.14**

There are some synapses that are purely electrical, with structural continuity between the two neurons so that action potentials can be directly transmitted between them. However, most synapses contain a narrow physical gap that does not permit direct electrical transmission.

The key point here is that in terms of sensory perception, all roads lead out from the sensory receptor neuron. A large number of interneurons then enter the picture and become involved in signal transmission and are processed by the nervous system. And therein lies the second means by which action potentials are generated. Each neuron must pass the signal on to the next one in the chain. However, most neurons are not physically connected, a fact that was recognized by Cajal himself. Therefore, an action potential cannot be directly conducted from one neuron to another but must go through an intermediate process that can generate membrane depolarization (not action potentials) in the next neuron. As with our original receptor neuron, if enough depolarization occurs in this next neuron to reach threshold, then an action potential will be generated here as well, as shown in Figure 2.12 (right).

4. SIGNAL TRANSMISSION BETWEEN NEURONS

What is the mechanism then by which electrical information is transmitted from one neuron to another? Recall that information flow in the nervous system is unidirectional in nature—signals flow out of axons and are usually transmitted to the dendrites of the next neuron. There is a very small physical gap called the **synapse** that exists at the junction where the two neurons meet (SideNote 2.14).

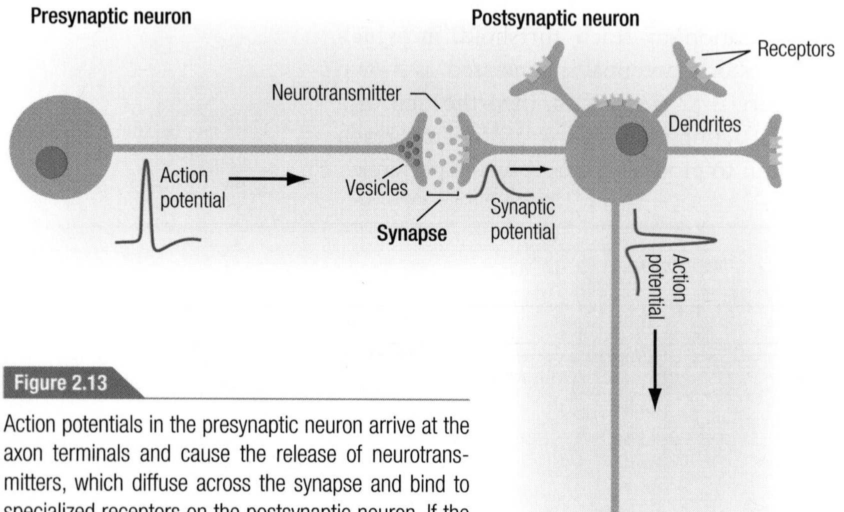

For this reason, an action potential coming down the **presynaptic** axon cannot directly produce an action potential in the dendrite of the **postsynaptic** neuron. Instead, the signals are transmitted across the synapse with the help of specialized chemicals (Shepherd, 1998; Squire et al., 2008).

Chemical mediators are involved in synaptic transmission

The presynaptic axon terminal contains numerous vesicles that are filled with chemical messengers, or **neurotransmitters**. When an action potential reaches the presynaptic terminal, a biochemical process is engaged that makes the vesicles fuse with the axon terminal membrane and release its contents into the synaptic space. As illustrated in Figure 2.13, neurotransmitter molecules then diffuse across the synapse where they bind to receptors on the postsynaptic neuron. The receptors, which are specialized proteins, have two properties that are important for signal transmission at the synapse. First, they have a high specificity for neurotransmitters and therefore readily bind the molecules that diffuse across the synapse. And second, these receptors are able to change the local membrane potential after neurotransmitter binding has taken place.

The synaptic potential

The membrane-bound receptors on postsynaptic neurons contain a pore that allows movement of ions into and out of the neuron. In this regard, they behave somewhat like the sodium and potassium ion channels that we discussed earlier but with two exceptions. The receptors are normally not permeable to ions until the precise moment that neurotransmitter binding occurs. As soon as this happens, the pore opens up and allows a net flux of Na^+ ions into the neuron. This will of course cause a slight depolarization and will be accompanied by a subsequent efflux of K^+ to return the membrane potential back to the resting level. We have just described the **synaptic potential**—a small change in the membrane potential caused by neurotransmitters binding to specialized receptors that then allows a momentary flux of ions into and out of the neuron. Figure 2.13 shows the synaptic potential that arises in a dendrite as a result of this process.

The second way in which these receptors differ from the ion channels is in the amount

Figure 2.13

Action potentials in the presynaptic neuron arrive at the axon terminals and cause the release of neurotransmitters, which diffuse across the synapse and bind to specialized receptors on the postsynaptic neuron. If the postsynaptic neuron is sufficiently stimulated at any given moment then an action potential will be generated there as well.

of depolarization that is allowed. The opening of the receptor pores is brief and limited by the availability of neurotransmitter substance. As a result, membrane depolarization is never sufficient to reach threshold and therefore these receptors by themselves cannot generate action potentials. And yet we need to do this somehow so that the signal can be propagated down the axon and on to the next neuron. Before describing how an action potential can be generated from synaptic potentials, we need to discuss one other feature of the synaptic potential.

Synaptic potentials can also be inhibitory

Although we have described the synaptic potential in terms of membrane depolarization, there are many instances when just the opposite happens. There are certain neurotransmitters that cause the membrane potential to become more negative, that is, to become hyperpolarized (SideNote 2.15) (Kandel et al., 2000; Squire et al., 2008). Whereas depolarization causes the neuron to become more excited, hyperpolarization makes the neuron more inhibited and reduces the likelihood that threshold potential will be reached to trigger an action potential. A hyperpolarizing synaptic potential can be produced if the receptor selectively allows only K^+ ions to leave the cell or if negative ions should enter the neuron. In both cases, the postsynaptic neuron around the synaptic zone will become more negative. Figure 2.14 illustrates the effects of excitatory and inhibitory neurotransmitters on the postsynaptic neuron.

Although it seems odd that an action potential in one neuron may hyperpolarize the next one, and therefore reduce the chances of propagating the signal, it turns out that much of the processing that takes place in the nervous system involves the interplay of excitatory and inhibitory signals. It is sometimes important to inhibit the activity of an interneuron at the next level in order to process sensory information effectively. In later chapters, we will further examine the role that inhibitory signals play in sensory processing. For now, let us assume that a postsynaptic neuron has to contend with both excitatory and inhibitory inputs from many different presynaptic neurons. The next question concerns how these different inputs influence the overall activity of the postsynaptic neuron and what determines whether an action potential will be generated there.

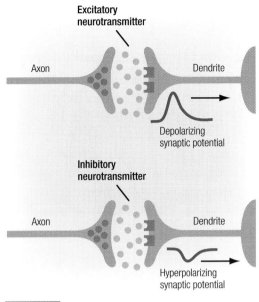

Figure 2.14

A presynaptic neuron can release either excitatory or inhibitory neurotransmitters. Excitatory neurotransmitters produce membrane depolarization at the postsynaptic neuron, whereas inhibitory ones produce a hyperpolarizing synaptic potential.

Integration of electrical signals by neurons

There are literally hundreds of synaptic connections on any given neuron, some of which are excitatory and some of which are inhibitory (SideNote 2.16). Thus, a key property of neurons is to integrate the various depolarizing and hyperpolarizing signals that occur at its many synaptic contacts at any moment in time (Matthews, 1997). If the depolarizing signals predominate, then the result of the integration will have a net excitatory effect on the neuron. And if that excitation is large enough to raise the membrane potential to threshold, then an action potential will be produced. However, this takes place only at the point where the axon emerges from the cell body—the so-called *axon hillock* (see Figure 2.12, right). This part of the neuron contains many Na^+ channels where membrane depolarization can cause the explosive sequence of events that leads to an action potential. If, however, the net effect of signal integration fails to reach threshold, then an action potential will not be generated and the subthreshold signal will simply fade away.

The important point to take away from this discussion is that each neuron acts as a miniature processing unit that surveys all of the incoming signals at any given moment. If the overriding consensus is to further propagate the signal, then action potentials will be

METHODOLOGY

Modifying Synapses and Encoding Memories

Harold Leslie Atwood at the University of Toronto has conducted a number of very important experiments, working with various crustaceans and drosophila, all focused on how individual synapses can be modified to encode memories of previous experiences. In one such technique by Atwood and his colleagues, three-dimensional reconstructions of neuron terminals were reproduced in order to count the individual synapses that were contributing to the local synaptic responses. This was accomplished using electron micrographs and led to the finding that there are differences in the structure of the synapse, depending on if it is "strong" or "weak" in nature.

generated at the axon hillock. Once those action potentials reach the axon terminal of that neuron, the entire sequence of events that we have described above will be replayed at the interface with the next neuron. In this way, sensory signals ultimately reach the brain where a massive, interactive circuit of literally billions of neurons, with trillions of synapses, will engage to produce the perceptual experience. The mere act of reading this page is generating vast numbers of action potentials at this very moment, ones that allow you to see the words, interpret their meaning, and perhaps appreciate the awesome complexity of the brain—assuming you are still awake.

5. GENERAL PRINCIPLES OF SENSORY CODING

Sensory systems gather information about the environment through specialized receptors, transform the energy in the stimulus into a biological signal, and then transmit that signal to the brain. However, what are the key features of the stimulus that are extracted by sensory systems? It turns out that despite their diversity, the principal sensory organs are all generally equipped to extract a similar set of information from the external stimulus.

Stimulus location coding

We have a keen awareness of the external location of a stimulus, especially in our visual and somatosensory systems. This occurs largely because topographic relationships are maintained from the sensory organ to the primary cortical site, as discussed earlier. The activity of each sensory neuron (or at least, a small cluster of neurons) is faithfully projected to the cerebral cortex. In other words, activity from say

touch receptors in the index finger does not mix with signals arising from other parts of the body. There are separate axonal fibres that conduct messages from different parts of the body, a separation that is maintained at the thalamus and cortex. We are therefore aware of a specific site of stimulation on the surface of our body or retina because neurons in a specific part of the cortex have become activated. In other words, each neuron in the cortical areas for touch or vision is therefore stimulated only if a particular site on the corresponding sensory surface is stimulated. This is the basis for a very important property of neurons—the so-called **receptive field**. Although we are also aware of the locations of sounds in our external environment, the coding for this is done somewhat differently, as discussed in Chapter 6. Location coding is not preserved in the chemosensory modalities (Wilson & Mainen, 2006).

Intensity coding

We learned in Chapter 1 that the intensity of a sensory stimulus must reach a certain threshold level before it can be detected. Furthermore, the precise relationship between perception and intensity at suprathreshold levels is complicated and depends on the modality in question. The most accepted explanation for these different behavioural observations relies on neural function at the level of the sensory receptors.

The transformation of stimulus energy into a biological signal is achieved somewhat differently by the different kinds of sensory receptors. However, they all share the common feature that the greater the intensity of the signal, the greater the final output. Given that an action potential is a fundamental entity and cannot be altered in size or duration, it is not possible to make a larger or longer action potential to code for a more intense stimulus. Sensory systems have therefore evolved a different strategy for encoding intensity.

Lord Edgar Adrian first showed in the 1920s that the frequency of action potentials increased with corresponding increases in stimulus intensity. However, there exists an absolute physiological threshold before receptors (or subsequent neurons) will show a discharge of action potentials, a fact that partly accounts for the behavioural absolute threshold. Beyond this level, the activity of sensory neurons can be described in frequency terms— the more intense the stimulus, the greater the receptor potential, which in turn generates a higher frequency of action potentials. Although the relationship between stimulus intensity and discharge rate of action potentials resembles the magnitude estimation relationship, they do not entirely overlap. Furthermore, a number of different nonsensory factors can affect the threshold such as fatigue, motivation, context, prior exposure, etc. This suggests that while sensory transduction can account for many aspects of the behavioural magnitude estimation function, there are other mechanisms, most likely cortical ones, that also play an important role in intensity coding and representation (Finger, 1994).

Duration coding

We are able to perceive the presence of a stimulus for fairly long periods of time. In some cases, receptor signalling persists as long as the stimulus is applied. However, one general feature of all sensory systems is that continued application of a stimulus makes us less aware of its presence. For example, we feel the surface of a chair as soon as we sit down. However, the continued mechanical pressure that is applied to that part of our somatosensory system leads to a diminished awareness until we are no longer aware of the stimulus. The term that is generally applied to this phenomenon is **adaptation**.

One explanation for sensory adaptation effect involves mechanisms right at the sensory receptor level. The continued presence of a sensory stimulus leads to an inactivation of the ion channels that are necessary to produce the receptor potential, resulting in a decreased firing of action potentials and therefore a reduced perception of the stimulus.

Sensory modality coding

Sensory receptors are only sensitive to a specific type of stimulus energy. As discussed in Section A.4, the *law of specific nerve energies* postulated by Johannes Müller in the 19th century stipulates that different sets of receptors and nerve fibres are dedicated to each of the sensory modalities. This specificity is a key property of the receptor and, as Table 2.3 shows, stimuli corresponding to the five principal modalities generate signals in specific types of receptors. We are able to perceive different kinds of sensations because the different types of receptors maintain a specific set of connections that ultimately stimulate parts of our cerebral cortex that are dedicated

Table **2.3**

Modality Representation by Different Types of Sensory Receptors

Stimulus	Receptor	Modality
Mechanical	Mechanoreceptor	Touch
Chemical (dissolved)	Chemoreceptor Gustatory receptor neuron	Taste
Chemical (airborne)	Chemoreceptor Olfactory receptor neuron	Smell
Sound	Mechanoreceptor Cochlear hair cell	Audition
Light	Photoreceptor Rods, cones	Vision

Note. Sensory receptors are specialized for transforming different kinds of external stimuli into a biological signal and represent the starting point for modality coding in the nervous system.

to each modality. This idea has come to be known as the *labelled-line* principle. As we will see in forthcoming chapters on the individual sensory systems, certain modalities are further composed of a set of constituent qualities, or submodalities. For example, the somatosensory modality can be parsed into different qualities that include the sensation of touch, heat, and pain—each of them being detected by different types of somatosensory receptors (Mountcastle, 1998; Siegel & Sapru, 2007).

C. Techniques for Studying Brain Function

Much of our current knowledge about the neural bases of sensory perception has emerged through direct studies on the nervous system. The 20th century saw dramatic developments in the field of neuroscience, ones that paralleled an increasing sophistication in techniques and instrumentation. Although our knowledge as to how brain activity produces higher mental functions continues to remain elusive, we now know much about the neural structures and mechanisms that are involved in the early processing of sensory signals. The advances from biological studies have evolved through efforts that can be broadly classified into two procedural categories—electrophysiology and functional brain imaging.

1. ELECTROPHYSIOLOGY

One way to study the nervous system has been to record the electrical activity generated by neurons. However, the cerebral cortex function that ultimately produces sensory perception depends on electrical activity across a very large number of neurons at any given site. One approach to understanding nervous system function is to probe the activity of one or a few neurons at a time and then use that information to decipher local processing at that cortical site. A second approach is to record the summated activity of large clusters of neurons using techniques that sample electrical changes over a larger part of the brain.

Single-unit recording

The technique for recording action potentials from single neurons was first introduced by Lord Edgar Adrian in 1926. Since then, electrophysiological (or single-unit) recording, as it

is known, has evolved from its original use in simple preparations to applications in the cerebral cortex of awake, behaving animals exposed to a sensory stimulus or engaged in some kind of behavioural task (SideNote 2.17) (Finger, 1994). Electrophysiological recordings have been used to answer detailed questions about the behaviour of individual neurons, or small clusters of neurons, and the roles they play in sensory, motor, and cognitive processing.

To observe the electrical changes that occur, a very thin electrode is placed in the neighbourhood of a neuron, as shown in Figure 2.15. This method of extracellular recording actually examines the electrical changes that occur around the tip of the electrode caused by activity in surrounding neurons. The changing ionic environment brought about by neural activity generates an electric current in the electrode. However, this current is typically very weak and needs to be amplified before being displayed, usually on some kind of monitoring device (SideNote 2.18). In this way, neuroscientists can examine the activity of neurons at a particular site in the nervous system in response to sensory stimulation.

One parameter that is usually assessed in such experiments is the number of action potentials that are produced in response to a stimulus and how altering the stimulus changes that frequency. The properties of many single units recorded in succession can then be pieced together to get a picture of signal processing in that particular part of the brain. In later chapters, we will examine the results of single-unit studies and the information they have provided in advancing our understanding of neural processing within specific sensory systems (Martin, 2002).

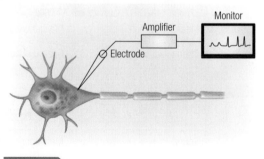

Figure 2.15

A standard way to record electrical activity in neurons is to place a fine electrode near the cell body or axon. Ionic changes in the extracellular fluid produced from neuronal activity will generate a small current in the electrode, which can be amplified and displayed on a monitor.

SideNote | 2.17

Anesthetized animals were generally used in early electrophysiological experiments. However, concerns about the effects of anesthesia and the inability to study neuronal activity during an active behavioural task paved the way for studies on awake animals.

SideNote | 2.18

The amplified current may be monitored by way of an oscilloscope, which provides a visual representation of the electrical signals. However, recent advances in computing technology have led to software programs that process, display, and analyze neural activity on computer monitors.

Electroencephalography

Despite the power and utility of single-unit recordings, there are a number of difficulties with this procedure that limits the information that can be obtained. The technique is invasive and can only be routinely applied in experimental animals, although there have been instances where recordings have been made in humans undergoing brain surgery. Single-unit experiments are also tedious and time-consuming. A typical experiment on say an awake, behaving monkey can take several months, or even years, to complete. Although single-unit recordings offer the best possible resolution of function—that is, at the cellular level—these drawbacks have imposed challenges.

An alternative approach to electrophysiological assessment that bypasses the single-unit level is the use of surface-based electrodes that sample electrical activity over a larger area. The technique of *electroencephalography* uses electrodes that are attached to the scalp. The number of electrodes can vary from a few to more than a hundred. Each electrode samples local voltage fluctuations in the underlying cortex that is believed to arise not from action potentials but from summated synaptic potentials in the cell body and dendrites of an ensemble of neurons. The **electroencephalogram**, or EEG, picks up changes in these potentials that occur when a stimulus is applied or a cognitive task is initiated. The electrical responses that are tied to a particular sensory stimulus or behavioural output are known as **event-related potentials (ERPs)**. These signals are generally of very low amplitude (voltage) and variable frequency (Luck, 2005).

There are two advantages of EEG recording: it is non-invasive and it offers excellent **temporal resolution**. However, its biggest drawback is that it offers poor **spatial resolution**. The localization of electrical activity in the underlying cortex can only be done in the broadest sense. This limits its use in particular situations where more precise function localization is required. Functional brain imaging techniques provide an alternative approach that allows the visualization of activated neuronal ensembles at a much greater resolution.

2. FUNCTIONAL BRAIN IMAGING

The guiding principle behind most functional brain imaging techniques is that neuronal activity creates a localized increase in blood flow. Increased neural activity in a particular area is accompanied by a greater demand in energy supply, waste production, and therefore a coincidental increase in blood flow to that area (Aine, 1995; Raichle, 1998). Although the precise mechanisms by which blood flow is coupled to neural activity remain poorly understood, this association has nevertheless served as a core foundation for imaging brain activity. The idea is simply this—find a way of measuring changes in blood flow and the result will be the identification of localized brain areas where increased electrical activity in an ensemble of neurons has just occurred.

Functional magnetic resonance imaging (fMRI)

The most commonly used technique for functional brain imaging is called **fMRI**. The principle behind fMRI is somewhat complex and based on magnetization properties associated with the spinning nuclei of atoms (Cabeza & Kingstone, 2006; Toga & Mazziotta, 1996). When placed in a strong magnetic field, these miniature magnets align with the external field. If a brief pulse of energy in the form of radio waves is applied, then the alignment of the spin axes is perturbed to produce a warbling effect. When the pulse is turned off, the nuclei return to their original orientation, a process known as *relaxation* that results in the release of energy in the form of radio waves. This is the fundamental basis of magnetic resonance—the resonating nuclei behave as miniature radio transmitters that emit signals at a characteristic frequency. These radio signals can then be picked up by detectors and are subjected to computer analysis to produce an image.

The actual physics and biophysics of this scenario are much more complex. However, for our purposes we only need to know that the resonance and relaxation process depends on the local molecular environment. For example, the magnetic qualities of **hemoglobin** that is deprived of oxygen are somewhat different than when oxygen is present. Since brain areas that are very active enjoy greater blood flow, more oxygenated blood is present in these areas. This actually increases the magnetic resonance signal compared to less active brain areas where there is less blood flow. By using these transient changes in the magnetic resonance signal, it is possible to image blood flow changes that presumably reflect accompanying changes in neural activity.

Although fMRI has been used to document sensory activation, from simple stimulus applications to complex constructs (e.g., see Figure 2.16), the use of this technique has evolved to the point where signal changes from cognitive tasks are now routinely measured (Kanwisher & Duncan, 2004). Studies on brain activity underlying diverse mental operations such as language tasks, reading comprehension, attention, memory, emotion, and mental imagery have been reported (Phan, Wager, Taylor, & Liberzon, 2002; Puce, Allison, Asgari, Gore, & McCarthy, 1996; Rajah & D'Esposito, 2005). Despite its advantages, fMRI does have its own share of problems. These include limited spatial resolution, image blurring caused by head or body movement, and very high instrumentation costs. Nevertheless, continued refinements in this technology, its growing availability for basic

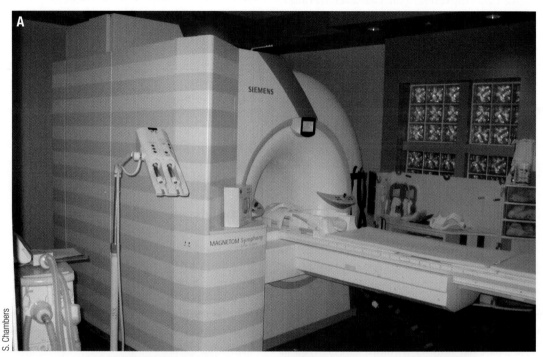

S. Chambers

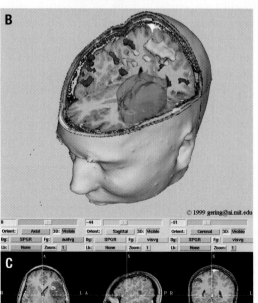

Oxford FMRIB Centre

© 1999 gering@ai.mit.edu

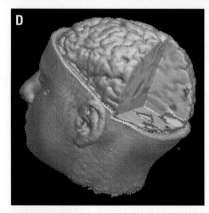

D. Gering, A. Nabavi, R. Kikinis, N. Hata, L. Odonnell, W. Eric L. Grimson, F. Jolesz, P. Black, W. Wells III. An Integrated Visualization System for Surgical Planning and Guidance Using Image Fusion and an Open MR. Journal of Magnetic Resonance Imaging, Vol 13, pp. 967–975, June, 2001

Figure 2.16

An MRI machine can be used to obtain images of functional activity in the human brain (A). Brain images may be obtained in response to sensory stimuli such as auditory stimulation (B) or more complex cognitive functions such as imagining the feeling of joy (C). Brain scans can also be rendered in 3D to provide more realistic volume-based images (D).

scientific studies, and the steady increase in applications to a wider set of research questions have propelled fMRI into an extremely valuable neuroscience tool.

Positron emission tomography (PET)

Positron emission tomography (PET) is also a non-invasive **in vivo** functional imaging technique. PET uses probes that are tagged with a special radioactive element that decays with time and releases highly energetic anti-electron particles (also known as *positrons*). The emitted positrons very quickly become annihilated when they come into contact with electrons in neighbouring atoms, a process that results in the production of a form of high-energy radiation known as **gamma rays** (Figure 2.17A) (Cherry & Phelps, 1996). These gamma rays shoot out from the point of positron–electron collision and can be picked up by an array of detectors to form an image of the functioning brain (Figure 2.17B).

The question then is "How can these positron-emitting probes actually be used to produce a functional image of the brain?" There is of course neural activity going on everywhere in the brain at any given time. The key though is to pick out the hot spots—brain areas that become highly activated as a result of sensory stimulation or some cognitive/behavioural task that the subject is performing. Recall that intense neural activity in a particular brain area is accompanied by increases in localized blood flow. If that blood flow can somehow be measured by PET, as was the case with fMRI, then it would allow a possible way of identifying those hot spots of neural activity.

In the majority of PET studies, the radioactive probe that is actually used is a special form of water, one in which the oxygen atom

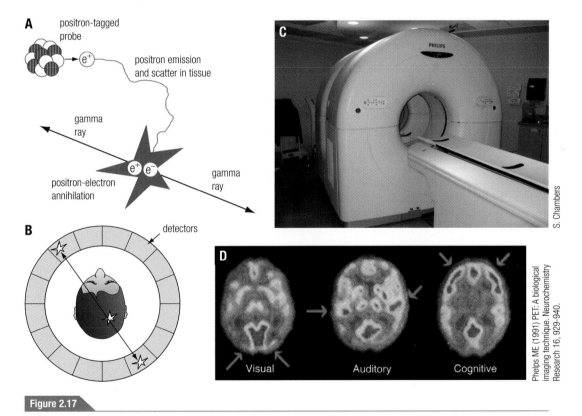

Figure 2.17

The principle and practice of PET imaging. Positrons are emitted from a tagged probe (A) that is administered to a human subject. The gamma rays that are produced by positron–electron collisions are picked up in a ring of detectors that surround the subject's head (B). The actual PET machine (C) is a large apparatus that scans gamma ray emissions along a given plane and, after computer analysis, can reconstruct the point at which the positron emission occurred. This information is used to produce a PET image as in these examples of cortical activation (D). Adapted from "Imaging Brain Function with Positron Emission Tomography," by S. R. Cherry and M. E. Phelps, 1996, in *Brain Mapping,* Eds. A. W. Toga and J. C. Mazziotta, San Diego, CA: Academic Press (A, B); "PET: A Biological Imaging Technique," by M. E. Phelps, 1991, *Neurochemistry Research, 16,* pp. 929–940 (D).

has been replaced by a positron-emitting form of oxygen [^{15}O]. In a typical PET experiment, the human subject is placed inside a large gamma ray scanner (Figure 2.17C), injected with [^{15}O] water, and exposed to a sensory stimulus or asked to perform a cognitive task. The increased blood flow to activated brain areas will carry with it some of this radioactive water. Therefore, those brain areas activated by the stimulus will emit more gamma rays compared to other areas or compared to control conditions in which no stimulus is applied. The gamma rays are picked up by the detector and computer to produce an image. Figure 2.17D shows examples of PET scans in response to selective visual or auditory stimulation and a cognitive task (Phelps, 1991).

Optical imaging

One of the earliest imaging techniques used voltage-sensitive dyes, which change their fluorescence properties in response to membrane depolarization (Kandel et al., 2000). This imaging procedure first required exposing the cortical surface in an experimental animal, giving that animal a sensory stimulus, and then observing the fluorescence changes in the exposed cortex. The fluorescent signals from the dyes are captured with a very sensitive video camera. It was later found that instead of using toxic dyes, it is possible to image just the intrinsic changes in light scattering that occur because of ionic movement and other associated consequences of electrical activity in neurons. It is also possible to use changes in localized blood flow as the basis for optical imaging. The signals in this case arise from the greater presence of hemoglobin itself and the changes in oxygen level that occur with blood rushing into an activated area. These alterations affect light absorption (or reflection), a parameter that can be easily tracked and used as a marker of enhanced neural activity.

Optical imaging studies have provided considerable information on architectural features of the cerebral cortex, especially in the visual cortex of cats and monkeys (Squire et al., 2008). These studies have benefited from the high spatial resolution that optical imaging offers. Furthermore, this technique allows separate images to be generated from the same cortical area in response to different stimulus applications. Thus, it is possible to see ensemble activity in the visual cortex in response to one stimulus *versus* another. In this way, it is possible to assess whether different stimulus conditions produce neural activity in different pools of neurons and, if so, to create a map of those separate areas of activation.

There are, however, a number of drawbacks to the use of optical imaging as well. First, the technique can only image activity from the surface of the brain, thereby preventing the sampling of large areas of the cortex that lie buried in the various sulci. And second, the technique is invasive in nature and requires direct visualization of the cortical surface. As a result, optical imaging studies have largely been limited to experimental animals.

Summary

1. There is a rich and interesting history of scientific thought on how the brain processes sensory information. An early idea proposed by Gall was that brain functions were localized to discrete areas that in turn created a localized expansion of the brain and a corresponding bump on the skull. The field of *phrenology* spawned by this idea gained considerable acceptance, though it was also met vigorously with contrary opinions. The opposing view was that the brain is a homogenous organ where sensory and other mental functions are broadly distributed.

2. Clinical studies on patients with wounds to various parts of the brain, as well as experimental studies on animals, later helped to show that there is indeed localization of function. Broca's and Wernicke's studies, for example, showed that there exists a dedicated module in the frontal and temporal lobes, respectively, for the production and comprehension of speech. Another significant development in localization studies came from Penfield, who directly stimulated various parts of the cerebral cortex in humans undergoing brain surgery. His studies showed that there is a precise map of the body in terms of somatosensory (touch) function that is accompanied by a similar map of motor function in a nearby brain area.

3. Sensory information processing is often mediated by parallel pathways, starting as early as the receptor level. Specific facets of a sensory modality are separately transmitted at the earliest levels of the neural pathways and even segregated to a certain extent in the higher cortical centres. The two hemispheres of the cerebrum provide overlapping functions, although certain sensory processes are lateralized, that is, undertaken in only one of the hemispheres (e.g., speech production and comprehension).

4. The central nervous system (CNS) is composed of the brain and spinal cord. Most of the grey matter (cells) is found in the cerebral cortex. It is in the cortex that the highest levels of sensory processing occur, leading to perceptual awareness. The cortex was subdivided into 52 discrete areas by Brodmann in the early 1900s based on anatomical criteria such as cellular composition and distribution. The human cerebrum had to expand throughout the course of recent evolution due to the progressively greater demands of sensory processing and higher mental functions in primates. The evolutionary answer to an expanding brain was to create a folded cortex, resulting in an expansion of cortical area within a confined cranial volume. The four general areas of the cortex are named after their overlying bony structures—that is, the occipital, temporal, parietal, and frontal lobes.

5. The brain is made up of specialized cells called *neurons*. There was a vigorous early debate as to whether or not the fibres that were visible in microscopic views of the brain represented an entirely separate entity, within which the neurons were enmeshed, or whether these structures actually belonged to neurons. Cajal showed that the fibrous structures were indeed associated with neurons, an idea that transformed neuroscience in the early 1900s by way of the *neuron doctrine*. The neuron is composed of a soma (cell body), a set of dendrites, and a single axon. Different types of neurons are distinguished by their dendrites, which can vary in number, density, and appearance. Electrical signals are received at the dendrites and then pass through the soma and axon onto the next neuron.

6. Electrical activity in neurons is based on the partition of ions, whereby an excess amount of K^+ is present inside the cell and an excess amount of Na^+ is present outside the cell. The resulting diffusive and electrical forces create a membrane potential of -55 to -85 mV (inside negative). Excitable cells such as neurons are able to change the membrane potential and thereby create a unitary electrical event known as an *action potential*. The process begins with sodium channels opening in response to stimulation, which in turn causes an influx of Na^+ into the neuron to cause depolarization (a positive shift in the membrane potential). This event is followed by an opening of potassium channels, resulting in the exit

of K^+ from inside the neuron and the re-establishment of the membrane potential to its original level. The ionic balances are restored by the sodium–potassium pump, which ejects Na^+ to the outside and brings K^+ back into the neuron.

7. Action potentials are all-or-none events and cannot be modified to become larger or last longer. They are the principal mechanism of neuronal signalling and are therefore responsible for all facets of sensory, perceptual, and cognitive function. Action potentials may be generated at the receptor by the transformation of physical energy, a process known as *transduction*. Action potentials then proceed through a cascade of neurons to reach the cerebral cortex.

8. The transmission of action potentials from one neuron to another occurs across a physical space called the *synapse*. Chemical mediators known as *neurotransmitters* are released at the axon terminal after the arrival of an action potential. The neurotransmitter then migrates across the synapse to either stimulate or inhibit the next neuron. If there is sufficient excitation of the next neuron, then an action potential will be generated. This entire sequence is repeated at all subsequent synapses and neurons.

9. There are different ways to measure brain function, with some focusing on recording the electrical activity from a few neurons (e.g., single-unit recordings) and others based on recording electrical activity from larger areas of the brain (e.g., electroencephalography). Other methods such as fMRI and PET are based on the assumption that neural activation causes increased localized blood flow. These methods are therefore aimed at monitoring changes in blood flow in the brain after human subjects are exposed to a sensory stimulus or engaged in some behavioural task.

Key Terms

action potential, 46
adaptation, 51
anion/cation, 44
aphasia, 33
astrocyte, 43
central nervous system (CNS), 36
cerebral cortex, 36
cerebrum, 36
cranial nerves, 38
cytoarchitectonics, 38
depolarization, 46
diffusion, 44
electroencephalogram (EEG), 53
event-related potentials (ERPs), 53
fMRI, 53

functional anatomy, 35
gamma rays, 55
gyrus (*gyri*), 37
hemoglobin, 53
histology, 34
hyperpolarization, 46
in vivo, in vitro, 55
interneurons, 42
lateralization, 36
lesion studies, 32
membrane potential, 44
modality, 39
multipolar and bipolar neurons, 42
myelin, 43
neuron doctrine, 41
neurotransmitters, 48
nucleus (*nuclei*), 38

oligodendrocyte, 43
parallelism, 35
peripheral nervous system, 36
phenomenology, 32
phrenology, 32
presynaptic, postsynaptic, 48
receptive field, 50
receptor potential, 47
Schwann cell, 43
sodium–potassium pump, 45
somatosensory, 35
spatial resolution, 53
sulcus (*sulci*), 37
synapse, 48
synaptic potential, 48
temporal resolution, 53
transduction, 47

1. Why is phenomenology an inadequate method for the study of perceptual function?

2. How did the ideas of Gall and other phrenologists differ from those who had contrary views of brain function? What were some of the major research developments of the 20th century that helped to resolve this debate?

3. What are the principal differences between each of the cerebral lobes in terms of sensory, perceptual, and cognitive function?

4. What was the basis for the dispute between Golgi and Cajal? How was this dispute resolved, and how did it advance the field of neuroscience?

5. What are the structural components of a neuron? What are the key features that make all neurons similar, and what makes them distinguishable?

6. Why is a neuron capable of altering its membrane potential, whereas most other cells are not? What is the process by which an action potential is produced? What is the role of the sodium–potassium pump?

7. What impact did the advent of electrophysiology have on our understanding of brain function? How does an electrode capture neural signals, and what equipment is required for detecting and displaying those signals?

8. Why does the brain injury suffered by Phineas Gage represent an interesting clinical case in the history of neuroscience? Why did it not help to resolve the debate on functional localization, and what new insights were provided by more recent examinations of his injury? What are the key properties of brain organization that prevented an early and conclusive determination of localization of function in the brain?

9. What is the *doctrine of specific nerve energies*, and how is it related to sensory processing by the nervous system? What is the fundamental basis for modality coding and the biological basis for the difference in sensory experience such as sight, hearing, touch, etc.?

10. How do excitatory and inhibitory neurotransmitters affect the postsynaptic neuron? Discuss the processes that are in play for determining whether or not an action potential is generated at a postsynaptic neuron. Why are action potentials unable to flow in the reverse direction—that is, from the postsynaptic to the presynaptic neuron?

11. What are the common features and principal differences between brain imaging technologies such as fMRI, PET, and optical imaging?

• Bear, M. F., Connors, B., & Paradiso, M. (2006). *Neuroscience: Exploring the brain* (3rd ed.). New York, NY: Lippincott Williams & Wilkins.

• Bennett, M., Dennett, D., Hacker, P., & Searle, J. (2007). *Neuroscience and philosophy: Brain, mind, and language.* New York, NY: Columbia University Press.

• Brodmann, K., & Garey, L. J. (2005). *Brodmann's: Localisation in the cerebral cortex* (3rd ed.). New York, NY: Springer.

• Finger, S. (1994). *Origins of neuroscience: A history of explorations into brain function.* New York, NY: Oxford University Press.

• Kandel, E. R., Schwartz, J. H., & Jessell, T. M. (2000). *Principles of neural science* (4th ed.). New York, NY: McGraw-Hill.

• Kanwisher, N., & Duncan, J. (2004). *Functional neuroimaging of visual cognition.* New York, NY: Oxford University Press.

• Purves, D. (2007). *Neuroscience* (4th ed.). Sunderland, MA: Sinauer.

• Squire, L. R., Berg, D., Bloom, F., & du Lac, S. (2008). *Fundamental neuroscience* (3rd ed.) San Diego, CA: Academic Press.

• Zeki, S. (2009). *Splendors and miseries of the brain: Love, creativity, and the quest for human happiness.* Malden, MA: Wiley Blackwell.

The Somatosensory System:
Touch, Feeling, and Pain

In this chapter . . .

- You will be introduced to the many types of skin receptors (mechanoreceptors, thermoreceptors, proprioceptors, and nociceptors) and will learn in detail how these receptors send their signals to the spinal cord and how exactly each type of fibre projects to area S-I of the brain and to associated sensory brain areas.

- You will learn how researchers devised tests to explore the ability to perceive touch and how it relies on a number of aspects such as the type of receptor, the intensity of the stimulus, where the stimulation occurs on the body, and how long the stimulus lasts. You will also discover that the somatosensory system can be used when vision is lost by taking advantage of tactile communication and the different forms this type of communication can take.

- You will explore the sense of proprioception and understand how very important it is to know where one's limbs are in space. It will become clear how it is that our brain gathers information on every movement we make and why it is important to do so.

- You will be introduced to the concept of pain, and understand why it is a difficult sense to quantitatively measure. You will learn to appreciate how important it is to study pain control, especially for those who suffer from chronic pain and have to use painkillers constantly.

A NEURAL BASIS OF SOMATOSENSORY PERCEPTION
1. The Skin and Its Receptors
2. Afferent Fibres
3. Spinal Mechanisms and Signal Transfer
4. The Somatosensory Cortex
5. Somatomotor Circuits

B PERCEPTUAL ASPECTS OF TACTILE SENSATION
1. Intensity and Sensation
2. Spatial Factors
3. Temporal Factors
4. Thermal Sensations
5. Tactile Communication

C PROPRIOCEPTION AND KINESTHESIS
1. Neural Foundations
2. Perceptual Aspects
3. Active Touch and Haptic Perception

D NOCICEPTION AND PAIN
1. Sensory Mechanisms of Nociception
2. Measurement of Pain
3. Control of Pain

I am sure that if a fairy bade me choose between the sense of sight and that of touch, I would not part with the warm, endearing contact of human hands or the wealth of form, the mobility and the fullness that press into my palms.

—Helen Keller

An example of tactile communication, Braille text is composed of a series of raised dots that can be read with the fingers by blind people or those whose eyesight is too poor for reading printed material. Photo: abalcazar/ iStockphoto.com

The somatosensory system is largely concerned with sensations that arise from stimulation of the skin and that are commonly referred to as touch. From the time of Aristotle until the middle of the 19th century, touch sensation had always been regarded as a unitary experience that formed one of the five primary senses. But there are many aspects to touch beyond the mere appreciation of mechanical pressure on the skin, a fact that became appreciated only in the last century. The feelings associated with touch, or tactile perception, encompass the attributes of pressure, vibration, warmth, and cold. When we interact with an object, we are usually aware of its many different features such as the shape, texture, elasticity, hardness, and temperature. In her 1923 monograph, Alice Sullivan wrote about how the basic touch attributes can blend together to produce a set of compound sensations—such as wetness, oiliness, gelatinousness, sliminess, mushiness, gumminess, sponginess, and so on (Sullivan, 1923). And yet, despite the wide variation in perceptions evoked by the various individual tactile attributes and their blends, we regard them all under the general sensory category of **touch**.

The unitary character of touch is just one of its many interesting facets. The experience of touch can be broken down into two fundamental features (Kruger, 1996). On one hand, we are aware of the point on our body where the interaction occurred with an object in the physical world. This localization feature forms the objective aspect of touch and deals with the question "Where was I touched?" This is accompanied by the subjective feeling of touch that allows for the classification and identification of the object and therefore deals with the questions "What did I touch and how did it feel?" While the objective component is similar to that found in the other sensory systems—vision for example—the subjective experience of touch is often regarded as being more highly developed. The sensations of warmth, cold, and pain are excellent examples, where the subjective side predominates and largely accounts for the perceptual experience. Indeed, the subjective experience of pain itself is so unique and pervasive that it is often considered separately from the other touch sensations.

Touch is therefore distinctive among the senses in that its multiple attributes can interact to produce compound sensations, having both objective and subjective qualities, and yet they are all part of a single kind of sensory experience. Another distinctive feature of touch is that the sensations arise from receptors that are distributed throughout the entire body rather than in discrete sensory organs, as is the case with all of the other senses (Kandel, Schwartz, & Jessell, 2000; Squire, Roberts, Spitzer, & Zigmond, 2002). Although **somatosensory** perceptions are largely associated with touch and pain, there are specialized receptors within muscles and joints that provide a further sensory dimension that is known as **proprioception** (Johnson, Babis, Soultanis, & Soucacos, 2008). Proprioceptive mechanisms allow us to be aware of the location of our limbs in space—a property that we will examine in detail later in this chapter. But first, we must understand the way in which touch signals are generated in the skin and then processed by the brain. This will be followed by an examination of some of the behavioural aspects related to touch as explored through psychophysical studies. The chapter will conclude with a discussion on the physiological and perceptual aspects of pain.

A. Neural Basis of Somatosensory Perception

The perception of touch occurs when we physically interact with an object in the environment. That object may emit energy, which we then capture through sensory receptors. Alternatively, we may have a situation where energy is reflected off the object and again captured by our receptors. Either way, we must possess a mechanism to capture that energy, whether it is in the form of mechanical pressure, vibration, heat, etc., and transform it into biological signals that can be processed by the central nervous system. Historically, two main ideas have been proposed to account for the way in which touch signals are generated and transmitted to the brain (Kruger, 1996; Morgan, 2009).

The *theory of receptor specificity* is borrowed directly from Johannes Müller's doctrine of specific nerve energies whereby individual receptors and nerve endings are selectively sensitive to a particular form of energy impinging on the skin. Each type of receptor not only produces a particular touch sensation but also indicates where on the skin surface the stimulation occurred. Influential German physiologist Max von Frey, who contributed much to the field of touch perception, took this concept one step further and proposed that there were specific receptors for heat, cold, pressure, and pain.

A somewhat different view was offered by the *pattern theory* in which the specificity of touch sensations was believed to arise not from individual receptors but rather through the overall pattern of activity across a broad spectrum of receptors. Different types of touch, according to this theory, generate different patterns of activity and somehow the brain is able to distinguish those patterns to produce the different touch perceptions.

We now know that touch signals are indeed highly specific and selectively generated by a particular type of receptor. These receptors, broadly classified as **mechanoreceptors**, are present in the skin throughout the body. Although we now accept receptor specificity as the basis for touch perception, it should be clear that most forms of touch usually involve stimulation of multiple types of receptors. Therefore, although the individual receptors convey a unitary tactile sensation, the total perception of touch is quite complex, often involving multiple attributes of the stimulus and, accordingly, a multitude of receptor types.

1.   THE SKIN AND ITS RECEPTORS

The skin is an architectural and functional marvel, though it often receives little respect from its owners (SideNote 3.1). It covers the entire body, having a surface area of close to 15 square feet and weighing about 10 pounds (Marieb & Hoehn, 2006). The skin is a highly complex organ composed of tiny glands, a rich network of blood vessels, and sensory receptors all interwoven within a matrix of **epithelial cells** and connective tissue. As Figure 3.1 shows, skin tissue can be anatomically divided into two principal divisions. The *epidermis*, which is the outermost layer, serves as a protective shield and is composed of several sublayers that are constantly being replenished. The underlying *dermis* makes up the bulk of skin tissue and contains most of the mechanoreceptors and nerve endings that generate touch sensations.

Skin tissue can be broadly classified into two general types—*hairy* and *hairless*—with each having its own structural makeup and

mechanoreceptor composition (Marieb & Hoehn, 2006). The structural differences impart different mechanical properties that affect the elasticity and resilience of skin that in turn affects the sensation of touch. Hairy skin, as the term implies, contains hairs and covers most of the body, whereas hairless skin is only found in certain distinct part of the body (e.g., palm, lips, etc.).

Types of mechanoreceptors

The human skin contains a variety of mechanoreceptors that can be classified into three types, as shown in Figure 3.2 on page 64. The so-called *encapsulated receptors* have a specialized capsule that surrounds a nerve ending (Kandel et al., 2000; Purves, 2007; Squire et al., 2002). The Pacinian, Meissner, and Ruffini corpuscles are examples of mechanoreceptors that fall into this category. The capsule itself serves specific functions that are ideally suited to the kinds of mechanical stimulation captured by that particular receptor. For example, the onion-like structure of the Pacinian corpuscle is believed to act as a mechanical filter, which aids in the transmission of vibrational stimuli, whereas the Meissner and Ruffini capsules are designed for transmitting light touch and steady pressure sensations, respectively.

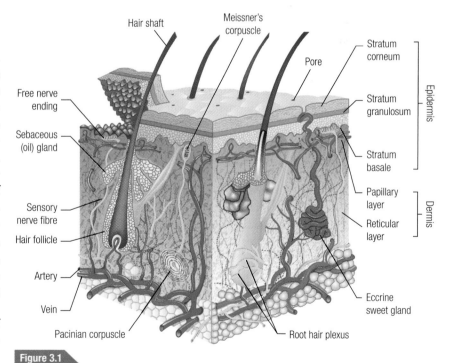

Figure 3.1

Cross-section of hairy skin showing the two principal divisions—epidermis and dermis. The majority of mechanoreceptors are located within the dermis. Adapted from *Human Anatomy and Physiology* (7th ed.), by E. Marieb and K. Hoehn, 2006, San Francisco, CA: Benjamin Cummings.

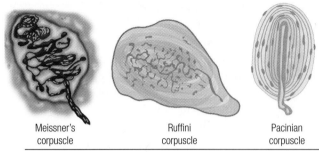

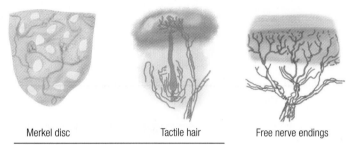

Figure 3.2

Drawings of several types of mechanoreceptors found in the skin. The receptors can be broadly classified as being encapsulated, having an accessory structure, or as free nerve endings. Adapted from *Histology*, by S. Ramón y Cajal, 1933, Baltimore, MD: William Wood & Co.

A second type of mechanoreceptor is composed of a sensory nerve fibre in conjunction with a separate accessory structure. The Merkel disc, for example, is a type of mechanoreceptor where the sensory nerve ending is associated with a type of epithelial cell (the so-called *Merkel cell*). This complex is responsible for the detection of light touch to the skin. Another example is the lanceolate endings, which are found in hairy skin where they run along the hair shaft and are therefore triggered only by movement of the hair follicles.

The third type of mechanoreceptor is made up of various types of free nerve endings that do not have any specialized terminal structures or other associations. These nerve endings are responsible for detecting thermal changes, such as warmth and cold, as well as pain. The pain receptors, also called nociceptors, can be further subdivided on the types of pain that are detected (e.g., mechanical, thermal, or mixed forms of pain).

The distribution of these different types of mechanoreceptors can vary with skin type. In general, the receptors are found either in superficial skin, near the interface of the dermis and epidermis, or more deeply in the dermis and even below it. Superficial receptors found in hairy skin include Merkel discs, hair receptors, and free nerve endings. Both Pacinian and Ruffini corpuscles are found in the deep zone of hairy and hairless skin (Marieb & Hoehn, 2006).

Signal transduction in mechanoreceptors

Our knowledge of transduction mechanisms in mechanoreceptors is somewhat limited because of the way in which they are embedded in skin tissue. It is difficult to isolate an individual receptor and study the way in which it generates electrical signals in response to mechanical stimulation. What we do know is largely derived from studies of the Pacinian corpuscle. Its relatively large size and location deep within the skin has helped it to serve as a model mechanoreceptor for tactile transduction studies.

When a mechanical stimulus is applied to the skin, the pressure is ultimately transmitted to the receptor itself where the strain produces opening of Na^+ channels (Lumpkin & Caterina, 2007; Smith, 2000). As we noted in Chapter 2, the resulting movement of Na^+ into the mechanoreceptor will result in a depolarizing receptor potential. If this potential is large enough, it will cause action potentials to be generated. But exactly where are these action potentials produced, given that all we have within the skin is a nerve ending, possibly with an accessory capsule? To answer that, we have to examine a rather unusual characteristic of the neurons that give rise to mechanoreceptors.

Mechanoreceptors are terminals of modified bipolar neurons

The vast majority of neurons in the brain have a multipolar structure whereby a single axon and various dendrites emerge from the cell body. As we saw in Chapter 2, the number and pattern of arborization of the dendrites is responsible for producing the diverse structural types of neurons within the central nervous system. Mechanoreceptors, however, emerge from a separate class known as *bipolar neurons*. These have a single axon and only a single dendrite that generally protrude from opposite ends of the cell body. At some point during development, the two processes fuse and produce a single emergent fibre that quickly splits into two just outside the cell body (Figure 3.3). One of the fibres is called the *peripheral branch* and proceeds to the skin where it ends up either as free nerve endings or in some kind of encapsulated form (e.g., a Pacinian corpuscle, as shown in Figure 3.3). The other fibre is called the *central branch* and carries touch signals to the spinal cord (Catania & Henry, 2006; Squire et al., 2002).

Where then is the cell body of the mechanoreceptor neuron located? It turns out that the cell body is actually situated quite far away from the skin in a structure called the **dorsal root ganglion** (DRG). The DRG itself is located right next to the spinal cord. We will return to this structure when we examine spinal mechanisms in Section A.3. For the moment, though, let us consider the flow of sensory signals that arise from tactile stimulation of the skin. As we have already noted, touch stimulation will produce a depolarizing receptor potential in the terminal end of the peripheral branch (i.e., the mechanoreceptor), the only site in the DRG neuron that is sensitive to stimulus energy (SideNote 3.2).

What makes the DRG neuron unusual is that once the receptor potential reaches threshold, an action potential is generated in the immediate vicinity of the end organ itself (Morley, 1998). That is, unlike conventional multipolar neurons where the depolarizing signal must first reach the cell body and can thereafter produce an action potential, DRG neurons are capable of producing action potentials right near the terminal end of the peripheral branch. These action potentials then flow along the peripheral and central branch to reach the spinal cord.

2. AFFERENT FIBRES

The nature of the sensory response to a tactile stimulus and the speed with which it is transmitted are determined in large part by the **afferent fibre**. DRG neurons come in many varieties, each suited to a particular role in

tactile sensation. This is evident in both the anatomical structure of the neuron and the physiological characteristics of its firing pattern and transmission. DRG neurons can be broadly classified into two groups based on the size of the cell body and the diameter of its fibres. Furthermore, the afferent fibres can be either myelinated or unmyelinated. These anatomical factors, along with the precise type of mechanoreceptor residing at the terminal end, determine the nature of the physiological response to touch.

Transmission speed

The speed at which afferent fibres conduct action potentials is determined by the diameter of the fibre and its degree of myelination (Morley, 1998; Smith, 2000). The larger the diameter, and the greater the degree of myelination, the faster the nerve signal transmission. Physiologists have designated sensory and motor nerve fibres by a lettering system—Aα, Aβ, Aδ, and C. Of these, only the latter three are associated with mechanoreceptors in the skin, the bulk being of the Aβ type. As Table 3.1 on page 66 shows, this fibre type is moderately myelinated and has a relatively large diameter compared to the others, making this a fast-conducting fibre. Both the Aδ and C fibres are thinner and contain either little or no myelination. Consequently, the transmission speed is much less in these fibres.

The speed at which tactile sensations are transmitted to the central nervous system is obviously important. A stimulus that is harmful requires a quick withdrawal response. If that response depended on the poorly conducting C fibres, then the response would likely be too slow to prevent physical damage. For example, it could take as long as four seconds for a signal to reach the spinal cord for a stimulus applied

SideNote | **3.2**

Strictly speaking, the end organ of the DRG neuron that serves as the transducing element is referred to as the *mechanoreceptor*.

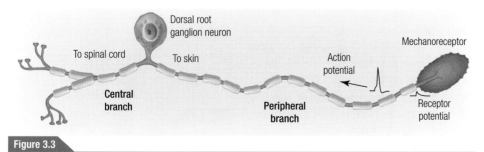

Figure 3.3

Mechanoreceptors belong to a specialized class known as *bipolar neurons*. The cell body, which is located in the dorsal root ganglion, gives off two processes—one that carries signals from the skin mechanoreceptor and another that transmits signals into the spinal cord.

Table 3.1

Characteristics of the Four Types of Afferent Fibres Associated with the Somatosensory System

Fibre Type	Myelination	Fibre Diameter	Transmission Speed
Aα	Heavy	15–20 μm	70–120 m/s
Aβ	Medium	5–15 μm	40–70 m/s
Aδ	Light	1–5 μm	10–35 m/s
C	None	0.2–1.5 μm	0.5–2.0 m/s

SideNote 3.3

The rapid withdrawal from a damaging stimulus is commonly referred to as a *reflex response*. We know from common experience that this occurs very fast and therefore the signals must be carried by fast-conducting fibres.

SideNote 3.4

Adaptability is largely determined by the structure of the receptor. Meissner corpuscles are physically attached to surrounding epithelial cells and therefore susceptible to rapid skin movements. Pacinian corpuscles have a fluid-filled capsule that mechanically filters out sustained pressures. As a result, both are FA-type receptors and respond transiently to changes in skin indentation.

to the soles of the feet. However, the more rapidly conducting Aδ could deliver the same signal in less than 60 milliseconds. The Aβ fibres would deliver the signal in half that time. The vast majority of skin mechanoreceptors are linked to fast-conducting afferent fibres to ensure rapid perception of tactile stimuli and a quick response if that stimulus is too intense (SideNote 3.3). In fact, as Table 3.2 shows, all of the encapsulated receptors are linked to the fast-conducting Aβ fibres. Only the free nerve endings are associated with the slower conducting fibres. Their roles in mediating painful stimulation will be taken up in detail in the last section of this chapter.

Response adaptation

Electrophysiological studies of tactile afferent fibres have shown that their responses can be placed in one of two classes in terms of how they adapt to ongoing or continuous stimulation. The studies, originally conducted by Roland Johansson and Åke Vallbo in Sweden during the 1970s, showed that touch signals can be either sustained or transient in nature (Johansson & Vallbo, 1983). The terms that they applied to these two classes were "slowly adapting (SA)" and "fast adapting (FA)." Response adaptation, in this case, refers to how the fibres respond to continuous touch stimulation, such as skin indentation due to pressure. A transient, or FA, response shows bursts of action potentials only when a stimulus is applied to the skin. This response is called *fast adapting* because neural firing subsides quickly during continued application of the stimulus (Figure 3.4). By contrast, SA-type fibres will fire as long as the stimulus in maintained, though at a somewhat reduced rate over time.

As Table 3.2 shows, afferent fibres associated with Merkel and Ruffini receptors show SA-type responses, whereas those linked to Meissner and Pacinian receptors show FA

responses. These are further subdivided on the basis of the receptors' location in the skin. Those receptors located in superficial areas are of type I (SA-I or FA-I), whereas receptors located in deep skin are of type II (SA-II or FA-II). The transient and sustained nature of the sensory response in tactile afferent fibres plays a crucial role in the kinds of touch stimuli that they can effectively transmit to the central nervous system (SideNote 3.4). The receptors with SA-type responses, for example, have low **temporal resolution** and therefore are best able to transmit tactile information that does not change with time (e.g., steady pressure). The receptors with FA responses, on the other hand, have much higher temporal resolution and are optimal detectors of physical stimulation that varies with time, such as vibration, motion, and flutter (Table 3.2).

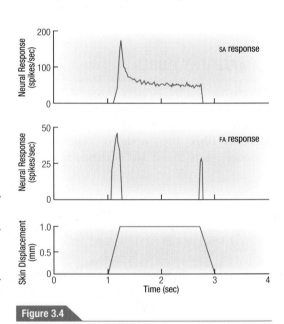

Figure 3.4

Sensory signals in tactile afferents can be either sustained (slowly adapting or SA) or transient (fast adapting or FA) in nature. SA-type fibres continue to generate signals as long as the stimulus is present, whereas FA fibres only produce a neural response at the beginning and end of skin indentation.

Table 3.2

Physiological Characteristics and Perceptual Impressions Produced by Different Types
of Skin Mechanoreceptors and Associated Afferent Fibres

Mechanoreceptor	Skin Location	Fibre Type	Response Type	RF Size	Perceptual Impression
Merkel	Superficial	Aβ	SA-I	Small	Steady pressure
Meissner	Superficial	Aβ	FA-I	Small	Flutter; motion
Ruffini	Deep	Aβ	SA-II	Large	Steady pressure
Pacinian	Deep	Aβ	FA-I	Large	Vibration
Free nerve endings	Superficial	Aδ	Mixed	Variable	Warmth; cold; sharp pain; burning pain

Receptive field size

The **receptive field** of a mechanoreceptor is determined by recording from its afferent fibre and surveying the area of skin that will generate electrical signals. The size of the receptive field is influenced by both the type of mechanoreceptor and its location on the skin (Kandel et al., 2000; Morley, 1998). Those receptors located in the superficial part of the skin have small receptive fields, whereas receptors in the deeper part generally have large fields. As Table 3.2 shows, both Pacinian and Ruffini receptors have large receptive fields, whereas the Meissner and Merkel receptors have small receptive fields with sharp borders (Figure 3.5). As noted on the previous page, sustained and transient responses among mechanoreceptors are further distinguished on the basis of skin location. Small field receptors in the superficial skin are denoted as type I (SA-I or FA-I), whereas the large field receptors in deeper skin are type II (SA-II or FA-II).

Our ability to resolve the spatial details of tactile stimuli is determined by the size of the receptive field. We distinguish closely spaced objects through receptors with small field sizes because they can capture more independent bits of information per unit space (SideNote 3.5). Therefore, the smaller the receptive field size, the greater our capacity for **spatial resolution**. The Merkel and Meissner receptors have small receptive fields and are used by the somatosensory system to resolve fine spatial differences among various tactile stimuli (Figure 3.5). The Ruffini and Pacinian receptors, on the other hand, have large receptive fields and therefore can only detect coarse spatial differences.

3. SPINAL MECHANISMS AND SIGNAL TRANSFER

We have come to learn that mechanoreceptors are actually terminal end organs of sensory axons that arise from dorsal root ganglion neurons (SideNote 3.6). As noted before, the cell bodies of these neurons reside in structures that are located just outside of the spinal cord. Each dorsal root ganglion gives off a fibre bundle that branches out to collect somatosensory

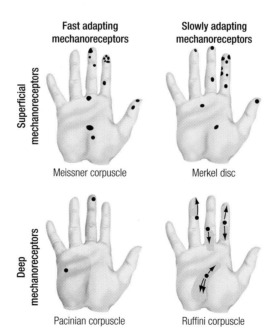

Fast adapting mechanoreceptors   **Slowly adapting mechanoreceptors**

Superficial mechanoreceptors

Meissner corpuscle   Merkel disc

Deep mechanoreceptors

Pacinian corpuscle   Ruffini corpuscle

Figure 3.5

Superficial mechanoreceptors, such as Meissner corpuscles and Merkel discs, have small, highly confined receptive fields. The Pacinian and Ruffini corpuscles, which are located in deeper skin, have large receptive fields, though with a zone of high sensitivity (black dot). Ruffini receptors can be excited by skin stretch (arrows).

SideNote | **3.5**

The ability to resolve the spatial layout of objects on skin is determined by receptive field (RF) size. Mechanoreceptors with small fields can distinguish two closely spaced objects better (i.e., high spatial resolution) than receptors that have a large field size (i.e., low spatial resolution).

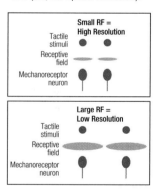

SideNote | **3.6**

Both the peripheral and central branches of the afferent fibre are considered to be a sensory axon because they are both capable of conducting action potentials. DRG neurons, therefore, have no dendritic elements and receive no synaptic stimulation from other neurons.

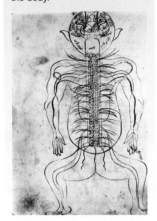

Image from the History of Medicine (NLM)

information from that side of the body. Action potentials generated by tactile stimulation flow along the afferent fibre, cross over from the peripheral to the central branch, and thereafter enter the spinal cord. In this section, we examine the details of how this information transfer occurs and how the signals ultimately reach the brain to produce tactile perception.

Spinal nerves and ganglia

The spinal cord is the only channel for the transmission of somatosensory and motor information to and from the brain. The spinal cord in turn receives and distributes these signals through a total of 31 pairs of spinal nerves that emerge out of the cord from top to bottom—one member of each pair innervating the right side of the body and the other, the left (SideNote 3.7). Each spinal nerve is made up of two roots—the dorsal and ventral, so named because of the way they emerge out of the spinal cord (SideNote 3.8). The two roots on each side emerge separately, proceed for a short distance, and then come together to form the spinal nerve on that side (see Figure 3.6A) (Smith, 2000; Squire et al., 2002).

The actual function of the nerve fibres contained in the two roots was established in the early part of the 19th century by Charles Bell and François Magendie. They showed that the dorsal root carries sensory signals into the spinal cord, whereas the ventral root carries motor signals out and into the muscles. This concept represented a major breakthrough in understanding the way in which two fundamentally different types of signals are coordinated by the nervous system and transmitted by the same fibre bundle to and from the periphery. This basic principle regarding the separation of function in the dorsal and ventral roots is referred to as the **Bell–Magendie law**.

Another important difference between the two roots of spinal nerves is the presence of the dorsal root **ganglion** and the absence of a similar collection of neurons in the ventral root. As Figure 3.6A and B show, the dorsal root fibres enter the spinal cord, proceed through the white matter, and terminate in the grey matter. Given that there is no ventral root ganglion, where then is the location of the motor neurons that give off the fibres contained in the ventral root? It turns out that these neurons

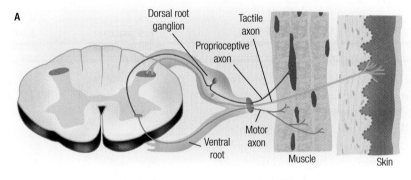

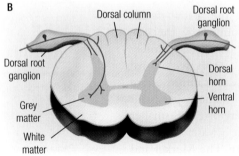

Figure 3.6

The organization of the dorsal and ventral roots of spinal nerves. A. Dorsal root fibres carry somatosensory signals from the periphery into the spinal cord, whereas ventral root fibres carry motor signals from the spinal cord to the muscles. The two roots join together to form a spinal nerve. B. The spinal cord is composed of white matter along the outer margins and a central, butterfly-shaped core of grey matter. The cell bodies of motor neurons are located in the ventral horn, whereas those of the somatosensory neurons are located in the dorsal root ganglion.

are located within the grey matter of the spinal cord itself in a part that is called the *ventral horn*.

Dermatomal map

All somatosensory information is sent to the central nervous system through spinal nerves and—in the case of the head, neck, and face region—through a set of cranial nerves that emerge out of the brain stem. The entire body surface can therefore be divided into discrete areas that are represented by a single nerve. Each of these areas is called a **derma-tome**, and the map representing the skin surface devoted to all spinal nerves is called the *dermatomal map* (Heller & Ballesteros, 2005; Lee, McPhee, & Stringer, 2008). As Figure 3.7 shows, the body areas portrayed in the derma-tomal map are designated by the segmental region of the spinal cord from where the nerve emerges. Although it appears that the bound-aries are exact in this representation, there is actually some overlap in innervation between adjacent spinal nerves. Dermatomal maps are valuable as a clinical tool in the event of injury or infection to a particular dorsal root.

Signal transmission through the spinal cord

We next follow the route taken by somato-sensory signals through the spinal cord and up to the brain. We should note at the outset that two dominant themes will emerge in this dis-cussion. The first is that there is a serial relay of signals from site to site as the signals ascend the hierarchy of neural structures to ultimately reach the cerebral cortex. And second, there is a parallel feature to this signal transmission such that the different qualities of touch that we have already remarked on are transmit-ted independently through separate pathways (Morley, 1998; Smith, 2000).

The route taken by afferent fibres after entering the spinal cord is largely determined by the type of fibre concerned and the kind of somatosensory information that is being trans-mitted. The large-diameter, myelinated fibres (Aα and Aβ), which carry tactile and proprio-ceptive signals, branch out soon after entering the spinal cord. As Figure 3.8 on page 70 shows, some branches proceed into the dorsal horn and synapse onto neurons there, whereas other branches take a sharp turn and proceed verti-cally up the white matter of the spinal cord within fibre tracts contained in the **dorsal column**. The second order neurons within the dorsal horn either synapse onto other neurons

locally, such as motor neurons in the ventral horn, or alternatively can send their projec-tions up the dorsal columns as well. In fact, almost half the dorsal column axons originate from these neurons with the remainder being branches of dorsal root ganglion neurons.

The route taken by the small-diameter, poorly or non-myelinated fibres (Aδ and C) that carry pain and temperature signals is quite different. These fibres first synapse in the dor-sal horn upon neurons that, instead of sending fibres up the dorsal columns, actually cross over to the other side of the spinal cord (Figure 3.8).

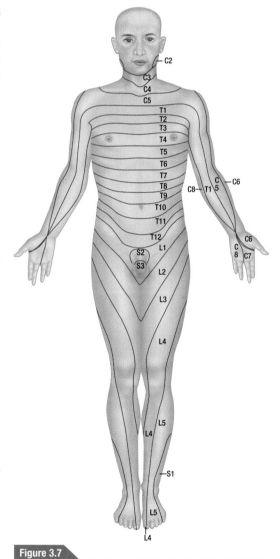

The frontal dermatomal map of a male human. The designa-tions reflect the skin representation of that particular spinal nerve. The spinal nerves are named in numerical order within the segmental regions of the vertebral column from which they emerge—eight from the cervical (C) segment, twelve from the thoracic (T) segment, five from the lumbar (L) seg-ment, and five from the sacral (S) segment. Based on a med-ical illustration by Frank H. Netter, MD.

SideNote | **3.9**

Apart from the olfactory (smell) system, ascending pathways from all other sensory systems are transmitted through relay nuclei in the thalamus on their way to the cerebral cortex.

Once there, they enter into fibre tracts that are part of the **anterolateral system**, which transmits the signals to higher levels in the central nervous system.

Serial arrangement of relay nuclei

The somatosensory system, like other sensory systems, transmits its signals to the cerebral cortex though a series of relay sites where synaptic transfer occurs onto neurons that in turn project to higher levels (Iwamura, 1998; Squire et al., 2002). The dorsal horn of the spinal cord itself is one such site of signal relay. The fibres of these neurons, as well as afferent fibres of DRG neurons, course upward within the dorsal column to terminate in nuclei located in the lower margin of the brain stem (medulla). These so-called **dorsal column nuclei** represent the second relay site. The axons of these neurons then arch over the midline to the

other side of the brain and ascend to the thalamus in a fibre bundle called the **medial lemniscus**. The fibres terminate in specific nuclei within the thalamus that serve as the next relay (SideNote 3.9). The thalamic relay neurons project directly to the cerebral cortex through a fibre bundle known as the **internal capsule**.

Signal relay in the anterolateral pathways that carry pain and temperature information is a bit more complicated. We have already seen that the first relay here occurs in the dorsal horn from where the projections cross the midline and proceed up through the anterolateral pathways on the opposite side of the spinal cord. Most of these axons terminate in relay nuclei that are distributed in three subcortical regions—the medulla, midbrain, and thalamus. The relay nuclei in the thalamus, which are different from the ones involved in the dorsal column–medial lemniscus pathway, project to the cortex in a diffuse manner. The variety in subcortical connections and the wide projection to the cerebral cortex of the anterolateral system reflect the complex physiological and perceptual nature of pain.

Parallel processing and modality segregation

The two pathways that we have just described—the dorsal column–medial lemniscus and anterolateral pathways—represent an important feature of signal transmission that is common to the somatosensory, auditory, and visual systems. These two ascending systems serve as examples of parallel pathways that mediate different types of information to the brain. The dorsal column–medial lemniscus pathway transmits tactile signals that are gathered from mechanoreceptors linked to Aβ fibres. As we have already seen, the signals present in these fibres can be either of SA or FA type and are triggered by steady or dynamic forms of touch, respectively. The anterolateral pathway, on the other hand, transmits signals from Aδ- and C-type afferent fibres, carrying information on warmth, cold, and pain.

This division of labour in signal transmission is not absolute. Each pathway carries some signals that are ordinarily carried by the other. For example, the anterolateral pathways can transmit some touch signals that are normally handled by the dorsal column–medial lemniscus system. However, this represents a small minority of its projections. The bulk of these fibres are used to carry somatosensory information that is specific to that pathway.

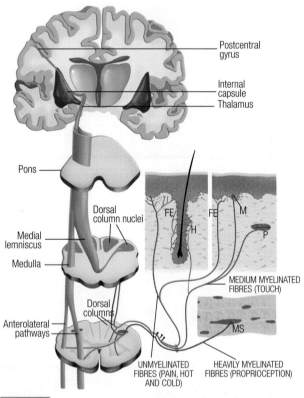

Labels: Postcentral gyrus; Internal capsule; Thalamus; Pons; Dorsal column nuclei; Medial lemniscus; Medulla; Anterolateral pathways; Dorsal columns; FE; FE; M; H; P; MEDIUM MYELINATED FIBRES (TOUCH); MS; UNMYELINATED FIBRES (PAIN, HOT AND COLD); HEAVILY MYELINATED FIBRES (PROPRIOCEPTION)

Figure 3.8

Tactile and proprioceptive signals from the periphery enter the spinal cord through the dorsal route and then follow one of two pathways to the brain. The dorsal column–medial lemniscus pathway transmits signals from medium and heavily myelinated afferent fibres, whereas the anterolateral pathway transmits information from poorly or non-myelinated fibres. Both pathways eventually cross over to the opposite side to produce contralateral mapping (i.e., the left side of the brain receives somatosensory information from the right side of the body and vice versa). There are a number of relay sites before somatosensory signals reach the cerebral cortex. Based on a medical illustration by Frank H. Netter, MD.

The presence of two parallel pathways permits independent transmission of different types of touch signals. This so-called **modality segregation** is advantageous because it allows the brain to process the two types of signals separately, something that may be necessary to produce the richness and diversity of perceptual experiences associated with different forms of somatosensory stimulation. Clearly, the processing needs of painful stimuli are different from other forms of touch, both in the noxious nature of the experience that is generated and the varied physiological, emotional, and even hormonal responses that follow.

Somatotopic organization

The projection fibres in both the dorsal column–medial lemniscus and anterolateral systems are precisely organized by function and body location. For example, axons that enter at the lowermost levels of the spinal cord are found near the midline of the dorsal columns, with axons at successively higher levels being displaced more laterally. As a result, an orderly representation of the body surface is contained in the fibre tracts that transmit somatosensory information to the brain. This so-called **somatotopic representation** is maintained in all structures along the way, such as the dorsal column nuclei and thalamus. The neural representation in these structures is such that neighbouring neurons process tactile signals from adjacent locations on the body surface.

4.   THE SOMATOSENSORY CORTEX

We have just seen how the organization of the somatosensory system at lower levels shows features that are common to other sensory systems and that can be generalized as follows. First, signal transmission is not direct but instead proceeds through a series of relay sites. Second, different aspects of sensation are coordinated through different pathways that are arranged in a parallel fashion and that display different anatomical and physiological properties. Third, the ascending fibres cross over to the opposite side so that ultimately the left side of the brain receives somatosensory signals from the right side of the body and vice versa. And finally, the afferent fibres are organized in a precise fashion within the ascending structures to produce an orderly representation of the body surface.

We will now see how these fundamental features observed at earlier levels of the somatosensory system are adopted by the cerebral cortex to ultimately yield the perceptual experience of touch and pain. It turns out that, rather than one area, several cortical areas are involved in the processing of somatosensory signals, further reflecting the general notion of parallelism and division of labour within the nervous system. The cortical areas that process these signals are located in the parietal lobe and are known as the *somatosensory cortex*.

Cortical processing begins in area S-I

The primary cortical areas that receive inputs from the thalamus through the internal capsule are located posterior to the central sulcus, a deep fissure near the top middle portion of the brain in each hemisphere. As Figure 3.9 shows, this so-called **primary somatosensory cortex** begins in the floor of the central sulcus,

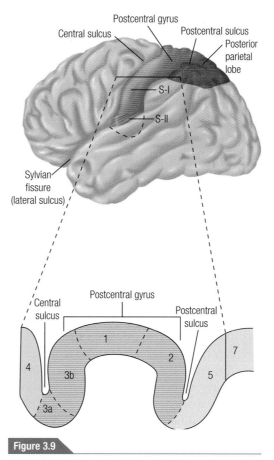

The primary and secondary cortical areas associated with somatosensory function are located in the parietal lobe. The cross-sectional view at the bottom shows the primary somatosensory cortex (area S-I), which in turn includes four anatomically distinct areas defined by Brodmann (3a, 3b, 1, and 2). Two other areas involved in somatosensory function are area S-II and the posterior parietal cortex (areas 5 and 7).

extends up the posterior wall of the sulcus, onto the mound of brain tissue located adjacent to the sulcus (**postcentral gyrus**), and down along the wall of the next fissure, the postcentral sulcus. This area of the brain serves as the starting point for cortical processing of somatosensory information. For this reason, it is referred to as the *primary somatosensory cortex* and denoted as *area S-I.*

It turns out that area S-I is actually a composite of four smaller areas that are distinguishable on anatomical grounds. In the early 1900s, anatomist Korbinian Brodmann made a microscopic survey of the entire cerebral cortex and subdivided it into regions of common histological appearance (see Chapter 2). The cortical region posterior to the central sulcus, according to his criteria, was composed of three such anatomically distinct subdivisions, which he named areas 1, 2, and 3 (Figure 3.9). Area 3 was subdivided by later anatomists into areas 3a and 3b.

Serial and parallel processing in the somatosensory cortex

Although all four anatomical subdivisions of area S-I receive projection fibres from the thalamus, the heaviest input occurs upon areas 3a and 3b. Neurons in both of these areas then project in a serial fashion to areas 1 and 2, thus forming a hierarchy of cortical modules within area S-I itself. The anatomical plan of serial connections that we observed in the ascending pathways is therefore also evident in the cortical regions that process somatosensory information.

The four anatomical subdivisions of area S-I are involved in basic processing of tactile and proprioceptive signals. Area 3a, for example, acts on proprioceptive signals arising from the muscles and joints, whereas area 3b processes tactile signals from the skin. The next pair of areas in the hierarchy also displays a similar division of labour with area 1 being particularly responsive to tactile signals and area 2 to both tactile and proprioceptive signals. In addition, neurons in area 1 process signals from FA– and SA-type mechanoreceptors in a separate manner. We therefore have a scheme where parallel processing of somatosensory signals is superimposed upon a serial arrangement of cortical areas. The parallel feature arises from the separate handling of tactile versus proprioceptive stimuli and also of FA versus SA signals within the tactile processing compartments.

The serial arrangement of cortical areas extends beyond area S-I as well. Two other cortical areas that process somatosensory signals are area S-II, a small area located just below area S-I, and the posterior parietal cortex. Although area S-II receives a small projection from the thalamus, its function is largely dependent on the heavy projection it receives from area S-I. Similarly, there are two areas in the region known as the *posterior parietal cortex* that are in turn dependent on signal processing in earlier somatosensory areas (Mountcastle, 1995). Areas 5 and 7, which lie adjacent to area S-I (see Figure 3.9), represent modules that are next in the hierarchy of cortical areas. As such, these areas represent higher-order sensory areas that integrate various aspects of somatosensory function. One example is the progressive integration of somatosensory signals whereby neural responses to both proprioceptive and tactile stimuli become more intertwined along each step in the hierarchy.

The somatotopic map

Another feature that the somatosensory cortex shares with the ascending pathways is the orderly representation of the body surface. In what is now regarded as a series of landmark studies in the history of neuroscience, Clinton Woolsey in Madison and Wilder Penfield in Montreal showed separately that the postcentral gyrus (area 1) contains a map of the entire body (Penfield & Rasmussen, 1950; Woolsey, Erickson, & Gilson, 1979). That is, neurons from different locations on the postcentral gyrus could be activated by somatosensory stimuli applied only to particular parts of the body, which when considered over the entire surface of the postcentral gyrus, represented an orderly and systematic body representation (Figure 3.10).

The details of this **somatotopic map**, however, were somewhat crude in the early studies because of the techniques available at the time. Woolsey used cats and monkeys for large-scale neural recordings (SideNote 3.10), whereas Penfield applied small electric currents in the postcentral gyrus of human patients undergoing brain surgery and asked them to indicate where on the body they felt a stimulus. More recently, single-unit studies in area S-I of monkeys by Michael Merzenich, Jon Kaas, and others have provided maps with much greater precision (Kaas, 2008; Kaas, Merzenich, & Killackey, 1983). These studies led to the

Wilder Penfield (1891–1976)
Image from the History of Medicine (NLM)

SideNote | 3.10

The organization of the somatosensory cortex in monkeys is similar to that of humans in terms of its layout and subdivision into anatomically discrete areas. Much of our current understanding of the neural bases of somatosensory function has therefore emerged from studies on monkeys.

surprising finding that each of the anatomical subdivisions of S-I actually has its own separate somatotopic map. That is, a separate and total body representation, often referred to as a **homunculus**, is found in each of areas 3a, 3b, 1, and 2. Similarly, a somatotopic map was later found to be present in area S-II, though not in any of the posterior parietal areas that have somatosensory function. Although it is likely that each of these maps contributes to a coherent perception of the nature and location of touched objects, their separate roles in this process are still not understood.

What are some of the notable features of the somatotopic map? As we have already seen, the map is an orderly representation of the opposite half of the body. This so-called *contralateral mapping* arises because of the crossover of the dorsal column–medial lemniscus fibre pathway in the medulla as well as the anterolateral system in the spinal cord. This arrangement is mirror symmetric so that the somatosensory cortex in the left hemisphere is activated by the right half of the body, whereas the cortex in the right hemisphere is activated by the left half of the body.

A second notable feature of the somatotopic map is the non-linearity of the representation. If the entire body surface were to be represented in an equivalent manner so that area S-I showed a uniform map, then we would have had a linear representation. However, as Penfield and Woolsey showed, each part of the body is represented in proportion to its relative importance. As Figure 3.10 shows, the distal sites—such as the trunk, toes, etc.—have only a small part of the somatosensory cortex devoted to them, whereas areas such as the face and index fingers are processed by a much larger cortical mass. In fact, the cortical representation of the digits is nearly 100 times greater than the cortical area devoted to the toes.

Receptive fields

The progressive complexity in somatosensory processing through the hierarchy of cortical areas is evident from the changes that occur in the structure of neuronal receptive fields (Goodwin & Wheat, 2004; Squire et al., 2002). As with the afferent fibres that we saw earlier, cortical neurons too can be driven by tactile stimulation applied only to discrete and confined regions of the body surface. This makes sense because cortical neurons after all are ultimately connected to afferent fibres that

innervate a particular part of the body. Each neuron in the somatosensory cortex, therefore, has a specific receptive field such that stimulation applied only in that location will activate the neuron.

Receptive fields are small and simple in the early cortical areas, such as areas 3a and 3b, and become larger and more complex as we proceed up the hierarchy to areas 1 and 2 and beyond. Receptive field size within each of these areas is highly variable and determined by its location in the somatotopic map. For example, the large amount of cortex devoted to the index finger means that many more neurons are sampling a given area of the skin surface than elsewhere in the body. This in turn is accounted for by a greater number of mechanoreceptors per unit area of skin tissue in the index finger

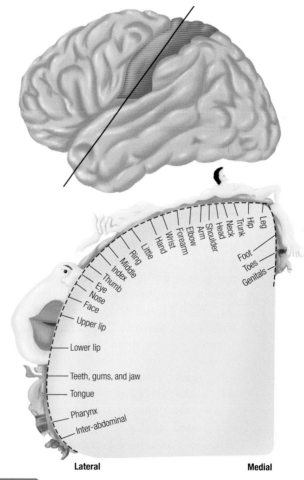

Figure 3.10

The somatotopic map of area 1 (postcentral gyrus) in the primary somatosensory cortex (S-I) shows an orderly representation of body areas. If the left cerebral hemisphere (top) is cut along the indicated line it would bisect the postcentral gyrus to reveal the section shown at the bottom. Neural activity from the medial to the lateral margins can be precisely mapped to a particular area of the body. Adapted from *The Cerebral Cortex of Man: A Clinical Study of Localization of Function,* by W. Penfield and T. Rasmussen, 1950, New York, NY: Macmillan.

SideNote | **3.11**

The fingertips in fact have the highest density of mechanoreceptors in the human body, a fact well suited to their function of probing and identifying objects during manipulation. There are more than 2,500 receptors per square centimetre, of which nearly two-thirds are Meissner's corpuscles.

SideNote | **3.12**

The cerebral cortex is composed of six layers that are distinct in terms of their cellular composition and input/output relationships compared to other parts of the brain.

SideNote | **3.13**

It was later shown in the 1960s that columnar organization is a fundamental feature of the primary visual cortex, the first cortical site where visual input arrives. Several other areas of the visual brain have subsequently been shown to have vertical columns of neurons that are largely devoted to processing a particular attribute of the visual stimulus.

(SideNote 3.11). As a result, each cortical neuron can sample from a much more confined surface area on the skin, which in turn produces small receptive fields. Cortical neurons that represent the extremities, such as the trunk and toes, have among the largest receptive fields.

Columnar organization

One of the major developments in the field of neuroscience came from the work of Vernon Mountcastle at Johns Hopkins University in the 1950s while he was exploring the receptive field properties of neurons in area S-I. It was well known by then that the different modalities of touch—such as pressure, vibration, temperature, etc.—were captured by different sets of mechanoreceptors and transmitted through FA- and SA-type fibres. It was originally assumed that these different modalities were separately processed in the different layers of the somatosensory cortex (SideNote 3.12). As Mountcastle showed, however, neurons in all six layers actually respond to the same modality in any given part of area S-I. Instead, the responses of the different types of receptors are organized in columns that run vertically from the cortical surface to the white matter (Mountcastle, 1997). As Figure 3.11 shows, some columns are activated by FA-type fibres, whereas others are activated by SA fibres.

Columnar organization quickly became accepted as a major architectural feature of the cerebral cortex and as another example of parallelism. The functional specialization of the peripheral mechanoreceptors and ascending pathways is further elaborated in the somatosensory cortex, first through area specialization (e.g., 3a vs. 3b) and then by way of the columns within any given area. The demonstration that columns of specialized neurons serve as elementary functional units in the somatosensory cortex has now been extended to other areas of the cerebral cortex that serve different sensory functions. As a result, neuroscientists now regard columnar organization as a basic structural principle of several cortical compartments (SideNote 3.13).

5. SOMATOMOTOR CIRCUITS

A major function of the somatosensory system is to provide information for the purposeful movement of our limbs and body in relation to objects in the external world with which we interact. The simple act of brushing

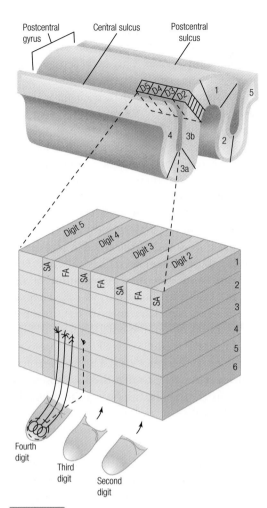

Figure 3.11

Tactile inputs from different parts of the body are arranged as columns of neurons that run from the surface to the white matter and encompass all six layers of the cortex. An example is shown here for a part of area 3b that represents the digits. The expanded view at the bottom shows that each digit is represented by a different column, which in turn is subdivided into inputs from FA- and SA-type afferents. Adapted from "Multiple Representations of the Body within the Primary Somatosensory Cortex of Primates," by J. H. Kaas, R. J. Nelson, M. Sur, C. S. Lin, and M. Merzenich, 1979, *Science, 204*, pp. 521–523.

our teeth, catching a baseball, or stroking our hair is actually the result of complex interactions between somatosensory input and motor output at multiple levels in the central nervous system. The motor output system itself is quite complex and involves many neural structures and circuits organized in a hierarchical and parallel fashion, an exhaustive review of which is outside the scope of this chapter. Rather, we briefly consider here two key sites of somatosensory and motor (somatomotor) interaction that are critical for a variety of functions, from simple reflexes to voluntary movements of the body.

Somatomotor control in the spinal cord

The spinal cord represents the lowest level in the hierarchy of somatomotor control. The neuronal circuits here produce a patterned output through the motor neurons in the spinal ventral horn that results in a number of stereotyped reflex movements (Kandel et al., 2000; Marieb & Hoehn, 2006). The motor signals emerge out of the spinal cord through the ventral roots and proceed through the spinal nerves to innervate the muscles (see Figure 3.6). The activity in the ventral horn motor neurons is modulated by interneurons, which in turn are controlled by two sources. The first source is the descending fibres within the spinal cord that carry motor commands issued by the cerebral cortex. Voluntary movements initiated by the motor cortex are therefore executed by the same network of spinal neurons that are involved in reflex behaviour.

The second source of input to the spinal motor networks is the somatosensory afferents from the dorsal roots. These neural circuits are responsible for the reflex withdrawal that we are so familiar with when we come into contact with a painful stimulus (SideNote 3.14). Even before we are aware of the noxious nature of the stimulus, we have already withdrawn our body from that source. The speed with which we are able to do this suggests that there is little time for the signals to proceed to the cerebral cortex and make us aware that damage is being done to our body before initiating the appropriate motor commands for withdrawal. Rather, a very simple set of neural circuits in the spinal cord—involving dorsal root afferents, interneurons, and motor neurons—are the only elements involved in generating the rapid withdrawal response.

Somatomotor control in the cortex

Another site where we see significant coupling between somatosensory input and motor output is in the cerebral cortex. We would expect to find the cortical areas involved in motor function to be located close to the cortical areas involved in somatosensory processing. This is indeed the case. The so-called *primary motor cortex*, which is located in the **precentral gyrus**, and associated areas located nearby represent the highest level of motor control. Here, the planning and coordination of complex voluntary movements is undertaken. The signals are then passed through relay sites where they are fine-tuned and ultimately reach the motor neurons in the spinal cord.

The primary motor cortex receives a large projection from all of the somatosensory processing areas. This is understandable given how closely the two systems must co-operate if we are to physically interact with an object—an interaction that relies on feedback signals from tactile receptors in the skin and proprioceptive receptors in the muscles. As we have already seen, those somatosensory signals are represented in the cortex in the form of an organized, somatotopic map. It turns out that the precentral gyrus also contains a similar map, but one representing motor output to muscles over the entire body. This **motor map** shares many similarities with the somatotopic map, including contralateral control and an expanded cortical area devoted to the muscles of the hand and face.

One advantage of having the motor and somatotopic maps in close proximity (i.e., on either side of the central sulcus) is that it permits a more precise registration in the connectivity. The somatosensory projections to the motor cortex are organized in a **homotopic** fashion—that is, a given part of the motor cortex receives projections from the same part on the body map of the somatosensory cortex. This specificity ensures that the somatosensory feedback that is crucial to guiding many of our movements is organized by body part and that neuronal ensembles representing the same part of the body are closely matched in terms of their connections.

B. Perceptual Aspects of Tactile Sensation

Much of the recent history of sensory research has been devoted to discoveries and insights that have emerged from the field of vision science. And yet, many of the fundamental laws of sensory science were actually first established by researchers working on the somatosensory system. Both Fechner and Weber, whom we discussed at length in Chapter 1, performed many psychophysical experiments on touch, the results of which were instrumental in the development of their ideas on sensory processing. Many of the more recent ideas on sensitivity, localization, persistence, and adaptation originated from somatosensory research as well. Even many of the neural underpinnings of sensory function such as receptive fields, parallel channels, and cortical columns were originally

SideNote | **3.14**

The common usage of the term *reflex* refers to the immediate withdrawal response that occurs after encountering a painful stimulus. The neural mechanisms for reflex action were first postulated by Descartes in the 17th century, as depicted in this figure from *De Homine*. The scientific usage of the term concerns any involuntary, stereotyped movement. An example is the back-and-forth motion of the arms during walking.

Image from the History of Medicine (NLM)

SideNote | **3.15**

To complicate matters further, it turns out that lifting a load attached to the skin is as effective a touch stimulus as having a force indent the skin. Therefore, skin movement itself is critical for generating the sensation of touch.

Max von Frey (1852–1932)
Image from the History of Medicine (NLM)

SideNote | **3.16**

The Semmes–Weinstein esthesiometer is often used as a clinical tool to evaluate loss of sensitivity in the lower extremities, especially the soles, that sometimes occurs in diabetic patients. Early detection of sensory loss can prevent a number of foot problems in these patients.

discovered in the somatosensory system. In the sections that follow, we will examine signal processing in the somatosensory system as revealed through psychophysical experimentation and the resulting insights that have been gained into the perceptual aspects of touch.

1. INTENSITY AND SENSATION

The first issue to consider in tactile psychophysics is the nature of the stimulus. Although it may seem straightforward to think of touch in merely mechanical terms, such as pressure applied to the skin, it turns out that the area of skin affected, the depth of skin indentation, and the rate at which the indentation occurs are also important factors that affect the touch sensation. Threshold values can be different depending on the velocity of indentation. For example, it is possible to indent the skin by as much as 2 mm without causing a sensation if it is done slowly enough. In many cases, however, it is sufficient to regard the touch stimulus only in terms of the force applied and the amount of skin depression that takes place (SideNote 3.15).

Esthesiometers—past and present

The question then is "How does one go about obtaining touch thresholds?" Whatever the procedure, it must be done in a way that allows

systematic application of different forces in a consistent and repeatable manner (Greenspan & Bolanowski, 1996). Around the end of the 19th century, Max von Frey discovered that horse hairs tend to apply a single downward force that depends on the thickness and stiffness of the hair. By using a set of calibrated hair fibres, von Frey created the first **esthesiometer**. The early studies by von Frey and others showed that human skin was very sensitive to touch and that small forces were sufficient to elicit sensation. The more recent work on touch thresholds relies on the use of nylon filaments, which were invented shortly after World War II. The Semmes–Weinstein esthesiometer is a set of 20 nylon fibres of different diameters attached to Plexiglas handles (SideNote 3.16). As with von Frey hairs, the nylon fibres can be used to determine the minimal force needed to elicit sensation and thereby determine the absolute threshold of touch over various parts of the body.

Absolute thresholds

The absolute threshold of touch is very small when considered in terms of the actual mechanical force that needs to be applied. However, touch is by no means the most sensitive among our sensory systems. The absolute thresholds of vision and hearing, for example, are nearly a billion times lower when considered in terms

METHODOLOGY

Tactile Automated Passive-Finger Stimulation (TAPS)

Daniel Goldreich and his colleagues have designed novel equipment in order to study tactile psychophysics in a more controlled manner. One of their devices, known as TAPS (the *Tactile Automated Passive-Finger Stimulator*), works to control the amount of pressure applied to the finger by knowing the exact force applied to the finger (through gravity and changes in mass and velocity, among other things). The participant's index finger is secured over a hole in a table, and the TAPS device applies stimuli to the finger (Figure 3.12). In one such experiment, the stimuli are gratings of different widths, and the participant must determine which presentation (first or second) was the horizontal grating. The results can be graphed, and a psychophysical curve can be determined in order to see what groove width corresponds to a 75% correct threshold detection.

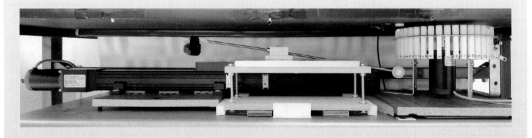

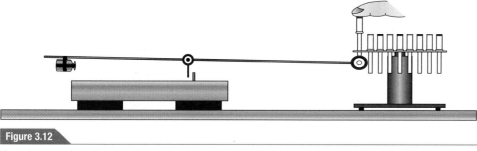

Figure 3.12

For a demonstration of the TAPS from its creators, please visit http://www.jove.com/index/details.stp?id=1374

of stimulus energy. As with all of the senses, the actual threshold value can depend on a number of different factors. One of the most important factors that affects touch threshold is the actual site on the body where it is measured.

In the 1960s, Sidney Weinstein undertook a detailed study using *von Frey hairs* to examine how absolute thresholds varied across the body surface (Weinstein, 1968). Table 3.3 shows the absolute threshold data, with the boxed values representing those at the lowest end. This data is graphically shown in Figure 3.13 on page 78. From here, it is clear that there is considerable variability in touch sensitivity across the body surface. Facial regions around the mouth and nose are among the most sensitive to pressure (i.e., have the lowest thresholds), whereas the extremities, particularly at the lower end of the body, require relatively large forces to produce a touch sensation. This is consistent with our everyday experience. A small puff of air, for example, will much more likely be detected if aimed at say our lips than our palms or soles.

The absolute threshold for pressure detection can also be influenced by age, gender, and condition of the skin. A reduction in skin elasticity will reduce sensitivity and therefore raise threshold. A **callus** is a good example where a marked increase in detection threshold occurs simply because the thickened skin is less elastic and therefore not as easily deformed by mechanical pressure. A more gradual loss of skin elasticity occurs with age, which in turn causes progressive increments in detection threshold. Interestingly, men and women differ in how the rate of detection threshold changes with age. It is not uncommon to hear that women are generally more sensitive than men. Weinstein found in his studies that pressure thresholds were generally lower in women than men in nearly all sites that he studied, with the exception of the tongue where they were nearly equal (SideNote 3.17).

Difference thresholds

It was the early studies by Ernst Weber on tactile perception that led him to formulate his now famous law. As reviewed in Chapter 1, Weber was primarily concerned with understanding

Table 3.3

Absolute Threshold and Two-point Threshold Values for Various Sites on the Human Body

Body Location	Absolute Threshold (g)	Two-point Threshold (mm)
Forehead	1.4	15.0
Nose	0.5	8.0
Lip	0.9	5.5
Cheek	1.0	7.0
Shoulder	10.0	41.1
Upper arm	16.0	44.5
Forearm	13.3	38.5
Thumb	9.0	3.5
Digit 1	11.4	3.0
Digit 2	6.8	2.5
Digit 3	7.9	4.0
Digit 4	5.7	4.5
Back	7.2	44.0
Belly	5.7	34.0
Thigh	21.1	45.5
Calf	40.3	47.0
Sole	35.9	22.5

Note. Boxed values represent areas of low threshold (high sensitivity). From "Intensive and Extensive Aspects of Tactile Sensitivity as a Function of Body Part, Sex, and Laterality," by S. Weinstein, 1968, in *The Skin Senses,* Ed. D. R. Kenshalo, Springfield, IL: Charles C. Thomas.

SideNote | **3.17**

There are certain parts of women's bodies that are especially sensitive, such as the belly and back, where the threshold values come close to those for the face. Men are not nearly as sensitive in these parts of the body.

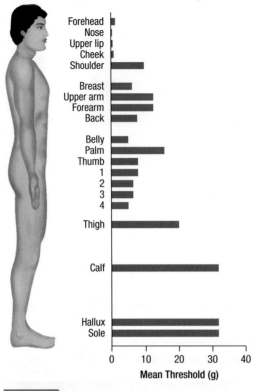

Absolute thresholds for pressure detection vary considerably over the body surface. The facial regions, especially around the nose and lips, have the lowest thresholds, whereas the lower extremities have among the highest thresholds. Adapted from "Intensive and Extensive Aspects of Tactile Sensitivity as a Function of Body Part, Sex, and Laterality," by S. Weinstein, 1968, in *The Skin Senses,* Ed. D. R. Kenshalo, Springfield, IL: Charles C. Thomas.

the relationship between perceived magnitude and stimulus intensity. He saw the need to establish the relationship between difference thresholds and stimulus intensity as a means of achieving this. The study of difference thresholds in the somatosensory system, therefore, began at the earliest moments in the history of experimental psychology.

We now know that difference thresholds for touch actually depend on a number of different factors (Kenshalo, 1978; Verrillo, 1993). One important finding has been that Weber's law actually holds true for only a limited range of tactile intensities. At very low or very high intensities, the constant in Weber's law can change dramatically, thereby leading to a failure in the law since Weber's constant no longer remains constant. Another factor that affects difference thresholds is the site on the body where the measurements are made. Skin areas that have low touch thresholds are

more sensitive to stimulus change and therefore have lower Weber constants. And finally, the actual experimental way in which difference thresholds are measured can have a bearing on the outcome. Over the past century, values in the range of 0.02 to 0.30 have been reported by various researchers. Given that many variables can influence the Weber constant, there is no one value commonly used to portray the tactile sense.

Sensory magnitudes

Many different magnitude estimation experiments have been performed on the somatosensory system. As with the difference threshold studies, these experiments have also produced different results. However, here the main distinctions arise from whether the stimulus is a single indentation or a vibrating one. Single indentations in hairless skin were shown to produce sensation magnitudes that increased linearly with depth of skin displacement. That is, the power law exponent of the function was close to 1.0. However, the same experiment on hairy skin produced an exponent value of 0.4. Clearly, the response characteristics of the two types of skin are different and yield different sensory magnitudes as stimulus intensity is increased.

2. SPATIAL FACTORS

The spatial resolution of the tactile sense has long been of keen interest. Starting with the early work of Ernst Weber in the 19th century, it was clear that our ability to resolve two different points of contact was very good on certain parts of the body and quite poor on others. The simple distinction of a *two-point threshold*, as Weber had called it, later gave way to more complex measures of the spatial parameters involved in form perception. It is now known that spatial discrimination is a very complex issue and one that needs more elaborate measures than a simple two-point discrimination procedure.

The two-point limen

The **two-point limen** was defined by Weber as the smallest separation of two points applied simultaneously to the skin that can still be discriminated (i.e., they evoke the sensation of two separate points). At spatial separations below this value, the sensations merge and therefore the two points feel as a single indentation. Weber used the **compass test** to probe the body for variations in threshold and quickly discovered that the hands, fingers, and facial regions were far superior in spatial discrimination ability than other parts of the body. This difference was also noted by fellow German physiologist Karl Vierordt, who found that the two-point limen improves by about twentyfold as one moves from the shoulder toward the fingertips—a finding that he formalized as the **law of outward mobility** (Figure 3.14) (Boring, 1942).

A systematic study of the two-point threshold was carried out by Sidney Weinstein in parallel with his study on detection threshold over the entire body (Weinstein, 1968). Table 3.3 also shows the two-point discrimination data, with the lowest values (highest resolution or acuity) shown in the boxed region. This data is graphically shown in Figure 3.15. A comparison between this figure and Figure 3.13 shows some striking differences. Weinstein had found that the two-point discrimination profile over the body does not exactly correspond to the pressure sensitivity profile. For example, although the facial regions are most sensitive to touch,

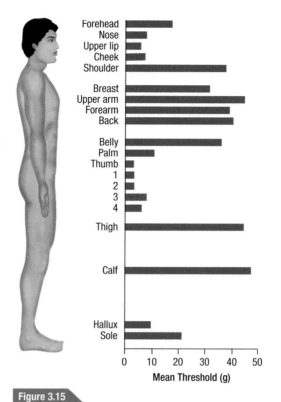

Figure 3.15

Two-point discrimination thresholds vary considerably over the body surface. The thumb and digits show the highest tactile acuity, followed by the lower facial regions. The upper arm, thigh, and calf have the lowest acuity. Adapted from "Intensive and Extensive Aspects of Tactile Sensitivity as a Function of Body Part, Sex, and Laterality," by S. Weinstein, 1968, in *The Skin Senses,* Ed. D. R. Kenshalo, Springfield, IL: Charles C. Thomas.

it is the fingers that show the highest spatial discrimination ability. Similarly, much of the upper torso is quite sensitive to touch but shows poor spatial resolution. The feet display just the opposite pattern—relatively good discrimination ability but poor sensitivity. It is worth pondering these data and how they relate to our own everyday experiences in tactile perception.

Mechanoreceptor properties related to two-point discrimination

The gradient of spatial acuity from the base of the palm to the fingertips, as shown in Figure 3.14, is quite striking. This region has been used to explore the neural basis of two-point discrimination function and the factors that underlie differences in the values. Åke Vallbo and Roland Johansson have carried out careful studies on the properties of mechanoreceptors in this region (Johansson & Vallbo, 1983). It is generally understood that

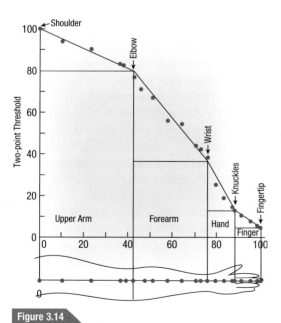

Figure 3.14

The two-point limen improves steadily from the shoulder to the fingertip, resulting in a near twentyfold reduction of the threshold. Threshold values are plotted as a percentage of the value at the shoulder. Adapted from *Sensation and Perception in the History of Experimental Psychology,* by E. G. Boring, 1942, New York, NY: Appleton.

INVESTIGATION

Mechanoreceptor Density and Receptive Field Size

This demonstration will illustrate the density of pressure receptors in different parts of the body such as the forearm, thigh, fingertips, and cheek. For this task, you will need a compass or a paper clip that has been unfolded, a ruler, and a piece of paper. For each body part, begin with the two points of your compass (or paper clip) fairly wide apart, and touch them to your skin. Do you feel one point or two? Repeat this, adjusting the two points closer together, until you can only feel one point. Measure the distance between the two points and jot it down. Continue testing other areas of the body. Are the distances the same? You should discover that certain parts of the body have larger distances than others, which translates into receptors that are less densely packed in that area. This makes sense because we do not need to know the exact location of a stimulus on our lower back but do need to know the location of a stimulus on our fingertips.

the smaller the receptive field's size, the greater the ability to discriminate two different points of stimulation. In other words, the field sizes should be much smaller for mechanoreceptors in the fingertip than say for those in the palm. Furthermore, this relationship should be especially apparent for mechanoreceptors linked to the FA-I and SA-I type afferents since these have the most superficial location.

Although there are systematic changes in FA-I and SA-I afferents in the manner expected, Vallbo and Johansson found that the change in receptive field size was not as great as the change in two-point discrimination across the hand. Therefore, an additional factor had to account for the superior tactile resolution in the fingertips. That factor turned out to be the actual density of mechanoreceptors. Both FA-I and SA-I afferents are densely packed in the fingertips and become much sparser outside of this region, a relationship that parallels the psychophysical gradient of two-point discrimination in the hand and fingers (SideNote 3.18). Therefore, differences in packing density of both types of mechanoreceptors play an important role in determining tactile acuity. The receptive field size and density of FA-II and SA-II afferents, however, does not change appreciably across the hand. It would be unlikely that these mechanoreceptors would play an important role in setting the limits of tactile acuity, given that they are located deep within the skin and have fairly large receptive field sizes.

Hyperacuity

It was known as early as Weber's time that certain spatial measures of tactile perception

produced superior performance in comparison to the two-point limen. Weber had developed a second spatial discrimination test, called **point localization error**, in which a person was required to identify the point in the body that was previously touched with a probe. The difference between this and the compass test is that the stimuli are presented simultaneously in the latter and successively in the localization test. It was soon discovered that the two methods produced consistently different results, with localization errors being 3–4 times smaller than two-point discrimination.

The two-point limen became increasingly viewed as only a single measure of spatial discrimination. By the 1970s, it was apparent that other means of assessing tactile resolution provided data that showed our tactile discrimination ability to be far superior than that obtained with the classical tests. For example, if human subjects were asked to discriminate size differences between two successively applied disks or edges, then the tactile spatial threshold became 4–10 times smaller than the classical two-point threshold. Similar threshold values were also found if subjects were tested on a line-separation task or asked to determine whether two bars were more or less separated than a comparison pair. The low threshold values that were found in these experiments suggested that there may be multiple forms of spatial discrimination ability depending on the type of stimulus used and the way in which the experiments are performed. The term **hyperacuity** has often been applied to spatial discrimination thresholds that are much lower than the traditional two-point limen.

SideNote | 3.18

The density of FA-I afferents is nearly 6 times greater in the fingertips than the palm, whereas the density of SA-I afferents is nearly 9 times greater. The average two-point threshold is nearly 5 times lower in the fingertips compared to the palm.

3. TEMPORAL FACTORS

The temporal factors affecting touch perception can be broken down into two forms based on duration—the effects of prolonged, steady stimulation and the effects of short, repetitive stimulation. The first kind produces the phenomenon of adaptation, whereas the second is referred to as *vibrotactile stimulation*. The perceptual characteristics of vibrotactile stimulation have long been studied and its consequences on tactile perception have generated much interest among psychologists.

Adaptation

We are constantly experiencing the phenomenon of **adaptation**. Actually, it is rather odd to think of it as an experience since adaptation is said to occur when the perceived intensity of a sensory stimulus is reduced, often to the point where it is no longer consciously *experienced*. This happens whenever a constant stimulus is applied for a prolonged period of time. A tactile stimulus becomes progressively less effective in producing a sensation the longer it is maintained. Adaptation becomes complete when the stimulus is no longer detectable (SideNote 3.19). The time required for complete adaptation depends on a number of factors: In general, the greater the area of the stimulus, the faster the adaptation; the greater the intensity or force, the slower the adaptation; finally, less sensitive areas of the body adapt the quickest, often within a few seconds.

It was originally thought that adaptation occurred due to reduced electrical discharges by mechanoreceptors. This has largely been rejected on two grounds. First, we now know that the sustained type of mechanoreceptors (SA-I and SA-II) continue to produce action potentials as long as the stimulus is applied. Therefore, a strictly neural explanation is unsatisfactory given that some mechanoreceptors at the site of stimulation are unlikely to become completely adapted. And second, there is now evidence that adaptation occurs largely because of mechanical reasons and that the key parameter is the lack of stimulus movement. In other words, we become less and less inclined to notice a stimulus if it is not dynamic enough or if the stimulus fails to remain in motion. Even though the peripheral receptors may be signalling a response to a constant tactile stimulus, the situation is not the same as at the time of its onset or say for a stimulus that changes with time. Both of these situations produce a contrasting condition that may elevate the sensory experience and our appreciation of it.

Vibrotactile stimulation

The importance of stimulus movement for tactile perception was recognized quite early, and this led to the idea that vibration provided a more suitable means for studying touch. **Vibrotactile stimulation** became the tool of choice for many studies on touch sensation during the 20th century. We have come to know that vibratory stimuli produce different threshold values than static stimuli. The two-point limen, for example, is lower if a vibrating probe is used. Magnitude estimation studies have also provided different results.

Nowhere is the effect of vibration frequency more apparent than when measuring the absolute threshold of detection (Kenshalo, 1978). Figure 3.16 summarizes the results of several studies that have shown the threshold value to be lowest for a certain vibrational frequency, typically in the range of 200–300 Hz. Furthermore, the threshold rises rapidly if lower or higher temporal frequencies are used.

SideNote | **3.19**

We rarely notice the constant pressure from a chair after sitting on it for a while or from the various garments and paraphernalia we wear, even though it was certainly apparent at the moment of our initial contact.

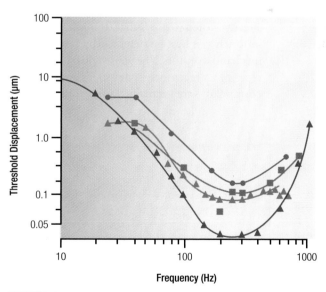

Figure 3.16

Tactile detection thresholds are strongly influenced by the vibration frequency of the stimulus. Threshold values are lowest in the range of 200–300 Hz and become elevated on either side of this range. The results from different studies are shown by the various symbols. Adapted from "Biophysics and Psychophysics of Feeling," by D. R. Kenshalo, 1978, in *Handbook of Perception, Vol. VIB: Feeling and Hurting* (pp. 29–74), Eds. E. C. Carterette and M. P. Friedman, New York, NY: Academic Press.

What is interesting is that this function appears to be true only if the stimuli encompass a fairly large area on the skin. In the 1960s, Ronald Verrillo at Syracuse University showed that if a more punctate stimulus is used instead, such as a vibrating pin, then the temporal frequency does not significantly affect threshold values (Verrillo, 1968, 1993). However, only low temporal frequencies, in the range of 20–40 Hz, were effective in this case. Beyond this frequency range, the detection threshold for punctate stimuli simply became too large. This finding led Verrillo to propose the duplex theory in which two separate and independent channels mediate the temporal nature of touch—a frequency-independent channel that operated only at low frequencies and a frequency-dependent channel that operated only at high frequencies. It is this latter channel that accounts for the peak sensitivity at around 200–300 Hz.

Mechanoreceptor properties related to vibrotactile processing

As sensory physiologists learned more about the details of mechanoreceptor function, it was quickly discovered that the psychophysical functions relating detection threshold to temporal frequency fit in very nicely with neural responses at the receptor level (Hollins, Bensmaia, & Roy, 2002). We have already noted before that temporal changes in touch can best be detected by fast-adapting mechanoreceptors. The sensitivities of the two types of FA receptors—Meissner's and Pacinian corpuscles—are actually quite different. As

Figure 3.17 shows, Meissner's corpuscles are more sensitive to low-frequency stimulation, whereas Pacinian corpuscles are sensitive to high-frequency stimuli. The low-frequency psychophysical responses described above are therefore best accounted for by Meissner's corpuscles. Furthermore, these receptors have small receptive fields due to their superficial location, which further accounts for the fact that the low-frequency response is optimally elicited by punctate stimuli. In contrast, stimulation of Pacinian corpuscles produces a more diffuse, poorly localized vibrational sensation. This system, however, can account for the detection of vibrotactile stimuli at higher frequencies, though it suffers from poor spatial resolution due to its large receptive fields.

The duplex theory was later refined to incorporate results from further psychophysical experiments with vibrotactile stimuli. These data led to the theory that tactile sensation is mediated by four different channels, each having separate properties and each being triggered by specific types of mechanoreceptors (Bolanowski, Gescheider, Verrillo, & Checkosky, 1988). In this model, a threshold stimulus is detected by the system that is most sensitive to the particular characteristics of the stimulus: (i) The channel mediated by Meissner's corpuscles produces the sensation of flutter in the low-frequency range (2–40 Hz); (ii) Pacinian corpuscles produce the sensation of vibration in the high-frequency range (40–600 Hz); (iii) Merkel receptors produce the sensation of pressure and respond best to static or near-static stimuli; and (iv) Ruffini receptors are also involved in steady pressure detection but can provide a buzz-like sensation at high temporal frequencies as well. Although tactile responses can be parsed into these separate receptor systems, it should be recognized that the suprathreshold experience of touch is mediated by neural activity generated by the various different types of mechanoreceptors.

Frequency discrimination and pitch perception

So far, our discussion has focused on the abilities of the tactile sense to detect different frequencies of vibrotactile stimulation and the bearing this has had on models of tactile perception. However, there has also been interest in our ability to discriminate the actual frequency of vibration. This research has been motivated in part by attempts to use the tactile system as a surrogate sensory device for communicating

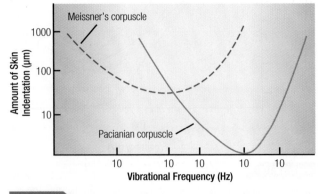

Figure 3.17

Excitation of Meissner's corpuscles produces a sense of flutter that can be highly localized on the skin surface, whereas Pacinian corpuscle excitation evokes a more diffuse, vibrational feeling in deeper tissue. The two types of mechanoreceptors differ in their peak sensitivities to temporal frequency, with Meissner's corpuscles being more sensitive to lower frequencies.

sound information in deaf people (Gilmer, 1966). If the tactile sense were too poor in this regard, then it would not be a viable alternative for this purpose.

The perceptual correlate of frequency is known as **pitch**. Psychophysical experiments have been conducted to obtain difference thresholds in pitch perception. However, the experiments are complicated by two factors. First, the threshold values depend on the actual frequency around which the discrimination task is conducted. And second, our appreciation of stimulus intensity can be affected by small changes in frequency, something we saw in Figure 3.16 (SideNote 3.20). Therefore, if changes in pitch perception are to be assessed by changing the vibration frequency, the stimulus intensity also has to be taken into account so that it does not interfere and cause an artifact. The various studies that have been conducted have reported somewhat different discrimination threshold values, generally falling in the range of 0.03–0.40. However, if intensity matching is carefully applied, then the difference threshold values are strongly influenced by the actual frequency level, approximately 0.20 at 25 Hz and 0.35 at 200 Hz (SideNote 3.21).

4. THERMAL SENSATIONS

The focus of our discussion on the somatosensory system has thus far revolved around pressure. However, a very important component of the tactile sense is the detection of heat and cold. This sensory parameter is responsible for producing a number of physiological effects in our body that allow us to adapt to **thermal** changes in our physical environment. Furthermore, the perceptual aspects related to thermal stimuli can interact with the other tactile qualities such as pressure, vibration, and pain to produce a multi-faceted sensory experience.

A particularly unique characteristic of the thermal quality of touch is that the perceived absence of heat or cold sensation occurs only when our body is exposed to a certain level of heat or thermal energy. We have seen that in all other cases, it is the absence of stimulus energy that produces no sensation. A total absence of thermal energy, however, occurs only at a temperature known as *absolute zero* (SideNote 3.22). And yet our ability to feel neither warmth nor cold occurs at considerably

higher temperatures, within a zone known as **physiological zero**, where the thermal energy bearing upon us is actually quite large. We only begin to feel warm or cool when our skin or body temperature deviates from this zone.

Thermoreceptors

Thermal energy is detected by our skin through specialized receptors known as **thermoreceptors**. The greater the deviation from physiological zero, the greater the feeling of warmth or cold generated by the firing of these receptors (Schepers & Ringkamp, 2009). Thermoreceptors can be divided into either warm or cold receptors, both of which are formed as unencapsulated nerve terminals. The axons of warm receptors are slowly conducting unmyelinated fibres, known as *C fibres* (see Tables 3.1 and 3.2). The cold receptors, however, have larger, lightly myelinated axons ($A\delta$ fibres) and therefore conduct action potentials somewhat faster.

The thermoreceptors are distributed throughout our body, as evidenced by the fact that we can experience both warmth and cold on all parts of our body surface. Our ability to experience these sensations through discrete points on the skin was taken, during the early history of tactile research, as proof for the existence of so-called *sensory spots*—tiny areas of skin that produce a sensation when stimulated. The basis for such localized sensory detection lies in the distribution of receptive fields of mechanoreceptors or thermoreceptors linked to a single afferent fibre. In the case of thermoreceptors, the receptive fields can be quite small—about 1 mm in hairless skin and 3–5 mm in hairy skin.

Thermoreceptors are very sensitive to local changes in temperature. The cold-type thermoreceptors increase their firing rate as temperatures are reduced from physiological zero. Similarly, the warm-type thermoreceptors fire when the temperature is increased. Figure 3.18 on page 84 shows the neural response profiles of these thermoreceptors as a function of temperature. The response is typically of a sustained nature within the range of temperatures to which the particular thermoreceptor type is responsive. However, the rate of temperature change can play an important role in how well these receptors fire. Slow changes in temperature produce little neural activity in thermoreceptors, whereas more rapid changes (e.g., about 5°C per minute or more) are very effective. As

SideNote **3.20**

Strictly speaking, Figure 3.16 showed the effects of vibration frequency on detection thresholds. However, the suprathreshold appreciation of intensity is similarly affected by frequency.

SideNote **3.21**

At 25 Hz, a 20% difference in frequency is required before it is perceived as being just noticeably different in pitch (i.e., the frequency would have to change to either 20 or 30 Hz). At 200 Hz, however, a 35% change in frequency would be required to produce a JND in pitch (i.e., the frequency would have to change to either 140 or 270 Hz).

SideNote **3.22**

Absolute zero (-273.16 °C) is defined as the temperature at which all molecular activity ceases, and therefore no thermal energy is present. Although this should be the temperature of null perception, the thermal sensory mechanism has adopted a much higher temperature—more suited to normal tissue physiology—as the null range for perception.

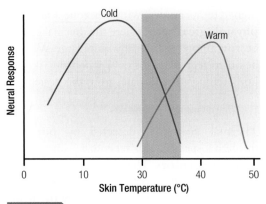

Figure 3.18

The neural response profile of warm and cold thermoreceptors overlap in the zone of physiological zero (shaded region).
Cold receptors increase their firing rate as the temperature
decreases, whereas warm receptors do the same when the
temperature increases. Both receptor types display peak
firing just outside the zone of physiological zero.

a result, thermoreceptors are more suited for
detecting changes in temperature rather than
being mere indicators of absolute temperature.

Perceptual aspects—detectability and scaling

The absolute threshold for detecting temperature change depends on a number of factors.
The rate of temperature change certainly plays
an important role, as noted on the previous
page with regard to thermoreceptor function
(SideNote 3.23). However, other important factors include the size of skin area that
is stimulated, the actual skin temperature at
the time of stimulation, and the body location where the measurement is made. Thermal
sensitivity varies widely over the body surface
in a manner similar to pressure. For example,
the temperature change required for detection in the extremities is higher, as much as a
hundredfold, compared to the more sensitive
facial regions.

The smallest detectable change in skin temperature has been reported to be a decrease of
0.0003 °C and an increase of 0.0001 °C. The
experiment that produced such small threshold
values involved stimulating a very large area of
the body. Stimulation of smaller skin areas typically yields much higher threshold values. We
know from everyday experience that perceived
intensity will be much less if we dip our finger into say a pot of warm water than if we
were to dip our entire hand. This illustrates the
phenomenon of **spatial summation**. As with
detection of vibrotactile stimuli, thermal sensitivity is also directly related to the area of skin

SideNote | 3.23

Objects that draw heat away
from the body faster than
others will feel cooler when
touched. The opposite is also
true—objects that impart heat
faster will feel warmer. This
property of objects is known as
thermal conductivity. A steel bar
feels warmer or cooler than a
bar made of wood because of
the higher thermal conductivity
of metals.

that is stimulated. The only caveat to this is if
a radiant source of heat is used instead, such as
an infrared lamp, where the thermal stimulus
does not make direct skin contact. In this case,
we are capable of making only feeble spatial
judgments, and any increase (or decrease) in
stimulation area is only registered in general
terms with respect to the warmth level. It turns
out that this is actually an important aspect of
the way we respond to thermal stimulation
because it allows us to have a stable perception
of radiant energy in our environment.

Magnitude estimation studies with warm
and cold probes have shown that thermal perceptions conform to the power law and have
exponent values of 1.6 and 1.0, respectively.
However, the actual exponent value can depend
on experimental factors. One important factor in scaling experiments for warmth, but not
cold, is the area of stimulation. It has been found
that the rate of growth of perceived warmth as
a function of temperature is inversely related
to area—very small stimulation areas produce
faster rates and vice versa. For example, a stimulation area of 2.5 cm^2 yields magnitude estimates that produce a power law function with
an exponent value of 1.7, whereas a stimulation
area of 22 cm^2 yields an exponent value of only
0.65. There is no similar effect of stimulation
area on cold perception.

Perceptual aspects—adaptation

Adaptation is a prominent feature of thermal
sensation and has therefore been well studied
(Green, 2004; Greenspan & Bolanowski, 1996).
The phenomenon is easily demonstrable by
placing your hand or foot into mildly warm
or cool water. With time, the resulting thermal sensation will fade in intensity until it is
no longer perceptible. The time required for
this to happen can vary among individuals but
is typically around 25–30 minutes. The actual
temperature will also have considerable bearing on the adaptation process and whether or
not it goes to completion. Temperatures in the
zone of physiological zero lead to complete
adaptation, whereas temperatures outside this
zone produce a persistent thermal response.
We have all experienced this in one way or
another, whether through the prolonged application of a cold pack; while being immersed
in a hot tub; or from exposure to extreme
environmental temperatures. Even though
the sensory magnitude may become reduced
with time due to adaptation, we nevertheless

continue to experience the feeling of warmth or cold in these situations.

The phenomenon of thermal adaptation led German physiologist Ewald Hering to propose in the 19th century that warmth and cold were really two dimensions of a single thermal sense. The following experiment illustrates this idea. Consider placing one hand in mildly cool water and the other in mildly warm water and waiting until each hand becomes completely adapted to that temperature. If both hands are then placed in water at an intermediate temperature, then the hand that was previously in the cool water will now feel warm, whereas the other hand will feel cool. This suggests that physiological zero can be shifted because the intermediate temperature, which would normally feel neutral, now evokes a different thermal sensation due to prior adaptation. Hering used this result as evidence for an **opponent process** in the somatosensory system, in which warmth and cold are different dimensions of the same sensory experience. Adaptation merely alters the null point within that continuum. We will see in Chapter 11 that the opponent process championed by Hering also forms a fundamental basis for colour vision in humans.

5. TACTILE COMMUNICATION

Due to a number of qualities related to tactile perception, the somatosensory system has served as a substitute for vision for blind people (Heller & Ballesteros, 2005). Vision and touch have an important property in common in that they are both spatial senses. The spatial information about an object in the outside world is accurately represented and encoded in both systems, whether by way of pressure on the skin or by the optical image created in the eye. The skin on certain parts of the body, such as the fingertips, are very sensitive and have high resolution—both properties that are important in sensing and representing the spatial dimensions of an object. The tactile system, however, does have one quality that it does not share with the visual system. The skin, unlike the eyes, is rarely "busy" and therefore allows blind individuals to use it solely for tactile communication. Following, we review some of the more common (and interesting) ways that the tactile system is used in sensory communication.

The Braille system

An important requirement for blind people is to become adept at a system that allows rapid reading of text. The most popular system used today was developed in the nineteenth century by Louis Braille. The story itself is quite touching. While playing in his father's shop at the age of three, Louis injured his eye on a sharp tool. Infection quickly set in and spread to the other eye, leaving him completely blind. Braille grew up to become a very intelligent young man who loved to read. While at the National Institute for Blind Youth in Paris, he experimented with different ways to use his fingers for reading text. The system of touch reading that Braille developed in 1829 was simple, practical, and elegant (SideNote 3.24). That system, which now bears his name, has become the standard means for reading and writing among blind people in virtually every language throughout the world.

Braille text is composed of a series of raised dots that can be read with the fingers by blind people or those whose eyesight is too poor for reading printed material. The Braille symbols are formed within units of space known as *Braille cells*. A full Braille cell can consist of up to six raised dots arranged in two parallel columns, each having three dots (see Figure 3.19). Sixty-four different combinations are possible using one or more of these six dots. Each letter of the alphabet is represented by a particular dot or a combination of dots arranged in different positions within the Braille cell. When every letter of every word is expressed in Braille, it is referred to as grade 1 Braille. Most textbooks and publications are transcribed in grade 2 Braille where the cells are used either individually or in combination with others to form a variety of contractions or whole words.

Louis Braille (1809–1852)
World History Archive/Alamy

SideNote | **3.24**

The system developed by Braille was actually based on the Ecriture Nocturne (night writing) code developed by a French army captain, Charles Barbier. This system, which was developed at Napoleon's command, was used for sending military messages that could be read on the battlefield without any light.

A	B	C	D	E	F	G	H	I	J

K	L	M	N	O	P	Q	R	S	T

U	V	X	Y	Z

Figure 3.19

The Braille alphabet is produced by different combinations of raised dots within a 2 x 3 grid, known as the *Braille cell*. A total of 64 different dot patterns are possible. These patterns are used to represent the full Roman alphabet as well as all standard punctuation marks.

SideNote | **3.25**

The phrase "You like him" would require 12 cells in grade 1 Braille, including cells to represent the spaces. However, it would only require 6 cells in grade 2 because the letters *Y* and *L* can be used to substitute the words *you* and *like*. The word *him* is formed by combining the letters *H* and *M*. There are 189 different letter contractions and 76 short-form words in grade 2 Braille. Contractions of this type are commonly used nowadays in text messaging (SMS), along with some very creative acronyms.

These shortcuts reduce the amount of paper needed for reproducing books in Braille text and allow for faster and more efficient reading (SideNote 3.25).

The Moon system

The majority of people who become blind in later life find it very difficult to master Braille because of its complicated system of dots. Most of these people, however, also rely on tactile sensing but with a system of embossed letters. A blind Englishman named William Moon developed a code in the 19th century that was initially quite popular. In the Moon system, a line-based tactile code is used in which many of the embossed letters either retain their actual structure or are presented in a slightly modified and less complex form. In a few cases, arbitrary shapes replace the actual letter. This simplified letter-based system is much easier for adults to learn than Braille because they are already familiar with the notational structure of the alphabet.

Why then has the Moon system, or embossed letter reading in general, not become the standard means for touch reading? One reason is that Braille text is much simpler, more flexible, and very economical to produce. Moreover, from a tactile sensory point of view, a system of raised dots offers a greater capacity for information transfer with less noise (Loomis, 1981). Figure 3.20 shows how this is so, with seven letters as an example along with the corresponding Braille type. As the fingertip is pressed on a Braille letter, each dot produces a momentary depression that affects surrounding areas of the skin. This can best be visualized as a form of mechanical blurring. The blur patterns for the Braille and embossed letters are shown in the bottom panels of Figure 3.20. The reason that Braille type is so effective is because its punctate nature allows individual cell patterns to be distinguished much easier than embossed letters, where minor changes in the contour can change a letter's identity. Indeed, the blur patterns produced by some of the embossed letters are so similar that they become nearly indistinguishable, unlike the Braille letters that retain their distinctive feature. Therefore, although it is more difficult to master the Braille alphabet, once done it allows a blind individual to read at much faster rates, often up to 100 words a minute, because less time is needed in tactile discrimination.

Tactile mapping systems

A tactile mapping system provides a pattern of stimulation on the skin that portrays the spatial information present in a visual stimulus. The first such system, called Optacon, is no longer in production though it remains one of the most talked about communication devices in the blind community. It was developed in the early 1960s by John Linvill to help his blind daughter. The Optacon, which stands for optical-to-tactile converter, is a small, 6 x 24 matrix of vibrating pins that directly maps the brightness inputs from an image into a corresponding vibrotactile pattern. The user tactually perceives the vibrating image by placing the index finger on the array. This device permitted blind people to read text and perceive simple geometrical objects by way of tactile stimulation. The growth of computer technology combined with low-cost speech synthesizers eventually led to reduced demand for the Optacon.

A device that was similar in principle to the Optacon was the Tactile Vision Substitution System (TVSS) developed by Paul Bach-Y-Rita and colleagues in the 1970s. The TVSS produced a tactile display of images from a video camera directly onto a vibrotactile belt that was worn around the abdomen. The system produced signals on the tactile array from black and white images with a resolution of 20 × 20 pixels. The TVSS and later systems were developed with the hope of giving "tactile sight" to blind people. The idea was to aim the camera in a particular direction and then experience a vibrotactile image of the visual scene. Although the tactile image was quite crude because of technical limitations, the early reports with this system showed that the TVSS produced an impressive degree of recognition and relative position sense of simple objects in the visual field of the camera.

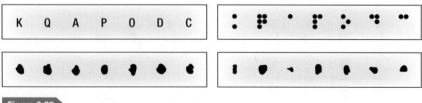

Figure 3.20

The mechanical blur produced by embossed letters, shown below the Roman type, reveals patterns that are very similar to each other and therefore not easily discriminated by tactile sensing. The blur produced by the corresponding Braille letters shows a more punctate profile that can be more easily discriminated. Adapted from "Tactile Pattern Perception," by J. M. Loomis, 1981, *Perception, 10,* pp. 5–27.

Tactile communication with deaf–blind individuals

The communication needs of people who are both blind and deaf are very different because they have to rely only on tactile means for gathering information. The world of the deaf–blind individual is best known through the story of Helen Keller, who was suddenly shut off from the world at the age of 18 months (SideNote 3.26) (Keller, 1903). Ms. Keller's early life was wild and unruly because the young girl had very little understanding of the world around her. However, her life began to take shape once she slowly learned to communicate with her teacher, Anne Sullivan. The celebrated teacher–student relationship between the two lasted a lifetime (Lash, 1980). The so-called *miracle worker* began by spelling out words on the young girl's palm for things that were easily identifiable. In time, the two could communicate effortlessly using this tactile method. Helen Keller went to Radcliffe College and eventually became a scholar in her own right, winning the praise of many around the world for her writings, philanthropy, and sheer triumph over adversity.

Some deaf–blind people are born deaf and become blind in later life. These people prefer to communicate by sign language. However, instead of watching the hands, they touch the hands during the signing process from which they can then understand what is being communicated. A similar principle is involved in the **Tadoma** method, which is also known as *tactile lip-reading*. In this method, the deaf–blind person places their hands and fingers over the speaker's lips and face. The lip and facial movements that arise during speech are sensed by the tactile system and interpreted. However, both the Tadoma and sign-reading methods are very difficult to learn and require many years of training. Once mastered, a Tadoma expert can comprehend speech at close to listening rates.

C. Proprioception and Kinesthesis

So far, we have taken the view of skin as a passive sensory organ, one that generates tactile sensations only when an object comes in contact with it. The somatosensory system, however, also encompasses proprioceptive function and its more dynamic counterpart, known as **kinesthesis**. These sensory dimensions share many anatomical, physiological, and perceptual features with the tactile senses. The neural elements that generate proprioceptive sensations, also known as **proprioceptors**, do not reside in the skin but in deeper structures such as the muscles, tendons, and joints. The sensory information from these receptors is critically important to the motor system in guiding our movement through the environment (Paterson, 2007). Furthermore, these are continuous sensations that produce a perceptual awareness within us as to where the different parts of our body are located in space and how they are moving at any given time (SideNote 3.27).

1. NEURAL FOUNDATIONS

As with the tactile signals, proprioceptive signals also begin with specialized receptors. However, these receptors sense only the position and movement of the various body parts. Proprioceptors are similar to mechanoreceptors in that they are found in the terminal ends of nerve fibres belonging to sensory neurons located in the dorsal root ganglion. These nerve endings, however, are specialized to detect the stretching or contraction of muscles and tendons (Proske, 2006). One type of receptor is a slowly adapting fibre that is wrapped around specialized muscle fibres known as *spindles*. As Figure 3.21 shows, spindles are encapsulated structures that are 4–10 mm in length and reside well within the muscle itself. The nerve fibre–spindle complex, which is called the *muscle spindle receptor*, is very sensitive to

Helen Adams Keller (1880–1968)
© INTERFOTO/Alamy

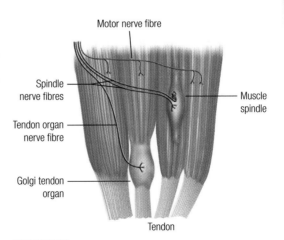

Figure 3.21

Muscle tissue contains elongated bands of muscle fibres and encapsulated structures such as spindles and Golgi tendon organs. These sensors detect changes in muscle tension due to contraction or elongation.

muscle stretch. Action potentials are generated in the nerve fibre from membrane depolarization caused by stretching of the entwined fibre around the spindle. Another type of receptor, the so-called *Golgi tendon organ*, is a slender encapsulated structure located at the junction of the muscle and tendon (see Figure 3.21). The free nerve fibres are intertwined around the tendon structure itself and are very sensitive to changes in muscle tension. Therefore, unlike the spindle receptors, these proprioceptors can indicate both contraction and extension of the muscle.

The nerve fibres that innervate both the spindle and Golgi tendon organs are of the Aα type (see Table 3.1). These fibres have large diameters and are among the most heavily myelinated of peripheral nerve fibres. Consequently, they are also among the fastest in terms of signal transmission to the spinal cord. As discussed in Section A.3 of this chapter, the large primary afferent fibres that carry tactile and proprioceptive signals synapse onto neurons in the dorsal horn of the spinal cord, which then send their fibres up the dorsal column. A small subset of these afferent fibres remains within the spinal cord and then synapses onto motor neurons in the ventral horn. As with the tactile afferent fibres, this proprioceptive channel is important for generating reflex actions (SideNote 3.28).

All proprioceptive information ultimately reaches the primary somatosensory cortex, the same brain region that processes tactile information. However, a functional separation is maintained in area S-I with regard to proprioceptive versus tactile processing. As we have already noted before, area S-I is actually a composite of four smaller areas that form a hierarchy of cortical processing modules. Of these four areas, area 3a acts primarily on proprioceptive signals, whereas the adjoining area 3b processes tactile signals (Squire et al., 2002). The separate processing of these two somatosensory functions is further maintained in higher cortical areas.

2. PERCEPTUAL ASPECTS

There have been fewer psychophysical studies of proprioception and kinesthesis compared to the tactile senses. Nevertheless, several studies have shown that we are remarkably good at detecting passive movement of the joints. Among the nearly 60 joints in our body, the

hip joint appears to be the most sensitive. Passive movement of the hip joint by as little as 0.2° can be detected by human subjects. Among the major limb joints, the following order has been reported in terms of decreasing sensitivity: shoulder, knee, ankle, elbow, wrist, and finger base. However, the data from kinesthetic experiments is complicated by several factors such as the direction of the joint movement, the degree to which the limb is stretched, and the precise way in which the measurements are made.

The receptors that mediate proprioceptive function are also responsible for the sensations of force, pressure, and weight through tension placed on the muscles. The psychophysical studies of these functions date back to the period of Fechner and Weber who, in the 19th century, showed that humans are exceedingly good at judging different weights. For example, the Weber fraction for weight discrimination is about 0.02. Magnitude estimation experiments have shown that there is a remarkable similarity in our appreciation of force regardless of how we exert it. The effort needed to exert a force produces similar power functions regardless of whether it is measured by way of a handgrip, finger squeeze, foot press, or biting. In all cases, the perceived effort can be fitted to a power function with an exponent value of 1.7.

Although we have spoken of proprioceptive function in this section as being mediated through specialized receptors, it turns out that another mechanism is also involved and can play an equal, if not greater, role in our perception of limb position, movement, and appreciation of applied forces. Every time we consciously move a part of our body, a command is issued from the motor centres of our brain to the appropriate muscles. If the perceptual centres in our brain could somehow get a copy of that command, then it would have the means to know what movement is taking place. Furthermore, this information would be independent of that being generated by the proprioceptors in the muscles and joints. German physicist and physiologist Hermann von Helmholtz advanced this idea in the 19th century by suggesting that a motor copy, called **corollary discharge**, was issued every time a voluntary movement was initiated. Although we do not know the precise neurological details of how this discharge is mediated, it is now widely accepted to be a key signal that combines with proprioceptor inputs

SideNote | 3.28

A notable example is the *knee jerk reflex*, which occurs after a sharp tap on the tendon just below the knee. The tap causes a momentary stretch of the spindle receptors in the quadriceps muscle (front thigh) that in turn relays through this spinal circuit to cause a reflexive contraction, producing the leg jerk.

to generate perceptions of limb position and movement (SideNote 3.29). The role of corollary discharge has been especially well studied in terms of eye movement function and will be taken up in greater detail in Chapter 13.

3. ACTIVE TOUCH AND HAPTIC PERCEPTION

Active touch results from physical manipulation of an object. This form of touch has traditionally received very little attention from researchers because of its complex and interactive nature. When we manipulate an object with our hands, we are of course using the passive tactile sensations that we have already discussed at length in this chapter. However, we are also using kinesthetic information that results from the wilful movements of our hands and fingers as we explore the object. The two combine to produce a more vivid impression of the physical attributes of an object, such as its shape and texture (Gordon, 1978). This combination of tactile and kinesthetic sensory experience is known as **haptic perception**.

Active touch is superior to passive touch

The field of haptics has become very important because of the greater interactions that are now necessary between humans and machines. An early pioneer in this field was American psychologist James J. Gibson, who showed the importance of movement in tactile perception in the 1960s. According to Gibson, our ability to identify an object only through tactile means becomes much greater if we can freely and actively touch that object (Gibson, 1962). The passive form of touch (e.g., by having the object pressed against our skin) is simply inadequate when it comes to identifying complex objects. Active touch, Gibson argued, was far superior for identification because it allows greater interaction and exploration that enhances our ability to gather information about the object (SideNote 3.30).

Gibson argued that two key factors form the basis for the superiority of active touch. First, it is wilful in nature and therefore engages the mind in purposefully exploring an unfamiliar object. Through active touch, we seek clues as to the identity of an object by manipulating it with our hands and analyzing the information in real time throughout this process. The second factor is the recruitment of proprioceptors that provide kinesthetic information. For example, the kinesthetic signals generated by having the fingers follow the contours of an object can provide important information about its three-dimensional structure. Both of these factors combine with the tactile sensations of pressure, texture, and temperature to provide the more complete experience of active touch.

Exploratory strategies in haptic perception

The manner in which we actively explore an object is very complex because of the integration that is necessary between the wilful actions of the mind in exploring that object and the sensory feedback provided by the mechanoreceptors and proprioceptors. The fidelity of this process is evident by the fact that we are able to identify most common objects within about two seconds. The actual process that underlies manual exploration was studied in the 1980s by two psychologists, Susan Lederman and Roberta Klatzky (Lederman & Klatzky, 1987). They found that the hand and finger movements of most subjects were very similar and could be categorized into a set of exploratory procedures such as lateral motion, contour following, pressure, and enclosure (Figure 3.22). The preferred use of these procedures depended on the type of object that was being handled. For example, if textural quality was being examined, then subjects mainly used lateral motion, whereas enclosure and contour following were the dominant procedures for judging the shape of an object.

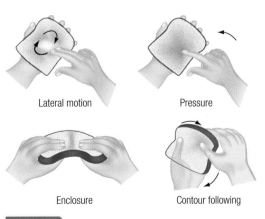

Lateral motion

Pressure

Enclosure

Contour following

Figure 3.22

Haptic perception arises from active manipulation of objects to identify their 3-D structure. A set of exploratory procedures have been identified that are typically used by humans. Adapted from "Hand Movements: A Window into Haptic Object Recognition," by S. J. Lederman and R. L. Klatzky, 1987, *Cognitive Psychology, 19*, pp. 342–368.

SideNote 3.29

Why do we only feel ticklish when someone else does the tickling, even though the same tactile and proprioceptive sensations can be generated through self-tickling? One explanation is that our brain can distinguish the two forms of stimulation because the latter is accompanied by corollary discharges that appear to nullify the tickling sensation.

SideNote 3.30

Gibson demonstrated the superiority of active touch with the use of cookie cutters. When his subjects were allowed to actively explore the cookie cutters, they could correctly identify the shape 95% of the time. If the cutters were only pressed against the skin, then shape identification dropped to 50%.

Loss of haptic perception

The possibility of losing a somatosensory quality, such as touch or haptic perception, is not as readily apparent as losing sight or hearing. Indeed, there is no word in the English language that serves as the tactile counterpart to *blindness* or *deafness* (SideNote 3.31). However, a rare condition known as **peripheral neuropathy** causes just such a sensory loss due to a widespread degeneration of the large myelinated fibres of the peripheral nervous system. The most striking result of this syndrome is the loss of proprioception that makes all body and limb movements nearly impossible to coordinate. The devastating nature of this disease is best known from the case of Ian Waterman who, at the age of 19, was suddenly struck by this illness and lost all proprioceptive sensation below the neck (SideNote 3.32) (Cole, 1995). He was unable to stand or coordinate any body movements because the proprioceptive signals that are so important to that process were now absent. Although the condition rarely improves, patients slowly learn to cope with the disease by using visual feedback to guide their limb and body movements. However, it turns out that the eyes are a very poor substitute for proprioceptive signalling. As a result, there is a slow and tedious learning process requiring a long period of therapy and persistence.

D. Nociception and Pain

We turn now to one of the most enigmatic and least understood perceptual experiences. Pain is very much a sensory-driven phenomenon, and yet our perception of it can be greatly affected by nonsensory events. Unlike other sensory qualities, there are situations where the perceived intensity of pain can be dramatically affected by factors that have nothing to do with the sensory signals. There are numerous anecdotal stories of soldiers in the heat of battle or athletes during sporting events who, despite having suffered serious injury, claimed not to have felt any pain. It has been argued that the diminished perception of pain in these cases represents an example of a self-defence mechanism that has evolved in animals. By reducing our normal response to painful events, an animal is better able to cope with a life-threatening situation involving an enemy or a predator. While the reduced perception of pain during instances of extreme stress may

be important for survival, it also illustrates the amazing influence that nonsensory factors can have on pain perception (Kruger, 1996).

Pain is a perplexing phenomenon in other ways as well. For example, the perceptual quality of pain can differ depending on the body part. A toothache feels very different from a stomach ache even though similar kinds of sensory fibres are stimulated in both cases. Sometimes pain that arises in deeper structures of the body is actually felt elsewhere, a phenomenon that is termed **referred pain**. And perhaps strangest of all, it is quite common for amputees to experience pain in a limb that they no longer have. This condition, known as **phantom pain**, is actually quite devastating because it feels very real and it lingers. The one common aspect to all of these examples is the distress and suffering that is produced by pain. In this regard, pain is a very different sensory experience from all of the others we will examine in this book (SideNote 3.33). We only associate pain with suffering, and it is therefore the only sensory quality that we go to great lengths to minimize or eradicate.

In the remainder of this chapter, we will explore the sensory aspects of pain signals and their transmission, the perceptual aspects of pain and how it is measured, and the various ways in which pain can be controlled. These are all very large topics, and our coverage of them will be brief. The bibliography contains references to several outstanding monographs on pain physiology, perception, and control.

1. SENSORY MECHANISMS OF NOCICEPTION

We should distinguish at the outset the difference between **nociception** and pain. The term *nociception* originated from the work of Sir Charles Scott Sherrington in the early part of the 20th century. Sherrington, who is regarded as one of the greatest neurophysiologists, suggested that the sensation of pain arises from activity in specialized pain receptors that were sensitive to noxious stimuli. The capture of noxious stimuli through these so-called *nociceptors* provides the brain with the sensory signals that indicate possible tissue damage. Pain is the perceptual experience that is generated by the brain from the incoming nociceptive signals. In this section, we examine the neural basis of nociception, whereas the next two sections will examine the perceptual aspects of pain.

SideNote 3.31

The closest term serving as the tactile counterpart to *blindness* or *deafness* is *numbness*. However, its common usage refers to a transient phenomenon rather than a permanent state of tactile deprivation.

SideNote 3.32

Waterman's case has been documented by his physician, Jonathan Cole, in a book titled *Pride and a Daily Marathon*.

SideNote 3.33

The early Greek philosophers did not regard pain as a sensation similar to vision, hearing, or even touch. Many of our current ideas about pain did not even emerge until as late as the 20th century.

Sir Charles Scott Sherrington (1857–1952)
LIBRARY OF CONGRESS/SCIENCE PHOTO LIBRARY

Neural pathways

There are many different kinds of painful stimuli—mechanical stress, extreme heat or cold, and noxious chemical agents (Lautenbacher & Fillingim, 2004; Squire et al., 2002). The identification of specific nociceptors that are triggered by these various stimuli came about largely through developments in electrophysiological recording. One of these techniques, called **microneurography**, compared electrical signals captured from individual nerve fibres with different kinds of sensory stimulation applied to the skin. From these and other studies, it was demonstrated that noxious stimuli trigger activity in some of the smallest nerve fibres that are present in our body—the so-called Aδ and C fibres. Both of these are very thin, contain either little or no myelination, and are slowly conducting fibres. Unlike mechanoreceptors, the nociceptors do not have any peripheral structures and instead exist as free nerve endings in the skin, joints, muscles, and many of the internal organs (SideNote 3.34). Different types of nociceptors exist that are sensitive to different kinds of noxious conditions such as mechanical, thermal, or chemical aggression.

As noted earlier in this chapter, the route that pain signals take to the brain is quite different from that of tactile signals. The small diameter fibres that carry pain signals first synapse in the dorsal horn of the spinal cord. Unlike the tactile fibres, which proceed up the dorsal column on the same side of the spinal cord, pain fibres cross over to the opposite side of the spinal cord and enter into the fibre tracts of the anterolateral system. This fibre tract system has a broad projection through various subcortical nuclei to ultimately reach the somatosensory cortex. The exact way in which pain signals are processed at the cortical level remains unknown. The complex physiological and perceptual nature of pain is reflected by the diffuse way in which the anterolateral system proceeds through the subcortical compartments and by its wide projection to the cerebral cortex (Willis Jr., 2007).

Referred pain

The way that pain fibres are wired in the dorsal horn of the spinal cord can be used to explain the rather unusual phenomenon of referred pain (Melzack & Wall, 1996). As noted before, there are instances where pain arising in deeper tissues often feels as if originating from a different location on the surface of the body. Perhaps the best-known example is the frequent complaint of pain in the shoulders and upper arms that is experienced during a heart attack. Although the nociceptive signals arise in the heart muscle due to reduced blood supply, the pain is actually referred to a different part of the body. There are many other examples of referred pain that involve various internal organs where the pain is experienced in a more remote and superficial location (SideNote 3.35).

The most accepted explanation for referred pain involves a well-known convergence of afferent fibres onto the spinal cord from different parts of the body. The example in Figure 3.23 shows how nociceptive fibres from the skin and gut converge upon a single neuron in the dorsal horn of the spinal cord. Since the projection from this neuron through the anterolateral pathway can carry information from both sources, it is easy for the brain to become confused as to the actual source of the nociceptive signals. Hence, an intestinal inflammation can sometimes be felt on the skin surface because the nociceptive fibres of the intestine and the skin share a common pathway to the brain.

Phantom pain

An unusual feature of dorsal horn neurons is that they become hyperactive when sensory input is removed. That is, if the tactile and nociceptive nerve fibres that are entering the spinal cord are cut, then the dorsal horn neurons upon which these fibres synapse will

SideNote | **3.34**

Interestingly, one of the organs that lacks nociceptors is the brain and spinal cord. This allows neurosurgeons to sometimes perform operations in these structures only under local anesthesia. The patients can therefore be awake and responsive throughout the procedure.

SideNote | **3.35**

Additional examples of commonly experienced referred pain include gall bladder pain referred to the shoulder, stomach problems referred to the spinal area, throat pain referred to the ear, and kidney stone pain referred to the testicles.

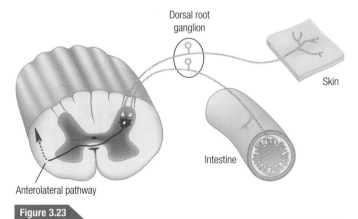

Figure 3.23

The phenomenon of referred pain likely arises due to the convergence of pain fibres from two different sites in the body onto the same neuron in the dorsal horn of the spinal cord. The same fibres in the anterolateral pathway are triggered by painful stimuli at either site (e.g., intestine or skin) and therefore produce errors in pain localization.

actually become hyperactive. In the event of traumatic injury to these nerves, or if a limb is amputated, the resulting chronic hyperactivity in the dorsal horn neurons can produce phantom limb sensation and pain. Phantom limb pain is an example of **central pain** where the nociceptive signals are not being generated at the peripheral nerve terminals but rather at a more central site (brain or spinal cord) due to increased spontaneous activity among neurons in the pain pathway (Melzack, 1989; Sherman, 1997) (SideNote 3.36). The suffering caused by pain of this nature is particularly devastating because it is internally generated within central compartments of the nervous system and therefore cannot be related to an external source.

The gate control theory

Sensory scientists have long known that one of the striking features of pain is that it can be modulated by central influences. The experience of pain can be heightened by expectation (e.g., a trip to the dentist) or lowered by intense stress, as in the case of the soldier injured during battle. By the 1960s, there was accumulating evidence that signals in the larger afferents (e.g., Aα and Aβ fibres) also interfered with transmission of pain signals and reduced pain perception in corresponding areas of the body. It was clear that the transmission and processing of pain signals at some point in the neural hierarchy was subjected to the influence of

non-nociceptive factors and that these factors subsequently influenced the magnitude of the pain experience.

In 1965, Ronald Melzack and Patrick Wall offered a provocative and now widely acclaimed theory of how these various influences were integrated (Melzack & Wall, 1965). According to their **gate control theory**, which is illustrated in Figure 3.24, descending influences from the brain as well as signals from large afferents converge upon the spinal cord and modulate the transmission of incoming nociceptive signals through the C fibres. The pain transmission circuit through the spinal cord has a gate—an inhibitory interneuron—that determines how effectively the nociceptive signals trigger activity in a projection neuron that transmits the signals up along the anterolateral pathway. As shown in Figure 3.24, signals in C fibres alone will stimulate the projection neuron and inhibit the interneuron. The negative influence of the C fibre on the interneuron enhances pain transmission through this circuit because any activity in the interneuron itself would have further inhibited firing in the projection neuron.

The way that the brain influences this circuit, according to this theory, is through descending pathways down the spinal cord that ultimately synapse onto the inhibitory interneurons. Because this influence is excitatory, the subsequent elevation of neural activity in

SideNote | **3.36**

The surgical removal of various other parts of the body (e.g., tongue, nose, breast) also lead to phantom pain. Liposuction, the surgical removal of fatty tissue, has also been known to cause lingering phantom pain due to damage to the afferent fibres innervating the affected area.

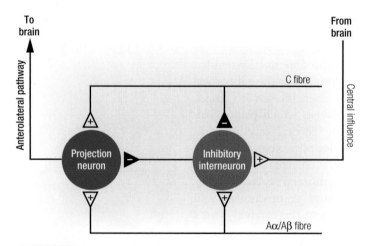

Figure 3.24

A hypothetical neural circuit in the spinal cord that controls pain transmission, according to the *gate control theory*. Nociceptive signals in the C fibres trigger activity in projection neurons while reducing activity in inhibitory interneurons. However, descending signals from the brain as well as those in the large afferents (Aα and Aβ fibres) trigger activity in the interneurons, which then inhibit the projection neurons. The interneuron gates the transmission of nociceptive signals depending on the degree of non-nociceptive influence.

the interneurons will inhibit firing in the projection neurons and therefore dampen the transmission of pain signals coming through the C fibres. In a similar way, neural activity in the large afferent fibres (Aα and Aβ) increases activity in the interneuron and therefore reduces pain transmission through the anterolateral pathway. The gate control theory provides an elegant explanation of several features of pain perception and offers clinical strategies for pain control (Wall, 2000; Wall & Melzack, 1999). For example, stimulation of peripheral nerves, which should suppress the transmission of pain signals in the spinal circuit, has been successfully applied in many cases for relieving pain.

2. MEASUREMENT OF PAIN

Pain is a very complex perceptual experience. Different strategies have therefore been devised to evaluate pain that take into account its multi-dimensional nature. The strategies can be broken down into two general approaches. In the first approach, the many dimensions of pain are not individually assessed but rather clumped together to form a unidimensional characteristic. In this univariate scheme, pain is treated in a manner similar to brightness or loudness perception and therefore similar psychophysical procedures are applied. The second is a multivariate approach to examine the different qualities of pain and assess them separately. These qualities can include perceptual intensity, unpleasantness, and emotional variables associated with pain. Below, we briefly review some general aspects of the univariate and multivariate approaches to pain measurement.

The univariate concept of pain

In this strategy, the experience of pain is measured in terms of its overall integrated impression, without considering the various sensory or emotional dimensions that make up the experience. As such, it is possible to use standard psychophysical approaches to determine threshold intensity levels and suprathreshold sensory magnitudes. There is one difficulty, however, in applying the standard threshold concept to pain. All cases of sensory detection rely on human subjects making a decision as to whether a sensation exists or not. In the case of pain, the sensation is always present, but the subject has to make a decision as to the quality of that sensation and whether or not it rises to

the definition of pain. This places certain limitations on how the data can be gathered, as shown in the following example.

Let us consider an experiment where electric current is applied to the tooth pulp within an intensity range of 0–50, as depicted by the intensity scale in Figure 3.25 (SideNote 3.37). We know from Chapter 1 that very low intensities will fail to yield a perceptual experience. The point at which a sensation is perceived (i.e., the detection threshold) can be estimated by classical psychophysical techniques, such as the Method of Constant Stimuli, that produce a psychometric function. The threshold for pain, which occurs at some point further along the intensity scale, is a bit more difficult to estimate. Because pain is such an unpleasant condition, we have to be careful that excessive intensities are not applied. Therefore, an ascending Method of Limits procedure is generally used whereby intensities are raised in discrete steps starting at a subthreshold pain level (SideNote 3.38). This procedure will also generate a psychometric function that can be used to estimate the threshold intensity for pain. As Figure 3.25 shows, both absolute detection and pain detection thresholds can be derived from psychometric functions obtained with separate stimulus parameters. In this example, three different pulse frequencies were applied to reveal that pain threshold is lowest at an intermediate frequency, whereas detection threshold remains relatively unaffected.

The experience of pain at suprathreshold intensities can be evaluated in several different ways. For scientific studies, magnitude estimation procedures have been used to reveal different power functions, depending upon the type of painful stimulus applied. For example, radiant heat produces power functions with an exponent value of 1.0, whereas electrical stimulation yields an exponent value of 1.8. Simplified versions of the magnitude estimation procedure have been developed for pain evaluation in clinical settings. These procedures typically use simple category scales that can be numerical (e.g., a range of 0–10) or descriptive (e.g., none, mild, moderate, severe). One of the most widely used descriptive scales for pain evaluation is the McGill Pain Questionnaire (MPQ) that was developed by Ronald Melzack (Melzack, 1975). The MPQ contains a checklist of 78 descriptive terms that are grouped into

SideNote | **3.37**

Not surprisingly, tooth pulp is heavily innervated with small-diameter fibres that generate a sharp painful sensation when stimulated. The cornea on the surface of the eyeball is another structure that gives rise to pain when stimulated. An interesting property of the cornea is that it is only innervated by Aδ and C fibres.

SideNote | **3.38**

Although there are inherent problems with the ascending Method of Limits approach, such as errors of expectation, it nevertheless avoids stimulus intensities that are beyond the tolerance level of the subject. Both human and animal studies on pain are among the most tightly regulated by university ethical review committees, whose approval is needed before any experiment can be initiated.

20 categories covering both the sensory and emotional aspects of pain.

The multivariate concept

Pain is a multi-dimensional experience that includes the attributes of location, duration, intensity, and quality. Unlike the univariate approach where the pain experience is only assessed along the sensory dimension, multivariate strategies seek to assess multiple pain dimensions. Although this makes for a more complex analysis, it has the advantage of more fully describing the complexity of the pain experience and in many instances provides a more accurate assessment of clinical pain. Of the different attributes, pain quality is perhaps the most

difficult to measure since pain is always accompanied by an unpleasant state of feeling that in turn generates an emotional component. These are not easy parameters to measure.

Multi-dimensional scaling techniques are generally used to assess the multiple qualities associated with pain. In practical terms, the scaling procedures we discussed above can be applied in multi-dimensional studies so long as they evaluate the different dimensions of pain separately. For example, the MPQ contains separate categories that address the sensory aspects of pain, the general intensity of the pain experience, and emotional factors that are associated with pain. The responses in each category can be quantified and therefore scaled

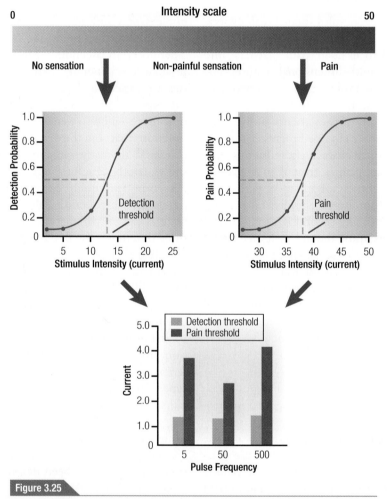

Figure 3.25

Electric current applied to the tooth pulp can be used to estimate both detection and pain thresholds. Current intensities in the range of 0–50 are shown on the scale at the top. Very low intensities fail to produce a sensation, whereas very high intensities produce pain; non-painful sensations arise at intermediate intensities. Detection thresholds for sensation and pain can be determined by standard psychophysical techniques to yield separate psychometric functions (middle). The actual threshold value for sensation and pain varies with frequency of electric pulse delivery (bottom). Data from "Non-pain and Pain Sensations Evoked by Tooth Pulp Stimulation," by P. A. McGrath, R. H. Gracely, R. Dubner, and M. W. Heft, 1983, *Pain, 15*, pp. 377–388.

METHODOLOGY

The McGill Pain Questionnaire

Ronald Melzack at McGill University developed the McGill Pain Questionnaire in order to try to better understand both the prothetic and the metathetic qualities of pain for clinical, chronic sufferers. The questionnaire has three major measures: (1) *pain rating index,* (2) *number of words chosen,* and (3) *present pain intensity.* By taking these three measures into account, pain is quantified in a way that can lead to statistical treatment. Throughout the many years of its use, this questionnaire has demonstrated that the English language has number of words to describe pain; that there is a high level of agreement when classifying those words for different pain dimensions or experiences; and that even with diverse backgrounds, people tend to use similar words at similar positions on the intensity scale.

to a particular intensity. A multi-dimensional map can then be constructed that portrays the magnitude of the different components of a particular pain experience.

3.   CONTROL OF PAIN

Pain plays an important role in survival because it alerts us to potential or actual tissue damage. It also affects our behaviour in that we are less inclined to engage in activities that will likely cause bodily harm. Simply put, pain is essential for survival because without it we would cause mortal damage to ourselves. There are, however, many instances of acute and chronic pain that cause needless suffering and that exert no biological or survival benefit (SideNote 3.39). It has been humankind's quest through the ages to find ways to relieve such pain and heal the wounded body.

Pharmacological approaches

Human experimentation with chemical substances that control pain has a long history. The early efforts to find cures for pain relied on the use of herbal extracts and plant products (SideNote 3.40). Although the actual remedies were arrived at through empirical means of trial and error, it turns out that many of the herbal agents that were popular in early times contain chemical substances that have now been shown to have striking **analgesic** function (Hwang & Oh, 2007; Wall & Melzack, 1999). The modern approach to pain control relies on the administration of a variety of drugs that fall into three general categories.

The first category of analgesics is anti-inflammatory drugs such as Aspirin, Tylenol, and ibuprofen. These drugs have both a peripheral and a central effect that reduce pain without affecting tactile signals. Their peripheral effect is to reduce inflammation that occurs as a result of tissue damage. Inflammation is responsible for sensitizing the nociceptors and thereby making them more active. The central effect of these drugs produces a more general analgesic response, though its precise mechanism is less well understood.

The second category includes a broad range of drugs that are not known for inflammatory control but that nevertheless have a potent analgesic function. Drugs such as antidepressants, anticonvulsants, and muscle relaxants can show significant analgesic effects under certain acute and chronic pain conditions.

The opioid analgesics form the third category and offer the most powerful means for pain control. The two most well-known examples are codeine and morphine. These drugs do not act at the level of the nociceptors but rather directly on the central nervous system. Opioid drugs bind to specific receptors (opiate receptors) in the brain where they modulate the activity of neurons that process pain signals. This effect is so potent that opioid-based drugs have become our main pharmacological defence against serious acute and chronic pain.

One of the most astonishing discoveries in pain research has been the demonstration that our own brains actually produce opiate-like substances. In the 1970s, neuroscientists showed that several endogenous substances called **endorphins** are synthesized in the brain. These substances are capable of binding to the same receptors that are targeted by morphine and other opioid drugs. Several such endogenous products have now been identified. It is believed that endorphins represent a self-defence mechanism and act to reduce pain

SideNote | **3.39**

Acute pain refers to the sudden onset of pain—from surgery, trauma, burns, etc.—or recurrent forms that are limited in duration (e.g., a headache). Chronic pain occurs in cases of progressive medical diseases (e.g., osteoarthritis, cancer, etc.). Some cases of chronic pain are evident even in the absence of any pathology and are attributable to psychological disturbances, known as *psychogenic pain.*

SideNote | **3.40**

Some of the most notable examples of herbal agents for curing pain are ginger root for internal pains, horseradish leaves for headaches, and willow plants, which contain salicyclic acid (the active ingredient in Aspirin) for arthritic pains.

SideNote | **3.41**

The ancient Chinese practice of acupuncture has been shown to relieve pain in some circumstances. One theory is that the insertion of fine needles at specific nerve junctions in the body triggers the release of endorphins, which then reduce the experience of pain.

SideNote | **3.42**

One of the more serious long-term side effects of opiate treatments is physical and psychological dependence. The possibility of addiction to painkillers is always present if taken for more than a few days. Another side effect of opiate drugs, such as codeine, is severe constipation that should normally require close monitoring if taken for a prolonged period.

in the same way as the external administration of morphine (SideNote 3.41).

Anesthetic, surgical, and neurostimulatory approaches

One particularly important approach to pain management is the use of anesthetic agents that block neural responses either at the local level or in the transmission of pain signals through the spinal cord. The application of local anesthetics—for example, during dental work—assures short-term numbing of the region by blocking nociceptive signal generation in peripheral pain receptors. The blockade of neural signals from a larger area, especially in the lower extremities, is accomplished by signal blockade through the spinal cord. The *epidural* procedure, which has become common during childbirth, involves the infusion of opiate agents in the space adjacent to the spinal cord where they act to block the transmission of pain signals through the anterolateral pathway to the brain.

The management of severe, chronic pain is somewhat difficult with pharmacological and anesthetic treatments because all pain-killing drugs have both short- and long-term side effects (SideNote 3.42). The surgical approach is only practised in very severe cases of pain and can include procedures at various levels, from peripheral nerves to the spinal cord (**cordotomy**), to surgical intervention in the frontal lobe of the brain (**lobotomy**). An alternative approach is to use neurostimulatory procedures where electrodes are used to deliver electric currents (Fregni, Freedman, & Pascual-Leone, 2007). For example, it has been shown that direct brain stimulation at certain sites can suppress pain. Several mechanisms may be involved in this process, including the active suppression of nociceptive signal transmission, endorphin production, and descending signals from the brain to control nociceptive signal gating in the spinal cord. A less invasive procedure based on the gate control theory involves the electrical stimulation of peripheral nerves, a procedure commonly known as **TENS**. Electrical signals in the Aα and Aβ fibres presumably activate inhibitory interneurons in the spinal cord, which then impair the transmission of pain signals.

Psychological approaches

Clinicians have found that management of chronic pain is best approached through a multi-pronged strategy. One effective component of that strategy involves behavioural therapy such as relaxation training, distraction techniques, and hypnosis. We have already seen that pain perception is very much controlled by factors beyond mere signal generation by nociceptors. The human mind itself can be a very potent controller of how much pain is felt. A nice example of that is the placebo effect, where patients proclaim striking benefits from medication they believe is effective in relieving their condition when in fact they have only consumed an inert substance. Given the powers of the mind, a comprehensive treatment plan can often include behavioural therapy that helps to reduce discomfort and often allows patients to cope with what would otherwise be a debilitating and traumatic pain experience.

Summary

1. The sensation of touch is multi-faceted, with the ability to detect pressure, vibration, and changes in temperature. Not only can humans determine objectively *where* touch occurs, but we can determine subjectively *what* was touched and *how* it felt.

2. The skin can be anatomically separated into two parts: the epidermis and the dermis. Touch sensation is mediated by mechanoreceptors, which can be placed into three categories:

   • encapsulated receptors—Pacinian corpuscle (vibration), Meissner corpuscle (light touch), and Ruffini corpuscle (steady pressure);

   • receptors with accessory structures—Merkel disc (light touch) and Lanceolate ending (in hair shaft; triggered when hair moves); and

   • free nerve endings, which detect changes in temperature and produce the sensation of pain.

3. Mechanoreceptors represent a unique type of neuron because they are able to transduce mechanical energy into an electrical signal by opening Na^+ channels. Furthermore, they are structurally unique, being a modified bipolar neuron with one branch leading from the dorsal root ganglion (DRG) to the skin and ending in a receptor. The other branch terminates at the spinal cord where it relays signals to the brain. Finally, action potentials are generated at the most peripheral site (i.e., at the mechanoreceptor itself) instead of at a later stage (i.e., close to the neuron body) as with most other neurons.

4. The spinal cord transmits somatosensory signals (via the dorsal root) and motor signals (via the ventral root) to and from the brain, respectively. This division is known as the *Bell–Magendie law*. The route that afferent fibres take up along the spinal column depends on the type of fibre and somatosensory information being carried.

5. Von Frey used horse hairs to determine the threshold pressure needed to detect skin impression. Absolute threshold depends on the site, age, gender, or condition of the skin (e.g., presence of calluses). The difference threshold is just as susceptible to a variety of factors. Other psychophysical tests include the two-point limen and point localization error.

6. There are different ways that the tactile system can be used for communication with blind people. Some examples are Braille and the Moon system. Braille can be read quicker, but the Moon system is useful for people who lose their sight in later life. Other more unusual systems are the Optacon, Tactile Vision Substitution System, and Tadoma method.

7. Proprioceptors provide important information about where one's limbs are in space by detecting the stretching or contraction of muscles and tendons. Psychophysical studies have examined how well people are at determining force, weight, or pressure. Von Helmholtz proposed that a neurological signal known as an *efference copy* (or corollary discharge) is sent to the perceptual centres of the brain so that we are aware of all our movements.

8. Nociceptors for different painful stimuli such as mechanical, chemical, and thermal energy are found throughout the body. Referred pain arises because of the way pain fibres are wired in the spinal cord. Phantom pain may occur after amputation and gives rise to the perception that the missing limb generates tactile or painful stimuli. Gate control theory is used to explain how pain perception can be affected by descending signals from the brain. Pain control by pharmacological means can be divided into three main categories: anti-inflammatory drugs, analgesic drugs, and opioid drugs.

Key Terms

Recall Questions

1. What are the different aspects or modalities of the touch sensation? Why is the somatosensory system considered to be a spatial sense?

2. What are the different categories of mechanoreceptors, and how do they differ from each other in terms of both structure and function? What are the different types of afferent fibres, and how are they related to mechanoreceptor type?

3. Why do mechanoreceptors represent a unique type of neuron? What is the receptive field of a mechanoreceptor?

4. What is the neural circuitry by which tactile signals reach the spinal cord and thereafter proceed to the cerebral cortex? How do touch and pain signals differ in terms of their transmission process?

5. What is the Bell–Magendie law? Why is it necessary to have a close coupling between sensory and motor processing, both at the spinal and cortical levels?

6. What are the different types of esthesiometers? How do the different parts of the body compare in terms of absolute and two-point threshold? In both regards, what are the most and least sensitive parts of the body?

7. What is meant by "physiological zero"? How do thermoreceptors differ from mechanoreceptors in terms of their structure and the fibres associated with them?

8. What are the different systems that have been developed for tactile communication? Why is Braille text superior to embossed letters in terms of readability?

9. What is the difference between proprioception and kinesthesis? What are the two main sites in the body where proprioceptors are located? How do their afferent fibres differ from those associated with mechanoreceptors? Why is active touch superior to passive touch for determining object identities?

10. What is the difference between *referred pain* and *phantom pain*? What is the multivariate concept of pain measurement, and how does it differ from the univariate concept? What are the three main approaches to the control of pain?

11. How do the adaptation properties of afferent fibres relate to the different qualities of tactile sensation? How do the FA- and SA-type fibres fit in with the concept of parallelism and modality segregation, at both low and high levels of processing?

12. What is corollary discharge, and how does it serve the somatosensory system? How does it differ from proprioceptive signalling?

13. Why do humans perform better point-localization than two-point discrimination? How is psychophysical performance on different spatial tasks related to mechanoreceptor distribution and function?

14. What is the gate control theory of pain? How can neurostimulatory approaches be used in the context of this theory to control pain?

Further Reading

- Grunwald, M. (2008). *Human haptic perception: Basics and applications*. Basel, Switzerland: Birkhäuser.

- Heller, M. A., & Ballesteros, S. (2005). *Touch and blindness: Psychology and neuroscience*. Hillsdale, NJ: Lawrence Erlbaum.

- Kruger, E. (1996). *Pain and touch, handbook of perception and cognition* (2nd ed.). San Diego, CA: Academic Press.

- Marieb, E., & Hoehn, K. (2006). *Human anatomy and physiology* (7th ed.). San Francisco, CA: Benjamin Cummings.

- Melzack, R., & Wall, P. D. (1996). *The challenge of pain*. Harmondsworth, UK: Penguin.

- Millar, S. (2008). *Space and sense*. New York, NY: Psychology Press.

- Morgan, M. J. (2009). *Molyneux's question: Vision, touch and the philosophy of perception*. Cambridge, England: Cambridge University Press.

- Paterson, M. (2007). *The senses of touch: Haptics, affects and technologies*. Oxford, England: Berg Publishers.

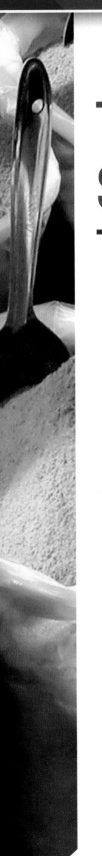

The Chemosensory Systems: Taste and Smell

4

In this chapter . . .

- You will discover that the chemosensory systems are unique in a number of respects, such as their ability to influence memories, mate selection, food preference, and many complex aspects related to socialization.

- You will learn that there are five primary taste qualities (sweet, sour, salty, bitter, and umami), and you will also learn how they interact with neurons within our taste buds to send taste information to the primary gustatory cortex.

- You will read about the difficulties one encounters when attempting to perform psychophysical experiments on taste. You will become familiar with the techniques that have been developed—such as electrogustometry, chemogustometry, and the whole-mouth technique—and how they are used to determine the absolute and difference thresholds for different tastants.

- You will learn about the path that odourants take to the olfactory epithelium to cause the sense of smell. You will also be introduced to odourant binding proteins (and understand their role in olfaction), the receptors that transduce olfactory signals, the mechanisms by which action potentials are produced in olfactory receptor neurons, and the pathways by which these signals reach the higher brain centres to yield olfactory perception.

- You will understand the many issues that must be addressed when conducting psychophysical experiments on smell, such as the time-sensitive nature of odourants, issues with adaptation, and the challenge of accurately delivering the stimuli. You will see how Fechnerian methods and direct estimation strategies are used to study the perceptual aspects of smell and individual differences that affect scent detection ability.

Although the scientific study of the chemosensory systems has a relatively short history, our preoccupation with these senses dates back to prehistoric times. The use of spices and other additives to enhance the taste of foods has been practised for thousands of years. Photo: horst72/iStockphoto.com

After the people are dead, after the things are broken and scattered, taste and smell alone, more fragile but more enduring, more unsubstantial, more persistent, more faithful, remain poised a long time, like souls, remembering, waiting, hoping, amid the ruins of all the rest.

— Marcel Proust, *Remembrance of Things Past*

SideNote 4.1

The Egyptians used perfume as part of their religious rituals, largely through burning incense and applying balms and ointments. Perfumed oils were also applied to the skin for either cosmetic or medicinal purposes. The use of perfumes quickly spread to the Greek and Roman empires where it enjoyed considerable popularity.

SideNote 4.2

The environment and climate of France provided ideal conditions for the plants and flowers used in making perfumes, leading to high production and demand by the 17th century. The use of perfumes in French society was so commonplace that there was a fragrance for every occasion, even one called *Parfum à la Guillotine.*

SideNote 4.3

The occurrence of taste receptors in fish has been known since the early 1900s. Many of their taste receptors are actually located on their body surface, which has led to the use of fish, especially the channel catfish, in physiological experiments on taste.

All animals are endowed with an ability to recognize chemical signals in their environment. In humans, this function is apparent in two forms. We are capable of detecting airborne chemicals through our **olfactory system**. The physiological processes involved in this detection ultimately produce the perceptual quality we call *smell*. In contrast, the **gustatory system** is involved in the detection of chemicals that dissolve in our saliva after we consume foods or beverages. The neural signals that are subsequently triggered in our tongue produce the sensation we call *taste*. In this chapter, we will examine the neural mechanisms that are involved in the operation of both of these chemosensory systems, and then we will discuss the various perceptual characteristics of these two systems in humans.

The systems that are specialized for chemosensory detection differ among different invertebrate and vertebrate species with regard to sensitivity and function. For humans, taste and smell are primarily important for food selection and, to a lesser extent, communication. We are keenly aware that the smell of a burning substance signifies fire and that a terribly bitter tasting substance is likely poisonous. In this regard, the chemosensory systems provide survival value to individual organisms. We now know that chemosensory communication, especially through smell, also plays an important role in sexual attraction and mate selection in many animal species. Whether or not chemical signals are important for sexual selection in humans remains an interesting though unresolved question (Brown, 1985; Kohl, 1995).

One characteristic that is well recognized is the extent to which chemosensory stimulation can affect our emotional state and alter our behaviour. The pleasures that we experience through smell and taste are unparalleled by any other sensory experience. Although the scientific study of the chemosensory systems has a relatively short history, our preoccupation with these senses dates back to prehistoric times. The use of spices and other additives to enhance the taste of foods has been practised for thousands of years. Indeed, much of the trade between societies on different continents during the Middle Ages was spurred by the quest for greater gastronomic delights. Similarly, the use of aromatic substances by ancient civilizations is well documented and played an important role in social interactions

(Genders, 1972; LaGallienne, 1928). The invention of perfume by the Egyptians quickly found its way to the Roman Empire and then, through the course of several hundred years, to a burgeoning industry centred in France (SideNotes 4.1 and 4.2) (Morris, 1984). Our preoccupation with the sensory delights that taste and smell bring to us illustrates the immense hedonic qualities that can be associated with these sensory experiences.

A. General Characteristics of Chemosensory Perception

The chemosensory systems are distinct from other sensory systems in several ways. In this section, we explore some of these differences and discuss the general characteristics of taste and smell. Our discussion will be centred on four pertinent questions.

What evolutionary factors led to the development of chemosensory systems?

Life on Earth began in the sea. The earliest organisms had not yet developed sensory mechanisms for vision or hearing but instead relied on the detection of chemicals in their environment for navigation, protection, and feeding. It seems that even the simplest organisms were capable of responding to chemical stimuli and altering their behaviour in response. And thus emerged the very first chemosensory systems. Of course, it is difficult to distinguish these systems as taste or smell in the way that we understand them now. Indeed, that distinction becomes somewhat arbitrary in a marine environment where all chemicals appear in dissolved form. However, one basis for the distinction lies on whether the mechanism is involved in the detection of chemicals emitted at a distant source, and therefore carried through the medium to the host, or whether chemical detection occurs only when the stimulus is in close proximity, as in the course of feeding (SideNote 4.3). This near-versus-far definition is applied as a simple way to distinguish between taste and smell.

The evolution of taste and smell was guided by the simple need for marine organisms to seek food and avoid predators. That requirement became further refined as terrestrial life forms emerged. With air as the new medium, the divergence of smell and taste soon began to take shape, with airborne chemicals now serving most species as a distant detector of chemical stimuli, whereas taste became specialized as a near detector (Beauchamp & Bartoshuk, 1997; Gibbons, 1986). American psychologist James J. Gibson regarded taste and smell together as a food-seeking and sampling system. Smell allows an animal to find its food, he argued, whereas taste provides a final check before consumption to ensure compatibility to that animal's nutritional needs. Certain foods that are useful in this regard yield a positive taste experience, whereas those that are poisonous produce a negative or unsavoury experience.

A number of sociobiological factors were also important in the evolution of chemosensory systems, particularly their role in terms of chemical communication. The emission of specific chemical signals allows members of a particular species to mark territorial boundaries, to interact with other species, and to signal sexual receptiveness (or, in some cases, repulsion). Territorial marking is usually accomplished through by-products of excretion, whereas sexual signalling largely occurs through the release of chemicals, known as **pheromones**, from specialized glands (SideNote 4.4). Although much remains to be known about how these chemicals work, their role in the sexual cycles of many species, from simple invertebrates to various mammalian species, is now well documented (Kohl, 1995; McClintock, 1971; Watson, 2000). Thus, in addition to food search and selection, the chemosensory systems evolved to play important roles in how animals develop, socialize, mate, and nurture their offspring—factors that in turn became critically important for their propagation as a species.

Why are we sensitive to chemicals?

The path of chemosensory evolution for humans, however, resulted in a bit of a quirk. Although chemical signals play a very important role for many mammalian species, humans rely much less on chemosensory stimulation. Instead, we have become largely visual creatures and depend on sight and sound for food acquisition, navigation, and communication. The decreasing importance of olfaction in humans and primates has been the source of much discussion (Brown, 1985; Van Toller & Dodd, 1988; Wilson & Stevenson, 2006). Sigmund Freud speculated that primate

evolution to an upright posture resulted in a diminished importance of smell. As we physically turned away from the earth, he argued, we psychologically turned away from the olfactory experience. It is somewhat ironic that the evolutionary forces that so clearly drove the differentiation of species through the sense of smell and its role in sexual reproduction ultimately produced a species where that very sense had become diminished.

Some have argued that taste and smell are no longer crucial to our survival and that the future course of humanity would be unaffected if these senses were to suddenly disappear. Although the importance of the chemical senses to humans is certainly less than to other animals, this does not necessarily mean that these senses are inconsequential. The social importance of chemical senses is quite significant when we consider the lengths to which we will go to create pleasant odours or, alternatively, to remove bad odours.

There is a lively debate among chemosensory scientists on the extent to which olfaction affects human sexuality and whether human pheromones exist and affect our behaviour in very subtle but real ways (SideNote 4.5) (Baxi, Dorries, & Eisthen, 2006; Watson, 2000). Human infants, for example, can detect the odours of their mother's breasts and are often attracted to those scents while being repulsed by the scents of strangers (Porter, 1999). Olfactory maternal attraction has been taken as evidence for the existence of a human pheromonal system, one that appears to operate from a very early age (SideNote 4.6). The well-known effect of menstrual synchrony among women in a college dormitory provides another striking example where specific odours emitted by people are believed to produce a behavioural response (SideNote 4.7) (McClintock, 1971). These examples have been used by some sensory physiologists to argue that certain emitted odours do indeed have pheromonal actions in humans, a notion that remains controversial largely because the actual scents and their functional mechanisms have remained elusive.

Humans' sense of taste has also been largely relegated to a hedonic role of enhancing the eating experience (Beauchamp & Bartoshuk, 1997; Taylor & Roberts, 2004). It can be argued that taste still provides survival value through its use in rejecting foods that are likely to be poisonous because of their bitter or sour taste. There is one substance that is critical for

SideNote **4.4**

The glands can be situated anywhere on the body, though for most mammalian species, they are concentrated around the genital area. The popular men's fragrance musk is derived from glandular secretions near the anus of the male musk deer of central Asia.

SideNote **4.5**

The connection between olfaction and sexuality was bolstered by a study in the early 1950s that showed exaltolide, an aromatic substance derived from plants, has a sexually stimulating effect. Women are very sensitive to the scent, especially during the ovulatory period, whereas men can barely detect the odour. Needless to say, exaltolide is a common ingredient in many perfumes.

SideNote **4.6**

The postulated sources of pheromones in adult humans are the oral cavity, vaginal emissions, and secretions from the apocrine glands found in the armpit. One theory asserts that the reason dancing is so common in all human cultures is that it stimulates the expression of pheromonal chemicals contained in armpit perspiration.

SideNote **4.7**

Martha McClintock found that when women house together, their menstrual cycles tend to synchronize and lengthen. A later study by Michael Russell showed that the so-called *McClintock effect* could be obtained if a group of women were exposed to the underarm scent of another woman that was unknown to them, suggesting that olfactory cues were involved in mediating the effect.

Methodology

Reducing Salt Content in Foods

Dérick Rousseau at Ryerson University in Toronto, Canada, is working with a team of researchers to figure out how to reduce the salt content in foods. They have decided to use a type of "slow release" technique that is already in use for different pharmaceuticals, and they plan on doing this by coating the salt molecules in a protein or carbohydrate shell. This will lead to an overall decrease in the amount of salt used (30%, according to the researchers) but with little perceived reduction in salty taste.

SideNote | **4.8**

Tracking ability has other functions besides predator survival. It is well known that salmon return to the stream in which they were spawned to reproduce and complete their life cycle. This migratory ability has been attributed to tracking olfactory cues that arise from the unique chemical composition of each stream due to the soil and vegetation that drain into it.

our survival, however, but whose intake must also be carefully controlled. The biological importance of salt is such that insufficient levels of it in our blood will rapidly produce disturbances in brain function and muscle contraction, leading to cardiac arrest. Our craving for salt may reflect the need for ensuring that adequate amounts of it are ingested every day. In fact, *saltiness* forms one of the four basic taste qualities that have been identified. And yet, we are also very sensitive to consuming too much salt. Our sensitivity to excessive salt intake through a negative taste experience provides a certain adaptive value because sudden increases in blood levels are also dangerous. Thus, the role of taste for this one substance reflects both our biological need for it as well as protection against excessive consumption of it.

How does human chemosensory function differ from that of other animals?

The difference between human chemosensory function and that of other animals appears to be most apparent within the domain of olfaction. We have already noted the important role that pheromones play in regulating a variety of behaviours in lower animals—including territory marking, maternal interactions with offspring, and sexual signalling. It appears that a separate chemosensory organ has evolved for the specific detection of pheromones—the so-called **vomeronasal organ** (Baxi et al., 2006; Keverne, 1999; Monti-Bloch, Jennings-White, & Berliner, 1998). The VNO, for short, is located in the nasal cavity but is separate from the main olfactory organ. The existence of the VNO is well established in many terrestrial mammalian species where it appears to serve as a parallel olfactory system for the specific detection of pheromonal scents. However, the presence of a functional VNO in humans remains controversial, though there is accumulating anatomical evidence for it. We

will review that evidence later in this chapter and speculate on the possible functions of a human vomeronasal system.

The sensitivity of the human olfactory system is also a major departure from that of many other animals. Given our reduced reliance on odour detection for daily survival, it is not surprising that this is accompanied by a reduction in our sensitivity to various scents. Most mammalian species are far more sensitive to a broad variety of odours than humans are. The ability to follow the scent tracks of potential prey is of great importance for the survival of all predators (SideNote 4.8) (Doty, 2003; Strausfeld & Hildebrand, 1999). The one example that is most often cited in this regard is the olfactory sensitivity of dogs. Compared to humans, dogs are up to 10,000 times more sensitive to particular scents. Certain breeds of dogs, such as German shepherds, are especially suited for tracking tasks because they not only have keen detection abilities but are also able to compare the strength of a scent from successive sniffs to determine whether the concentration is increasing or decreasing. This is useful in police work for following the olfactory traces of criminals or victims.

How do taste and smell differ from the other sensory systems?

The chemosensory systems differ from our other senses in several ways. At the most elemental level, the very nature of the stimulus that triggers our various taste and smell experiences remains unknown (Schiffman, 2000; Scott, 2005; Serby & Chobor, 1992). This is not true for the other sensory systems where a particular perceptual quality can be precisely associated with the stimulus quality. For example, we know exactly what physical qualities of light are necessary to obtain the perceptual impression of a certain colour. Similarly, the physical nature of a sound or touch stimulus can be associated with the perceptual impressions that they create. However, the connection between stimulus and perception is very complex for the chemosensory systems.

Another major difference from the other sensory systems, but at a much higher level, concerns the way in which the chemosensory systems can affect our emotions. We have all experienced first-hand the recollection of a past moment in our life through re-exposure to a particular scent, or the effect that certain scents can have on changing our mood, or the very fact that the most common description we place on any taste or smell stimulus is its pleasantness or unpleasantness (Doherty, Brewer, Castle, & Pantelis, 2006; Wilson & Stevenson, 2003). The notion that odours can trigger memories from the distant past, especially those charged with emotional significance, has sometimes been called the Proust phenomenon (SideNote 4.9). This special ability of olfaction arises because of the unique connections that the olfactory organ has within the brain. Smell is the only sense that has direct contact with the limbic system—a set of brain structures responsible for the neural processes that trigger emotion, mood, motivation, and sexual behaviour. The fact that these structures can be directly stimulated only by the olfactory system seems to account for the strong connection between certain fragrances and their effect upon emotion, memory, and sexual desire.

A particularly unique distinction of the chemosensory systems is the role they have played in early thinking on evolution and anthropology—a role that is far more pervasive than for any of the other sensory systems. We have already discussed the importance of smell in the evolutionary process and especially within the context of sexual selection. Odours play an important role in sexual development as well, and according to Freudian logic, they form the critical stimuli for ushering in the Oedipus complex (SideNote 4.10). However, it was the paradox of diminished human olfaction through the course of evolution that generated some of the most bizarre ideas from the 19th century (Harrington & Rosario, 1992). The anthropological response to this paradox was rooted in concepts of savage or *primitive* cultures—non-white races who had superior olfactory ability and therefore served as an evolutionary bridge between lower animals and *advanced* humans belonging to modern

European civilization. The scientific literature of this period contained many anecdotal accounts of the keen olfactory ability among non-Europeans, a trait that many linked directly to the level of skin pigmentation (SideNote 4.11).

It should be clear from the general background contained in this section that the chemosensory systems have a rather unique role in human biology, culture, and society. Their many diverse (and peculiar) qualities also offer substantial challenge to a fuller scientific understanding of how they function. In the remainder of this chapter, we expand on many of the functional aspects of both taste and smell by discussing their operational details and various characteristics of the perceptual impressions they create.

B. The Gustatory System— Biological Mechanisms

Humans' taste system has traditionally been thought of as having four basic qualities—sweet, sour, salty, and bitter (Finger, Silver, & Restrepo, 2000; Tortora & Derrickson, 2008). More recently, a fifth category of taste stimuli, called **umami**, has been added to the list of primary taste sensations (SideNote 4.12). The signals that produce these primary sensations arise from specialized sensory organs that reside in the oral cavity. It has been known since the middle of the 19th century that tiny structures in the tongue that resemble flower buds are responsible for producing taste sensations. In addition to the tongue, these so-called **taste buds** are also found in the roof and in the back of the mouth, though in much smaller numbers. We have only recently come to learn the remarkable way in which these taste organs function and how they produce the signals that ultimately generate the different types of taste qualities that we experience.

1. TASTE RECEPTION IN THE TONGUE

We begin our exploration of the neural substrates of taste by first looking at the tongue in some detail (Doty, 2003). A close examination of the human tongue reveals that it is composed of numerous bumps and grooves that are arrayed over its entire surface. Each small mound or projection of tissue is called a **papilla**. As Figure 4.1 shows, there are several

SideNote | 4.9

The Proust phenomenon is named after French novelist Marcel Proust for his description of childhood memories that were triggered by certain tastes or smells. A particularly famous passage is in his novel *Swann's Way*, where the author describes the memory unlocked by tasting a madeleine cake dipped in tea which he used to have as a child: "Once I had recognized the taste of the crumb of madeleine soaked in her decoction of lime flowers which my aunt used to give me, immediately the old gray house upon the street, where her room was, rose up like the scenery of a theater."

SideNote | 4.10

This phase of psychosexual development in boys, thought to occur between the ages of two and three, is believed to be triggered by sensitivity and aversion to male odour (usually that of the father) and initiates feminine heterosexual reactivity (usually toward the mother).

SideNote | 4.11

Olfactory sensitivity was considered to be highest among dark-skinned races, which was thought to help in predatory behaviour as well as identifying gender and tribal affiliation. The *civilized* Europeans, according to this view, dispensed with such needs and therefore gradually lost their olfactory prowess.

SideNote | 4.12

Umami is the Japanese term for the flavour enhancer monosodium glutamate (MSG), which is believed to be responsible for a fifth primary taste sensation. Although used by Oriental cooks for over 1,200 years, it was not until the early 1900s that a Japanese scientist discovered that the distinctive flavour of seaweed broth was caused by this chemical substance.

different kinds of papillae that are distributed over the surface of the tongue. The *fungiform papillae*, so called because of their mushroom-like appearance, are found primarily near the front tip of the tongue, although a somewhat larger kind is found toward the back. The much larger *vallate papillae* are found along a V-shaped line at the very back of the tongue. As shown by the insets in Figure 4.1, the grooves that encircle the vallate mounds are quite deep in comparison to those of the fungiform papillae. And finally, the *foliate papillae* are found at the back and along the sides of the tongue where they create a set of deep ridges.

An important feature of these papillae is that the vast majority of our taste buds are embedded within their grooves. Food substances dissolved in saliva are carried into the grooves where they interact with the taste buds to initiate the first sequence of events that leads to taste. All of our gustatory sensations arise in this manner through a total of approximately 4,600 taste buds that are located within the walls of the various papillae. As can be seen in Table 4.1, nearly one-half of this total is located within the vallate papillae, with the remaining taste buds being divided among the fungiform and foliate papillae.

Table 4.1

Distribution of Taste Buds According to Papilla Type in Adult Human Tongue

Fungiform Papillae	
3.4 taste buds/papilla	1,120 taste buds
290 papillae/tongue	(24%)
Vallate Papillae	
240 taste buds/papilla	2,200 taste buds
9.2 papillae/tongue	(48%)
Foliate Papillae	
118 taste buds/papilla	1,280 taste buds
10.8 papillae/tongue	(28%)
	4,600 taste buds

Note. From "Anatomy of the Peripheral Taste System," by I. J. Miller, Jr., 1995, in *Handbook of Olfaction and Gustation*, Ed. R. L. Doty, New York, NY: Marcel Dekker.

Taste receptor cells are located inside the taste bud

Although taste buds are considered to be the primary sensory organ of taste, it is the specialized receptor cells within them that are responsible for transducing the chemical stimuli into electrical signals. The dissolved chemicals, also known as **tastants**, infiltrate the taste buds through a narrow pore that opens into the grooves (see Figure 4.2). The receptor cells inside the taste buds are similar to the cells found in skin tissue, though with one important difference. Taste receptor cells actually behave as neurons in that sensory stimulation—in this case the binding of a tastant molecule—produces a change in the membrane potential that leads to neurotransmitter release (Breslin, 2000; Chandrashekar, Hoon, Ryba, & Zuker, 2006).

Each taste bud contains 50–150 receptor cells. There are two general types of receptor cells that can be distinguished by their appearance under a microscope—the so-called *dark* and *light cells* (Squire, Roberts, Spitzer, & Zigmond, 2002). As Figure 4.2 shows, both types become tapered at the pore where the cell's membrane becomes invaginated into a series of folds or **microvilli**. Once tastants enter the taste bud, they interact with the receptor cell membrane at the microvilli. The ensuing transduction process unfolds through a

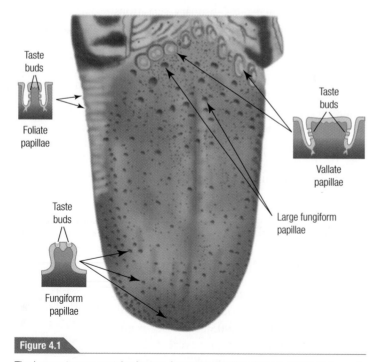

Figure 4.1

The human tongue contains bumps, known as *papillae*, that are distributed over its entire surface. There are regional variations in the size and depth of the papillae. The smaller fungiform papillae are found near the tip of the tongue, whereas the larger vallate and foliate papillae occur toward the back.

series of molecular events that results in neuro-transmitter release at the opposite end of the receptor cell.

Taste receptor cells are innervated by sensory neurons

A synapse is present at the interface between the receptor cell and gustatory nerve fibre where the release of neurotransmitter substance leads to action potentials in the nerve fibres. These fibres then carry the action potentials along one of two cranial nerves, depending on the part of the tongue in question. As Figure 4.3 shows, gustatory signals from taste buds in the front two-thirds of the tongue are transmitted through the **facial nerve** (also known as *cranial nerve VII*), whereas signals from the back one-third of the tongue are carried by fibres that belong to the **glossopharyngeal nerve** (also known as *cranial nerve IX*). Another cranial nerve, the **vagus nerve** (*cranial nerve X*), carries gustatory signals that arise from the few taste buds located at the back of the throat (Breslin, 2000; Miller, Jr., 1995).

The organizational layout of these three cranial nerves is similar to that of the spinal nerves we discussed in the last chapter with regard to somatosensory signalling. The major difference, however, is that these cranial nerves emerge from the brain stem rather than the spinal cord. Associated with each nerve is a ganglion, or collection of neurons. It is these sensory neurons that give rise to the gustatory fibres that innervate the tongue and throat (see Figure 4.3). It should be noted that in addition to transmitting taste messages, the fibres in these nerves also carry non-taste signals such as touch and pain. Although these facets of sensation are often not discussed within the context of gustation, they are nevertheless very important in delivering the total experience of food ingestion.

2. SIGNAL TRANSDUCTION MECHANISMS

We return to the picture at the receptor cell level to explore the events by which tastants produce a neural signal in these cells. This process had remained a mystery until recent advances in electrophysiological recording techniques coupled with the explosive developments in molecular technology. The picture that has emerged is that the primary taste qualities each have their own transduction mechanism.

These mechanisms fall into two general categories—ionic channel and receptor-mediated (Chandrashekar et al., 2006). Regardless of the specific mechanism involved, the end result

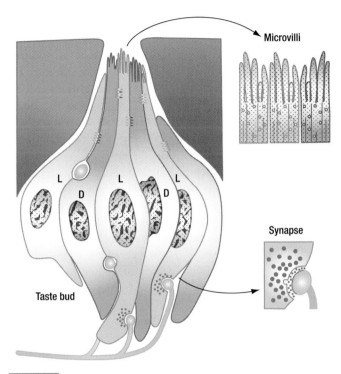

Figure 4.2

Light (L) and dark (D) cells are among the types of receptor cells found in the taste bud. The receptor cells become tapered toward the pore through which tastants enter and then interact with the cell's microvilli, leading to neurotransmitter release at the other end of the receptor cell.

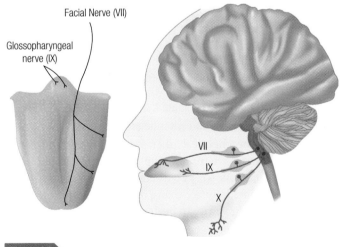

Figure 4.3

Gustatory signals from taste buds in the tongue are carried by nerve fibres that travel within two cranial nerves. A branch of the facial nerve (cranial nerve VII) innervates the anterior two-thirds of the tongue, whereas a branch of the glossopharyngeal nerve (cranial nerve IX) innervates the posterior one-third of the tongue. The cranial nerves emerge from the brain stem and have their cell bodies located within a ganglion just outside the brain stem.

of chemical stimulation upon a receptor cell is the same—membrane depolarization that results in neurotransmitter release upon the gustatory fibre.

Ionic channel mechanisms code for salty and sour tastes

The taste of salt is mediated by certain free ions, the most potent of which is sodium (Na^+). The transduction of sodium ions by taste receptor cells is fairly straightforward. As we noted in Chapter 2, all cells in the body have a lower concentration of Na^+ inside the cell than outside, creating an electrochemical gradient that favours the entry of Na^+ into the cell. This is precisely what happens in receptor cells when we ingest salt. Figure 4.4A shows the entry of Na^+ into the taste receptor cell through a sodium channel in the membrane, an event that results in a brief membrane depolarization that travels to the opposite end of the cell where it causes neurotransmitter substance to be released into the synaptic space (SideNote 4.13) (Beauchamp & Bartoshuk, 1997; Finger et al., 2000).

Sour taste is produced by acidic substances, which release free hydrogen ions or protons (H^+) in solution. The H^+ ions enter the receptor cells simply by proceeding through the sodium channels in the microvilli (Figure 4.4). As with Na^+ ions, H^+ also depolarizes the receptor cell once inside and therefore leads to neurotransmitter release. However, the sodium channel can only be used for this purpose if the Na^+ concentration in saliva is quite low. Otherwise, the two ions compete for the channel, and one ion can block the entry of the other. It is well known that acids from sour foods reduce the perceived taste of salt.

Receptor-mediated mechanisms code for sweet and bitter tastes

The chemicals that produce sweet and bitter tastes are more complex than the simple ionic tastants we just discussed (SideNote 4.14). In fact, there are many different compounds that can give rise to both taste sensations. The sweet taste, for example, can be generated by simple sugars such as glucose, fructose, and sucrose (ordinary table sugar) as well as more complex compounds such as various amino acids, peptides, and artificial sweeteners (e.g., aspartame, saccharine). However, it is the way in which sweet and bitter chemicals generate taste signals that provides the major framework for

our discussion here (Finger et al., 2000; Squire et al., 2002).

Sweet tastants in general bind to specific receptors that are found in the membranes of taste receptor cells at the microvilli. These receptors, which are large protein molecules that actually span the cell membrane, are coupled

SideNote 4.13

It is not clear what specific neurotransmitters are released into the synaptic space when the taste receptor cell depolarizes, although a number of candidates have been proposed such as acetylcholine, serotonin, and various amino acids.

SideNote 4.14

The molecular structures of two receptor-binding tastants, sucrose and quinine, that produce sweet and bitter tastes, respectively, are shown below.

DR TIM EVANS/SCIENCE PHOTO LIBRARY

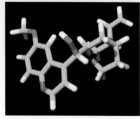

PROF. K. SEDDON & DR T. EVANS, QUEEN'S UNIVERSITY BELFAST/SCIENCE PHOTO LIBRARY

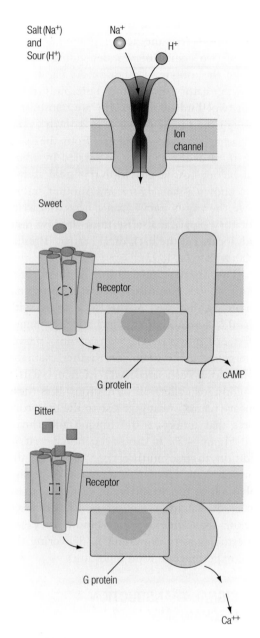

Figure 4.4

The primary taste sensations are transduced by either ionic channel mechanisms (salty and sour) or receptor-mediated mechanisms (sweet and bitter). The movement of Na^+ or H^+ through a pore in the receptor cell membrane produces depolarization and neurotransmitter release. The same occurs when sweet or bitter tastants bind to specific receptors. A cascade of biochemical events is then triggered by way of a G protein within the receptor cell.

with a so-called *G protein* (see Figure 4.4B and C). The binding of a sweet tastant to the receptor triggers the G protein, and this ultimately results in the production of a molecule known as *cAMP* within the receptor cell. The cAMP serves as a so-called **second messenger**—that is, it triggers a further set of biochemical events within the cell. In this case, it is believed that cAMP works directly upon the ionic channels to produce membrane depolarization, an event that leads to neurotransmitter release and hence signal generation in gustatory fibres.

Bitter tastes can be produced by a variety of chemicals, especially a family of nitrogen-containing compounds called *alkaloids*. These complex chemicals are usually found in plants. The most commonly cited example is quinine, an extremely bitter compound that is obtained from the bark of the South American cinchona tree and was first used by Amerindians for the treatment of malaria. Some other plants that contain high levels of alkaloids are periwinkles, California poppies, wolfberries, yellow pond lilies, and tobacco.

As with sweet tastants, bitter-tasting chemicals first bind to specific receptors, which then produces a series of G protein coupled intracellular events. In this case, the events appear to culminate in the release of Ca^{++} ions, which in turn trigger the release of neurotransmitters into the synaptic space. It is likely that different transduction mechanisms may be involved for different types of bitter substances. One compound that is particularly effective in unleashing this cascade is denatonium benzoate, the bitterest substance known (SideNote 4.15).

Umami

The umami taste, which is produced by the flavour enhancer monosodium glutamate, is considered by many to represent a fifth primary taste (Doty, 2003; Finger et al., 2000). If true, then there should be a specific receptor that mediates the transduction process in taste cells. A specific receptor for umami has indeed been identified—one that specifically binds glutamate molecules and, as with the receptors for sweet and bitter tastants, triggers a series of biochemical events in the taste cell. The identification of the umami receptor has given further credibility to establishing it as a primary taste similar to the other four. It would make sense that umami would have evolved to be a primary taste because glutamate is among the most abundant of amino acids and is found

at high levels in most food proteins. As we learned in Chapter 2, glutamate also serves as an important excitatory neurotransmitter in the brain. Therefore, the presence of a specific taste mechanism that leads to enhanced ingestion of glutamate would produce important physiological benefits for the organism.

3. CODING OF GUSTATORY SIGNALS

The way in which different aspects of a particular sensory dimension are processed has long fascinated physiologists and psychologists. We all know from personal experience the rich and multi-faceted nature of the taste experience. It is not surprising therefore that the complexity of the taste experience is reflected by a similar complexity in the way that information is encoded and transmitted by the different elements of the gustatory system. The attempt to unravel this complex process has produced much debate and controversy along the way, with a complete understanding of it still eluding us.

"Labelled-line" versus "cross-fibre" coding

The problem confronting the gustatory system is simple—how to distinguish among a variety of taste stimuli. In the somatosensory system, we discovered that the different characteristics of touch (e.g., pressure, heat, pain, etc.) are detected by different receptor types, transmitted through different channels, and processed by the brain in a segregated and independent manner (Squire et al., 2002). These are precisely the characteristics of a **labelled-line coding** system where each nerve fibre is responsible for transmitting information that is highly specific and restricted to a particular sensory modality. Throughout the 19th century, it was assumed that taste processing occurred in a labelled-line fashion where the four primary taste qualities—whose identity was already established from psychophysical studies—were encoded by distinct receptors and transmitted separately to the brain (Breslin, 2000; Doty, 2003). Indeed, the prevailing attitude of early scientists in all sensory domains was heavily tilted in favour of labelled lines, an idea whose origins can be traced to Johannes Müller's *law of specific nerve energies*, which we discussed in Chapter 2.

One would thus predict that a single taste receptor cell should be sensitive to only one of the four primary taste qualities and that the

SideNote | **4.15**

Adding as little as 30 parts of denatonium benzoate to one million parts of a liquid would make it too bitter to be tolerated by most human subjects. Because of its aversive reaction, denatonium benzoate is commonly added to items such as toiletries, pesticides, antifreeze, and many other products to avoid accidental poisoning. The commercial name for denatonium benzoate is Bitrex.

Carl Pfaffmann (1913–1994)
Image from the History of Medicine (NLM).

nerve fibre to which it synapses would faithfully carry only this signal to the brain. However, this does not appear to be the case. We now know that individual receptor cells are fully capable of responding to several taste stimuli through the various transduction mechanisms that we discussed in the previous section (Schiffman, 2000; Smith, John, & Boughter, 2000). To make matters more complicated, a single nerve fibre can receive signals from more than one taste bud, and each taste bud can send its signals through more than one gustatory fibre.

It was the pioneering work of Carl Pfaffman at Brown University during the middle of the 20th century that led to a significant revision in our thinking of gustatory coding. Pfaffman conducted electrophysiological studies of gustatory nerve fibres and found that a single fibre could respond to multiple taste qualities. The fact that the neural messages contained in single fibres were broad, rather than narrowly tuned to a specific taste, provided a major challenge to the labelled-line theory. The solution proposed by Pfaffman was that a certain taste quality was encoded by the pattern of firing in a large set of nerve fibres (Doty, 2003; Squire et al., 2002). According to this so-called **cross-fibre coding** scheme, the different taste qualities are distinguished not by neural discharges within dedicated nerve fibres but rather by the pattern of discharges across a large population of fibres. The higher taste centres of the brain have the task of decoding this pattern to generate a specific taste percept.

Taste quality and intensity coding

The notion that taste quality, whether it is simply the primary tastes or more complex mixtures, is encoded by the response profile of a large number of gustatory fibres is now generally accepted. However, many gustatory fibres do show a preference for a particular taste primary even though they may be stimulated by several different tastes as well. It has been argued that despite this preference, taste quality appears to be best represented by the cross-fibre pattern of firing. Physiological studies have shown that stimuli that produce similar tastes, such as different types of sweeteners, yield very similar patterns of firing. Conversely, chemical stimuli that generate similar patterns of firing are perceived to be closer in taste than those that generate different firing patterns.

Another dimension that must be encoded by gustatory fibres is the intensity of the stimulus. In the case of taste, stimulus intensity is reflected by the concentration of the chemical dissolved in saliva (Squire et al., 2002). It is common experience that increased concentration of any tastant is accompanied by an increase in the perceived taste intensity. The dimension of intensity is encoded by the firing rate of action potentials in gustatory fibres. All neurons that respond to a taste stimulus show increased firing rates in response to increased tastant concentration.

Regional differences in taste across the tongue

It was once believed that the tongue was subdivided into discrete regions where each of the taste qualities enjoyed exclusive processing by a highly selective set of taste buds. The old textbook pictures showed that the processing of bitter tastants occurred along the very back of the tongue, sour along the sides at the back, salty along sides at the front, and sweet at the very anterior tip of the tongue. We now know that this is not the case and that all four primary qualities are processed by taste buds located throughout the tongue. Nevertheless, there does appear to be some regional preference for certain taste qualities that produces an uneven distribution across the tongue (Collings, 1974).

It turns out that our sensitivity for sweet and salty stimuli is higher at the tip of the tongue, whereas sensitivity to sour and bitter stimuli is higher near the back of the tongue. This difference in taste sensitivities across the tongue, though small, nevertheless reveals a hint of organization in the layout of the taste primaries—something that has been referred to as **chemotopic organization**. The consequence this has for signal transmission to the brain is rather interesting. Recall that taste signals from the anterior portion of the tongue are carried in the facial nerve and the posterior portion in the glossopharyngeal nerve. The fibres that travel within the facial nerve are therefore generally more responsive to sugar and salt, tastes that we prefer, whereas the fibres in the glossopharyngeal nerve are more responsive to adverse taste qualities, such as sour and bitter.

4. GUSTATORY PROCESSING IN THE BRAIN

We have already discussed that taste signals are transmitted to the brain through three cranial nerves. The neural processes that ultimately lead to the perceptual experience of taste occur in cortical areas that are devoted to this sensory dimension. However, gustatory signals are first relayed through two different subcortical sites before arriving at the cerebral cortex (Finger et al., 2000; Tortora & Derrickson, 2008).

Subcortical relay sites for gustatory signals

The first subcortical structure that serves as a relay station for gustatory signals is the **nucleus of the solitary tract (NST)**. The NST is a collection of neurons located in the brain stem that acts as a relay station for other non-gustatory signals as well (Squire et al., 2002). As Figure 4.5 shows, the NST receives gustatory fibres from neurons whose cell bodies are located in ganglia associated with the three cranial nerves (nerves VII, IX, and X) emerging on each side of the brain stem. Single-unit physiological studies of NST neurons have shown that they, like the signals in the incoming gustatory fibres, are responsive to a broad range of taste stimuli. However, in most cases the neurons respond best to a particular taste primary. There is some evidence—the way that different taste-preferring neurons are spatially distributed—that a rough chemotopic arrangement also exists in the NST. It has been suggested that this organization reflects the preferential input of sour/bitter tastes through the glossopharyngeal nerve and sweet/salty tastes through the facial nerve.

The second subcortical relay site is located further up along the taste pathway within a segment of the thalamus known as the **ventral posterior medial nucleus (VPMN)**. The neurons here are generally small and densely packed. Single-unit studies of VPMN neurons have shown that they are also broadly tuned and therefore show responses to multiple taste primaries. However, responses to sweet and salty are the most common, followed by sour and bitter. VPMN neurons send fibre projections to the primary gustatory cortex, the first site in the cerebral cortex where taste signals are processed (see Figure 4.5).

Primary gustatory cortex

The projections from the thalamus arrive into an area of the frontal lobe that is buried within the sylvian sulcus, the large fissure that bisects each hemisphere along the lateral margin (see Figure 2.4 on page 37). The first hint that this cortical area was involved in taste processing came from studies in the 1940s from patients with bullet wounds to the head suffered during

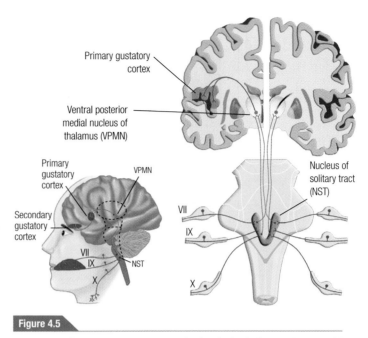

Figure 4.5

Taste signals from the tongue are transmitted to the brain through three cranial nerves. The signals are relayed by the nucleus of the solitary tract and thalamus before reaching the primary gustatory cortex. Higher aspects of taste function are processed in the secondary gustatory cortex.

the Second World War. It was found that some of the patients suffered a loss of taste sensation, a finding that could be tied to brain damage within a specific area known as the **insula**. Further studies through experimental brain lesions in monkeys clearly established the insula and surrounding cortex as a pure taste area, one that is now referred to as the *primary gustatory cortex* (SideNote 4.16).

Single-unit studies have shown that neurons in the primary gustatory area are responsive to all taste primaries, including umami. As with earlier structures of the gustatory pathway, the majority of neurons here have preferences for particular taste primaries (Scott & Plata-Salaman, 1999). Figure 4.6 on page 112 shows that the majority of neurons are tuned to sweet and salty tastes. One interesting aspect of neural coding at the cortical level is that the preference for a particular taste appears to be more selective. We noted earlier that gustatory neurons in general have broad tuning such that they can be triggered by multiple taste primaries. It appears that as we ascend the taste pathway, the preference for particular tastants becomes sharper. British neuroscientist Edmund Rolls has shown that neurons in the primary gustatory cortex are actually more specifically tuned to the individual primary tastes than neurons in earlier structures (Rolls, 1995).

SideNote | **4.16**

Experimental brain lesions followed by behavioural testing have often been used to establish the details of sensory function, especially in monkeys. Once an area has been clearly defined with regard to a particular sensory function, it is then possible to undertake single-unit studies to further characterize the details of neural processing.

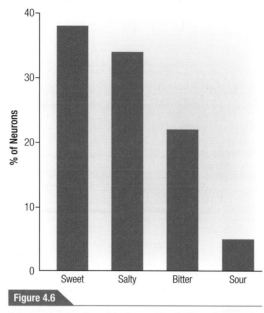

Figure 4.6

Functional properties of taste neurons in the primary gustatory cortex show a strong preference for sweet and salty tastes and a reduced preference for bitter and sour tastes. Adapted from "Taste in the Monkey Cortex," by T. R. Scott and C. R. Plata-Salaman, 1999, *Physiology and Behavior, 67*, pp. 489–511.

One interesting finding from single-unit studies concerns neural responses under the conditions of hunger and satiety. It turns out that neither of these conditions affects the firing of neurons in the primary gustatory cortex. Rather, these neurons appear to be involved only in the pure sensory processing of taste information. Since we know from common experience that taste perception can be modulated by motivational factors that are affected by our level of hunger or satiety, it is likely that the integration of these factors at the neuronal level must occur at some other site in the brain.

Secondary gustatory cortex and beyond

It appears that such high-level factors do influence taste signals in an entirely separate brain area in the frontal lobe, known as the **orbitofrontal cortex**, a part of which has been dubbed the *secondary gustatory cortex* (Doty, 2003; Squire et al., 2002). Here, gustatory neurons have been found to process higher aspects of taste function. One such aspect is the enhanced sensation of taste under conditions of hunger. Neurons in the secondary gustatory cortex of monkeys show reduced firing if the animal is fed to satiety and increased firing if the animal is hungry. Thus, although the sensory aspects of the stimulus remain unchanged,

the motivational state of the animal can have significant effects upon neural activity in the orbitofrontal cortex.

The orbitofrontal cortex also appears to be a gateway by which taste signals reach other areas of the brain. Two of these areas are the hypothalamus and amygdala, as shown in Figure 4.7. Neurons in these areas are well known for encoding behavioural features that include emotion, desire, motivation, and memory. While we know very little about the actual way these features are processed by the brain, it appears that at least some of these factors interact with taste signals in the hypothalamus and amygdala. It may be that neuronal activity here plays a role in determining whether a particular food tastes pleasant, whether it should be eaten at all, and whether to build positive or negative learning associations for future reference.

We know that the eating experience encompasses multiple sensory facets that can strongly influence taste. These include the way the food smells, its texture, and even how it looks. Thus, it would seem that signals from these various sensory modalities should be combined at some point in the brain. There is evidence that the secondary gustatory cortex may indeed be one of those sites. As shown

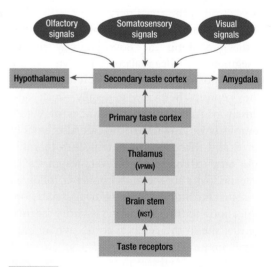

Figure 4.7

Sensory pathways of the gustatory system show a hierarchical arrangement of brain areas. Signals from taste receptors reach the primary taste cortex via two relay stations (NST and VPMN) and then proceed to the secondary taste area where higher aspects of taste function are elaborated. The secondary taste cortex is a gateway for taste signals to other areas of the brain such as the hypothalamus and amygdala. It is also a site for the integration of sensory signals from other modalities such as smell, touch, and vision.

in Figure 4.7, there are anatomical pathways that provide inputs of olfactory, somatosensory, and visual signals from the respective parts of the brain to the orbitofrontal cortex. The convergence of signals from these other sensory systems onto taste neurons may provide the neural basis for combining the sight, smell, texture, and taste of food into a comprehensive sensory experience that is so common during eating.

C. The Gustatory System—Perceptual Characteristics

The taste system is endowed with a unique role among all of the sensory modalities. The act of eating and drinking is necessary for all animals to survive. And yet, the consumption of anything poisonous could have catastrophic consequences. An animal must therefore make a quick decision as soon as something is placed in its mouth as to whether or not it should be ingested or rejected. The taste signals generated by a particular substance can therefore produce an immediate reflexive response based on an innate understanding of whether that food is appropriate to sustain life or would end up destroying it (SideNote 4.17). As we noted earlier, sweet, salty, and umami foods are generally beneficial, whereas bitter and sour substances are less so and can even be toxic. It is widely believed that these perceptual features have evolved to guide and enforce the acceptance/rejection decision.

There are two key perceptual aspects of taste—intensity and quality. Although intensity is directly related to the amount or, more specifically, **concentration** of the tastant being sampled, there are many complex issues that impact this sensory parameter. Among these are the lingering effects of the tastant over time, differences in detection sensitivity over the tongue, and the very way in which the psychophysical test is administered. However, it is the perception of taste quality that provides the greatest challenge for objective analysis because of its complex nature and the fact that any attempt at measurement must rely on a subjective description of the sensory experience. Before addressing these issues, we first examine the principal techniques by which gustatory function is measured.

1. PSYCHOPHYSICAL TECHNIQUES FOR TASTE MEASUREMENT

The perceptual characteristics of gustatory function have been explored using a variety of techniques. It should be noted at the outset that all of these techniques are problematic in one way or another. In general, the difficulty arises because of a lack of agreement on the nature of taste qualities and the finding that different methods can yield different results. The biggest problem, though, arises from the fact that the stimulus cannot be effectively controlled because chemical substances are difficult to apply and remove in a precise manner on the tongue (Halpern, 1997). For this reason, one approach that has often been used is to apply electrical stimulation, a technique known as **electrogustometry**.

Electrogustometry

This technique relies on the delivery of a small electrical current through an electrode or metal disk to a specific point or region of the tongue and oral cavity (Doty, 2003). The main advantage here is that the electrical stimulus can be applied in a highly discrete manner with respect to both time and space, something that is not easy with chemical solutions. The disadvantage is that taste sensations evoked by electrical stimulation are limited to the sour–salty dimension and therefore cannot be used to explore any of the other taste qualities. It is believed that electrical stimulation delivers ions to the taste buds, which in turn stimulates the sour and salt ionic channel mechanisms in the receptor cells. Despite this limitation, electrogustometry has been used to obtain taste detection thresholds from various parts of the tongue. It is also often used in clinical settings to assess taste dysfunction.

Regional and whole-mouth chemogustometry

The use of chemical solutions to assess taste function is known as **chemogustometry**. There are two standard approaches with this technique (Doty, 2003). The regional technique requires application of the chemical solution to a restricted part of the tongue by way of a small filter paper or cotton swab containing the solution. This technique is routinely used to assess detection thresholds, or to obtain an estimate of sensory intensity, or to identify taste quality. Another regional technique is based on a solution flowing over a limited extent of the

SideNote | **4.17**

The reflexive action to consume or reject food is present at the prenatal stage and, as any new parent knows, very much so at the newborn stage. Adult humans can make taste-dependent decisions within as little as 50 milliseconds of tasting.

SideNote | **4.18**

Vincristine and amitriptyline, two drugs used in treating cancer and depression, respectively, are notorious for causing significant losses in taste sensitivity.

tongue. The advantage is that the stimulation area is kept constant and interference effects of saliva are minimized. These regional techniques have been used to probe both the basic aspects of gustatory function and the clinical aspects of gustatory dysfunction (Collings, 1974; Halpern, 1997). Figure 4.8 shows an example of how this kind of testing can be administered.

Another method for delivering chemical solutions during a taste test is the whole-mouth technique. As the name suggests, the purpose here is to use the entire taste apparatus of the tongue and mouth to make an assessment of gustatory function. There are several ways to carry out the test, the main difference being the actual volume of the test sample. In the *three-drop test*, the subject has to distinguish which one of three drops of a liquid contains the stimulus—the other two contain only water. The detection threshold is defined as the concentration at which the subject can identify the correct drop three trials in a row. In general, thresholds obtained with this technique tend to have high values, probably because of the small volume that is used. An alternative technique is the so-called *eight-cup test* where subjects have to identify which of four cups among eight contains the taste stimulus. The threshold is defined as the concentration at which the subject can make the perfect separation between *stimulus* and *water-only* cups.

Assessment of taste abnormalities

Any of the above techniques can be applied in a clinical setting to determine a reduction or loss of taste function. A total loss of taste is known as

Figure 4.8

An example of how psychophysical testing of gustatory function can be administered. The subject is seated behind a screen and, through a flow tube, samples various solutions provided by the experimenter.
Photo courtesy of B. Halpern, J. Delwiche, and Cornell University Photography.

ageusia, a condition that can arise from injury to any of the gustatory nerves or as a side effect of certain medications (SideNote 4.18) (Seiden, 1997). A less severe form of taste loss occurs with **hypogeusia**, which is simply a reduction in taste sensitivity. This can occur with dry mouth, smoking, or as a symptom of diseases such as influenza, diabetes, and hypertension. The parameter that is typically assessed in clinical testing is the detection threshold of a certain taste primary, usually salty or sweet. Clinical assessments to identify alterations in taste quality perception, however, are often carried out in cases of **dysgeusia**. This is a particularly annoying disorder where taste distortions occur. As a result, foods that normally fall under a particular taste quality are perceived under a different category. Quality assessment is more demanding and less precise than the more standard assessment of detection threshold.

2. PERCEPTION OF INTENSITY

Psychophysical assessments of taste intensity are generally concerned with deriving absolute detection thresholds, discrimination thresholds, and suprathreshold perceptual ratings (Doty, 2003). The primary goal of these experiments is to obtain quantitative relationships of a perceptual dimension that are generally described through a set of qualitative terms. This imposes an added burden for determining a signal from background noise, especially given that different individuals have different inherent sensitivities to taste. Furthermore, an accurate depiction of gustatory function should be carried out in the absence of saliva, with absolute purity of water, and exactly the same set of methods from study to study. Because these conditions are generally difficult to attain, an understanding within the scientific community is to use published psychophysical values in a more comparative than exact manner (e.g., differences among the taste primaries, location on the tongue, temperature, etc.). With this caveat in mind, next we explore the data obtained for various aspects of gustatory intensity perception.

Detection thresholds

Table 4.2 shows absolute detection thresholds for various substances categorized by taste quality (Breslin, 2000). A close look at these values reveals an interesting trend among the different primaries. It appears that bitter

Table 4.2

Gustatory Detection Thresholds for Some Common Tastants in Each of the Primary Taste Categories

Sweet	
Saccharin	0.009
Aspartame (artificial sweetener)	0.02
Sucrose (table sugar)	0.65
Salty	
Calcium chloride	0.008
Sodium chloride	1.0
Potassium chloride	6.3
Sour	
Citric acid	0.07
Acetic acid (vinegar)	0.1
Bitter	
Quinine	0.001
Caffeine	0.05
Urea	15.0
Umami	
Monosodium glutamate	0.05

Note. The numbers represent concentration values (millimoles per litre) of the dissolved substance in water.

substances generally have the lowest detection thresholds, followed by sour, salty, and sweet. However, there are examples within each category that deviate from this trend. The artificial sweetener saccharin, for example, shows an extremely low threshold value, whereas the threshold for the bitter substance urea is very high (SideNote 4.19).

One interesting aspect of taste thresholds is that they are affected by other primary tastants in a mixture such that the presence of one might alter the threshold of the other, a phenomenon known as *masking* (Stevens, 1997; Stevens & Traverzo, 1997). For example, the presence of sucrose or citric acid in a salt solution can raise the detection threshold for salt nearly three times, and the presence of both maskers raises the salt threshold nearly nine times. We know from everyday experience that, in order to be detected, more seasoning has to be added to foods that contain complex mixtures.

Another factor that has an impact on detection threshold is temperature (McBurney, Collings, & Glanz, 1973). As Figure 4.9 illustrates, the relationship between threshold and temperature shows a U-shaped function for

the four taste primaries. Oddly, the temperature at which sensitivity is highest (i.e., lowest threshold) is not body temperature (37 °C) but somewhere between it and room temperature (22 °C). Detection thresholds increase if the temperature is either below or above the optimal value for that particular taste primary. It is believed that such a temperature preference reflects an optimal thermal condition for binding of the tastant molecule to the gustatory receptor cell (Schiffman, 2000).

There has been considerable interest as to how taste detection thresholds change with age. Most studies have shown that threshold values increase for each of the taste primaries, reflecting a general decrease of taste function with age. This appears to be especially true for bitter and salty taste primaries. Despite such reductions in taste sensitivity, the pleasure of eating does not appear to diminish with age, as is evident from the common experience of seeing elderly people enjoying food. However, there is one potentially harmful consequence of the reduced taste sensitivity that does occur with age. There is a tendency among elderly people

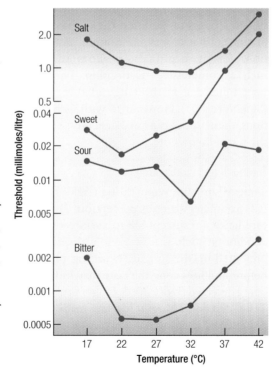

Figure 4.9

Detection threshold values can vary with temperature. Each of the four primary taste qualities has an optimal temperature value that lies somewhere between room and body temperature. From "Temperature Dependence of Human Taste," by D. H. McBurney, V. B. Collings, and L. M. Glanz, 1973, *Physiology and Behavior, 11*, pp. 89–94.

SideNote 4.19

The two most common artificial sweeteners are saccharin and aspartame. Saccharin contains zero calories but may have a bitter aftertaste and produce health risks if consumed in high quantities. Aspartame contains nearly as many calories as table sugar. However, because of its significantly lower detection threshold, much less is needed to produce the same degree of sweetness.

SideNote | **4.20**

Excessive salt intake has been linked to high blood pressure that in turn can cause stroke and heart disease.

to add excessive salt to foods because of its elevated detection threshold. This is especially true with complex foods where the medley of tastes produces a masking effect that in turn further elevates the threshold (SideNote 4.20).

Suprathreshold intensity perception

Difference thresholds for taste have not been studied extensively. However, it appears that the smallest detectable concentration change, or Weber fraction, is in the range of 15–25% (Doty, 2003). The exact value depends on the particular tastant in question and the way the test is carried out. Nevertheless, taste appears to be the least sensitive of our sensory functions in terms of discriminability. The Weber fraction for sweet taste (0.15) remains relatively unaffected with age, whereas the fraction for bitter taste can increase dramatically.

A greater effort has been made at the direct scaling of perceived taste intensity by way of magnitude estimation. Recall from Chapter 1 that the resulting power law relationship that derives from such studies reveals the nature of suprathreshold intensity perception. An exponent value that is less than 1.0 shows a negatively accelerating function where the nervous system appears to compress the physical information into a sensory continuum. Taste functions for most primary qualities show just such a compressive relationship. The exponent values fall in the range of 0.85 to 0.93 (SideNote 4.21). However, as with Weber fractions, these values can vary depending on how the test is carried out.

Temporal and spatial factors

Time is an important, though seldom studied, parameter in taste perception. Detection thresholds are susceptible to various temporal conditions, such as how rapidly the tastant is presented on the tongue, what was presented before, and how long the taste may linger after being detected (Doty, 2003; Finger et al., 2000). Taste detection thresholds are made in the presence of saliva, which contains sodium and other ions that can have an interfering effect. A residual background due to saliva or the lingering effects of a prior tastant can therefore affect both detection and discrimination thresholds. While most tastes are short-lived, there are some that do exert a long-lasting effect, such as artificial sweeteners. One way to reduce the influence of background factors is to increase the flow of the solution on

SideNote | **4.21**

The exponent value for sucrose is 0.93. The power law that relates perceived intensity (I) to sucrose concentration (C) is therefore $I = k \cdot C^{0.93}$.

the tongue. This has been shown to reduce detection threshold, perhaps because a greater number of tastant molecules are presented on the tongue per unit of time.

The spatial extent of stimulation on the tongue can also affect taste intensity perception. In general, the greater the area of stimulation, the lower the threshold. This is most likely due to the recruitment of additional taste receptors that add to the neural signal for that particular taste. Another spatial aspect of taste function is the topography of gustatory responses over the tongue. As we noted earlier, all taste qualities can be detected throughout the tongue. However, there are small regional differences in the detection threshold, as shown in Figure 4.10. Detection thresholds are shown here in a relative manner for the four taste primaries in various parts of the tongue (Collings, 1974; Schiffman, 2000). The threshold values for salty and sweet are somewhat lower at

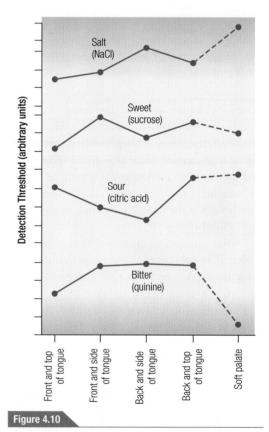

Figure 4.10

Detection threshold values can vary with location on the tongue. Although all four primary taste qualities can be detected throughout the tongue and parts of the soft palate, there are regional differences in their threshold values. Adapted from "Human Taste Response as a Function of Locus of Stimulation on the Tongue and Soft Palate," by V. B. Collings, 1974, *Perception and Psychophysics, 16*, pp. 169–174.

the front end of the tongue than elsewhere, whereas the sour threshold is lowest at the back of the tongue. Detection threshold for bitter is actually lowest in the soft palate. An interesting aspect of bitter taste sensation is that although its detection threshold is lower at the front of the tongue than at the back, the suprathreshold relationship between perceived intensity and stimulus concentration shows a steeper function at the back of the tongue than at the front. This finding is consistent with the commonly held notion that a regional preference for bitter sensations occurs at the back of the tongue.

Adaptation and cross-adaptation

A fundamental characteristic of all sensory systems is that signal strength is affected by prior or ongoing stimulation. In gustation, this can decrease the perceived intensity or sensitivity to a tastant, a condition known as **adaptation**. The fact that saliva contains many ions though remains tasteless represents one example of adaptation. Total adaptation to a particular taste quality can only occur under controlled conditions where that taste is applied continuously over the tongue. The time required for adaptation depends on the concentration of the adapting substance, though generally it can occur within a matter of minutes. Adaptation to food normally does not occur because of its continuous movement over the tongue.

The phenomenon of **cross-adaptation** occurs when the perceived intensity of a compound decreases due to the adaptation to a different one. This occurrence likely reflects complex interactions between the two compounds at the receptor cell level. If two different tastants do not cross-adapt, then they likely stimulate different receptor and signalling mechanisms. It has been shown that compounds representing the four classical taste qualities do not actually cross-adapt each other—a result that is consistent with the notion that a separate and independent transduction mechanism exists for each quality.

PTC/PROP thresholds—non-tasters, tasters, and supertasters

An interesting aspect of bitter taste perception concerns the detection threshold for a substance known as **PTC** and its synthetic counterpart **PROP**. While synthesizing PTC in 1931, a chemist accidentally released some of it into the air. Although the chemist could not detect the taste of this chemical, his colleagues complained about its intense bitterness. Subsequent research has shown that approximately 25% of people who have normal taste sensitivity cannot detect the bitter taste of PTC/PROP. These people are known as *non-tasters*, a term not meant to be disparaging but one that merely reflects their very high detection thresholds to these bitter compounds. Linda Bartoshuk at Yale University has shown that among the remaining group of *tasters*, approximately one quarter are so-called *supertasters*—individuals who are hypersensitive to PTC/PROP (Bartoshuk, Duffy, & Miller, 1994). These individuals also display elevated sensitivity to other bitter substances (e.g., caffeine, saccharin) as well as other taste qualities (e.g., sweet, sour), which suggests that supertasters may experience a higher overall level of tasting ability than others (SideNote 4.22).

3. PERCEPTION OF QUALITY

We noted earlier that there are no straightforward chemical or physical dimensions along which the molecular properties of tastants can be related to the subjective quality of taste. This has led to the view that taste is a *categorical* sensory dimension where the different taste qualities can be regarded in the same way as say the different modalities of touch perception such as pressure, warmth, pain, etc. This is quite different from the perceptions that arise from sound and light stimulation where changes along a particular physical dimension give rise to a systematic change in sensory perception (SideNote 4.23). As a result, much effort has been placed on finding ways to represent the psychological dimension of taste quality (Doty, 2003). We begin with a general discussion of this issue and then take up various other aspects of taste quality perception, such as complex mixtures and interactions with other sensory systems.

Representing taste quality

One of the earliest schemes for representing taste quality was proposed by Hans Henning in 1916. Henning suggested that the four standard taste primaries can be represented at each corner of a three-sided pyramid, as shown in Figure 4.11 on page 118, leading to the conjecture that all complex tastes arise from mixtures of these primaries. Thus any taste, regardless of its complexity, can be represented as some point within this three-dimensional geometric

SideNote | **4.22**

Supertasters are quite sensitive to tastes and as such tend to dislike a number of foods including some fruits and vegetables, fatty and sweet foods. Non-tasters, on the other hand, enjoy rich, fatty, sweet foods due to their lower perception of flavours. Finally, even things like wine preference and alcohol consumption are partially related to the number of papillae, with supertasters drinking less than non-tasters in general.

SideNote | **4.23**

Changes in sound frequency, for example, produce a qualitative change in pitch perception, whereas a systematic change in light wavelength causes a change in colour perception.

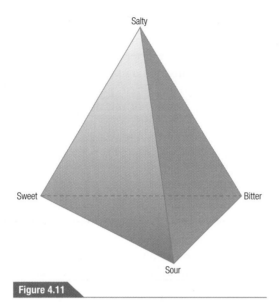

Figure 4.11

Taste representation proposed by Henning shows the four classical taste qualities occupying the corners of a three-sided pyramid. Any perceived taste is presumed to arise from some combination of these primaries and therefore occupies a point somewhere within this three-dimensional geometric space.

SideNote **4.24**

Umami taste represents one example of a quality that falls outside the geometric boundaries of the Henning taste pyramid.

space by virtue of its being composed of some mixture of each primary taste quality.

Although the notion of taste primaries has been around since Aristotle's time, it remains one of the more contentious issues among sensory psychologists today. The very idea that human gustation can be specified by four classical taste qualities—and that complex tastes are based on mixtures of these—has been called into question. Some scientists have proposed that taste is really a sensory continuum and therefore cannot be represented by a simple geometric figure such as Henning's pyramid (Taylor & Roberts, 2004). There are compelling arguments on both sides of this issue, however. On the one hand, it is difficult to dismiss the categorical nature of taste, and just as mixed colours cannot be broken down into their constituent components, studies have shown that human subjects do a very poor job of identifying the constituent primaries in taste mixtures. Furthermore, the well-accepted cross-fibre theory of gustatory processing is difficult to reconcile with the notion of taste primaries because the very independence of taste qualities is not maintained in the transmission of neural signals up the chain of brain areas. On the other hand, the existence of taste primaries is supported by neural considerations as well, from independent receptor coding mechanisms in the taste buds to chemotopic organization in brain stem gustatory areas.

Furthermore, psychophysical evidence based on cross-adaptation studies, as discussed earlier, has provided a powerful argument for the existence of primary taste qualities.

It has been suggested that a more suitable way to represent the complex nature of taste quality is through multi-dimensional scaling. As we noted in Chapter 1, this psychophysical technique is ideally suited for representing metathetic sensations such as taste. Subjects are asked to make judgments of their sensation along some scale—such as similarity—for a pair of taste stimuli. The numerical results are mapped on a geometric space where close proximity represents similarity of taste quality. Susan Schiffman at Duke University has carried out extensive studies on taste quality with this method (Schiffman, 2000). Figure 4.12 shows the spatial arrangement of 19 compounds obtained by multi-dimensional scaling procedures. Although many of the tastants fall within the outline of Henning's pyramid, there are clearly several compounds that lie outside of it as well. Given the fact that these tastes are not fully contained within the space of the four classical qualities, Schiffman has argued that the restrictive boundaries established by such a scheme do not encompass the totality of human gustatory perception (SideNote 4.24).

Another way of representing taste quality is by using a rating system for a set of taste descriptors. This has been widely practised

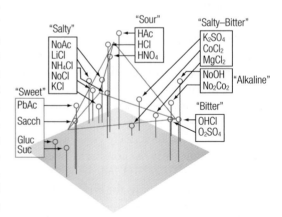

Figure 4.12

Three-dimensional space of taste quality obtained from multi-dimensional scaling studies of perceptual similarity. Although the outline of Henning's taste pyramid contains many of the tastants shown here, there are clearly many that fall outside the geometric space outlined by the four taste primaries. From "Taste Quality and Neural Coding: Implications from Psychophysics and Neurophysiology," by S. S. Schiffman, 2000, *Physiology & Behavior, 69*, pp. 147–159.

in the brewing industry since the 1970s. An example is shown in Figure 4.13 where two different beers are represented on a taste map consisting of 19 descriptors that brewers have adopted. A panel of expert tasters provides ratings of taste impressions that are generated along each of these dimensions and then plotted on a scale of 0–10. The resulting taste maps are used to make comparisons among different beers and establish certain guidelines for acceptable taste qualities.

Taste quality in mixtures

Another contentious issue in taste research is whether a mixture of two or more compounds produces a sensation where the quality of each is retained or whether an entirely new taste sensation arises. There are valid arguments on both sides of this debate as well, one that goes back to the 19th century. It has been somewhat difficult to resolve this question because scientific research in this area must contend with the very subjective nature of the taste experience. We do know, however, that there are specific interactions between different taste compounds that can generally be broken down in terms of either a positive or a negative effect (Stevens, 1997).

Mixtures of substances that are similar in taste quality, known as *homogeneous mixtures*, generally show enhancement or synergy. That is, together the compounds elicit a more intense sensation of that quality, the magnitude depending on the exact nature of the mixture and the concentrations of the compounds involved. This is typically the effect observed if say two different types of sweet or two different types of salty compounds are mixed together. However, there are examples of cross-quality enhancement, such as when sodium chloride (NaCl) and arginine, which is bitter tasting, are mixed together. In the resulting mixture, arginine enhances the salty taste of NaCl. Perhaps a more common example is that of monosodium glutamate (MSG), which is often added to foods to enhance flavour. The umami taste of MSG enhances other taste qualities (SideNote 4.25).

Mixtures of substances that are dissimilar in taste quality, known as *heterogeneous mixtures*, generally show the opposite effect (i.e., suppression or masking). A good example of this occurs when combining sweet and sour components, as when making lemonade. The sourness of lemons and the sweetness of sugar will have a mutually suppressive effect so that

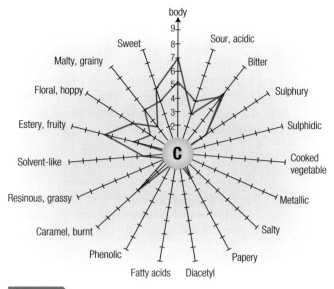

Figure 4.13

Taste quality can be represented by sensory analysis for a set of descriptors, a practice common in the brewing industry. This map shows the ratings for two beers, Carling and Tuborg. Expert tasters provide ratings on a scale of 0–10 for each of the 19 descriptors. The resulting taste map provides a standard tool for making comparisons and establishing quality goals in beer production. Reprinted by courtesy of Carling Brewing Company, Denmark.

the resulting mixture does not taste either as sour or as sweet as the individual components would by themselves. Furthermore, the perceptual quality of the resulting taste mixture can often be different, though there are instances (lemonade is a good example) where the constituent tastes can be separately identified. To complicate matters further, it appears that sometimes there is no firm relationship between the physical complexity of the stimulus and the complexity of the mixture percept. It has been found that unmixed stimuli are sometimes judged as being composed of more than one taste quality and mixtures are often identified as being composed of a single quality. Thus, there is necessarily no one-to-one relationship between complexity of taste mixtures and the resulting complexity of the taste experience.

Interactions with other sensory systems

We know from common experience that smell plays an important role in eating. The taste of food is either altered or reduced when we have a reduced capacity for smell (e.g., during a cold). As Figure 4.14 on page 120 shows, our ability to correctly identify the tastes of a broad range of foods is quite high under normal circumstances. However, if subjects are prevented from smelling the tastants, then the identification rate

SideNote | 4.25

Although MSG is often applied as a food additive, its use has been controversial. MSG is the sodium salt of glutamate, a pervasive and powerful excitatory neurotransmitter. There have been reports of neurological disturbances after excessive consumption of MSG. It has been shown, however, that dietary glutamate does not cross the blood–brain barrier and therefore does not likely pose a threat to brain function.

Epicurus (341–270 BCE)
© INTERFOTO/Alamy

drops significantly. This result illustrates the extent to which higher gustatory functions, such as taste preference and identification ability, rely upon the contribution of olfactory influences. However, our perception of taste is also affected by other sensory factors such as touch and sight. This combination produces the so-called **flavour** of foods, where multiple sensory dimensions such as texture, temperature, and even visual appeal together modulate the perceptual impression of taste (SideNote 4.26) (Doty, 2003; Small & Prescott, 2005).

The somatosensory aspects of flavour impression under normal eating conditions are largely driven by the form and texture of food, although irritant chemicals in spicy foods such as chili peppers can trigger pain signals through nerve fibres that wrap around each taste bud. These nerve fibres in general transmit multiple aspects of touch sensation that include simple

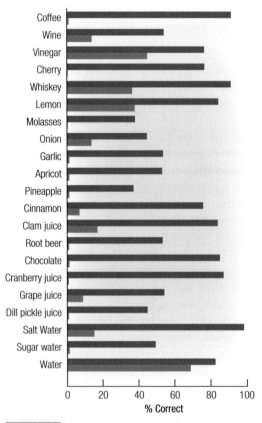

Figure 4.14

Taste identification for a variety of foods and beverages is quite high under normal sensing means involving both taste and smell (red bars). However, if subjects are prevented from smelling the compounds, then identification ability drops, in some cases quite dramatically (green bars). From "Nasal Chemoreception in Flavor Identification," by M. M. Mozel, B. Smith, P. Smith, R. Sullivan, and P. Swender, 1969, *Archives of Otolaryngology, 90*, pp. 367–373.

tactile detection to heat and pain. The active ingredient in chili peppers, **capsaicin**, binds to receptors in these nerve fibres. It turns out that many of these same fibres also encode thermal sensations, which explains the characteristic burning feeling that arises from eating chili peppers and why that sensation has been dubbed *hot*. Thus, the sensation of hot/spicy is not really a true gustatory quality but rather arises as a result of chemical irritation to thermal and nociceptive fibres (SideNote 4.27). It has been shown that this chemical irritation can interact with true gustatory sensations, especially bitter and sour tastes, to produce suppression and masking.

Taste hedonics

In closing this section, we return to the argument that the gustatory system evolved as measure of protection and survival, accepting foods that are nutritious and rejecting those that are poisonous. A particularly delightful aspect of this evolutionary consequence is the sheer enjoyment we derive from the experience of eating. This facet of human existence has even taken on a philosophical importance that started with the ideas of Epicurus, a Greek thinker from the 3rd century BCE, who proposed that humans should seek only a simple life that is devoid of physical pain and instead maximizes pleasure from the senses. The consumption of delicious foods and beverages is taken as one of those Epicurean delights, and to this end, numerous chapters and societies can be found throughout the world dedicated to the pursuit of this philosophy.

The **hedonic** aspects of taste perception concern the evaluation of foods with regard to its positive or negative appreciation (Taylor & Roberts, 2004). This is perhaps one of the most difficult parameters to measure in taste perception because of the large variability that arises from subtle changes in composition. For example, a particular food that is ordinarily judged to be terrific may become distasteful with even the smallest addition of seasoning or salt. A further complication arises from cultural differences in taste preference. In North American societies, eating insects is widely considered to be disgusting even though the same societies have no trouble devouring large crustaceans such as shrimp, crawfish, and lobster. Conversely, foods such as peanut butter, avocado, and flavoured yogurt are considered to be distasteful by some Asian and European societies.

The complex nature of taste hedonics is further illustrated by the fact that prior experience and taste history can play an important role as well. In fact, taste history can begin in early life. It has been shown that newborns show a significant preference for the taste of carrot juice if their mothers had consumed it during pregnancy. Among adults, the consumption of bitter substances such as beer and coffee is commonplace, even though bitter taste generally has a negative hedonic quality. It has been argued that our generally positive appreciation of these beverages is acquired through continued taste experience.

D. The Olfactory System— Biological Mechanisms

We now turn our attention to the second chemosensory system—smell perception, or olfaction. It was generally believed throughout much of history that our sense of smell occurred via direct access of odours to the brain. This notion was not questioned until the 17th century, although the finer details only began to appear around the middle of the 1800s. It was shown then that human olfaction occurred through a structure, the so-called **olfactory epithelium**, that was located at the upper margins of the nasal cavity. It is here that airborne or volatile chemicals, known as **odourants**, trigger the neural signals that ultimately reach the brain to produce olfactory perception (Beauchamp & Bartoshuk, 1997; Squire et al., 2002; Tortora & Derrickson, 2008). However, to get to the epithelium, odourants must pass through the complex conduits of the nasal channels. As Figure 4.15 shows, there are two possible routes. The orthonasal route allows odourants to reach the epithelium through the nostrils, up the two nasal passages, and around a set of bony protuberances or turbinates. The retronasal route is a separate channel at the very back of the throat. In the remainder of this section, we examine what happens next by discussing the neural processes that underlie olfactory perception.

1. OLFACTORY EPITHELIUM

The very first events in olfactory signal processing occur in the olfactory epithelium. This sense organ is composed of several layers of cells and is located at the uppermost recesses

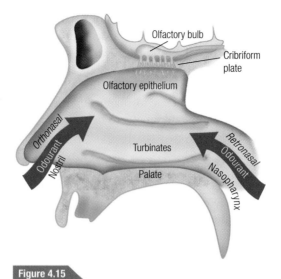

Figure 4.15

Schematic diagram showing two routes by which airborne odourants can reach the olfactory epithelium: the orthonasal route originating at the nostrils or the retronasal route at the back of the throat.

of the nasal cavity, as shown in Figure 4.16. Airborne odourants must first pass through a thin mucous barrier that covers the epithelium before reaching the sensory neurons. The mucus—which serves a protective function—is composed of water, electrolytes, and protein. Because of its high water content, the mucous layer provides a barrier for hydrophobic or fat-soluble odourants. It turns out, however, that a chemical must have a certain amount of fat solubility in order for it to be

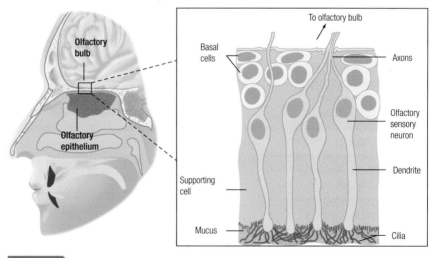

Figure 4.16

The olfactory epithelium is located at the uppermost margins of the nasal chamber and is composed of three main cell types—olfactory sensory neurons, supporting cells, and basal cells. The cilia belonging to the sensory neurons protrude into a thin layer of mucous substance that coats the lower margins of the epithelium. Axons belonging to the sensory neurons project to the olfactory bulb.

odourous. Thus, without some assistance, most odourants will not easily reach the epithelium. A special protein known as **odourant binding protein (OBP)**, which is found in fairly high concentration within the mucus, is believed to attach to many different kinds of hydrophobic odourants to help them across the mucous layer.

Cellular composition of the epithelium

Once the odourants pass through the mucous layer, they encounter the *olfactory sensory neuron*, one of three kinds of cells found in the epithelium (SideNote 4.28). There are approximately 12 million sensory neurons within the roughly 5 cm^2 area of the olfactory epithelium (Doty, 2003). These sensory cells are bipolar neurons—that is, they have one dendrite and one axon that emerge from opposite sides of the cell body. The axons from several neurons join together to form a small nerve bundle that projects to the *olfactory bulb*, which is the next structure in the neural hierarchy of olfactory processing. The dendrites of the sensory neurons proceed toward the lower margin of the epithelium. Projecting from the terminal ends of the dendrites are minute hair-like filaments, or **cilia**. The cilia from all the dendrites together form an intricate matted arbor that invades the mucous layer. The interaction between odourants and olfactory sensory neurons occurs at the cilia.

One particularly interesting property of the olfactory sensory neuron is its rapid turnover, or lifetime, approximately 30–60 days (Finger et al., 2000; Serby & Chobor, 1992). Unlike elsewhere in the nervous system, dying neurons in the olfactory epithelium are rapidly replaced by new sensory neurons, a unique feature of this process (SideNote 4.29). The other notable exception is that of the gustatory receptor cells where a similar, though more rapid, turnover occurs. However, there is one striking difference between the two chemosensory neurons in this respect. Gustatory receptor cells merely release neurotransmitter substance onto a nerve fibre and therefore its replacement can be easily envisioned, whereas olfactory sensory cells have an axon that projects to another brain area. One of the major unresolved questions in this field concerns the mechanisms by which newly generated sensory neurons establish functional connections that maintain the integrity of prior olfactory circuits.

The second type of cell found in the olfactory epithelium is the *basal cell*. These cells provide the source for the continuous replacement of the dying sensory neurons. The basal cells make up less than 5% of the total cellular population in the epithelium. The third type of cell is the *supporting cell*. It is believed that these cells are partly responsible for producing the mucus and regulating its ionic content. Additional functions of the supporting cell include both the degradation of odourant molecules and other substances that may penetrate the mucous barrier and the removal of dead or dying neurons in the epithelium.

Sensory transduction in the olfactory epithelium

The interaction between odourants and sensory neurons occurs at the cilia. It has been shown that the entire transductional machinery resides within these thin filaments. It is here that odour molecules become bound to specific receptors. There are approximately 1,000 different types of receptors, each being sensitive to a broad set of odourants, though there appears to be some affinity for a specific chemical structure. Each olfactory sensory neuron expresses only one type of receptor, and it therefore produces a signal only when that receptor is stimulated. The painstaking work of uncovering the nature of olfactory receptors and their associated genes was carried out by American neuroscientists Richard Axel and Linda Buck, for which they received the Nobel Prize in 2004 (Buck, 2000; Buck & Axel, 1991).

The manner in which olfactory receptors function is similar to the process we saw earlier for sweet taste transduction. The receptors in the olfactory sensory neuron are large protein molecules that span the cell membrane and are coupled to a G protein (Laurent, 1999; Mombaerts, 1999). As Figure 4.17 shows, the binding of an odourant molecule to the receptor triggers the G protein, and this results in the production of a second messenger (Finger et al., 2000). As with the sweet taste receptor system, the second messenger in olfactory sensory neurons is cAMP. It is believed that cAMP then works directly upon the ionic channels to increase the entry of Na$^+$ ions into the neuron and produce membrane depolarization. An action potential can be produced if odourant binding should cause sufficient membrane depolarization to reach threshold. Once produced, action potentials are then transmitted via the **olfactory nerve** to the olfactory bulb.

SideNote | **4.28**

Sensory neurons in the epithelium are also known as *olfactory receptor cells.*

SideNote | **4.29**

Smell perception is sometimes reduced or can disappear entirely after a head injury causing trauma to the olfactory epithelium. However, because of the rapid turnover of sensory neurons, olfactory function is usually re-established after some time. Boxers commonly complain that they lose their sense of smell after a fight.

2. OLFACTORY PROCESSING IN THE BRAIN

As with taste signals, the neural processing of smell encompasses a broad set of subcortical and cortical structures. This ensures the processing of not only the sensory aspects of olfaction but also the emotional and cognitive features of smell-related behaviour. Neuroscientists have made considerable progress in identifying olfactory circuits and their function over the last decade. However, as with other sensory systems, we are still far from achieving a thorough understanding of the neural processes that lead to olfactory perception.

Signal processing in the olfactory bulb

The olfactory bulbs are paired oval structures that reside just below the frontal lobe of the brain against the bony base of the skull (SideNote 4.30) (Squire et al., 2002; Tortora & Derrickson, 2008). As Figure 4.18 shows, the unmyelinated axons from olfactory sensory neurons congregate into bundles, pierce the bony cribriform plate, and arrive into the olfactory bulb. The olfactory bulb in vertebrates therefore represents the site where neural signals triggered by odourants are first processed before being transmitted to higher centres in the brain.

All incoming axons converge upon a discrete spatial unit in the olfactory bulb called the **glomerulus**. There are approximately 2,000 glomeruli, each being about 0.1 mm in diameter, per olfactory bulb. Each olfactory sensory neuron projects to only one glomerulus, but each glomerulus can receive axons from sensory neurons over widespread areas of the olfactory epithelium. Upon arriving into a glomerulus, an axon can synapse with one of three different types of neurons—the *mitral, tufted,* or *periglomerular* cells. The first two serve as relay neurons and transmit signals out of the olfactory bulb through the olfactory tract to higher centres in the brain. The third type of cell serves as an interneuron that encircles the glomerulus.

It is believed that information about different odourants is mapped onto different glomeruli (Mori, Nagao, & Yoshihara, 1999). The experimental support for this view has emerged from studies showing that each glomerulus largely processes odour information mediated by a specific odourant receptor from sensory neurons distributed throughout the epithelium. This has led to the notion that

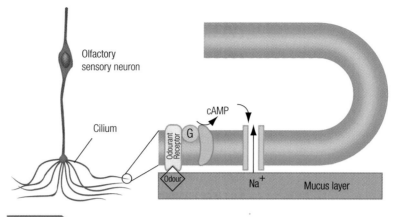

Figure 4.17

Odourant binding to a membrane receptor in a cilium triggers a G protein and leads to the production of cAMP. The cAMP then increases Na⁺ entry through an ionic channel that produces membrane depolarization and, if threshold is reached, action potentials in the olfactory sensory neuron.

each glomerulus serves as an independent coding unit, similar in its functional scope to the cortical columns that were described in the last chapter for the somatosensory cortex (Xu, Greer, & Shepherd, 2000). The several thousand glomeruli in each olfactory bulb together represent a broad spectrum of functional units that are necessary to receive, process, and transmit information about a large set of smells.

Signal processing in higher cortical areas

The mitral and tufted cells of the olfactory bulb, usually referred to as *M/T cells*, send their axons through the olfactory tract to several discrete areas of the brain (Doty, 2003; Finger et al., 2000). The **primary olfactory cortex**

SideNote | **4.30**

The olfactory bulbs in humans are quite small in relation to the size of the brain, especially when compared to other mammals, reflecting the reduced dependence humans have on olfaction.

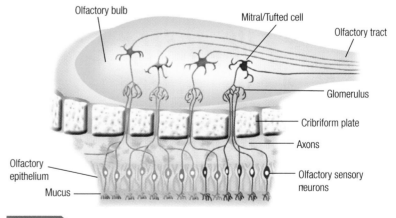

Figure 4.18

Axons from several olfactory sensory neurons cluster together and pierce the bony cribriform plate to reach the olfactory bulb that overlies it. The inputs into the bulb converge to form a glomerulus, which is considered to be a fundamental processing unit of olfaction. The mitral and tufted cells transmit the output of the glomerulus to higher olfactory centres through the olfactory tract.

METHODOLOGY

A Breakthrough in Smell Perception

Richard Axel (Howard Hughes Medical Institute) and Linda Buck (Fred Hutchison Cancer Research Center) won the Nobel Prize in Physiology or Medicine in 2004 for elucidating many aspects of smell perception in mice. One big discovery was made by using molecular techniques, which found that there are roughly 1,000 genes that encode our olfactory receptors, and when activated, each gene triggers a G-coupled protein, which leads to a signal that travels to the olfactory epithelium. Next, they independently found that the axons from neurons expressing the same type of odourant receptor lead to the same glomerulus (i.e., micro-region) in the olfactory bulb, creating a kind of spatial map. From there, mitral cells send the signals to different parts of the brain, which are combined into a specific pattern of activation, depending on the scent.

encompasses those brain areas that receive a direct axonal projection from the olfactory bulb. There are five areas that fit into this definition. Their anatomical locations within the brain are shown in Figure 4.19. The closest of these to the olfactory bulb is the anterior olfactory nucleus, a sheet of neurons that mediates the transmission of signals from one olfactory bulb to the other. However, it is the piriform cortex, where the bulk of the M/T projection fibres arrive, that is considered to be the main olfactory processor. Located in the frontal lobe, the piriform cortex is a three-layered structure with an extensive network of circuits. Although neurons in the piriform cortex respond to a wide range of odourants, very little is known about the processing details in this structure. The three other areas that compose the primary olfactory cortex are the olfactory tubercle, parts of the amygdala, and entorhinal cortex. In the larger areas, such as

the amygdala and entorhinal cortex, olfactory tract axons innervate only small sub-regions that are dedicated to olfactory processing.

While the piriform cortex is believed to process fundamental sensory aspects of olfaction, the amygdala and entorhinal cortex are largely concerned with higher aspects of smell sensation. A schematic diagram of the interconnections among these different brain areas is shown in Figure 4.20. As can be seen here, there are two other areas that belong to the smell system—the hippocampus and orbitofrontal cortex. The hippocampus receives olfactory signals through the entorhinal cortex, whereas the orbitofrontal cortex receives its olfactory input either directly from the hippocampus or indirectly from the piriform cortex through the thalamus. The olfactory pathways leading to the amygdala and hippocampus, both of which belong to the **limbic system**, are believed to mediate the emotional and

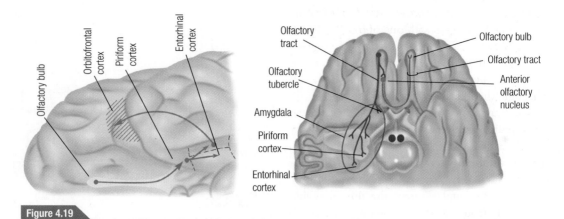

Figure 4.19

A side view of the brain containing the major areas that process olfactory information (left). The image on the right shows a bottom view of the brain overlaid with pathways that carry olfactory signals from the olfactory bulb. The primary olfactory cortex contains the anterior olfactory nucleus and the four areas within in the oval outline (olfactory tubercle, amygdala, piriform cortex, and entorhinal cortex).

memory-related facets of olfactory experience (Wilson & Stevenson, 2006). The orbitofrontal cortex is thought to be responsible for the actual perception and discrimination of odours (SideNote 4.31). Recall from Section B.4 of this chapter that the orbitofrontal cortex is also the area involved in processing higher gustatory functions and where smell–taste integration occurs in flavour perception.

3. CODING OF OLFACTORY SIGNALS

We face the same challenges with the olfactory system that we encountered in encoding and representing taste signals (i.e., how to construct a system that can distinguish among a variety of chemical stimuli). Consider the following. Somehow the brain must encode thousands of different chemical substances that have diverse molecular structures through a detection system that expresses thousands of different membrane-bound receptors, the outputs of which are transmitted through only a limited number of cables to the brain. The system must maintain fidelity by virtue of being able to generate the same perceptual experience through repeated exposure to a particular odourant and yet be capable of differentiating subtle differences among odourants to yield different olfactory sensations. To put it simply—we do not know how this is accomplished. Nevertheless, it is important to consider some of the postulated mechanisms of olfactory coding, as will be done in this section.

Chemical coding of odourants

The purpose of the olfactory system is to detect volatile chemicals. There are a multitude of different possible combinations by which the structural properties of different compounds can be defined. One of the long-sought issues in olfactory coding has been to determine exactly what features of an odourant molecule are necessary to trigger a neural response (Buck, 2000; Laurent, 1999). These features are collectively known as the **odotope**. There is evidence to indicate that the standard features generally used to describe chemical properties—such as molecular weight, polarity, solubility, and **isomerism**—are all critical for determining the odourous characteristics of a compound. However, at present there is no well-established relationship between the chemical properties of an odourant molecule and the perceptual quality of olfaction that it generates. Chemicals that often have little

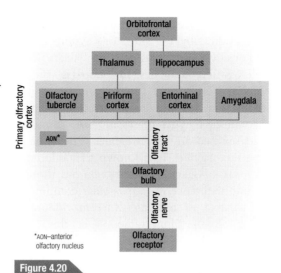

Figure 4.20

Sensory pathways of the olfactory system show a hierarchical arrangement. There is a convergence of olfactory signals from several million olfactory receptor cells upon several thousand glomeruli in the olfactory bulb. Signals from the olfactory bulb are transmitted to five areas that together make up the primary olfactory cortex. Limbic structures, such as the amygdala and hippocampus, process emotion- and memory-related aspects of smell, whereas the actual perceptual representation of smell is believed to take place in the orbitofrontal cortex.

SideNote | **4.31**

Patients who have suffered lesions of the orbitofrontal cortex due to stroke or traumatic injury have considerable difficulty identifying and discriminating odours.

resemblance to each other can smell alike, whereas other chemicals that are structurally very similar may smell very differently.

Despite much effort at trying to uncover the coding relationship between odourant chemistry and olfactory perception, our present knowledge is limited to only a few fundamental principles (Finger et al., 2000; Squire et al., 2002). Odourant molecules generally need to be small so that they are easily capable of being airborne. Second, to be effective, an odourant must have some fat solubility. And third, the three-dimensional structure of the odourant molecule determines how effectively and to which receptor it will bind. Scientists who study the chemical qualities of fragrances continue to search for the *olfactophore*—the minimum set of structural features that will produce a particular olfactory percept. If such a fundamental property truly exists, and if it is known, then a significant advance will have taken place in our quest to understand the olfactory system.

Coding strategies in olfactory processing

The ways in which odourant information is successively processed in neural structures, from the olfactory bulb onward, remains just

SideNote **4.32**

Chemical communication includes reproductive and social behaviours, such as mother–litter interaction, territorial marking, and detection of other species, especially in the context of predator–prey relationships.

as much of a mystery. We discussed earlier that taste coding by the gustatory system could be considered in terms of either labelled-line or cross-fibre strategies. The same is true of olfactory processing. One argument against labelled-line coding in gustation is the fact that multiple types of tastants can stimulate receptor neurons in taste buds. The same is true in olfaction. It is known that odourant receptors in olfactory sensory neurons, though having preference for a particular compound, are capable of binding different odourants (Buck, 2000). Thus, olfaction at this level appears to be multi-dimensional due to the broad tuning of the receptor neurons, a feature that would support a cross-fibre coding strategy. And yet, there appears to be a precise anatomical relationship between receptor neurons and individual glomeruli in the olfactory bulb. This specificity is consistent with a labelled-line strategy where exact connections between one neural structure and another are necessary to maintain the precise transmission of sensory information.

At a functional level, however, signal processing in the olfactory bulb does not appear to be consistent with the labelled-line model. For example, it has been found that a single odourant can activate several different glomeruli. Furthermore, different odourants recruit different sets of glomeruli to produce different patterns of activation across the olfactory bulb. The characteristic pattern of glomerular activation that appears for each odourant has been considered as an *odour image*—that is, a neural representation of olfactory identity (Mori et al., 1999).

If different patterns of activity across a neural structure are involved in characterizing the distinctions among odours, then does this reflect some sort of chemotopic organization? That is, is there an orderly representation or map of odourant properties in the olfactory bulb and beyond, similar in nature to the somatotopic map that we discussed in the last chapter? Perhaps, but it is not a map that can be easily deconstructed. In the somatosensory system, we saw a simple spatial code by which different parts of the body had an orderly relationship to neural activity in various brain structures. In olfaction, that relationship is not at all straightforward because of the very fact that we know so little about odourant properties and how they relate to perception. Thus, although there is no chemical counterpart to

the spatial topography we saw in the somatosensory system, the fact that there are distinct patterns of activation across the olfactory bulb suggests that some kind of chemotopic relationship that we have yet to uncover may indeed exist (Hawkes & Doty, 2009).

4. THE VOMERONASAL SYSTEM

A separate sensory apparatus exists in many species that deals with detection of pheromones and other chemicals involved in chemical communication (SideNote 4.32). Unlike the odourants involved in smell perception, pheromonal chemicals are often large molecules, such as proteins, and are generally non-volatile. The presence of these large molecules in urine and vaginal fluid have been shown to elicit sexual behaviour in a number of mammalian species. The detection of pheromonal compounds occurs through the vomeronasal system—a chemosensory pathway that exists in parallel to the main olfactory system.

Neural substrates of vomeronasal function

Sensing pheromones begins with the vomeronasal organ (VNO), which can be thought of as the counterpart to the olfactory epithelium (Keverne, 1999; Monti-Bloch et al., 1998). The VNO is present in most terrestrial mammals, amphibians, and reptiles. In non-human species, the VNO is a tube-shaped structure that is located on both sides of the bone or cartilage (nasal septum) that separates the two nasal chambers. The cellular composition of the VNO is similar to that of the olfactory epithelium in that it contains sensory, supporting, and basal cells (Mombaerts, 2004). The sensory cells are bipolar neurons that express receptor proteins on their surface. However, the identity of the VNO receptors remains unknown, although there is evidence that the transduction mechanism is linked to a G-protein system but involves second messengers other than cAMP. Another difference between the two types of sensory cells is that the VNO neurons do not have cilia.

After stimulation, neural signals generated in sensory neurons of the VNO epithelium travel through axons that course their way up the nasal septum (vomeronasal nerve), penetrate the cribriform bone, and synapse in the accessory olfactory bulb (AOB). This structure is the vomeronasal counterpart to the main olfactory bulb and is located nearby. The AOB contains glomerular circuits that are similar to those found in the main olfactory bulb. The M/T cells project out of the AOB and carry neural signals to higher brain centres. However, unlike the projections of the main olfactory bulb, the AOB's projections are largely targeted to the limbic system, amygdala, and hypothalamus. Thus, stimulation of the vomeronasal pathways initiates activity in brain regions that have well-known roles in reproductive function and provides a neurobiological basis for the observed behaviours in response to pheromones (SideNote 4.33).

Do humans have a functional vomeronasal system?

It is clear that the vomeronasal system is anatomically and functionally distinct from the main olfactory system in many species and that it represents a parallel stream for conveying chemosensory information (Baxi et al., 2006). However, the existence of the VNO and accessory olfactory system in humans and other higher primates is not entirely clear. It is believed that an anatomical structure similar to the VNO is present at birth and that there are functional connections to the olfactory bulb. However, those connections begin to degenerate and then disappear by the time a child is five months old. In adults, an anatomical depression is sometimes found in the nasal septum and has been interpreted by some to correspond to a human VNO. These claims have remained controversial because, despite the anatomical appearances, there is no convincing evidence that these structures are actually functional. At the beginning of this chapter, we discussed some tantalizing accounts of possible pheromonal action in humans. However, at present there is little conclusive evidence to favour the existence of a functional VNO or accessory olfactory system in humans.

E.   The Olfactory System—Perceptual Characteristics

Smell perception is present shortly after birth; newborns consistently demonstrate odour sensitivity, including a strong preference for maternal odours. The subsequent developmental profile of olfaction is not entirely understood, though most scientists believe that olfactory experiences in early life can shape future perceptual function. It is clear that, despite our reduced dependence upon olfaction, we are still extremely good detectors of certain odours and that many of our behavioural conditions—such as mood, emotion, and memory—are inextricably linked to the sense of smell (Wilson & Stevenson, 2006). We will complete this chapter with a short review of some of the known characteristics of olfactory perception.

1.   DETECTION AND SENSITIVITY

Psychophysical measures of olfactory function are somewhat difficult to carry out. As noted above, we have not yet uncovered a clear relationship between the nature of the stimulus (odourant chemistry) and olfactory perception. Furthermore, there are a vast number of chemicals that yield different olfactory experiences, making the selection of any one chemical a somewhat arbitrary choice for studying such a complex process. Perhaps the biggest obstacle in olfactory psychophysics lies in the fact that our sensitivity to an odourant is very much a time-dependent process. For example, the longer we inhale an odourant, the more reduced our olfactory sensation becomes to that particular odour. This phenomenon of adaptation, which is significantly less in taste sensation by comparison, must be kept in mind when undertaking threshold studies.

In practical terms, olfactory psychophysics is also hampered by the difficulty in control and delivery of the stimulus. One of the simplest ways of performing a detection task is to ask a subject whether an odour is perceived after sniffing two or more vials, only one of which contains the odourant. However, this is a rather crude procedure due to variability that can inevitably occur in stimulus delivery, for example, due to different rates or intensities of sniffing. To avoid such problems, current studies of olfactory function rely on the use of an **olfactometer**. This is a mechanical device that can deliver very brief, controlled pulses of air containing a fixed odourant concentration at a constant temperature and humidity.

Absolute threshold

Detection thresholds in olfaction are measures of the lowest odourant concentration that can produce a reliable judgment of its presence. A human subject has to merely say whether or

SideNote | **4.34**

One way to convey concentration values is by ppm—parts per million. Thus, mercaptan can be detected if just one molecule is present in 50 billion molecules of air.

SideNote | **4.35**

Olfactory detection ability is affected by the number of olfactory receptors that are present to detect a particular compound. Dogs have nearly 20 times more olfactory sensory neurons and therefore in general are superior in detecting most chemical substances.

not a smell was perceived. In some cases, individuals are asked to name the identity of the odourant. The resulting recognition thresholds provide a measure of a subject's sensitivity, not just to the presence of an odour but also to their capacity to associate that odour with a prior olfactory experience. In general, recognition thresholds are susceptible to **criterion effects** whereby pre-existing biases, such as a tendency to favour a particular odour quality, can influence the results. Classical Fechnerian methods such as the Method of Constant Stimuli or Method of Limits, as well as newer techniques, have been used to obtain detection and recognition thresholds (Doty, 2003; Doty & Kobal, 1995).

Detection threshold values for a variety of ordinary odourants are shown in Table 4.3. The wide range of threshold values seen here attests to the vast range of human olfactory sensitivity. As with gustatory thresholds, these values are mere approximations because of their susceptibility to testing conditions and methodology. Nevertheless, it is apparent that human olfaction can be quite sensitive to certain chemical substances. One example that is usually cited in this regard is the foul-smelling chemical mercaptan. It has been estimated that its detection threshold can be as low as 2×10^{-5} ppm (SideNote 4.34). For this reason, mercaptan is often added to odourless toxic or dangerous gases, such as propane or natural gas. Thus, even though humans rely much less on olfaction than many other species, it is clear that our sensitivity is quite high for certain odours and can actually approximate the detection abilities

of many animals that are well known for their keen olfactory sense (SideNote 4.35).

Factors that affect detection thresholds

A number of different factors are known to affect detection thresholds (Hawkes & Doty, 2009; Serby & Chobor, 1992). Gender differences have been particularly intriguing, especially for certain chemicals that seem to affect mood. One example is exaltolide, an aromatic compound that has a sexually stimulating effect (see SideNote 4.5 on page 103). Studies have shown that women are much more sensitive to exaltolide, especially around the midpoint of the menstrual cycle. It has been suggested that estrogen levels can affect the mucous layer in the olfactory epithelium and thereby produce changes in accessibility of certain chemicals to the sensory neuron. Although female superiority for the detection of certain chemicals has been linked to hormonal factors, there is also evidence that gender differences exist among prepubertal boys and girls.

The relationship between olfactory detection thresholds and age is now well known for a number of chemical substances (Doty et al., 1984). In all cases, increasing age is accompanied by a reduction in sensitivity. The corresponding increase in detection threshold can vary among different chemicals. For example, thresholds for various organic compounds can be 2–5 times higher in persons over 65 than those under 30. The detection threshold for other chemicals, such as phenyl ethyl alcohol, can be more than 10 times higher among middle-aged subjects compared to those who are very young. Similarly, recognition thresholds for food additives and other flavouring agents can be at least 10 times higher among elderly subjects. Recognition thresholds in general are lowest between the ages of 20 and 40 and increase thereafter. One of the major reasons for the increase in thresholds with age is a reduction in the number of olfactory sensory neurons.

There are two other factors that were generally believed to affect olfactory thresholds (Doty, 2003). One of those is smoking, which had been previously thought to increase detection thresholds. Although there is some evidence that this might be the case for certain chemicals, studies have shown that smokers do not experience a reduced ability to detect exaltolide, vanillin, and a number of other odourants. Another factor thought to affect olfactory thresholds is blindness,

Table **4.3**

Detection Thresholds for Various Odourant Substances

Musk	0.00007
Lemon	0.003
Vanilla	0.002
Rotten eggs	0.2
Bitter almond	3.0
Perspiration	9.0
Banana	39.0
Wintergreen	100.0

Note. The threshold values are expressed in micrograms per litre.

the logic being that the loss of one sensory modality results in increased, compensatory performance within another. It is now clear that blind subjects are no more sensitive to a variety of odourants than are sighted subjects. However, blind people display somewhat better recognition ability, which suggests that they are better able to process the olfactory information they encounter.

Abnormalities of olfactory function

There is considerable variability in olfactory detection and recognition thresholds among humans, in some cases by as much as a thousandfold, even though there may not be any overt signs of olfactory abnormality. In cases where there is true olfactory dysfunction, sensory measures can often show dramatic reductions in psychophysical performance (Seiden, 1997). There are more than 2.5 million people in the United States who suffer from some form of olfactory dysfunction. The most common disorder is **hyposmia**, or reduced smell perception. This condition can arise from infection or inflammation of the nasal passages, which in turn produces physical obstruction of the airways. Hyposmia can also result from traumatic injury to the olfactory apparatus, such as chemical (e.g., ammonia inhalation) or physical injuries (e.g., head impact). In most of these cases, the reduction in olfactory sensation is transient. There are, however, cases where a more long-lasting or chronic impairment can occur. Some conditions that produce this are persistent sinus infection, development of scar tissue after injury, or tumours that impact any of the olfactory structures.

A total loss of all smell sensation, which fortunately is quite rare, is called general **anosmia**. This condition can arise due to a genetic condition whereby the olfactory bulbs do not fully develop and therefore cannot make functional connections with the olfactory epithelium. The more common occurrence is the loss of smell for a particular odour, known as *specific anosmia* (SideNote 4.36). This condition has intrigued sensory scientists for some time. Given the hereditary link that is usually observed in such cases, it has been argued that specific anosmias arise due to genetic suppression of a particular odourant receptor. In addition to the two types of anosmias, there are a number of other conditions that can lead to altered olfactory function (SideNote 4.37).

2. SUPRATHRESHOLD OLFACTORY FUNCTION

Suprathreshold measures of olfactory function are generally much easier to obtain from an experimental point of view. However, there are many complex aspects of olfactory sensation that now come into play, such as the interaction of smell with higher cognitive and emotional conditions. The complexity of olfactory function continues to challenge both neurobiologists and behavioural scientists, from developing an understanding of the perceptual representation of odour quality to the intricate ways in which smell can influence a broad range of human behaviours.

Representation of odour quality

The classification of odour quality has remained one of the vexing problems of chemosensory science largely because it is difficult to agree on a set of primary odours that is universally accepted. Given the categorical nature of smell perception, it is quite difficult to distill the 10,000 or so odours that we can perceive into a small set of fundamental qualities (Wise, Olsson, & Cain, 2000). Nevertheless, several attempts have been made at constructing just such a classification scheme. As with taste quality representation, Hans Henning was also instrumental in the early development of this idea in olfaction. Henning relied on verbal labels that people most often used for a variety of odours. Based on the results of sampling several hundred different odourants, Henning reduced the perceptual judgments to six categories—*putrid, flowery, fruity, spicy, resinous,* and *burnt.* As with the taste pyramid, Henning believed that these qualities could be represented in some geometric form. Figure 4.21 on page 130 shows the so-called *Henning smell prism,* where each of the six primary qualities is located at a corner. According to this view, all perceived smells can be represented somewhere on this prism as a blend of two or more of the primary odours.

Needless to say, the Henning smell prism and all other such schemes suffer from the same problem we found in gustation—that is, the representation may be too simple and therefore not encompass the totality of olfactory experience. Furthermore, the very notion that olfactory perception is based on a small set of fundamental odours suggests that something about their chemistry is responsible for triggering that particular primary quality. As

SideNote | **4.36**

One example of a specific anosmia involves the detection of musk, a condition that was reported in one study to affect as many as 12% of the people sampled. It is believed that musk anosmia is linked to a genetic condition.

SideNote | **4.37**

The following conditions are also recognized forms of olfactory dysfunction (dysosmia): parosmia—distortions in odour quality; phantosmia—odour perception in the absence of volatile odourants; and cacosmia—olfactory hallucination of repugnant smells.

SideNote | **4.38**

Some scientists have suggested that there are no real odour primaries, which is certainly consistent with the idea that olfactory perception is the result of complex interactions among a variety of odourant receptors.

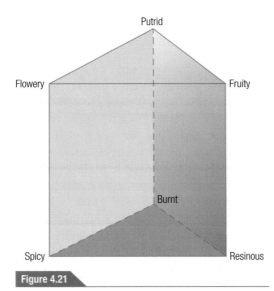

Figure 4.21

The Henning smell prism is defined by six odours, each presumed to represent a primary quality. According to this scheme all perceived odours, regardless of their complexity, are believed to correspond to some mixture of these primaries and therefore should be represented somewhere within the volume of this prism.

previously discussed, the relationship between odourant chemistry and olfactory perception is very complex and presently unknown. Thus, a scheme that distinguishes odour qualities on the basis of verbal descriptions and contains as an underlying principle the notion that each

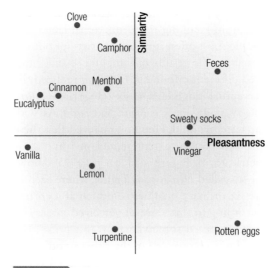

Figure 4.22

An odour map showing a representation of various odourants obtained by multi-dimensional scaling. Odour pleasantness is mapped along the x-axis, pleasant being to the left and unpleasant to the right. Odour similarity is mapped along the y-axis. Although rotten eggs and feces are both highly unpleasant odours, they are also considered to be very dissimilar in terms of their perceived smell. The same can be said of cloves and vanilla, though in this case both are considered to be quite pleasant.

primary has its own chemical coding feature is simply not supported by current scientific data (SideNote 4.38).

An alternate classification strategy is based on multi-dimensional scaling where two or more parameters are used in assessing various odours. The use of numerical values to rate the sensory impact along a particular dimension allows a map to be created where the respective values for each odour can be plotted. Susan Schiffman used this procedure to create a smell map containing several common odours, as shown in Figure 4.22 (Schiffman, 1974). In this example, odours are rated according to how pleasant or unpleasant they are, with the actual values being plotted along the x-axis. Within each of these categories, the odours can be further considered according to how similar they are in their perceived smells. Thus, two odours may be perceived as being equally pleasant but highly dissimilar in their quality (e.g., turpentine and camphor).

One particular advantage to this type of classification scheme is that it allows further exploration of odours that are perceptually similar. Using this strategy, Schiffman has verified that there are no straightforward chemical characteristics of odours that fall neatly into this space. That is, there is little or no relationship between the molecular structures of different odourant chemicals and where they may appear on this odour map.

Suprathreshold intensity perception and odour recognition

When we are exposed to a particular odour, the two features that strike us right away are a sense of how strong that odour is and a general ability to identify it (Serby & Chobor, 1992). These two facets of olfactory experience have been studied in some detail. Odour discrimination tests, for example, are often used in making comparisons between different fragrances. Although it is generally accepted that odour discrimination thresholds are approximately 25%, it has been shown that if odourant delivery to the olfactory epithelium is carefully controlled then the threshold actually comes down to around 7%, which is close to that seen in other sensory systems.

The suprathreshold parameter that has been studied to a greater degree is intensity perception (i.e., how our perceptual rating of intensity varies with concentration for a particular odour) (Doty, 2003). These measures are carried out by way of magnitude estimation tasks whereby a subject sniffs different concentrations of a particular odour and assigns a numerical value on the basis of its perceived intensity. The application of this method has revealed a power law relationship between odour concentration and perceived intensity with exponent values in the range of 0.2–0.7. An exponent value that is less than 1.0 means that perceived odour intensity grows more slowly than concentration, thereby allowing a large range of odourant concentrations to be compacted into a more restricted perceptual range.

One of the more unique features of the olfactory system is odour recognition ability (Buck & Axel, 1991; Doty et al., 1984). We are able to identify a truly vast number of different odours, an ability that only becomes better with experience and training (SideNote 4.39). Some tantalizing results have emerged from studies on individual and gender differences in emitted odours. All humans emit a distinctive set of odours that serve as a characteristic *smell signature* for that individual (SideNote 4.40). It appears that we are quite capable of distinguishing our own odour from those of others. Furthermore, it has been shown in studies with college students that it is possible to identify whether a person is male or female by smelling their hands or being exposed to the odour of that person's breath. It has also been claimed that humans are able to identify the emotional state of an individual on the basis of that person's body odour.

We noted in the previous section that detection and recognition sensitivities are generally higher in females and that these functions decrease with age. The same is true for odour identification at suprathreshold levels. Figure 4.23 shows performance data for odour identification among males and females for 80 common stimuli (Cain, 1982). As can be seen here, identification ability among females (denoted by the open bars) is greater than males for a vast majority of the odours in this sample. A number of interesting examples pop up in this survey. Females are better at correctly identifying the smells of cigar butts, machine oil, turpentine, and rubber, whereas males are better at identifying molasses, black pepper, and Ivory bar soap. Regardless of gender, our ability to correctly identify odours declines with age. Identification performance remains steady up to one's sixties and then begins to decline quite sharply. In many instances, an

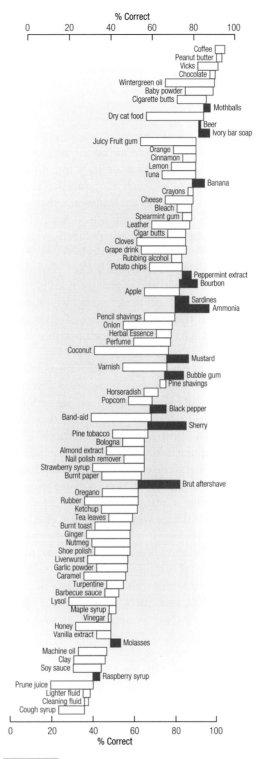

Figure 4.23

Odour identification ability for males and females among a sample of 80 common stimuli. The filled bars show examples of stimuli where identification ability was greater in males; open bars show the corresponding examples for females. The length of the bar indicates the size of the gender difference. Odour identification ability is superior in females for a significant majority of the odourants in this sample, as evident by the large number of open bars. From "Odor Identification by Males and Females: Predictions Versus Performance," by W. S. Cain, 1982, *Chemical Senses, 7*, pp. 129–142.

SideNote 4.39

Perfume makers are able to discriminate and categorize odours to a much greater degree, an ability that comes not only with training but may also be influenced by inborn or genetic factors. A fascinating fictional account of this can be found in the novel *Perfume* by Patrick Süskind.

SideNote 4.40

The highly individual nature of human odour allows hound dogs, for example, to trace that scent in police work, even in the presence of odours from other individuals. Certain diseases also emit distinctive odours and are used by doctors for diagnostic purposes.

age-related decrease in olfactory neural processing accounts for these deficits. These results also explain why some elderly people complain about the bland taste of foods since olfactory signals have considerable impact on flavour.

Adaptation and cross-adaptation

We know from everyday experience that continued exposure to an odour reduces our perceptual appreciation of it. While this has certain advantages, such as reduced olfactory sensation in physical environments that smell bad, it also presents certain unwelcome effects. Some examples include the reduced awareness of our own body and breath odours, excessive application of perfume or other fragrances, and the reduced appreciation of odours while cooking. In all of these cases, we become adapted to these odours, whereas other individuals who have not had that opportunity are keenly aware of them.

The phenomenon of olfactory adaptation produces temporary increases in detection threshold and reduces responses to suprathreshold sensations (Dalton, 2000). The two main factors that affect adaptation are the intensity of the adapting odour and the length of adaptation. In general, the effects of adaptation decline rapidly after removing the adapting stimulus, often within a matter of minutes. However, there are situations where adaptation effects are more long-lasting. It is believed that short-term adaptation occurs due to desensitization at the receptor level in olfactory sensory neurons. However, the long-term effects likely occur at more central sites, such as the olfactory bulb and cortex, where a persistent physiological change produces decreased olfactory sensation (Zufall & Leinders-Zufall, 2000).

It is also possible to produce cross-adaptation whereby sensitivity to one odourant is reduced by exposure to a different one. It is usually necessary that the two odourants be similar, though there are instances where cross-adaptation can occur with compounds that are structurally and perceptually dissimilar. It was once believed that cross-adaptation might be a suitable means for classifying odour qualities in much the same way that gustatory sensations show cross-adaptation effects among similar compounds. However, this approach is problematic because of the sheer number of different odourant chemicals that can be independently perceived. Furthermore, we currently know

SideNote | 4.41

The term *deodorizer* is often mistakenly used for masking effects, especially with air fresheners. A true deodorizer actually removes the foul-smelling odourants entirely rather than just covering them up.

very little about the physiological mechanisms of olfactory cross-adaptation.

Perception of odour mixtures

Mixing two or more odours can produce complex effects in addition to cross-adaptation. We do know that mixing odours does not result in a simple addition of the components' odourant intensities. Rather, the different odours can interfere with each other and produce suppression or masking effects. This knowledge has been used for centuries to produce perfumes and fragrances that mask offensive body odours or suppress foul smells in the air (SideNote 4.41). The rich history of experimentation in odour mixtures for precisely this purpose has led to the identification of many fragrances such as jasmine, lavender, and rose oil, which continue to be used in the production of perfumes and air fresheners (Serby & Chobor, 1992; Van Toller & Dodd, 1988).

There are two other perceptual effects that are possible in odour mixtures. In some cases, a mixture of two or more odourants can blend together and create an entirely new fragrance that bears little relationship to the original components. Another possibility, however, is that the components may retain their individual qualities and be perceived as such. In other words, it may be possible to sort out the various odours in a mixture, especially if the components are quite distinct and dissimilar. Recall that the corresponding ability in gustation can be extremely difficult. Our ability to identify odour components in a mixture may be due to the fact that odours are sensed through nearly 1,000 different types of receptors, whereas taste is only sampled through four to five receptor types. It is this difference that may endow the olfactory system with a greater ability to distinguish the odourant compounds in a complex mixture.

Olfaction, emotion, and memory

The relationship between olfactory perception and higher functions such as emotion and memory is well known, not just from our ordinary experiences but also from the very way in which the olfactory structures are wired in the brain (Doty, 2003; Wilson & Stevenson, 2003). As we noted earlier, there is a direct neural link between the olfactory bulb and the limbic system. Two major components of the limbic system are the amygdala and hippocampus, where emotional experience and memory traces are respectively consolidated. These pathways provide a neural basis for the immediacy of emotional responsiveness that often accompanies odour stimulation. Certain odours—such as the smell of a forest or beach or, oddly enough, spearmint—are known to elicit a positive emotional response. The mood enhancing qualities of various odours has been used in the practice of **aromatherapy**.

It is also well known that odours can elicit vivid emotional memories, a fact that was powerfully portrayed in the writings of Marcel Proust. Indeed, odours can become intricately associated with certain events so that re-exposure to that odour, even many years later, will immediately bring forth the earlier association. It has been suggested that certain odour memories persist largely because of their emotional significance. However, despite the strong access that olfaction has to memory, we cannot wilfully recall a particular odour. For example, it is impossible to evoke the smell of a particular flower or perfume in our mind, even though we can do this easily for the auditory and visual systems by simply recalling a tune or imagining the face of a close friend. Thus, even though the olfactory sense has direct access to our core emotions and memories, the odours themselves are not maintained in a declarative form where they can be recalled at will without direct sensory input (SideNote 4.42).

3. THE COMMON CHEMICAL SENSE

During the early 1900s, research on the behaviour of catfish showed that they tended to stay away from noxious chemicals, even when their normal chemosensory systems had been disabled. Further research has shown that most animals, humans included, are easily aroused by noxious chemicals and that these chemicals are detected by mechanisms that are quite distinct and separate from the olfactory system.

Trigeminal chemoreception

A separate system for the detection of irritating chemicals has come to be known as the *common chemical sense*. However, in reality this system is not specialized for detecting chemicals in the way we have seen for the gustatory or olfactory systems. Rather, it is the free nerve endings in the olfactory epithelium that are involved in the detection of irritating chemicals. These nerve endings are normally sensitive to pain and temperature. However, they are also stimulated by noxious chemicals and hence produce the characteristic irritating sensations. In the facial region, it is the trigeminal nerve (cranial nerve V) that gives rise to the free nerve endings that innervate the oral and nasal chambers (SideNote 4.43). For this reason, noxious chemical stimulation of these fibres has been referred to as **trigeminal chemoreception** (Squire et al., 2002).

We have already considered the effects of noxious stimulation in the gustatory system through the effects of capsaicin and other spices such as black pepper, horseradish, mustard, cloves, and ginger. Although these items will stimulate nasal chemoreception as well, the more volatile chemicals, such as ammonia and vinegar, will produce an especially rapid and intense irritation in the nasal passages. Such chemical stimulation is often confused with olfactory sensation. While noxious chemicals can modulate neural activity in some structures such as the olfactory bulb, our perception of chemical irritants is mediated almost exclusively through trigeminal mechanisms. The chemicals act directly on ion channels within the free nerve endings where they cause membrane depolarization. If the depolarization is sufficient to reach threshold, then action potentials are generated and transmitted through the brain stem to somatosensory processing areas of the cerebral cortex (SideNote 4.44).

SideNote 4.42

An interesting extension of this idea arises from the fact that we routinely experience visual and auditory stimuli while dreaming and yet rarely experience an olfactory dream where a vivid smell is experienced.

SideNote 4.43

The effects of irritating chemicals are not just restricted to the oral and nasal chambers. Chemosensitive fibres are found throughout the skin, especially in the mucous membranes of the mouth, respiratory tract, eye, and anal/genital areas. The chemical chloracetophenone, commonly known as *tear gas*, has a highly specific action on the chemosensitive fibres of the eyes.

SideNote 4.44

Excessive stimulation by chemical irritants produces reflex reactions—such as coughing, sneezing, and hiccupping—as a means of rejecting the offending agents.

Summary

1. The ability to detect chemicals likely represents the first sensory system to have emerged in the course of evolution. Detection of dissolved chemicals is mediated by the *gustatory system* and produces the perception of taste, whereas detection of airborne chemicals is mediated by the *olfactory system* and produces the perception of smell. Both sensory systems are unique in terms of the diverse interconnections they have with different brain structures, leading to striking effects on memory and emotion.

2. The chemosensory systems are used in territorial marking, food seeking and sampling, and in many species—possibly including humans—mate preference or selection. The latter function is mediated by a parallel chemosensory system that includes the vomeronasal organ and associated neural pathways. Although the sense of smell is well developed in most animals, humans have comparatively reduced smell sensitivity, likely due to our greater reliance on the visual and auditory systems.

3. Taste sensation is represented by five qualities—sweet, sour, salty, bitter, and umami. Ionic channels are responsible for signal transduction in the case of salty and sour sensations, whereas receptor-mediated mechanisms are involved in the others. Gustatory receptor neurons release neurotransmitters after stimulation, causing action potentials to generate in nerve fibres that carry the signals to the cerebral cortex via two relay stations in the brain stem and thalamus. Taste signals are encoded across a broad set of fibres in the gustatory pathway.

4. Two general techniques are used for the psychophysical studies of taste function—probing the tongue with an electrical current (electrogustometry) and with chemical substances (chemogustometry). Bitter substances generally have the lowest detection threshold, followed by sour, salty, and sweet. Taste thresholds are affected by other primary tastants in mixtures. Other factors that affect taste detection and discriminability include temperature, age, temporal and spatial aspects of stimulation, adaptation to similar or other tastants, and the precise psychophysical technique used in the study.

5. Taste quality is best represented using multi-dimensional scaling techniques. A combination of factors including smell, sight, texture, and temperature are responsible for producing the flavour experience. Taste hedonics depends on prior experience as well as cultural factors. Abnormalities in gustatory function can include a total loss of sensation (ageusia), reduced sensation (hypogeusia), or distorted sensation (dysgeusia).

6. Airborne chemicals can travel through either the orthonasal or the retronasal route to reach the olfactory epithelium where the transduction process occurs. Odourants must first pass through a mucous layer with the help of odourant binding proteins, after which they bind to specific receptors on olfactory receptor neurons. There are over 1,000 different receptor types that show a high degree of specificity in terms of what chemical can be bound. The transduction process involves a series of intracellular events that leads to the production of action potentials, which are then transmitted to the olfactory bulb.

7. Olfactory processing in the bulb takes place within discrete spatial units (glomerulus). Different odourants produce different patterns of glomerular activation. The precise relationship between the chemical nature of an odourant and its activation profile in the bulb, as well as the smell sensation that is produced, remains unknown. The neural output of the olfactory bulb is directed at a number of cortical sites, which together are referred to as the *primary olfactory cortex*.

8. Detection threshold for smell varies, depending upon the odourant as well as nonsensory factors such as age, gender, prior exposure, criterion effects, and smoking. As with taste, the representation of odour quality is similarly challenging. Multi-dimensional scaling techniques can

be used to create a smell map. A total loss of olfactory function (anosmia) is relatively rare, whereas reduced olfactory function (hyposmia) can occur more frequently and usually develops after head impact, inhalation of strong chemicals, or infection of the sinus passages.

9. The common chemical sense (trigeminal chemoreception) arises from the stimulation of free nerve endings in the olfactory epithelium by noxious chemicals (e.g., ammonia, vinegar, etc.). The resulting irritating sensation usually produces a reflexive withdrawal from the stimulus.

Key Terms

adaptation, 117
ageusia, 114
anosmia, 129
aromatherapy, 133
capsaicin, 120
chemogustometry, 113
chemotopic organization, 110
cilia, 122
concentration, 113
criterion effects, 128
cross-adaptation, 117
cross-fibre coding, 110
dysgeusia, 114
electrogustometry, 113
facial, glossopharyngeal, and vagus nerves, 107
flavour, 120

glomerulus, 123
gustatory system, 102
hedonics, 120
hypogeusia, 114
hyposmia, 129
insula, 111
isomerism, 125
labelled-line coding, 109
limbic system, 124
microvilli, 106
nucleus of the solitary tract (NST), 111
odotope, 125
odourant binding protein (OBP), 122
odourants, 121
olfactometer, 127

olfactory epithelium, 121
olfactory nerve, 122
olfactory system, 102
orbitofrontal cortex, 112
papilla, 105
pheromone, 103
primary olfactory cortex, 123
PTC, PROP, 117
second messenger, 109
tastants, 106
taste bud, 105
trigeminal chemoreception, 133
umami, 105
ventral posterior medial nucleus (VPMN), 111
vomeronasal organ (VNO), 104

Recall Questions

1. What are some of the unique characteristics of the chemosensory systems? What evolutionary factors were involved in the emergence of these systems? Why do humans have a reduced smell sensitivity compared to other animals?

2. What are pheromones, and why are they useful? What are the arguments for and against the idea that humans are capable of emitting and using pheromones? What is the vomeronasal system?

3. What are the different kinds of papillae, and how are they distributed across the tongue? How do tastants interact with taste buds to produce a neural signal? How are those signals then transmitted to higher centres of the brain?

4. What are the advantages and disadvantages of electrogustometry? How are the techniques of regional and whole-mouth chemogustometry conducted?

5. What factors can affect taste sensitivity? How can taste quality be assessed and represented in graphical form? What is the difference between *taste* and *flavour*?

6. What is the composition of the olfactory epithelium? What is the role of olfactory binding proteins? What happens after an odourant binds to an olfactory receptor cell, and what subsequent processes are unleashed?

7. What are the challenges in undertaking olfactory psychophysics experiments? What is an olfactometer?

8. What are the different factors that can affect smell detection thresholds? How can multi-dimensional scaling techniques be used in research on olfaction? What are the different abnormalities of olfactory function, and how do they occur?

9. What is trigeminal chemoreception, and what mechanisms are involved in producing it? Can you think of some examples of noxious chemicals, other than ammonia and vinegar, that can stimulate this system?

10. What are the transductional features that differentiate the signalling of sour/salty tastants from sweet/bitter ones? What are the two different intracellular mechanisms underlying G-protein mediated signalling, and which tastants are involved in their activation?

11. What is the difference between labelled-line *versus* cross-fibre coding? Why would it be difficult to have labelled-line coding in the olfactory system?

12. How does chemotopic organization differ from somatotopic organization in terms of modality segregation and spatial organization?

13. What is the difference between taste and odour mixtures in terms of the resulting perceptions? Why is the olfactory system superior to the gustatory system when it comes to identifying the components in a mixture?

Further Reading

- Brown, R. (1985). *Social odours in mammals.* London, England: Oxford University Press.

- Doherty, P., Brewer, W. J., Castle, D., & Pantelis, C. (2006). *Olfaction and the brain.* Cambridge, England: Cambridge University Press.

- Finger, T. E., Silver, W. L., & Restrepo, D. (2000). *Neurobiology of taste and smell.* New York, NY: Wiley-Liss.

- Genders, R. (1972). *A history of scent.* London, England: Hamish Hamilton.

- Harrington, A., & Rosario, V. (1992). Olfaction and the primitive: Nineteenth-century medical thinking on olfaction. In M. J. Serby & K. L. Chobor (Eds.), *Science of olfaction.* New York, NY: Springer-Verlag.

- Hawkes, C. H., & Doty, R. (2009). *The neurology of olfaction.* Cambridge, England: Cambridge University Press.

- Morris, E. T. (1984). *Fragrance—The story of perfume from Cleopatra to Chanel.* New York, NY: Charles Scribner's Sons.

- Taylor, A. J., & Roberts, D. D. (2004). *Flavor perception.* London, UK: Wiley-Blackwell.

- Watson, L. (2000). *Jacobson's organ and the remarkable nature of smell.* New York, NY: W. W. Norton.

- Wilson, D. A., & Stevenson, R. J. (2006). *Learning to smell: Olfactory perception from neurobiology to behavior.* Baltimore, MD: Johns Hopkins University Press.

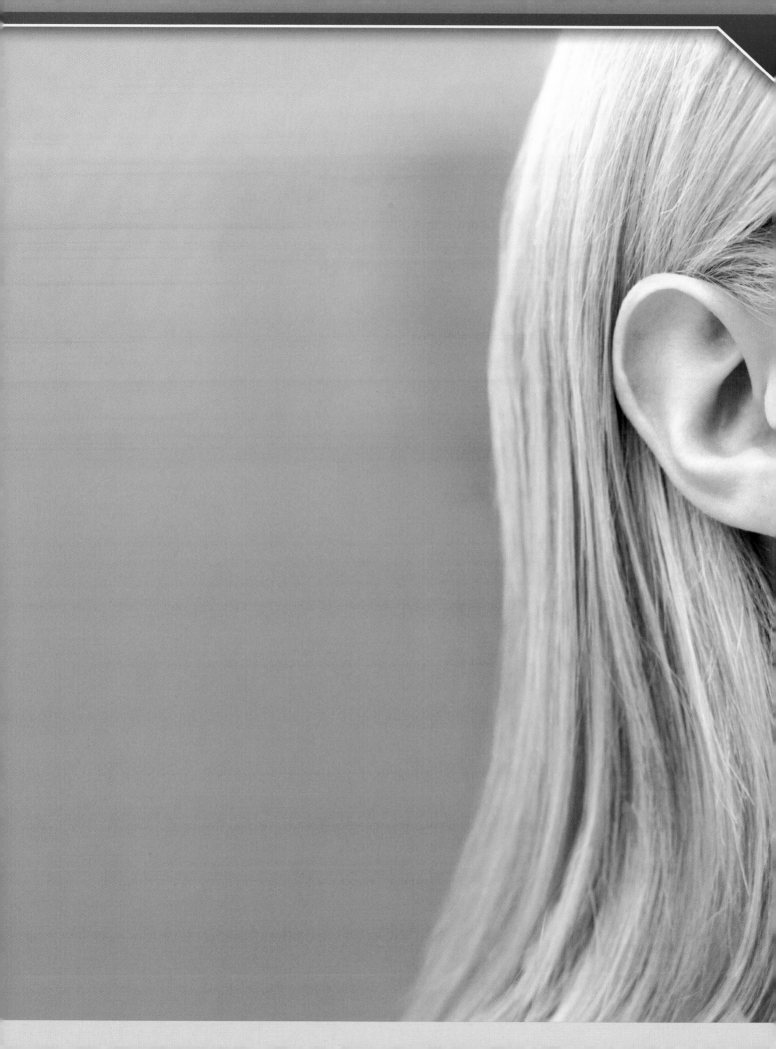

The Auditory System: Sound and the Ear

5

In this chapter . . .

- You will learn about the physical properties of sound—such as amplitude, intensity, and frequency—and what is created when these properties are combined. You will explore the properties needed for an object to produce sound and other factors that contribute to our ability to hear.

- You will explore the intricacies of ear anatomy and how its parts are designed to maximize hearing—from the outer ear that captures sound, to the middle ear that transfers sound waves into liquid signals, to the inner ear that converts the liquid waves into a neural signal.

- You will discover how sound energy is transformed into a biological signal when the ossicles hit the oval window, causing waves whose amplitude will peak in a particular area on the basilar membrane. Further, you will learn how these waves cause a shearing motion between the basilar membrane and the tectorial membrane and how this in turn causes a depolarization that travels to the auditory cortex.

- You will explore the types of hearing loss and how a simple bone conduction test distinguishes between the different types. Finally, you will learn how research has helped to design devices to recapture hearing.

Among humans, there is a broad range of auditory perceptual experience. We are captivated by rhythmic sounds such as those in a melody. We derive meaningful information through the structured and periodic sounds contained in speech. We are quickly irritated by noise in our surroundings. And we recoil from sounds as diverse as thunder and fingernails on a chalkboard.
Photo: MentalArt/iStockphoto.com

No matter how eloquently a dog may bark, he cannot tell you that his parents were poor but honest.

—Bertrand Russell

In the last chapter, we learned about the many ways that chemosensory information can be used for communication among animals. For many species, the sensory system best suited for this purpose is **audition**. The detection of sound and an ability to determine its source are essential requirements for locating food, finding mates, and avoiding predators. The auditory system is especially well suited for these purposes for two reasons. First, unlike the somatosensory and chemosensory systems, audition is truly a *distant sense* in that a stimulus can be detected from quite far away. This provides an animal with the means to plot a kill, forge an escape, or hear the distant calls of a potential mate. And second, among all the sensory systems, the auditory system operates on the fastest time scale. As we will see later in this chapter and the next, minute differences in the oscillations of sound waves or even their difference in arrival to the ears by mere fractions of a second are important sensory features of auditory function.

Among humans, there is a broad range of auditory perceptual experience. We are captivated by rhythmic sounds such as those in a melody. We derive meaningful information through the structured and periodic sounds contained in speech. We are quickly irritated by noise in our surroundings. And we recoil from sounds as diverse as thunder and fingernails on a chalkboard. Needless to say, our preoccupation with hearing and how it occurs has a long history. The Egyptians around 1500 BCE were among the first to have regarded the ear as the organ of hearing, though they believed it was also responsible for respiration. Greek philosophers also pondered the role of the ear in hearing and made modest attempts at understanding its function (SideNote 5.1). However, much of our knowledge about the auditory system has emerged from studies since around the mid-1800s when the anatomy of the ear began to be described in detail. Auditory research during the 20th century accelerated due to rapid technological developments in both the physical and the biological sciences. Current research on hearing is carried out by scientists from various fields including physics, electronic engineering, marine science, neuroscience, and psychology.

We begin this chapter with a discussion of the properties of sound followed by a description of the anatomical and physiological characteristics of different parts of the ear, the process by which sound energy is transduced into biological signals, and parts of the brain that are involved in auditory processing. We conclude the chapter with a discussion of auditory dysfunction and hearing loss. Our emphasis throughout this chapter will be on the physical properties of sound and how they relate to early sensory processing within the auditory system. This will lay the groundwork for a fuller discussion of the perceptual characteristics of hearing in the next two chapters.

A. The Physics of Sound

Any effort to understand auditory function must begin with a study of the nature of sound—how it is produced, what its physical characteristics are, how it travels, and how it interacts with other objects. For us to hear a sound, there are three essential requirements. First, there must be something that creates the sound. Second, the sound must propagate through a medium from its source. And third, there must be a mechanism to translate sound energy into a biological signal that ultimately generates the perceptual experience we refer to as *hearing*. In this section, we will deal with the first two issues. However, to understand them more thoroughly, we need to first come to grips with exactly what sound is.

It was not until the 16th century that humanity first began to understand sound (SideNote 5.2). The first major advance originated with Galileo whose interest in sound was inspired by his father who was a mathematician, musician, and composer. Galileo believed that sound is a vibrational event and that alterations in the frequency of those vibrations correlate with differences in pitch perception (Deutsch & Richards, 1979; Rossing & Fletcher, 2004). His idea that sound occurred due to waves in the air was quite contentious because of the view held by many philosophers and scientists of that time that sound was created by invisible particles which originated at its source and interacted with the ear to produce hearing. The dispute was resolved by the famous *bell jar experiment* conducted by British chemist Robert Boyle in 1660. The experiment, which even today remains common in high-school physics classes, showed that the sound produced by a bell becomes less audible if enclosed in a jar from which the air is slowly pumped out, eventually becoming silent when the jar is free of air. Although the actual reasons for the reduction in sound intensity are somewhat complicated, this experiment nevertheless convincingly demonstrated that air was required to serve as a medium for the transmission of sound.

1.   THE CREATION OF SOUND

If we were to seek a definition of the term *sound*, it is likely that we would obtain two different answers. Psychologists tend to define *sound* within the context of hearing. In other words, sound is considered to be a certain physical event that produces the perceptual experience we know as hearing. In this context, sound can be described by a set of qualities, such as loudness and pitch, which we distinguish entirely within the perceptual domain. To a physicist, however, sound is a vibrational disturbance of a medium and is therefore associated with certain physical qualities that can be exactly described. There is no requirement to perceive the sound, and therefore its existence is independent of perception (SideNote 5.3). Although air is the most common medium for sound transmission, any medium—gas, liquid, or solid—can serve this purpose. However, the initial requirement in all cases is that there be a source that creates the vibrational disturbance in the first place (Rossing, Moore, & Wheeler, 2001).

Vibrational properties of objects

For an object to create sound, the one necessary condition is that it be able to vibrate and thereby impart a corresponding vibrational disturbance to air. Although it may seem that any object should be capable of doing so, there are actually two essential properties that it must, by definition, possess—**inertia** and **elasticity** (Berg & Stork, 2004). All physical objects have mass and therefore either resist being moved if at rest or resist coming to rest if in motion. The greater the mass of an object, the greater its inertia.

The first condition for vibration is that once force is applied, the movement of an object is sustained due to the property of inertia. To simplify the picture, let us consider the situation where an object is anchored so that it cannot move in its entirety when force is applied. Rather, the force now causes the object to become distorted due to a change in its shape. The property of inertia will still apply because there will be a tendency for the object

to resist becoming deformed. But once started, the inertial force will ensure that deformation continues, something that can only be halted or reversed if an opposing force comes into play. This is indeed what happens because the distortion in the shape of the object is quickly met by an opposing tendency to return the object to its original state. This is the property of elasticity, and it ensures that the object's deformation does not continue beyond a certain extent. Consequently, the interaction of two opposing forces, inertia and elasticity, makes the object move back and forth after a force is applied, resulting in vibration.

The tuning fork as a sound source

Any elastic object can serve as a sound-producing device as long as it is capable of vibrating (SideNote 5.4). Although we commonly think of musical instruments, loudspeakers, and the human vocal apparatus as convenient examples in this regard, the sounds they make are quite complex and therefore not suitable for our analysis at this point. Rather, the simple device known as a **tuning fork** is more convenient and often used to understand the physical characteristics of sound (Berg & Stork, 2004; Hartmann, 1998). The properties of inertia and elasticity apply to the tuning fork as well and account for its behaviour when it is struck. Initially, the applied force causes the prongs (or tines) of the tuning fork to move in the direction of the force, as illustrated in Figure 5.1 on page 142. As the prongs move, the elasticity of the metal produces a restoring force that opposes this motion and causes the prongs to return toward equilibrium (Gulick, Gescheider, & Frisina, 1989). However, the inertial force of this return movement makes it pass through its equilibrium point in the opposite direction. The elastic force then opposes this motion, and so the prongs are then set into motion in the opposite direction (SideNote 5.5).

The resulting vibration of the tuning fork occurs in a very simple and elegant way. As Figure 5.1 shows, the back and forth displacement of the prongs over time from one extremity to the other occurs in a smoothly varying manner that physicists refer to as **simple harmonic motion**. If we look at the positional trace of one of the prongs as it vibrates, we see that from a starting displacement of zero the prong moves outward to a maximum displacement and then moves in the opposite direction, only to be reversed again

SideNote **5.3**

Recall the famous query, "If a tree falls in a forest and no one is there to hear it, will it still create a sound?" Of course it will, according to the physicists, though psychologists may argue otherwise.

SideNote **5.4**

Elasticity can also be thought of as the ability to resist deformation. This is a property shared by all objects, though different objects have different degrees of elasticity. For example, the elasticity of steel is about 1.2 million times greater than that of water.

SideNote **5.5**

The vibration of the tuning fork's prong eventually decays with time due to friction of the prong's movement against air, a process known as *damping*.

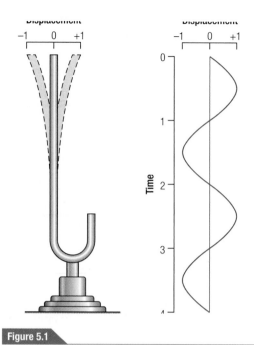

Figure 5.1

The displacement profile of a tuning fork, shown here for one of its prongs, follows a sinusoidal function. The initial force on the prong is toward the right, resulting in a rightward displacement. The smoothly varying back and forth motion of the prong is the consequence of two competing forces—inertia and elasticity. Adapted from *Hearing: Physiological Acoustics, Neural Coding, and Psychoacoustics*, by W. L. Gulick, G. A. Gescheider, and R. D. Frisina, 1989, New York, NY: Oxford University Press.

SideNote 5.6

Prior to the motion of the tuning fork, the air molecules are evenly distributed and in constant but random motion, maintaining an average distance from each other. This random motion causes air to exert pressure on any object, which at sea level amounts to approximately 14.7 lbs/in.^{2}

SideNote 5.7

An analogy is often made between sound waves and the vibrational effects seen when a pebble is thrown into a pond, although the waves in the two conditions are actually somewhat different. In sound waves, the air particles move back and forth in the direction of wave propagation. In water waves, the particles move up and down at right angles in the direction of wave propagation. In both cases, there is a travelling wave of energy—that is, the medium does not move with the wave.

by the elastic nature of the metal arms. The displacement trace that is made in such cases of simple harmonic motion takes the form of a **sinusoidal function** (Berg & Stork, 2004; Rossing & Fletcher, 2004). We will return to sinusoids in a moment, but we must first analyze the effect a vibrating tuning fork has on the surrounding air.

Impact of a sound source on the medium

The simple harmonic motion of a tuning fork imparts a corresponding vibrational disturbance to the air particles that surround it (SideNote 5.6). Because air also has the properties of inertia and elasticity, the effect of the vibrating tuning fork will cause effects similar to that which we described above. The outward movement of a tuning fork's prongs will cause the air molecules immediately surrounding it to become crowded, resulting in a momentary increase in air pressure known as **compression** (Rossing & Fletcher, 2004). When the prong begins to move in the opposite direction, the compression is relaxed. As the prong passes the equilibrium point toward the opposite

extremity, the air molecules thin out to produce a momentary decrease in air pressure known as **rarefaction**. As the tuning fork continues to vibrate, the same group of air molecules in its immediate vicinity will go through alternating states of compression and rarefaction.

As Figure 5.2 shows, the alternating pressure changes move outward through the air mass away from the tuning fork (Speaks, 1999). This occurs because each air particle acts as a separate vibrator, which then collides with neighbouring particles and causes them to vibrate. As a result, the momentary compressions and rarefactions are passed from region to region and result in a wave of outward vibrational changes in air pressure. It is this moving vibrational energy that actually forms the sound wave (SideNote 5.7). It is important to understand that there is very little actual outward displacement of the air molecules themselves throughout this process. Rather, the air molecules are merely oscillating back and forth in register with the vibration of the tuning fork.

We now return to the sinusoidal movement of the tuning fork, and we can see through Figure 5.3 that the vibrational sequence in air also takes on a similar form (Gulick et al., 1989). It is a fundamental principle of physics that because air is an elastic medium, each air molecule will mimic the original pattern of vibration. The propagating regions of increased and decreased air pressure therefore also show a sinusoidal profile of pressure change that is

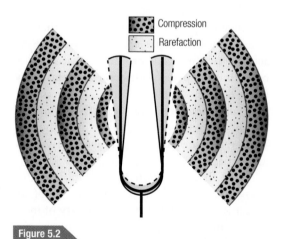

Figure 5.2

A vibrating object such as a tuning fork produces alternating regions of increased and decreased air pressure known, respectively, as *compression* and *rarefaction*. These alternating pressure regions radiate outward from the source to produce a travelling sound wave that is conducted through the medium.

a direct consequence of the sinusoidal simple harmonic motion of the tuning fork. The resulting sound wave is the simplest that can be produced in nature—a so-called **pure tone** that is characterized by a single sinusoidal function of air pressure change over time (Rossing & Fletcher, 2004).

2. THE PROPERTIES OF SOUND

Sound is a **longitudinal** travelling wave of pressure disturbance within a medium. It is these pressure changes that are detected by our auditory system and allow us to hear. Once it was recognized that sound is in fact a wave, a number of parameters related to wave functions were soon established. We first review two parameters of sound waves—amplitude and frequency—that have great importance for hearing followed by a discussion of the speed of sound.

Amplitude and its relationship to sound intensity

If we strike the same tuning fork again but this time much harder, the prongs will vibrate as before but with much greater displacement from one end to the other. This will cause the momentary changes of air pressure to be greater. The sound wave profile in this condition compared to a light tapping of the prongs is shown in Figure 5.4. The difference in the two waveforms is apparent from the height and depth of the troughs and crests. In a pure tone, the pressure change from the baseline to the peaks of the sinusoidal function is referred to as the **amplitude**. A loud sound has a waveform in which the pressure changes are greater, and therefore has greater amplitude, than a soft sound (Berg & Stork, 2004; Hartmann, 1998).

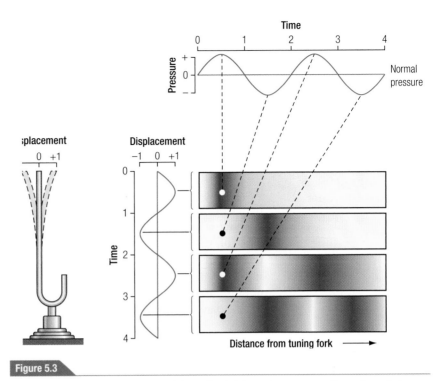

Figure 5.3

The sinusoidal displacement pattern of the tuning fork imparts a corresponding pattern of air pressure change. With each rightward displacement of the prong, air pressure in its immediate vicinity increases. As the prong swings to the other side, air pressure decreases momentarily. The pressure changes occur in a smoothly varying manner and display a sine-wave pattern if plotted as a function of time. Adapted from *Hearing: Physiological Acoustics, Neural Coding, and Psychoacoustics,* by W. L. Gulick, G. A. Gescheider, and R. D. Frisina, 1989, New York, NY: Oxford University Press.

The actual pressure values can be given in a number of different ways depending on the unit of measure that is applied. One of the units used in the metric system is newtons per square metre or pascal (Pa). The atmospheric pressure at sea level is 100,000 Pa. As we will see in a moment, the pressure changes caused by compression and rarefaction in sound are tiny fractions of normal atmospheric pressure. Therefore, sound pressures are sometimes denoted in millionths of a pascal, or micropascal

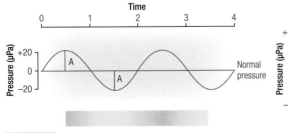
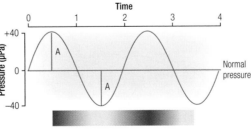

Figure 5.4

Sinusoidal waveforms of two sounds of different amplitudes are created by a light versus strong tapping of a tuning fork. The pressure changes from baseline values during compression and rarefaction are given in micropascals (μPa). The amplitude (A) is the difference in air pressure between baseline and the maximum peak or trough values of the sound wave (20 and 40 μPa in the two examples shown here). A pictorial account of the changes in air pressure is shown below each sound wave.

(μPa). In considering the loudness produced by a particular sound, we rarely speak in terms of the actual air pressure modulations produced by that sound. Instead, the term we are most familiar with in describing the physical characteristic of sounds in terms of their loudness is **intensity**.

Intensity is related to the square of sound pressure (SideNote 5.8). When referring to the intensity of a sound, we seldom consider the absolute intensity but rather the intensity in relation to a reference level (Luce, 1993; Rossing et al., 2001). Specifically, we take the ratio of the intensity of a particular sound (denoted as I_s) to the intensity of an accepted standard reference (i.e., I_s/I_r). Relating this to pressure, this ratio can be written in the following way:

$$P_s^2/P_r^2$$

where P_s is the peak pressure (amplitude) of the sound we wish to measure, and P_r is the peak pressure of the reference sound. The question then is "What is the reference sound?" One sensible choice would be the lowest sound level that can be heard by humans under optimal circumstances. That way, all other sounds whose intensity we wish to consider can be related to this reference, and the ratios above would be interpreted in terms of the minimum audible sound level. Therefore, a common way to express sound levels is to use a P_r

value of 20 micropascals, the lowest sound level that can be heard.

If we examine the pressure values of some common sounds in our environment, as shown in Table 5.1, we quickly see that we have to deal with some pretty staggering numbers. It is not so much that the absolute pressure values themselves are so large but rather the ratio of these sound pressures to that of the minimum audible sound (P_r) encompasses a vast range, spanning a factor of 10 million from the faintest sound to that which is intense enough to produce pain. Furthermore, if we think in terms of intensity rather than pressure, recalling that intensity is related to the square of pressure, then the range of values becomes truly enormous.

Representing sound intensities

One way to reduce this range into a manageable set of values is to convert the linear ratio scale into a logarithmic one (Gulick et al., 1989; Hartmann, 1998). If we take the logarithm of the intensity ratio, we can then compress this scale into the so-called **bel** (B) scale, named in honour of Alexander Graham Bell. The intensity ratio in terms of the number of bels is therefore log (I_s/I_r). Looking again at Table 5.1 this means that the entire range of intensity ratio values shown here can be collapsed into a range spanning 0–18 (i.e., log 1 to log 10^{18}). Unfortunately, the compression produced by such a logarithmic transformation is

SideNote 5.8

More precisely, $I = P^2$ where I is intensity and P is the air pressure.

Table 5.1

Sound Level of Some Familiar Noises Shows the Vast Range of Values That Are Possible

Sound	Pressure Level (pascals)	Pressure Ratio (P_s/P_r)	Intensity Ratio (I_s/I_r)	dB$_{SPL}$
Minimal audible sound	0.00002 (P_r)	1	1	0
Soft whisper	0.0002	10	100	20
Quiet office	0.002	10^2	10^4	40
Average conversation	0.02	10^3	10^6	60
Vacuum cleaner	0.2	10^4	10^8	80
Subway train	2	10^5	10^{10}	100
Loud thunder	20	10^6	10^{12}	120
Jet engine at takeoff (pain threshold)	200	10^7	10^{14}	140
Wind tunnel	2,000	10^8	10^{16}	160
Space shuttle	20	10^9	10^{18}	180

Note. The pressure and intensity ratios are taken with respect to the minimum audible sound as the reference point (P_r).

a bit too excessive because the scale is so small that minor changes in intensity would be difficult to relate on the bel scale.

The solution to this problem is to convert the scale to one-tenths of a bel, or **decibel** (dB). Thus, 1 bel equals 10 decibels, and the formula above can be rewritten as follows:

$$dB = 10 \log (I_s/I_r) \quad \text{(SideNote 5.9)}$$

When the reference intensity (I_r) is taken to be the minimum audible sound level, which in terms of pressure is 20 μPa, we can then specify the decibel level as dB$_{SPL}$, where the notation *SPL* stands for *sound pressure level*. This is simply a convention that has been adopted. Of course, any reference value can be used as long as it is specified. Therefore, when dB values are shown as dB$_{SPL}$, we know right away that the minimal audible reference value was used.

As Table 5.1 shows, the range of human hearing spans from the minimum audible level or threshold of 0 dB$_{SPL}$ to 140 dB$_{SPL}$, at which point pain and damage result. Each tenfold increase in pressure ratio or hundredfold increase in intensity ratio is equivalent to an increase of only 20 dB$_{SPL}$. Although the advantage of the decibel scale is that it removes the burden of dealing with very large numbers, it should also be kept in mind that this is a logarithmic scale and therefore cannot be treated in terms of linear mathematics. For example, two sounds that are each 40 dB$_{SPL}$ do not together make an 80 dB$_{SPL}$ sound but rather a 46 dB$_{SPL}$ sound. And each decibel value corresponds to a greater change in intensity or pressure the higher the dB$_{SPL}$ (SideNote 5.10).

Sound frequency

A second primary property of a pure tone is its frequency. In the previous section, we noted that striking a tuning fork with greater force increases the amplitude of vibration. However, if we examine the resulting sound waveforms in Figure 5.4 again, we see that the cyclic pattern of the pressure changes remain the same along the x-axis. That is, the time scale of the pressure change was not affected, only its amplitude. This will always be true as long as the same tuning fork is used, no matter how strongly or lightly it is tapped. In other words, the **frequency** of the sound produced by any given tuning fork is always the same.

The sound waveforms of two different frequencies are shown in Figure 5.5. In both examples, a single **cycle** is represented as a complete vibration containing one instance of compression and one of rarefaction. In the first example, we see that one complete cycle required a 1-second duration. One way to define the frequency of a repetitive pattern is by the number of complete cycles per second, also known as *hertz* (Hz). The first waveform in Figure 5.5 therefore has a frequency of 1 Hz. The second waveform required a 2-second period to complete a single cycle and therefore has a frequency of 0.5 Hz. Although sounds can encompass a large range of frequencies, humans are only capable of hearing sounds under optimal conditions in the range of 20–20000 Hz (Howard, 2000; Speaks, 1999).

Sound frequency is governed by the vibrational properties of a sound source. A given tuning fork has a single vibrational property and therefore can create a pure tone of only one frequency. To create a different sound frequency, we will need to obtain a tuning fork with different physical characteristics. Not surprisingly, the two properties that specify the vibrational frequency of a sound source are its mass and stiffness (elasticity). As the stiffness or tension increases, so does the vibrational frequency. However, an increase in the mass of the

SideNote | **5.9**

The same formula in terms of pressure is

$$dB = 10 \log (P_s^2/P_r^2), \text{ or}$$

$$dB = 10 \log (P_s/P_r)^2$$

Since the logarithm of a number raised to a power is algebraically equivalent to the power multiplied by the log of the number, our equation can be rewritten as

$$dB = 20 \log (P_s/P_r)$$

This is the standard equation relating sound decibel in terms of pressure.

SideNote | **5.10**

Some values for the loudest recorded sounds in dB$_{SPL}$ include the loudest insect—song of the African cicada (106.7); loudest finger snap (108); loudest burp (118.1); loudest scream by a crowd—Party in the Park (Hyde Park, London), 1998 (126.3); loudest animal sound—low-frequency pulses by blue whales (188); loudest sound ever—volcanic eruption of Krakatoa in 1883 (dB level not known, but the sound could be heard up to 5,000 kilometres away).

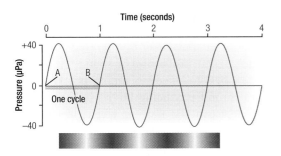
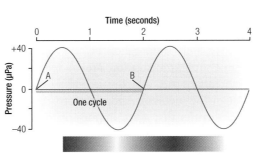

Figure 5.5

The frequency of a sound wave is defined by the number of cycles in a second (Hz). A complete cycle occurs when it begins and ends at the same point of displacement (e.g., points A to B). In the first example, a complete cycle spans a 1-second duration, whereas the second example spans 2 seconds. The two respective frequencies are therefore 1 Hz and 0.5 Hz.

SideNote 5.11

On a piano, lower frequency sounds are created by striking longer, thicker wires, whereas higher frequencies are created by striking shorter, thinner wires. A guitar can be tuned by changing the tension on the strings—the greater the tension, the higher the frequency.

SideNote 5.12

For this reason, temperature is usually specified when the speed of sound is given, especially if the medium is a gas or liquid.

object results in a decrease in vibrational frequency. The vibrational frequency that results from the combination of these two factors for any given object is known as its natural or **resonant frequency**. The length of an object must also be taken into account. Increasing the length also decreases the object's vibrational frequency (SideNote 5.11). To create a tuning fork with a higher vibrational frequency, we must either decrease its mass or the length of its prongs. Alternatively, we can increase the tension on the prongs, for example, by using a stiffer metal. In so doing, we will change the physical properties of the tuning fork, which in turn will alter its resonant frequency.

Speed of sound

Attempts to measure the speed of sound began in the 17th century with the simple procedure of measuring the time difference between the onset of a sound and its arrival some distance away. Since it was known by then that light travels much faster than sound (nearly one million times faster, to be precise), several experimenters used the flash of a gun as the cue for when the sound was generated. Although this might appear to be quite crude, the values obtained through such early efforts were actually quite accurate. Currently, the accepted value for the speed of sound in air at a temperature of 0°C is 331.5 metres/second or 742 miles/hour (Rossing & Fletcher, 2004).

We saw in the preceding sections that sound frequency depends on the physical characteristics of the sound source and that intensity depends upon its vibrational amplitude. The speed of sound, on the other hand, has nothing to do with the sound source but is entirely dependent upon the characteristics of the medium. Sounds of all frequencies and amplitudes travel at the same speed in a given medium. What then are the characteristics of the medium that affect sound speed? Again, the two main factors turn out to be inertia and elasticity. This should not be too surprising because sound propagation after all relies upon a sequential series of acoustic energy transfers through the medium. And therefore, the same characteristics that were important for sound generation should be expected to play a role in sound propagation as well.

The inertial property of the medium is usually expressed by way of its density, or mass per unit volume. The speed of sound is inversely related to the density of the medium—as the density increases, sound speed decreases (Berg & Stork, 2004; Rossing & Fletcher, 2004). For any given medium, one condition that affects this relationship is temperature (SideNote 5.12). As the temperature increases, a corresponding expansion in the medium causes a decrease in density, especially for a gaseous medium. As a result, the speed of sound increases because of the inverse relationship between sound speed and density. For air, each 1°C rise in temperature results in a 0.6 metres/second increase in sound speed.

Any astute student of physics (or a movie buff) knows that one way to tell if a train is coming before it can be heard is to sense the vibrations in the tracks. We noted before that sound can travel in any medium, and steel rails are no exception. It turns out that the speed of sound is much greater in steel than in air (Berg & Stork, 2004). This is surprising because steel is certainly much more dense than air and yet conducts sound almost 18 times faster, something that would not have been predicted from the inverse relationship between sound speed and density. However, the dominant factor here is the second parameter that determines sound speed in a medium—elasticity. Sound speed is directly related to elasticity. Thus, the greater the elasticity of the medium, the greater the speed of sound propagation. Although it is not intuitively obvious, steel has much greater elasticity than air because of its far greater tendency to return to its original shape if deformed. Similarly, water has greater elasticity than air, though not as much as steel. For this reason, sound waves will travel faster in steel than in water and faster in water than in air. Table 5.2 shows the speed of sound in several different gas, liquid, and solid media. In each example, the twin factors of density and elasticity govern the speed values shown.

3. COMPLEX SOUNDS

It has been convenient thus far to describe the fundamental properties of sound by way of pure tones produced by a tuning fork. However, most sound-producing bodies do not display simple harmonic motion when they vibrate; instead, the vibrational sequence that commonly occurs is quite complex. Most of the sounds in our environment—whether a note on a musical instrument, the sound of a human voice, or the noise of a busy city street—are characterized by pressure waveforms that are

Table **5.2**

The Speed of Sound in Different Media

Medium	Sound Speed (metres/second)
Gas	
Carbon dioxide	268
Air	331
Helium	972
Liquid	
Ethanol	1,130
Fresh water	1,402
Sea water	1,522
Solid	
Brass	4,700
Steel	5,790
Aluminum	6,420

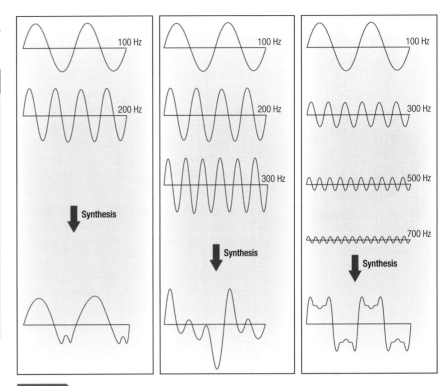

Figure 5.6

Complex periodic sound waves can be constructed by algebraically summing the amplitudes of two or more individual pure tones at each moment in time. The first example shows the synthesis of a complex periodic wave from two component sine waves of 100 and 200 Hz. The second example shows the result of combining waves in a harmonic series (100, 200, 300 Hz). In the third example, odd integral multiples of the first waveform, each with a progressively reduced amplitude, are combined.

far more complicated than the simple sinusoidal patterns that we have discussed. In general, these complex sounds can be classified as periodic and aperiodic.

Complex periodic sounds

A periodic sound occurs when the pattern of pressure change repeats itself at regular intervals over time (Rossing et al., 2001; Speaks, 1999). A pure tone is an example of a simple periodic wave. A complex periodic wave is a repeating wave that does not have a sinusoidal profile. Figure 5.6 shows three examples of how we can create a complex periodic pattern by combining a set of sinusoidal waveforms that differ in frequency. In the first example, we take two sine waves, one having a frequency of 100 Hz and another of 200 Hz and add them together algebraically. That is, at any given point in time, we simply add the respective amplitudes of the two sine waves to produce the compound wave shown at the bottom. In the second example, three waves with a frequency of 100, 200, and 300 Hz are similarly added together. In the third example, four sine waves with a frequency of 100, 300, 500, and 700 Hz are added together. However, in this example, the four sine waves differ not only in frequency but also in their amplitude (SideNote 5.13). The resulting compound wave in each of the three examples contains discrete patterns that are exactly duplicated in a cyclic manner, hence the term *complex periodic sound*.

What does complex periodic vibration sound like? That would of course depend on the nature of the waveform. Many of the sounds made by the human voice, especially vowel sounds, have a periodic waveform. Similarly, the notes on a musical instrument have a highly periodic profile characterized by the summation of a precise series of sine waves known as the **harmonic series** (Howard, 2000). A sound-producing musical body such as the string on a guitar vibrates as a whole at a **fundamental frequency**. However, parts of the string also vibrate separately but simultaneously to produce the so-called *overtone harmonics*. The overtone frequencies are whole number multiples of the fundamental frequency known as the *second, third, fourth harmonic* and so on. The middle panel in Figure 5.6 is an example of a harmonic series where the first waveform can be taken as the fundamental frequency (also known as the *first harmonic*) followed by two waveforms that represent the second and third harmonics. (We will have a more expanded discussion on the nature of musical sounds in Chapter 7.)

SideNote **5.13**

If a large number of waves in such a series are added together, the resulting composite wave appears to have abrupt modulations in pressure similar to turning a sound on and off in a periodic manner. This kind of a waveform is known as a *square wave*.

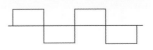

Baron Jean-Baptiste-Joseph
Fourier (1768–1830)
SCIENCE PHOTO LIBRARY

SideNote | **5.14**

A fuller understanding of
Fourier analysis requires
advanced mathematics and is
beyond the scope of this book;
excellent accounts can be
found in Yost (2000) and
Hartmann (1998).

Complex aperiodic sounds

The second category of complex sound is characterized by aperiodic patterns. The sounds produced by aperiodic vibration are also known as **noise** (Speaks, 1999). An example of noise is shown in Figure 5.7. As can be seen here, the vibrations appear to be random in nature, and it is virtually impossible to find any two time intervals where the changing pressure profile is exactly the same. An aperiodic waveform can be created by combining a large set of sound frequencies that have random, varying amplitudes. However, if the noise pattern is composed of all the frequencies within a particular range, such as the range of human hearing, then the sound is referred to as **white noise**. Some examples of sounds that approximate white noise are the roar of traffic, the whirling of a fan, the interference on a radio, and the noise from a large crowd. Although generally considered to be undesirable, there are examples of noise patterns that are soothing, such as the sound of waves breaking on a beach or the cascading sound of a waterfall. Many speech sounds, such as fricative sounds (e.g., "sh," "th," "ph," etc.), also have an aperiodic waveform.

Fourier analysis

It should be clear from our discussion thus far that the sinusoidal waveform can be viewed as a fundamental building block of sound. Regardless of how complex a sound pattern appears, it can always be considered to be the result of a combination of different sine waves, each of a particular frequency and amplitude. This leads to the following question: "Is the reverse also possible?"—that is, "Is it possible to deconstruct a complex periodic or aperiodic pattern into its constituent sinusoidal components?" Such a

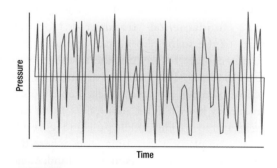

Figure 5.7

An example of a complex aperiodic waveform that can be constructed by adding sine waves encompassing a broad range of frequencies. There are no two time intervals in this noise pattern where the pressure fluctuations are identical.

process means that we would have to proceed in the reverse direction of that shown in Figure 5.6, starting with a complex pattern such as those shown at the bottom of the figure and then deriving the individual sine waves that serve as its building blocks.

A procedure for performing just such an operation was developed in the early 1800s by French mathematician Joseph Fourier (Berg & Stork, 2004; Rossing & Fletcher, 2004; Rossing et al., 2001). Fourier was interested in studying heat diffusion through solid bodies. During the course of that work, he came to the conclusion that any function, regardless of its complexity, can be decomposed into a series of sine-wave functions. The mathematical process for doing so, named **Fourier analysis** in his honour, has since been widely used in pure mathematics, applied physics, and engineering. The implications of Fourier analysis in acoustic research is that *any* complex waveform can indeed be decomposed into a series of sine-wave patterns without prior knowledge of exactly what those constituent patterns are (SideNote 5.14).

If we apply Fourier analysis to the complex periodic patterns in Figure 5.6, we would expect to obtain the same set of sinusoidal functions that were used during their synthesis. However, it would be rather cumbersome to portray all of the constituent sine waves in each case, especially if a complex pattern was made up of a large set of sine-wave functions. Figure 5.8 shows an alternate and more efficient way by which the Fourier components can be represented. We have thus far illustrated both simple and complex sounds as time-domain waveforms (i.e., in terms of pressure fluctuations over time). The set of sine-wave functions derived through Fourier analysis can instead be represented in terms of amplitude and frequency. Such a frequency-domain plot is called a *spectrum*, or more specifically, the **Fourier spectrum**, where the location of each vertical line along the x-axis shows the frequency of a particular sine-wave component, whereas its height gives its amplitude.

The first two examples in Figure 5.8 show the Fourier spectra as being composed of two and three frequencies, respectively, all of equal amplitude. The third pattern shows a Fourier spectrum composed of four frequencies of different amplitude. The use of a frequency-domain spectrum removes the need to plot out each of the component sine-wave functions, as in Figure 5.6. Essentially the same data is portrayed in both, though much more succinctly by way of a spectrum. The final example in Figure 5.8 shows the noise pattern from Figure 5.7. Fourier analysis results in a continuous spectrum composed of all frequencies within the range at equal amplitude. Therefore, this is an example of white noise.

Ohm's law of hearing

Our interest in Fourier analysis goes beyond the mere technical aspects of being able to represent complex sound patterns. The auditory system is faced with a similar problem—that is, how to decompose a complex sound into its constituent sinusoidal waves so that it can be processed more efficiently. Because there are an infinite variety of complex sound waveforms, it would be far easier to analyze their spectral components. As early as 1843, shortly after Fourier's work became widely accepted in Europe, German physicist Georg Ohm suggested that complex sound waves could also be subjected to Fourier analysis and that just such an operation occurs in hearing (Gulick et al., 1989; Speaks, 1999). This is now known as **Ohm's law of hearing**. As we will see later in this chapter, the ear actually does function as a type of Fourier analyzer in that it decomposes complex sound waveforms into their spectral components.

4.   SOUND TRANSMISSION

We have thus far regarded sound in terms of a sinusoidal or complex wave of pressure change as a function of time. It was implicit that the pressure was being measured immediately adjacent to the sound source. Since sound is also a travelling wave of pressure fluctuation through space, the obvious question that arises is how these pressure fluctuations persist as we move away from the sound source. In general, there are two factors that sound waves must contend with. The first is that sound intensity becomes dissipated with distance. The second is that sound waves must interact with objects in their path. The placement of various objects in the path of a sound can interfere with it in many complex ways, either enhancing or dampening it. We briefly explore these issues in this section.

The inverse square law

We know from common experience that sound intensity diminishes with distance. One way to understand this phenomenon is to

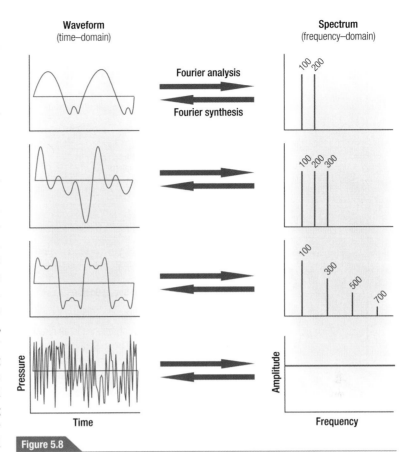

Figure 5.8

The complex sound patterns in Figures 5.6 and 5.7 can be decomposed into its constituent sine-wave functions by Fourier analysis. The resulting Fourier spectrum is represented by discrete lines whose position along the x-axis provides the frequency and whose height gives the amplitude. The individual frequency values are given above each line. The noise pattern at the bottom shows a continuous spectrum of equal amplitude among all of the frequencies. The reverse operation whereby the data in a Fourier spectrum is used to produce the complex waveform is known as *Fourier synthesis*.

consider an example where the sound originates from a point source, as shown in Figure 5.9 on page 150. The sound waves emerging from this source will radiate outward in all directions within the three-dimensional space. The moving wave front can be thought of as a sphere that progressively grows in diameter as the wave front moves outward. However, the energy contained in the sound is dissipated over a larger and larger area because the surface area of the sphere becomes progressively larger as we move away from the sound source. Since the area of the sphere grows by the square of that distance, sound intensity must decrease by a corresponding amount (Berg & Stork, 2004). Let us assume that a particular intensity value, denoted simply as "I," is apparent at a distance, "r," away from the sound source. As Figure 5.9 shows, doubling the distance (2r) would mean that intensity is reduced to one-quarter, and tripling the

Georg Simon Ohm (1789–1854)
© The Print Collector/Alamy

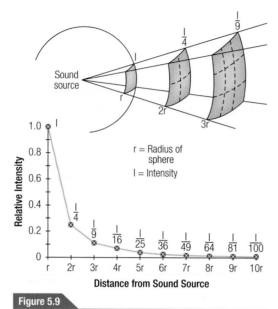

Figure 5.9

A point source produces sound that radiates in all directions to create a moving spherical wave front. Sound intensity dissipates with distance because the energy contained in the sound must be distributed over progressively larger areas of the sphere as the sound propagates outward. Since the area of a sphere increases by the square of its radius, sound intensity must be reduced by a corresponding amount. The graph shows how the relationship between sound intensity and distance obeys the inverse square law.

distance (3r) means a reduction to one-ninth of the original intensity. Sound intensity is therefore inversely related to the square of the distance from the sound source. This relationship is known as the **inverse square law**.

Interaction of sound with objects

The inverse square law is strictly true only if sound travels in a medium that is totally free of all other matter. However, this is rarely the case in our ordinary environment. By the time a particular sound reaches our ears, it will likely have interacted with several different obstacles in its path. The result of this interaction can take one of three forms—reflection, absorption, or diffraction.

When light hits a reflective surface, much of the incident light bounces back in a manner that can be predicted in precise geometric terms. The same is true of sound. A boundary can serve as a reflective surface if the second medium offers a greater resistance to sound transmission (SideNote 5.15). Although it is common to think of hard objects as being good sound reflectors, a considerable amount of reflection also occurs at an air–water interface where up to 99.9% of the incident sound

energy is reflected back toward the source. Reflected sounds are also called *echoes* or *reverberations*. A room with highly reflective walls is known as a *reverberant room*.

The sound that is not reflected at an interface between two different media is absorbed and may be transmitted through the second medium (Hartmann, 1998; Howard, 2000). The magnitude of absorption for any object is given by its absorption coefficient, which is simply the proportion of sound energy absorbed to that contained in the incident wave (Everest, 2000). Water, for example, has a very low absorption coefficient, whereas other objects such as Styrofoam, rubber, and certain kinds of ceiling tile can absorb upwards of one-third of the incident sound. A room whose walls are made of material with high sound absorbance is known as an *anechoic room*.

A third type of interaction occurs when sound waves encounter an object that is too small for either reflection or absorption to occur. In such cases, the sound waves bend around the object in a process that physicists call **diffraction**. A simple way to picture this is to think of the ripples in a pond and how they bend around small objects only to reform and continue. A large object would have the effect of halting the wave. Thus, the size difference between the wave and the object determines whether diffraction can occur efficiently. Sound waves of high frequency have more compressed undulations of pressure change and therefore cannot be diffracted as easily as sounds of lower frequency by a given object. In other words, a single cycle of low-frequency sound spans a greater amount of space and therefore can be diffracted more easily by a small object (SideNote 5.16).

Architectural acoustics

The properties of absorption and reflection discussed above become especially important considerations in the design of auditoriums and concert halls, where the goal is to maximize the quality of sound perceived by the audience (Beranek, 2003; Long, Levy, & Stern, 2005). Although acoustic concepts have been applied in structural design in a rudimentary way since ancient Greek civilization, it was not until the pioneering work of Wallace Sabine at Harvard University in the 19th century that the field of architectural acoustics matured fully. People in an enclosed space will hear not only the sound directly from the source

SideNote 5.15

The term generally used to convey resistance to sound transmission is *acoustic impedance*. Different materials have different degrees of acoustic impedance. The greater the impedance difference or mismatch at a surface, the greater the amount of sound reflection.

SideNote 5.16

As any stereo buff knows, high-pitched (high-frequency) sounds tend to be more directional because they bend less around objects (i.e., they are diffracted less). The low-pitched bass sounds spread out more and can be easily heard around corners because of their greater diffraction ability.

but also the various reflections from the floor, walls, and ceiling. Sabine noted that the most important factor in acoustic suitability is sound reflection, a factor that he quantified using the so-called **reverberation time**.

It comes as no surprise that considerable effort is made to take into account the acoustic factors that would be optimal for a particular concert hall. Certain concert halls are characterized by greater reverberation and are said to have more *fullness*, while other halls have less reverberation and are said to have greater *clarity*. There is no ideal reverberation for all applications. A hall that provides a fuller sound, for example, is better for musical performances from the Romantic period, whereas a hall with greater clarity is optimal for the rapid passages in the music of Bach and Mozart. Another consideration is *intimacy*—the impression of being physically close to the sound source, which occurs if the reverberant sound reaches the listener very quickly. Designers of music halls incorporate layers of sound-reflecting panels in the ceiling to achieve this effect. A number of other acoustic qualities such as *warmth*, *brilliance*, *texture*, and *blend* also become factored into the overall design of an auditorium (SideNote 5.17).

B. Auditory Processing of Sound—Physical Characteristics

The sound waves that arrive at our ears are detected by an apparatus that is as elegant as it is complex. The sensory systems that we have discussed in earlier chapters were responsible for signal detection at short range, whether it was in the form of pressure applied to the skin or chemicals that entered specific chambers in our body. The detection of sound represents the first example of a sensory process that captures signals originating far away and which display a very brief temporal quality. The ear accomplishes this by transmitting the acoustic pressures that arrive at the outer ear through a series of structures, ultimately causing a similar wave pattern to be generated within a fluid-enclosed chamber located near the middle of the head. In so doing, the ear must not only detect sound and convert it into a biological signal but must also find a way of encoding amplitude and frequency.

Our current understanding of exactly how this occurs has emerged from numerous competing theories that have been advanced over the last 150 years. Before describing the fascinating process of sound transduction, we first undertake an anatomical exploration of the human ear and describe the physical mechanisms by which sound is transmitted through it.

1. ANATOMICAL COMPONENTS OF THE HUMAN EAR

Sound waves are systematically transmitted through a series of structures within the ear. Each of these structures must retain the frequency characteristics of the original sound stimulus and transmit it in a way that causes the least disruption in amplitude. Although we usually refer to the ear by the flap of cartilaginous tissue on the side of the head, the human ear actually encompasses many more structures that are contained in one of three well-defined structural segments—the outer, middle, and inner ear (see Figure 5.10).

The outer ear

The outer ear consists of three parts—the visible part of the ear or **pinna**, the **external auditory canal**, and the eardrum or **tympanic membrane** (Bear, Connors, & Paradiso, 2006;

SideNote | **5.17**

Smaller concert halls in general have better acoustics because clarity declines once the seating capacity exceeds 2,000. London's famous Royal Albert Hall built in 1871 is well known for its acoustic problems that stem from its large seating capacity of over 5,000. One of the concert halls renowned for its excellent acoustics is the Stadt-Casino in Basel, Switzerland, which has a seating capacity of only 1,400.

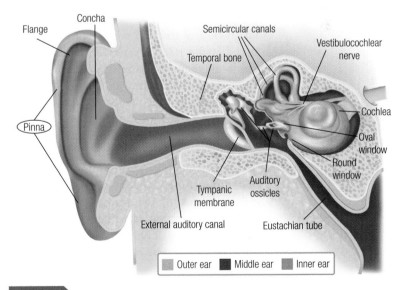

Figure 5.10

The structural components of the ear can be placed into one of three compartments—the outer, middle, or inner ear. The outer ear is composed of the pinna, external auditory canal, and the tympanic membrane (eardrum). The middle ear contains three tiny bones (ossicles). The inner ear contains two separate functional components that are integrated within a common bony structure (the semicircular canals, which are used in vestibular function, and the cochlea, which is used in hearing).

SideNote | **5.18**

A common example of reduced outside pressure occurs in an airplane after takeoff. The cabin pressure declines slightly as the plane gains altitude, producing an outward force on the eardrum due to the pre-existing higher pressure in the middle ear chamber. The dull hearing sensation that this produces can be relieved by swallowing or yawning, which opens the narrow eustachian tube that usually remains closed.

SideNote | **5.19**

The malleus, incus, and stapes are commonly referred to as the *hammer, anvil,* and *stirrup.* The malleus resembles a club more than a hammer, and the incus looks more like a premolar tooth. The stapes is the smallest bone in the body (3 mm in length).

Musiek & Baran, 2006). The pinna is composed of cartilage and serves as a sound funnel. In certain animals, it contains muscles that allow it to move in the direction of incoming sound. However, the human pinna lacks any musculature and is therefore a passive receptor of sound. It is composed of several visible bumps and grooves that together enhance the transmission of certain sounds. Sound waves are funnelled by the pinna into the external auditory canal. This canal is mildly S-shaped and approximately 25 mm in length and 5 to 7 mm in diameter. The outer half of the canal is lined by cartilage, whereas the remaining inner part is covered by skin lining the temporal bone (see Figure 5.10). The wax-secreting glands that line the canal protect the eardrum from small foreign objects.

The external auditory canal is covered at its innermost end by the eardrum, which by definition serves as the interior boundary of the external ear. The eardrum is a thin elastic membrane that is approximately 10 mm in diameter. It is attached to the skin of the external auditory canal and completely seals it off. The incoming sound waves set off a similar vibrational pattern in the eardrum. This vibrational sequence is then passed on to the components of the middle ear. In addition to its role in sound transmission, the eardrum also provides protection to the middle ear against intrusion by foreign bodies.

The middle ear

The next area through which sound is transmitted is the middle ear—an air-filled space within the temporal bone located immediately adjacent to the eardrum (see Figure 5.10). The middle ear is a roughly rectangular chamber with the eardrum forming one wall and the remainder being formed by thin plates of bone. The only exception is the front wall of the chamber, which opens up into the narrow **eustachian tube** that connects the middle ear with the back of the throat. If the middle ear was a completely closed airtight chamber, then the vibrational properties of the eardrum would be significantly compromised by changes in outside air pressure. For example, increased outside pressure would push the eardrum inward, whereas decreased pressure would do the opposite. The added tension caused by such forces upon the eardrum would reduce its vibrational response to incoming sound waves, resulting in reduced hearing. Because the eustachian tube is connected to the outside air,

it provides a means for equalizing any pressure differences across the eardrum and therefore allows it to operate efficiently under different atmospheric pressures (SideNote 5.18).

Sound waves arriving at the eardrum may be subsequently transmitted through the middle ear in one of three ways. First, the sound can be transmitted through the bony matrix of the head. Second, it can be conducted through the air that is present in the middle ear space. Although both of these mechanisms can theoretically play a role in sound transmission, their effect is quite negligible due to considerable dampening of the sound stimulus. Instead, a third mechanism has evolved that physically conducts the sound vibrations through a series of bony levers to the inner ear. The three bones involved in this process from the outside-in are called the *malleus, incus,* and *stapes.* Together they are known as the auditory **ossicles** (SideNote 5.19).

The ossicles are shown in detail in Figure 5.11. They are suspended in the middle ear space by ligaments and connected to each other to form what is commonly referred to as the *ossicular chain.* The malleus is made up of a long bony protrusion called the *handle.* It is this part of the malleus that is physically attached to

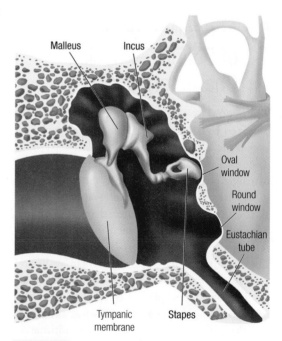

Figure 5.11

An expanded view of the middle ear chamber containing the three ossicles. The connection order of the ossicles starting from the eardrum is the malleus, incus, and stapes. The latter is directly connected to the oval window of the cochlea. The middle ear is ventilated by the eustachian tube.

the eardrum. The *head* of the malleus is tightly connected to the *body* of the second bone, the incus. The shaft of the incus, called the *long process*, forms a joint with the *head* of the third bone, the stapes. The stapes, which lies horizontally and at a right angle to the incus, has an oval-shaped *footplate*, which makes a tight connection with the *oval window* of the inner ear. The vibration of the eardrum is conducted through this ossicular chain and transferred to the inner ear at the oval window. The suspension of the ossicles in the middle ear chamber permits these bones to vibrate freely and therefore provide an efficient and faithful transmission of the original acoustic pattern.

The inner ear

The temporal bone contains a cavity known as the *bony labyrinth*. The labyrinth has two structural subdivisions, each of which contains different functional organs. One of them is the *semicircular canals*, which are fluid-filled bony cavities that are part of the **vestibular system** and are used to transmit information about balance and body position in space (Moller, 2006). We will not discuss the vestibular system here but rather devote our attention to the second component of the inner ear, the **cochlea**, which is part of the auditory system. As Figure 5.12 shows, both structures are part of an integrated physical complex that makes up the inner ear (Yost, 2000). They both have similar operational properties even though they serve different sensory functions.

The cochlea is a coiled fluid-filled bony structure that contains the sensory transduction apparatus of hearing (SideNote 5.20) (Deutsch & Richards, 1979; Moller, 2006; Yost, 2000). It is here that the physical energy contained in sound waves gives rise to the electrochemical signals that are transmitted to the brain. The spiral form of the cochlea begins at its basal end and makes almost two-and-a-half turns before ending at the apex. If the cochlea were to be uncoiled and stretched out, it would be about 35 mm in length. The diameter at the base would be about 9 mm and somewhat less at the apex due to its tapering nature.

The interior of the cochlea is divided into three separate fluid-filled channels, as shown in Figure 5.12 (Deutsch & Richards, 1979). The largest of the three is the *scala vestibuli*. In a cross-sectional view of the cochlea, it would appear as the uppermost of the three channels

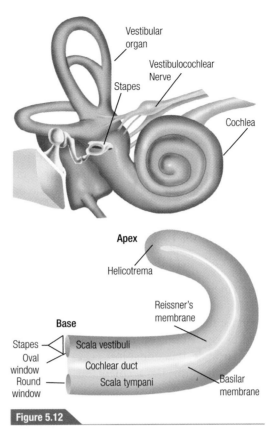

Figure 5.12

The cochlea is embedded within the temporal bone. The internal structure of the cochlea is shown in uncoiled form (bottom).

extending from the base to the apex. The oval window, which we described as being connected with the stapes, can be found at the basal end of the scala vestibuli. The lowermost of the three channels is the *scala tympani*. The basal end of this channel contains a very thin membrane that forms the *round window*.

The scalae vestibuli and tympani are actually connected to each other through a small aperture at the apex known as the *helicotrema*. Thus, both of these channels contain the same watery fluid. Sandwiched between these two channels is the *scala media*, often referred to as the *cochlear duct*. This is the smallest of the three channels and occupies only about 7% of the total volume of the cochlea. A very thin and delicate membrane known as *Reissner's membrane* separates this channel from the scala vestibuli; the *basilar membrane* separates the cochlear duct from the scala tympani (see Figure 5.12). Unlike the other two channels, the cochlear duct is a self-contained chamber filled with a different fluid. The two fluids do not come into contact with each other. They both have similar consistency, though somewhat different ionic concentrations.

SideNote | **5.20**

Cochlea is derived from the Greek word for *snail* in reference to its spiral structure. The cochlea is not a freestanding structure but rather a spiral cavity within the temporal bone, considered to be one of the hardest in the body.

Sound transmission through the ear

We can now present a complete picture of sound transmission through the various components of the ear, especially the inner ear, using the illustration in Figure 5.13 (Hartmann, 1998; Moller, 2006; Yost, 2000). We have already noted that sound waves are funnelled by the pinna and transmitted through the external auditory canal to the eardrum, where a similar vibrational pattern is set off. This pattern is then conducted by the auditory ossicles into the cochlea through the oval window. The back and forth movement of the stapes upon the oval window makes it act like an accordion. This sets off a compressional sound wave in the fluid of the scala vestibuli. The vibrational properties of the wave pattern in this fluid environment mimic the original sound stimulus except that it is now characterized by oscillations of liquid molecules rather than air molecules (SideNote 5.21).

An inward displacement of the stapes upon the oval window creates a momentary increase in pressure that is immediately distributed throughout the cochlear fluids. The increased pressure generated within the scala vestibuli is transmitted across Reissner's membrane, through the cochlear duct, and across the basilar membrane into the scala tympani. This is shown in Figure 5.13 by the series of arrows within the cochlea. The increased pressure within the scala tympani must then be dissipated somehow. This is the function of the round window, which is an elastic membrane found at the basal end of the scala tympani. Any increase in fluid pressure in the scala tympani

is relieved by an outward distension of the round window. This entire sequence occurs in the opposite direction during those moments when the stapes moves outward.

The result of the pressure fluctuations in the cochlear fluids is to cause movement of the membranes that separate the three channels. In particular, the up and down movement of the basilar membrane turns out to be the critically important outcome in this entire sequence because the neural transduction apparatus rests upon this membrane. One feature of this entire mechanism is to maintain the fidelity of incoming signals with respect to the two principal characteristics of sound—amplitude and frequency. The challenge for the auditory structures of the ear is to ensure that the vibrational pattern ultimately produced in the cochlear fluid accurately portrays the sound stimulus with regard to these two parameters. Any loss, disruption, or modification of either to a significant degree would have negative consequences for hearing. In the next two sections, we discuss how the remarkable design of the auditory system ensures that sound amplitude is adequately preserved and that sound frequency is properly represented within the cochlea.

2.   AMPLITUDE PRESERVATION

The evolution of animals from the sea to land produced vertebrates with an inner ear that remained filled with fluid (SideNote 5.22). However, the neural sound detectors residing within this fluid-filled chamber were now

SideNote | **5.21**

The speed of sound conduction is considerably higher in liquid than in air. As a result, the sound stimulus travels about four times faster within the cochlea, taking a mere 25 millionths of a second to traverse its length.

SideNote | **5.22**

Marine animals possess very specialized systems for detecting vibrational events in their environment. For example, the *lateral line* system in fish is a network of sensory receptors located around the head and extending down both sides of the fish to its tail. This system detects pressure changes in the surrounding water.

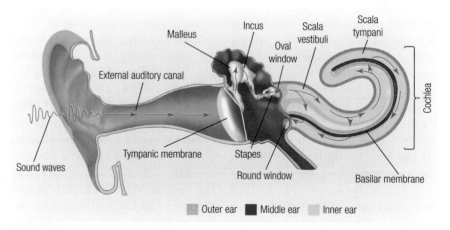

Outer ear ■ Middle ear Inner ear

Figure 5.13

Sound waves are captured by the pinna and funnelled into the external auditory canal. Sound vibration is conducted through the auditory ossicles to arrive at the oval window where it is transmitted to the fluid environment of the cochlea.

required to detect pressure changes taking place in a different medium—air. It turns out that sound waves are almost entirely reflected back at an air–water interface, resulting in minimal sound transmission into the liquid. It has been estimated that there would be a 30 dB pressure loss if the sound waves were delivered directly through air to the oval window (SideNote 5.23). A particular evolutionary challenge for the terrestrial auditory apparatus therefore was to develop mechanisms that overcame the large vibrational amplitude loss that would occur with sounds reaching the cochlear interface on their own. There are four key physical features of the human auditory system that make up for this potential loss (Deutsch & Richards, 1979; Geisler, 1998; Moller, 2006).

The lever effect

The transmission of acoustic energy through the bones of the middle ear produces a certain amount of amplification. As the sound energy is transferred from the malleus to the incus, there is a small increment in mechanical force because of the difference in the relative sizes of the two ossicles. This is known as the *lever effect*, and it accounts for an estimated amplification of 2 dB. However, this means that much of the 30 dB loss that would otherwise occur at the cochlear interface still needs to be made up somehow.

The condensation effect

Much of that potential loss is made up by the so-called *condensation effect* that occurs from the design of the auditory components. The sound collected by the eardrum is channelled through the ossicles onto the footplate of the stapes. The surface area of the eardrum is nearly 20 times larger than the surface area of the footplate. As a result, the vibrational pressures condense from a large area to a small area, producing an amplification that is nearly related to the ratio of two surface areas. The net effect of the condensation property is to provide a pressure gain of almost 25 dB. Thus, the lever and condensation effects together produce sufficient amplification to nearly offset the loss that would have otherwise occurred during sound transmission from air to a liquid environment.

The resonance effect

The sound gain offered by the above two effects is maximal in the frequency range of 500 to 2000 Hz. Much of the acoustic energy

that strikes the eardrum within this range is therefore effectively transmitted by the middle ear to the cochlear fluids. However, there is some boosting of sound frequencies outside of this range as well due to the resonant properties of the outer ear. As we noted earlier, all objects have a certain resonant property that is related to its mass and elasticity. An enclosed tube such as the external auditory canal is no exception. In this case, the resonant frequency is about 2500 Hz, and therefore sounds of this frequency are boosted somewhat as they travel down the canal (SideNote 5.24). Similarly, the resonant properties of the pinna account for a gain in sounds in the 4000 to 5000 Hz frequency range. The two parts of the pinna that contribute most to this are the flange and concha (see Figure 5.10). The resonant properties of these various outer ear components together can produce a net pressure gain of about 10 to 15 dB in sound frequencies spanning 2500 to 5000 Hz.

The directional effect

The ossicular chain of the middle ear provides another key contribution in that it channels all of the incoming sound energy only upon the oval window. This is sometimes referred to as the *directional effect*. The sound energy delivered to the oval window causes a reciprocal movement of the round window. As the stapes moves the oval window inward, the round window moves outward to relieve the pressure, and vice versa. In the absence of an ossicular chain, both the oval and round windows would be equally affected by incoming sound waves, resulting in no real net movement of cochlear fluid. As a result, the vibrational amplitudes within the cochlea would be effectively reduced by as much as a thousandfold (60 dB), thus having a dramatic impact upon hearing. This is precisely what happens in certain diseases of the middle ear where the function of the ossicles is impaired (SideNote 5.25).

3.   FREQUENCY REPRESENTATION

The second key sound parameter that needs to be faithfully encoded by the mechanical components of the ear is frequency. We have already noted that the conductive structures of the ear, from the eardrum to the stapes, show a vibrational pattern that mimics the sound stimulus in terms of its frequency content. This is also true of the compressional waves

SideNote | **5.23**

This value is derived from the fact that only 0.1% of the incident sound energy is transmitted across an air–water interface. Because water is a dense and incompressible medium relative to air, much greater pressures would be needed to cause vibrational sequences in the cochlear fluid, something that cannot be effectively achieved by sound waves in air.

SideNote | **5.24**

The external auditory canal's vibrational properties can amplify the sound if it has a frequency that matches the canal's own resonant frequency (i.e., 2500 Hz). This phenomenon is an example of a well-known law in physics concerning the interaction of sound waves with an object.

SideNote | **5.25**

The net result of all the mechanical properties of the human ear is to produce considerable auditory sensitivity within a range of middle frequencies. It has been estimated that we are capable of hearing sounds under optimal conditions that cause movement of the eardrum by as little as 1 angstrom (1/10,000,000 of a millimetre).

SideNote 5.26

The resonance theory cannot account for the full range of frequencies that are audible to humans. Furthermore, the fine frequency discrimination that is possible by humans cannot be physically accounted for by a series of resonating fibres that also signal rapid changes in frequency, such as those that occur in speech or music. And finally, it turned out that the basilar membrane was a continuous membrane rather than a series of individual fibres.

SideNote 5.27

Proponents of the *frequency theory* regarded the cochlea merely as an energy transducer that was involved in converting physical signals to biological ones. Accordingly, the interpretation of the neural code is left entirely up to the brain, which deciphers the frequency and amplitude of the electrical waveform into a meaningful perceptual representation of pitch and loudness.

Ernest Rutherford (1871–1937)
© The Print Collector/Alamy

that occur in the cochlear fluids from the movement of the oval window. The critical question therefore concerns how cochlear fluid movement subsequently affects the basilar membrane and whether it too is capable of moving up and down at the same frequency as the sound stimulus.

This has been one of the fundamental questions in auditory research since the mid-1800s, by which time it was well established that the neural elements involved in sound processing lie on top of the basilar membrane and within the cochlear duct. Movement of the basilar membrane therefore represents the key end-product of the sequence of mechanical events in the ear. As a result, there was much theoretical and experimental research aimed at trying to understand the nature of the basilar membrane, how it responds to fluid movement in the cochlea, and the frequency characteristics of that response. The scientific problem at hand was to figure out how the auditory system contends with a large range of sound frequencies that are audible to humans and what mechanisms can best accommodate this range in the most effective manner.

An early idea proposed by Hermann von Helmholtz, an influential 19th-century German physicist and physiologist, was that the basilar membrane was composed of a series of fibres tuned to different frequencies. According to his resonance theory, the sound of a particular frequency would set an appropriate fibre in motion that would then stimulate a dedicated nerve fibre projecting to the brain. Although this idea was appealing at first, it had to be abandoned because it failed to account for a number of properties of hearing (SideNote 5.26). The two main theories that were proposed afterwards became ingrained within the auditory field (Musiek & Baran, 2006; Yost, 2000). What is particularly striking about these two theories is that they are completely different from each other.

The *frequency* theory

The most radical challenge to the resonance theory was offered in 1886 by Ernest Rutherford, the famous British physicist and Nobel laureate who correctly described the structure of the atom. According to Rutherford, the basilar membrane was capable of vibrating within the full range of frequencies that are audible to humans (i.e., 20 to 20000 Hz). His so-called **frequency theory** asserted that

auditory nerve fibres were stimulated by the basilar membrane and that it was their firing rate that conveyed sound frequency information to the brain. Thus, the mechanical structures of the ear not only vibrated in synchrony with the sound stimulus, so did the electrical firing rate of neurons at multiple levels within the auditory system. However, the question of how sound intensity could be encoded was left unanswered. Rutherford proposed that more intense sounds produced an electrically larger response in auditory neurons. Thus, according to the frequency theory, the electrical discharge profile in these neurons mirrored the sound stimulus—that is, neural firing rate mirrored sound frequency, and neural firing amplitude mirrored sound intensity (SideNote 5.27).

Although Rutherford did not know it at the time, the firing properties of neurons were squarely at odds with his theory. It was later shown that neurons always fire in an all-or-none manner and that the size of the neural impulse was always constant. This meant that the amplitude of electrical discharges in auditory neurons cannot encode sound intensity. Furthermore, the discharge rate of all neurons is constrained by the time required to complete an action potential. Consequently, neuronal firing rates rarely exceed 500 impulses per second, well below the 20000 that would be needed to signal the upper frequency limit in humans. A final problem with the frequency theory was that it assumed the width of the basilar membrane was uniform, for only then would it have the physical property necessary to oscillate in its entirety at the same frequency as the sound stimulus. However, the width of the basilar membrane is actually uneven, a fact that had great bearing for the second, and more acclaimed, theory of frequency coding.

The *place* theory

The fundamental idea behind the **place theory** is that sounds of different frequencies produce a vibrational pattern whose maximum amplitude occurs at different places along the basilar membrane. This idea, which was proposed by Georg von Békésy in 1928, represents one of the most striking examples in science where a theory is advanced on the basis of fundamental physical principles and then confirmed through an exquisite series of experiments (SideNote 5.28).

Von Békésy was aware that the basilar membrane had an uneven width (Deutsch

& Richards, 1979; Gulick et al., 1989). This is a somewhat peculiar aspect of the cochlea. Even though it becomes narrower toward the apex, the basilar membrane contained within it actually becomes wider. Furthermore, the tension on the basilar membrane is higher at the basal end. Both of these factors together suggested to von Békésy that the basilar membrane could not show the same vibrational response to sounds of different frequencies. The reason for this is based on the fact that the gradient in width and tension from one end to the other produce a systematic change in the natural or resonant frequency of the basilar membrane throughout its length. Von Békésy proposed that vibrational disturbances in the cochlear fluids set up a travelling wave within the basilar membrane whereby a pure tone of a particular frequency produces maximum displacement only at the point where it coincides with the resonant frequency of the basilar membrane. The concept of the travelling wave is illustrated in Figure 5.14 along with an uncoiled depiction of the basilar membrane (Yost, 2000).

The experimental side of Békésy's research was carried out by way of direct observation of the cochlea and through simulations in a mechanical model that he constructed. The model confirmed that there was indeed a direct relationship between sound frequency and the point of maximal displacement along the

basilar membrane. Further support came from direct observations of the basilar membrane within cochlea that were intact and obtained from human cadavers. Békésy discovered that sinusoidal movement of the oval window by artificial means produced a displacement pattern on the basilar membrane that could best be described as a travelling wave. However, a detailed analysis of the basilar membrane's physical response to sound stimulation had to await the development of more sensitive techniques, such as laser interferometry and the Mössbauer technique (SideNote 5.29).

We noted in Section A.2 that sound frequency is closely related to the size and tension of an object. The larger the size, the lower the resonant frequency. However, the greater the tension, the greater the resonant frequency. These two general relationships apply to the basilar membrane as well and are in fact responsible for producing its vibrational response characteristics. The smaller width (size) and higher tension at the basal end produce a higher resonant frequency in this part of the basilar membrane. As we proceed toward the apex, the increasing width and decreasing tension progressively lower the resonant frequency. As a result, a high-frequency sound stimulus will produce maximum vibration at the basal end of the basilar membrane, whereas low-frequency sound will yield maximum displacement toward the apical end. As Figure 5.15 on page 158 shows, there is a systematic decrease in the resonant frequency of the basilar membrane with increasing distance toward the apex (Gulick et al., 1989).

Tonotopic organization

The most important consequence of the place theory is that the basilar membrane's resonant frequency is organized in a topographic manner. The actual way that frequency is represented is called the **tonotopic map** (Musiek & Baran, 2006; Syka & Merzenich, 2005). We have seen in earlier chapters that sensory information is often systematically represented (e.g., body surface in a somatotopic map and chemical features in a chemotopic map). In the auditory system, it is sound frequency that is mapped onto a key sensory structure. In this case, the vibrational response of the basilar membrane changes systematically to encompass nearly the full frequency range that is audible to humans. Figure 5.16 shows the tonotopic map of the basilar membrane

Georg von Békésy (1899–1972)
© The Print Collector/Alamy

SideNote | **5.28**

Békésy became interested in human hearing while working on problems of long-distance communication at the Hungarian telephone system laboratory. He received the Nobel Prize in 1961 for his research contributions to auditory coding.

SideNote | **5.29**

Laser interferometry is carried out by analyzing the reflection of a laser beam from the surface of a membrane. The Mössbauer technique relies on the analysis of changes in the emitted radiation of a radioactive probe placed on the basilar membrane. Both techniques have confirmed that the mechanical response function of the basilar membrane best fits the place theory.

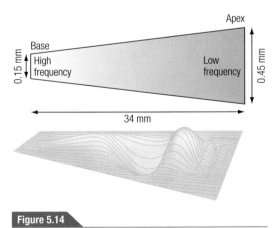

Figure 5.14

The width of the basilar membrane is smallest at the basal end (toward the oval window) and expands gradually toward the apex, where it is nearly three times as wide. The effect of this non-uniform width is to produce a travelling wave of displacement in the basilar membrane in response to cochlear stimulation by a pure tone. The maximum amplitude of the travelling wave occurs at a point where the stimulus frequency coincides with the natural (resonant) frequency of the basilar membrane.

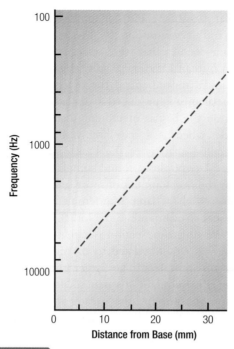

The physical properties of the basilar membrane produce a systematic preference for sound frequencies along its length. The smaller width and higher tension at the basal end make this part of the basilar membrane more sensitive to higher frequencies. The gradient of increasing width and decreasing tension toward the apex results in a progressive sensitivity toward lower sound frequencies. Adapted from *Hearing: Physiological Acoustics, Neural Coding, and Psychoacoustics,* by W. L. Gulick, G. A. Gescheider, and R. D. Frisina, 1989, New York, NY: Oxford University Press.

Place theorists believe that the cochlea is responsible not only for auditory transduction but also for frequency analysis. Thus, frequency coding by the basilar membrane can simply be passed on to the neural elements. In the frequency theory, however, the basilar membrane was just a passive vibrator and therefore the neural elements had to encode the full frequency range.

This idea was originally proposed by Georg Ohm (see Ohm's law of hearing in Section A.3), although the actual details of how it could be achieved were not known at the time.

within the coiled cochlea. The upper frequency limit of human hearing is represented at the base, whereas the lower limit is represented at the apex, with all intermediate frequencies in between. An important outcome of this systematic representation is that neural coding of frequency can be accomplished quite effectively if it is linked to the tonotopic organization of the basilar membrane (SideNote 5.30). We will shortly return to this idea and take it up more fully in our discussion of auditory transduction.

Frequency analysis of complex sounds

We noted before that the vast majority of sounds that we commonly hear are composed of mixtures of different frequencies. The place theory provides an elegant means for processing such complex sounds (Gulick et al., 1989; Luce, 1993; Yost, 2000). Any sound regardless of the complexity of its waveform can be theoretically decomposed into a set of sinusoidal functions by way of Fourier analysis. It

turns out that the auditory system performs a filtering operation that ends up producing a similar kind of frequency decomposition. When the ear is exposed to a complex sound, a vibrational disturbance is created in the cochlear fluid that follows the complex waveform of the sound stimulus exactly. However, because of the vibrational restrictions placed upon the basilar membrane by its physical characteristics, it is the sine-wave components of the complex sound that produce the vibrational disturbance there. Furthermore, these only occur where the frequencies in the sound's spectrum match the resonant frequency of the basilar membrane.

Figure 5.17 shows an example of how this occurs. The complex sound wave shown here has a spectrum containing four sine waves of differing frequencies (1000, 3000, 5000, and 7000 Hz). The basilar membrane operates as a filter when exposed to this sound pattern whereby a maximal vibrational disturbance is produced by each of the frequency components only at the corresponding tonotopic locations. In effect, the basilar membrane functions as a sort of frequency analyzer. This operation can be thought of as a physical counterpart to the mathematical procedure of Fourier analysis (SideNote 5.31). The distribution of vibrational perturbations across the basilar membrane can then be analyzed by the neural components of the auditory system. The physical properties of the basilar membrane, therefore, provide a highly effective means for encoding and representing complex sounds.

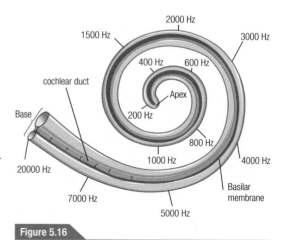

The tonotopic map of the basilar membrane as it appears within the coiled cochlea. The frequency preference of the basilar membrane changes systematically along its entire length to encompass the full frequency range of human hearing.

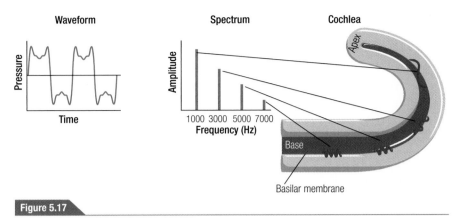

Figure 5.17

The Fourier spectrum of the complex sound pattern shown on the left reveals four sine waves of differing frequency and amplitude. When the complex sound stimulus arrives at the ear, the individual sine-wave constituents produce maximum vibrational amplitude only at the point in the basilar membrane where their frequencies coincide with the tonotopic frequency.

C. Auditory Processing of Sound—Biological Mechanisms

We have thus far concentrated on the physical interactions of sound with the anatomical components of the ear but have said nothing about how the sound energy is converted into signals that are biologically relevant. At some point, the sound stimulus must be transduced into a neural signal, which the brain can then interpret to produce the perceptual impression of hearing. This section will be devoted to understanding the processes that underlie sensory transduction, the nature of the neural signals that are produced in the cochlea as a result, and the paths taken by those signals to reach the auditory cortex.

1. AUDITORY TRANSDUCTION

The conversion of vibrational to neural signals occurs within a structure that lies on top of the basilar membrane. The **organ of Corti**, named after Italian anatomist Alfonso Corti who first described it in 1851, is a group of cells and associated structures that spans the entire length of the cochlea (Bear et al., 2006; Luce, 1993; Spoendlin, 1974). Because of its close proximity to the basilar membrane, any vibrational disturbance there is imparted onto the organ of Corti. It is this mechanical stimulation that produces the initial bioelectric response through a remarkable process, thereby generating the first event in the neural processing of sound.

Organ of Corti—structural features

The organ of Corti is located entirely within the cochlear duct and is therefore immersed in the fluid contained in that chamber. Figure 5.18 on page 160 shows a cross-section of the cochlea, revealing the relationship of the organ of Corti with respect to other cochlear structures. The finer structural elements within the organ of Corti are shown in the bottom panel. One of the most prominent features is the *arch of Corti*, a rigid inverted "V" structure. The pillars rest upon the basilar membrane in a longitudinal series that runs the length of the cochlea. The arches divide the organ of Corti into an inner and outer portion (SideNote 5.32).

There are several different cell types within the organ of Corti, most of them serving a supporting function. The most important cells with regard to auditory signal processing are the **hair cells**, of which there are two types (Hudspeth, 1997). There is a single row of *inner hair cells* located on the inner side of the arch and extending the full length of the cochlea. In humans, there are approximately 3,000 to 3,500 inner hair cells. The second type is the *outer hair cells*. These are located on the outer side of the arch and arranged in three separate rows, also spanning the entire length of the cochlea. There are approximately 12,000 outer hair cells in each human cochlea. As their name implies, both types of hair cells contain fine filaments, called **stereocilia**, that protrude from their upper surface. Inner hair cells have about 40 such filaments arranged in two or more parallel rows. The outer hair cells have about 150 filaments that form a V-shaped arrangement (see Figure 5.19 on page 160).

SideNote | **5.32**

Corti looked at the arches from above and reported them as free-standing rods. Von Helmholtz and others took this mistaken description as evidence of tuned resonators whose stimulation by sound triggered nearby nerve fibres. The correct arch-like description was later provided by Otto Deiters in 1860, which then produced uncertainty about the tuned-resonator theory (see Section B.3).

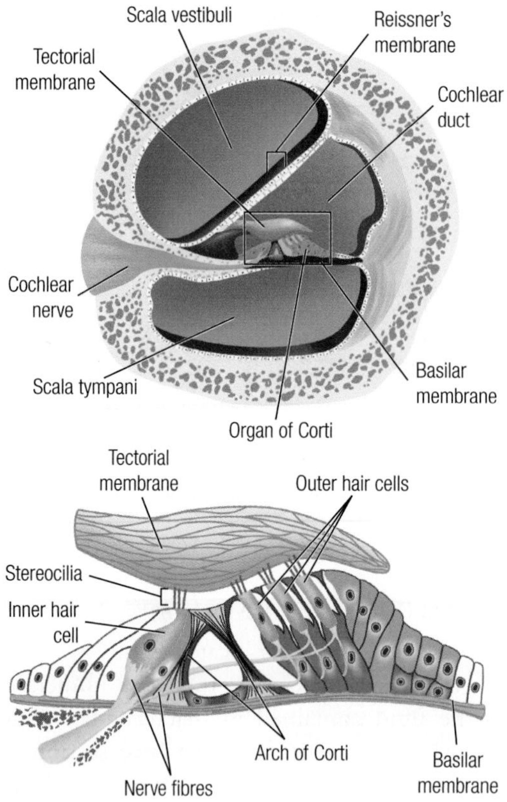

Scala vestibuli

Reissner's membrane

Tectorial membrane

Cochlear duct

Cochlear nerve

Scala tympani

Basilar membrane

Organ of Corti

Tectorial membrane

Outer hair cells

Stereocilia

Inner hair cell

Nerve fibres

Arch of Corti

Basilar membrane

Figure 5.18

A cross-sectional view of the cochlea showing all three fluid chambers (top panel). The organ of Corti rests on the basilar membrane within the cochlear duct. The cochlear nerve emerges from the organ of Corti and follows the coiled excursion of the cochlea. The area within the rectangular outline is shown in higher magnification in the bottom panel, revealing the cellular and structural elements of the organ of Corti.

A soft gelatinous structure called the **tectorial membrane** lies above the cellular components of the organ of Corti (Luce, 1993; Richardson, Lukashkin, & Russell, 2008). It too runs the entire length of the cochlea, attached to its inner margin. The stereocilia of the outer hair cells are connected with the tectorial membrane. Both the tectorial membrane and the arch of Corti serve a critical function in transferring the vibrational energy in the basilar membrane throughout the organ of Corti, with important consequences for the hair cells where that energy is ultimately transduced into a neural signal.

Organ of Corti—mechanical response to sound stimulation

The propagation of a travelling wave in the basilar membrane produces a complex set of mechanical events within the organ of Corti (Hudspeth, 1999). The result of the up and down movement of the basilar membrane is to produce lateral shearing forces by the tectorial membrane and arches of Corti. To understand how this occurs, two facts must be kept in mind. First, movement of the basilar membrane also produces movement in the tectorial membrane because of their attachment through the stereocilia of the outer hair cells. And second, as Figure 5.20 shows, the hinges (fulcrum) of the tectorial and basilar membranes are laterally displaced. Since this is the point through which these membranes pivot, there will be different relative motions of the two membranes depending upon whether the deflection is upward or downward. The two membranes do not move in concert but actually slide in opposite directions of each other, thereby producing a shearing motion between the cells in the organ of Corti and the tectorial membrane. An upward deflection of the basilar membrane will produce a shearing force toward the outer margins of the cochlea (shown by the rightward arrow in Figure 5.20), whereas a downward deflection will produce a shearing force in the opposite direction. The net effect upon the stereocilia of the hair cells is that they will bend in the direction of the force—outward for an upward deflection and inward for a downward deflection. These different movements of the stereocilia have a dramatic effect upon signal generation by the hair cells.

Transductional mechanism in hair cells

The shearing forces serve as the ultimate event that triggers a neural signal. Although we have thus far spoken of both the inner and the outer

Figure 5.19

A high magnification surface view of the hair cells obtained with a scanning electron microscope. The three rows of outer hair cells with their V-shaped stereocilia are shown in the top part of this figure. The single row of inner hair cells are shown at the bottom.

STEVE GSCHMEISSNER/SCIENCE PHOTO LIBRARY

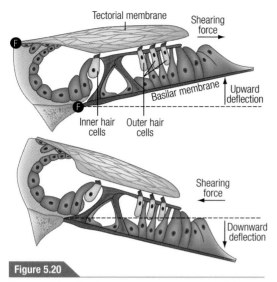

Figure 5.20

The tectorial and basilar membranes rotate about their fulcrum (F), or point of attachment, in response to a travelling wave. Both membranes move in the same direction because of their attachment through the stereocilia of the outer hair cells. The mechanics of this system produces an outward shearing force in response to an upward deflection of the basilar membrane. An inward shearing force is produced when the basilar membrane moves downward. An important outcome of these two possible events is that the stereocilia on the hair cells are deflected in the direction of the shearing force.

hair cells as a fundamental unit, most of the neural output from the cochlea actually arises from the inner hair cells. Thus, it is here that the transformation of mechanical energy into neural events will have the greatest consequences for signal transmission to the higher stages of the auditory nervous system. We will return to the function of the outer hair cells in a moment.

Sensory transduction in general involves the production of a bioelectric current in response to some sort of external stimulation (Bear et al., 2006; Gulick et al., 1989). In the case of hair cells, it is the bending of the stereocilia that leads to the opening of ionic pores and subsequent depolarization. Our knowledge of the remarkable way that this happens has been advanced largely through the work of James Hudspeth at Rockefeller University (Hudspeth, 1999). The individual filaments of the stereocilia are themselves connected to each other by way of a very thin fibre known as a **tip link**. Rightward bending of the stereocilia due to upward movement of the basilar membrane increases the tension on the tip links. As Figure 5.21 illustrates, these minute fibres are actually connected to gates on ionic pores that are normally in the closed position. Hudspeth showed that these gates serve as a trap door

that controls the flow of ions into the hair cell. Increased tension on the tip links opens the gates, thereby allowing ions such as potassium (K^+) and calcium (Ca^{2+}) to flow into the hair cell through the stereocilia (SideNote 5.33). Increased intracellular levels of K^+ in the hair cell have the effect of depolarizing its membrane potential. If the stereocilia are bent in the opposite direction due to downward movement of the basilar membrane, then the tension on the tip links is reduced and the ionic gates remain closed. This has the effect of hyperpolarizing the hair cell since even spontaneous openings are less likely to occur.

This unusual mechanism has one key advantage that is of great importance to hearing—rapidity (Vollrath, Kwan, & Corey, 2007). We noted earlier that the auditory system must contend with rapid changes in the stimulus that typically occur with high sound frequencies. Such rapid events imposed by the very nature of the sound stimulus also require that the transductional mechanisms show an extremely rapid response. Recall from Chapter 4 that signal transduction in the chemosensory systems can involve membrane-bound proteins and second messengers. Such a mechanism would be too slow for the auditory system and simply not allow the hair cells to provide the necessary rapid response. Instead, the direct gating action on ionic pores through the tip links provides the fastest possible response to mechanical deflection of the stereocilia.

The initial depolarization caused by bending of the stereocilia causes two things to happen. First, depolarization leads the ionic gates within the hair cells to open further, thereby producing greater depolarization (SideNote 5.34). And second, depolarization along with the increased Ca^{2+} levels lead to neurotransmitter release at the base of inner hair cell. The neurotransmitter, believed to be glutamate, crosses the synaptic space to depolarize cochlear nerve fibres that innervate the hair cells (see Figure 5.21). The resulting action potentials produced in these nerve fibres carry auditory information out of the cochlea to higher centres in the auditory nervous system.

Role of outer hair cells

The cochlear response to sound can be considered to occur in two ways—passive and active. The processes we discussed above whereby sound stimulation produces depolarizing events in the inner hair cells represent

SideNote | **5.33**

The cochlear duct fluid has a much higher concentration of potassium ions than other fluid compartments of the body. Therefore, when the ionic gates in the stereocilia open, it is potassium rather than sodium ions that enter the hair cells. Nevertheless, the hair cell becomes depolarized.

SideNote | **5.34**

The normal resting potential of inner hair cells is about –60 millivolts (mV). The greater the bending of the stereocilia, the greater the depolarization up to a maximum level.

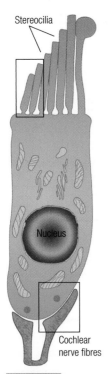

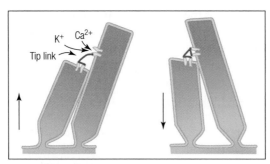

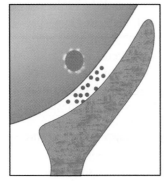

Figure 5.21

Auditory hair cells are cylindrical in shape and have stereocilia that appear as a bevelled set of filaments. Each hair cell is innervated by cochlear nerve fibres at its base. The top inset shows movement of the stereocilia in response to deflection of the basilar membrane. Upward deflection produces bending of the stereocilia toward the taller edge, which opens ionic pores to allow potassium (K^+) and calcium (Ca^{2+}) ions to enter the hair cell. This produces depolarization leading to neurotransmitter release upon cochlear nerve fibres (bottom inset). A downward movement of the basilar membrane bends the stereocilia in the opposite direction, thereby closing the ionic pores. Adapted from "Sensory Transduction in the Ear," by A. J. Hudspeth, 1999, in *Principles of Neural Science,* 4th ed., Eds. E. R. Kandel, J. H. Schwartz, and T. M. Jessell, Norwalk, CT: Appleton & Lange.

mechanical coupling is sensitized by motile changes in the outer hair cell to enhance the cochlear response to sound, especially at higher frequencies (SideNote 5.35).

The electrical mechanism by which outer hair cells influence cochlear transduction is somewhat more complicated. The movement of outer hair cells in response to basilar membrane vibration produces an electrical response across the organ of Corti known as the **cochlear microphonic**. The unusual ionic properties of the fluid in the cochlear duct create a steady current flow across the organ of Corti through the hair cells. This current is modulated by movement of the stereocilia in the outer hair cells to produce the cochlear microphonic. A striking quality of this electrical response is that its waveform follows the sound waveform exactly. For example, a sinusoidal sound wave produces a sinusoidal change in voltage. Similarly, a complex stimulus such as speech will produce an identical voltage waveform in the cochlear microphonic (SideNote 5.36). It is believed that the lateral spreading of the cochlear microphonic enhances the passive electrical response functions of the inner hair cells, though the precise mechanism remains unknown.

2. NEURAL CAPTURE OF AUDITORY SIGNALS

The transmission of auditory signals out of the cochlea to the central nervous system occurs via the **vestibulocochlear nerve** (also known as *cranial nerve VIII*) (Ehret & Romand, 1996; Musiek & Baran, 2006). There are two distinct components of this nerve—the vestibular branch that innervates the vestibular apparatus and the cochlear branch (also called the *cochlear nerve*). Each cochlea is innervated by approximately 30,000 cochlear nerve fibres. These fibres are responsible for transmitting intensity and frequency information—the two principal qualities of sound—to the central nervous system. Before discussing how this is accomplished, we first survey the layout and some important features of the nerve fibres that enter the cochlea.

Anatomical organization

The fibres of the cochlear nerve originate from cell bodies that are located in the cochlear ganglion. This collection of nerve cell bodies is found just outside the body of the cochlea.

SideNote | 5.35

The motility of outer hair cells is believed to be the source of sound emissions by the ear. These are known as *cochlear* or *otoacoustic emissions.* Spontaneous emissions are sometimes produced in the total absence of external sounds. These emissions can actually be detected if a sensitive microphone is placed in the external auditory canal. The energy generated by active processes in outer hair cells is believed to be transmitted by all of the ears' elements in the reverse direction and ultimately upon the eardrum, which then acts as a speaker.

the passive response to auditory stimulation. A more active process is mediated through the outer hair cells (Fettiplace & Fuchs, 1999; Manley, 2000). The active mechanism in turn is believed to occur in one of two ways—mechanical or electrical.

The mechanical response of outer hair cells involves actual physical changes in its structure when sound stimuli are applied. Outer hair cells contain contractile elements similar to those found in muscle tissue. The actual physical changes can occur very fast and in synchrony with the vibrational sequence of sound waves. A second and slower response occurs through nerve stimulation of the outer hair cells. This will be discussed in further detail in the next section. It is believed that the net effect of these mechanical changes is to influence the movement of the tectorial membrane. Recall that the stereocilia of the outer hair cells provide a physical connection between the basilar and tectorial membranes. This

It follows the cochlear spiral and is therefore also called the **spiral ganglion**. The neurons of the spiral ganglion are of the bipolar type and therefore give rise to a single fibre that quickly breaks off into two branches. The shorter branch perforates the bony cochlea to innervate the hair cells (see Figure 5.18). The longer branch becomes part of the cochlear nerve and carries auditory signals to higher centres in the brain.

Approximately 90% of cochlear nerve fibres terminate upon the inner hair cells. The remaining fibres proceed around the arch of Corti to innervate the outer hair cells. In both cases, these nerve fibres conduct action potentials generated at their nerve endings by the release of neurotransmitter following hair cell depolarization. Therefore, these are termed *afferent fibres* because they transmit neural signals from the cochlea to the central nervous system. A separate set of fibres exist within the cochlear nerve that do the opposite—that is, they carry messages from the brain to the cochlea. These so-called *efferent fibres* largely terminate on the outer hair cells, though there is a sparse innervation of the inner hair cells as well (Moller, 2006; Musiek & Baran, 2006).

Afferent versus efferent nerve fibres

Figure 5.22 provides a map of how the afferent and efferent nerve fibres terminate upon the two types of hair cells. As can be seen here, each afferent fibre terminates upon a single inner hair cell. This produces a large neural divergence, given that the 3,000 or so inner hair cells end up stimulating the vast majority of the 30,000 afferent fibres. Thus, each inner hair cell can direct its output through nearly 10 separate nerve fibres. The benefit of such multiple projections from a single transduction site is that differences in processing can occur at each of the synapses by controlling how much neurotransmitter is released there. This allows the stimulus to be separately represented in subtle ways and transmitted via independent fibre pathways to the brain. Although there is some innervation of afferent fibres upon the outer hair cells, the sparseness of this projection makes it unlikely that outer hair cells make a major transductional contribution in the auditory analysis of sound.

If the afferent fibres carry neural signals out of the cochlea to the central nervous system, then what can be said of the role of the efferent fibres? The innervation scheme in Figure 5.22

shows an opposite pattern whereby most of the efferent fibres terminate on the outer hair cells. Electrophysiological studies have shown that the sparse projection upon the inner hair cells has an inhibitory function. That is, increased activity in the efferent fibres reduces the firing rate of action potentials within afferent fibres in response to the same sound stimulus, which may allow inner hair cells to respond over a larger range of sound intensities than would have been otherwise possible. The role of the efferent fibres on the outer hair cells is also speculative. One likely possibility is that efferent nerve activity changes the response characteristics of the outer hair cells (Eatock, 2000; Manley, 2000).

Neural coding of sound intensity

The greater the amplitude of the sound stimulus, the greater the deflection of the basilar membrane, organ of Corti, and tectorial membrane resulting in greater deflection of

SideNote | **5.36**

The cochlear microphonic was first described in 1930 and was immediately believed to be responsible for directly stimulating the cochlear nerve fibres. This idea was abandoned when it was discovered that it was the inner, rather than outer, hair cells that were primarily responsible for generating the output signals of the cochlea.

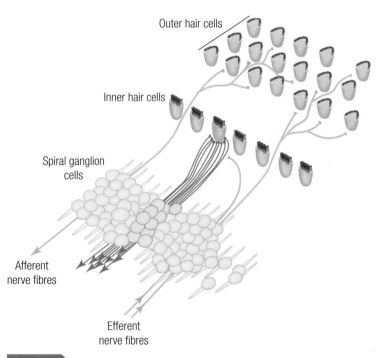

Figure 5.22

The organ of Corti is innervated by both afferent and efferent fibres. The afferent fibres belong to neurons whose cell bodies reside in the spiral ganglion. These fibres largely terminate on the inner hair cells in such a way that each afferent fibre makes contact with only a single inner hair cell. There is approximately a 10:1 ratio in the number of afferent fibres to the number of inner hair cells, resulting in considerable divergence of information outflow from the cochlea. The efferent fibres originate from the brain stem and make contact largely with the outer hair cells, though there is a sparse innervation of the inner hair cells as well. Adapted from "Neuroanatomy of the Cochlea," by H. Spoendlin, 1974, in *Facts and Models in Hearing*, Eds. E. Zwicker and E. Terhardt, New York, NY: Springer-Verlag.

the stereocilia, greater depolarization of inner hair cells, and finally greater neurotransmitter release upon the afferent fibres. The entire dynamic range of these events allows human hearing in turn to span a truly incredible range of sound pressure levels, amounting to nearly 120 dB$_{SPL}$. The challenge for the auditory nervous system is to find a way of allowing neural signals in the afferent fibres to encode this vast intensity range (SideNote 5.37).

An elegant solution to this problem has evolved that uses different sensitivities of afferent nerve fibres (Hartmann, 1998; Yost, 2000). As Figure 5.23 shows, some nerve fibres have a high level of spontaneous neural activity, probably caused by greater spontaneous release of neurotransmitter by the inner hair cells. These fibres are also very sensitive to sound and can show response thresholds around 0 dB$_{SPL}$. However, these fibres also saturate quite rapidly and therefore rarely show increased neural firing beyond 40 dB$_{SPL}$. At the opposite extremity are afferent fibres that show very low levels of spontaneous activity. These fibres generally have much greater firing thresholds and therefore saturate at much higher sound levels, typically around 100 dB$_{SPL}$ and beyond. The full range of audible sound intensity is therefore coded by afferent fibres whose response profiles lie between these two extremes.

The mechanism that likely generates such differences in response sensitivity is the amount of neurotransmitter released by the inner hair cell. We saw earlier that each inner hair cell is innervated by close to 10 afferent fibres. A key advantage of this multiple innervation scheme is that any given inner hair cell can respond to a particular sound intensity by releasing different amounts of neurotransmitter at its different synapses. This systematic difference in neurotransmitter release means that the output from an inner hair cell can trigger different levels of neural activity among a parallel set of fibres, whose sensitivity and response profile in turn are determined by the nature of its synaptic interaction with the hair cell (SideNote 5.38).

Neural coding of sound frequency—place theory mechanisms

The central nervous system obtains information about sound frequency from the afferent fibres in two different ways. The first is based on the place theory that was discussed in Section B.3. Recall that the basilar membrane shows maximum vibrational amplitudes at different places along its length in response to different sound frequencies. The innervation pattern of hair cells by the afferent fibres also occurs in a systematic and topographic manner throughout the cochlear span of the organ of Corti. Thus, a particular afferent fibre carries signals from a hair cell that was depolarized only by the particular sound frequency associated with its place in the tonotopic map (Luce, 1993; Warren, 1999; Yost, 2000). Frequency information, according to this place code, can simply be interpreted by the brain by noting which fibre contained the neural discharge. The cochlear nerve, therefore, simply preserves the place coding of frequency selectivity that is found along the basilar membrane (SideNote 5.39).

The relationship between sound frequency and neural response in a particular afferent fibre can be portrayed by its **tuning curve**, which shows a plot of the minimum sound intensity required to obtain a sufficient neural response as a function of sound frequency (Figure 5.24). The lowest point in the curve occurs at the so-called **characteristic frequency**. This is the frequency where the least sound pressure is required to evoke a neural response (i.e., the frequency at which that fibre is most sensitive). As the frequency shifts away from the characteristic frequency, greater sound levels are required to obtain a sufficient neural response (SideNote 5.40). Another way to show the response properties of auditory nerve fibres

SideNote 5.37

The temporal properties of action potentials limit the maximum firing rate within most neurons to about 200–300 spikes/second and rarely beyond 500 spikes/second. No single neuron can therefore represent the 120 dB$_{SPL}$ intensity range that is audible to humans.

SideNote 5.38

Another way that firing rates in afferent fibres can be modulated is through the inhibitory action of efferent fibres that terminate on the inner hair cells. The response profile shown in Figure 5.23 shifts to the right with increased activity in efferent fibres. This mechanism serves an important role in detecting sounds that occur in the presence of noise.

SideNote 5.39

Tonotopic mapping must therefore also be preserved in the cochlear nerve. Afferent nerve fibres that run along the outer margins of the cochlear nerve innervate hair cells at the basal end of the cochlea and therefore code for high frequencies. Afferent fibres located toward the middle of the cochlear nerve bundle innervate hair cells located progressively toward the apex and therefore encode correspondingly lower sound frequencies.

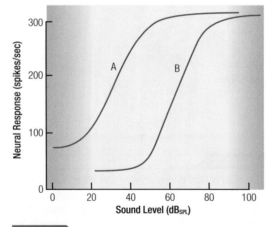

Figure 5.23

Neural coding of sound intensity is accomplished by afferent fibres that show different sensitivity profiles. Very sensitive fibres (A) typically have high spontaneous firing rates and become saturated at low intensities. Afferent fibres that have a higher threshold of activation (B) become saturated at much higher intensities.

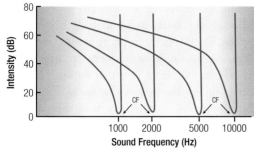

Figure 5.24

Tuning curves of cochlear nerve fibres show a function that relates sound frequency to the minimum intensity required to evoke a measurable increase in neural discharge. The four examples shown here each have a different characteristic frequency (CF). The intensity values on the y-axis indicate the decibel values relative to the fibre's threshold at the CF.

is by way of a **frequency response curve** (Figure 5.25). Frequency response curves, or FRCs, portray essentially the same information with regard to frequency selectivity (Gulick et al., 1989). However, because the dependent measure is the neural discharge rate (i.e., action potentials per second), it is possible to show the frequency response at different sound levels as well.

The tuning curves and frequency response functions show that auditory fibres in the cochlear nerve are narrowly tuned to a particular frequency. For some time there was debate as to whether this tight tuning was a property of the neural system (i.e., something occurring within the organ of Corti) or whether it simply reflected the mechanical properties of

the basilar membrane. It was hard to believe that the basilar membrane alone could display such sharpness in vibration at any given locus, especially since it was assumed that a certain blurring would occur due to simple mechanical forces. The accumulated experimental evidence shows that the basilar membrane indeed displays extremely sharp vibrational patterns and that it alone is largely responsible for generating the narrow frequency tuning functions that are observed in cochlear fibres.

Neural coding of sound frequency—frequency theory mechanisms

A second way that frequency information is encoded by cochlear nerve fibres is related directly to the frequency of the sound stimulus. We noted in Section B.3 that the properties of the basilar membrane do not allow frequency-based mechanisms to operate over the full span of the audible frequency range. However, there is experimental evidence to suggest that the auditory system does rely on some form of neural frequency encoding that is directly linked to the pressure undulations of the sound wave. According to this view, an action potential may be produced during each cycle of the sound wave. Furthermore, the neural discharge occurs in a stereotyped manner, such as during the compressive phase of the sound waveform (SideNote 5.41). This type of response by an auditory fibre is known as a **phase-locked response** (Yost, 2000).

Given the upper limit of neural discharge rates, it would seem that phase-locking can

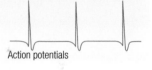
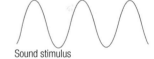
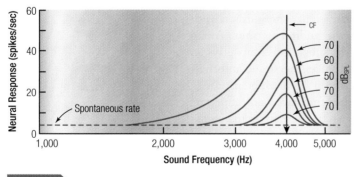

Figure 5.25

Frequency response curves for a single auditory fibre in the cochlear nerve. The neural discharge rate is shown as a function of sound frequency for a series of different intensities (dB$_{SPL}$). Each response curve is centred on the characteristic frequency (4000 Hz in this example) and shows progressively greater responsiveness with increasing sound intensity. Adapted from "Patterns of Activity in Single Auditory Nerve Fibers of the Squirrel Monkey," by J. E. Rose, J. F. Brugge, D. J. Anderson, and J. E. Hind, 1968, in *Hearing Mechanisms in Vertebrates,* London: Churchill Livingstone.

SideNote | **5.42**

A general theory of how this might occur was proposed in 1949 by Ernest Wever, who called it the *volley principle*. Wever believed that co-operative firing by multiple fibres, each with its own phase-locking characteristics, could convey frequency information to the brain. However, this principle would only operate beyond the upper limit of neural firing (500 Hz) up to approximately 4000 Hz. Wever believed that a combined place and frequency mechanism was responsible for encoding the full range of audible sound frequencies.

SideNote | **5.43**

The auditory portion of nerve VIII joins the vestibular portion that carries signals from the vestibular apparatus. They travel together before the auditory portion branches out to the cochlear nucleus.

theoretically occur only up to frequencies of about 400 to 500 Hz. However, it is now clear that phase-locking persists up to frequencies of about 4000 Hz. Since action potentials cannot be produced at such high rates of firing, it is believed that a fibre may fire once every few cycles of the sound wave, thereby still retaining some form of phase-locking though at a more dispersed manner (SideNote 5.42). If a pure tone at or below 4000 Hz is applied, then not only will those nerve fibres that have the corresponding characteristic frequency (place code) fire, but so will all other nerve fibres through phase-locked responses (frequency code). The central nervous system can therefore obtain information about stimulus frequency by way of both a place code and a frequency code. However, only the place code is believed to apply at sound frequencies above 4000 Hz.

3. SUBCORTICAL AUDITORY STRUCTURES

We have just seen how the neural output from the cochlea effectively encodes the two major characteristics of sound—frequency and intensity. These signals serve as the basic input to higher levels of the auditory system where significant additional processing occurs. Until now, we have devoted our analysis to the mechanical operations and neural output of a single cochlea. The more advanced aspects of hearing, such as localization of the sound source, require the interaction of neural signals from both ears. That interaction begins in the **subcortical auditory structures** that together form a hierarchical set of neural processing units in the signal transmission path from cochlea to the auditory cortex. Along the way, each of the subcortical units plays an important role in processing sound information that is relayed to it (Vollrath et al., 2007). These structures therefore have a dual function. First, they serve as a relay mechanism that transmits information from one site to another. And second, through their active role they enhance, modify, and further process the auditory signals, thereby imparting significant consequences for the perceptual experience of hearing.

Ascending pathways

The ascending transmission pathway begins at the point of neurotransmitter release by inner hair cells upon cochlear nerve fibres (Musiek & Baran, 2006). These fibres make up the peripheral processes of bipolar neurons that reside in the spiral ganglion (SG), as discussed before. The longer central processes of the SG neurons come together to form a twisted nerve trunk (cranial nerve VIII) that enters the brain stem and terminates in the cochlear nucleus (SideNote 5.43). It is here that the auditory signals encounter the first synapse in the central nervous system. As Figure 5.26 shows, the cochlear nucleus is also the point at which auditory signals begin to branch out. Each of the subcortical structures in this pathway is bilaterally represented. The interconnections may therefore be directed to structures on the same side of the brain or they may cross over to connect with the same structure on the opposite side (Read, Winer, & Schreiner, 2002; Schreiner & Winer, 2007). For simplicity, only the projections of auditory structures on the right side of the brain are shown in Figure 5.26.

The cochlear nucleus has two major subdivisions containing some neurons that act largely as relay cells and others that are involved in enhancing and sharpening the signals. The neurons in the cochlear nucleus on either side of the brain only receive inputs from the cochlea of that side alone. There is no crossover of auditory signals at this level, and therefore

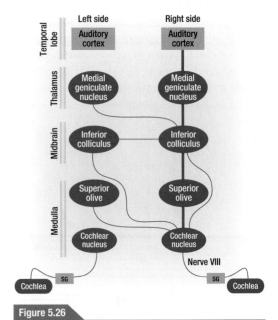

Figure 5.26

Neural signals in the cochlea are captured by nerve fibres, whose cell bodies reside in the spiral ganglion (SG), and are then transmitted to the cochlear nucleus. Signal transmission in the ascending pathways occurs through a number of different subcortical structures before arriving at the auditory cortex. These structures are located in the thalamus and at different levels of the brain stem.

these neurons are considered to be **monaural**. From the cochlear nucleus, the projections diverge into two higher areas—the superior olive and the inferior colliculus. As Figure 5.26 shows, the cochlear nucleus projections may be directed to the same side of the brain as well as to the opposite side. The implication of this crossover is that neurons at these levels, and higher, display **binaural** responses because they are able to integrate auditory signals from both ears (SideNote 5.44).

The superior olive is a complex of several small nuclei among which two serve in auditory processing. The nuclei also provide a major output to the inferior colliculus (IC) on the same side of the brain. The IC is a multi-layered structure that is located in the midbrain with functions related to the auditory signal relay and coordination of acoustic reflexes. Both monaural and binaural neurons are present in the IC. There are three sets of projections from the inferior colliculus, the most important being to the medial geniculate nucleus (MGN) on the same side and minor projections to the IC and MGN on the opposite side. The MGN is a thalamic nucleus that largely serves a relay function and represents the last in the series of hierarchical subcortical structures. From here, there is a large radial projection of fibres to the auditory cortex.

Response characteristics of subcortical structures

There are three general themes that emerge when considering neural function in the subcortical structures—response modification, tonotopicity, and laterality (Winer & Lee, 2007; Winer, Miller, Lee, & Schreiner, 2005). The first relates to the fact that auditory signals are processed to a certain degree in some structures, especially the cochlear nucleus, by way of excitatory and inhibitory influences within a localized neural network. As a result, the response profile as a function of sound frequency can undergo some modification. One result of this operation is that it helps to sharpen the neural representation, which in turn is thought to be important for sound localization, perceiving sounds in a complex field, and detecting sounds that are present in noisy backgrounds.

A second feature of the subcortical structures—especially the cochlear nucleus, inferior colliculus, and medial geniculate nucleus—is the presence of a tonotopic map.

Earlier, we discussed the tonotopic arrangement in the basilar membrane. Through the place code, individual cochlear fibres retain a precise frequency selectivity that is in turn imparted to the subcortical nuclei in a systematic way. As a result, a topographic organization is evident whereby a progressive change in the characteristic frequency occurs along a particular spatial dimension. This is most prominent in the IC where each layer of neurons is believed to display the same characteristic frequency, resulting in the so-called **isofrequency sheets** (SideNote 5.45). The presence of a tonotopic arrangement in these structures means that the place code propagates through the subcortical pathways all the way up to the cortex. It also ensures that frequency information is retained in much the same manner at multiple levels of the auditory system.

A final characteristic of subcortical neurons is laterality—that is, the extent to which they can be separately driven by the two ears. Auditory neurons that reside in structures above the cochlear nucleus integrate information from the two ears because of the crossover of projection pathways. The binaural response of such neurons can be evaluated by the degree to which sound input from the contralateral (opposite) side is mixed with sound input from the ipsilateral (same) side. In general, binaural neurons are excited by contralateral sound stimulation, whereas ipsilateral inputs can produce either excitation or inhibition. The dominant excitation from the contralateral side is consistent with the general body plan that we observed in the somatosensory system whereby neural structures on one side of the brain represent the opposite side of the body (SideNote 5.46).

Descending pathways

Auditory signal transmission up the hierarchy of subcortical structures is accompanied by information flow in the opposite direction as well (Knig, Hall, Scheich, Budinger, & Konig, 2005; Musiek & Baran, 2006). These signals originate in the cortex and proceed through essentially the same structures, though the participating neural elements are kept separate from the ascending pathways. This so-called *descending system* is largely involved in modulating the auditory response to sound. There are two ways in which this is accomplished.

Earlier we described the efferent fibres that innervate the cochlea and their role in

SideNote | **5.44**

Binaural signal processing is critically important for sound localization in space and will be discussed at length in the next chapter.

SideNote | **5.45**

Frequency representation in the IC and other subcortical structures generally spans the audible range for that particular animal. An interesting case is found in echolocating bats, which use a particular frequency. Neural responses in these animals show an over-representation of the echolocating frequency throughout their auditory system.

SideNote | **5.46**

Lesion studies have shown that damage to the auditory structures on one side of the brain produces a selective impairment in sound localization on the opposite side. This has been taken as evidence for functional laterality in the auditory system.

inhibiting inner and outer hair cell function. The neuronal cell bodies that give rise to the efferent fibres reside in the superior olive and are termed **olivocochlear neurons**, or OC neurons. These neurons in turn are controlled by descending pathways from higher auditory centres. The descending system can exert considerable influence upon firing rates in the ascending system, especially at high sound intensities. It is believed that outer hair cell inhibition by efferent fibres, through the mechanisms we discussed in Section C.1, allows the auditory system to encode a higher range of sound intensities by preventing early saturation of discharge rates. The OC system functions in a somewhat reflexive manner as evidenced by its sudden recruitment at relatively high sound intensities.

A second way in which cochlear function is modulated by the efferent system involves the motor activation of two small muscles located in the middle ear. These muscles, called the *tensor tympani* and the *stapedius*, are very small and also function in a largely reflexive manner. Motor neurons in the brain stem stimulate contractions of these muscles in the event of sudden sound bursts. The muscular contractions lead to decreased sound transmission through the middle ear, thereby protecting the middle and inner ear components from damage. This role is especially well tailored to sounds of low frequencies and therefore complements the reflexive action of the OC system, which largely operates in the middle and high frequency ranges.

4. THE AUDITORY CORTEX

Whereas the subcortical areas are involved in coding and transmitting the basic qualities of the sound stimulus, the auditory cortex assembles the incoming neural signals into meaningful acoustic events. The higher perceptual functions that we discuss in the next two chapters arise through signal processing in neural networks at the cortical level. In this section, we review some of the basic features of the auditory cortex. Much of our understanding of this area has been derived through single-unit studies in cats and monkeys. More recently, the advent of non-invasive imaging procedures has greatly expanded our insight into the functional anatomy of human cortical areas, especially with regard to speech and music processing.

SideNote 5.47

The temporal lobe on each side of the brain has an anatomically defined area A1 that receives fibres from the MGN only on that side. There is no crossover of projections from the MGN to the auditory cortex.

Anatomical organization

The ascending pathway emerges from the medial geniculate nucleus and terminates in a small segment of the temporal lobe. The discrete area that receives the incoming fibres is termed the primary auditory cortex, or **area A1** (SideNote 5.47) (Bear et al., 2006; Musiek & Baran, 2006; Winer & Lee, 2007). The actual location of area A1 in humans, shown in Figure 5.27, is along a mound on the surface of the temporal lobe and extends into an adjacent deep groove called the *Sylvian fissure*. This area of the brain was originally described by Korbinian Brodmann in the early 1900s as two distinct cytoarchitectonic zones, which he named *areas 41* and *42*.

There are a number of other auditory areas that surround area A1. These have been identified largely in cats and monkeys on the basis of auditory responses at the single neuron level as well as through their separate projection patterns from the MGN. These areas are also interconnected with each other. Auditory area A2 immediately surrounds the primary auditory cortex and is believed to process higher order acoustic information. Although there is some evidence for the existence of other auditory areas in primates, these areas have generally not been mapped out in detail nor are their functional roles entirely clear.

One area in humans that has a distinctive auditory function is Wernicke's area, which is also located in the temporal lobe (see Figure 5.27). The important role that Wernicke's area plays in speech comprehension has been known for some time, largely through the disruptive effects that occur in humans with brain lesions in this area. As such, Wernicke's area can be considered to be an auditory association area that is specialized to serve the unique role of speech analysis in humans. A further distinctive aspect of Wernicke's area is its restriction to the dominant (usually left) hemisphere. The lateralization of language production and comprehension functions in humans to one cerebral hemisphere represents a rare example of anatomical and functional asymmetry (Knig et al., 2005).

Functional organization

The functional characteristics of the auditory cortex have been uncovered largely from studies of area A1 (Musiek & Baran, 2006; Read et al., 2002). The two key features that stand out

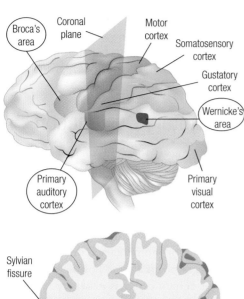

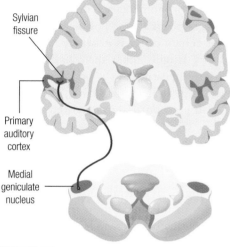

A second functional feature of area A1 concerns the way binaural inputs are combined. The crossover of auditory signals from one side of the brain to the other at earlier levels of the brain stem means that neurons in the auditory cortex receive inputs from both ears. One type of neuron in area A1 shows a **summation response** (i.e., the inputs from both ears are excitatory and therefore the neuron can be driven by sound stimulation of either ear, though there is usually a stronger preference for the ear on the opposite side). A second type of neuron shows a **suppression response** (i.e., the neuron is excited by sound input from the opposite side but is inhibited by stimulation on the same side).

The striking aspect of this arrangement is that it appears the two types of neurons are clustered into separate sets of cortical columns. Single-unit studies have shown that area A1 is functionally organized into discrete vertical columns of neurons that span the thickness of

Figure 5.27

The location of the primary auditory cortex and two areas related to language function, Broca's area and Wernicke's area, are shown in a lateral view of the left cerebral hemisphere. A coronal view of the brain through area A1 (shaded plane) is shown in the bottom illustration. Area A1 extends from a mound on the temporal lobe into the Sylvian fissure. Neurons in this area receive signals directly from the medial geniculate nucleus.

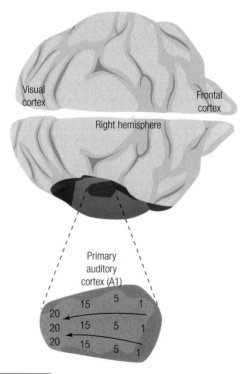

Figure 5.28

The tonotopic map in the primary auditory cortex (area A1) of monkeys shows a systematic representation of sound frequency. Neurons stimulated by low frequencies are found toward the anterior segment, whereas higher frequencies are represented toward the opposite end. The numbers depict sound frequency in kilohertz. Adapted from "Representation of the Cochlear Partition on the Superior Temporal Plane of the Macaque Monkey," by M. M. Merzenich and J. F. Brugge, 1973, *Brain Research, 50*, pp. 275–296.

are tonotopic organization and the clustering of binaural features (Schreiner, Read, & Sutter, 2000; Schreiner & Winer, 2007). The tonotopic arrangement is a straightforward result of the tonotopic projection pattern found in the subcortical structures. The systematic arrangement of neurons with regard to characteristic frequency is shown in Figure 5.28 for area A1 of monkeys. Neurons that are tuned to low sound frequencies are present toward the anterior end of this area, whereas those preferring higher frequencies are found more toward the opposite end. This systematic arrangement produces the so-called *isofrequency sheets* whereby auditory neurons tuned to the same frequency are segregated along narrow strips.

the cortex. Within each column, neurons show either a summation or a suppression response. Furthermore, the columns are organized perpendicular to the isofrequency sheets. Thus, area A1 can be thought of as a two-dimensional sheet where sound frequency is represented along one axis and binaural mixing is represented along the other (SideNote 5.48). According to this scheme, neurons within any given column display a similar characteristic frequency and are driven by a similar type of binaural interaction (either summation or suppression).

Parallel auditory pathways

The organizing principles of area A1 thus appear to be directed at representing sound frequency and binaural interaction. This architecture reflects the key role that the auditory cortex plays in sound localization and in the processing of temporal patterns for the analysis and identification of complex sounds. An emerging idea in this field is that the twin functions of sound analysis and localization are reflected by processing in separate but parallel neural pathways of the higher auditory system (Rauschecker & Scott, 2009; Rauschecker & Shannon, 2002). We saw in Chapter 3 that a similar idea is invoked to explain different aspects of information processing within the somatosensory system. In the auditory system, it appears that neural circuits involved in sound pattern analysis are segregated from those involved in sound localization analysis. Josef Rauschecker at Georgetown University has argued on the basis of cat and monkey single-unit data that higher auditory areas appear to be segregated into two streams that

reflect a functional specialization for processing sound localization and complex auditory patterns (Rauschecker & Scott, 2009; Rauschecker, Tian, Pons, & Mishkin, 1997).

D. Auditory Dysfunction

There are more than 30 million people in North America who suffer from some sort of hearing loss, ranging from moderate impairment to total deafness (SideNote 5.49). In addition to the magnitude of the loss, hearing disorders may show different time courses as well. A brief or momentary reduction of hearing, as might occur after exposure to an intense sound or certain drugs, is generally referred to as auditory fatigue rather than loss. In operational terms, hearing loss is best described as a reduction in auditory sensitivity. The impact this has on perceptual aspects related to hearing will be taken up in the next chapter. Here, we discuss the different forms of hearing loss in relation to the auditory structures covered in this chapter.

Hearing loss is generally discussed in terms of the two major sites within the ear where damage typically occurs (Moller, 2006; Musiek & Baran, 2006). **Conductive loss** occurs when the outer or middle ear is affected, leading to reduced transmission of sound to the cochlea. **Sensorineural loss** occurs when there is damage to the cochlea or to the nerves of the inner ear. Both conditions result in reduced auditory perception due to a deficiency of sound processing by the ear. The onset of hearing loss is also an important parameter because of the

SideNote | **5.48**

There is also evidence that neurons within any given column display ear preference. That is, a particular column may be driven predominantly by the opposite or same-side ear. A similar situation exists in the primary visual cortex where vertical columns of neurons are driven by only one of the eyes.

SideNote | **5.49**

Of this number, nearly 80% have irreversible hearing loss. The incidence of hearing loss climbs rapidly with age and represents the third most prevalent chronic condition among the elderly. Whereas 14% of individuals between 45 and 64 have hearing loss, the number rises dramatically to 54% for people over the age of 65 (National Institute on Deafness and Other Communication Disorders [NIDCD]).

METHODOLOGY

Principle of the Telephone

As we all know, Alexander Graham Bell has been credited with inventing the telephone, but what you may not know is that his motivation for researching sound was to help educate deaf people (most likely because his mother was deaf). In this vein, he first invented the microphone, and in 1876 he invented what we call the *telephone* (Bell called it an *electrical speech machine*). The principle behind the telephone is that speech sounds are converted into electrical signals and then sent down to the opposite end of a wire. The earpiece of a telephone contains a loudspeaker, and the mouthpiece contains a microphone, which has a flexible plastic diaphragm attached to an iron coil and a magnet close by. Speech sounds cause the diaphragm to vibrate, moving the iron coil closer and then farther from the magnet, transducing the sound energy from our voice into an electrical current. The loudspeaker transforms the energy in the opposite way—from electrical current to sound energy.

role that hearing plays in language development. Congenital hearing loss occurs due to either a genetic cause or a problem associated with the birth process, whereas acquired hearing loss develops later in life. Any hearing loss that is present in prelingual children will hinder speech development simply because hearing sounds is a critical requirement for learning speech and developing vocalization skills (Kral & Eggermont, 2007; Turkington, 2000). Speech sounds that are muffled due to hearing loss at this important developmental period will produce a similar distortion in vocalization. If it is not accompanied by special training, a total loss of hearing in early childhood will lead to **deaf-mutism**, the absence of language vocalization ability.

1.   CAUSES OF HEARING LOSS

Damage to the auditory system can occur in many ways—from the simple mechanical blockage of the auditory canal to the complex and unrelenting effects of aging. We briefly consider some of the more common causes of hearing loss and note that an exhaustive discussion of this topic could easily fill an entire textbook.

Conductive loss

The distinguishing feature of all types of conductive loss is that it affects the mechanical conduction of sound through the ear (Moller, 2006). Although simple wax buildup or a perforation of the eardrum will have this effect, it turns out that there are many other causes of conductive loss. One of the most common is a middle ear infection, also known as **otitis media**. An inflammation of the eustachian tube often accompanies this condition and leads to an imbalance in pressure across the eardrum. The subsequent changes in the vibrational characteristics of the eardrum reduce sound transmission through the middle ear. A more serious condition occurs when there is actual fluid buildup in the middle ear due to an infection. This can interfere with the conductive operation of the ossicles and may become quite problematic if the fluid persists for prolonged periods in the middle ear chamber. The prevalence of otitis media is greater in children because the eustachian tube is smaller and more inclined along the horizontal plane, making it especially susceptible to an upper respiratory infection.

Another major cause of conductive loss is **otosclerosis**, an inherited bone disease that produces abnormal development and function of the ossicles. The ossicles become impaired because of increased accumulation of calcium, which in turn leads to problems in the movement of these tiny bones. The stapes is especially susceptible because it is the bone that transfers sound energy to the oval window. The reduced function of the ossicles in this condition fails to provide adequate amplification and transfer of sound energy, resulting in as much as a 30 dB loss of sound pressure. Recent advances in microsurgery now make it possible to either repair the ossicles or replace them with artificial implants (SideNote 5.50).

Sensorineural loss

Any impairment in cochlear function or in the neural elements of the inner ear will cause a loss or reduction in auditory function (Jesteadt, 1997; Moller, 2006). In most cases, the effect occurs at the hair cells, which are extremely sensitive to damage. Furthermore, mammalian hair cells do not regenerate after damage, thereby producing a permanent loss. One common way that damage to hair cells occurs is through the ingestion of **ototoxic** drugs. Certain antibiotics, such as neomycin and streptomycin, are toxic to the hair cells because they destroy the stereocilia. Even Aspirin in large doses can cause ototoxic effects leading to **tinnitus**—the perception of "ringing in the ears" in the absence of any external sound (Puel & Guitton, 2007; Viirre, 2007). A similar effect occurs with large does of quinine-based drugs, which are used to combat malaria.

Some other causes of sensorineural loss include traumatic injury, tumours, and disease. Any kind of head injury, such as a fracture of the temporal bone, can affect cochlear function. The inner ear can also be afflicted by tumours, especially in the cochlear nerve, which are known as *acoustic neurinomas*. Among diseases, the presence of rubella (German measles) in a pregnant mother can cause severe damage to her child's organ of Corti. A particularly insidious condition called *Ménière's disease* is caused by the excessive formation of cochlear fluids (Sajjadi & Paparella, 2008). The result is an increased pressure throughout the cochlear duct leading to a general stimulation of auditory nerve fibres. This disease initially produces tinnitus and can progress to a debilitating set of auditory and vestibular symptoms.

SideNote | **5.50**

One particularly successful procedure is known as *stapedectomy*, which involves cutting one side of the eardrum, removing the stapes and replacing it with an artificial implant. This procedure has close to a 90% success rate.

A final cause of major injury to the inner ear is exposure to intense environmental noise (Caitlin, 1986; Kryter, 1996). The mechanical impact of intense sounds causes injury to the hair cells and damage to the transductional mechanisms, leading to a condition that has been termed *noise-induced hearing loss* (NIHL). Both the amount of noise and the duration of exposure determine the degree of hearing damage. In general, damage arises because the elastic limits of the organ of Corti are exceeded with accompanying effects upon the stereocilia of the hair cells and structural damage to the tectorial and basilar membranes. Sounds greater than 80 dB are potentially dangerous, and those over 120 dB are considered to be painful. The presence of intense sounds in the workplace has become an issue of occupational safety, and appropriate measures are often needed to insulate the ears from its effects. Nevertheless, the greater presence of environmental noise in our society has led to an increased incidence of hearing loss and its appearance much earlier in life than a mere generation ago (SideNote 5.51).

Hereditary factors and aging

The more complex causes of auditory dysfunction generally involve age-related changes to the hearing apparatus and genetic factors (Turkington, 2000). The two major genetic causes of hearing loss are Usher syndrome and Waardenburg syndrome. Usher syndrome, named after British eye doctor Charles Usher, is caused by a defective gene that is passed on in an autosomal recessive manner (SideNote 5.52). Usher syndrome causes variable degrees of deafness either at birth or later in life. The syndrome is often accompanied by visual problems, leading to a dual sensory deficit of both hearing and sight. The use of tactile or somatosensory communication in such deaf–blind individuals was discussed in Chapter 3.

Waardenburg syndrome, named after Dutch eye doctor Petrus Waardenburg, is a rather unusual genetic disorder that causes hearing loss and changes in skin and hair pigmentation. A common characteristic of this syndrome is that affected individuals often have two different coloured eyes, one brown and the other blue. Hearing loss in these individuals can vary from moderate to severe. The affected gene, which is believed to control aspects of inner ear development, is passed from parent to child.

Unlike Usher syndrome, Waardenburg syndrome occurs in a dominant manner. Thus, only one defective gene is required for the syndrome to occur, and there is a 50/50 chance of it being passed from an affected parent to their child.

Hearing loss that occurs gradually due to the effects of aging is known as **presbycusis** (Cohn, 1999). The loss initially occurs with high-pitched sounds and progresses to the point where ordinary conversation becomes difficult to hear. Although the condition arises as a natural consequence of aging, it is aggravated by prolonged exposure to high noise intensities in earlier life. The main culprit in presbycusis is sensorineural hearing loss largely due to the loss of inner hair cells. In some cases, presbycusis is caused by conductive loss arising from abnormalities of ossicular function. Although there are no cures for this condition, there are ways of at least partially restoring hearing capacity in affected individuals, as discussed in the next section.

2. DIAGNOSIS AND TREATMENT

The evaluation of hearing function is carried out by *audiologists*, whereas the clinical diagnosis of auditory disorders is carried out by medical specialists known as *otolaryngologists* (SideNote 5.53) (Turkington, 2000). Although there are many tools employed in the modern diagnosis of hearing disorders, there is a very simple way of distinguishing between conductive and sensorineural loss—the *bone conduction test*. This test involves applying a vibrating tuning fork somewhere on the skull, usually just behind the ear (Stenfelt & Goode, 2005). As we noted in Section A.2 of this chapter, any solid object can conduct sound, and the bony skull is no exception. A person with normal hearing capacity would be able to hear the tuning fork in air and when applied to the skull. A person with a conductive loss would not be able to hear the vibrating tuning fork in air but should be able to when applied to the skull because it would conduct the vibrations to the cochlea directly rather than through the middle ear components. Finally, a person with sensorineural loss would not be able to hear the tuning fork in either application because of damage to the cochlea. This very simple qualitative test continues to be used because of its simplicity and power in quickly diagnosing the two most common sources of hearing loss.

SideNote | **5.51**

To increase public awareness of the hazardous effects of noise, the last Wednesday in April has been declared *International Noise Awareness Day*. The festivities include a "quiet diet," which includes observing 60 seconds of no noise between 2:15 p.m. and 2:16 p.m.

SideNote | **5.52**

A person must inherit a defective copy of the gene from both parents for this disease to occur. The parents are generally unaware that they have a defective gene because no symptoms are present unless both copies of the gene are defective.

SideNote | **5.53**

Ear treatments were originally carried out by eye specialists. In the late 19th century, the connection between the ear and throat became known, and therefore otologists (ear specialists) merged with laryngologists (throat specialists). Otolaryngologists are also known as *ear–nose–throat specialists*, or ENT specialists.

Hearing aids

A hearing aid is a device that amplifies incoming sounds and delivers them to the ear (Dillon, 2000). The basic concept of amplifying sounds to the hard of hearing has been around for some time. In the late 1700s, ear trumpets were used to collect sounds from a large area and funnel them into a narrow opening that was guided into the ear—essentially the reverse operation of the bullhorn (SideNote 5.54). Fortunately, the technology for hearing aids has advanced considerably. Modern hearing aids are battery-operated miniature amplifiers that can fit into the auditory canal or can be placed behind the ear. All hearing aids have the same essential components—a small microphone to collect the sound, an electronic amplifier, and a small speaker to deliver the sound into the ear. Hearing aids are particularly useful for improving speech comprehension within a fairly large range of hearing loss.

Cochlear implant

A hearing aid can only be effective as long as sensory function in the cochlea is not lost. Although hearing aids are often used in cases of sensorineural damage (e.g., effects of aging, NIHL, etc.), the hair cell transduction mechanisms must still be intact to a certain degree for these devices to be effective. But what happens in cases of sensorineural damage where hair cell function is totally lost? Under these circumstances, the use of a hearing aid will not generate any neural impulses in the cochlear nerve—no matter how much the sound is amplified.

Such cases of deafness could not be treated until the development of the **cochlear implant** in the 1970s (Erickson, 1990). The principle behind the cochlear implant is quite different from that of the hearing aid. A cochlear implant consists of a small microphone and a processor that converts the sound signal into an electric current that is actually then delivered to the inner ear through a set of fine wires. The idea is for the implant to take over the transductional functions of the cochlea and directly stimulate the auditory nerve fibres (Laszig & Aschendorff, 1999). There are two types of cochlear implants—single channel and multi-channel. A single channel implant delivers the electrical signal through a single electrode to the auditory nerve. Given what we already know about the transmission properties of auditory nerve fibres, this type of device would not be expected to provide a rich content of sound frequencies. This limitation is especially cumbersome in trying to decode the auditory signals in speech. A single channel implant, therefore, is not meant to restore normal hearing quality but rather to provide a simple and effective acoustic warning system.

A multi-channel cochlear implant can resolve a number of these problems. The idea behind this type of device is to decode the incoming sound into a set of parallel channels, each with its own characteristic frequency representation (Clark, 2006). Typically, the processor is tuned to accentuate the frequencies found in ordinary speech so that most of the channels are carriers of those dominant frequencies. The output of this processor is sent though several electrodes, typically more than 20, that run longitudinally along the cochlea and activate nerve fibres at selective points along its length. Those electrodes that stimulate the basal portion of the cochlea are carriers of high-frequency information, whereas the electrodes terminating at the apical portion transmit lower frequencies. In this scheme, the cochlear implant not only simulates the transductional properties of the cochlea but also does so in a tonotopic manner that the auditory system can decipher (Kral & Eggermont, 2007). Multi-channel cochlear implants have now been used in thousands of individuals—with a high success rate—bringing sound and speech comprehension ability to individuals who would otherwise have had no alternative to lifelong deafness.

SideNote | **5.54**

A late 18th-century etching, titled *Friends by the Ears*, illustrating the use of an ear trumpet.

Image from the History of Medicine (NLM)

Summary

1. The ability to perceive sound is based on three fundamental requirements—the creation of sound by an object, the propagation of that sound through a medium, and finally a biological mechanism that transforms the sound stimulus into a neural signal. The vibrational property of an object is influenced by two factors—inertia and elasticity—that act in opposing ways to determine the nature of the sound produced. A vibrating object causes repeated compression and rarefaction on the surrounding air molecules, which in turn creates a propagating sound wave.

2. Sound is characterized by two properties. Sound *intensity* is related to the amplitude of a sound wave (i.e., pressure difference between the peak and trough). The range of audible amplitudes is very large, and therefore a logarithmic scale has been developed to denote sound intensity. The decibel level of a sound's intensity is obtained by the formula $dB = 20 \log (P_s/P_r)$, where P_s is the pressure level of the sound stimulus, and P_r is a reference sound. By convention, the reference is usually taken as the minimum pressure audible to humans.

3. The second property of sound is *frequency*—that is, the number of complete cycles of the pressure waveform in one second. Every object has an intrinsic resonant frequency that is governed by its mass and stiffness (or elasticity), which in turn determines the frequency of the sound emitted by it. The frequency range of human hearing under optimal conditions spans 20–20000 Hz (or cycles per second). A pure tone is characterized by a pressure wave with a sinusoidal profile of a single frequency. Complex periodic tones are repetitive patterns of sound waves made up of multiple sinusoidal frequencies. Noise is characterized by aperiodic vibrations of sound waves with multiple frequencies that span a broad range of the audible spectrum.

4. Complex waveforms can be deconstructed into a set of sinusoidal functions by way of a mathematical technique known as *Fourier analysis*—that is, any waveform, regardless of its complexity, can be broken down into a set of sine-wave functions. The frequency and amplitude of the constituent sine waves is known as the *Fourier spectrum*. The opposite process (i.e., the creation of a complex waveform from a set of sine waves) is known as *Fourier synthesis*. According to Ohm's law of hearing, the ear serves as a Fourier analyzer because it can decompose complex sound waves into its constituent sinusoidal functions so that they can be more easily processed.

5. The ear has three anatomical divisions, each being made up of further components. The *outer ear* is composed of the pinna (which funnels sound), external auditory canal, and the tympanic membrane (which vibrates in a manner similar to the incoming sound). This vibrational pattern is transmitted to the *middle ear*, which contains three small bones—the malleus, incus, and stapes. These bones amplify and transfer the vibration of the tympanic membrane to the fluids within the cochlea of the *inner ear*. The cochlea is a spiral-shaped chamber containing the auditory transduction apparatus.

6. The resulting vibrations in the cochlear fluid, which replicate the wave pattern of the original sound stimulus, are transmitted to the basilar membrane. This membrane separates two of the fluid chambers within the cochlea. The transduction apparatus, known as the *organ of Corti*, rests above the basilar membrane and therefore experiences a similar vibrational disturbance as the cochlear fluids. The auditory *hair cell*, which is a component of the organ of Corti, represents the cellular site where signal transduction occurs. Filaments (or cilia) on these cells bend in response to the vibrational disturbance, which in turn opens ionic channels to produce depolarization and neurotransmitter release. Action potentials are subsequently transmitted through the cochlear nucleus and other subcortical structures to the primary auditory cortex (area A1).

7. Sound intensity is encoded by the firing rate of auditory neurons. The encoding of sound frequency, however, is best explained by the *place theory*. The basilar membrane is of uneven width and thickness. Its resonant frequency therefore varies in a continuous manner, with the highest frequencies being represented at the basal end and the lowest frequencies at the apex. An incoming sound wave triggers a corresponding wave on the basilar membrane. Complex sounds trigger vibrations only at those locations where the intrinsic resonant frequency of the basilar membrane corresponds to the Fourier components of the sound signal. Neural signals from those locations represent the place code (i.e., the location of stimulation on the basilar membrane conveys the frequency information to the auditory brain). This so-called *tonotopic map* is maintained at later brain structures involved in auditory processing.

8. Auditory dysfunction can be due to conductive loss (impairment in sound transmission) or sensorineural loss (impairment in neural capture or processing). The *bone conduction test* is a simple procedure that can distinguish between these two causes. Conductive loss can be treated with hearing aids, whereas the use of a cochlear implant can be helpful in cases of sensorineural damage.

Key Terms

Recall Questions

1. What is the difference between *inertia* and *elasticity*? How do they influence the vibrational property of an object? How does a tuning fork create sound waves, and why is it a convenient tool for understanding sound creation?

2. Why is the decibel scale a convenient way of representing sound intensity? How is the decibel mathematically defined in terms of sound intensity and pressure? What are the decibel levels of some common sounds?

3. What is the difference between a simple harmonic wave and a complex periodic wave? What is noise? Why is Fourier analysis a convenient tool to represent complex sounds, and why is it important for understanding auditory function?

4. What properties of the outer ear help to capture and transmit sound? How are sound waves in air transferred into the cochlea to create sound signals in liquid? What are the four factors involved in preserving sound amplitude through the transmission process from an air to a liquid environment?

5. What is the difference between the *frequency theory* and the *place theory* of sound frequency representation? Why can the frequency theory not account for encoding the full range of audible frequencies? What is the tonotopic map, and how is it related to the basilar membrane? How does the ear function as a Fourier analyzer?

6. What is the organ of Corti, and where is it located? What is the mechanism by which a sound signal is transduced by the *hair cell*? What is the pathway by which neural signals are transmitted from the cochlea to the auditory cortex?

7. How is sound intensity encoded by the auditory system? How is the place theory used in explaining the neural coding of sound frequency? Why do individual auditory fibres exiting the cochlea have such sharply tuned frequency response curves?

8. What is the difference between conductive loss and sensorineural loss? How can the two conditions be differentiated using the *bone conduction test*? How does a cochlear implant work?

9. What is the speed of sound in air? Why does a rigid material, such as steel, conduct sound so much faster than air or water? How does the temperature of the medium influence sound speed?

10. What are different ways that sound can interact with an object? What implications does the impedance mismatch between air and water have for sound transmission through the air? How does the auditory system solve this problem?

11. What are the different roles of the inner and outer hair cells? How is the tectorial membrane involved in the transduction process? What are some functional similarities and differences between the different subcortical and cortical structures involved in auditory processing?

Further Reading

- Ehret, G., & Romand, R. (1996). *The central auditory system.* New York, NY: Oxford University Press.

- Geisler, G. C. (1998). *From sound to synapse.* New York, NY: Oxford University Press.

- Gulick, W. L., Gescheider, G. A., & Frisina, R. D. (1989). *Hearing: Physiological acoustics, neural coding, and psychoacoustics.* New York, NY: Oxford University Press.

- Knig, R., Hall, P., Scheich, H., Budinger, E., & Konig, R. (2005). *Auditory cortex: Synthesis of human and animal research.* Hillsdale, NJ: Lawrence Erlbaum.

- Luce, R. D. (1993). *Sound and hearing.* Hillsdale, NJ: Lawrence Erlbaum.

- Moller, A. R. (2006). *Hearing: Anatomy, physiology, and disorders of the auditory system* (2nd ed.). San Diego, CA: Academic Press.

- Musiek, F. E., & Baran, J. A. (2006). *The auditory system: Anatomy, physiology, and clinical correlates.* Boston, MA: Allyn & Bacon.

- Rossing, T. D., & Fletcher, N. H. (2004). *Principles of vibration and sound* (2nd ed.). New York, NY: Springer-Verlag.

- Syka, J., & Merzenich, M. M. (2005). *Plasticity and signal representation in the auditory system.* New York, NY: Springer.

The Auditory System: Perceptual Aspects of Hearing

6

In this chapter . . .

- You will learn that there is a difference between the physical stimulus known as *intensity* and the perceptual experience of loudness. You will explore how the experience of loudness can be influenced by anatomical and physical factors, and you will learn about the experimental methods that were designed by classical psychophysicists to determine the absolute and difference thresholds. You will discover the minimal audibility curve and how this profile shows the range of hearing for different frequency levels.

- You will come to recognize that sound has many qualitative aspects and that researchers have developed different scales to quantify these more metathetic qualities. You will learn about the sone and mel scales and how each of these describes the relationship between the sound stimulus and the perception that is produced.

- You will explore the association between frequency and pitch and how the tonotopic arrangement of the basilar membrane contributes to our ability to make pitch judgments.

- You will realize why it is that humans are quite good at locating sounds in space, and you will explore how two phenomena known as *interaural time difference* and *interaural intensity difference* contribute to this performance.

A INTENSITY AND LOUDNESS
  1. Audibility Thresholds
  2. Difference Thresholds
  3. Loudness Perception—Relationship to Intensity
  4. Loudness Perception—Relationship to Frequency
  5. Masking and Noise

B FREQUENCY AND PITCH
  1. Frequency Thresholds
  2. Acoustic Pitch
  3. Coding Mechanisms in Pitch Perception

C AUDITORY SPACE PERCEPTION
  1. Acoustic Cues for Localization
  2. Neural Mechanisms
  3. Binaural Hearing and Perceptual Organization

Although individual abilities differ among people, it is generally accepted that the frequency range of hearing among humans is 20 to 20000 Hz. The perception of intensity is intricately related to the frequency of sound within this range. Photo: indianeye/iStockphoto.com

I like hearing myself talk. It is one of my greatest pleasures. I often have long conversations all by myself and I am so clever that sometimes I don't understand a word of what I'm saying.

—Oscar Wilde

In the last chapter, we learned about the physical characteristics of sound and the biological mechanisms of sound processing by the ear. The neural signals that emerge out of the cochlea are ultimately transformed in the brain to produce the experience of **hearing**, a perceptual dimension characterized by a truly impressive set of qualities. Among them is our keen ability to identify the exact locations of sounds in our environment using simple acoustic cues. We are also able to easily distinguish the identity of a sound even when it is present in the midst of a very noisy environment. These properties of the auditory system are present in addition to its normal role in providing a meaningful representation of the twin physical characteristics of sound—intensity and frequency. As we noted in Chapter 5, the stimulus in all of these cases is merely a travelling wave of air pressure change that in turn sets up a fluttering motion of the two eardrums. It is this simple mechanical operation that leads to such impressive properties as sound identification and localization as well as the auditory experiences we associate with speech and music perception.

The goal of this chapter is to describe the perceptual characteristics of hearing. Our technical ability to generate or reproduce precise sound stimuli is a relatively recent development in the history of this field. Thus, much of what we will discuss has emerged from studies that were largely undertaken in the 20th century, though there are certainly numerous examples of insightful observations by scientists from an earlier era (Boring, 1942). Two particularly notable examples are the elegant work of Galileo, who showed the relationship between sound frequency and pitch, and the contributions made by Lord Rayleigh in the late 1800s toward understanding the mechanisms of sound localization (SideNote 6.1). We begin this chapter with a discussion of sensitivity and loudness perception and conclude with a discussion of sound localization and auditory space perception.

A. Intensity and Loudness

We frequently talk about the **loudness** of sound to convey our mental impression of its intensity. It is important to distinguish at the outset that *loudness* always refers to the magnitude of the perception created by the sound of a particular physical intensity. Therefore, sound itself cannot have a particular value of loudness, only intensity (or pressure). This distinction is important because quite often the term *loudness* is used interchangeably with the physical intensity of sound.

The characteristics of loudness perception in humans are related to several factors, the most important being the frequency of the sound. Although individual abilities can differ among people, it is generally accepted that 20 to 20000 Hz characterizes the frequency range of hearing among humans. The perception of intensity, as we will shortly see, is intricately related to the frequency of sound within this range. Some other factors that have a bearing on loudness perception include the use of one ear or both, the duration of the sound stimulus, and the presence of other stimuli such as noise. We begin by examining the lowest limits of sound perception—that is, absolute detection thresholds—and the factors that affect them.

1. AUDIBILITY THRESHOLDS

One of the fundamental issues of auditory function concerns the absolute sensitivity of the ear and how it relates to sound frequency (Deutsch & Richards, 1979; Emanuel & Letowski, 2007). Knowledge of this relationship can provide insight into how sound interacts with the auditory structures as well as how perceptual mechanisms are affected by the sensitivity of the auditory system at different frequencies. Furthermore, the use of auditory thresholds to establish cases of hearing loss makes it necessary to obtain a standard set of values for normal hearing function. Attempts to measure auditory thresholds began in the early 1900s, with the first detailed account appearing from Leon Sivian and Samuel White in 1933.

Procedural aspects

The manner in which sound stimuli are delivered to the ear can affect the actual threshold values that are obtained (Fletcher & Munson, 1933; Gulick, Gescheider, & Frisina, 1989). Two general procedures are used. One is to provide the sound through a loudspeaker located directly in front of the subject seated in an enclosed room (SideNote 6.2). Absolute threshold values obtained by this *open-ear* method are called **minimum audible field (MAF)** thresholds. The advantage of MAF thresholds is that they are obtained by

SideNote | **6.1**

The earliest contributions to our understanding of musical pitch are from the ancient Greeks who observed the qualities of vibrating strings and related them to waves in water. In the 6th century BCE, Pythagoras showed that integral ratios of string lengths produced common intervals in vibrational frequency.

SideNote | **6.2**

By convention, the sound source is placed directly in front of the subject, along his or her midline and exactly one metre away. The position of the head must be maintained so that neither ear has an advantage. The room in which the measure is done should minimize sound reflection.

free-field measurement and therefore represent a natural way of listening. The disadvantage is that a number of factors, such as head position and the environmental quality of the room, can influence sound detection.

A second procedure is to have the subject listen to sounds presented to both ears through earphones (Gulick et al., 1989; Moore, 2003). The sound pressure at the eardrum is either estimated or measured directly through a detailed **calibration** procedure. Absolute threshold values obtained by this *closed-ear* method are known as **minimum audible pressure (MAP)** thresholds. The advantage of MAP thresholds is that they can be related to the exact pressure values at the eardrum. It is also easier to ensure that sound stimulation is equally applied to both ears. The disadvantage, however, is that individual differences in the size and shape of the ear canal mean that the pressures exerted upon the eardrum will not necessarily be the same among different people.

The general procedures used to determine the absolute threshold of hearing can be based on any one of Gustav Fechner's classical methods, as discussed in Chapter 1 (SideNote 6.3). In a typical experiment, a subject would be asked whether or not a sound presented at a particular intensity was heard. The sound itself may be presented by either an open-ear or a closed-ear method, as discussed above. After gathering the data from a large number of trials at various subthreshold and suprathreshold intensities, a psychometric function can then be plotted to show the relationship between detection performance and intensity. Typically, the sound intensity that produces 50% detection level is chosen as the criterion for threshold.

Absolute detection thresholds

It has been known for a long time that hearing sensitivity is very much dependent upon frequency (Emanuel & Letowski, 2007; Yost, 2006). Therefore, this is the one critical parameter that needs to be specified at the outset for any threshold measurement. Typically, a pure tone of a certain frequency is used to obtain a psychometric function. This process is then repeated at a different frequency until enough frequencies have been sampled to provide a comprehensive picture of hearing sensitivity. Figure 6.1 shows four psychometric functions, each obtained at a different tone frequency.

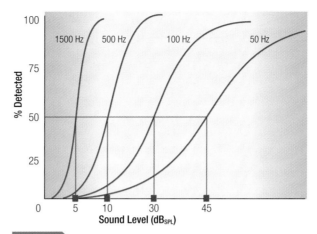

Figure 6.1

Absolute threshold estimates can be obtained from psychometric functions, as shown in these four examples, by taking the sound level that produces 50% detection performance. Detection thresholds are highly dependent upon tone frequency, revealing psychometric functions that shift with respect to each other. In these examples, a 1500 Hz tone yields the lowest absolute threshold value, whereas a 50 Hz tone produces the highest.

The more sensitive the ear is to a particular frequency, the more the psychometric function will be shifted to the left because the threshold level will occur at a lower sound intensity. As shown in this figure, a tone of 1500 Hz requires the least sound level to reach 50% detection performance. Therefore, this frequency yields the lowest detection threshold (about 5 dB$_{SPL}$) in this group, whereas a tone of 50 Hz yields the highest threshold (about 45 dB$_{SPL}$).

Once a set of threshold values is obtained in this manner, they can be plotted with respect to the frequencies at which they were obtained. Such a relationship, known generally as a **psychophysical function**, provides a portrayal of how sensory thresholds vary in relation to a particular stimulus parameter. In the auditory domain, a highly useful psychophysical function is one that relates threshold sound detection levels in terms of frequency. This function, which is shown in Figure 6.2 on page 182, is also known as the **minimal audibility curve**. The threshold values specified by the four psychometric functions in Figure 6.1 are shown by the small squares in Figure 6.2 at their respective frequency points along the x-axis. In order to obtain this profile, a further set of threshold values must be derived in the same manner through their respective sets of psychometric functions at other frequency values within the range shown in Figure 6.2. Since each psychometric function by itself requires a large amount of data

SideNote | **6.3**

Recall that the three principal methods that Fechner introduced were the *Method of Adjustment*, the *Method of Limits*, and the *Method of Constant Stimuli*. Of these, the first is the most straightforward and the third is the most time-consuming, though it is considered to be the most dependable. A quick review of Sections B.1 and B.2 of Chapter 1 may be helpful.

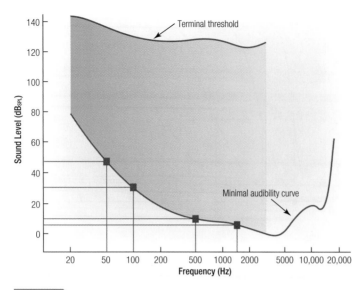

Figure 6.2

The absolute threshold for hearing in humans (minimal audibility curve) shows that sound detection ability is best at frequencies around 2000 to 4000 Hz. Detection performance deteriorates as sound frequencies deviate from this range. The data points on the minimal audibility curve represent the threshold values depicted in the four psychometric functions in Figure 6.1. At the opposite extreme of loudness perception, the sound intensity values that produce a painful sensation occur around 130 to 140 dB$_{SPL}$ and do not appear to rely as much on the sound frequency (terminal threshold). Adapted from *Hearing: Physiological Acoustics, Neural Coding, and Psychoacoustics,* by W. L. Gulick, G. A. Gescheider, and R. D. Frisina, 1989, New York, NY: Oxford University Press.

Anatomical and physiological determinants of the minimal audibility curve

What factors are responsible for the U-shaped profile of the minimal audibility curve? The possibilities can be divided into three sources—the conductive elements of the outer and middle ear, the mechanical response function of the cochlea, and the physiological properties of the auditory nervous system (Moore, 2003; Yost, 2006). The cochlear source can be eliminated because it has been shown that its mechanical response function, particularly that of the basilar membrane, is largely similar across a broad range of sound frequencies. Thus, the determinants of the minimal audibility curve can only be attributed to the other two factors.

We learned in Chapter 5 that the resonant properties of the outer ear (pinna and auditory canal) are such that maximal enhancement occurs at the middle frequencies (SideNote 6.5). It is generally accepted that the low threshold values in the middle frequency range largely occur due to the enhancement of sounds as they are transmitted through the outer and middle ear. However, it is clear that even if these effects are accommodated, there is still another factor at play that causes further threshold reduction in the middle frequencies.

Jozef Zwislocki at Syracuse University has shown that the added threshold reduction occurs due to physiological factors related to the neural processing of sounds (Zwislocki, 1965). He suggested that as sound frequency increases, neurons are better able to summate the responses that are triggered by each complete cycle of the sound wave. Thus, higher frequencies in general produce a stronger neural signal because the rapidity of pressure fluctuations allows them to be more efficiently integrated by the nervous system. This in turn results in reduced detection thresholds. However, this process can only be applied up to a certain limit and therefore does not prevail at very high frequencies. The rise in threshold with frequency to the right of the minimum point in Figure 6.2 illustrates the reduced capacity of the auditory system for signalling rapid pressure changes associated with high frequencies.

Factors that affect absolute sensitivity

The minimal audibility curve can be affected by a number of factors, such as the way in which the data are collected (Gulick et al., 1989). In general, thresholds obtained with the MAF

collection, it should be evident that a psychophysical function such as the minimal audibility curve requires considerable research effort.

A close examination of the minimal audibility curve shows several important features. First, the lowest detection thresholds (highest hearing sensitivities) are found in the range of 2000 to 4000 Hz, the so-called *middle frequencies*. Threshold sound pressures in this frequency range are so low that they nearly approximate the limits imposed by the laws of physics (SideNote 6.4). Second, sounds at frequencies below the optimal range display progressively higher detection thresholds. The absolute lowest frequency that can be detected is a bit difficult to assess because very low frequencies produce a fluttering or tingling and therefore can be felt as well as heard. The lowest frequency that can be heard appears to lie somewhere between 10 and 20 Hz. And third, sound frequencies higher than the middle range also display progressively higher threshold values. Although the upper end of audible sound frequency is generally taken to be 20000 Hz, there have been reports of hearing ability in young subjects with sounds of up to 23000 Hz.

technique are lower by about 6 dB than those obtained with the MAP technique, though the profile of the audibility curve is very similar for both. Whereas the MAP method uses sound pressure values at the eardrum, the MAF method uses pressure values at the outer ear. The lower MAF values can be attributed to the fact that sounds are augmented by the resonance properties of the outer and middle ear. In fact, when these factors are taken into account, much of the threshold discrepancy is eliminated.

Two other factors that affect detection thresholds are the duration of the sound stimulus and whether the sound is applied to both ears (binaural) or just one ear (monaural) (Algom, Ben-Aharon, & Cohen-Raz, 1989). Monaural stimulation yields thresholds that are on average 6 dB higher than binaural thresholds, a value that corresponds to a doubling of sound pressure. Thus, it is the total sound pressure applied to the auditory system that appears to be the relevant factor. That sound pressure can be given to one ear alone or halved and applied to both ears, assuming that both ears are equally sensitive. The fact that the auditory system appears to integrate sound energy from both ears is known as **binaural summation**.

Another type of summation occurs in the time domain. As discussed above, the auditory nervous system can integrate neural excitation generated by successive cycles of sound stimulation. However, it appears that this integration can only occur over a limited time, about 200 milliseconds. This means that if the duration of the sound stimulus is greater than this value, then the auditory system can take full advantage of the integration property. However, if the stimulus duration is less than 200 milliseconds, then the efficiency of the neural capture is compromised. Increasing the sound intensity can offset this deficit. Thus, progressive reductions of sound duration below 200 milliseconds are accompanied by a corresponding increase in detection threshold, as shown in Figure 6.3. Stimulus durations above 200 milliseconds yield a constant threshold value. The fact that the auditory system appears to integrate sound energy over time is known as **temporal summation**.

Terminal thresholds

Thus far we have discussed the properties of hearing at the lowest limits of detection. Beyond this level, we enter into the suprathreshold range where much of our daily

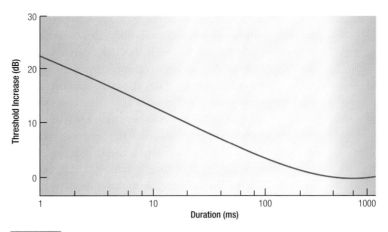

Figure 6.3

The temporal summation properties of the auditory system are revealed when detection thresholds are measured for different stimulus durations. The detection threshold increases progressively as duration is reduced below 200 milliseconds. The threshold is unaffected for stimulus durations above 200 milliseconds. Adapted from "Analysis of Some Auditory Characteristics," by J. J. Zwislocki, 1965, in *Handbook of Mathematical Psychology,* Eds. R. D. Luce, R. R. Bush, E. Galanter, New York, NY: Wiley.

hearing function occurs. However, what happens if sound intensities are increased well beyond our normal level of exposure? Very intense sounds are felt as well as heard, causing either discomfort or pain at the highest limits (Punch, Joseph, & Rakerd, 2004; Sherlock & Formby, 2005). The upper curve in Figure 6.2 shows the **terminal threshold** profile, the maximum sound pressure that we can tolerate. As shown by this profile, sound pressures of around 130 to 140 dB_{SPL} are taken to represent the upper limit of auditory function, regardless of sound frequency.

The range of intensities for normal hearing function therefore occurs within the space bounded by the minimal audibility curve and the terminal threshold profile. This is known as the **dynamic range** of hearing and is shown in Figure 6.2 by the blue shaded area (SideNote 6.6). The dynamic range is highly dependent upon sound frequency. For example, the dynamic range is approximately 135 dB at 4000 Hz, whereas it is only about 80 dB at 100 Hz. This variation with frequency can largely be attributed to the minimal audibility curve, which shows a greater modulation with sound frequency than the relatively flat terminal threshold profile.

2.   DIFFERENCE THRESHOLDS

We are constantly required to discriminate subtle changes in sound signals in our everyday experience with hearing. This requirement

SideNote **6.6**

The range over which terminal thresholds are evaluated does not extend to very high frequencies because of the technical difficulty of producing very intense, high frequency sounds. For this reason, the dynamic range (shaded region) shown in Figure 6.2 does not encompass the full frequency range of the minimal audibility curve.

is especially important in speech perception where fine discrimination ability is essential. One of the well-studied hearing parameters is our ability to discriminate changes in sound intensity. The effort to obtain difference thresholds dates back to the very early days of psychophysical experimentation when Ernst Weber established the general relationship between difference thresholds and signal intensity. Recall from Chapter 1 that according to Weber's law, stimulus intensity had to be changed by a constant proportion, regardless of the intensity level, in order to detect the change. Hence, the difference threshold (ΔI) is related to stimulus intensity by a constant value (k)—that is, $\Delta I = k \cdot I$.

SideNote | **6.7**

It is now known that Weber's law holds true for only a limited range of intensities, within which the Weber constant does not fluctuate. However, at very low or very high intensities, Weber's law breaks down, and the Weber constant can vary with intensity. This condition is known as the *near miss* to the Weber fraction. It appears that much of the intensity range for sound level discrimination can be characterized as a near-miss condition when studied with single tone frequencies.

Weber's law—relationship to sound intensity and frequency

As with detection thresholds, difference thresholds must be separately evaluated for different sound frequencies (Gulick et al., 1989; Jesteadt, Wier, & Green, 1977). Figure 6.4 shows how the Weber constant (k) varies with sound intensity for a number of different tone frequencies. There are two important points contained in this graph. First, the Weber constant for sound intensity discrimination varies from approximately 0.1 to 0.4. This is somewhat

surprising because Weber's notion of a proportional relationship for threshold discrimination was considered to apply across a broad range of intensities. That is, if the Weber constant was say 0.1 at one level then it should remain the same at another level, meaning that a 10% change in stimulus intensity would be required to detect the change across a broad range of intensities. And yet, Figure 6.4 shows that the Weber constant for sound intensity discrimination is higher at low intensities and gradually declines as the intensity increases. Thus, a larger proportional difference is needed at higher than lower sound intensities to produce a just noticeable difference (SideNote 6.7).

The second important point to be taken from Figure 6.4 concerns the role of sound frequency (Jesteadt et al., 1977). Each of the discrimination functions shown here was evaluated with sound tones of a single discrete frequency. There appears to be no functional relationship between sound frequency and the Weber constant because each curve in Figure 6.4 shows a similar profile. Thus, it appears that intensity discrimination is not affected by sound frequency when single tones are used.

Determinants of intensity discrimination ability

Our ability to discriminate sound intensity is based on the response properties of auditory neurons. Although it is possible for individual neurons to signal changes in intensity, it is likely that this function occurs in a broader fashion (Gulick et al., 1989). The reason is that for sound of any given frequency, a greater intensity produces a travelling wave of greater magnitude, as shown in Figure 6.5. This is turn produces an increased spread of excitation along the basilar membrane. We saw in the last chapter that the basilar membrane is mapped in a tonotopic fashion so that a greater spread of excitation essentially means that auditory neurons across a broader range of frequencies will be stimulated. Indeed, our current view is that increased sound intensities produce not only increased discharge in auditory neurons whose characteristic frequency (CF) matches the stimulus but also increased discharge of neurons encoding other nearby frequencies as well. Thus, at low intensities, only neurons with CFs matching the stimulus show increased firing. As the intensity of the tone increases, a larger number of neurons with different CFs are recruited and begin to fire. Our perceptual ability to discriminate sound intensity is likely

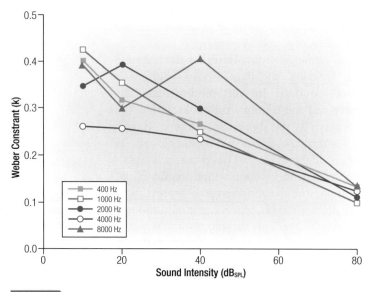

Figure 6.4

The Weber constant (k) for intensity discrimination declines in a steady manner as the sound level increases. However, sound frequency does not appear to influence the Weber constant because the same function is evident across a broad range of frequencies. Adapted from "Intensity Discrimination as a Function of Frequency and Sensation Level," by W. Jesteadt, C. C. Wier, and D. M. Green, 1977, *Journal of the Acoustical Society of America, 61,* pp. 169–177.

derived from a comparison of the discharge patterns across a range of auditory neurons that encode different sound frequencies, as illustrated in Figure 6.5.

3. LOUDNESS PERCEPTION— RELATIONSHIP TO INTENSITY

We now turn to the perception of sounds at suprathreshold intensity levels. As we noted above, the psychological dimension of sound intensity perception is referred to as *loudness*. The effort to understand the fundamental relationship between intensity and loudness has a long and controversial history (Boring, 1942). The controversy can be traced back to the very beginning of psychophysical experimentation in the 19th century when Fechner asserted that sensory magnitudes can only be estimated by indirect means through a series of difference thresholds, as discussed in Sections B.3 to B.5 of Chapter 1. The logarithmic relationship between stimulus intensity and sensation that Fechner derived was believed to apply to all sensory processing, including sound intensity. However, subsequent research with the direct scaling methods developed by S. S. Stevens established the now accepted power law relationship between intensity and loudness (Gulick et al., 1989).

The quest for this fundamental relationship of auditory function began in the early part of the 20th century when the technology became available for precise amplitude control of sound stimuli (SideNote 6.8). Although it was obvious that loudness grows with intensity, the early research quickly showed that there is no exact correspondence between the two—that is, loudness sensation grows at a different rate than intensity. If there really were a one-to-one correspondence, then loudness perception would double when sound pressure doubled. Although a doubling of sound pressure is equivalent to a 6 dB increase (SideNote 6.9), it turns out that a greater amount of intensity change (10 dB to be precise) is required to double loudness sensation. It is worth examining the experimental basis for this result in further detail because it illustrates one of the more elegant investigations in perceptual science.

The sone scale of loudness

Stevens' new psychophysics, which guided much of the research on loudness perception, was based on the direct assessment of sensory

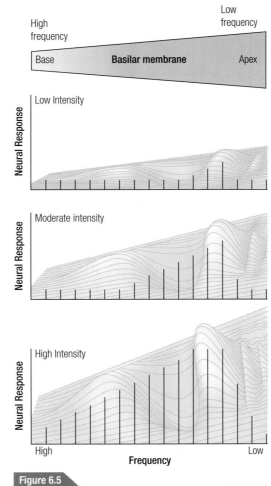

Figure 6.5

Higher intensity sounds produce travelling waves of greater magnitude that in turn produce a greater spread of excitation along the basilar membrane. As the intensity increases, the spread of excitation increases the discharge of neurons at different points along the basilar membrane. Intensity discrimination of single tones is therefore based on a comparison of the discharge patterns across a broad range of auditory neurons. Adapted from *Hearing: Physiological Acoustics, Neural Coding, and Psychoacoustics*, by W. L. Gulick, G. A. Gescheider, and R. D. Frisina, 1989, New York, NY: Oxford University Press.

magnitudes (Gulick et al., 1989; Moore, 2003; Yost, 2006). The experimental procedures required subjects either to rate the perceived intensity of the stimulus (**method of magnitude estimation**) or to identify pairs of stimulus intensities that generated a certain ratio of loudness sensations, such as half, double, etc. (**method of fractionation**). However, in order to carry out these experiments effectively, it was necessary to first define a standard unit of loudness.

Even though loudness cannot be directly measured because it is a perceptual quality, Stevens assumed that its magnitude could

SideNote 6.8

There were a few creative attempts in the 19th century to control sound intensity. One of them involved striking a metal plate with a falling object. The intensity was controlled by raising the object to different heights before its release.

SideNote 6.9

Recall that the decibel scale is based on the logarithm of two sound pressures and can be formally stated as follows—20 log (P1/P2). Thus, doubling pressure from one sound level to another can be written as 20 log (2). This is equal to 6 dB.

nevertheless be quantified. This led him to establish the so-called **sone** scale. By definition, 1 sone is equal to the loudness sensation produced by a 1000 Hz tone at 40 dB_{SPL}. The use of a 1000 Hz tone has therefore become common as a standard stimulus in loudness perception studies. The sone scale by definition is confined to this frequency and all comparisons are made in terms of this standard. For example, a sound of 10 sones is perceived as being 10 times louder than a 1000 Hz tone at 40 dB_{SPL}.

The intensity–loudness function

Let us consider an experiment by which we can establish the relationship between sound intensity and loudness sensation (Gulick et al., 1989). All stimuli in this experiment are of 1000 Hz frequency. We begin by presenting a 40 dB_{SPL} tone, which we now know produces 1 sone of loudness sensation. A human subject is then asked to adjust the physical intensity of a second stimulus until it is perceived as being exactly twice as loud (i.e., 2 sones). After noting the actual intensity (decibel level) of the second stimulus, we now make it the reference stimulus and ask the subject to adjust the intensity level of a third stimulus until it is perceived as being twice as loud (i.e., 4 sones). This procedure is conducted several times, with each iteration representing a doubling in loudness compared to the previously perceived reference. The same procedure can be applied in the opposite direction as well. For example, the subject may be asked to adjust the intensity of the 1000 Hz tone until it is perceived as being half as loud as the 1-sone stimulus. The intensity data from a set of such loudness ratio settings can then be shown in graphical form, as in Figure 6.6 where the x-axis represents sound intensity and the y-axis shows loudness on the sone scale. For the present moment, we will confine our discussion to the binaural function (bold line in Figure 6.6), since both ears were used to listen to the stimuli in this experiment.

Several important points can be taken from this result. First, we see that 40 dB_{SPL} corresponds to 1 sone, which is not surprising since this must be the case by definition. However, in order to perceive a loudness of 2 sones, the stimulus intensity had to be set at 50 dB_{SPL}. And in order to perceive a further doubling of loudness (4 sones), the stimulus had to be set at 60 dB_{SPL}. Thus, an increase of

SideNote 6.10

The 10 dB increase, when converted to sound pressure, corresponds to a factor of 3.2. Thus, slightly more than 3 times the sound pressure is needed to produce a doubling of loudness sensation.

10 dB_{SPL} was required for every doubling of loudness and a 10 dB_{SPL} decrease was required for halving the loudness. This is sometimes referred to as the *10 dB rule*. The interesting fact here is that a perceptual doubling of loudness required sound pressure to be more than doubled (recall that 6 dB is equivalent to a doubling of sound pressure), thus providing us with the basis for our earlier statement that loudness and intensity grow at different rates. To be precise, loudness grows at a lower rate than intensity because relatively more sound intensity is required to produce a given increase in loudness (SideNote 6.10).

The power law relationship

The second interesting feature in Figure 6.6 is that there appears to be a simple relationship between intensity and loudness (Gulick et al., 1989). Except at the very low end, much of the function can be described as a straight line. However, this conclusion would be wrong because the functions in Figure 6.6 are not plotted on linear axes. A careful look at the y-axis shows that the loudness values here increase by multiples of 10 sones along

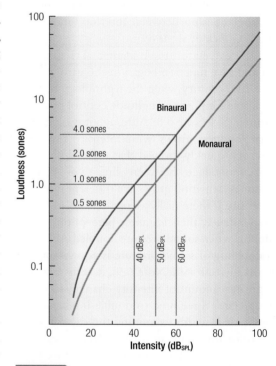

Figure 6.6

The relationship between sound intensity and perceived loudness in sones for a 1000 Hz stimulus. From *Hearing: Physiological Acoustics, Neural Coding, and Psychoacoustics,* by W. L. Gulick, G. A. Gescheider, and R. D. Frisina, 1989, New York, NY: Oxford University Press.

equivalent distances. In other words, this is a logarithmic axis. The x-axis, which represents stimulus intensity, is also logarithmic because it is inherent in the definition of the decibel. Thus, the data in Figure 6.6 are shown in the format of a **log–log plot**.

It turns out that a straight line on a log–log plot is mathematically equivalent to a **power function**. Thus, what appears as a simple straight line in Figure 6.6 actually represents a power function between loudness and sound pressure (SideNote 6.11). The most recent version of that power function was provided by Stevens in 1972 when he derived the following relationship:

$$L = k \cdot P^{0.67}$$

In this equation, loudness (L) is given in sones and the constant (k) depends on the actual units used for sound pressure (P).

The intensity–loudness relationships in Figure 6.6 appear to have two segments. Below approximately 20 dB$_{SPL}$, the function rises rapidly before taking the form of a straight line. It is this straight-line portion that is described by the power law relationship above. The exponent value of 0.67 stipulates that this is a negatively accelerating function. In other words, although loudness increases with intensity, it does not grow as rapidly. This has certain implications for our everyday hearing experience. If two persons are talking at the same intensity, then the perceived loudness will not be twice the loudness produced by their individual voices but only 60% more. This becomes especially important in situations where many more people are all speaking at the same time—for example, in a university lecture hall before a class begins. Just as doubling sound intensity fails to double the loudness, in this situation the perceived loudness will not be a multiple of the individual voices but rather much less, a fact that surely brings some measure of auditory comfort in very noisy environments.

Binaural summation

We saw earlier that absolute detection thresholds were higher by 6 dB with monaural stimulation compared to binaural stimulation. In other words, a doubling of the sound pressure was required, and we concluded from this finding that the auditory system is capable of near-perfect binaural summation at threshold

intensities. It turns out that a similar situation exists at suprathreshold levels with regard to loudness perception (Algom et al., 1989; Fletcher & Munson, 1933; Moore, 2003). This can be seen in Figure 6.6 by comparing the binaural and monaural loudness functions. For any given stimulus intensity, the loudness sensation with binaural presentation is always judged to be twice that of the monaural condition. For example, a 60 dB$_{SPL}$ sound produces 4 sones of loudness according to the binaural function but only 2 sones according to the monaural function. Simply put, sounds are perceived to be louder when they are heard through both ears rather than just one. And the fact that they are judged to be twice as loud has led to the notion that the auditory system is capable of near-perfect binaural summation at suprathreshold intensities. The total loudness sensation generated by any given stimulus is therefore the sum of the loudness resulting from the stimulation of each ear separately.

Determinants of loudness perception

We have previously discussed the neural processes involved in intensity coding and discrimination. As sound intensity increases, the electrical activities of cochlear neurons also increase (see Section C.2 of Chapter 5). However, auditory neurons are only capable of signalling within a restricted range of about 40 dB, far less than the 120 dB that represents the dynamic range of human hearing. The solution to this problem is to have cochlear neurons that encode discrete intensity regions within this span. Therefore, any intensity will only stimulate a subset of the auditory neurons whose operating range contains that intensity. The brain can map sound intensity into loudness by assessing which pool of neurons are responsive to a stimulus and what the firing rate is within that pool.

A second means for intensity coding was presented in the previous section where we saw that higher sound intensities produce a spread of excitation along the basilar membrane (see Figure 6.5) (Deutsch & Richards, 1979; Yost, 2006). That excitation in turn recruits auditory neurons of different characteristic frequencies. For example, a 1000 Hz tone will trigger activity largely within cochlear neurons that receive signals from the corresponding part of the tonotopic map. As the intensity of this tone increases, the spread of excitation along the basilar membrane will

SideNote | **6.11**

The power law relationship between loudness and sound pressure takes the form shown below. This function is equivalent to the straight-line portion in Figure 6.6.

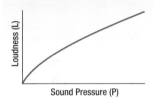

SideNote | **6.12**

Cochlear neurons are responsive within a small range of frequencies even though they fire maximally to a particular *characteristic* frequency (CF). A more intense stimulus will therefore trigger activity in auditory neurons from adjacent parts of the tonotopic map because those neurons may be partially responsive to that sound frequency.

Harvey Fletcher (1884–1981)
Courtesy of Tom Fletcher

SideNote | **6.13**

Harvey Fletcher is regarded as one of the pioneers of hearing research. He played a major role in developing the electronic hearing aid and was the first to demonstrate stereophonic recording and transmission technology. Fletcher was involved in presenting the first stereophonic concert at Carnegie Hall in 1939. He undertook experiments on loudness and frequency as part of a larger effort to understand the properties of hearing, especially in the context of speech and communication technology.

induce activity from adjacent segments of the tonotopic map and therefore trigger signals in cochlear neurons with somewhat different frequency preferences (SideNote 6.12). The brain can examine the total signal envelope from a range of frequency-tuned fibres to construct a loudness percept. Thus, the greater the range of active frequency-tuned fibres, the larger the sound stimulus was likely to have been.

4.   LOUDNESS PERCEPTION— RELATIONSHIP TO FREQUENCY

Just as intensity and frequency represent the twin fundamental qualities of the sound stimulus, a similar idea holds true for the perceptual aspects of hearing. This is the case, for example, with regard to absolute thresholds where the minimum intensity needed for detection is tightly coupled to frequency. Thus, it should not be surprising that the suprathreshold experience of loudness perception is also dependent upon the frequency content of the stimulus. Until now, we have discussed loudness perception largely with regard to the sound of a single frequency (i.e., 1000 Hz). Next, we discuss how loudness perception is affected as the frequency is altered.

Equal loudness contours

Our understanding of how loudness is related to frequency is based largely on the classic work of Harvey Fletcher and Wilden Munson (SideNote 6.13). During the early 1930s, they carried out a series of experiments where subjects had to match the loudness of single tones at various frequencies to a standard reference stimulus. The reference tone was always set at 1000 Hz and presented at a constant intensity level. For each presentation, subjects had to adjust the intensity of a different tone until its loudness was judged to be the same as the reference stimulus. In this way, Fletcher and Munson were able to determine how frequency affected loudness perception across a range of suprathreshold intensities.

Figure 6.7 shows the relationships that were derived when the 1000 Hz reference tone was set at three different intensity levels (38, 68, and 98 dB$_{SPL}$) (Gulick et al., 1989). We first analyze the results of the 38 dB$_{SPL}$ profile as an example. By definition, the ordinate (y-axis value) at 1000 Hz must be equal to 38 dB$_{SPL}$, as shown by the stippled line, since these values

correspond to the intensity and frequency content of the standard stimulus. However, what are the intensity settings at other frequencies that are needed to match loudness to this reference? Figure 6.7 provides this answer for two frequencies—80 and 6000 Hz. As shown by the thin solid lines, an 80 Hz stimulus requires an intensity setting of 70 dB$_{SPL}$, whereas a 6000 Hz stimulus needs to be set at 47 dB$_{SPL}$. A similar procedure can be used to find the intensity values needed to make a loudness match anywhere along the frequency scale of this curve or within any of the two curves that lie above it. In case of the latter, the 1000 Hz reference tone is set at 68 or 98 dB$_{SPL}$, and the same protocol for loudness matching is repeated. The functions derived in this manner and shown in Figure 6.7 are referred to as **equal loudness contours** (Gulick et al., 1989; Suzuki & Takeshima, 2004).

There are several important points to be taken from Figure 6.7. First, each of the equal loudness curves provides a comprehensive set of data on the intensity values that produce equal loudness perception across a range of frequencies. Thus, even though the curves are labelled according to the intensity value used for the 1000 Hz reference tone, the relationship portrayed by each curve is binding on all other frequencies with respect to each other. Using the examples above, we would know that a 6000 Hz tone at 47 dB$_{SPL}$ would be matched for loudness by an 80 Hz tone at 70 dB$_{SPL}$. Second, it can be seen that progressively higher intensities are needed to achieve equal loudness perception as we move toward the extreme ends of the frequency spectrum (SideNote 6.14). The equal loudness contours in Figure 6.7 rise sharply for low and high frequencies, a relationship that is similar to threshold sound detection, as illustrated by way of the minimal audibility curve. And third, the equal loudness contours appear to become flatter at higher intensities. In other words, the intensity setting required to match loudness is similar across a broad range of frequencies. This implies that very loud sounds are perceived as being equally loud irrespective of frequency.

The appearance of the minimal audibility curve in Figure 6.7 as a smooth U-shaped function is somewhat different from the minimal audibility curve we saw earlier in Figure 6.2 (SideNote 6.15). The main difference is that the earlier function displayed some perturbations

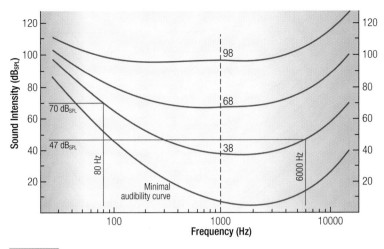

Figure 6.7

Loudness matching of sound intensities across frequency shows a characteristic U-shaped profile. These so-called *equal loudness contours* are obtained through loudness matches to a 1000 Hz tone at a particular intensity level. This figure shows the functions obtained at three such suprathreshold intensities (38, 68, and 98 dB$_{SPL}$) along with the minimal audibility curve. Adapted from "Loudness, Its Definition, Measurement and Calculation," by H. Fletcher and W. A. Munson, 1933, *Journal of the Acoustical Society of America, 5,* pp. 82–108.

at the high frequency end. The reason for this is based on the way the two functions were derived. The earlier function was obtained from measurements in a free field, such as an enclosed room, whereas the minimal audibility curve and the similarly shaped equal loudness curves in Figure 6.7 were obtained by Fletcher and Munson using an earphone. A free-field approach is preferable in many ways because it simulates hearing under natural conditions.

The phon scale of loudness

A later study of equal loudness matches was conducted in a free field. The results of that study are shown in Figure 6.8 on page 190 (Gulick et al., 1989). The various equal loudness contours in this figure all have a similar appearance in that there is a notch at about 4000 Hz accompanied by a steep rise at 8000 Hz. These perturbations are believed to be the result of artifacts caused by the listener's head, which alters the sound pressure reaching the eardrum within this set of frequencies. Consequently, the perturbations in the equal loudness contours are only evident in free-field measurements (Figure 6.8) and not when earphones are used (Figure 6.7).

As noted earlier, the equal loudness curves are derived by using a reference tone of 1000 Hz set at a particular intensity. Thus we can label each equal loudness curve by the intensity value of the reference as a way of distinguishing them. This was the implication in Figure 6.7. However, this becomes somewhat cumbersome because we have to be absolutely explicit in noting that the intensity value refers only to the 1000 Hz standard. Furthermore, we cannot use that value as a general descriptor of the entire equal loudness curve because the intensity needed for a loudness match varies with frequency. We cannot use the sone scale either because that is restricted to sounds of only 1000 Hz and therefore cannot be used as a loudness scale for other frequencies.

The unit of measurement used to indicate loudness level across frequencies is the **phon**. The number of phons at any frequency is simply equal to the intensity in dB$_{SPL}$ of the 1000 Hz standard tone when the two are judged to be of equal loudness. For example, the three equal loudness contours in Figure 6.7 can be denoted as 38, 68, and 98 phon curves. Similarly, the equal loudness contours in Figure 6.8 are given by the phon level of each curve. The use of the phon scale makes it easier to convey loudness information. For example, all tones specified by the frequency and intensity values on the 40 phon curve in Figure 6.8 produce the same loudness sensation as a 1000 Hz tone at 40 dB$_{SPL}$—that is, they are all 40 phons of loudness.

SideNote **6.14**

Low and high frequency sounds are perceived as being much less loud than mid-frequency sounds, hence the need to use greater intensities. This has certain implications. For example, music is normally played at intensity levels between 30 and 100 dB$_{SPL}$. If the intensity level of all frequencies is decreased by the same amount, then bass (low) and treble (high) frequencies can fall below the threshold of hearing. This is why the loudness control on a stereo system boosts the intensity of very low and high frequencies relative to others so that the music will have the same proportion of treble and bass to the ear as when it is played at a higher level.

SideNote **6.15**

The minimal audibility curve can also be thought of as an equal loudness contour except that it represents the threshold of detection (i.e., the minimum perception of loudness). For this reason, it is usually shown along with the set of suprathreshold equal loudness contours.

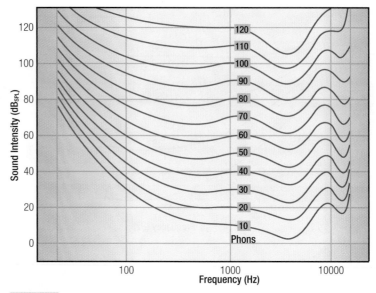

Figure 6.8

Equal loudness contours obtained for pure tones matched to a 1000 Hz stimulus. Each curve is labelled by the loudness measure in phons (i.e., the intensity in dB$_{SPL}$ of the 1000 Hz standard tone). Adapted from *Hearing: Physiological Acoustics, Neural Coding, and Psychoacoustics,* by W. L. Gulick, G. A. Gescheider, and R. D. Frisina, 1989, New York, NY: Oxford University Press.

5. MASKING AND NOISE

Our ability to hear sounds is highly affected by the presence of other background sounds. Thus far, we have discussed the sensory capacities of hearing only when single tones were used and under the condition that there was no background noise. However, this kind of auditory stimulation is generally restricted to laboratory settings. Our normal world contains sounds with a mixture of many different frequencies, thereby producing an auditory signal that is far more complex than in the case of a single tone. Furthermore, our auditory system has to deal with the ongoing challenge of distinguishing a signal from irrelevant sounds that make up the background noise. In this section, we will discuss some of the more complex features of loudness perception that arise when the sound signal contains more than a single tone.

Masking—general properties

The most common perceptual consequence of listening to sound mixtures is **masking**. We encountered this phenomenon previously in the chemosensory system where we saw that the detection threshold of a taste primary or an odourant can be raised if they are presented in a mixture. After all, this is the basis for how fragrances and deodorants mask unpleasant

body odours. A similar effect of sound interaction occurs in the auditory system. Our perception of a particular sound is affected by the presence of other sounds through the phenomenon of masking. We know from ordinary experience that low to moderate intensity sounds are often not heard if in the presence of more intense sounds. When the detection threshold of a particular sound is raised because of other sounds, it is said to masked. The amount of masking is given by the amount of threshold elevation and usually expressed in decibels. For example, if the normal threshold for a particular tone in a silent background is 20 dB$_{SPL}$ but becomes 60 dB$_{SPL}$ in the presence of noise, then there is a 40 dB masking effect from the noise (SideNote 6.16).

The study of masking effects has played an important role in our understanding of auditory perception and physiology (Moore, 2003; Yost, 2006). In fact, many of the early masking studies were quite influential in providing clues to the biological processing of sound signals. As a result, there has been much effort to study the various aspects of auditory masking. These efforts can be broken down into two general categories—masking effects of single tones and masking by noise. Both sets of studies have revealed considerable insight into auditory function, such as the properties of the

SideNote | **6.16**

There is no set rule as to which sound serves as the signal or the masker. For example, if we happen to be talking to someone while there is an interesting song in the background, then either the person's speech can be masked by the music or vice versa, depending on which signal we wish to attend to. Furthermore, this can change from moment to moment. Thus, the signal in one instance can become the masker in the next.

basilar membrane and the way that sound frequency information is transmitted to the brain. The interesting point here is that many of these insights were provided by psychophysicists well before the advent of technological developments in biology that permitted direct functional studies of the auditory system.

Tonal masking—frequency effects

The masking effects of a single tone by another is known as **tonal masking**. A typical experiment would be carried out by choosing a tone of a fixed frequency (the test tone) and determining how its audibility is affected by another tone (the masking tone) (Vogten, 1974). If the test and masking tones are of the same frequency, then the experiment can be thought of as a mere intensity discrimination study. In other words, the extra sound intensity required to just make a tone audible over and above a tone of the same frequency represents a difference threshold measure. This is illustrated in the top panel of Figure 6.9 where a brief test tone must be distinguished when applied in the presence of a masking tone. A composite sound waveform is created where the two tones overlap (shown in bold), and it is this portion of the sound pattern that must be distinguished from the background masking tone. A more interesting situation arises when audibility of the test tone is determined for a masking tone of a different frequency, as shown in the middle panel of Figure 6.9. In this example, a brief 1000 Hz test tone is presented with a 500 Hz masking tone. The task in a psychophysical experiment would be to detect the sound produced by the composite waveform (shown in bold) that arises from the overlap of the test and masking tones.

The effects of varying the masking frequency upon the audibility of a single test tone provide a classic example of the power of psychophysical experimentation (Vogten, 1974; Wegel & Lane, 1924). Let us consider a 1000 Hz test tone that is presented at an intensity of 10 dB above its threshold detection level. The objective is to take a different frequency masking tone and find the intensity level at which the test tone can just be detected when the two are presented together. The test tone intensity in this experiment is always constant, and it is the masking tone intensity that is varied until the test tone can just be heard. The results are shown in the bottom panel of Figure 6.9. It is evident from this data

that different masking frequencies have different effects upon the audibility of the 1000 Hz test tone. The most effective masking occurs, not surprisingly, when the masking and test tone frequencies are the same. This is apparent from the fact that the least amount of intensity is needed when the masker frequency is 1000 Hz. Masking tones of other frequencies are less effective because they require higher intensities to mask the 1000 Hz test tone sufficiently to make it just audible.

Tonal masking—psychophysical tuning curves

The masking profile in Figure 6.9 presents an important relationship because it shows how effectively sound at a particular frequency is processed by the auditory system in the presence of other tones. Masking, after all,

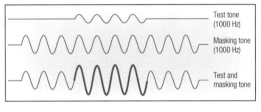

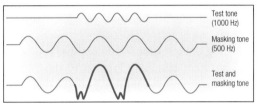

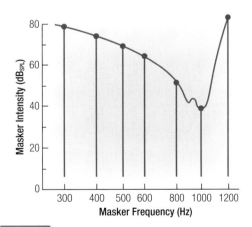

Figure 6.9

Tonal masking effects are evaluated with test and masking tones at a single frequency. The test and mask frequencies may be identical (top panel) or different (middle panel). The bold component represents the composite waveform when the two tones are presented together. The bottom panel shows the masking intensities that are needed at different frequencies to reduce the audibility of a 1000 Hz, 10 dB test tone so that it is barely detectable.

SideNote | **6.17**

The importance of the psycho-physical tuning curve in Figure 6.9 is that it shows the frequency selectivity characteristics of the human auditory system as revealed by the masking capacity of tones at different frequencies. The only similar measure we have seen is the neural response functions related to frequency (see Figure 5.24). However, that data was obtained from animals by single-unit recording techniques that cannot be applied to humans.

SideNote | **6.18**

It was first observed in 1876 that sounds are more easily masked by lower frequency sounds than higher frequency ones. The psychophysical tuning curves reflect this fundamental property of masking and show that there is an inherent asymmetry in how sound frequencies are transmitted through an internal filter.

represents the perceived interference effects of two different tones. If a particular tone requires a high intensity level for its masking function, then it interfered poorly with the principal tone being considered. This in turn implies that less effective masking frequencies are simply processed at lower efficiency by the functional units responsible for coding and transmitting the test tone. Using this logic, the masking profile can be thought of in terms of an internal filter. The filter shown in Figure 6.9 is most effective at transmitting sounds of 1000 Hz and less so at other adjacent frequencies. For these reasons, the masking profile is more commonly referred to as a *psychophysical tuning curve* (SideNote 6.17).

A psychophysical tuning curve essentially portrays the frequency selectivity of an internal filter that is centred around some frequency (Gulick et al., 1989). A narrow tuning curve means that the filter has a high degree of frequency selectivity, whereas a broad curve implies a lower selectivity such that other frequencies are also efficiently transmitted. The next question then concerns the tuning characteristics of internal filters at other frequencies and whether they are comparable to the one shown in Figure 6.9. We can obtain tuning curves related to other frequencies by changing the test tone frequency and repeating the above experiment. Figure 6.10 shows a set of such psychophysical tuning curves that were obtained with various test tones and frequencies. Although tuning curves are generally all

U-shaped, they differ in terms of their frequency selectivity. At low frequencies, for example, the tuning curve is quite broad compared to the tuning curves representing higher frequencies. Furthermore, the placement of these profiles along the intensity scale (y-axis) follows the general trend of the minimal audibility curve. This is not surprising because the masking effectiveness of any tone is related to its perceived loudness, which as we saw in the previous section is related to frequency in a manner that is similar to the minimal audibility curve.

Tonal masking—asymmetric response profile

A closer look at the psychophysical tuning curves in Figure 6.10 shows a rather odd property (Gulick et al., 1989). Each of these profiles has an asymmetric shape in that the high frequency end shows a steep rise, whereas the low frequency end rises more gently and can even plateau. This is especially evident in the tuning curve shown in Figure 6.9, which can be used as a reference in the following discussion. The upshot of this asymmetry is that masking tones whose frequencies are higher than the test tone frequency lose their masking effectiveness much more rapidly than masking tones of a lower frequency (SideNote 6.18). This suggests that there is an inherent asymmetry in the way that sounds are processed by the auditory system.

It turns out that the source of this asymmetry can be traced to the travelling wave that is produced on the basilar membrane by sound stimulation (Recanzone & Sutter, 2008; Yost, 2006). We saw in Chapter 5 (Section B.3) that the travelling wave proceeds from the base of the cochlea to its apex and shows maximum displacement at a point on the tonotopic map of the basilar membrane that corresponds to the sound frequency. It turns out that the travelling wave shows a gradual buildup and then a sudden decay after reaching the maximum displacement. This can be seen in the top panel of Figure 6.11 where a travelling wave generated by a 1000 Hz tone is shown in grey. The undulation of the basilar membrane can be thought of as producing a certain level of excitation in the auditory neurons (shown by the bold line). Accordingly, the excitation level follows the general trend of the travelling wave in that it too shows a gradual buildup along the basilar membrane and then decays very fast after the signal has crested. Because

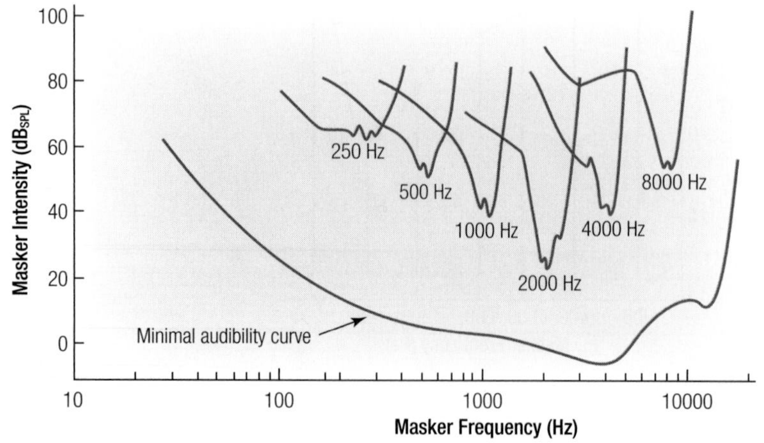

Figure 6.10

Psychophysical tuning curves obtained with test tones of various frequencies show a common U-shaped profile. Tuning curves at lower frequencies generally show a broader selectivity. The blue profile represents the tuning curve from Figure 6.9. Adapted from "Pure Tone Masking: A New Result from a New Method," by L. L. M. Vogten, 1974, in *Facts and Models in Hearing*, Eds. E. Zwicker and E. Terhardt, Berlin: Springer-Verlag.

this represents a general property of basilar membrane response, all tonal sounds will show a similar excitation profile, although the actual peak will occur at different points depending on the frequency.

We are now armed with the necessary background to understand the asymmetric nature of psychophysical tuning curves. Let us first consider a 1000 Hz test tone and an 800 Hz masking tone. The excitation levels produced by the two tones in response to their respective travelling waves are shown in the middle panel of Figure 6.11. Recall that high frequencies are represented toward the base of the cochlea and low frequencies toward the apex. Thus, the masking tone (the grey profile in the middle panel of Figure 6.11) will crest further along the basilar membrane than the test tone. This means that the test tone will have to be distinguished against a fairly high background excitation level produced by the masking tone, as shown by the closeness of the two arrowheads. For this reason, a relatively low intensity is sufficient for an 800 Hz tone to effectively mask the 1000 Hz test tone. On the other hand, if the masking tone frequency is 1200 Hz, then the crest of its travelling wave occurs before that of the test tone (grey profile in the bottom panel of Figure 6.11). The test tone must now be distinguished against a fairly low background excitation level because of the sharp decay in the masking tone's travelling wave. For this reason, a higher masking frequency has reduced effectiveness and therefore requires a greater intensity setting to produce the same masking effect. It is this fundamental difference in masking effectiveness between higher and lower frequencies that produces the asymmetry in the masking profile.

Noise masking—asymmetric response profile

We have thus far considered the masking effects of tones at different frequencies upon the audibility of a single test tone. Another way of evaluating masking effects is to do the opposite—that is, use a single masking tone and evaluate its effect upon the audibility of test tones of different frequencies. The results of such an experiment should theoretically show an asymmetric profile similar in nature to the one we saw before. In general, this is true, although the results are cleaner if *noise* is used instead of a single masking tone. We learned in Chapter 5 that noise simply refers to sounds composed of multiple frequencies.

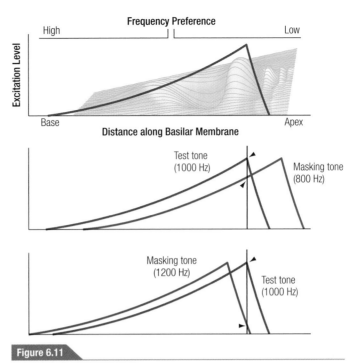

Figure 6.11

Neural excitation level in response to stimulation by a 1000 Hz tone (top panel) shows a gradual increase along the basilar membrane that suddenly decays after reaching its peak. This profile mimics the travelling wave on the basilar membrane (shown in green). The presence of two tones of different frequencies produces two separate excitation profiles that crest at different points (middle and bottom panels). The excitation signal generated by a 1000 Hz test tone must be processed against a fairly high masking signal when the mask frequency is lower (arrowheads in middle panel), whereas the same test tone is less affected if the mask frequency is higher (arrowheads in bottom panel).

If the noise happens to encompass a large segment of audible frequency range then it is referred to as **broadband noise**. On the other hand, if the noise stimulus contains a limited range of frequencies, then it is called **bandpass noise**.

Let us consider an experiment where we observe the masking effects of *narrow-band noise* upon test tones of various frequencies. The narrow-band noise is centred at 410 Hz and has a **bandwidth** of 90 Hz (SideNote 6.19). The effect that this noise pattern has on the threshold elevation of different test tones is shown in Figure 6.12 on page 194 (Gulick et al., 1989). The greatest effect is seen for test tones in the frequency range of the noise band. The threshold elevation effect rapidly diminishes for test tones of lower frequency. However, the drop-off is much more gradual for higher test tone frequencies. In other words, the test tone is masked to a greater degree when it has a higher frequency than the masking stimulus, resulting in elevated detection thresholds. Thus, we again find evidence for an internal filter with

SideNote **6.19**

The masking noise stimulus, which is shown below, has a centre frequency of 410 Hz and contains energy in the range of 365–455 Hz (i.e., it has a bandwidth of 90 Hz).

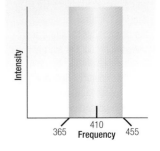

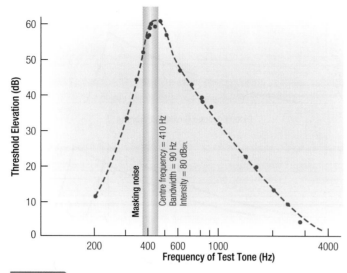

Figure 6.12

The use of narrow-band noise reveals different degrees of masking depending upon the test tone frequency. The masking effect (detection threshold elevation) is greatest when the test tone frequency is similar to that of the noise band. At lower test tone frequencies, the masking effect shows a sharp decline, whereas the masking effect is comparatively greater when test tone frequencies are higher than the masking band. Adapted from "On the Masking Pattern of a Single Auditory Stimulus," by J. P. Egan and H. W. Hake, 1950, *Journal of the Acoustical Society of America, 22*, pp. 622–630.

SideNote | 6.20

These filters are based on psychophysical data and represent individual channels through which signal transmission is thought to occur in the auditory system. They are similar in nature to the neural tuning functions we saw in Chapter 5. However, the psychophysical filters are likely the product of activity in a number of neighbouring cochlear neurons. Sensory filters represent a common theme in perceptual science, as noted in our treatment of the various sensory systems.

an asymmetric profile. As before, this asymmetry can be attributed to the properties of the travelling wave in the cochlea and exactly the same logic can be applied to explain the relative degrees of masking provided by sounds of different frequencies.

Noise masking—critical band

We have now seen two ways in which psychophysical tuning functions can be derived—first, through tonal masking where the effects of different masking tones were evaluated on the audibility of a fixed test tone and, second, through noise masking where threshold detection was evaluated for different test tones in the presence of a fixed narrow-band noise. Both procedures revealed a tuning function whose properties can be considered to represent those of an internal filter. These results have led to the idea that the basilar membrane operates as a bank of filters covering the entire audible range, as shown in the top panel of Figure 6.13 (SideNote 6.20). Each filter is centred on a particular frequency and transmits a sound within a limited range of frequencies (i.e., its bandwidth).

The next question concerns just how large the effective bandwidth of these internal filters is. Psychophysical efforts to estimate

the bandwidth have also made use of masking noise and its effects upon the detection of single tones. To understand this, we consider a 500 Hz test tone and examine the influence of noise bands on its detection threshold. In a typical experiment, subjects are tested on how much the test tone's detection threshold is elevated when it is presented with noise of different bandwidths. From a theoretical perspective, let us assume that there is an internal filter whose maximum output is centred on the tone frequency, as represented by the bold tuning curve in the top panel of Figure 6.13. Given that the internal filter has a certain bandwidth, it is reasonable to assume that only those components of noise that are passed through this filter will affect test tone detection. Any noise frequencies that fall outside the filter should not affect its detection threshold.

This is precisely the result observed, as shown in the middle panel of Figure 6.13. The left graph in this panel shows that detection threshold of the test tone rises with increasing noise bandwidth. However, the masking effects of the noise only occur up to a certain bandwidth after which there is no further threshold elevation. To understand this, we consider three different noise bands and their relationship to the tuning function in question (bottom panel in Figure 6.13). The three noise bands are all centred on the test tone frequency (shown as the white line) but encompass different portions of the tuning curve. Noise Band 1 produces only a slight elevation of the tone threshold, whereas Noise Band 2 produces the maximum threshold elevation. Noise Band 3 does not produce further threshold elevation because the additional frequencies it contains largely fall outside the range of the internal filter. Thus, only sound stimuli that have frequencies within the bandwidth of the same filter can mask each other. By definition, the noise bandwidth that can elevate the tone detection threshold is known as the **critical band**. The critical band, in turn, provides a measure of the effective bandwidth of the internal filter.

B. Frequency and Pitch

The perceptual quality that we associate with sound frequency is **pitch**. The subjective experience of pitch is most often described along a *high–low* dimension—that is, two sounds of different frequencies are usually described in terms of one being higher or lower in pitch than the other (Plack, Oxenham, Fay, & Popper, 2005). Our long-standing interest in pitch stems largely from its association with music. Studies of musical pitch can be traced back to the ancient Greeks who used differences in pitch as the basis for musical intervals. Pythagoras showed in the 6th century BCE that the pitch generated by different strings is related to differences in their vibrational pattern and that differences in pitch are related to simple ratios in the lengths of the strings.

The modern study of pitch perception began largely around the middle of the 19th century and included important early contributions by von Helmholtz, Ohm, and Seebeck on the relationship between pitch and sound frequency. This paved the way for significant advances in our understanding of frequency processing and pitch perception throughout the 20th century. In this section, we will discuss many of the insights that emerged from these studies, including the various attributes of pitch and its relationship to frequency. However, we first begin with a description of the fundamental limits of sound frequency perception in humans.

1. FREQUENCY THRESHOLDS

In physical terms, sound can theoretically vary in frequency from just above zero to about 10^{13} Hz (SideNote 6.21). Human hearing, however, is sensitive to a very small segment within this vast range. By now we are well familiar with the fact that human auditory function usually encompasses a frequency range that spans from 20 to 20000 Hz. As we noted earlier in Section A.1, sound detection may be possible under exceptional cases up to a limited extent above and below these values.

Limits of sound frequency detection

Sounds that have a frequency below 20 Hz are called **infrasonic** and are often found in nature—thunder, waves, waterfalls, volcanoes, and earthquakes. It is thought that certain animals have developed an early warning mechanism for detecting weather disturbances because of their sensitivity to low frequency sounds. A comparison of the effective range of hearing among various animals in Figure 6.14 shows that elephants (and cows and horses) have the lowest frequency detection capability in this list.

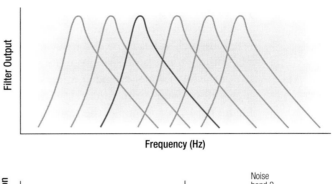

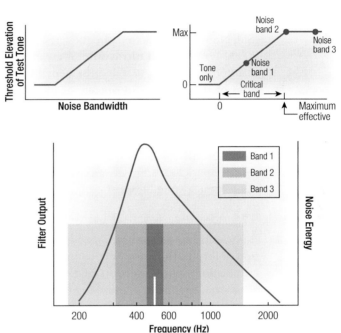

Figure 6.13

A set of tuning functions that can be considered internal filters spanning the frequency range of the auditory system (top panel). The detection threshold of any given test tone is governed by a specific filter (shown in bold) and affected only by masking noise frequencies that are transmitted through the same filter. A limited range of noise frequencies, known as the *critical band*, can affect tone detection (middle panel). The bottom panel shows the relationship between the internal filter and three different noise bands that are centred on the tone frequency (white line).

Even though outright hearing may not be possible in humans for sounds below 20 Hz (i.e., there is no discernible pitch), such sounds nevertheless produce a fluttering or thrusting quality that can often be felt as a tactile stimulus. Low frequencies in general, even when they are within the audible frequency range, tend to produce a pressure sensation on the body. This is apparent from our routine experience with low frequency (high bass) musical beats played at high intensity. The resulting boom that is felt on our body occurs largely because of the high intensity needed in the signal to overcome our low sensitivity for low frequency sounds. It has been reported that a flutter sensation can be felt with infrasonic frequencies down to about

Pythagoras of Samos (572–490 BCE)
© Lebrecht Music and Arts Photo Library/Alamy

10 Hz. Prolonged exposure to infrasonic sound at high intensity produces a number of adverse reactions, such as headache and nausea.

Although human hearing is quite impressive at the low frequency end, it is less so at the high end in comparison to other animals (see Figure 6.14). For example, the upper limit of 20000 Hz in humans is quite modest in comparison to say bats and marine mammals such as dolphins and whales, which are all capable of hearing sounds in excess of 100000 Hz (SideNote 6.22). Sound frequencies above 20000 Hz are called **ultrasonic**. It is believed that both the mechanical and the neural functions of the cochlea can operate at ultrasonic frequencies. The upper limit in humans is largely imposed by pain that is produced due to the high intensities needed at high frequencies. Nevertheless, it has been reported that sounds up to 23000 Hz are audible under special laboratory conditions.

Difference thresholds

It is possible to estimate frequency discrimination ability in the same way as intensity discrimination, which we discussed earlier. The question here concerns how much of a change in frequency is required to produce a detectable difference. From a procedural point of view, the question is complicated by the fact that sounds of two slightly different frequencies cannot be simultaneously applied because they will then produce a composite sound wave that will itself be different from either of the two tones. Frequency discrimination studies are therefore carried out by the successive presentation of two different tones, after which the subject must judge whether they were the same or different (Deutsch & Richards, 1979; Plack et al., 2005).

There are two general trends that emerge from these studies. First, the difference threshold (Δf) has a constant value of around 3 Hz for tone frequencies less than 1000 Hz. In other words, only a 3 Hz change is required in order for human subjects to notice a difference in pitch. Second, at frequencies above 1000 Hz, the difference threshold rises progressively. However, the important parameter to consider here is the Weber constant (k)—that is, $\Delta f/f$—because it relates the difference threshold to the actual frequency at which it is measured. By now we know that for most sensory processes, the Weber constant remains stable over a fairly broad range of the sensory dimension in question. The same is true for frequency difference thresholds. The value we just noted (i.e., $\Delta f = 3$ Hz at $f = 1000$ Hz) produces an extremely low Weber constant value of 0.003, implying a very high sensitivity to detecting changes in frequency (SideNote 6.23).

2. ACOUSTIC PITCH

The characteristics of the auditory system have both a positive and negative impact on the study of *acoustic pitch* perception (SideNote 6.24). The way that sound frequency is coded by the basilar membrane and related neural elements produces a major advantage when it comes to making pitch judgments. We know from our discussion in the last chapter that sound signals across the full auditory range are transmitted through cochlear neurons that are sensitive to only a discrete range of frequencies. The net effect of this setup in terms of sensory function is that a large series of internal filters is responsible for separately processing and transmitting discrete bands of frequency information across the full auditory spectrum. As a result, our capacity to make differential pitch judgments is extremely

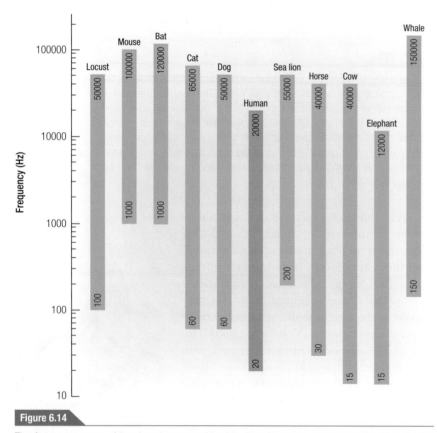

Figure 6.14

The frequency range of hearing shows considerable diversity across animal species. The species are presented here from left to right by increasing body weight. There is no consistent relationship between animal size and the frequency range of hearing.

good and in fact accounts for the very high frequency discrimination sensitivity noted above. The fact that sound frequency information is being sampled simultaneously through a large number of parallel channels allows us to make exquisite judgments based on a comparison of signals from a large number of independent transmission cables to the brain.

The negative dimension that pitch perception studies must contend with concerns the fact that pitch perception is a highly qualitative sensory experience (Plack et al., 2005). We already know from our previous discussion that loudness sensation can vary in a quantitative manner—that is, the sensory quality is the same at all levels but the magnitude of the experience can vary depending on the sensation level. Different levels of pitch, however, are difficult to quantify along any single dimension. As the pitch changes, we experience a different kind of perception that appears to be related to multiple dimensions at once. Another sensory experience that is somewhat similar in nature is that of colour vision. Although perceived colour is related to light wavelength, changing the stimulus along this dimension produces an entirely different sensory experience. Perceptual qualities that allow us to make a judgment of "how much" are termed *prothetic*, as is the case with loudness sensation. Pitch and colour perceptions, however, represent *metathetic* qualities, whereby the sensory experience cannot be related to the stimulus in a precisely quantitative manner (see Section C.2 of Chapter 1).

Relationship between frequency and pitch

Even though sound frequency cannot be mapped onto the sensory dimension of pitch in an exact manner, there is nevertheless a correlation between the two. We know, for example, that higher frequencies sound "higher" in pitch, whereas lower frequencies sound "lower." Indeed, it may seem that this perceptual correlation with sound frequency forms the basis for the "high–low" dimension of pitch sensation. However, it is more likely that these descriptors of pitch arise from the feelings they generate in the listener. High-pitched tones, for example, give the impression that they have a higher localization in space than low-pitched tones.

The relationship between sound frequency and pitch is complicated by a number of other factors. For example, the intensity of

a tone can affect its pitch even when the frequency remains unchanged. Furthermore, this intensity effect is different for low versus high frequency tones. Perhaps the most perplexing of all is that a pitch sensation that normally corresponds to a particular frequency is reported even when there is no signal at that particular frequency. This well-known effect has important implications for the neural coding of pitch. Thus, even though there is a correlation between tone frequency and pitch sensation, it is clear that there are a number of effects that complicate this relationship.

The mel scale of pitch

The relationship between the psychological impression of pitch and the physical parameter of frequency can be explored through psychophysical means (Stevens & Volkmann, 1940; Stevens, Volkmann, & Newman, 1937). If we start with a tone at a particular frequency, say 1000 Hz, we can then ask a listener to adjust the frequency until the pitch sensation is judged to be half as much (SideNote 6.25). However, how do we actually convey a pitch value that is half as much as the one produced at 1000 Hz? One way to do so would be to come up with a unit of pitch. In 1937, S. S. Stevens defined the **mel** scale of pitch and proposed that the pitch sensation generated by a 1000 Hz tone be arbitrarily given a value of 1,000 mels. Thus, a pitch sensation that is half of this would be 500 mels, whereas a pitch sensation that is twice as high would have a value of 2,000 mels. The question now is "What are the corresponding sound frequencies that produce such pitch sensations?"

Figure 6.15 on page 198 shows the relationship between sound frequency and pitch sensation in mels (Gulick et al., 1989). The important point to be taken from this graph is the non-equivalent relationship between pitch and frequency. For example, pitch sensation rises rapidly with frequencies up to 1000 Hz. Above 1000 Hz, pitch sensation rises much less rapidly (SideNote 6.26). Returning to the question above, we see from Figure 6.15 that a pitch of 500 mels is produced by a tone frequency of 400 Hz, whereas a pitch of 2,000 mels requires a tone of 3000 Hz. Thus, sound frequencies do not have an exact correspondence to pitch in terms of the mel scale, even though we began by assigning 1,000 mels to a tone of 1000 Hz. The importance of Figure 6.15 is that it portrays a general function between pitch and

SideNote **6.23**

A value of 0.003 is in fact the lowest Weber constant found across all sensory processes. A quick glance at Table 1.1 provides a comparison of the Weber fraction for pitch (i.e., frequency discrimination) with some other sensory dimensions.

SideNote **6.24**

At this point, we distinguish pitch produced by single tones as *acoustic pitch* and that produced by complex tones as *musical pitch*. We will take up musical pitch in the next chapter.

SideNote **6.25**

This procedure, known as the *method of fractionation*, is similar to that used for determining the sone scale of loudness, as discussed in Section A.3. The first set of experiments to relate the stimulus qualities of intensity and frequency to the psychological dimensions of loudness and pitch were carried out by Stevens and his colleagues.

SideNote **6.26**

Although this point may not be obvious from looking at Figure 6.15, keep in mind that the pitch scale (y-axis) is plotted on a linear dimension, whereas the frequency scale (x-axis) is logarithmic. Thus, although the curve looks quite steep beyond 1000 Hz, the rise in pitch sensation actually grows less rapidly in relation to frequency.

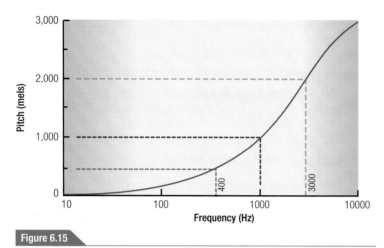

Figure 6.15

Pitch sensation increases with tone frequency, although the relationship between the two is not exact. By definition, a 1000 Hz tone at 40 dB$_{SPL}$ produces a pitch of 1000 mels. Adapted from "The Relation of Pitch to Frequency," by S. S. Stevens and J. Volkmann, 1940, *American Journal of Psychology, 53*, pp. 329–353.

frequency because a true quantitative relationship between the two is difficult to attain.

Intensity and pitch

We have thus far been careful to avoid bringing intensity into the picture because it can complicate matters considerably. In general, the pitch of a pure tone is influenced by intensity (SideNote 6.27). However, this effect is different for sounds of different frequencies. Above 2500 Hz, increasing the intensity produces an increase in acoustic pitch. Furthermore, this intensity effect upon pitch becomes progressively greater for higher frequencies. Below 2500 Hz, the opposite effect takes place. That is, the perceived pitch actually declines as tone intensity increases. For middle frequencies around 2500 Hz, there is no appreciable effect of intensity on pitch perception. These varied effects together illustrate the fact that pitch and frequency have a complex relationship, one that is made more complex by the further influence of intensity.

3. CODING MECHANISMS IN PITCH PERCEPTION

We are now well aware that sound frequency is represented in an orderly fashion by way of a tonotopic map on the basilar membrane (Warren, 1999; Yost, 2006). The advantage of this layout is that complex sounds composed of multiple frequencies can be transformed into an orderly representation of peak wave undulations at specific points on the basilar membrane. High

SideNote 6.27

Luckily, the intensity effect only applies to the pitch of pure tones and not to complex tones found in music. Otherwise, the pitch of musical instruments would be different depending on the intensity at which they were played.

frequency sounds trigger such undulations near the base of the cochlea, whereas low frequency sounds do so toward the apex. This process is physically analogous to the mathematical principles of Fourier analysis such that any complex sound can be decomposed into a fundamental set of sinusoidal functions that are transformed into a representation in space (tonotopic layout) (Gulick et al., 1989; Plack et al., 2005). Implicit in this transformation is the idea that sound frequencies are captured by discrete neural populations associated with the entirety of the basilar membrane. Earlier in this chapter, we saw that the very notion of independent channels, each with its own particular tuning curve and critical band, represent a functional extension of the place coding theory.

Given that pitch is associated with frequency, it would be appealing to extend the above idea and assert that pitch coding is also based on the place theory. In other words, our subjective experience of pitch arises through the stimulation of specific points on the basilar membrane—for example, stimulation near the basal end (high frequency) produces high pitch, whereas stimulation toward the apex yields lower pitch. We will return to this idea in a moment. However, we will first see that this simple and elegant view of pitch coding does not hold true because of some tantalizing observations that were made as early as the mid-1800s. These observations also complicate our understanding of the way pitch coding occurs in the auditory system (Deutsch & Richards, 1979; Moore, 2003).

The problem of the missing fundamental

Let us consider a complex sound in which a pure tone of 200 Hz is combined with a series of tones at other frequencies. These other frequencies are restricted to being exact multiples of the first tone (400, 600, 800 Hz, etc.). The spectral distribution of these various components is shown in Figure 6.16. By definition, the first tone in this series is called the **fundamental** and each successive component is called a **harmonic**. These frequency components together represent a harmonic series—that is, the fundamental (or 1st harmonic) and the later harmonics (2nd, 3rd, 4th, etc.)—whereby each harmonic can take on a somewhat different intensity value. Thus far, we have used the term *tone* to generally refer to pure tones where the sound stimulus is composed of a signal at one particular frequency. We now distinguish this from a **complex tone**, which is made up of an orderly set of harmonic components that have a precise relationship to each other.

What does a complex tone, such as the one depicted in Figure 6.16, sound like? Oddly, we do not hear all of the individual components separately under normal conditions. In other words, the pitch of this complex tone is not perceived as a conglomerate of individual pitch sensations representing the various harmonics. Rather, a single pitch is perceived corresponding to the fundamental frequency (200 Hz). It is as if the higher harmonics simply meld into a single perceptual event that is triggered by the fundamental component in this harmonic series (SideNote 6.28) (Deutsch & Richards, 1979; Gulick et al., 1989; Plack et al., 2005).

A remarkable facet of complex tone perception occurs when the fundamental component is removed. This can be done by a number of means, and in fact, the advent of electronic signal generators makes it quite easy with modern technology. When a harmonic series is presented to a listener with the fundamental component removed, the pitch does not appear to be altered. In other words, the perceived pitch continues to correspond to the fundamental frequency even though it is not present in the signal. This result, which itself provides evidence for a dissociation between frequency and pitch, has come to be known as the **problem of the missing fundamental**. The problem in this case concerns a perceptual event that is linked to a signal that does not even exist.

Place versus frequency theories

The case of the missing fundamental also has significant consequences for pitch coding by the auditory system, especially with regard to the place theory. Because there is no energy on the basilar membrane corresponding to the fundamental frequency, the place theory cannot account for the pitch sensation that is attributed to this frequency. In the absence of stimulation at the corresponding place on the basilar membrane, it has been argued that some other mechanism must be involved in generating the *fundamental* pitch sensation.

One mechanism that has been proposed is that neural firing in auditory fibres occurs in synchrony with the waveform of the complex tone (Schreiner, Read, & Sutter, 2000; Tramo, Cariani, Koh, Makris, & Braida, 2005). This is in accord with the basic principles of the frequency

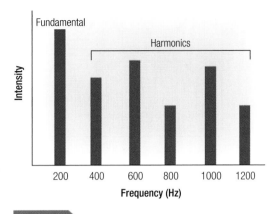

Figure 6.16

The spectrum of a 200 Hz tone and its harmonics. The 200 Hz tone is called the *fundamental frequency* (or 1st harmonic). Each multiple of this frequency is called a *harmonic*, starting with the second (400 Hz) and ending in this example with the sixth (1200 Hz). The intensity value of each harmonic can vary.

theory (SideNote 6.29). The idea behind this principle can be appreciated by examining Figure 6.17 on page 200. The waveform shown on the left represents a complex periodic sound that repeats every 5 milliseconds. The Fourier spectrum on the right shows that this waveform can be decomposed into three pure tones with frequencies of 800, 1000, and 1200 Hz. This represents the fourth, fifth, and sixth harmonics of the spectrum shown in Figure 6.16. When presented, this sound produces a distinct pitch that corresponds to the missing 200 Hz fundamental. Again, there is no real signal at this frequency and therefore no significant undulation should occur in the basilar membrane at the corresponding tonotopic location.

An important point to note is that the 5-millisecond periodic nature of the waveform does correspond to a frequency of 200 Hz. If cochlear neurons are indeed synchronized to the timing of the pressure changes in the waveform, then these neurons will also fire at this rate and therefore convey the 200 Hz repetition rate of this complex signal to higher centres in the brain. Thus, according to this theory, the precise timing of the periodic pressure fluctuations is responsible for driving the firing rate of cochlear neurons rather than the precise tonotopic stimulation by the constituent Fourier components. In this example, therefore, the frequency theory provides a more suitable explanation than the place theory in terms of the pitch generated by the complex tone.

The story, however, is not quite that simple because there are several counter-examples

SideNote | **6.28**

The same phenomenon occurs with complex tones that have a different fundamental. If the fundamental frequency is very high (e.g., 4000 Hz and above), some of the harmonics begin to reach the limit or fall outside of the frequency range of human hearing.

SideNote | **6.29**

Recall from Chapter 5 that according to the frequency theory, neural firing occurs in synchrony with sound frequency. However, this theory had its limitations because action potentials cannot fire at rates high enough to encode the full frequency range. Therefore, the frequency theory can only be invoked for encoding low frequency sounds.

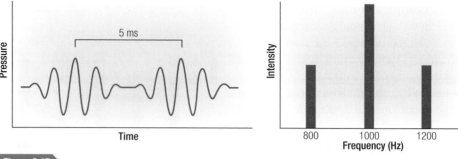

The waveform of a complex sound that shows periodic pressure fluctuations every 5 milliseconds at a frequency of 200 Hz. The perceived pitch of this sound corresponds to 200 Hz, possibly due to neuronal firing that is synchronized to the periodicity of the pressure fluctuations. The Fourier spectrum on the right shows that the complex waveform is only composed of three frequency components, none of which occur at 200 Hz. Adapted from *Hearing: Physiological Acoustics, Neural Coding, and Psychoacoustics,* by W. L. Gulick, G. A. Gescheider, and R. D. Frisina, 1989, New York, NY: Oxford University Press.

where the place theory provides a more suitable explanation for pitch perception. One such example occurs when the harmonics are presented to both ears separately. This experimental procedure is known as *dichotic* listening (Algom et al., 1989; Deutsch & Richards, 1979). If a 1000 Hz tone and a 1200 Hz tone are presented to the left and right ears, respectively, it turns out that the pitch corresponds to a 200 Hz tone. In other words, the two dichotically presented stimuli, which correspond to the fifth and sixth harmonics of a 200 Hz fundamental, somehow end up generating a pitch that conforms to the fundamental frequency. The curious fact here is that the two dichotic stimuli are not allowed to combine to produce a complex waveform. Thus, there is no periodic repetition in the sound profile that mimics the fundamental frequency and to which the cochlear neurons can fire in synchrony. Instead, the pitch is generated from the separate stimulation of each cochlea at frequencies believed to be encoded by the place theory.

Pitch coding mechanisms have come to represent one of the enduring disputes in auditory science, given the convincing evidence that appears to favour both the place and the frequency theories (Gulick et al., 1989; Plack et al., 2005; Schreiner, 2000). A central thorn in this debate has revolved around the case of the missing fundamental. One idea that presents a compromise of sorts is that the brain reconstructs the missing fundamental based on an analysis of the harmonic components. The idea is that the auditory system somehow finds the best common denominator of the harmonics and generates a corresponding pitch

percept. The harmonic components themselves may be conveyed by the place coding mechanism or, if the frequency values are low enough, by the frequency coding mechanism. Thus, pitch coding in general likely involves place mechanisms for much of the frequency spectrum except at very low frequencies where neural synchrony mechanisms may operate instead (SideNote 6.30).

C. Auditory Space Perception

We conclude this chapter with a discussion of another remarkable property of the auditory system—our perceptual ability to localize sounds in space. In the visual and somatosensory systems, the perceptual operations for localizing stimuli are rather straightforward because extra–personal space is mapped onto the sensory surface in an exact manner. As we learned in Chapter 3, touch stimulation can be precisely localized through the spatial coordinates of the somatotopic map. Similarly, we know exactly where an object lies in our visual world because its optical image in our eye is formed according to precise geometric rules. It is similarly important for us to know where a stimulus originates from in auditory space. The evolutionary drive for an accurate sound localization mechanism in animals was based on the survival advantage of being able to know the source of food or predators in the environment.

The fundamental problem the auditory system faces in localizing a sound source is that the acoustic signal contains no information

SideNote | 6.30

The place coding mechanism is believed to have a lower limit of 150 Hz, below which frequency coding mechanisms are believed to encode pitch. There is likely a range of intermediate frequencies at which both mechanisms are responsible for pitch coding. The upper limit of the frequency coding mechanism is believed to occur around 300 to 400 Hz.

about its spatial origin. Thus, unlike somato-sensory and visual processing, auditory processing is inherently non-spatial in nature (SideNote 6.31). The solution to this problem requires taking advantage of the fact that we have two laterally spaced ears, and that as a result, there are subtle differences in how sound arrives at each ear. As early as 1796, Italian physicist Giovanni Battista Venturi proposed that the slight difference in the intensity of sound delivered to the two ears is a cue for localization. Venturi also noted that people who were deaf in one ear had great difficulty localizing sounds. The intensity hypothesis, however, was not rigorously tested for nearly a century and was confirmed largely through the efforts of Lord Rayleigh in England. We now know that in addition to intensity differences, time differences in the arrival of sound also serve as an important cue. In the remainder of this section, we will examine the precise way by which such mechanisms provide localization information, how they are processed by the auditory nervous system, and some interesting perceptual facets related to binaural hearing.

1. ACOUSTIC CUES FOR LOCALIZATION

The study of sound localization ability is rather straightforward in principle. Human subjects are asked to listen to a sound stimulus placed at various positions in space and then asked to point to or indicate in some manner the spatial location of the source. The simplicity of this procedure and the fact that it is independent of sophisticated technology sets it apart from other studies of auditory function such as loudness perception, frequency processing, etc. As a result, localization studies have a fairly long history. More recent scientific studies have used headphones to examine the effects of various acoustic cues upon localization, such as intensity and time difference. Although the use of headphones has revealed important information about acoustic cues, these studies are complicated by the fact that perceptual localization becomes difficult in such situations because the sound appears to originate within the listener's head (SideNote 6.32). It appears that the complex changes that occur in the acoustic stimulus under natural conditions—due to interactions with the head, pinna, or other structures in the environment—are factors that we have become accustomed to (Gulick et al., 1989; Moore, 2003). Apparently we use these

complex factors in perceiving auditory space, something that cannot be easily done under the restrictive stimulation conditions of headphone use.

Physical considerations

The first issue that comes up in any effort to understand auditory space perception is the manner by which the physical location of the sound can be specified. The source may be located along any direction with respect to the head. That direction is given by two angular values—the **azimuth** and the **elevation**. As shown in Figure 6.18 on page 202, the azimuth specifies the horizontal angle around the head, with the straight-ahead position denoted as 0°. The angle increases in a clockwise fashion such that the sound source has an azimuth angle of 90° when in line with the right ear, 180° when directly behind the head, and 270° when in line with the left ear. The elevation value specifies the vertical angle with respect to the head. All sound sources in space can be given by an azimuth and elevation angle, though we are primarily interested in the azimuth value because it represents the more important horizontal location. Figure 6.18 also shows two axes that are used as a frame of reference—the mid-sagittal axis (front to back) and the binaural axis (connecting the two ears).

The location of the sound source relative to the head can produce one of two general situations (Deutsch & Richards, 1979; Konishi, 2003). If the source is directly in front or directly behind the head along the mid-sagittal axis, then the path distance of the emitted sound will be the same to the two ears. This is shown by points A and B in Figure 6.19 on page 202. The equal path length means that all of the physical parameters of the sound will be identical to the two ears, a condition known as **diotic stimulation**. On the other hand, if the source is located off the mid-sagittal axis, then the path length to the closer ear will be less than the farther ear. Two examples of this condition are shown by points C and D in Figure 6.19. For both of these sources, the right ear is closer than the left, and hence there will be a difference in the physical quality of the sound reaching the two ears. More precisely, sound intensity will be slightly greater in the right ear and will arrive earlier. A condition that causes such a binaural difference in sound quality is known as **dichotic stimulation** (Gulick et al., 1989).

Giovanni Battista Venturi (1746–1822)
SCIENCE PHOTO LIBRARY

Interaural intensity difference

An important consequence of dichotic stimulation is that the sound reaching the farther ear will be slightly less intense than the sound reaching the closer ear. This so-called **interaural intensity difference (IID)** arises for two reasons. First, sound pressure decreases with increasing distance. For example, the sound emitted by the object located in position C in Figure 6.19 will have a greater path length to the left ear than to the right, thereby causing the intensity to be slightly reduced by the time it reaches the left ear. The second, and more important, reason for an IID effect is the *sound shadow* produced by the head. This phenomenon, which is known as the **head shadow effect**, arises from the simple fact that the head reflects incoming sounds (SideNote 6.33 on page 203). As a result, the ear closer to the sound source in a dichotic situation will hear a more intense sound than the farther ear (Gulick et al., 1989).

The situation, however, is somewhat complicated because the effectiveness of the head shadow effect in creating an interaural intensity difference is not the same for all sound frequencies. High frequency sounds display a much higher amount of reflection when they interact with the head, whereas low frequency sounds can actually bend around the head and continue. This effect, which is depicted in Figure 6.20, occurs because low frequency sounds have a long wavelength in relation to the size of the head. As a result, the IID is much greater with high frequency sounds (Campbell & King, 2004; Carlile, Martin, & McAnally, 2005; Deutsch & Richards, 1979).

The IIDs that occur for sound sources placed at various azimuth angles is shown in Figure 6.21. As expected, the IID is negligible at azimuth angles of 0° and 180° for all sound frequencies because these represent a diotic condition. The greatest IID occurs when the sound path difference between the two ears has the largest value—that is, an azimuth angle of 90° (and 270°) when the source is directly in line with one ear. The effectiveness of the head shadow can be seen in this figure because the greatest IID values occur when the sound is of high frequency. A low frequency sound creates comparatively little IID because much more of it reaches the farther ear by bending around the head.

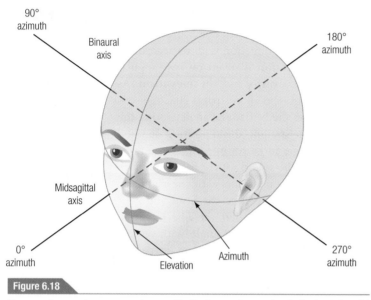

Figure 6.18

The sound source in space can be specified by two angles—azimuth (horizontal angle) and elevation (vertical angle). A sound source is said to be at a 0° azimuth when it is straight ahead and 180° when it is directly behind the head along the mid-sagittal axis. Azimuth angle values increase in a clockwise manner.

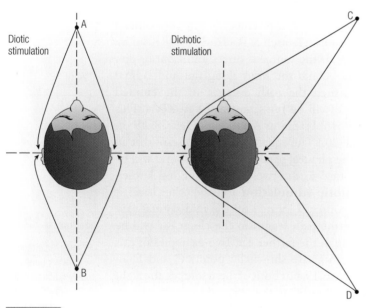

Figure 6.19

Sound sources that are directly in front of or behind the head result in an equal path length to the two ears, a condition known as *diotic* stimulation (points A and B). When the sound source is to one side, there is a greater path length to the farther ear, a condition known as *dichotic* stimulation (points C and D). Adapted from *Hearing: Physiological Acoustics, Neural Coding, and Psychoacoustics,* by W. L. Gulick, G. A. Gescheider, and R. D. Frisina, 1989, New York, NY: Oxford University Press.

Interaural time difference

The lateral separation of the ears produces another cue that can be used to localize sounds in space (Konishi, 2003; Warren, 1999; Yost, 2006). The extra distance means that sounds require extra time to travel to the farther ear, thereby creating a time cue known as **interaural time difference (ITD)**. A number of important facts must be kept in mind with

High frequency sound

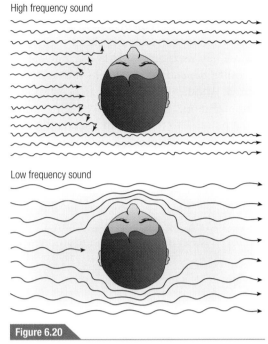

Low frequency sound

Figure 6.20

An illustration of the head shadow effect. High frequency sounds are reflected when they interact with the head, whereas low frequency sounds simply bend around the head and continue. Adapted from Deutsch, L. J., & Richards, A. M. (1979). *Elementary hearing science.* Baltimore, MD: University Park Press.

regard to ITDs. First, only dichotic stimulation can produce an ITD. As with IIDs, diotic stimulation produces negligible ITDs since the path length of the sound to the two ears is the same. Second, the time difference in the arrival of the sound at both ears will be very small because sounds travel fast in air (331 metres/second), and the lateral separation of the two ears is relatively small (about 0.22 metres). Thus, the maximum extra time needed for sound to travel to the farther ear is only in the range of 0.65 to 0.70 milliseconds.

The third, and most important, fact is that the path difference of sound transmission to the two ears will depend on the azimuth angle. The maximum difference should occur at 90° and 270° azimuth when the sound source is lined up with one of the ears. As the source moves from this point toward the mid-sagittal axis, the difference in the path length to the two ears becomes progressively reduced and with it so should the value of the ITD. This is precisely the effect seen in Figure 6.22, which shows a plot of ITD as a function of azimuth angle (Feddersen, Sandel, Teas, & Jeffress, 1957). The data points in this figure were taken from actual measured values at the two ears from a sound source placed several feet away. Sound

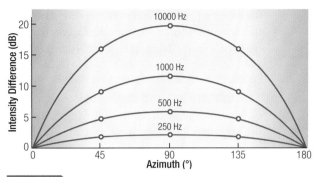

Figure 6.21

IID values are zero for diotic conditions (0° and 180° azimuth) and maximal when the source is placed on the binaural axis (90° and 270° azimuth). The IID values under dichotic conditions increase with higher sound frequencies because of the head shadow effect. Adapted from *Hearing: Physiological Acoustics, Neural Coding, and Psychoacoustics,* by W. L. Gulick, G. A. Gescheider, and R. D. Frisina, 1989, New York, NY: Oxford University Press.

sources off the mid-sagittal axis show progressively greater ITD values, reaching a maximum at 90° azimuth. Thus, the actual measured values agree with what would be predicted from the path length difference to the two ears from various points on the horizontal plane.

A final point with regard to ITDs is that they are much less susceptible to changes in frequency than IIDs. Indeed, it was recognized quite early that IID could not serve as the only cue for localization because it is not very effective for low frequency sounds. And yet, it was well known that humans are quite capable of effectively localizing such signals. The tandem effects of ITD and IID ensure that we are able

SideNote **6.33**

Very little sound actually penetrates the head because of the large difference in density and elasticity between the head and the surrounding air medium. For this reason, much of the sound will actually reflect off the head, thereby creating an interaural intensity difference for dichotic sources.

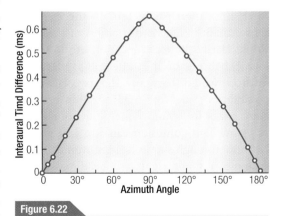

Figure 6.22

ITD is zero for diotic sources (0° and 180° azimuth) and increases to reach a maximum when the sound source is aligned with the binaural axis (90° and 270° azimuth). The actual ITD values are mere fractions of a millisecond. Adapted from "Localization of High Frequency Tones," by W. E. Feddersen, T. T. Sandel, D. C. Teas, and L. A. Jeffress, 1957, *Journal of the Acoustical Society of America, 29,* pp. 988–991.

SideNote | **6.34**

It is possible to fool the auditory system by presenting an ITD that favours one ear with an IID that favours the other. Such experiments have been carried out under precise conditions with the use of headphones. The two cues will balance out, and the person will perceive the sound source to be located along the mid-sagittal axis.

SideNote | **6.35**

Assume that a 5° rightward head rotation is made. If the source had originally been at 60° azimuth, then the rotation would now shift the ITD from 0.48 to 0.45 milliseconds (as obtained from Figure 6.22 for a 55° azimuth). However, if the source had originally been at 120°, then the rotation would shift the ITD value to 0.52 milliseconds instead (the ITD data point for a 115° azimuth). The brain can presumably interpret this difference to distinguish between the two original possibilities.

SideNote | **6.36**

The work of McCulloch and Pitts set forth the idea that neuronal operations can be considered in terms of computations. This idea along with the rapid development of computer hardware led to an explosion of later efforts to model various neurological and perceptual phenomena. Artificial neural networks are now entrenched in a broad range of modelling efforts, from predicting weather patterns to stock prices.

to obtain a precise perceptual representation of the acoustic source in space for a broad spectrum of sound frequencies (SideNote 6.34).

Localization under ambiguous conditions

The fact that IID and ITD values change in a systematic way with azimuth angle means that the auditory nervous system can use these natural cues to determine the location of the sound source on the horizontal plane. The advantage of this setup is that the cues arise due to simple laws of physics—that is, sound reflection by the head (IID) and difference in sound arrival due to a fixed transmission speed (ITD). The way in which the brain uses these cues to obtain a spatial map of the sound source will be taken up in the next section. However, a closer look at the IID and ITD functions in Figures 6.21 and 6.22 shows that there are two possible azimuth angles for any given value (Gulick et al., 1989; Warren, 1999). For example, an ITD value of 0.48 milliseconds can be interpreted by the auditory system as coming from a sound source at an azimuth angle of either 60° or 120°, since both will produce this ITD value. Similar ambiguities are possible at all other ITD values as well, except at the peak of the function, which only occurs for a source at 90° (or 270°) azimuth.

The confusion between two possible angles for a particular IID or ITD value must be resolved somehow, which we know occurs because we can easily distinguish a sound source from either being directly in front of or behind us. One solution is to turn the head along the vertical axis so as to change the binaural stimulation parameters. In the example above, a small rightward rotation of the head would clarify the exact location of the sound source because of the differential effect the rotation would have on the two alternate possibilities (SideNote 6.35). A similar ambiguity exists for sounds emerging from above or below. This confusion can also be resolved but now through tilting head movements. For example, a slight rightward head tilt would favour the left ear for sounds from above, whereas the right ear would be favoured for sounds from below.

Perhaps the most perplexing situation arises with diotic stimulation when the auditory system is faced with the challenge of determining whether the source is directly ahead or behind in the absence of any binaural cues. Recall that both ITD and IID are

zero under these situations. However, here too, slight head movements can help to distinguish whether the source is ahead or behind because any rotation would favour one ear or the other depending on where the source is located. Another factor that has been shown to resolve diotic ambiguity is the contribution of the pinna. The sound from a source located directly ahead can proceed in an unimpeded manner to the ears. However, the sound from a source located from behind must first interact with the pinna, which itself can cast a sound shadow, producing a reduction in intensity. This cue may be taken into account by the auditory system in resolving diotic ambiguity.

2. NEURAL MECHANISMS

The previous section has shown how binaural cues are made available to the auditory system due to the simple laws of physics and the fact that a small distance separates our two ears. It is up to the auditory nervous system to exploit these cues to construct an auditory space map—that is, an internal representation of where external sounds are located in space. We now know quite well the fundamental neural mechanisms by which this feat is accomplished. An interesting facet of this story is that it serves as an excellent example of a case where an influential theoretical model of a neural mechanism is first proposed and then later verified by experimental evidence.

The binaural cross-correlation model

The origins of modern theoretical neuroscience date back to the early 1940s when Warren McCulloch and Walter Pitts showed that an interacting network of neurons can perform any computational operation (SideNote 6.36). A key feature of their model was that a single neuron can integrate inputs in a multiplicative fashion such that it only fires when its inputs are positive (McCulloch & Pitts, 1943). This work served as the foundation for many later models of neural processing, including auditory function. In 1948, Lloyd Jeffress proposed a highly influential **cross-correlation** model of binaural localization based on the coincident detection of neural signals, an idea that was borrowed from the general theories set forth earlier by McCulloch and Pitts.

The Jeffress model, which is shown in Figure 6.23, was based on interaural time differences (ITDs) in a neural network that receives inputs from both ears (Jeffress, 1948). The inputs from each ear arise from discrete segments of the basilar membrane and are therefore restricted to sound frequencies in that portion of the tonotopic map. A series of discrete frequency-specific inputs is shown by the dark bands along the sound frequency axis in Figure 6.23. The neural signals from each ear are progressively delayed along the input lines. The farther the signal proceeds along the line, the longer the delay before it stimulates the neuron. This is shown by the arrows in the bottom part of the figure. Thus, each neuron in this network, shown by the small circles, receives a binaural input that has a specific delay value from each side. We know from our discussion above that a dichotic signal will produce a specific ITD that depends on the azimuth angle. According to this model, when the ITD value of the sound signal coincides with the neural delay in a particular circuit, the neuron associated with that circuit will become activated because of correlated input from both ears (SideNote 6.37) (Gulick et al., 1989; Hyakin & Chen, 2005; Jeffress, 1948).

We consider three examples to see how this theoretical model may work to yield perceptual localization of the sound source. In the first case, assume that the sound source produces diotic stimulation (e.g., it is located directly in front). Thus, the ITD is zero, and therefore the signal will proceed equivalently along the input lines from each ear. As can be seen in the top right panel of Figure 6.23, only the neuron shown by the filled circle will be activated because its inputs (D and D') represent the same delay value for each ear. In the second case, assume that the sound source is located on the right side directly in line with the right ear. We know from our previous discussion that this will produce the greatest ITD value and that the right ear will be stimulated first. As the middle panel shows, the neuron represented by the filled circle will now become activated because only its inputs (A and A') will provide a correlated signal. This is because the extra time needed for the neural signal to proceed along its input line to point A' in the network will be compensated by the time required for the sound to travel to the left ear and then along its shorter input route to point A. For the third case, we assume that the source is placed on the left side at some point between the binaural axis and the mid-sagittal axis. Thus, we already know that we will have

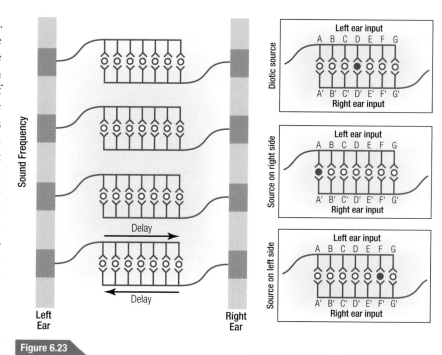

Figure 6.23

The Jeffress cross-correlation model is based on a network of binaural neurons receiving inputs from the two ears with different delay values. The delay from each ear becomes progressively greater along its input line (arrows at bottom). The right panels show the neurons that would become activated (filled circles) in three situations—sound source–producing diotic stimulation, sound source at right in line with the right ear, and sound source at left at an intermediate azimuth angle. The location of the activated neuron in this network can provide information on the spatial source of the sound-emitting object. Adapted from *Hearing: Physiological Acoustics, Neural Coding,* and *Psychoacoustics,* by W. L. Gulick, G. A. Gescheider, and R. D. Frisina, 1989, New York, NY: Oxford University Press.

an ITD situation that favours the ear on that side but that will not be as excessive as in the previous case. The neuron that will receive correlated inputs is now shown by the filled circle in the bottom panel. The increased neural delay from the left side to point F in the network will now coincide with the later arrival of the sound to the right side and its shorter route to point F'. This neuron will therefore code for an intermediate ITD value and therefore specify a sound source to the left side but not quite in line with the left ear. If that had been the case, then the correlated inputs would arrive through points G and G'.

Neural correlation mechanisms in the brain stem

The Jeffress model provides an elegant theoretical mechanism by which the auditory nervous system can conceivably code for sound source locations at various azimuth angles. The network as shown in Figure 6.23 can be thought of in terms of an auditory place model. That is, a particular ITD value produced by a dichotic sound source will only trigger a neuron at a certain place in this

SideNote | **6.37**

The convergence of the binaural inputs is believed to be multiplicative. Thus, a particular neuron in the network will only fire strongly when both of its inputs are active. This will occur when the neural delay compensates exactly for the interaural delay in the arrival of the dichotic sound signal.

network (SideNote 6.38). Thus, if a higher centre in the brain is informed of the place of activation in the network, it would then have a way of decoding the ITD value and with it ultimately generate a perceptual impression of where the sound source was located in space. The advantage of this setup is that progressively greater values of ITD are sequentially represented along this network. This means that azimuth angle is in effect mapped onto this network of neurons in a faithful way to produce an auditory place map (Pressnitzer, Sayles, Micheyl, & Winter, 2008; Recanzone & Sutter, 2008; Yost, 2006).

The question that emerges is "Where in the brain can such a network of ITD detectors be found?" We know that the cochlear nucleus can be ruled out because it only receives inputs from the ear on that side. Thus, all neurons here are monaural, whereas the neurons in the Jeffress model must be binaural. There is now considerable physiological evidence for the existence of neurons coding for binaural time difference at multiple sites in the auditory pathway, including the inferior colliculus, the medial geniculate nucleus, and even the primary auditory cortex. However, an auditory nucleus located in the lower part of the brain stem known as the **superior olive** is the primary site where binaural differences are coded in a systematic way (SideNote 6.39). The superior olive has two segments, known as the *medial* and *lateral* divisions. Neurons in the lateral superior olive (LSO) code for interaural intensity difference, whereas neurons in the medial superior olive (MSO) respond to interaural time difference.

The neural pathways to the MSO and LSO are shown in Figure 6.24. The MSO is the first site in the auditory pathway where binaural time differences are systematically represented (Zigmond et al., 1999). The evidence for this has emerged from electrophysiological studies of neuronal activity in a variety of species (SideNote 6.40). A given neuron within the MSO responds best at a particular ITD value and less so at others. For example, the neuron located at the bottom of the MSO shown in Figure 6.24 will respond best when the sound source is located on the right side because of the longer neural delay in the input line from that ear. There is a systematic layout of the ITD preferences within the MSO in a manner that reflects the predictions made in the Jeffress model. In general, the MSO on a particular side optimally codes various azimuth angles of a sound source on the opposite side. This means that the right MSO is specialized for localizing sounds on the left side and vice versa.

3. BINAURAL HEARING AND PERCEPTUAL ORGANIZATION

Our world contains sounds with a mixture of many different frequencies, thereby producing an auditory signal that is far more complex than in the case of a single tone. Furthermore, the auditory system has to deal with the ongoing challenge of distinguishing a relevant signal from background noise. An often-used example of this problem is that of a crowded party. The so-called **cocktail party effect** refers to our ability to follow what a particular person is saying despite the fact that there

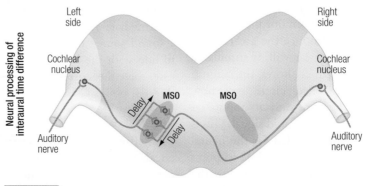

Figure 6.24

The medial superior olive (MSO) contains an orderly representation of ITD values. The delay in the contralateral input line produces a preference for coding azimuth angle values of sound sources on the opposite side. Adapted from *Fundamental Neuroscience*, by M. J. Zigmond, F. E. Bloom, S. C. Landis, J. L. Roberts, and L. R. Squire, 1999, San Diego, CA: Academic Press.

INVESTIGATION

Studying the Cocktail Party Effect

Colin Cherry examined the cocktail party effect in 1953. He set up a series of experiments using head-phones that played two different messages at the same time, under different conditions. One experiment involved the same speaker giving two different messages simultaneously; the task involved following one message and ignoring the other. Subjects performed well on this experiment, although it was found to be a difficult task. Another experiment involved one message being played to one ear and another message being played to the other ear; in this case, the ability to follow one conversation was quite simple due to the apparent spatial separation of the two messages. Although we are quite good at attending to one stimulus, if asked about the stimulus we were ignoring, humans are quite poor at remembering much, including changes in language or even sentences played backwards, but we do, however, notice when the gender of a speaker switches.

---

is usually a lot of surrounding noise (Hyakin & Chen, 2005). Furthermore, by shifting our attention, we can focus in on the conversations of various other people in the room in a selective manner. This is a remarkable feat when one considers that the speech signal is embedded in a considerable amount of noise and that, as in the problem of sound localization, there is really no information contained in the acoustic signal that distinguishes itself from the rest of the background noise.

Masking effects of background noise

A clue as to how the auditory system is able to distinguish a signal from surrounding noise comes from the well-known fact that people who are deaf in one ear have considerable difficulty in this task. Unilateral deafness produces a profound loss in our ability to listen to a signal, such as speech, in the midst of background noise. To understand how the auditory system can use binaural hearing to distinguish signal from noise, consider the following. In nearly all cases, the source of the noise occurs at a different point in space than the signal. For example, a person may be talking to us at a cocktail party from just to our right, whereas the bulk of the background noise originates from everywhere else.

The spatial separation of the sound signals that originate from different locations can allow us to better hear the signals because they produce binaural differences in stimulation of the two ears (Campbell & King, 2004; Carlile et al., 2005; Yost, 2006). Indeed, the masking effect of the noise is minimal when it has a different spatial location from the signal. Therefore, the

binaural mechanisms that we discussed above with regard to sound localization play a further important role in separating the various acoustic sources in space and reducing the masking effects of the different sounds upon each other. The improvement in hearing that occurs through the masking reduction due to binaural hearing is known as the **binaural masking level difference (BMLD)**. Studies with earphones in which the binaural characteristics of the sound signal can be systematically altered have shown that the BMLD can be as much as 15 dB. This means that the detection threshold for a signal in the presence of noise can be reduced by 15 dB under appropriate conditions of binaural stimulation (SideNote 6.41).

Auditory scene analysis

It is indeed remarkable that our auditory system is able to distinguish different sets of incoming sounds and produce separate perceptual representations in a continually faithful manner. For example, our environment may be filled with sound sources that can include music, speech, or other sounds. These various sources usually interfere with each other at multiple points in the auditory system—from the vibrations produced in the tympanic membrane to the travelling waves in the basilar membrane, to the electrical stimulation produced by hair cells. And yet, we usually obtain a separate perceptual impression of each of the sound elements as well as their source in space.

An influential account of this problem and a possible solution has been proposed by Canadian psychologist Albert Bregman. He suggested that the challenge faced by the

SideNote 6.41

A similar 15 dB improvement in sound detection was first noticed during a wartime project on the detection of underwater sonar signals. Nobel chemist Irving Langmuir showed that when the sonar tone and masking noise appeared to be at different locations, there was considerable improvement in signal detectability (Warren, 1999).

METHODOLOGY

Auditory Scene Analysis

Albert Bregman at McGill University has completed much research on the auditory system and was first to coin the term *auditory scene analysis* (ASA). Bregman stumbled across this phenomenon during a study when he found that the perception of a fast string of unrelated sounds was not in the same order as the actual stimuli. This led to a career studying ASA, which we now know is a process whereby complex sounds in the environment (composed of many frequencies) are "packaged" together by sound source. Three important aspects of ASA are sequential grouping cues (over time), simultaneous grouping cues (over frequencies), and schemas (learned patterns). When we hear a complex sound, that sound is first segregated into different streams (called *stream segregation*) and then put back together. This affects our perception of many properties of sound—including timbre, loudness, and spatial location—as well as our understanding of speech and music.

auditory system is similar in many ways to that faced by the visual system in analyzing a scene (Bregman, 1994). The visual world is filled with objects that at any given moment have a precise spatial relationship to each other. Bregman proposed that a similar situation arises in hearing with multiple sound-emitting objects at different locations in space. The manner by which the ear achieves an effortless segregation of concurrent sounds has been called **auditory scene analysis (ASA)**.

Bregman suggested that the mixture of sounds reaching the auditory system is analyzed by a two-stage ASA process. In the first stage, *primitive grouping*, the mixture of sounds is decomposed into separate auditory streams. The individual streams generally share common acoustic parameters such as frequency, intensity, and location. All of these are aspects of normal auditory processing that we have reviewed throughout this chapter. The auditory signal can then be grouped according to a number of characteristics that are described by the Gestalt principles of perceptual organization. One of these principles is *proximity*, the notion that acoustic signals appearing close together in time will be grouped as a perceptual unit. The Gestalt principle of *similarity* applies the same logic but with regard to the acoustic characteristics of the signal such as frequency and intensity. Thus, sound signals that are grouped in terms of their acoustic similarity can form a distinct auditory stream. The

Gestalt principle of *common fate* stipulates that common changes occurring over time can be used to segregate signals. This principle can also be used in primitive grouping processes in ASA to separate the mixture of incoming sounds into distinct streams. For example, sequential changes in pitch or intensity, something that commonly occurs in music, would provide a powerful cue for stream segregation.

A subsequent processing stage, known as *schema-driven grouping*, uses knowledge of familiar patterns and concepts (Bregman, 1994). This higher-level process is dependent upon prior experience with various types of acoustic signals. The recognition of certain patterns allows us to identify the sound signal and therefore plays an important role in the perceptual organization of the auditory scene. For example, a walk through a forest will reveal a multitude of easily recognizable sounds: the wind rustling through the leaves, the rushing water of a nearby stream, or the sounds of various birds and insects. In this midst, the appearance of a faint noise from a distant airplane is immediately recognized and perceptually segregated from all of the other ongoing sounds, even though its acoustic spectrum is quite similar to the low frequency rumble of the rushing stream. The role of higher-level cognitive influences plays a critical role in parsing the incoming auditory signals and creating a perceptual experience that corresponds faithfully to the sensory input.

Summary

1. The factors that influence loudness (i.e., the perceptual correlate of sound intensity) include the sound duration, the presence of other stimuli, and whether the sound is heard through monaural (one ear) or binaural (both ears) means. There are two procedural ways to deliver sound stimuli during threshold experiments—through the open-ear method (minimum audible field) or through headphones (minimum audible pressure). The general procedures used to obtain detection and discrimination thresholds of hearing can be based on Fechner's classical methods. Detection thresholds depend upon sound frequency, with the lowest thresholds occurring in the range of 2000 to 4000 Hz. The mechanical properties of the outer ear, such as its resonance, along with physiological factors account for the low threshold values at these frequencies.

2. Studies of auditory perception at suprathreshold levels are aimed at determining discrimination thresholds and the intensity–loudness relationship. The Weber constant for sound intensity varies from 0.1 to 0.4. In general, Weber's law holds true only over a limited range of sound intensities. Our perceptual ability to discriminate sound intensity is likely derived from a comparison of the discharge patterns across a range of auditory neurons that encode different sound frequencies.

3. The relationship between sound intensity and perceived loudness was derived from magnitude estimation experiments, originally conducted by Stevens. Although loudness grows with intensity, there is no exact correspondence between the two (i.e., doubling sound does not double loudness). Stevens established a loudness rating scale in which 1 sone is equal to the loudness sensation produced by a 1000 Hz tone at 40 dB_{SPL}. He derived the relationship between loudness sensation and sound pressure, which takes the form of a power law ($L = k \cdot P^{0.67}$). Loudness perception is also governed by sound frequency and can be studied by way of loudness matching experiments that reveal *equal loudness contours*. In general, low and high frequency sounds require higher intensity levels in order to be judged as being equally loud in comparison to the middle frequencies.

4. The lower limit of sound detection in terms of frequency is generally taken to be 20 Hz, and the upper limit, 20000 Hz. The perceptual correlate of sound frequency is *pitch*, which is a metathetic sensation—that is, changing the sound frequency produces a qualitative change in the perceived sound. Humans are extremely good at discriminating changes in pitch—for example, a 3 Hz change of 1000 Hz tone can be detected. The Weber constant at 0.003 is among the lowest in the sensory systems.

5. The pitch sensation produced by a single tone (frequency) is known as *acoustic pitch*, whereas the sensation produced by a complex tone is referred to as *musical pitch*. To study the relationship between acoustic pitch and sound frequency, Stevens developed the mel scale, in which a 1000 Hz tone produces a pitch sensation of 1,000 mels. Even though sound frequency cannot be mapped onto the sensory dimension of pitch in an exact manner, there is nevertheless a correlation between the two—that is, increasing the sound frequency yields a *higher-pitched* sound.

6. The relationship between sound frequency and pitch perception suggests that the tonotopic layout of the basilar membrane plays an important role. It has been proposed that the place of stimulation on the basilar membrane triggers activity in a precise set of auditory nerve fibres that is in turn used by the auditory brain to construct a pitch sensation. Although this theory may hold true for acoustic pitch sensations, difficulty arises in explaining the pitch produced by complex tones in which exact multiples of a fundamental frequency are mixed together. In such cases, the complex tone yields a single pitch sensation even though multiple points on the basilar membrane are stimulated. Perhaps most perplexing is that the pitch sensation is not altered if the fundamental frequency is removed from the complex tone. This fascinating phenomenon has significant relevance to pitch perceptions produced

by musical notes and will be taken up in detail in Chapter 7.

7. The localization of sounds in our physical environment represents a significant challenge for the auditory system because there is no information about spatial origin contained in the sound signal. The physical location of a sound source is specified by its azimuth value (angle along the horizontal plane) and its elevation (vertical angle). The physical separation of the two ears can produce a difference in the quality of the sound arriving at each ear (known as *dichotic stimulation*) if the path length from the sound source to one ear is different than the other. This condition has its maximum impact when the source is directly aligned with one ear (i.e., azimuth value of 90° or 270°). In situations where the path length is the same to both ears (known as *diotic stimulation*), such as when the sound source is directly in front of or behind the head (i.e., azimuth value of 0° or 180°), then there is no difference in sound quality at the two ears.

8. Dichotic stimulation produces a difference in the time of arrival of the sound to each ear, known as the *interaural time difference* (ITD). Similarly, a difference arises in the intensity of sound at each ear due to the different path lengths, a phenomenon known as the *interaural intensity difference* (IID). Both ITD and IID values depend on the azimuth angle. The auditory brain is able to exploit these two signal qualities that arise strictly due to physical factors in order to derive the sound's location in space. The neural networks for mapping ITD and IID values are based on a cross-correlation model that detects the coincident arrival of binaural signals. These networks reside in auditory structures within the brain stem.

Key Terms

1. What is the difference between sound intensity and loudness? What are the advantages and disadvantages of the *open-ear* and *closed-ear* methods for obtaining detection thresholds? What are the anatomical and physiological factors that account for the shape of the minimal audibility curve?

2. What is the difference between the method of magnitude estimation and the method of fractionation? How is the sone scale defined, and what are its uses? What is the 10 dB rule?

3. What is the general relationship between sound frequency and loudness perception? How are equal loudness contours derived?

4. What is the accepted range of audible sound frequencies in humans? What are the factors that affect this range?

5. What is the difference between acoustic pitch and musical pitch? What is the *problem of the missing fundamental*? Why does the pitch perception of complex tones represent a challenge to the place theory as an explanation for pitch coding?

6. What is the fundamental problem the auditory system faces in localizing a sound source? What are the cues available to help in sound localization? What impact does sound frequency have on ITD and IID values?

7. What is the binaural cross-correlation model of sound localization, and how does it explain sound localization ability? What brain structures are believed to be involved in correlating binaural signals for the spatial localization of sound sources?

8. What factors affect the absolute sensitivity of hearing? How does the minimal audibility curve affect the dynamic range of hearing? What are the different ways that binaural hearing can influence auditory function?

9. What is the difference between tonal masking and noise masking? Why does a masking tone whose frequency is lower than the test tone have a greater effect than one of a higher frequency? How does the critical band reveal information on the physiological bandwidth of auditory nerve fibres?

10. How does the auditory system resolve ambiguities in diotic and dichotic stimulation? What is auditory scene analysis, and how does it help to segregate sound signals in a complex auditory environment?

- Bregman, A. S. (1994). *Auditory scene analysis: The perceptual organization of sound.* Cambridge, MA: MIT Press.

- Deutsch, L. J., & Richards, A. M. (1979). *Elementary hearing science.* Baltimore, MD: University Park Press.

- Emanuel, D. C., & Letowski, T. (2007). *Hearing science.* Baltimore, MD: Lippincott Williams & Wilkins.

- Moller, A. R. (2006). *Hearing: Anatomy, physiology, and disorders of the auditory system* (2nd ed.). San Diego, CA: Academic Press.

- Moore, B. C. J. (2003). *An introduction to the psychology of hearing* (5th ed.). London, England: Academic Press.

- Plack, C. J., Oxenham, A. J., Fay, R. R., & Popper, A. N. (2005). *Pitch: Neural coding and perception.* New York, NY: Springer-Verlag.

- Warren, R. M. (1999). *Auditory perception: A new analysis and synthesis.* Cambridge, UK: Cambridge University Press.

- Yost, W. A. (2006). *Fundamentals of hearing: An introduction* (5th ed.). San Diego, CA: Academic Press.

- Yost, W. A., Fay, R. R., & Popper, A. N. (2007). *Auditory perception of sound sources.* New York, NY: Springer.

The Auditory System: Music and Speech Perception

In this chapter . . .

- You will explore how the harmonic components of music activate the basilar membrane in regularly repeating ways and where on the basilar membrane the fundamental frequency and successive harmonics activate. You will learn about a basic unit of music known as the octave and the different ways each octave can be split up. You will become familiar with how musicians represent their musical pitch sequences on paper. You will see how different timbres represent different intensity distributions of the harmonics and how they differ across musical instruments.

- You will learn about the debate on what evolutionary purpose could have resulted in the development of music, for every culture as well as ancient civilizations produced music in one form or another. You will also be introduced to two phenomena that contribute to music perception, known as *tonal superpositions* and *tonal sequences*.

- You will discover areas of the brain that are involved in the processing of pitch perception and what happens when those areas are damaged by stroke or injury. You will also see how functional imaging studies have helped to locate particular areas of the brain that are associated with aspects of music perception.

- You will learn about the many body structures that contribute to speech productions and the different ways to represent (and thus study) speech sounds.

- You will come to understand that all human languages have three things in common and that although there are many levels to speech comprehension, there is only one that falls under sensory perception: isolating and recognizing words, pauses, and non-speech sounds. You will appreciate that formant identification is categorical in nature and how our perception changes when the voice onset time is altered.

- You will learn that there are areas of the brain dedicated to speech, such as Wernicke's area and Broca's area.

Music and speech perception, arguably the two most sophisticated hearing-related functions, represent fundamental and unique aspects of human existence.
Photo: Jan_Kowalski/iStockphoto.com

A MUSIC PERCEPTION
1. Musical Pitch and Timbre
2. Perceptual Aspects of Music
3. Music and the Brain

B SPEECH PERCEPTION
1. Speech Production
2. Speech Comprehension
3. Language and the Brain

It appears probable that the progenitors of man, before acquiring the power of expressing their mutual love in articulate language, endeavored to charm each other with musical notes and rhythm.

—Charles Darwin

We conclude our exploration of the auditory system with a review of music and speech perception, arguably the two most sophisticated functions related to hearing. The impact and significance of music rests on the fact that it is intertwined with our daily lives, producing powerful impressions of pleasantness (and sometimes disgust). Music can be uplifting, provoke creativity, induce elation, or evoke sad or happy memories. Research in music perception has a long and storied history, some of which will be covered in this chapter. The complex phenomena related to music perception and cognition, however, are only now unravelling through the efforts of psychologists and neuroscientists, due in part to technological advances that allow imaging of functional activity in the human brain (Patel, 2007).

Speech and language behaviour also represent a fundamental and unique aspect of human existence. Speech perception research, however, has a more recent historical timeline than most other areas of perceptual science. Although it has been known for several centuries that damage to selective parts of the brain leads to speech impairment, much of the pioneering work in understanding speech perception followed recent technical developments in speech analysis and synthesis. For example, the actual hardware necessary for studying speech patterns began to emerge only around the Second World War (SideNote 7.1). This early research was guided by military applications and followed by commercial interests in developing machines capable of speech synthesis and voice recognition. As we will see later, the complexity of speech imposes severe limitations on the capacity of modern computers to perform these functions—a limitation that is even now being grappled with by scientists and engineers.

A. Music Perception

Our discussion of complex tones in the previous chapter provides the needed introduction to musicality and music perception. It turns out that the tones generated by musical instruments conform to a harmonic series. Musical instruments do not produce pure tones but rather complex tones made up of a fundamental frequency and a series of harmonics (SideNote 7.2). As a reminder, the pitch sensation produced by a complex tone is identical to

the pitch of its fundamental frequency. In other words, if a pure tone of a particular frequency were presented, then under normal conditions its pitch would be perceived to be the same as a complex tone containing the same fundamental frequency along with its related harmonics (Gulick, Gescheider, & Frisina, 1989; Roederer, 1995). This remarkable fact forms the basis for **musical pitch** and represents the starting point of our discussion on music perception.

1. MUSICAL PITCH AND TIMBRE

It is indeed fortunate that complex tones produce a single pitch sensation, for without it music perception as we know it could not exist. There has been some effort in trying to understand why it is that complex tones produce a single pitch sensation. One idea is that a pitch processor somewhere in the auditory system examines the spatial arrangement of the wave patterns on the basilar membrane produced by the various harmonics of a complex tone (Peretz & Zatorre, 2005; Roederer, 1995). Take for example the middle C key on a piano. Pressing this key causes a particular string inside the piano to be struck. The fundamental frequency of that string, and hence the middle C note, is about 261 Hz. However, the string simultaneously vibrates at a series of higher harmonic frequencies as well, each contributing sound energy to make up the complex tone. The pressure waveform of the first 10 harmonics is shown in the top left panel of Figure 7.1. We learned in the previous chapter that it is much more informative to display the Fourier spectrum (top right panel), where the intensity and vibrational frequency of each harmonic is plotted (SideNote 7.3).

Pitch sensations from complex tones

Each of the harmonic components associated with the middle C note produces a travelling wave in the basilar membrane whose peak occurs at a point where its frequency corresponds to the tonotopic frequency. As shown in the bottom panel of Figure 7.1, the various harmonic components together produce an orderly pattern of peak wave activity on the basilar membrane. The fundamental frequency (f) is represented toward the apex, with each successive harmonic (2 f, 3 f, etc.) represented further toward the base. The interesting point about this representation is that there is

SideNote | 7.1

Research during World War II was aimed at producing machines that made visual patterns of speech signals. Acoustic scientists suggested that enemy radio voices could be identified by such patterns. The research was kept a military secret and became known only after the war.

SideNote | 7.2

This occurs due to the multiple resonant qualities of the sound-producing element in a musical instrument. A piano or guitar, for example, has a number of different preferred states of vibration or resonance, as shown by the sample waveforms below. When it is struck by the hammer (piano) or plucked (guitar), all of the resonant vibrational modes are simultaneously activated, each one producing sound at its characteristic frequency. These multiple resonances together produce the complex tone.

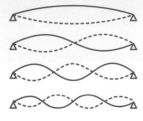

a certain regularity to the spatial arrangement because all of the harmonics produce their peak undulation according to the layout of the tonotopic map. As a result, the individual harmonic representations on the basilar membrane all have a fixed distance relationship to each other.

Our current view is that the brain somehow registers this spatial relationship such that the neural activity triggered at each of these regions forms a coherent signal that is transformed into a pitch sensation (Ciocca, 2008; Loui, Wu, Wessel, & Knight, 2009; Patel, 2007). Thus, it is the actual spatial pattern of peak wave activity on the basilar membrane that forms the critical factor in producing a single pitch sensation by a complex musical tone. A different tone would produce another regular pattern on the basilar membrane, though the actual locations of wave activity would be different depending on the fundamental frequency of that tone and its associated harmonics. Although the exact mechanisms by which the brain recognizes the spatial pattern of wave activity is unknown, it appears that a unique pitch sensation is the end result from each such pattern. The perceptual consequence of this remarkable process is that each musical tone, despite containing multiple frequency components, ends up producing a single, unique pitch sensation.

Musical scales—general concepts

Given that different musical tones produce different pitch sensations, the next question that arises is how these different pitch sensations can be scaled and represented in a standardized manner. We learned in the last chapter how the sensation of acoustic pitch relates to sound frequency through the so-called *mel scale*. A corresponding format is needed as well for musical pitch so that it can be effectively related to musical tones produced by a broad range of instruments. Indeed, this is a mandatory requirement in any formal musical system. For example, there would be considerable confusion if two musicians sat down to play on different instruments without prior agreement on the pitch sequences they were about to produce, a problem that would only be amplified manyfold in an orchestral setting.

The effort to create a practical **musical scale** has a long history, beginning with the Greeks as early as the 4th century BCE. By that time it was understood that tones having

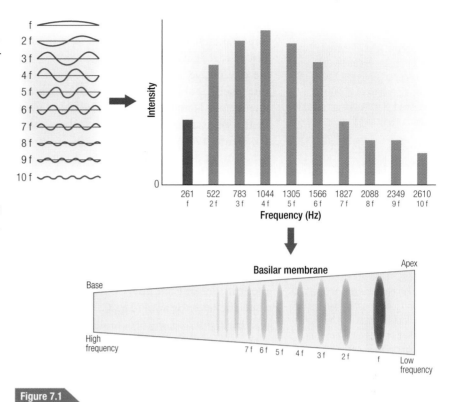

Figure 7.1

The top left panel shows the wave profiles of the first 10 harmonics of the middle C key in a piano. The Fourier spectrum in the top right panel shows the specific frequency values of the harmonics and their relative intensities. The fundamental frequency (f) is 261 Hz (red bar), whereas the harmonics are exact multiples of this frequency (lighter bars). The bottom panel shows the spatial arrangement of the peak wave patterns corresponding to each harmonic component on the basilar membrane.

a twofold relationship to each other produced similar pitch sensations. Nearly all cultures have since employed the 2:1 frequency ratio as the fundamental interval of musical pitch. This basic unit has come to be known as the **octave**. To move one octave higher in pitch, the fundamental frequency must be doubled, whereas to move one octave lower it must be halved. A tone with a frequency of 522 Hz, for example, is one octave higher than a tone of 261 Hz (i.e., middle C). The effective range of musical pitch spans about 7 octaves, even though the frequency range of human hearing spans 10 octaves (SideNote 7.4 on page 216). This is because tones with a fundamental frequency above 4500 Hz are not suitable as musical sounds (SideNote 7.5 on page 216) (Pierce, 1983; Roederer, 1995).

Musical scales—chromatic intervals and tone height

It is not customary to speak of musical tones in terms of their frequency content even though that is what determines the quality of pitch sensation. Instead, musical tones are represented by an alphabetic notational system that has

SideNote | **7.3**

The actual sound produced by the middle C key on a piano is a composite of all of these harmonics. Its waveform, shown below, is the sum of all the individual harmonic components in the top left panel of Figure 7.1.

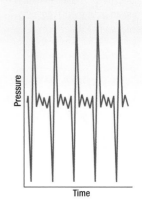

SideNote 7.4

Starting at a low frequency limit of 20 Hz, there can be only 10 doubling intervals before the upper limit of 20000 Hz is reached. Hence, human hearing spans 10 octaves.

SideNote 7.5

Among orchestral instruments, the deepest note of the bass viol (41 Hz) represents the lower limit, whereas the highest note of the piccolo (4500 Hz) represents the upper limit. Musical tones with higher fundamental frequencies do not sound too appealing because of the limited number of harmonics that can be accommodated within the frequency limits of human hearing.

SideNote 7.6

The songs made by whales and dolphins are composed of continuously changing pitches. However, the music made by humans contains distinct pitch transitions based on musical scales. This is preferable because pitch transitions produce musical patterns that are more easily processed and stored by the brain.

SideNote 7.7

Different cultures have developed different sets of oral scales. For example, the Indian system uses the syllables *sa, ri, ga, ma pa, dha, ni*; the Balinese system uses *ding, dong, deng, dung, dang*; and the Korean system uses *tong, tung, tang, tong, ting*.

evolved over several centuries. There are two important characteristics of this system. The first is that it is repetitive. Musical tones that are one octave apart sound similar, and therefore each doubling of the fundamental frequency produces tones that can be represented by the same alphabetic character (Olson, 1967; Roederer, 1995). The entire pitch spectrum can thus be divided into a series of octaves of repeating characters. The second important characteristic is that musical pitch within an octave is not defined as a continuous parameter but instead forms a series of discrete transitions (SideNote 7.6). Any given octave is therefore divided into smaller intervals in a precise manner that is largely culture dependent. The musical tone at each interval is represented by a specific letter or note (e.g., C, D, E, F, G, A, B, and back to C again to complete the octave). The relative position of the tones within an octave is known as **tone chroma** and is represented in a circular manner, as shown in the upper diagram of Figure 7.2. The vocal counterpart of musical intervals in the modern European tradition, known as **solmization**, is the familiar *do-re-me-fa-sol-la-ti* scale, where *do* corresponds to the C note (SideNote 7.7).

The actual intervals of the chromatic scale in Western musical culture are based on simple frequency ratios among the various notes, as shown in Table 7.1. The currently accepted scale was originally sponsored by Johann Sebastian Bach and is known as the **equally tempered scale**. Each octave is broken up into 12 equal divisions when plotted on a logarithmic frequency scale. These divisions, known as **semitones**, can be further divided into 100 cents to signify minor alterations in pitch. Thus, each tempered semitone is separated by 100 cents and each octave by 1,200 cents (see Table 7.1). The octave division into 12 semitones is repeated for each successive octave along the entire musical pitch spectrum. This repeating sequence is referred to as **tone height** and is usually depicted as a spiralling series of octaves that appears in graphical form similar to a barber pole (see lower diagram in Figure 7.2).

The appearance of a series of octaves along the musical spectrum leads to the question of how to differentiate similar notes among the different octave registers. In other words, "How can we distinguish a particular note, say G sharp (G#), from belonging to one octave versus another?" The adopted convention has

been to attach numerical subscripts to notes according to their tone height. For example, the C note in the lowermost octave is C_1; in the next octave it is C_2, etc. The middle key on a piano, middle C, is denoted as C_4. Exactly the same convention applies to all of the other notes in an octave, as shown in Figure 7.2.

Musical scales—staff notation

Given that the most important element in music is pitch, it is not surprising that over

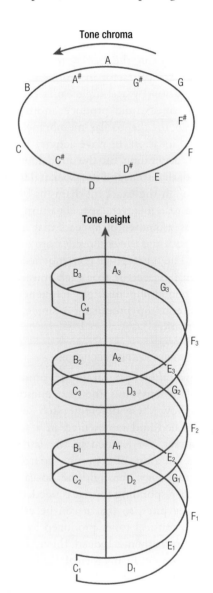

Figure 7.2

An octave is divided into 12 pitch intervals that can be represented in a circular manner and denoted with alphabetic characters or notes. The entire musical pitch spectrum is divided into a series of such octaves. The repeating sequence of octave registers is known as *tone height* and is shown as an ascending series of spirals. Musical notes are given numerical subscripts according to the octave register to which they belong.

Table 7.1

Musical Pitch Intervals According to the *Equally Tempered* Chromatic Scale

Interval	Example	Frequency Values (Hz)	Frequency Ratio	Cents
Minor third	C, D#	261, 311	6:5	300
Major third	C, E	261, 330	5:4	400
Perfect fourth	C, F	261, 349	4:3	500
Perfect fifth	C, G	261, 392	3:2	700
Minor sixth	C, G#	261, 415	8:5	800
Major sixth	C, A	261, 440	5:3	900
Octave	C, C	261, 522	2:1	1,200

Note. The full octave is divided into 12 semitones, each being 100 cents apart. The frequency values refer to the octave containing middle C.

Johann Sebastian Bach
(1685–1750)
© Lebrecht Music and Arts Photo Library/Alamy

the centuries much effort has been devoted to develop a written system to communicate musical pitch sequences (North & Hargreaves, 2008; Pierce, 1983). The purpose was to permit others to replicate the same pitch sequence and therefore allow musical performance. The current Western **staff** notation is based on graphical signs that have their origins from the 12th century. Any student of music is aware of the various complex properties of musical notation. However, at its core, the different notes in staff notation essentially represent different musical pitch sensations, each of them in turn being comprised of a certain fundamental frequency. Figure 7.3 shows the relationship between a series of notes spanning the bass and treble clefs and their fundamental frequencies, and the inset shows the exact frequency values for selected notes within an octave starting with middle C. Musicians, however, do not have to worry about these frequency details because a precise set of norms for pitch tuning has been established through a musical scale that uses alphabetical characters instead.

Perfect pitch

Musical composition arises from a sequence of tones that emphasizes pitch transitions. As a result, humans have developed a common ability, known as **relative pitch**, to accurately identify tonal intervals. Musicians especially have a well-developed sense of relative pitch because of their extensive training in playing and listening to tonal sequences. However, the ability to actually identify an isolated

tone by name is much more difficult, even among trained musicians. This ability, known as **perfect pitch**, is so rare that it is present in about one in 10,000 people (SideNote 7.8 on page 218) (Levitin & Rogers, 2005). Because we are more concerned with pitch transitions in music, it may be that the actual pitch value is not processed or retained even though it reaches our brain. Thus, we find it difficult to associate a single pitch by name because that

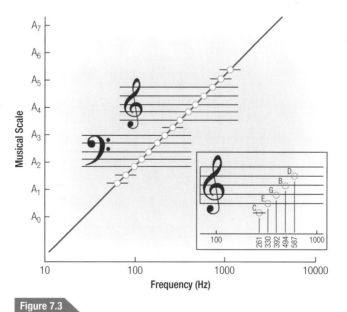

Figure 7.3

In Western musical notation, a set of five parallel horizontal lines along with a clef (bass or treble) is used to indicate the pitch of musical notes. That pitch in turn is related to the fundamental frequency and the associated harmonics of the note. The inset shows specific frequency values for a set of notes in an octave starting at middle C (261 Hz). Note that the horizontal axis is logarithmic.

A famous story of Wolfgang Amadeus Mozart, who was blessed with perfect pitch, claimed that by age 7 he could identify when his violin was tuned half a quarter of a tone sharper than his friend's, which he had played several days earlier.

A musical tone can therefore be characterized by three different attributes—pitch, loudness, and timbre. In fact, musical notes can be distinguished from noise because they have a clear association with these three qualities. Although noise can have loudness, it is much more difficult to assign a unique pitch quality to it.

information is not directly relevant to the cognitive processes underlying music perception.

There is a lively debate among specialists as to whether perfect pitch is genetic or whether it can be learned (Patel, 2007; Peretz & Zatorre, 2005; Zatorre, 2003). The idea of a genetic origin arose from early findings that perfect pitch tends to run in families. More recent studies have shown that perfect pitch is more common in identical twins than in fraternal twins. However, there is evidence to suggest that musical training in early life is also associated with a greater incidence of perfect pitch, suggesting that it is more of a learned phenomenon. It may be that a combination of both genetic and environmental factors is responsible for perfect pitch. For example, some form of perfect pitch may be present in a large segment of the population but disappears early in the absence of musical training.

Tone quality

By now we know that a musical note is composed of a fundamental frequency and a set of harmonics, each having a particular intensity value. What would be the perceptual consequence for a complex tone if only the intensity values of the harmonics were altered but the same frequencies were retained? To begin with, we would expect the same pitch sensation to occur because the same spatial pattern of activity would be evoked along the basilar membrane. This is precisely what happens when the same note is played on two different instruments. However, the perceptual impression created by the two instruments is not the same. We can easily distinguish a difference in tone quality even though the pitch sensation is judged to be identical. This difference in tone quality, which is known as **timbre**, arises from the different intensity distributions of the harmonics (Pierce, 1983; Roederer, 1995).

Different musical instruments produce different intensity distributions among their harmonics for the same note because each instrument favours certain harmonics over others. Figure 7.4 shows the pressure waveform of the middle C note played on a guitar and an alto saxophone, along with their respective Fourier spectra (Olson, 1967). The fact that the two spectra show the same harmonic frequency distribution means that the exact same distance relationships should occur between peak wave activities on the basilar membrane. The difference in tone quality therefore arises from subtle differences in neural activation at each point of the basilar membrane due to intensity differences among the harmonics. It is this difference that allows us to distinguish the timbre of musical tones that otherwise produce the same pitch sensation (SideNote 7.9) (Fletcher & Rossing, 1991; Pierce, 1983).

There is no formal manner by which timbre sensation is characterized other than through

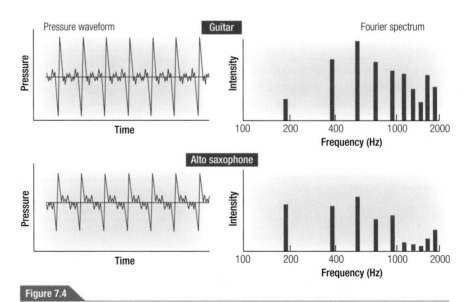

Figure 7.4

The middle C note played on a guitar and an alto saxophone produces a pressure waveform that appears quite similar. The Fourier spectra, however, show a difference in the intensity values of the various harmonics. This difference is responsible for producing the characteristic timbre sensation associated with each musical instrument. Adapted from *Music, Physics, and Engineering*, by H. F. Olson, 1967, New York, NY: Dover.

INVESTIGATION

Exploring Musical Notes and Timbre

To investigate sounds and the fundamental frequencies of complex sounds, download the following program: http://audacity.sourceforge.net/. Next, visit the following website to utilize the sound samples of different instruments playing certain notes: http://www.philharmonia.co.uk/thesoundexchange/make_music/samples/library/.

First, press Record in Audacity and then select a particular musical note played by a certain instrument. When the sound is complete, stop the recording in Audacity and explore the options—for example, select Analyze/Plot Spectrum from the toolbar to see the note broken down into its fundamental frequencies. You can also use Audacity to generate different sounds by selecting Generate from the toolbar and choosing a sound option. Finally, you can experience the phenomenon "timbre" just by listening to the different instruments playing the same note and detecting the qualitative changes.

---

such vague terms as *shrill*, *mellow*, or *full*. In general, timbre sensations are usually referred to by the instruments responsible for producing them. As such, differences in timbre can be as varied as the number of musical instruments. There are three general categories under which musical instruments can be classified—chordophones (string instruments), aerophones (wind instruments), and percussions. There are further subgroups within each class. For example, string instruments can be broken down by the manner in which the sound is produced (i.e., bowing, plucking, or striking). Table 7.2 provides a short list of instruments that belong to each group.

Table **7.2**

Three Major Categories of Musical Instruments

	Chordophones			Aerophones			Percussions
Bowing	Violin Viola Cello Double bass		Brass	Bugle Trumpet Cornet French horn Trombone Tuba		Idiophones	Xylophone Cymbal Steel drum Gong Triangle
Plucking	Guitar Harpsichord Banjo Mandolin Ukulele Zither Lyre Lute		Woodwind	Flute Clarinet Recorder Saxophone Oboe English horn Bassoon Piccolo		Membranophones	Timpani Bongo Side drums Tabla
Striking	Piano Dulcimer Clavichord		Free Reed	Accordion Harmonica Harmonium			

Note. Chordophones (string instruments) are further broken down according to the way the strings are set in motion. Aerophones use air movement to produce sound and include the brass, woodwind, and free reed types. Percussion instruments include those that produce sound when they vibrate (idiophones) and those in which a membrane vibrates after being struck (membranophones).

The manner by which each instrument produces musical sounds is quite complex. These mechanisms, which are now well understood, are responsible for the characteristic resonant qualities that in turn produce the specific timbre and range of pitches associated with each musical instrument. For example, the different timbres produced by different brass instruments—such as the trumpet, French horn, and tuba—result from differences in the way their mouthpieces are shaped, the material from which they are made, and the manner in which they are played. The pitch of musical tones is largely a function of the physical characteristics of aerophones and of strings in chordophones (SideNote 7.10). As a result, each musical instrument produces complex tones with fundamentals that fall within a restricted range. The piano shows an especially impressive range of fundamentals, spanning from about 27 to over 4000 Hz. Another impressive instrument in this regard is the harp, from which the piano was originally developed in the early 1700s. Figure 7.5 shows the full piano keyboard along with the range of fundamentals produced by various other musical instruments (Pierce, 1983).

2. PERCEPTUAL ASPECTS OF MUSIC

We have thus far discussed the composition and characteristics of musical tones. But we have not really discussed music per se. The pleasure and enjoyment we experience from musical sensation arises from truly complex psychological events that still remain poorly understood. To begin with, there is no generally accepted view of musical perception in evolutionary terms (Trebub, 2003; Wallin, Merker, & Brown, 2000). One theory asserts that both music and language evolved from a common ancestor. Whereas language subsequently evolved into a specialized communicative tool, music became associated with emotive processes. But why did evolution produce a brain with the musical ability of such masters as Mozart or Beethoven? Pleasure, after all, is not an adaptive function that drives evolution. Rather,

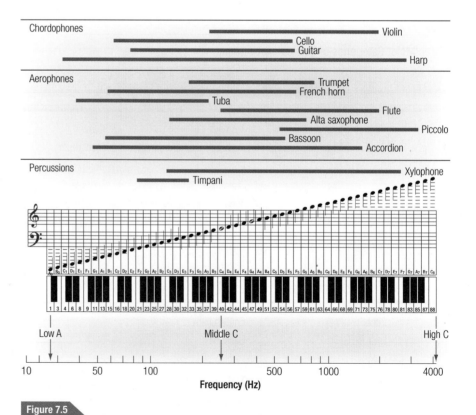

Figure 7.5

The fundamental frequency range of the piano keyboard spans 27.5 Hz (low A) to 4186 Hz (high C). The range of the fundamentals for various other musical instruments is shown in relation to the piano keyboard. The tuba and piccolo are examples of instruments whose sounds dominate the low and high ends of the spectrum, respectively. Adapted from *The Science of Musical Sound*, by J. R. Pierce, 1983, New York, NY: Freeman.

adaptations occur either through natural selection for individual survival benefit or through sexual selection for reproductive benefit. With regard to the latter point, Charles Darwin took the view that human music evolved as a courtship function to attract sexual mates, an idea that has been largely ignored (SideNote 7.11).

At the other extreme are the suggestions that the evolution of music was accidental because there is no biological cause or effect for which music is useful. As linguist Steven Pinker puts it, music is "auditory cheesecake" (SideNote 7.12). And yet, the universality of music is astonishing. Every known human society practises music in one form or another. There is compelling evidence for the presence of music in ancient civilizations as well, such as the Sumerians and Babylonians who flourished around 3,000 BCE. The oldest musical instrument in the archeological record, a flute carved from an animal bone, dates back to the Neanderthal period nearly 50,000 years ago. Whether music originated due to survival benefits or merely as an accident of evolution will likely remain debated for years to come. What is certain though is that music has a profound ability to transform emotions and thereby exerts enormous influence upon humans.

What then are the characteristics of the music signal that produce such stunning effects on our psyche? Music perception relies on two distinct qualities—tonal superpositions and tonal sequences. In tonal superposition, different musical tones are sounded together in unison to produce a compound sound. In tonal sequences, different musical tones (or sometimes the same one) are sounded in rapid succession. The corresponding events in terms of pitch sensation are ultimately responsible for the phenomenon of music perception. In this section, we discuss some key characteristics of tonal superpositions and sequences that form the underlying basis for music perception.

Tonal superpositions—monophonic versus polyphonic tones

The musical tones that we have discussed up to now were made of single or monophonic tones. Although it is possible to have musical composition based on a series of monophonic tones, Western music is generally composed of superpositions of multiple tones, known as **polyphonic** tones. For example, a chord is formed when three or more single tones are played simultaneously. The basic triad is formed by superpositions of three tones at intervals of a third. Any student of music can testify to the routine requirement of having to name the components (i.e., the trio of notes) that make up a particular triad. A truly remarkable property of the auditory system is that despite the complexity of the sound signal in a chord or triad, we are still able to define its constituents, an ability that is especially well developed in trained musicians (Ciocca, 2008; Jackendoff & Lerdahl, 2006; Thompson, 2009).

The brain's ability to disentangle the complex sound waveform of a chord is especially impressive because of all the possible harmonic interactions. Two examples of the confounding possibilities in a simultaneous two-tone (doublet) combination are shown in Figure 7.6 (Roederer, 1995). The top panel shows the

INVESTIGATION

Benjamin Franklin and the Armonica

All material has a frequency with which it vibrates, known as the *resonance frequency*. In 1761, Benjamin Franklin took advantage of this natural property when he invented the Armonica (also known as the *glass harmonica*). It consists of a series of 37 glass bowls in graduated sizes on a horizontal spindle rotated by a flywheel and a foot pedal. The music is produced by the friction created when the rotating bowls are "played" with a wet or powdered finger. The range of frequencies that the armonica plays is between 1000 and 4000 Hz. This range of frequencies is difficult to locate in space, which led people in the 18th century to believe the armonica caused insanity, depression, and even marital problems. You can see how the armonica works and even try playing it for yourself by accessing the following website: http://sln.fi.edu/franklin/musician/virtualarmonica.html

SideNote | 7.13

Recall that differences in timbre are created when the intensity values of the harmonic distribution are altered. This is precisely the situation that arises due to the superposition of certain harmonics when two notes that are an octave apart are played simultaneously, as shown in Figure 7.6 (top panel).

SideNote | 7.14

The concepts of consonance and dissonance have largely remained stable over several centuries in terms of the tonal combinations. However, from time to time, certain musical styles that have made use of dissonant combinations have appeared.

situation that arises when the fundamental frequency of one tone corresponds to one of the harmonics of another tone. In this example, the A3 note coincides with the second harmonic of the A$_2$ note when the two are played together. Indeed, several of the frequency components of the two notes are reinforced, producing a new harmonic distribution indicated by the dashed line. The important point here is that we are able to identify the presence of both tones in this doublet even though the expected outcome from the profile in Figure 7.6 should be a sensation of a single tone with a different timbre (SideNote 7.13).

A related intriguing case arises when exactly the same note is played simultaneously on two different musical instruments. We know from our previous discussion on timbre that both tones would produce the same harmonic frequency distribution but that their respective intensity values would be somewhat different. Again we would have a situation where the intensity values at each harmonic frequency are reinforced to produce a new compound intensity distribution. However, we do not

hear a single note at a higher intensity or different timbre but instead correctly perceive two notes of the same pitch but different timbre. Thus, we are somehow able to discriminate the timbre of the two notes in this superposition even though there is nothing inherent in the frequency distribution that should permit this. One cue that may allow this function is the time element regarding the onset of the two tones. The initiation or *attack* of two tones played on different instruments is rarely synchronized due to physical differences in the way they produce sounds. This extremely small timing asynchrony may help the brain to bind the harmonic components of one musical tone and distinguish it from a second. This phenomenon is all the more astonishing when one considers the complexity of the sound profile emerging from an orchestra where the same note from a multitude of musical instruments is played simultaneously, producing a massive superposition of harmonic frequencies.

Another confounding situation arises when two notes producing a different pitch are superimposed, as shown by the example in the bottom panel of Figure 7.6 (Roederer, 1995). Here, the A$_2$ and C$_3{}^{\#}$ notes are played in unison to produce a staggered set of harmonic distributions. Each of these harmonic components in turn produces peak wave activity in the basilar membrane at the corresponding point on the tonotopic map. However, there is nothing in this distribution to bind the harmonic components so that one sequence should belong to a specific note. The brain is somehow able to make that connection and assign the relevant harmonics to each note to produce two simultaneous but distinct pitch sensations.

Tonal superpositions—consonance and dissonance

The next question that arises is "Exactly what are the perceptual consequences with tonal superpositions?" Common experience with the piano keyboard tells us that certain combinations of notes sound pleasant, whereas others do not. Two or more simultaneously played notes are said to generate a **consonant** sensation if they are deemed to be pleasant. The alternative is an unpleasant or **dissonant** sensation. The subjective feeling of consonance is associated with calm and stability, whereas dissonance is associated with tension and harshness (SideNote 7.14) (North & Hargreaves, 2008; Thompson, 2009).

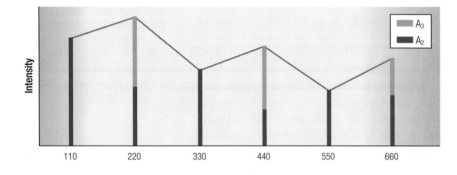
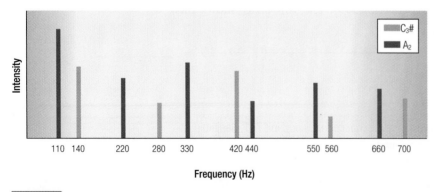

Figure 7.6

Simultaneously playing two notes that are one octave apart reinforces the intensity values of certain harmonics (top panel). The resulting compound intensities at these harmonics produce a new intensity distribution (green line). Another confounding situation arises when two different notes are played simultaneously to produce a staggered distribution of harmonics (bottom panel). Adapted from *The Physics and Psychophysics of Music. An Introduction,* by J. G. Roederer, 1995, New York, NY: Springer-Verlag.

What are the musical intervals of tonal superposition that produce consonant and dissonant sounds? The answer to this question becomes self-evident once we understand the factors that contribute to these opposite musical sensations. It turns out that both consonance and dissonance can be explained largely in terms of the frequency content of musical tones. Consonant sounds occur when two or more tones contain harmonic frequencies that coincide and therefore reinforce each other. The best example of this occurs with notes that are an octave apart, as in the example presented in the top panel of Figure 7.6. In this case, the harmonics of the second note coincide with every alternate harmonic of the first note. There are no frequency components that lie in between. The octave is the only musical interval that gives rise to this perfect coincidence and therefore accounts for its special status and the fact that despite differences in pitch, all notes that are an octave apart appear to have a similar sound.

The musical intervals shown in Table 7.1 all produce consonant sounds. For some of the intervals, such as the fourth and fifth, only a partial set of harmonics among the two tones will have a coincident frequency. For example, at an interval of a fifth, the fundamental frequencies of the two tones have a 3:2 ratio. This means that all even numbered harmonics of the upper tone will coincide, whereas the odd ones will not, as illustrated in the top panel of Figure 7.7. Two notes that have an interval of a fourth, where the fundamental frequencies have a 4:3 ratio, will produce coincidence at every third harmonic of the upper tone (see middle panel in Figure 7.7). As the ratio of fundamental frequencies takes on more complex values, the incidence of overlapping harmonics becomes further reduced, and with it, so does the likelihood of consonance (Roederer, 1995).

This does not, however, mean that tones with very few overlapping harmonics will necessarily be dissonant. A musical interval spanning a major third largely produces non-overlapping harmonics (SideNote 7.15). And yet, this interval is considered to be consonant. The reason for this lies in the fact that the harmonics of the two tones are well separated and therefore produce distinct activation patterns on the basilar membrane. Thus, a second determinant of consonance is that a distinct and separable frequency pattern be present among two or more tones that are played

simultaneously. A dissonant sensation will occur if the harmonic representations are too close, especially for the lower harmonics. An example of this is when the interval between two tones is a major second (e.g., two adjacent white keys on a piano). The frequency distribution in this case shows that the initial harmonics of the two tones are nearly adjacent (bottom panel in Figure 7.7). This results in interference between their activations on the basilar membrane that in turn produces a clashing or dissonant sensation.

Tonal sequences—melody, tempo, and rhythm

We next turn to the second major characteristic of music—tonal sequences. The rhythmic properties of music do not arise from the frequency content of individual musical tones but rather from their sequential appearance

SideNote 7.15

The A_2 and $C_3^\#$ notes, whose harmonic distributions are shown in the bottom panel of Figure 7.6, span a major third interval.

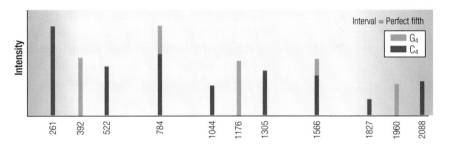

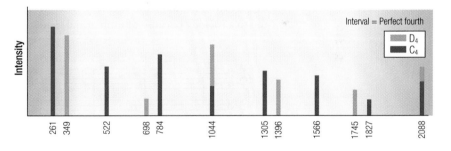

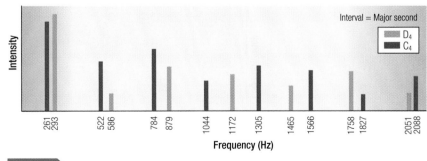

Figure 7.7

The superposition of two musical tones at various intervals produces different harmonic relationships relative to each other. Two tones that are a perfect fifth apart produce a periodic set of coincident harmonics that reinforce each other (top panel). The coincidence frequency becomes reduced at an interval of a perfect fourth (middle panel). Both of these intervals produce consonant sensations. A major second interval (bottom panel) produces a dissonant sensation because of the clashing effect that arises from the close proximity of the lower harmonics.

SideNote | **7.16**

Rhythm is the one indispensable component of music because no melody can exist without it. Different concepts of rhythm have produced a large variety of musical styles over the centuries. The trend in the 20th-century was to experiment with a variety of rhythmic structures, producing such recognizable musical forms as jazz, rhythm and blues, hip hop, and rap—just to name a few.

in time (Gulick et al., 1989; Roederer, 1995; Thompson, 2009). A group of musical tones that forms such a sequence is called a **melody**. While the frequency characteristics of an individual tone determine its pitch, it is the melodic sequence that somehow harmonizes with the emotional centres in our brain to produce pleasure (Meyer, 1956; Thompson, 2009).

The two key parameters that come up in any discussion of a tonal sequence are *time* and *contour*. The perception of music is strongly influenced by time-dependent variables, such as the duration of the tones and their rate of presentation. The notes in a melody usually occur at rates that are comparable to syllables in speech. The fastest presentation rate can reach 150 milliseconds per note, although the notes are still recognizable at rates of up to 50 milliseconds. The perceived speed of tonal presentations in a melodic sequence is known as **tempo**. Subtle changes in tempo can produce a grouping effect whereby a sequence of tones that occur close together in time are perceptually separated and grouped as a separate subunit. A similar effect can occur by introducing a brief time gap between a group of notes. The perceptual organization of a melody into subunits based on the temporal character of the sequence is responsible for producing **rhythm**. Rhythmic organization occurs spontaneously when listening to a melody because of our natural tendency

to allocate tonal elements into perceptually organized subunits (SideNote 7.16) (Loui et al., 2009; Pierce, 1983).

The **contour** of a tonal sequence refers to the nature of pitch changes with time. All melodies are characterized by sequential rises and drops in frequency that together produce a pattern of sound. An example is provided in Figure 7.8 where the first line of the familiar tune "My Bonnie lies over the ocean" is shown in terms of its musical notation along with the corresponding fundamental frequency value of each note. As with all melodies, this particular one is characterized by a precise set of pitch changes as a function of time and shown by the contour in the bottom segment of Figure 7.8. We noted earlier that it is the *relative* pitch relationships that we attend to in music rather than the *absolute* pitch values. A melody retains the same perceptual identity even if played in a different key or shifted by an octave, as long as the pitch contour remains the same (see Figure 7.8, right). Thus, we are able to identify a melody regardless of a transposition to a different pitch range as long as it is applied equally to all of the notes.

Tonal sequences—cognitive theories

A melody produces a global percept where the individual tones are rarely recognized as a distinct sequence of sounds but instead meld

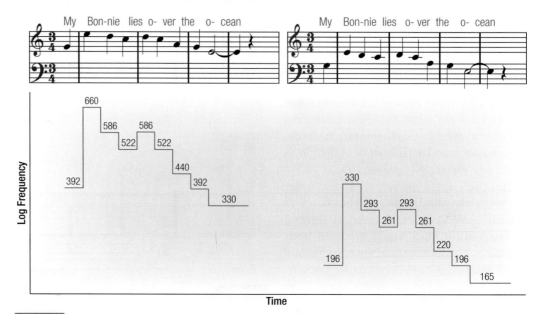

Figure 7.8

A melody is characterized by a precise set of pitch changes with time, known as the *pitch contour*. The contour of a familiar tune is shown along the top in notional format and along the bottom in terms of the fundamental frequencies of the individual notes. A transposition by one octave changes the actual frequency values but retains the same relative pitch relationships.

together into a cohesive whole. This raises the question as to what underlying features in a melodic contour are responsible for generating the perceived wholeness of music. It is believed that the grouping of musical tones to form a melodic structure occurs in the higher cognitive centres of the brain according to a set of basic organizational principles (Lerdahl & Jackendoff, 1983; Peretz & Zatorre, 2005; Warren, 2008). These principles, which were first set out in the early part of the 20th century, have come to be known collectively as **Gestalt theory** (SideNote 7.17). The principles were deduced largely on the basis of intuitive reasoning and observations gathered from simple experiments on visual perception.

The basic tenets of Gestalt theory have been used to account for the wholesome and cohesive quality of melodic perception. There are three Gestalt principles that can be applied to group musical sequences. The first is the principle of *proximity*, which states that tones appearing close together in time will be grouped as a perceptual unit. Thus, a sequence of notes that follows each other very closely in time will form a perceptually separable group from another such sequence. Another Gestalt principle, known as *similarity*, uses the same logic but applied to pitch and timbre. Musical tones that have a similar pitch or timbre are therefore perceptually bound together in the same group. Symphonic music provides an elegant example where instruments that have a similar timbre appear to be perceptually grouped and distinguishable from other instruments. The third Gestalt principle of grouping is known as *common fate*. Given that music is sequential pitch movement either up or down in scale, it would seem reasonable that tonal sequences whose pitch changes in the same direction would form a common unit. The same principle can be applied to common changes in the intensity pattern as well. Thus, perceptual grouping under this principle is based on the similarity of the pattern of change with time, whether it be with regard to pitch or intensity.

3. MUSIC AND THE BRAIN

Music enjoys a special status among sensory qualities because of the emotional response it creates. An understanding of the precise way by which music activates the brain remains elusive. Musical stimulation has been thought of as a cyclically changing flux of neural signals that propagates through the auditory centres and triggers neural circuits that may have a periodic or cyclical response pattern. One idea is that the rhythmic sound pattern of music resonates with some internal rhythm in the brain that in turn leads to the activation of higher emotional centres.

It has been known for some time that specific brain areas are likely involved in the processing of pitch sequences (Peretz & Zatorre, 2005; Zatorre & Gandour, 2008; Zatorre, Chen, & Penhune, 2007). There are cases where a stroke or traumatic injury has left a musician with a specific inability to perceive or express musical sounds (Stewart, von Kriegstein, Warren, & Griffiths, 2006). Brain imaging studies have revealed some tantalizing clues about the neural substrates of pitch perception. It has been found that a particular brain region near the auditory cortex called the *planum temporale* is significantly enlarged in the left hemisphere of professional musicians and those who have perfect pitch. This area of the brain is also responsible for processing speech sounds and has been postulated to be responsible for the analytical tasks common to both language and music perception, even though musical function is generally regarded as being dominated by the right hemisphere. It may be that musicians develop a certain specialization in the left hemisphere for processing pitch sequences that are largely the domain of the right hemisphere in non-musicians.

Brain imaging studies have also shown that a distinct pattern of neural activity is evident when human subjects listen to tonal melodies as opposed to non-melodic sequences. Figure 7.9 shows a brain scan obtained with the *functional magnetic resonance imaging* or fMRI technique. The image on the left shows sparse brain activity in the temporal lobe in response to non-melodic stimulation. Musical stimulation, however, produces much greater brain activity in the same regions as well as new ones in the auditory areas of the temporal lobe (Figure 7.9, right). Increased brain activity here may arise due to the richer meaning and rhythmic quality of music. Other studies have shown distinct patterns of brain activity to emerge during musical imagination, pitch memory tasks, music score reading, and music performance (Peretz & Zatorre, 2005; Warren, 2008; Zatorre et al., 2007).

SideNote | **7.17**

Gestalt theory makes an attempt to understand various psychological phenomena such as perception, learning, and thinking as structured wholes. The ideas were originally developed by three Czech- and German-born psychologists: Max Wertheimer, Kurt Koffka, and Wolfgang Köhler. Gestalt theories have had a major influence on our attempts to understand the visual perception of objects and will be discussed in greater detail in Chapter 10.

METHODOLOGY

Music Therapy and Well-being

The idea of using music as a healing medium began in ancient times; however it was not until the First World War that music therapy was implemented in the form we use today. Kenneth Bruscia is a music therapist who wrote that music therapy has three main aims: to facilitate general development, to remediate specific developmental disabilities, or to return a client to a recurring developmental problem in order to resolve the issue. Music therapy has been found to ameliorate the quality of life for those suffering from physical disorders such as cerebral palsy, multiple sclerosis, and Alzheimer's disease as well as those suffering from psychological disorders such as depression, autism spectrum conditions, schizophrenia, and attachment disorder. The Canadian Association of Music Therapy states that its accredited therapists act to promote, maintain, and restore mental, physical, emotional, and spiritual health. Research has shown that music therapy has been found to decrease depression, improve mood, and reduce anxiety, as well as improve quality of life. By coupling music therapy with traditional therapies, many improvements have been seen.

B. Speech Perception

In the last section, we discussed the possible origins of musical perception and the arguments as to how it may have been an accidental consequence of evolution. There is no doubt, however, that speech perception had a very powerful evolutionary force—survival benefit through communication. Indeed, it is our communicative ability that was partly responsible for the astounding development of our species through the course of hominid evolution. And that in turn is believed to have occurred due to an expansion of our brain, and more specifically, particular chambers that are responsible for both speech production and perception (Jackendoff, 2003; Patel, 2007).

Speech perception represents a very large field of inquiry within perceptual science. It can be broadly divided into three areas—speech production, speech comprehension, and the brain structures responsible for both of these functions. Each of these three general areas in turn is responsible for covering a wide array of topics. For example, speech comprehension research deals with a range

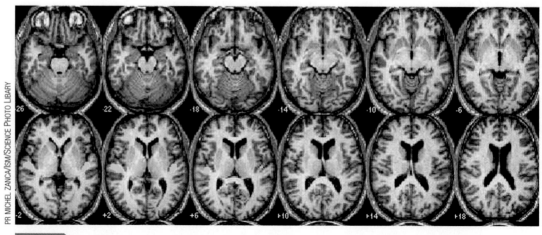

Figure 7.9

Functional MRI (fMRI) imaging shows areas of the brain that are activated while listening to music. A series of transverse sections through different levels of the brain shows specific regions of the temporal lobe that are responsive (coloured areas). The front of the brain is at top.

of issues that include the interpretation of speech signals, how the meanings of words are determined, information derived from sentence structure, and various issues surrounding written and non-verbal language schemes. Similarly, speech production research deals not only with the mechanistic aspects of vocalization but also with the many clinical issues surrounding this process, such as speech errors, stuttering, etc. Given that volumes can be (and have been) written on the various topics surrounding speech perception, our goal here will be to condense the current knowledge into an introductory account that focuses on the fundamental biological and perceptual aspects of this fascinating phenomenon.

1. SPEECH PRODUCTION

Language evolved as a means of communication among humans. At present, there are about 7,000 different languages in the world, and more than half of them are practised by small bands of people concentrated in two tropical zones—central Africa and Papua New Guinea (Ladefoged, 2001; Ladefoged & Maddieson, 1996; Pisoni & Remez, 2007). It is important to distinguish between *language* and *speech* at the outset. Language can encompass any form of communication, including non-verbal methods such as alphabetic writing, symbolic writing (e.g., Braille), hand communication (e.g., sign language), or other less conventional methods (e.g., Morse code, semaphoric signalling, etc.). The most common way of using language is through **articulation**, a process that uses the vocal apparatus, the output of which is referred to as *speech*. All spoken languages use outgoing air from the lungs to produce the distinctive vocal sounds that constitute speech.

The unique aspect of speech is that it is the only sensory stimulus that is actually produced by humans. All other sensory signals have a non-human origin that we capture and process to understand something about our environment. Of course, we are capable of pinching ourselves, releasing various odours, etc., that do have a sensory impact on us and others. Nonetheless, speech represents the only structured stimulus that we produce to form an active sensory signal.

The process of vocalization

Human speech sounds are produced by the vocal apparatus, which is made up of a number of structures in the chest, throat, and mouth (Gleason & Ratner, 1998; Pickett, 1999; Warren, 2008). These structures can be roughly divided into three major systems—the **subglottal system**, the larynx, and the vocal tract, as shown in Figure 7.10. The subglottal system is composed of the windpipe (trachea), the lungs, and the muscles that are responsible for expansion and contraction of the chest that moves air in and out. The air moves into the lungs from the nasal and oral cavities through the pharynx, larynx, and finally the trachea.

As air proceeds through the larynx, it must pass through an opening in the **vocal folds** known as the **glottis**. The vocal folds are made up of two strips of ligaments that can be controlled through a set of muscles to change the size of the glottis. During inhalation, the glottis remains open to allow the air to flow into the lungs. During exhalation, however, rapid opening and closing of the glottis interrupts the airflow and causes a buzz-like sound. The vibrations in the vocal folds, shown in Figure 7.11 on page 228, are caused by fluctuations of air pressure similar to that in a whistling kettle. The pressure of the air in the lungs separates the vocal folds, and then as the air

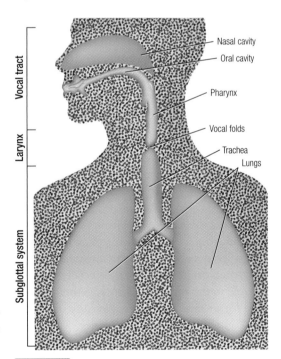

Vocal tract

Larynx

Subglottal system

Nasal cavity

Oral cavity

Pharynx

Vocal folds

Trachea

Lungs

Figure 7.10

The structures involved in speech production can be divided into three major components—the subglottal system, the larynx, and the vocal tract. The vocal tract is composed of a number of structures within the oral and nasal chambers. Adapted from *Auditory Perception: A New Analysis and Synthesis*, by R. M. Warren, 1999, New York, NY: Cambridge University Press.

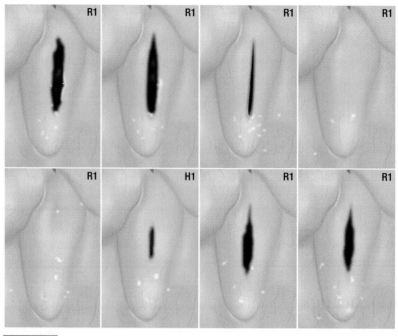

Figure 7.11

A sequence of vocal fold positions starting with an open glottis. This entire sequence occurs in fractions of a second due to rapid fluctuations in air pressure. Based on pictures captured with a mirror in the back of the throat from *Vowels and Consonants. An Introduction to the Sounds of Languages,* by P. Ladefoged, 2001, Malden, MA: Blackwell.

SideNote | **7.18**

The vocal folds can also be lengthened or shortened to influence the frequency characteristics of the buzz-like sound, also known as the *laryngeal buzz.* The folds can also be maintained at a fixed position for a prolonged period, as during whispering when the glottis is kept nearly closed.

SideNote | **7.19**

The actual fundamental frequencies of voice that result from these numbers are men—120 Hz, women—250 Hz, and children—400 Hz.

SideNote | **7.20**

Most phonemes are symbolically represented by a single character. By convention, a slash (/) is placed before and after the character. The English language has around 40 different phonemes.

passes through, the folds close because of the drop in pressure. The closing of the vocal cords sets the air in the throat into vibration that in turn causes the initial vocal sound (SideNote 7.18) (Conway & Pisone, 2008; Warren, 2008).

It is this sound that is modified by the vocal tract structures to ultimately produce recognizable speech sounds. The vocal tract, which includes the lips at one end and the larynx at the other, is composed of the tongue, teeth, **palate**, lips, and various cavities and structures within the nasal and oral chambers. Different speech sounds are produced by either contorting the structures within the vocal tract or producing a constriction somewhere along the pathway to modulate the movement of air. The tongue and lips play an especially important role in this process and are together responsible for producing the great variety of speech sounds in all the world's languages.

All speech sounds can be generally characterized by a particular pitch that contains the fundamental frequency of the voice signal. The rate at which the glottis opens and closes is primarily responsible for the fundamental frequency (Conway & Pisone, 2008; Warren, 2008). The vibrational frequency of the glottis is about 125 pulses per second for adult males, 200 pulses per second for adult females,

and about 300 pulses per second for children (SideNote 7.19). It is this difference in the frequency of glottal pulsing that accounts for the difference in voice pitch between men, women, and children. The lower vibrational frequency for males is attributed to a thickening and lengthening of the vocal folds at puberty.

The nature of speech sounds

Speech can be broken down into words. Words in turn can be broken down into syllables. And even syllables can be considered in smaller terms, known as **phonemes**, which in linguistics are considered to be the smallest units of speech. A phoneme is the basic speech sound that distinguishes one word element from another (Gleason & Ratner, 1998; Jackendoff, 2003; Pickett, 1999). A subtle change in a phoneme can alter the entire meaning of a word. The /p/ phoneme in *map*, for example, can be changed to create entirely new words with different meanings, such as *mat, man, mad,* etc. (SideNote 7.20). The term *phoneme* is generally restricted to **vowels** and **consonants**, though it may sometimes be used to indicate alterations in pitch or rhythm.

Vowels and consonants represent the two major classes of phonetic sounds. Vowels are not produced by constrictions in the vocal tract but rather through changes in the shape of the mouth and lips. Consonants require more articulatory movement and almost always require either a constriction or impediment somewhere within the vocal tract, usually by way of tongue movement (SideNote 7.21). The different consonants can therefore be described on the basis of two characteristics—their place of articulation and the manner in which the constriction is made. Table 7.3 shows some English consonants that are classified according to the place of articulation, whereas Table 7.4 shows various different manners of articulation. Both of these descriptors together provide the necessary information as to how a particular speech sound is made. A systematic representation of the various phonemes was developed in the late 19th century and formalized into a standard set of symbols that has come to be known as the **International Phonetic Alphabet (IPA)**. The symbols

represent a shorthand way of describing how each sound is made. The IPA theoretically contains all of the distinct speech sounds made in the world's languages.

Acoustic properties of speech sounds—general principles

There are two general ways of describing speech sounds (Gleason & Ratner, 1998; Ladefoged, 2001). The first is by the way the sound is articulated and therefore essentially describes the details of how it is made. This is the case for the descriptions of the various consonants in Tables 7.3 and 7.4. A second way of describing speech is through its acoustic properties. This would require us to consider the physical characteristics of the sounds. Speech is a time-varying signal in which the twin properties of sound—intensity and frequency—are both changing in complex ways as the speech signal unfolds.

SideNote | **7.21**

There are nearly 200 different vowels in all of the world's languages and over 600 different consonants. The variety of consonants are produced by different points of articulation, constriction, and even inhalation sounds such as the clicks made in !Xóõ, a Bushman language of southern Africa.

Table **7.3**

A Classification of English Consonants Based on Place of Articulation within the Vocal Tract

Place	Description	Example
Bilabial	The two lips coming together at the beginning or closing at the end.	[p], [b], [m]
Labiodental	The top teeth against the bottom lip.	[f], [v]
Interdental	The tongue protruding between the teeth or lips.	[th]
Alveolar	The tongue placed behind the upper teeth.	[t], [d], [n]
Palatal	The tongue against the hard palate.	[ch], [sh]
Velar	The back of the tongue touching the soft palate [velum].	[k]

Note. Adapted from *Vowels and Consonants. An Introduction to the Sounds of Languages,* by P. Ladefoged, 2001, Malden, MA: Blackwell; *Psycholinguistics,* by J. B. Gleason and N. B. Ratner, 1998, Fort Worth, TX: Harcourt Brace.

Table **7.4**

A Classification of English Sounds Based on Manner of Articulation

Manner	Description	Example
Oral stop	Closure of the vocal tract. Air blocked from going out through mouth.	bin, pin
Nasal stop	Closure of the vocal tract. Air blocked from going out through nose.	map
Fricative	Constriction of the vocal tract so that a noisy airstream is formed.	fin, thin
Affricate	A stop followed by a fricative made at the same place of articulation.	gin, chin
Liquid	Airflow that is minimally constricted.	raw, law

Note. The relevant consonants are underlined and shown in the context of a word example. Adapted from *Vowels and Consonants. An Introduction to the Sounds of Languages,* by P. Ladefoged, 2001, Malden, MA: Blackwell.

One way to represent the acoustic nature of speech is by way of its pressure waveform (Moore, 1997; Pickett, 1999; Warren, 2008). Figure 7.12 shows an example where the sound pressure waveform (i.e., pressure change over time) is shown for the word *poor*. The pressure changes depicted over approximately 200 milliseconds in this example provide a visible record of the acoustic properties of this particular spoken word. An advantage of the pressure waveform representation is that it can be stored and later used to recreate the exact sound by way of a mechanical device. This was precisely the principle involved in encoding sound information in vinyl records of recent past.

The major problem with representing speech by way of pressure waveforms is that they do not reveal details of the frequency content in the stimulus (Moore, 2008; Pisoni & Remez, 2007). Speech is composed of a complex sound wave that contains many different frequencies simultaneously. We already know that it is the individual frequency components that are of great importance for the way sounds are processed by the auditory system. However, the Fourier components in the speech signal are impossible to determine from the pressure waveforms. And yet, if we were to understand anything about how the speech stimulus is processed, we would need to analyze its frequency content since that represents the basic foundation of cochlear functioning.

One possible solution to this problem is to identify the principal frequency components associated with various phonemes. Figure 7.13 shows just such a representation for several vowels and consonants in the English language. As we can see here, the frequency values span a range of about 250 Hz to nearly 8000 Hz (SideNote 7.22). English vowel sounds tend to be clustered more toward the lower frequency range, whereas the consonants cover a much wider range of frequencies. Furthermore, there

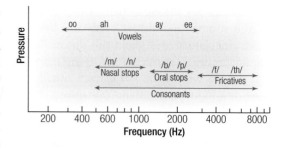

Figure 7.13

Frequency characteristics of some English vowels and consonants. Vowel sounds are largely represented in the lower frequency end, whereas consonant sounds cover a wider range and can reach fairly high frequencies, as is the case with fricatives.

is considerable variability among the consonants. For example, nasal stop consonants have a lower frequency content than oral stops. The highest frequencies associated with speech occur with fricatives. (See Table 7.4 for further examples of these various consonants.) Although it is of interest to know the frequency content of individual speech sounds, this representation cannot provide a full picture of how the frequencies actually change with time during speech.

Acoustic properties of speech sounds—spectrographic representation

Neither of the two forms of signal representation that we have seen thus far is of great value in conveying information about sound patterns that change over time, such as speech. The pressure waveform representation (Figure 7.12) provides no information about frequency content, whereas the second form, frequency representation of various speech sounds (Figure 7.13), provides no information as to how these frequencies change with time as the speech signal is executed.

A far more effective way of depicting the speech stimulus is by way of the **sound spectrograph** (Pickett, 1999; Raphael, Borden, & Harris, 2006; Tatham & Morton, 2006). This is an instrument that analyzes audio signals and determines the distribution of sound frequencies contained within the signal. An important feature of the spectrograph is that it can perform this function repeatedly over time as the speech signal is unfolding, thus providing a readout of how the frequencies change with ongoing speech. The problem though is how to represent all of this information in a graphical format because there are now three pieces of information that need to be

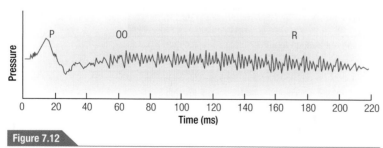

Figure 7.12

The spoken word *poor* is represented here by way of its pressure waveform as a function of time. Adapted from *Auditory Perception: A New Analysis and Synthesis,* by R. M. Warren, 1999, New York, NY: Cambridge University Press.

represented—sound intensity, sound frequency, and time. The solution is to plot the last two variables with respect to each other such that frequency is represented on the y-axis and time, on the x-axis. Sound intensity is shown by the darkness of the markings on the graph. Figure 7.14 shows an example of such a plot, which is known as a **spectrogram**, for the sentence "Sheep like soft grass."

A spectrogram provides a stationary display of all the important components in a speech signal. A closer look at Figure 7.14 shows a number of important features. The frequency content of the individual phonemes in this passage span a range of frequencies, as seen by the vertical smears along the various time points. We know from Figure 7.13 that vowels largely contain low frequencies, and therefore appear toward the bottom of the spectrogram, whereas consonants and especially fricatives are made up of higher frequencies and therefore appear near the top. The interesting feature of a spectrogram is that it displays the changing nature of sound frequencies and associated intensity values throughout the duration of the speech signal.

Another important characteristic of a spectrogram is that the frequency content of a particular phoneme can sometimes appear in the form of bands of resonant frequencies, called **formants** (Pickett, 1999; Warren, 2008). The formants, which appear in a spectrogram in the form of a dark (high intensity) band, arise due to a resonance in the vocal tract. As we noted before, the sound signal that emerges from the glottis is further modified by the various components of the vocal tract. These components act like a complex filter and introduce resonances (formants) at certain frequencies. Figure 7.15 on page 232 shows several examples of vowel formants that can be clearly seen in a spectrogram (Ladefoged, 2001). The formants are numbered—the one at the lowest frequency is called the *first formant* (F1); the next one is called the *second formant* (F2), and so on. A spectrogram that compares several words alongside each other provides useful information on the frequency bands associated with changing speech sounds. For example, the four words in Figure 7.15 differ only in the middle vowel. The shifts in formant frequency, especially the first (F1), can often be directly related to the pitch of the words when spoken.

Sound spectrograms represent a powerful tool for describing speech. The early motivation behind their development was to use them for identifying individual speakers in military settings. The spectrogram of every individual was believed to be as unique to that person as her or his fingerprints. However, the so-called **voiceprint** never became a popular means for identifying individuals, though it is frequently used with other animals such as birds, where individual species can often be identified by the spectrogram of their call (Hennessy & Romig, 1971). Another potential use of the spectrogram was in the area of visual speech (i.e., permitting deaf individuals to see and comprehend spoken language). However, spectrograms were disappointing in this regard also and never fulfilled their potential for use with the hearing impaired (SideNote 7.23). Nevertheless, spectrographic analysis has been used to provide valuable insight into aspects of the sound signal that may be important for the comprehension of speech segments.

2. SPEECH COMPREHENSION

Speech signals are extremely complex because they contain information across the frequency, intensity, and time domains simultaneously. Despite the fact that speech signals can be ultimately broken down into a set of phonetic segments, the sensory events that underlie speech perception are far more complex than the mere detection and assembly of a set of phonemes (Liberman, Cooper, Shankweiler, & Studdert-Kennedy, 1967; Moore, 2008). Indeed, speech perception involves special auditory processing mechanisms that have evolved for the specific perception of speech sounds. Our progress toward understanding some of

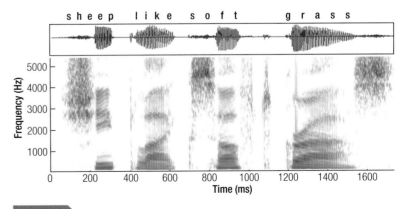

Figure 7.14

A spectrogram provides a convenient way of showing the frequency and intensity content for sound patterns that change over time. Sound frequency is plotted as a function of time with sound intensity shown by the darkness of the markings. The pressure waveform for the spoken sentence "Sheep like soft grass" is shown in the box above its spectrogram.

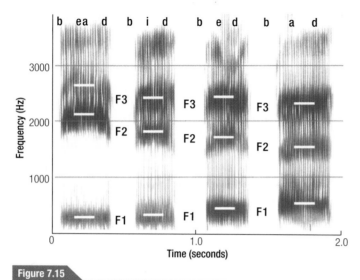

Figure 7.15

A spectrogram of four words (*bead*, *bid*, *bed*, *bad*) reveals discrete bands of resonant frequencies known as *formants*. The formants are indicated by white lines and numbered from the lowest frequency set (e.g., F1, F2, etc.). The four words in this example differ only in the middle vowel sounds. From Ladefoged & Maddieson, The Sounds of the World's Languages, Wiley-Blackwell.

SideNote | **7.24**

Contemporary terms such as *cool, heavy, hip, gay, honey, trip,* and many others are sometimes used to convey meanings that are quite different from their original intended use. Similarly, many words that are now commonly used to convey a specific meaning once enjoyed a more popular use with an entirely different meaning. Some examples, along with their original meanings, are *shambles* (marketplace), *bowels* (affections), *pardon* (allowance), and *mate* (conquer).

these mechanisms has come through research in multiple fields of science, such as linguistics, telecommunications, computer science, experimental psychology, and neuroscience. In this section and the next, we will examine some of the insights that have appeared from research in these various fields. However, we must first ask a fundamental question before we can proceed to a fuller discussion of the mechanisms underlying speech comprehension.

What exactly is a language?

We noted earlier that speech represents one of many forms of communication. A specific set of signs, symbols, structures, or gestures of human communication make up a language. Our daily lives are filled with effortless exercises in reading, listening, writing, and speaking. In all of these behaviours, we are employing a vast set of skills in one or more languages that we have mastered, usually from childhood. And yet, even the simplest use of a language is based on complicated processes that require us to come up with words from a large reservoir and then link them together according to an established format so as to project the exact meaning that was intended (Martin, 2003; Tatham & Morton, 2006). This really is an amazing and natural skill that is unique to humans, both in terms of execution and comprehension.

All human languages are structured, symbolic, and arbitrary systems. By arbitrary, we do not mean that they are changeable, although there are many examples where certain words do change in their meaning, or add new meaning, due to prevailing circumstances of social discourse (SideNote 7.24). Rather, words are merely arbitrary symbols that convey a particular concept or meaning. For example, there is no reason why a chair should be called a chair. It is an arbitrary term that came to be during the course of English language development, conveying a thing with four legs that we sit on. Similarly, the structural nature of language specifies a precise format for combining words to produce a certain intended meaning (Ladefoged, 2001; Liberman et al., 1967; Moore, 2008). All languages are governed by organizational rules. For example, the English language follows a basic wording rule termed SVO (subject–verb–object) order (i.e., subjects precede verbs and objects follow verbs).

METHODOLOGY

Non-verbal Communication Devices

Tom Chau, who is a researcher at the University of Toronto, has undertaken studies to aid and improve the lives of children with disabilities. He and his team have designed many helpful technologies for these children, including the aspirometer and virtual musical instrument, and have helped make advances in the prosthetic arm. A newly developed non-verbal communication device uses an infrared camera that captures changes in heat levels. One use of this technology is to present users with a screen and keyboard that scrolls through the alphabet; when the correct letter is highlighted, the users open their mouth, which increases the heat level. The camera captures this heat change and types the appropriate letter. Another use is to aim the infrared light at the frontal lobes of the brain; changes in blood flow correspond to auditory or visual stimuli, with the goal of differentiating between the "resting" brain and one that is making decisions.

Even if these rules are followed, a precise understanding of what was said is often modified by inferences, expectations, and contextual linkage. For example, the string "My wife is a lot of fun" has a straightforward meaning. However, a mere transposition of two words to produce the string "My fun is a lot of wife" reveals an obscure though potentially more interesting message. Even a technically accurate sentence is often interpreted differently based on the context. We clearly understand what is meant when someone utters "Nobody said nothing about that," despite the fact that a strict interpretation would actually generate the opposite meaning.

The science of psycholinguistics

The rules and conventions that govern the use of a language have been studied extensively by linguists and psychologists. The goal of **psycholinguistics** research is to understand the precise mechanisms by which humans use language (Gleason & Ratner, 1998; Pisoni & Remez, 2007). For our purposes here, the specific aspects of language use that we are interested in are those that underlie speech perception and, more specifically, the signal qualities in the speech stimulus that serve as important parameters for that process. Even a very simple sentence is interpreted through a complex sequence of mental events that can be broken down into a series of processing stages. First, the words, pauses, and non-speech sounds that make up the speech signal must be isolated and recognized. Second, the words must then be identified along with their meanings. Third, the grammatical rules by which that language operates must be applied to the sentence to derive meaning from the sequence of words. And fourth, the derived meaning must be interpreted in terms of the current situation or context (SideNote 7.25). The latter three are issues that fall more within the domain of linguistics and cognitive psychology, whereas the first is directly relevant to sensory perception. Therefore, the remainder of our discussion will be oriented toward the specific sensory mechanisms that underlie speech comprehension.

Perception of phonetic segments—vowels

Much of the progress in our understanding of speech perception has emerged from studying artificial forms of speech synthesis. During the 1950s, three pioneering scientists named Franklin Cooper, Alvin Liberman, and Pierre Delattre developed a speech synthesizer that was to reveal much about the **acoustic cues** that play important roles in deciphering speech signals (Liberman et al., 1967; Schmalhofer & Perfetti, 2007; Tatham & Morton, 2006). The machine worked by recreating speech sounds from visual patterns such as spectrograms. One of the first findings was that much of the information contained in a spectrogram, such as that in Figure 7.14, was not really needed in order to perceive speech accurately. It was found that high frequencies in general were not needed to identify vowel sounds and that the same was true for low frequencies with regard to consonants. Thus, it appeared that much of the spectrographic signal was actually redundant and that our auditory system is capable of understanding many speech sounds with only a limited amount of the actual frequency information contained in speech signals.

This finding meant that if spectrograms could be simplified, they should produce an intelligible sound when fed into a speech synthesizer. Figure 7.16 shows just such a simplified spectrogram for several examples of vowel sounds. When these signals were fed into a synthesizer, the resulting sound could be accurately identified in most instances (SideNote 7.26). Although individual vowel sounds are in reality characterized by several formants, it turned out that only the first two formants were critical for accurate identification. In some cases, the first formant alone was sufficient to provide its identity. Beyond the second formant, the acoustic cues become redundant, and although they may accentuate the sound, they are not absolutely necessary for vowel identification.

SideNote | **7.25**

These levels of analysis have been formalized into the following terms: *phonology*—analysis of language in terms of its sounds; *morphology*—rules for word formation; *lexicon*—word meanings or vocabulary; *semantics*—study of word meanings and how they are related to each other; *syntax*—rules and conventions for combining words into grammatically correct sequences; *pragmatics*—interpretation of language based on context.

SideNote | **7.26**

In the early days of speech research, the simplified spectrograms were actually hand painted on acetate film. The paintings would then be fed into a synthesizer, which would work like a reverse spectrograph to convert the pattern into an acoustic signal. Those signals could then be used in psychophysics experiments to identify the sound or discriminate it from others.

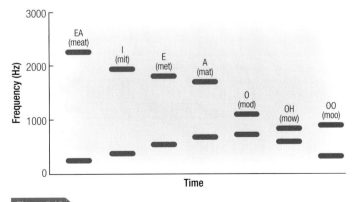

Figure 7.16

A highly simplified spectrogram is produced by using discrete bands to illustrate the formants. The two formants of the various vowels shown here are usually sufficient to correctly identify them when heard in isolation.

The situation becomes somewhat more complicated when vowels are considered within the context of adjacent consonants rather than in isolation, as was the case above (Ladefoged, 2001; Tatham & Morton, 2006). In isolation, vowels can be visualized on a spectrogram as discrete formants. However, in the presence of consonants, the vowel formants have fairly sharp transitions with the spectrographic components of the neighbouring consonants. The examples in Figure 7.17 show the abrupt shifts in frequency that occur with consonant–vowel pairings (Liberman et al., 1967). These frequency shifts, which are known as **formant transitions**, provide important cues to the identity of vowels during speech. Thus, unlike isolated vowels, where the placement of the formants alone is sufficient, vowel identification in mixed sounds requires spectrographic information on the transition with neighbouring consonants.

Perception of phonetic segments—consonants

Formant transitions also play an important role in consonant identification (Liberman et al., 1967; Pickett, 1999; Warren, 2008). Figure 7.17 shows the transitions that occur with the phoneme /d/ in association with two different vowels. The first formant transition in both cases is identical. However, it turns out that a similar pattern is also found in the first formants of two other consonants, /b/ and /g/. It is the second formant transition that actually identifies this sound as the /d/ phoneme and therefore separates it from the others. And yet,

SideNote | 7.27

Some consonants are only acoustically meaningful when present with a vowel. For the syllable [ga], it is impossible to separate the [g] portion from the [a] portion because the consonant by itself has no meaningful sound; in fact, it sounds like a chirp. Thus, the acoustic signal from the consonant along with the transition into the next vowel are both necessary to fully hear the consonant.

the nature of the second formant transitions are quite different in the two examples, downward for the syllable [di] and upward for [du]. This difference between the two sounds illustrates the concept of **co-articulation**, that is, the context-dependent relationship between adjacent phonetic sounds that result from overlapping articulatory movements. Even though both sounds begin with the phoneme /d/, their acoustic signals are quite different and depend on the phonetic segment that follows. In other words, the sounds that occur before or after can actually affect the way any given phoneme is perceived (SideNote 7.27).

Another perceptually important feature of some phonetic sounds is the timing sequence during the articulation of certain consonants. This is especially true with the oral stop consonants such as /b/ and /p/ (see Table 7.4). Both phonemes are articulated in the same manner, though with one important difference. The /b/ sound is produced by a release of air that is simultaneously accompanied by a vibration of the vocal folds. This type of consonant is called +*voice* (**voiced**). For the /p/ sound, however, there is a brief time gap between the release of air and the onset of vibration in the vocal folds. This type of consonant sound is called −*voice* (**voiceless**). In this particular example, the interval between the release of air and the onset of vocal fold vibration, which is known as the **voice-onset time (VOT)**, is about 50 milliseconds.

The importance of the VOT as an acoustic cue can be seen through artificially synthesized sounds in which the VOT value is systematically changed (Gleason & Ratner, 1998; Warren, 2008). Starting with a zero VOT value, the sound perceived in all cases is that of a /b/. This continues to be the case as the VOT increases, and then at a certain point called the **phonetic boundary**, the perceived consonant suddenly changes to /p/. The phonetic boundary therefore serves as the marker for two distinct phonetic sounds. The range of VOTs for various stop consonants in the English language span from 0 to about 60 milliseconds. In all cases, the VOT value appears to play an important role in both the perception and the identification of that specific consonant.

A sufficient change in the VOT value can therefore alter the sound, causing it to be perceived as an entirely different phoneme. This sharp transition suggests that phonetic perception is categorical in nature because a slight

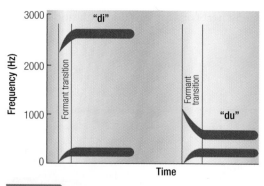

Figure 7.17

Formant transitions that are found in two examples of a consonant–vowel pairing. The transitions represent abrupt shifts in frequency content of the spectrographic pattern, shown here by way of a simplified representation. Adapted from "Perception of the Speech Code," by A. M. Liberman, F. S. Cooper, D. P. Shankweiler, and M. Studdert-Kennedy, 1967, *Psychological Review, 74,* pp. 451–461.

shift across the phonetic boundary will create an entirely different category of perception. This has led many scientists to consider speech as an example of **categorical perception**. A fundamental feature of categorical perception is that discrimination ability for sounds within a particular category is worse than for sounds across categories. For example, we are quite poor at discriminating two different versions of the voiced stimulus [da] and two different versions of the voiceless stimulus [ta], as shown in Figure 7.18 (Gleason & Ratner, 1998). In each of these examples, subjects were asked whether the two versions in each category, which differ by a VOT of only 20 milliseconds, are the same or different. As long as the sounds are within the same phonetic category, discrimination performance is quite poor—that is, subjects were unable to distinguish the two sounds as being different. However, we get perfect discrimination performance as soon as the VOT straddles the phonetic boundary (30 milliseconds) where the two sounds are now members of different perceptual categories. Even though the VOT difference is still the same, there is a dramatic improvement in our ability to differentiate the two sounds, something that was not possible as long as they belonged in the same category (SideNote 7.28).

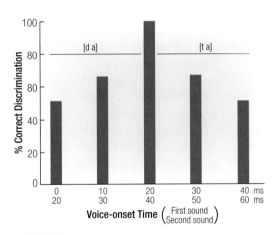

Figure 7.18

The voiced sound [da] becomes transformed into the voiceless [ta] at a VOT value of 30 milliseconds. Discrimination ability for two sounds that differ in their VOTs is quite poor if those values fall within the same category (e.g., 0 and 20, 10 and 30 milliseconds for the [da] category; 30 and 50, 40 and 60 milliseconds for the [ta] category). However, if the two VOT values fall in different categories (i.e., 20 and 40 milliseconds) because they occur on either side of the phonetic boundary, then discrimination performance becomes excellent. Adapted from *Psycholinguistics*, by J. B. Gleason and N. B. Ratner, 1998, Fort Worth, TX: Harcourt Brace.

Perception of words and word sequences

Although we have little difficulty in segmenting speech into its units of vowels and consonants, the fact that we are able to perform the same feat with words is quite remarkable. The reason for this is that speech is a continuously flowing signal where the transitions between individual words are really not that apparent when considered in purely acoustic terms (Martin, 2003; Raphael et al., 2006). This can be seen by way of the spectrogram in Figure 7.19, which shows the acoustic pattern of a simple sentence. Unlike the sentences that appear in written form, there are no clear boundaries between the acoustic signals of individual words in free-flowing speech. Thus, a **segmentation problem** arises in speech because normal articulation is a smooth and continuous process. Furthermore, the fact that individual people have somewhat different speech mannerisms and accents can give rise to considerable variability in the way that individual words are articulated. This **variation problem** can cause significant changes in the acoustic properties of many words. And yet, we are very good at being able to understand a given sentence under a broad set of such acoustic circumstances. And finally, a **co-articulation problem** arises because speech is contextual in nature (Pisoni & Remez, 2007; Warren, 2008). The various word segments in a sentence are embedded and mixed with sounds around it. Thus, the pronunciations of a given segment are very much affected by neighbouring segments, leading to overlapping movements of speech (SideNote 7.29).

Given these problems, there has been much effort to try to understand the mechanisms by which the individual components in a speech signal are segmented and appropriately

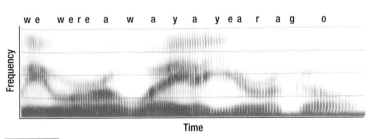

Figure 7.19

A spectrogram of the sentence "We were away a year ago" shows the continuous nature of free-flowing speech. There are no pauses within the spectrographic pattern to serve as boundaries for the individual words. Rather, the acoustic signals of the words appear to be merged together into a continuous pattern. From KENT. The Speech Sciences, 1E. © 1998 Delmar Learning, a part of Cengage Learning, Inc. Reproduced by permission, www.cengage.com/permissions.

SideNote | **7.28**

Subtle variations of the same phoneme are known as *allophones*. Allophonic variations are common with many consonant sounds. For example the /t/ in *toy* is articulated with a puff of air. This type of sound is known as *aspiration*. However, the /t/ in *dirt* is crisp and non-aspirated.

SideNote | **7.29**

This means that any segment of an acoustic pattern in speech can carry information about neighbouring phonetic segments. Along with the problems of segmentation and variation, these facts represent the key obstacles that speech recognition systems such as modern computers must face.

identified. One clue to a possible mechanism can be found when an individual is exposed to a foreign language (Ladefoged, 2001; Moore, 2008; Ziegler & Goswami, 2006). In this instance, word boundaries are difficult to identify and instead the language appears as a continuous stream of unbroken utterances. However, the same speech signal can be parsed into individual words and correctly interpreted by someone who is familiar with that language. Indeed, the greater the familiarity with the language, the greater the ease with which individual words can be identified. A crucial element in mastering a foreign language therefore is to acquire a sufficient lexical database (i.e., knowledge of the words and their meanings).

A vast vocabulary by itself, however, is not sufficient for the perception of fluent speech. Prior knowledge of the correct word relationships (semantics) and grammatical rules (syntax) also plays a critical role in speech perception. Indeed, the mere perception of a word is influenced by the context in which it is presented. For example, words presented in an isolated manner are perceived less accurately than when they are embedded in a sentence. It has also been shown that single words mixed with noise are better recognized when contained in a sentence than when presented alone. It is therefore apparent that speech perception is very much influenced by higher-level cognitive factors relating to semantics and syntax.

There are two interesting demonstrations that speech perception is determined by factors beyond the mere processing of acoustic signals. In 1970, Richard Warren showed that when a phonetic segment in a sentence was replaced by an irrelevant sound, such as a cough, most subjects were still able to accurately perceive the affected word (Warren, 1970, 2008). It was as if the word was heard in its entirety and the cough merely appeared as background noise. Known as the **phonemic restoration effect**, this result showed that a phoneme that was not acoustically present could nevertheless be perceptually restored due to some higher-level cognitive mechanism, presumably because it was expected to be present within the context of the speech segment.

Another demonstration that speech perception can be affected by factors beyond mere acoustics is based on conflicting visual and acoustic cues. It is not uncommon to be able to decipher certain speech patterns by only looking at the movement of the lips

(SideNote 7.30). In 1976, British psychologist Harry McGurk reported an interesting illusion (Gleason & Ratner, 1998; Jackendoff, 2003; Moore, 1997). When a subject was exposed to the sound /ba ba/ and at the same time viewed a videotape in which the lips were making the sound /ga ga/, the actual sound perceived by the subject appeared somewhere in between, as in /da da/. This illusion, which is known as the **McGurk effect**, shows that speech sounds are perceived through a pooling of multiple cues that apparently also includes visual information on the manner of articulation. Most importantly, the McGurk effect provides a powerful example of the influence of non-auditory factors in the perception of speech sounds.

Interpretation of the speech signal

The correct interpretation of speech requires both the auditory processing of the signal (i.e., the phonological sequences) and the expectation of the speech pattern based on our prior knowledge of the semantic and syntactic structure of that language. These two processes are respectively distinguished as bottom-up (based on auditory signal processing) and top-down (based on the recruitment of cognitive factors). Current models of speech perception propose that an interactive mechanism incorporating both factors is involved in word recognition (Dehaene-Lambertz & Gliga, 2004; Patel, 2007; Schmalhofer & Perfetti, 2007).

In one such model, the acoustic signal is used in a bottom-up manner to process the phonetic information contained in speech. However, a number of similar words can be activated in memory as soon as signal processing begins (e.g., *truck, track, trick*, etc.). The rapid time course of speech makes it difficult to consistently extract the full phonetic signal and therefore identify a specific word only on the basis of the acoustic input. Additionally, there are many variations among individual speakers, and also, we do not always pay close attention to every single phonetic element. To eliminate the various ambiguities and false associations, a top-down process is then recruited to identify which of the word possibilities is appropriate given the available semantic and syntactic context. The coordination of both bottom-up and top-down processes is currently believed to be responsible for the rapid and accurate perception of speech.

Although this process serves us well most of the time, we are sometimes painfully aware of errors in speech perception that can lead to embarrassing misunderstandings. Misperceptions sometimes occur in word associations where an ambiguous relationship may exist (e.g., meaty urologist, rap city, new cooler, etc.). A misheard phrase is known as a **mondegreen**, a term that was coined by writer Sylvia Wright who mistook the lyric "Oh, they have slain the Earl o' Morray and laid him on the green" as "Oh, they have slain the Earl o' Morray and Lady Mondegreen." The most common occurrence of mondegreens is found in popular music where an entirely different meaning can sometimes be derived from a set of lyrics (SideNote 7.31). Mondegreens are especially common among children because they have not yet developed extensive context experience in speech comprehension (Gleason & Ratner, 1998; Schmalhofer & Perfetti, 2007).

The converse circumstance where speech errors occur through mistakes in production has also been the source of much study. Speech comprehension and production represent two strikingly different goals. During speech production, the speaker knows in advance the words that are to be articulated and will formulate a sentence prior to the actual act of vocalization. During speech comprehension, however, the process is reversed. The listener does not know the details of the speech signal in advance and must wait until it is fully received. Comprehension errors often occur due to misperceptions caused by difficulties in identifying the context (Schmalhofer & Perfetti, 2007; Warren, 2008). Speech production errors, however, are usually spontaneous slips of the tongue. There are, however, cases in which certain individuals are prone to making such errors. The most famous example is that of Reverend William Spooner, an Oxford University warden during the early 1900s. His frequent transpositions of words have led to a compilation of amusing **spoonerisms** (SideNote 7.32). Speech production errors have been studied by psycholinguists to gain insight into the processes that underlie the planning and execution of spoken sentences.

3.   LANGUAGE AND THE BRAIN

It has been argued that language is what sets humans apart from all other species. This does not mean that other animals are incapable of communicating (Trout, 2001). Chimpanzees, for example, use screeches and hoots to signal danger, approach, and various social communications. Songbirds use extended vocalizations for mate attraction and territorial defence. And even honeybees communicate information about food location through an intricate dance. What sets human language apart, however, is that we use symbols that have meanings. As such, it is theoretically possible to express an infinite set of ideas through the combination of various speech sounds made into words. We are unrestricted in terms of what we can express through language, a fact that has generated boundless linguistic creativity (SideNote 7.33).

The primary reason for our unique ability is the presence of specialized brain regions that are dedicated to language (Jackendoff, 2003; Patel, 2007). The Greeks provided the earliest clues that specific parts of the human brain were involved in language processing. They observed that certain types of brain injury led to a loss of language function, a condition now generally known as *aphasia*. By the 16th century, it was known that brain injury caused specific speech disorders that were unrelated to any motor disturbances of the tongue or mouth. The most detailed attempts to understand how language functions are organized in the brain came in the 19th century by directly studying the brains of individuals who suffered from speech disorders. Current studies of brain function and language ability, known as **neurolinguistics**, are based on research involving psychophysical measures, functional brain imaging, and clinical analysis.

Neural processing of language

The two main centres of the brain that concern language processing are separately devoted to language comprehension and production (Grodzinsky & Santi, 2008; Martin, 2003; Schmalhofer & Perfetti, 2007). German neurologist Carl Wernicke described an area in the upper part of the left temporal lobe that was critically important for understanding language. Any damage to this so-called *Wernicke's area* produces a striking deficit in understanding language, a loss that is known as **Wernicke's aphasia**. People affected by this condition are able to speak clearly but the words do not make sense because of the grammatical structure or the use of nonsense words that are strung together in long, complicated utterances. Some have referred to this type of speech as *word salad* because all of the words appear to be mixed up. It is important to note

SideNote **7.31**

Some notable examples of mondegreens from popular music include "The girl with colitis goes by" ("The girl with kaleidoscope eyes," The Beatles); "Scuse me while I kiss this guy" ("Scuse me while I kiss the sky," Jimi Hendrix); "The ants are my friends" ("The answer my friends," Bob Dylan); "There's a bathroom on the right" ("There's a bad moon on the rise," Creedence Clearwater Revival).

SideNote **7.32**

Some examples of famous spoonerisms include "You hissed my mystery lecture" ("You missed my history lecture"); "You've tasted two worms" ("You've wasted two terms"); "We'll have the hags flung out" ("We'll have the flags hung out"); "Our queer old dean" ("Our dear old queen").

SideNote **7.33**

There have been various claims that certain non-human primates, such as gorillas and chimpanzees, are capable of developing limited language ability—expressed through hand signalling or even cursory vocalization. Although intriguing, the scientific validity of such studies has been questioned by most psychologists and linguists.

Carl Wernicke (1848–1905)
Image from the History of Medicine (NLM).

SideNote | 7.34

There can be isolated disorders of writing, known as *dysgraphia*, that are not accompanied by any specific losses of speech production or comprehension ability. A similar disorder can occur only with reading ability, known as *dyslexia*. However, these conditions occur due to disruptions of neural processes other than those required for language.

SideNote | 7.35

The dominance of the left hemisphere for language function did not receive widespread attention until Broca reported his findings in 1861. As a result, most people began to associate the hemispheric asymmetry for language with Broca, even though Dax had first suggested it nearly 25 years before. The correct recognition of this fact was later forcefully made by his son, Gustave Dax.

that Wernicke's aphasia is characterized by a generalized loss of language understanding and not just speech comprehension. For example, these patients also show deficits in writing and reading ability (SideNote 7.34).

A severe loss of speech production ability is characterized as **Broca's aphasia**, named after French surgeon Paul Broca. People affected with this condition are unable to speak fluently and instead display slow and slurred speech in which the words are not properly formed. There is, however, little loss in language comprehension ability. Broca was able to identify the brain region responsible for this syndrome. By studying the brains of affected individuals postmortem, Broca discovered an area that appeared to be damaged in the frontal lobe of the left hemisphere, which is now known as *Broca's area*. Damage to Broca's area also produces a generalized deficit in language production ability that extends beyond speech. For example, these aphasics also have difficulty in language production through writing and the use of gestures (i.e., sign language).

The interplay between the various neural structures involved in speech processing and production is shown in Figure 7.20. When a speech signal is heard, the first process must necessarily involve the elemental analysis of the acoustic signal, something that at the

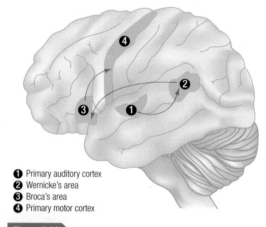

1 Primary auditory cortex
2 Wernicke's area
3 Broca's area
4 Primary motor cortex

Figure 7.20

Neural processing of spoken language begins with the initial processing of the acoustic signal in the primary auditory cortex (1). The signal is then fed to Wernicke's area (2), which is a key site for language comprehension. This language area in the temporal lobe is connected to Broca's area (3) in the frontal lobe, an area responsible for the production of fluent speech. Broca's area is connected to the primary motor cortex (4), the site where the actual motor signals for mouth and tongue movements in speech originate.

cortical level begins in the primary auditory cortex. Damage to this area will abolish all auditory perceptual function, including speech analysis and comprehension. Neural signals from the primary auditory cortex are then sent to Wernicke's area. This area, as noted above, is considered to be the classical language comprehension centre. Damage to this area will disrupt language understanding, though more basic auditory functions such as sound detection, discrimination, and localization will remain relatively unaffected. A prominent fibre tract connects Wernicke's area to Broca's area and provides the important language inputs necessary for speech and other types of language production. Damage to this tract produces a disorder in which the individual can understand and produce speech but cannot easily repeat what is said. This condition occurs because even though both the comprehension and production areas are spared, information cannot be shuttled from one site to the other. On the other hand, damage to Broca's area only will be accompanied by a selective deficit in language production. Broca's area in turn provides an important input to the primary motor cortex. The act of vocalization requires the movement of a set of muscles in the mouth and tongue. The primary motor cortex generates the initial signals for the coordinated movement of these muscles, based on the language output from Broca's area.

Brain asymmetry and lateralization

We noted above in passing that both Broca's area and Wernicke's area are located in the left hemisphere. Although the actual movement of the muscles involved in vocalization is controlled by the motor cortex of both hemispheres, much of the neural processing underlying language production and comprehension is restricted to the left hemisphere in most people (Jackendoff, 2003; Rasmussen & Milner, 1977; Tatham & Morton, 2006). French physician Marc Dax discovered in the early 1800s that all of his patients who displayed severe language difficulties had damage to the left side of the brain (SideNote 7.35). The current view is that linguistic function is not entirely confined to the left hemisphere but rather dominated by it. The right hemisphere does perform a variety of linguistic tasks, particularly related to high-level functions such as language interpretation, drawing inferences, and resolving linguistic ambiguities.

The different processing abilities of the two hemispheres showcase the larger picture of an asymmetric brain. The fact that the two halves are not identical is now well established. There are certainly physical differences. For example, the right hemisphere is heavier, has a larger parietal lobe, and even enjoys a greater volume of blood flow. In functional terms, the dominance of the left hemisphere for language is the clearest example of brain **lateralization**. It is often argued that a number of other functions also show an asymmetry, such as analytical thought, spatial awareness, mathematical ability, and artistic creativity. The lateralization of these and other behavioural functions is widely discussed in popular science forums and generates a lively debate with regard to the possible influence of gender and handedness.

The role of handedness in hemispheric dominance for language is particularly interesting. It was believed that all right-handed individuals had a left dominance for language, with the opposite being true for right-handed people. Indeed, early neurosurgeons often used handedness as the basis for deciding which hemisphere language function was localized in and therefore were especially careful to spare those parts of the brain. The actual situation is somewhat more complicated and was revealed through a remarkable experimental procedure (Pisoni & Remez, 2007; Warren, 2008). Japanese neurosurgeon Juhn Wada developed a test for language dominance that involved injecting a small amount of anesthetic into an artery in the neck. The effect of this injection was to anesthetize the side of the brain in which the injection was given. While one

Table 7.5

Lateralization Estimates Obtained with the Wada Test

Speech Representation	Handedness	
	Left	Right
Left hemisphere	70%	96%
Bilateral	15%	0%
Right hemisphere	15%	4%

Note. Lateralization estimates obtained with the Wada test reveal a left hemisphere dominance for speech representation regardless of handedness. From "The Role of Early Left-brain Injury in Determining Lateralization of Cerebral Speech Functions," by T. Rasmussen and B. Milner, 1977, *Annals of the New York Academy of Science, 299,* pp. 355–369.

half of the brain is asleep, the other half can be tested for language function. The drug wears off after a few minutes and the procedure can then be repeated on the other side. This so-called *Wada test* has shown that language lateralization does not have a simple relationship to handedness. In fact, the left hemisphere is the dominant source for language function in the majority of both right- and left-handed individuals. As Table 7.5 shows, lateralization estimates obtained through the Wada test show that 96% of right-handed individuals have left hemisphere dominance for language, whereas 70% of left-handed individuals also show similar lateralization. The remainder have either a right hemisphere or a bilateral representation of language function (SideNote 7.36).

SideNote | 7.36

Removing an entire brain hemisphere is a radical surgical procedure undertaken in patients who display severe seizure disorders. The procedure, which is usually carried out in children, produces a shifting of language function to the remaining hemisphere if the language-dominant hemisphere was removed. There are reports that such shifts can take place up to the age of 14.

Summary

1. Musical instruments have multiple resonant qualities and therefore produce complex tones that contain a fundamental frequency and a set of harmonics that are exact multiples of the fundamental. Despite their multi-frequency composition, musical notes produce a single pitch sensation (known as *musical pitch*) that is equivalent to the pitch associated with the fundamental frequency. It is believed that the spatial arrangement of wave patterns on the basilar membrane produced by the harmonics is responsible for their coherence into a single pitch sensation.

2. An octave, which is a 2:1 frequency ratio, represents the fundamental interval of musical pitch. The effective range of musical pitch spans about seven octaves, beyond which the harmonics are no longer suitable as musical sounds. Any given octave is further divided into smaller intervals that are represented by a specific note. The positions of the notes within an octave are known as *chroma*. In Western musical culture, the intervals of the chromatic scale, which was established by Bach and known as the *equally tempered scale*, is broken up into 12 equal divisions known as *semitones*.

3. Musical notes are represented by *staff* notation, allowing musicians to play them without worrying about the actual pitch composition. Musicians have an especially well-developed sense of relative pitch as a result of listening to and playing tonal sequences. Perfect pitch, which is the ability to identify an isolated tone by name, is much more difficult and only present in about one in 10,000 people. An important quality of music is *timbre* (i.e., a difference in tone quality), which arises from different intensity distributions of the harmonics. Each musical instrument has its own characteristic intensity distribution for each harmonic of a note, which in turn causes subtle differences in neural activation at the respective points in the basilar membrane. The three major categories of musical instruments are chordophones, aerophones, and percussions.

4. Music perception relies on two distinct qualities—tonal superpositions (simultaneous appearance of musical tones) and tonal sequences (sequential appearance of musical tones). The auditory system is somehow able to disentangle the individual components of a musical note in a superposition, such as a chord, and associate them with an individual note. Consonant superpositions occur when they sound pleasant, whereas dissonance arises from harsh and clashing combinations, which arise when two or more tones produce interference among their activation patterns on the basilar membrane. Tonal sequences are responsible for the melodic quality of music, which in turn creates rhythm and tempo. The sequential sound pattern of music resonates with some internal rhythm in the brain that in turn leads to the activation of higher emotional centres.

5. Research on speech perception can be divided into three main areas—speech production, speech comprehension, and the brain structures responsible for each. Speech is the only structured sensory stimulus produced by humans. The vocalization process leading to speech (articulation) involves the subglottal system, larynx, and vocal tract. The vocal folds (or glottis) are controlled by muscles during exhalation to produce a buzz-like sound that is then shaped by the different structures of the vocal tract to produce the audible sounds of speech. Speech can be broken down into words, which in turn are composed of syllables that can be considered in terms of *phonemes*. These are the smallest units of speech and are represented symbolically by a single character.

6. Speech can be represented by its pressure waveform, though it does not contain information on the frequency content. A convenient format is the sound spectrograph, which provides a visual display of frequency as a function of time, with intensity being represented by the darkness of the markings on the graph. Specific phonemes appear as bands of resonant

frequencies called *formants*. Vowel sounds are composed of low frequencies and therefore appear near the bottom of the spectrograph, whereas consonants (and especially fricatives) are made up of higher frequencies that appear near the top.

7. All human languages are structured, symbolic, and arbitrary systems. The goal of psycholinguistics research is to understand the mechanisms that underlie human language use. Sentences are broken down into four different processing stages:

   • Words, sounds, and non-speech sounds must be isolated and recognized.

   • Words must be identified and their meanings understood.

   • Grammatical rules must be applied to derive meaning from a sequence of words.

   • Meaning must then be interpreted within the specific context.

   The latter three fall in the domain of linguistics (cognitive psychology), whereas the first falls under the rubric of sensory perception.

8. The unique human ability of speech expression and comprehension arises due to the presence of specialized brain areas dedicated to language. It has long been known that certain types of brain injury affect language function in specific ways. Wernicke's aphasia (the ability to speak, but an inability to understand language) and Broca's aphasia (slurred and slow speech, but a maintenance of language understanding) are two examples of speech disorders, each being linked to damage in a particular area of the left hemisphere.

Key Terms

Recall Questions

1. What is the difference between *acoustic pitch* and *musical pitch*? What is the relationship between the fundamental frequency in a complex tone and its harmonics? How do complex tones affect the basilar membrane in terms of its activation profile?

2. What is an octave, and why does it have a special quality in terms of musical pitch? What is the difference between *tone chroma* and *tone height*? How many divisions are there in the *equally tempered scale*? Why is staff notation a useful way to represent musical pitch?

3. What is the difference between *relative pitch* and *absolute pitch*? What is *timbre*, and how does it relate to the auditory signal in musical tones?

4. How can consonant and dissonant superpositions be explained in terms of basilar membrane activation? How are the concepts of melody, tempo, and rhythm related to tonal sequences?

5. What are the different anatomical components involved in the process of vocalization? How do the different parts of the vocal tract cause the different speech sounds? Why is a spectrogram an efficient way of visually representing speech? What are formants?

6. What is the difference between language and speech? What are the different areas of research in the field of psycholinguistics?

7. What is *neurolinguistics*? What is the difference between Wernicke's aphasia and Broca's aphasia?

8. What arguments can be put forth for a Darwinian view of music development? What are the arguments for the opposing view that music perception was an accidental outcome of evolution?

9. How do vowels, consonants, and fricatives differ in terms of their articulation process? What is *co-articulation*? How is the concept of categorical perception related to structural aspects of speech, such as the *voice-onset time*?

Further Reading

- Jackendoff, R. (2003). *Foundations of language: Brain, meaning, grammar, evolution.* New York, NY: Oxford University Press.
- Ladefoged, P., & Maddieson, I. (1996). *The sounds of the world's languages.* Malden, MA: Blackwell.
- North, A. C., & Hargreaves, D. J. (2008). *The social and applied psychology of music.* Oxford, UK: Oxford University Press.
- Patel, A. (2007). *Music, language, and the brain.* New York, NY: Oxford University Press.
- Peretz, I., & Zatorre, R. J. (2003). *The cognitive neuroscience of music.* New York, NY: Oxford University Press.
- Pisoni, D., & Remez, R. (2007). *The handbook of speech perception.* Oxford, UK: Wiley-Blackwell.
- Roederer, J. G. (1995). *The physics and psychophysics of music: An introduction.* New York, NY: Springer-Verlag.
- Sacks, O. (2008). *Musicophilia: Tales of music and the brain.* New York, NY: Vintage.
- Schmalhofer, F., & Perfetti, C. A. (2007). *Higher level language processes in the brain: Inference and comprehension processes.* Mahwah, NJ: Lawrence Erlbaum.
- Tatham, M., & Morton, K. (2006). *Speech production and perception.* New York, NY: Palgrave Macmillan.
- Thompson, W. F. (2009). *Music, thought, and feeling: Understanding the psychology of music.* New York, NY: Oxford University Press.

The Visual System: Light, Optics, and the Eye

In this chapter . . .

- You will learn about the properties of light and how those properties contribute to vision by interacting with objects in the environment to allow us to see them (by being reflected, absorbed, transmitted, or scattered).

- You will learn about the properties of lenses and how they can alter the path of light rays. You will explore the components of the eye and how they are involved in capturing images of our external world. You will discover how the eye's two refractive lenses work together to ensure that the images created on the retina are in focus. You will also come to understand how the eye changes its optical power to focus objects at different distances.

- You will realize that optical disorders can occur from birth, or with old age. You will come to understand that there is an optimal eyeball size, and if the eyeball is too long (myopia) or too short (hyperopia), the image will be blurred, and specialized lenses are needed to correct those problems. You will learn that presbyopia occurs when the lens loses its elasticity and becomes less able to accommodate images that are too close.

A THE NATURE OF LIGHT
1. General Properties of Light
2. Interaction of Light with Objects
3. Basic Principles of Optics

B THE HUMAN EYE
1. Structure of the Eye
2. Optical Properties of the Eye
3. The Retinal Image

C OPTICAL DISORDERS OF THE EYE
1. Presbyopia
2. Refractive Errors

Vision allows sensory perception to occur from the greatest distance because it uses light as the carrier of information. The unique properties of light along with the sensitivity of our visual system even allow us to see objects at celestial distances. Photo: Choreograph/iStockphoto.com

Light consists of rays that acting like feelers, travel in straight lines from the eye to the object, and the sensation of sight is obtained when these rays touch the object.

—Pythagoras

The idea that sensory systems can be thought of as being either *near* or *far* in terms of their ability to detect external stimuli reaches its uppermost limit with vision. The somatosensory (touch) and gustatory (taste) systems lie at the *near* end of this spectrum because they are only involved in sensing stimuli that are directly in contact with the body. We then move to the olfactory and auditory systems, both of which permit sensing more distant stimuli. Indeed, with audition the distance limit is imposed only by physical factors of sound transmission, and in cases where the sound is loud enough, the source can indeed be many miles away. Vision allows sensory perception to occur from the greatest distance because it uses light as the carrier of information. As we will see later in this chapter and the next, the unique properties of light along with the sensitivity of our visual system even allow us to see objects at celestial distances, such as Eta Ursa Minoris, one of the dimmest stars visible to the naked eye (SideNote 8.1).

The importance of vision in evolutionary terms is quite easy to understand, given the enormous survival benefits that it provides to all species. For humans, vision is the dominant sensory system. We are truly *visual* animals, a fact that has been stressed in previous chapters. The complexity and sheer magnitude of the information processed by the visual system imposes considerable computational requirements when compared to other sensory systems. As a result, nearly one-half of the human brain is directly dedicated to processing visual information. The many different aspects of vision also require that we consider these different facets carefully and independently. For this reason, nearly one-half of this book is devoted to the study of vision and visually guided behaviour.

We start with an examination of light and the laws of optics. Our visual experience begins with the production of an optical image at the back of the eye. Thus, a fuller understanding of the nature of light and way that this optical image is formed will greatly help us understand several fundamental aspects of visual perception. The next two chapters will provide detailed descriptions of how visual information is processed—from transduction of the optical image into a set of neural signals in the **retina** to the early and intermediate levels in the visual brain where the elemental aspects of vision are processed, to the highest levels of visual processing where objects come

to life through the magic of perceptual experience. The final three chapters of this book will be devoted to a fuller understanding of three fundamental aspects of vision—colour perception, depth and space perception, and finally motion perception.

A. The Nature of Light

We begin with a fundamental question: Exactly what is it that we are seeing? For centuries, humans believed that light was made up of particles emitted by certain objects, such as the sun or a candle flame, which travelled through the **ether** in straight lines (SideNote 8.2). This basic idea made sense because it accounted for a number of simple phenomena involving light. For example, it was known early on that light reflects off a smooth surface, such as a mirror, in geometrically predictable ways and that it bends when going from one medium to another, such as air to water. These simple observations could easily be explained by the particle theory and straight-line motion of light (Guenther, 1990; Waldman, 1983).

Around the middle of the 17th century, the particle theory of light began to be questioned, and a wave theory began to emerge. It was shown by then that many of the basic properties of light can also be explained if light is considered to travel in a wave-like manner. However, it was not until the early 1800s that it became clear that certain phenomena, such as **diffraction**, clearly could not be accounted for by the particle theory and that light must indeed have wave-like motion. The only problem with this theory was that all waves must necessarily occur as a deformation of a medium and therefore there must be a medium through which light is conducted. It was not clear exactly what that medium was, though it was generally accepted that the ether was involved in some way. However, this also meant that the ether must truly have some unusual properties (SideNote 8.3). We learned in Chapter 5 that the more rigid the medium, the greater the speed with which it conducts sound. It was thought that the same must be true of light. Therefore, the ether would have to be extremely rigid so as to permit light to travel through it at an incredibly fast speed, a fact that was already well known to early scientists. And yet, it was not clear how this ether, which was believed to permeate through empty space,

SideNote | **8.1**

The farthest individual star that can be seen is about 4,000 light years away. The farthest object in the universe visible to the naked eye is M-31 (the Andromeda Galaxy), appearing as a faint cloud but containing billions of stars located nearly 2.5 million light years away. The light from M-31 reaching us now originated at a time when early hominids such as Lucy and Ardi were walking the Earth.

SideNote | **8.2**

The actual origins of this idea can be traced back to the early Greeks. The particles were also called *corpuscles*, and hence this idea became known over the centuries as the *corpuscular theory of light*.

SideNote | **8.3**

The idea of an *ether* dates back to Aristotle, who called it the fifth element. Aristotle believed that the heavens were made of this element, an idea that carried through for centuries in the thought that the fabric of outer space was made up of this material.

nevertheless allowed the planets to move effortlessly through it and without much resistance.

The pendulum swung back in favour of the particle theory early in the 20th century when it was found that a light beam can produce an ejection of electrons from an object under appropriate conditions (Waldman, 1983). This phenomenon, which can only be explained if light consists of particles, was worked out by Albert Einstein, for which he received the Nobel Prize. The idea began to take hold that light travelled in small packets or *photons* that also had a wave-like quality to them. That is, even though the energy in light is actually concentrated in these particles, it was believed that the photons themselves travelled in a wave-like manner through space. This so-called **dual-theory of light** provided an explanation for a number of wave phenomena, such as diffraction, and yet also accounted for particle phenomena, such as electron emission when light strikes an object. Thus, the propagation of light was best explained by the wave theory, whereas the interaction of light with matter was best explained by the particle theory. To this day, the dual-theory remains as the cornerstone of our current understanding on the nature of light (Freeman, 1990; Meyer-Arendt, 1998; Welford, 1990).

1.   GENERAL PROPERTIES OF LIGHT

A major advance in understanding the wave properties of light emerged from the work of Scottish physicist James Clerk Maxwell. In 1873, he showed that an oscillating charged particle produced **electromagnetic radiation**—a type of moving energy field that is found everywhere in nature. We now know that all electromagnetic radiation is characterized by the flow of photons. Furthermore, the movement of photons through space produces an oscillating electric and magnetic field that together move in the same direction as the photon. This phenomenon is illustrated in Figure 8.1. The moving electric and magnetic fields are mutually linked to each other and vary in intensity over time (Hecht, 2001; Jenkins & White, 2001). Specifically, the two fields lie perpendicular to each other. Thus, if the intensity of the electric field is oscillating say along the vertical axis, then the magnetic field will oscillate along the horizontal axis (SideNote 8.4).

The fluctuating electric and magnetic fields essentially represent the waves that are

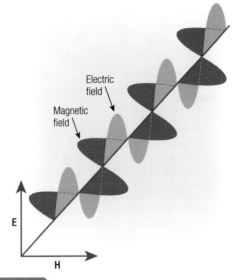

Figure 8.1

Electromagnetic radiation is composed of two moving wave forms—an electric and a magnetic field that are mutually linked. The two fields are always oriented perpendicular to each other. The waveform of the electric field (E) is shown here with the intensity varying along the vertical axis, whereas the intensity of the magnetic field (H) varies along the horizontal axis.

moving through space. Since the two fields always have a fixed relationship to each other, it is sufficient to show just one of them. The example in Figure 8.2 on page 248 shows only the electric field. The first point to note is that the waveform is similar to that we saw in Chapter 5 with regard to sound waves in that there is a sinusoidal fluctuation of some parameter. For sound, that parameter was air pressure changing as a function of time. The difference here is that the electromagnetic waves represent a fluctuation in the electric (or magnetic) force field as a function of space or distance. As Figure 8.2 shows, a single cycle represents that segment of the wave before it repeats itself. The distance covered by a full cycle, and hence separating two identical points in the waveform, is known as the **wavelength** and is commonly denoted by the Greek letter lambda (λ). The wavelength can vary considerably, and it is this parameter that sets the different types of electromagnetic radiation apart (SideNote 8.5).

Visible light is an example of electromagnetic radiation

The full range or **spectrum** of electromagnetic radiation that can be produced by both natural and artificial sources is truly impressive. Figure 8.3 shows the wavelength

James Clerk Maxwell (1831–1879)
© The Print Collector/Alamy

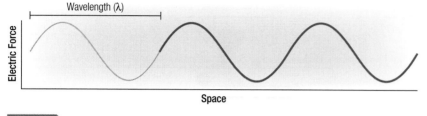

Figure 8.2

The electric field component of an electromagnetic wave is shown as a snapshot in time. A single cycle (shown in grey) encompasses a complete segment of the wave before it repeats itself. Three full cycles are shown here. The distance covered by a full cycle representing two identical points in the wave is known as the *wavelength* and denoted by the Greek letter lambda (λ).

SideNote | **8.6**

ELF, which stands for *extremely low frequency* radiation, can have wavelengths spanning several thousand kilometres. There has been some debate as to whether background ELF radiation, especially from power lines, can affect human health. There are various conspiracy theories of a giant ELF generator in Alaska that can be secretly used by the military to affect the Earth's magnetic field, change weather patterns, or even cause mood fluctuations.

SideNote | **8.7**

Although human vision does not extend outside of the visible light spectrum, this is not necessarily true of other animal species. Various insects, for example, can detect low-wavelength light that extends into the ultraviolet region. Certain reptiles, such as snakes, are able to sense infrared rays.

values associated with the different forms of electromagnetic radiation. A number of different units are often used to express wavelength values across this vast range, such as metres for long-wavelength radiation all the way down to **nanometres** for the short-wavelength end of this spectrum. To maintain consistency, the

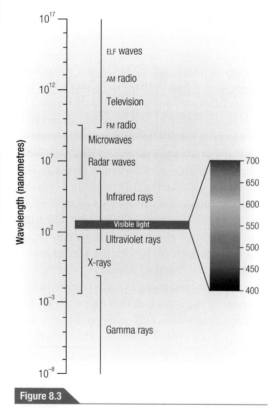

Figure 8.3

The electromagnetic spectrum contains radiation spanning a very large range of wavelengths. The shortest wavelength radiation is that of gamma rays, whereas the longest are the so-called *ELF waves*. Visible light represents a very small segment of this entire spectrum, spanning only 400 to 700 nanometres. The various colours that are perceived by the human visual system are governed by the actual wavelength of light, as shown by the expanded representation of the visible spectrum.

entire range of wavelength values in Figure 8.3 is expressed only in nanometres. As can be seen in this figure, the shortest wavelength radiation is that of the gamma rays, a type of cosmic radiation that travels vast distances from the hottest regions of the universe to reach the Earth. Near the opposite end of the **electromagnetic spectrum** lie some of the more familiar types of radiation used in electronic communication, such as radar, microwaves, radio, and television. At the uppermost end of the spectrum lie the ELF waves, which are produced by various sources such as household appliances and power lines (SideNote 8.6).

The most important point to take from Figure 8.3 is that only a very small segment of the electromagnetic spectrum is actually used for sensory function (i.e., the narrow band of radiation known as **visible light**). Indeed, visible light is a type of electromagnetic radiation that is nestled in between ultraviolet and infrared rays and spans a wavelength of 400 to 700 nanometres (nm) (Pedrotti, Pedrotti, & Pedrotti, 2006; Welford, 1990). Our visual system is responsive to the energy contained in light in ways that are now well understood. One of the fascinating phenomena related to light stimulation is that different wavelengths produce different perceptual impressions that we label in terms of the various colours. The relationship between light wavelength and perceived colour is shown by the expanded representation of the visible light spectrum in Figure 8.3. We will discuss this relationship in much greater detail in Chapter 11. For now, it is sufficient to note that blue colours are associated with short wavelengths; green and yellow, with middle wavelengths; and red, with long wavelengths. Human vision is practically non-existent outside these boundaries (i.e., outside the wavelength range of visible light) (SideNote 8.7).

This brings us to a rather interesting question: Why is it that visible light is the only type of electromagnetic radiation that we can see? After all, the electromagnetic spectrum is quite vast and encompasses many different types of radiation. Thus, it is somewhat curious that nearly all animal life on Earth is only sensitive to a very small segment of this entire spectrum. The answer becomes apparent when we consider that the major source of electromagnetic radiation reaching the Earth is the Sun (Minnaert, 1993; Williamson & Cummins, 1983). Figure 8.4 shows that the **emission**

spectrum of the Sun is restricted to a narrow band of radiation spanning from 100 to about 4,000 nanometres. This region contains the ultraviolet, visible, and infrared bands. Nearly all of the Sun's electromagnetic radiation is contained within this region, and in fact, there is very little emission in other portions of the electromagnetic spectrum (SideNote 8.8).

The Sun's emitted radiation must then reach the surface of the Earth, and therefore the transmission properties of the atmosphere also become an important factor. The bottom panel in Figure 8.4 shows that the **transmission spectrum** of the atmosphere has a similar profile to the Sun's emission spectrum and indeed overlaps it significantly within the same wavelength range. What is especially important is that the visible light spectrum falls comfortably within these emission and transmission spectra, as shown by the blue bar. Thus, the reason that life on Earth evolved to take advantage of light as a sensory stimulus is that much of the Sun's emission includes this band of electromagnetic radiation. Furthermore, nearly 80% of that radiation band is transmitted through the atmosphere and allowed to reach the Earth's surface.

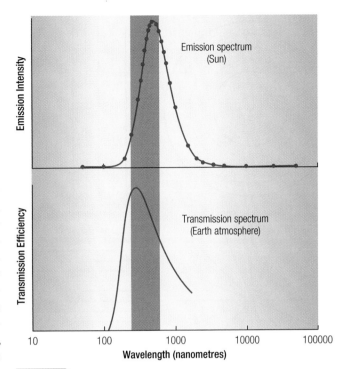

Figure 8.4

The radiant energy emitted by the Sun falls within a restricted range of the electromagnetic spectrum (top panel). This range also happens to include the visible light spectrum (blue bar). Much of the Sun's radiation can reach the Earth's surface because the transmission efficiency of the atmosphere is highest in this range (bottom panel). The visual system has evolved to take advantage of the availability of this narrow band of electromagnetic radiation for sensory function.

Speed of light

An important property of light that has immense bearing on visual perception is the fact that it is transmitted along straight lines and at a truly awesome speed. For this reason, vision is an almost instantaneous sense in that it allows us to perceive environmental events, even distant ones, with little delay. The rapid transmission of light information to our eyes allows the visual system to assume the role as our most *distant* sense. Even though we are also able to hear sounds at great distances, the distance limit in vision is simply incomparable to that of hearing. We are all familiar with the oft-cited example of "seeing lightning before hearing thunder," a fact that merely reflects the far greater speed of light than sound. Although this observation had been noted for many centuries, the first serious attempts at measuring the speed of light only began in the late 1600s (SideNote 8.9). Since then, a number of different figures have been offered for the actual speed of light. It is now widely accepted, from both theoretical and experimental accounts, that the speed of light in vacuum is 299,792 kilometres per second (186,282 miles per second) (Waldman, 1983).

This value represents one of the fundamental constants of nature.

Apart from the great velocity of light, there is another important factor that allows vision to sample more distant stimuli. Whereas sounds require a medium for transmission, light energy can travel in the absence of a medium, such as the emptiness of outer space. This is because the nature of electromagnetic radiation is such that propagation of the electric and magnetic fields can occur in a total vacuum. In fact, when light does pass through a denser medium, such as air or glass, its speed actually slows down somewhat.

Light propagation

We now turn to some basic features of light propagation through space and their implications for visual processing. To understand how light spreads out from a source, it is often convenient to collapse the light source down to an imaginary point (Guenther, 1990; Jenkins & White, 2001). As Figure 8.5 on page 250 shows, light waves emanate from this **point source**

SideNote **8.8**

The band from 100 to 400 nanometres corresponds to *ultraviolet radiation* and represents 7% of the Sun's total emission. About 48% of the total emission is in the form of visible light. Much of the remainder, about 48%, is contained in the band from 700 to 4,000 nanometres, known as *infrared radiation*.

SideNote **8.9**

In 1675, Danish astronomer Olaf Roemer used the time interval between consecutive eclipses of one of Jupiter's moons to calculate a rough figure of 132,000 miles per second for the speed of light. He was largely ridiculed for his work because the prevailing attitude was that the speed of light was infinite.

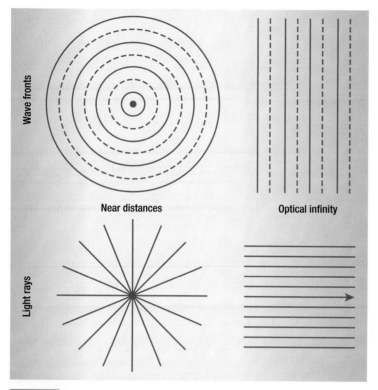

Wave fronts

Light rays

Near distances

Optical infinity

Figure 8.5

The emission of light from a point source can be considered in terms of spreading wave fronts (top diagrams). The wave fronts are represented as concentric circles radiating outwards at positions close to the point source. At optical infinity, the wave fronts have such a large diameter that they essentially flatten and proceed as a train of plane waves. Light emission can also be represented by a set of rays that are drawn as straight lines perpendicular to the wave fronts (bottom diagrams). A single ray can be thought of as the path followed by a photon. Light rays appear as a parallel set of lines at optical infinity.

SideNote **8.10**

The idea of optical infinity is sometimes confused with the notion that the light source is situated at a truly great distance, such as the stars seen in the night sky. Although the light rays arriving to the eyes from the stars are certainly parallel, the same is achieved if the light source is merely 20 feet away.

and spread out in all directions. The **wave fronts** are very small in the immediate vicinity of the point source and expand progressively as they radiate. A typical representation shows a concentric series of wave fronts of increasing diameter. At a sufficient distance from the point source, the diameter of the wave front becomes so large that its curvature essentially flattens out. The distance at which this happens, known as **optical infinity**, is about 6 metres (20 feet) from the source (Freeman, 1990). The flattened wave fronts at optical infinity and beyond can be considered as a train of plane waves, as shown in the top right diagram of Figure 8.5.

It is usually more convenient to represent light propagation in terms of rays rather than waves. We can consider a **light ray** as the particle analog of a travelling wave (i.e., the straight-line path followed by a photon). Thus, what emerges from a point source can be depicted as a radiating pattern of straight lines, as shown in the bottom left diagram of

Figure 8.5. Beyond optical infinity, the flattened wave fronts are portrayed by a series of parallel lines in terms of light rays. In optics textbooks, the term *parallel incident light* is often used to describe the nature of light rays at optical infinity and beyond (see bottom right diagram in Figure 8.5) (SideNote 8.10).

Effect of distance on light intensity

The divergence of light rays with increasing distance is also responsible for a reduction in intensity (Freeman, 1990; Jenkins & White, 2001). We know that a light source will appear to be dimmer the farther away it is from an observer. This reduction, however, is not linear but instead is related to the square of the distance. Figure 8.6 shows that light rays passing through an imaginary square area at a distance of "1d" away from the source will diverge enough so as to pass through 4 times that area at a distance of "2d." Similarly, at a distance of "3d," the light will have diverged enough to cover 9 times the area of the initial square. The reduction in light intensity comes from the fact that any given bundle of rays must be distributed over an area that increases with the square of the distance. Thus, the total number of photons per unit area decreases with increasing distance. The relationship between light intensity and distance, which is known as the **inverse square law**, stipulates that the intensity is inversely proportional to the square of the distance. The graph in Figure 8.6 shows how the intensity diminishes with distance according to the inverse square law function. The reduction is especially apparent at first and then tails off because further decrements occur on progressively reduced intensity values.

2. INTERACTION OF LIGHT WITH OBJECTS

We learned above that what we actually *see* is a restricted band of electromagnetic radiation. Most life forms on Earth have over the course of evolution developed sensory structures that capture light and transduce it into neural signals. The importance of vision as a sensory mechanism, however, comes from the fact that light interacts with objects in our environment in meaningful ways, thereby producing a pictorial scene. Our visual system uses that pictorial information to reconstruct a mental image of our external space. Depending on the nature of the object, light can bounce off it, be absorbed by it, be transmitted through it, or be scattered by it in various directions. Thus, the interaction of light with an object and the nature of that physical relationship have considerable bearing on visual perception. After all, we see an object because it interacts with light in a different way than its surround, thus making it stand out as a distinct coherent entity. We will briefly discuss some of the essential ways in which light interacts with matter.

Absorption, reflection, and transmission

One of two things can happen when light strikes the surface of an opaque object—the light is either absorbed or reflected (Keating, 2002; Masud, 2002). An object absorbs light only when its atoms can convert the energy contained in light into vibrational motion (SideNote 8.11). The vibrational energy in the atoms is then dissipated by way of heat, which is why an opaque material can feel warmer under certain conditions after a period of absorbing light. It may be the case, however, that the incident light fails to create significant vibrational motion in the atoms because of the nature of the object and the precise way in which it interacts with light. In such cases, much of the light fails to be absorbed and instead is reflected by the object. The atoms in this case simply re-emit the energy back as reflected light. In cases where the object is transparent, the light, rather than being reflected, simply passes through (transmits) the object.

The way that objects interact with light is also responsible for the colours we perceive (Keating, 2002; Pedrotti et al., 2006). As noted in the previous section, visible light is composed of a range of wavelengths that are responsible for producing the different impressions of colour. An object may only reflect a certain segment of the visible spectrum while absorbing the rest, a property that is responsible for producing its colour appearance. For example, if an object reflects long-wavelength light but absorbs the rest, then the object will appear red. If it should only reflect short-wavelength light, then it will appear blue. The colour of an object can thus be attributed to the wavelengths of light reflected back and then captured by our eyes. Objects that fully reflect all visible light will appear white, whereas those that fully absorb all wavelengths will appear black. We will return to an expanded discussion of object properties and colour appearance in Chapter 11.

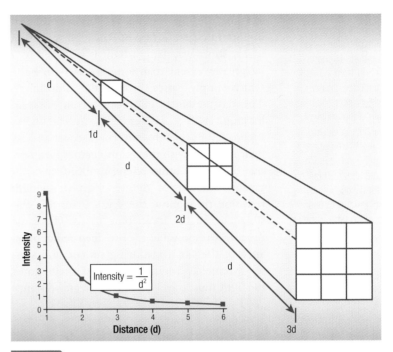

$$\text{Intensity} = \frac{1}{d^2}$$

Figure 8.6

Light divergence is responsible for the progressive reduction in intensity with increasing distance. Light rays that just fill an imaginary square at a distance "d" from the source will diverge enough to fill 4 times that area at a distance of "2d" and 9 times the area at "3d." As a result, the total number of photons per unit area becomes smaller with distance. The graph at the bottom shows the relationship between intensity and distance, known as the *inverse square law*.

Light scattering

A different phenomenon, known as *light scattering*, occurs when light interacts with gaseous particles. In this case, light is first absorbed by a particle and then re-emitted in a random direction. The best example of this is atmospheric scattering, which occurs when sunlight interacts with various particles and gas molecules that are present in the Earth's atmosphere. The random re-emission that occurs as a result of atmospheric scattering produces a diffuse radiation that fills the atmosphere. How much scattering takes places depends on the types of particles that interact with sunlight as well as the distance travelled through the atmosphere. It is worthwhile to briefly describe the different forms of atmospheric scattering because of the visual effects they produce when we look up at the sky.

There are three different types of atmospheric scattering (Keating, 2002). The most notable is **Rayleigh scattering**, which occurs when the particles are of a very small size compared to the wavelength of light, such as the gaseous molecules of nitrogen and oxygen. This type of scattering is the dominant form above

SideNote | **8.11**

All atoms have a resonant frequency of vibration. When the frequency of the incoming light, which is related to its wavelength, matches the resonant frequency, the atoms in that object are set into vibrational motion, resulting in the absorption of light.

The presence of sulfur-based aerosols in the atmosphere, most commonly from industrial pollution, produces greater amounts of light scattering, resulting in the oddity of beautiful sunsets in industrial settings. The 1991 eruption of Mount Pinatubo in the Philippines injected about 20 million tons of sulfur dioxide into the atmosphere, producing beautiful sunsets around the globe for many months.

The Sun has a yellowish appearance because more of its radiant energy is contained in the upper part of the visible spectrum (see Figure 8.4, top panel). Also, the short-wavelength component of sunlight is reduced because it is dissipated in various directions due to Rayleigh scattering.

4.5 km (i.e., in the upper atmosphere). An important characteristic of Rayleigh scattering is that short-wavelength light is scattered to a far greater extent than long-wavelength light, which simply passes through the atmosphere. This has certain implications for an observer looking at the daytime sky, as shown in Figure 8.7. Rayleigh scattering occurs as sunlight interacts with the gas molecules throughout the upper atmosphere, resulting in a far greater amount of diffuse short-wavelength radiation throughout the sky. It is for this reason that the sky looks blue to us. The same process is responsible for the deep red appearance of the horizon during sunrise and sunset (Meinel & Meinel, 1983). At these times, the light must travel through a greater distance

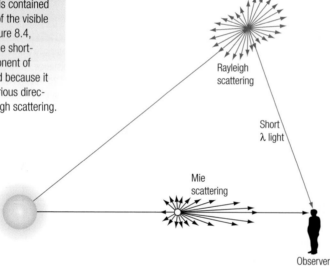

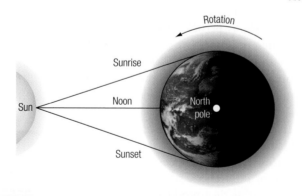

Figure 8.7

An observer on Earth looking directly at the Sun at midday (top diagram) will see a whitish halo that is caused by Mie scattering. The remainder of the sky appears blue because of Rayleigh scattering, which strongly favours only short-wavelength light that in turn reaches the observer. Sunlight must travel through a greater amount of the atmosphere at sunrise and sunset (bottom diagram), resulting in a greater degree of Rayleigh scattering. Thus, only the longer wavelengths are allowed to penetrate the atmosphere and reach the observer, producing the deep red appearance of the horizon at these times.

within the atmosphere, thereby resulting in greater scattering. Thus, more of the short-wavelength light is scattered away, leaving a greater proportion of longer wavelengths to penetrate the atmosphere and reach our eyes (SideNote 8.12).

A second type of scattering, known as **Mie scattering**, occurs due to larger particles such as dust, smoke, and water vapour. In general, these larger particles do not reach the upper parts of the atmosphere, and therefore Mie scattering only occurs below about 4.5 km. Unlike Rayleigh scattering, Mie scattering is not strongly wavelength dependent. Furthermore, much of the scattering occurs in the direction of light propagation. As Figure 8.7 shows, the impact of atmospheric Mie scattering is therefore greatest when looking toward the Sun. The white glare seen around the Sun is attributed to Mie scattering (SideNote 8.13).

The third type of atmospheric scattering is known as *non-selective scattering*, which occurs when the particles are much larger than the wavelength of light. This type of scattering is also wavelength independent and therefore equally affects radiation from across the visible spectrum. Clouds appear white to us because the water droplets and ice crystals contained in them produce a non-selective scattering of sunlight.

Polarization

Another property of light that can affect visual perception under certain conditions is polarization (Guenther, 1990; Hecht, 2001; Meyer-Arendt, 1998). To understand this phenomenon, we must reconsider a fundamental wave property of light (i.e., its electric and magnetic fields). Figure 8.8 shows three diagrams representing different compositions of light in terms of these two fields. The leftmost diagram is taken from Figure 8.1. In this example, the electric field is only oscillating in the vertical plane and the magnetic field, by definition, is restricted to the horizontal plane. This kind of light is known as **plane-polarized light** because the electric (and magnetic) fields are restricted to only one plane. A common convention among physicists is to describe polarized light only in terms of the plane containing the electric field. Hence, this is an example of vertically polarized light and is depicted by way of a vertical line with arrowheads. The middle diagram in Figure 8.8 shows an example of horizontally polarized light.

The two examples above represent a rather unusual case and occur only under certain conditions. The more common occurrence is for the incident light to have an array of electric fields in all possible orientations, as shown in the right diagram of Figure 8.8. Indeed, the electric fields may be contained in any one of the nearly infinite number of arbitrary planes in space. The cross-sectional representation of such **unpolarized light** would therefore contain many lines with arrowheads, each representing one of the planes containing the electric field. Direct sunlight and nearly all forms of artificial light are unpolarized.

This brings us to the following question: If nearly all forms of incident light are unpolarized, then how do we obtain plane-polarized light? It turns out that polarization occurs only under certain conditions when light interacts with an object (Meyer-Arendt, 1998; Waldman, 1983). There are three common ways that polarization can be achieved, as shown in Figure 8.9. The light that is scattered by a particle can be polarized along a certain plane, depending on the direction of the scattered light. Thus, although direct sunlight is unpolarized, much of the peripheral skylight is polarized because it reaches us only after having been scattered in the upper atmosphere. The human visual system is not capable of distinguishing polarized from unpolarized light or, for that matter, differentiating the different planes of polarization. Thus, we see skylight as a uniform blend of blue light. Certain insects, however, are able to separately detect the different planes of polarized light and use this ability to navigate through space (SideNote 8.14).

A second way to obtain polarized light is by transmission through certain crystals that absorb more light in one plane than another (see middle diagram in Figure 8.9). The light that emerges out of the crystal has an electric field that is oscillating in only one plane because light oscillating in all other planes is absorbed. There are several such naturally occurring crystals, such as the mineral *tourmaline*. Many people are familiar with the trade name *Polaroid*, which is given to the most commonly used polarizing material. The breakthrough made by the inventor, Edwin Land, in the 1920s was to place a polarizing material on vinyl sheets, thereby making it both flexible and economical. Polaroid is a very effective polarizer, typically transmitting more than 80% of light in a particular plane and less than 1% in the remaining planes.

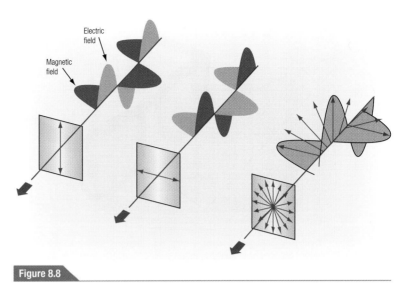

The electric field in polarized light is restricted to either the vertical or the horizontal plane (left and middle diagrams, respectively). The magnetic field by definition must oscillate in a perpendicular plane. Most incident light is unpolarized such that the electric field can oscillate in any one of many possible planes in space (right diagram). Polarized light, also referred to as *plane-polarized*, is usually depicted by a line with arrowheads representing the plane containing the electric field.

The third manner by which polarization can be achieved is through reflection. Under certain conditions, unpolarized light that is incident on a surface will become polarized after reflection, with the electric field oriented along the plane causing the reflection. This natural law of physics is used very effectively in the design of polarizing sunglasses (see Figure 8.10). The polarizing material in these glasses absorbs light in all planes except the vertical, which is transmitted through to the eyes. Consequently, there is a reduction in the overall intensity of direct sunlight passing through it because much of the incident light is not transmitted except for the small fraction

SideNote 8.14

Many social insects, such as bees, crickets, and certain kinds of desert ants, use the polarized skylight as a celestial navigational device. These insects have evolved specialized visual mechanisms that allow them to separately detect the different planes of polarized light. Thus, they are able to travel very large distances and return by using polarized skylight as a compass.

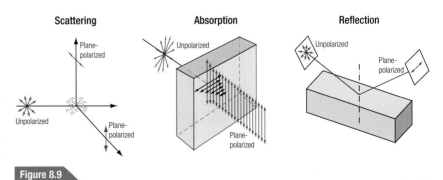

Polarization can be achieved through light scattering, absorption, or reflection. The electric fields in scattered light are restricted to only one plane (left diagram). Certain polarizing materials transmit light in only one plane while absorbing all other planes of electric field oscillation (middle diagram). Polarization can also occur when unpolarized incident light is reflected off a surface (right diagram). The reflected light is plane-polarized with the electric vector contained in the horizontal plane.

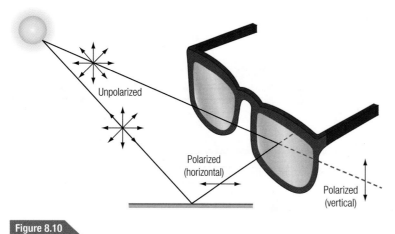

Figure 8.10

Polarizing sunglasses reduce the intensity of direct sunlight because they only allow light in one plane (vertical) to be transmitted to the eyes while filtering out light in all other planes. These sunglasses also effectively filter out the glare of reflected light because it is horizontally polarized and therefore absorbed by the vertically oriented polarizing filters.

SideNote 8.15

A simple experiment can be performed with polarizing sunglasses to demonstrate that skylight is polarized. Rotate a Polaroid sunglass (or any polarizing material) in front of the eyes while looking at the sky. At different rotational points, different amounts of the skylight will come through the lenses, depending on the orientation of the sunglass with respect to the polarized skylight.

contained in the vertical plane. Another useful property is that they reduce the transmission of glare (i.e., the light reflected off surfaces such as a road or the hood of a car). Polaroid sunglasses block the glare of reflected light because its horizontal plane of polarization does not match the orientation of the polarizing material in the glasses and is therefore not transmitted to the eyes (SideNote 8.15).

3. BASIC PRINCIPLES OF OPTICS

The eye has two essential functions—to form an image of the outside world upon the retina and to transduce the light energy in that image into neural signals. To understand the properties of the eye that allow it to serve as an optical device, we must first discuss some of the basic aspects of image formation by a lens. These principles will also be important for acquiring a thorough understanding of the optical abnormalities that form the basis for near- and far-sightedness in humans. To understand how an optical device such as a lens or the human eye forms images, we must first learn some fundamental principles of physics relating to how light rays behave when moving from one medium to another.

Refraction

The final property that we consider in regard to light interaction with an object is **refraction**, which refers to the bending of light that occurs when it travels from one medium to another (Freeman, 1990; Guenther, 1990). We are familiar with the common

occurrence of a straight stick that appears bent when immersed in water or the kaleidoscopic appearance of the world when viewed through a glass prism. The bending of light that occurs in these instances is due to a change in speed as light moves from one medium to another. Light travels at its fastest speed in vacuum and slows down when it enters a denser medium. In air, the speed of light is only marginally less than in vacuum. However, the reduction in speed is more significant in denser media such as water or glass. One way to indicate the speed of light in a particular medium is through its **refractive index**. The greater the refractive index of a medium, the slower the speed of light within it (Hecht, 2001). Table 8.1 lists the refractive index values of some common materials as well as the various structures that make up the human eye.

There are three important properties of refraction that we need to consider (Hecht, 2001; Keating, 2002). First, the medium must be transparent otherwise light will not be transmitted through it and no refraction will be apparent at the boundary. Second, the greater the difference in refractive index between the two media, the greater the refraction. For example, a greater amount of refraction will occur when light crosses an air–glass interface than an air–water interface. And third, refraction will only take place if an incident light

Table 8.1

Refractive Index Values for Some Representative Items

Object	Refractive Index
Vacuum	1.0000
Air	1.0003
Water	1.333
Glycerine	1.473
Crown glass	1.50–1.62
Flint glass	1.57–1.75
Diamond	2.42
Human eye	
Cornea	1.376
Aqueous humour	1.336
Crystalline lens	1.386–1.406
Vitreous humour	1.337

ray strikes the boundary at an angle away from the **normal**, which is an imaginary line that is perpendicular to the boundary separating the two media, as shown in Figure 8.11. Although light will slow down when entering into glass from air, there will be no refraction if light rays hit the boundary straight on (i.e., at a normal to the surface). However, if light strikes the surface at an angle, then it becomes bent toward the normal when entering a higher refractive index medium and away from the normal when entering a lower refractive index medium.

Divergence and convergence of light by a lens

The refractive property of an object becomes especially important when we consider the function of a lens. The earliest known lenses consisted of glass spheres filled with water. During the time of the early Greeks and Romans, these were used as "burning lenses" to start a fire. True glass lenses only became available in Europe around the 13th century. A common early use for glass lenses was in magnifying glasses and later in telescopes and spectacles.

A lens may have one of two general properties—divergence or convergence—with regard to its effect on light (Keating, 2002; Welford, 1990). A diverging lens, such as a **concave lens**, is usually made of glass and has its two surfaces bowed inward. As shown in Figure 8.12, incident light bends or diverges at the first refractive surface (air–glass) and then again at the second surface (glass–air). The result is that the light rays emerging from the lens are diverted away from the **optic axis**, which is an imaginary line connecting the midpoints of the two refracting surfaces. The outward refraction at the first surface occurs because light rays bend toward the normal when entering a higher refractive index medium. A further outward refraction occurs at the second surface because light rays bend away from the normal. Figure 8.12 illustrates these effects at the two surfaces in relationship to the normal, causing the emergent light rays to diverge from the optic axis.

The refractive conditions become just the opposite in a converging lens, such as a **convex lens**, because of the outward bowing of the two refractive surfaces. This causes the normal to become oriented in such a way that light rays encountering the first surface become converged as a result of refraction toward the

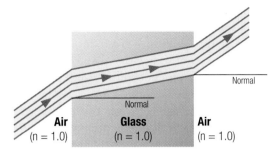

Figure 8.11

Light rays bend (refract) as they move across an interface between two different transparent media. The rays refract toward the normal when entering a medium of higher refractive index and away from the normal when entering a medium of lower refractive index. The refractive index, denoted as *n*, indicates the relative speed of light in the two media (higher the refractive index, lower the speed of light).

normal. Similarly, refraction away from the normal at the second surface causes further convergence. In the examples shown in Figure 8.12, the incident light hitting the two lenses originated from a point source at optical infinity. The converging property of a convex lens redirects the rays toward the optic axis where they

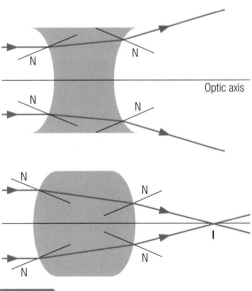

Figure 8.12

Light rays bend toward the normal (N) at the first surface because they are entering a higher refractive index medium, whereas they bend away from the normal at the second surface because they are entering a lower refractive index medium. Light rays are refracted away from the optic axis after passing through a concave (diverging) lens. With a convex (converging) lens, however, light rays are refracted toward the optic axis, producing an image (I) at some distance away from the lens. In both examples, the incident light originated from a point source at optical infinity.

SideNote | **8.16**

A diverging lens does not produce a real image because the light rays are diverted away from the optic axis and therefore never come together.

ultimately meet to produce an image of the point source. This is a *real image* in that placing a film at this location will produce an image of the very point source that gave off the light rays to begin with (SideNote 8.16). The actual location of the image point, I, is dictated by two factors—the refracting power of the lens and the distance at which the light-emitting object is placed from the lens (i.e., the object distance).

Lens power affects image location

The **refractive power** of a lens is determined simply by how much refraction will occur at its two surfaces. We learned before that the greater the refractive index of a material, the greater the amount of refraction at its boundaries. Thus, a lens made of flint glass will have more refractive power than one made of crown glass, though a diamond lens will have the greatest refractive power of them all (see Table 8.1 for their respective refractive index values).

Changing the lens material is not a convenient way to alter the refractive power of a lens. A more practical way of changing the refractive power is to modify the curvatures of the two surfaces. A lens with a greater surface curvature will have greater refracting power than a lens with flatter surfaces (Jenkins & White, 2001; Mouroulis & Mcdonald, 1997). This is because light undergoes greater refraction if it hits a surface at a greater angle away from the normal. Figure 8.13 shows three examples of lenses with different surface curvatures and hence different refractive powers. The relatively flat lens at the top allows a small amount of refraction to take place, producing

an image at a fairly large distance away from the lens. Lenses with greater surface curvatures produce greater refraction and thereby create an image closer to the lens. This leads us to the following rule: The greater the refractive power of a lens, the smaller the image distance.

Object distance affects image location

In all of the examples we have considered thus far, the object (point source) was placed at optical infinity. This is generally the default condition when discussing the image forming ability of a lens. However, objects are not always placed at optical infinity. The question then arises as to what happens to the image if the object is moved closer to the lens? Figure 8.14 shows the image created at different object locations for a fixed convex lens (Jenkins & White, 2001). At the top, the object emitting the light is placed at optical infinity. The lens therefore receives parallel light, which it converges to produce an image (I) at a certain distance. In the middle diagram, the object has been moved closer to the lens and therefore it receives a divergent set of light rays. Since we are dealing with the same lens as the one above, the refractive power remains the same. Therefore, the same amount of convergence is applied to the incoming light, which is now a diverging cone. This results in a shift of the image location farther away from the lens (Jenkins & White, 2001; Masud, 2002). This idea can be taken one step

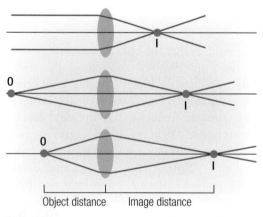

Object distance   Image distance

The closest image location for a given lens occurs when it receives parallel light from an object (O) at optical infinity (top diagram). As the object distance is reduced, the same lens receives a divergent cone of light rays to which it applies the same fixed amount of refractive (convergence) power (middle diagram). This causes the image point (I) to move farther from the lens. As the object moves even closer, the greater divergence of the incident rays causes the image to move even farther away (bottom diagram).

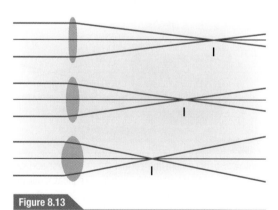

The surface curvatures of a lens determine its refractive power. A relatively flat convex lens (top) produces an image (I) at a fairly distant location away from the lens, whereas a more curved lens (bottom) places the image much closer. The greater the refractive power of the lens, the smaller the image distance.

further by moving the object even closer, as in the bottom diagram. The lens again applies the same fixed amount of converging power to the incoming light. Given the greater divergence of the incident light bundle, the image point is shifted even farther away from the lens. Because a convex lens of a given refractive power can only apply a fixed amount of converging ability, changing the object distance will therefore affect the image distance. This leads us to the following rule: The smaller the object distance, the greater the image distance for any given lens (Mouroulis & Mcdonald, 1997; Pedrotti et al., 2006). In the next section, we will apply these fundamental principles of optics to provide an understanding of image formation by the human eye.

B. The Human Eye

The human eye has been regarded by scientists, philosophers, and theologians throughout the centuries as one of the most astounding anatomical creations among all of the organs in the body. This realization by a broad group of thinkers has also led to an intense debate as to how such a phenomenal device could have been created. As usual, the debate centres on whether evolution could have produced an instrument of such complexity through the slow cumbersome process of natural selection or whether the eye is the product of divine

creation (Ings, 2008; Nilsson & Pelger, 1994). Even Charles Darwin admitted an initial sense of doubt in *The Origin of Species*: "To suppose that the eye [. . .] could have been formed by natural selection, seems, I freely confess, absurd in the highest degree." However, Darwin did reach the conclusion that a slow and gradual series of multiple incremental changes ultimately led to a complex, and nearly perfect, visual sensing apparatus (SideNote 8.17). Each small step in the evolution of the eye conferred added survival advantage to that species. It has been theorized that a complete fish eye could have evolved in less than 350,000 years and that eyes in general have separately evolved more than 40 times.

1. STRUCTURE OF THE EYE

A full appreciation of the elegant structure of the human eye was apparent several centuries ago when early anatomists began to study and describe it in detail. What they could not fathom, however, was how the different parts of the eye contributed to the visual experience. It was only around the middle of the 16th century that the various parts of the eye were described in sufficient detail and that their role in the optical process of image formation was gradually understood. To understand that ourselves, we have to begin with a description of the individual components that make up the human eye.

SideNote | **8.17**

A possible sequence of evolutionary developments leading to a human eye is shown below, with each step occurring gradually and improving the quality of the eye. The process begins with an eye spot, a flat patch of light-sensitive cells (1). A slight variation then produces an inward dimple, which protects the light-sensitive cells (2). This process continues through a series of steps (3, 4) that leads to an enclosed eyeball-like structure with a clear jelly filling that further protects the light-sensitive cells and helps to keep debris out. Finally, a lens appears, most likely due to a mutation (5), which gradually becomes thicker and moves inward to improve the clarity of vision (6). Adapted from "A Pessimistic Estimate of the Time Required for an Eye to Evolve," by D-E Nilsson and S. Pelger, 1994, *Proceedings of the Royal Society London B, 256,* pp. 53–58.

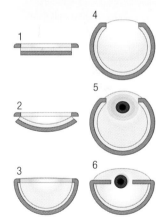

METHODOLOGY

Diversity of Eyes among Animal Species

The structure and evolution of the eye have been studied quite intensively, for it is fascinating to understand how different species "see." The most primitive type of eye is actually flat (known as a *stigma*), which means that the light-sensing cells cannot determine the direction of light, only its presence or absence. Unicellular organisms such as the euglena posses this type of visual system, which is unable to determine any shapes. When the light sensors began to sink into the head in a sort of cup shape (known as *pit eyes*), the ability to determine the spatial location of light began in its most rudimentary sense. Species such as the planaria and some snails still have this type of visual system. The next main evolution of the eye was with the "pinhole camera" model, which had a small opening for light to enter, allowing for directional sensing and a somewhat rudimentary shape-sensing detection. This visual system is still in use today by species such as the nautilus (a type of marine creature that looks somewhat like a snail). Each type of eye up to this point is basically a hole, which is open to the environment, and does not contain a cornea or lens. Another interesting type of eye is compound eyes, which are composed of repeating arrays of light-sensing units (each containing a lens, crystalline cone, sensing cells, and pigment cells). The increase in ommatidium leads to an increase in discrimination of detail (although not nearly as detailed as our vision).

SideNote 8.18

The cornea continually absorbs fluid from the interior of the eye. Specialized cells in the cornea then pump this fluid back out, an act that requires considerable energy. This pumping action fails shortly after death, causing the cornea to become cloudy. After death, the cornea can be kept transparent if placed in a warm sugar solution, which maintains the action of the pump. This simple procedure is used to store corneas destined for transplantation.

SideNote 8.19

This pressure is normally maintained at a steady level by the continuous production and elimination of the liquids. A defect in this process may lead to elevated pressure within the eye, a condition known as *glaucoma*. Prolonged glaucoma can disturb retinal function, eventually leading to blindness. Because there is no pain associated with glaucoma, it is important to get regular eye checkups during which the pressure can be measured through a simple and painless procedure.

Peripheral components of the eye

The human eye can be broadly divided into two sets of components—those that make up the outer or peripheral elements and those that are contained inside the eye (see Figure 8.15) (Oyster, 1999). The eyeball itself is a nearly spherical structure of about 1 inch in diameter. It is held together by a very tough outer membrane called the **sclera**, which is essentially a continuation of a similar membrane known as the *dura mater* that serves as the outer covering of the brain. The sclera is most conspicuous at the front of the eye where it appears as the white part of the eyeball. The opaque appearance of the sclera occurs because the protein fibres within it are arranged in an irregular manner that causes light to be scattered and reflected. However, this situation changes considerably as the sclera continues forward to the front of the eye where the same protein fibres become organized in a highly parallel manner. This arrangement is crucial for vision because it makes the front part of the sclera transparent, thereby allowing light to enter inside the eyeball. The transparent front part of the eye, which is known as the **cornea**, serves as the first of two refractive elements in the human eye (SideNote 8.18).

The next layer within the peripheral rim of the eye is known as the *choroid*. This structure contains a very rich blood supply that nourishes all of the cells in the immediate vicinity. An additional component of the choroid is a pigmented layer of cells that provides a dark background to help absorb any light scattered

within the eye. Along the inside wall of the choroid lies the retina, the so-called *film of the eye*. The refractive elements of the eye focus all incoming light to create an optical image on the retina. As Figure 8.15 shows, the retina covers much of the inside back wall of the eye, extending forward to just a little past the midline along both the vertical and horizontal axes. Thus, the retina can be considered to be similar to the inside surface of half a ping-pong ball. The retina is made up of several layers of specialized neurons which transduce the light energy in an image into a set of neural signals. These signals are carried in nerve fibres that penetrate the back of the eyeball to form the optic nerve. The optic nerve transmits the retinal output to the brain.

Internal components of the eye

The inside of the eye is largely made up of two different kinds of liquids that together exert an outward pressure from within the eyeball (SideNote 8.19) (Oyster, 1999; Smith & Atchison, 1997). The region immediately behind the cornea contains a liquid called the **aqueous humour**, whereas a much larger region in front of the retina contains a more gelatinous liquid called the **vitreous humour**. Naturally, both of these are clear liquids that allow light rays to proceed through them with minimal scattering and absorption. Otherwise, the optical image formed on the retina would be compromised, leading to degraded visual function.

The two liquid chambers are separated by the **crystalline lens** along with its related structures. Known simply as the *lens*, this convex structure represents the second refractive element in the eye. It is held in place by a set of thin ligaments that are attached to a small muscle (see Figure 8.15). The lens is a highly elastic structure made up of protein fibres arrayed in a parallel format, similar to the cornea. This explains its transparency, which is an important property because the lens must allow light rays to penetrate through it and in so doing allow refraction to occur at its front and back surfaces. Lying immediately in front of the lens is an opaque curtain-like structure known as the **iris**. The iris is essentially a forward extension of the pigmented layer contained in the choroid. The iris is dark brown in the vast majority of people, though in some it can take on different shades of blue and green, thereby accounting for differences in eye colour. The iris has a hole in its centre known as

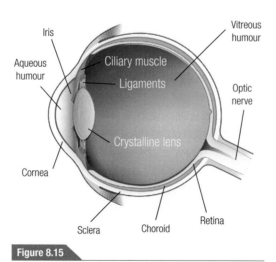

Figure 8.15

A cross-section of the human eye showing its various components. The cornea and the crystalline lens are the only two refractive elements in the eye, focusing incoming light rays onto the retina.

the **pupil** that allows light to proceed through it and then into the lens. By changing the size of the pupil, the iris can control how much light reaches the retina. Under dim lighting conditions, the pupil size is at its largest so as to allow maximum light entry, whereas under bright lighting conditions the pupil is at its most constricted form.

2. OPTICAL PROPERTIES OF THE EYE

Although we now take for granted that light enters into the eye to form an image, this seemingly obvious process remained poorly understood while humanity grappled to understand the fundamental nature of light. Some of the greatest philosophers of early Greek civilization, such as Euclid and Plato, argued that light actually emanated from the eyes and seized objects with its rays. This idea persisted for several centuries. Even Leonardo da Vinci in the 15th century initially believed in this so-called *extromission theory*, though he later reversed his position and came to accept that light must indeed enter into the eyes. A comprehensive (and correct) explanation of optical image formation by the eyes was provided in the early 1600s by Johannes Kepler and later by René Descartes (SideNote 8.20).

The emmetropic eye

A considerable advance toward understanding the optical properties of the human eye was made in 1908 when Swedish ophthalmologist Allvar Gullstrand introduced the **schematic eye**, a theoretical model that takes into account the optical properties of the cornea and lens to arrive at details of image location and quality (Keating, 2002; Schwartz, 2002). Gullstrand later received the Nobel Prize for his achievement in understanding the optical functions of the human eye. In pictorial terms, a schematic eye is represented by its key elements—the cornea, lens, and retina (see Figure 8.16). The simplicity of this diagram makes it easier to follow the path of light rays as they travel through the eye, something that we will take advantage of from here on.

The human eye is a complex system consisting of two refractive components—the cornea and lens. Nearly two-thirds of the total refraction in the eye occurs at the air–cornea boundary (Smith & Atchison, 1997; Waldman, 1983). This is because the refractive index difference between air and cornea is considerably greater than the difference seen at any of the other refractive boundaries within the eye (see Table 8.1 for a list of refractive index values of the eye's components). The remaining one-third of the total refraction occurs in the lens. The net result of these refractive processes is to converge incoming light rays toward the optic axis. By definition, an optically normal eye is one where parallel light rays from an object at optical infinity are focused just enough to form an image on the retina. In other words, the optical power of the cornea–lens combination must be sufficient for parallel incident rays to be imaged exactly on the retina. This situation is shown in the bottom diagram of Figure 8.16. The term **emmetropia** is often applied to an optically normal eye. The important point to note here is that an eye is said to be emmetropic based only on the requirement that incoming parallel light be brought to a sharp focus on the retina. We noted before that parallel light rays are generally used as a default condition when discussing the optical properties of a lens, and in this regard, the eye is no different.

The problem of near distances

What happens though if the object is not at optical infinity but instead is moved closer to the eye? We have encountered this problem before in our discussion of simple lenses where

SideNote | **8.20**

The Renaissance period marked an effort to fuse anatomy and geometry. An example of this movement can be found in the illustration below from Descartes' *Dioptrics*, which shows light rays from a vertical object being focused by the eyes and then projected to the brain.

Image from the History of Medicine (NLM)

Allvar Gullstrand (1862–1930)
LIBRARY OF CONGRESS/SCIENCE PHOTO LIBRARY

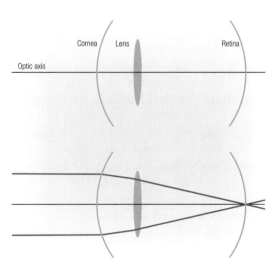

Cornea   Lens   Retina

Optic axis

Figure 8.16

A pictorial representation of a schematic eye shows the two optical elements and the retina. The optic axis connects the centres of the refractive surfaces. The bottom diagram shows how an optically normal or emmetropic eye focuses parallel incoming light rays to form an image on the retina. The projection of the refracted light rays beyond the retina is shown in grey, though in reality light rays cannot penetrate the choroid and sclera.

we found that a near object produces a corresponding backward shift in the image. This phenomenon is illustrated in the top diagram of Figure 8.17 for a point source that is moved closer to the eye. Let us assume that the refractive power of the eye (cornea and lens together) remains fixed (i.e., the optical power is only sufficient to refract incoming parallel light from optical infinity onto the retina). That same amount of optical power now becomes insufficient to place the image on the retina because it is applied to a set of diverging rays from the closer light source. Instead, the image point is shifted behind the retina, though in reality, no such image will be formed because light rays do not penetrate the sclera. What will actually appear on the retina is a blur spot resulting from a defocused image of the object point source.

A convenient way of approaching this problem is to see how other optical instruments deal with focusing near objects. As an example, it is quite common to make comparisons between the optical functions of the human eye and those of a camera. Indeed, there are many similarities because the camera too uses a lens to focus incoming light onto a film plane, and therefore both must deal with the challenge of focusing objects at different distances, especially those that are placed closer to it than optical infinity. The more expensive cameras allow users to focus the image by turning a ring on the lens turret. This action physically moves the lens either closer or farther from the film plane (actually nowadays, it is an image sensor on digital cameras). This movement has the result of changing the effective image distance from lens to film and therefore allows a sharp image to be formed on the film plane for a range of object distances (SideNote 8.21). Thus, back and forth movement of the lens along the optic axis may represent one possible mechanism that the eye can use to focus near objects.

The process of *accommodation*

For a long time, it was believed that the physical movement of the lens was indeed responsible for focusing by the human eye because it worked so well for a variety of optical instruments, such as the telescope. However, it turns out that such a focusing mechanism is only used by a few animal species, such as certain types of fish. This left only one other possible means by which the eye could focus on near

objects—changing the curvature of its optical surfaces. But which ones? The cornea itself was ruled out because a change in its surface curvature would not account for a number of observed phenomena (SideNote 8.22). In 1793, English scientist Thomas Young postulated what turned out to be the correct focusing mechanism in the eye—a change in the surface curvatures of the lens in response to changing object distances (Charman, 1991; Goss & West, 2001). This mechanism has been termed **accommodation**.

The blur spot created on the retina by changing the object distance serves as the stimulus for accommodation. A neural blur processor located in the brain stem immediately sends signals to the so-called **ciliary muscle** that is associated with the lens (see Figure 8.15). When neural signals arrive at the ciliary muscle, one of the consequences is that it constricts, thereby causing the lens to become more rounded. This is shown in the middle diagram of Figure 8.17, with the original flattened shape of the lens shown in grey. The result of the more rounded form of

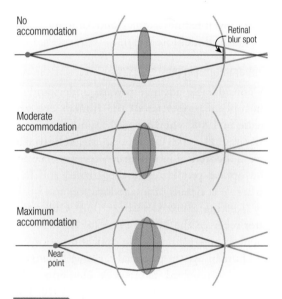

Figure 8.17

Retinal blur is created when an object is moved closer to the eyes from optical infinity (top diagram). The blur spot then serves as the stimulus for accommodation, a fast reflexive constriction of the ciliary muscle that allows the lens to become more rounded (middle diagram). The eye now benefits from added refractive power, allowing the nearby object to be brought into sharp focus on the retina. An even closer object will produce greater accommodation, reaching its limit when the object is brought to the near point (bottom diagram). The inner blue outline of the lens shows its most flattened state, which is the default state for objects at optical infinity.

---

the lens is an increase in its surface curvatures, which in turn gives the eye the added refractive power needed to focus divergent rays from a near object onto the retina (Oyster, 1999; Smith & Atchison, 1997).

The lens can assume an even more rounded form if the object is placed still closer to the eyes, as shown in the bottom diagram of Figure 8.17. The greater divergence of incident rays from this source places a greater demand on the eye to focus the image on the retina. Thus, a greater amount of ciliary muscle contraction will have to occur. However, there is a natural limit to this process because of the limited extent to which the lens can become rounded. For most young people, that limit of maximum accommodation is reached at object distances of about 20 centimetres (8 inches). This is known as the **near point**. An object placed any closer to the eye will exceed the accommodative limit and therefore will appear blurred because it can no longer be brought to a sharp focus on the retina. This fact can be demonstrated by simply bringing this book closer and closer to the eyes until the text becomes blurry.

A person with optically normal eyes will therefore have a dynamic range of clear vision that spans from the near point to optical infinity. As we change our gaze from object to object in our visual environment, the accommodative system is continually adjusting the shape of the lens through the ciliary muscle in an extremely precise manner to ensure that a sharp image is placed on the retina. In some cases, this will mean greater constriction of the ciliary muscle if the object is closer, whereas in others it will mean greater relaxation if the object is farther. This mechanism is so fast that we do not even detect the temporary blur spot that produces the accommodative adjustment in the lens. Furthermore, the entire process represents an involuntary reflex and therefore occurs automatically as soon as the retinal image becomes blurred (SideNote 8.23).

3. THE RETINAL IMAGE

We have thus far discussed retinal image formation for only point source objects. The real world, however, is made up of a mosaic of objects that have to be faithfully imaged over the entire surface of the retina. At any given point in time, we are staring at a visual world composed of multiple things located in different points in space. In this section, we discuss how such a complex visual scene is actually imaged over the entire retina along with the optical characteristics of that image.

Extended objects and their retinal image

A useful way of thinking about a complex visual scene is that any given object is made up of a large number of point sources. For example, the arrow object in Figure 8.18 can be thought of as a series of point sources located adjacent to each other along the entire extent of the arrow (Keating, 2002; Pedrotti et al., 2006). Each of these point sources emits light, which is refracted by the optical elements of the eye to produce a corresponding retinal image point. The point source defining the very tip of the arrow emits a cone of light rays that produce a corresponding retinal image at the retinal location shown in the figure. Similarly, light rays emitted from the most bottom point of the arrow produce a corresponding image at a different location in the retina. All of the intervening point sources, which have been left out to avoid cluttering up this diagram, will be similarly imaged to produce the entire image of the arrow. In reality, only the two endpoints are actually needed to define the retinal image because it is assumed that all of the intervening points will line up accordingly. In this way, even the most complex visual scene can be broken down into a simple series of point sources whose rays can be easily traced through a schematic eye to define the resulting retinal image.

SideNote | **8.23**

Although accommodation is a reflexive involuntary process, it is possible to change the shape of the lens voluntarily by wilfully crossing the eyes. This fools the brain into thinking that one's gaze has been redirected to a nearby object, and hence the accommodative state changes accordingly, leading to blurred vision of distant objects.

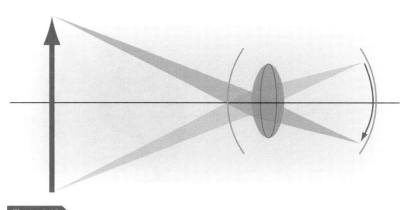

Figure 8.18

Image formation of an extended object follows the same principles of refraction as a point source. Each tiny segment of the arrow object in this figure can be treated as a point source. The light rays emerging only from the head and tail points are shown as they go on to produce an inverted retinal image. The eye in this figure is in an accommodated state because the object is located at a near distance.

SideNote | 8.24

The inversion of the optical image has been well known since Kepler's time, and it generated a lot of debate among early philosophers as to how we can still perceive an upright world. This quandary was more or less resolved after it became accepted that *up* and *down* are relative and that sensory processing in the brain determines the manner by which the world is perceived.

SideNote | 8.25

In the human eye, the nodal point is located on the optic axis about 7 mm behind the cornea (i.e., near the back surface of the lens). The nodal point can be used to provide an extremely useful shortcut in finding the retinal image by way of the procedure described in Figure 8.20.

Optical transformations in the retinal image

One of the geometric consequences of light refraction by an optical system such as the eye is that the image is transformed in two ways (Charman, 1991; Keating, 2002; Welford, 1990). First, the image is inverted, as shown in Figure 8.18. All objects in the real world thus appear upside down on the retinal image (SideNote 8.24). Second, the image is horizontally flipped (i.e., all objects in the left part of our visual world are imaged on the right part of the retina and vice versa). Both of these transformations are evident in Figure 8.19, which shows an example of an environmental scene along with the corresponding retinal image. The actual scene from the perspective of an observer is shown in the left frame. The right frame shows the retinal image as viewed from behind the eyes. That is, we assume that the retina is a curved screen upon which the image is placed, and we are viewing this screen from behind. Both optical transformations are clearly apparent here—the right-leaning, upright coconut tree in the real world appears in the retinal image as left-leaning and inverted. Despite the transformations in the retinal image, the relationship between various objects in the visual world is retained in the image. Thus, the retinal image is a faithful replica of the natural world scene, except that it is inverted and flipped horizontally.

The faithful projection of the real world upon the retina is demonstrated in Figure 8.20. The five object points, A–E, are equivalently spaced out along the left–right axis. To find their respective image points on the retina, we can assume as before that each point emits a cone of rays that are refracted by the cornea–lens system. However, it turns out that a more straightforward ray-tracing solution can be applied to find the retinal images. There exists an imaginary point near the back surface of the crystalline lens that serves as the optical centre of the eye. According to optical theory, an entire cone of rays emitted from a point source can be collapsed into a single ray that passes through this so-called **nodal point** (SideNote 8.25). Thus, all we have to do is take a single ray from each of the five sources, draw a straight line through the nodal point, and see where it ends up on the retina. The resulting ray traces for the five object points in this figure confirm two important claims made earlier. First, that there is a left–right transformation of the retinal image and, second, that the retinal image is a faithful replica of object space because the image points seen here on the retina are equally spaced out and therefore no distortion occurs in their layout.

Retinal image quality

Returning to Figure 8.19, a careful inspection of the right frame shows that the image in peripheral parts of the retina are slightly blurred compared to the actual scene shown in the left frame. For example, the leaves on the coconut tree do not appear quite as sharp as in the original image. In general, image quality in the centre is always sharpest because all lens systems refract rays with their highest fidelity in

Visual scene (observer perspective)   **Retinal image (rear view)**

Figure 8.19

The retinal image is transformed in two ways—inversion and left–right reflection. The visual scene on the left shows an observer's perspective. The retinal image of this scene (right frame) shows the effect of the two transformations. The quality of the retinal image is reduced in the periphery because of optical aberrations produced by the cornea and lens.

and around the optic axis (Pedrotti et al., 2006; Welford, 1990). The farther away one gets from the optic axis, the greater the degradation in the image. This is because the combined effects of various types of **lens aberrations** have a more serious impact in peripheral parts of the image. One of the reasons that professional photographers will pay a much higher price for a premium camera lens is that its optical quality is superior, especially in the periphery where less image blur and distortion is produced in comparison to the cheaper lenses (SideNote 8.26).

Object distance and retinal magnification

We have thus far restricted our discussion to image formation for objects at a fixed distance, whether at optical infinity or at some point close to the eye. What happens to the retinal image when the same object is viewed from different distances? We know from everyday experience with photography that nearby objects produce a much larger image than objects located farther away. The retinal image is susceptible to exactly the same phenomenon, a fact that yields different sized images depending upon the object distance (Keating, 2002; Pedrotti et al., 2006). Consider the following example. A 6-foot tall person standing just 2 metres away will produce a 1.65 cm retinal image. The same person at a 6 metre distance will produce a 0.55 cm image, whereas at 10 metres they will produce a 0.33 cm image. In all cases, the image will of course be inverted. These numbers show that the distance between the observer and the object will greatly influence retinal image size (both height and width). As an object moves closer to the eye, the **retinal magnification** begins to increase rapidly, and at some point the image can spread over the entirety of the retina (SideNote 8.27).

Depth of field

We often have to deal with multiple objects in the real world that may be located at different distances from us. Our accommodative system always focuses on a single object at any given time, usually the one we wish to scrutinize in great detail and hence look at directly. This means that other objects located at different depth planes will produce a blurred image on the retina since the optical power of the eye is not optimized for those object distances. This situation is illustrated in the top diagram of Figure 8.21 on page 264. The schematic eye is

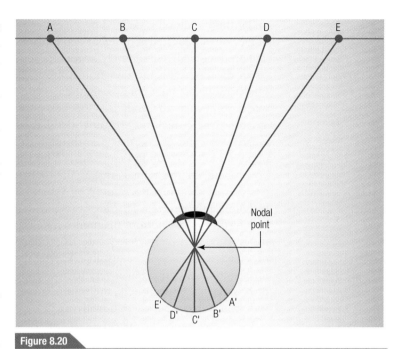

Nodal point

Figure 8.20

A top-down view of a human eye looking at an array of five object points (A–E) that are equally spaced out along the left–right axis. According to optical theory, the cone of rays emitted by each point can be collapsed into a single ray that passes through an imaginary point, known as the *nodal point*. The intersection of this ray with the retina defines the image point. The resulting images (A'–E') show the left–right transformation as well as the non-distorted optical replication of object space in the retinal image.

shown in an accommodated state with respect to Object 1—that is, light from this object is refracted just enough to produce a sharp image on the retina (black light rays in diagram). This means that Object 2 located in front of Object 1 will not be refracted enough and will therefore produce a blur spot on the retina (grey light rays in diagram). This condition can easily be demonstrated by looking through an overhead acetate containing some writing and focusing on a distant object. The writing on the acetate will appear blurred because the accommodative system is tuned to the more distant object. If attention is suddenly changed to the writing on the acetate, then accommodation will switch accordingly, and the objects situated behind it will now be blurred (SideNote 8.28).

It turns out that under certain situations, the retinal blurring from objects at different depth planes may be reduced (Meyer-Arendt, 1998; Mouroulis & Mcdonald, 1997). We have to follow the diagrams in Figure 8.21 to understand this. The top diagram shows the path of light rays through the eye when the iris is fully open—that is, the diameter of the pupil (**aperture**) is at its largest. This will occur under dim light conditions so as to maximize light entry into the eye. Because the retinal image

SideNote 8.26

We do not notice the slightly degraded image in the peripheral parts of the retina because our visual system is much more concerned with analyzing the visual image in the centre. It is for this reason that we orient our eyes upon an object of interest in such a way that its image falls in the centre of the retina. This issue is discussed in much greater detail in the next chapter.

SideNote 8.27

The advantage of viewing close objects is that the larger retinal image permits a more detailed analysis, whereas the same object placed at a larger distance yielding a smaller image cannot be similarly scrutinized. For example, the colour of a person's eyes are apparent at a distance of 2 metres but not when that person is 10 metres away.

SideNote **8.28**

This implies that at any given time, much of the retinal image is actually blurred since we can only accommodate a single object at a given distance. While this is certainly true, its impact is reduced because we are generally much less concerned with the visual details of objects we are not directly looking at. Also, the brain filters out irrelevant information so the blurring is less apparent.

SideNote **8.29**

It is well known that vision can be made sharper under dim light conditions by squinting. Even though the pupil itself may be widely open under dim light, squinting reduces the opening through which light enters the eye and therefore helps to increase the depth of field.

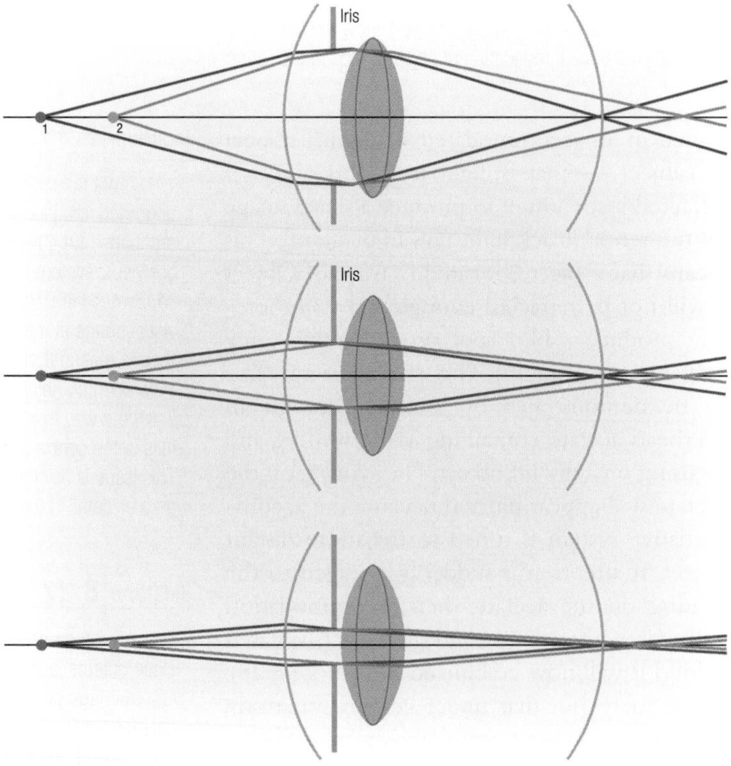

under this condition is defined by a large cone of rays, objects located at different depth planes will produce a correspondingly larger blur spot (as in the case with the rays from Object 2). Under moderate light conditions, the iris constricts somewhat to produce a smaller pupil aperture. The retinal image is now defined by a narrower cone of rays that pass through the pupil (middle diagram in Figure 8.21). This has no bearing on the retinal images themselves except that the blur spot caused by Object 2 is significantly reduced. This idea is taken one step further in the bottom diagram where the iris is in its most constricted state to produce the smallest pupil aperture possible. The retinal images are now defined by a very narrow cone of rays. As can be seen here, the resulting blur spot from Object 2 is exceptionally small.

We interpret the illustrations in Figure 8.21 in the following way. For any given optical condition (i.e., object distance and accommodative state), pupil size can determine the degree to which retinal blurring occurs. Blurring is at its greatest with wide pupils and least with narrow pupils (Goss & West, 2001; Keating, 2002). This means that two objects located at different depth planes will both be seen at their sharpest when the pupil diameter is at its smallest. Another way of stating this is to say that the **depth of field** is at its greatest with small pupils and least with large pupils. Experienced photographers know this fact well and always go with the smallest lens aperture possible when they want to maximize the focus for objects at different distances. In terms of our own visual system, we have the poorest depth of field under dim light and the best depth of field under bright daylight conditions (SideNote 8.29).

C. Optical Disorders of the Eye

We now turn our attention to various optical problems that affect the eye and which together are responsible for abnormal vision in more than half of the world's population. Fortunately, proper vision can be restored through the use of various types of spectacle or contact lenses that are of sufficient optical precision to exactly correct the refractive problem. As we will see in this section, refractive problems in the eye can occur for several reasons. We begin our discussion with the one condition that afflicts nearly everyone around middle age and thereafter—a gradual impairment in accommodation that soon hinders near vision and therefore greatly reduces reading ability.

1. PRESBYOPIA

One of the consequences of aging is that many of the body's tissues begin to lose their elasticity. The crystalline lens is no exception. We noted earlier that the process of accommodation depends on the elastic quality of the lens, which allows it to assume a more spherical shape for viewing close objects when greater refractive power is needed. With increasing age, the lens begins to harden due to changes in the protein fibres within it (Michaels, 1985; Newell, 1996). This condition, which is known as **presbyopia**, is a very natural process and afflicts everyone, usually beginning in the 40s. The gradual loss in lens elasticity means that

Figure 8.21

Retinal blurring of objects at unaccommodated distances depends on the pupil diameter (aperture). In all of these examples, the eye is accommodated to Object 1, and we consider the retinal blurring caused by Object 2. A wide pupil aperture (top diagram) allows a large cone of rays to enter the eye and thereby produce a large blur spot. A moderate aperture (middle diagram) reduces the blur spot because the images are defined by a narrower cone of rays. The least blurring occurs with the smallest pupil diameter (bottom diagram). These results imply that the eye's depth of field is greatest under bright light conditions (narrow pupil) and least under dim light conditions (wide pupil).

there is a progressive loss in its accommodative ability. Although this does not affect viewing distant objects, near objects will appear blurred, and people often find themselves holding reading material at an increasingly greater distance. In other words, the near point gradually moves farther away with advancing presbyopia. Figure 8.22 shows how the near point changes with age (SideNote 8.30).

The treatment of presbyopia is quite straightforward. A presbyopic eye needs additional refractive power, which can be easily provided by a convex lens. In other words, the additional refractive ability needed by the eye for viewing close objects is precisely what a convex lens of appropriate optical power can provide. However, because distance vision is not affected in presbyopia, such glasses cannot be used for viewing objects at all distances. The familiar **reading glasses** provide the additional refractive power necessary for viewing close objects, yet allow a person to avert their eyes outside of the glasses in order to view distant objects. The increasing loss of accommodative ability with age means that progressively stronger corrective lenses are needed for near work with advancing presbyopia.

2. REFRACTIVE ERRORS

The most common visual disorder is an inability to focus light exactly upon the retina. Refractive errors exist in all populations and represent the predominant need for wearing glasses. More than a thousand years ago, glasses in India were actually made out of metal. The metal plates contained numerous small holes and therefore served as pinhole glasses. The principle behind these glasses, though probably not known at the time, is that the small apertures of the individual holes served to increase the depth of field and therefore restored much of the refractive error in the eye. The modern idea of using curved glasses to alter the convergence or divergence of light rays entering the eyes emerged around the 13th century. In this section, we will consider how these corrective lenses work in restoring normal vision. We will largely concentrate on two main types of refractive error—hyperopia and myopia.

Hyperopia (far-sightedness)

Refractive errors of the eye arise due to a mismatch between the length of the eyeball

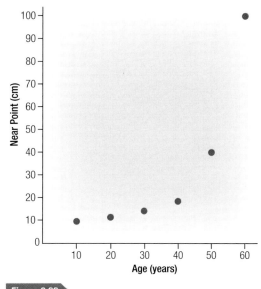

Figure 8.22

The near point moves farther away with increasing age due to a progressive loss of accommodative ability. However, the greatest decline in accommodation begins around the age of 40–45 when the lens starts to harden and lose its elasticity, a condition known as *presbyopia*.

and its optical power (Goss & West, 2001; Schwartz, 2002; Waldman, 1983). In the case of **hyperopia**, the eyeball is too short, and therefore the retina lies ahead of where it should normally be, given the optical power of the eye. This situation is illustrated in the top diagram of Figure 8.23 on page 266. As with all other optical situations we have examined in this chapter, we first consider the refractive condition in terms of parallel light rays emerging from a source at optical infinity. The shorter-than-normal length of the hyperopic eye means that parallel light rays will not converge enough to focus on the retina and will therefore produce a blur spot (SideNote 8.31). The grey outline in the top diagram of Figure 8.23 shows the location of the retina in a normal eye for comparative purposes.

In optical terms, the hyperopic eye lacks sufficient refractive power to focus parallel light onto its retina. One solution to this problem is simply to provide additional optical power through accommodation, as shown in the middle diagram of Figure 8.23. In fact, this is precisely what happens when a hyperopic person looks at distant objects. The blur spot on the retina is very quickly eliminated through a reflexive accommodative response, thereby allowing parallel light rays to come to a sharp focus on the retina. The problem with this solution is

SideNote **8.30**

Many vision scientists do not consider presbyopia to be an optical disorder because it is caused by a natural aging process. In fact, everyone at some point in their life will become presbyopic to a certain degree, even if they have never had any other visual problems.

SideNote **8.31**

Most babies are born with a slight degree of hyperopia. This condition decreases with age. The normal variation in eyeball length can end up causing a situation where the refractive power of the eye simply does not match the length of the eyeball. In fact, a mere 1 mm deviation in the placement of the retina will require optical correction.

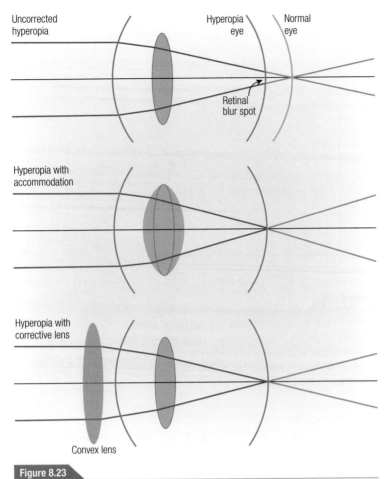

Figure 8.23

Hyperopia (far-sightedness) is characterized by an eyeball that is too short for its optical power. Light rays from optical infinity create a blur spot on the retina because it is located closer to the lens in comparison to a normal eye (top diagram). A hyperopic person can accommodate to correct this situation (middle diagram), though this will cut into the accommodative range for viewing near objects. The preferred solution is to wear convex lenses that provide additional optical power to image parallel rays on the retina and therefore simulate a normal eye (bottom diagram).

SideNote | 8.32

Myopia is the most common optical disorder and affects nearly 30% of Canada's population. In most cases, myopia develops between the ages of 5 and 10. Some scientists consider myopia to be a hereditary disorder because in many cases it runs in families. Others argue that though myopia may be inherited, its actual development may result from various environmental factors, such as close work and eye strain.

that by using up some of the eye's accommodative ability just to look at distant objects, there is going to be less accommodative range left for viewing nearer objects. In other words, since there is only a fixed amount of accommodative ability because of the limitation in the elasticity of the lens, a hyperopic person exhausts that ability much sooner since the lens already had to accommodate to view distant objects. As a result, the near point in these people will be located farther away. Thus, a hyperopic individual will have little problem viewing distant objects, but near objects become out of focus. It is for this reason that hyperopia is also commonly referred to as *far-sightedness*.

A more preferable solution is to use an optical means of correcting the refractive error. The need for additional refractive power to view a distant object means that a hyperopic person would have to be fitted with glasses containing convex lenses, as shown in the bottom diagram of Figure 8.23. The exact amount of the refractive error in each eye is first determined by an optometrist after which glasses are prescribed containing the precise amount of additional optical power needed to restore a sharp image on the retina for distant objects. A hyperopic person wearing such corrective glasses does not need to accommodate for distant objects and therefore can use the full accommodative range for viewing objects closer than optical infinity. In other words, a convex lens allows the hyperopic eye to optically function as a normal eye.

Myopia (nearsightedness)

The opposite condition of hyperopia is **myopia**. In this refractive disorder, the eyeball is too long given the refractive power of the eye (SideNote 8.32) (Goss & West, 2001; Schwartz, 2002). As a result, parallel light is focused onto a point that lies in front of the retina, as shown in the top diagram of Figure 8.24. Unlike hyperopia, there is no relief through accommodation because that will only increase the myopic eye's optical power and therefore move the image point even farther away from the retina. The natural solution in this case is to move the object closer to the eye. The greater divergence of the light rays will now move the image point backward until a certain object distance will cause the image to fall exactly on the retina. This means that the **far point** for myopes is not optical infinity but is located somewhat closer to the eye (middle diagram in Figure 8.24).

The exact location of the far point depends on the severity of the disorder. Objects located closer than the far point are imaged on the retina through additional accommodative power, as needed. However, the accommodative response only kicks in for objects that are located closer to the eye than the far point. Since the far point itself is located closer than optical infinity, the full accommodative response allows myopes to view objects much closer (i.e., the near point too is located closer to the eye than in an optically normal person). It is for this reason that myopia is commonly referred to as *nearsightedness*.

The optical solution to myopia is to prescribe concave lenses of appropriate optical power to allow parallel light rays to focus on the retina (bottom diagram in Figure 8.24)

(Michaels, 1985; Schwartz, 2002). In other words, a sufficient amount of divergence must be added to the incoming parallel rays to allow the image point to move backward and fall exactly on the retina. The optical power of the concave lens that is needed is based on the severity of the refractive disorder. Once a correct lens is applied to each eye, all objects at optical infinity will be imaged on the retina, whereas those located closer than optical infinity will induce an accommodative response. Thus, a concave lens allows the myopic eye to optically function as a normal eye.

Comparison of various optical disorders

The impact of the various optical disorders that affect the human eye is summarized in Figure 8.25. This figure provides a top-down schematic view of four eyes (normal, presbyopic, hyperopic, and myopic) looking out into space. Each of the optical disorders causes vision to be restricted within a range of space ahead of it. Starting with the normal eye, a clear range of vision is apparent from its far point (FP) of optical infinity all the way up to its near point (NP) of around 12 cm. The normal eye in this figure represents that of a 20-year-old individual, and therefore a full range of normal accommodation will allow this person to clearly see all objects within this depth range. As this person develops presbyopia with advancing age, the dynamic range of vision will become constricted due to progressive limitations in accommodative ability. As a result, the near point will move farther away with advancing presbyopia, though the far point will remain relatively unaffected.

A similar situation is found in those individuals with hyperopia, though here the

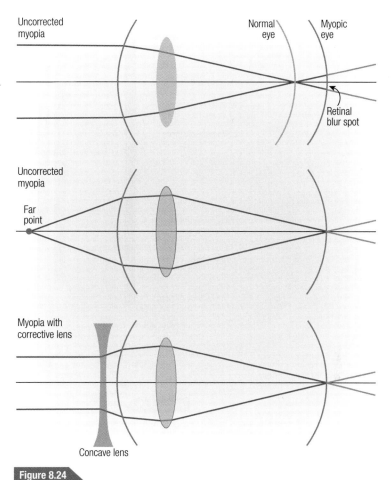

Figure 8.24

Myopia (nearsightedness) is characterized by an eyeball that is too long for its optical power. Light rays from optical infinity create a blur spot on the retina because it is located farther away from the lens in comparison to a normal eye (top diagram). An object must therefore be moved closer to the eye in order to create a sharp image on the myope's retina—that is, the far point is located closer than optical infinity (middle diagram). The optical correction needed is a concave lens of appropriate power to allow parallel light rays to diverge just enough so as to focus on the retina (bottom diagram).

cause is due to the refractive mismatch with a shorter-than-normal eyeball. Nevertheless, hyperopes have a normal FP because they are

INVESTIGATION

Comparing Prescription Glasses

For this investigation, you will need a few sets of prescription glasses in different strengths (which can be purchased at a dollar store or pharmacy). Prescription glasses measure strength in dioptres; negative numbers are associated with concave lenses and are used for myopic individuals (i.e., nearsighted), and positive numbers are associated with convex lenses and are used for hyperopic individuals (i.e., far-sighted). Concave lenses will cause light rays to diverge, and convex lenses will cause light rays to converge. Take a flashlight and cover the light with opaque tape, leaving only a slit of light uncovered. Remove the lenses from the frames and hold one perpendicular to a table. Turn off the lights and shine the flashlight at the lens. Observe what happens to the light ray's path when you increase the dioptre strength.

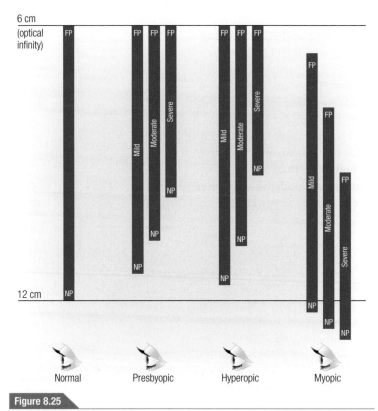

Figure 8.25

A schematic top-down view of the dynamic range of clear vision for the normal eye and those with various refractive disorders (without optical correction). The normal eye of a 20-year-old has a near point (NP) of 12 cm and a far point (FP) of optical infinity. This represents the dynamic depth range where all objects will be focused exactly on the retina. In presbyopia, the FP remains unchanged, but the NP moves progressively farther away from the eye depending on the severity. A similar situation exists with hyperopia, though the underlying cause in these two conditions is quite different. In myopia, both the FP and NP move closer to the eye, their exact location depending on the severity of the refractive error. Corrective eyeglasses will restore the dynamic range in all of these disorders to simulate that of a normal eye.

SideNote | 8.33

Certain types of astigmatism along with the more common disorders of myopia and hyperopia can be treated by laser surgery. Also known as *refractive surgery*, techniques such as *laser-assisted in situ keratomileusis* (LASIK) and the older procedure of radial keratotomy (RK) are based on altering the shape of the cornea through small laser-induced incisions.

able to accommodate for distant objects. In doing so, however, they end up reducing their accommodative range. This results in a farther-than-normal NP, the exact location of which depends on the severity of the hyperopia. The opposite situation occurs in myopia where a longer-than-normal eyeball means that distant objects must be moved closer in order to be imaged on the retina. As a result, the FP moves closer to the eye, and since the accommodative process begins at that point, the NP also moves closer to the eye. The exact locations of the FP and NP in myopia will depend on the severity of the disorder. All of the situations illustrated in Figure 8.25 show the depth range of vision without optical correction. Each of these disorders can be resolved through corrective lenses that optically convert the affected eye into a normal one.

Astigmatism

We have thus far treated the optical surfaces of the eye as being symmetrical along all directions. In fact, we have assumed that the cornea and lens are effectively spherical and therefore have an equivalent degree of curvature all around. While this is ordinarily true, there are situations where one of the refractive components, especially the cornea, may be more curved along one direction than another (e.g., the horizontal axis may be more curved than the vertical) (Keating, 2002; Michaels, 1985). This situation, known as **astigmatism**, results in partial blurring of the retinal image along the affected direction. Astigmatic vision can be fixed with special lenses that correct the refractive deficit along a particular orientation while sparing the remaining ones (SideNote 8.33).

Summary

1. It was believed for many centuries that light is made up of particles. However, there are many aspects of light that are better explained if it is considered to travel in a wave-like manner. The currently accepted *dual-theory* asserts that light is composed of particles (photons) that travel in a wave-like manner, thus explaining many phenomena associated with light.

2. Light is an example of electromagnetic radiation, that is, a moving energy field composed of both oscillating electrical and magnetic fields. A full cycle of the electrical field is referred to as the *wavelength*. Visible light spans a wavelength of 400–700 nm. Within this spectrum, blue colours are associated with short wavelengths, green and yellow with middle wavelengths, and red with long wavelengths.

3. It is often convenient to consider light as emanating from a point source when describing its interaction with objects. At a distance of 20 feet (or 6 metres) from the point source, the divergence of light rays becomes so negligible that they can be considered parallel. This distance, which is referred to as *optical infinity*, represents the initial condition when examining the interaction of light with objects.

4. In general, light can be absorbed, reflected, or scattered by an object. Light may also undergo transmission through transparent objects. The phenomenon of refraction can arise at the boundary between two different media (e.g., air and water, air and glass, etc.), which causes the light rays to either converge or diverge away from the normal (the plane perpendicular to the boundary). The greater the difference in refractive index between the two media, the greater the refraction at the boundary.

5. The curved surfaces of a lens are ideally suited for refraction. With a concave lens, light rays refract in such a way at both surfaces that they emerge in a divergent manner and therefore can never create a true image of the point source. A convex lens, however, converges the incoming light to produce a true image a certain distance away from the lens. That distance depends on the optical power of the lens, which in turn is determined by the curvature of its surfaces and the refractive index of the lens. Another factor that affects image distance is the location of the object—image distance increases as the object is brought closer to the lens.

6. The eye is made up of many components, notably the cornea, crystalline lens, aqueous and vitreous humours, and retina. The eye is both an optical instrument and a device that converts the energy in visible light into neural signals. The optical properties arise at the air–cornea surface by way of the crystalline lens. An *emmetropic* eye is one whose optical power is precisely sufficient to converge light rays from an object at optical infinity into an image on the retina. The retinal image is inverted and horizontally flipped.

7. Objects located closer than optical infinity require the eye to increase its optical power in order to create a focused image on the retina. This is accomplished by the process of *accommodation*, that is, an increase in the curvature of the lens surfaces to provide the extra optical power needed. Accommodation is a reflexive process driven by the blur signal on the retina. There is a limit to how much accommodation is possible. As a result, objects closer than the *near point* cannot be accommodated and remain out of focus.

8. *Presbyopia* arises from reduced elasticity of the lens with increasing age, leading to decreased accommodative ability. *Farsightedness* (hyperopia) arises when the eyeball is too short for the optical power of the eye. For distant objects, the eye can accommodate to provide the additional optical power, which is not a favourable solution because it reduces the accommodative range of the eye. The proper solution is to wear glasses with positive optical power (convex lens) sufficient to overcome the refractive error of the eye. *Nearsightedness* (myopia) arises when the eyeball is too long for the optical power of the eye, a situation that can be corrected by wearing glasses with negative optical power (concave lens).

Key Terms

accommodation, 260
aperture, 263
aqueous humour, 258
astigmatism, 268
ciliary muscle, 260
concave lens, 255
convex lens, 255
cornea, 258
crystalline lens, 258
depth of field, 264
diffraction, 246
dual-theory of light, 247
electromagnetic radiation, 247
electromagnetic spectrum, 248
emission spectrum, 248-9
emmetropia, 259

ether, 246
far point, 266
hyperopia, 265
inverse square law, 250
iris, 258
lens aberrations, 263
light ray, 250
Mie scattering, 252
myopia, 266
nanometre, 248
near point, 261
nodal point, 262
normal, 255
optic axis, 255
optical infinity, 250
plane-polarized light, 252
point source, 249
presbyopia, 264

pupil, 259
Rayleigh scattering, 251
reading glasses, 265
refraction, 254
refractive index, 254
refractive power, 256
retina, 246
retinal magnification, 263
schematic eye, 259
sclera, 258
spectrum, 247
transmission spectrum, 249
unpolarized light, 253
visible light, 248
vitreous humour, 258
wave fronts, 250
wavelength, 247

Recall Questions

1. What is the dual-theory, and how does it account for the observed behaviour of light? What are the different components of the electromagnetic spectrum? Why did evolution not create a sensory system to detect other parts of the electromagnetic spectrum, such as x-rays or radar waves?

2. What is optical infinity, and why is it important in discussions of optics? What are the different ways that light can interact with an object?

3. What are the properties of a lens that determine how much refraction will take place? How does a convex lens differ from a concave lens? What is the relationship between object distance and image distance with regard to lenses?

4. What are the different anatomical components of the human eye? What are the refractive elements of the eye? Why is it important to form a clear and focused image on the retina? How does the eye accommodate for objects at near distances?

5. What is the nodal point, and why is it important in optics? What are the characteristics of the retinal image in terms of its orientation and quality?

6. What causes presbyopia? What kind of lens should be prescribed for hyperopia? Why should a correcting lens be used at all when accommodation can correct the refractive error?

7. How does myopia affect the near point? What kind of correcting lens should be prescribed in this condition?

8. What are the different types of light scattering? What are some examples of Rayleigh and Mie scattering?

9. What are the different ways that polarized light can be produced? Under what conditions does scattering produce polarized light?

10. How does astigmatism differ from ordinary refractive error? Under what conditions would a bifocal spectacle be useful (i.e., a spectacle with a different optical power on the top half versus the bottom half)?

- Greenler, R. (1980). *Rainbows, halos, and glories*. Cambridge, UK: Cambridge University Press.

- Jenkins, F. A., & White, H. E. (2001). *Fundamentals of optics* (4th ed.). New York, NY: McGraw-Hill.

- Meinel, A. B., & Meinel, M. (1983). *Sunsets, twilights, and evening skies*. Cambridge, UK: Cambridge University Press.

- Minnaert, M. G. J. (1993). *Light and color in the outdoors*. New York, NY: Springer-Verlag.

- Mouroulis, P., & Mcdonald, J. (1997). *Geometrical optics and optical design*. New York, NY: Oxford University Press.

- Pedrotti, F. L., Pedrotti, L. S., & Pedrotti, L. M. (2006). *Introduction to optics* (3rd ed.). San Francisco, CA, and New York, NY: Benjamin Cummings.

- Welford, W. T. (1990). *Optics* (3rd ed.). New York, NY: Oxford University Press.

- Williamson, S. J., & Cummins, H. Z. (1983). *Light and color in nature and art*. New York, NY: Wiley.

Further Reading

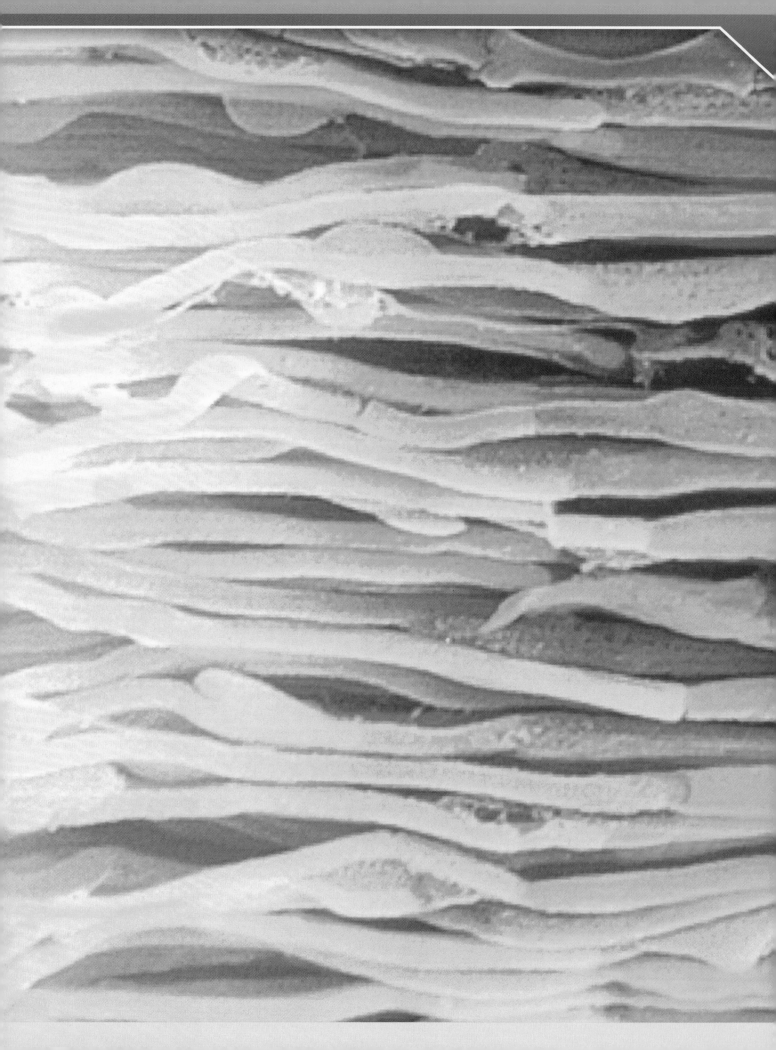

The Visual System: Retinal Processing and Early Vision

9

In this chapter . . .

- You will learn about the three neuronal layers that make up the retina; the outermost layer contains the photoreceptors (rods and cones), which capture light and transform it into a neural signal; the innermost layer contains the retinal ganglion cells, which serve as the output neurons of the retina; and the middle layer contains three types of neurons whose circuitry creates the properties displayed by the retinal ganglion cells.

- You will come to understand the properties of a ganglion cell, such as its receptive field, which is circular and made up of two parts—a centre and a surround. You will come to know that some ganglion cells have an ON (excitatory) centre and will only fire when light falls within a restricted circular zone of the retina, along with an OFF (inhibitory) surround that will offset any excitatory effect. You will learn how this feature contributes to the visual property of contrast detection.

- You will learn about the two types of vision—scotopic and photopic—and how each serves different purposes.

- You will learn about how the biological setup of the retina is responsible for visual properties such as sensitivity and resolution. You will also come to appreciate that our retinal function gives rise to lightness contrast, lightness constancy, and certain visual illusions.

When this net-like body is removed from the eye and its parts are collected, he who looks with persistent attention at them thinks that they are a part of the brain and cannot believe that they were in the eye.

—Hunain ibn Is-hâq (ca. 850)

A colour-enhanced scanning electron micrograph of rods and cones in the human retina. Photo © Ralph C. Eagle Jr./Photo Researchers Inc.

SideNote | **9.1**

The term *retina* is derived from the Latin *réte*, meaning *net*. The net-like appearance of the retina may explain the origin of this term.

SideNote | **9.2**

The retina is somewhat loosely attached to the back wall of the eyeball and can become detached if the head experiences rapid forces, such as in an automobile accident. Many of the neurons in a detached retina can die because they are separated from their blood supply, leading to irrecoverable vision loss or blindness. It is therefore important to seek immediate medical attention after any kind of forceful trauma to the head, even if the person appears unaffected.

The **retina** is a thin film of cells that lines the inside back wall of the eyeball (SideNote 9.1). We noted in the last chapter that the retina can be thought of in three dimensions as one-half of a sphere that extends from the back of the eyeball all the way forward to just a little past the midline along both the vertical and horizontal axes. An optical image is cast upon this entire area by the refractive elements of the eye. All vertebrates have a retina that is made up of similar types of cells, though there is variability in the composition and layout of these cells. The dominant cells in the retina are actually neurons. In fact, the retina forms as an outgrowth of the central nervous system that invades the eyeball during embryonic development. As such, any kind of disease or traumatic injury to the retina that destroys these cells will lead to permanent blindness because neurons do not regenerate and new neurons cannot be created in the retina (SideNote 9.2).

In historical times, the retina was thought of as having a largely nutritional role by providing essential nourishment to the inner eye elements such as the vitreous and lens. In fact, the lens itself was thought to be the main instrument of vision rather than the retina. A key advance took place when we finally understood the optical nature of the eye and the fact that an image is formed on the retina itself. However, this only invited many new ideas on what the retina actually did with the optical image. Isaac Newton, for example, believed that light produced vibrations in the retina, much as sound does in the auditory structures, and that these vibrations were transmitted to the brain through the fibre tracts.

The actual mechanisms by which an optical image produces electrical signals in the retina are now well understood. We will discuss those mechanisms in this chapter and go on to see how the different neural elements within the retina process the signals to produce a final output that is transmitted to the visual brain. We will conclude this chapter with a discussion on various perceptual aspects of vision that can actually be attributed to retinal processing mechanisms.

A. The Photoreceptor Array

An optically normal human eye is designed to cast a visual image exactly on the retina. More precisely, the image is actually projected on the very outer margins of the retina just within the inside wall of the eye. It is along this margin that an array of **photoreceptors** is found (Rodieck, 1998; Tessier-Lavigne, 2000). As illustrated in Figure 9.1, the photoreceptors are embedded within the fibrous matrix that holds the eyeball together. Photoreceptors serve as the light-absorbing elements of the retina, and it is in these cells that the very first events in vision occur—that is, absorption of light to produce a neural signal. Thus, photoreceptors function as the transducing elements of the visual system, converting the energy in the light distributed across the retinal image into a series of signals that are then processed by other neurons in the retina (MacLeish, Shepherd, Kinnamon, & Santos-Sacchi, 1999).

The photoreceptors lie immediately in front of a layer of cells known as the **pigment epithelium**. As the name suggests, these cells contain pigmented material that absorbs stray light, that is, light that did not get captured by the photoreceptors. This is a very important function because, as it turns out, a certain amount of the incident light bypasses the photoreceptors and is then absorbed by the pigment epithelium. Visual function can be impaired in cases where the pigment is reduced or absent in these cells because unabsorbed stray light

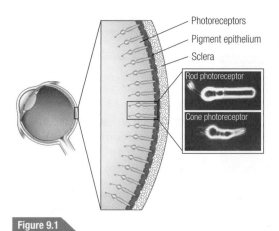

Photoreceptors
Pigment epithelium
Sclera
Rod photoreceptor
Cone photoreceptor

Figure 9.1

The retina contains an array of photoreceptor neurons that is located along the outermost margins of the retina. The photoreceptors are actually embedded within the fibrous matrix of the eyeball and located next to the pigment epithelium. An inspection of the photoreceptor array at high magnification shows that these cells can be divided into two different types based on their shape—that is, rod and cone photoreceptors. Photoreceptors transmit their signals to other neurons within the retina (not shown in this figure). Adapted from "Sensory Transduction," by MacLeish et al., 1999, in *Fundamental Neuroscience,* Eds. M. J. Zigmond, F. E. Bloom, S. C. Landis, J. L. Roberts, and L. R. Squire, San Diego, CA: Academic Press. Photos: Michael Zigmond, Fundamental Neuroscience, pp. 673 © Elsevier, 1998.

interferes with the normal processing of visual information. This is precisely what happens in albino individuals who generally lack pigmented material in the pigment epithelium as well as skin tissue (SideNote 9.3).

1. RODS AND CONES

The human retina contains two types of photoreceptor cells—rods and cones. Rod photoreceptors are by far the more numerous. The retina in each eye typically contains around 120 million rods and about 6 million cones (Rodieck, 1998). The names of these photoreceptors were originally given because of their physical shape. Figure 9.1 shows microscopic images of the two types of photoreceptors. It can be seen here that rod photoreceptors have a slender, cylindrical (rod-like) appearance, whereas cone photoreceptors taper off at one end, giving them a more conical appearance.

Rod and cone photoreceptors mediate different visual functions

The difference between these two photoreceptor classes, however, is far more profound than merely their physical appearance. Rods and cones serve as the front-end of two fundamentally different visual systems. As diurnal animals, we must be able to function across a wide range of light conditions, from the highly intense levels of a very sunny day to the dimmest levels that are present on a moonlit night (Bruce & Georgeson, 1996; Wolken, 1995). It turns out that no single type of photoreceptor can function across this vast range of light levels, and therefore there exists a division of responsibility. Rod photoreceptors serve as the front-end of a visual mechanism that mediates **night vision**, whereas cone photoreceptors serve a second visual mechanism that mediates **day vision**. Our visual system automatically switches from one mechanism to the other as we move from daylight to nighttime conditions and vice versa. This fundamental dichotomy of day *versus* night vision should be kept in mind as our discussion of retinal processing unfolds over the remainder of this chapter.

Photoreceptor distribution across the retina

To further understand how visual processing occurs under day and night conditions, we begin by looking at the distribution of the two photoreceptor classes across the retina. Danish anatomist Gustav Østerberg made a systematic survey to see how the density of both rod and cone photoreceptors changes from one end of the retina to the other (Østerberg, 1935). The results of this classic study are shown in Figure 9.2. In order to properly interpret this data, we have to first become better acquainted with the major retinal landmarks. The top diagram in Figure 9.2, which provides a schema of the right eyeball, shows that the retina can be divided into two halves—a nasal (toward the nose) half and a temporal (toward the temple) half. The midpoint dividing these two halves contains a small pit called the **fovea**. The other physical landmark of importance is the **optic disk**, which represents the point in the nasal retina through which retinal nerve fibres exit the eyeball (SideNote 9.4).

The distribution of rods and cones throughout the retina becomes more meaningful if we now look at the data in terms of these landmarks. Figure 9.2 shows how the retina from this eyeball can be portrayed in an unfolded manner. The distance along this

SideNote | **9.3**

A genetic disorder known as *ocular albinism* results in reduced pigmented material only within the pigment epithelium cells. Individuals with this disease suffer from a variety of visual disorders, including a reduced ability to see fine detail, due to the presence of large amounts of stray light in the retina.

SideNote | **9.4**

The same scenario depicted in Figure 9.2 for the right eye applies to the left eye as well. The fovea lies in the centre of its retina, and the optic disk can be found in its nasal retina.

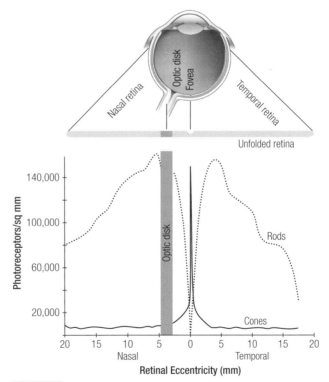

Figure 9.2

A schematic figure of the right eyeball in the top diagram shows two important retinal landmarks—the fovea and the optic disk. The retina can be divided into a nasal and a temporal half, starting at the fovea. The bottom diagram shows the distribution of rod and cone photoreceptors at increasing distance (eccentricity) in both directions from the fovea. The optic disk located in the nasal retina is also known as the *blind spot* because it does not contain photoreceptors.

unfolded retina represents the x-axis of the graph below it, with the "0" point denoting the fovea. There are three important points to take away from this figure (Tessier-Lavigne, 2000). First, there are no photoreceptors (rods or cones) whatsoever at the optic disk. This makes sense because if the nerve fibres of the retina are to exit the eyeball at this location, there cannot be any photoreceptors in the way. The fact that there is no light absorption due to a lack of photoreceptors means that this small part of the nasal retina is effectively blind. For this reason, the optic disk is more popularly called the *blind spot*.

The second important point is that the density of cone photoreceptors (shown by the solid curves) is quite low in the peripheral parts of the retina on both the nasal and temporal sides but shoots up and reaches its maximum value at the centre of the fovea. The difference in the numbers is quite dramatic, about 7,000 cones per square mm in the periphery but rising close to 150,000 at the fovea.

The third point is that an opposite pattern is seen with regard to the density of rod photoreceptors (shown by the dotted curves). Rods are much more numerous in the periphery and reach their peak at around 5 mm on either side of the fovea. However, their numbers drop dramatically near the centre of the retina, and in fact, there are absolutely no rods present within the fovea itself. This means that all of our night vision functions occur only through the peripheral parts of the retina, starting from just outside the fovea. Day vision, on the other hand, can be mediated throughout all parts of the retina since cones are found everywhere. However, this raises a couple of interesting questions. Why does the cone density simply not remain the same across the entirety of the retina, and why is there such a large concentration of cones in the fovea?

The foveal retina is specialized for detailed vision

We know from common experience that we always direct our gaze toward an interesting object so that it falls on our line of sight. Thus, whenever we want to scrutinize something in detail, we direct our eyes so that its image falls on the fovea. The large concentration of cones in the fovea is dedicated to processing image detail, primarily because of the way the cones are connected to the other neurons in the retina (Boycott & Dowling, 1969; Dowling, 1987;

Rodieck, 1998). Thus, although day vision is served by all parts of the retina, it is the fovea that is further specialized for scrutinizing the details of a given object. The answer as to how this is actually accomplished will have to come in stages as we begin to understand the various aspects of retinal function, including neural processing that takes place beyond the photoreceptor level.

The peripheral retina is specialized for low light detection

Given the absence of rods in the fovea, this part of the retina becomes severely handicapped under very low light conditions or when the object being viewed is very dim. The peripheral retina, however, compensates for this loss through its large concentration of rod photoreceptors. Visual function under such low light conditions is therefore mediated only by the peripheral retina (SideNote 9.5) (Rodieck, 1998; Tessier-Lavigne, 2000). In terms of the camera analogy, the retina can be thought of as being composed of two types of film—a very light-sensitive film in the peripheral parts and a much less sensitive film in the central part that is specialized for resolving fine image detail. This too represents a fundamental dichotomy of retinal function, and something we will revisit throughout this chapter. However, next we turn our attention to understanding how photoreceptors absorb light and convert that event into a neural signal.

2. VISUAL TRANSDUCTION

In previous chapters we reviewed the various different ways by which external stimulation can trigger neural activity at the very first stages of sensory processing. This so-called process of *transduction* is unique for each sensory system. The way that mechanical stimulation induces neural activity in mechanoreceptor neurons, for example, is quite distinct from the way that chemicals trigger activity in gustatory and olfactory receptor neurons, which in turn is very different from the vibrational triggering of electrical activity in cochlear hair cells. The neural processing of visual information must also begin with the very first act of transforming energy in the stimulus (light) into neural activity within those neurons (photoreceptors) located at the very first stage of the visual pathway. This process, which is known as **phototransduction**, is far different from any

SideNote | **9.5**

An oft-used example of this fact is drawn from gazing at stars in the night sky. A very dim star will disappear from view if one gazes at it directly (i.e., it is imaged on the fovea) but becomes immediately visible if the line of sight is shifted slightly to one side so that its image now falls on the rod-rich part of the retina. Astronomy buffs call this *averted vision* and used this technique to look at the comets Hyakutake and Hale-Bopp when those comets visited Earth in 1996 and 1997, respectively.

of the others we have covered thus far in that it produces a very unconventional outcome in terms of electrical activation.

Photoreceptors contain photopigment material

The first event in phototransduction is the capture of light photons by photoreceptors to generate an electrical signal. This is accomplished by a special material, known generically as *photopigment*, which is found in high concentration within both rods and cones. The photopigment in all mammalian photoreceptors is called **rhodopsin**. Figure 9.3 shows that rod and cone photoreceptors can be divided into two segments, an inner and an outer segment (Batschauer, 2004; Tessier-Lavigne, 2000). It is the outer segment that is embedded within the fibrous matrix of the eyeball and that contains a large concentration of rhodopsin molecules. The outer segment of rods contains a stack of discs, whereas in cones, the outer segment is invaginated by a series of infoldings. The rhodopsin molecules are located within the membrane of each of the discs or infoldings, as shown in the right diagram of Figure 9.3 (SideNote 9.6). American biochemist George Wald was responsible for much of our understanding on the chemical makeup and function of rhodopsin in absorbing light, for which he received the Nobel Prize in 1967 (Wald, 1968).

The dark current

In total darkness, rhodopsin molecules are maintained in an inactive form. However, there are still a number of very interesting things going on inside the photoreceptor cells, as outlined in Figure 9.4 on page 278. In the absence of any light whatsoever, there is a steady flow of sodium ions (Na+) into the outer segment through what are known as *cGMP-gated sodium channels* (MacLeish et al., 1999; Wensel, 2008; Yau K-W, 1994). cGMP is an organic molecule found in high concentration within the outer segment. The sodium channels located here are somewhat special in that they need to bind cGMP in order to allow sodium to flow in. In other words, the sodium gates are only open when there is enough cGMP around. The entry of sodium ions into the outer segment by this mechanism in the absence of light is known as the **dark current**.

 The entry of positively charged sodium ions into the photoreceptor is accompanied by an outward flow of potassium ions (K+) in

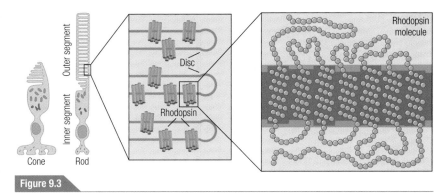

Figure 9.3

Rod and cone photoreceptors can be broadly divided into two compartments—the inner and outer segment. The outer segment of rods contains a set of membranous discs that are stacked like pancakes. Each disc in turn contains millions of molecules of the photopigment known as *rhodopsin*. Light absorption by rhodopsin triggers a cascade of events that leads to the production of a neural signal in both rods and cones. Adapted from *Principles of Neural Science,* 4th ed., by E. R. Kandel, J. H. Schwartz, and T. M. Jessell, 2000, New York, NY: McGraw-Hill.

the inner segment. This maintains a net balance of ionic charges. However, continued inflow and outflow of these two ions will result in an excess accumulation of Na+ inside and K+ outside the cell. To prevent this from happening, a sodium–potassium pump exchanges these ions in an opposite manner—that is, sodium ions are ejected from the photoreceptor, and potassium ions are brought back inside. The net result of this entire series of ongoing events is that the photoreceptor membrane potential is maintained at a steady level of around −40 mV (SideNote 9.7).

Phototransduction involves a cascade of biochemical events

The ionic exchanges described above take place as long as rhodopsin remains in an inactive state due to darkness. We now turn to the events that take place when photoreceptors are exposed to light (Batschauer, 2004; Fiesler & Kisselev, 2007). Figure 9.5 on page 278 shows the activation of a single rhodopsin molecule after light absorption and the subsequent sequence of events that takes place in its immediate vicinity. Light photons have to pass through the inner segments of the photoreceptors before reaching the stack of discs in the outer segment containing the rhodopsin molecules. The large number of discs ensures that a light particle will likely be absorbed at some point. When this happens, the energy in the photon is imparted to a rhodopsin molecule causing a slight change in its physical structure or conformation. Rhodopsin is now in its activated state. The activated rhodopsin then interacts with a so-called *G protein*,

George Wald (1906–1997)
© SCIENCE PHOTO LIBRARY

SideNote 9.7

Ionic channels, pumps, and membrane potentials were covered in Section B.3 of Chapter 2. We noted there that the membrane potential for neurons ranges from −55 to −85 mV (the negative value refers to the inside of the neuron). Thus, the resting membrane potential for photoreceptors (−40 mV) is quite a bit higher (i.e., more depolarized) than most neurons.

SideNote 9.8

Both the ionic and biochemical mechanisms described here require a considerable amount of energy. In fact, photoreceptors have the highest energy requirements of all known cell types in the body and therefore need to be constantly well nourished.

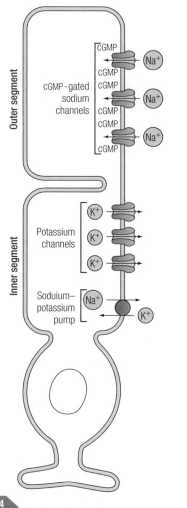

Figure 9.4

Photoreceptor outer segments contain cGMP-gated sodium channels that allow sodium ions to flow into the cell in the absence of light. This constitutes the so-called *dark current*. To maintain charge balance, potassium ions are ejected from the inner segment. A sodium–potassium pump exchanges these ions in the opposite direction to maintain their concentrations both inside and outside the cell.

which also resides in the disc membrane. The G protein that is activated by this interaction in turn activates a specific enzyme. The function of this enzyme is to convert the cGMP within the outer segment into ordinary GMP, which are unable to bind to the sodium channels. Thus, the cascade of biochemical events that takes place in quick order after light absorption by rhodopsin results in the removal of cGMP within the outer segment (SideNote 9.8).

Light absorption leads to photoreceptor hyperpolarization!

We saw above that cGMP is essential for the sodium channels to remain open, thereby allowing a steady stream of sodium ions into the photoreceptor outer segment (the dark current). The removal of cGMP by the activated enzyme means that there is less of it available to bind to the sodium channel. This in turn causes the sodium channels to shut down, preventing the entry of sodium ions and thereby abolishing the dark current. However, the potassium ions are continually ejected from the inner segment. Recall that the potassium outflow was necessary to offset the sodium influx and therefore maintain the charge balance. With the sodium channels now closed, the continued outflow of the positively charged potassium ions means that the membrane potential will become more negative. In other words, the photoreceptor actually becomes hyperpolarized after absorbing light (Baylor, Lamb, & Yau, 1979; Yau, 1994).

This is an astonishing result. The standard view of neuronal activation is for it to become depolarized (i.e., for its membrane potential to shift toward the positive end).

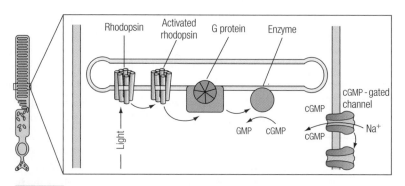

Figure 9.5

Rhodopsin molecules in the outer segment are activated after light absorption. This in turn causes a membrane-bound G protein to become activated. This is followed by the activation of an enzyme that converts cGMP into GMP. The reduction in cGMP means that less of it is available to bind to the sodium channels that need it in order to remain open. Thus, light activation causes the sodium channels to shut down, thereby reducing the dark current (inward sodium flow).

Indeed, the transducing neurons in all of the other sensory systems behave in this manner. And yet, photoreceptor activation following light absorption actually produces membrane hyperpolarization, an effect we normally associate with inhibition. The greater the amount of light absorbed, the greater the impact of the above series of biochemical events, leading to a greater hyperpolarization. The normal resting membrane potential of −40 mV in photoreceptors can become as low as −70 mV under bright light conditions.

Light activation of photoreceptors causes less neurotransmitter release!

Perhaps just as surprising as the electrical behaviour of photoreceptors after light absorption is the subsequent effects on neurotransmitter release. We normally associate neuronal activation with greater neurotransmitter release. However, the hyperpolarization of photoreceptors causes just the opposite effect at its synaptic junction with the next level of neurons in the retina. Both rod and cone photoreceptors produce and release the excitatory neurotransmitter *glutamate* (Fiesler & Kisselev, 2007; Tessier-Lavigne, 2000). Under dark conditions, photoreceptors display a steady release of glutamate. Light absorption and subsequent hyperpolarization of photoreceptors actually causes them to release less glutamate. Thus, the next level of neurons in the retina must somehow interpret the reduction in glutamate release as a signal that photoreceptor activation has occurred. A description of exactly how that happens will be given in Section B after we complete our discussion of photoreceptor function.

3. SPECTRAL RELATIONSHIPS

How much light is absorbed by a photoreceptor depends on two factors—the intensity of the incoming light and its wavelength. Naturally, the greater the light intensity, the greater the amount absorbed because there are simply many more photons present. However, the relationship between absorption and light wavelength is more complex. We know that human vision operates only within the wavelength range of 400 to 700 nm. Therefore, as a starting point, we would want to know the efficiency with which rod and cone rhodopsins absorb light within this **spectral** range. It would then be interesting to compare the visual sensitivity of humans (i.e., our sensory capacity to detect light) as a function of wavelength for both rod and cone vision.

Absorption spectrum of rod rhodopsin

Let us consider a simple experiment. Assume that we are able to obtain some retinal tissue from a nocturnal animal (e.g., a raccoon or an owl) (SideNote 9.9). Such tissue is largely if not entirely made up of rod photoreceptors. After the photoreceptors have been separated from the rest of the retinal neurons, rhodopsin molecules can then be released and collected with the simple addition of a mild detergent. Let us now put that rhodopsin in a test tube, as shown in Figure 9.6 on page 280, and then place it in the path of a light beam whose wavelength

METHODOLOGY

Restoring Vision with Retinal Implants

The Boston Retinal Implant Project (BRIP), begun in the early 1980s by Joseph Rizzo and John Wyatt, focuses on creating an alternative to seeing and targets diseases that affect the rod and cone photoreceptors (i.e., retinitis pigmentosa and age-related macular degeneration). It has been found that even when there is photoreceptor loss, many of the other nerve cells are still intact. This means we can directly stimulate those cells to then be transmitted to the brain. The two key teams working on this project are the biology and engineering teams. The biology team focuses on the optimal parameters of electrically stimulating the retina and biocompatible materials to create the retinal prosthesis. The engineering team focuses on the actual design and fabrication of the electrode array to ensure it will be viable for a number of years. Human testing has begun and has resulted in patients seeing spots of light, sometimes after being legally blind for decades. In the meantime, continued research on the mechanisms of vision will be invaluable to the BRIP and will hopefully lead to at least partial restoration of vision in some types of blindness.

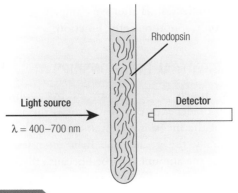

When plotted in relative terms, the peak absorption point is given a value of 100%, and all other values are plotted relative to this. The advantage to this type of plotting is that it is easier to compare the nature of the profile with those of other photopigments, something that will be important when we get to the cone rhodopsins.

Figure 9.6

The absorption spectrum of rod rhodopsin can be determined by first extracting it from the outer segments and placing it in solution inside a test tube. A narrow beam of light at a particular wavelength is then passed through this solution. The amount of light that emerges from the other side is measured and can be used to determine how much was absorbed at that particular wavelength. This process can be repeated for other wavelengths across the visible spectrum.

can be changed. The light that is not absorbed by the rhodopsin will emerge out of the other side of the test tube where it can be measured with a simple detector. In our experiment, we systematically change the wavelength of the incoming light in the range of 400 to 700 nm and measure how much of the light is absorbed by rhodopsin at each wavelength. This procedure is known as **spectrophotometry**.

A typical result from such an experiment involving rod rhodopsin is shown in the left panel of Figure 9.7. The curve, known as an **absorption spectrum**, shows how much light is absorbed by rod photopigment across the entire visible spectrum (Batschauer, 2004;

MacLeish et al., 1999; Wolken, 1995). The upside-down U-shaped absorption profile reflects the different efficiencies by which rod rhodopsin molecules absorb light photons of different wavelengths. It is customary to display the data in terms of *relative absorption*, as shown on the y-axis, in order to make comparisons among different photopigments and conditions (SideNote 9.10). The most important point to note from the profile shown in Figure 9.7 is that light absorption by rods is not uniform across all wavelengths but shows a maximum at around 500 nm (bluish-green light). Absorption drops rather dramatically on either side of this peak, and beyond 650 nm, there is no appreciable absorption of light at all. This means that vision at wavelengths beyond this limit must be accomplished by the cone rhodopsins, which is indeed the case.

Spectral sensitivity of rod (scotopic) vision

Given that the peak efficiency of light capture occurs at 500 nm, this suggests that rod photoreceptors would also produce their greatest signal at this wavelength compared to other wavelengths of equal intensity. This in turn means that human vision under nighttime conditions should be most sensitive to 500 nm light. To test this prediction, a simple experiment can be conducted in which human observers are asked to detect a light spot whose wavelength is systematically changed (Schwartz, 1999; Valberg, 2005; Wandell, 1995). The objective is to find the absolute threshold of light detection for each wavelength tested. The only important requirement to keep in

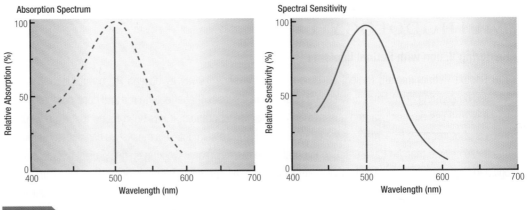

Figure 9.7

The absorption spectrum (left panel) shows a profile of the relative efficiency by which rod photopigment absorbs light at different wavelengths across the visible spectrum. This function looks very similar to the visual sensitivity function of rod (scotopic) vision that is obtained from behavioural measures of light detection ability in humans across the visible spectrum (right panel). Both profiles show a peak at 500 nm and decline to negligible levels around 600 nm.

mind is that the experiment should be conducted so that only rod vision is tested.

At this point, we introduce the term **scotopic vision**, which refers to visual processes that are mediated only by rod photoreceptors. One way to ensure that it is indeed scotopic vision that is being tested is to conduct the experiment under very dim light conditions and to apply the light spot in the peripheral part of the retina where there are lots of rods. A typical result from such an experiment is shown in the right panel of Figure 9.7. The profile shown here depicts the human visual system's sensitivity to light of different wavelengths and is known as the scotopic **spectral sensitivity function** (SideNote 9.11).

The important point to note here is that this function is derived from experiments conducted with human observers and therefore reflects the sensitivity of the visual system in behavioural terms. Thus, the peak of the sensitivity function, which is also seen to be at 500 nm, means that scotopic vision is most sensitive to bluish-green light and that it is not functional beyond 650 nm (red light). This is precisely the prediction that we would make from the absorption spectrum because if light is not even absorbed by rod photoreceptors beyond a certain wavelength, then we simply should not be able to see it (SideNote 9.12). Indeed, the degree to which the scotopic sensitivity function as a whole mimics the absorption spectrum of rod photopigment is quite striking (compare the right and left panels in Figure 9.7). In other words, our sensitivity to different light wavelengths under scotopic conditions can be explained entirely by the absorption spectrum of rod photopigment (Rodieck, 1998).

Absorption spectrum of cone rhodopsins

We now apply the same sequence of experimental approaches to visual function driven by the cone photoreceptors. On the basis of both theoretical and experimental studies, it had been known early on that the retina contains more than one type of cone photoreceptor. For the time being, let us proceed with the idea that there are indeed multiple types of cones, each containing a slightly different type of photopigment. This assumption unfortunately presents a technical difficulty in that we cannot undertake the same spectrophotometry experiment as above for rods because even if we were to obtain an animal with an all-cone retina, we would end up with a mixture of different cone photopigments in our test tube. This means that we would not be able to derive the individual absorption spectra for each of the cone photopigments because they would all be mixed together.

A technical breakthrough in the 1970s allowed the procedure of spectrophotometry to be miniaturized so that it could be applied to individual, isolated cone photoreceptors (Bowmaker, 1984). Known as **microspectrophotometry**, this technique confirmed the existence of three different types of cone photoreceptors, each having its own characteristic absorption spectrum. The three profiles, which are shown in the left panel of Figure 9.8, have a similar shape but are offset with respect to each other. The

SideNote | **9.11**

The term *sensitivity* is used here to reflect the ease with which light of a particular wavelength can be detected. In experimental terms, the absolute threshold for detection is evaluated at different wavelengths (see Section B.2 in Chapter 1 for a review). The inverse value of *threshold* is sensitivity. Thus, the lower the threshold, the greater the sensitivity.

SideNote | **9.12**

A simple experiment can demonstrate this fact. Place a blue, green, yellow, and deep red object in a room and then dim the lights until the objects can barely be seen. Wait about five minutes. Your visual system is now operating only through the scotopic system. The blue, green, and yellow items will be visible in shades of grey, whereas the red one will be invisible.

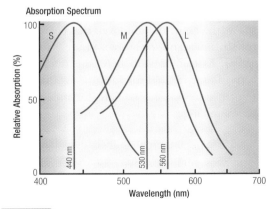

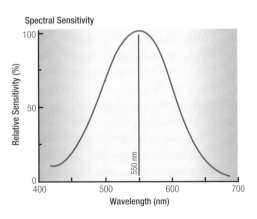

Figure 9.8

The absorption spectrum (left panel) shows the profiles of three cone photoreceptors—S-, M-, and L-cones—in terms of their relative efficiency at absorbing light across the visible spectrum. Each cone photopigment absorbs maximally at a different wavelength. The spectral sensitivity function for cone (photopic) vision has a peak at 550 nm (right panel), suggesting that light detection by this system when obtained from behavioural measures is largely mediated by the M- and L-cones.

cone photoreceptor with the lowest-wavelength absorption spectrum is known as *short-wavelength* absorbing cone, or **S-cone**. It has a peak absorbance at 440 nm. The next cone type is known as *middle-wavelength* absorbing cone, or **M-cone**, with a peak absorbance at 530 nm. The third type of cone photoreceptor is known as *long-wavelength* absorbing cone, or **L-cone**, with an absorbance peak at 560 nm (SideNote 9.13). It turns out that the rhodopsin photopigment in these three types of cones is slightly different in molecular terms, which in turn is responsible for causing the peak absorbance to occur at different wavelengths (Kochendoerfer, Lin, Sakmar, & Mathies, 1999; Rodieck, 1998; Wolken, 1995).

Spectral sensitivity of cone (photopic) vision

Together, the three types of cones are responsible for mediating **photopic vision**, the scientific term used to refer to day vision. Visual processing under photopic conditions is regulated only by the collective output of these three types of cones, and there is no input whatsoever from rods (Rodieck, 1998). One of the consequences of photopic vision is that the brain is able to take the separate output of the three cone types to construct a perceptual phenomenon that we know as colour vision. The details of how this occurs will be discussed at length in Chapter 11. What we are presently interested in knowing is how signals from cone photoreceptors account for light sensitivity under photopic conditions.

The right panel in Figure 9.8 shows the photopic spectral sensitivity function, which is merely the counterpart to the scotopic function we saw in Figure 9.7 except that this relationship is obtained under photopic conditions. Photopic vision can be assured by simply restricting a small light patch to the fovea, where only cones are present, and finding the minimum intensity required for detection. The objective in such an experiment is to have the subject merely indicate when a light is visible, regardless of its perceived colour. The detection threshold values are then collected at different wavelengths across the visible spectrum to produce the resulting photopic sensitivity function. This profile has a peak around 550 nm, suggesting that light intensity detection at the behavioural level is largely regulated by the output of M- and L-cones (Tessier-Lavigne, 2000; Valberg, 2005; Wandell, 1995). Unlike scotopic vision, where visual sensitivity

could be attributed to the light-capturing ability of only a single photopigment (rod rhodopsin), light sensitivity under photopic conditions occurs due to the light-capturing ability of multiple photopigments (cone rhodopsins).

4. SENSITIVITY, BLEACHING, AND RECOVERY

The most important point to emerge from our discussion in the previous section is that visual function in humans is executed by two independent mechanisms—one mediated by rod photoreceptors (known as *scotopic vision*) and another mediated collectively by the three types of cone photoreceptors (known as *photopic vision*). This duality of visual processing in turn is regulated by the light intensity of the image on the retina. Only the rods are functional at low light intensities, whereas only the cones are functional at relatively higher intensities. This leads us then to an obvious question—what happens to cones under scotopic conditions and to rods under photopic conditions?

Rods have a lower activation threshold than cones

Both rod and cone photoreceptors are extremely sensitive in terms of their absolute ability to capture photons. In fact, both are able to reliably absorb even a single light photon under ideal conditions (Baylor et al., 1979). However, rods are much more efficient than cones at converting photon absorption into a neural signal. As a result, the threshold for rod activation is considerably lower, and this fact allows for them to function at extremely low light levels. Under such conditions, cones do not produce a neural signal at all, and therefore they remain functionally inactive. Figure 9.9 shows the range of light levels that corresponds to scotopic and photopic vision (Rodieck, 1998). As can be seen here, the much lower activation threshold for rods means that cones remain unresponsive to light for much of the scotopic range.

Rods become bleached at moderate intensities

The very high sensitivity of rods under dim light conditions comes at a price—it turns out that rods can only remain active for a limited range of light levels. Beyond moderate light intensities, rod photoreceptors can no longer absorb any photons because much of their photopigment is converted to an inactive form. The reason for this is as follows. After a

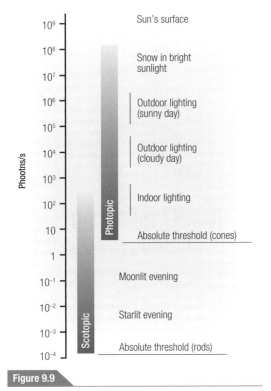

Figure 9.9

The light levels under which scotopic and photopic vision operate cover the range from the dimmest possible visual conditions to the brightest. The y-axis shows the light level in terms of the number of photons absorbed by a photoreceptor per second. Photopic vision begins to take over around the light level at which scotopic vision tails off.

Cones continue to respond at all daylight intensity levels

The activation threshold for cone photoreceptors fortuitously occurs around this light level (see Figure 9.9). This means that cones become functional around the level at which rod vision tails off, thus marking the beginning of photopic vision (SideNote 9.14). At higher levels within the photopic range, rods remain non-functional, whereas cones continue to respond effectively (MacLeish et al., 1999; Rodieck, 1998; Tessier-Lavigne, 2000). It would seem logical that the cone rhodopsins should also become increasingly bleached with increasing light levels. While this does indeed happen, it turns out that cone photoreceptors do not become completely bleached under ordinary daylight conditions. Indeed, complete **bleaching** only happens under extremely intense light conditions, such as looking briefly at the sun, where prolonged viewing will actually damage the photoreceptors. This situation can also be simulated by looking briefly at a household tungsten light bulb. Subsequent viewing of other objects then becomes difficult because the cone photopigments are momentarily bleached, causing a temporary blind spot at the fovea.

Visual recovery from bleaching

Let us assume that photopic vision becomes momentarily blinded as a result of looking at an intense light source. We know from our own experiences that the resulting blind spot quickly disappears, and we are able to see through the fovea again. This illustrates an important aspect of cone photoreceptor function—rapid recovery from bleaching. One way to find out the actual time course for such recovery is to conduct a **dark adaptation** experiment in which the detection threshold for a small light spot is

SideNote | **9.14**

As Figure 9.9 shows, the switch from scotopic to photopic vision is not abrupt. In fact, there is a small range of light levels at which both rods and cones are functional and can produce a signal. This small overlapping region is called *mesopic vision*.

rhodopsin molecule absorbs light, it temporarily becomes unable to absorb any more photons until the photopigment molecule is regenerated. During this period, the rhodopsin molecule is said to be bleached (Rodieck, 1998). As the light level increases, a greater proportion of rod rhodopsin becomes bleached until it reaches a stage where any additional light simply cannot be detected. This represents the upper limit of scotopic vision, beyond which rod photoreceptors are effectively blind.

INVESTIGATION

Switching from Photopic to Scotopic Vision

In bright light conditions our vision is driven exclusively by our cones (photopic vision) because the rods are bleached. In dim or dark conditions, however, our vision is driven exclusively by our rods (scotopic vision). Due to the fact that rods and cones have different absorption spectra (and therefore different peak wavelengths), the switch from photopic vision to scotopic vision will actually alter your perception of the colour swatches you see. To test this, dim the lights until you can barely see the colour patches on the right. The red patch will disappear, and the blue, green, and yellow patches should appear to be different shades of grey.

measured at various times after bleaching (Fain, Matthews, & Cornwall, 1996; Fain, Matthews, Cornwall, & Koutalos, 2001; Schwartz, 1999). Figure 9.10 shows the dark adaptation profiles for both cones and rods.

Looking first at the cone profile, we see that the initially high threshold levels following bleaching rapidly decline such that by about 5 minutes, the detection threshold for cone vision is essentially at its lowest level. This explains why the dark spot goes away fairly quickly after looking at a bright light bulb. The recovery time for rod photoreceptors, however, is considerably longer—the lowest threshold levels are reached only around 20 minutes or more after bleaching. This means that as we move from photopic to scotopic lighting conditions, we will not be able to see with our rod photoreceptors until they gradually become unbleached. This sluggish recovery in rod

SideNote | 9.15

Experiments have shown that when measured psychophysically, as in the curves of Figure 9.10, dark adaptation recovery corresponds closely to the rate of rhodopsin pigment regeneration after bleaching. Thus, rod rhodopsin shows a regeneration time-course that can explain the rod dark adaptation curve, whereas cone rhodopsin recovery can explain the cone dark adaptation curve.

function is responsible for a common experience we all share upon entering a movie theatre. As we move from a much brighter (photopic) visual environment to the scotopic conditions of a theatre, we are unable to see anything because the rods are initially bleached and therefore non-functional. However, the rods become unbleached with time, and the interior of the theatre gradually becomes more visible (SideNote 9.15).

B. Neural Processing in the Retina

We now turn to the processes that take place in the retina beyond the photoreceptor level. The electrical signals that are created in the photoreceptor after light absorption are further processed by a network of interacting neurons. The ultimate result of this interaction is to produce a final electrical output that is sent to the visual brain. The complexity of the retinal analysis that takes place is truly astounding and has led to the view among some scientists that much of visual processing is actually done in the retina, with the brain just filling in the details. While this is not true, we will come to see that many fundamental aspects of visual function can be fully explained by neural processing that occurs strictly within the retina.

Our approach to understanding retinal function will be somewhat unconventional. We will begin first by looking at the output neurons of the retina—the so-called **retinal ganglion cells**. These are the only neurons in the retina whose axons actually leave the eyeball and therefore carry electrical signals to the brain. Once we understand the nature of those signals, we will be in a better position to examine how they are created and influenced by the intermediate-level neurons—that is, those residing between the ganglion cells and the photoreceptors. We will conclude this section by examining how retinal function varies across the retina, from the fovea to the periphery.

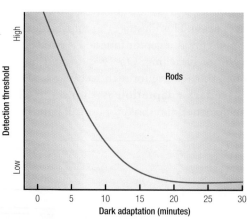

Figure 9.10

Dark adaptation curves are generated by measuring the detection threshold of a small light spot in the dark at various times following photoreceptor bleaching. Cone photoreceptors recover quite fast and show their lowest thresholds within 5 minutes after bleaching. Rod recovery is much more sluggish and only becomes complete after nearly 20 minutes in the dark following bleaching.

1. THE RETINAL GANGLION CELL

The retinal ganglion cell (RGC) represents the site in the retina at which a number of features first emerge (MacLeish et al., 1999; Tessier-Lavigne, 2000). As noted above, this is the only retinal neuron whose axon leaves the eye, whereas the axons of all other neurons remain within the retina. Second, ganglion cells represent the first site within the retina where action potentials are generated. Electrical activity in all other retinal neurons occurs by way of transient changes in the membrane potential, either depolarization or hyperpolarization, which spreads throughout the cell but never quite triggers an action potential. It is only at the ganglion cell level that we encounter the first set of neurons that is able to produce an action potential, which is quite important because these signals have to be transmitted along relatively large distances to the next structure in the visual pathway. And finally, ganglion cells represent the site at which we observe the emergence of parallel visual streams, an idea that will be introduced here and more fully elaborated in successive chapters.

Structure and layout of RGCs in the retina

The layout of the various retinal neurons is usually described in terms of three layers—the photoreceptor layer occupying the outermost margins, the **inner nuclear layer** lying within the middle segment of the retina, and the ganglion cell layer resting along the inside margin of the retina. Figure 9.11 shows a small segment of the retina that has been stained to reveal these layers and placed alongside a schematic diagram showing the various cell types (SideNote 9.16) (Boycott & Dowling, 1969). The arrangement of these layers in this sequence means that the ganglion cells are located closest to the crystalline lens. Thus, the incoming light rays have to first pass through the ganglion cells, then through the inner nuclear layer, before finally reaching the photoreceptors. This is a seemingly backward arrangement because one would expect the light-absorbing photoreceptors to be the first set of neurons to interact with incoming light rays. As it turns out, the transparency of retinal neurons means that there is little disruption in the passage of the photons through these cells on their way to the photoreceptor layer (SideNote 9.17).

American anatomist Stephen Polyak is credited with providing the first detailed structural description of ganglion cells in the primate retina (Polyak, 1957). Each human retina contains approximately 1.25 million ganglion cells. Polyak described several different classes of RGCs that differed in terms of their shape, size, and pattern of dendrites. Among the different types of RGCs, two are particularly important because they are present in relatively large numbers, and they play a major role in visual information processing. The so-called **midget ganglion cell** is characterized by its relative small size and compact **dendritic**

SideNote | **9.16**

The cell bodies of neurons are quite transparent and therefore cannot be directly visualized under a microscope unless the retinal tissue has been specially processed. A number of histological procedures have been developed to stain neurons so that their structures can be easily seen, as discussed in Chapter 2.

SideNote | **9.17**

A particular advantage to the photoreceptors being located along the outer margins of the retina is that they can be better anchored compared to those neurons that lie in front of it. Since photoreceptors are the "film" of the eye, it is necessary for them to be as stable as possible.

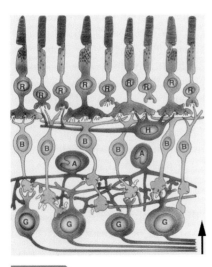 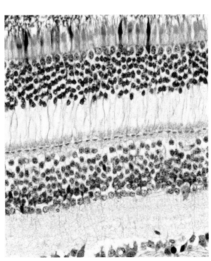

Pigment epithelium

Photoreceptor layer

Inner nuclear layer

Ganglion cell layer

Figure 9.11

The layout of retinal neurons is generally described in terms of three specific layers—the photoreceptor layer, the inner nuclear layer, and the ganglion cell layer. The right panel shows a small segment of the retina where the arrangement of these layers is displayed. The left panel shows a corresponding schematic drawing of the connections between the various retinal neurons. R—photoreceptor (rod and cone); B—bipolar cell; H—horizontal cell; A—amacrine cell; G—ganglion cell. The arrow shows the direction of incoming light rays. Adapted from "Organization of the Primate Retina: Light Microscopy," by B. B. Boycott and J. Dowling, 1969, in *Philosophical Transactions of the Royal Society B, 255*, pp. 109–184. Photo on right: STEVE GSCHMEISSNER/SCIENCE PHOTO LIBRARY

field. These cells are the most numerous of the ganglion cells, representing about 70% of the total, and are found in especially high densities in and around the fovea. The so-called **parasol ganglion cell** represents the second major cell type and accounts for about 10% of the total ganglion cell pool. These neurons are characterized by a relatively large size and dendritic field (Watanabe & Rodieck, 1989). The axons from both the midget and the parasol ganglion cells form the major output of the retina through the optic nerve and project to separate segments within the next structure along the visual pathway. We now know that visual function in primates is largely mediated through two separate but parallel pathways all the way to the brain, starting with these two ganglion cell types in the retina (Callaway, 2005; Lee, 2008; Wassle, 2004).

Electrical activity in ganglion cells

The most direct way to understand how ganglion cells respond to light stimulation is to place an electrode in the retina and record the electrical activity of these cells. As shown in Figure 9.12, electrical signals captured by a **microelectrode** are amplified and displayed on a device such as an oscilloscope. We are

particularly interested in detecting and counting the number of action potentials that are generated over a period of time. Early studies of retinal ganglion cells showed that these cells fire action potentials even in the total absence of light (Bruce & Georgeson, 1996; Rodieck, 1998). This is known as **spontaneous activity** and occurs at a rate of about 20–50 action potentials/second. What is especially surprising is that the random firing of action potentials in the dark persists even when the retina is flooded with uniform light. This is an odd result because it means that the very purpose of the retina, to detect light, does not affect the electrical state of ganglion cells under uniform illumination because they continue to discharge at the spontaneous rate.

The solution to this problem lies in the fact that retinal ganglion cells are not set up to signal overall light levels but rather are optimized for the detection of differences in light stimulation in adjacent parts of the retina. Hungarian-American physiologist Stephen Kuffler was the first to show precisely how this occurs (Kuffler, 1953). The very fact that ganglion cells have a high spontaneous discharge of action potentials means that their firing rate can go in two directions—a sudden increase or decrease in activity. By using very small spots of light, Kuffler showed that single ganglion cells can be excited when light falls in one part of the retina, whereas the same neuron can be inhibited when the light spot is moved to surrounding parts (SideNote 9.18). The area of the retina that influences a neuron, by way of either excitation or inhibition, is known as its **receptive field**. Kuffler found that every ganglion cell is affected by only a limited region of the retina that is roughly circular in shape. Figure 9.12 shows a flattened profile of a retina where a hypothetical receptive field of a ganglion cell is displayed.

Receptive field structure of ganglion cells

The idea that a neuron can only be activated by a limited region of a sensory surface is not new. We encountered this very idea in Chapter 3 where we found that mechanoreceptor neurons in the somatosensory system can only be stimulated by touch through a limited patch of skin surface. Exactly the same principle applies in the visual system except here the stimulus is light, and the sensory surface is the retina. Kuffler showed that the receptive field of ganglion cells can be divided into

SideNote | **9.18**

The term *excitation* here means that the number of action potentials/second is greater than the spontaneous firing rate for the same neuron, whereas *inhibition* implies that the firing rate is below spontaneous firing.

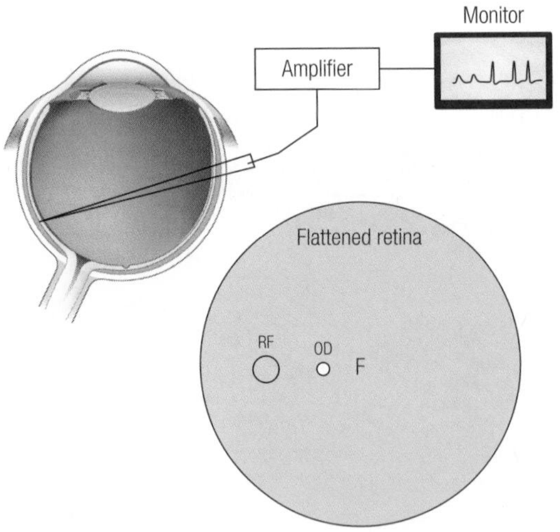

Monitor

Amplifier

Flattened retina

RF   OD   F

Figure 9.12

Electrical activity in ganglion cells can be recorded with a microelectrode placed in the retina. The signals are then amplified and displayed on a monitor to reveal any action potentials that take place in response to light stimulation. The area of retina that influences the activity of a visual neuron such as a retinal ganglion cell is known as the *receptive field*. The flattened profile of the retina in the bottom diagram shows the fovea (F) in the centre, the optic disk (OD), and the receptive field (RF) of a single ganglion cell.

METHODOLOGY

Electroretinograms and Their Functions

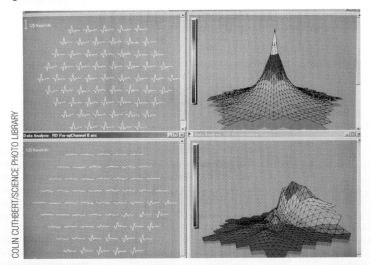

COLIN CUTHBERT/SCIENCE PHOTO LIBRARY

It has been known for over a century that a light stimulus presented to the eye can cause a change in photoreceptors' electrical potential, but it was not until Holmgren and Dewar began to study these visual properties in the late 1800s that the electroretinogram (ERG) was developed for lab use. Then, in the 1940s, an alternative use (besides research) was discovered for the ERG—to clinically diagnose different visual disorders. Electroretinograms work by measuring the electrical responses of the different cells in the retina by electrodes near the eye and sometimes through contacts with electrodes on the cornea. This can be done in dark-adapted or light-adapted conditions, depending on whether you want to measure the rods or cones. By knowing the precise amount of light entering the eye, and the exact amount of electricity produced for that light, we can determine if the photoreceptors are working properly. Not only are ERGs used to diagnose inheritable diseases, but they are also used to determine if retinal surgery is an option to try and restore visual function.

two zones—an area of excitation and an area of inhibition based on the response to light. If a light spot should fall on the excitatory part of the receptive field, then the ganglion cell displays a burst of action potentials over and above its spontaneous discharge rate. If, however, the light should fall on the inhibitory part of the receptive field, then the ganglion cell displays a sudden decrease in firing that is well below its spontaneous rate. Neuroscientists usually refer to these two types of responses as *ON* and *OFF*.

Kuffler showed that virtually all retinal ganglion cells have a receptive field that is made up of both an excitatory and an inhibitory component. The spatial arrangement of the ON and OFF areas is shown in Figure 9.13 on page 288 (Kuffler, 1953; Ratliff, 1974). This figure shows a schematic eye looking out at a screen, where "x" marks the fixation point that

is imaged on the fovea. The receptive field of the ganglion cell we are recording from can be extended into space and projected onto this screen, as shown by the white disk. In other words, light falling within this circular region on the screen will be imaged onto the retinal patch that defines the receptive field of this particular ganglion cell (SideNote 9.19). Further probing of the receptive field shows that the circular excitatory and inhibitory areas overlap each other, as shown in the boxed panel of Figure 9.13. In one type of cell, a centre circular region is excited by light stimulation (ON area), whereas the surrounding zone is inhibited by light (OFF area). A second type of cell is arranged in exactly the opposite manner. By convention, the first cell is referred to as an **ON/OFF** type, whereas the second is referred to as an **OFF/ON** type. All ganglion cells display either an ON/OFF or an OFF/ON

SideNote | **9.19**

The receptive field is mapped in this way during an actual experiment. An electrode is placed in the retina or optic nerve to examine the activity of a single ganglion cell. A light spot is then placed in various parts of the screen until an area is found that influences the activity of the cell being recorded. The receptive field is defined as the part of the screen where a light probe will have either an excitatory or an inhibitory influence on the neuron.

type receptive field, and there are roughly equal numbers of both in the retina.

Retinal ganglion cells are optimized for detecting contrast

The concentric spatial arrangement of the ON and OFF sub-regions in the receptive field leads to a property known as **centre–surround antagonism**. In other words, the two fields oppose each other in terms of how they influence the firing rate of ganglion cells (Tessier-Lavigne, 2000; Trobe & Leonello, 2001). A simple example with an ON/OFF ganglion cell can illustrate this point (see Figure 9.14). If a light spot should fall only on the centre of its receptive field, then the cell will show a burst of action potentials. However, if the light spot is enlarged so that it encroaches into the surrounding OFF region, then there will be a reduction in the number of action potentials because of the inhibitory influence from the surround. When the light spot is made large enough to cover the entire receptive field, the ganglion cell will theoretically fire at its spontaneous rate because the excitation through its centre is exactly counterbalanced by the inhibition from the surround (SideNote 9.20). It is this fact that accounts for the observation we noted above in which uniform diffuse light does not lead to increased neural activity in retinal ganglion cells over and above their spontaneous firing rate.

SideNote | 9.20

We assume that the ganglion cell receives an equal influence from the centre as well as the surround. While this may be the case, there can be subtle differences in the weighting of the two inputs so that the influence of one sub-region may dominate the other.

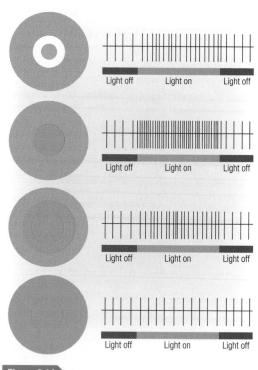

Figure 9.14

The firing rate of an ON/OFF ganglion cell is shown in response to light spots of different sizes. Action potentials are shown by vertical line segments over a brief period in which the light spot is on, in between two periods when there is no light stimulation. The discharges during the "light off" periods correspond to the spontaneous firing rate. A small light spot placed in the centre of the receptive field, shown by the light blue disk, produces a mild increase in the firing rate (top diagram). The ganglion cell is maximally stimulated when the light spot fills the excitatory centre. The firing rate declines if the light spot is enlarged to encroach into the inhibitory surround. When the light spot fills the entire receptive field, there is no discernible change in firing from the spontaneous rate (bottom diagram).

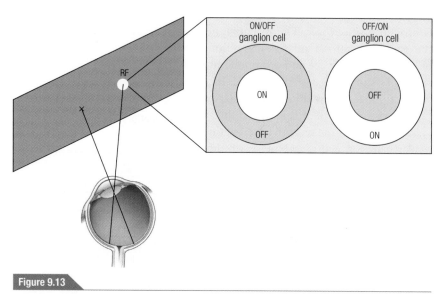

Figure 9.13

The receptive field of a retinal ganglion cell can be projected onto a screen where the presence of light within a roughly circular region will affect the firing rate. The receptive field can have one of two arrangements—a central excitatory area with a surround inhibitory zone (ON/OFF cell) or vice versa (OFF/ON cell).

The centre–surround antagonistic property of these receptive fields has an important consequence—the retinal output sent to the brain by ganglion cells is driven by light contrast (Kaplan & Shapley, 1986; Tessier-Lavigne, 2000; Westheimer, 2007). An ON/OFF ganglion cell, for example, will maximally fire to a light spot that precisely fills its centre excitatory region in the presence of a dark surround. Similarly, an OFF/ON ganglion cell will maximally fire to a dark spot that fills its centre in the presence of a light surround. Both types of cells therefore prefer contrasting stimuli to be placed in the centre and surround segments of their receptive fields. The fact that neurons this early in the visual pathway display a strong preference for light contrast is not surprising. Our natural visual world is made up of objects that differ considerably in their light reflectance. Hence, the retinal image at any given time is a mosaic of components that differ in their intensity. A key objective of the visual system is to distinguish these various objects from their surround so that they can be recognized. The best way to segment an image is on the basis of light contrast (i.e., to detect borders separating two different regions of light intensity). Our visual system is very efficient at this task largely because it has such robust contrast detectors placed very early in its processing pathways.

2.   ELECTRICAL CIRCUITS IN THE RETINA

Our discussion above leads us to the following question—how does a ganglion cell's receptive field arise in the first place? Naturally, the first step is the absorption of light by photoreceptors, which in turn generates an electrical signal. That signal is then processed by an intermediate set of neurons located within the middle band of cells in the retina, known as the *inner nuclear layer*, before arriving at the ganglion cells. The electrical circuitry within this set of intermediate-level neurons is what endows ganglion cells with their properties. We now examine the electrical circuits that create the centre–surround antagonistic receptive fields of the ganglion cells.

Bipolar cells mediate the centre response

The two major retinal cell classes we have covered thus far include the photoreceptors and the ganglion cells. We now introduce a third class whose cell body is situated between these two. The main function of these so-called **bipolar cells** is to transmit signals between the photoreceptors and ganglion cells (SideNote 9.21) (Dowling, 1987; Dowling, 1979; Masland, 2001). However, in so doing, the bipolar cells produce some interesting consequences, which we can understand by way of the schematic diagram in Figure 9.15. As shown here, a cone photoreceptor is connected to two different bipolar cells—an ON bipolar and an OFF bipolar. We first look at the sequence of events that occur if a light stimulus falls on this particular photoreceptor (left panel in Figure 9.15). We already know two things that will happen right away after it absorbs this light—there will first be a brief hyperpolarization followed by a sudden drop

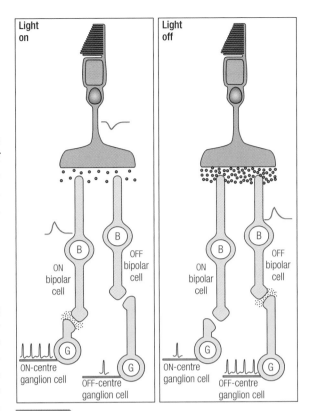

Figure 9.15

A schematic diagram of a simple retinal circuit shows that the transmission of signals from photoreceptors to ganglion cells occurs through either an ON or an OFF bipolar cell. These two types of bipolar cells behave differently in response to glutamate release by photoreceptors. This differential effect is responsible for producing either an excitatory (ON) or an inhibitory (OFF) centre response within the receptive fields of ganglion cells.

in the photoreceptor's release of the neurotransmitter glutamate.

The reduction in glutamate release has an odd effect on the ON bipolar cell—it actually becomes depolarized (stimulated) (Rodieck, 1998). This is an unexpected result because glutamate is an excitatory neurotransmitter that is usually associated with postsynaptic depolarization (i.e., it stimulates the next neuron). Thus, a reduction in glutamate release by the photoreceptor should certainly not stimulate the ON bipolar cell. The reason this happens is because ON bipolars have the odd property of becoming spontaneously depolarized in the absence of glutamate. In fact, glutamate actually turns off this spontaneous depolarization. Thus, light ends up stimulating the ON bipolars but through a rather unconventional manner. The OFF bipolars, on the other hand, do not show such an effect and therefore are not depolarized in the presence of light (Rodieck, 1998). Rather, as the right

SideNote 9.21

It would be worthwhile to take a brief look back at Figure 9.11 to review the cellular components of the retina, especially the inner nuclear layer where bipolar cells are located.

panel in Figure 9.15 shows, the OFF bipolar cell is stimulated when the light spot is turned off. In this case, the photoreceptor is no longer hyperpolarized, and it returns to a state where much greater glutamate is being released. The OFF bipolars behave like conventional neurons in that increased glutamate release causes them to become depolarized. Thus, the OFF bipolars that are linked to a particular photoreceptor are stimulated only when that photoreceptor is not absorbing light.

The impact of these two scenarios can now be evaluated in terms of ganglion cell function. We know that each of the two types of bipolar cells is in turn linked to a separate ganglion cell. Whenever an ON or an OFF bipolar cell is stimulated, it will release glutamate that will in turn stimulate the ganglion cell connected to it. We have thus created two separate types of ganglion cells—one that is stimulated by a light spot through an intermediate ON bipolar cell and another that is stimulated by a dark spot through an intermediate OFF bipolar cell. What we have just described is the centre response property of the two types of ganglion

cells we were introduced to earlier—the ON/OFF and the OFF/ON response types. A ganglion cell with an ON centre receptive field will only be stimulated when a light spot is present in a circular patch directly below it, whereas a ganglion cell with an OFF centre will only be stimulated if no light falls upon that circular patch (SideNote 9.22). Ganglion cells behave as typical neurons in that a sufficient amount of depolarization will create action potentials that are then transmitted through their axons.

Horizontal and amacrine cells mediate the surround response

Although the precise details of how the centre response is generated in ganglion cells are now fairly well known, it remains unclear as to exactly how the surround response is produced. It is apparent that two other types of intermediate neurons situated between the photoreceptors and ganglion cells are involved. The so-called **horizontal cells** are thought to play a major role because they display processes that branch out in a lateral manner and make contact with adjacent photoreceptors, as shown by the schematic diagram in Figure 9.16 (Boycott & Dowling, 1969; Dowling, 1979; Tessier-Lavigne, 2000). It is this lateral sampling that allows horizontal cells to gather signals over a fairly large area of the retina, which is precisely what would be needed for them to play a role in generating the surround response. The signals produced by light absorption in the surrounding photoreceptors are passed onto the horizontal cells, which in turn inhibit the photoreceptors linked to the centre response. In this way, the firing rate of an ON/OFF ganglion cell is reduced if a light spot falling on its excitatory centre is enlarged sufficiently to encroach into the inhibitory surround.

Another group of neurons that may participate in generating the surround response are the **amacrine cells**. There are a large number of amacrine cell types, and most of their functions are poorly understood. As shown in Figure 9.16, amacrine cells also make lateral connections (Dowling, 1979). However, these connections are entirely at the level of the bipolar and ganglion cells, and therefore the lateral interactions are quite distinct from those of the horizontal cells. Both the horizontal and the amacrine cells are examples of neurons that are responsible for one of the most fundamental and commonly observed properties of the nervous system—**lateral**

SideNote | **9.22**

The circuit described here shows the simplest form possible (i.e., one cone linked to one bipolar cell linked to one ganglion cell). While this does happen in the fovea, the circuit in much of the retina shows many photoreceptors converging upon a single bipolar cell and in turn many bipolars converging upon a single ganglion cell. Thus, the centre response of a ganglion cell is usually driven by the summed outputs of many photoreceptors lying below it.

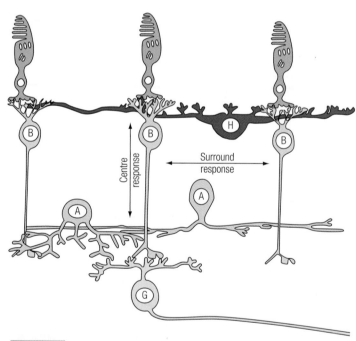

Figure 9.16

The surround response in a ganglion cell emerges as a result of lateral interactions within the retina. These interactions occur at the level of the photoreceptors by way of the horizontal cells (H) and at the level of bipolar (B) and ganglion (G) cells by way of the so-called *amacrine cells* (A). The lateral interactions are always opposite in nature to the centre response, thereby setting up the property of centre–surround antagonism in the receptive fields of ganglion cells. Adapted from "Information Processing by Local Circuits: The Vertebrate Retina as a Model System," by J. E. Dowling, 1979, in *The Neurosciences: Fourth Study Program*, Eds. F. O. Schmitt and F. G. Worden, Cambridge, MA: MIT Press.

inhibition. It is through this mechanism that ganglion cells inherit the property of centre–surround antagonism and become endowed with a receptive field that is optimized for the detection of light contrast (Dowling, 1979; Ratliff, 1974; Tessier-Lavigne, 2000).

Retinal processing of rod photoreceptor signals

The retinal circuits involved in the transfer of rod photoreceptor signals show many similarities to the cone circuits discussed above. For example, rod signals are also transmitted to bipolar cells, and there are similarities in the way that horizontal cells mediate lateral interactions among neighbouring rods. However, there do not appear to be any ganglion cells that are specifically dedicated to transmitting rod signals out of the retina. Instead, these signals merge into the cone signal pathway and arrive at the same set of ganglion cells (Blomfield & Dacheux, 2001; Rodieck, 1998). The precise circuit is now well known and involves a specific type of amacrine cell that connects the two pathways. As a result, all of our scotopic visual functions are ultimately handled by the same set of ganglion cells used by the photopic system (SideNote 9.23).

3. VISUAL PROCESSING ACROSS THE RETINA

Centre–surround antagonism is a hallmark of retinal processing and can be seen throughout the retina. However, this does not mean that the electrical circuits are identical throughout all parts of the retina. We have already seen how photoreceptor distribution can vary. For example, the fovea has a very high concentration of cones and no rods, whereas the peripheral retina contains far more rods than cones. Thus, ganglion cells in the fovea are exclusively driven by cones, whereas those in the periphery are driven by a mixture of rods and cones. Furthermore, the number of photoreceptors that feed into a ganglion cell differs systematically across the retina, a fact that has considerable impact on visual function.

The retina is not of uniform thickness

The cellular components of the retina have a fixed spatial relationship to each other that accounts for its relatively uniform thickness, approximately 250 micrometres. However, the thickness at the centre of the retina is

considerably less because of a small depression known as the **foveal pit**. The pit arises because all of the neurons (except photoreceptors) are shifted to one side, as shown in Figure 9.17 (Tessier-Lavigne, 2000). This arrangement allows for incoming light rays to have unimpeded access to the photoreceptors. Consequently, the quality of the optical image is enhanced at the fovea because there is less chance of light distortion or scatter, which might happen in other parts of the retina where light rays have to first pass through a number of neurons before reaching the photoreceptor layer. The high quality of the optical image is one reason why the foveal region is able to process fine details in the visual image.

Retinal wiring differs with eccentricity

The main reason for our visual system's ability to see fine detail through the fovea, however, rests on the way that neurons are wired (Dowling, 1987; Field & Chichilinisky, 2007;

SideNote | **9.23**

The major difference between the scotopic and photopic visual systems therefore rests at the photoreceptor level. Also, some of the early retinal elements, such as the bipolar and horizontal cells, have subclasses that selectively process rod signals. However, the same output neurons (i.e., ganglion cells) are used by the two systems.

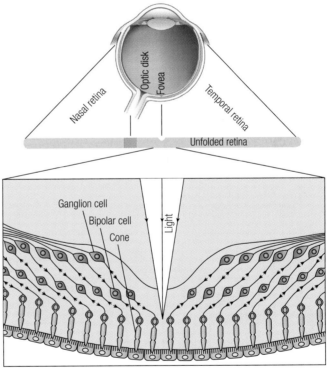

Figure 9.17

Retinal neurons, with the exception of photoreceptors, shift to one side in the fovea. This creates a pit that allows light to have unimpeded access to the photoreceptor layer. Furthermore, the neurons in the fovea are finely wired and can reach their lowest limit where one photoreceptor is connected to one bipolar cell that in turn is connected to one ganglion cell. Both of these properties endow the foveal retina with the ability to sample fine detail in the visual image. Adapted from "Visual Processing by the Retina," by M. Tessier-Lavigne, 2000, in *Principles of Neural Science* (4th ed.), Eds. E. R. Kandel, J. G. Schwartz, and T. M. Jessell, New York, NY: McGraw-Hill.

SideNote **9.24**

The description here of course refers to the neural elements that produce the centre response in a ganglion cell. A similar tight arrangement is in place for generating the surround response by way of the cells in the *inner nuclear layer*.

SideNote **9.25**

The small receptive field size in the fovea is exactly what would be needed for sampling fine detail in the visual image. A ganglion cell with a small receptive field is able to detect differences in light contrast over a smaller area compared to a ganglion cell with a large receptive field.

Rodieck, 1998). As Figure 9.17 shows, the cells lying above the photoreceptor layer are connected to each other in an exclusive manner. Thus, a single photoreceptor is connected to a single bipolar cell that is in turn connected to a single ganglion cell. This is as good as it gets in terms of **spatial sampling** because one light detector (photoreceptor) is ultimately connected to one output neuron (ganglion cell) in this part of the retina (SideNote 9.24). The visual brain is therefore receiving signals through a dedicated electrical wire for the smallest possible patch of the retinal image that can be sampled. Accordingly, our ability to see fine detail becomes especially enhanced in the fovea because no information is lost, as would happen, for example, if the signals from several photoreceptors converged upon a single ganglion cell.

A one-to-one relationship between photoreceptors and ganglion cells is a special feature of the fovea and not seen elsewhere in the retina. Recall that there are a total of 126 million photoreceptors in each eye (120 million rods + 6 million cones). However, there are only 1.25 million ganglion cells. Thus, given these numbers alone, a one-to-one relationship simply cannot be maintained throughout the retina. The solution to this problem lies in signal convergence (i.e., signals from multiple photoreceptors converging upon a single ganglion cell). This is precisely what happens outside of the fovea, as shown in Figure 9.18. In the immediate vicinity of the fovea, there are a few photoreceptors that converge upon a single ganglion cell. At more peripheral parts of the retina, the convergence is much greater, such that each ganglion cell is receiving input from a much larger array of photoreceptors. In general, the greater the retinal **eccentricity**, the greater the number of photoreceptor signals feeding into a ganglion cell.

There are two aspects of this eccentricity relationship that are worth noting (Dowling, 1979; Rodieck, 1998). First, the dendritic field of the ganglion cells must also increase with eccentricity so as to allow them to receive signals from a greater number of bipolar cells (see Figure 9.18). This is indeed what happens. The dendrites of ganglion cells around the fovea are very constricted, whereas those in the peripheral retina cover a much greater area. Second, the receptive field of ganglion cells must also show systematic changes with retinal eccentricity. This would be expected simply because the receptive field is defined by the extent of the retina that influences a visual neuron. As Figure 9.18 shows, a ganglion cell located near the fovea has a much smaller receptive field compared to one located in the periphery. The smallest receptive fields are of course found in the fovea (SideNote 9.25).

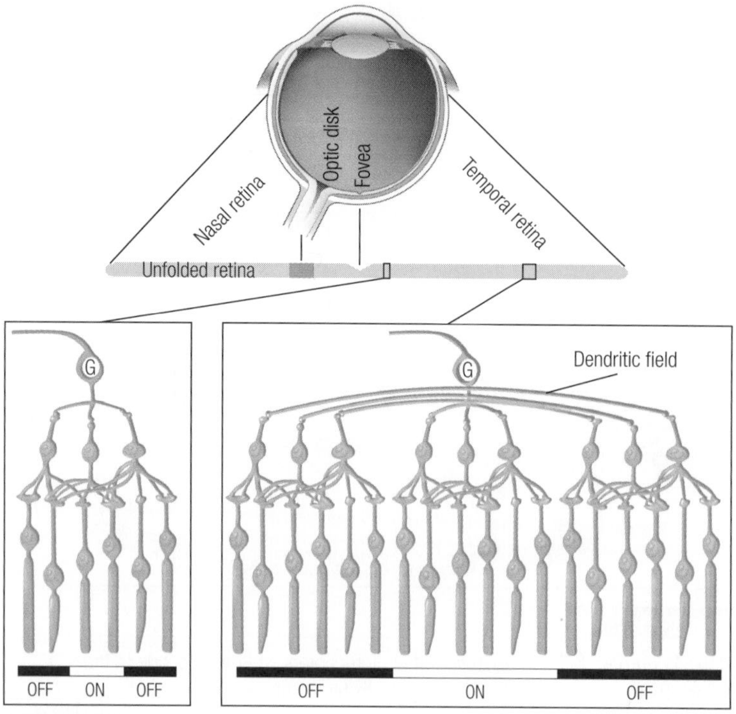

Midget and parasol ganglion cells show different sampling properties

We noted earlier that there are two major types of ganglion cells—midget and parasol (Silveira et al., 2004; Wassle, 2004; Watanabe & Rodieck, 1989). Both types display centre–surround receptive fields with ON/OFF and OFF/ON arrangements. Although both types are found throughout the retina, the midget type is more dominant in terms of numbers. Another difference between the two concerns the dendritic field size. As Figure 9.19 shows, midget ganglion cells have a smaller dendritic field than those of the parasol type at all retinal eccentricities. This means that at any given point in the retina, a parasol ganglion cell will have a larger receptive field than a midget ganglion cell. These anatomical and functional differences

Figure 9.18

Ganglion cells in the periphery are fed by signals from a larger part of the retina compared to those located in the more central parts of the retina. As a result, peripheral ganglion cells must have a larger dendritic field in order to sample from a larger area. This also causes the receptive fields of ganglion cells to become progressively larger at increasing retinal eccentricities.

set the stage for the emergence of two distinct and separate signal pathways to the brain.

C. Perceptual Aspects of Retinal Function

The neural signals that emerge out of the retina are used by the brain to create the perceptual impression that we know as vision. Although a considerable amount of neural processing must take place in the brain before we can *see*, it turns out that many aspects of visual perception can be explained simply in terms of retinal function. Visual information in any given part of the real world is sampled through a small set of ganglion cells whose receptive fields can be mapped onto that point in space (SideNote 9.26). We can therefore think of the retinal output as a sampling of the visual world through a multitude of ganglion cells. Thus, many aspects of our visual experience are regulated by the properties of ganglion cells and, in particular, their predisposition for contrast detection.

A number of visual phenomena can be explained at an elemental level by way of rod and cone function. We noted before how some of the properties of photoreceptors, such as their preference for certain light wavelengths, can account for various perceptual properties when assessed at the behavioural level. In fact, the division of visual function into the scotopic and photopic ranges is largely derived from the signalling abilities of rod and cone photoreceptors. Those properties along with the way photoreceptor signals converge onto the ganglion cells account for such fundamental perceptual qualities as how well we can see spatial detail (resolution) and how little light is actually required for a visual stimulus to be detected (sensitivity).

The goal of this section is to discuss a broad range of perceptual phenomena in human vision that can be tied directly to the biological aspects of retinal function. The important point to keep in mind is that two factors are at work—the nature of photoreceptor function (i.e., rods *versus* cones) and the way their signals arrive at the ganglion cells though an intermediate plexus of retinal neurons. Both factors have considerable impact on the output signals produced by ganglion cells, which in turn account for a range of perceptual properties that are collectively referred to as *early vision*.

1. SENSITIVITY

Visual sensitivity simply refers to our ability to detect light stimuli, either something as simple as seeing a point of light under optimal conditions or when more complex situations are present, such as a flickering stimulus. As a general rule, there is a trade-off between sensitivity and resolution. The conditions under which visual sensitivity is enhanced also represent the conditions under which visual resolution is reduced. For example, the scotopic system shows far greater light sensitivity than photopic vision because of the lower activation threshold of rod photoreceptors (Bruce & Georgeson, 1996; Schwartz, 1999). However, that superior sensitivity is offset by a much poorer ability of the scotopic system at resolving image detail, something that the photopic system is particular good at (Cornsweet, 1970). Much of our understanding of the relationship between these twin facets of vision—sensitivity and resolution—arose during the 20th century through the tireless work of many gifted vision scientists.

The absolute threshold of vision

An oft-cited example is the work of Selig Hecht who, along with his colleagues Simon Schlaer and Maurice Pirenne, undertook the first detailed experiments on light sensitivity (Hecht, Schlaer, & Pirenne, 1942). Much of the impetus for this research arose as a result

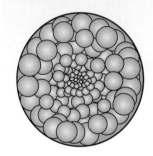

SideNote 9.26

There is some overlap among the receptive fields of ganglion cells within a particular part of the retina. The visual scene is therefore sampled by an array of overlapping receptive fields, as shown in the schematic figure below of a flattened retina. Note how receptive fields become progressively larger in the periphery.

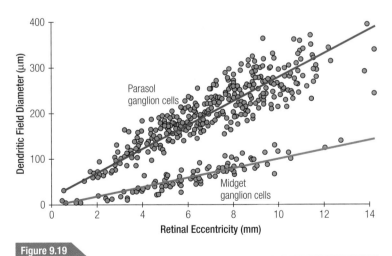

Figure 9.19

The relationship between dendritic field diameter and eccentricity shows two broad clusters. At any given eccentricity, parasol ganglion cells have larger dendritic fields, and therefore larger receptive fields, than those of the midget ganglion cells. The output of these two ganglion cell types forms the front end of two distinct visual pathways. Eccentricity values are measured from the fovea. Adapted from "Parasol and Midget Ganglion Cells of the Primate Retina," by M. Watanabe and R. W. Rodieck, 1989, *Journal of Comparative Neurology, 289,* pp. 434–454.

of practical questions that needed to be addressed during the Second World War (SideNote 9.27). Hecht and his colleagues tested visual sensitivity under optimal conditions, such as complete dark adaptation, placing the light spot in the peripheral retina with the highest density of rods and using a stimulus wavelength close to the peak of the rod absorption spectrum. Under these conditions, they found that the absolute detection threshold was as low as a mere 90 photons delivered to the surface of the cornea. Of these, they assumed that only 10 or so photons actually arrived at the retina because of reflection at the corneal surface as well as absorption and scattering within the various chambers of the eye. Given the size of the light spot, it was calculated that these 10 photons had to be spread over a retinal patch that contained around 350 rods. A statistical analysis based on these numbers led Hecht and his colleagues to the astounding conclusion that rod photoreceptors are capable of responding to single photons under such ideal conditions. This result was verified in 1979 by Denis Baylor and his co-workers at Stanford University, who showed by way of physiological experiments that rods from the toad retina are able to respond to a single photon (Baylor, Lamb, & Yau, 1979).

Scotopic vs. photopic sensitivity

The data reported by Hecht and his colleagues represent the lowest possible threshold limit because the experiments were conducted under ideal conditions. A small alteration that would cause a dramatic increase in the threshold value is to present the light spot on the fovea, where there are no rods. The higher activation threshold of cones suggests right away that there would be a corresponding increase in light detection threshold at the fovea. This resulting difference would therefore be due solely to the photoreceptor class involved in mediating the detection of light.

A comprehensive way of looking at the sensitivity differences between rod- and cone-mediated vision is to compare their spectral sensitivity curves. Recall from Section A.3 that light sensitivity shows an upside-down U-shaped relationship with wavelength and that the scotopic and photopic functions peak at different wavelengths (SideNote 9.28). Figure 9.20 shows these two functions again but this time in relation to each other. The scotopic sensitivity profile is higher throughout the visible

spectrum except at very long wavelengths, where photopic vision is actually more sensitive. This is because the absorption spectrum of rod rhodopsin declines rapidly at long wavelengths (Hood & Finkelstein, 1986; Tessier-Lavigne, 2000). In fact, there is very little light absorption by rod photoreceptors beyond 650 nm, and therefore all visual functions are mediated only by the photopic system. One way that photopic vision can dominate at wavelengths below 650 nm is under certain pathological conditions such as night blindness (**nyctalopia**).

Taking a closer look at Figure 9.20, we see that the two sensitivity curves are shifted both vertically and horizontally with respect to each other. This has certain consequences for visual function (Cornsweet, 1970; Davson, 1990; Wade & Swanston, 2001). Assume that you are looking at a subthreshold patch of light that is exactly 450 nm. As the light intensity increases, you will first see it with your scotopic system because it is far more sensitive at this wavelength. However, you will not be

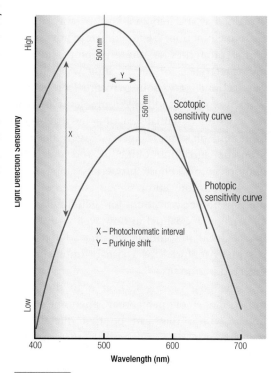

Figure 9.20

The scotopic and photopic spectral sensitivity curves show both a vertical and a horizontal shift. The vertical difference between the two functions at any given wavelength is known as the *photochromatic interval*, whereas the horizontal shift of peak sensitivity between 550 nm and 500 nm is known as the *Purkinje shift*. The scotopic system is far more sensitive at all wavelengths except the upper end (> 650 nm) where all visual functions are mediated only by the photopic system.

able to tell its colour because rod vision is colour-blind. It is only after the light intensity is further increased so as to reach the cone activation threshold that its colour will become apparent. The vertical distance between the scotopic and photopic curves at this wavelength, shown by the arrow marked "x" in Figure 9.20, indicates the sensitivity difference between just seeing a light (scotopic vision) and just being able to tell its colour (photopic vision). This so-called **photochromatic interval** is greatest at low wavelengths and decreases at longer wavelengths.

We know that the two systems operate optimally at different wavelengths, as indicated by the horizontal difference between the two curves in Figure 9.20. Assume that we are looking at a visual scene and the overall illumination is reduced so that our vision shifts from photopic to scotopic processing. All coloured objects will now appear as different shades of grey. However, there will also be a shift in the perceived brightness of various objects depending on their previous colour. Those objects that were green under photopic conditions will actually appear brighter with scotopic vision, whereas yellow and red objects will appear dimmer. This is because the shift from photopic to scotopic levels is accompanied by a transition of the peak wavelength of sensitivity from 550 nm to 500 nm, as shown by the arrow marked "y" in Figure 9.20 (Rodieck, 1998; Valberg, 2005; Wandell, 1995). Thus, objects whose colours are associated with lower wavelengths, such as green, appear brighter because the scotopic system is more sensitive at those wavelengths. This transition in visual sensitivity is called the **Purkinje shift** in honour of Czech physiologist Johannes (Jan) Purkinje, who first described it in the early 1800s (SideNote 9.29).

Sensitivity and retinal eccentricity

Another factor that has considerable bearing on visual sensitivity is the amount of signal convergence upon a ganglion cell. We noted before that the peripheral retina contains ganglion cells with larger dendritic fields, and therefore they are able to collect information from a larger array of photoreceptors (Rodieck, 1998). The principle by which greater signal convergence leads to greater light sensitivity is illustrated in Figure 9.21. Let us assume that signals from five cone photoreceptors converge upon a ganglion cell in the central part of the

retina (left image), whereas in the periphery, the signals from 15 rod photoreceptors converge upon a ganglion cell (right image). In the latter case, a dim light spot that is spread over this array (stimulus 1) will have a better chance of triggering a signal out of the ganglion cell because the entire photoreceptor output is pooled (or summated). On the other hand, the ganglion cells that are sampling from a smaller central array are handicapped because the energy from the same dim light spot is now divided among three ganglion cell inputs, resulting in far less signal summation. Hence, in this instance it is likely that we will not be able to perceive the presence of the dim light spot.

The trade-off between sensitivity and resolution referred to earlier is also apparent in Figure 9.21. Although ganglion cells located in the retinal periphery have greater light sensitivity, they are less able to convey image detail. If a trio of smaller light spots is now placed in the same part of the retina (stimulus 2), they will be indistinguishable because the entire array of rod photoreceptors stimulated by these three spots converges upon one ganglion cell. Therefore, the signal sent to the visual brain cannot distinguish between a large light spot or three smaller ones. That is not true in the more central parts of the retina where the smaller degree of signal convergence allows ganglion cells to be independently stimulated by a smaller array of cone photoreceptors. Thus, the convergence factor alone has a considerable impact on light detection sensitivity

SideNote | **9.29**

The perceptual effect accompanying the Purkinje shift can be easily demonstrated in a garden at dusk. As the overall light level changes from photopic to scotopic levels, yellow and red flowers appear to become much dimmer, whereas green foliage will appear relatively brighter.

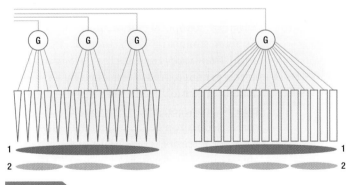

Figure 9.21

The ganglion cells on the left are handicapped in detecting a dim light spot (stimulus 1) due to the limited amount of signal pooling from the convergence of only a few cones. However, they are better suited at distinguishing a series of smaller light spots (stimulus 2) as long as they are of sufficient intensity to drive the cones. In the periphery, greater signal convergence from rods allows greater signal pooling and therefore enhanced light sensitivity (right image). The cost here is that the ganglion cells have poor spatial resolution because they cannot distinguish between a series of smaller spots over the same array.

and resolution and accounts for our relative abilities in these facets of visual function across the retina (Rodieck, 1998; Wandell, 1995).

Integration over space and time

The same principles of signal pooling by ganglion cells can be used to explain the relationship between detection threshold and area of stimulation (Cornsweet, 1970; Davson, 1990). Assume that we have a very small light spot that is of sufficient intensity to be just detected. We would expect that threshold intensity value to be reduced if the light spot is enlarged. The reason is that as the spot size becomes larger, a greater number of photoreceptors are stimulated, and therefore more signals converge upon a ganglion cell. Hence, the overall intensity needed to generate the same output from the ganglion cell becomes smaller. This idea of spatial summation is formalized by way of **Ricco's law**, which states that the product of light intensity and stimulation area (i.e., the total amount of light) must reach a critical level for detection to occur (SideNote 9.30). It turns out, however, that any increase in stimulation area beyond a certain size does not yield a further reduction in threshold intensity because the enlarged light spot now presumably exceeds the summation area for the ganglion cells.

Our visual system displays an analogous property in terms of stimulation time. Consider a simple example from photography, where the standard rule is to increase the exposure time under conditions of weak lighting. This allows the photons to integrate over time and thereby expose the film sufficiently to produce an acceptable photo. The visual system also shows a similar temporal summation of photons. As with stimulation area, there is a trade-off with stimulation time such that any increase in this parameter is accompanied by a decrease in light intensity needed for threshold detection (Cornsweet, 1970; Davson, 1990). If the stimulus duration decreases, on the other hand, a greater intensity is needed to make it detectable. This idea is formalized by way of **Bloch's law**, which states that the product of light intensity and duration must reach a critical value to produce threshold detection. There is, however, an upper limit to how well time and intensity can be combined in a co-operative manner. For photopic vision, that limit is about 30 milliseconds, whereas for scotopic vision, it is around 100 milliseconds. Beyond these times, there is no further benefit to increasing

stimulus duration in terms of reducing threshold intensity.

Increment threshold and contrast detectability

It is fitting that we end our discussion on visual sensitivity with a brief review of the perceptual aspects of contrast detection, given that ganglion cells are ideally constructed for that purpose. It is for this reason that ganglion cells are maximally stimulated when light spots are presented upon a dark background or vice versa. This leads to the question "How sensitive is the centre–surround arrangement in conveying contrast information?" In terms of perceptual function, this can be determined by the **increment threshold** or minimum contrast needed for a light spot to be detected against a background of a particular intensity (Amesbury & Schallhorn, 2003; Davson, 1990; Hood & Finkelstein, 1986). This question is also of historical interest because of the early work by psychophysicists, such as Ernst Weber, who explored this issue as part of a broader agenda to understand the relationship between stimulus intensity, contrast, and sensation (SideNote 9.31).

An increment threshold experiment is carried out by simply finding the extra intensity (ΔI) that is just needed to detect a small light spot against a background of a particular intensity (IB), as shown in the inset of Figure 9.22. As the background intensity increases, it is expected that a greater change will be needed to detect the light spot. In other words, the increment threshold should increase as the background intensity increases. This is precisely what happens, as shown by the threshold versus intensity (TVI) relationship given in Figure 9.22. When this experiment is conducted with a small spot placed just outside the fovea, the TVI relationship shows two branches—one attributed to rod function and the other to cone function. At a low background intensity, visual function is mediated only by rod photoreceptors, and therefore the TVI curve here represents the contrast detectability profile of scotopic vision. As the background intensity rises, cone photoreceptors are activated and become responsible for retinal output through the ganglion cells. The second branch of the TVI curve therefore represents the contrast detectability of photopic vision.

The TVI relationship in Figure 9.22 is a somewhat complicated function. At very low background intensities, the increment threshold

SideNote | **9.30**

Another way of thinking about Ricco's law is by way of the centre response of a ganglion cell with an ON/OFF receptive field arrangement. An increase in spot size stimulates more of the excitatory centre, and therefore a smaller intensity is needed to accomplish the same effect.

SideNote | **9.31**

This topic was covered in depth in Section B of Chapter 1. Recall that Weber undertook a series of experiments on incremental and decremental intensities needed for the detection of a target over a background. His results led to the relationship that is now known as *Weber's law*.

remains constant despite changes in background intensity. Thus, perceptual sensitivity is unaffected by background intensity over a very small range before the TVI curve swings upward. As this happens, the function enters a linear region where the increment threshold is equal to a constant proportion of the background intensity (boxed regions in Figure 9.22). This is precisely what Ernst Weber found, a relationship that is formalized in terms of Weber's law. That is, the contrast or increment threshold (ΔI) is equal to a constant factor (k) multiplied by the background intensity (IB). The important point to note is that within a broad intensity range, k is an important parameter because it stipulates the amount of contrast needed for distinguishing a visual stimulus against its background. For rod-mediated vision, the value of k is 0.14, whereas for cone-mediated vision, it is only 0.02. Thus, a 14% increase in intensity is needed to detect a light spot over its background under scotopic conditions, whereas only a 2% increase is needed under photopic conditions. Although rods are far more sensitive in terms of absolute light detection, it turns out that cone-driven retinal output is actually better in terms of contrast detection or sensitivity (SideNote 9.32).

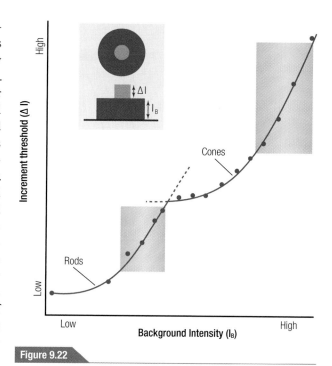

Figure 9.22

An increment threshold experiment reveals how much extra intensity (increment threshold, or ΔI) is needed to detect a light spot placed over a background (IB), as shown in the inset. As the background intensity increases, so does the increment threshold. The lower threshold versus intensity (TVI) curve can be attributed to rod function, whereas the upper curve is based on cone function. The boxed regions of the two curves show a constant response region as specified by Weber's law.

2. RESOLUTION

Visual resolution simply refers to our ability to detect fine detail in the optical image. As with visual sensitivity, a number of factors can affect **acuity**, the term usually applied synonymously with resolution. The best acuity occurs in the rod-free foveal region for reasons that have already been discussed (i.e., a high-quality optical image in the centre of the retina, the least amount of signal convergence upon retinal ganglion cells, etc.). We will see shortly that a number of other factors can also affect spatial resolution. We begin, however, with a brief discussion of the physical and biological parameters that affect visual acuity.

Physical and biological limits to resolution

The maximum resolution of human vision is a function of both physics and biology. Although we have previously mentioned that point light sources create point light images on the retina, in reality the actual image is slightly blurred because of optical distortion inherent in the laws of physics that govern image formation (Davson, 1990; Hood &

Finkelstein, 1986; Wandell, 1995). Thus, our maximum ability to resolve two individual points of light is limited by the extent of the blur spots they produce, which are known as **point spread functions** (PSFs). As shown in the right diagram of Figure 9.23, the two PSFs must be sufficiently spaced apart from each other before they can be physically distinguished. In other words, if the two points of light are placed any closer than shown here, their PSFs will overlap sufficiently so that it becomes physically impossible to distinguish them.

The other limiting factor in acuity concerns the biological construction of the retina by which these point images are detected. We can think of this detection mechanism in two ways—either in terms of the photoreceptors or the ganglion cells. Ultimately, resolution is limited by the spatial sampling ability of ganglion cells since they produce the output fibres to the visual brain (Gregory, 1997; Kolb, Ripps, & Wu, 2003; Wandell, 1995). We already know that ganglion cells in the fovea are fed in a rather exclusive manner by individual photoreceptors. Therefore, the limit to resolution in the fovea, in biological terms,

SideNote **9.32**

As with absolute light detection performance, we can consider sensitivity to be the inverse of threshold. Thus, the fact that the contrast detectability thresholds are always less for photopic vision means that it is more sensitive in detecting light contrast compared to scotopic vision.

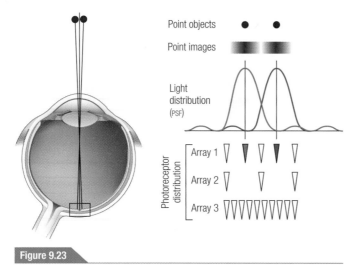

Figure 9.23

The lower limit to two-point resolution is affected by both physical and biological factors. Two-point objects in visual space produce slightly blurred point images on the retina, whose light distributions are called *point spread functions* (PSFS). The two PSFS need to have the minimum separation shown in the right diagram in order to be physically distinguishable. The photoreceptor distribution in the fovea (Array 1) is optimized to detect this minimal point image separation because a receptor (shaded) is spatially lined up with the peak of each PSF and separated by an unstimulated receptor. A hypothetical photoreceptor array that is too sparse (Array 2) or too dense (Array 3) would not adequately sample these two PSFS.

SideNote | **9.33**

If photoreceptor packing in the retina was actually similar to the hypothetical Array 2 shown in Figure 9.23, then the physical resolution limit would exceed the biological capacity for two-point detection. If packing was similar to Array 3, then the biological resolution limit would exceed that imposed by physics.

is stipulated by the packing density of the photoreceptor array. German physiologist and philosopher Hermann von Helmholtz argued that our ability to resolve two-point images requires that at least one unstimulated detector lies in between two stimulated detectors. Of the three hypothetical photoreceptor arrays shown in Figure 9.23, the top row serves this purpose and would therefore be sufficient for the detection of the two-point images that are located as close together as physically possible. It turns out that the actual photoreceptor distribution in mammals generally follows this scheme. In other words, the biological construction of the retina matches the limits of two-point resolution imposed by the physics of image formation. Thus, the resolving capacity of human vision in the fovea is about as good as it can possibly get (SideNote 9.33).

Resolution and retinal eccentricity

We always turn our eyes toward an object we wish to scrutinize so that its image falls on the fovea. The neural capacity to resolve image detail rapidly deteriorates outside of the fovea. As a result, peripheral objects are always perceived with considerably less resolution, something that can be easily demonstrated. While fixating on a particular word on this page, try to guess the identity of neighbouring words

at progressively farther distances. It becomes quite clear that even nearby words become indistinguishable and that the eyes have to be moved in order to identify them.

The rapid decline of visual acuity with eccentricity is graphically shown in Figure 9.24 (Anstis, 1974). We have previously described retinal eccentricity in terms of spatial distance, in millimetres, from the fovea (e.g., Figures 9.2 and 9.19). A better way to measure eccentricity when considering the locations of peripheral images is to stipulate the angle subtended by a light ray from that object in relation to a central ray being imaged on the fovea. The fovea by definition has a retinal eccentricity of 0°, and all peripheral locations toward either the nasal or the temporal side will have higher angular values. The graph in Figure 9.24 shows visual acuity as a function of retinal eccentricity when plotted in angular terms.

The acuity–eccentricity relationship in Figure 9.24 shows a sharp rise in the fovea accompanied by a rapid and symmetrical decline on either side. This is reminiscent of the cone density distribution across the retina (see Figure 9.2) and reinforces the point that cone-mediated retinal output is largely responsible for conveying information about image detail. We now know that not only is the reduction in cone density an important factor but so is the increase in signal convergence that allows ganglion cells to expand their sampling territory of the retina at progressively higher eccentricities. The combined impact of these two factors on visual perception is demonstrated in the right diagram of Figure 9.24. The letters in the immediate vicinity of the fixation spot in the centre of this diagram are easily identified. However, the letters have to be made considerably larger at peripheral locations in order to overcome the progressive loss of spatial resolution at greater eccentricities in all directions.

Measures of spatial resolution—Snellen chart

The idea that alphabetic characters need to be sufficiently large in order for their identity to be resolved forms the basis for a fast and common eye test. Routine eye examinations are important for early detection of many visual abnormalities, from the onset of optical disorders to more serious **ocular** pathologies. An important requirement in any eye test is to identify deficits in spatial resolution (Bruce & Georgeson,

1996; Jenkin & Harris, 2005; Schwartz, 1999). Although two-point discrimination would be a valid test for such purposes, it is not a straightforward parameter to assess in a routine manner because it requires specialized equipment, conditions, and personnel to carry out the psychophysical experiments.

A far simpler and faster procedure is to use an eye chart developed in the late 19th century by Dutch ophthalmologist Hermann Snellen. This so-called *Snellen chart*, which is shown in Figure 9.25, presents rows of alphabetic characters that become sequentially smaller. The strokes of each letter subtend a precise angle, known as the *minimum angle of resolution* (MAR), when measured at the testing distance of 20 feet (6 metres). By definition, a person with normal visual acuity will be able to resolve a MAR value of 1.0 **minute arc** when viewed with one eye (SideNote 9.34). This is more commonly referred to as 20/20 vision—that is, the testing distance (numerator) divided by the distance at which the letter subtends a MAR value of 1.0 minute (denominator). Thus, someone with 20/50 vision has poor visual acuity because they can only resolve at 20 feet what is normally resolvable at 50 feet. Legal blindness is defined as 20/200 vision or worse. The advantage of the Snellen chart test is that it can rapidly establish whether any visual deficits exist that need to be further explored by a clinician (SideNote 9.35).

Measures of spatial resolution—contrast sensitivity function

The major drawback to the Snellen test is that it provides only a rough assessment of visual acuity. This is because the letters are all made of high contrast characters, whereas vision normally operates over a large range of contrast values. A more detailed analysis of visual acuity should therefore include a test of contrast perception as a function of spatial detail. Although the Snellen test can theoretically be conducted with letters of varying contrast values, a far more effective approach is to use an interdigitated set of light and dark bars, known as a **grating** (Cornsweet, 1970; Olzak & Thomaas, 1985; Schwartz, 1999). The advantage of using gratings is twofold—first, the width of the bars can be increased or decreased so as to provide a stimulus with different degrees of spatial detail, and second, the intensity values of the light and dark bars can be changed relative to each other to produce different values of contrast. By

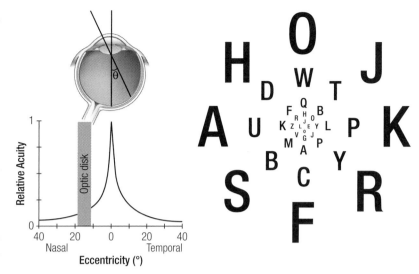

Figure 9.24

Retinal eccentricity is best represented by the angular subtense (θ) of peripheral light rays in relation to the central ray defining the foveal image. A plot of visual acuity as a function of retinal eccentricity shows a sharp rise in the fovea accompanied by a rapid and symmetric decline on either side. The loss of spatial resolution with increasing eccentricity means that letters have to be made progressively larger in order for them to have the same resolving capacity (right diagram). Letter chart adapted from "A Chart Demonstrating Variations in Acuity with Retinal Position," by S. M. Anstis, 1974, *Vision Research, 14*, pp. 589–592.

SideNote **9.34**

One minute of arc is equal to 1/60 of one degree.

SideNote **9.35**

Some people have supernormal vision such that they are able to read finer print than should be normally resolvable. Such people display Snellen notation values that are less than 20/20 (e.g., a person with 20/15 vision can see at 20 feet what a person with normal vision can see at 15 feet).

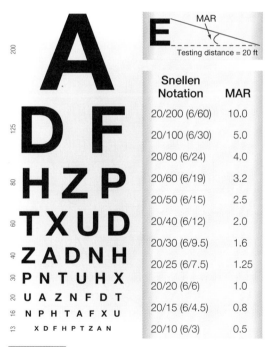

Snellen Notation	MAR
20/200 (6/60)	10.0
20/100 (6/30)	5.0
20/80 (6/24)	4.0
20/60 (6/19)	3.2
20/50 (6/15)	2.5
20/40 (6/12)	2.0
20/30 (6/9.5)	1.6
20/25 (6/7.5)	1.25
20/20 (6/6)	1.0
20/15 (6/4.5)	0.8
20/10 (6/3)	0.5

Figure 9.25

The Snellen eye chart contains sequential rows of characters of declining size. Each letter is characterized by the angle it subtends at the testing distance of 20 feet (top right panel). People with normal visual acuity can resolve a *minimum angle of resolution* (MAR) of 1 minute arc. This is normally referred to as *20/20 vision*. The Snellen notation accompanying each row and its respective MAR value is given in the table (metric values in metres are given in parentheses).

systematically changing these two parameters, it is possible to estimate the contrast needed in order to visualize gratings with progressively higher values of spatial detail.

To conduct such an experiment in a precise and quantitative manner, we have to be more specific about exactly what we mean by spatial detail in a grating. One way to do this is to specify its frequency—that is, the number of light and dark bars in a given unit of space. Figure 9.26 shows three gratings of different frequencies. An important point to note here is that the intensity values change in a gradual manner between the light and dark bars. The intensity profile, which is shown below each grating, follows a sinusoidal pattern. In fact, these are called *sine-wave gratings* for that reason. A full cycle of a grating includes both a light and a dark bar.

Let us for the moment assume that we view the gratings in Figure 9.26 at a distance such that each complete grating subtends 1° of visual angle at the eye (SideNote 9.36). Since

the leftmost grating contains three full cycles within that span, this would mean that it has a **spatial frequency** of 3 cycles/deg. Similarly, we can specify the spatial detail in the other two gratings by their spatial frequencies of 6 cycles/deg and 12 cycles/deg, respectively. The greater the spatial frequency of a grating, the narrower the bars, and therefore it can be thought of as having more spatial detail. Regardless of the spatial frequency, the contrast value of a grating can be independently modulated. The inset in Figure 9.26 shows the same grating with two different contrast values. The only difference is that the intensity maxima (light bar) and minima (dark bar) are compressed as the contrast is reduced, and therefore there is less difference between these extremes.

We can now describe how gratings are used to assess visual function (Hood & Finkelstein, 1986; Lamming, 1991; Wade & Swanston, 2001). Standard psychophysical procedures are employed to find the minimum contrast (contrast threshold) that is needed to make a grating

SideNote | **9.36**

A simple way to get a sense of how much space is spanned by 1° of visual angle is to hold out your thumb with your arm fully extended. The width of the thumb at this distance will subtend about one degree at the eye.

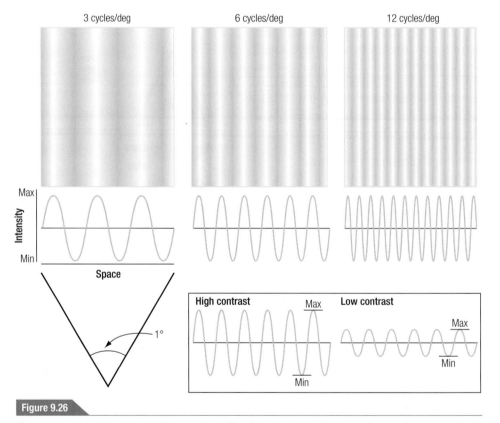

Figure 9.26

Sine-wave gratings have a sinusoidal intensity profile when plotted as a function of space. One full cycle of a grating includes a light and dark bar together (grey outlines in the intensity profiles). The spatial frequency of each grating specifies the number of cycles per degree of visual angle at the eye. The contrast of each grating can be independently modulated by compressing or extending the maximum and minimum intensity values (inset). In a typical contrast sensitivity experiment, the minimum contrast (threshold) needed to just visualize a sine-wave grating is determined across a range of spatial frequencies.

of a particular spatial frequency just visible. This experiment is then repeated across multiple spatial frequencies, and the threshold data are plotted in terms of sensitivity—that is, the reciprocal or inverse of the threshold data—to produce the **contrast sensitivity function (CSF)**. Figure 9.27 shows an example of a typical CSF obtained under photopic conditions in humans. As a general rule, the lower the contrast threshold, the better the visibility of the grating, a fact that is reflected by a higher contrast sensitivity value. Thus, the peak of the CSF, which occurs around 8–10 cycles/deg, represents the optimal spatial frequency for human visual function. The fact that the least amount of contrast is needed to detect a grating at these spatial frequencies means that our visual system is optimized to process this level of spatial detail.

Properties of the CSF in terms of retinal function

As Figure 9.27 shows, there is a small decline in the visibility of gratings at frequencies lower than the peak value and a rapid decline at higher frequencies. To explain this profile, we must examine grating detection in terms of the centre–surround receptive field structure of retinal ganglion cells (Campbell & Green, 1965; Cornsweet, 1970; Lamming, 1991). The inset at the top of the CSF shows that a low spatial frequency grating (on the left) is optimally detected by a receptive field large enough to accommodate the relatively wide light and dark bars within its ON and OFF fields. If we assume that retinal ganglion cells have an upper limit in terms of their receptive field size, then there will come a point at which further reductions in spatial frequency will produce light bars of increasing width that encroach into the OFF areas (or dark bars encroaching into the ON areas). The resulting inhibitory effects will reduce the neural output of the ganglion cells and therefore produce a decline in grating visibility at very low spatial frequencies.

The rapid decline in visibility with increasing spatial frequencies can also be tied to ganglion cell function. As we know already, the central retina displays the highest capacity for resolving spatial detail. Thus, our sensitivity for high spatial frequencies is largely mediated by the foveal retina. This is consistent with our earlier discussion that receptive field sizes of ganglion cells within the central retina are smaller than elsewhere. This is

precisely what would be needed to optimally detect high spatial frequency gratings so that the light and dark bars fall within the smaller spatial constraints of their ON and OFF areas (see top inset in Figure 9.27). However, there is also a limit as to how small a receptive field can get, and this in turn imposes an upper limit to the visibility of very high spatial frequency gratings. Because of the fact that a single ganglion cell may be fed by a single photoreceptor in the fovea, the limit to resolution is ultimately dependent on the density of the photoreceptor array (Campbell & Green, 1965; Cornsweet, 1970). The highest spatial frequency that can be theoretically sampled, known as the **Nyquist limit**, is therefore determined by the spacing of the photoreceptor array. The Nyquist limit for the fovea, based on the centre-to-centre spacing of the cone photoreceptors, is 60 cycles/deg. As Figure 9.27 shows, the high frequency cutoff in the human CSF occurs around this frequency. This is an astounding result because

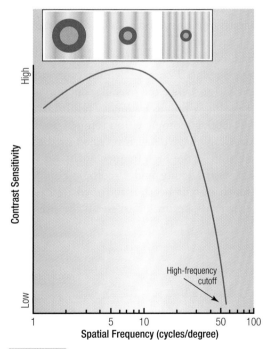

Figure 9.27

The human contrast sensitivity function (CSF) shows peak grating visibility at intermediate frequencies (8–10 cycles/deg). Grating visibility declines mildly at lower spatial frequencies and rapidly at higher frequencies. The inset shows that the optimal receptive field size of ganglion cells becomes smaller for gratings of higher spatial frequencies in order to accommodate the light and dark bars within the spatial margins of their ON and OFF fields.

SideNote | **9.37**

A grating beyond the Nyquist frequency can still produce a visual effect. However, because all of the grating components cannot be individually detected, there is an under-sampling that effectively misrepresents the stimulus as a lower frequency grating. This sampling error is known as *aliasing*.

SideNote | **9.38**

The early formative years are known as the *critical period* when the impact on neurological development due to a sensory deficit is especially severe. A permanent reduction in spatial vision, known as *amblyopia*, results if early visual disorders are not detected and resolved while a child is still in the critical period of development.

it means that our capacity to resolve spatial detail reaches the maximum value that is theoretically possible given the layout of the photoreceptors in our retina (SideNote 9.37).

Factors affecting visual acuity and the CSF

The CSF is very useful because it portrays the broad spatial capacities of visual processing by providing information on the relative visibility of gratings at different spatial frequencies. The human CSF shows that our visual system is less sensitive to very low and very high spatial frequencies than it is to intermediate frequencies. The utility of the CSF becomes apparent when we consider how it changes under various conditions. This information is not only useful for furthering our fundamental knowledge of visual function, but it is also used by clinicians when they wish to evaluate the impact of a particular visual disorder on spatial processing.

The three major factors that affect the human CSF are light level, age, and disease (Bruce & Georgeson, 1996; Tessier-Lavigne, 2000). As Figure 9.28 shows, reducing the light level from photopic to mesopic and then to scotopic levels results in a systematic decline in contrast sensitivity and a shift toward the low frequency end. This makes sense because as we discussed earlier, scotopic vision displays a more reduced contrast sensitivity than photopic vision, hence the overall reduction in the CSF profile within its frequency response range. The fact that scotopic vision is much poorer at processing image detail is revealed by the leftward shift in the high frequency cut-off value. Thus, visual acuity under scotopic conditions is much poorer because rod-mediated retinal mechanisms are unable to signal the presence

of high spatial frequencies and therefore are fundamentally unable to convey image detail.

Another important factor is age. The standard photopic CSF represents data gathered from a young adult. With increasing age, a combination of both optical and neural factors creates a progressive reduction in the high frequency cut-off. The low spatial frequency end is relatively unaffected, meaning that only our ability to process image detail becomes selectively reduced with age. The CSF profile in a young infant is even more compressed largely because the neural mechanisms that encode high spatial frequencies have not yet matured. Neural maturation is a steady process that is largely directed by ongoing visual experience during the first few years of life. It is therefore very important that any visual defects at this stage, such as optical anomalies, are detected and quickly resolved. Otherwise, the neural mechanisms involved in visual processing cannot attain normal adult capacities, and the result is a lifelong deficit in spatial vision and other visual functions (SideNote 9.38).

The final major factor that can affect the human CSF is disease. The right panel in Figure 9.28 shows some examples where the CSF deviates from the normal adult photopic profile. Optical disorders such as myopia produce a blurred retinal image. Consequently, the impact of retinal blur is greatest at high spatial frequencies, and accordingly, the high frequency cut-off in the CSF becomes reduced. Cataract, on the other hand, causes a broad reduction in the CSF because the impaired transmission of light through the crystalline lens affects all spatial frequencies. One of the conditions that affects the low frequency end

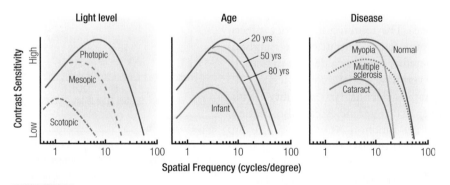

Figure 9.28

Light level, age, and disease can all affect the human CSF, at either all spatial frequencies or only a particular range of frequencies. Any reduction in the high frequency cut-off, such as with increasing age, reduces the visual system's ability to process image detail. Clinicians use the CSF to evaluate the impact of various diseases on spatial vision.

selectively is inflammation of the optic nerve caused by multiple sclerosis. A number of other diseases, such as glaucoma and diabetic retinopathy, are also accompanied by changes in the CSF. The CSF, therefore, is an important tool in determining the precise visual impact of a disease and is often used as part of an overall assessment strategy in low-vision clinics.

3.   SCOTOPIC VERSUS PHOTOPIC VISION

The retina is a duplex processor in that one type of photoreceptor (rod) is used under dim light conditions, whereas the other (cone) is used under daylight conditions. The physiological differences in rod and cone function and the way they feed into ganglion cells largely account for the perceptual differences that arise under scotopic versus photopic conditions. We have examined the properties of scotopic and photopic vision at various points throughout this chapter. It would be useful now to directly compare and contrast those properties in order to attain a more comprehensive perspective of their relative functions. Table 9.1 provides a summary of the major features that we have discussed, along with the sections of this chapter where a fuller description was given.

There are four key points to keep in mind when comparing scotopic and photopic visual function. First and foremost, scotopic vision is extremely sensitive and therefore operates only under dim light conditions, whereas photopic vision has a lower sensitivity that allows it to operate only under more intense light conditions. Second, although there is a narrow light range over which both systems operate together (mesopic vision), they largely function independently of each other within their preferred light levels. This means that the scotopic system is functionally blind under photopic conditions (due to bleaching), and the photopic system is functionally blind at scotopic levels (due to its higher activation threshold). Third, the visual attributes of each system are tailored to meet their individual functional requirements. For example, the fact that the scotopic system operates only under very dim light conditions means that it need not be concerned with image detail (resolution), precise encoding of contrast, or colour. In fact, the neurobiological mechanisms that endow the scotopic system with such high sensitivity, such as the greater degree of signal convergence upon ganglion cells, actually work against it in terms of encoding image detail. Rather, that is left up to the photopic system, which is especially well suited for that purpose because of the nature of the cone photoreceptors and the way they are wired to the ganglion cells.

Table **9.1**

Summary of Key Properties of Scotopic and Photopic Vision

Scotopic Vision	Photopic Vision	
Night vision	Day vision	(A.1)
Rod-mediated (single type)	Cone-mediated (3 types)	(A.1)
Grey-scale vision	Colour vision	(A.3)
Dominant in peripheral retina	Dominant in central retina	(A.1, B.3)
Peak sensitivity = 500 nm	Peak sensitivity = 550 nm	(A.3)
Low activation threshold	High activation threshold	(A.4)
Slow recovery from bleaching	*Fast recovery from bleaching*	(A.4)
High neural convergence	Low neural convergence	(B.2, B.3)
High sensitivity	Low sensitivity	(C.1)
Low resolution	High resolution	(C.2)
Low contrast sensitivity	*High contrast sensitivity*	(C.1, C.2)
Sluggish temporal summation	*Rapid temporal summation*	(C.1)

Note. Parentheses show section numbers of this chapter where that property was discussed; advanced topics shown in italics.

The term *brightness* is usually reserved for specific spatial locations, such as a room or a general environment. The term *lightness* refers to the appearance of a specific object or surface that reflects light. The lighter the object, the more it reflects light.

And finally, the photopic system imposes a far greater **computational load** on the nervous system, not only because of the high degree of image detail that it can process but also because of the fact that three types of cones sample different parts of the visible spectrum and in so doing allow the visual brain to create colour impressions. Although the photopic system remains operational at all retinal eccentricities, it is especially dominant in the central retina. This allows the visual brain to process a large amount of information in terms of image detail through a very small part of the retina (fovea), something that would simply not be possible throughout the entirety of the retina because the computational load on the nervous system would then be overwhelming. The division of labour between the central retina, with its devotion to image detail, and the peripheral retina, with its devotion to low light conditions, therefore provides us with a perfect blend of two independent systems that permit visual function under a truly vast range of sensory and survival demands.

4. CENTRE–SURROUND EFFECTS

We know from our discussion in Section B that the optical image is detected by an array of photoreceptors whose signals converge upon ganglion cells in a way that produces a centre–surround antagonistic receptive field. The biological property of centre–surround antagonism is fundamentally responsible for our visual system's preference for analyzing the retinal image in terms of light contrast. This in turn accounts for a number of perceptual phenomena in vision. Indeed, the visual brain processes all of its information based on the collective output from the retinal ganglion cells, and therefore the receptive field properties of these cells largely determine the way we see the world. To close this chapter, we examine some of the perceptual consequences that can be directly attributed to the property of centre–surround antagonism in retinal ganglion cells.

Lightness contrast

The neural output from a ganglion cell reflects the summated response from the centre and surround components of its receptive field. One of the consequences of this interplay is a perceptual phenomenon by which the **lightness** of an object can appear to

be altered under different background conditions (SideNote 9.39) (Cornsweet, 1970; Hood & Finkelstein, 1986; Wandell, 1995). The left panel in Figure 9.29 shows such an example of **lightness contrast**. The central disks in both stimuli reflect the same amount of light and therefore in physical terms have the same light intensity. However, it is clear that the central disk in stimulus A appears considerably lighter than the one in stimulus B. The only difference between these two stimuli is the background upon which the central disks are located. This deception in lightness value is somewhat problematic because it means that the perceived lightness of an object surface is not stable but instead can be affected by different background conditions. Unfortunately, this is something we have to live with because it occurs as a direct consequence of centre–surround antagonism in our visual neurons.

To understand the reason behind this, we first consider a simple experiment where we measure the neural output of a retinal ganglion cell under different conditions of centre and surround light stimulation. The left panel in Figure 9.30 shows the neural response of a retinal ganglion cell to a light spot of increasing

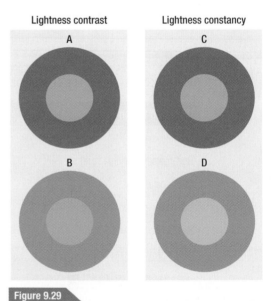

Lightness contrast   Lightness constancy

A   C

B   D

Figure 9.29

An example of the *lightness contrast* and *lightness constancy* phenomena. Both centre disks in the left panel reflect light equally and therefore have the same intensity. The disk in stimulus A appears considerably lighter than the one in stimulus B because of the different influences from the surround. However, if an equivalent increase in intensity is applied to both the centre and the surround to produce stimulus D, the perceived lightness of the centre disk remains relatively unaffected.

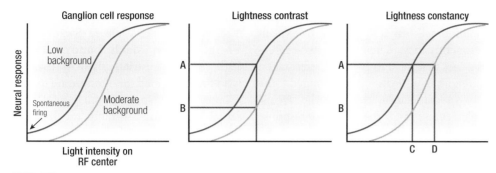

Figure 9.30

Retinal ganglion cells increase their firing rate as the light intensity on the receptive field (RF) centre increases. As the background level increases, the response curve shifts to the right due to a surround inhibitory influence that counteracts the centre response. This is a natural result of centre–surround antagonism and can account for both lightness contrast and constancy, as shown by the middle and right panels. The neural response to stimuli A and B from Figure 9.29 is different because only the background intensity changes. The neural response to stimuli C and D is the same because both the centre and surround light intensities change in an equivalent manner.

intensity placed only upon the centre (we assume that we are recording from an ON centre–OFF surround neuron). If we conduct this experiment in the presence of a low background, the surround inhibitory influence will be minimal, and the ganglion cell will likely respond according to the curve shown on the left. The response profile begins at the spontaneous firing rate and increases progressively as the light intensity on the centre increases until it saturates at some point because the neuron is incapable of responding to further light increments. The same neuron will show a similar response profile if we increase the background illumination except that the curve will be shifted to the right. The greater inhibitory influence from the surround will now counteract the excitatory signals from the centre, and therefore a greater amount of light intensity will be required before the neuron begins to respond. This explains the reduction in the spontaneous firing rate and the overall rightward shift of the response curve. In general, the greater the background illumination, the greater the surround inhibition and therefore the more rightward shifted the curve becomes.

The general description above of the behaviour of retinal ganglion cells can now be used to explain the phenomenon of lightness contrast. The middle panel in Figure 9.30 shows that the same centre light intensity generates two different response levels depending on the background. In the case of stimulus A, the lower background illumination stipulates that the ganglion cell responds according to the left curve. Consequently it fires at a relatively high rate compared to stimulus B, whose

response is much lower because it is dictated by the right curve due to the higher background illumination. Thus, the same degree of stimulation through the receptive field centre produces two very different response levels. Although the perceptual experience of lightness contrast ultimately requires neural activity within a relatively large set of neurons in the visual brain, this exercise demonstrates that the simplicity of centre–surround antagonism at a very early part of the visual pathways can theoretically account for this very robust visual illusion (SideNote 9.40).

Lightness constancy

The centre–surround mechanism is also responsible for a somewhat different phenomenon that has considerable survival advantage—**lightness constancy** (Bruce & Georgeson, 1996; Schwartz, 1999). Imagine a situation where the clouds move across the Sun and thereby significantly reduce the overall environmental or ambient illumination. There should logically be a corresponding downward shift in the lightness of objects in our visual world, making them appear darker. This would be extremely troublesome because of the perceptual instability it would cause. Fortunately, an overall change in the ambient illumination affects both objects and surround in equal measure, resulting in a relative constancy of lightness perception. This effect is simulated by the right panel in Figure 9.29. The two centre disks in stimuli C and D provide a similar lightness appearance under two different conditions of ambient illumination that affect the background level as well.

SideNote 9.40

Lightness contrast, which is sometimes referred to as *brightness contrast*, has been documented since the early Greek period. Leonardo da Vinci understood the important role that background plays and suggested that this illusion can be used to manipulate relative brightness values in paintings. From *A Natural History of Vision*, by N. J. Wade, 1999, Cambridge, MA: MIT Press.

The centre–surround mechanism of retinal ganglion cells can also be used to explain lightness constancy. There are two inter-related issues that need to be considered when the ambient illumination is changed—the intensity of stimulation through the receptive field centre and the specific response curve dictated by the background intensity. As the ambient illumination changes, both of these factors change equally, and therefore the net impact upon retinal ganglion cell firing becomes negligible. This is shown by the neural response to stimuli C and D in the right panel of Figure 9.30. Although the centre spot in stimulus D has a greater intensity, the accompanying higher background level means that the ganglion cells respond according to the right curve and therefore the benefit of greater centre stimulation is diminished. The ratio of centre to surround responsiveness does not change, and therefore the ganglion cells fire at about the same level. As with lightness contrast, the centre–surround mechanism of retinal ganglion cells can also account for lightness constancy—a phenomenon that is of considerable importance because of the stability in visual perception that it provides under a wide range of ambient light conditions (SideNote 9.41) (Walsh & Kulikowski, 1998; Zdravkovic, Economou, & Gilchrist, 2006).

Mach band illusion

Another phenomenon that can be explained by centre–surround principles is our tendency to see light and dark bands at boundaries where the intensity changes abruptly (Lu & Sperling, 1996; Wade & Swanston, 2001). These so-called **Mach bands**, named after 19th-century Austrian physicist Ernst Mach who first described this illusion, are quite compelling and can be seen in Figure 9.31. The actual bars in this stimulus are separated by boundaries where there is an abrupt transition in the intensity value. However, there is a false impression of a narrow dark band immediately to the left and a narrow light band immediately to the right of each boundary. This is simply an illusion because there are no such bands, and in fact, each bar has a constant intensity value across its entire width.

The Mach band illusion can be explained if we consider the output of a select group of retinal ganglion cells (Gregory, 1997; Schwartz, 1999; Wade & Swanston, 2001). Because this is a fairly large stimulus, it will cast an optical image that will stimulate a large number of ganglion cells. However, we need to consider the output of only four of them to understand how this illusion is generated. We will conduct this analysis with ON/OFF cells, though the same conclusion can be reached with OFF/ON cells as well.

Among all of the ganglion cells stimulated by the Mach band image, we first consider the relative outputs of only two of them—those having receptive fields that interact with the stimulus at positions 1 and 2 (Figure 9.31). The ganglion cell at position 1 will fire at a spontaneous level because it receives equal light stimulation in its centre and surround regions. The situation is somewhat different for the ganglion cell at position 2. Here, the receptive field straddles the boundary in such a way that its centre region is entirely filled by the bar to the left of the boundary. Thus, the centre stimulation in both ganglion cells is the same. However, a portion of this ganglion cell's OFF surround is filled by the adjacent lighter bar in the stimulus. Now, compared to the first ganglion cell, this cell will be somewhat more inhibited because it receives slightly more light in its surround.

The output of these two cells will be sent to the brain where they will be compared. The logical conclusion to be drawn from this comparison is that a slightly darker spot exists just to the left of the boundary, thereby accounting for the difference in the relative outputs of the two ganglion cells. Now assume that this relative difference in activity is repeated

Figure 9.31

The Mach band illusion can be seen at each of the borders separating the bars in this stimulus. A narrow dark band appears to the left and a narrow light band to the right of each boundary, even though the physical transition in intensity is actually quite abrupt. The illusion can be explained by considering the relative output of ganglion cells whose receptive fields interact with the stimulus at the positions shown.

among an array of ganglion cells whose receptive fields are located up and down this entire bar at similar horizontal positions. The total output will coalesce to produce an impression of a dark band just to the left of the physical boundary. The same analysis can be applied to each of the other boundaries in this stimulus, thereby explaining the illusory dark bands seen throughout the stimulus.

The illusory white band can be explained by similar principles, this time drawing on the relative outputs of ganglion cells at locations 3 and 4. The stimulus interacts with the ganglion cell at position 3 in such a way that its entire receptive field is filled by the bar, leading to a spontaneous level of neural firing. We assume that the image of the bar falls on the ganglion cell at location 4 in such a way that it straddles the boundary, with the bar filling its centre region entirely. Thus, the centre stimulation in both ganglion cells will again be the same. However, because the surround region of the ganglion cell at location 4 receives slightly less light in its surround, due to the adjacent darker bar, it will fire at a relatively higher rate because of reduced surround inhibition. The output of the two ganglion cells will be compared at the perceptual centres in the visual brain with the logical conclusion that a light spot must exist just to the right of this boundary due to the

relatively greater output of the ganglion cell at location 4 compared to location 3. Again, the relative output of a series of such ganglion cells up and down this bar will produce the illusory impression of a light band located just to the right of the boundary.

These effects show that although the physical intensity relationship is precise at each of the boundaries, the perceptual consequence is quite different because of the biological properties of the neurons that detect these stimuli. In general, lightness perception is directly related to the physical intensity of light reflected by an object. However, the Mach band phenomenon shows that under certain circumstances, perceptual impressions do not exactly match the physical conditions (SideNote 9.42).

Hermann grid illusion

Another compelling illusion, which was originally described by German physiologist Ludimar Hermann, is shown in Figure 9.32. While looking at these **Hermann grids**, one gets the fleeting impression of a set of spots at each of the intersections (Schiller & Carvey, 2005; Wade & Swanston, 2001). The spots in the left stimulus appear dark, whereas they appear to be white in the right stimulus. Interestingly, a spot disappears from an intersection if the eyes are shifted directly to it.

SideNote | **9.42**

There are a number of other examples of lightness illusions, such as the circular version of the Mach band below (showing an illusory light ring at the periphery). The middle stimulus contains a series of expanding squares that shows two oblique illusory bands. A more captivating illusion is shown at the bottom. Try moving closer and further to this stimulus.

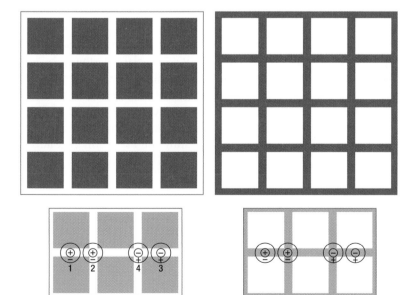

Figure 9.32

The Hermann grid illusion can be seen as a series of spots at the intersections of a grid pattern. The stimulus on the left produces black spots, whereas the one on the right produces white spots. These illusory spots can be explained by the relative firing levels of a select group of ganglion cells whose receptive fields interact with the stimulus at the positions shown in the bottom panels.

SideNote | **9.43**

The same conclusions are reached if the output of a ganglion cell located along one of the vertical bars is compared with that from an intersection. Due to circular symmetry, a ganglion cell responds in the same fashion regardless of whether a horizontal or vertical light bar is centred on it.

SideNote | **9.44**

The same principles in ganglion cell output at different locations can be used to explain the illusory white spots in the Hermann grid stimulus on the right-hand side of Figure 9.32. The panel below this grid contains the same types of ganglion cells at the same locations, except that they now interact with a reverse pattern of light intensity values. An analysis of their relative outputs here is left as an exercise to the student.

The Hermann grid illusion can also be explained by the centre–surround properties of retinal ganglion cells (Schwartz, 1999; Wade & Swanston, 2001). The retinal image of the grid is sampled by a large number of ganglion cells at any given time. As with our analysis of the Mach bands, we consider the output of only a select few among the stimulated ganglion cells, as shown in the bottom panels of Figure 9.32. We first consider a hypothetical ganglion cell whose receptive field interacts with the stimulus at position 1. Here, the horizontal light bar fills the centre of this ON/OFF cell, and therefore it has a strong stimulatory effect. The surround regions are largely filled by the dark segments of the stimulus, and therefore there is little inhibitory influence. This cell on the whole should therefore fire at a fairly high rate. The ganglion cell located at one of the intersections, as in position 2, behaves somewhat differently. The surround region of its receptive field receives greater illumination compared to the cell at position 1, and therefore the greater inhibition makes it fire at a reduced rate. When the output of these two cells is compared at the higher visual centres of the brain, the logical conclusion is that a dark spot exists at the intersection because of the comparatively reduced firing rate of the cell sampling this part of the grid (SideNote 9.43).

The same conclusions are reached if we consider the relative outputs of the second class of ganglion cells—those with an OFF/ON receptive field structure. A ganglion cell of this type that interacts with the grid image at a point away from an intersection, as in position 3, will be strongly inhibited. This is because the horizontal light bar fills the centre inhibitory region, whereas the surround excitatory region is largely covered by the dark segments of the stimulus. The ganglion cell at position 4, however, will fire at a slightly higher rate because it receives more light in the surround excitatory region. Thus, again a comparison of the two cells' firing rates will lead to the logical conclusion that a dark spot exists at the intersection because of the relatively higher firing rate of an OFF/ON cell located there (SideNote 9.44).

These analyses again show how our visual system can sometimes be fooled by the biological properties of centre–surround antagonism. Of course, these spots are not really there—but it sure seems like they are. One reason for implicating the centre–surround operation of ganglion cells is that the illusion disappears under very dim light conditions, a situation in which surround antagonism is known to become ineffective. Also, as noted earlier, staring directly at an intersection makes the spot there disappear. Presumably, this occurs because the receptive fields in the fovea are among the smallest and therefore can be filled by the entire segment of an intersection, resulting in spontaneous neural activity. This would eliminate any relative differences with the output of neighbouring ganglion cells whose receptive fields would also be filled entirely by a horizontal (or vertical) light bar.

Although the receptive field properties of ganglion cells do account very nicely for this illusion, there are some facets of it that are not as easily explained. One of them is the fact that the strength of the illusion increases with the number of intersections, something that cannot be explained simply by centre–surround antagonism. The spots are also affected by the regularity in the pattern of intersections. These effects suggest that more complex neural operations beyond the retina also play a role in generating the Hermann grid illusion.

Summary

1. An optically normal eye creates a visual image directly on the retina and, more specifically, upon the retinal layer that is lined with photoreceptors. Photoreceptors are able to capture light photons and subsequently create a neural signal. Rod photoreceptors are specialized for low light conditions (night or scotopic vision), whereas cone photoreceptors function at much higher light levels (day or photopic vision). Rods and cones have different distribution profiles: rod density is highest in the periphery, whereas cone density is highest in the centre of the retina (fovea). There are three kinds of cone photoreceptors that are together responsible for generating colour vision.

2. The absorption spectrum of rods shows a maximum at 500 nm, which coincides with the maximum spectral sensitivity of scotopic vision. The three cone subtypes have different peaks of absorption—S cones at 440 nm, M cones at 530 nm, and L cones at 560 nm. The three cone subtypes together provide the foundation for photopic vision, which has a peak spectral sensitivity at 550 nm. Rod photoreceptors have a lower activation threshold than cones and become bleached at moderate to high light intensities. Cone bleaching only occurs at high light intensities.

3. The retina is anatomically composed of three layers—the photoreceptor layer, the inner nuclear layer, and the ganglion cell layer. The axons of ganglion cells leave the eye and carry retinal signals to higher centres of the brain. There are two major types of ganglion cells—midget (small cell size and dendritic field) and parasol (large cell size and dendritic field). The area of the retina that can influence a ganglion cell is referred to as the *receptive field*. Ganglion cells display circular receptive fields with either a central excitatory and surround inhibitory zone (ON/OFF) or vice versa (OFF/ON). The antagonistic nature of this arrangement is optimally suited for visual contrast detection.

4. The central retina has a foveal pit where the neurons of the inner nuclear layer and ganglion cells are shifted to one side, giving light rays more direct access to the photoreceptors. The wiring pattern of photoreceptors to ganglion cells varies across the retina. In the central retina, the wiring is so fine that it may be possible to have a single photoreceptor connected through a bipolar cell to a single ganglion cell. This arrangement is responsible for the finest degree of spatial sampling and largely accounts for the high resolution (and poor sensitivity) of central vision. In the peripheral retina, there is great convergence whereby a single ganglion cell is driven by a much larger array of photoreceptors. This arrangement is largely responsible for the high sensitivity (and poor resolution) of peripheral vision.

5. Visual resolution (or acuity) can be affected by a number of factors, including point-spread functions and image location (e.g., fovea versus periphery). In general, acuity declines with retinal eccentricity. The simplest measure of spatial resolution in a clinical setting is the *Snellen chart*. A more detailed test involves contrast detection for gratings of different spatial frequencies. The resulting *contrast sensitivity function* (CSF) shows a peak around 8–10 cycles/deg for normal vision.

6. The following key features differentiate scotopic (rod) vision from photopic (cone) vision. Scotopic vision is mediated by one photoreceptor type and therefore generates monochromatic (grey-scale) vision. It is dominant in the peripheral retina, has a low activation threshold, and a peak spectral sensitivity around 500 nm. Rods have a high degree of neural convergence and therefore produce vision that is of low resolution but high sensitivity. Photopic vision, on the other hand, is driven by three different cone subtypes and therefore generates colour vision. It is dominant in the central retina, has a higher activation threshold, and a peak spectral sensitivity around 550 nm. Cones have a much lower degree of neural convergence and therefore produce vision that is of high resolution but low sensitivity.

7. The centre–surround properties of ganglion cells are responsible for a number of perceptual phenomena. Lightness contrast, which arises when an object appears to be of different lightness depending upon the background, is a direct consequence of the

surround inhibitory influence upon the neural output of a ganglion cell. Another phenomenon is lightness constancy, which is responsible for the similarity of lightness appearance of an object under different environmental light conditions. In this case, the coincident effect on both the centre and surround response of a ganglion cell under varying light levels is responsible for the constancy in signal output.

Key Terms

absorption spectrum, 280
acuity, 297
amacrine cell, 290
bipolar cell, 289
bleaching, 283
Bloch's law, 296
centre–surround antagonism, 288
computational load, 303
contrast sensitivity function (CSF), 301
dark adaptation, 283
dark current, 277
day vision, 275
dendritic field, 285–6
eccentricity, 292
fovea, 275
foveal pit, 291
grating, 299
Hermann grid, 307
horizontal cell, 290
increment threshold, 296

inner nuclear layer, 285
lateral inhibition, 290–1
L-cone, 282
lightness, 304
lightness constancy, 305
lightness contrast, 304
Mach bands, 306
M-cone, 282
microelectrode, 286
microspectrophotometry, 281
midget ganglion cell, 286
minute arc, 299
night vision, 275
nyctalopia, 294
Nyquist limit, 301
ocular, 298
OFF/ON ganglion cell, 287
ON/OFF ganglion cell, 287
optic disk, 275
parasol ganglion cell, 286
photochromatic interval, 295
photopic vision, 282

photoreceptor, 274
phototransduction, 276
pigment epithelium, 274
point spread function, 297
Purkinje shift, 295
receptive field, 286
retina, 274
retinal ganglion cell (RGC), 284
rhodopsin, 277
Ricco's law, 296
S-cone, 282
scotopic vision, 281
spatial frequency, 300
spatial sampling, 292
spectral, 279
spectral sensitivity function, 281
spectrophotometry, 280
spontaneous activity, 286

Recall Questions

1. What is the difference between the fovea and the optic disk? How do the rod and cone distribution profiles differ across the retina, especially with regard to the fovea? What is the difference between the fovea and peripheral retina in terms of visual sensitivity and resolution?

2. Why can the standard procedures of spectrophotometry not be applied in deriving the cone absorption spectra? How do the rod and cone absorption spectra differ in terms of their peak wavelength of light absorption?

3. How do rods and cones differ in terms of their activation threshold and bleaching properties? What is mesopic vision?

4. What are the two major types of ganglion cells, and how do they differ from each other in anatomical terms? What is the definition of a receptive field? What is the difference between an ON/OFF and an OFF/ON receptive field?

5. What are the key differences between the fovea and peripheral retina in terms of anatomical connections between the photoreceptor and ganglion cell? How do these differences account for the different sensitivity and resolution characteristics of the two parts of the retina?

6. What is a Snellen chart, and how is it used in clinical assessment? What is a grating, and how is it used in clinical assessment? How is the contrast sensitivity function derived?

7. How does scotopic vision differ from photopic vision in terms of sensitivity and resolution? Why does the photopic system impose a greater computational load on the visual brain?

8. How does the centre–surround receptive field structure of ganglion cells account for lightness contrast and lightness constancy?

9. What is the *dark current*? How does the capture of a photon by rhodopsin lead to electrical signalling in the photoreceptor? What is the role of cGMP in producing photoreceptor hyperpolarization?

10. What factors would have to be taken into account in designing experiments to obtain the spectral sensitivity function of scotopic versus photopic vision? How do the two functions differ in terms of their peak sensitivity and profile? What is the difference between the Purkinje shift and the photochromatic interval?

11. What is the role of bipolar cells in creating the receptive field structure of a ganglion cell? How do the two types of bipolar cells separately influence a ganglion cell? What are the roles of the horizontal and amacrine cells in the retina?

12. How does the centre–surround receptive field structure of ganglion cells account for the Mach band and Hermann grid illusions?

Further Reading

- Dowling, J. E. (1987). *The retina: An approachable part of the brain*. Cambridge, MA: Harvard University Press.

- Farah, M. J. (2000). *The cognitive neuroscience of vision*. Malden, MA: Wiley-Blackwell.

- Gregory, R. L. (1997). *Eye and brain*. Princeton, NJ: Princeton University Press.

- Kolb, H., Ripps, H., & Wu, S. (2003). *Concepts and challenges in retinal biology*. Amsterdam, Netherlands: Elsevier.

- Rodieck, R. W. (1998). *The first steps in seeing*. Sunderland, MA: Sinauer Associates.

- Valberg, A. (2005). *Light vision color*. Chichester, UK: Wiley.

- Wade, N. J., & Swanston, M.T. (2001). *Visual perception: An introduction* (2nd ed.). Philadelphia, PA: Taylor and Francis.

- Wandell, B. A. (1995). *Foundations of vision*. Sunderland, MA: Sinauer Associates.

- Wolken, J. J. (1995). *Light detectors, photoreceptors, and imaging systems in nature*. New York, NY: Oxford University Press.

The Visual System: Cortical Processing and Object Perception

In this chapter . . .

- You will explore the path travelled by visual signals, from the retina to the lateral geniculate nucleus (LGN) and then to area V1. You will see the details of how retinal fibres travel to the LGN, and you will learn about the structure of the six-layered LGN itself. You will come to understand that the bottom two layers (1 and 2) are made up of one type of cell (known as *magnocellular* [M] *neurons*) and that the top four layers (3–6) are made up of another type of cell (known as *parvocellular* [P] *neurons*). You will learn to distinguish the properties of M-neurons versus P-neurons and the separate roles they play in visual processing. You will also come to appreciate the role that the superior colliculus (SC) plays by integrating somatosensory, visual, and auditory information.

- You will investigate the anatomical structure of the six layers of area V1 and where the LGN projects its fibres. You will learn about four important aspects of vision (binocularity, orientation selectivity, directional motion selectivity, and colour contrast detection) that emerge for the first time in area V1. You will learn about the organization of area V1 into ocular dominance columns, as well as about hypercolumns and how they are structurally organized.

- You will come to grasp the sheer number of higher cortical areas (known as the *extrastriate cortex*) and understand how these are organized anatomically into two "streams": the dorsal stream and the ventral stream. You will go on to discover the functional characteristics of the ventral stream in considerable detail, especially in terms of its role in object and face perception.

A complex set of mental processes enable us to visually organize objects in the environment even when the objects are similar. Photo: hkratky/iStockphoto.com

The most learned authorities state that the eyes are connected with the brain. For my own part, I am inclined to believe that they are also thus connected with the stomach. It is unquestionable that a man never has an eye knocked out without vomiting.

—Pliny the Elder (77 CE)

We learned in the previous chapter that the retinal output is sent through a nerve bundle comprising more than a million fibres. This output is directed at the visual brain, where the incoming signals are processed through multiple stages along a hierarchy of cortical areas. The signals carried in the retinal fibres are produced by local contrast detection (i.e., a light spot detected over a dark background or vice versa). The visual brain takes these incoming signals and transforms them into progressively more complex representations. One of the greatest challenges facing vision scientists is to understand the precise way in which visual information is encoded through these transformations to ultimately yield the perceptual experience of vision. We will examine some of the possible coding strategies that the visual system may use later in this chapter.

The first item on our agenda, however, is to understand precisely how the retinal output arrives at the brain. We will then proceed to a discussion of the neural processes that take place in cortical areas devoted to visual analysis. There are many of these areas, which are collectively referred to as the **visual cortex**. We learned in Chapter 2 that the brain can be physically and functionally divided into four lobes—occipital, parietal, temporal, and frontal. Visual information is processed in one way or another in all four of these lobes, starting in the occipital lobe at the very back of the brain and proceeding forward. The current thinking is that visual information processing beyond the occipital lobe occurs along two major cortical pathways (see Figure 10.1): the *dorsal stream*, which proceeds into the parietal lobe, where neural structures are primarily involved with the dynamic and spatial aspects of vision, such as motion perception, spatial orientation, and visuomotor behaviour; and the *ventral stream*, which proceeds into the temporal lobe, where neural structures are primarily involved with encoding structural details of the visual image, leading ultimately to a complete representation of various object classes (SideNote 10.1).

In this chapter, we will take a gradual approach to the topic of cortical processing while weaving in what we understand of how we perceive visual objects. We will thus follow the neural processing cascade along the ventral stream and integrate our knowledge of the biological mechanisms in those areas with various theories of object perception. We will

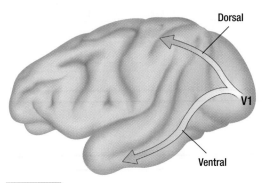

Figure 10.1

Visual information processing in the brain begins in the occipital lobe (area V1) at the very back of the brain and thereafter occurs along one of two major cortical streams. The dorsal stream encompasses areas of the parietal lobe and is responsible for processing dynamic visual events that guide action. The ventral stream proceeds into the temporal lobe and is responsible for processing the structural details of objects, leading to visual object perception.

examine the dorsal stream and the perceptual consequences of neural processing in those areas in Chapters 12 and 13.

A. The Retinal Projection to the Brain

For much of the early history of neuroscience, very little attention was paid to the actual projection of nerve fibres from the eye for the simple reason that the brain was generally thought to be of little importance. That view changed gradually with time, though much of the focus remained on the ventricles, which are fluid-filled chambers within the brain where, according to the prevailing belief, the animal spirits interacted with the visual spirits that arrived through the optic nerves (Wade, 1998). Even Leonardo da Vinci's early anatomical drawings showed a projection of the optic nerves extending directly into one of the brain's ventricles (SideNote 10.2).

A correct understanding of the retinal projections to the brain began with Renaissance anatomist Andreas Vesalius of Padua, and continued to develop over the next three centuries. Along the way, one of the perplexing issues that generated much discussion was why the two optic nerves come together and become briefly fused just behind the eyes. As we will soon see, this fusion has a considerable impact on the projection pattern of retinal fibres and how the brain analyzes our visual environment.

SideNote | **10.1**

David Milner and Mel Goodale, in an influential account of this dichotomy in information processing, proposed that the dorsal stream is primarily involved in the online control of action, whereas the ventral pathways are responsible for the sensory processing of objects and their identity (Milner & Goodale, 1995). An expanded discussion of this issue will be taken up in Chapter 13.

SideNote | **10.2**

An early drawing by Leonardo da Vinci (below) shows the optic nerves entering directly into the first of three fluid-filled cerebral ventricles (Wade, 1998).

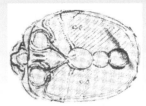

A Natural history of Vision by Nicholas J. Wade. MIT Press, 1998

Andreas Vesalius (1514–1564)
© The Print Collector/Alamy

1. GENERAL LAYOUT OF THE RETINAL PROJECTION

The retinal nerve fibres emerging from each eyeball quickly become myelinated so as to provide maximum insulation for the electrical signals that are being conducted within them. This is especially necessary because the vast majority of these signals have to travel several centimetres before arriving at the next neural structure, where they undergo further processing. The projection pattern in Figure 10.2 shows the pathway out of the eyes and into the major **subcortical** structures (Rosenzweig, Leiman, & Breedlove, 1999). The remainder of this section will be devoted to a fuller discussion of this pathway.

Subcortical targets of the retinal output

The interior part of the brain is largely made up of two components—white matter (i.e., the nerve fibres carrying signals for the various sensory and motor systems) and neuron clusters that vary from very small to large and well organized, such as the *thalamus*. We saw in earlier chapters that the thalamus is a major site for the relay of sensory information (e.g., in the somatosensory and auditory systems). Similarly, the visual system contains, on each side of the brain, a major thalamic structure known as the *lateral geniculate nucleus*, or LGN. In fact, as Figure 10.2 shows, the LGN is the principal subcortical target of the retinal projection and therefore plays a critical role in the transfer of visual information to the visual cortex (Bear, Connors, & Paradiso, 2006; Kandel, Schwartz, & Jessell, 2000; Rosenzweig et al., 1999). We will shortly look at the LGN in detail. The other major target of the retinal projection is the *superior colliculus*, which is a paired structure sitting just below the LGN and close to the midline of the brain.

The cortical projection of retinal signals

Retinal signals reach the visual cortex only after they have passed through the LGN. The retinal fibres synapse onto LGN neurons, and it is the axons of these LGN neurons that in turn carry visual signals to the cortex. As Figure 10.2 shows, there is a massive fibre projection, known as the *optic radiation*, that transmits the LGN signals to the visual cortex in the occipital lobe. There is no crossover of the fibres at this level, and therefore the right and left LGN project only to the visual cortex on

their respective sides. In primates, this pathway serves as the main route for visual information travelling to the cortex.

Signal splitting at the optic chiasm

The general rule governing sensory projections to the brain is that a crossover takes place at some point along the fibre pathway so that the right side of the brain samples sensory information from the left side of the body and vice versa (Kandel et al., 2000; Squire, Roberts, Spitzer, & Zigmond, 2002). We learned in Chapter 3, for example, that the right side of the brain receives somatosensory information only from the left half of the body and vice versa. If we were to apply this rule to the visual system, we would predict that the optic nerve emerging from the left eyeball should project entirely to the right side of the brain, and that, correspondingly, the right optic nerve should project entirely to the left side of the brain. But it turns out that this is only half true. To

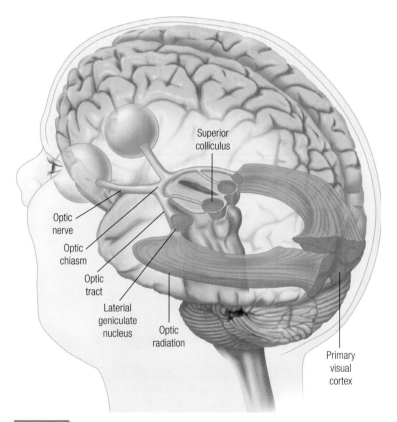

Figure 10.2

The retinal output carried by the two optic nerves merge at the optic chiasm, where roughly one-half of the retinal fibres cross over to the opposite side. The emerging fibre bundle, known as the *optic tract*, projects to two subcortical structures—the lateral geniculate nucleus (LGN) and the superior colliculus (SC). Visual signals from each LGN are then sent to the primary visual cortex through a major fibre tract known as the *optic radiation*. From *Biological Psychology*, by M. R. Rosenzweig, A. L. Leiman, and S. M. Breedlove, 1999, Sunderland, MA: Sinauer Associates.

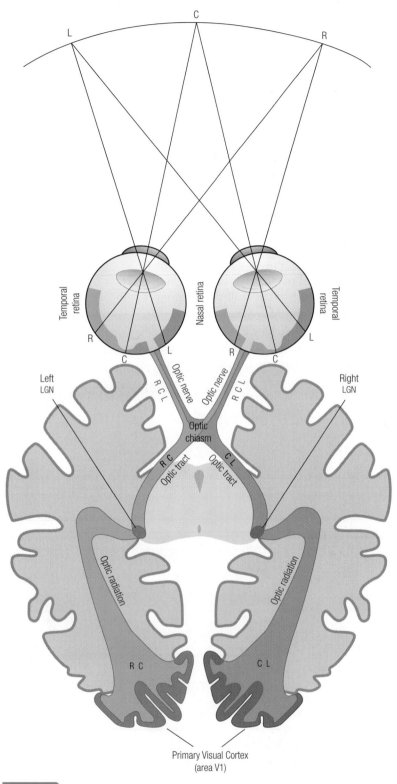

Figure 10.3

A top-down view of the retinal projection patterns from the eyes to the visual cortex. Retinal fibres from the nasal half of each retina cross over to the opposite side at the optic chiasm, whereas fibres from the temporal retina project to the same side. This anatomical arrangement ensures that information from the left visual field (L), which is imaged in the right retinal field of each eye, is ultimately transmitted to the right visual cortex. Similarly, visual information from the right visual field (R) is transmitted to the left visual cortex. The centre of the visual field (C), which is imaged on the fovea, enjoys a bilateral representation through its projection to both sides. Adapted from *The First Steps in Seeing,* by R. W. Rodieck, 1998, Sunderland, MA: Sinauer Associates.

understand why, we must take a close look at Figure 10.3, which provides a top-down view of a pair of eyes looking out at the visual world, along with their projection pathways to the brain (Rodieck, 1998).

As we learned in the previous chapter, the retina can be divided into a temporal and a nasal half, with the fovea serving as the midpoint. Each optic nerve contains axons from all of the ganglion cells in that eye. However, when the two optic nerves come together at the **optic chiasm**, the nasal and temporal fibres of each eye begin to follow different routes (Rosenzweig et al., 1999; Tovée, 1996). The axons from all of the ganglion cells in the temporal half of the retina project to the LGN on the same side, whereas the nasal fibres actually cross over and project to the opposite LGN. This fundamental rule applies in exactly the same way to the retinal fibres of both optic nerves. Whereas the optic nerve carries retinal fibres from only one eye, the fibre bundle emerging after the optic chiasm contains fibres from both eyes—that is, the temporal fibres from the **ipsilateral** (same side) eye and nasal fibres from the **contralateral** (opposite side) eye. This nerve bundle is called the **optic tract** in order to distinguish it from the optic nerve, given the important transformation in its fibre composition. The fibres in the optic tract terminate in the LGN on the same side (SideNote 10.3).

This is a rather unusual arrangement, and one that is certainly not predictable from the central projection patterns of other sensory systems. The reason the visual system projects in this manner becomes apparent if we look at the situation in terms of the visual analysis of objects in the real world. At any given time, both of our eyes are fixated on a particular object so that it is imaged upon the fovea of both eyes. As Figure 10.3 shows, the fixated object defines the centre of our visual field (C), while all objects to the left of it (e.g., object L) define the left visual field, and all objects to the right of it (e.g., object R) define the right visual field. Object L and all other objects from the left visual field fall on the right half of each retina, whereas object R and all other right visual field objects are imaged on the left half of each retina. Each optic nerve carries signals from R, C, and L (i.e., the entire retinal surface). However, because of signal splitting at the optic chiasm, the optic tract carries information from only one-half of the retina of each eye. Specifically, the right optic tract transmits signals from the right retinal halves of each eye, and the left optic tract conveys signals from the left retinal halves. In our earlier coverage of optical laws and principles (Chapter 8), we learned that there is a left–right transformation, meaning that all objects in the left part of our visual world are imaged on the right half of each retina and vice versa. Each optic tract therefore transmits visual information that represents the opposite, or contralateral, half of the visual field, as shown in Figure 10.3. Since the optic tract signals are transmitted to the LGN and then directly to the visual cortex, both of these structures must also process contralateral visual information only. In short, the right side of our brain processes the left half of our visual world and vice versa (SideNote 10.4).

The foveal representation

The left–right crossover of visual information means that neural signals from the foveal retina should theoretically become split right down the middle, since the fovea straddles the midline of the retina. Such an arrangement would require a precise anatomical partitioning of the left and right **retinal fields**. This means that ganglion cells residing immediately on either side of the midline should follow their appropriate course according to the projection rules through the optic chiasm. However, it has long been thought that such an exact partitioning is highly unlikely, because biological systems rarely show such precise boundaries. One controversial proposal, based on anatomical studies, is that the projection pattern along the entire vertical midline, and through the fovea, is somewhat fuzzy (Bear et al., 2006; Hubel, 1995; Rodieck, 1998). In other words, some of the ganglion cells within this fuzzy zone project along the ipsilateral pathway and others along the contralateral pathway. If true, this would mean that the optic tracts, in addition to containing retinal fibres from the opposite retinal field, also contain fibres from ganglion cells throughout the entire fovea. The bilateral representation of the midline has an important perceptual consequence in that it binds together the two visual halves of our world into a unified and seamless representation (SideNote 10.5).

2.   THE LATERAL GENICULATE NUCLEUS

The LGN is a six-layered neural structure that serves as the main projection target of the optic tract. Even though it is one of the smaller neural structures, being roughly the size of a dime, its anatomical and physiological properties have been intensely studied because of its importance in visual transmission and processing. Early accounts of the LGN characterized it as merely a relay station within the visual transmission pathways to the brain. It was believed that the retinal fibres synapsed onto LGN neurons that in turn projected to the primary visual cortex. Although this is still widely considered to be a key functional property of the LGN, recent studies have shown that it also plays an important role in organizing visual inputs to the brain and even in selecting which visual signals are to be enhanced and therefore given greater priority (O'Connor, Fukui, Pinsk, & Kastner, 2002; Sherman, 2005).

Structural and functional properties of the LGN

The LGN is a bell-shaped neural structure that receives approximately 90% of the retinal fibres contained in the optic tract. The six layers are numbered from the bottom up. Figure 10.4 on page 318 shows the location of the LGN within a cross-sectional view of the brain; the six layers are shown in greater detail in the inset pictures at the bottom. Early neuroanatomists noticed that neurons in the lowest two layers (i.e., layers 1 and 2) have large cell bodies, and so these came to be known as **magnocellular neurons**; neurons in the upper four layers, which have comparatively smaller cell bodies, are called **parvocellular neurons**.

It is possible to record electrical activity from these neurons by inserting a microelectrode through the brain all the way down to the LGN. The early pioneering studies of the LGN were carried out in cats and monkeys by David Hubel and Torsten Wiesel at Harvard University (Hubel & Wiesel, 2004). As with retinal ganglion cells, it is possible to map which parts of the retina need to be stimulated in order to obtain a neural response. In other words, just as ganglion cells display a receptive field, so do LGN neurons. Hubel and Wiesel found that all LGN neurons, regardless of which layer they are located in, display receptive fields that have an organization similar to that of the ganglion cells. That is, LGN neurons also show concentric circular receptive fields with an ON centre response and an OFF surround or vice versa. Thus, the centre–surround antagonism that was a key property of ganglion cells is still maintained at the level of the LGN (Hubel,

SideNote **10.3**

Some of the retinal fibres contained in the optic tract send off branches, known as *collaterals*, to other subcortical visual structures, including the superior colliculus. Thus, a subset of the visual signals proceeding to the LGN are copied to these other structures.

SideNote **10.4**

The retinal projection makes sense when considered in terms of visual analysis of the real world. If all of the retinal fibres crossed over to the opposite side (similar to what happens in the somatosensory system), then each cortical hemisphere would separately process the entire visual field. The partial crossover at the optic chiasm means that each hemisphere can make a detailed analysis of only the opposite visual field. The importance of this arrangement will become apparent in our discussion of depth perception in Chapter 12.

SideNote **10.5**

It is presumably because of this dual representation across the midline that we do not perceive any discontinuities between the right and left halves of our visual world.

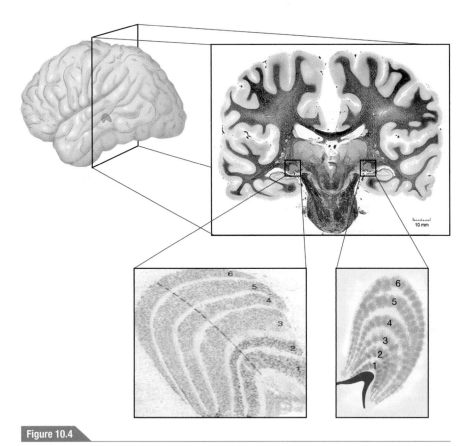

Figure 10.4

The lateral geniculate nucleus is a paired neural structure located deep inside the brain, as shown in the cross-sectional picture taken from the plane indicated in the schematic diagram. A magnified view of the LGN at the bottom left shows the neurons to be largely confined to six distinct layers. These layers are numbered from the bottom up, as shown in the schematic diagram of the LGN at the bottom right. Photo top right: Courtesy of http://www.msu.edu/user/brain and the U.S. National Science Foundation. Photo bottom left: Courtesy of Frank Werblin.

1995; Rodieck, 1998). This is not too surprising because LGN neurons receive a direct input from ganglion cells and so their properties are expected to be similar.

Organization of visual signals—retinotopy

A major function of the LGN is the organization of the visual signals flowing through it. This organization can be found in two forms—retinotopy and functional segregation. We noted that each LGN receives inputs from both eyes through the optic tract. The anatomical layout of the two eyes' inputs are shown in the schematic diagrams of the LGN in Figure 10.5. The first point to note is that each of the six layers represents only a single eye. The retinal fibres from the contralateral eye arrive into layers 1, 4, and 6, whereas fibres from the ipsilateral eye arrive only into layers 2, 3, and 5. Thus, the LGN neurons in each layer are strictly **monocular** and can be driven only by light stimulation through the appropriate eye (Rosenzweig et al., 1999; Squire et al., 2002).

The retinal inputs to each layer are not haphazard; they occur in an organized manner that reflects the spatial layout of the retina. Figure 10.5 shows a pair of eyes looking out at a series of objects around a fixation point (F). These objects trigger neural activity at precise points within the retina that in turn project to precise locations within the LGN. Thus, objects A, B, and C trigger activity at specific points in each of the six layers of the right LGN, while objects G, H, and J trigger activity at specific points within the left LGN. It is apparent that the spatial layout of activated neurons along each of these layers is related to the retinal site where the stimulation arose. The LGN therefore displays a precise **retinotopic organization**, whereby a topographic layout of the retina is formed in each of the layers. Thus, adjacent points in the retina are mapped onto adjacent points in all of the layers of the LGN.

The retinotopic layout arises because ganglion cells project in an orderly manner throughout the LGN to produce a complete representation of the contralateral half of the visual field. This does not mean, however, that all parts of the retina are exactly equal in their representation throughout the LGN. The foveal retina has a much higher density of ganglion cells and therefore enjoys greater LGN territory in terms of representation. This is shown in Figure 10.5 by way of the enlarged foveal representation (F) in each LGN. The neurons in each layer of the LGN are fairly evenly distributed, meaning that a greater physical territory is needed to encompass the much higher number of ganglion cells in and around the fovea. The peripheral parts of the retina have much lower ganglion cell density and therefore require less LGN territory.

Organization of visual signals—functional segregation

It may seem surprising that there are actually six LGN layers, each with an identical retinotopic layout. Taking into account the fact that each LGN separately processes information from the two eyes, we are still left with the redundancy of three layers being devoted to each eye. It turns out that this can be accounted for partly by a further level of organization within the LGN that relies on the distinction between magnocellular and parvocellular layers. Recall from the last chapter that there are two major types of retinal ganglion cells—the so-called *midget* and *parasol* cells. Midget ganglion cells, as the name suggests, are characterized by their relatively small size and compact dendritic field, whereas the parasol ganglion cells are larger with a relatively large dendritic field (Rodieck, 1998). The axons from both the midget and the parasol ganglion cells form the major output of the retina through the optic nerve.

We now know that visual function in primates is largely mediated through two separate but parallel pathways all the way to the brain, starting with these two ganglion cell types in the retina (Kandel et al., 2000; Callaway, 2005). A functional segregation of these two pathways is also maintained at the level of the LGN by way of a precise projection pattern between the two groups of ganglion cells. The parasol ganglion cells project only to the magnocellular layers of the LGN, while the midget ganglion cells project only to the parvocellular layers. A review of Figure 10.5 shows that magnocellular neurons in layer 1 receive parasol input

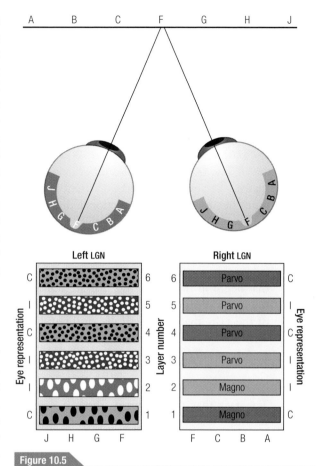

Figure 10.5

The LGN organizes visual information according to three principles—eye source, retinotopy, and functional segregation. Each of the six LGN layers is driven by visual information from the contralateral half of the visual field through either the contralateral (C) or the ipsilateral (I) eye. The given points in visual space are represented throughout each LGN layer as shown at the bottom of the schematic diagrams. There is a precise retinotopic organization so that adjacent points in the retina are mapped onto adjacent points in all layers of the LGN. The foveal (F) retina, however, enjoys greater LGN territory than the periphery. A third level of organization occurs in terms of the magnocellular (large cell) and parvocellular (small cell) layers. The two layers corresponding to the magnocellular division are located at the very bottom of the LGN (layers 1 and 2), whereas the parvocellular division occupies the upper four layers. These two divisions transmit different aspects of the visual information.

from the contralateral eye, whereas the magnocellular neurons in layer 2 receive their input from parasol cells of the ipsilateral eye. In terms of parvocellular processing, there are two layers devoted to each eye—layers 3 and 5 receive midget cell input from the ipsilateral eye, and layers 4 and 6 receive their input from the contralateral eye.

Although the physical distinction between magnocellular and parvocellular LGN neurons had been known for over a century, it was not until neuroscientists were able to probe the electrical activity of the LGN that the separate roles of its neurons became clearly understood. We now know that magnocellular neurons are more highly tuned to light contrast levels, whereas only parvocellular neurons are able to convey information about colour contrast, specifically the differences between red vs. green and blue vs. yellow (Kandel et al., 2000; Tovée, 1996). The LGN neurons also differ in terms of spatial and temporal aspects of visual processing. The details of the functional differences between these two pathways will be covered in Section B.4 of this chapter. For now, it is enough to understand that visual information is processed through two parallel pathways that begin in the retina and that are transmitted to the visual cortex through separate layers of the LGN that are physically distinguishable as the magnocellular and parvocellular layers (SideNote 10.6).

Regulation of information flow

The fact that LGN neurons show a centre–surround receptive field profile had been taken as evidence that these neurons serve merely as a conduit for information flowing from the retina to the visual cortex. However, it has recently been shown that LGN neurons may serve an important gatekeeping function by controlling what information actually flows through them. To understand this function, it is important first to know that the fact there is a major fibre tract between the LGN and the primary visual cortex does not mean that there is only a one-way flow of information. In fact, there is a very large return flow of signals from the visual cortex back down to the LGN as well. This seems perplexing, given that all of the higher operations pertaining to visual processing are known to occur in the cortex. Why then should there be a reverse projection back to the LGN?

A clue to the function of this backward projection was found in studies showing that LGN neurons are affected by our attentional state (Bundesen & Habekost, 2008; O'Connor et al., 2002). These results are consistent with a series of discoveries made during the 1990s, which showed that early visual structures are affected by higher-level cognitive states. LGN neurons appear to show enhanced neural activity when we are paying close attention to a visual object and reduced activity when the object is neglected. It makes sense that

attentional factors should affect neural activity in a low-level visual structure such as the LGN. There would be no point for the brain to undertake the extensive neural computations necessary for processing a visual object through the various parts of the cortex only to discard the end product because we are not interested in the information. If we are keenly attending to an object, the neurons involved in processing that stimulus would be expected to have greater activity. By modulating the activity at the LGN level, the visual system can be more efficient because it makes a selection, early in the neural pathways, as to which signals to amplify in response to a greater attentional interest (SideNote 10.7).

3. THE SUPERIOR COLLICULUS

Residing below the LGN and closer to the midline is a paired structure known as the *superior colliculus*, or SC. The SC is functionally divided into two major zones—the superficial layers and the deep layers. A subset of the retinal fibres projecting to the LGN sends a branching or collateral fibre to superficial layers of the SC (Bear et al., 2006; Chalupa & Werner, 2003). Thus, retinal fibres project directly to this structure and form a retinotopic layout of the contralateral visual field in the superficial layers. However, unlike with the LGN, there is no fibre output directly from the SC to the visual cortex. This does not mean that the SC cannot influence cortical activity. There is a pathway out of the SC through another subcortical structure within the thalamus, known as the *pulvinar*, that in turn projects to a wide part of the visual cortex. This pathway is nowhere near as dominant as the main **geniculocortical pathway**. For example, destroying the LGN or the optic radiation produces a total loss of visual sensation (blindness). Interestingly, patients suffering this kind of blindness retain an ability to locate a source of light by pointing or orienting themselves toward it. This interesting phenomenon, which was first reported in 1905, has been termed **blindsight**. It is believed that the pathway through the SC and pulvinar is responsible for this rudimentary visual ability, though it is unable to generate true visual sensory experience that we know as sight (SideNote 10.8) (Squire et al., 2002; Weiskrantz, Warrington, Sanders, & Marshall, 1974; Wurtz, Sommer, & Cavanaugh, 2005).

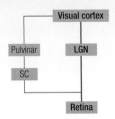

Methodology

The Blindsight Phenomenon

Blindsight is the ability to respond to visual stimuli in the absence of perceptual awareness or sight. Many psychophysical tests have looked at this surprising finding in both humans and monkeys. Monkeys with blindsight were able to discriminate shapes, had some visual acuity, and were sensitive to movements. One of the earliest tests on human patients was conducted in 1974 by Weiskrantz and Warrington. They found that, when using simple two-alternative forced-choice paradigms, their patient, D.B., could discriminate both the orientations of gratings and whether an object was moving or stationary, had some residual visual acuity, and could indicate approximately where in space an object was located, sometimes at an accuracy of >80%. Other research has focused on the physiological aspects of blindsight to determine how these rudimentary visual aspects remain. From the retina, axons project mainly to the lateral geniculate nucleus (LGN), but some information is sent to the superior colliculus (which controls how the eyes move toward a target), the suprachiasmatic nucleus (which controls daily circadian rhythms such as the sleep–wake cycle, and many hormones), and the pretectum (which coordinates the pupillary light reflex). These three areas have been implicated in the residual functioning of patients such as D.B.

Like the LGN, the SC receives a large descending input from the visual cortex that arrives into the superficial layers. However, the more interesting inputs into the SC actually arrive from two other sensory systems—the somatosensory and the auditory. The cortical areas for these systems send their fibres into the deep layers, where they are coordinated with the visual information processed in the superficial layers. In fact, the deep layers of the SC have the same map of the visual field that is found in the superficial layers. The integration of visual, auditory, and somatosensory cues makes the SC an unusual neural structure and one that has been of major interest to the neuroscientific community. It has been widely studied, especially with respect to how it integrates the various kinds of sensory information.

The integrative role of the SC begins to make sense when its main function is considered (Chalupa & Werner, 2003; Squire et al., 2002). The SC has a major output to motor areas of the brainstem, through which it controls the **saccades**, the rapid orienting movements of the eyes. We make a saccadic eye movement whenever we shift our gaze from one object to another. The visual, auditory, and somatosensory maps in the SC are all in register so that when a stimulus is in a particular part of space with respect to our body, we are able to coordinate the information from these cues to make an appropriate saccadic eye movement.

For example, consider a sound-emitting object that is present in the right visual field. The location of this object from both of these cues will be in register within the SC maps, and this information can be used to generate a motor signal to drive an appropriate saccadic eye movement so that our gaze is shifted to that object.

4.   OTHER SUBCORTICAL VISUAL STRUCTURES

We are able to effortlessly alter the shape of the crystalline lens to accommodate to near objects or change the size of the pupil to control how much light is allowed into the eye. Optical image defocus and light level directly affect the retinal mosaic. However, there must be a neural mechanism somewhere in the visual pathways to process this information and compute an appropriate response to be carried out by either the lens or the iris. It is unlikely that the necessary neural computations are carried out in the visual cortex because they are fairly straightforward. Furthermore, because lens control and iris control are involuntary reflexes, the computations must be carried out rapidly to ensure that an appropriate response is made as quickly as possible. It is therefore not surprising that there are dedicated neuronal clusters located in the brainstem just a short distance away from the eyes where both the accommodative and the pupillary reflexes are processed.

The midbrain controls reflex operations

A small subset of the retinal fibres proceeding toward the LGN sends off branches that are directed toward two areas known as the midbrain *pretectum* and the *Edinger-Westphal* nucleus. Both of these are small collections of neurons that process specific aspects of visual information (Chalupa & Werner, 2003). For example, if the light level in the retinal image is too low or high, this information is quickly computed in these structures and a motor signal is sent back to the eyes through a separate nerve (not the optic nerve, which only carries retinal signals out of the eye). The motor signal affects tiny muscles in the iris that adjust the diameter of the pupil, allowing either more or less light to enter the eye (SideNote 10.9). Similarly, optical image defocus is detected in these neural structures, and an appropriate signal is sent to the ciliary muscle to change the accommodative state of the eyes. For example, if we shift our gaze to a nearby object, then the exact need for added optical power is quickly determined, and a signal is sent to the eyes so that a positive accommodative response occurs before we are even perceptually aware of the retinal blur that triggered this response.

The suprachiasmatic nucleus drives circadian rhythms

All animals display behaviour that is linked to the day–night cycle, such as feeding, mating, and sleeping. It has long been believed that these cyclical patterns, known as **circadian rhythms**, are driven by an internal clock that is regulated by environmental light levels. A major advance in our understanding of these patterns occurred in the early 1970s, when researchers showed that a small nucleus located just above the optic chiasm serves as the circadian oscillator (Bear et al., 2006; Chalupa & Werner, 2003). The aptly named *suprachiasmatic nucleus* receives a small subset of retinal fibres that processes information about light levels in the environment. The neurons from this structure project to the *pineal gland*, which is responsible for producing and secreting the hormone **melatonin**. Light activation of the suprachiasmatic nucleus has an inhibitory effect on melatonin production, which therefore occurs mostly at night. Melatonin, which is released into the bloodstream, exerts wide influence on the nervous system. The fact that much of it is produced at night may in fact be the trigger for the onset of sleep (SideNote 10.10).

B. The Primary Visual Cortex

We now arrive at the primary visual cortex, which is located in the occipital lobe at the very back of the brain. The processing of visual information here takes a significant jump in complexity. As we will see, the centre–surround contrast detection that was a major feature of neurons in earlier parts of the visual pathway now gives way to more complex aspects of vision. Indeed, there is a stepwise increase in receptive field complexity as we proceed through the hierarchy of cortical areas. All visual signals from the LGN are directed only at the primary visual cortex and therefore this structure serves as the gateway for all later cortical processing. Consequently, visual neuroscientists over the past four decades have been especially preoccupied with the primary visual cortex because of its central role in receiving and processing visual signals.

The localization of visual function in the cerebral cortex was not without its fair share of controversy and even some fierce scientific debate (Gross, 1999; Hubel, 1995; Zeki, 1993). It appears that the first person to attribute the posterior cortex to visual function was an Italian anatomist named Bartolomeo Panizza in the mid-19th century. However, his observations went largely unnoticed, and soon thereafter began a decade-long battle between several scientists debating the actual location of the visual cortical area. The claims and counterclaims were based on research on monkeys in which the posterior part of the brain was surgically removed and the behaviour of the monkeys observed. Among the participants in this quarrel were noted English physiologist David Ferrier, who suggested that the visual cortex was localized to a part of the parietal lobe, and German physiologist Hermann Munk, who claimed that the occipital lobe was actually the seat of visual function. The quarrel became so serious that the combatants even brought their brain-lesioned monkeys to scientific meetings so that they could be examined by other scientists. In the end, the evidence pointed clearly to the occipital lobe as being a principal visual area, a conclusion that was eventually accepted by much of the scientific community (SideNote 10.11).

The primary visual cortex derives its name from being the first cortical area to process visual information. A distinctive anatomical feature of this part of the cortex is a band of fibres, quite visible in cross-sections of the brain, that runs through the middle layers (Chalupa & Werner, 2003). Because of its striated appearance, the primary visual area is also commonly referred to as the **striate cortex**. Another name that has been frequently applied is *area 17*, a term that derives from the systematic naming of cortical areas based on the careful anatomical studies of Korbinian Brodmann in the early 1900s. The most recent name to appear in the scientific literature is **area V1** ("vee-one"), a simple derivative of its role as the primary visual cortical area. This term now widely appears in the scientific literature, and it is the one we will use exclusively from here on.

1. STRUCTURE AND LAYOUT OF AREA V1

Like the LGN, area V1 is made up of six layers. It differs, however, in that its layers are numbered in the reverse order, so that layer 1 is found at the top and layer 6 at the bottom (see Figure 10.6). Immediately below layer 6 lies the white matter containing nerve fibres that carry visual information to and from area V1. The six layers of neurons together create a cortical band of grey matter that is approximately 2 mm in thickness. Considerable effort has been devoted to understanding the characteristics of the various V1 layers through both anatomical and physiological studies. Much of what we now know about area V1 derives from studies of animals, such as the cat and the monkey.

Anatomical characteristics of the various layers

The neurons within each layer of area V1 can be visualized by cutting thin sections of brain tissue and applying a staining procedure (SideNote 10.12). The right panel in Figure 10.6 shows the individual layers as revealed by way of two commonly applied staining procedures—Nissl and cytochrome oxidase staining. Nissl staining reveals an internal component of neurons, whereas cytochrome oxidase staining reveals a specific protein that is present at varying concentrations in different neurons. Both show that individual layers differ in the density of their neurons, creating a staggered pattern with cell-dense layers interspersed between less dense ones (Chalupa & Werner, 2003; Squire et al., 2002). Cytochrome oxidase staining also shows an interesting pattern in the upper layers (layers 2 and 3), indicated by the arrows in Figure 10.6, where dense zones of cytochrome oxidase staining are separated by areas of less staining. These discrete zones of rich staining, which have been termed *cytochrome oxidase blobs*, have been shown to have an important role in visual information processing. This will be taken up in Section B.3.

SideNote | **10.12**

Normally, brain cells are fairly transparent and cannot be seen in sections under a microscope unless a stain is applied. There are various stains that can be applied to label selective parts of the cells, thereby making them visible. A quick review of Section B in Chapter 2 may be helpful.

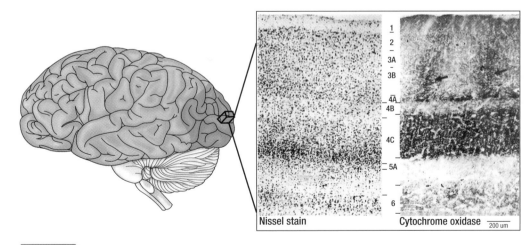

Figure 10.6

The primary visual cortex (area V1) is located in the occipital lobe, at the back of the brain (left panel). A small segment of area V1 is magnified and shown by way of two different staining procedures—Nissl and cytochrome oxidase (right panel). Both stains show that area V1 contains six major layers that differ in terms of neuronal density. Cytochrome oxidase staining also shows patches of rich staining in the upper layers (arrows) that have been termed *cytochrome oxidase blobs*.

Layer 4 is the thickest of area V1 and is divided into a set of sublayers—4A, 4B, and 4C. Layer 4C is distinctive as the site where LGN fibres terminate and synapse onto area V1 neurons. Visual information processing in area V1 therefore begins with the arrival of LGN signals in layer 4. The neural signals then propagate upward to layers 2 and 3 and downward to layers 5 and 6. There are rich sets of connections between the various layers so that any given vertical segment can be considered an interactive functional unit. The upper and lower layers perform specific communication functions with other parts of the brain. In general, neurons in layers 2 and 3 are responsible for coordinating information with other visual cortical areas, while neurons in layers 5 and 6 transmit information to subcortical structures such as the LGN and SC (SideNote 10.13).

The neurons in area V1 can be broadly classified into two groups—projection neurons and interneurons (Kandel et al., 2000). Projection neurons, as their name suggests, send information to other areas of the brain. All projection neurons are pyramidal in shape (i.e., they have a cell structure that appears triangular in cross-section and displays large dendrites that receive and integrate information from other neurons). All pyramidal neurons are excitatory in nature. Interneurons are non-pyramidal cells and are largely responsible for local connections within and between neighbouring layers in area V1. They can be either excitatory or inhibitory in nature and are found throughout the various layers in area V1. The largest pyramidal neurons are situated in the lower layers, while small- to medium-sized pyramidal neurons are found in the upper layers.

The retinotopic layout of area V1

Each point on the retina is represented in a particular part of area V1. As with the LGN, there is a systematic layout of the retina in the cortex as well. The retinotopic map of area V1, however, is not a uniform representation because the fovea enjoys greater cortical territory than the peripheral parts of the retina (Bear et al., 2006; Chalupa & Werner, 2003; Tovée, 1996). This distortion is evident from the schematic drawing in Figure 10.7. A flattened profile of the retina in the right eye is shown here with equally spaced hash marks. The retinotopic layout of area V1, shown as an unwound cross-sectional profile, depicts the foveal region (F) with an expanded

representation, whereas the peripheral retina is represented as much more compressed. The hash marks in the cortical profile correspond to the retinal ones starting at the fovea and proceeding toward the periphery.

There are two reasons for the distorted retinotopic layout in area V1. The first is the fact that the density of ganglion cells in the foveal retina is much higher than in the periphery. Therefore, the greater numbers of retinal fibres from a small central part of the retina must be accommodated by way of greater physical territory in area V1. The second reason concerns the way that cortical territory is allocated to the incoming fibres. It turns out that ganglion cells located in the fovea are given 3 to 6 times more cortical volume than are ganglion cells located in the periphery. The functional consequence of this distortion in cortical representation is that much greater neuronal computational power is available to central vision. This is precisely what would be expected given the foveal retina's much greater capacity for visual resolution, which in turn imposes the need for greater capacity in information processing in the brain.

2. PROPERTIES OF AREA V1 NEURONS

Visual information processing becomes considerably more complex once the retinal signals arrive in area V1. The neural circuits here are wired to produce more elaborate visual representations at the single cell level. As a result, receptive fields of neurons in area V1 take on more complex properties than the simpler centre–surround contrast detection that was evident in earlier areas (SideNote 10.14). Indeed, the large size of area V1 in comparison to the LGN can be explained by the need to house the many extra neurons that participate in networks responsible for the new functions. There are four important new features that appear for the first time in area V1—binocularity, orientation selectivity, directional motion selectivity, and colour contrast detection. In this section, we discuss the first three of these features, leaving the colour-coding properties of area V1 for the next chapter.

The emergence of binocularity

One of the new features to emerge in area V1 is the intermingling of eye inputs at the single cell level. We know that LGN neurons are driven exclusively by one eye, and that each LGN

SideNote | **10.13**

Layer 1 contains almost no neurons. Instead, it is filled with nerve fibres from neurons that lie in the layers below it.

SideNote | **10.14**

Receptive fields have exactly the same meaning for area V1 neurons as they did for LGN and retinal neurons (i.e., they are maps of the retina that influence the firing of a neuron). Thus, when we speak of cortical neurons having more complex properties, it is with regard to the kind of visual stimulus falling on the retina that makes those neurons optimally responsive.

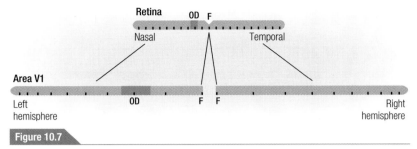

Figure 10.7

The retina from the right eye is shown in schematic form by way of a flattened profile containing 10 equally spaced hash marks. A similar flattened profile of area V1 (both hemispheres) shows that the retinal points are not equally distributed. The foveal retina enjoys much greater cortical territory than the peripheral retina, leading to a distorted retinotopic map. F = fovea; OD = optic disk.

layer is composed only of monocular neurons. Given that these monocular LGN neurons send their axons to layer 4C of area V1, we can assume that monocular neurons should also be present in area V1, and that there should exist a roughly equal distribution of such neurons driven by either the left or the right eye. This is because each LGN receives separate inputs from both eyes and in turn transmits that input into area V1 on the same side.

While both of these properties hold true, it also turns out that many area V1 neurons display convergent input from both eyes. One of the important discoveries made by David Hubel and Torsten Wiesel, whose studies of the LGN were described earlier, was that many area V1 neurons can be activated by light stimulation of either eye or of both eyes simultaneously (Hubel & Wiesel, 1962, 2004). Hubel and Wiesel undertook a large series of electrophysiological studies of area V1 in cats and monkeys starting in the 1950s. They discovered very early in their research that, whereas LGN neurons are exclusively monocular, area V1 neurons are characterized by their **binocularity**, a key feature that distinguishes them from neurons in earlier parts of the visual pathway.

The response properties of monocular and binocular neurons are compared in Figure 10.8 on page 326. Each activity profile here shows action potentials—represented as discrete vertical bars—in response to light stimulation of the left eye only, of the right eye only, and of both eyes together. Monocular neurons in area V1 show a preference for a particular eye and will respond with a vigorous discharge of action potentials only when the preferred eye is stimulated. When both eyes are stimulated, the response is similar to that seen with light

stimulation of the preferred eye alone. These profiles are similar to what would also be observed with monocular neurons in the LGN. A binocular neuron in area V1, on the other hand, shows increased firing when either eye is stimulated (see bottom set of activity profiles in Figure 10.8). However, its strongest discharge occurs when both eyes are simultaneously stimulated, because the responses for either eye alone are now summated. A perfectly binocular neuron will show precise summation, so that the response to stimulation of both eyes is twice that of the response to stimulation through either eye alone (SideNote 10.15) (Hubel & Wiesel, 1962; Squire et al., 2002).

The profiles in Figure 10.8 show the response patterns of neurons that are either strictly monocular or perfectly binocular. Hubel and Wiesel found that there was more to area V1 neurons than this simple dichotomy; instead, there was a gradient of binocularity. In other words, although strictly monocular neurons were certainly present, the binocular neurons displayed a range of responses in terms of how the two eyes' inputs were summated. In order to classify these different types of neurons, Hubel and Wiesel established the **ocular dominance** scale, which defined type 1 neurons as being driven exclusively by the contralateral eye and type 7 neurons as being driven exclusively by the ipsilateral eye. In between were neurons that showed different degrees of preference for either eye, with type 4 representing equal preference (i.e., perfectly binocular). Figure 10.9 on page 326 shows a histogram of neurons belonging to each category, based on a sample of response properties gathered by Hubel and Wiesel (1962). As one can see, the strictly monocular neurons (types 1 and 7) represent a minority. Indeed, most neurons in area

SideNote | **10.15**

Primates are born with binocular functions in area V1. However, the response properties of the binocular neurons are fairly weak and become mature only through visual experience in early life. If one eye is blind throughout early development, then binocularity is permanently lost, even if visual function is restored to the blind eye in adulthood. Thus, the maturation of binocular responses in area V1 is critically dependent on normal visual input through both eyes in early development.

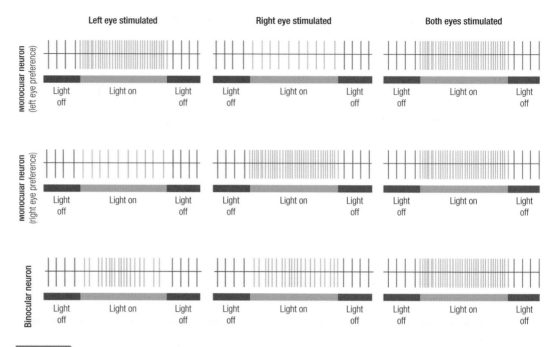

Figure 10.8

Monocular neurons in area V1 show a vigorous discharge of action potentials (represented by the vertical bars) when stimulated through the preferred eye—that is, a neuron with a preference for the left eye will fire only when that eye is stimulated with light; it remains unresponsive when the other eye is stimulated (top panel). A right eye–preferring neuron displays the opposite pattern of responses (middle panel). A binocular neuron shows an increase in action potentials when either eye is stimulated and a summation of the two responses when both eyes are stimulated together (bottom panel).

V1 show some degree of binocular influence, with type 4 being the most common.

The question that arises at this point concerns the role of the binocular neurons and, specifically, what functions they serve in terms of visual perception. We have known since the time of Euclid, the famous Greek mathematician of the 4th century BCE, that vision with two eyes offers distinct advantages over vision with just one eye (Wade, 1998). However, it was not until the elegant work of Charles Wheatstone in the 19th century that we began to understand how images from the two eyes can be combined to provide an impression of the relative depth of different objects in our visual world. Binocular neurons, because they receive visual signals from both eyes, are perfectly suited to undertake comparisons of the two retinal images. We will see in Chapter 12 how the binocularity feature of area V1 neurons ultimately allows us to perceive the relative depths of different objects in the environment.

Orientation selectivity

The receptive field layout of both retinal ganglion cells and LGN neurons displays a centre–surround antagonistic arrangement in which

the centre is either excitatory (ON) or inhibitory (OFF). We have learned in earlier chapters that this layout is perfectly suited for the local

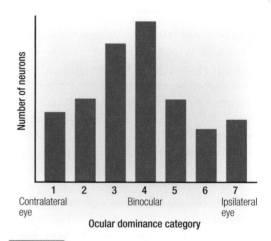

Figure 10.9

A histogram showing the distribution of area V1 neurons according to ocular dominance category. Type 1 and type 7 neurons are strictly monocular, preferring the contralateral and ipsilateral eyes, respectively. The majority of area V1 neurons show some degree of binocular influence, with type 4 (equal influence from both eyes) being the most numerous. Adapted from "Receptive Fields, Binocular Interaction and Functional Architecture in the Cat's Visual Cortex," by D. H. Hubel and T. N. Wiesel, 1962, *Journal of Physiology, 160,* pp. 106–154.

detection of contrast. However, one of the disadvantages for a neuron having a circular receptive field is that it is not well suited for detecting the orientation of an extended light stimulus. For example, a light bar, whether it be vertical, horizontal, or lying at some oblique angle, would generate the same rate of action potential firing in a centre–surround LGN neuron because of its circular receptive field symmetry.

This limitation presents a potential problem for the brain when deciphering the orientation of an extended object because visual neurons with circular receptive fields are fundamentally unable to encode orientation (SideNote 10.16). And yet, most objects in our world are oriented edges or elements, so there must be some way by which the visual brain can obtain this information. A crucial discovery was made in the early 1960s, again by Hubel and Wiesel, as to just how orientation is encoded by visual neurons (Hubel & Wiesel, 1962, 1968, 2004). While exploring the properties of area V1 by way of electrophysiological experiments, they discovered that many neurons displayed receptive fields that were elongated along a particular axis. Many of the neurons nevertheless continued to display response antagonism if light fell on different areas. Yet the ON and OFF subfields were now found to be rectangular rather than circular, as shown in Figure 10.10.

The elongated profile of area V1 receptive fields naturally led researchers to question how the same process could occur from inputs with circular fields. Hubel and Wiesel proposed that neurons with centre–surround receptive fields, such as those in the LGN, feed onto area V1 neurons in a very precise manner. For example, consider three LGN neurons whose receptive fields are staggered vertically with respect to each other (Figure 10.10). An area V1 neuron receiving convergent input from these three neurons will display a vertically elongated receptive field owing to summation of its inputs. In other words, the elongated profile of the centre and surround components of the three LGN neurons when considered together would account for the vertical orientation of the cortical neuron's receptive field. In a similar way, area V1 neurons whose receptive fields are oriented at other angles (see the examples in Figure 10.10) can be generated by convergent input from LGN neurons whose receptive fields are arrayed along the corresponding axes (SideNote 10.17).

Neurons with all possible receptive field orientations have been reported in area V1. The capacity of these neurons to detect orientation arises from the fact that an elongated light stimulus will trigger maximum activity only in those neurons with a similar receptive field orientation (Chalupa & Werner, 2003; Palmer, 2002; Squire et al., 2002). This property, known as **orientation selectivity**, is described in greater detail in Figure 10.11 on page 328, which features a neuron with a vertically elongated receptive field as an example. A horizontal light bar will elicit the smallest response

SideNote | **10.16**

The best stimulus for a neuron with a centre–surround receptive field structure is a doughnut-shaped light stimulus with a dark centre (optimal for an OFF/ON neuron) or vice versa (optimal for an ON/OFF neuron). A quick inspection of your visual surroundings will show that there are not too many such stimuli. Instead, most visible objects are oriented along a particular axis.

SideNote | **10.17**

There are other arrangements in addition to the ones shown in the box in Figure 10.10. For example, the ON and OFF areas can be reversed so that the central zone is inhibitory. Also, there may be only one ON and one OFF zone appearing side by side. Such a neuron is considered to be an edge detector, since it optimally fires to a light bar situated adjacent to a dark one.

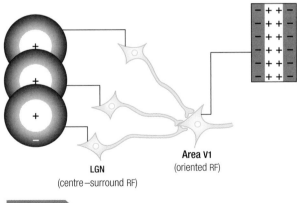
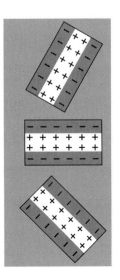

LGN
(centre–surround RF)

Area V1
(oriented RF)

Figure 10.10

According to a model originally proposed by Hubel and Wiesel, visual neurons organized with circular receptive fields (RF) converge upon cortical neurons in area V1. The cortical neuron in this example becomes endowed with a vertically elongated receptive field owing to summation of the input neurons' receptive fields, which are arrayed along this axis. Cortical neurons display receptive field orientations along many different axes (some examples are shown in the box).

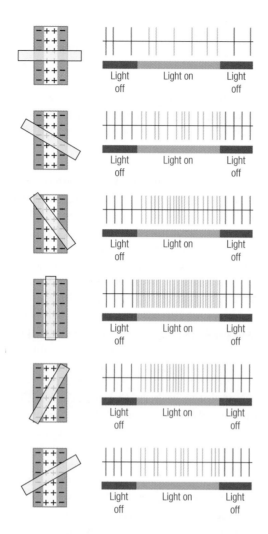

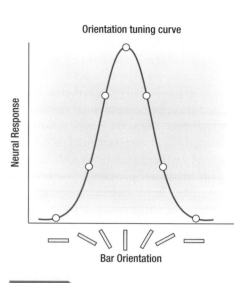

Orientation tuning curve

Bar Orientation

Figure 10.11

The neural response of an orientation-selective neuron depends on the relationship of the light bar's orientation to that of the receptive field. The series of firing profiles along the left shows that maximum firing will occur when the light bar is vertical and therefore coincident with the vertical orientation of the receptive field. Minimum firing will occur with a horizontal light bar. The orientation tuning curve provides a summary of firing rate data as a function of bar orientation.

from this neuron because it will affect the ON and OFF subfields equally. As the orientation of the light bar becomes more vertical, the firing rate will increase correspondingly, achieving a maximum rate when the light bar is perfectly vertical. The neuron's response profile (i.e., its action potential firing rate), which is shown along the left side of this figure, can be plotted in terms of the light bar's orientation to reveal its **orientation tuning curve**. In this example, we see a symmetric decline in the firing rate as the orientation is changed from its peak response for bars oriented vertically. The location of the peak for any given neuron's tuning curve will, of course, depend on the orientation of its receptive field. For example, a cortical neuron with a receptive field elongated horizontally will display maximum response for light bars at this orientation and minimal response for bars oriented vertically.

Directional motion selectivity

The mere fact that we live in a dynamic world where we and many of the objects around us

are in motion brings us to the idea that there must be motion-detecting neurons within our visual system. This requirement exists because the direction of movement of an image across the retina needs to be efficiently encoded by visual neurons in order to create a vivid perceptual impression of motion. Although movement detectors have been reported in the retina of some species, it turns out that neurons specialized for detecting the direction of motion appear in primates for the first time only in area V1. Given the importance of motion information in our daily lives, it is not surprising that these specialized neurons are found at such a relatively early site in the entire hierarchy of visual brain structures.

The property of motion detection that is readily apparent in area V1 is **directional selectivity**, whereby a neuron shows significantly greater firing to stimulus movement in a particular direction compared with all others (Palmer, 2002; Rosenzweig et al., 1999; Squire et al., 1999). This property is easily illustrated by plotting the neuron's firing rate in a radial manner, as shown in Figure 10.12. The firing rate is plotted on a particular axis for stimulus movement in either direction along that axis. The resulting response profile provides a neat way to visualize a neuron's directional preference. For example, the left diagram shows that this particular neuron responds equally well regardless of which direction the light bar is moving because the **directional tuning curve** shown here has a circular profile. A circular tuning profile is characteristic of non-directional neurons because they fire equally well to all directions of stimulus movement.

The neuron shown in the right diagram, on the other hand, has a strong directional preference. It displays a vigorous response only when the light bar moves at an angle of 45° and a greatly reduced response at other angles. In fact, the narrow tuning curve indicates that this is a neuron that displays strong directional selectivity. Other directionally selective neurons may show a broader tuning curve, where the preference for one direction is only moderately greater than that for other directions. There is a broad range of such directionally selective neurons, covering all possible directions of movement, in area V1. Together, these directionally selective neurons represent the initial stages of a complex series of neural operations underlying motion perception. We will return to this topic in Chapter 13, where we will take a much closer look at biological motion processing.

3. FUNCTIONAL ARCHITECTURE OF AREA V1

The emergence of binocularity, orientation, and directional selectivity leads to the question of how these new features are organized throughout area V1. One possibility is that neurons that process these stimulus qualities are located throughout area V1 in a somewhat random manner. Under this scheme, any two neighbouring neurons may differ considerably in terms of their direction, orientation, or eye preference. On the face of it, such an arrangement would seem unlikely because neurons with similar properties are likely to be concentrated in one location so that the brain can more effectively create the elementary neural circuits needed for perception. This is indeed the case, and again, it was the groundbreaking work of David Hubel and Torsten Wiesel that paved the way to more than four decades of subsequent research on the **functional architecture** of area V1.

Ocular dominance columns

We saw in Section B.2 that area V1 neurons have a range of preferences in terms of binocularity, with some preferring the contralateral eye and others the ipsilateral eye, a feature known as *ocular dominance*. Hubel and Wiesel, in the course of their electrophysiological studies, discovered that there was a systematic shift in eye preference among neurons throughout area V1 (Hubel, 1995; Hubel & Wiesel, 2004). This shift became especially prominent when their recording electrode passed through area V1 at an oblique angle with respect to the surface of the cortex. Interestingly, no such shift was apparent when a recording electrode entered the cortex vertically. Hubel and Wiesel took this information to mean that area V1 was organized functionally into a set of columns, with each column containing neurons that preferred one eye to the other (SideNote 10.18).

The columns, which are about 400 μm (0.4 mm) thick, are arranged in an interdigitated manner with "left-eye preferring" and "right-eye preferring" columns repeating throughout much of area V1. The existence of these so-called **ocular dominance columns** did not come entirely as a surprise because columnar organization was already known to exist in the somatosensory cortex. American neuroscientist Vernon Mountcastle had shown in the 1950s that neurons responsive to the different modalities of touch were arranged in columns in the primary somatosensory cortex (area S1),

SideNote | **10.18**

Each column of area V1 contains neurons with a stronger preference for either the left (L) or the right (R) eye. An electrode that enters the cortex in an oblique manner will pass through a series of such columns and will therefore display a periodic shift in eye preference among the neurons it encounters. An electrode that enters the cortex vertically will likely be restricted to just one of the columns and will therefore display neurons that prefer only one of the eyes.

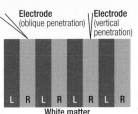

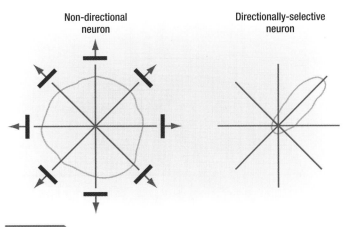

Non-directional neuron   Directionally-selective neuron

Figure 10.12

Directional preference for a visual neuron can be shown by way of a radial plot in which the firing rate is shown at two points on an axis for stimulus movement in either direction along that axis. The circular directional tuning curve in the left diagram is typical for a non-directional selective neuron because a similar neural response is seen along all directions of movement. The tuning curve in the right diagram indicates that this neuron is highly directional-selective, given its strong preference for motion at 45° and a much reduced response at all other angles.

as described in Chapter 3. The findings in area V1 reinforced the idea of cortical columns as elementary structures and led to their broad acceptance as a major architectural feature of the cerebral cortex (Gross, 1999; Zeki, 1993).

How do ocular dominance columns arise in the first place? The top diagram in Figure 10.13 shows how LGN projections arriving into layer 4C of area V1 become separated in terms of eye representation. Recall that the LGN is divided into six layers, with three layers representing each eye. The separation of inputs in area V1 occurs because neurons from LGN layers representing the right and the left eyes project into alternating sectors of layer 4C. It is this anatomical separation in LGN inputs that sets up the ocular dominance architecture. Once the inputs arrive into layer 4C, their influence extends to other layers by way of vertical signal projections above and below,

as indicated by the arrows in Figure 10.13. As a result, neurons in the other layers favour the same eye, thereby creating a series of vertical ocular dominance columns that span the entire thickness of the cortex.

Orientation columns

Hubel and Wiesel discovered yet another important architectural feature of area V1—that neurons with similar orientation preferences are clustered together in vertically oriented columns similar to the ones described above for ocular dominance (Hubel & Wiesel, 2004). These so-called **orientation columns** are approximately half the width of the ocular dominance columns. Neurons within each orientation column are largely tuned to a specific bar orientation. Hubel and Wiesel discovered that the orientation preference changed in a systematic fashion among

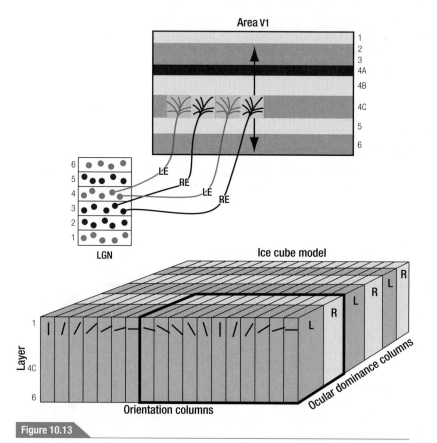

Figure 10.13

Neural projections from the LGN arrive into discrete, interdigitated sectors of layer 4C of area V1. The patches alternate in terms of eye preference owing to "right eye" versus "left eye" LGN layer projections (top diagram). Signal transfer out of layer 4C in a vertical manner (as indicated by the arrows) is responsible for setting up the vertically oriented ocular dominance columns. According to the original model proposed by Hubel and Wiesel, these columns coexist in a perpendicular fashion with a second system, the so-called *orientation columns* (bottom diagram). The three-dimensional arrangement of these two columnar systems has been referred to as the *ice-cube model*. A hypercolumn (shown in bold outline) is made up of one pair of ocular dominance columns in conjunction with a complete series of orientation columns.

neurons that were encountered during oblique electrode penetrations (see SideNote 10.18). This finding led them to conclude that there was a discrete shift in the orientation preference from one column to the next and that a series of such columns together represented all possible orientations.

The discovery of orientation columns presented a bit of challenge in terms of accommodating them physically with the ocular dominance columns. Hubel and Wiesel suggested that the two columnar systems exist in a somewhat independent manner, with one system running perpendicular to the other. This scheme, which is illustrated in the bottom diagram of Figure 10.13, became known as the **ice-cube model** because of its three-dimensional similarity to an ice cube. According to this model, the ocular dominance columns run in one direction while the orientation columns are arrayed along a perpendicular axis (Hubel, 1995; Kandel et al., 2000; Squire et al., 2002). Each ocular dominance column contains a series of orientation columns whose orientation preference changes in a regular manner until all possible orientations are represented. The entire series then repeats. Similarly, each single orientation column contains repeated alternations of "left eye" and "right eye" ocular dominance columns.

Hubel and Wiesel recognized that there existed a higher form of organization in the repeating series of orientation and ocular dominance columns. They suggested that one pair of ocular dominance columns in conjunction with one complete series of orientation columns represented a discrete module, which they termed a **hypercolumn**. The bold outline in Figure 10.13 shows an individual hypercolumn (SideNote 10.19). According to this view, area V1 is composed of a mosaic of hypercolumns containing neurons that are driven by both eyes and representing all possible orientations (Bear et al., 2006; Chalupa & Werner, 2003).

What then is the difference between one hypercolumn and the next? Recall that area V1 is characterized by a retinotopic organization in which neighbouring locations in the retina are systematically laid out. A hypercolumn therefore represents a small portion of cortex in which all visual functions are accommodated for a very small part of the retinal (and visual) field. From the brain's perspective, a hypercolumn is like a tiny window looking out into a discrete part of the world. Because an object in the real world can be of any orientation, the hypercolumn "cortical window" must be able to encode all possible orientations. A large array of such hypercolumn windows covering all of area V1 is responsible for processing visual information throughout all parts of the real world.

Cytochrome oxidase blobs

Return for a moment to Figure 10.6. The right panel in this figure shows a thin section of area V1 that has been stained for the protein *cytochrome oxidase*. This protein not only is present at high concentration along a continuous band through layer 4C but also appears in an intriguing patch-like manner in the upper layers. These patches, which are also called **blobs** because of their appearance, show up as darkened spots due to the heavy concentration of the protein in those areas. The blobs are arranged not in a random manner but along the centres of the ocular dominance columns. The intervals between the blobs, which appear pale in comparison due to reduced cytochrome oxidase staining, are referred to as the interblob regions (SideNote 10.20).

Although the cytochrome oxidase protein does not play a specific role in visual function, it is known to be generally correlated with regions of high neuronal activity. The heavy concentration of this protein in layer 4 is understandable because of its key role in receiving LGN inputs. However, it is the patch-like appearance of cytochrome oxidase in the upper layers that has led to much speculation about the possible functional roles of the blob and interblob cortical regions (Bear et al., 2006; Chalupa & Werner, 2003; Squire et al., 2002). One controversial theory is that blob areas are largely responsible for coordinating colour information. However, even nocturnal primates that do not perceive colour display cytochrome oxidase blobs in area V1, suggesting that an exclusive association between blobs and colour processing may not hold true.

It does appear, though, that the blob and interblob areas are anatomically distinct. First, the horizontal neural connections within the upper layers of area V1 maintain a blob/interblob preference (e.g., neurons within blobs are largely connected to neurons in nearby blobs). Second, the blob and interblob regions receive a somewhat different mixture of inputs from earlier layers of area V1, notably layer 4C. And

SideNote | **10.19**

The hypercolumn is just a conceptual entity in that it encompasses one pair of ocular dominance columns and a full series of orientation columns. There are no physical boundaries actually separating one hypercolumn from the next.

SideNote | **10.20**

The cytochrome oxidase protein participates in the biochemical pathways involved in cellular energy. Thus, cortical areas of high cytochrome oxidase are believed to be more active because of the higher energy requirements of the neurons there. The patch-like appearance of cytochrome oxidase staining in the upper layers, shown in the schematic diagram below, represents such discrete areas of higher neural activity.

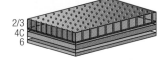

2/3
4C
6

third, neurons from the blob and interblob regions show different patterns of projection to higher areas of the visual cortex. It would be natural to ask what purpose is served by these regional differences between blob and interblob areas. It turns out that the anatomical differences can be linked to visual processing through two principal systems—the magnocellular and parvocellular channels. This relationship will be explored in detail in Section B.4.

Visualizing the architecture of area V1—functional anatomy

The early suggestions of columnar architecture within area V1, based on electrophysiological recordings, quickly led to efforts to actually visualize the columns through anatomical and imaging techniques. There is a considerable history of work in this area, and many of the developments that occurred in the 1970s and 1980s galvanized the neuroscience community. A new term, **functional anatomy**, became a popular way to describe the new efforts at understanding the functional aspects of cortical architecture. This emerging area of neuroscience was stimulated by rapid technical advances in visualizing brain activity, first in animal models and later in humans. One of the new techniques that generated considerable excitement was **optical imaging**, an elegantly simple procedure that produces maps that display areas of high neural activity in the visual cortex in response to activation by a specific stimulus (Kandel et al., 2000).

The principle behind optical recording is illustrated in Figure 10.14. An animal views a monitor on which the visual stimulus is presented. The activity generated in the visual cortex by this stimulus is captured by a sensitive LCD camera. The technique is based on the fact that brain areas that are more active reflect less light than inactive areas (SideNote 10.21). The part of the brain that is of interest is exposed and illuminated. The changes in the pattern of light reflection across this small part of the cortex are captured by a camera and then processed digitally. The optical signals from the brain can be used to visualize areas that were directly activated by the stimulus. The main advantage of this technique is that once an optical image is captured, the stimulus to which the animal is exposed can be changed and the brain activity imaged again. This allows multiple patterns of activity to be obtained in response to a series of different stimuli.

This last point is especially important for imaging the architectural features of area V1, given the differences in its columnar systems. An example of the power of this approach is shown in Figure 10.15. The left panel shows a digitally enhanced optical image of the visual

SideNote | **10.21**

Neural activity causes local changes in metabolic activity and blood flow. The change in local blood volume, oxygen level, and movement of ions and water produces changes in light scattering and reflection. These effects, which are collectively called *intrinsic signals*, make active brain regions reflect less light, something that can be captured by a sensitive imaging system.

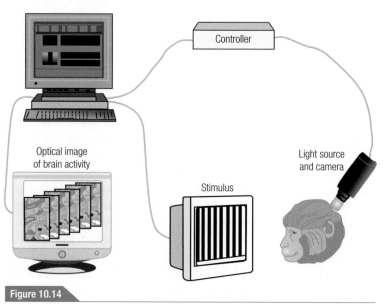

Figure 10.14

Optical imaging involves presenting an awake, behaving animal with a specific visual stimulus. The resulting neural activity in the cortex is observed through a small viewing window in the skull. The pattern of light reflection, which changes with increased brain activity, is captured by a video camera. The computer-processed optical image provides a functional map of brain activity generated in response to the visual stimulus.

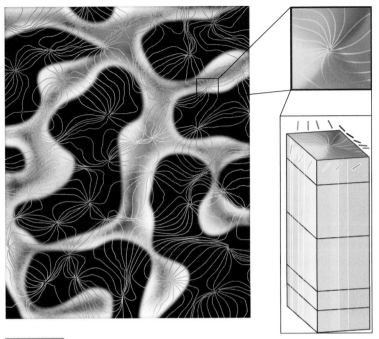

Figure 10.15

The left panel shows a superimposed pattern of the ocular dominance and orientation maps of area V1. The composite is taken from optical images in a top-down view through a small window in the skull. The broad dark and bright stripes represent the ocular dominance columns, whereas the coloured lines represent borders of the various orientation columns. An enlarged view in the right panel shows that the system of orientation columns appears as a pinwheel pattern on the surface of the cortex, where multiple columns converge into a central core. The pinwheel segments extend down through the thickness of the cortex to make up a series of vertical orientation columns.

cortex. The broad set of light and dark stripes represents the two sets of ocular dominance columns as seen from above. The optical image in this figure was gathered by having the animal look at a visual stimulus through one eye only. The topography shown here is somewhat different from the schematized version of the ice-cube model. Ocular dominance columns do not run in straight lines but in fact have a meandering quality. It is important to bear in mind that the viewing window into the cortex in optical imaging studies is very small, typically about 1 cm in diameter. As a result, this image shows only a small segment of the overall ocular dominance pattern across area V1.

A top-down view of the system of orientation columns can be obtained in the same animal by exposing it to a series of differently oriented bars and capturing the optical signal in response to each (Bonhoeffer & Grinvald, 1991). The superimposed pattern in the left panel of Figure 10.15 shows a series of lines that demarcate the borders of the different orientation columns. These columns are usually colour-coded to facilitate comparison. As

with the ocular dominance columns, orientation columns do not run in straight lines but in this case appear as a series of pinwheel patterns. The right panel in Figure 10.15 shows an enlarged topographic view of one such pinwheel where it can be seen that the different orientation columns converge into a central core, or *singularity*. Every orientation is represented once in this pinwheel fashion. The superimposed image of the ocular dominance and orientation systems in the left panel shows that their relationship is quite complex, though they both retain a columnar quality in that neurons within vertical slabs do show similar ocular or orientation preferences.

4.   PARALLEL VISUAL CHANNELS

We are now in a position where we can revisit our earlier discussions on parallel visual channels to see how they are represented in the visual cortex. Recall that the visual system is divided into two well-characterized parallel networks (or channels) by which visual information is transmitted, starting as early as the

SideNote | **10.22**

There is a third network of neurons starting as early as the retina, known as the *koniocellular* pathway. The neurons in the LGN belonging to this pathway are situated largely between the M- and P-layers. Compared with what is understood about the function of the two main pathways, much less is known about the koniocellular channel.

SideNote | **10.23**

Although there is a strict physical segregation of the two channels up to the input layers of area V1, there is now evidence that a mixing of neural signals begins to occur slowly from there on. The blob zones represent one site for this mixture. It is therefore more appropriate to think of neural structures at these levels and beyond as being dominated by M or P influence than as being processors of either one of them exclusively.

SideNote | **10.24**

The lesions can be performed by different means. One is to simply physically remove the portion of brain tissue that is of interest. Other methods involve injecting either anaesthetics that briefly inactivate the area (e.g., lidocaine) or chemical agents that produce a toxic degeneration (e.g., ibotenic acid).

retina. We learned in Section A.2 that the two networks remain segregated at the level of the lateral geniculate nucleus (SideNote 10.22). The two objectives of this section are as follows: to describe the neural pathways by which the magnocellular (M) and parvocellular (P) channels coordinate visual information through the cortex and to understand the different visual perceptual functions that are mediated by these two channels.

Anatomical aspects

The M- and P-channels actually originate at the level of the retina, where two different classes of retinal ganglion cells—the parasol and midget cells—can be anatomically differentiated largely by the size of their dendritic fields (Rodieck, 1998). The parasol neurons project exclusively to the magnocellular layers of the LGN, whereas the midget ganglion cells project exclusively to the parvocellular layers. The projection patterns from these two parts of the LGN to the visual cortex are shown in Figure 10.16. As can be seen here, the two channels remain anatomically segregated throughout area V1 in two ways—arrival of inputs and projection through the various parts of area V1.

The axons that arrive from the LGN through the optic radiation terminate in different parts of layer 4C, the main recipient layer of the primary visual cortex (Rodieck, 1998; Squire et al., 2002). Neurons from the M–LGN layers project to the upper half of layer 4C, whereas neurons from the P–LGN layers project to the lower half. For this reason, the two halves are differentiated, respectively, as layer $4C_\alpha$ and $4C_\beta$ (see Figure 10.16). From there, the two channels remain segregated by way of specific neural connections among the different subcompartments of area V1. For example, M-channel neurons from layer $4C_\alpha$ display specific projections to layer 4B and to the cytochrome oxidase blobs in the upper layers. The P-channel neurons in layer $4C_\beta$, on the other hand, project to both the blob and the interblob areas of the upper layers. In functional terms, this means that the blob zones process a mixture of M- and P-channel information, while the interblob zones appear to be dedicated to P-channel processes (SideNote 10.23).

It would be appropriate at this point to ask what advantages are produced by continued physical segregation of the two visual channels at this level of the visual pathway. One distinct

advantage is the fact that each pathway is dedicated to a particular type of visual information processing, as we will see in the next section. Is has been argued that by compartmentalizing neural assemblies to a particular function, the brain is able to perform its operations more efficiently. For example, assume that a particular neural network is involved in processing information about the shape of an object. From a computational point of view, it would be more efficient to have the network be dedicated solely to that function rather than being involved as well in, say, processing information about the movement of the same object, a task that can, in turn, be processed more efficiently by a different network of neurons. We now know that early vision is indeed parsed in this manner, so that different aspects of the visual stimulus are separately encoded and then later recombined. The M and P division provides a broad-based anatomical basis for the separation of duties at the early stages of visual information processing.

Functional aspects

What then are the functional differences between the M- and P-pathways in early vision? This question has been addressed by a number of techniques, including direct electrophysiological recordings from the brain, visual psychophysical studies on humans, and selective lesion studies in animal models. This last group of studies has been especially revealing. In any lesion study, the objective is to inactivate or remove a part of the brain and then observe the consequences on perception or behaviour (SideNote 10.24) (Chalupa, 2003; Kandel et al., 2000; Tovée, 1996). Lesion studies were carried out on monkeys by American neuroscientists Peter Schiller, John Maunsell, and William Merrigan in order to better understand the different roles of the M- and P-systems in visual processing. The best site to separately inactivate the M- and P-systems is at the LGN, where there is a clear physical separation of the two visual channels (i.e., layers 1 and 2 representing the M-channel and layers 3 to 6 representing the P-channel).

The results from these studies have revealed that the M- and P-channels are quite distinctive, and that each is responsible for a particular set of visual processing functions (Alonso, Yeh, Weng, & Stoelzel, 2006; Rodieck, 1998; van Essen, Anderson, & Felleman, 1992). The different properties of the two channels, as

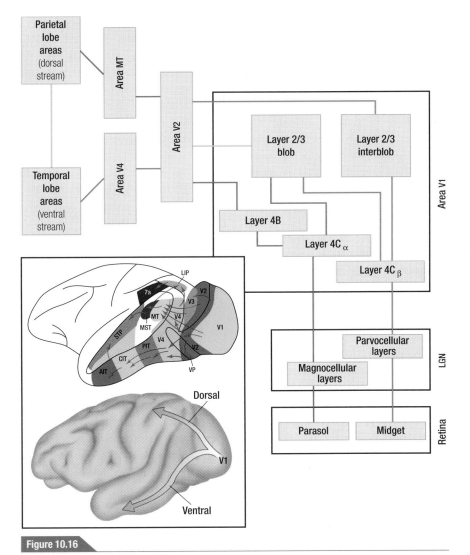

Figure 10.16

Early visual processing takes place through two major channels. The M-channel (red lines) and P-channel (green lines) are anatomically segregated in early visual structures, such as the retina, the LGN, and the input layers of area V1. This early segregation gives way to two major cortical processing streams, where visual signals become more intertwined due to cross-projections and mixed M- and P-inputs (yellow lines). The dorsal cortical stream, composed of parietal lobe structures, receives a preferential M-channel input through area MT. The ventral cortical stream, composed of temporal lobe structures, receives a more dominant P-channel input through area V4. The two general streams and the various extrastriate cortical structures that compose it are shown in the inset box.

revealed through electrophysiological, behavioural, and lesion studies, are set out in Table 10.1. To begin with, the M-channel is involved in processing visual information from the peripheral retina to a greater degree than the P-channel, which in turn is largely devoted to central vision (SideNote 10.25). Consistent with this division is the fact that receptive field sizes for parvocellular neurons are smaller than those of the magnocellular ones. Recall that in general, visual neurons in the central retina have smaller receptive fields than those in the periphery. Therefore, the general finding

that magnocellular neurons have larger receptive fields originates from the greater degree of retinal convergence upon parasol ganglion cells in the peripheral retina.

In terms of visual function, the parvocellular system shows significantly higher sensitivity in two areas (see Table 10.1 on page 336). The first is colour sensitivity, which is now known to be an almost exclusive function of the P-channel. The second is related to spatial aspects of the visual stimulus. In general, parvocellular neurons have higher spatial resolution and therefore a greater ability to resolve image

SideNote **10.25**

It should be stressed that this is not an exclusive relationship, as the converse also holds true to some degree (i.e., there is some parvocellular function in peripheral vision and magnocellular function in central vision).

detail in the stimulus. Lesion studies carried out in the P-layers of the LGN in monkeys have shown striking deficits in shape, pattern, and texture sensitivity. Monkeys that were trained to make visual discriminations along these parameters displayed reduced abilities after lesions to the parvocellular LGN layers but not after lesions to the magnocellular ones. Thus, aspects of vision related to the processing of form, colour, and object detail are largely carried by the P-channel. The M-channel, on the other hand, displays greater sensitivity to image contrast and temporal aspects of the stimulus, such as flicker. Of particular importance is the finding that lesions to the magnocellular LGN layers significantly impair motion sensitivity, something that is spared with parvocellular LGN lesions.

The findings summarized in Table 10.1 provide us with a picture of the different functional roles of the two visual processing channels (Palmer, 2002; Zeki, 1993; Tovée, 1996). The P-channel is unable to efficiently process the dynamic aspects of the visual stimulus, such as object movement in the real world. Its preference for static stimuli makes sense given its predominant role in analyzing image detail. In photography, for example, object stability is an absolute requirement in order to obtain information about the object's fine structure and composition. Similarly, the P-channel is devoted to processing the fine details of an object but only in instances where it is relatively stationary. A contrasting demand occurs when an object is rapidly moving through our visual field. This situation represents a different challenge for our visual system, which must quickly compute the trajectory of the object (e.g., to see if it is heading on a collision course toward us) or use that information to effectively coordinate a motor reaction (e.g., to move our body or guide our eye movements). As the last line in Table 10.1 shows, signal transmission in the M-system is quite rapid compared with that in the relatively sluggish P-system. This feature allows the M-system to quickly compute and transmit essential information about the movement details of an object, but at the sake of discarding its structural and compositional details (SideNote 10.26).

Parallel processing through extrastriate areas

Early vision can therefore be considered in terms of a spatial and temporal dichotomy. The P-system is devoted to the spatial details of an object, whereas the M-system is devoted to its temporal details and, most importantly, its movement characteristics. We have discovered that these two sets of operations are carried out more or less independently in the early stages of visual processing, starting with the retinal ganglion cells and proceeding all the way to the various layers and compartments of area V1. The question then becomes "What happens

SideNote 10.26

This does not necessarily mean that we cannot observe the fine detail of a moving object. A special case arises if we begin to track the object with our eyes. This causes the image on the retina to be held steadily on the fovea. The stability of this image then allows the P-system to provide us with considerable detail about the object's colour and structural composition. On the other hand, an insect that is buzzing around in our peripheral visual field generates a strong percept of motion through the M-channel but we are unable to discern the fine detail in this instance.

Table **10.1**

Key Properties of the Magnocellular and Parvocellular Systems

Visual Function	Magnocellular	Parvocellular
Retinotopic emphasis	Peripheral vision	Central vision
Receptive field size	Large	Small
Contrast sensitivity	High	Low
Colour sensitivity	Low	High
Spatial resolution	Low	High
Shape sensitivity		
Pattern sensitivity		
Texture sensitivity		
Temporal resolution	High	Low
Flicker sensitivity		
Motion sensitivity	High	Low
Neural transmission	Rapid	Sluggish

beyond area V1 in terms of the processing of these separate visual functions?"

The visual brain beyond area V1 remained poorly understood for much of the 20th century, when it was commonly described vaguely as *visual association areas*. In anatomical terms, Korbinian Brodmann identified two broad regions on the basis of microscopic appearance; he named them *area 18* and *area 19* (area 17 being equivalent to area V1). It was believed that all of the elemental visual processes were more or less completely undertaken in area V1 and then sent to the association areas, where more complex operations were responsible for creating the perception of vision. The arrival of modern electrophysiological techniques and sophisticated methods for tracing anatomical connections among different brain areas led to a revolution in our view of the visual brain beyond area V1. In the 1970s, neuroscientists began to systematically study the association areas and quickly discovered that the two general areas identified by Brodmann were actually composed of many small cortical regions, each being distinct by virtue of its anatomical characteristics, its pattern of connections to other areas, and its functional specificity (i.e., its way of processing specific aspects of the visual stimulus) (Chalupa & Werner, 2003; Hubel, 1995; Squire et al., 2002). The newly discovered areas were named either sequentially, as V2, V3, V4, etc., or by acronyms that reflected their anatomical location in the brain. In all, more than 40 distinct areas have now been identified as being involved in some kind of visual processing function beyond area V1. Together, they are collectively referred to as the **extrastriate areas** (i.e., areas that lie beyond the striate cortex, area V1).

The circuit diagram in Figure 10.16 shows signal transmission out of area V1 on to these higher areas. One of the first things we notice is that the separation of visual processing by way of the M- and P-pathways is retained to some degree throughout the higher areas. The first area beyond area V1, known as *area V2*, is compartmentalized into different repeating segments, with each receiving preferential inputs from the blob zones, the interblob zones, or layer 4B of area V1. Thus, the M and P distinction appears to carry forward through area V2 and then on to at least two higher areas, area V4 and area MT. Area V4 receives a dominant input through the P-channel (indicated by the green lines in Figure 10.16), while area MT receives a dominant input through the M-channel (shown by the red lines). The known functions of these two areas are also consistent with this preferential input. For example, neurons in area V4 are known to process information pertinent to the form of an object, such as image contours, texture, and colour—functions that are expected on the basis of area V4's P-channel link. Similarly, the functional role of area MT is supported by its M-channel link, because neurons here are highly sensitive to object motion and have been shown to be responsible for processing various aspects of movement detail (SideNote 10.27).

C. Higher Cortical Functions and Object Perception

Areas MT and V4 serve as major gateways to a host of visual areas located in the parietal and temporal lobes, respectively. The circuit diagram in Figure 10.16 shows that signal output from area MT is directed at the areas of the parietal lobe that together make up the so-called **dorsal cortical stream**. Signals from area V4 are directed at the areas of the temporal lobe that together make up the **ventral cortical stream**. The inset box in Figure 10.16 shows the different parietal and temporal lobe structures as well as the general pathways of the two cortical processing streams.

There are a number of important issues to take into account concerning the layout and functional roles of these pathways. The first concerns the integrity of the M and P division at these higher cortical levels. Although early visual structures, such as the retina, the LGN, and the input layers of area V1, display a strict segregation of the two streams, that physical separability becomes more and more blurred at the higher levels. Extrastriate visual areas are not usually thought of as having an exclusive M or P association but rather as being preferentially influenced by either of the two channels. The blurring of the M and P distinction can also be attributed to a second feature of the extrastriate visual areas—bidirectional information flow. The different visual areas laid out in Figure 10.16 are interconnected in such a manner that neural signals flow in both directions. This is referred to as *feedforward* and *feedback* projections. As a result, the crosstalk among the different cortical areas means

SideNote | **10.27**

The circuit diagram of visual brain areas in Figure 10.16 is highly simplified, given that over 40 extrastriate visual areas have been identified. The purpose of this figure is to show the key routes of M and P information flow through the hierarchy of visual areas.

that whatever preferential input any given area receives from either the M- or the P-channels becomes mixed to a certain degree.

The wide-ranging interconnections and bidirectional information flow among these many visual areas means that there is significant integration of different types of visual information. This makes sense because although the M-channel may be ideally suited to capture early visual information related to motion, ultimately we do not have separate perceptual experiences of the structure, colour, and motion of an object. Rather, we experience a unified percept, where the different facets of a visual stimulus are perceived in a cohesive manner. For that to occur, there must be considerable neural integration between the higher cortical areas that process different components of a visual stimulus. A particularly noteworthy example of this concept can be found in the interconnections between the parietal and temporal lobe areas, as shown in the circuit diagram of Figure 10.16.

The final major issue in higher visual function concerns the nature of the two cortical streams (Ungerleider & Mishkin, 1982). The dominant input into the parietal lobe areas (dorsal stream) from area MT means that these areas display qualities consistent with an M-channel link (SideNote 10.28). Again, this is not to say that the parietal visual areas are to be thought of as driven exclusively by the M-channel; rather, it could be said that they receive a more influential input from the M-channel. The operations that are carried out in the parietal (dorsal) areas are certainly consistent with this notion. We now know that many of the areas linked to the dorsal cortical stream are involved in the visual coordination of body and eye movements, a function that in turn is highly dependent upon visual input related to object motion in the real world (an M-channel function). Furthermore, many of the parietal areas are concerned with encoding extrapersonal space and the spatial relationships of external objects with respect to one's own body coordinates. For this reason, the dorsal stream has been dubbed by some as the *where* pathway because of its role in processing object locations, their spatial relationships, and movement.

We will cover the operation of the dorsal stream in greater detail in Chapter 13, where we will discuss the neural and psychophysical aspects of motion processing and eye movements. For the remainder of this chapter, we will devote our attention to the ventral cortical stream and the role it plays in visual information processing related to object detail and identity.

1. THE VENTRAL CORTICAL STREAM

The ventral cortical stream is composed of a hierarchy of visual areas found in the temporal lobe. As Figure 10.16 shows, the dominant input into the temporal lobe areas is through area V4. This means that the ventral stream can be thought of as displaying qualities that are consistent with a preferential input from the P-channel. The operations carried out in the temporal lobe areas are therefore quite distinct from those in the parietal lobe. The temporal lobe structures are largely concerned with processing visual information related to object detail, such as shape, structure, and composition. These operations are consistent with a preferential P-channel link that provides early visual input devoted to spatial detail and colour (see Table 10.1). Our perception of visual objects, from the simplest to the most complex, arises from neural operations that are largely carried out in the temporal lobe. The ventral stream has been dubbed by some as the *what* pathway, a term that aptly expresses its dominant role in processing the structural and compositional details of visual objects (Kandel et al., 2000; Milner & Goodale, 1995).

Visual areas in the temporal lobe

The temporal lobe comprises two major segments that are divided by a deep groove called the **superior temporal sulcus (STS)**. Because the temporal lobe curves downward as it arches forward, the two segments can be thought of in anatomical terms as a forward, upper region and a backward, lower region. The upper margin is called the *superior temporal cortex* and is responsible for a range of perceptual functions, most notably auditory information processing. It is the lower margin, known as the **inferior temporal cortex (area IT)**, where higher visual functions are processed. The visual areas here collectively make up the ventral cortical stream.

As Figure 10.17 shows, area IT is a large swath of cortical territory that extends from the upper boundary with the occipital lobe all the way down to its bottom-most margin, which is known as the *temporal pole* (Seltzer & Pandya, 1991). This expanse of cortex is

SideNote 10.28

We refer to the M- and P-systems as "channels" because of their strict anatomical segregation in early visual structures. The two main cortical systems are referred to as "streams" because of their more integrative characteristics. The general idea of parallel visual *channels* (M and P) in early vision therefore gives way to the notion of cortical *streams* (dorsal and ventral) in higher vision.

generally divided into three functional areas—posterior IT (PIT), central IT (CIT), and anterior IT (AIT). Although these areas are arranged in a physically declining sequence, the opposite is true of their functional sophistication. For example, area PIT receives neural inputs directly from area V4 and therefore represents the first site for complex visual processing within the temporal lobe. Neural signals from area PIT are then sent to areas CIT and AIT, where more complex visual analysis is performed. The organization and processing of complex information at these levels is referred to as *high-level* vision, in contrast to the more elemental processing that occurs at earlier cortical and subcortical levels. One of the current goals in visual neuroscience research is to understand how early signals are combined at progressively later stages in the cortical hierarchy to yield complex visual representations.

Processing schemes in high-level vision

It is undoubtedly a major challenge to understand how the brain pieces together visual signals that originate with the simple centre–surround contrast detection properties of retinal ganglion cells into a cohesive perceptual phenomenon that synthesizes these elemental signals in our mind to form complex images (Boothe, 2002; Milner & Goodale, 1995; Rock, 1984). Although we may be able to address this issue more fully in future editions of this text, for now we can summarize the key facets by way of a simple outline shown in Figure 10.18. The retinal image, as we know from our discussion in the last chapter, can be thought of as a point-by-point re-creation of light distribution in the real world. As such, the retinal image is formed according to the laws of optics, and each point of light in that image contributes to the so-called **image raster** (SideNote 10.29). This is the earliest and simplest level in terms of visual analysis, and it is from here that a stepwise set of operations begins that synthesizes the point-light distributions into cohesive representations of form and structure in area IT.

The journey to achieve that begins with the centre–surround contrast detection carried out by retinal neurons. This elegantly simple process represents the basis for creating the **form primitives** in early visual cortical structures, such as area V1. An example of this early synthesis can be drawn from the orientation-selective properties of cortical neurons, as was described earlier in this chapter. We now know

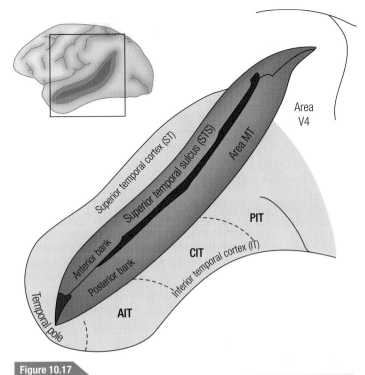

Figure 10.17

Visual processing in the temporal lobe occurs largely within the inferior temporal cortex (area IT) and much of the cortical mass that extends down into the superior temporal sulcus (STS). The STS, which is shown here in a retracted manner, extends all the way down the temporal lobe and includes several discrete visual modules, most notably area MT. High-level visual processing along area IT can be divided functionally into three broad segments—posterior IT (PIT), central IT (CIT), and anterior IT (AIT).

that extrastriate areas, such as areas V2, V3, and V4, take these operations to higher levels of sophistication by integrating information about colour, motion, and form. The net result is to create the elementary tokens of visual form analysis that then serve as the input for more complex visual operations in the inferior temporal cortex.

As Figure 10.18 on page 340 shows, visual operations in the temporal lobe begin with area PIT and then proceed to areas CIT and AIT. Together, these areas represent the major components of the ventral cortical stream and are responsible for constructing complex mental representations (Pasupathy, 2006; Schwartz, 2004; Squire et al., 2002). However, there is an interesting twist as to how information is processed in this advanced part of the visual brain. It appears that image processing at this level becomes segmented into two further streams—one dedicated to complex objects and another to faces. The evidence for this is based on single-unit studies in monkeys, brain imaging of the temporal

SideNote | **10.29**

The retinal image can be thought of as a matrix of light points (raster) by way of its optical formation characteristics as well as detection through a set of photoreceptors, which are in effect point light detectors.

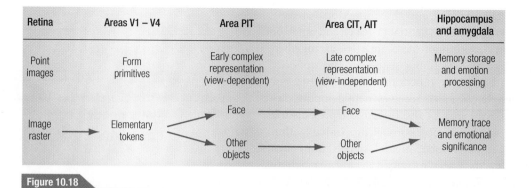

Retina	Areas V1 – V4	Area PIT	Area CIT, AIT	Hippocampus and amygdala
Point images	Form primitives	Early complex representation (view-dependent)	Late complex representation (view-independent)	Memory storage and emotion processing
Image raster	Elementary tokens	Face / Other objects	Face / Other objects	Memory trace and emotional significance

Figure 10.18

Visual analysis begins with the simple optical point-light image in the retina and proceeds to the gradual construction of more elaborate primitives to ultimately produce complex image representations within neurons of the inferior temporal cortex. There appears to be segmentation at higher cortical levels into neural systems dedicated to analysis of objects and faces. The output of these systems in the temporal lobe is directed at the hippocampus and amygdala, where memory traces and emotional significance are generated.

lobe in humans, and behavioural studies of patients with temporal lobe damage (Farah, 1990; Gross, Rocha-Miranda, & Bender, 1972; Kanwisher, McDermott, & Chun, 1997). Together, these studies have revealed the existence of separate neural systems dedicated to processing faces as well as non-face complex objects within the inferior temporal cortex. As noted before, the processes become more sophisticated as we descend through the areas of the temporal lobe (Chalupa & Werner, 2003; Gross, 1999). For example, area PIT is believed to encode early complex representations whereby object and face stimuli must have specific configurations in order to trigger activity in single neurons. However, neurons in later areas, such as areas CIT and AIT, are believed to encode late complex representations. An example of this level of complexity involves *view invariance*, the notion that neurons will fire to objects or faces under different perspective conditions. Such encoding endows us with the capability to recognize objects and people regardless of the direction from which we view them.

The output of the temporal lobe structures is directed at several neural compartments, most notably the *hippocampus* and the *amygdala*. These structures are involved in transforming the perceptual impression into a memory trace and in generating emotional significance, both of which take us into the realm of cognitive function. It is not surprising that the linkage between perception and memory takes place at this level because it is the end-product of visual processing, where we have elaborated the highest and most complex mental representations, that requires storage into long-term

memory. For example, it is only after we have fully derived the representation of an individual person's face in terms of its structural and compositional details that we would be interested in storing it for future reference and recall.

The above is a very general view of how visual processing proceeds along the ventral cortical stream. For the remainder of this chapter, we will discuss further details of the two dominant forms of higher-order visual processing—objects and faces. Although we will refer to neurobiological mechanisms where appropriate, our goal will be to concentrate on the perceptual characteristics of high-level vision within these two domains.

2. OBJECT PERCEPTION

The understanding that neural processing in the temporal lobe is responsible for object perception comes from case studies of patients who have suffered damage to this part of the brain. In the past, clinical studies have been very important for localizing the neural substrates of specific perceptual and behavioural functions, as we saw early in Chapter 2. Selective damage to the ventral visual pathways produces a disorder in which people have difficulty recognizing objects, a condition that is termed **agnosia**, but with no deficits in early visual functions or motor control (Chalupa & Werner, 2003; Farah, 1990; Schwartz, 2004). It is only the later visual functions, such as the ability to recognize and identify objects, that are selectively impaired. Some examples of this impairment are shown in Figure 10.19. In one type of agnosia, individuals are unable to recognize or copy drawings of common objects, while in another type, they are unable to unify the parts of an object or match them with shapes stored in memory. In the latter case, patients can copy and match shapes but are unable to identify them (SideNote 10.30).

Although agnosia is a relatively rare condition, its consequences highlight the critical role played by the ventral cortical stream in the analysis of structure and form. The two kinds of agnosia described above suggest that different brain areas within the ventral stream may be responsible for the analysis of structural information versus the interpretation of structural information. In other words, there is an early (perceptual) and later (interpretive) division in form perception, and that selective damage to brain areas associated with those processes produces the respective deficits. This idea is consistent with our neurobiological discussion in the preceding section, where we saw that there is a gradual progression in terms of complexity of function along the hierarchy of visual areas.

Structuralism—origins and importance

It may therefore be the case that form perception arises from the stepwise assembly of primitive visual tokens to produce successively more complex representations (Bundesen & Habekost, 2008; Chalupa & Werner, 2003; Rock, 1984). As it turns out, this idea actually has its origins from the very early days of research in experimental psychology. Nineteenth-century German psychologist Wilhelm Wundt introduced the perceptual theory known as **structuralism** as a way to explain conscious experience. Wundt is a legendary figure in psychology because he was the first to introduce a truly experimental approach that was rooted in physiological principles (SideNote 10.31). His approach was to use introspective methods (i.e., to turn one's mind inward and carefully assess the mental experiences that arose in response to a particular kind of stimulus).

The basic tenet of Wundt's structuralism was that mental experiences result from a core set of elementary building blocks that are somehow assembled together in the mind. According to this view, visual perception arises from the coalition of a set of simpler definable components. The goal of the new science of structuralism was to understand the building blocks in terms of the simplest definable components—the so-called *sensory atoms*—and then to find ways in which these components

could be fit together to produce complex forms. The problem of understanding object perception therefore boiled down to a necessity of understanding the elementary building blocks of form vision.

Structuralism represented the very first **paradigm** in experimental psychology and therefore had a major influence over how this new field of science unfolded. The methods for introspective analysis were carefully defined, and individuals were trained to become expert observers of their own mental experiences. The logic behind this approach rested on the belief that outside observers simply could not obtain information on the subjective experiences of another person. The idea that the complexity of perception could be well understood by cataloging its constitutive sensory units represented the first major theoretical foray in the new science of psychology. This early attempt, however, quickly met with some major failures. The introspectionists could not, for example, agree on the data they gathered, and therefore a bedrock scientific principle—data confirmation—could not be met. Furthermore, the many ways that a perceptual representation could be built and the sheer number of elemental sensations that could exist represented a significant challenge for the early structuralists

SideNote | **10.30**

The first type is known as *apperceptive agnosia* and is characterized by a purely perceptual loss (e.g., inability to recognize shapes or copy drawings). The second type is known as *associative agnosia* and is characterized by an inability to identify or name an object although there is no deficit in the ability to copy and draw an object.

SideNote | **10.31**

The scientific tradition of experimental psychology can be largely credited to the work and writings of Wilhelm Wundt, who is often credited as the founder of modern psychology. Wundt borrowed from the earlier philosophical principles of empiricism and introduced them to the study of conscious experience. His ideas on structuralism were popularized in the West by his English-born student Edward Titchener.

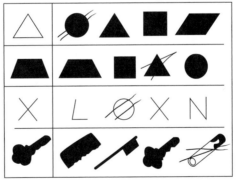
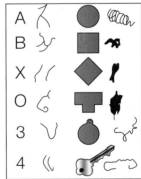

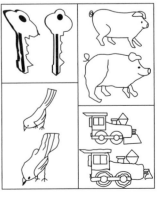

Figure 10.19

One type of agnosia results in a visual deficit of form perception. A patient with this type of agnosia is unable to compare and match different structures, as in the top left panel, where the task was to cross off the figure in the right-hand column that matched the sample figure on the left. Such patients also have difficulty in copying and drawing alphabetic characters or simple shapes (top right panel). A second type of agnosia produces a sparing of perceptual function but an inability to name the structures. Such patients are able to copy and draw even complex figures (bottom panel) but cannot compare them with shapes stored in memory in order to identify them.

Wilhelm Max Wundt (1832–1920)
© INTERFOTO/Alamy

SideNote 10.32

We previously encountered
Gestalt grouping principles in
Chapter 7, in our discussion
of tonal sequences underlying
music perception. The same
Gestalt principles discussed
here for visual perception may
be applied to the global structure of tonal forms to explain
the holistic perception of music.

attempting to catalogue them all. As a result, the doctrine of structuralism began to fade in its influence and effectively came to an end with the death of Wundt. Another major factor behind the demise of structuralism was the emergence of a new and very different theory of object perception.

Gestalt theory of object perception

The movement arose as a direct challenge to the analysis-by-parts approach that was championed by the structuralists. The origins of the Gestalt movement can be traced to the early part of the 20th century, when three psychologists—German-born Wolfgang Köhler and Kurt Koffka and Czech-born Max Wertheimer—began to promote the view that object perception simply did not occur by an assembly of elemental parts (Kanizsa, 1979; Köhler, 1969). Indeed, they rejected all aspects of structuralism, from its basic foundations to its theoretical assumptions and even its method of data collection by introspection. Instead, the Gestaltists proposed that object perception had an intrinsic quality that was based on the *wholeness* of structure, something that could not be reduced to its constituent parts or even to the relationship among those parts. This notion is perhaps best captured by the oft-cited mantra of the Gestalt school: "The whole is different from the sum of its parts."

The idea that object perception arises from the overall structure of a visual image led the Gestaltists to propose a number of rules that governed the global interactions within a stimulus. They called them "laws" of perceptual organization. The *law of similarity* asserted that similar items appear to be grouped together because they share common features in terms of shape, size, orientation, colour, or lightness. The top left panel in Figure 10.20 shows how the arrangement of dots placed against a background of smaller squares makes them stand out to form the letter *A* (Köhler, 1969). The similarity of the dots in terms of their size and shape is what causes them to be grouped together to produce the form. Another grouping principle formulated by the Gestaltists is that of *closure*, which asserts that a single closed pattern can obscure its components. This is illustrated by the bottom panel in Figure 10.20. In the top part of this box, the letters *M* and *W* stand out quite clearly, but they become less apparent when the two become intertwined (middle) and even less so when they completely

overlap (bottom). In the latter case, the closure of the elements produces the impression of three linked *X*s, although the original letters can be made out if careful attention is paid to the contours. Another example can be found in the top right panel of Figure 10.20. The pattern shown here is actually a hand-written version of the word *men*; however, it is shown in conjunction with its mirror image in such a way to produce a closed pattern that makes it appear instead as a series of heart-like forms (SideNote 10.32).

A number of other Gestalt laws have been proposed but are not discussed here in detail. These include the *law of proximity* (near items appear to be grouped together), the *law of simplicity* (items are organized into figures in the simplest way possible), the *law of good continuation* (clusters of individual elements are perceived as forming a single contour), and the *law of common fate* (items moving in the same direction are grouped together). In all of these cases, the laws were derived not through formal experimentation but rather through the simple reporting of phenomenal events (i.e., straightforward demonstrations that produced perceptual impressions that were universally accepted). An elegant example of this common experience can be drawn from the so-called *subjective contours*, or Kanizsa figures (Kanizsa, 1979). These demonstrations, which were originally introduced by Italian psychologist Gaetano Kanizsa, produce a strong perceptual impression of form in the absence of any physical contours. Two examples of such illusory figures are shown in Figure 10.21 (Bradley & Petry, 1977; Kanizsa, 1979). The triangle and cube that form in the background do not really exist but are perceived because of the way that the black discs are segmented and arranged with respect to each other. The Gestaltists would argue that only a **holistic** mechanism can be responsible for the perception of these figures because sensory analysis of the figures at the elementary (structural) level cannot account for their emergence in our mind.

The Gestalt principles have also been used to explain perceptual organization in terms of **figure–ground segregation**. In Gestalt terms, this notion is based on the observation that a salient figure or foreground impression stands out and is therefore distinguishable from background stimulation. This concept is easily understood in vision, where any object appears

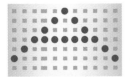

Figure 10.20

The Gestalt law of similarity proposes that items that are similar in nature appear to be grouped together to create form, as in the round dots against a background of smaller squares (top left panel). The Gestalt principle of closure explains how interacting items can create a closed pattern that obscures its components (bottom panel). The same phenomenon can be observed by the example in the top right panel, showing the word *men* placed in conjunction with its mirror image to produce a series of heart-like shapes. Adapted from *The Task of Gestalt Psychology*, by W. Köhler, 1969, Princeton, NJ: Princeton University Press.

distinct from some kind of a background, whether it is structured or homogeneous. A common example used in such discussions is the famous vase-face image that was popularized by Danish psychologist Edgar Ruben (Figure 10.22, left panel). There are two possible interpretations of Ruben's figure—a central white vase stands out over a dark background, or two opposing dark faces appear over a white background. One of the consequences of figure–ground organization is that the figure is perceived as a holistic (Gestalt) ensemble that lies in front of the ground. What is interesting about Ruben's vase is that the figure and

ground can alternate in time, with both versions producing equally plausible perceptions. There are many different examples of such illusions that are generated by differing interpretations of figure and ground (SideNote 10.33).

A final factor in perceptual organization that is worth discussing is the value of past experience (Bundesen & Habekost, 2008; Rock, 1984; Schwartz, 2004). Max Wertheimer, one of the founders of **Gestalt psychology**, believed that prior interaction with an object can affect the way it is perceived in later instances. Consider the right panel in Figure 10.22, which is an inverted version of Ruben's vase. The vase in this instance appears more salient because the upside-down faces are difficult to

SideNote 10.33

Is the figure below that of an attractive young woman or a man with a very large nose playing a saxophone?

Figure 10.21

The holistic (Gestalt) nature of form perception is apparent in these two examples of Kanizsa figures. Neither the white triangle nor the cube actually exists in either image; both are created in the mind because of the way the black discs are segmented and arranged with respect to each other. A structural analysis of the two images based on the arrangements of the discs fails to account for the perception of the illusory images. (Left) Adapted from *Organization in Vision: Essays on Gestalt Perception*, by G. Kanizsa, 1979, New York, NY: Praeger. (Right) Adapted from "Organizational Determinants of Subjective Contour: The Subjective Necker Cube," by D. R. Bradley and H. M. Petry, 1977, *American Journal of Psychology, 90*, pp. 253–262.

Figure 10.22

The relationship between figure and ground can alternate in ambiguous situations, such as the Ruben's vase figure (left panel). There are two alternative percepts—a white vase in the foreground over a uniform black background, or two opposing black faces over a white background. An inverted version of this figure (right panel) largely invokes a foreground vase percept because upside-down faces are difficult to perceive as such.

perceive as such. Once we are convinced that this is indeed an inverted Ruben's vase figure, then the inverted face images become more salient and appear to pop into our mind with greater frequency. Another example of the effect of past experience is given in Figure 10.23, which shows what initially appears to be a random array of black marks over a white background. However, it is immediately apparent to those familiar with this image that the black marks in the middle right part of the image cohere into that of a Dalmatian that is sniffing the ground. To those who are seeing this figure for the first time, it is worth making the effort to ensure that a convincing image of the Dalmatian is perceived (the dog's head is located exactly in the middle of the figure). Although familiarity is not one of the fundamental Gestalt principles, it nevertheless has a profound effect on object perception in ambiguous situations. It is a certainty that those who have now been able to observe the Dalmatian in this figure will in all future occasions perceive it instantly when viewing this image.

Modern structural theories—introduction

The Gestalt laws were formulated to account for the holistic nature of perception by describing the global interactions that lead to the *wholeness* of objects. In scientific terms, however, it is really not appropriate to refer to the Gestalt formulations as "laws" but as "principles." A law must account for a comprehensive set of observations that have their

basis in a firm set of predictions. The Gestalt principles, therefore, are usually regarded not as laws but as **heuristics** (i.e., the most plausible solution to a particular problem given the circumstances). Although Gestalt principles do account for many aspects of object perception, they are not robust enough to account for visual impressions under all possible stimulus configurations.

The major problem with Gestalt theory, however, lies in the fact that it is difficult to reconcile it with our current understanding of visual analysis by biological systems. We have come to see how neural processing in the primate visual system involves a stepwise approach to complex representations from the assembly of early level visual tokens. The entirely holistic concept of Gestalt psychology is therefore at odds with the structured nature of biological analysis. Although the Gestalt approach had been influential for its ability to account for numerous aspects of perceptual experience, current views on object analysis have reverted more to structural concepts of perceptual organization.

Modern structural theories—FIT

One of the modern structural theories that has been quite influential is **feature integration theory (FIT)**, which was proposed by British psychologist Anne Treisman. According to FIT, visual processing begins with the capture of elemental features across the retinotopic map. These early level tokens are conceptually similar to the physiologically defined primitives, such as contrast, colour content, and orientation. This so-called *feature map* is what our visual system has to work with at the earliest levels, before any of the higher cognitive factors such as attention begin to have their influence. In fact, one way in which Treisman and others have identified the basic characteristics of the features in this pre-attentive elemental map is through simple demonstrations of **pop-out phenomena**. As Figure 10.24 shows, certain features such as oriented line segments or contrast differences immediately pop out regardless of the number of distracters (other tokens). The elementary features at this pre-attentive stage represent the alphabet of the visual system and can be contrasted with later complex features that require greater analysis, such as the more intricate patterns contained in numerical forms (Figure 10.24, right panel). In this

Figure 10.23

The effect of familiarity can have a profound effect on object perception. A prior knowledge of this figure leads to instant identification of a Dalmatian sniffing the ground. However, those seeing this figure for the first time generally have to search through the jumble of black marks before being able to delineate the dog's profile.

case, a token that is of a different numerical identity is not immediately apparent (i.e., it does not pop out, suggesting that it does not represent one of the core elemental features). It is only when we focus our attention and search through the field of tokens that we eventually find the number that is different from the rest of the field.

Attentional mechanisms, therefore, play a central role in FIT and actually dominate the next level, where feature integration is believed to take place (Bundesen & Habekost, 2008; Gross, 1999; Palmer, 2002). Consider the following problem. Our visual system extracts a set of early form primitives from the optical image on the retina (the pre-attentive stage) but is then faced with the challenge of correctly assembling them into object forms. The dilemma of how elementary tokens are assembled into a visual object has been named the **binding problem**. We are obviously very good at solving this problem because in nearly all cases we correctly perceive the structural makeup of an object and seldom bind features in the wrong way. According to FIT, feature binding occurs when attention is introduced into a specific location in the visual field. Focused attention on a single part of the retinotopic map allows the features at that location to be selected and assembled into a unified perceptual object. The important point to note here is that the binding of elementary features into an object occurs only through focused attention. Our attentional focus shifts from one location to another to create a perceptual impression with multiple objects in our visual world. Once the features are bound together, the resulting object is then compared to memory, where a positive match then leads to identification (SideNote 10.34).

Modern structural theories—RBC

Another formidable problem in understanding object perception has to do with the different perspectives by which an object can be viewed. It is common experience that most objects are correctly recognized regardless of the viewpoint. For example, a telephone is always perceived as such regardless of the angle that we view it from. The challenge for our visual system is to be able to generalize across multiple views, with each producing a different optical image on the retina and yet consistently yielding correct recognition. One solution that has been proposed is that multiple representations

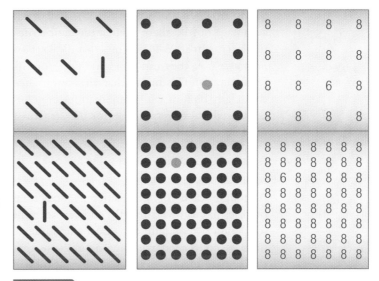

Figure 10.24

The three vertical panels in this figure show clusters of visual features at either low or high density. The first two panels show that differences in elementary features such as orientation and contrast are immediately perceptible (i.e., they "pop out," regardless of the number of other similar features [distracters] in their surround). Because there is no need to undertake a careful attentional search to identify the one feature that is different in each of these fields, these primitive features are believed to be part of an elemental *pre-attentive* map in vision. The numerical features in the right panel, however, represent a higher level of complexity that now requires an attention-driven search to identify the one numeral that is different from all of the others (i.e., there is no "pop-out"). The greater the number of distracters, the greater the time needed to find the unique numeral. The features at this stage represent an attentive level of object analysis whereby the binding of elemental features occurs only through focused attention.

generated by different views of a given object are stored in memory. In this case, any given view of an object will quickly create a match with a stored representation of that same object, leading to correct recognition.

A more generalized solution to this problem was proposed by Irving Biederman, who suggested that visual objects are initially parsed into simple geometric volumes that are later assembled to create a 3-D representation. This theory is known as the **recognition-by-components (RBC)** solution (Biederman, 1987). A key difference between RBC and other structural theories is that the basic features are volumetric primitives (i.e., they are made up of various three-dimensional shapes). Biederman named these primitives **geons**, which is short for *geometric ions*. Figure 10.25 shows how a small set of geons can be assembled into several common objects. Biederman proposed a basic set of 36 geons, each with different volumetric properties. It turns out that close to 75,000 different objects can be generated by combining one pair of geons from this set, and that over 150 million objects can be generated if three

SideNote | **10.34**

The flowchart below outlines the processes involved in object perception according to Treisman's feature integration theory.

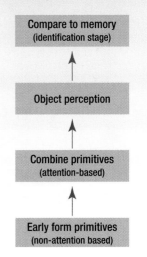

SideNote | **10.35**

How many different objects can humans distinguish? One liberal estimate suggests that there are approximately 3,000 object categories, such as dogs, cups, chairs, etc. Within each category, there are a variable number of types (or exemplars). Some have more (e.g., dogs), while others fewer (e.g., cups). If a mean number of 10 types per category is assumed, then the total number of readily discriminable objects turns out to be approximately 30,000. Thus, RBC theory can easily accommodate this estimate in terms of the number of objects that can be created by various geon combinations.

geons are used (SideNote 10.35). The main advantage of RBC theory is that the basic structural elements are 3-D volumes that display *view invariance* (i.e., they can be identified from different angles). This means that view invariance is similarly built in with combinations of geons that in effect are responsible for the structural makeup of visual objects (Biederman, 1987).

Analytical approaches—Marr's computational algorithm

Although each of the different structural theories has its own strengths and can account for a number of different visual phenomena, none is concerned with the actual way that the retinal image is segmented to produce the primitive features that serve as the building blocks of vision. We know from biological studies that geons are not processed at the retinal level. And yet, there must be some mechanism that extracts edge information initially to produce the primitives that are shown in Figure 10.25. One way that edge analysis can be carried out is through the operation of early level visual neurons, such as those in area V1 that are responsible for detecting line orientation and local contrast. The emerging knowledge of physiological mechanisms in early visual neurons sparked much research on the actual mechanisms by which the retinal image is segmented and reconstructed to provide form vision. The first stage in that analysis, it was believed, required identification of the edges that are inherent in an image (Marr &

Hildreth, 1980).

Much of the progress in understanding image segmentation using edge-detection procedures was driven by scientists who viewed visual analysis as really a computational problem, not unlike the challenge faced by a computer in deconstructing an optical image into its contents. These scientists knew that the very first operation that needs to be performed on an image is to find the lines and edges that both provide the internal details of an object and allow it to be separated from the background. The *brain-is-a-computer* metaphor led various groups to propose different *algorithms* for segmenting and analyzing the visual image.

One of the most influential analytical theories of vision was proposed by David Marr and his colleagues at the Massachusetts Institute of Technology (Marr, 1982; Vaina, 1991). Marr proposed that the visual system implements an edge-detection algorithm at the first stage to create spatial primitives composed of edges, lines, blobs, and terminations. Marr even proposed a specific algorithm that computes changes in light intensity across the image to create this collection of primitives, which he termed the **raw primal sketch**. One reason for the appeal of Marr's theory was that his edge-detection algorithm appeared to fit closely with the known contrast-detecting functions of early visual neurons.

One of the problems in a strict intensity-based segmentation scheme stems from the fact that intensity changes in the real world occur over multiple spatial scales (e.g., abrupt intensity changes at borders as well as gradual intensity changes over broad areas such as in shadows and highlights). One proposed solution to this problem was to analyze the image at different levels of resolution, from coarse to fine. An application of this approach is shown in Figure 10.26, where Marr's algorithm is applied at different resolution levels on a sculpture to show both the gradual and the abrupt changes in intensity. Again, the advantage of Marr's approach is that it is consistent with the biological properties of the visual system where contrast detection is known to be carried out in both a coarse and a fine manner by visual neurons with different-sized receptive fields.

As with the feature integration theory, there must exist some mechanism for assembling the features in the raw primal sketch into more organized structures. Marr proposed

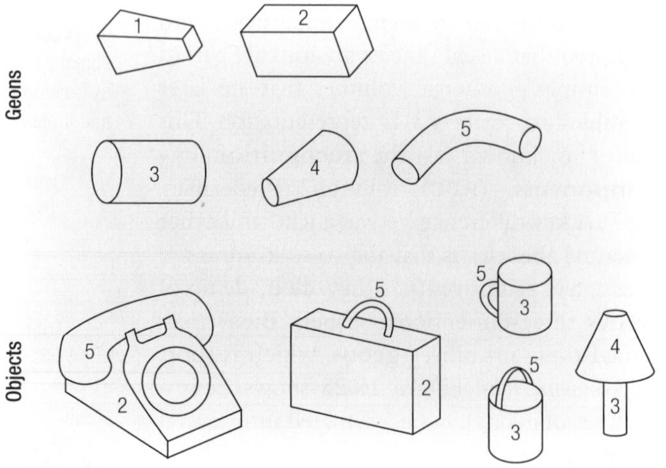

Figure 10.25

Five examples of geons are shown along the top, together with some common objects that can be assembled by various combinations of these particular geons. Adapted from "Recognition-by-Components: A Theory of Human Image Understanding," by I. Biederman, 1987, *Psychological Review, 94*, pp. 115–147.

that the next stage in the visual brain's computational algorithm was to link the primitive features into larger ones and group similar elements together, the result of which was to produce a representation of an object's surface and layout. The information in this so-called *full primal sketch* is then transformed into a 3-D representation that we perceive. Although much of the emphasis in Marr's theory was devoted to the early stages of image segmentation, his algorithmic approach based on a computational analysis of vision had a considerable impact on this field and paved the way for further advances while stimulating the introduction of alternative computational theories (SideNote 10.36).

3. FACE PERCEPTION

We now arrive at the second, and undoubtedly the most complex, level of form processing. Human faces represent the most complex objects that we view, process, retain, and recall from memory. In terms of sensory processing, faces represent a considerable challenge because of the many different and subtle variations of the internal features that together are responsible for defining an individual. And yet, our visual system is very efficient at processing such highly complex object forms, a fact that has led many to bestow a special status to face processing.

Neural processing of faces

One of the more remarkable developments in neuroscience was the discovery that face processing in the primate brain can be traced down to the level of single neurons in the temporal lobe. In the early 1970s, American psychologist Charles Gross began investigating this area of the brain with single electrodes in an attempt to understand the complex visual processes that are undertaken in this area (Gross, 1999; Gross et al., 1972). There was a valid reason to explore the ventral visual pathway in this regard. Psychological studies on brain-damaged patients had previously shown that damage to this part of the brain produces a variety of agnosias, as discussed at the beginning of Section C.2. One type of agnosia is a marked inability to recognize faces (Farah, 1990; Zeki, 1993). The specificity of this disorder, which is known as **prosopagnosia**, is quite stunning because in many instances the patients are simply unable to recognize faces

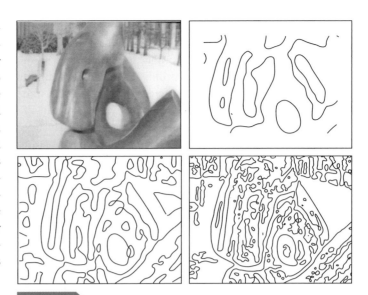

Figure 10.26

The image of a sculpture by Henry Moore is analyzed by an edge-detection algorithm at three different spatial scales. Broad changes in intensity level in the image are outlined at coarse resolution (top right), whereas abrupt intensity changes are identified at fine resolution (bottom right). Intermediate-level intensity changes are detected at medium resolution (bottom left). The three spatial levels of intensity analysis allow an algorithm to pick out both sharp borders and broad intensity changes such as in shadows and highlights. Adapted from "Theory of Edge Detection," by D. Marr and E. C. Hildreth, 1980, *Proceedings of the Royal Society of London, B 207*, pp. 187–217.

even though other visual functions are spared, including the ability to recognize complex non-face objects. In some cases, a patient may be unable to recognize close family members or even his or her own face in a mirror. This problem cannot be attributed to a deficit in cognitive function, such as memory recall, nor to a generalized visual dysfunction. Indeed, prosopagnosics usually display normal visual capacities in terms of other non-face-related stimuli. Thus, it appears that prosopagnosia is caused by impairment in sensory processing of high-level visual functions in the temporal lobe that specifically targets the ability to recognize faces.

Gross and his colleagues found that single neurons in the temporal lobe of monkeys were responsive to face stimuli in a very specific manner. That is, the same neurons show reduced firing when the face images are degraded or when other complex object forms are shown. An example of the response specificity of a face-selective neuron is shown in Figure 10.27 on page 348 (Bruce, Desimone, & Gross, 1981). These findings showed that single neurons in the temporal lobe are responsible for coding visual information at the most complex possible level of representation and stimulated

SideNote | 10.36

David Marr's contribution to the field of vision research was cut short by his untimely death due to leukemia at the age of 32. He wrote a highly influential book, titled *Vision*, during the last two years of his life.

SideNote | **10.37**

The idea of *grandmother* cells originated in the influential work of Polish scientist Jerzy Konorski, who suggested that neural systems form hierarchical clusters that terminate in so-called *gnostic units*. These units were postulated to represent complex stimuli that an animal would encounter in its environment. The grandmother cell is an extension of this idea, whereby the neural representation of an individual (e.g., the grandmother) is coded at the level of a single neuron in the temporal lobe.

an interesting debate on whether the long-sought-after *grandmother* cells had indeed been found. Gross and others argued that the neural representation of individual faces is highly unlikely to be restricted to single cells. Rather, they argued, the face-selective neurons in the temporal lobe are components of a much larger interactive network of neurons that together are responsible for the sensory representation and coding of faces (SideNote 10.37).

Where in the human brain would such a face-processing network reside? Electrophysiological studies cannot be carried out in humans, and so the answer had to await the development of non-invasive brain imaging techniques, such as the *functional MRI* (fMRI). Research in the 1990s began to show that a small, well-defined area within the ventral extrastriate stream was consistently activated when human subjects were shown images of faces. This turned out to be a highly specific response, because the same area showed significantly reduced responses to other object categories. Figure 10.28 shows an

illustration of this activated region, which was termed the **fusiform face area** (FFA) because of its anatomical location on the so-called *fusiform gyrus* in the temporal lobe (Kanwisher et al., 1997; Kanwisher & Yovel, 2006; Tsao & Livingstone, 2008). This area may be thought of as the functional equivalent, or homologue, of the inferotemporal cortex in monkeys. The existence of the FFA and its specificity for processing facial stimuli provides another piece of evidence that visual processing at the highest levels is parsed into neural networks that are separately devoted to the analysis of objects and faces.

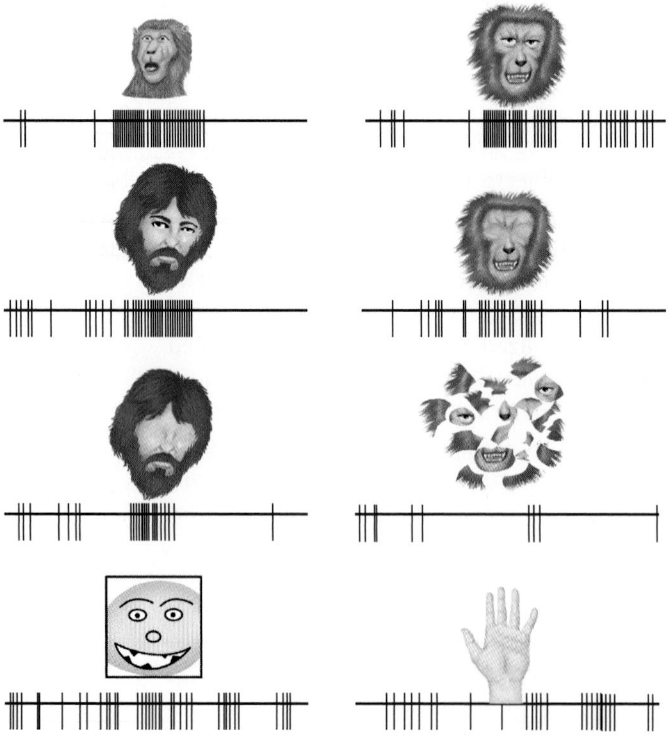

Perceptual aspects of face processing

The remarkable quality about face perception is that we are able to distinguish literally thousands of different individuals in our lifetime, and remember a good number of them as well. This is all the more impressive because the complexity of the structural information contained in a face is stunning. Human faces differ owing to differences in their physical qualities (pigmentation, texture, uniformity, etc.), differences in the size of the individual components (eyes, nose, mouth, eyebrows, etc.), differences in the intrinsic layout of these components (curvature, fullness, continuity, etc.), and finally, differences in the geometrical layout of these components with respect to each other (SideNote 10.38). It would be a truly amazing feat if our visual brain separately analyzed all of these features independently when we are in the midst of trying to recognize a face. In other words, if we are called upon to name a familiar face, say in a photograph, then a feature-by-feature analysis of that face with a similar image stored in our memory would represent such a daunting challenge in computational terms that it would make the recognition process both slow and error-prone. And yet, we recognize people instantly and nearly always, correctly.

One of the ways that face perception is believed to be distinct from object perception is that, whereas the latter is believed to rely heavily on feature analysis and integration, face perception is believed to rely on psychological processes that have evolved one important step further—to produce a mental representation that is fundamentally holistic in nature (Boutet & Chaudhuri, 2001; Farah, 1990; Fox, Iaria, & Barton, 2008). Indeed, face perception provides one of the greatest pieces of support

Figure 10.27

Neuronal activity in the inferior temporal lobe of the monkey shows specificity to face and face-like stimuli. The highest level of activity is seen when the monkey is shown facial images of other monkeys or even humans. The same neuron shows reduced levels of firing when the face image is degraded (e.g., if the interior components are erased or scrambled). The neuron barely responds to other complex forms, such as a hand. Adapted from "Visual Properties of Neurons in a Polysensory Area in the Superior Temporal Sulcus of the Macaque," by C. Bruce, R. Desimone, and C. Gross, 1981, *Journal of Neurophysiology, 46*, pp. 369–384.

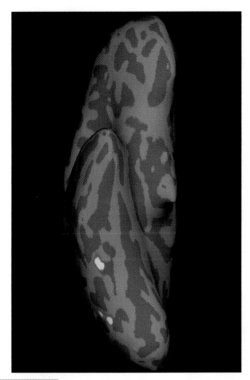

Figure 10.28

Functional activity in the brain in response to faces shows a focus of neural activation in an area on the fusiform gyrus. This area, which has been termed the fusiform face area (FFA), is consistently activated when humans are shown facial images as opposed to non-face objects. Another area in the occipital lobe to the left is also activated in responses to faces. Image courtesy of Nancy Kanwisher, MIT.

for the Gestalt theory. Of course, the path to a holistic representation is based on early processing of elemental features that all visual objects must be subjected to (e.g., detection of

contrast, orientation, colour, etc.). However, the ultimate sensory representation of faces appears to be based not on the concatenation of the individual features themselves but rather on the configuration of these features in a holistic manner to produce a gestalt. It has been argued that a holistic mental representation of a complex stimulus such as the human face forms a key reason behind our ability to quickly make comparisons with stored memories (SideNote 10.39).

The simple demonstration in Figure 10.29 shows that faces and objects may indeed be treated differently by our visual system (Boutet & Chaudhuri, 2001). The left panel shows two superimposed faces that are arranged at right angles to each other. In purely stimulus terms, the various internal features of the two faces should blend together to produce a jumbled image. For example, the nose of one individual merges with the cheek of the other, the eyes with the forehead and nose, etc. And yet, when viewing this image, it is clear that two salient images—one of each face—clearly stand out in our mind. This likely happens because our visual system treats each face in a holistic manner so that there are only two entities here that alternate in terms of our perceptual experience. The same does not hold true with two non-face objects, such as the overlapped houses shown in the right panel. Although the individual elements of each house can be delineated with some effort, those elements do not cohere into a complete holistic entity that allows us to perceive each house in its full form.

SideNote **10.38**

Hair provides a powerful clue in identifying people in our daily lives. However, most studies of face perception are conducted with images that have been cropped along the hairline, thereby limiting the focus strictly to features of the face.

SideNote **10.39**

Many arguments have been offered in support of belief in the evolution of a specialized face-processing mechanism that creates holistic representations. Faces form a special object category in that social interactions are so heavily driven by the need for rapid identification of individual faces (e.g., of parents, children, friends, mates, etc.) and correct interpretation of facial expressions (e.g., happiness, anger, sadness, lust, etc.).

Figure 10.29

The holistic nature of face perception can be demonstrated with two overlapped face images. Although the facial features of one individual blend in with those of the other, our visual brain analyzes each face in a global manner so that only one face is perceived in its entirety at any given time. However, when images of two non-face objects (houses) are superimposed in the same way, it becomes difficult to distinguish them because all of the individual features become perceptually intertwined. Adapted from "Multistability of Overlapped Face Stimuli Is Dependent upon Orientation," by I. Boutet and A. Chaudhuri, 2001, *Perception, 30,* pp. 743–753.

INVESTIGATION

Face Recognition Experiments: Contrast Reversal and Inversion

Face recognition is most accurate when we are viewing upright, contrast-normal faces. This makes sense because this is the most common view we have of other peoples' faces, and so our face recognition mechanisms have become optimized for this view. We know from common experience that contrast-reversed images, as in a photographic negative, pose a considerable challenge to recognition ability, even with highly familiar faces such as close family members. The top row in Figure 10.30 shows three contrast-reversed images of famous people. Although it may be possible to name them after spending some effort, it is clear that their identity is not immediately apparent, as it would have been (at least for most people) had these been contrast-normal images. Similarly, inverted images also pose a challenge to recognition ability, as illustrated by the bottom row of images in Figure 10.30 (Rossion & Gauthier, 2002).

Figure 10.30

A holistic representation of faces seems to require upright, contrast-normal images. When the contrast is reversed, as in a photographic negative (top row), face recognition becomes very difficult. The same is true when a face is inverted, even if its contrast is normal (bottom row). Can you recognize these familiar faces?

Top: l) © Allstar Picture Library/Alamy; c) © Allstar Picture Library/Alamy; r) © The Print Collector/Alamy
Bottom: l) © Panthera / Alamy; c) © Photo Researchers/Alamy; r) © Redcarpetpress/Alamy

Top panel (left to right): Denzel Washington, Jim Carey, Sigmund Freud; bottom panel (left to right): Hillary Clinton, Albert Einstein, Oprah Winfrey.

1. The major target of the retinal fibres emerging out of the eye is the lateral geniculate nucleus (LGN), which is a six-layered subcortical structure located in the thalamus. From here, signals are carried by the optic radiation to the primary visual cortex in the occipital lobe. The retinal output is split into a nasal half and a temporal half; the temporal fibres project to the LGN on the same side, whereas the nasal fibres cross over at the optic chiasm before projecting to the opposite LGN. This layout ensures that the right visual field is represented in the left cerebral hemisphere and vice versa.

2. The bottom two layers of the LGN (layers 1 and 2) have large cell bodies and are known as the *magnocellular* (M) *layers*. The top four layers (layers 3 to 6) contain smaller-sized neurons and are referred to as the *parvocellular* (P) *layers*. LGN neurons have a similar receptive field structure as the retinal ganglion cells—that is, centre–surround antagonism with ON/OFF and OFF/ON organization. The LGN displays a precise retinotopic organization. The superior colliculus (SC) also receives projections from the retina, as do a number of other subcortical structures. The SC is involved in integrating sensory and motor information for the guidance of eye movements.

3. The primary visual cortex (area V1) also has six layers, which are labelled from top (layer 1) to bottom (layer 6). There is a somewhat distorted retinotopic map in area V1, with a much larger foveal representation. There are four new features that arise in area V1:

   • Binocularity. Area V1 neurons integrate retinal output from the two eyes. Binocular neurons fire optimally when both eyes are stimulated as opposed to a single eye. Binocular neurons are important for depth perception.

   • Orientation selectivity. Area V1 neurons have elongated receptive fields that are optimally suited for coding the orientation of a light bar or edge. Different area V1 neurons have different degrees of orientation selectivity. Hubel and Wiesel theorized that the summated input of neurons with circular receptive fields oriented along a particular axis likely represents the basis for orientation selectivity.

   • Directional selectivity. A subset of area V1 neurons displays a preference for stimuli moving in a particular direction, although the majority of neurons are equally responsible to all directions of movement.

   • Colour contrast sensitivity. This too is a feature that arises for the first time in area V1, in which a subset of neurons can distinguish pure colour differences in the stimulus. This property is taken up in greater detail in Chapter 11.

4. The functional architecture of area V1 is such that a vertical set of ocular dominance columns is arrayed in conjunction with another vertical set of columns for orientation preference. According to Hubel and Wiesel's *ice-cube model*, the two sets of columns have a perpendicular relationship. A hypercolumn spans a full set of orientation columns and one pair of ocular dominance columns.

5. The M- and P-channels originate in the retina and remain segregated through the LGN and into the input layers of area V1. Lesion studies of the M- and P-layers of the LGN have revealed that the two pathways serve different functional requirements. For example, the M-pathway is characterized by low colour sensitivity, low spatial resolution, and high temporal sensitivity. The P-pathway, on the other hand, is optimized for high colour sensitivity, high spatial resolution, and low temporal sensitivity. Consequently, the M-channel is best suited to process dynamic stimuli, whereas the P-channel is optimized for static stimuli upon which a considerable amount of image (and colour) detail can be processed.

6. The general characteristics of the M- and P-channels appear to be maintained to some degree throughout the extrastriate cortical areas. Areas MT and V4 serve as major gateways to a host of visual areas located in the parietal and temporal lobes that together make up the dorsal and ventral cortical streams, respectively. The dominant input into the parietal lobe areas (dorsal stream) from area MT means that these areas display qualities consistent

with an M-channel link. The dominant input into the temporal lobe areas (ventral stream) through area V4 means that these areas display qualities that are consistent with a preferential input from the P-channel.

7. The inferior temporal cortex (area IT) is a large swath of cortical territory that extends from the upper boundary with the occipital lobe all the way down to its bottom-most margin at the temporal pole. Visual operations in the temporal lobe begin with area PIT and then proceed to areas CIT and AIT. Together, these areas represent the major components of the ventral cortical stream and are responsible for constructing complex visual representations. It appears that image processing in the temporal lobe becomes segmented into two further streams—one dedicated to complex objects and another to faces. The evidence for this is based on single-unit studies in monkeys, brain imaging in humans, and behavioural studies of patients with temporal lobe damage.

8. Selective damage to the ventral visual pathways produces a disorder in which people have difficulty recognizing objects, a condition called *agnosia*. In one type of agnosia, individuals are unable to recognize or copy drawings of common objects, while in another type, they are unable to unify the parts of an object or match them with shapes stored in memory. One important theory of object perception is *structuralism*, which is based on the idea that mental experiences result from a core set of elementary building blocks that are somehow assembled in the mind. The Gestalt movement offered an opposing view, which asserted that object perception simply did not occur by an assembly of elemental parts but rather the holistic nature of the object itself.

9. One type of agnosia is a marked inability to recognize faces, known as *prosopagnosia*, which arises from selective damage to the temporal lobe. Clinical findings in conjunction with physiological studies have shown that area IT is specialized for processing faces. Neuroimaging studies have subsequently shown dedicated face processing modules, such as the fusiform face area, in the human brain.

Key Terms

1. What is the pattern of ipsilateral versus contralateral projection of retinal fibres to the LGN? How does signal splitting at the optic chiasm affect cortical processing of vision? Which LGN layers are referred to as *magnocellular* and *parvocellular*?

2. Why is area V1 also known as the *striate cortex*? How is the retinotopic layout of area V1 different from the LGN?

3. What are the four new properties that arise in area V1? What is the ocular dominance scale? What role do binocular neurons play in vision?

4. Why are retinal ganglion cells and LGN neurons unable to provide information on object orientation? How are directionally selective neurons functionally different from orientation-selective neurons?

5. What is the relationship between ocular dominance columns and orientation columns according to the *ice-cube model*? What is a hypercolumn?

6. How are magnocellular and parvocellular neurons segregated in the LGN and area V1? What are the key distinctions between these two channels with regard to visual

processing? What is the difference between the dorsal and ventral visual streams in terms of anatomical layout and function?

7. What is the role of the temporal lobe in vision? What are the different types of agnosia? How is the theory of *structuralism* different from the Gestalt theory of object perception?

8. What is the fusiform face area? What is the evidence for the holistic representation of faces?

9. What role does the backward projection to the LGN play in vision? Why is it important for the visual system to control information flow to the cortex as early as possible? What are the roles of some of the other subcortical structures in vision?

10. What are cytochrome oxidase blobs, and where are they located? How has optical imaging contributed to our understanding of the functional anatomy of area V1?

11. What are some of the problems with the Gestalt theory of object perception? What are the different modern structural theories? What are the different aspects of Marr's computational theory of vision?

- Boothe, R. G. (2002). *Perception of the visual environment.* New York, NY: Springer-Verlag.
- Gibson, J. J. (1979). *The ecological approach to visual perception.* Boston, MA: Houghton Mifflin.
- Gross, C. G. (1999). *Brain, vision, memory.* Cambridge, MA: MIT Press.
- Hubel, D. H, & Wiesel, T. N. (2004). *Brain and visual perception: The story of a 25-year collaboration.* New York, NY: Oxford University Press.
- Legéndy, C. (2009). *Circuits in the brain.* New York, NY: Springer.
- Marr, D. (1982). *Vision: A computational*

investigation into the human representation and processing of visual information. San Francisco, CA: W.H. Freeman.
- Palmer, S. E. (2002). *Vision science: Photons to phenomenology.* Cambridge, MA: MIT Press.
- Rock, I. (1984). *Perception.* New York, NY: Scientific American Books.
- Schwartz, S. H. (2004). *Visual perception.* New York, NY: McGraw-Hill.
- Wade, N. J. (1999). *A natural history of vision.* Cambridge, MA: MIT Press.
- Zeki, S. (1993). *A vision of the brain.* New York, NY: Wiley.

The Visual System: Colour Perception

In this chapter . . .

- You will learn about the different physical processes that influence colour vision, starting with an examination of Newton's discovery on the chromatic nature of light, to understanding an object's reflective qualities, to deriving the colour signal that largely determines an object's perceived colour. You will also learn about the details behind additive and subtractive colour mixing. You will come to understand how to represent a metathetic quality like colour and the different uses of a *colour space*.

- You will learn how colour signals arise in the visual system and how two very different theories were formulated to explain early colour processing. You will discover how the LGN is organized for colour vision and learn about the types of retinal ganglion cells that project to this structure. You will learn that it was not until the biological aspects of colour were understood that we could resolve the debate over how we see colours. You will explore different levels of colour deficiency and learn the biological properties of each.

- You will come to appreciate the different perceptual aspects associated with colour vision and how they arise.

Colour is an entirely psychological property of our visual experience and not an inherent property of light itself or objects that reflect light. Simply put, objects do not have colour; they only reflect light in a way that produces the psychological phenomenon of colour. Photo © dbimages/Alamy

The laws of colour are unutterably beautiful, just because they are not accidental.

—Vincent Van Gogh

Sir Isaac Newton (1643–1727)
© Lebrecht Music and Arts Photo
Library/Alamy

We must now deal with one of the most complex topics in sensory science. Colour is something that we normally take for granted because it is such a fundamental aspect of our visual experience. The seeming simplicity of colour vision, however, is governed by physical and psychological processes that are so intertwined that unravelling it required the effort and intellect of true scientific geniuses over several centuries. The physics of colour vision is rooted in the very nature of light itself, something that remained obscure until Newton conducted his famous prism experiments, though controversy over some of his claims remained for another 200 years. Newton showed that the experience of colour has its origin in the nature of light entering our eyes. We now know that it is the wavelength of the incoming light that plays a key role in determining the colour we perceive.

The conundrum however lies in dissociating the physical property of light from our psychological experience of colour. A red object is not red at all. In other words, there is nothing fundamentally *red* about that object. It only emits (or reflects) long-wavelength light. Similarly, the sky is not *blue* at all; it just scatters light in a way that only the short-wavelength component reaches us. The physical nature of the light that enters our eyes (i.e., its wavelength) is responsible for producing a psychological phenomenon (colour perception) that occurs only after considerable neurological processing in our visual brain. Colour is an entirely psychological property of our visual experience and not an inherent property of light itself or objects that reflect light. Simply put, objects do not have colour; they only reflect light in a way that produces the psychological phenomenon of colour. Even then, a host of factors can affect both the nature and the quality of colour perception. For example, if we were to drastically dim the amount of light falling on the red object, its *redness* would disappear even though the wavelength composition will not have changed. Indeed, nothing about the light coming from that object will change except for its intensity, and yet the colour will disappear (SideNote 11.1).

In this chapter, we will discuss the physical, biological, and psychological facets of our colour experience. An animal is said to have **colour vision** if it has the ability to discriminate different lights only on the basis of its spectral (wavelength) content. A large number of animal species are known to possess this ability to varying degrees. Some examples include various types of insects, coral reef animals, reptiles, and a host of mammals including dogs, cats, and monkeys (SideNote 11.2 on page 357). It has been argued that colour vision evolved because it provided both survival and reproductive advantages, which are the two adaptive elements in Darwinian natural selection. The ability to distinguish objects in the natural world improves substantially if the visual scene can be surveyed through different spectral channels. As a result, the ability to discriminate objects on the basis of their wavelength emission allows an animal to better hunt, spot a predator, or search for edible fruits. Many animals also use colour to indicate sexual availability and thereby perpetuate their species through reproduction (SideNote 11.3 on page 357). The evolution of colour vision was therefore highly beneficial in terms of natural selection, something that in turn produced a perceptual phenomenon that adds immense richness and beauty to our visual experience.

A. Colour Science

Colour science is a very broad term that encompasses the study and measurement of both the physical and the psychological factors that govern colour perception. Our discussion on the physical foundations of colour vision and **chromaticity** will initially centre on the spectral characteristics of light and the reflective nature of objects. The psychological dimension will then be incorporated to describe how colour information can be represented and categorized. We will conclude this section with a description of how early efforts at combining physical principles and psychological measurement led to striking theoretical insights into how spectral information may be encoded by biological systems to produce colour vision.

1. THE CHROMATIC NATURE OF LIGHT

The idea that colour is an inherent property of objects remained ingrained in the human psyche for at least 2,000 years of recorded history (Lynch & Livingston, 2001; Waldman, 2002). This is not difficult to understand, and

SideNote | **11.1**

This is easily verified by looking into a closet filled with colourful clothes and then turning down the lights. The transition from photopic to scotopic vision, explained in Chapter 9, is responsible for the loss of signal from cone photoreceptors, whose function is necessary to produce colour vision.

even today the lay explanation that an object appears to be coloured because *it is coloured* is often encountered. The notion that the colour of an object is intrinsically associated with that object made perfect sense because the perception of an object's form and colour are so intertwined. Such a strongly held belief would therefore require a colossal shift in thinking.

The history of science contains a number of major landmarks where deeply held beliefs become shattered. Such was the case when Sir Isaac Newton demonstrated in 1666 that colour perception was actually generated by light itself and that sunlight was made up of a number of discrete components that each produced a different colour experience. Although the scientific detail and precision of Newton's work eventually convinced many scientists of his generation, the idea that light itself was responsible for generating perceived colour remained highly contentious for some time, especially among a circle of philosophers (SideNote 11.4 on page 358).

Newton's breakthrough

The famous prism experiment that led to this breakthrough is shown in Figure 11.1 (Nassau, 2001; Palmer, 2002). Newton placed a glass prism in the path of a beam of sunlight that came into his laboratory through a small hole in the window shade. The beam of light passed through the prism and fell upon a white screen where a rainbow of colours appeared. As Figure 11.1 shows, the incident light is refracted at both surfaces of the prism in such a way that violet light is refracted the most, red light the least, and the other colours to various degrees in between, thus producing the gradient of colours on the screen. Newton himself noticed seven different colours in the following order—red, orange, yellow, green, blue, indigo, and violet, a pattern that some schoolchildren remember using the mnemonic *Richard Of York Gave Battle In Vain*.

Newton was convinced that sunlight is actually composed of different colours of light and that, when they were combined, they produced white light. He verified this by taking the rainbow of coloured lights emerging from a prism and passing it through additional prisms in such a way that a beam of white light was reproduced. Newton did not really know the reason why white light became separated into the different constituent colours, though he came close to understanding the relationship between colour and wavelength

Human view

Cat view

Rat view

OGphoto/iStockphoto.com

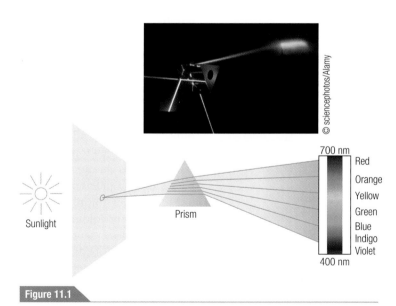

Figure 11.1

In Newton's famous prism experiment, sunlight was passed through a small hole in a screen and directed at a glass prism. The light passing through the prism was refracted in a graded manner according to wavelength, producing a gradient of colours on a white screen. The lowest visible wavelength (around 400 nm) is refracted the most, whereas the longest visible wavelength (around 700 nm) is refracted the least. The inset shows white light being refracted by an actual prism to produce a rainbow of colours.

SideNote | 11.4

One of Newton's fiercest critics was German poet and philosopher Johann von Goethe. Goethe was convinced of the purity of white light and argued that it simply could not be "contaminated" by other colours. He also argued that accepting Newton's conclusion would mean that human sensory perception was fundamentally unreliable.

SideNote | 11.5

Later developments in our understanding of the wave nature of light explained the separation of colours by a prism. The bending of light (refraction) as it proceeds through a transparent material depends upon the wavelength—the shorter the wavelength of light, the greater the amount of refraction. This wavelength-dependent gradient of refraction is what caused the rainbow of colours to appear in Newton's experiment.

(SideNote 11.5). He did understand, however, that the colours we perceive are not that of the light itself. In other words, there is no colour inherent in light but rather we see colour only after a particular light interacts with our visual system. This remarkable insight that Newton took away from his experiments represented a major departure from the way people had regarded colour for many centuries before him.

Spectral nature of light sources

If sunlight can be dissociated into a continuous band of colours by a prism, then that must mean that it contains sufficient photons at all wavelengths across the visible spectrum—that is, the 400 to 700 nm band of electromagnetic radiation that is visible. This is easily verified by an instrument that can measure the intensity or energy content of light at a particular wavelength. Using such a device, a plot of the energy content of sunlight at each visible wavelength can be made, as shown in the top left panel of Figure 11.2 (Palmer, 2002; Waldman, 2002). This so-called **emission spectrum** indeed shows a continuous profile of energy across the full range of visible wavelengths. In fact, natural sunlight contains relatively similar numbers of photons across the full visible spectrum. This permits sunlight, when passed through a prism,

to be refracted along a gradient of wavelengths, thereby producing the different visible colours.

The emission spectrum of sunlight is continuous in that photon energy is present at all visible wavelengths. Another light source that displays a continuous spectrum is tungsten light bulbs. However, the spectrum in this case is biased toward the higher wavelengths in terms of energy content, thereby giving ordinary household light bulbs their yellowish appearance. A somewhat different profile is seen with light sources that have discrete spectra. The fluorescent light bulb, for example, contains just a few such discrete spikes of energy at different wavelengths within the visible spectrum. Most lasers have just a single spike, such as the example in Figure 11.2 showing the spectrum of a helium–neon laser. The energy spike of this common and inexpensive laser occurs at precisely 632.8 nm, giving the deep red appearance commonly seen in laser pointers.

Additive colour mixtures

If sunlight is composed of energy at various wavelengths that individually trigger a unique colour sensation such as red, green, indigo, etc., then why does a mixture of energy at all of these wavelengths produce a **neutral colour** appearance? Simply put, why does sunlight appear white? The answer to this question requires that we consider the additive properties of light at different wavelengths—that is, the perceptual result of superimposing two or more such lights upon each other (Kuehni & Schwarz, 2008; Lee, 2009; Nassau, 2001).

The first foray into this area was actually made by Newton. To understand how coloured lights can be added together to produce new colours, Newton relied on his analytical skills and his strong belief that the laws of nature can be precisely defined in mathematical terms. Newton reasoned that the addition of two different coloured lights would produce an intermediate sensation from within the rainbow of colours that he discovered through his prism experiment. However, it was difficult to come up with precise rules governing the quality of this intermediate colour. To solve this problem, Newton simply joined the two ends of the colour spectrum to create a circular arrangement, as shown in the left diagram of Figure 11.3 (Palmer, 2002; Wade, 1998). This figure is a depiction of the original **colour circle** made by Newton, a development that

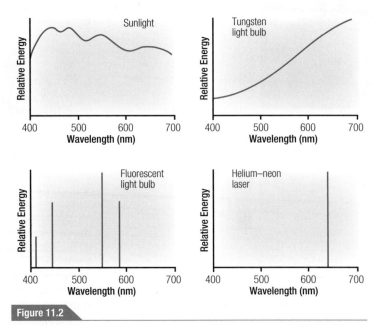

Figure 11.2

The emission spectrum of four different light sources. Both sunlight and tungsten light bulbs show a continuous spectrum with energy content at all wavelengths. Some light sources such as fluorescent light bulbs and lasers show discrete spectra, with energy contained only at certain wavelengths.

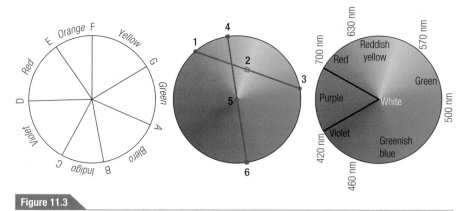

Figure 11.3

The first graphic model of colour perception was developed by Newton (left diagram). The seven spectral colours were depicted as wedges within a circle and considered to be analogous to the seven tones on a musical scale. The middle diagram shows a colour circle but with a continuous blend of the spectral colours. Newton showed that the colour produced by mixing any two lights together can be predicted to lie on a straight line between them (e.g., if lights evoking colours at points 1 and 3 in the circle are mixed together in equal amounts, the predicted colour sensation would lie midway, at point 2). Any two colours that lie at opposite ends (e.g., points 4 and 6) produce a whitish sensation, as indicated by point 5 in the middle of the circle. A modified version of the colour circle (right diagram) takes into account the fact that purple, which results from mixing red and blue lights, is not a spectral colour. The wedge in this circle separates purple from the true spectral colours, which are arranged around the remainder of the circle.

stands out as the first graphic model of colour perception. In it, the seven original spectral colours observed by Newton are arranged as pie-shaped wedges to make up the circle. One of the interesting features of Newton's colour circle is the association he made between colour and the musical scale. Newton believed that vision and hearing were closely related sensory functions, and therefore the seven colours in the spectrum had to be related to the seven tones on the musical scale (SideNote 11.6).

The colour circle paved the way for a simple geometric procedure by which intermediate colours could be predicted from the mixture of any two coloured lights (Nassau, 2001; Plamer, 2002; Waldman, 2002). According to Newton's scheme, mixing two coloured lights of equal intensity would produce a colour that lies precisely midway between them on the colour circle. This idea is illustrated by way of a more modern version of the colour circle, which is shown in the middle diagram of Figure 11.3. The different colours here smoothly blend into each other rather than being depicted as discrete wedges. If we mix two equally intense coloured lights, say red and green (shown as points 1 and 3 in the figure), then the resulting mixture would be predicted as being in the middle of a straight line between these points in the colour circle. Through a careful series of light-mixing experiments, Newton showed

that this was indeed true (i.e., the predicted yellow colour based on the graphical scheme [point 2 in the figure] was the correct result of mixing red and green lights together). Similar predictions with other pairs of colours were also borne out through his experiments. Furthermore, the location of the colour mixture in the circle could be accurately predicted even if one of the two lights was of greater intensity. In this case, the point representing the intermediate colour would shift along the line toward the light having the greater intensity.

In general, the colour circle can adequately predict the perceived colour that results from mixing any pair of lights (SideNote 11.7). This fact can now be used to answer the question posed at the beginning of this section—why does sunlight appear white? Let us return to the colour circle in the middle of Figure 11.3 and consider a pair of lights that lie exactly opposite to each other, such as reddish yellow and greenish blue (points 4 and 6). The resulting mixture rests exactly at the centre of the colour circle (point 5). It is the neutral colour "white" that appears in the centre and is the predicted result of combining any two colours that lie exactly opposite each other in the circle (e.g., red and cyan, green and magenta, blue and yellow, etc.). An actual experiment would verify that mixing such pairs of coloured lights does indeed produce light with a whitish

SideNote | **11.6**

It is thought that Newton originally observed only five colours in his prism experiment but later added two more, orange and indigo, so that he could make the analogy between spectral colours and the seven musical tones.

SideNote | **11.7**

The notion that the colour produced by different light mixtures can be predicted through a simple geometric procedure is really quite amazing when we consider that colour is a purely perceptual phenomenon. Given that the lights themselves are not "coloured," the colour circle therefore provides a convenient tool to represent not only colours but also perceptions that arise when different lights are mixed together.

appearance. Any pair of colours that produces white when mixed together is referred to as being **complementary**. All spectral colours represented along the circumference of the colour circle therefore have a complementary counterpart at the opposite end (Lynch & Livingston, 2002; Waldman, 2002). Thus, all possible complementary colour pairings from the visible spectrum will produce a whitish appearance. Because sunlight is made up of all of the spectral colours mixed together, the end result of that mixture produces a point in the middle of the colour circle—white.

Nonspectral colours

If white light is made up of a series of spectral colours, then is white itself also a spectral colour? The answer is *no*. Although white is produced by combining pairs of complementary spectral colours (or even combining all of the spectral colours together), white would not appear anywhere in the spectrum of Newton's prism experiment. Another way to consider this is the fact that there is no single wavelength of light that would trigger the sensation of white. This is not true of the spectral colours such as red, yellow, green, etc., all of which can be triggered by electromagnetic emission at a single wavelength (e.g., helium–neon laser) or a small range of wavelengths (e.g., blue skylight) within the visible spectrum. Thus, white light can be dissociated into spectral colours, but white is considered to be a **nonspectral colour**.

Another example of a nonspectral colour is purple, which is produced by mixing red and blue lights together. Purple does not appear anywhere in the visible spectrum, and there is no wavelength that can be associated with this colour sensation. The colour circle presented in the middle diagram of Figure 11.3 however shows that the transition from red to blue goes through purple. Given that purple is a nonspectral colour, the colour circle needs to be revised if it is to accurately portray spectral colours. A revised and more accurate version of the colour circle is shown in the right diagram of Figure 11.3. A notch has been placed in the circle between the red and blue segments to exclude purple from the true spectral colours, which are arranged around the circumference of the remainder of this figure. A number of wavelength values have been placed here for reference. The colour wheel therefore incorporates both the spectral colours that are directly linked to light wavelength as well as the nonspectral colours that do not actually appear in any part of the visible spectrum (Lynch & Livingston, 2002; Malacara, 2002; Waldman, 2002). Our visual brain creates colours such as purple and white only when our eyes are exposed to certain mixtures of wavelengths.

Additive primary colours

If purple can be created by mixing two different coloured lights, then the same principle should be applicable to other light pairings or even multiple combinations to produce a variety of other colours. The sheer number of colours that we are able to perceive makes it clear that colour vision is not limited to just the spectral and nonspectral colours. Newton believed that the seven colours he observed in his prism experiment represented the fundamental colours because they could not be broken down any further. All other colours were thought of as being composites that were created by different mixtures of these seven spectral colours.

It turned out Newton's conclusion in this regard was incorrect. There are only three basic colours that cannot be separated into any other colour—red (R), green (G), and blue (B). In other words, lights that evoke these three colour sensations cannot be decomposed into any other colour, and for this reason they are referred to as the **primary colours**. More specifically, the term *additive primary colours* is used because nearly all other colours of light can be derived by adding either two or three of these colours from the RGB palette (Kuehni & Schwarz, 2008; Lee, 2009; Malacara, 2002). Figure 11.4 shows the various colours that result from additive mixing of the RGB set of primaries. As we noted before, an equal mixture of red and green lights will produce yellow, whereas red and blue mixtures will produce purple. A mixture of all three primaries in equal amounts will yield white. All of these colours, and the many more that can result from unequal mixtures of the RGB primaries, are referred to as *secondary colours* (SideNotes 11.8 and 11.9).

2. THE CHROMATIC NATURE OF OBJECTS

The additive properties of light discussed above only apply under circumstances where light from different emitting sources are blended

SideNote | **11.8**

Colour television and computer monitors provide excellent examples of additive colour mixing where three different light-emitting systems (red, green, and blue) produce a wide array of colours.

SideNote | **11.9**

How many different secondary colours are there? There is no simple answer to this because of the large number of additive possibilities. The National Institute of Standards and Technology in the United States has created the Universal Color Language that is made up of 267 blocks of colours, with each block having up to six finer subdivisions. The Pantone Matching system, which is widely used by graphic artists, contains over 1,200 discernible colours. The RGB model, with 256 intensity levels per primary, can theoretically produce over 16.7 million colours (256 R x 256 G x 256 B).

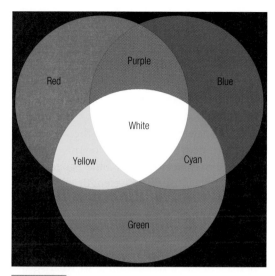

Figure 11.4

Additive colour mixing can be demonstrated by superimposing three light beams that evoke each of the primary colours—red, green, and blue. The superposition of all three produces white, whereas the mixture of two primaries in equal amounts evokes the colour sensations of purple (red + blue), yellow (red + green), and cyan (blue + green). There are many other such secondary colours that can be produced by mixing the primaries in unequal amounts.

together. For example, the mixture shown in Figure 11.4 can be thought of as being produced by three different projectors that send their light output through a coloured filter and then become superimposed in the manner shown. In the real world, we rarely look directly at light-emitting objects. Indeed, the most common source—the sun—is simply too intense to look at directly, and artificial sources such as light bulbs, which have been available since their first public demonstration in 1879, are discrete light emitters that are used to provide general illumination of our environment rather than objects to be viewed.

Light reflection by objects

The vast majority of stimuli that produce colour perception are objects that reflect light, whether from the sun or from artificial sources. The precise way that an object reflects light has a considerable impact on the colours we perceive. Figure 11.5 shows that light reflection from an opaque object can occur in two ways (Nassau, 2001; Waldman, 2002; Wandell, 1995). The first is reflection at the surface, which is also known as **specular reflection**. This is a simple mirror-like reflection that affects all wavelengths of incident light in an equal manner. Objects that display a large amount of

specular reflection are glossy in nature, whereas those that display little reflection at the surface take on a matte appearance. A perfectly matte surface is also known as a *Lambertian surface.*

The second type of reflection is a bit more complex. As Figure 11.5 shows, light entering the object is dispersed by its molecules and after some internal scattering, emerges out of the object in all directions. This phenomenon, which is known as **body reflection**, is actually responsible for giving an object its perceived colour. Objects that reflect all wavelengths equally in this manner will take on a whitish appearance, whereas those that reflect very little light across all wavelengths will appear black. Intermediate levels of reflection across all wavelengths will create various levels of grey, depending on the amount of light reflected.

An object takes on a specific colour appearance when it reflects unequal amounts of light across the visible spectrum. For example, an object that displays body reflection dominated by the long wavelengths will appear red when illuminated by white light. In this case, only the longer wavelength light will enter the observer's eyes because the other wavelengths are absorbed by the object. The same logic can be applied to materials that appear to be of a different colour, except in those cases a different segment of the visible spectrum will appear in the body reflection.

The perceived colour of an object

A scientific approach to this discussion requires that we be more exact in describing the reflectance properties of an object. A precise

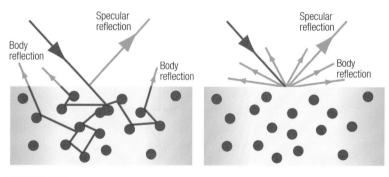

Figure 11.5

The interaction of light with an object produces two types of reflection—specular reflection at its surface and body reflection. The latter occurs after light enters the object and becomes dispersed by its molecules before being re-emitted (left panel). Specular reflection, which is mirror-like in nature, is confined to a small angle and therefore appears to be more intense, whereas body reflection is more random and diffuse and produces a less intense emission but equally in all directions (right panel). Adapted from *Foundations of Vision*, by B. A. Wandell, 1995, Sunderland, MA: Sinauer Associates.

description of the nature of body reflection is given by an object's **reflectance spectrum** (i.e., a plot of the amount of reflection as a function of wavelength) (Kandel, Schwartz, & Jessell, 2000; Palmer, 2002; Wandell, 1995). Figure 11.6 shows the reflectance spectra of four different objects. The important point to note in these figures is that the spectra are all continuous and show peaks at different points within the visible spectrum. Thus, the red colour of a tomato arises not from a single, discrete spike at a particular wavelength but a more generalized emission at long wavelengths accompanied by reduced emission at short and middle wavelengths.

Does this mean that a tomato will always look red no matter what the lighting conditions? Consider what would happen if the light source illuminating this tomato only emitted blue light. In this case, the tomato would appear quite dark because it does not reflect the incident blue light, and furthermore, its preferred wavelengths of reflection are not contained in the incident light (SideNote 11.10). This simple example shows that the chromatic appearance of an object is a function of not only its reflectance properties but also the wavelength content in the incident light.

This point is illustrated in Figure 11.7 where a sheet of blue paper (reflectance spectrum in

the top right panel of Figure 11.6) is illuminated by a tungsten light bulb (emission spectrum in the top right panel of Figure 11.2) (Wandell, 1995). At each wavelength, the amount of energy contained in the light is multiplied by the amount reflected by the object to produce a new plot that accurately portrays the **colour signal**. The perceived colour of the object will be determined by the nature of this signal. It now becomes clear that the blue paper, which largely reflects short-wavelength light, will appear somewhat different when viewed under a tungsten light source, which contains little energy at short wavelengths. The higher energy content of the tungsten light at longer wavelengths will add a reddish tinge to what would otherwise appear purely blue under white light.

Subtractive colour mixtures

The principle of additive colour mixing discussed in Section A.1 showed that it was possible to obtain a vast range of secondary colours from a mixture of three primary colours of light. Can the same principle be used with coloured objects, most notably inks, paints, and dyes? The answer is *yes*, but the results of such mixing are quite different than mixing lights (Lee, 2009; Malacara, 2002; Nassau, 2001). To begin with, paint takes on a particular colour because it absorbs light from certain segments

SideNote | **11.10**

This can be easily verified by looking at a tomato under blue light, such as that emitted by a common garden bug zapper. Similarly, blue objects appear dull under yellow light, such as the sodium vapour lamps found along many highways.

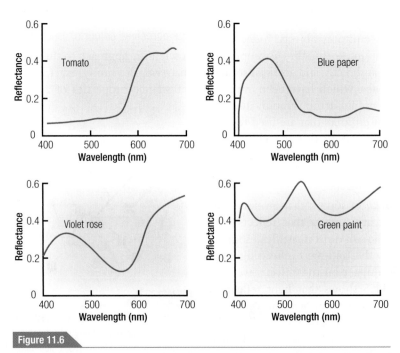

Figure 11.6

The reflectance spectrum is a plot of the degree to which light is reflected as a function of wavelength across the visible spectrum. The four examples here each show the spectrum to be continuous in nature and peaking at a certain point. The perceived colour of an object is largely determined by its reflectance property.

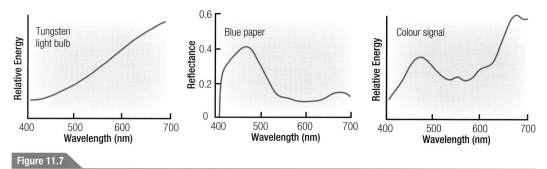

Figure 11.7

The colour signal from an object depends on both its reflectance spectrum and the emission spectrum of the light illuminating it. The colour signal is obtained by taking the energy contained in the light at each wavelength and multiplying it by the reflectance of the object at that wavelength. The resulting profile (right panel) determines the colour that will be perceived by an observer. Adapted from *Foundations of Vision,* by B. A. Wandell, 1995, Sunderland, MA: Sinauer Associates.

of the visible spectrum. The colour we perceive is associated with body reflection of the non-absorbed wavelengths. In other words, the paint subtracts light of particular wavelengths from the incident light, and the remaining light that is reflected produces the colour appearance. Figure 11.8 illustrates the subtractive principle of object colours through three objects that each absorb one of the primary colours of light. Note the following—cyan paint absorbs red light while reflecting both green and blue, magenta paint absorbs green light while reflecting both red and blue, and yellow paint absorbs blue light while reflecting both red and green (SideNote 11.11).

These three paint colours should sound familiar because they are the secondary colours that were produced by pairwise mixtures of coloured lights (see Figure 11.4). These three colours also serve as the subjective primary colours, that is, a triplet of colours from which all others can be obtained through mixture. To understand this concept, let us assume that cyan (C) and magenta (M) paints are mixed together. As Figure 11.9 on page 364 shows, this mixture

will produce a blue coloured paint. The reason for this is that paints, inks, and dyes retain their absorption characteristics even when mixed together. Therefore, the mixture of cyan and magenta paints will absorb red and green lights, respectively, leaving blue to be reflected back to our eyes. Similarly, a mixture of yellow (Y) and magenta will yield red, whereas mixing yellow and cyan will produce green.

The interesting fact that emerges from mixing C, M, and Y colours in a pairwise manner is that in each case the resulting colour is one of the additive primaries—red, green, or blue. And just as we were able to obtain a broad range of colours through light mixtures of these additive primaries, the same logic underlies the fact that a full range of colours can be produced by varying the proportions of the subtractive primaries in paint mixtures (Lee, 2009; Waldman, 2002). For this reason, CMY printing uses dyes of these three colours that can be mixed in various combinations to produce colours that are not absorbed by the mixture. When all three are mixed in equal amounts, however, the result is black because theoretically no light is

SideNote | 11.11

Magenta is a nonspectral colour, similar to purple but with a slightly more reddish appearance. It is named after a dye that was discovered soon after the Battle of Magenta, fought near the northern Italian town by that name.

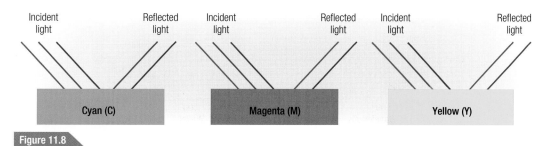

Figure 11.8

Coloured objects absorb light of certain wavelengths and reflect the non-absorbed light to produce the perceived colour. The following are the absorption and reflection properties of objects that appear as one of the three subtractive primary colours when illuminated by white light: cyan—absorbs red, reflects blue and green; magenta—absorbs green, reflects red and blue; yellow—absorbs blue, reflects red and green.

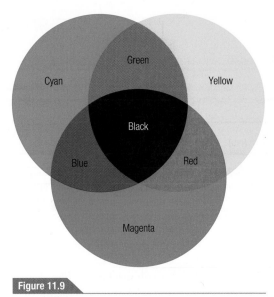

Figure 11.9

Subtractive colour mixing can be demonstrated by superimposing three paints that evoke each of the primary subtractive colours—cyan, magenta, and blue. The superposition of all three produces black, whereas the mixture of two primaries in equal amounts evokes the colour sensations of red (magenta + yellow), green (yellow + cyan), and blue (cyan + magenta). There are many other colours that can be produced by mixing the primaries in unequal amounts.

reflected. In reality, the *black* generated by mixing CMY primaries is not as deep as that of a genuine black dye or ink. Therefore, modern printing processes use four-colour mixtures that include black (K). Indeed, CMYK mixtures

permit superior print qualities because a broad range of colours can be generated along with a deep black.

Coloured lights on coloured surfaces

Earlier we discussed the example of viewing a red tomato under a blue light and concluded that the tomato would appear quite dark. This example raises the general issue of how coloured objects appear when a coloured light, rather than a white light, is used as the illumination source. The colour appearance of the object in this case must take into account not only the subtractive properties associated with body reflection but also, in some cases, the additive properties of the reflected light mixture (Lee, 2009; Nassau, 2001). Table 11.1 provides several examples that are worth considering. In the first set of examples, white light is used to illuminate a trio of object colours comprising the three subtractive primaries. The absorption and reflection properties given here are the same as those seen in Figure 11.8.

The remaining examples in Table 11.1 deal with non-white light sources. A blue object illuminated by red light or a red object illuminated by blue light will both create a situation where little light is reflected, making the object appear black. Magenta light falling on a white object will simply produce a reflection of the two component colours in the light source,

Table **11.1**

The Effect of Coloured Lights on Coloured Objects

Light Colour	Object Colour	Object Absorbs	Object Reflects	Colour Perceived
White (R, G, B)	Cyan	Red	Green, Blue	Cyan
	Magenta	Green	Red, Blue	Magenta
	Yellow	Blue	Red, Green	Yellow
Red	Blue	Red, Green	Nil	Black
	Yellow	Blue	Red	Red
Blue	Red	Blue, Green	Nil	Black
	Magenta	Green	Blue	Blue
Magenta (R, B)	White	Nil	Red, Blue	Magenta
	Yellow	Blue	Red	Red
Yellow (R, G)	Cyan	Red	Green	Green
	Green	Red, Blue	Green	Green

Note. The effect of coloured lights on coloured objects yields reflected light that is a function of both the wavelength content of the light as well as the absorption properties of the object. The perceived colour of the object depends on the nature of the reflected light that reaches the eyes.

making the object appear magenta. However, magenta light falling on a yellow object will make it appear red because the object will absorb the blue component of the magenta light (remember, yellow objects absorb blue light). The final two examples are quite interesting because they show what happens when yellow light is used to illuminate a cyan and a green object. In both cases, the object will appear to be green. Thus, a cyan-coloured object under white light will appear green under yellow light, whereas green-coloured objects remain unaffected (SideNote 11.12).

3. REPRESENTING AND CATEGORIZING COLOURS

Newton's colour circle represented a significant development because it used a simple geometrical form to represent the complex property of colour vision. This is not an easy task because colour perceptions do not arise from physical aspects of the stimulus in a predictable way. Perceptual qualities such as brightness or loudness are directly linked to the physical value of light or sound intensity. However, there is no quantitative difference between say the colours red or green. They produce two entirely different kinds of perception that, though linked to the wavelength of light, cannot be scaled to wavelength in a meaningful way. Increasing the wavelength of light does not add to the magnitude of the sensory experience but rather changes it entirely. As such, colour vision is an example of *metathetic* perception, as discussed in Section C.2 of Chapter 1.

Physical versus psychological descriptions of colour

We have by now developed a sufficient understanding of the basics of colour vision and can undertake a more meaningful discussion of the physical and psychological representations of colour. A physicist would describe light by way of two specific parameters—its intensity and its wavelength. Light, whether reflected by an object or emitted from a source, can be described in physical terms by its energy content (which is related to intensity) at each and every wavelength within the visible spectrum. Thus, the physical spectrum provides a neat description of the total information available from the physical realm. The left panel in Figure 11.10 shows three different spectra, each indicated by a numeric label (Palmer,

2002). As we will soon discover, it is the nature of the physical spectra that in turn gives rise to the different psychological experiences of colour perception.

If a physicist can describe light in terms of its physical spectrum, then how does a psychologist describe light in terms of the colour it evokes in the human mind? As noted earlier, the first foray into this area was undertaken by Newton, who proposed that a colour wheel best depicts the psychological dimension of colour when laid out in terms of perceptual similarity. Metathetic qualities such as colour perception cannot be scaled directly in terms of a physical parameter, in this case wavelength, and therefore have to be evaluated in a qualitative way (Malacara, 2002; Palmer, 2002). This means that psychologists must introduce the notion of similarity and dissimilarity when evaluating metathetic percepts. For example, subjects presented with three colours at a time may be asked to judge which pair is the most similar. Alternatively, subjects may be asked to indicate how similar two colours are to one another using a numerical scale (SideNote 11.13). After enough data has been collected with a sufficient number of colours, it is possible to represent the information by way of a similarity map where those colours that are perceived to be similar occupy nearby positions, and those that are dissimilar are placed farther apart. Thus, psychological similarity can be represented by physical distance in a spatial map to produce a so-called **colour space**.

Returning to Figure 11.10, we see that the perceptual dimension of colour is indeed best represented by a circular colour space, as suggested by Newton. The circular arrangement

SideNote | 11.12

This is a striking example of why the colours of different objects should be compared under full-spectrum white light (e.g., sunlight). For example, cars parked at night under the strong yellow lamps of many auto dealerships will often appear to be a different colour during daylight conditions.

SideNote | 11.13

Similarity experiments do not require subjects to actually name the colour but rather to make comparisons between colours and then reach a judgment about how similar or dissimilar they are. A numerical approach, such as a scale of 1–10, can be used to quantify similarity.

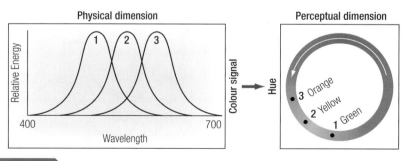

Figure 11.10

A physical description of light is given by its emission spectrum—that is, energy content at each wavelength across the visible range (left panel). The perceptual parameter that corresponds to wavelength, which is known as *hue*, can be represented in a circular manner where the distance around the circle corresponds to the changing hue sensations (right panel). The three colour signals generated by the three emission spectra each produce a distinct hue sensation that can be mapped onto the respective points in the colour circle.

shows a gradual transition between the different colours. At this point we need to introduce a new term. Strictly speaking, the perceptual quality that we speak of as *colour* actually encompasses three distinct psychological dimensions. One of them concerns the chromatic quality that we indicate by certain names, such as *blue, green, yellow, indigo, red, purple*, etc. This psychological dimension is referred to as **hue**. Looking at Figure 11.10 again, we see that the three different physical spectra (1, 2, and 3) produce three distinct hues, which can be mapped onto the colour space (i.e., the perceptual dimension) at the points indicated by the respective numerical values. The physical spectrum of a particular stimulus, whether it is a light source or body reflection from an object, will produce a distinct hue. One of the interesting (and confusing) facets of colour vision is that the reverse is not true. That is, a specific hue need not be associated with a unique physical spectrum. In fact, there can be a very large number of different spectra that will actually produce the same hue (Waldman, 2002; Wyszecki & Stiles, 2000). Our understanding of this, however, will have to wait until the next section of this chapter.

Saturation and value

In his colour mixing experiments, Newton observed that the intermediate colour produced by mixing a pair of spectral lights had a washed-out appearance. In other words, the hue of the mixture did not have the same degree of purity as the original two spectral lights. In general, any hue can vary in terms of its purity or **saturation** (i.e., the vividness of its chromatic quality). A highly saturated colour is one that evokes the most intense quality of hue, whereas colours that are less saturated appear washed out or more whitish in nature. A fully desaturated (unsaturated) colour is in fact a shade of grey. Saturation, therefore, represents the second psychological dimension of the colour experience.

Figure 11.11 illustrates the physical basis of colour saturation and its corresponding psychological representation (Palmer, 2002; Wyszecki & Stiles, 2000). In physical terms, a highly saturated colour is generated by light whose energy is contained within a very narrow range of wavelengths, as shown in the left panel (e.g., spectrum 1). As the spectrum flattens out, the dominant wavelength identity of this stimulus becomes diluted because it incorporates energy from a progressively broader range of wavelengths (e.g., spectra 2 and 3). Although all three stimuli shown here will evoke the same hue sensation, there will be a progressive loss of saturation as the spectrum flattens out, the result being a more washed-out colour that becomes whitish in appearance. A perfectly flat energy profile would induce a grey hue.

The right panel in Figure 11.11 shows how the perceptual dimension of saturation can be incorporated into the same colour space that depicts hue. Recall that hue is represented in a circular manner whereby the distance around the circle indicates the changing hue sensations. As Newton had shown, the intermediate colour that results from mixing two pure spectral colours will be represented by a point that is midway between them on the colour circle (see middle diagram in Figure 11.3). This

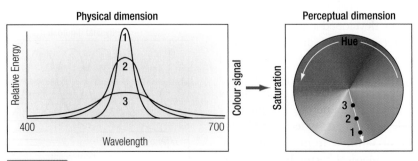

Figure 11.11

Physical spectra centred upon a particular wavelength can have various degrees of sharpness (left panel). The flatter the profile, the more the signal encompasses neighbouring wavelengths. This change in the physical profile does not affect the hue but does alter its perceived vividness (saturation). Saturation is represented in a radial manner in colour space, where the centre occupies a neutral colour and the edges represent the most saturated hues (right panel). The three colour signals each produce a different saturation sensation that can be mapped onto the respective points in the colour space.

point will actually be inside the circle, meaning that the purity of its hue is degraded in comparison to the original pair in the mixture. Whereas the purest (maximally saturated) hues are found along the periphery of the colour circle, the more desaturated colours are represented by points within the circle. The colour circle therefore becomes a colour disk once the parameter of *saturation* is incorporated. The centre of the disk is a pure neutral colour—white. Returning to the three physical spectra shown in the left panel of Figure 11.11, we see that the perceptual quality of saturation is represented by radial distance from the centre of the colour disk. The corresponding locations of the three physical spectra in this space show that decreasing the saturation places the colour more toward the centre of the disk.

The third and final perceptual parameter that we need to take into account is the **brightness** or **lightness** of colour (Lee, 2009; Nassau, 2001; Wyszecki & Stiles, 2000). A stimulus of a particular hue and saturation can be generated at multiple levels of intensity. The left panel in Figure 11.12 shows the physical spectra of three lights that contain different amounts of energy, which is related to the physical parameter known as *intensity* (Palmer, 2002). However, all three spectra are centred on a particular wavelength and encompass the same range of neighbouring wavelengths. Therefore, the hue and saturation produced by these three lights should be similar, but the perceived intensity or **value** would be different (SideNote 11.14).

How can the perceptual dimension of value be represented in colour space? As the right panel in Figure 11.12 shows, the colour disk can occupy a particular position along the vertical dimension to represent the perceptual quality of *value*. The colour disk will be located at a lower position for stimuli having low value (brightness/lightness), such as the stimulus indicated by numeral 3. Stimuli having high value will be found within a colour disk that is placed at correspondingly higher points along the vertical dimension (e.g., stimuli 1 and 2).

The HSV colour space

Although hue is the primary psychological dimension that we usually refer to when discussing colour, we have just learned that a full description of colour requires the two additional perceptual parameters of saturation and value (brightness/lightness). We saw above how these three qualities are generated by physical aspects of the light stimulus and how they in turn can be represented in a psychologically defined colour space. These three parameters—hue (H), saturation (S), and value (V)—provide the complete psychological description of colour.

In our discussion above, we gradually built up the HSV colour space one parameter at a time. The complete HSV colour space forms a cylinder when all three parameters are combined, as shown in the left panel of Figure 11.13. This is not surprising because as we have already noted, hue is represented in a circular manner, saturation in a radial manner, and value in a vertical manner. Assembling all three of these parameters together results in a cylindrical colour space—a three-dimensional solid volume that portrays how humans describe the colour experience (Malacara, 2002; Palmer, 2002; Wyszecki & Stiles, 2000).

SideNote | **11.14**

Brightness concerns the perception of intensity from a luminous source (e.g., a light-emitting object). However, the light we see arises for the most part from body reflection off objects, the perceived intensity of which is referred to as *lightness*. The term *value* also refers to the perceptual correlate of intensity but without distinguishing between emitted versus reflected light. The shape of the colour space for both emitted and reflected light is the same; hence the term *value* can be used as a generic term of perceived intensity.

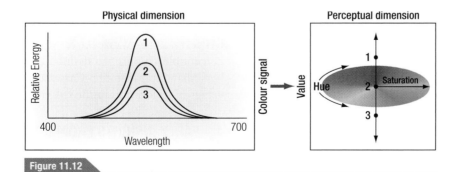

Figure 11.12

Colour signals can be centred on the same wavelength and encompass the same range of wavelengths but have different levels of energy content (left panel). The hue and saturation remain unaffected in this case, but each stimulus produces a different perceived value (brightness or lightness). Value is represented along the vertical dimension in colour space (right panel). The three colour signals each produce a different value sensation that can be mapped onto the respective points along the vertical dimension of the colour space.

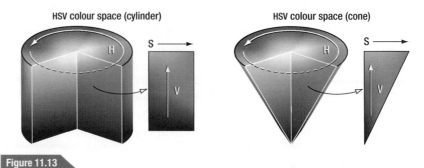

HSV colour space (cylinder)   HSV colour space (cone)

Figure 11.13

A three-dimensional colour space can be generated by incorporating the three perceptual parameters of colour—hue (H), saturation (S), and value (V). The HSV colour space can take the form of a cylinder where hue is represented in a circular manner, saturation in a radial manner, and value in a vertical manner. A rectangular slice through this colour space provides the full range of saturation and value for any given hue. A more accurate colour space, however, is conical in shape because decreasing the value of the stimulus produces a reduced range of perceived hue and saturation. A wedge-shaped segment within this colour space provides the full range of saturation and value for any given hue (right panel).

We must, however, make one modification to this colour space. We know from perceptual experience that the number of visually distinct hues and saturation levels decrease as the value approaches black. Thus, as we go down the value axis, the size of the disk becomes smaller so as to encompass a smaller range of hue and saturation. The HSV colour space is therefore best described as a cone (right panel in Figure 11.13). Exactly the same logic applies as a stimulus becomes lighter, leading again to a reduced colour disk with increasing value. Therefore, the full HSV colour space can best be described as a spindle-shaped volume where the two vertical ends become tapered, the bottom point being black and the top point being white (SideNote 11.15).

Other colour systems

The HSV colour space is a useful and commonly used model of human colour perception. There are, however, several other colour systems in use as well. One of the earliest was developed at the beginning of the 20th century by painter Albert Munsell. This system is similar to the HSV model in that it incorporates the three perceptual parameters of colour vision. The Munsell system is derived from a book of carefully prepared colour chips, the so-called *Munsell Book of Colour*. The chips (more than 1,600) are arranged according to hue and are laid out in a two-dimensional array on each page according to deviations in value and saturation (which is called *chroma* in this system). Each colour chip is specified by a decimal notation for the three colour parameters, rather than a colour name. The Munsell

colour space is similar to the HSV colour space in terms of its three-dimensional layout. An important departure, however, is that certain hues (such as red) display a broader saturation range, whereas others (such as green) are comparatively weaker with a reduced saturation range (Waldman, 2002; Wandell, 1995).

Although three-dimensional colour spaces are conceptually useful, there is an obvious drawback when it comes to representing them on a flat page. A commonly used colour system developed in 1931 by the International Commission on Illumination, which goes by the acronym CIE from the French translation of its name, gets around this problem by defining its colour space in terms of proportions of light rather than absolute levels of light. The CIE model uses a standardized system for representing colour that is widely used by colour scientists and technologists. The result is the CIE chromaticity diagram—a two-dimensional plot of colours that represents hue and saturation at constant intensity (value) (Lee, 2009; Malacara, 2002; Wyszecki & Stiles, 2000). All perceptible colours are defined by two numbers that represent the Cartesian coordinate values of its location in the CIE diagram.

4. EARLY INSIGHTS FROM COLOUR MATCHING EXPERIMENTS IN HUMANS

The principles of colour mixing that we have learned in preceding sections will now be pivotal in understanding how the first correct theories of colour vision were developed. By the early 1800s, the basic principles of

SideNote | **11.15**

In physical terms, light can vary along only two parameters—intensity and wavelength. These two physical parameters generate the three perceptual qualities of hue, saturation, and value (HSV). The complete HSV colour experience can be mapped onto a three-dimensional spindle-shaped colour space where any perceived colour can be represented by a point somewhere within that solid.

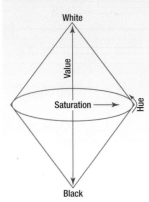

additive colour mixing were fairly well established, and it was known that overlapping three
primary lights (such as red, green, and blue–
violet) in varying amounts created mixtures
that produced virtually all of the other perceptible colours. There was something about this
number, three, that impressed these early scientists. One in particular was Thomas Young,
an English physicist widely acknowledged to
be one of the great scientific geniuses of all
time (SideNote 11.16) (Young, 1802). Young
postulated that there were *three* separate light-
capturing elements in the eye whose ability to
detect light coincided with the primary colours.
Young reasoned that the physical limitations of
the retina did not permit an indefinite number
of detectors for colour, and therefore these had
to be limited to the three principal colours.

The *three-colour* or **trichromatic theory**
represented a tour de force of scientific insight,
for here was a scientist who did not even know
about the nature of cone photoreceptors, and
yet through simple experimentation on colour mixing, he advanced a provocative idea on
how colour is encoded by the visual system.
Young's trichromatic theory was also ahead of
its time and therefore did not immediately gain
wide acceptance. It would require the careful
experimental work by another great physicist
50 years later, combined with the influence of

a legendary figure in vision science, before the
trichromatic theory would become accepted
as a fundamental tenet of colour vision.

Colour matching and metameric mixtures

The idea that at least three primary colours are
necessary to obtain a perceptual match with
virtually any other colour was firmly established through the experiments of James Clerk
Maxwell in the mid-1850s (SideNote 11.17)
(Nassau, 2001; Waldman, 2002). Maxwell demonstrated that most colours can be matched by
superimposing three separate coloured lights
on a black screen. The experiment worked
best if the three colours were sufficiently
spaced apart in colour space. The principle
behind this requirement is shown in the left
diagram of Figure 11.14. The three primaries
in this example—simply named red (R), green
(G), and blue (B)—are located at maximally
separable points in the colour disk so as to
produce the largest possible triangle. The goal
is to maximize the distance between any given
pair of primaries by placing them at the very
edge of the colour disk. This means that the trio
of lights must each produce highly saturated
colours. The corresponding physical spectra in
Figure 11.14 show that this is indeed the case
because the energy content of the R, G, and
B primaries is restricted to a single wavelength

Thomas Young (1773–1829)
© Classic Image/Alamy

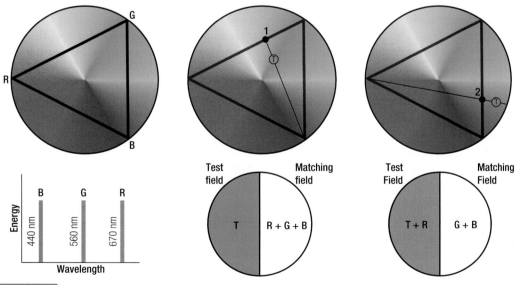

Figure 11.14

Colour matching experiments provide the best results with a trio of colours (primaries) that are sufficiently spaced apart in
colour space (left diagram). The R, G, and B primaries shown here are highly saturated colours whose physical spectra show
them to be monochromatic lights. A mixture of these three primaries will yield any colour contained within the triangle (middle
diagram). A bipartite field can be used to find the proportion of R, G, and B primaries needed in a mixture (matching field) to
exactly match the colour in the test field (T). An exact colour match can still be made if the test colour appears outside the
triangle by adding one of the primaries to the test field (right diagram).

(670 nm, 560 nm, and 440 nm, respectively). Each of these so-called **monochromatic lights** therefore has the physical characteristics to produce a highly saturated hue.

We learned earlier that additive mixing of any pair of colours from this disk produces an intermediate colour that lies somewhere along a straight line connecting them (e.g., see Figure 11.3). The exact location depends upon the relative amounts of each light in the mixture. We can now expand this idea to state that additive mixing of three primaries will produce a colour that will fall somewhere within the triangular boundary defined by the locations of the primaries. This idea is illustrated in the middle diagram of Figure 11.14 by way of a colour matching experiment (Malacara, 2002; Palmer, 2002; Waldman, 2002). The bottom part of this diagram shows a circular patch with two half-fields—a so-called *bipartite field*—in which the left half is named the *test field* and contains a colour (T) of hue and saturation corresponding to point "T" in the colour disk above. In a colour matching experiment, subjects are told to combine the three colour primaries in any proportion in the right half, or *matching field*, to make an exact colour match with the test field (i.e., the two fields must appear to be identical in colour). At the end of this experiment, the relative proportions of R and G primaries in the matching field will by themselves produce a colour that will appear at the position indicated by the numeral "1" in the colour disk. The addition of the third primary (B) to this mixture will then change the colour so that it moves along a straight line toward its position in the triangle. Adding just the right amount of B primary will move the mixture to the "T" position in the colour disk and therefore produce a matching field colour that will exactly match the test field colour.

We have just seen something quite astounding. The test field colour is a somewhat desaturated greenish hue that is produced by a light whose physical spectrum is likely to be fairly broad in nature, such as spectrum 2 in Figure 11.11. And yet, an exact perceptual match was achieved experimentally by combining three monochromatic lights in a certain proportion. Although the two halves may appear to be perceptually identical, they are actually physically different in terms of their energy distribution across the visible range of light wavelengths. Any pair of lights or surfaces that are perceptually identical but physically

different are called **metamers** (Malacara, 2002; Waldman, 2002; Wandell, 1995). What is perhaps even more astounding is that there are many possible metameric mixtures for any given test colour. Returning to our example in Figure 11.14, consider another trio of primaries other than the ones used here. This new set will map out a different triangle in the colour disk and therefore predict a completely new set of proportions needed for a metameric match to the same test colour. Metamers can thus be produced by any trio of primaries, leading to the conclusion that a specific hue need not be associated with a unique physical spectrum. In fact, there can be a very large number of metamers—different spectra that will actually produce the same hue. In all cases though, the number *three* is an essential requirement in terms of the set of primaries needed to achieve a metameric mixture (SideNote 11.18).

Colours outside the mixture triangle

We end our discussion of colour matching with a problem—how do we make metameric matches with a trio of primaries if the test colour lies outside the boundaries of the triangle defined by them in colour space? This situation is illustrated in the right diagram of Figure 11.14 where the test field contains a fairly saturated bluish hue that can be mapped onto the colour space above it at the position denoted by the letter "T." How is it possible to make a metameric match in this case, given that all possible additive mixtures of the three primaries will produce a colour that lies only within the triangle? The solution lies in the use of a little trick. First consider mixing the G and B primaries at a certain proportion that will yield a colour along this axis at the position indicated by the numeral "2." The addition of the R primary to this mixture will only move the colour location along that axis toward its triangular apex, which does not help us in achieving a match with the test colour. However, if a small amount of R is added to the test field itself, then it will move its colour location along the same straight line until it coincides with the G–B mixture. As a result, a metameric match will occur between the colour at position 2 in the colour disk and a small addition of the R primary to the test colour (T). Thus, the rules of colour mixture remain valid for all colours, including those outside the mixture triangle, by allowing for this small modification.

SideNote | **11.18**

The RGB set of primary colours is well known to produce a wide gamut of colour mixtures. Indeed, these three lights can create just about any hue when mixed in various proportions. This fact forms the basis for colour technology, such as the images on television and computer monitors, where the different colours are produced by additive mixing of three saturated shades of red, green, and blue.

5. THEORETICAL FOUNDATIONS OF HUMAN COLOUR VISION

By the middle of the 19th century, two brilliant physicists—Thomas Young and James Maxwell—had weighed in with their theoretical and experimental contributions, which suggested that a three-channel mechanism was responsible for encoding colour. However, it required the extraordinary clout of a person many regard as the greatest vision scientist ever to firmly establish the trichromatic theory. That scientist was Hermann von Helmholtz, a German physiologist and physicist whose contributions to the field of vision science were monumental (von Helmholtz, 1911/2000).

The Young–Helmholtz theory of trichromacy

Von Helmholtz resurrected Young's trichromatic theory because he felt that it served as the correct explanation for Maxwell's, as well as his own, colour matching experiments. The fact that three colour primaries can be used to generate any other perceptible colour provided an elegant proposition that the visual system must also have three primary detection mechanisms, whose combined output can similarly generate any other colour experience (Bowmaker, 1983; Gegenfurtner & Kiper, 2003; Wandell, 1995). Von Helmholtz even went one step further. He proposed that there were three sets of fibres that emerged from the eye, each with its own distinct profile of excitation according to the wavelength of incoming light (SideNote 11.19).

According to von Helmholtz, compound colours would excite these three fibres to different extents, some feebly and others strongly, and it is this relative degree of excitation among the three fibre sets that in turn generates the perceived colour we associate with a given light. As with Young, von Helmholtz too did not

know about the nature of cone photoreceptors and therefore described colour vision in terms of fundamental sensations carried by the three types of fibres. Nevertheless, the notion that colour sensations are generated by a trio of separate wavelength-dependent light detectors in our eye finally became a cornerstone of vision science and went on to be known as the *Young–Helmholtz theory of trichromacy*.

Colour afterimages

The trichromatic theory soon became hailed as one of the fundamental theories in vision. However, the party did not last long. Around the end of the 19th century, another German physiologist, Ewald Hering, began to question the trichromatic theory. Unlike von Helmholtz, Hering undertook careful studies of the way colours actually appeared in the perceptual domain (Chalupa & Werner, 2003; De Valois & De Valois, 1990; Graham, 1965). One of the perplexing phenomena that Hering grappled with was the colour reversal that occurs after viewing an object for an extended amount of time. This phenomenon can be experienced by way of the illustration in Figure 11.15. The left panel of this figure looks very similar to a well-known flag, except that the colours are incorrect. The true colours in this flag can be produced by following a simple procedure—stare at the white spot in the middle of the left panel for approximately 30 seconds, being careful not to deviate your gaze to any other part of this figure. Then, abruptly shift your gaze to the black spot in the middle of the right panel. The true colours of the *Stars and Stripes* should now appear for a brief moment. This fleeting image is an example of a **colour afterimage**, a transient impression whereby previously green areas now appear red (and vice versa) and previously yellow areas now appear blue (and vice versa).

Hermann Ludwig Ferdinand von Helmholtz (1821–1894)
© INTERFOTO/Alamy

SideNote 11.19

The three distinct sets of detectors, according to von Helmholtz, were each sensitive to different parts of the visible spectrum, as can be seen from the figure below. The different spectral colours (B to R) would be sampled (or detected) by each of these detectors in different amounts.

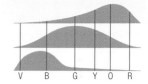

V B G Y O R

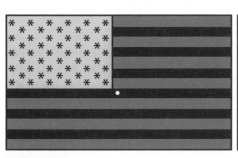

Figure 11.15

The true colours of the *Stars and Stripes* can be obtained by staring at the white spot in the left panel for about 30 seconds and then abruptly shifting your gaze to the black spot in the right panel. The fleeting impression of the American flag occurs due to a colour afterimage in which a substitution of colour takes place.

Ewald Hering (1834–1918)

Hering's theory of colour opponency

Colour afterimages represented just one of several perceptual facets of colour vision that Hering could not reconcile with the trichromatic theory. There is nothing about the trichromatic mechanism that would offer an explanation for the colour reversals seen in an afterimage. Prolonged viewing of a green stimulus, for example, should not produce a red afterimage. In other words, there is no basis in trichromatic theory for expecting greater activity in the *red* channel following stimulation of the *green* channel.

Hering was also intrigued by the fact that mixing red and green lights does not yield an intermediate reddish green (or greenish red), as would be expected from trichromatic theory, but rather something completely different—yellow. Similarly, mixing blue and yellow lights does not yield an intermediate hue but rather white (or grey). Thus, there is something fundamentally different about these two colour pairings—red versus green and blue versus yellow—that stands out from any other pairings. For example, mixing red and yellow lights produces an intermediate colour (orange) within which the original two colours can still be perceived. The same is true of mixing red and blue lights to produce magenta. And yet, red–green and blue–yellow pairings completely destroy the perceptual quality of either of the constituent colours.

The trichromatic theory cannot account for any of these phenomena. Furthermore, whereas the trichromatic theory was based on three colours, Hering proposed that colour perception is fundamentally based on four— the fourth being yellow. The subjective appearance of yellow is as unique as the other three primaries in that we do not perceive any other colour to be contained within it. Therefore, in perceptual terms, yellow is as much a primary colour as are the other three that were adopted from trichromatic theory.

Hering used these observations to propose a somewhat different, and at the time radical, view of how colour was encoded by the visual system (Backhaus, Kleigl, & Werner, 1998; Chalupa & Werner, 2003; Kandel et al., 2000). He was absolutely convinced that the four chromatic primaries are structured in opposite pairs. Hering's **opponent colour theory** asserts that red and green are not simultaneously processed by the visual system and

therefore should be thought of as representing opponent colour mechanisms. The same is true of blue and yellow. A spatial representation of the opponent theory is shown in Figure 11.16.

It is important to appreciate how fundamentally different the opponent colour theory is from the trichromatic theory. Instead of assuming that a colour is triggered by the pattern of activity in three different sensory detectors at any given time (trichromatic theory), we now have a scheme that places two colour pairs at polar opposites such that they are never simultaneously processed (opponent theory). Whereas the trichromatic theory is useful in explaining and predicting metameric matches, the opponent theory provides a convincing explanation for various subjective phenomena, such as the presence of four perceptual colour primaries, the subjective appearance of colour in various mixtures, and the colour afterimage phenomenon (SideNote 11.20) (Palmer, 2002; Valberg, 2005).

For von Helmholtz and other physicists of his time, the subjective appearance of colour was considered to be of little scientific importance. As a result, Hering's views were largely ignored by mainstream scientists of his era, and so the trichromatic theory continued in its supremacy. The challenge to the trichromatic theory did remain, however, and was not fully resolved until the advent of physiological recording techniques in the next century, which explored colour processing right down to the neuronal level. The resolution of this debate represents one of the fascinating outcomes in modern science and will be taken up in the next section when we explore the biological facets of colour processing.

B. Biological Aspects of Colour Vision

Now that we have come to learn many of the physical and perceptual properties of colour vision, it is worthwhile to first ask why such a system would have evolved in the first place. It is generally believed that early mammals either lacked or at best had a crude form of colour vision because they were nocturnal creatures whose visual systems were well adapted for night vision (Osorio & Vorobyev, 2008; Waldman, 2002). According to the *nocturnal bottleneck* hypothesis, the impetus for evolving

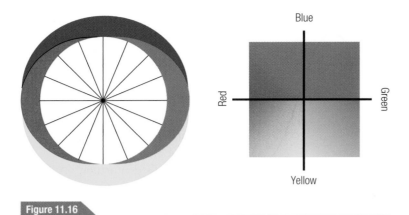

Figure 11.16

Hering proposed that two opponent colour pairs (red/green and blue/yellow) are organized in polar opposites in colour space (left panel). The opponent colours do not overlap because their mixtures neutralize each other to produce dull hues or colourless greys. A modern representation of Hering's circle (right panel) shows the transitional colours as well as the middle of the colour space fading to grey.

full colour vision among mammals, and more notably in primates, arose due to survival challenges for those species that made a transition to daylight life. Colour vision confers an entirely new dimension to vision by providing a wavelength-based system for distinguishing objects in the real world. The result in terms of survival advantage is quite striking because animals with full colour vision are simply better able to identify objects from the background. For example, the ability to distinguish red from green allows an animal to more easily identify ripe edible fruits, which tend to be reddish, against a background of green foliage. A wavelength-based visual discrimination system also provides for better detection of camouflaged predators.

What is involved in creating a biological system that can produce colour perception? To begin with, a colour vision system would require that wavelength information in the retinal image be captured through different detectors that are optimally sensitive to different parts of the visible spectrum. However, merely having different detectors would not be helpful if they all happened to feed into the same set of neurons at the next stage. Therefore, the wavelength sampling that must occur through different detectors also has to be transmitted through independent cables to the brain. This means that a colour vision system must develop the proper circuitry to allow independent processing and transmission of separate colour signals (Hurvich, 1981; Kaiser & Boynton, 1996; Palmer, 2002). And finally, the visual brain must establish the necessary

neural networks to transform these signals into the perceptual representation that we experience as colour. In this section, we will see how the biological structures in our visual system accommodate each of these needs.

1. TRICHROMACY

How many independent sets of detectors are needed to produce colour vision? We learned from the preceding segment of this chapter that a three-detector (trichromatic) system can theoretically account for the full gamut of colours that are normally experienced by humans. Although a considerable amount of psychophysical data pointed to the existence of trichromatic vision in humans, it required a technological breakthrough in the 1960s to finally confirm this theory. Using very small beams of light, a group of scientists in the UK demonstrated the existence of three different types of cone photoreceptors, each having a distinct absorption spectrum for light (see Section A.3 of Chapter 9 for a review of this topic) (Bowmaker, 1983; Bowmaker & Dartnall, 1980). The absorption spectra of the three cone classes in humans are shown in Figure 11.17 on page 374 (Schnapf, Kraft, & Baylor, 1987). The important point to note from this figure is that the three profiles overlap to a certain extent, though each has a different peak of maximum light absorption. This difference in absorption preference forms the basis for naming them *short-wavelength* (S), *medium-wavelength* (M), and *long-wavelength* (L) cones.

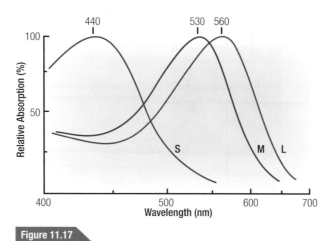

Figure 11.17

Absorption profiles (spectra) of the three types of cone photoreceptors in humans show that each has a different range of wavelength preference and, correspondingly, a different wavelength of peak absorption. The S, M, and L cones maximally absorb light at 440 nm, 530 nm, and 560 nm, respectively. Adapted from "Spectral Sensitivity of Human Cone Photoreceptors," by J. L. Schnapf, T. W. Kraft, and D. A. Baylor, 1987, *Nature, 325*, pp. 439–441.

The principle of univariance

The biological mechanism for colour perception begins with light absorption in these three types of cone photoreceptors. They are the actual entities that are responsible for trichromatic vision and therefore represent the pillar of the Young–Helmholtz theory that all perceptible colours are generated by light activation of three separate detector systems. The major issue that remains before us is to understand how this is so.

It is tempting to assume at the outset that each of the three classes of photoreceptors transmits actual wavelength information to the brain. In this scenario, the S cones would be expected to transmit wavelength information over its absorption range, with the same being true of the M and L cones but over a respectively longer set of wavelengths. This conjecture is simply not true. The cone photoreceptors do not register information about the actual wavelength of light. Rather, the signal that emerges out of each cone is related only to how much light is absorbed at a given moment (Chalupa & Werner, 2003; Hurvich, 1981; De Valois & De Valois, 1993). The greater the amount of light capture, the greater the electrical signal. It just so happens that each of the three cone classes is optimally suited for capturing light over a particular segment of the visible spectrum, which we now know is due to molecular properties of the rhodopsin molecules inside each cone

photoreceptor (Gegenfurtner & Kiper, 2003; Neitz, Neitz, & Jacobs, 1993). Another way of stating the same idea is that the absorption of each photon in a cone produces exactly the same response regardless of its wavelength. It is only the efficiency with which photons are captured that is wavelength-dependent, not just within an individual cone but across the three classes of cones (De Valois & De Valois, 1975; Gegenfurtner, 2000; Hurvich, 1981). This bedrock principle of colour vision is known as the **principle of univariance** (SideNote 11.21).

An application of the principle of univariance in the context of trichromatic theory is shown in Figure 11.18. The first example shows how cone signals are generated in response to light reflected by a sheet of red paper (top diagram). The physical spectrum of the stimulus (the colour signal) shows that most of the energy content is restricted to the long-wavelength end of the visible range, as would be expected. The photons making up this light stimulus strike all three classes of cone photoreceptors in the retina. However, the electrical signal generated by each of the cones will depend upon how much energy—that is, the number of photons—is contained within its preferred wavelength range of absorption. The S cones will absorb very little of this light because there is simply not much energy in the stimulus at the lower wavelengths. Light absorption by the L cones, on the other hand, would be much higher because its absorption spectrum is better matched to the physical spectrum of this stimulus. The M cones, using the same logic, will have an intermediate level of photon absorption. The bar graph in the top right panel shows the resulting signal strengths of the three types of cones caused by their relative levels of photon capture.

According to a modern version of trichromatic theory, all perceptible colours are generated by the activation pattern of the three cone classes. Any change in the physical spectrum of the stimulus will also cause the relative outputs of the three cones to change, resulting in a new colour sensation. The second example in Figure 11.18 (bottom diagram) shows how the cone activation pattern becomes reversed if, instead, a blue stimulus is imaged on the retina. The S cones now provide the largest signal because their absorption spectrum more closely matches the low-wavelength energy content of the stimulus. Thus, more photons will be

SideNote | **11.21**

The principle of univariance predicts that the same electrical response will be produced by a cone photoreceptor if the intensities of two different wavelength lights are adjusted to take into account the difference in their absorption efficiency. The figure below shows the response produced by a cone to 659 nm and 550 nm light at a 9:1 intensity ratio, which matches the difference in their absorption at these wavelengths. The electrical response to a flash of the two lights is indistinguishable (black vs. grey curves).

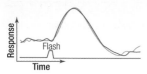

Adapted from Baylor et al. (1987).

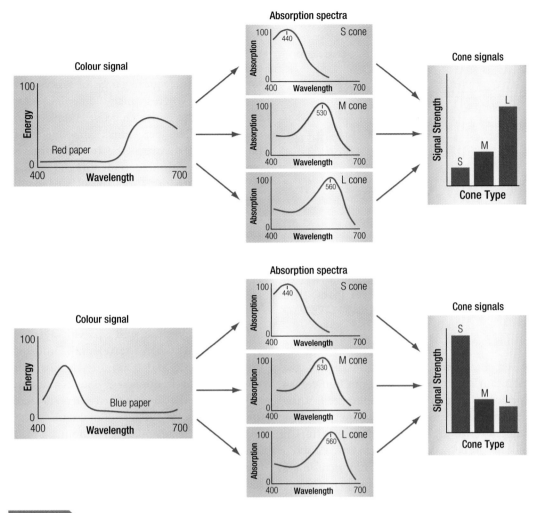

Figure 11.18
The output signals from each of the three cone classes can be obtained by integrating the physical spectrum of the stimulus with the individual cone absorption spectra. A red stimulus (top diagram) will produce an activation pattern among the three cones that is weighted toward the L cones, whereas a blue stimulus (bottom diagram) will produce a greater signal in the S cones. The visual brain, according to trichromatic theory, generates a subjective impression of colour on the basis of the output pattern of the three cones.

captured by the S cones compared to the M and L cones. Our visual brain interprets this output pattern of the three cone classes to create a colour impression that we know as blue (SideNote 11.22).

Metameric mixtures—revisited

The two examples in Figure 11.18 show how cone photoreceptor signals are generated by integrating the physical spectrum of the stimulus with the absorption spectra of cone pigments. Cone signals represent the output of the trichromatic system, which are then fed to the next stage in the neural processing of colour. One of the great triumphs of the trichromatic theory was its predictive success and explanation of metameric matches (Backhaus, et al., 1998; Hurvich, 1981; Kaiser

& Boynton, 1996). We learned earlier that an exact perceptual colour match can occur with two different stimuli having very different physical spectra. We can now explain this phenomenon with our understanding of biological trichromacy.

Let us assume that a metameric match to the blue paper stimulus in the bottom diagram of Figure 11.18 is obtained with a trio of saturated primary colours, as defined in Figure 11.14—that is, monochromatic lights of 440 nm, 560 nm, and 670 nm. A colour matching experiment will reveal the exact proportion of the three primaries that would make such a metameric match. This outcome is shown in Figure 11.19 on page 376. Among the three primaries, the blue primary makes a dominant contribution combined with reduced amounts

SideNote | 11.22

According to the principle of univariance, the brain receives no information about the actual wavelength of light that is absorbed but merely how much light was absorbed by a particular class of cone photoreceptor. In order for our brain to generate colour perception, it must also have knowledge about the type of cone that absorbed the light in the first place. In other words, the brain must be able to distinguish the signals as having originated from a particular cone class (S, M, or L); otherwise it will be unable to use the incoming information in a meaningful way to create colour perception.

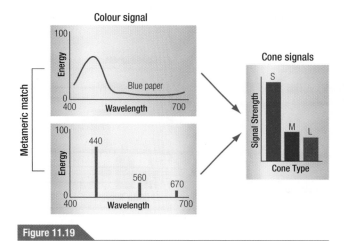

Figure 11.19

A metameric match occurs when two physically different stimuli yield the same perceived colour. Although the blue paper stimulus shows a continuous spectrum, the cone outputs are identical to that produced by the discrete spectra of a trio of primary matching lights. The two stimuli appear perceptually identical because they create the same trichromatic activation pattern.

SideNote | **11.23**

A different trio of primary colours will also create a metameric match using the same principles applied here. In fact, there are a vast number of possible primary colour trios that will yield an exact colour match because some combination of their proportions will produce the same cone output signals as the blue paper stimulus. This is why the number of metamers to a given colour signal is truly quite vast.

SideNote | **11.24**

"The eye cannot separate combined colours from each other; it sees them as an unresolvable, simple sensation of one mixed colour. There is no harmony in the same sense as with the ear; there is no music" (von Helmholtz, 1857).

of red and green primaries. There are two important points to note from this figure. First, a perceptual match occurs despite the fact that the physical spectra of the metamers are very different—that is, a continuous spectrum in the case of the paper stimulus versus a discrete spectrum containing a trio of monochromatic energy sources in the case of the primary colours. Second, both continuous and discrete spectra produce exactly the same cone output signals. And this is precisely why a metameric match occurs in this situation. The two stimuli appear perceptually identical because they create the same trichromatic activation pattern. We are unaware of the actual physical difference between the two stimuli because our brain can only create a colour impression based on the cone output signals, which are identical (SideNote 11.23).

Why trichromacy?

The trichromatic nature of colour vision has a considerable impact on how we actually perceive colour. Von Helmholtz was among the first to recognize this by way of contrasting colour vision with pitch perception in hearing (Palmer, 2002; Thompson, 1995; Valberg, 2005). It is quite natural to make this analogy because the underlying physical factors in both cases are similar—light wavelength versus sound frequency (which is directly related to wavelength). The difference however is that colour vision is encoded at the earliest stages by a set of three broadly tuned detectors, whereas

sound frequency is encoded by a large set of narrowly tuned detectors (see Section C.2 of Chapter 5 for a brief review). In other words, only three types of detectors are responsible for sampling the entire range of visible light wavelengths, whereas many different detectors sample the entire range of audible sound frequencies. The perceptual consequence of this difference between the two sensory systems is that we are able to identify the separate elements of a complicated sound, such as the individual notes in a musical chord, but cannot similarly differentiate the components of a mixed colour. This limitation is best exposed through two colours—yellow and white. We are simply unable to identify them as red–green or red–green–blue mixtures, respectively (SideNote 11.24).

Naturally, the question that arises now is "Why did we not end up with a colour vision system where wavelength information is captured and transmitted in a similar way to sound frequencies?" Such a system, as shown by the hypothetical set of detector profiles in the top diagram of Figure 11.20, would have the advantage of sampling a more discrete range of wavelengths and therefore provide similar advantages to colour vision as those we enjoy with sound perception. The reason for not having such a colour vision system is twofold. First, it would be very difficult to construct a set of biological pigments that have very sharply tuned absorption spectra and whose peaks occur at the multiple locations shown in Figure 11.20. This limitation occurs because the chemical nature of the rhodopsin pigment endows it with a broadly tuned absorption spectrum. It would have been an immense evolutionary challenge to produce a set of narrowly tuned light detectors with an entirely new class of biological pigments whose absorption profiles were staggered with respect to each other.

The second reason for rejecting a colour vision system with many narrowly tuned detectors is that we would have been saddled with a major functional problem. Consider a situation where this hypothetical visual system is exposed to a stimulus with a narrow physical spectrum, say around the middle of the visible range (e.g., 550 nm). This stimulus would maximally excite the receptor shown in bold in the top diagram of Figure 11.20. However, because all of the other types of receptors must be accommodated within the spatial confine of the retina, the actual physical spacing for any given receptor is quite large. The profile of the retina in the top right diagram of Figure 11.20 shows several circular patches that each contain the full complement of the 11 receptors in our hypothetical visual system. The coarse spacing of the receptor we need to detect this stimulus, which is filled in dark red, means that we would have a crude capture of the light signal from the retinal image. This in turn means that visual resolution would greatly suffer for an object that emits light at or around 550 nm. Although a visual system with many independent detectors would offer terrific colour discrimination ability, similar perhaps to what we enjoy in hearing, the major drawback is that it would come at the expense of much poorer visual resolution. Thomas Young recognized this fact at the turn of the 19th century and used it to argue that trichromacy offers the following advantage—all of the needed receptors for colour vision can be packed into a physically small retina. As the bottom right diagram in Figure 11.20 shows, a much greater degree of image resolution is possible with a trichromatic retina because the same small circular patches contain many M and L cones, both of which would be involved in detecting the stimulus discussed above.

Monochromacy—colour blindness

Given that a retina with many different types of receptors provides severe drawbacks in terms of resolution, why not go to the other extreme and create a system where colour vision is generated from the output of only a single type of detector (Kandel et al., 2000; Kuehni & Schwarz, 2008; Squire, Roberts, Spitzer, & Zigmond, 2002)? This would certainly endow the eye with maximum resolution since only one photoreceptor class would have to be accommodated within the retina. The idea is that the neural output of this single detector would vary according to the wavelength of incoming light and therefore be used to create colour impressions.

One possible absorption spectrum for such a hypothetical detector is shown in Figure 11.21, which will serve as the basis for our discussion of a **monochromatic** colour system. Let us first consider the response of this receptor to two different light sources having the same intensity—one at 450 nm (stimulus 1) and another at 570 nm (stimulus 2). The relative absorption of this detector at the

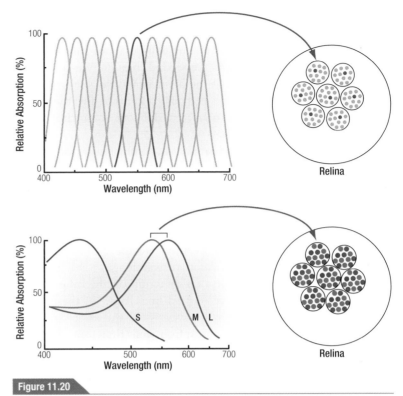

Figure 11.20

A hypothetical colour vision system with many independent light detectors would provide excellent wavelength discrimination ability (top diagram). However, this advantage would come at the expense of poor visual resolution because any given detector would have a coarse distribution in order to accommodate all of the other receptor types. A trichromatic retina offers poorer wavelength discrimination (bottom diagram). However, the major advantage gained is that it produces a much higher retinal density for any given type of detector, resulting in far greater visual resolution.

two wavelengths is different, being twice as much for the first stimulus. According to the principle of univariance, the neural output is

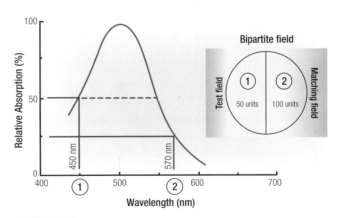

Figure 11.21

A monochromatic colour system is made up of a single type of light detector, such as the one shown here. The output of this detector cannot be used to reliably generate colour signals because there are always situations where pairs of lights at two different wavelengths will produce an identical signal, especially when their intensities can be manipulated. The bipartite field (inset) shows that the two light sources in this example provide an exact match when one has twice the intensity of the other.

proportional to the amount of light absorbed, and therefore the signal sent to the brain by the first stimulus will be approximately twice as great as the second stimulus. We could then argue that the brain would be able to use this difference in signal outputs at the two wavelengths to create a different colour impression for each.

The above reasoning, however, has a major flaw because there are many instances that would cause the receptor to produce exactly the same output when the stimuli are clearly very different. The stimulus at 450 nm, for example, is absorbed at about 50% efficiency by the detector. But the same is true for another wavelength that intersects the absorption spectrum on the other arm of the curve (dotted line). Both of these wavelengths will always yield the same degree of photon absorption and therefore the same neural output. The same is true of many other pairs of wavelengths, especially if the intensity of the stimuli can be manipulated. This is shown for the two stimuli in Figure 11.21 by way of the bipartite field (inset). The same number of photons will be absorbed by this detector at both wavelengths whenever stimulus 2 has twice the intensity of stimulus 1. This is simply to offset the greater photon capturing efficiency at 450 nm. In general, a stimulus at any wavelength can always be matched by a stimulus at any other wavelength if we are able to adjust its intensity.

All of the above caveats produce an immense problem for a monochromatic system—there are simply too many instances when it can be fooled into producing an identical neural output when the wavelength content of two stimuli are quite different. This does not bode well for a monochromatic system because the visual brain would be unable to properly generate colour impressions when there is no reliable correlation between the signals it receives and the wavelength composition of the stimulus. For this reason, a monochromatic visual system is fundamentally colour-blind. To end this section, it is worthwhile noting that the absorption spectrum shown in Figure 11.21 is not a hypothetical one at all but the actual profile of rod photoreceptor absorption. The exact same logic we have used in our discussion above can now be applied to explain why we are unable to see colour under scotopic conditions, when only the rods are active (SideNote 11.25).

Dichromacy—colour deficiency

Let us now raise the number of independent colour detectors to two and see what happens. The resulting **dichromatic** colour vision system would be driven by the output of these two detectors from which all colour experiences would be formed. We can extend the logic for monochromacy—that only one colour primary is needed to match any other colour—to assume that two colour primaries would be sufficient to match any other colour in a dichromatic system. This is illustrated in Figure 11.22 where three light sources, shown at their respective wavelengths, are used in a colour matching experiment. For the purposes of this discussion, let us assume that the two detectors in this hypothetical scenario represent the S and M cone photoreceptors.

The colour stimulus in the test field (stimulus 1) is absorbed at high efficiency by the M cones and less so by the S cones, as indicated by the points of intersection with the two respective absorption profiles. The challenge now is to exactly duplicate the neural output of these cones with a combination of two other colours. Let us assume the two stimuli in the matching field are those indicated at positions 2 and 3 along the wavelength axis. Stimulus 2 would be absorbed quite effectively by the S cones and less so by the M cones, due to the relative position of their absorption spectra at this wavelength. Stimulus 3, on the other hand, is a long-wavelength stimulus that is only absorbed by the M cone system. By adjusting the intensities of these two matching stimuli, an exact setting can be found at which their combination will be perceived as being identical to the colour of stimulus 1 in the test field. Although we used a specific set of test and matching stimuli in this example, it is generally true that any two different chromatic stimuli can be used to exactly match another colour in a dichromatic system.

It turns out that dichromacy due to the presence of only the S and M cones is not that unusual (Jacobs, 1981, 1993). A small segment of the human population actually lacks the L cone system and therefore is functionally dichromatic. This condition, which is known as **protanopia**, is present in slightly more that 1% of males but very few females (about 0.02%) (Chalupa & Werner, 2003; Gegenfurtner, 200; Kaiser & Boynton, 1996). The same is true for individuals who are dichromatic because they lack the M cone system but have a preserved

SideNote | 11.25

A rare genetic condition occurs in about one in 50,000 people where cone photoreceptors do not develop normally, and therefore these individuals have a visual system made up only of rods. These so-called *rod monochromats* can only detect differences in light intensity and are therefore truly colour-blind. The greatest concentration of *rod monochromacy* occurs in the Pacific atoll of Pingelap, where as many as 1 in 12 suffer from this condition. This interesting story is described in a book by Oliver Sacks titled *The Island of the Colourblind*.

set of S and L cones. This condition, known as **deuteranopia**, is also present to a much greater degree in males (about 1.1%) than females (0.01%). The reason for the gender difference in both conditions is quite simple—the genes that encode the L and M photopigments are located on the X chromosome. Given that males have only one copy of this chromosome, they are much more susceptible to a disturbance of the genes that produce either the L or the M rhodopsin in these cones (SideNote 11.26). The third form of dichromacy occurs due to a loss of the S cone system, known as **tritanopia**. This condition is quite rare and occurs with roughly equal frequency (0.002%) in males and females because the gene in this case is located on a different chromosome.

It is common to refer to dichromatic individuals as being colour-blind. This is not correct. The only true form of colour-blindness occurs in monochromatic individuals. Dichromats are able to perceive a range of colours, though this range is quite restricted in comparison to colour-normal, or trichromatic, individuals (Chalupa & Werner, 2003; Rosenthal & Phillips, 1997). It is therefore more appropriate to refer to dichromacy as a form of colour deficiency rather than blindness. As noted above, the most common type of dichromacy occurs due to the absence of M or L cone photopigment. These two types are collectively referred to as red–green colour deficiency because it is the red–green axis in the colour space that is affected. Although it would be impossible to know exactly what

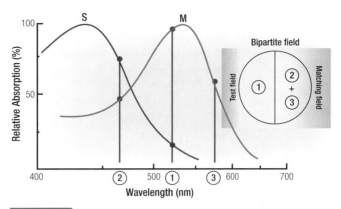

Figure 11.22

A dichromatic colour system is made up of two different light detectors that sample different portions of the visible spectrum. The combined output of the two detectors is responsible for generating all colour perceptions. A dichromatic system requires two primary colours to match any other given colour. For example, a combination of colours 2 and 3 with appropriately adjusted intensities will exactly match the appearance of the colour generated by stimulus 1 in a colour matching experiment (inset).

the world looks like to such types of dichromats, it is reasonable to assume that their blue–yellow axis in the colour space is preserved but that hues along the red–green axis appear more as neutral greys. It is as if the normal colour disc that trichromats experience has been squashed along the red–green dimension to produce an oval-shaped colour space. Their colour world is therefore largely composed of different shades of blues, yellows, and greys. Tritanopes (those lacking the S cone system), on the other hand, have a preserved red–green axis of colour experience but fail to discriminate blues and yellows. Their colour

SideNote | **11.26**

In addition to a total loss of the M or L photopigment, causing true dichromacy, there exists a range of conditions in which either pigment is defective to a certain extent. Individuals with one of these conditions lie somewhere between being dichromatic and fully trichromatic. Altogether, more than 8% (1 in 12) of males suffer some form of colour deficiency associated with the M and L photopigments.

METHODOLOGY

Restoring Full Colour Vision in Squirrel Monkeys

Among primates, the male squirrel monkey happens to be dichromatic because it lacks a functional L-cone system. A group of American scientists have found a way to restore trichromacy in male squirrel monkeys using gene therapy. Gene therapy works by injecting the missing gene into a virus that has been genetically altered. The viruses can then be inserted into human cells. The injected gene can theoretically begin to produce the missing protein, restoring the loss of function that the patient experienced. In the case of colour-deficient squirrel monkeys, the males naturally lack the gene responsible for L-cone rhodopsin, making them unable to distinguish between red and green. The researchers injected a virus carrying the gene that makes the missing photopigment into the monkeys' eyes. They then tested the monkeys on behavioural tasks that required them to distinguish between blue/yellow and red/green dots on a screen. For the first five months after gene therapy, the monkeys were unable to distinguish between the red and green dots, yet after that became able to distinguish between the two colours.

world is therefore a blend of reds, greens, and greys. Figure 11.23 provides a summary of the colours experienced by the three types of dichromats as a function of light wavelength (SideNote 11.27) (Palmer, 2002).

Why trichromacy?—revisited (briefly)

Monochromacy is associated with total colour blindness. Dichromacy yields only a crude and limited form of colour vision. Trichromacy, however, generates a much richer palette of perceived colours and creates fewer instances of colour confusion—that is, when a particular stimulus can appear to be identical with another but whose physical spectrum is totally different (Bowmaker, 1983; Palmer, 2002). This is because a colour match to any particular stimulus requires three primary colours with exactly the correct intensity combination. This is a much more difficult undertaking in natural viewing conditions, and therefore the number of physically different stimuli that can fool us in the real world by creating the same colour impression is much less compared to a dichromatic visual system. Of course, tetrachromacy (four receptors), pentachromacy (five receptors), and so on would be expected to produce even greater benefits in terms of colour discrimination and perhaps even the richness of colour perception. However, this would come at a price—the more independent colour detectors, the greater the impact on spatial resolution. Through the process of evolution, the right balance had to be found between two opposing factors—a requirement for sufficient colour discrimination ability *versus* the need to preserve visual resolution. The best solution for many primates, including humans, ended up being *trichromacy*.

2. COLOUR OPPONENCY

The Young–Helmholtz theory of trichromacy provides an example of where a theoretical account of behavioural data is later verified by experimental data from the domain of neuroscience. Indeed, the convergence of theoretical and biological trichromacy represents one of the glorious stories in the history of science. We learned earlier, however, that all behavioural data in colour vision could not be accounted for by trichromatic theory alone and that many phenomena, such as colour afterimages and the subjective appearance of colour, were better explained by Hering's

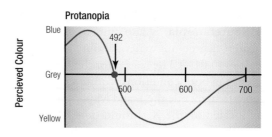

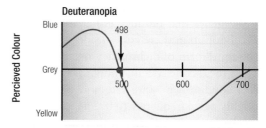

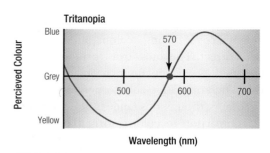

Wavelength (nm)

Figure 11.23

The colour experiences of the three types of dichromats as a function of light wavelength shows that their colour space is largely restricted to one dimension (blue–yellow or red–green). Protanopes and deuteranopes perceive only shades of blues, yellows, and greys, whereas tritanopes experience only shades of reds, greens, and greys. The point of transition between the two extremes of their colour space is known as the *neutral point*, where only a pure grey is experienced. The wavelength of the neutral point differs among the three types of dichromats (shown by arrows). Adapted from *Vision Science: Photons to Phenomenology*, by S. E. Palmer, 2002, Cambridge, MA: MIT Press.

theory of colour opponency. Recall that according to this theory, two pairs of colours (red/green and blue/yellow) are not simultaneously processed but instead thought to represent opponent colour mechanisms. Thus, instead of assuming that colour perception is triggered by the output of three different sensory receptors, the opponent theory asserts that colour vision is mediated by a subtractive process that somehow pits the opponent colour pairs against each other.

Resurgence of Hering's opponent colour theory

The idea that only the trichromatic theory explained all aspects of colour vision started losing steam in the 1950s when vision scientists seriously began to ponder the possibility that colour opponency may also exist in the visual system. The re-emergence of this thinking did not occur at the expense of discarding trichromatic theory, which already had a solid foundation, but in the idea that an additional feature of visual processing existed beyond the trichromatic stage of photoreceptors. Although a neurobiological account for this postulate would have to await later developments, the emerging psychophysical evidence was already paving the way for some tantalizing insights. Two American vision scientists, Dorothea Jameson and Leo Hurvich, argued against the dominant orthodoxy at the time that subjective colour appearance could not be studied by rigorous scientific means (Hurvich & Jameson, 1957). Working at the Eastman Kodak Laboratories, this husband-and-wife team developed the psychophysical technique of *chromatic cancellation* as a method of quantitatively measuring opponent colour processes and in so doing ushered in a new era in colour vision research.

Chromatic cancellation is based on Hering's idea that certain hues cancel each other due to the opponent nature of colour processing. For example, a 600 nm light source appears orange and incorporates both red and yellow hue components. If a green-appearing stimulus is progressively added to this mixture, then the reddish appearance will gradually be cancelled until there comes a point where only a yellow hue will exist. The red and green components completely cancel each other out at this point. Similarly, adding blue light to an orange stimulus will gradually cancel the yellow component until only a reddish field appears. By carefully measuring the amounts of the cancelling stimuli, Jameson and Hurvich not only provided psychophysical evidence for the existence of opponent mechanisms but also an elegant quantitative method for evaluating the strength of a particular hue within a mixture.

Neurobiological evidence for colour opponency

The opponent colour theory became firmly established when it was revealed that neurons in the visual system actually do process chromatic information in accordance with red/green and blue/yellow opponent pairings. This pioneering work was carried out by Russell De Valois at Berkeley during the 1960s. Using coloured stimuli, De Valois and his colleagues recorded the activity of neurons in the LGN of monkeys (De Valois & De Valois, 1975, 1990, 1993). They discovered that a subset of LGN neurons were excited by light at some wavelengths but inhibited at others. Through careful studies of these neurons, De Valois showed that four types of colour selective cells existed in the LGN, as shown in Figure 11.24. These four cell types can be summarized as follows—excitation by green but inhibition by red light (G+/R−), excitation by red but inhibition by green (R+/G−), excitation by blue but inhibition by yellow (B+/Y−), and excitation by yellow but inhibition by blue (Y+/B−). In short, LGN neurons showed excitation and inhibition to light in exactly the same opponent colour pairings originally predicted by Ewald Hering.

Colour opponency at the neural level emerged as a new concept in terms of information processing by early visual neurons. It turned out that the way in which this opponency was structured had similarities to the spatial centre–surround opponency found in retinal ganglion cells, as discussed in Chapter 9. Recall that the receptive field of retinal ganglion and LGN cells is such that light stimulates these neurons through a central part of their receptive field but produces an inhibitory effect when it falls on the surround. Another group of neurons has exactly the opposite arrangement (i.e., inhibiting the neuron through its centre and exciting it through the surround). As

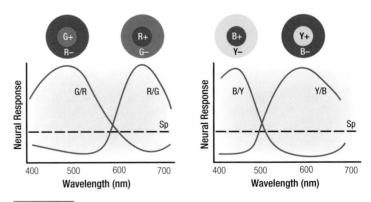

Figure 11.24

Colour-opponent neurons in the LGN show an elevated response to a particular range of wavelengths and an inhibitory response to another range. The original description of these neurons by De Valois placed them in four categories—G/R, R/G, B/Y, and Y/B. The first letter describes the colour-specific centre response and the second the surround response. The centre–surround nature of colour opponency is shown by way of the receptive fields of these neurons above each profile. The dashed line approximates the level of spontaneous (Sp) activity in these neurons. Adapted from *Vision Science: Photons to Phenomenology,* by S. E. Palmer, 2002, Cambridge, MA: MIT Press.

Figure 11.24 shows, the receptive field arrangement of the so-called **colour-opponent neurons** in the LGN also have a centre–surround profile. However, a key difference here is that the centre–surround antagonism is now chromatic in nature. For example, one set of LGN neurons (G/R) was found by De Valois to have an excitatory centre but only to green light, with the surround being inhibited by red light (SideNote 11.28). The opposite arrangement (R/G) was also present. Therefore, these two types of neurons participate in red–green opponency—that is, they are stimulated by one and inhibited by the other. Exactly the same holds true for blue–yellow opponency, with one set of neurons having its receptive field centre excited by blue light accompanied by an inhibitory surround to yellow light and another set having the opposite arrangement (SideNote 11.29).

Colour opponency and colour perception

To understand how colour-opponent neurons contribute to colour perception, we need to first consider the nature of the signal being sent by these cells to the visual brain. The neural response profiles of the four colour-opponent subtypes show that they respond vigorously to a discrete range of wavelengths but are actually inhibited by others (Figure 11.24) (De Valois & De Valois, 1975; Gegenfurtner & Kiper, 2003; Palmer, 2002). For example, an R/G neuron is maximally stimulated by long-wavelength light, but at shorter wavelengths, neural activity actually drops below spontaneous firing (i.e., the neuron is inhibited). The same is true for the other three subtypes, though of course the wavelength range for excitation and inhibition differs. Therefore, we can think of colour-opponent neurons as being selective for a particular wavelength range and anti-selective for another range of wavelengths. An R/G cell will fire if red light fills its entire receptive field but will be inhibited if replaced by green light. The opposite is true for G/R cells. Similarly, B/Y and Y/B cells are excited and inhibited if their receptive fields are filled by light with wavelengths that are associated with blue and yellow hues (SideNote 11.30).

Can the neural signals from colour-opponent cells be used by our visual brain to generate colour perception? To answer this question, let us first examine the top panel in Figure 11.25, which shows the relative contributions of each colour-opponent neuron subtype to a light flash at a particular wavelength (De Valois & De Valois, 1990). At very long wavelengths, the R/G subtype is largely responsible for generating the neural output from the LGN. At progressively lower wavelengths, the cell type with the dominant neural output shifts, first to the Y/B subtype, and then to the G/R subtype. At very short wavelengths, the B/Y subtype begins to provide a greater overall signal. Think of these curves as comparing the neural signals delivered to the visual brain by each opponent cell type across the visible spectrum.

Now turn to the bottom panel in Figure 11.25, which shows behavioural data gathered from human subjects who had to specify a colour name to a light flash of a particular wavelength (SideNote 11.31). The results were then combined to provide an account of the proportion of colour names used to describe light flashes across the visible spectrum. As expected, long-wavelength light was most often referred to as *red*, followed by *yellow*, *green*, and *blue* at progressively lower wavelengths. Think of these curves as comparing how our perceptual experience of hue is associated with light wavelength.

The most astonishing aspect of these two sets of figures becomes evident by simply glancing back and forth between them—that is, their similarity. The top and bottom panels in Figure 11.25, which represent two entirely different data sets—one neural and the other perceptual—are nearly identical in terms of their overall layout (De Valois & De Valois, 1975). Perhaps the most astounding element in this similarity is the implication that the neural output of colour-opponent cells is indeed largely responsible for generating perceptual impressions of the primary hues. According to this idea, the perception of *red* is largely the result of activity in R/G neurons, the perception of *yellow* in Y/B neurons, etc. Of course, a considerable amount of neural processing must occur in the visual cortex before hue perception is actually produced. Nevertheless, it is truly striking that the output of neurons at such an early level in the visual system can so neatly correlate with a high-level behavioural parameter such as colour naming. The excellent correspondence between neural signal and colour naming data suggests that the visual cortex does indeed use the output of colour-opponent neurons in the LGN as a first step toward generating colour perception.

Colour afterimages—revisited

The colour afterimage phenomenon, where prolonged viewing of a coloured stimulus produces an afterimage of its opponent colour, can now be explained. According to our discussion above, a particular colour-opponent neuron would be strongly triggered in response to a colour stimulus. For example, G/R colour-opponent neurons are activated when a green stimulus is viewed. However, if this stimulus is viewed for a long time, then the G/R neurons reach a state of **adaptation** whereby they respond in a more sluggish manner over a subsequent period. As a result, the opponent colour (red) will briefly dominate because R/G neurons are able to give a more robust response than the adapted G/R neurons. Prolonged viewing of the flag stimulus in Figure 11.15 resulted in an adapted state of G/R and Y/B neurons such that their opponent colours appeared afterwards to produce a fleeting impression of the true colours of the American flag.

The dual process theory

The controversy over whether trichromatic theory or colour-opponent theory provided the best explanation for colour vision raged for decades. The data gathered through colour matching experiments provided strong objective evidence for the trichromatic camp, whereas the subjective experience of colour and its associated phenomena, such as colour afterimages, supported the colour-opponent camp. De Valois's discovery of colour-opponent neurons in the monkey LGN in the 1960s represented a breakthrough in our understanding of early colour processing because it provided the critical piece of evidence to establish colour opponency in physiological terms. And yet, this was also the period in which a group in the UK firmly established the trichromatic theory through the demonstration of the existence of three different types of cone photoreceptors, each having a distinct absorption spectrum for light (Gegenfurtner & Kiper, 2003; Solomon & Lennie, 2007; Wandell, 1995).

The problem of having two competing theories to account for colour vision had a very surprising solution—both theories were correct! It is certainly true that the initial mechanism for capturing spectral information occurs through light absorption in three separate types of cone photoreceptors (trichromatic

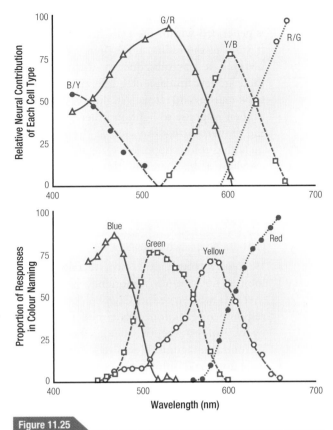

Figure 11.25

The visible spectrum is parsed into discrete wavelength regions that optimally stimulate each colour-opponent subtype (top panel). Similarly, colour naming experiments show that perceptual impressions of hue are also parsed into discrete wavelength regions (bottom panel). The correspondence between these two sets of data suggest that the output of LGN colour-opponent neurons plays a prominent role in generating colour perception. Adapted from "Neural Coding of Color," by R. L. De Valois and K. K. De Valois, 1975, in *Handbook of Perception, Vol. 5*, Eds. E. C. Carterette and M. P. Friedman, New York, NY: Academic Press.

theory). However, the output of the trichromatic stage then undergoes further processing to produce opponent signals between red–green and blue–yellow colours at a later stage (colour-opponent theory). Thus, both theories are correct but for different stages of colour processing, leading to what is now referred to as the **dual process theory**. This naturally leads to the following question—how does the neural output from the trichromatic stage (cones) go on to produce colour opponency in the LGN? The answer to this question will become apparent in the next section.

3.   COLOUR PROCESSING IN EARLY VISION

An interesting historical fact about colour opponency is that its physiological existence was first shown in the LGN. This naturally led to the question of whether colour opponency is generated within the LGN itself or whether it arises in the retina and is then fed into LGN neurons. It was subsequently discovered that there are few fundamental differences between LGN neurons and retinal ganglion cells in terms of their response to light. In other words, all of the properties that are seen at the LGN level, including colour opponency, are also present in ganglion cells. Therefore, the neural circuitry responsible for transforming the trichromatic photoreceptor output into opponent colour signals must actually reside in the retina.

From trichromacy to opponency

We return to the retina now to take a closer look at how colour opponency is generated there. As we learned in Chapter 9, the neural response of ganglion cells is best represented by way of its receptive field, whose centre–surround antagonistic nature shows separate excitatory and inhibitory responses to light (Kandel et al., 2000; Squire et al., 2002). In our prior discussion of ganglion cell receptive fields, there was no mention that action potentials were triggered by specific wavelengths but rather the excitation or inhibition occurred to light along its entire spectrum in general. The two types of ganglion cells were dubbed ON/OFF and OFF/ON to distinguish their respective centre–surround responses to light.

With colour-opponent cells, the centre–surround opponency occurs not only in terms of excitation and inhibition but also in a colour-specific manner (Chalupa & Werner, 2003; Gegenfurtner, 2000; Wandell, 1995). Figure 11.26 shows a schematic diagram of how this may be achieved with respect to the red–green colour-opponent subclass (R/G and G/R neurons). The left portion of this figure shows long-wavelength (L) cones feeding into a retinal ganglion cell in an excitatory manner. The surround inhibition upon this same ganglion cell, however, arises only from the output of middle-wavelength (M) cones. As a result, the receptive field of this neuron shows a classic centre–surround excitation and inhibition profile, but with a key difference—each is driven by a separate cone class (SideNote 11.32). The result is to produce what we have come to know as an R/G neuron. A reversal of the cone inputs produces a G/R colour-opponent neuron (right portion of Figure 11.26).

This simple circuit involving selective inputs from the photoreceptor layer is all that is theoretically needed to produce colour-opponency at the ganglion cell level. Such precision of cone inputs is also apparent when we consider how blue–yellow colour opponency is generated. As Figure 11.27 shows, a central input of S cones in an excitatory manner along with a peripheral inhibitory input from both L and M cones can account for the receptive

SideNote | **11.32**

Figure 11.26 shows a simplified diagram where cone photoreceptors feed directly into a ganglion cell. In reality, the neural output from cones is transmitted through three intermediate cell types—bipolar, horizontal, and amacrine cells—as discussed in Chapter 9. The excitatory and inhibitory colour-opponent properties of a ganglion cell are actually produced by the neural circuitry that involves these intermediate cells.

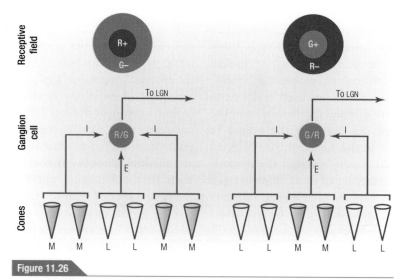

Figure 11.26

Colour opponency in the retina is generated by selective input of cone signals upon a ganglion cell. An R/G colour-opponent cell (left portion) receives input from a central group of L cones in an excitatory manner (E) and a peripheral group of M cones in an inhibitory manner (I). The receptive field of this R/G neuron will show centre–surround colour opponency (i.e., red centre, green surround). Exactly the opposite arrangement of cone inputs will produce a G/R colour-opponent neuron (right portion).

field properties of a B/Y cell. The central excitatory blue response in this case is driven by S cone input, whereas the combination of L and M input produces the yellow inhibitory surround. A reversal of this input pattern, shown in the right portion of Figure 11.27, can account for the colour-opponent response of Y/B neurons (SideNote 11.33). Thus, each of the four subtypes of colour opponency can be explained by selective inputs of cone photoreceptors upon a particular ganglion cell. The colour-opponent property of ganglion cells is then transmitted through a direct connection to LGN neurons.

Encoding light intensity

The existence of colour-opponent cells in the retina does not mean that they serve as a replacement for the classical ON/OFF and OFF/ON neurons. In fact, colour-opponent cells coexist with these two other cell types. Whereas the colour-opponent neurons are responsible for encoding chromatic information, the ON/OFF and OFF/ON cell types are responsible for encoding **luminance** information (i.e., the intensity of an emitted or reflected light source). Thus, there are two major channels that emerge out of the retina from a functional point of view—the **chromatic channel** (represented by four neuronal subtypes: R/G, G/R, B/Y, Y/B) and the **achromatic channel** (represented by two subtypes: ON/OFF, OFF/ON). The chromatic

and achromatic channels are responsible for transmitting the early signals that respectively produce two essential qualities of colour perception—hue and brightness (or lightness) (Kandel et al., 2000; Palmer, 2002; Rodieck, 1998; Valberg, 2005).

We have seen how colour-opponent signals can be generated by selective cone inputs. To conclude our consideration of this topic, next we review how achromatic signals are generated in the retina. An achromatic signal in essence means that the excitatory and inhibitory responses are not confined to a particular range of wavelengths. Figure 11.28 on page 386 shows how a central excitatory input from both M and L cones combined with a similar input from the periphery, but in an inhibitory manner, can produce an achromatic ON/OFF (+/−) type cell (left portion). The excitatory and inhibitory influences in this case arise from the tandem input of both M and L cones, and therefore there is no colour differentiation between the centre and surround. Instead, one part of the receptive field is excited by light and another is inhibited simply because of the way the cone photoreceptors are wired to the ganglion cell. A slight change in the nature of this wiring so that the central input is now inhibitory and accompanied by a peripheral excitatory input results in an OFF/ON (−/+) cell (right portion).

Both of the achromatic subtypes transmit contrast information, as discussed extensively

SideNote | **11.33**

There is some evidence that the B/Y and Y/B colour-opponent subtypes do not have well-defined centre and surround regions but rather that the two are spatially co-extensive. In other words, the excitatory and inhibitory colour responses occur over the entirety of the receptive field, but in a colour-specific manner. The overriding factor in these cells, however, concerns the nature of their colour opponency, which remains the same regardless of the exact details of their underlying receptive field organization.

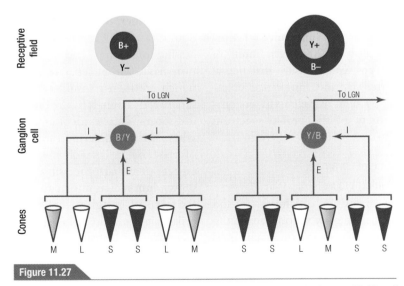

Figure 11.27

Colour opponency in B/Y and Y/B ganglion cells is produced by selective inputs of S, M, and L cones. A central excitatory input of S cones combined with a peripheral inhibitory input of both M and L cones is responsible for B/Y colour-opponency (left portion). The opposite pattern of inputs produces the Y/B cell type (right portion).

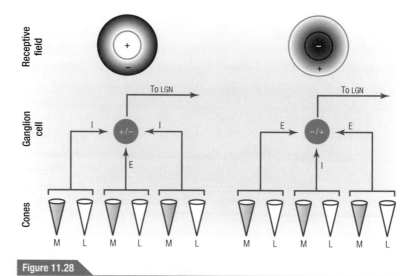

Figure 11.28

Achromatic neurons show excitatory and inhibitory responses in a broad spectral manner and without any colour opponency between the centre and surround regions of their receptive fields. ON/OFF (+/−) neurons receive central excitatory inputs from a combination of M and L cones and a similar surround input, but in an inhibitory manner (left portion). The opposite is true for the second subtype—an OFF/ON cell (right portion). There is some evidence that S cones may also provide a very small input into these cells (not shown).

in Chapter 9, and therefore convey the luminance component of the visual signal. Indeed, the achromatic channel is also referred to as the *luminance channel* for this reason. The signals in this channel are believed to be combined with those from the chromatic channel to produce an overall perceptual impression of colour that encompasses both hue and brightness/lightness. An interesting facet of the luminance channel is that it appears to be largely driven by M and L cones. However, it was shown by American neuroscientist Ed Callaway that S cones do indeed provide a small input into the neurons that are part of the luminance channel (Chatterjee & Callaway; 2002). An input of all three cone types would ensure that neural signals transmitted by the luminance channel are driven by light wavelengths encompassing the entirety of the visible spectrum (SideNote 11.34).

Parallel processing of chromatic and achromatic information

The foregoing discussion of chromatic and achromatic channels in early vision leads to the following question—how are these channels organized in terms of information flow out of the retina and ultimately to the visual cortex? The answer to this question has emerged after nearly four decades of intense research by anatomists and physiologists, many of whom have dedicated their entire scientific lives to

understanding the organizational details of early visual pathways. Figure 11.29 summarizes our current knowledge, which will form the basis for our discussion at each of the three different levels—retina, LGN, and area V1 (Rodieck, 1998).

The most important feature of early visual organization to keep in mind is that the functional channels are organized in a parallel but anatomically segregated fashion (see Sections A.2 and B.4 of Chapter 10 for a review of this topic) (Dacey & Packer, 2003; Gegenfurtner & Kiper, 2003; Palmer, 2002; Squire et al., 2002). In other words, the processing of colour and luminance information arises within separate classes of neurons, which are then transmitted through separate functional channels to the brain. This anatomical separation is evident as early as the retina where we can describe three different classes of ganglion cells, each involved in different aspects of visual processing. As Figure 11.29 shows, luminance information is encoded by the **parasol ganglion cells** (i.e., the types of cells that show the ON/OFF and OFF/ON receptive field structures). Colour information, on the other hand, is processed by two different types of ganglion cells. The **midget ganglion cells** are responsible for red–green colour processing and therefore display the R/G and G/R types of receptive fields (Dacey, 1993; Rodieck, 1998). A separate class, known

The three types of cone photoreceptors together capture light across the entirety of the visible range of wavelengths (400–700 nm). Even a small input of S cones into the luminance channel would imply that short-wavelength light can exert an influence in the physiological processing of light intensity.

as **bistratified ganglion cells**, is responsible for blue–yellow colour processing and therefore displays the B/Y and Y/B types of receptive fields (Dacey & Packer, 2003; Rodieck, 1998). The latter two ganglion cell types form the early elements of the chromatic channel, whereas the parasol cells and their projections give rise to the achromatic channel.

At the LGN level (middle diagrams in Figure 11.29), we find that the anatomical separation of colour and luminance processing persists, but in a somewhat different way. Whereas the three types of ganglion cells are relatively intermixed within the retina, the layout in the LGN is such that there is a physical separation of neurons among different layers, each dedicated to processing a certain type of information (Chalupa & Werner, 2003; Gegenfurtner, 2000; Kandel et al., 2000). The bottom two layers (1 and 2) of the LGN, which are known as the *magnocellular layers*, receive input from the parasol cells. Therefore, these layers are exclusively dedicated to processing luminance information

and therefore are part of the achromatic channel. The top four layers of the LGN (3 to 6), which are known as the *parvocellular layers*, receive input from the midget cells. Therefore, these neurons are largely involved in processing red–green chromatic information. And finally, a very thin layer of neurons resides in between the six major LGN layers. The cells in these layers, which are known as *koniocellular neurons*, receive input from the bistratified neurons of the retina and are therefore involved in processing blue–yellow chromatic information. The parvocellular and koniocellular LGN layers are part of the chromatic channel, though they are involved in processing different chromatic aspects of the stimulus.

The layout of neurons and their interconnections in the retina and LGN have revealed that early visual processing occurs in a segregated and parallel fashion (SideNote 11.35). It turns out that this segregation actually persists all the way to the first cortical structure, area V1, as shown in Figure 11.29 (right diagram)

SideNote | **11.35**

An interesting historical fact about the LGN is that its laminar structure was well known around the turn of the 20th century when anatomists described it in detail and named the layers according to their constituent cell size (e.g., magnocellular for large-cell body and parvocellular for small-cell body). It was only after the advent of electrophysiological techniques that the functional difference between these layers was fully appreciated, and then, through advanced anatomical tracing techniques, it was demonstrated that the different subdivisions are actually linked to certain cell types in the retina.

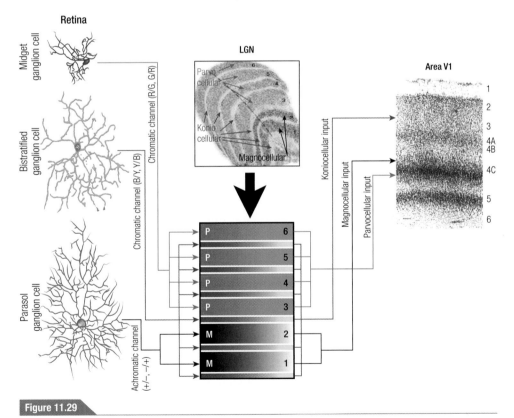

Figure 11.29

Visual processing is mediated by a variety of anatomically distinct retinal ganglion cells, including the parasol, midget, and bistratified subtypes (left diagrams). Parasol cells process luminance information and provide input into the magnocellular layers of the LGN. Colour processing occurs by way of the midget and bistratified neurons, which provide input into the parvocellular and koniocellular LGN layers, respectively (middle diagrams). The parallel channels involved in chromatic and achromatic processing remain segregated right up to area V1, where the parvocellular, magnocellular, and koniocellular channels arrive into separate physical regions of the cortex (right diagram).

(Kandel et al., 2000; Orban, 2008; Rodieck, 1998; Squire et al., 2002). The magnocellular input, carrying luminance information, is delivered to the upper parts of layer 4C of area V1, whereas the parvocellular input, carrying chromatic information, is delivered to the lower parts of the same layer. Chromatic information by way of the koniocellular input arrives into layer 3 of area V1. Thus, the chromatic and achromatic channels show segregated input into area V1. The next section of this chapter will be devoted to understanding colour processing at the cortical level.

4. CORTICAL PROCESSING OF COLOUR

Parallel visual processing is now recognized as a fundamental aspect of the anatomical organization of early visual pathways (Hubel, 1989; Orban, 2008; Sincich & Horton, 2005; Yantis, 2001). In many mammalian species, including primates, this organizational structure is responsible for the separate processing and transmission of colour and luminance information. Anatomical segregation in early visual structures is advantageous because separate neural elements can be exclusively devoted to capturing, processing, and transmitting elementary but important aspects of visual stimuli. By keeping the processes separate, the chromatic and achromatic channels can transmit visual information to the brain with maximum fidelity. The signals from these two channels are believed to combine at a later level to produce a gestalt perceptual impression.

A complete understanding of colour processing in the visual cortex remains elusive. The remainder of this section will therefore summarize only some key aspects of cortical processing. We begin with an interesting perceptual condition that poses a dilemma in terms of what we already know about colour processing at the early levels. As it turns out, the solution to this dilemma arises only at the visual cortex level by way of a new and more elaborate kind of colour-opponent neuron.

The problem of isoluminance

Our visual world is made up of objects that can be distinguished from their immediate background largely on the basis of differences in light reflectance. The most salient aspect of figure–ground discrimination is therefore light intensity difference. It is this form of contrast that allows our visual system to delineate an object and its internal components. But what happens if an object and its surround reflect the same amount of total light but differ only in terms of chromaticity? In this case, we have what is known as an **isoluminance** condition (i.e., the luminance is constant across the stimulus and background but the colour varies, leading only to differences in perceived hue) (SideNote 11.36).

The colour grating in Figure 11.30 is an example of a stimulus that is often used in laboratory studies of isoluminance (SideNote 11.37) (De Valois & De Valois, 1990). The components of an isoluminant grating vary only in terms of wavelength and therefore generate a stimulus that differs only in terms of perceived hue. Isoluminant stimuli pose an interesting dilemma—they do not generate neural activity in colour-opponent neurons that are found in the retina and LGN. Consider a situation where an isoluminant colour grating falls on the retina in such a way that it interacts with the receptive fields of an R/G and a G/R colour-opponent neuron in the manner shown in Figure 11.30 (top panel, bottom left). In the first case the red bar falls exactly on the centre of the R/G neuron's receptive field, and the adjacent green bars fall exactly on the surround. Given what we know of the behaviour of colour-opponent neurons, we can assert that this interaction would not produce a significant neural response because the excitatory input through the centre would be negated by the inhibitory signal from the surround. The G/R neuron also would not fire under similar stimulation conditions because the red bar would not generate an excitatory signal through its centre nor would there be any inhibition from the surround. In both cases, the expected response of the neuron is that it would fire at a steady state, similar to its spontaneous firing rate (see neural activity profile below each neuron). Exactly the same logic can be applied if these two types of colour-opponent neurons interacted with other parts of the isoluminant grating, say by having the green bar fall on the centre and the red bars on the surround. Again, there would be no discernible neural response, as shown in Figure 11.30 (top panel, bottom right).

This situation is somewhat baffling because it is counter-intuitive to find that colour-opponent neurons do not actually provide a response to a coloured stimulus. This, however, is one of the paradoxical aspects of the way colour-opponent neurons behave. They

SideNote | 11.36

Isoluminance is quite rare in natural environments because it requires an exact equivalence of light emerging from various objects and their background. Instead, small parts of a scene, such as local regions in dense foliage, may only differ in chromaticity and therefore be isoluminant. Studies with isoluminant stimuli are carried out under precise laboratory conditions.

SideNote | 11.37

Strictly speaking, this stimulus is not isoluminant because it would be difficult to achieve that in printed format. However, pure colour or chromatic gratings can be produced in a laboratory, where the various wavelengths are equated for luminance, and therefore the stimulus varies only in terms of the perceived hue.

are really just detectors of colour in that they provide an excitatory response to one set of wavelengths and an inhibitory response to another. Under isoluminant conditions, colour-opponent neurons are silenced because the coloured light falling on the inhibitory surround cancels the excitatory response from the coloured light falling on the centre. In spite of the way they are named, red–green colour-opponent neurons are fundamentally unable to detect colour contrast such as the pure colour boundaries created by isoluminant red and green bars (SideNote 11.38).

It is clear, however, that we are able to see isoluminant colour gratings (i.e., we can make out the red, green, and yellow components). Therefore, the question arises as to how this happens when early colour detectors in our visual system are simply unable to respond to these stimuli. In effect, we should be blind to pure colour contrast created by isoluminant stimuli, unless of course there is another mechanism involved in their detection.

Double-opponent neurons

The solution to this problem is found by way of a higher form of colour-sensitive neuron that provides an excitatory signal to both colours that are on either side of a border. This can be achieved by neurons that are both spatially and chromatically opponent (Hubel, 1989; Palmer, 2002; Wandell, 1995). It turns out that exactly such types of neurons have been found to exist, though not in the retina or LGN. In the 1970s, several researchers demonstrated the existence of what has been termed **double-opponent neurons** in the primary visual cortex (area V1) of the monkey. Unlike the single-opponent colour detecting neurons at earlier levels, which only show colour opponency, these higher-level double-opponent neurons display both spatial and chromatic opponency. For example, one type of double-opponent neuron has a receptive field centre that is excited by red light but inhibited by green. The receptive field surround shows exactly the opposite effect (i.e., it is excited by green light but inhibited by red). This dual specificity in terms of space and colour means that the shorthand notation for double-opponent neurons becomes a bit more complicated. A neuron that shows the responses just described would be labelled as an R+ G–/G+ R– neuron.

The bottom panel in Figure 11.30 shows that unlike single colour-opponent neurons,

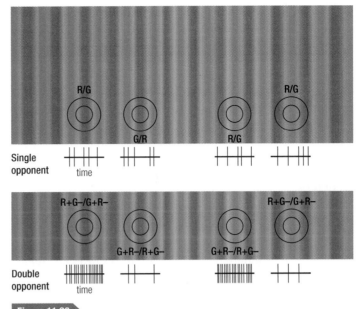

Figure 11.30

An isoluminant colour stimulus, such as a red–green grating, does not trigger neural activity in colour-opponent neurons because the excitatory and inhibitory responses from the centre and surround parts of their receptive fields offset each other. This is seen by way of the four examples in the top panel. Unlike these single-opponent neurons, double-opponent neurons display both spatial and chromatic opponency. Their receptive field organization permits an isoluminant grating to have a reinforcing excitatory effect through both the centre and the surround, resulting in a strong neural response (bottom panel). These neurons may also be inhibited if the colour components of the stimulus do not match the colour specificity of the response from the centre and surround. Adapted from Figure 7.1 in De Valois RL, De Valois KK (1990) *Spatial Vision*. Oxford University Press, New York.

such as those in the retina and LGN, double-opponent neurons are able to provide a strong response when exposed to an isoluminant colour stimulus. For example, an R+ G–/G+ R– neuron that interacts with the grating in such a way that a red bar falls on the centre and green bars fall on the surround will trigger a strong neural response because each stimuli produces excitation through the respective parts of its receptive field. However, this same neuron will be strongly inhibited if instead a green bar falls on the centre and red bars fall on the surround because now these bars produce an inhibitory response through both parts of the neuron's receptive field. A double-opponent neuron with the opposite configuration (i.e., a G+ R–/R+ G–) would also show strong excitation and inhibition when the green and red bars interact appropriately with its receptive field, as shown in the bottom panel of Figure 11.30. Whereas single-opponent neurons are unresponsive to isoluminant stimuli, the examples in this figure show that double-opponent neurons are able to provide a robust response and therefore may account for our ability to perceive

SideNote **11.38**

An isoluminant condition provides a stimulus with colour contrast but no light contrast. Colour-opponent neurons are unable to detect colour contrast for the reasons discussed. This situation is quite different from the achromatic pathway neurons (i.e., ON/OFF and OFF/ON cells) which are robust detectors of light contrast.

SideNote | **11.39**

Double-opponent cells are not restricted to the red–green variety. As expected, blue–yellow double-opponent neurons also exist in area V1. The receptive field is similarly organized except that both centre and surround double opponency is restricted to the blue–yellow combination.

objects that are distinguishable from their background only on the basis of colour differences (SideNote 11.39) (De Valois & De Valois, 1990; Hubel, 1989; Palmer, 2002).

Cytochrome oxidase blobs

The existence of double-opponent neurons elevates the processing complexity of colour information. We have previously discussed the remarkable fact that single colour-opponent neurons are found as early as the retinal ganglion cell level and then within the parvocellular and koniocellular layers of the LGN. Single-opponent cells are also present in area V1. However, it is only at this stage that the double-opponent neurons are first seen, where they are believed to arise through the inputs of single-opponent neurons.

The presence of double-opponent neurons in area V1 leads to the question of exactly where they are found within this cortical structure. In Chapter 10 we learned that the upper layers of area V1 display an interesting pattern of patchy staining for a protein known as *cytochrome oxidase*, or CO for short (Kandel et al., 2000; Palmer, 2002; Squire et al., 2002). The patches of high CO staining have been referred to as *blobs*. Neurons within the CO blobs have a higher concentration of this protein compared to neurons in the intervening parts, known as

interblobs. Figure 11.31 shows a schematic representation of the blob and interblob zones in area V1. Although the CO protein itself does not play a specific role in visual function, it is known to generally correlate with regions of high neuronal activity.

The patch-like appearance of CO in the upper layers of area V1 has led to much speculation about the possible functional roles of the blob and interblob cortical regions. One idea that has been proposed is that blob areas are largely responsible for coordinating colour information. It has been shown that the CO blobs get a direct input from the koniocellular layers of the LGN, which are known to process blue–yellow colour-opponent information (Figure 11.31). The most tantalizing aspect of the idea that CO blobs may be associated with colour processing comes from reports that they have a high presence of double-opponent neurons. As far as we know, these neurons represent the most sophisticated form of colour processing within area V1.

Colour processing beyond the primary visual cortex

The neurobiological mechanisms that are needed to create colour perception arise through further processing in brain areas beyond area V1. Unfortunately, the precise details

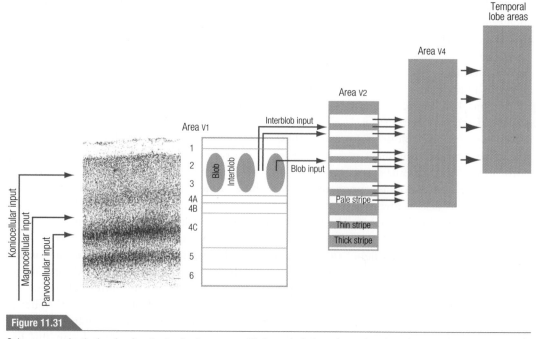

Figure 11.31

Colour processing in the visual cortex begins in area V1 with the arrival of LGN inputs into specific layers. The upper layers of area V1 can be segmented on the basis of CO staining into blob and interblob regions, which in turn show preferential inputs into the next cortical structure, area V2. Colour processing is believed to be carried out at later cortical stages within area V4 and then integrated into a generalized object and form processing mechanism in the temporal lobe.

of the later cortical processing of colour remain elusive. We do, however, have some idea of the interconnections among the brain areas. As Figure 11.31 shows, the next stage of visual processing occurs within area V2. Interestingly, CO staining of area V2 does not reveal blobs but instead a pattern of thin and thick stripes, where there is a higher presence of the CO protein, interspersed with areas of low presence that are known as *pale stripes* (Figure 11.31) (Gegenfurtner, 2003; Sincich & Horton, 2005).

An interesting feature of the CO staining pattern in area V2 is that there seems to be some precision as to how it is wired to area V1. Neurons from the CO blobs of area V1 send a preferential projection to the thin CO stripes of area V2, whereas the interblob neurons in area V1 are connected to both the thin and the pale stripe zones of area V2. This pattern of connections, along with data from electrophysiological and optical imaging studies, have led to the idea that the thin CO stripe zones of area V2 represent a higher area of colour processing. The pale stripes, on the other hand, have been implicated in form processing (i.e., as part of a mechanism in object perception) (SideNote 11.40).

As Figure 11.31 shows, both the thin and the pale stripe zones of area V2 project to the next area in the hierarchy of visual areas, area V4 (Gegenfurtner & Kiper, 2003; Orban, 2008; Zeki, 1994). This area has been implicated in various higher functions related to colour vision, which will be discussed in the next section within the context of the perceptual aspects of colour. The colour and form inputs that area V4 receives are then forwarded to the temporal lobe areas which, as we learned in Chapter 10, are primarily involved in object perception. It therefore makes sense that colour information, which provides so much richness in terms of object detail, should be coordinated with neurobiological mechanisms underlying form perception, starting in area V4 and extending down into the temporal lobe.

C. Perceptual Aspects of Colour

We have already discussed various perceptual aspects of colour vision throughout this chapter. These included the early Newtonian view of a colour wheel to describe the psychological dimension of colour, colour matching

functions that led to early theoretical views on trichromacy, colour cancellation experiments and their impact on the resurgence of opponent colour theory, and the role that isoluminant colour perception played in the search for complex colour coding mechanisms. All of these examples highlighted the remarkable role that perceptual science played in framing the issues that needed to be addressed by physiologists and often predicted the correct biological mechanisms that were later discovered in the brain.

In the last section of this chapter, we now deviate somewhat from the close coupling of perceptual and neural science in our discussions of early colour vision to describe some of the more fundamental and complex aspects of colour perception. Although all of these facets of colour vision arise through early encoding mechanisms of wavelength information, some of the more complex colour phenomena are the result of high-level neural processing, which are only now being slowly unravelled.

1. COLOUR DISCRIMINATION ABILITY

An early effort to understand the details of human colour perception concerned the fundamental question of how much change in wavelength is needed to detect a difference in hue, saturation, or brightness. The data from these experiments generated discrimination functions that provided important insights into the human visual system's capacity to process colour information (Davson, 1962; Graham, 1965).

Hue discrimination

The trichromatic visual system is capable of producing a vast number of perceived hues. But how good is it at discriminating one hue from another? To address this question, we can turn to the familiar procedure of using a bipartite field, as shown in the inset of Figure 11.32 on page 392. One side of this field emits light of a particular wavelength, whereas the other half emits the same light plus a small increment in wavelength ($\Delta\lambda$). The graph in Figure 11.32 shows how much the wavelength needs to be changed (i.e., the value of $\Delta\lambda$) in order to produce a perceptible difference in hue. As can be seen here, for much of the visible spectrum, that amount is quite small. Indeed, less than a 2 nm change in wavelength is needed to detect a change in hue for much of the spectrum

SideNote | **11.40**

The thick CO stripes of area V2 project to areas that are associated with the parietal (dorsal) stream where spatial relationships and visual information related to motion are processed. The details of this pathway will be discussed in Chapter 13.

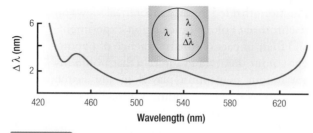

Figure 11.32

The wavelength discrimination function shows that humans with normal colour vision have an excellent ability to perceive changes in hue for much of the visible spectrum, except at the ends (blue light and red light). Adapted from *The Eye: The Visual Process, Vol. 2*, by H. Davson, 1962, New York, NY: Academic Press.

except for the lower and upper ends (i.e., blue and red light) (Davson, 1962). Thus, the trichromatic human visual system is capable of detecting very small changes in the wavelength content of a coloured stimulus.

Saturation discrimination

Recall that saturation refers to the purity of a colour (i.e., the vividness of its chromatic quality). A highly saturated colour is one that evokes the most intense quality of hue, whereas colours that are less saturated appear washed out or more whitish in nature. A fully desaturated (unsaturated) colour is in fact a shade of grey. As with hue discrimination, the question arises as to how good a trichromatic visual system is in terms of saturation discrimination. A bipartite field can again be used, but this time one side of it emits white light, whereas the other half emits white light in combination with light of another wavelength. The task of the experiment is to determine the quantity of the coloured light that needs to be added before an observer can distinguish the two fields (SideNote 11.41).

Figure 11.33 shows the nature of the bipartite field that is used in such experiments (inset) along with the saturation threshold data obtained for two observers. The threshold peaks around 570 nm (yellow light) and then declines on both sides, reaching its lowest levels for blue light. This means that a greater amount of yellow light must be added to a white patch to make it appear coloured and therefore distinguish it from the adjacent pure white patch (Graham, 1965). In other words, yellow has low **saturating power**. Red and blue lights, on the other hand, have high saturating power because only a small amount needs to be added to white light to make it appear coloured.

SideNote 11.41

Hue and saturation discrimination experiments must be conducted very carefully to ensure that both halves of the bipartite field are isoluminant for all stimulation conditions. Otherwise luminance information will provide a cue to the observer and lead to false results.

Brightness discrimination

A straightforward way to obtain brightness discrimination data was discussed in Chapter 1. A small light patch of variable luminance is compared to another patch of fixed luminance. In this way, we can obtain the Weber fraction, which under photopic conditions is approximately 2%. In other words, the light level needs to be changed by this much to make it just distinguishable (discriminated) from a neighbouring or background patch. These experiments are typically carried out with neutral (grey) lights. But what happens if both light patches are coloured? It turns out that the same Weber fraction is obtained as long as the light levels are at photopic levels and the same colour is used for both patches.

2. COLOUR CONTRAST

The concept of sensory contrast is not new to us. We encountered it as early as the somatosensory system where we noted that exposure to one type of stimulus followed by its opposite quality will enhance the sensory experience. For example, jumping out of a sauna and into a cold pool significantly accentuates the feeling of coldness. In terms of vision, we saw in Chapter 9 how a patch of light surrounded by a dark background appeared much lighter than

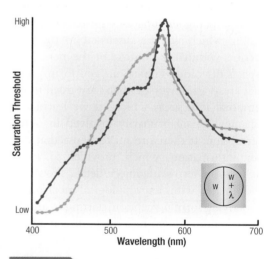

Figure 11.33

Saturation discrimination experiments are conducted by comparing a white patch with another in which the white is mixed with a spectral colour (inset). The results for two observers show that the saturation threshold is highest around 570 nm (i.e., compared to other colours, a greater amount of yellow light must be added to white to make it distinguishable). Adapted from *Vision and Visual Perception*, by C. H. Graham, 1965, New York, NY: John Wiley and Sons.

when the same patch was placed upon a light background, something we came to know as *lightness contrast*.

Colour contrast is a similar phenomenon that is evoked when there is a simultaneous juxtaposition of different colours (Hurvich, 1981; Kaiser & Boynton, 1996; Thompson, 1995). Put simply, the colour appearance of a light or object depends on the surrounding colours (SideNote 11.42). The adjacent colours interact to alter the perceived appearance of an object. The significance of this phenomenon is that because we rarely look at objects in total isolation, the colour content of the surround can have a considerable impact on the perceived colour of objects in our visual world. That impact is greatest when a particular coloured object is surrounded by its complementary colour—for example, blue against yellow, red against green, and vice versa. In such situations, a particular colour is actually accentuated by its complementary surround and therefore appears more vivid.

An excellent example of the complementary accentuation of colours is found in works of art (Enns, 2004; Gage, 2000). For centuries, artists have used the technique of juxtaposing complementary colours without fully understanding the underlying mechanisms. One of the most creative artists in this regard

was Vincent Van Gogh. The painting shown in Figure 11.34 (left panel) illustrates how yellow and blue accentuate each other. An even earlier example of the same use of complementary colours can be found from mummy cases of ancient Egypt, such as the mask of Tutankhamun, which is inlaid with gold and blue pigment (right panel). Modern artists, decorators, and architects often use these concepts in choosing colour combinations that highlight the perceptual salience of their creative work (SideNote 11.43).

3. COLOUR CONSTANCY

Whereas colour contrast comes into play when a coloured object is placed in the context of different coloured backgrounds, an entirely different phenomenon occurs when the light source that illuminates a group of objects or a scene changes. Again, we can draw on our earlier discussion of *lightness constancy* in Chapter 9 where we discovered that the perceived lightness of an object remains stable despite widely changing the intensity of an illuminating source. Because changes in illumination affect the object and its surround, our visual system is able to account for those simultaneous changes to create perceptual stability in terms of lightness sensation.

SideNote **11.42**

A number of excellent examples of this phenomenon have been introduced by artist Josef Albers, such as the one below. The light reflected off the two "Xs" is identical, and yet their colour looks so different when placed against the two separate backgrounds. The fact that they are the same lines can be seen at the bottom where they are connected.

SideNote **11.43**

Nineteenth-century German philosopher Johann von Goethe was among one of the early thinkers who appreciated the nature of complementary colours. He illustrated this concept by way of the drawing below, which he made after gazing at a girl in a pub. After staring at this drawing for a minute or so and then turning to a blank wall, he observed an afterimage with complementary colours, revealing the true likeness of the girl. Try it!

WebExhibits.org/IDEA.org

Figure 11.34

The painting *Café Terrace on the Place du Forum, Arles* by Vincent Van Gogh shows how two complementary colours, blue and yellow, can be used effectively to produce a vivid impression of the scene. Artists have used complementary colours for thousands of years, as evidenced by the mask of Tutankhamun with its striking use of gold and blue pigment. Photos: (Left) © Peter Horree/Alamy; (Right) © Russell Kord/Alamy

There is a striking benefit to such perceptual constancy in that we do not experience wide fluctuations in visual intensity sensation (lightness or brightness) due to physical variations in illumination intensity.

We can now broaden this concept to encompass colour perception as well. **Colour constancy** is the phenomenon by which coloured surfaces appear relatively unchanged despite changes in the lighting conditions (Ebner, 2007; Hurvich, 1981; Thompson, 1995). For example, changing the illumination source from fluorescent to tungsten light bulbs will alter the nature of the light falling on a multi-coloured surface. We know that the light reflected from each part of this surface will also change in terms of its wavelength composition as a result (see Section A.2 for a quick review). However, the different colours will appear similar under both lighting conditions. Just as lightness constancy confers many benefits to the observer, the same can be said of colour constancy. Consider what would happen if our visual world appeared to change in its chromatic makeup simply because the light source was changed or that we went from one part of the day to another, such as the rosy light of dawn to the broader spectral light of high noon. Our visual world would be at the mercy of changes in the illuminant, and we would no longer be able to make reliable judgments of object colours.

Constraints on colour constancy

Colour constancy also presents us with a puzzle in terms of how it arises. We learned earlier that the chromatic property of *an object* is derived from its physical spectrum, which in turn is based on two factors—the reflectance property of the object and the wavelength composition of the light falling upon it. The physical spectrum can be altered by changing the incident light, and as we learned in Section A.2, this in turn can affect the perceived colour of the object. The key term here is "an object." If we look at objects in isolation, then the colours that they evoke are most certainly altered by changing the incident light. By the same token, if a visual scene is observed through a narrow tunnel, whereby only a small part of that scene is observed in isolation, then the perceived colour of an object is also affected by changing the light source. Thus, colour constancy does not arise when objects are viewed in isolation or when a scene is viewed under

aperture conditions (Ebner, 2007; Palmer, 2002; Thompson, 1995).

Theories of colour constancy

Colour constancy prevails only with visual scenes containing multiple objects such that any given object can be placed in the context of a surround (SideNote 11.44). Several theories have been proposed as to why the perceived colour of a scene is relatively unaltered by changes in illumination. One explanation that has received considerable attention was proposed by American inventor Edwin Land (SideNote 11.45) (Land, 1977). Land studied colour constancy by way of large collages of multi-coloured geometric shapes, known as a *mondrian*, because of its resemblance to the works of Dutch painter Piet Mondrian (see SideNote 11.44). Among his interesting findings, Land showed that a given segment of a collage would continue to produce the same colour appearance even if the projectors that illuminated it were manipulated so that the physical light that reflected off this segment would in isolation yield an entirely different colour.

The work with mondrians along with earlier research on colour constancy led to the view that the visual system does not judge absolute wavelength information from an object but rather compares it with different parts of the scene. Thus, it is the relative rather than the absolute spectral distribution of light in a scene that determines the perceived colour. And therein lies a possible explanation for colour constancy. If the illumination source is changed, then the light energy reflected off all objects will be similarly affected. Therefore, as with the phenomenon of lightness constancy, a neural process that is based on relative comparisons among objects will continue to produce the same perceived colour. It is not possible, however, to make relative comparisons with an isolated object or when viewing a scene under aperture conditions. In this case, colour constancy is lost and colour perception is driven entirely by the spectral nature of the light that is reflected off the object (Land, 1977; Zeki, 1994).

A relative comparison process by itself may not be enough to explain colour constancy. It is theoretically possible that an entirely different kind of colour experience is produced when a visual scene is affected by changing the illuminant. In other words,

SideNote | **11.44**

It is difficult to illustrate colour constancy because it requires changing the light source in order to observe the phenomenon. One easy way to demonstrate it is to simply put on a pair of sunglasses. Even though the nature of the light entering the eye has now changed, the colour of objects in the visual scene are not significantly altered. Colour constancy has been studied in the laboratory by way of collages of multi-coloured geometric shapes that resemble the paintings of Piet Mondrian.

Peter Horree/Alamy

SideNote | **11.45**

Edwin Land invented the first inexpensive filters capable of polarizing light and later went on to establish the Polaroid Corporation. He also helped design the optics of the U-2 spy plane and invented the instant camera, apparently because his daughter complained that it took too long to develop ordinary film.

colour constancy is not necessarily an automatic outcome. One way to get around this problem is to assume that we have some prior knowledge about the typical colours of objects. We may then use this intrinsic knowledge to recover the normal colour associated with various objects when all parts of a scene are similarly affected. It is clear that early vision alone (i.e., retinal-based mechanisms) cannot account for colour constancy and that higher cortical mechanisms, which are involved in making local comparisons, must also be engaged. This dual requirement for both early and high-level vision led Edwin Land to formulate the **retinex theory**, which holds that the eye (retina) and brain (cortex) are both involved in colour constancy processing (Land, 1977).

4.   COMPLEX COLOUR PHENOMENA

We remarked earlier in this chapter that colour is an example of metathetic perception. There is no definable relationship between the stimulus (light wavelength) and the nature of the perception (hue). Changing the wavelength does not add to the magnitude of hue sensation but rather alters it entirely. Thus, the very relationship between colour as a perceptual phenomenon and the stimulus that gives rise to it is complex to begin with. Even though colour perception arises from early processes that encode wavelength information, it turns out that wavelength sometimes plays an astonishingly small role in determining the colour appearance of objects in complex scenes. This is precisely what we learned in our preceding discussion on colour constancy. The many other examples of the complex qualities of colour vision can fill an entire book. We conclude this chapter with a brief review of just a few, including a visual illusion that remains as enigmatic today as when it was discovered more than 40 years ago.

Hue depends on intensity

We have come to appreciate the close interaction that light wavelength has on hue perception. It turns out that in certain situations, hue is additionally affected by light intensity (Bruce, Green, & Georgeson, 2003; Gegenfurtner, 2000; Lythgoe, 1979). We saw an example of this in Chapter 9 with the transition from photopic to scotopic conditions where green hues appear to become brighter

and yellows become dimmer, a phenomenon known as the *Purkinje shift*. Another intensity-related phenomenon, which occurs under strictly photopic conditions, is known as the **Bezold–Brücke effect**, first reported by two German scientists in the 19th century in terms of how hue perception is affected by changing light intensity. Increasing the intensity of coloured lights with wavelengths greater than 510 nm causes the hue to shift toward a more yellowish appearance, whereas wavelengths less than 510 nm produce a shift toward a more bluish appearance. Although hue perception is largely governed by the wavelength composition of light, this is clearly a complex relationship given that light intensity may also play a role.

Hue depends on saturation

Another factor that has an impact on hue perception is saturation. It is well known that adding white light to a coloured light will make it appear washed out or desaturated. However, it turns out that a shift also takes place in terms of hue. For example, a mixture of white and 650 nm light produces a hue shift in the direction of purple. Thus, to maintain the same redness, a shorter wavelength light (say around 610 nm) has to be mixed with the white light. The hue change that accompanies changes in saturation is known as the **Abney effect**, which becomes especially pronounced in colour monitors where variations in saturation produce discernible changes in hue.

Hue depends on size and duration

The size of an object may also affect colour perception. In general, perceived hue grows with stimulus size for any given part of the retina up to the far periphery, where colour vision is quite poor. This effect has been reported for all four primary perceptual colours. Colour vision therefore suffers with very small objects, where even highly saturated hues are perceived as being whitish in nature (SideNote 11.46). There is a similar effect with regard to exposure time. Hue perception is severely affected when the duration of a stimulus is less than 200 milliseconds.

The McCollough aftereffect

Earlier in this chapter, we discussed colour afterimages, which are fleeting impressions that arise after viewing a coloured stimulus for a prolonged period of time. An afterimage

SideNote | **11.46**

Size effect on hue has certain implications in various situations, such as astronomy. The many reddish features of Mars, for example, often appear greyish because of their small size.

has some very precise attributes, such as being short-lived and always complementary in colour to the original stimulus. Indeed, this complementarity was one of the pieces of evidence used to formulate the opponent theory of colour perception.

It turns out that not all colour afterimages are short-lived. In 1965, Celeste McCollough described a colour aftereffect that was truly stunning (McCollough, 1965). The McCollough aftereffect is unlike standard colour afterimages, which are based on retinal mechanisms. The reason is simple—viewing two different oriented gratings through the same part of the retina generates completely different colour afterimages (see Figure 11.35). This phenomenon is an example of a **contingent aftereffect**, which is dependent on two different aspects of the stimulus. In this case, the conjunction of colour and orientation leads to the specificity of the illusion. Perhaps an even more remarkable aspect of contingent aftereffects is that they are long-lasting (SideNote 11.47).

A widely accepted and satisfactory explanation for the McCollough aftereffect remains elusive to this day (Humphrey & Goodale, 1998; Webster & Malkoc, 2000). One theory is that alternate viewing of the two gratings selectively adapts only those neurons that jointly process both colour and orientation information. In the example of Figure 11.35, the vertical green grating stimulates only those neurons that are triggered by both of these properties of the stimulus. The same is true for the horizontal red grating. Given that orientation selectivity is a property that arises for the first time in the primary visual cortex (area V1), one conclusion is that this aftereffect is a cortical property, unlike ordinary colour afterimages, which are

SideNote | **11.47**

One way to demonstrate this is to make a copy of just the bottom panel in Figure 11.35 and carry it around. The McCollough aftereffect should still be present several days after the original adaptation experiment was done.

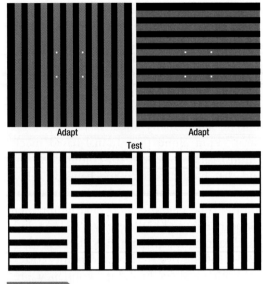

Figure 11.35

The McCullough aftereffect phenomenon can be demonstrated by viewing each coloured grating (top panels) for about 15 seconds and then shifting your gaze to the other grating. Fixation should be alternated between the four white points at the centre of each image. This process should be repeated for as long as possible, but at least 5 minutes. Viewing the achromatic gratings afterwards (bottom panel) reveals an orientation-specific colour aftereffect. The vertical gratings show a reddish afterimage (complementary to green), whereas the horizontal gratings show a greenish afterimage (complementary to red).

attributed to neural adaptation at lower levels such as the retina. However, it has also been proposed that the McCollough aftereffect is not related to selective adaptation at all but is merely a form of associative learning. According to this theory, prolonged viewing of the two gratings creates a firm association between the twin properties of the stimulus, which then lasts for many days afterwards, explaining the long-lasting afterimage.

Summary

1. The notion that colour perception is associated with the spectral nature of light was demonstrated by Newton in the seventeenth century through his famous prism experiment. The differential refraction of light as a function of wavelength creates a continuous band that appears as a rainbow of colours, leading to Newton's conclusion that colour is associated with light rather than being an intrinsic property of objects. Newton created a colour circle to represent the seven spectral colours contained in sunlight, which in turn provided a simple geometric way to predict intermediate colours that arise from the mixture of any two coloured lights. A pair of colours that produces white when mixed together is referred to as being *complementary*. Because sunlight is made up of all of the spectral colours mixed together, the end result of that mixture produces a point in the middle of the colour circle—white.

2. An object can absorb, scatter, or reflect light. Objects that display a large amount of specular reflection are glossy in nature, whereas those that display little reflection at the surface take on a matte appearance. A second type, known as *body reflection*, influences the perceived colour of an object. Objects that reflect all wavelengths equally will take on a whitish appearance; those that reflect very little light will appear grey or black. A precise description of the nature of body reflection is given by an object's *reflectance spectrum*. The actual perceived colour of an object is determined by this parameter in conjunction with the spectrum of the incident light, which together generates the *colour signal* of the object.

3. A physical description of light is given by its emission spectrum—that is, energy content at each wavelength across the visible range. The perceptual parameter that corresponds to wavelength is known as *hue* and can be represented in a circular manner where the distance around the circle corresponds to changing hue sensations. The flatter the emission spectrum, the more the signal encompasses neighbouring wavelengths, leading to changes in perceived vividness, or *saturation*. Saturation is represented in a radial manner in colour space, where the centre occupies a neutral colour, and the edges represent the most saturated hues. The emission spectra of two sources can have similar profiles but different levels of energy content. Hue and saturation remain unaffected in this case, but each stimulus produces a different perceived *value* (brightness or lightness). Value is represented along the vertical dimension in colour space.

4. Additive colour mixing of three primaries (red, green, and blue-violet) in varying amounts can produce virtually all of the other perceptible colours. Young postulated that there were three separate light-capturing elements in the eye whose ability to detect light coincided with the primary colours. Any pair of lights or surfaces that are perceptually identical but physically different are called *metamers*. Metamers can be produced by any trio of primaries, and in fact, there can be a very large number of metamers. Von Helmholtz resurrected Young's postulate of three primary colour detection mechanisms in the eye—that is, the visual system can create all colour experience from the output of three primary detectors. This idea became known as the *Young–Helmholtz theory of trichromacy*.

5. Biological trichromacy arises from the presence of three different types of cone photoreceptors—S, M, and L cones. Photoreceptors, however, do not register information about the actual wavelength of light. The signal that emerges out of each cone is related only to how much light is absorbed at a given moment, as specified by the *principle of univariance*. All perceptible colours are generated by the activation pattern of the three cone subtypes. Any change in the physical spectrum of a stimulus will also cause the relative outputs of the three cones to change, resulting in a new colour sensation. A reduced palette of colour sensations (colour deficiency) is present in those individuals who have only two functional cones, leading to the condition of dichromacy. The presence of only one functional photoreceptor (monochromacy), as with rods under scotopic conditions, leads to colour-blindness. Trichromacy represents an ideal compromise between the need to generate a rich palette of colours and the need to preserve adequate spatial resolution.

6. All behavioural data in colour vision cannot be accounted for by trichromatic theory alone, and many phenomena (e.g., colour afterimages and the subjective appearance of colour) are better explained by Hering's theory of colour opponency. According to this theory, two pairs of colours (red/green and blue/yellow) are never simultaneously processed but instead represent opponent colour mechanisms. Psychophysical research in the 1950s (chromatic cancellation) and neurobiological studies on monkeys in the 1960s that found LGN neurons with R/G, G/R, Y/B, or B/Y receptive fields firmly established the colour-opponent theory. The neural output of colour-opponent cells correlates well with the perceptual impressions of the primary hues; for example, the perception of *red* is largely the result of activity in R/G neurons, the perception of *yellow* in Y/B neurons, etc. Both the trichromatic and opponent process theory are correct but at different levels of visual processing, leading to the *dual process* theory.

7. Colour opponency in the retina is generated by selective input of cone signals upon a ganglion cell. An R/G colour-opponent cell receives input from a central group of L cones in an excitatory manner and a peripheral group of M cones in an inhibitory manner. The receptive field of an R/G neuron shows centre–surround colour opponency (i.e., red centre, green surround). A similar selective nature of cone inputs is responsible for generating the other subtypes of colour-opponent cells. The retinal output can be parsed into two channels—a chromatic output (composed of signals from the four colour-opponent subtypes) and an achromatic output responsible for encoding luminance information (composed of signals from the two light-opponent subtypes—ON/OFF, OFF/ON). The chromatic output of the retina arrives at the four upper (parvocellular) layers of the LGN and the achromatic output at the two lower (magnocellular) layers.

8. Wavelength discrimination studies have shown that humans with normal colour vision have an excellent ability to perceive changes in hue for much of the visible spectrum (less than a 2 nm change in wavelength), except at the extreme ends of the visible spectrum. The colour appearance of a light or object depends on the surrounding colours, which can alter the perceived appearance of an object. That impact is greatest when a particular coloured object is surrounded by its complementary colour—for example, blue against yellow, red against green, and vice versa. In such situations, a particular colour is actually accentuated by its complementary surround and therefore appears more vivid. The opposite phenomenon is known as *colour constancy*, in which coloured surfaces appear relatively unchanged despite changes in the lighting conditions.

Key Terms

1. What is the order of colours that appeared in Newton's prism experiment? Why was this experiment so important in the history of science? What are complementary colours, and what do they produce when mixed together?

2. What is the difference between *specular* and *body* reflection? How does the reflectance spectrum of an object help to determine its colour? What is the colour signal of an object, and how is it derived?

3. How is *hue* represented in colour space? What is the difference in physical spectra between two stimuli that differ in terms of saturation? How are saturation and value represented in colour space?

4. What are metamers, and how did they influence the development of our ideas on colour vision? How did the results of colour matching experiments give rise to the idea of trichromacy?

5. How does the Hering theory of colour opponency differ from the Young–Helmholtz theory of trichromacy? What are the different pieces of evidence that support each theory?

6. What is the principle of univariance, and why is it important for understanding colour vision? Why is scotopic vision colour-blind? What are the names of the different types of colour deficiency, and how do they arise? What is the argument that trichromacy represents the best evolutionary solution for human vision?

7. What were the two key advances that led to a resurgence of the opponent colour theory? What are the different subtypes of colour-opponent neurons? What is the evidence to support the notion that perceptual impressions of colour are generated from the neural output of colour opponent neurons?

8. How do colour-opponent neurons arise in the retina from the three cone subtypes? What are the different types of neurons that make up the chromatic and achromatic channels?

9. How can a hue discrimination experiment be conducted, and what are the general findings for humans? What are the ideal colour contrast conditions in terms of foreground versus background colours? What is *colour constancy*, and why is it important?

10. What are some examples of non-spectral colours? How is subtractive colour mixing different from additive mixing?

11. How does the opponent theory account for colour afterimages, and why does the trichromatic theory fail in this regard? Why are colour-opponent neurons unable to signal isoluminant colour contrast? How do double-opponent neurons resolve this problem?

12. How can colour constancy be explained? What is the McCollough aftereffect, and how can it be explained by known mechanisms of visual cortex function?

• Backhaus, W. G. K., Kleigl, R., & Werner, J. S. (1998). *Color vision: Perspectives from different disciplines*. Berlin, Germany: de Gruyter.

• Ebner, M. (2007). *Color constancy*. Chichester, UK: Wiley.

• Gegenfurtner, K. R. (2000). *Color vision: From genes to perception*. Cambridge, UK: Cambridge University Press.

• Hurvich, L. M. (1981). *Color vision*. Sunderland, MA: Sinauer Associates.

• Kuehni, R. G., & Schwarz, A. (2008). *Color ordered: A survey of color systems from antiquity to the present*. New York, NY: Oxford University Press.

• Livingstone, M. S. (2002). *Vision and art: The biology of seeing*. New York, NY: Harry N. Abrams.

• Lynch, D. K., & Livingston, W. (2001). *Color and light in nature*. Cambridge, UK: Cambridge University Press.

• Thompson, E. (1995). *Colour vision: A study in cognitive science and the philosophy of perception*. London, UK: Routledge Press.

• Waldman, G. (2002). *I ntroduction to light: The physics of light, vision, and color*. Mineola, NY: Dover Publications.

• Wandell, B. A. (1995). *Foundations of vision*. Sunderland, MA: Sinauer Associates.

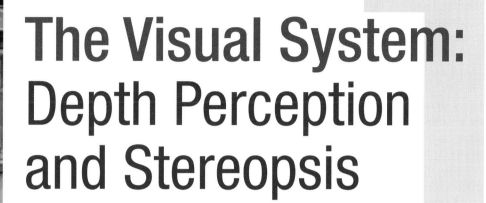

The Visual System: Depth Perception and Stereopsis

In this chapter . . .

- You will learn that all objects in space have a specific relationship to us, based on distance and direction, and how our brain manages to register movement (both our own movement and that of objects) in order to function well in the environment. You will come to understand the different frames of reference used when looking at objects in space, and how our body and its many systems accommodate for our own movements to ensure that everything else appears stable. You will explore the cues needed to master depth perception, such as retinal image size, accommodation, and vergence.

- You will discover the many monocular cues we use to help determine relative depth; you will also explore in detail the different types of cues, such as pictorial cues (used for two-dimensional images), dynamic cues (used for moving objects), size perception and constancy (the interplay of object size, retinal image size, and perceived size), and different illusions that have been created to trick our perception of both size and depth (such as the moon illusion).

- You will learn to understand why binocular vision is superior to monocular vision. You will learn about stereopsis and how the difference between the nasal retinal image and the temporal retinal image is used by the brain to determine if there is retinal disparity. You will also learn how area V1 encodes disparity selectivity and about the disorder that occurs if one cannot fuse the two images together.

- You will come to appreciate the various solutions to the correspondence problem and learn about a phenomenon known as *binocular rivalry*, as well as the breakthroughs in our understanding of vision that this technique has made possible.

Humans are quite good at distance perception—that is, judging how far away from us a particular object is located. In order to judge distance accurately, however, our brain must have information that is not ambiguous.
Photo: © Bill Gozansky/Alamy

Vision with two eyes is better than with one.

—Claudius Ptolemy (circa 150 CE)

Visual perception endows us with a single, unified awareness of our external world. What is so striking about this phenomenon is that it arises from separate input of visual information through the two eyes. And yet each of our eyes sees the world in a slightly different way—a fact that can be easily demonstrated by alternately closing one eye at a time. The resulting small shift in the scene occurs because each eye views the world from a different horizontal position. It is clear, though, that closing one eye does not change the actual nature of visual perception. We still see all the objects, their colour, detail, location, and even depth. This fact had philosophers perplexed for nearly 2,000 years, and it was not until the 19th century that the true benefits of **binocular vision** were clearly understood.

So why do we have two eyes? One simple answer is that many organs in our body are paired and therefore the eyes should be no exception. A more scientifically refined answer could draw on evolutionary theory—two eyes would represent a survival advantage if one of them happened to be damaged. In terms of sensory function, however, we now know that many fundamental aspects of vision are actually better with two eyes. For example, basic light detection and discrimination, visual resolution, object detection, eye-hand coordination, and even attention to fixated objects are all better with two eyes. The greatest benefit of binocular vision, however, is that it gives us an outstanding ability to differentiate the relative depths of objects in our visual world.

That is the main topic of this chapter. In the path to understanding how the images from the two eyes are combined, creating that remarkable ability to judge depth, we will also come to appreciate why vision with two eyes ends up producing **cyclopean perception**—that is, a single, unified vision of the world (SideNote 12.1).

A. Extrapersonal Space

All objects in the external world have a particular spatial relationship to us. There are two parameters that define this relationship—object direction and object distance. To complicate matters, our spatial relationship to external objects is highly dynamic because we ourselves are not stationary creatures. Every time we move our body, we change our spatial relationship with respect to all external objects.

Therefore we need first to understand how we can specify that spatial relationship. Then we need to understand how we obtain and process information about the changing orientation of our own body in a three-dimensional world. Both components are crucial to obtaining a spatial sense of the directional location of external objects. Finally, we need to obtain the depth component and add it to the directional component to provide a complete perceptual impression of our extrapersonal space. It will therefore be essential to develop an understanding of what types of information are at our disposal for perceiving the **absolute depth** of an object.

This section of the chapter is devoted to understanding all three facets of information processing that underlie our perception of external space.

1. SPATIAL FRAMES OF REFERENCE

A *frame of reference* is a set of axes by which the position or placement of an object is described. There are two general ways of classifying the spatial location of objects (Howard, 1982). One way is simply to specify an object's location independent of the viewer. In this **allocentric** frame of reference, spatial positions or directions are defined in an external manner. Thus a wall clock can be located exactly 1 metre above a blackboard, a Ford van can be parked just behind a red Corvette, and a statue can be located 10 metres due west of a fountain. In each of these examples, the objects are represented only in relation to each other and would maintain their specified relationship regardless of where the viewer was situated.

Allocentric frames of reference have certain advantages in that they provide spatial and directional information in unambiguous terms. For example, the two cars would maintain exactly the same spatial relationship in the environment regardless of who was viewing them. The drawback to this reference system is that space perception in humans is actually *viewer-centred*. In other words, we perceive our extrapersonal space only in relation to our own body and self. Therefore, specifying the direction of an object with respect to the viewer would be much more meaningful. A viewer-dependent system is referred to as an **egocentric** frame of reference and object positions in this system are specified in terms of *egocentric direction*.

SideNote **12.1**

The term *cyclopean* perception is derived from "Cyclops," the name of a race of one-eyed giants in Greek mythology. The most famous Cyclops was Polyphemus (below), whose only eye was destroyed by Odysseus in his bid to escape from the giant's ruthless grip.

© The Art Gallery Collection/Alamy

An egocentric frame of reference in turn implies that we must have a reference point on our body for judging the directions of objects—this reference point is called the **visual egocentre**. Psychophysical tests on directional judgments have shown that visually fixated objects are generally perceived to be projected to a point midway between the two eyes, as shown by the illustration in Figure 12.1 (Howard, 1982; Howard & Rogers, 1995). The visual egocentre, which has also been called the *cyclopean eye*, serves as the common point of reference when the two eyes operate together, so that the direction of an object is judged as if seen through a single eye at the midpoint between the two (SideNote 12.2).

2.   HEAD AND BODY MOVEMENTS IN SPACE

If directional judgments are made by way of an egocentric frame of reference, then what happens if we turn our head or body? Presumably the *cyclopean eye* would also move with our body, changing the visual perspective and raising the possibility that the world would appear to move in the opposite direction. This idea is comparable to panning a camcorder in one direction. The resulting video would show the world moving in the opposite direction. If the same were true for the human visual system, then head movements should change the perceived direction of all external objects as well.

Does the world appear to move every time we turn our head or body? We know from everyday experience that our visual impression of the world is extremely stable in spite of frequent head and body movements. Furthermore, we always seem to have an accurate sense of object direction with respect to ourselves regardless of any head turns, tilts, or slants (SideNote 12.3). Our brain somehow registers self-motion, which is then taken into account by the brain to produce stable space perception. We will first look at the different ways the body can move and then proceed to examine how self-motion is registered.

Human dynamics

As with directional judgments, any movement of the body must also be defined within a particular frame of reference. The accepted convention is to define the principal axes of the body with respect to gravity in an upright stance. Movement of the head and body can then be defined with respect to these axes. As Figure 12.2 shows, the principal axes X, Y, and Z are defined as being contained within the transverse, coronal, and median planes, respectively (Howard, 1982). The *transverse plane* containing the X-axis

SideNote **12.2**

Young children up to the age of 2 behave as if they are actually seeing the world through the cyclopean eye. When told to sight an object through a tube, they generally place the tube midway between the eyes. This effect diminishes with age and is rarely found by the age of 4.

SideNote **12.3**

It had been predicted on theoretical grounds that the visual egocentre is actually located inside the head on its axis of rotation. This would be consistent with the fact that head rotations along the vertical axis do not affect directional judgments. Although initial studies supported this idea, carefully conducted experiments showed the visual egocentre to be located midway between the eyes.

Figure 12.1

The direction of an object in space viewed through both eyes is perceptually referred to a point midway between the eyes (dashed line). This visual egocentre or cyclopean eye provides an egocentric reference point for directional judgments, resulting in a unified sense of visual direction. Adapted from *Binocular Vision and Stereopsis,* by I. P. Howard & B. J. Rogers, 1995, New York, NY: Oxford University Press.

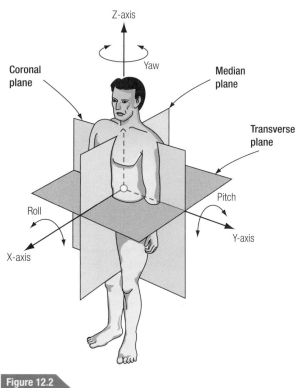

Figure 12.2

Principal planes, axes, and directions of rotation of the human body in three-dimensional space. Adapted from *Human Visual Orientation,* by I. P. Howard, 1982, New York, NY: John Wiley & Sons.

is the only horizontally oriented plane and divides the body into two halves, upper and lower. Head and body rotations around this axis produce a tilting movement or *roll*. The *coronal plane* is a vertically oriented plane that separates the body into a front and back half and contains the Y-axis. Head and body rotations around this axis produce forward or backward slanting movements, also known as *pitch*. And finally, the *median plane* separates the left and right sides of the body and contains the Z-axis. Rotations along this axis produce head and body turns, also known as *yaw*.

Proprioceptive and efferent signals

The question then arises as to how these three types of movements are registered so that we know which direction our body has moved in. Some movement information is provided by the receptors located in our joints and muscles, which detect any local movement (Frith, 2007; Mather, 2006; Squire, Bloom, & Spitzer, 2008). These receptors together form what is known as the *proprioceptive system*—an elegant and highly accurate system of detectors of muscle contraction and movement around a joint. Proprioceptive perception, or **proprioception**, is a key aspect of the somatosensory system and was discussed in detail in Chapter 3, Sections C.1 and C.2.

Proprioception is accompanied by another mechanism that provides information on body position and movement. Every time we consciously move a part of our body, a command is issued from the motor centres of our brain to the appropriate muscles. It is believed that the perceptual centres of our brain receive a copy of this command. This signal is referred to by two names, which are synonymous—**efference copy** and **corollary discharge**. Although we do not know the precise neurological details of how this discharge is mediated, it is now widely accepted to be a key signal that combines with proprioceptor inputs to generate knowledge and perception of limb position and movement.

The vestibular system

Another extremely sensitive detector of head and body movement is the **vestibular apparatus**, often referred to as the *balance organ*. Located within the inner ear, the vestibular apparatus consists of two sets of receptor organs that register self-motion—the *semicircular canals* and the *otoliths* (Squire et al., 2008). As Figure 12.3 shows, the vestibular apparatus is located adjacent to the cochlea. Indeed, the operation of the vestibular organs is similar in principle to the cochlea in that it is based on fluid movement that stimulates specialized neurons (hair cells) located within them. Fluid movement within the vestibular organs is in turn generated by movements of the head and body. Rotational body movement produces fluid displacement within the semicircular canals, whereas linear body movement (e.g., forward, backward, or vertical) stimulates the otolith organs.

A key requirement for initiating fluid movement in the vestibular organs is acceleration, either rotational or linear. This is precisely what happens when our head or body suddenly moves from one position to another.

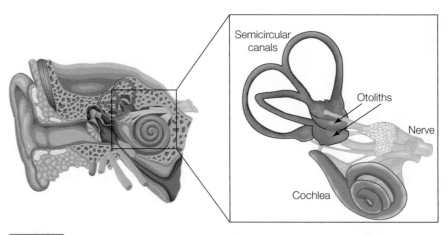

Figure 12.3

The vestibular apparatus is a fluid-filled organ located within the bony matrix of the inner ear, adjacent to the cochlea. It is made up of the semicircular canals and the otoliths. Fluid movement within these chambers produces neural impulses that convey information about head and body movements.

There are three semicircular canals, each oriented differently so as to detect motion along that plane (Mather, 2006; Squire et al., 2008). The vestibular organs on both sides of the head work in conjunction to provide highly precise information on self-motion. Our perception of the world as being stable is due to one simple fact—our brain is aware that it is *we* that have moved rather than the world itself. This awareness is the marvellous outcome of high-level integration of visual, vestibular, and proprioceptive signals. The perceptual stability produced in this way is also responsible for the fact that perceived object directions in the world remain stable in spite of self-motion as well (SideNote 12.4).

3. PERCEPTION OF ABSOLUTE DEPTH

Our visual brain can easily determine an object's direction because it can recover the information from the object's image position on the retina. This fact is illustrated in Figure 12.4, where the retinal location of image A' exactly specifies the directional location of object A in external space. A different object would be imaged at a different retinal position, enabling the visual brain to deduce that object's location as well (SideNote 12.5).

Although object direction is easily recovered from the retinal image, the same is not true of the second parameter that defines an object's location in space—distance from the observer. This parameter represents a much thornier problem, as Figure 12.4 shows. The object being fixated (F) produces an image (F') on the fovea. However, the fixated object can be moved forward or backward along its projection axis (arrows) without changing its foveal image. The unchanging image position in this situation makes it difficult to recover information about absolute depth. In fact, depth perception based on retinal image position is inherently ambiguous. The reason for this ambiguity is that the world has three dimensions, but the retinal surface has only two—therefore retinal image position cannot encode the third dimension (depth).

Yet we are usually quite good at distance perception—as long as our brain has information that is not ambiguous. There are three cues available to the visual brain that enable us to tell how far away a particular object is (Ebenholtz, 2001; Howard & Rogers, 1995; Schwartz, 1999).

Optical cue—retinal image size

Let us return to the example above of moving an object closer or farther from the observer. Although the position of the retinal image is not affected, changing the object distance does affect the size of the retinal image, as shown in Figure 12.5 (Palmer, 2002). The fact that a near object casts a larger retinal image than one located farther away allows the brain to interpret object distance. Thus, retinal image size represents an optical cue (in fact, the only one we have) for judging absolute depth.

In order to estimate distance with any accuracy, however, we must already know something about the size of the object. Otherwise we could not tell whether we were looking at a small object nearby or a large one far away, because both would yield similar-sized images. If we are familiar with the object, we can easily deduce its distance based on the retinal image size. We know, for instance, that most adults are somewhere between 1.5 and

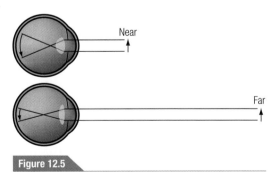

Figure 12.5

A near object casts a larger retinal image than one farther away. This difference in retinal image size may be used as a cue for absolute depth. Another cue is provided by the accommodative state of the eye. A near object requires greater accommodation (a thicker crystalline lens), while one that is far away requires less (a thinner crystalline lens). Adapted from *Vision Science: Photons to Phenomenology*, by S. E. Palmer, 2002, Cambridge, MA: MIT Press.

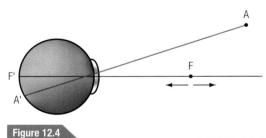

Figure 12.4

The direction of an external object (A) can be recovered from the position of its retinal image (A'). However, the same cue cannot be used to obtain the distance of an object from the observer. For example, the retinal image (F') of a fixated object (F) will be the same regardless of its absolute depth, that is, its position along the axis (arrows).

2 metres tall, that a typical car is 4 to 5 metres in length, and that most chairs have a seat that is roughly half a metre off the ground. Our brain uses size assumptions such as these, acquired through visual experience, in order to deduce absolute depth.

What happens, though, when we look at an unfamiliar object, one on which there is no size information in our brain's database? Even with familiar objects, the value of optical cues depends on our ability to accurately discern the viewed object. How can we tell that we are looking at a car parked across the road rather than a toy model located only an arm's length away? Our visual brain could theoretically be fooled in many situations if it relied only on optical size cues to generate absolute depth perception. Fortunately, in addition to the optical cue, we have at our disposal two **ocular cues** that provide unambiguous information about absolute depth (Ebenholtz, 2001; Palmer, 2002).

Ocular cues—accommodation

When we turn our gaze to different objects located at different distances, we immediately and reflexively change the optical power of our eyes through a process known as *accommodation* (SideNote 12.6). Near objects require greater optical power than more distant ones in order to produce a sharp retinal image, as illustrated in Figure 12.5 (Palmer, 2002). Additional optical power is provided by increasing the thickness of the crystalline lens. Alternatively, distant objects require less optical power, hence a thinner crystalline lens, to produce a clear, focused retinal image. The thickness of the lens is controlled by the *ciliary muscle*.

The accommodative state at any given moment is an important cue to the visual brain for generating distance perception. Furthermore, there is no ambiguity in this cue because accommodation is directly related to object distance. The only requirement is that the information regarding the accommodative state of the eye be transmitted to the higher centres of the brain for interpretation. There is one limitation, however, to the use of accommodation as a depth cue. The accommodative mechanism is more engaged for near than far objects because it is at close range that the need for additional optical power arises (Howard & Rogers, 1995; Palmer, 2002; Sekuler & Blake, 2002). Indeed, the accommodative state of the eyes changes very little for objects beyond about 3 metres (10 feet), and therefore makes a

negligible contribution to distance perception for faraway objects (SideNote 12.7).

Ocular cues—vergence

Accommodation represents an ocular cue because it signals a particular state or condition of the eyes (i.e., the refractive state at a given moment). Another ocular cue for distance perception occurs when our eyeballs rotate horizontally within our eye sockets to ensure that a fixated object falls on the fovea, as shown in Figure 12.6 (Ogle, 1950; Schwartz, 1999; Squire et al., 2008). When viewing a distant object (O_1), as in the left diagram of this figure, both eyeballs are positioned in such a way that the image falls on the foveal retina (F) of both eyes. However, if we wish to turn our gaze to a closer object (O_2), then the eyes must change their position; otherwise the object would be imaged at peripheral retinal locations (grey outline). Both eyes therefore need to rotate inward (or converge) just enough that the fovea is aligned with the image of the closer object, as shown in the right diagram of Figure 12.6. This type of eye movement is known as **convergence**. The distant object now becomes imaged on the peripheral retina (the nasal portions, to be exact). In order to shift our gaze back to the distant object, an outward rotation of the eyes, or **divergence**, is needed so that its image will return to the fovea (SideNote 12.8).

These two types of eyeball rotation—convergence and divergence—are together known as *vergence* eye movements. These eye movements are under the control of brain structures

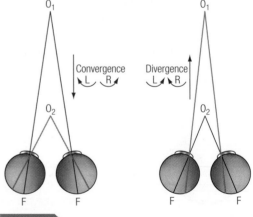

Figure 12.6

An inward rotation of both eyes (convergence) occurs when view is shifted from a distant to a near object (left diagram). This allows the near object to be imaged on the fovea of both eyes (right diagram). Changing the gaze back to the distant object now requires an outward movement of both eyes (divergence), so that the object will be imaged on the fovea.

that calibrate eye position precisely to ensure that objects fixated at different distances will be imaged exactly on the fovea.

Afference, efference, or both?

As with accommodation, it has been argued that the vergence state of the eyes can provide the brain with cues for distance perception. This idea is quite old, having originated with Descartes in the 17th century (SideNote 12.9). If the visual brain is aware of the rotational state of the eyes at any given moment, then it should be able to deduce how far away in space the fixated object is located. Furthermore, there should be no ambiguity in this signal because vergence is directly related to object distance. The question then is, how can the brain obtain information on both the vergence and the accommodative state of the eyes?

Let us first consider what is required for a change in accommodation to occur. A blur spot occurs on the retina if the refractive state of the eye is not matched for object distance. Once the blur is detected, a motor command is issued from the brainstem to the ciliary muscle to change the shape of the crystalline lens so that the object can be brought into focus. Now let us assume that a copy of this motor command to the ciliary muscle is sent to higher centres of the brain that deal with perceptual function, as shown in Figure 12.7. In this way, the visual brain is kept abreast of the accommodative state while viewing the object and therefore can generate an impression of object distance (Howard & Rogers, 1995; Mather, 2006; Sekuler & Blake, 2002). Exactly the same logic applies in the case of vergence, which is triggered by the need to rotate the eyes so as to place an image on the fovea. This situation requires that the motor centres in our brainstem send a command to our eye muscles to converge or diverge. A copy of this command may also be sent to the higher centres of the brain where distance information is processed.

The idea that a carbon copy of a motor signal may be sent to other parts of the brain is nearly a century old, having originated with British physiologist Charles Sherrington (Ogle, 1950; Wade, 1999). A neural signal that is discharged from the brain and carried to the periphery is known as an *efferent* signal; therefore Sherrington used the term *efference copy* to refer to the copy of the motor signal. Although the exact neural mechanisms that underlie this process remain unknown, studies on monkeys

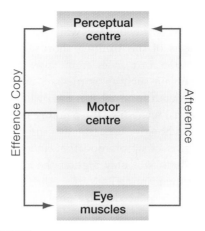

Figure 12.7

Information about the accommodative and vergence state of the eyes can be relayed to the perceptual centres of the brain by way of either an efference copy or an afference signal. In the latter, the actual contraction state of the eye muscles is detected locally and then sent to the brain. Alternatively, the motor centres of the brain that issue a command to the eye muscles in the first place may send a copy of this signal to the perceptual centres.

suggest that an efferent copy may be relayed to the frontal cortex and other parts of the brain.

A second way to transmit information on accommodation and vergence is based on our earlier discussion of proprioceptive function. The brain is constantly aware of the contraction state of our various muscles by way of stretch detectors that lie within the joints and muscles themselves. The muscles that control accommodation and vergence are known to have similar built-in detectors and therefore can indicate their contraction state to the brain. In this case, the signal arises directly at the site of the muscles themselves and is forwarded to the perceptual centres (see Figure 12.7). A neural signal sent from the periphery to the brain is known as an **afferent signal**.

It is believed that both these signals play important roles in registering the moment-to-moment state of accommodation and vergence and thereby allowing the visual brain to determine the absolute distance of objects in space.

B. Monocular Depth Perception

French post-impressionist painter Paul Cézanne created a compelling sense of depth and structure in a work titled *The Abduction* (Figure 12.8 on page 408). This painting is just one of

SideNote | **12.9**

Descartes even came up with a procedure that could allow blind people to estimate object distance using natural geometry (see his illustration below). The angle of the two rods with respect to each other would be sufficient to determine the object's distance. The same geometric principle underlies the use of ocular vergence to estimate changes in absolute depth.

© World History Archive/Alamy

SideNote | **12.10**

The effective use of pictorial cues was not present in paintings until around the 15th century. In earlier paintings, the size of objects was not associated with distance but rather the importance of the figures. The painting below exemplifies how the relative depths of the various people are not captured effectively because of the work's emphasis on the two central characters. A useful exercise would be to re-examine this image after reading Section B.1 to figure out which pictorial cues are not used properly.

numerable examples where the third dimension is captured so vividly. We will examine various aspects of this painting shortly. However, the question that arises right away is "How do we obtain such an immediate and strong sense of depth from what is essentially a two-dimensional scene (i.e., the painting or its replica in this book)?" We certainly cannot use the ocular cues of accommodation and vergence because both will only register the actual distance to the painting itself.

We are also faced with a similar problem in the real world. Let us assume that we are looking at a particular object. There will likely be many other objects in the scene as well, some closer than others. In the last section, we discussed the cues that are used by the visual brain to endow us with distance perception and learned that we are especially good at judging absolute distance when we are directly gazing at an object. Although we can use ocular cues to provide a sense of how far a particular object is located, how is it that we also obtain a strong and instantaneous impression of the depths of all other objects in the scene at the same time, without looking at them directly?

One of the major challenges faced by our visual system is sorting out the **relative depths** of objects (i.e., where they are located with respect to each other in terms of distance along the third dimension). In this and the next section, we will explore the visual cues and mechanisms that allow us to obtain an impression of the relative depths of objects in

our visual scene. We will come to discover that having two eyes endows us with significant benefits in this regard. However, we also know from everyday experience that we can easily obtain relative depth information through just one eye—a phenomenon that arises because we have a number of *monocular depth cues* at our disposal. That is the topic of this section, which as we will shortly discover, also provides the basis for depth perception in paintings, photographs, and movies.

1. PICTORIAL CUES

Pictorial cues are based on stationary optical information contained in two-dimensional scenes or pictures. These cues are also involved in relative depth perception during monocular viewing. Pictorial cues are effective because they are based on physical factors that govern object relationships and their appearance at different depths. Indeed, these cues are so effective that painters rely on them to create a compelling sense of depth in their artwork (SideNote 12.10). However, in order to be effective, our visual brain must interpret pictorial cues and make inferences as to what they represent in terms of depth information.

Occlusion

One of the very simple inferences we can make is through image **occlusion** (Palmer, 2002; Schwartz, 1999). If one object covers another, then our immediate sense of relative depth holds that the occluded object must lie behind or farther away than the occluding object. This is obvious in Cézanne's painting where the woman being abducted is clearly perceived to be in front of the man and therefore farther away from us. Object occlusion is common in our visual scene and represents one of the most fundamental pictorial cues for relative depth perception. Nevertheless, we are not born with this ability, and therefore the correct interpretation of this cue depends upon visual experience and learning. There is evidence that we acquire the skill to interpret occluding images in terms of relative depth somewhere between the ages of 5 and 7 months.

Relative size

Let us turn again to Cézanne's painting. The two bathers on the left are perceived to be far away along the banks of the river. We attain this impression immediately upon viewing

Figure 12.8

The Abduction (1867) by Paul Cézanne contains a number of pictorial cues that together create a vivid impression of relative depth.

this painting because of the relative size of the bathers, who are much smaller than the two individuals in the foreground. The automatic inference in this case is that because the two people are smaller, they are situated farther away, an obvious fact of physics. Distant objects cast smaller images, and therefore our visual brain has learned to associate image size in terms of relative object depth in pictorial situations.

Texture gradient

A more complex circumstance arises when image size applies broadly to a large number of objects. In this case, the texture of the scene can provide an important cue to depth. An excellent illustration of this concept can be found in an image of the Martian surface taken during the Pathfinder mission in the late 1990s. As Figure 12.9 shows, the boulders, rocks, and pebbles in the foreground are quite large, whereas those farther away are much smaller. In other words, the foreground texture is quite coarse, whereas image texture for distant objects becomes much finer. This difference in texture, which is referred to as **texture gradient**, provides a strong depth cue to the visual brain (Howard & Rogers, 1995; Mather, 2006; Palmer, 2002). We interpret coarse texture in images as arising from objects that lie closer to us, whereas finer texture is presumed to be caused by distant objects. Texture gradient is a powerful cue and generates strong impressions of relative depth in a two-dimensional picture.

We do not need to go to Mars to find examples of texture gradient. A systematic change in both the size and the shape of large collections of objects occurs in our own environment. Some common examples include shingles, brick buildings and streets, floor patterns, trees, crowds, etc. In all these examples, the size of the visual elements decreases with distance and, when taken together, causes the image texture to become finer. We have learned through experience to interpret diminished visual texture as a result of increased relative depth.

Linear perspective

The geometrical rules of image formation cause the third dimension to be represented in precise and well-defined ways on a flat surface. For example, an outdoor scene when viewed through a window can be etched on the glass surface through **perspective projection** to recapture the third dimension. One of the rules of perspective is taken from the very idea that objects become smaller as they recede. This rule forms the basis for the pictorial cue known as **linear perspective** (Palmer, 2002; Sekuler & Blake, 2002).

We are accustomed to the notion that parallel lines appear to converge with increasing distance, such as the familiar image of railway tracks as they fade into the horizon. The reason for the convergence of the lines is quite simple—with increasing depth, the distance in the image must become smaller if it is to faithfully represent equal physical distance in reality. This idea is simply borrowed from the fact that near objects appear larger than distant ones in a pictorial format. Therefore, the physical space between the railroad tracks when it is nearby can be thought of as an imaginary object, which must progressively cast a smaller image as the tracks recede in depth (SideNote 12.11).

Again, we can turn to the art world to see an excellent example of the use of linear perspective as a pictorial cue for depth. The painting *Paris Street: A Rainy Day* by 19th-century French impressionist Gustave Caillebotte represents one of the best artistic examples of perspective projection (Figure 12.10 on page 410). This carefully arranged painting provides an eye-level view of a street scene that blends all of the major pictorial cues discussed thus far to provide a striking impression of depth (SideNote 12.12). The use of linear perspective contributes to the depth impression of the buildings, especially the triangular building in the central background. Such use of linear perspective did not arise until about the 15th century, after which it began to flourish

SideNote 12.11

Parallel lines that recede in depth in the real world project onto a 2-D image as converging lines. An important feature of this perspective projection is that the lines converge toward a *vanishing point* on the horizon. The linear perspective represented in the image below provides a powerful impression of depth.

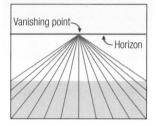

SideNote 12.12

A useful exercise would be to try and identify the various pictorial cues in Caillebotte's painting, such as the use of occlusion, relative size, texture gradient, and linear perspective.

NASA/JPL

Figure 12.9

A texture gradient arises from diminishing image texture with distance. The boulders, rocks, and pebbles in the foreground of this image of the Martian surface are larger and therefore together are responsible for the coarse image texture. Distant objects appear smaller and hence lead to finer image texture. Texture gradient serves as a powerful pictorial cue for relative depth.

© Burstein Collection/CORBIS

Figure 12.10

Paris Street: A Rainy Day (1877) by Gustave Caillebotte provides a rich blend of pictorial cues, including linear perspective, to produce a striking impression of depth.

in Renaissance art. Indeed, the transition from medieval to modern art occurred when painters began to make effective use of linear perspective and other pictorial cues for capturing depth information.

Aerial perspective

Distant objects when viewed through the atmosphere appear fuzzy and washed out. The reason is that image contrast decreases because of light scattering caused by the atmosphere. This hazy quality of distant environmental objects serves as a pictorial depth cue known as **aerial perspective**. We are most accustomed to seeing this effect when viewing tall structures from a distance, such as mountains, skyscrapers, etc. An example of this effect can be seen in Figure 12.11. The mountaintops in the foreground appear sharp, whereas those in the distance appear much fuzzier. We use this information in conjunction with other pictorial cues to make inferences about relative object depth.

Shading and shadows

Another useful source of depth information arises from the way light is reflected off curved surfaces (Palmer, 2002; Ramachandran, 1988). In such situations, curved surfaces vary

in terms of their shading quality. Some scientists have argued that this cue should more properly be called a *shape* rather than a *depth* cue because it provides structural information about the object itself, hence the oft-used term *shape-from-shading*. The four disks in the left panel of Figure 12.12 have a shading pattern that becomes progressively darker from top to bottom. Because the surfaces take on a convex appearance, we might assume they are being lit from above by the sun, hence the shadow at the bottom. Only the outside surface of a sphere would be consistent with this shading pattern. If, however, the shading pattern is reversed so that the shadow appears at the top (right panel of Figure 12.12), then the assumption of a sunlit surface no longer holds true. As a result, the three-dimensional shapes of these disks are not as vivid and instead appear concave.

Image blur

The last pictorial cue we will discuss pertains to the optics of image formation on the retina. At any given time, we are gazing at an object located at a particular depth plane in relation to us. The optical power of the eye is adjusted so that the object's image is sharply focused on the retina. However, objects that lie in front of or behind this plane will be out of focus and

Figure 12.11

"Aerial perspective" occurs when the image of distant objects becomes hazy due to greater atmospheric light scattering. This information is used in conjunction with other pictorial cues to generate relative depth impression.

therefore create a blur spot. The greater the blur, the greater the relative depth in relation to the object we are fixating on. There is some evidence that retinal image blur acts as a pictorial cue and therefore contributes to relative depth perception (SideNote 12.13) (Mather, 1996).

2.   DYNAMIC CUES

The monocular cues discussed in the previous section concerned static or stationary information that is available to the visual brain in terms of pictorial content in the retinal image. We do not, however, live in a static world but rather one in which things are moving, we are moving, or both. The dynamic cues discussed in this section change over time and confer information about the relative depth of objects. These cues are extremely powerful, and in fact, dynamic information alone can provide considerable data for our visual brain to recover complete information about the relative depth of objects in the visual world (Palmer, 2002). There are two general categories of dynamic cues that arise from image motion on the retina—one based on object motion and one based on observer motion.

Kinetic depth

We first discuss a dynamic cue that arises from object motion when viewed by a stationary

observer. Imagine looking out the window on a windy day and seeing the leaves on a tree blowing around. All things being equal, the closer leaves will be perceived to have moved a greater distance than those farther away. This difference in movement provides rich information on the

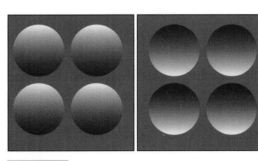

Figure 12.12

Shading patterns and shadows can serve as cues to three-dimensional shapes. The left panel shows four disks that are assumed to be illuminated from above because the shading becomes darker toward the bottom, creating the impression of a set of convex surfaces. If the shading pattern is reversed (right panel), the disks appear hollow. The visual system uses shading cues and shadows to recover information about the three-dimensional nature of objects. These cues become especially useful with complex objects such as sculptures. The directional nature of shadows can also be used by the visual system to determine the relative depth of various objects. For example, if a scene is illuminated from a particular direction, then objects that create a large shadow must be closer to the light source than objects that cast a smaller shadow.

SideNote | **12.13**

We are not consciously aware of the retinal image blur caused by near and distant objects because we are usually fixating on the main object, and therefore neural mechanisms filter the blur. It appears that, somehow, retinal blur may still be registered to provide a depth cue even though we are not overtly aware of its presence.

relative depth of the leaves with respect to each other. The term **kinetic depth** is used to refer to the motion cues generated by the movement of objects in different depth planes. This cue is especially effective for the movement of a rigid object, such as the rotation of a sphere, where the differential motion of its various parts contributes to a vivid impression of the three-dimensional structure of the object.

Motion parallax

A somewhat different situation arises when the observer is moving but gazing at stationary objects. The most familiar example is a passenger looking out the window from a moving train. The relative movement of passing objects in this situation is an example of **optic flow**. This kind of differential movement is especially intriguing because objects at different depth planes not only produce different degrees of

motion, but their perceived movement may actually be in opposite directions. The change in an object's direction of movement caused by self-motion is known as **motion parallax**. An explanation of this phenomenon and how it can provide information on relative object depth is given in Figure 12.13. The discussion that follows is based on this figure (Palmer, 2002; Rogers, 1993).

Let us assume that the observer is moving from right to left and gazing out the window at a particular object (say a tree), as represented by the fixation spot in the figure. Object A lies farther away from the fixated object and object B lies closer to the train. This arrangement is depicted in the top left panel of Figure 12.13, showing the line of sight through the fixated object. To simplify this discussion, the left eye is covered, and only the view through the right eye is shown. As the observer moves leftward,

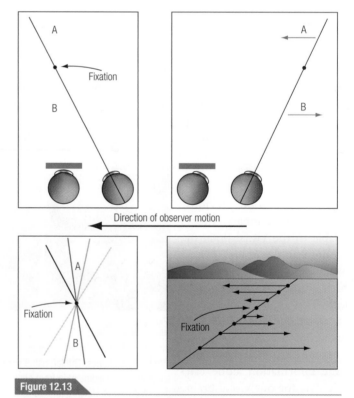

Figure 12.13

Motion parallax occurs when an observer moves in one direction while fixating on a particular object (top left panel). Objects located farther than the fixation point (A) are perceived to move in the same direction as the observer, whereas objects located closer (B) appear to move in the opposite direction (top right panel). This differential movement, known as *parallax*, arises due to the geometric relationship between the objects and the changing line of sight, as shown by the set of progressively lighter grey lines in the bottom left panel. The greater the relative distance between the objects and the fixation point, the greater the magnitude of the parallax (bottom right panel). Bottom right panel adapted from *Vision Science: Photons to Phenomenology,* by S. E. Palmer, 2002, Cambridge, MA: MIT Press.

all objects are displaced to the right. However, something interesting happens if the observer keeps fixating on the same object, as shown in the top right panel. Even though all objects are displaced to the right as the train moves, the more distant object (A) actually appears to move to the left with respect to the line of sight, whereas the nearer object (B) moves in the opposite direction (i.e., in tandem with the true direction of displacement).

This perplexing outcome is explained in the bottom left panel of Figure 12.13. As the observer moves leftward and the fixated object moves rightward, the eyes rotate in the same direction as the object in order to maintain its image on the fovea (Palmer, 2002). Therefore, the line of sight rotates progressively from left to right. This is shown by way of the four progressively lighter lines in the bottom left panel, with the darkest line representing the starting position. As the line of sight rotates to follow the rightward displacement of the fixated object, the closer object (B) is seen to have a relative rightward displacement, whereas the more distant object (A) has a leftward displacement in relation to the line of sight. This means that an object that is closer than the fixation point will flow in the opposite direction to the observer's direction of movement, whereas a more distant object will flow in the same direction as the observer's motion.

This is not surprising if we look closely at the geometry of the situation. As the line of sight rotates to the right, the relative displacements of near and far objects will be in opposite directions with respect to this reference and hence will appear to move in opposite directions on the retina. It is this differential movement of far versus near objects that is known as *motion parallax* and serves as a potent cue for relative depth. Furthermore, the extent of this relative motion will depend on an object's actual distance from the fixated object, as shown in the bottom right panel of Figure 12.13. The length of the arrows in this figure shows that the greater the distance of an object from the point of fixation, the greater the magnitude of the relative movement. Thus, motion parallax allows our visual brain not only to determine whether an object lies in front of or behind the fixation point but also to generalize how far away the object is (SideNote 12.14).

Expansion and looming

Motion parallax is an example of optic flow

that occurs with translational motion (i.e., when we move sideways in relation to the visual scene). A somewhat different situation arises when we move toward or away from a visual scene. Motion toward a scene generates an expanding pattern of object movements, as shown in Figure 12.14 (Sekuler & Blake, 2002; Warren, Morris, & Kalish, 1988). To make things easy, let us assume that we are fixated on a particular object that is at the centre of this scene. Movement toward this object will not cause any shift in its retinal image because it will be maintained on the fovea. The images of more peripheral objects, on the other hand, will be displaced on the retina as we continue to move through the environment. The actual magnitude of peripheral movement will in turn depend on how far an object is located from the fixation point. Those objects that are located nearby will have only a small amount of peripheral movement, whereas others that are farther away will undergo greater image movement on the retina. The differential expansion or looming that occurs in this case is an example of optic flow and is shown by the motion gradients in Figure 12.14 (SideNote 12.15).

The role of motion in depth perception has long been appreciated by vision scientists. It was the famous American psychologist James Gibson who coined the term *optic flow* and showed how global patterns of retinal motion were generated as observers moved through their visual environments. Gibson argued that motion gradients caused by looming and expansion provide a rich source of depth information (Gibson, 1950). Similarly,

SideNote **12.14**

Parallax is very useful in astronomy, where the apparent displacement of a nearby star in relation to more distant ones can be used to determine how far away it is. In this case, the movement of the Earth is the cause of the parallax, which is usually very small and measured in *seconds arc* (1 arc second is 1/3600th of 1°). This has led to a distance measurement known as the *parsec* (parallax of 1 arc second), which is equal to about 3.3 light years. The closest star to Earth is *Proxima Centauri* at a distance of 1.3 parsecs.

SideNote **12.15**

The expansion pattern shown in Figure 12.14 will only occur if one's eyes are stationary and fixated on the central object. The optic flow pattern changes if the gaze shifts toward another object. A new and more complex set of motion gradients emerges in this case.

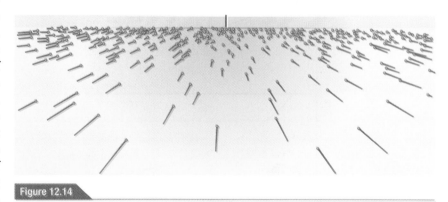

Figure 12.14

Motion gradients in the retinal image produced by objects in the visual field as an observer moves in a straight line toward the flagpole (top centre). The dots represent various elements in the field, and their associated lines represent the magnitude of the motion vector. Objects that lie close to the fixation point (flagpole) show a small degree of image movement, whereas those objects farther away display much larger motion vectors. Adapted from "Perception of Translational Heading from Optical Flow," by W. H. Warren, Jr., M. W. Morris, and M. L. Kalish, 1988, *Journal of Experimental Psychology: Human Perception and Performance, 14,* 646–660.

movement away from a scene produces a contraction of motion gradients. Psychophysical studies have shown that optic flow is not only used in depth perception but also serves as an important cue for the control of balance and heading during locomotion.

Accretion and deletion

Another dynamic source of depth information arises from the appearance (accretion) or disappearance (deletion) of objects behind an edge, such as dancers moving on and offstage behind a partially drawn curtain. According to the rules of occlusion, the curtain is automatically judged to be the closer object. As an occluded object (dancer) moves behind a nearby object (curtain), either more or less of the moving object will become visible, depending on the direction of movement. A similar situation will arise if, instead, the observer is moving while looking at two partially overlapped objects. Thus, **accretion and deletion** are really dynamic versions of occlusion whereby more or less of the distant object becomes visible, depending on the circumstances of the relative movement.

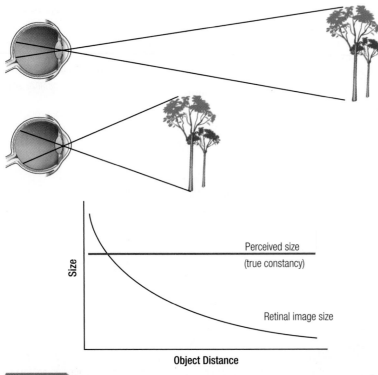

Figure 12.15

Retinal image size depends on object distance, as illustrated in the top diagram. The actual relationship between image size and object distance (black curve in bottom diagram) shows that as the distance increases, there is initially a dramatic reduction in size. However, this rate of image reduction tails off with large distances. The grey line shows that the perceived size of the object will remain unchanged with distance in the case of true constancy.

3. SIZE PERCEPTION AND CONSTANCY

In earlier sections, we saw how retinal image size can serve as a cue for depth perception. We now turn our attention to the other side of this relationship (i.e., how object distance can affect size perception). It is important to note the different terms that we will use—object size, retinal image size, and perceived size. A given object is defined by a particular set of physical dimensions and therefore has constant object size. The size of the retinal image created by that object, however, depends on the distance from which it is viewed. It is with the perceived size of the object, on the other hand, that things become much more interesting.

The size–distance relationship

The actual size of an image created by a given optical device, such as the eyeball, depends entirely on how far the object is situated. This fact is illustrated in Figure 12.15 in terms of the retinal image (top diagram). An object that is located close to the eye casts a larger image on the retina than when it is located farther away. The precise relationship between object distance and image size is shown at the bottom of Figure 12.15 (solid black curve). As object distance increases, there is a dramatic reduction in retinal image size. With increasing distance, the image continues to get smaller, but the rate of change is reduced. Therefore, much of the impact of object distance in terms of retinal image size occurs around the near point of vision (SideNote 12.16).

Size constancy—basic aspects

The question that now arises is "What is the relationship between object distance and the perceived size of that object?" A straightforward answer would reason that perception is closely related to the retinal image. If so, then the relationship between the perceived size of an object and its physical distance should follow the same profile as that in Figure 12.15 for retinal image size.

A simple experiment will illustrate that this is not actually the case. Hold one index finger at arm's length away and the other index finger at half the distance. With both eyes open, shift gaze from one finger to the other. Despite the fact that one finger is situated twice as far away, the perceived size of both fingers is virtually identical. And yet, the closer finger casts a much larger image on the retina. This simple experiment shows that size perception is not evidently related directly to the size of the retinal image. There are many other examples that we can draw from to illustrate this fact, such as looking at a crowd of students in a classroom, gazing at a receding automobile, or even staring at a steak on the dinner table. As we move our head closer to the plate, the steak does not suddenly appear to be much larger, nor do individuals in a classroom appear to be of different sizes based on where they are seated, nor do receding automobiles suddenly appear to be tiny cars.

These examples show that our visual brain perceives objects as they are in terms of their physical reality and not on the basis of their retinal image size. This phenomenon is known as **size constancy**, which in effect means that the mental impression of perceived size conforms to actual object size regardless of the distance at which it is located (Boring, 1964; Ebenholtz, 2001; Ings, 2008; Schwartz, 1999). If we think about it for a moment, this has enormous advantages. Long before we could eat steak from a dinner plate, humans (and our predecessors) had to go out and hunt for food. As predatory creatures, we relied primarily on vision and had to navigate effectively through the environment to locate prey. Without size constancy, visual perception would not conform to objects as they really are but would be at the mercy of the changing retinal image size as we moved closer or farther away from them. A small rodent could in effect suddenly appear to be a large voracious man-eater as we approached it, whereas a man-eating lion would appear to be a harmless pussycat from a distance.

Size constancy—mechanisms

The phenomenon of size constancy implies that perceived size should not theoretically be affected by object distance. This possibility is shown by the grey line in Figure 12.15 for the case of *true constancy*. We will return momentarily to whether or not true constancy exists. However, we first turn to the question of how size constancy arises in the first place.

Psychologists have largely relied on two explanations for the size constancy phenomenon (Ebenholtz, 2001; Howard & Rogers, 1995; Palmer, 2002). The most widely accepted theory is that we come to learn about the true physical size of objects through visual experience and use absolute depth information to

calibrate a mental impression. For example, we know the real size of our index finger. Therefore, in the small experiment we just conducted, a large retinal image does not automatically lead to the perception of a gigantic finger. Instead, we take into account the distance of the two fingers and correlate them with the retinal image size to arrive at a perceived size. Object distance can be obtained from various cues, such as accommodation and vergence. Apparently, our visual brain takes into account the actual object distance obtained through these cues to offset the variable nature of retinal image size to generate a perceived size that accurately reflects the object's true physical nature.

Another explanation for size constancy is based on the relative sizes of all other objects in the environment. As the distance changes, according to this theory, all objects embedded in the scene also change in terms of their retinal image size. Therefore, a particular object retains the same relative size when viewed in relation to its surrounding objects. For example, say we are on a boat approaching a dock. As we get closer to the dock, the people, cars, trees, etc., all retain the same perceived size because their retinal images are changing in tandem. Therefore, the perceived size of any given object in the environment does not grow disproportionately in relation to the others. Our visual brain may also use this cue to create stable size perception and constancy.

If size constancy were absolutely perfect, then the relationship between perceived size and object distance would be given by the grey line in Figure 12.15, as noted before. That is, regardless of the actual object distance, perceived size would remain unaffected. In reality, this is not the case. Although size constancy works relatively well over ordinary distances, it does break down under extreme conditions—for example, if the visual system is unable to infer object distance due to environmental conditions or pictorial interference that leads to distance misjudgment. The latter is especially interesting in terms of size illusions, which will be taken up in the next section. However, the most common cause for size constancy breakdown is when object distance becomes very large. In this case, information about distance is imprecise, and therefore the visual system cannot undertake the computation necessary to create a perceptual impression of the correct object size (SideNote 12.17).

SideNote | **12.16**

An example of how the size–distance relationship becomes inexact at very large distances can be taken from the cosmic domain. One of the brightest stars is Vega, from the Lyra constellation, located about 25 light years away. Several other stars in the same constellation lie at much greater distances, such as Zeta Lyrae at 160 light years. Despite this vast difference, the two stars appear only marginally different when viewed from Earth.

© Science Photo Library/Alamy

SideNote | **12.17**

This phenomenon occurs when looking at objects from a large distance, such as from the viewing deck of a tall building or from an airplane. The people, cars, and other objects do not retain their true size because size constancy breaks down at such large viewing distances.

Emmert's law

An intriguing phenomenon of size constancy occurs with afterimages, which are fleeting impressions of an image that arise after the prolonged viewing of a particular object. For example, staring at a light bulb for 30 seconds will create a dark afterimage in the same shape as the bulb. In the late 1800s, psychologist Emil Emmert discovered that the perceived size of the afterimage depended on the distance at which it was projected. In this example, if the afterimage arises when looking at a sheet of paper held at arm's length, then it will be perceived to be much smaller than when looking at a distant wall (SideNote 12.18). This phenomenon, which has been dubbed **Emmert's law**, occurs because we take into account the distance of the plane on which the afterimage is projected in arriving at a perceived size of the afterimage (Gregory, 2008; Howard & Rogers, 1995; Palmer, 2002). The true sensory nature of the afterimage itself does not change in size because it arises as a purely retinal phenomenon of local neuronal adaptation. However, when projected on a distant surface, we perceive the afterimage to be much larger because only then would the condition of constancy be satisfied—that is, a larger object viewed at a greater distance to produce a retinal image of the same size.

4. ILLUSIONS OF SIZE AND DEPTH

We now delve into a fascinating topic that has captivated people for centuries. The notion that illusions are common sensory experiences has led many philosophers and scientists to disassociate them from real events, and even to ponder the very meaning of reality. Albert Einstein's famous quote that "Reality is merely an illusion, although a very persistent one" captures the essence of this idea. We are often susceptible to illusions of depth that are so compelling as to fool us into believing them to be a depiction of reality. For example, all 2-D pictures that produce depth impressions are nothing but illusions. There is of course no depth at all in a flat picture, and it is only through the interpretation of various pictorial cues that our visual brain re-creates an impression of a third dimension that simply does not exist.

There are many types and examples of depth illusions, and therefore an exhaustive review of them all is beyond the scope of this book (SideNote 12.19). In this section, we

discuss three specific illusions because each reveals something about the underlying mechanisms or assumptions that lead to the illusion. All three reflect the close relationship between depth and size. These illusions arise because our brain is led to believe that a depth parameter has been altered or is assumed to be different, giving rise to the illusion. We begin with an extremely compelling example, which has baffled people for thousands of years.

Misconception of absolute depth— the *moon illusion*

The first known description of this illusion dates back to the 7th-century BCE. We know that Greek philosophers, Aristotle and Ptolemy in particular, later tried to explain this phenomenon (Wade, 1996, 1999). The **moon illusion** is the vivid appearance of a very large moon on the horizon, especially during a full moon, compared to when it is directly overhead (zenith moon). Figure 12.16 (left panel) illustrates the abnormally large appearance of the horizon moon. No one who has observed this occurrence needs to be convinced of its striking nature. For those who have not yet experienced this visual phenomenon, it is well worth the effort to view a full moon as it rises above the horizon and then compare it to the zenith moon several hours later.

The abnormally large size of the horizon moon is simply an illusion, a fact that can be easily verified by taking photographs of the horizon and zenith moons and comparing them. The moon is no different in size at these locations nor is there any kind of an atmospheric magnifying effect, as was once thought. Rather, the effect is entirely due to psychological factors, though there remains some debate as to the exact cause. The most commonly accepted explanation is the *apparent-distance theory*, which is based on the idea that humans generally believe the horizon to be located farther away than the sky overhead (Hershenson, 1989; Ross & Plug, 2002). Some have referred to this intrinsic belief as the *flattened heavens*, whereby the moon appears to take a trajectory that we conceive to be farther away at the horizon than when directly overhead. This perceived path of the moon is shown in the right diagram of Figure 12.16. However, the true path is such that the distance to the moon at its horizon and zenith locations is actually identical, which in turn creates an identical retinal image in both instances.

SideNote | **12.18**

This illusion is quite compelling and well worth trying. Stare at a light source or bright object on a computer monitor. Then stare at a nearby plane (such as a blank part of the computer monitor) and then quickly shift gaze to a more distant plane (such as a wall at the end of the room). The afterimage will appear to be much larger in the latter case.

SideNote | **12.19**

Apart from illusions that arise due to normal misconceptions of size and depth, neurological conditions, such as the so-called *Alice in Wonderland syndrome*, exist in which subjects perceive the world to be substantially smaller than it is. The syndrome has been associated with migraine headaches, epilepsy, and drug use. Some scholars have speculated that Lewis Carroll, the author of *Alice's Adventures in Wonderland*, may have composed his story because he suffered from this condition as a result of his migraines.

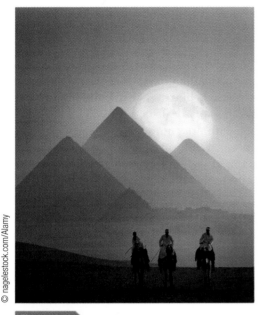

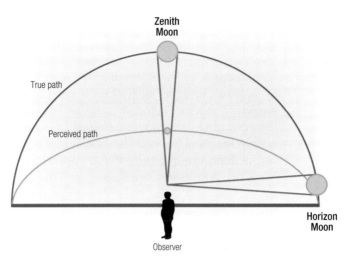

Figure 12.16

The moon illusion occurs when the moon is perceived to be much larger on the horizon (left panel) than overhead. This striking phenomenon is believed to arise from our intrinsic belief that the sky overhead is closer than the horizon. Thus, the perceived path of the moon follows a more flattened arc than the true path, which is equidistant at all points (right diagram). An object casting the same-sized retinal image from all locations will be perceived to be much larger when we believe it is farther away (horizon moon) than when we perceive it to be closer (zenith moon).

The question that arises then is "Why should the moon appear larger simply because we believe the sky to be farther away at the horizon than overhead?" Recall the *size–distance relationship* specifying that retinal images become progressively smaller as the distance increases. The moon, however, casts the same-sized retinal image from everywhere in the sky, and yet we have an intrinsic belief that it is physically farther away on the horizon. Our visual brain therefore interprets the moon to be of a much larger size on the horizon because only in this case is the *size–distance relationship* satisfied—that is, a larger object viewed at a greater distance to produce the same-sized retinal image (SideNote 12.20). Thus, the moon illusion appears to be based on a misconception of absolute distance of the horizon versus the sky overhead.

Misconception of relative depth—the *Ponzo illusion*

We now turn to an illusion that arises due to a misconception of relative distance. Consider the left panel in Figure 12.17 showing a set of railroad tracks projecting off into the distance. Superimposed on this picture are two white lines. Despite the fact that both are identical in length, there is a strong impression that the

lower line is smaller than the upper one. A simpler version of this illusion was first shown by Italian psychologist Mario Ponzo. The *Ponzo illusion* is shown in the right panel of Figure 12.17. Again, the lower line clearly appears to be smaller than the upper one despite the fact that they are identical.

Ponzo suggested that our visual system makes size judgments based on background information contained in the scene. In the

SideNote | **12.20**

The moon illusion is similar in principle to that of Emmert's law. An image that is believed to be located far away is perceived to be larger than when it appears to be closer, though in reality the retinal image does not actually change.

Figure 12.17

The lower horizontal line appears smaller than the one above, even though both are of identical length. This so-called *Ponzo illusion* arises because the two lines are taken to be at different relative distances when compared to the pictorial cue of the converging lines. The upper line is perceived to be larger in order to satisfy the size–distance relationship. Photo on left © Ian Dagnall/Alamy

example in Figure 12.17, the linear perspective effect of the parallel railroad tracks receding into the background provides an important pictorial depth cue. The horizontal line segments are captured within that context to yield an impression of the lower line being closer to us than the upper one. What is especially impressive about this illusion is that apart from the obvious fact that both horizontal lines are exactly the same physical distance away from us, the difference in relative depth impressions of the two is generated by a simple pictorial cue that in turn produces a vivid conscious perception of a difference in their size (Palmer, 2002).

The illusion itself can be explained by the same mechanism as the moon illusion. An object that casts an identical retinal image but that is believed to lie farther away will be perceived to be larger because only then can it satisfy the *size–distance* relationship. The difference with the Ponzo illusion is that it arises due to a perceived difference in the relative depths of two objects, whereas the moon illusion arises due to a perceived difference in its absolute depth of a single object at different locations (SideNote 12.21).

Misperception of relative size— the *Ames room illusion*

The third illusion is explained by a curious misperception of relative size. The Ames room illusion occurs when looking into a specially designed trapezoidal room through a pinhole. The room is unusual in that the left wall is almost twice as long as the right and also almost twice as high (solid outline in left panel of Figure 12.18). However, when looking through the pinhole, the trapezoidal construction of the room is not apparent, and instead it falsely appears as a normal rectangular room (dashed outline in Figure 12.18). This is known as an *Ames room* in honour of American ophthalmologist Adelbert Ames who first constructed it in the mid-1940s. There are various science museums around the world, such as the Exploratorium in San Francisco, which have excellent replicas of this room.

An extremely compelling illusion arises when looking at people in this room through a pinhole, as shown in the left panel of Figure 12.18 (Mather, 2006; Palmer, 2002; Sekuler & Blake, 2002). The individual in the right corner of the room appears to be larger than the two people in the left corner. One explanation is that this illusion occurs due to a breakdown of size constancy. Normally, our visual system factors in depth cues to provide a stable size perception of people in real world situations. In this instance, the observer is not aware that the people on the left are twice as far away and instead assumes they are in line with the person on the right. However, the individuals on the left cast a much smaller retinal image because in reality they are twice as far away. In the absence of this depth information, our visual system misinterprets their size and scales them to the retinal image, as if they really were tiny people standing in the corner of a normal room. Thus, the Ames room illusion in effect represents a breakdown of size constancy because of the peculiar way in which the room is constructed.

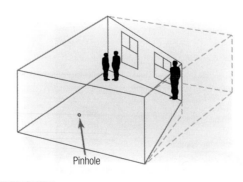

Pinhole

Figure 12.18

The Ames room is trapezoidal—twice as far and high on the left side compared to the right (left panel). However, a false impression of a normal rectangular room occurs when looking at this room through a pinhole. The misperception of true depth in this room leads to a breakdown in size constancy such that people standing on the right side of the room appear to be very large, whereas those standing on the left appear to be very small. The photo on the right provides a nice illustration of this so-called *Ames room illusion*. Photo on right © Mauro Fermariello/Science Photo Library.

METHODOLOGY

The Ames Room

The Ames Room was created by Adelbert Ames Jr. in 1946 (based on plans designed by Hermann von Helmholtz). Its effect depends on two different visual illusions. First, when viewed through a pinhole, the trapezoidal room appears cubic. Second, when viewing people in the room walk from one corner to the other, they appear to grow or shrink, overriding our perception of size constancy. The room is set up so that the left corner is actually twice as far from the pinhole than the right corner, yet some researchers state that our visual system resolves this ambiguity by using past experience (i.e., top-down processing) to "see" the room as a cube. When our eyes try to accommodate the differently distanced corners, we experience an "odd" feeling, yet this is not enough to break the visual illusion.

C. Binocular Depth Perception

We learned earlier that accurate perception of the third dimension can occur under monocular viewing conditions through the use of various pictorial and dynamic cues. This is easily demonstrated by simply covering one eye. The objects in the visual scene still appear to retain their relative depths with respect to each other. However, something happens when we uncover the eye and look at the same scene using binocular vision. Suddenly, there seems to be greater richness in the quality of the depth impression and a more acute sense of the relative depths of various objects (SideNote 12.22).

Our perceptual impression of relative object depths with monocular vision is pretty good. However, depth perception with binocular vision is absolutely outstanding, to the point where we can be up to 10 times better at distinguishing the relative depths of objects with both eyes than with one. What is it about binocular vision that endows us with such outstanding depth discrimination ability? The answer is *stereopsis*. Before we learn more about stereopsis, we must first discuss some of the general advantages of binocular vision.

1. ADVANTAGES OF BINOCULAR VISION

The idea that two eyes are better than one because the second eye can serve as a spare if the first is lost or damaged is unarguable. However, having two eyes also provides some distinct advantages in terms of visual function.

Binocular interaction and summation

The two eyes can have a strong influence upon each other, especially in terms of eyeball position and optical power (Ebenholtz, 2001; Palmer, 2002). Both accommodation and convergence reflexes occur in a binocular manner, though the stimulus can arise from only one of the eyes. For example, changing gaze to a nearby object with just one eye open will alter the accommodative and vergence states of the closed eye as well. Another example of binocular interaction concerns pupil diameter. When the light input to one eye increases, the diameter of the pupils in both eyes is jointly affected. These examples show how the two eyes are linked so that changing stimulus conditions have a reinforcing effect due to binocular interaction.

We discovered in Chapter 10 that neurons in area V1 possess binocular receptive fields. An important property of these neurons is that visual stimulation through both eyes triggers greater activity than stimulation through just one eye. This kind of neural summation of responses is a well-known property of binocularity. One result of such summation at the perceptual level is that visual detection with both eyes is superior to one eye alone. Psychophysical experiments have shown that detection thresholds are indeed lower with binocular compared to monocular viewing. As a result, there are significant advantages under low light viewing conditions because **binocular summation** confers greater visual sensitivity (SideNote 12.23).

Binocular versus monocular visual fields

Another advantage of binocular vision is immediately apparent upon closing and opening

SideNote 12.22

In spite of Ptolemy's view that "Vision with two eyes is better than with one," many philosophers of the time believed that vision was actually superior with one eye. One of the underlying assumptions was that more "visual spirits" could concentrate in one eye under monocular viewing, thereby giving better vision.

SideNote 12.23

Although one would think that sensitivity should double with binocular versus *monocular* viewing, this is not the case because noise is also doubled. After factoring in noise, there should be a 1.41 (square root of 2) increase in sensitivity when using both eyes. This statistical advantage has been verified by psychophysical experiments carried out in the mid-1960s.

one eye. It becomes obvious that we see less of the world through one eye than with both. Simply put, the **visual field** is larger with binocular vision, as illustrated in the left diagram of Figure 12.19 (Howard & Rogers, 1995; Sekuler & Blake, 2002). This figure shows a top-down image of the visual field of a human. The right eye's visual field extends approximately 150°, starting with right edge of the hemifield (three o'clock) toward the left (about ten o'clock). The reverse is true for the visual field of the left eye. However, the two eyes together provide nearly 180° of visual field coverage. A large portion of this field is simultaneously viewed by both eyes (i.e., the binocular field), whereas the extreme edges are only visible to the eye on that side (i.e., monocular field).

A somewhat different situation arises with animals that have laterally placed eyes (i.e., near the sides of the head). The right diagram in Figure 12.19 shows the visual field of a rabbit, one of many animals in this category (Sekuler & Blake, 2002). In this case, the visual field extends behind the animal to cover approximately 315° of visual space. This arrangement provides a significant advantage to the animal because it can detect a predator that is approaching from behind. The drawback, however, is that much less of the visual field is captured by both eyes, and accordingly, there is a small binocular field accompanied by much larger monocular fields. The advantages of binocular vision are therefore less apparent to animals with laterally placed eyes than to those with frontally placed eyes, such as humans.

SideNote | 12.24

It goes without saying that comparing two retinal images is not possible with monocular vision, hence the need to rely on pictorial and other so-called *monocular cues* to generate depth impressions.

SideNote | 12.25

Many different formats for vision have evolved, each optimally suited for the living conditions of that particular species. Although this distinction is not absolute, frontally placed eyes are more useful to predatory animals, whereas laterally placed eyes are more useful to those that are preyed upon, thereby providing a greater survival advantage to both types of animals.

Binocular fusion and stereopsis

The benefit of having frontally placed eyes in the context of binocular vision is especially striking with regard to depth perception. The presence of frontal eyes allows optical capture of the same visual scene through two slightly different viewpoints. It is as if two laterally placed cameras took a picture of the same scene, but from slightly different angles. The two pictures will be similar but not identical. Our visual brain does wonders with this information. First, it combines the two retinal images to produce a unified picture of the visual scene, an outcome that is referred to as **binocular fusion**. In other words, we do not actually perceive the two different views but instead obtain a single, coherent mental picture. This singleness of vision has been referred to as *cyclopean perception*.

The second remarkable aspect of binocular vision is that the visual brain can obtain information on the third dimension by comparing the two views from each eye. Subtle differences in the retinal image of each eye, which we will discuss in detail in the next section, endow us with the capacity to deconstruct the relative depths of different objects in the visual field. This remarkable process, which is referred to generally as **stereopsis**, is entirely responsible for the outstanding depth perception that occurs under binocular viewing conditions (SideNote 12.24) (DeValois & DeValois, 1988; Gibson, 1950; Mather, 2006; Ogle, 1950).

So, why would a rabbit not want to have this benefit? Unfortunately, stereoscopic depth perception does have its costs. As we noted above, only animals with frontally placed eyes have sufficient binocular coverage of the visual field to permit effective stereopsis, which in turn means that such animals are unable to view anything behind them. For those species that are especially vulnerable to predators, such as rabbits, a panoramic view of the world is an important survival advantage. For predatory animals, on the other hand, a greater binocular field provides a better ability to reconcile the relative depths of different objects, a feature that is more important for a hunter (SideNote 12.25).

2. STEREOSCOPIC CUES AND BINOCULAR DISPARITY

How does stereoscopic depth perception arise? There are two elements to this process—the

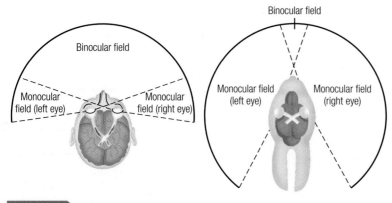

Figure 12.19

Animals with frontally placed eyes, such as humans, have a visual field that covers approximately 180°—much of which enjoys binocular overlap (left diagram). Animals with laterally placed eyes have wider visual coverage (right diagram). However, much of the visual field is viewed monocularly, leaving a small central field with binocular overlap. Adapted from *Perception,* by R. Sekuler and R. Blake, 2002, New York, NY: McGraw-Hill.

availability of stereoscopic cues (i.e., the fundamental pieces of information that arise from binocular viewing of a scene) and the brain's ability to decipher those cues to generate depth perception. This section is devoted to exploring the first topic, whereas the next section will cover the second.

In the 2nd century, astronomer Claudius Ptolemy provided the first written account that the images formed by each eye were slightly different and yet somehow produced a singleness of vision (Wade, 1999). By carefully observing vertical cylinders, Ptolemy noted that each eye sees a slightly different view, and yet we obtain a single visual percept of the cylinders. Then followed nearly 17 centuries of little or no advancement in our understanding of binocular vision. Australian psychologist Nicholas Wade has proposed that the reason for this gap was the lack of development of a theoretical link between two seemingly irreconcilable phenomena—the disparity of the two eyes' optical images and the singleness of vision that was experienced (Wade, 1987, 1996). It was not until the mid-1800s that a British physicist named Charles Wheatstone invented the *stereogram* to show how the disparity of retinal images is responsible for the vivid perception of relative depth. To understand Wheatstone's *stereogram*, we first need to discuss some fundamental issues in binocular visual imaging (Wheatstone, 1838).

Horopters

In the early 1800s, two physiologists showed that when both eyes are fixated on an object at a particular distance, there exists a theoretical circle in space that has a special property—all objects situated on this circle produce optical images at analogous retinal points in the two eyes (Howard & Rogers, 1995; Palmer, 2002). This so-called **Vieth–Müller circle**, named after Gerhard Vieth and Johannes Müller, is illustrated in Figure 12.20. This figure shows a top-down view of a pair of eyes fixating on object F. Consider object A located in the left visual field at a point in space through which the Vieth–Müller circle passes. Light rays from this point will be refracted by both eyes to produce an image on the two retinae, as shown. However, all the light rays can be collapsed into a single ray that projects through the *nodal point* of the eye, which is the standard way of illustrating object–image relationships (see Section B.3 in Chapter 8 for a quick review).

The important point here is that the image of object A is formed at analogous sites in both retinae. The same is true of all other objects located on the Vieth–Müller circle, including the fixation point, F (SideNote 12.26). In general, the set of environmental points that produce an image at analogous retinal sites for a given fixated object is called the **horopter**. The Vieth–Müller circle is a *theoretical horopter* because it is constructed from basic geometric and optical principles. While it is true that all objects on the Vieth–Müller circle project onto analogous points of the retinae, does this mean that all objects on this circle are actually perceived as stimulating analogous retinal points?

To answer this question, psychophysicists have carried out experiments with human subjects who were required to move objects at various peripheral locations back and forth in space until a certain criterion was met, such as aligning them in terms of relative depth. Different procedures and criteria have been used to question whether the perceptual and theoretical horopters are identical. It turns out that they are not. The experimentally determined horopter based on human perception, called the *empirical horopter*, deviates somewhat from the Vieth–Müller circle, for reasons that are not entirely clear. As Figure 12.20 shows, the empirical horopter is flatter (less convex) than the theory would predict. However, the difference between the two is actually quite

SideNote | **12.26**

The Vieth–Müller circle is a theoretical circle that passes through the fixation point and the nodal points of both eyes. Any given pair of analogous points in the retinae, when projected out into space in a straight line through their respective nodal points, will intersect at the Vieth–Müller circle.

Sir Charles Wheatstone (1802–1875)
© Alan King engraving/Alamy

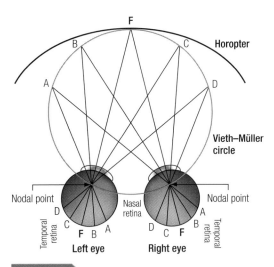

Figure 12.20

A top-down view of a pair of eyes fixated on object F. This, along with all other objects situated on the Vieth–Müller circle, projects to analogous or corresponding points on the retinae. The Vieth–Müller circle is known as the *theoretical horopter*. Psychophysical experiments have shown the *empirical horopter* to be flatter than the Vieth–Müller circle.

SideNote | **12.27**

Given that the horopter describes all the points in space that yield corresponding retinal images for a particular fixation, the question arises as to how the empirical horopter changes for fixation points at different depths. The horopter for a nearby fixation point (e.g., 20 cm) is quite convex. With greater fixation distances, the empirical horopter flattens out and actually becomes slightly concave at optical infinity, as shown below.

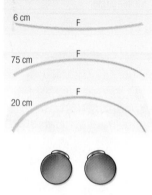

small, and therefore we will refer to the empirical horopter (or just *horopter* for short) as representing the sum of points in space that produce analogous retinal images (SideNote 12.27).

Corresponding retinal images

It is somewhat unconventional for vision scientists to refer to the retinal image points shown in Figure 12.20 as being on *identical* or *analogous* parts of the retina. For example, image point A is formed on the temporal retina of the right eye and on the nasal retina of the left eye. For this reason, the images in this figure are referred to as **corresponding retinal images**, which means they form at optically analogous points of the two eyes (Mather, 2006; Ogle, 1950; Schwartz, 1999). For example, object A's two images are formed at corresponding points, object B's are formed at corresponding points, and so on. Based on our discussion above, we can now assert that all objects located on the horopter produce corresponding retinal images.

The relative locations of the two images in each eye for any given object have significant consequences for stereoscopic depth perception. It is therefore important to come up with a way of quantifying their relative positions in each eye, and a good place to start is with corresponding retinal images. To begin, imagine yourself standing behind the pair of eyes in Figure 12.20 and somehow being able to see where the various retinal images are formed, as if the retinae were translucent screens. Figure 12.21 shows the locations of

the retinal images when viewed from behind. This perspective is advantageous because you can see what the two eyes see as they gaze out into space. Next, we go through a sequential analysis of this viewpoint to set the framework for understanding stereo vision.

The fixation point will be imaged on the fovea, which itself is located at the intersection of the horizontal and vertical axes of the retinae, as shown in Figure 12.21. The images of the other objects will appear as shown. For example, the images of both A and B will be formed in the nasal retina of the left eye but the temporal retinae of the right eye; the opposite arrangement is true for objects C and D. If we wish to compare the relative locations of the same image between the two eyes, then we have to use a certain point in the retina that can serve as a frame of reference. The most obvious reference point would be the fovea because it is located in the centre of the retina. We can therefore specify the position of any given retinal image by measuring its distance (d) from the fovea. This has been done for the two images of object A. Rather than refer to them as *left* and *right* eye images, it is better to label them in terms of whether they are situated in the *nasal* (n) or *temporal* (t) retina. Thus, we first need to determine where a particular image is located.

The position of image A in the right eye, which is situated in the temporal retina, is specified as d_t (read as *d sub t*); the position of image A in the left eye is specified as d_n (read as *d sub n*) because of its location in the nasal retina. Exactly

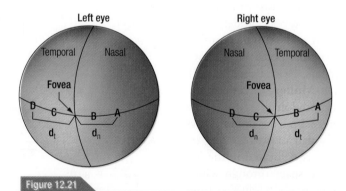

Figure 12.21

A representation of the retinal surface from behind the two eyes shows the relative locations of images of the four peripheral objects shown in Figure 12.20. The locations of the images can be specified by their distance (d) from the fovea and whether they are situated in the nasal (n) or temporal (t) retina. Each of the four pairs of images is formed on corresponding retinal points such that their distance from the fovea is identical in the two eyes—that is, $d_t = d_t$ (as shown for the binocular images A and D). The same is true for images B and C (not shown).

the same notations would apply for image B, though the actual distance values in this case will be smaller because they are located closer to the fovea. The reverse is true for images C and D. The position of image D in the temporal retina of the left eye must be denoted as d_t, whereas the position of image D in the nasal retina of the right eye is denoted as d_n.

Retinal disparity

What is the purpose of going to such lengths to specify the retinal images? Quite simply, it allows us to describe the locations of the images in each eye in exact terms (SideNote 12.28). Since all the images in Figure 12.21 are located at corresponding retinal points, this must mean that their distances from the fovea are identical (i.e., $\mathbf{d_t} = \mathbf{d_n}$). This is a general fact, and thus the same relationship would hold true for the binocular images of any object located on the horopter (Howard & Rogers, 1995; Ogle, 1950). The two important points to take away from this discussion are that any given pair of *corresponding retinal images* is defined by the fact that $\mathbf{d_t} = \mathbf{d_n}$ and that this relationship is true only for those objects that lie on the horopter.

Recall that depth perception from stereoscopic vision is based on differences in the two retinal images that arise due to the lateral displacement of the two eyes. Therefore, we need to come up with a way to compare the binocular images with respect to each other. Our attempt to specify the exact location of the image in each eye is a good start, but we have not yet compared the two images in a quantitative manner. One way to do so is to define a new term, **retinal disparity**, which specifies the difference in the location of the binocular images. We denote *retinal disparity* by the letter D and define it mathematically as follows:

$$\mathbf{D} = \mathbf{d_t} - \mathbf{d_n} \text{ (``d sub t'' minus ``d sub n'')}$$
(SideNote 12.29)

The value of D for corresponding retinal images is zero by virtue of the fact that $\mathbf{d_t} = \mathbf{d_n}$. Thus, all objects on the horopter yield zero disparity because they give rise to corresponding retinal images. However this is not true for objects that lie in front of or behind the horopter, as we will see in the next two sections.

Stereoscopic cues—crossed binocular disparity

We now turn to the situation that arises when objects are not situated on the horopter. Figure 12.22 shows the same situation that was

illustrated in Figure 12.20, but with a major difference—objects A and C are now situated in front of the horopter. Thus, from the perspective of the person whose eyes are illustrated in this figure, these two objects are now located closer than objects on the horopter (such as the fixation point). The other two objects, B and D, have been moved farther back and are also off the horopter. We first analyze what happens to the retinal images when objects are situated closer than the horopter.

The top panel in Figure 12.22 shows ray traces from the two closest objects to the retinal surface. A close look at this figure reveals that the binocular images for each object are no longer situated on corresponding retinal points. This is best seen for object A, where it is clear that the temporal image in the right eye is farther away from the fovea than its counterpart in the nasal retina of the left eye. Thus, we

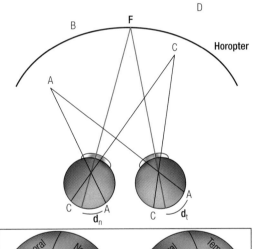

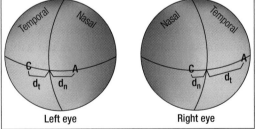

Figure 12.22

Objects located in front of the horopter create binocular images on non-corresponding retinal points such that the temporal image distance is greater than the nasal image distance ($d_t > d_n$), as shown in the top panel for object A. This is known as *crossed disparity*. The retinal surface representation (bottom panel) shows the retinal image distributions in this situation. The farther an object is in front of the horopter, the greater the disparity between the two images. For example, the disparity in the retinal images for object C (i.e., d_t versus d_n) is less because it is closer to the horopter than object A.

SideNote | **12.28**

As discussed in Chapter 9, the convention adopted by vision scientists is to specify object locations in space and their associated retinal images in terms of visual angle. However, the advantage of adopting a strategy for specifying images in terms of their exact retinal position will become clear when we discuss the neural processes that underlie binocular vision.

SideNote | **12.29**

We can easily reverse the variables so that $\mathbf{D = d_n - d_t}$. Indeed, the notion of disparity would remain conceptually unchanged. However, the advantage of retaining the original definition of *D* will become clear when we discuss non-corresponding images.

have a situation where the value of d_t is greater than d_n. In other words, we now have disparity between the two retinal images of the same object. This situation is illustrated in the retinal surface view (bottom panel in Figure 12.22), where the temporal image of object A clearly shows a greater distance from the fovea than the nasal image (i.e., $d_t > d_n$).

An object located in front of the horopter is imaged on non-corresponding retinal points and therefore introduces disparity between the respective binocular images. Given the way we have mathematically defined retinal disparity (D) above, we can now say that objects situated closer than the horopter *have a value of D that is greater than zero*. Objects lying in front of the horopter can therefore be thought of as giving rise to *plus disparity*, though the more conventional term applied in this case is **crossed disparity**.

The actual magnitude of the disparity—that is, how much d_t differs from d_n —depends on how far the object is actually located from the horopter. The greater this distance, the greater the disparity between d_t and d_n. Returning to Figure 12.22, we see that object A is located farther away from the horopter than object C. Although in both cases we have a situation that creates crossed disparity, the magnitude of the disparity (D) is greater for object A than for object C. This is evident upon comparing the projected retinal images (bottom panel of Figure 12.22), where the difference between d_t and d_n is clearly quite large for object A and much less for object C. Therefore, object C also creates a crossed disparity situation but with a lower magnitude—that is, the value of D is less compared to object A. As an object moves closer to the horopter, the retinal disparity decreases until it reaches a value of zero when actually on the horopter itself.

Stereoscopic cues—uncrossed binocular disparity

Next, we examine what happens to retinal images for objects located farther away from the horopter. We again begin with the situation where an observer is fixating on object F, but now two other objects, B and D, are placed behind the horopter, as shown in Figure 12.23. The ray traces to the retinal surface show that a disparity arises, as illustrated for object D in the top panel of this figure. However, there is now one notable difference. The temporal image of object D in the left eye is closer to the fovea

than its counterpart in the nasal retina of the right eye. In other words, d_t is now less than d_n (bottom panel of Figure 12.23).

An object that is located farther away than the horopter therefore creates a disparity situation as well, though now the conditions are reversed (i.e., $d_t < d_n$). Given the way we have mathematically defined retinal disparity (D), we can say that objects situated outside the horopter have a value of D that is less than zero. Objects lying behind the horopter can therefore be thought of as giving rise to *minus disparity*, though the more conventional term in this case is **uncrossed disparity** (SideNote 12.30).

As with crossed disparity, the actual distance an object is located away from the horopter determines the magnitude of the retinal disparity value (D). For example, object B in Figure 12.23 is located closer to the horopter than object D, and although both will produce

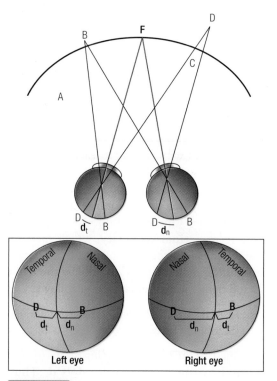

Figure 12.23

Objects located behind the horopter create binocular images on non-corresponding retinal points. However, the temporal image distance is now smaller than the nasal image distance ($d_t < d_n$), as shown in the top panel for object D. This is known as *uncrossed disparity*. The retinal surface representation (bottom panel) shows the retinal image distributions in this situation. The farther an object is from the horopter, the greater the disparity between the two images. For example, the disparity in the retinal images for object B (i.e., d_t versus d_n) is less because it is closer to the horopter than object D.

uncrossed disparity, the actual difference between d_t and d_n is less for the first object. Therefore, object B also produces uncrossed disparity but with a lower magnitude (i.e., the value of D is less).

3. NEURAL PROCESSING OF BINOCULAR DISPARITY

The preceding section outlined three situations that arise in terms of relative object depths—that is, a location on, in front of, or behind the horopter. As we discovered, the relative depth of an object in relation to the horopter has important consequences for the spatial relationship of the retinal images between the two eyes. It is important to understand that this relationship is governed entirely by the physical principles of optics and geometry. In other words, there is absolutely nothing about the eyes or the visual system that creates disparate retinal images. The exact optical situation would arise if objects situated at different depths were photographed by two horizontally separated cameras. A comparison of the images from each camera would reveal similar instances of image disparity and an identical relationship between the nature and magnitude of the disparity and object location in space (SideNote 12.31).

It is a gift of physics that we are provided with a robust optical framework for encoding relative object depth. It is one thing, however, to have disparity cues at our disposal and yet quite another to be able to use that information effectively. Thus, we must possess the biological means to both capture and decode disparity cues in order to yield relative depth perception. In one of the great triumphs of modern neuroscience research, we now know how this is accomplished by our visual brain. This section will be devoted to understanding the fundamental neural mechanisms that govern stereoscopic depth perception.

The role of binocular neurons

We first need to briefly review the visual pathway from the eyes to the brain. Recall from Chapter 10 that the temporal and nasal halves of each eye project to opposite brain hemispheres (Squire et al., 2008). For example, the temporal half of the right eye's retina and the nasal half of the left eye's retina both project to the right cerebral hemisphere; the opposite is true for the left hemisphere. As Figure 12.24 shows, the implication of this anatomical setup

is that an object in the left visual field (e.g., A) is imaged on the eyes' retinae in such a way that it triggers neural activity in the right visual cortex, starting in area V1. Similarly, objects in the right visual field (e.g., D) trigger neural activity in the left visual cortex.

The anatomical layout of the visual brain is important because it is only at area V1 that we first encounter binocular neurons (i.e., neurons activated by the simultaneous visual stimulation of both eyes). Without binocular integration, it would not be possible to compare light activation of the two eyes at the neuronal level. This is an important requirement because the retinal image distribution changes between the two eyes depending on the relative depth of the object. We therefore need a way to capture retinal disparity information, which at the neuronal level would require binocular activation in the first place.

Let us examine this concept further by way of an example. The right diagram in Figure 12.24 follows the activation sequence for object A, starting with retinal stimulation of both eyes and leading to neural activity in area V1 of the right hemisphere. The bottom portion of this figure shows the retinal views of both eyes,

SideNote | **12.31**

There are many situations where stereoscopic imaging is undertaken for scientific purposes (e.g., studying the 3-D structure of objects, satellite imagery, etc.) and entertainment (e.g., 3-D movies). The way in which these images are captured and processed are discussed in Section C.4, where you will see a stunning stereoscopic image taken from a satellite.

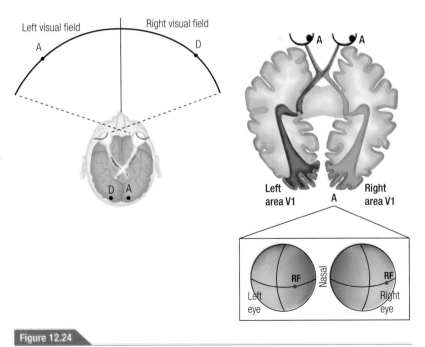

Figure 12.24

The layout of the visual system is such that all objects in the left visual field (i.e., to the left of the fixation point) trigger neural activity in the right visual brain and vice versa for objects in the right visual field (left diagram). Binocular neurons, which first arise in area V1, are stimulated by light. For example, object A stimulates binocular neurons in area V1 (right diagram), which in turn are driven by ganglion cells situated in the exact locations of the nasal and temporal retinae of the two eyes where the optical image is formed. The receptive fields (RF) of the ganglion cells are shown in the retinal surface representation (bottom right panel).

SideNote 12.32

This is not as surprising as it seems. The ganglion cell fibres that pass through the optic nerve of each eye must be connected to a pair of LGN neurons that in turn converge upon a particular neuron in area V1. If we were to record electrical activity from this binocular neuron, we would expect it to be stimulated only when light falls on the receptive field of the ganglion cell in each eye.

similar to those in previous figures. A particular binocular neuron in area V1 can be thought of as being driven by retinal ganglion cells from both the right and the left retinae whose receptive fields are located at the positions shown by the shaded circles in the diagram. Therefore, the ganglion cells of the two retinae, when stimulated by the image of object A, will in turn trigger neural activity in a particular binocular neuron located in area V1.

Disparity selectivity in the visual cortex

The example in Figure 12.24 shows a situation of zero disparity because the object is located on the horopter. Thus, in order for a binocular neuron in area V1 to be stimulated by object A, the two ganglion cells have to be located at corresponding retinal points because only then can they be stimulated by the optical image that is formed in each eye for this object.

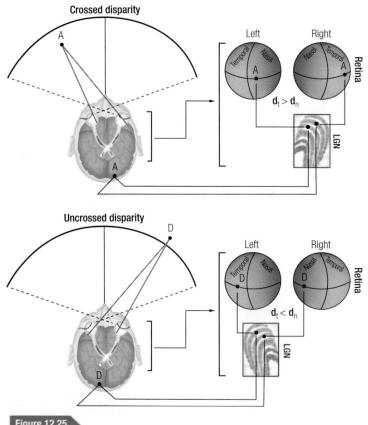

Figure 12.25

An object situated closer than the horopter (A) creates crossed retinal disparity ($d_t > d_n$), whereas an object located farther than the horopter (D) creates uncrossed disparity ($d_t < d_n$), as shown by the top and bottom diagrams, respectively. Retinal ganglion cells whose receptive fields are spatially offset to coincide with such optical disparity feed into the LGN and then converge upon binocular neurons in area V1. The disparity condition therefore becomes encoded at the neuron level in area V1, leading to the emergence of a new property—*disparity selectivity*. The activation of either circuit, and the binocular neurons linked to them, is ultimately responsible for our perception of near or far *relative depth* perception.

What implication does this have for depth perception? For starters, let us look at this situation from the perspective of the visual system. A neural circuit is somehow created whereby two ganglion cells at corresponding retinal points feed into a particular binocular neuron in area V1 (SideNote 12.32). When this neuron becomes activated, it will send information to higher parts of the visual brain, which will decode the incoming firing as having originated from an object on the horopter (i.e., a situation of zero disparity). Other disparity conditions will not activate this circuit because their optical images will not coincide with the receptive fields of the two ganglion cells. Therefore, stimulating this particular circuit will allow our brain to interpret the physical situation as it exists—that of a zero disparity object at a precise location in the left visual field. This will cause us to perceive the object at the same relative depth as others on the horopter, including the fixation point.

What we have just learned is that a simple circuit created by feeding the output of two ganglion cells into a binocular cortical neuron forms the fundamental basis by which we ultimately perceive relative depth. However, we have only covered one depth condition (i.e., no relative depth or zero disparity). Are there binocular neurons that encode crossed and uncrossed disparity conditions as well? It is safe to assume that such neurons must theoretically exist because we not only perceive these depth conditions, but we are actually very good at judging whether an object is in front of or behind the horopter. The scientific confirmation came about through a series of elegant electrophysiological experiments that started in the 1960s and showed that different binocular neurons in area V1 actually encode all three categories of retinal disparity—zero, crossed, and uncrossed (Barlow, Blakemore, & Pettigrew, 1967; Poggio & Fisher, 1977). Therefore, we can now add **disparity selectivity** as another property that emerges in area V1 (SideNote 12.33).

Crossed disparity selectivity occurs in binocular neurons when the receptive fields of the ganglion cells are located at non-corresponding retinal points to coincide with the optical condition of crossed (plus) disparity (i.e., $d_t > d_n$). This means that there must actually be a slight spatial offset in the receptive fields of the two ganglion cells that feed into this circuit with respect to each other. Figure 12.25 illustrates how an object located in front of the horopter (A) can stimulate the two ganglion cells. A particular binocular neuron in area V1 is fed by these two ganglion cells (through the LGN), and therefore when it fires, our brain will interpret its activity as having been caused by an object located in front of the horopter. Although optical disparity arises strictly because our eyes are laterally displaced, it is the neural convergence of the resulting disparate stimulation of the two retinae upon individual binocular neurons in the visual cortex that is responsible for stereoscopic depth perception (Hubel & Wiesel, 1979; Parker & Cumming, 2001; Poggio, 1995).

If crossed disparity-selective neurons are responsible for generating near depth perception with stereoscopic vision, then what kind of circuitry is responsible for perceiving objects located farther than the horopter? The bottom diagram in Figure 12.25 shows how an *uncrossed* disparity-selective neuron is constructed. As before, ganglion cells from non-corresponding retinal points feed into the LGN and then converge upon binocular neurons in area V1. The difference in this case is that the receptive fields of the ganglion cells are spatially offset according to the rules of uncrossed disparity (i.e., $d_t < d_n$) and therefore optimized for objects situated farther than the horopter (SideNote 12.34). Our visual brain generates a perception of far relative depth when binocular neurons linked to circuits such as this are activated.

Panum's fusional area

Several types of disparity-selective neurons have now been discovered in the visual cortex of mammals. The left panel in Figure 12.26 shows the three major types discussed above (LeVay & Voigt, 1988; Poggio, 1995). Binocular neurons in area V1 are generally tuned to a particular disparity value (**optimal disparity**), whether it is *zero* or a *crossed* or *uncrossed* value. Neurons that are driven by uncrossed disparity are sometimes referred to as "far" tuned, whereas those that are driven by crossed disparity are termed "near" tuned, in recognition of their respective roles in encoding object depth relative to the horopter. A given binocular neuron will only be triggered when its disparity preference is matched by the optical disparity in the retinal image. Furthermore, maximal firing will occur when the magnitude of that retinal

SideNote | **12.33**

The optical images in each eye must be independently controlled in a very careful manner in order to see whether a binocular neuron is selective for retinal disparity. The original experiments that showed disparity selectivity in area V1 were carried out in cats by Horace Barlow, Colin Blakemore, and Jack Pettigrew at the University of California, Berkeley. Disparity selectivity was later verified in monkeys by Gian Poggio at Johns Hopkins Medical School in the 1970s.

SideNote | **12.34**

The retinal disparity illustrated in these situations between the two ganglion cells' receptive fields is one of *horizontal disparity*. This is necessary because the slight spatial misalignment between the two optical images is also one of horizontal disparity, due to the horizontal separation of our eyes.

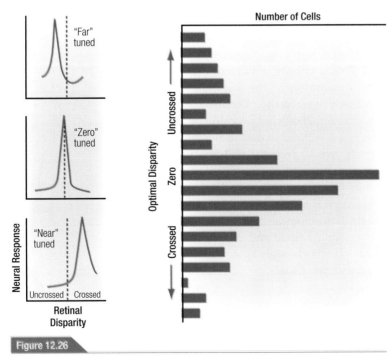

Figure 12.26

Binocular neurons can be tuned to zero disparity or a crossed or uncrossed disparity value (left panel). The optimal disparity is the value at which peak firing occurs. The majority of binocular neurons are tuned around zero disparity, with progressively fewer neurons encoding higher values of crossed or uncrossed retinal disparity (right panel). Adapted from "Mechanisms of Stereopsis in Monkey Visual Cortex," by G. F. Poggio, 1995, *Cerebral Cortex, 3,* 193–204; "Ocular Dominance and Disparity Coding in Cat Visual Cortex," by S. LeVay and T. Voigt, 1988, *Visual Neuroscience, 1,* 395–414.

disparity coincides with the optimal disparity at which the neuron is tuned.

The right panel in Figure 12.26 shows the range of optimal disparities found in the visual cortex. The majority of neurons are tuned around zero disparity, with progressively fewer neurons encoding higher values of either crossed or uncrossed disparity. As this figure suggests, the range of disparity values encoded by the visual system is finite. This means that there are simply no neurons available in the visual cortex that are binocularly driven beyond a certain disparity value (SideNote 12.35).

This has certain consequences for depth perception. Imagine an object situated so far in front of the horopter that the magnitude of retinal disparity is outside the range covered by neurons of the visual system. The resulting failure to stimulate any binocular neurons means that the retinal image in each eye will simply not be integrated at the neuronal level. Instead, each of the images will be processed independently, yielding two separate visual percepts of the same object, akin to double vision or **diplopia**. In a similar manner, any object that lies too far beyond the horopter will fail to stimulate any binocular neurons and will therefore also yield two separate images (SideNote 12.36).

As shown in Figure 12.27, only a limited depth range both in front of and behind the horopter exists in which objects are perceived as single or fused. This is known as **Panum's fusional area**, in recognition of the Danish physiologist who first described the phenomenon (Ogle, 1950; Palmer, 2002). Single vision within this depth range is possible due to the fact that an object's retinal disparity will be within the range encompassed by the visual system and will therefore successfully stimulate binocular neurons to yield stereoscopic depth perception. It is this neurological reality that is responsible for creating a fused and unified awareness of visual objects through binocular stimulation, or *cyclopean perception*.

The problem of midline stereopsis

An interesting situation arises when an object is located off the horopter and between the lines of sight of the two eyes, as illustrated in Figure 12.28. With the eyes fixated on point F, the image of object A is formed on the temporal side of each retina. As we know from the anatomical layout of the brain, this situation is problematic for the visual system because the images now project separately to the two

cerebral hemispheres, making direct convergence upon binocular neurons difficult (see top right box in Figure 12.28).

It turns out, however, that binocular neurons that are activated under such conditions do exist. The integration of visual information between opposite hemispheres occurs through the *corpus callosum*—a large band of nerve fibres that transmits information from one hemisphere to the other and that serves to integrate sensory information across the midline (see bottom right box in Figure 12.28) (Squire et al., 2008). As a result, normal stereoscopic depth perception occurs for objects located along the midline, a phenomenon that is referred to as **midline stereopsis**.

Stereo-blindness

Stereoscopic depth perception is easily lost by simply closing one eye. We know from earlier sections of this chapter that we are still able to perceive the relative depths of objects in our visual environment through the use of monocular cues. However, the fine ability to discriminate depth due to stereopsis is not possible with monocular vision. Closing an eye is a voluntary act, and therefore stereopsis can be quickly restored by reopening the eye. This is not the case for individuals who are blind in one

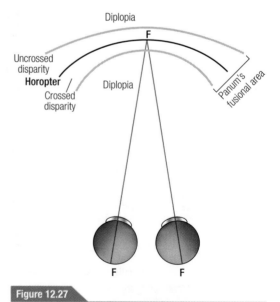

Figure 12.27

The finite range of disparities encoded by binocular neurons means that only a limited range of relative depths can be effectively captured by the visual system. Panum's fusional area defines the depth range in front of and behind the horopter within which an object is visually fused and capable of generating stereoscopic depth perception. Objects outside this area are diplopic.

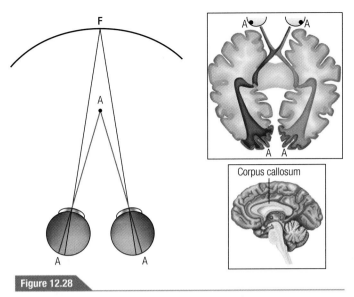

Objects situated along the midline produce retinal images that project to both cerebral hemispheres. The two retinal images of object A therefore fail to directly converge on binocular neurons in the visual cortex (top right box). Such objects are nevertheless fused and yield stereoscopic depth perception due to the integration of visual signals by way of the corpus callosum (bottom right box).

eye and therefore suffer from a permanent loss of stereoscopic depth perception, or **stereo-blindness**. A similar situation arises in individuals whose binocular vision was disrupted during childhood—for example, due to a cataract in one eye. In such cases, the neural circuits mediating disparity selectivity do not form. Another condition that leads to stereo-blindness is *strabismus*—a visual disorder where the eyes are misaligned and point in different directions. This results in a failure to fuse the two retinal images, which if not corrected in early childhood, leads to a permanent failure to produce the binocular circuits that mediate stereoscopic depth perception (SideNote 12.37).

4. BINOCULAR CORRESPONDENCE

The act of combining the two retinal images into a fused visual percept has perplexed scientists and philosophers for centuries. It was not until the invention of the **stereoscope** by Sir Charles Wheatstone in the 19th century that binocular disparity became firmly established as the basis for stereoscopic depth perception (Wheatstone, 1838). At the time, this development was widely hailed by scientists as well as the general public. People became fascinated by the vivid depth that was seen in essentially flat drawings or photographs by way of a simple device that helped to optically combine a pair

of images. The simplicity of the device combined with its entertainment value generated wide public sensation, similar to modern-day toys (such as the View-Master) and 3-D movies (SideNote 12.38).

Stereographic images, or **stereograms**, have provided significant insight into binocular vision and how visual information from each eye is combined to produce depth perception. An excellent example of the scientific use of stereograms concerns the so-called *correspondence problem*, which we will discuss shortly. In order to better understand how stereograms have advanced our understanding of binocular vision, we must first discuss how they produce such compelling depth perception in the first place.

Stereograms

The original Wheatstone stereoscope was an elegantly simple device, as shown in the left diagram of Figure 12.29. A pair of mirrors situated in the middle of the device reflect light from two separate photographs that are placed on either side. As the schematic diagram shows, the optical arrangement of the device is such that each eye obtains a separate and independent view of the picture on that side. This forms a separate image on each retina—the left picture in the left eye, the right picture in the right eye.

It is sometimes helpful for artists to close one eye to yield a flatter perception of a scene in order to capture it more effectively. It has been suggested that Rembrandt may have been stereo-blind because some of his self-portraits reveal an individual with strabismic characteristics.

There have been many variations of stereoscopic devices since Wheatstone introduced the original, and all of them have been based on the principle of displaying a separate image to each eye. The slight offset in the components of each image creates retinal disparity and thus vivid depth perception. One example is the View-Master, which has been popular since its introduction in 1939.

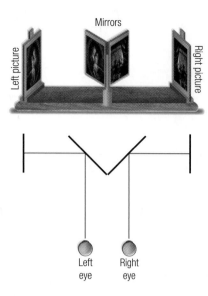

Figure 12.29

The Wheatstone stereoscope (left) uses a pair of mirrors to project two separate images on each eye, as shown by the schematic diagram below. The stereoscopic photographs above are of the smaller temple at Philae, Egypt and were taken in 1859 by Francis Frith. The small displacement of the various pictorial components in these images produces retinal disparity when viewed through a stereoscope, which in turn yields a striking impression of relative depth. Photo: SSPL via Getty Images.

SideNote | **12.39**

The midpoint of each picture in Figure 12.29 contains an "x." The distance from this centre point to the temple or trees is different in the two images. The actual magnitude of an image component's displacement may be fairly small and yet still produce depth in a stereoscope.

SideNote | **12.40**

British psychologist John Frisby referred to free fusion as "the poor man's stereo-scope" to reflect the fact that any individual can use this technique to fuse a pair of images that have been appropriately designed to produce retinal disparity of its contents.

Wheatstone's stereoscope impacted vision science because of what it revealed about binocular correspondence and stereoscopic depth perception. Wheatstone showed that a small deviation in a particular image component's location between the two pictures would cause it to stand out in front of or behind the other parts of that picture. In other words, if the various contents were not at identical locations in the two pictures, then this in turn produced disparity in their retinal images that were fused by the visual system to yield relative depth perception. An example of a stereographic picture can be found in the right panel of Figure 12.29. Viewing these two pictures through the Wheatstone stereoscope produces vivid depth perception—the rocky landscape in the background, the temple somewhere in the middle, and the palm trees in the foreground. Although there is no real depth in either picture, the small deviations in the contents of each image produce a disparity in the two retinal images because each picture is independently projected to each eye (SideNote 12.39).

To better understand how depth perception arises in stereograms, we need to engage in further analysis of the pictorial information itself and its consequences on the retinal image. An alternative approach to the Wheatstone stereoscope for seeing depth is **free fusion**, wilfully crossing (or uncrossing) the eyes (see left diagram in Figure 12.30). If two pictures are placed side by side, crossing the eyes sufficiently will produce an overlapped and fused image. Many people have

difficulty voluntarily crossing their eyes, and therefore it often helps to place a small object, such as a pencil, between the pictures and then gradually move the object toward the eyes. Although both eyes should follow the movement of the object, it is important to pay attention to what is happening to the images in the background. As the object moves closer to the eyes, there will come a point at which the two separate pictures will fuse and the eyes will lock onto it. The object can now be removed, and the splendor of depth perception from free fusion becomes immediately apparent (SideNote 12.40). Try this exercise with the images in Figure 12.29.

How is depth generated by crossing the eyes to fuse a pair of pictures? The simple answer is that disparity in the pictorial elements of the two images creates retinal disparity in the same way as the Wheatstone stereoscope. However, this explanation by itself is not enough, and therefore we need to go through the process in detail to fully understand it. Let us consider two items in the temple images as part of our analysis—the hillside in the left half of the background and the rubble in the right foreground. These two components are represented by icons A and B, respectively, in the schematic diagram of Figure 12.30. Crossing the eyes (convergence) rotates the right eyeball toward the left picture while the left eyeball rotates toward the right picture. At some point, there is sufficient convergence such that the midpoint of each picture, represented by the "x," is imaged on the fovea. The two pictures are now fused because they each optically

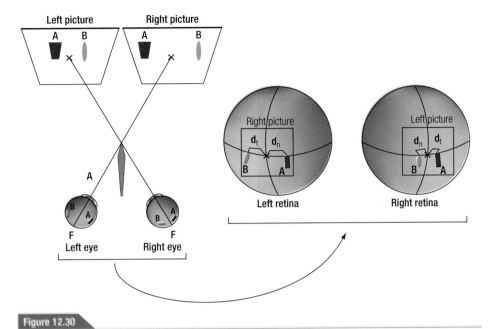

Figure 12.30

Free fusion of stereographic images (a stereogram) can be produced by crossing the eyes, often with the aid of a pencil or similar object (left diagram). Icons A and B refer to the hillside and rubble from the stereogram in Figure 12.29. The lateral displacement of these two components in the two pictures in turn produces disparity in their retinal images when fused. The exact nature of this disparity can be seen in the retinal projections (right diagram). The rubble's image produces crossed disparity, whereas the hillside's image produces uncrossed disparity, resulting in their respective depth impressions.

project onto the eyes in a symmetric manner around the fovea.

Still, this does not explain the exact nature of the retinal disparity that is created by free fusing the two pictures. To understand this, we must first appreciate that there is a disparity in the original pictures to begin with in terms of where the two objects are located. For example, icon A (the hillside) is located slightly closer to the midpoint in the *left* picture, as is icon B (the rubble). Free fusing these two pictures produces a spatial offset in their retinal image locations, as shown in the schematic diagram of each eye. For example, icon A is imaged closer to the fovea in the right eye than the left, and the opposite is true for icon B. A closer inspection of the nature of this disparity is more revealing, as shown by the projected images on the retinae (right diagram in Figure 12.30). The disparity in the retinal images can now be specified exactly— for icon A we have an uncrossed disparity situation ($d_t < d_n$), whereas for icon B we have a crossed disparity situation ($d_t > d_n$). As a result, the hillside should appear in the distance, and the rubble should stand out in front, which is exactly the impression that arises from free fusing the stereogram (SideNote 12.41).

The disparities produced in a stereogram are simply a trick of geometry. The small displacements in the actual pictorial content are transferred to the retinal image upon fusing the stereogram, either freely or through an optical device such as a stereoscope. Even though there is no real depth in the pictures, a vivid 3-D impression appears by taking advantage of our visual system's ability to transform the optical disparity in retinal images into a perception of relative depth (Palmer, 2002). This artificial way of re-creating the third dimension has been of great commercial value, from the sale of stereographic images to its importance in many fields of science (e.g., medical imaging, visualizing the three-dimensional structure of crystals and other objects). Satellite imaging of the Earth has also taken advantage of stereographic technology because of the detail with which geographic undulations are revealed. An excellent example is found in Figure 12.31 on page 432, which shows a stereoscopic satellite image taken by NASA.

The correspondence problem

Binocular matching of the two retinal images in area V1 creates an interesting problem for the visual system. We learned in Chapter 8 that visual objects in the real world can be considered,

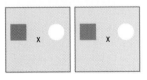

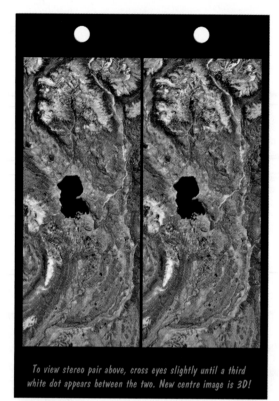

To view stereo pair above, cross eyes slightly until a third white dot appears between the two. New centre image is 3D!

Figure 12.31

A stereogram of Lake Palanskoye, which is located in the northern Kamchatka peninsula of Russia. The lake was formed when a large landslide triggered by an earthquake disrupted the drainage pattern and formed a natural dam. This stereoscopic image pair was generated from images captured by the Landsat 7 satellite. Merging the images through free fusion generates a stunning three-dimensional view of this region. © NASA/JPL/NIMA http://visibleearth.nasa.gov

in optical terms, to be made up of a mosaic of point light sources. In Chapter 9 we learned that the visual system samples the retinal image through a mosaic of photoreceptors that converge upon a set of ganglion cells whose output is transmitted to the visual cortex. The problem that arises for the visual system is matching one set of optical point sources to the other. In biological terms, this requires matching the output of a set of ganglion cells from one eye with the output from the other. If an exact point-to-point match between the two retinal outputs is not attained, then the visual system will fail to create a coherent and correct depth representation of the object being viewed (Howard & Rogers, 1995; Ogle, 1950).

This dilemma is illustrated in Figure 12.32. The eyes in the left image of this diagram are gazing at a dog sitting in a field. The retinal image of the dog in each eye is shown on the right-hand side of the figure. The two ganglion cells in each eye, shown by the pair of black and white dots, occupy corresponding retinal points. There are three different possibilities by which the "black" ganglion cell can be wired to a binocular neuron in area V1 (shown in the bottom right box). One is that it can be coupled with its counterpart from the other eye, in which case the binocular neuron receiving this feed will be selective for zero disparity. Alternately, the "black" ganglion cell may be coupled with the "white" ganglion cell from the other eye. In one case, the

INVESTIGATION

How Does Binocular Vision Improve Depth Perception?

In order to better understand how binocular vision aids depth perception, here are a few activities to try:

1. Hold a pencil (or pen) in each hand and stretch your arms out in front of you with the tip of the pencils facing each other. Close one eye, and try to move the pencils toward each other until they touch. Next, try with both eyes open.

2. Place a coin on a flat surface such as a desk and crouch so that you are at eye level with the desk. Close one eye and try to pick up the coin. Repeat with both eyes open.

3. Make your own stereogram at http://graphicssoft.about.com/library/uc/oransen/uc_stereo.htm. Notice that the photographic film is analogous to what is projected onto each of your retinas. The slight differences are what give the image a three-dimensional quality.

To view some pre-existing stereograms, please visit http://www.brianharte.co.uk/blog/archives/tag/stereogram.

binocular neuron in area V1 will be selective for crossed disparity, and in the other, it will be selective for uncrossed disparity.

So, which of these three wiring possibilities is actually in place? In fact, the answer is all three (Julesz, 1971; Palmer, 2002). This is precisely what we learned earlier in this chapter—that there are three broad categories of disparity selectivity based on how ganglion cells from the two retinae feed (through the LGN) into a particular binocular neuron in area V1. The problem is that only one of the neural circuits shown in Figure 12.32 will provide the correct disparity value and therefore correspond to the true depth of that part of the object. The other pairings will produce false matches, and therefore a misperception of depth relative to the other components of the object. A correct point-to-point binocular correspondence must be made, which is a difficult task because, at this early level, the visual system does not know what part of the object a given point belongs to until it is reconstructed by the brain. From the retina's point of view, the image is nothing but a mosaic of point light sources.

One possible solution to this so-called **correspondence problem** is to first extract the structure of the object or its internal components and then undertake the binocular matching process to derive disparity (Julesz, 1971). This would mean that the visual system in this example would first delineate parts of the dog's face at some level of the visual cortex and then match those parts between the two retinal images to obtain disparity information. According to this explanation, form vision (or at least some rudimentary aspect of it) must first occur in order to derive correct stereo depth information. But the problem with this is that the earliest neurons that show disparity selectivity are those in area V1, a level that is too early for complex object representation. A major advance in our understanding of binocular correspondence came from a brilliant demonstration by Hungarian-born engineer and vision scientist Béla Julesz.

The breakthrough occurred with the use of **random-dot stereograms**, which are created by randomly assigning either a black or a white spot to any location in the stimulus (Julesz, 1971; Mather, 2006; Palmer, 2002; Sekuler & Blake, 2002). A stereogram is created by using identical pairs of the same image, but with a

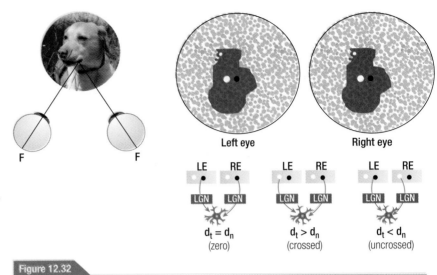

Left eye   Right eye

LE RE	LE RE	LE RE
LGN LGN	LGN LGN	LGN LGN
$d_t = d_n$	$d_t > d_n$	$d_t < d_n$
(zero)	(crossed)	(uncrossed)

Figure 12.32

The correspondence problem arises from a matching uncertainty between image points in the two retina. The retinal representation of an object (right panel) illustrates how a particular image point can be matched to its counterpart in the other eye or mismatched to another point. Both the black and the white dots represent ganglion cells at corresponding retinal points. Different wiring patterns between these ganglion cells to a binocular neuron in area V1 can lead to zero, crossed, or uncrossed disparity selectivity (bottom right box). The challenge for the visual system is to ensure that a particular object point stimulates the correct circuit so that its true depth, relative to other parts of the object, can be captured correctly.

twist. Julesz showed that if an internal patch in one member of the random-dot stimulus is slightly displaced in the other, then fusing the two images creates a vivid depth impression of the displaced segment. This remarkable phenomenon can be seen upon free fusing the example in Figure 12.33 on page 434. A rectangular patch on the right is seen to float above a background pattern of random dots, whereas another rectangular patch on the left appears to be recessed into the pattern. Both of these patches create an impression of relative depth because of their spatial arrangement within the two members of the random-dot pair, producing crossed and uncrossed disparities, respectively (SideNote 12.42 on page 434).

By using these and other similar stimuli, Julesz showed that the visual system can extract disparity information by undertaking a point-by-point match between the two retinal images (Julesz, 1971). Because random-dot stereograms contain no shape information, it is clear that the visual system does not need to extract structural information about the object before deriving its disparity through binocular matching. For example, the two rectangular segments in Figure 12.33 are not visible in either pattern but emerge only after binocular fusion. Interestingly, this demonstration shows the

Béla Julesz (1928–2003)
Photo by Nick Romanenko, Rutgers
Photo Services.

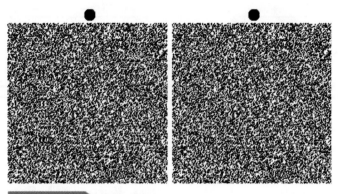

Figure 12.33

A random-dot stereogram is constructed by randomly assigning black or white dots across the image. Both halves of the stereogram are identical except that two internal rectangular patches of dots are slightly displaced in one of these images. In one case, the displaced dots produce crossed disparity and uncrossed disparity in the other when the two halves are binocularly fused. Free fusing this stereogram produces an impression of one rectangular patch floating out over the background while the other appears recessed.

SideNote | 12.42

For those who are unable to free fuse Figure 12.33, one of the rectangular sets of dots is shown in shaded form below. This set of dots creates crossed disparity when the stereogram is fused by crossing the eyes and will therefore appear to float out above the background.

opposite—that it is possible to extract the disparities between the mosaic of dots that make up an object before combining them to generate its structure. The question that remains unanswered is how the visual system is capable of this remarkable feat.

Binocular rivalry

The experiments with random-dot stereograms show that the visual system is capable of solving the correspondence problem in the absence of shape information. However, this result does not remove the possibility that shape analysis is entirely absent, only that it is not mandatory. It is possible that some kind of elementary shape processing, such as contour analysis, may actually help in the correspondence process. The fact that neurons in area V1 are selective for stimulus orientation suggests that at least this particular parameter may play a role.

Experiments on **binocular rivalry**—a phenomenon that arises when the two eyes are presented with different images—revealed the importance of the role of orientation in binocular correspondence (Blake, 2001; Ooi & He, 1999). The top panel in Figure 12.34 shows a stereogram in which one part is made up of vertical bars, whereas the other is filled with horizontal bars. Binocular fusion of this stereogram (e.g., free fusing by crossing the eyes) presents the visual system with a problem, which is illustrated in the bottom panel of this figure. The right and left eyes, which view each component of the stereogram independently

after binocular fusion, are presented with conflicting orientations at corresponding retinal points. Binocular neurons in area V1 would have difficulty processing this information because they are also orientation selective. For example, an area V1 neuron that is selective for vertical orientation would be stimulated by one eye but inhibited by the other because the corresponding parts of its retina are feeding horizontal bar information (Palmer, 2002; Tong, Meng, & Blake, 2006).

The result of this binocular mismatch is that at any given time, only one orientation will be perceived, and only briefly, before the other orientation takes over. It is as if one eye were suppressing the other, and for this reason, binocular rivalry has also been referred to as *binocular suppression*. For large stimuli such as the one in Figure 12.34, the pattern breaks up so that some parts are briefly visible as vertical bars, whereas others are horizontal. The rivalry between the two stimuli creates an oscillation in visual perception between the two orientations. At no time are the two orientations perceived simultaneously.

Binocular rivalry has fascinated scientists because visual awareness fluctuates, even though the stimulus is unchanged, thereby

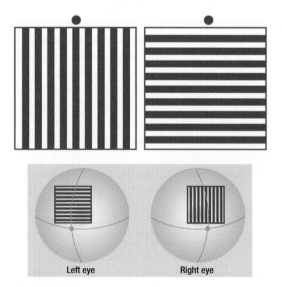

Figure 12.34

Binocular rivalry for simple geometric figures can be demonstrated by fusing this stereogram composed of vertical and horizontal bars. The resulting percept is a patchwork of the two whereby only one orientation is briefly visible before the other one appears. The visual system is confronted with two alternate orientations at corresponding retinal locations after fusing this stereogram (bottom panel), which leads to a perceptual oscillation between the two.

providing a tool for psychophysical and physiological explorations of perception (Crick & Koch, 1998; Ooi & He, 1999). Current explanations of binocular rivalry have benefited from physiological studies in the visual cortex of awake, behaving monkeys (Logothetis, 1998; Logothetis & Schall, 1989; Pettigrew, 2001). It was long believed that binocular rivalry occurs due to competition between monocular neurons tuned to different stimulus features (e.g., orientation), with only one set dominating at any given time while suppressing the other. However, it has been shown that the visual neurons that correlate with perception occur largely at later stages of the visual system, such as the temporal lobe, whereas neurons in early areas, such as area V1, are less susceptible to perception-related changes in activity.

These findings suggest that rivalry occurs due to a competition between alternative perceptual interpretations at a much higher level of analysis than simply the competition between monocular visual neurons at lower cortical areas. An example of high-level perceptual rivalry is shown in Figure 12.35. Binocular fusion of the two components of this stereogram—an image of a building (Jefferson Memorial in Washington, DC) and an image of a woman's face—produces a perceptual oscillation between the two. At times the building is visible in its entirety, and at others, only the woman's face stands out. This example shows that the perception of complex visual structures is also unstable when we are confronted with two alternate possibilities. Rather than merge the two into a composite percept, the competition between the two causes the visual system to select only one of the images, which is then perceived in its entirety before a shift to the alternate one (SideNote 12.43). The fact that binocular rivalry can suppress the awareness of a stimulus to which we are fully exposed has led some scientists to use it to study visual consciousness.

The singleness of vision

We close this chapter by revisiting an intriguing phenomenon that was brought up at the very beginning. How is it that we see the world through two eyes and yet we obtain a single and unified perception of our surroundings? Although this had baffled scientists and

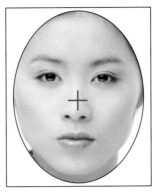

Figure 12.35

Binocular rivalry of complex geometric figures can be seen after fusing the stereogram above. Perceptual oscillation between the building and the woman's face works best when fixation is restricted to the central cross mark. At any given time, only one of the figures stands out in its entirety before the alternate image appears. Photos: (l) uschools/iStockphoto.com; (r) iconogenic/iStockphoto.com

philosophers for centuries, Wheatstone's early work combined with the later contributions of many psychologists and physiologists has given us the answer.

We now know that the integration of visual signals from the two eyes first occurs in the primary visual cortex (area V1). However, this integration is limited in scope because only a certain range of disparities can be encoded by the binocular neurons at this site. Thus, true single vision is really a phenomenon that is restricted to a small range of depths—the so-called *Panum's fusional area*. The rest of the visual world lying outside this area cannot be binocularly fused and therefore produces diplopia (or double vision). And yet, we do not ordinarily perceive double images of such objects, which is quite fortunate because of the confusion and perceptual chaos that it would create. This situation is avoided by high-level processes that underlie binocular suppression, as discussed above. The rivalry between alternative image representations in the two eyes for objects that cannot be binocularly integrated leads our visual system to choose only one to be perceived at any given time.

The singleness of vision therefore arises because we are endowed with the twin processes of *binocular integration*, which fuses objects within a given disparity range, and *binocular suppression*, which ensures that we perceive only a single object when confronted with two equally plausible alternatives.

SideNote | **12.43**

A simple way of demonstrating perceptual instability is through geometric figures that can be interpreted in more than one way. An excellent example is the *Necker cube*, shown below. There are two equally plausible perspectives—the shaded side at the back of the cube or on top of the cube. Staring at this figure will lead to a perceptual oscillation between these two perspectives.

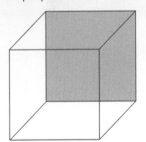

Summary

1. The spatial relationship of any external object with regard to an individual observer is specified by its direction and absolute depth. The directional component can be described by way of either an *allocentric* or an *egocentric* frame of reference. For the latter, there must be an internal reference centre, known as the *visual egocentre*. Head and body movements, however, must be continually registered and taken into account in specifying egocentric direction. Proprioceptive signals, corollary discharge, and vestibular system output together provide important information on self-motion.

2. The visual system relies on various cues to obtain information on an object's depth in space (i.e., absolute depth). Optical cues, such as retinal image size, can help to differentiate between near and far objects. Ocular cues, such as the state of accommodation and vergence, also play an important role because they provide unambiguous information on the absolute depth of an object being fixated on. The contraction of the ciliary muscle (accommodation) and oculomotor muscles (vergence) can be transmitted to the perceptual centres of the brain. Similarly, a copy of the motor signal to these muscles (known as *efference copy* or *corollary discharge*) can also provide information on changes in accommodation and vergence.

3. One of the major challenges faced by the visual system is to sort out the *relative depths* of objects (i.e., where they are located with respect to each other in terms of distance along the third dimension). A set of monocular cues can be used to provide this information. For example, *pictorial cues*, which are based on physical factors that govern object relationships at different depths, can be extremely effective and are used routinely by artists. Some examples of pictorial cues include occlusion, relative size, texture gradient, and linear perspective. Dynamic cues, such as *kinetic depth*, are extremely powerful and are based on object and observer motion.

4. Humans perceive object depths that are consistent with their physical reality and not merely on the basis of their retinal image size. This phenomenon is known as *size constancy*. It is likely that humans come to learn about the true physical size of objects through visual experience and use absolute depth information to calibrate the mental impression that is generated. The visual brain apparently takes into account the actual object distance to offset the variable nature of retinal image size to generate a perceived size that accurately reflects the object's true physical size. Size constancy may also be produced by comparing the relative sizes of all other objects in the environment. As absolute distance changes, all objects embedded in the scene also change in terms of their retinal image size, and therefore a particular object retains the same relative size when viewed in relation to its surrounding objects. A number of visual illusions can arise due to misconceptions of absolute depth, the most famous of which is the *moon illusion*.

5. Depth perception with binocular (stereoscopic) vision is outstanding, to the point where humans can be up to 10 times better at distinguishing the relative depths of objects with both eyes than with one. The presence of frontal eyes in primates, and various other species, allows the same visual scene to be captured through two slightly different viewpoints. The visual brain is able to combine the two retinal images to produce a unified picture of the scene, which is referred to as *binocular fusion*, leading to singleness of vision (*cyclopean perception*). Another remarkable aspect of binocular vision is that the visual brain can obtain information on the third dimension by comparing the two views from each eye. Subtle differences in the retinal image of each eye endow us with the capacity to deconstruct the relative depths of different objects in the visual field.

6. The set of environmental points that produce an image at analogous retinal sites (known as *corresponding images*) is called the

horopter. By definition, there is no *retinal disparity* between these images. An object that lies in front of the horopter, however, produces retinal disparity in which the temporal image is located at a slightly greater distance from the fovea than the nasal image in the other eye, a situation that is referred to as *crossed disparity.* Objects that are situated behind the horopter produce *uncrossed disparity,* in which the nasal image is located slightly farther from the fovea than the temporal image in the other eye. Wheatstone showed that it is this disparity of the retinal images that is actually responsible for generating a vivid perception of relative depth.

7. Retinal disparity arises as a geometric consequence of having two laterally displaced eyes. The temporal half of the right eye's retina and the nasal half of the left eye's retina both project to the right cerebral hemisphere; the opposite arrangement is true for the left hemisphere. This creates a situation where binocular neurons in area V1 are able to encode retinal disparity. There are three general types of *disparity selective* neurons in area V1—that is, those capable of encoding the *zero, crossed,* and *uncrossed* retinal disparity conditions. The neural circuitry underlying this construction is based on converging retinal input from corresponding and non-corresponding retinal locations. Together, the different classes of disparity-selective neurons form the initial neural substrate for deconstructing the relative depths of objects.

8. Wheatstone developed the first stereogram, which apart from its entertainment value, revealed much about the visual processing of disparity. A small deviation in a particular image component's location between the two pictures causes it to stand out in front of or behind the other parts of that picture. The small displacements in the actual pictorial content are transferred to the retinal image upon fusing the stereogram, either freely or through an optical device such as a stereoscope. Even though there is no real depth in the pictures, a vivid 3-D impression arises by taking advantage of the visual system's ability to transform the optical disparity in retinal images into a perception of relative depth.

Key Terms

Recall Questions

1. What are the two main spatial frames of reference, and how do they differ from each other? What is the *visual egocentre*? How are head and body movements registered by the visual brain? What is the difference between an efferent signal and a proprioceptive signal?

2. What are the different cues available to the visual system for encoding absolute depth? Why do the ocular cues provide unambiguous depth information?

3. What is the difference between *relative depth* and *absolute depth*? Why are pictorial cues so effective in monocular depth perception? What are the different pictorial cues that might be present in a painting producing a vivid depth percept? What is an example of a dynamic cue for relative depth?

4. What is *size constancy*? What are the two main explanations for this phenomenon? How is the *moon illusion* related to mechanisms underlying size constancy? Why does this illusion arise?

5. What are the advantages of binocular as opposed to monocular vision? What are the pros and cons of having frontally placed eyes versus laterally placed eyes? What is *cyclopean perception*?

6. What is a *horopter*? Where do objects have to be in relation to the horopter to produce crossed and uncrossed disparities?

What is the retinal image relationship between the two eyes for an object that produces crossed disparity, uncrossed disparity, and zero disparity?

7. What features of the anatomical projection to the cortex underlie the creation of binocular neurons? What are the different types of *disparity selective neurons*, and how are they related to processing relative depth information?

8. What is a stereogram? How is stereo depth generated by crossing the eyes while viewing a pair of pictures? What is the correspondence problem, and what important insight was produced through the study of random-dot stereograms? What is binocular rivalry, and why does it arise?

9. Historically, why was it so difficult to understand binocular fusion and cyclopean vision? What was the major breakthrough?

10. How is the problem of midline stereopsis resolved? What is stereo-blindness, and what impact could it have on say navigating through the real world? How is Panum's fusional area related to cyclopean perception, and what happens outside this area?

11. What are some examples of depth illusions? What is Emmert's law? How is motion parallax used as a cue to depth perception?

Further Reading

- De Valois, R. L., & De Valois, K. K. (1990). *Spatial vision*. New York, NY: Oxford University Press.

- Gibson, J. J. (1950). *The perception of the visual world*. Westport, CT: Greenwood Press.

- Howard, I. P. (1982). *Human visual orientation*. New York, NY: Wiley.

- Howard, I. P., & Rogers, B. J. (1995). *Binocular vision and stereopsis*. New York, NY: Oxford University Press.

- Ings, S. (2008). *A natural history of seeing: The art and science of vision*. New York, NY: W. W. Norton.

- Julesz, B. (1971). *Foundations of cyclopean perception*. Chicago, IL: University of Chicago Press.

- Ogle, K. N. (1950). *Researches in binocular vision*. London, UK: Saunders.

- Peterson, M. A., Gillam, B., & Sedgwick, H. A. (2007). *In the mind's eye: Julian Hochberg on the perception of pictures, films, and the world*. New York, NY: Oxford University Press.

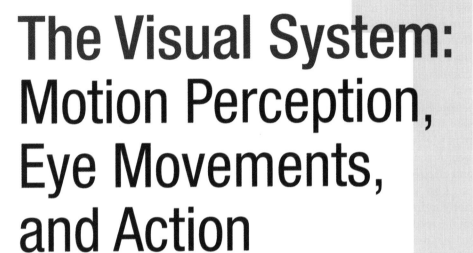

The Visual System: Motion Perception, Eye Movements, and Action

In this chapter . . .

- You will learn about the many ways that motion and motion detection are useful (e.g., to identify friends, catch prey, avoid collisions, etc.) and the many types of motion we encounter on a daily basis. You will come to understand that motion is a *spatiotemporal event*. You will discover the temporal aspects of vision in order to understand how it is that we see motion and how motion perception differs under photopic and scotopic conditions.

- You will explore how elementary motion detectors work and where they are situated in the visual pathway. Additionally, you will come to see that different motion detectors have different degrees of directional selectivity and tuning.

- You will learn about the different perceptual facets related to motion, such as detection thresholds and differences in sensitivity across the retina. You will come to appreciate how psychophysical studies are designed, using moving bars, gratings, and correlated dot motion. Finally, you will discover the consequences of lesions to cortical sites, such as area MT, that are devoted to motion analysis.

- You will explore the mechanisms behind the phenomenon of apparent motion as well as how different motion illusions have given us insight into how we process motion. You will see how we track motion and how we maintain stable vision as we move around.

- You will learn about the different types of involuntary eye movements such as microsaccades, the vestibulo-ocular reflex, and optokinetic nystagmus as well as voluntary eye movements such as smooth pursuit and saccades. Finally, you will discover a provocative theory on the function of parietal lobe structures that make up the dorsal stream in vision.

We live in a highly dynamic world, one in which either objects are in motion or we ourselves are in motion, or usually a combination of the two. It is therefore important that we capture and interpret this dynamic information so that we attain a perceptual impression of the real world as it unfolds in real time.
Photo: Aflo Foto Agency/Alamy

The secret to film is that it's an illusion.

—George Lucas

Up to now, we have discussed visual processing in terms of object qualities that are static in nature, such as form, colour, location in space, etc. However, we live in a highly dynamic world, one in which objects are in motion or we ourselves are in motion, or usually a combination of the two. It is therefore important that we capture and interpret this dynamic information so that we attain a perceptual impression of the real world as it unfolds in real time. The final chapter of this book is devoted to motion perception. As we will see, this is a field that has truly benefited from the major technological advances of 20th-century neuroscience research, such as neuroimaging and electrophysiological brain recording.

Our visual system uses motion information for diverse purposes. The most fundamental use is to recreate the true motion of objects in the real world so that we know exactly what is moving and how it is moving. In addition to generating an accurate perceptual impression of our dynamic surrounding, such knowledge also helps us to avoid collisions as objects move toward us or we move toward an object. A moving object can also help to define its shape and set it apart from the background. For example, a camouflaged leopard can remain barely detectable until it begins to move, at which point the coherent movement of the spots on its body reveals the outline and full form of the animal (SideNote 13.1). Complex image motion can also be used by our visual system to deduce object identity. An example is our ability to identify a friend simply by observing his or her gait or some other characteristic movement that is peculiar to that individual. And finally, motion signals are used to direct eye movements, either in a reflexive manner (e.g., the *nystagmus* that occurs when gazing out the window of a moving train) or in a purposeful manner (e.g., when attempting to track a moving object).

These are only some of the features of motion that play an important role in our lives, all of which we will come to learn more about throughout this chapter. We begin by exploring some fundamental issues that are pertinent to this topic, such as the biological mechanisms that mediate motion perception, and then proceed to discuss the various psychological qualities associated with motion. We will then examine eye movements, their relationship to motion signals, and their effect on motion perception. We conclude the chapter with a discussion of the dorsal cortical stream and examine a provocative theory about its role in perception and behaviour.

A. Fundamental Aspects of Motion Processing

Although animals differ widely in their ability to see colour, depth, and detailed form vision, it is clear that all animals—from invertebrates to mammals—have an ability to process and use motion information. It is likely that the fundamental way by which motion information is captured is very similar across species, and indeed, as we shall see, much of our insight into this mechanism actually arose from early experiments on an annoying little creature—the common housefly.

1. WHAT IS MOTION?

Although we all know what is meant by the term *motion*, it is nevertheless important to have an explicit definition. In the scientific domain, motion is described as a **spatiotemporal** event (Adelson & Bergen, 1985; Epstein & Rogers, 1995). Quite simply, an object moves across a certain amount of space in a given amount of time. The greater the space covered, the greater the *speed* of the object. The one other quality necessary to describe motion is *direction*. These two parameters—speed and direction—define the **velocity** of an object.

The nature of object motion can be depicted in a space–time diagram, as shown in Figure 13.1. The top panel actually shows a motionless object because its spatial position remains unchanged in time. The middle panel shows an object moving at constant speed in a certain direction. In order to determine what that direction is, it would have to be specified on the y-axis, (e.g., for vertical motion, the axis would state "Vertical position"). The bottom panel shows an object whose position oscillates in space in a manner that we recall as simple harmonic motion from our analysis of auditory signals. As a result, the spatiotemporal profile shows a sinusoidal shape. The horizontal movement of a pendulum would be an example of such motion. Space–time diagrams provide a useful way of displaying the nature of object motion and are often used by vision scientists to analyze how image structure changes over time.

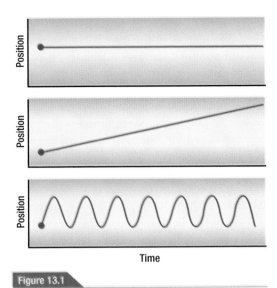

Figure 13.1

Space–time diagrams show the nature of an object's movement. The top panel shows a motionless object because its position does not change over time. The middle panel shows an object moving at a steady speed in a particular direction, whereas the object in the bottom panel is undergoing an oscillation such that its position changes in a sinusoidal manner over time.

2. TEMPORAL VISION

The perception of motion requires the visual system to process and integrate both spatial and temporal information. Although we have dealt with spatial vision in considerable detail in earlier chapters, especially Chapter 10, the temporal dimension of vision is something new and therefore needs to be understood before we proceed to discuss motion processing by the brain.

The speed of sight

One of the most fundamental questions that students often ask is "How quickly do I see something after it appears?" Although there is no exact answer to this question, we can reach some pretty reasonable estimates. The neural pathways mediating visual experience are now well known to us (Kandel, Schwartz, & Jessell, 2000). From the moment light photons reach the photoreceptors, a series of cumulative delays are introduced, beginning with the conversion of light energy into biological signals and then the transmission of those signals, through a hierarchy of visual pathways, to the temporal cortex and beyond where the neural processes that mediate object recognition are presumed to take place (Keysers, Xiao, Földiák, & Perrett, 2001).

The total time for visual signals to reach the higher areas of the visual cortex can be 80–120 milliseconds, depending on various factors such as the nature of the stimulus and the precise brain area in question (Chalupa & Werner, 2004; Enns, 2004; Kandel et al., 2000). It generally takes another 80–100 milliseconds to make a motor response to that stimulus. Thus, the speed of sight is rather slow in part due to the complex set of processes that must unfold at the neurological level before we are able to perceive the stimulus. Given the sluggish speed of sight, an interesting question arises—do we ever obtain visual experience in real time? It seems that we are always living in the immediate past by experiencing something that happened more than 100 milliseconds ago (SideNote 13.2).

Temporal resolution

It is one thing for the visual system to be somewhat slow in transmitting and interpreting visual signals and yet another to be slow at detecting changes in the stimulus. This is an important distinction because the visual system may be somewhat slow at registering incoming information, but if it is slow at detecting changes that occur in the stimulus sequence, then that can have an impact on other aspects of vision that rely on temporal processing, including motion perception. For example, if it was true that we could not detect visual stimuli that changed faster than say 100 milliseconds, then we would have had a very difficult time watching television in the old days because in that time three frames would have zipped by. It is not difficult to imagine how this would produce a rather jittery appearance.

The rate of change of a visual stimulus is called **temporal frequency** and is specified in terms of cycles of change per second (or hertz). A simple way to study how fast we are able to follow a changing stimulus is to undertake an experiment on **flicker** perception (Chalupa & Werner, 2004; Enns, 2004). The visual stimulus typically used is a simple pattern (e.g., a filled square or a disk) that is presented in an alternating fashion at different temporal frequencies (SideNote 13.3), with the goal of determining the frequency at which flicker perception disappears. Such studies have shown that we are capable of detecting stimulus alternations at frequencies up to 60 Hz, after which the stimulus appears to be uniform in nature—that is, the stimulus blends into the background so that the appearance of flicker disappears. Vision

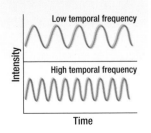

SideNote | **13.4**

Recall that *sensitivity* is the inverse of *threshold*. Thus, the lower the contrast threshold needed to just detect flicker, the greater our sensitivity at that temporal frequency.

SideNote | **13.5**

The time to collision can be calculated by simply dividing the distance by the rate of movement. Consider the example of a baseball thrown from a pitcher's mound that is 60 feet (18 metres) away at a speed of 90 miles per hour (40 metres/second). The time to collision with the batter is only 0.45 seconds (18/40). Thus, if the ball is thrown right at the batter, a collision will take place in less than half a second unless there is quick evasive action.

scientists have come to refer to the frequency at which temporal changes are undetectable as the **critical flicker fusion** frequency, or CFF.

A flicker perception experiment such as the one described above provides only a superficial account of temporal vision because it does not give information on how sensitive our visual system is to different temporal frequencies. To find out more about the **temporal resolution** characteristics of the visual system, a somewhat more sophisticated experiment needs to be performed. One way to proceed is to obtain the contrast threshold of a flickering stimulus (usually a sine-wave grating) at different temporal frequencies (Adelson & Bergen, 1985; Hart, 1987; Kelly, 1974). The greater our temporal resolving ability at a particular frequency, the lower the contrast needed to just observe the flicker. Figure 13.2 shows the human **temporal contrast sensitivity function** that can be derived from such threshold measures (SideNote 13.4) (Hart, 1987). This figure also reinforces the notion that the CFF frequency occurs around 60 Hz under photopic conditions. However, an important new insight offered by this figure is

that our visual system optimally detects temporal frequencies in the 10–15 Hz range and that our temporal sensitivity declines on either side of this range. Furthermore, scotopic vision is much more sluggish compared to photopic vision at all frequencies and displays a much lower CFF frequency. Night vision is therefore not well suited for detecting temporal changes in a visual stimulus.

Time to collision

We have all had the experience of having to quickly duck out of the way either because an object was rapidly approaching us or because we were approaching it. The critical behavioural requirement under such circumstances is to avoid a collision, often under split-second circumstances. The question that arises is "How does our visual system process the trajectory of an incoming object and quickly determine the time to collision?" We know that we are extremely effective in this regard from commonly observed human behaviours—for example, a professional boxer eluding a rapidly thrown punch, or a baseball player following a fastball in order to make a precise swing of the bat, or the more personal experience of having to quickly brake while driving because the car ahead had suddenly stopped.

In all of these cases, it can be argued that the visual system merely needs to evaluate the absolute depth of the incoming object, make an estimate of its speed of approach, and from these two parameters proceed to obtain the **time to collision**, or TTC (SideNote 13.5). The only problem with this solution is that the visual system is not very good at estimating the absolute distance of objects. Thus, any TTC processing system that relies on such a sluggish and inaccurate ability would simply not be able to give the precise values that allow us to react with such rapidity.

It has been suggested that instead we derive TTC values from the way the retinal image changes as an object approaches us (or vice versa) (Lee, 1976). In purely optical terms, the retinal image rapidly becomes much larger for an approaching object. The ratio of the retinal image size to the rate at which it is expanding at any given moment is referred to as **tau**. There are two important features of tau. First, it provides an accurate estimate of TTC, and second, it does so without the need for obtaining object distance or its rate of movement toward us. All of the information for determining TTC is thus

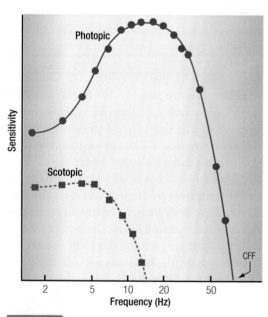

Figure 13.2

The human temporal contrast sensitivity function (TSF) shows a peak around 10–15 Hz, with declining sensitivity on either side. Temporal changes are undetectable beyond the critical flicker fusion (CFF) frequency of about 60 Hz. Scotopic (rod) vision has much poorer temporal sensitivity compared to photopic (cone) vision. Adapted from "The Temporal Responsiveness of Vision," by W. M. Hart Jr., in *Physiology of the Eye: Clinical Application*, 1987, Eds. R. A. Moses and W. M. Hart, St. Louis, MO: Mosby.

contained in the retinal image and how it changes with time. The tau hypothesis asserts that optical image analysis can be undertaken very quickly in computational terms and is therefore responsible for our amazing ability to make split-second reactions to avoid collisions.

3.   LOW-LEVEL MOTION DETECTORS

The preceding sections revealed that the human visual system is extremely sensitive to the dimension of time and, in particular, to temporal changes in a stimulus. This ability becomes critically important in motion detection, where very subtle changes of stimulus position over time must be detected to generate an accurate perception of true object motion in the real world. The fact that motion is such a fundamental aspect of our visual experience suggests that the neural mechanisms for movement detection must be robust and integral to early visual information processing. Both of these facets of motion detection are true, the details of which we shall explore next.

Directional selectivity

One way for the brain to produce motion awareness is to sample the physical position of objects in a visual scene at different points of time and then interpolate any changes to generate the corresponding motion percepts. In this scenario, the brain would capture snapshots of the visual scene from which changes in the physical location of different objects are used to generate a sense of their motion. Such a situation is analogous to what happens under stroboscopic lighting, which was the rave at nightclubs during the disco era of the 1970s and possibly still in use in remote places, ostensibly with an entertainment value (SideNote 13.6). In such cases, objects in a room are intermittently visible and therefore the change in their position with each successive light exposure creates a sense of movement.

The problem with generating motion perception in this manner is that it does not lead to an appreciation of smooth movement but rather of jittery displacement, something that can be appreciated by anyone who has experienced stroboscopic lighting (Epstein & Rogers, 1995; Hart, 1987). If our brain similarly derived movement signals from an analysis of the visual scene at different times, then we would not likely be endowed with a robust and salient perception of object motion. An

argument can be made in evolutionary terms of the need for generating motion perception that truly captures object motion, given the survival advantage that follows when animals are able to recreate a faithful impression of their dynamic world.

It had thus long been appreciated that motion detectors must exist very early in the visual pathways so that dynamic information could be captured and integrated with other aspects of visual function. The twin qualities required of a low-level motion detector are the ability to differentiate both the direction and the speed of a moving object. We learned in Chapter 10 that **directional selectivity**—the ability of a neuron to distinguish one direction of motion from all others—is found in primates as early as area V1 (Chalupa & Werner, 2004; Kandel et al., 2000). This finding in turn leads to the question of how such a selectivity for movement direction is generated in early visual neurons.

The Reichardt detector

Let us assume that we have two neurons (A and B) that detect visual stimuli through adjacently placed receptive fields and that both feed into another higher-level neuron (D), as shown by the leftmost panel in Figure 13.3. The three neurons along with their connections are

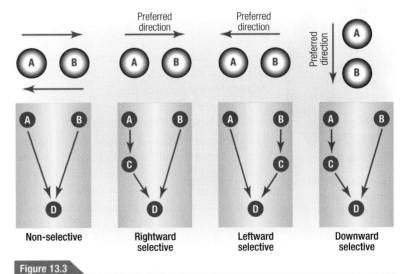

Preferred direction   Preferred direction   Preferred direction

Non-selective   Rightward selective   Leftward selective   Downward selective

Figure 13.3

Simple convergence of two neurons upon a third (leftmost panel) does not endow it with the property of directional selectivity. The insertion of an interneuron in one path of this circuit (second panel), however, creates a delay that when matched to the delay of stimulus movement in the correct direction produces a synchronized convergence of neural signals, thus conferring directional selectivity upon neuron D. Directional preference can be changed by moving the interneuron (third panel) or by appropriate placement of the detectors' receptive fields (rightmost panel). Neuronal circuits are shown within the shaded boxes; receptive fields of the detectors are shown above.

shown within the shaded box; the receptive fields of the two detectors are shown above the box. This very simple circuit would certainly activate neuron D as a stimulus moves across the receptive fields of the two detectors, though it would not be able to distinguish the direction of motion because it will be similarly activated for both rightward and leftward stimulus movement. Indeed, there is nothing in this circuit that allows neuron D to differentiate these two movement directions, and therefore it cannot have the property of directional selectivity.

It turns out that a small change to this circuit can have a huge impact—that being the insertion of a separate neuron within one of the two pathways. As the second panel in Figure 13.3 shows, placing a so-called *interneuron* (C) in the path from neuron A to D creates an asymmetrical circuit and imposes a delay along this route. Signal transmission from neuron B to D remains unaffected. The result of the delay is the following. Assume that we have a rightward moving visual stimulus, which will first trigger neuron A and then a short time later, neuron B. If the delay in transmission through the interneuron matches the delay in the arrival of the stimulus to neuron B, then the signals from both sides of this circuit will converge upon neuron D at the same time. The resulting summation of signals will cause enhanced firing in this neuron. If, on the other hand, the visual stimulus is moving in the opposite direction, then neuron B will first be stimulated followed by neuron A. In this case, the signal from neuron B will immediately proceed to neuron D, whereas the signal from neuron A will be delayed by the interneuron. The asymmetrical placement of the interneuron in this circuit is no longer beneficial for this direction of movement because it causes the signals from the two sides to arrive out of phase. As a result, we have conferred the property of directional selectivity upon neuron D by making it more reactive to rightward over leftward stimulus movement.

The existence of the circuit outlined above and its role in creating directional selectivity was proposed by German physicist and physiologist Werner Reichardt (Reichardt, 1969, 1986). In recognition of his influential work in this field, this circuit has come to be called the **Reichardt detector**. Reichardt was able to obtain physiological evidence for this circuit from an unlikely model—the common housefly (SideNote 13.7). There are several key advantages to the Reichardt detector. Most notably, this extremely simple circuit relies only on temporal summation of signals from two detectors to produce directional selectivity. Furthermore, a preference for another direction of movement can be easily created by either placing the interneuron in the other pathway or by linking detectors that have different receptive field placements. For example, the third panel in Figure 13.3 shows that moving the interneuron to the right side of the circuit now makes neuron D selective for leftward movement, whereas a Reichardt detector constructed with vertically placed receptive fields, in the way shown in the rightmost panel of Figure 13.3, can create a directional preference for downward motion.

Another key advantage to the Reichardt detector scheme is that it provides a simple way of encoding the second important aspect of motion detection—speed selectivity. The delay imposed by the interneuron must be matched to the delay in stimulus movement from one detector to the other (e.g., from the receptive field of neuron A to B) because only then will the signals from the two pathways arrive simultaneously upon neuron D. There will be a temporal mismatch if the stimulus is moving too fast or too slow because the interneuron's delay will no longer coincide with stimulus movement. In such cases, a simple alteration is needed to create a Reichardt detector that is suitably reactive. By changing the value of the delay in the interneuron—for example, by having either a faster-acting or a more sluggish response—we can create a Reichardt detector that is tuned for faster and slower speeds, respectively. Indeed, it may be the case that motion signals in the brain are encoded through a range of Reichardt-type detectors tuned to various speeds and directional preferences so as to encompass the widest range of stimulus movement possibilities in the real world.

Elaborated low-level detectors

The Reichardt model by itself may be too simplistic to account for motion signal generation in mammalian visual systems. Physiological experiments have shown, for example, that directionally selective neurons are excited by stimulus movement in the preferred direction but inhibited by movement in the opposite direction (Albright, 1984; Born & Bradley, 2005). The elementary nature of the Reichardt detector allows only for a multiplication of signals arriving on the directionally selective neuron

Werner E. Reichardt (1924–1992)
Max Planck Institute for Biological Cybernetics, Tübingen, Germany

SideNote 13.7

Insects represent an excellent model for studying motion because of their need to rapidly navigate through complex environments; therefore they must rely on simple and robust motion processing systems.

and therefore by itself cannot explain inhibition in the anti-preferred direction. One way to achieve this, however, would be to take two Reichardt detectors that are tuned to opposite directions and have their outputs subtracted to form a bidirectional motion detector. Further elaborations to this basic structure involve spatial filtering at the input level to accommodate the known behaviour of early visual neurons (van Santen & Sperling, 1984; Watson & Ahumada, 1985). Although the fundamental strategy of *delay-and-compare* is retained, the elaborated versions of later models of low-level motion detection are better suited to the known physiological properties of the visual system.

4.   CORTICAL MOTION MECHANISMS

The next question that arises is "Where in the visual pathway would we find directionally selective neurons similar to the Reichardt detectors described above?" A reasonable place to start looking would be the retina, which we learned in previous chapters is already capable of undertaking important visual computations, including contrast detection, spatial frequency filtering, and opponent colour processing. It would be natural to assume that directional selectivity should also be observed in retinal ganglion cells, given the simplicity of the Reichardt scheme.

Despite much effort, there have not been any electrophysiological studies to demonstrate convincingly the presence of directionally selective neurons in the primate retina. It has been shown that retinal ganglion cells in rabbits and mice do display directional responses (Chalupa & Werner, 2004; Weng, Sun, & He, 2005). However, the same does not appear to be true in monkeys and therefore unlikely in humans as well, nor have there been any reports of directional selectivity in the LGN of any primate species. Rather, the first site at which this property arises in the primate visual pathway is area V1 (primary visual cortex).

Motion processing in area V1

The first demonstration of directional selectivity in area V1 neurons was by David Hubel and Torsten Wiesel in the 1960s. Since then, there have been many detailed studies of the primary visual cortex that have led to a greater understanding of the physiological aspects of motion processing in this area as well as uncovering many important anatomical details.

In terms of the physiological properties, directionally selective neurons in area V1 display a vigorous response only when a light bar moves along the direction preferred by that neuron (Gur & Snodderly, 2007; Sincich & Horton, 2005). These neurons often show inhibition when the stimulus moves in the opposite direction. Different neurons display different degrees of directional tuning preference. Some are extremely specific for a particular direction such that any deviation from the preferred direction leads to a near silencing of action potentials. Other directionally selective neurons show a broader tuning curve where the preference for one direction is only moderately greater than that for other directions (SideNote 13.8). There is a broad range of directional preferences among area V1 neurons that cover all possible directions of movement. These directionally selective neurons together represent the initial stages of a complex series of neural operations underlying motion perception.

The anatomical details of motion processing in area V1 concern two general issues—the precise location of directionally selective neurons and their connections to higher areas of the visual cortex. The first issue has been addressed through several careful studies in which the property of directional selectivity was assessed among the different layers of area V1 (Hawken, Parker, & Lund, 1988). As Figure 13.4 shows, electrode penetration through area V1 during

SideNote 13.8

This property of directional selectivity is portrayed by plotting the neuron's firing rate in a radial manner (shown below). The firing rate is plotted on a particular axis for stimulus movement in either direction along that axis. The top profile shows a non-directional neuron (i.e., one that responds equally well regardless of which direction the light bar is moving, resulting in a near circular tuning curve). The profile at the bottom is typical of neurons with a strong directional preference. In this case, a vigorous response is seen when the light bar moves at an angle of 45° and a much reduced response at other angles.

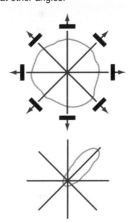

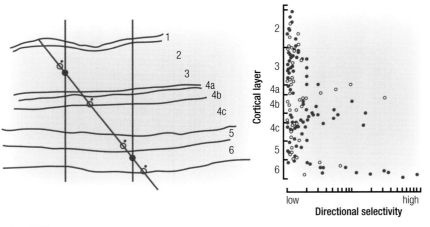

Figure 13.4

Electrophysiological experiments typically require an electrode to penetrate through many layers of the visual cortex (area V1). Neural responses can be sampled at any point during such an experiment (left panel). Directionally selective neurons have largely been found to reside within a middle band (layer 4b) and at the bottom (layer 6) of area V1. The other layers show low or weak directional selectivity (right panel). Adapted from "Laminar Organization and Contrast Sensitivity of Direction-selective Cells in the Striate Cortex of the Old-world Monkey," by M. J. Hawken, A. J. Parker, and J. S. Lund, 1988, *Journal of Neuroscience, 8*, pp. 3541–48.

SideNote | **13.9**

It is difficult to identify which layer a given neuron belongs to in the midst of an electrophysiological study. This problem can be resolved by leaving a mark at the recording site. For example, it is possible to inject current through the electrode to produce a lesion (small hole) after surveying the neurons at a given site. After the experiment, the cortical site is then examined under a microscope and the layer containing the lesion is identified. In this way, it was possible to identify the precise layers containing directionally selective neurons in area V1.

a physiological study will sequentially traverse all layers before arriving at the white matter. It is possible to identify the various layers after an experiment so that the presence (or absence) of directionally selective neurons can be documented in a layer-specific manner (SideNote 13.9). The right panel in Figure 13.4 shows that the majority of neurons with high directional selectivity are found in the bottom layer (6) and along a middle band (4b). All other layers in area V1 show either an absence or at best a weak selectivity for movement direction.

The second anatomical issue concerning directionally selective neurons in area V1 is their connection with higher cortical areas. Area V1 represents only the first stage of motion processing and given the many different aspects and perceptual qualities related to motion, it would be expected that the more advanced properties are relegated to the later stages of the visual pathway. This is indeed the case, as discussed in the next section.

Motion processing beyond area V1

The visual brain has been characterized as being modular in nature such that many of the cortical areas beyond the primary visual cortex are specialized for a given property (Zeki, 1993). We saw this earlier, for example, with regard to colour processing in area V4 and object processing in the temporal lobe areas. One of the major developments in understanding higher visual function took place in the 1970s with the discovery of a specific area in the monkey brain that seemed almost exclusively dedicated to motion processing. This area, which was independently discovered in two different species of monkeys, by John Allman in the U.S. and Semir Zeki in the U.K., came to be known as **area MT** (and later, *area V5*). The property of area MT that fascinated neuroscientists was the fact that the vast majority of neurons within it were directionally selective, leading some to dub it "the motion area."

The discovery of area MT also propelled a great amount of research in trying to understand how motion signals are processed by the primate brain (Albright, 1984; Born & Bradley, 2005; Newsome & Pare, 1988). It was soon discovered that area MT is just one of several motion areas in that part of the brain. A small area lying just next to it, area MST, was shown to process more advanced properties of the motion signal and, together with

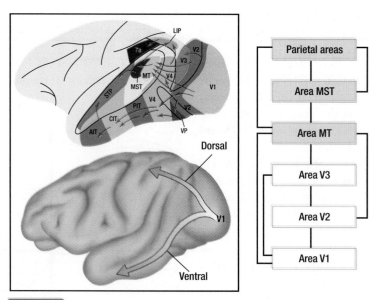

Figure 13.5

Visual areas in the monkey brain are known to be interconnected in complex ways. A guiding principle behind these connections is that they compose two major channels of visual information processing—the ventral and dorsal streams (left panel). The latter is responsible for processing spatiotemporal relationships and dynamic aspects of vision. The areas of the dorsal stream are interconnected in complex ways via both feedforward and feedback connections (right panel). Areas MT, MST, and various parietal lobe areas are primarily responsible for processing more complex aspects of motion. Adapted from *Principles of Neural Science* (4th ed.), by E. R. Kandel, J. H. Schwartz, and T. M. Jessell, 2000, New York: McGraw-Hill.

area MT, to connect to various areas of the parietal lobe. The left panel in Figure 13.5 shows the locations and interconnections of these various areas. We saw in Chapter 10 that several of the visual areas involved in object processing within the temporal lobe together make up the so-called *ventral visual stream*. The counterpart to this channel is the set of visual areas in the parietal lobe that, along with the motion areas, form the so-called **dorsal visual stream**. The brain areas that belong to this stream are largely involved in computing the dynamic aspects of vision and the spatial relationships of objects so as to guide motor function (SideNote 13.10).

We now know that directionally selective neurons in area V1 have a **feed-forward projection** to higher cortical areas. As shown in the right panel of Figure 13.5, there is a series of connections from area V1 through areas V2, V3, and up to the motion areas (MT and MST) (Kandel et al., 2000; Sincich & Horton, 2005). Although the scheme shown in this connectional diagram reveals a hierarchical organization, it should be noted that they are not merely connected in a sequential way. For example, there are direct projections from area V1 to area MT. Indeed, it is the directionally selective neurons in the middle layers of area V1 that project directly to area MT. Furthermore, there are direct connections from area V1 to V3, from area V2 to MT, and so on. The anatomy of higher visual areas becomes further complicated by the fact that these are not just unidirectional connections from a lower area to one of greater complexity but rather reverse, or **feedback connections**, exist as well. Thus, it appears that the various higher visual areas are interconnected in complex ways with the added feature of both forward and reverse lines of communication. In later sections of this chapter, we will come to understand the precise roles that the various brain areas play in terms of motion perception and guiding eye movements.

Although much of our understanding of the neurobiology of motion perception has been attained through studies of the monkey brain, the question always remained as to whether similar structures and mechanisms operate in the human brain as well. There is now substantial evidence to believe that this is indeed the case. The development of advanced neuroimaging techniques has shown that many of the cortical areas identified in the monkey brain also exist in the human brain. With regard to motion processing, the identification of area MT in humans, as shown in Figure 13.6, has been a major development to reinforce the idea of analogous neural structures between monkeys and humans for motion processing (Tootell et al., 1995).

B. Perceptual Aspects of Motion

In this section, we take up the various behavioural and perceptual qualities associated with object movement. An important requirement for the brain is to generate accurate perceptions of object movement in the real world. However, this operation is not quite as simple as merely sampling image movement across the retina because the eyes are themselves often in motion, thereby complicating the interpretation of the retinal signal alone. Furthermore, object motion in depth is not easily represented in the retina, and yet we see objects moving toward us (or away from us) in a faithful way. As we will come to appreciate, the visual system has developed a remarkable bag of tricks to get around these problems and endow us with an accurate mental impression of true object movement.

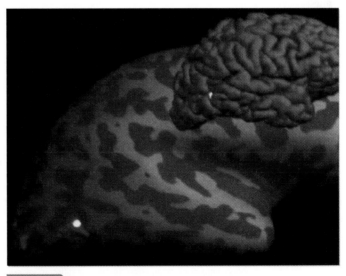

SideNote | **13.10**

The parallel nature of visual processing is known to begin at the very early stages with the magnocellular and parvocellular channels. Based on anatomical connections and physiological function, American neuroscientists Leslie Ungerleider and Mortimer Mishkin proposed that the higher cortical areas can be distinguished in terms of two parallel streams—the dorsal (parietal) and ventral (temporal) pathways. This idea enjoyed wide acceptance, though there is considerable interplay between the higher brain areas to allow for the integration of object identity (ventral stream function) with spatiotemporal and dynamic qualities (dorsal stream function).

Figure 13.6

Neuroimaging studies in humans have revealed a small area in the lateral part of the brain that is activated by moving stimuli. The three-dimensional reconstruction of the human brain shows an area of enhanced activity (white patch) representing area MT (V5). Adapted from "Visual Motion Aftereffect in Human Cortical Area MT Revealed by Functional Magnetic Resonance Imaging," by R. B. H. Tootell et al., 1995, *Nature, 375*, pp. 139–41.

SideNote | **13.11**

From a biological perspective, there exists only a limited range of Reichardt-type detectors in terms of the delay value in the circuit. Motion detectors with a small delay value are optimized for high-speed sensing, whereas those with long delay interneurons are involved in low-speed detection. Stimulus speeds that are outside the physiological detection range simply do not generate perceived motion.

SideNote | **13.12**

Some studies of motion perception use a stimulus that is a variant of the sine-wave grating. Known as a *gabor patch* (image below), the stimulus is created by combining sine-wave patterns with a bell-shaped curve, producing a pattern that fades with distance and is therefore more consistent with the nature of receptive fields of visual neurons.

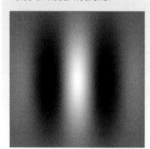

1. PSYCHOPHYSICAL STUDIES OF MOTION PERCEPTION

A fundamental requirement for all biological operations underlying motion perception is that our visual brain be capable of detecting motion to begin with. The scientific effort to determine motion thresholds began in the late 1800s with German physiologist Hermann Aubert and has been followed up by various researchers during the past century. Aubert showed that the speed of a moving object plays a critical role in our ability to detect its motion.

Motion thresholds—speed

An object that moves too slowly does not generate perceived movement, as is the case, for example, with the moving hands of a clock or celestial bodies such as the moon or stars. As Figure 13.7 shows, the slope of the space–time plot for a moving object must reach a critical height before movement is perceived. On the other hand, if the slope is too large, which would be the case when an object is moving very fast, then motion perception again deteriorates because the signal cannot be effectively captured by the brain's motion detectors (SideNote 13.11). There are several other factors that also play a role in affecting motion thresholds (Chalupa & Werner, 2004; Epstein & Rogers, 1995; Hart, 1987). For example, we are better at picking up motion signals when an

object is moving against a background of other objects than against an empty field. Similarly, the longer we are able to view a moving object, the lower the motion detection threshold will be.

Motion thresholds—eccentricity

Another factor that affects motion thresholds is retinal position or eccentricity. Aubert was among the first to show that objects moving across the central visual field have lower motion thresholds than those in the periphery. It turns out that there is a steady deterioration of motion detection ability with increasing retinal eccentricity. One reason for this may be the fact that retinal ganglion cells in the peripheral retina have progressively larger receptive fields. A moving object therefore must traverse a greater distance in order to stimulate successive ganglion cells. Thus, slower moving objects are at a disadvantage in the periphery compared to the central retina. An interesting twist to this picture is that when objects move relatively fast, the periphery is actually superior at detecting movement than the central retina. We have all experienced situations where a fly buzzing around in the periphery is quickly detected and draws our attention.

Motion stimuli

Any non-fixed object can have movement associated with it, and therefore, not surprisingly, many different types of moving stimuli have been used in the study of motion perception. The early physiological studies of directionally selective neurons relied on moving bars, as shown in the left panel of Figure 13.8. The bars, which can be oriented at any angle, seemed appropriate given the preference of area V1 neurons for oriented stimuli. In fact, most directionally selective neurons also have an orientation preference and therefore fire strongly when the bar is moving perpendicular to the preferred axis. An elaborated version of the simple bar stimulus is a sine-wave grating, as shown in the centre panel of Figure 13.8. An advantage to using gratings is that their spatial frequency can be altered to suit a particular neuron's preference. The grating in this example will appear to move rightward because each successive presentation is accompanied by a slight rightward shift of its components, as shown by the arrows (SideNote 13.12).

Another stimulus that has been very useful in both physiological and psychophysical studies is known as **correlated dot motion**

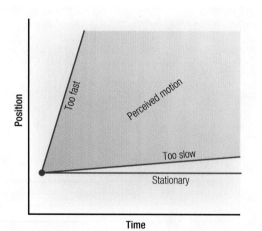

Figure 13.7

A space–time diagram showing the various different speeds at which an object, indicated by the dot at the lower left, can move. In order to perceive motion, a minimum speed must be attained, as shown by the lower diagonal line. On the other hand, if an object moves too fast, as shown by the upper diagonal line, then its motion is also not detectable. Motion perception occurs in the space–time domain that lies between these extremes.

(Newsome & Pare, 1988). The stimulus, which is shown in the right panel of Figure 13.8, is created quite simply with a set of moving dots. One extreme situation is to have each of the dots move in a random direction. This situation causes *visual dynamic noise*, and although we would see the individual random dot movements, there is no coherent movement of the dots in a given direction that stands out. At the other extreme, we can have a situation in which all of the dots move in the same direction (100% coherence). Naturally, in this case we will perceive a global rightward movement of all the dots.

The more interesting situation arises when an intermediate number of dots are moving coherently in one direction, whereas the remaining dots are moving randomly. Depending on the experimental situation, it may be possible to discern a global movement direction. By changing the percent of correlated dot movements, it is possible to arrive at a threshold figure that yields a coherent motion percept. The advantage to this stimulus is that the threshold can be measured under different experimental circumstances and also track perceptual loss in clinical conditions that affect motion perception. This stimulus was also used in a series of elegant studies by American neuroscientist Bill Newsome and his colleagues at Stanford University to show that correlation thresholds increase dramatically after area MT is removed in monkeys, thereby reaffirming the important role that this cortical area plays in motion perception (Newsome & Pare, 1988).

2. ROLE OF MOTION IN PERCEPTION AND BEHAVIOUR

Motion signals are extremely important in vision and visually guided behaviour for a variety of reasons. One use of motion signals occurs in support of perceptual organization. An excellent example is that of a camouflaged animal, such as a leopard hiding in a tree. The structural characteristics of the animal are barely visible until it begins to move. At this point, the moving spots on its body cohere to define the shape and outline of the leopard. Motion signals are also important for helping to deduce the three-dimensional structure of objects, providing guidance and stability during running or walking, and judging the impact time of an approaching object. Motion signals serve a crucial role in guiding our eye movements, the

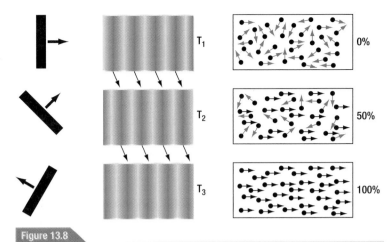

Figure 13.8

Motion stimuli for psychophysical and physiological studies can be very simple, such as a bar moving perpendicular to its oriented axis (left panel). Sine-wave gratings have also been used in various studies. Grating movement is shown in the centre panel by way of snapshots at three different time-points at which the components are shifted slightly to the right. Correlated dot motion stimuli (right panel) are created from a random field of dots in which a certain percentage of the dots move coherently in one direction, whereas the remainder move in random directions. A range of correlations is possible, from 0% (random motion of all dots) to 100% (coherent movement of all dots in a particular direction).

details of which are discussed later in this chapter. And finally, motion signals help to determine the identity of complex objects, and even people. For example, we have often experienced the phenomenon of being able to identify friends or relatives by the characteristics of their body movement, such as their gait, even if we cannot see their face (Loula, Prasad, Harber, & Shiffrar, 2005). This type of recognition, sometimes referred to as *identity-from-motion*, occurs very fast and is usually very accurate.

Biological motion perception

It is quite remarkable that we should be so good at being able to identify an individual merely by the nature of that individual's walking pattern or other body motions. An early theory proposed that our visual brain interprets moving points as though they were attached to a rigid body, and therefore the motion signals associated with a few critical points may be sufficient to provide considerable information on structural identity. The studies by Swedish psychologist Gunnar Johansson were especially important in showing just how good we are at obtaining form perception from motion information (Johansson, 1973). Johansson created point-light displays by fitting people with small lights at various joints of the body, such as the ankles, knees, shoulders, etc., and then filming their movements in a dark room so that only the motion of the lights was visible.

An example of Johansson's setup is shown in Figure 13.9 through an image of famous actor and dancer Gene Kelly. The points of light by themselves, as shown in the right panel of this figure, are meaningless when stationary and convey no useful information. In fact, it is not even clear that they are connected to a person. However, as soon as the actor begins to move (or in this case, dance), the trajectory of each of the light points provides a real-time trace of the movement of that particular joint. Johansson discovered that the constellation of point-light movements led to an immediate and vivid perception of the person's movement. This finding, which has been called **biological motion perception**, paved the way for many subsequent psychophysical experiments and has spawned many theoretical studies on just how our visual system is able to extract complex form information from the movement of a few points of light (often referred to as *motion capture*). For example, computer scientists have made tremendous advances in understanding the biomechanics of this phenomenon, which in turn has had a wide impact in the fields of robotics and entertainment. A considerable amount of motion capture technology was used to produce the 2009 blockbuster movie *Avatar* (SideNote 13.13).

One of the most intriguing findings is that we are extremely sensitive to subtle differences in human body movement. The observers in biological motion experiments are often able to identify a specific individual that they are acquainted with, and even the gender of an unknown individual. The latter ability presumably arises from our innate assumption that men generally have broader shoulders and more slender hips than women, which in turn leads to a difference in the trajectory of the light points at these joint locations. Our ability to identify a friend presumably also arises from the specific characteristics of the way their body moves in space, and quite remarkably, our visual brain can extract this information from only the movement of a small number of points on the body.

Kinetic depth effect

Biological motion perception is an example of a general ability to construct the three-dimensional structure of complex objects from motion signals alone. This property of the visual system was revealed in the 1950s through the studies of Hans Wallach and his colleagues (Wallach & O'Connell, 1953). Wallach showed that movement can enhance the three-dimensional appearance of objects in space, a phenomenon that is referred to as the **kinetic depth effect**, or KDE. A simple illustration of the KDE is given in Figure 13.10. The left panel of this figure shows a wire that is bent along all three dimensions and projected onto a screen. The shadow, when viewed from behind the screen, appears as a mere 2-D curved figure and does not by itself reveal the depth dimension associated with the object. However, if this wire figure is rotated as indicated by the arrow, the dynamically changing shadow now creates an immediate visual impression of the true three-dimensional nature of the object.

The motion signals associated with the changing retinal image of the moving shadows is used by our visual system to re-create the depth dimension of the rotating wire. A fundamental assumption made by our visual system is that such movements are associated with a rigid object. As with biological motion perception, depth dimension can be recovered from merely a limited set of moving points, as shown by the rotating cylinder example in the right panel of Figure 13.10. Here, a small set of points is attached to a transparent cylinder and illuminated the same way to cast their shadows on the screen. The dots on the various parts of

SideNote | **13.13**

It is difficult to fully appreciate how powerful biological motion perception is by merely reading about it because a textbook cannot show the dynamic nature of these stimuli. The following websites show animated sequences of "biological motion," which reveal the vividness of the perceptual impression that is generated by the mere movement of a sparse set of light points.

www.biomotionlab.ca/

www.michaelbach.de/ot/mot_biomot/index.html

www.youtube.com/watch?v=1wK1lxr-UmM&feature=related

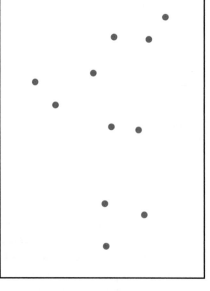

Figure 13.9

Biological motion perception is studied by attaching small points of light at various joints of the body, as shown in this image of famous actor and dancer Gene Kelly. The movement of the point-light sources are captured in real time as the dancer moves in the dark so that no part of the body is visible except the movement of the light sources (right panel). The point sources provide a spatial trace of the trajectory of the respective joints, which in turn provide a vivid perception of the actor's movements.

METHODOLOGY

Visual Biological Motion

The term *visual biological motion* was coined by Swedish psychologist Gunnar Johansson in 1973 and refers to movements made by animals and humans, which, he states, are "characterized by a far higher degree of complexity than the patterns . . . usually studied in our laboratories." This movement can be studied by attaching lights to the body's main joints and then observing only the light points to discern what is occurring. Johansson needed to represent the skeletal movements without having the overall human form aid the subjects in determining what the moving lights represented. Up to 1973, most motion perception tasks involved a few spots of light moving together, or displays of dots with a particular coherence. Biological motion, however, is not quite the same, for although certain lights are moving relative to each other (i.e., the left elbow and wrist), they are moving opposite to other light points (i.e., the right elbow and wrist). However, it has been found that subjects are quite accurate at perceiving human motion, rather than a series of disparate dots. In fact, in 1976, Johansson found that by seeing only the point-light walkers for 0.2 seconds, 100% of the subjects saw a human form moving in a particular way. Many studies have adopted Johanssons's technique to determine which brain areas correlate with biological movement, how infants perceive biological motion, strategies used to identify this motion, and even whether different species (such as cats) can integrate the points of light into a whole.

the cylinder will move at different speeds, and even directions, when the cylinder is rotated. Our visual system assumes that the moving dots are attached to a rigid object, and therefore the only correct interpretation that can be derived from the nature of their movement is that the dots belong to a rotating cylinder. The recovery of 3-D information and its use in producing form perception, as illustrated through these two examples, is also referred to by vision scientists as **structure-from-motion**, or SFM (SideNote 13.14).

Guiding locomotion

Another example of how motion signals can influence our behaviour is based on the retinal image changes that take place with self-motion. James Gibson argued that the retinal image changes in a highly systematic way as we move through the environment (Gibson, 1979). An oft-cited example of the changing pattern of retinal motion is that of forward movement toward a specific object. The left panel in Figure 13.11 on page 454 shows the general nature of this moving field as a car heads forward in a straight line. The lateral displacement of objects that lie straight are minimal. The objects that lie in the periphery, on the other hand, are displaced to a much greater extent, as depicted in the photograph.

The nature of image displacement on the retina is very similar as we walk in a straight

line toward an object. An object that lies directly ahead will not be laterally shifted so long as it is fixated and therefore maintained on the fovea. The actual magnitude of peripheral movement will depend on how far an object is located from the fixation point. Those objects that are located nearby will only have a small amount of peripheral movement, whereas others that are far away will undergo greater image movement on the retina. The differential expansion or looming that occurs in this case is an example of **optic flow** and is shown by the motion gradients in the right panel of Figure 13.11.

SideNote | **13.14**

The assumption of object rigidity is central to theories that seek to explain how SFM arises perceptually. If an object is prone to deformation during movement, then the points of light that are structurally associated with it will also deform in an infinite number of ways. Thus, our visual system has learned to avoid potential confusion by applying the rigidity assumption in order to create a correct perceptual impression of the object.

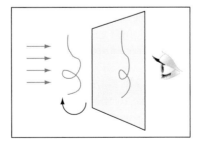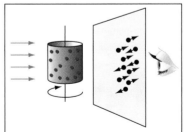

Figure 13.10

The kinetic depth effect arises when viewing the shadow of a rotating three-dimensional figure, such as a bent wire (left panel) or a transparent cylinder with spots (right panel). Even though the shadow image is cast on a two-dimensional surface, the visual system is able to obtain depth information from the moving images to re-create a correct structural impression of the object in three dimensions. This phenomenon is also referred to as *structure-from-motion*.

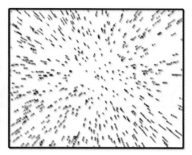

WendellandCarolyn/iStockphoto.com

Figure 13.11

Self-motion through an environment produces predictable changes in the retinal image. Objects at the centre of the field deviate little from the centre of the retina in terms of their image, whereas peripheral objects appear to zoom by (left panel). This optic flow pattern can be illustrated with motion vectors where the individual lines correspond to retinal image motion associated with objects in the scene (right panel). The differential motion of peripheral objects sets up a motion gradient over the entire retina.

SideNote | 13.15

Individuals with mild to moderate Alzheimer's disease are impaired in navigating their surroundings. Several studies have shown that a deficit in this group arises from a reduced ability to process optic flow information and to construct form perception from motion signals.

SideNote | 13.16

The vision science community has been indebted to certain individuals who, through a twist of medical fate or genetics, have developed a neurological condition that leads to specific perceptual or behavioural deficits. The motion-blind patient (pictured below) has given us insight into a perceptual world that is devoid of motion. Merely riding an escalator, for example, can be an extremely difficult experience because of her inability to process the motion signals needed to perceive self-motion and coordinate the precise timing and body movement sequences needed to step off.

Joe McNally/Getty Images

Psychophysical studies have shown that the motion gradients in optic flow serve as an important cue for the control of balance and heading during locomotion (Chalupa & Werner, 2004; Noë, 2005; Vaina, Beardsley, & Rushton, 2004). The visual expansion on the retina during forward locomotion helps to coordinate and guide the movement of the body, to maintain heading direction, and steer around obstacles. The importance of vision and motion signals on locomotion can be appreciated when there is a failure to use this information, such as in trying to navigate with the eyes closed and in certain clinical conditions (SideNote 13.15).

Collision avoidance

The movement of oneself toward an object, or conversely, the motion of an object toward us, sets up the need to avoid an imminent collision. Our visual system has built-in mechanisms that rapidly detect the likelihood of a collision and ensure that immediate motor steps are taken to avoid it. Indeed, collision avoidance represents another striking example of how motion signals impact our daily behaviour. The need to rapidly calculate the *time to collision* (TTC) was taken up in Section A.2, where we also discussed how the visual system possibly computes the ratio of the retinal image size to the rate of expansion (the so-called *tau* parameter) to derive an accurate estimate of the TTC (Lee, 1976).

As with optic flow processing, certain clinical conditions such as Alzheimer's disease can impair collision avoidance due to a generalized loss in motion processing ability. One of the most striking cases of motion loss, however, was reported by a German woman, who is known in scientific literature as the *motion-blind* patient

(Enns, 2003). The cause in this case is not a neurodegenerative disease such as Alzheimer's but rather a stroke that caused damage to both sides of her brain around the site where area MT is located. The resulting motion deficit in this patient is total—she has no ability whatsoever to perceive motion—and yet her other visual functions in terms of form, colour, depth, etc., remain relatively intact.

There are numerous accounts of what a visual world without motion means for this patient and a few others like her. The smooth perception of object translocation that we take for granted is replaced by snapshot perceptions of moving objects that suddenly appear at different places, somewhat similar perhaps to the example of stroboscopic motion discussed at the beginning of this chapter. The simple task of pouring a cup of tea becomes a burden because the rising level of the cup is not detected until the tea spills over. An even more harrowing task is navigating outdoors, especially when crossing a street. The motion of cars after all is invisible to her. A vehicle can therefore suddenly appear out of nowhere because a moment ago it was seen at a more distant location. The ability to track the trajectory of a moving object and avoid a collision, which appears so effortless to us, is simply absent in this patient (SideNote 13.16).

3. MOTION SENSING AND ADAPTATION

Throughout this book, we have tried to intertwine the various facets of perceptual experience with the underlying biological properties of the sensory system in question. We continue that exploration now with a closer look at three specific aspects of motion perception and how they are intrinsically related to the neurobiology of motion sensing. The first issue we take up is an interesting phenomenon that arises as a direct consequence of the nature of motion circuits in the brain. The second and third issues are more complex but nevertheless represent fundamental problems that our visual brain must face in processing motion signals, and for which it must come up with a biological solution.

The motion aftereffect

As early as 350 BCE, Greek philosopher Aristotle noticed that a stationary object will appear to move when looked at immediately after viewing a moving scene, such as a flowing river. The critical point in this observation is that one must look at a moving object for a prolonged period, say about a minute or so. Afterwards, a stationary object will appear to move in a direction opposite to the previously viewed moving scene. This so-called **motion aftereffect** is a very compelling phenomenon, which has been described in various forms throughout the ages, most notably by Czech physiologist Jan Purkinje in the early 1800s. A later description of this phenomenon was provided by Robert Addams after viewing a waterfall in Scotland (see Figure 13.12). When Addams then turned his gaze to the vertical face of the rocky cliff immediately to the side of the waterfall, it appeared to move upward in a very vivid and realistic manner (SideNote 13.17). The phenomenon has subsequently been dubbed the *waterfall illusion* based on this historical account.

The waterfall illusion is really an example of **motion adaptation**, a phenomenon that is now well known and highly studied (Mather, Verstraten, & Anstis, 1998). In previous chapters, we have seen that the responsiveness of sensory systems becomes altered after being exposed to a stimulus for some time. In this case, the prolonged viewing of a moving stimulus, such as a waterfall, produces strong firing within downward-preferring directionally selective neurons. Once this stimulation ceases, such as by changing gaze toward a stationary object, those neurons that previously fired at a high level now enter a temporary period of reduced responsiveness that is sometimes characterized as "fatigue." It is believed that the motion aftereffect arises due to such neural adaptation in one set of motion detectors (downward preferring) such that when a stationary object is viewed, a motion impression

Figure 13.12

The Falls of Foyers is ideal for producing the waterfall illusion because of the surrounding rock cliffs. The falls are part of the River Foyers that feeds into Loch Ness in Scotland. Photo © Brian Parkes/Alamy

in the opposite direction arises (Kandel et al., 2000). Recall that neurons in the central nervous system usually discharge at a certain level, known as *spontaneous firing*. Thus, if say upward-preferring directionally selective neurons continue to fire at their spontaneous level but are not counterbalanced by the downward-preferring ones (due to adaptation), then there will be a brief period when stationary objects will be perceived to be drifting upward until the adaptation effect wears off (SideNote 13.18).

The preceding is just one possible explanation for the motion aftereffect, but one that is widely accepted within the vision science community. The question that arises is "Where exactly in the visual system does neural adaptation take place to trigger the perceived motion aftereffect?" It would be reasonable to assume that area V1 is a leading candidate because this is the first site where directionally selective neurons are found. An interesting, and simple, experiment seems to confirm this idea. If adaptation to a stimulus is undertaken by monocular viewing, say the right eye only, then the motion aftereffect will still arise when a stationary object is viewed through the other eye only

SideNote | **13.17**

The words of Robert Addams have often been cited as an excellent description of the phenomenon: "Having steadfastly looked for a few seconds at a particular part of the cascade . . . and then suddenly directed my eyes to the left, to observe the face of the sombre age-worn rocks immediately contiguous to the water-fall, I saw the rocky surface as if in motion upwards, and with an apparent velocity equal to that of the descending water, which the moment before had prepared my eyes to behold that singular deception."

Jan Evangelista Purkinje (1787–1869)
© LIBRARY OF CONGRESS/SCIENCE PHOTO LIBRARY

SideNote | **13.18**

In the absence of sensory adaptation, a stationary object does not create differential firing in neurons with opposing directional preferences (i.e., both upward- and downward-preferring neurons discharge at their spontaneous rate). However, neural adaptation leads to reduced spontaneous firing in one set (the downward-preferring neurons in this example), whereas the upward-preferring neurons continue to fire at their normal spontaneous rate. This misbalance in the two opposing neural circuits caused by adaptation is what presumably leads to perceived upward movement.

INVESTIGATION

The Waterfall Illusion

For this investigation, you will need to visit the following website: http://www.michaelbach.de/ot/mot_adapt/index.html. Follow the instructions there, and then afterwards, read the explanation below.

The first image (black and white) is the adapting stimulus. As you watch this image (which appears to be moving inwards toward a centre point), you are causing particular neurons to become adapted. For example, the neurons that are coding for downward movement in the top area of the circle fire for the entire duration of the downward motion. In the next picture (the figure of Buddha), the image is still, however we see upward (expanding) motion near the figure's head. This can be explained due to the opponency set up between the downward-preferring and upward-preferring neurons. The downward-preferring neurons adapt after firing during the adapting stimulus and suppress their firing (to below baseline levels) when the stationary stimulus appears. Due to this suppression, the upward-preferring neurons in the same area *appear* to be firing more, for the spontaneous level of firing they are emitting is still stronger than the suppressed downward-preferring neurons. The result is movement in the opposite direction, even when there is no movement.

To view another afterimage, please see the following website: http://www.michaelbach.de/ot/mot_adaptSpiral/index.html. Stare at the image for about 20 seconds, and then look somewhere in the room. See if you can use the explanation above to understand what happens!

(the left eye, in this case). This phenomenon, which is known as **interocular transfer**, demonstrates that the adaptation effects responsible for the motion aftereffect do not occur at the level of the retina or LGN, where only monocular neurons exist. That is, the effects of the adaptation cannot transfer from one eye to the other at these points because there is no interaction between them at the neural level. Rather, the fact that interocular transfer occurs with the motion aftereffect means that it can only arise at a level where neural output from the two eyes are combined, which we know happens for the first time in area V1.

The aperture problem

Consider a situation where a moving object is viewed through a round window or aperture, as illustrated in Figure 13.13. We know from ordinary experience that the object's movement will be clearly observed even if only a small part of it is visible through the window. However, it turns out that the global motion of the object is not faithfully represented by the motion that is only visible through the aperture. In the example here, the view through the two apertures will capture the downward movement of the two edges belonging to a diamond. The restricted aperture views in this

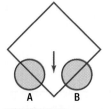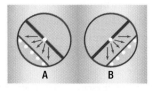

Figure 13.13

The global movement of an object may be sampled through small apertures that capture only the local motion of its components (left diagram). However, there happens to be a range of theoretical directions at which these edges may move, and yet all of them will only generate motion that is perpendicular to the edge within the aperture (middle diagram). The inability to derive the true motion of an object in such cases is known as the *aperture problem*. One way to derive the correct direction of the object's movement is to integrate information from multiple apertures by combining the local component vectors to derive the global motion vector (right diagram).

case will actually portray a direction that is perpendicular to the axis of the edge, and therefore it will not coincide with the correct global movement of the object (SideNote 13.19).

This situation has been characterized as the **aperture problem** and is further illustrated in the middle diagram of Figure 13.13 where the two edges of the diamond are shown within the two apertures. Although in this particular case the edges are physically moving downward, consider what would happen if each edge actually moved in one of several different directions, as indicated by the arrows. The centre point of the edge (shown by the white dot) would then end up at one of several different locations depending on the movement direction of the edge. However, none of these correct movement directions will actually be observed through the aperture and instead the edge will appear to move only perpendicular to its axis. At the next moment in time, the edge will therefore be seen to have arrived at the position shown in the figure. Thus, the aperture actually constrains the view we obtain, and therefore the line of arrival at the next time-point, know as the *constraint line*, remains the same regardless of the actual direction of motion.

The aperture problem is not merely a curious phenomenon but one that has significant biological relevance. We know that the visual world is captured by retinal neurons that have circular receptive fields. Therefore, in a sense we view the world through many small apertures, and it is this view that is transmitted out of the retina to our visual brain. Hence, the aperture problem remains fundamental to the acquisition of visual information and therefore must be solved by the brain if we are to obtain a correct impression of global object motion, which we do.

The most widely accepted solution to the aperture problem is one that has been advanced by American neuroscientist Anthony Movshon and his colleagues (Adelson & Movshon, 1982). Given that a single aperture view constrains the true direction of object motion, Movshon argued that the solution must rely on integrating information from two or more apertures. If two non-parallel edges are part of the same moving object, then they must also be moving in the same direction, though each will have its own constraint line within each aperture. However, only one of the many possible movement directions of each edge within an aperture will be common to the object's true global

motion. A simple method called *intersection of constraints* can solve the problem. As shown in the right diagram of Figure 13.13, the true motion of the object (arrow) is derived from the one motion vector that is common to all the constraint lines. Movshon has shown that this level of integration arises in area MT where, in addition to neurons that process component motion (i.e., the constraint lines), a separate pool of neurons exist that integrate locally analyzed motions of a single rigid object to generate signals corresponding to its true global motion. The aperture problem is therefore solved by integrating multiple component motions into a single, and correct, global motion signal (Stoner & Albright, 1992; Adelson & Movshon, 1982).

Higher-order motion processing

Our treatment of motion signals thus far has assumed that a luminance difference exists between a moving object and its background. In other words, the moving edge itself is defined by a difference in light level compared to its immediate surroundings, as in the case of a moving bar, a dancing actor, or a cascading waterfall. Luminance-defined object movement is the most commonly occurring type of motion in our natural world. Vision scientists refer to this as **first–order motion**.

Consider, however, a situation in which an object blends in with the background so that there are no luminance-defined edges. There are many instances where this occurs in nature, such as in aquatic environments, with various types of marine animals, as well in various terrestrial situations. Figure 13.14 on page 458 shows a few such examples of animal camouflage where the lightness and colour composition of an animal mimics the background. The question that arises is—would we not detect the movement of these animals? In fact, we do indeed detect the movement of isoluminant objects (i.e., those in which the light reflected off the object and its immediate background are similar or identical). The problem though is "How can the visual brain process isoluminant motion through the classical motion detectors that are structured to detect moving, light-defined edges?"

This problem represents a special situation in motion processing and has been dubbed **second–order motion**. There are different aspects of second-order motion in which a moving border is defined by isoluminant texture difference, isoluminant colour difference, illusory contour, or flicker difference (also

SideNote | **13.19**

The situation is further illustrated by way of the example below. The light bar is actually moving downward and to the right (shown by the arrow). However, when the bar's movement is viewed exclusively through the aperture, it will be seen to be moving only rightward (i.e., the downward component is obscured, thereby generating a misleading impression of the object's true direction of motion).

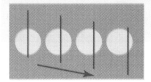

Figure 13.14

Camouflaged animals blend with their background, making it difficult for predators to detect their presence. The camouflage process works by ensuring that the lightness and colour composition of an animal mimics its surroundings, as in these examples of terrestrial (left side) and aquatic (right side) animals. Photos clockwise from top left: bbuong/iStockphoto.com; DurdenImages/iStockphoto.com; semet/iStockphoto.com; tamer/iStockphoto.com

SideNote | 13.20

We previously discussed the example of a moving leopard in terms of camouflage. Most animals that rely on camouflage do not have such distinctive body patterns, and instead, their movement is detected by second-order motion mechanisms. The presence of such advanced circuits presumably arose as a survival advantage due to the ability to detect moving camouflaged prey.

Max Wertheimer (1880–1943)
© NATIONAL LIBRARY OF MEDICINE/
SCIENCE PHOTO LIBRARY

known as *temporal texture*) (Chalupa & Werner, 2004; Enns, 2004; Epstein & Rogers, 1995). Although the classical low-level detectors are unable to detect the movement of such boundaries, there is now considerable evidence of the existence of high-level motion detectors that are capable of processing second-order motion. It appears that much of the circuitry that permits movement perception in such cases is situated in areas MT and MST. The study of these special neural circuits and how they integrate first-order motion is currently an area of considerable physiological and computational vision research (SideNote 13.20).

4. ILLUSORY MOTION

The quote by George Lucas at the beginning of this chapter sets the stage for our discussion in this section. Motion illusions are extremely compelling and occur all around us—from the curious reversal of movement of the spokes of a tire as a car speeds up to the very way in which animated sequences create a smooth perception of motion, even though there is no real movement of the characters. These illusions arise because the visual stimulus is very effective in triggering our motion detectors. In some cases, however, the illusions are so baffling that they defy explanation. We will conclude this section with one such example.

Apparent motion

The phenomenon of **apparent motion** arises when a stimulus is presented at one location, turned off, and then shown at a different location shortly afterwards (Chalupa & Werner, 2004; Epstein & Rogers, 1995; Palmer, 2002). This sequence produces a vivid impression of movement from the first point to the second (SideNote 13.21). In fact, the motion impression is so convincing that it cannot be distinguished from real motion; it is as if the object really did move from one point to the next. This illusion was originally described in detail by Gestalt psychologist Max Wertheimer in the early 20th century. Wertheimer discovered that when two lights flicker on and off in close proximity, it appears as if the light moves back and forth between the two locations. The Gestalt psychologists called this *phi movement* and used it as an important example of their *law of minimum principle*—that is, that we do not necessarily perceive the real world as it is but instead organize our perceptual experiences to be as simple as possible.

From a biological perspective, apparent motion is easily explained by way of the classical motion detector. If we assume that the two stimuli sequentially stimulate the two sensors of a Reichardt detector, then a motion signal will be generated in the same way as if the stimulus actually moved between the two sensors in real time. In other words, the detector cannot distinguish true movement from apparent movement because insofar as it is concerned, the stimulation sequences are no different. It is perhaps for this reason that apparent motion creates such a vivid perception of movement. And that vivid perception in turn has formed the basis for literally the entire visual arts entertainment industry. Apparent motion, quite simply, is the foundation for all movement in television and film. A simple example is shown in Figure 13.15 in which an action sequence is captured by an overlapping collage of still images. If these images were presented consecutively in time then the effect would be to produce a compelling movement of the basketball players. As George Lucas remarked, film is truly an illusion.

There are certain requirements for an apparent motion stimulus to be effective (Kolers, 1972). Again consider the problem from the point of view of the Reichardt detector. Any given detector is optimized for a certain time delay between the stimulation of one sensor and the next. As we learned earlier in

Figure 13.15

An action sequence captured by a series of still images showing the successive movement of a basketball player.

this chapter, there likely exists a broad range of detectors with different delay preferences so as to encode different stimulus speeds. Thus, the delay between the offset of one stimulus and the onset of the next in an apparent motion display must fall within the range of these delays. Otherwise a motion signal will either not be generated or at best be very weak. Similarly, there is only a limited range of distances over which the apparent motion display will work. If the distance between the two stimuli becomes too large, then the motion signal will be degraded. The importance of space and time was appreciated by the Gestalt psychologists, who went to great lengths to understand the optimum conditions for generating apparent motion (SideNote 13.22).

The wagonwheel effect

The effect of stimulus distance in an apparent motion display becomes especially clear when we consider an intriguing visual illusion that we have all witnessed in movies or TV, especially in Westerns that typically show horse-drawn carriages. As soon as a moving stagecoach reaches a certain speed, the large spoked wheels suddenly appear to rotate in the opposite direction. This illusion, which has been given various names including the **wagonwheel effect**, is very striking because at one moment a wheel

will appear to be turning in one direction and then suddenly reverse itself and begin rotating in the opposite direction (Palmer, 2002). The same effect can be observed with any rotating object, such as an airplane propeller, a helicopter rotor, or the tires of a car under ordinary viewing conditions.

The solution to this puzzle is actually quite straightforward and is explained in Figure 13.16. Let us assume that a four-spoked wheel is rotating clockwise and captured on film at a certain frame rate. The top panel shows what happens when the wheel is rotating at a relatively slow speed. The next frame will capture the new position of the wheel in which the spokes have moved clockwise by a small extent (previous frame position is shown in grey). We therefore have an apparent motion stimulus between the spokes when the two frames are presented sequentially, resulting in the perception of clockwise rotary movement. If, on the other hand, the wheel happens to be rotating very fast, then the next frame will show that the spokes have advanced quite far around the circle (bottom panel in Figure 13.16). But now, an interesting event occurs. The spokes from the previous frame

SideNote | **13.21**

A space–time plot of an apparent motion stimulus is shown below. A stimulus (shown by the black dot) appears at one position and then reappears at a different location a short while later. If the space and time parameters are within certain limits, then a vivid impression of smooth motion occurs between the two locations of the stimuli.

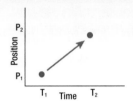

Frame 1   **Frame 2**

Figure 13.16

A clockwise rotating wheel in a movie is perceived to move in the correct direction at low speeds (top panel) because the spokes that appear in the next frame have moved only a short distance, leading to an apparent motion signal in the clockwise direction. If the same wheel is moving very fast (bottom panel), then the spokes have moved around a much greater distance, and therefore a counter-clockwise motion signal represents the shortest motion path, creating an illusory rotation of the wheel in the opposite direction.

SideNote | **13.22**

The space–time parameters that guide apparent movement were formulated by Gestalt psychologist Adolf Korte in 1915 and are now referred to as *Korte's laws*.

(again shown in grey) need to traverse a much shorter distance in the counter-clockwise direction to match the spokes in the second frame. Our visual system prefers this shorter distance in associating image components in an apparent motion stimulus, and therefore an illusory counter-clockwise motion will be generated, even though the wheel is actually rotating clockwise (SideNote 13.23).

The correspondence problem

The wagonwheel effect introduces us to an important issue in apparent motion—the matching or *correspondence* between image components in the different frames of a sequential display. A slowly rotating wheel produces a correct correspondence between the image components because the spatial parameters coincide with true directional motion. However, the correspondence at faster speeds is still technically accurate in that the correct objects are being matched in generating the motion signal; it is just that the perceptual movement direction does not match the physical direction because of the closer proximity of counter-clockwise correspondence.

A question that arises with more complex images concerns how the visual system makes a correct match between the individual components from one frame to another in an apparent motion display. If we take a sequence, such as the one in Figure 13.15, we know that smooth motion perception occurs in which the correct components appear to move from one frame to their counterpart in the next. But why is it that the player's head in the left sequence does not jump and meld with the basketball in the next frame? After all, our visual system re-constitutes the overall scene based on early elemental parsing of the components and therefore low-level mismatches are seemingly plausible. The exact matching of image components in such displays presents a challenge from a computational point of view, and vision scientists have dubbed it the **correspondence problem** (SideNote 13.24) (Epstein & Rogers, 1995; Kolers, 1972; Palmer, 2002).

It is not yet known what precise rules the visual system uses to solve the correspondence problem. One important factor is certainly *space*. In other words, our visual system will match an image component to another that is closer rather than another that is farther away. The wagonwheel effect makes this clear. There are other factors that have also been shown

to be important, such as similarity in terms of colour, orientation, and spatial frequency. Our visual system will create a motion path between object tokens that are similar in terms of these parameters compared to those that are very different. Thus, the basketball player's head in the example in Figure 13.15 will be correlated with his own head in the next sequence and not be perceived to move toward any other structure because there are no similarities in any of the fundamental features. Instead, apparent motion will be properly generated to produce movement between similar objects in the scene, leading to vivid animated movement that makes sense.

Complex motion illusions

The motion illusions that we have taken up thus far in our discussion arise from the activation of low-level detectors. For example, we saw how apparent motion can be partly explained by sequential activation of the sensors of a Reichardt-type detector, much as with a real moving stimulus. Similarly, the motion aftereffect could be attributed to the adaptation of low-level motion detectors to yield illusory motion in the opposite direction. The vivid quality of these illusions is the consequence of tapping into motion circuits at the earliest levels of the visual pathway.

A wide variety of motion illusions exist that go well beyond the ones we have discussed so far. In general, these illusions have more complex origins and can usually be attributed to interpretational mistakes at a more cognitive level. One such class of illusions is based on object–object interactions; in other words, the movement of one object imparts an illusory movement upon another. One such type of illusion is that of **induced motion**, in which a large moving object or background induces movement in a smaller stationary object (Enns, 2004; Palmer, 2002). This illusion can occur when looking at the moon through moving clouds. It often appears as if the moon itself is moving rather than the clouds. One explanation for this effect is that our visual system makes an assumption that the larger object, which in visual terms is the cloud, is likely to be stationary and therefore assigns relative motion to the visually smaller object (the moon).

Another class of complex visual illusions occurs when moving objects impart a sense of self-motion. We have all experienced this

SideNote | **13.23**

The wagonwheel effect also occurs under natural viewing, such as directly looking at the propeller of a plane when it starts up. As it speeds up, there comes a point when the propeller appears to rotate in the opposite direction. The illusory reversal of rotational movement under normal viewing conditions has also been referred to as *subjective stroboscopy*.

SideNote | **13.24**

We previously encountered a similar correspondence problem in stereoscopic vision (Chapter 12, Section C.4) where the visual system had to solve an image matching problem. In that case, the correspondence problem related to image associations between the two eyes rather than two successive images in time, as is the case with apparent motion.

illusion in various forms, such as in a stationary car, train, or airplane. The movement of another vehicle outside leads to a momentary **vection illusion** (i.e., the movement of oneself in the opposite direction) (Palmer, 2002). Our visual brain interprets the movement of the periphery to generate a false sensation of self-movement. The illusory movement in this case happens to arise from a false cognitive interpretation of the retinal image movement. There are indeed many situations where vection can create a compelling visual effect, a fact that has been used in virtual reality displays and by the gaming industry to create enticing arcade games. Vection illusions have also been studied in aviation settings because of the many types of illusions that arise from visual interaction with the environment during flight (SideNote 13.25).

A final class of motion illusions is dependent upon eye movements while viewing a visual stimulus. In all cases, the stimulus itself is stationary, though the effect of moving the eyes over it generates a sense of illusory movement. There are many examples of these illusions that include linear and circular movement as well as illusory movement in depth. One particularly powerful illusion is the *rotating snakes*, which was created by Japanese psychologist Akiyoshi Kitaoka and is shown in Figure 13.17. The illusion appears strongest when scanning the image and becomes very weak and almost negligible if fixation is maintained on any one part of the image, such as one of the central black dots. Kitaoka and his colleagues have shown that the amplitude of eye movements correlate well with the saliency of the illusion (Kuriki, Ashida, Murakami, & Kitaoka, 2008). The property of eye movements in general and how they affect visual perception are topics that are taken up in the next section.

C. Eye Movements

In the preceding sections we discussed how moving objects in our physical world produce vivid motion perception. Object movement also introduces a separate challenge in that we need to be able to keep track of the object's motion trajectory through the environment. There are three ways we can do this—orient our body with the moving object, move our head, or track the object by moving our eyes. In reality, all three are used though the efficiency

Figure 13.17

The *rotating snakes* illusion created by Akiyoshi Kitaoka generates a compelling sense of rotational movement in this static image. The illusion disappears upon maintaining strict fixation on any components of the image, suggesting that eye movements play a role in producing the illusory effect. Image courtesy of Akiyoshi Kitaoka.

and exactness of the response depends on the circumstances. For example, if we were to visually follow a foul ball hit into the stands during a baseball game, then we would invariably turn our body to see where it landed. A tennis match, on the other hand, usually requires lateral head movements to follow the back and forth movement of the ball, whereas a ping-pong match would normally require mere tracking movements of the eyes.

The exact type of response that we make therefore depends on many factors but is primarily driven by how the object itself is moving. In general, various combinations of eye, head, and body movements are usually involved in tandem. The **oculomotor** response, however, is the most sensitive in terms of **object tracking**. In some cases, there is a direct relationship between object motion and the oculomotor response, whereas in other situations, eye movements are aimed at reorienting gaze upon a different object of interest (Land, 1999). The scope, use, and biological mechanisms underlying these various types of eye movements are taken up in this section of the chapter.

1. BIOLOGICAL FOUNDATIONS

The two notable features of mammalian eye movements are that they are binocular in nature and extremely precise (SideNote 13.26). The latter feature is a necessity because a sloppy

SideNote | **13.25**

A number of aviation-specific illusions have been described that are of visual origin and often involve a false illusion of self-motion that is at odds with the correct heading, tilt, or incline of the aircraft. Some examples of these include the following: black-hole approach illusion, autokinetic illusion, false visual reference illusion, and linear perspective illusion.

SideNote | **13.26**

There are rare instances when binocular eye movement is compromised. The two eyes may move slightly differently due to the nature of visual stimulation or diseases affecting the brain stem or cerebellum. Certain amphibians and reptiles (e.g., chameleons) are well known for their ability to move their eyes independently.

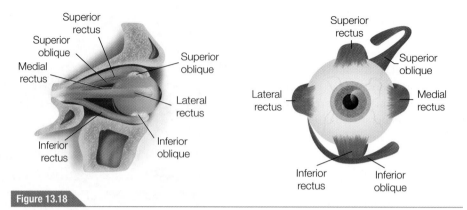

The six extraocular muscles are tightly packed within the bony socket containing the eyeball (left diagram). The four rectus muscles insert into symmetrical points around the eyeball at its midline (right diagram). The superior and inferior rectus muscles move the eyes up and down, respectively, whereas the medial and lateral rectus muscles are responsible for horizontal movements. The two oblique muscles produce rotational eye movements.

oculomotor system would not allow us to make the minute eye movements that are often necessary to ensure proper fixation upon moving objects or to accurately redirect our gaze. Indeed, the outstanding precision of eye movements has made this a model system for study by engineers and physicists. The biological aspects of oculomotor function have similarly captivated the neuroscience community, leading to significant insight over the past five decades into how sensory and motor functions are intrinsically intertwined (Ebenholtz, 2001; Epstein & Rogers, 1995; Optican, 2005).

The oculomotor muscles

The physical placement of each eyeball within a bony *orbital socket* gives it considerable freedom of movement. One reason for the outstanding accuracy of eye movements is that each eyeball is controlled by six **extraocular muscles**, as shown in Figure 13.18. These muscles, which are among the smallest in the body, are tightly packed into the orbital socket and insert into the eyeball just around its midline. The four so-called *rectus muscles* move the eyeball along the horizontal and vertical axes (Carpenter, 1988; Kandel et al., 2000). The medial and lateral rectus muscles, which are placed toward the nasal and temporal sides, respectively, are responsible for left–right movements, whereas the superior and inferior rectus muscles are responsible for up–down movements. The two oblique muscles take a somewhat horizontal path before inserting into the eyeball. This unusual trajectory allows these muscles to produce small rotational movements of the eyeball.

Eye movements involved with gaze shifts and object tracking are symmetrical in nature (i.e., both eyes move together in the same direction, which is referred to as **conjunctive eye movements**). Imagine a situation where the eyes are fixated upon an object straight ahead and then a moment later the observer shifts gaze to an object lying to the right. The two eyes in this case will move in tandem and to the same horizontal extent to fixate on the new object. To accomplish this task, the lateral rectus muscle of the right eye will contract in synchrony with the medial rectus muscle of the left eye to produce equivalent rightward movement of both eyeballs. A similar situation arises when we track a moving object, as can be easily demonstrated by moving a finger in front of a friend's eyes and watching the conjunctive movements as the eyes follow the motion of the finger.

A somewhat different situation arises with vergence eye movements that occur due to gaze shifts between objects at different depth planes (see Section A.3 of Chapter 12 for a quick review). The act of shifting gaze to a closer object is accompanied by the inward rotation of both eyes, or *convergence*. In this case, the medial rectus muscles of the two eyes are simultaneously contracting to produce the inward rotations. The opposite movement occurs when we shift gaze to a farther object. The lateral rectus muscles of both eyes in this case contract in order to swing both eyes outward (i.e., *divergence*). Oculomotor responses in which the eyes rotate in opposite directions are referred to as **disjunctive eye movements** and generally occur during vergence.

Neurobiological mechanisms

There are a number of areas in the brain stem, cerebellum, thalamus, and cerebral cortex that together are responsible for processing eye movement functions, as illustrated in Figure 13.19 (Chalupa & Werner, 2004; Krauzlis, 2005; Trillenberg, Lencer, & Heide, 2004). The left part of the connection circuit shows the pathway by which signals from the retina reach the lateral geniculate nucleus (LGN) and then the visual cortex. The cortical structures beyond area V1 involved in eye movement function include several areas in the parietal cortex (such as **area LIP**) and the frontal cortex (such as **area FEF**) (Catz & Their, 2007; Ilg & Their, 2008). The ascending visual signals also reach the superior colliculus (SC), which is a paired structure located just below the LGN. However, unlike the LGN, there is no fibre output directly from the SC to the visual cortex.

There are major descending projections from the three major cortical areas noted above back to the SC, as well as two other areas—the cerebellum and the brain stem. The projection to the SC is particularly interesting because it allows this structure to integrate sensory information from the retina with the descending cortical output (Catz & Their, 2007; Wurtz, Sommer, & Cavanaugh, 2005). The integrative role of the SC begins to make sense when its main function is considered. The SC has a major output to motor areas of the brain stem and through these areas controls the rapid orienting movements of the eyes. The brain stem also receives a direct projection from the frontal cortex and the cerebellum. These projections play a prominent role in guiding the tracking movements of the eyes. It is the brain stem that contains the motor neurons that innervate the extraocular muscles (SideNote 13.27) (Ebenholtz, 2001; Ilg & Their, 2008; Trillenberg et al., 2004).

Neuroscientists have studied the SC in considerable detail, not only because of its role in guiding eye movements but also as a key example of a neural structure where signals from different sensory domains appear to converge. It has been shown that in addition to visual signals, the SC also processes auditory and somatosensory functions as well. Indeed, a subset of SC neurons simultaneously process signals from these different sensory domains, a feature that has been dubbed **multi-sensory integration**. There are other areas of the brain, most notably parts of the parietal and frontal cortex that also display similar properties. Multi-sensory integration by the SC allows gaze shifts to take place in response to incoming information other than just the visual signals, such as a sound impulse or tactile stimulation, thereby ensuring that visual feedback is immediately initiated.

Oculomotor control and position constancy

The visual brain is faced with a significant challenge in that it must be able to generate motion perception arising from true object movement but not from movement of the eyes. For example, the trajectory of a tennis ball

SideNote | 13.27

Figure 13.19 is a highly schematized diagram and does not contain many connectional details and brain structures involved in generating eye movements. The full neural circuitry of oculomotor function is extremely complex and is beyond the scope of this section.

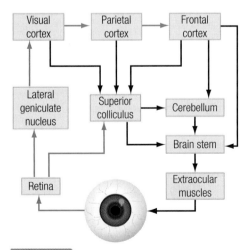

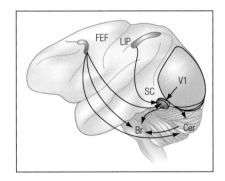

Br – brainstem
Cer – cerebellum
FEF – frontal eye fields
LIP – lateral intraparietal area

SC – superior colliculus
V1 – primary visual cortex
(area V1)

Figure 13.19

The neural structures that are important in generating eye movements involve various cortical and subcortical structures. The ascending information (red arrows) carries visual input upon which motor signals are computed and flow in a descending manner (black arrows). The interaction of multiple brain areas (inset) results in a final set of motor commands on the extraocular muscles to produce an oculomotor response.

during a match represents true object movement and must be faithfully captured as such. However, if we intentionally move our eyes to scan the stadium, then that too produces retinal image movement, which should also theoretically generate motion signals. In the latter case, however, the people seated in the stadium are not moving at all, and therefore any such perception would create a false representation of reality. We know from everyday experience that moving our eyes does not create such false movement impressions. The stability of the visual world during self-generated eye movements is referred to as **position constancy**.

How does the visual system dissociate retinal image motion arising from true object motion versus retinal image motion due to eye movements? One way to achieve this is for the sensory quarters of our brain to somehow obtain motor information associated with eye movements and then compare those signals with the actual retinal image motion (Carpenter, 1988; Buttner-Ennever, Konakci, & Blumer, 2006; Wurtz et al., 2005). Such a scheme is illustrated in Figure 13.20. We saw in Chapter 12 how motor commands associated with accommodation and vergence eye movements are monitored by the brain to obtain a perceptual representation of object depth. In a similar manner, the motor signal sent to the oculomotor muscles during conjunctive eye movements is accompanied by a carbon copy.

The idea that a carbon copy of a motor signal (also known as **corollary discharge**) may be sent to other parts of the brain is nearly a century old, having originated with Charles Sherrington.

As Figure 13.20 shows, the motor signal acts on the oculomotor muscles of the eyeball to create an eye movement that in turn produces a shift in the retinal image. The corresponding visual signal is sent to sensory areas of the brain (visual cortex), which can in turn be used to calibrate the motor signal, as shown by the connection between sensory and motor brain areas. However, an important point to note here is that a copy of the sensory signal is sent to brain structures that also receive the motor copy. As a result, this so-called *comparator* is then able to correlate the sensory and motor signals to create the sense of position constancy (Wurtz et al., 2005). The implications of this correlation and its role in generating position constancy will be taken up in succeeding sections when we discuss the different types of eye movements. Figure 13.20 will serve as an important reference for this later discussion (SideNote 13.28).

2. MICROMOVEMENTS OF THE EYES

The purpose behind fixating on an object in our visual world is to ensure that its image is placed on the fovea, which in turn allows the

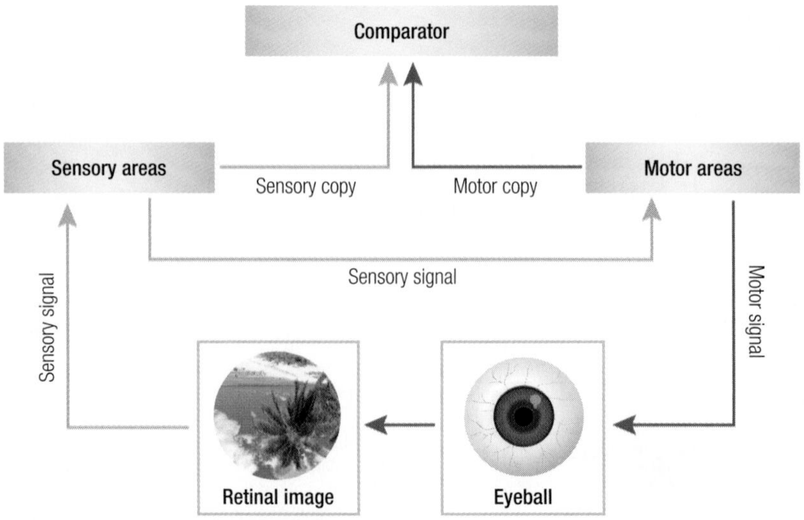

SideNote | **13.28**

It is also believed that sensors in the oculomotor muscles monitor the contraction state and send signals to higher brain centres. This so-called *afference copy* likely serves as an additional mechanism over that of the corollary discharges to inform the visual brain as to when the eyes have moved.

Figure 13.20

Eye movements are initiated by motor signals that in turn produce a shift in the retinal image. The associated retinal signals are transmitted to the higher sensory areas as well as a comparator, which also receives a carbon copy of the motor signal. A comparison is then made between the sensory and motor signals to compute the true physical characteristics of environmental objects.

visual system to capture its fine spatial details. Although we may think that our eyes have perfectly locked onto an object when we are scrutinizing its details, it actually turns out that there are small jittery movements that are causing its image to continually shift ever so slightly over the retina. Vision scientists refer to these as *fixational micromovements*. The advent of new technologies in the 1950s allowed researchers in the U.S. and the U.K. to show that micromovements are essential for vision and that without them we would effectively become blind.

The perils of retinal stabilization

There were two technological developments that paved the way to a greater understanding of fixational micromovements. First, the ability to detect extremely small eye movements remained elusive until new instruments with greater sensitivity were developed. It was subsequently shown that the eyes are actually in continuous motion even during what seems to be perfectly stable fixation (Ratliff & Riggs, 1950; Riggs, Armington, & Ratliff, 1954). These involuntary movements have been divided into further subclasses called **microsaccades**, *microdrifts*, and *tremors*. A full understanding of the role that these micromovements play in visual perception had to await a second technological development—an optical system to counteract these movements to produce **retinal stabilization**. The objective of these studies was to determine what happens to vision as a result of a perfectly stabilized image, which could be artificially created by quickly shifting the image in a precise manner to compensate for any micromovement.

An astonishing result is produced when an image is made to be perfectly stable by such means on the retina—the image disappears! It begins to fade within about a second and thereafter completely disappears to yield a blank space (SideNote 13.29). The early work by Lorrin Riggs and his colleagues at Brown University established that micromovements of the eyes are actually necessary to prevent visual fading (Riggs et al., 1954). These tiny eye movements, which we are totally unaware of and cannot even detect in another individual, serve an important purpose by continually shifting the image of a fixated object over a few photoreceptors. It is known that persistent stimulation of any given photoreceptor will cause it to become rapidly adapted (i.e., the neural output will diminish). Microsaccades

and other ocular micromovements serve to avoid photoreceptor adaptation by continually shifting the image of a fixated object onto new sets of photoreceptors, which in turn prevents visual fading (Martinex-Conde, Macknik, Troncoso, & Dyar, 2006).

The Purkinje tree

An interesting phenomenon related to visual fading concerns the shadow cast on the photoreceptors by the network of retinal blood vessels that are present in each eye. Figure 13.21 shows these blood vessels, which enter the eye through the optic disk and arborize extensively to cover the entire retina. The blood vessels actually lie in front of the photoreceptor plane and therefore give rise to an interesting situation. As light rays proceed through the eyeball, they must interact with the blood vessels on their way to creating the retinal image. Consequently, there must be a shadow of these vessels cast upon the photoreceptors, which has been named the **Purkinje tree** to describe the branching vessel network.

It goes without saying that we never see this Purkinje tree during normal visual experience. The question therefore arises as to what mechanisms may be responsible for its perceptual absence. One clue to the answer arises from the fact that the shadow is always fixed. In other words, the same pattern of shadows appears on the photoreceptors because the light is always entering through one fixed aperture, the pupil. Hence, this shadow does

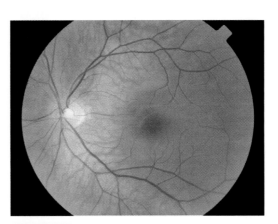

Figure 13.21

Retinal blood vessels enter and leave the eye through the optic disk. The blood vessels give rise to a branching network that lies in front of the photoreceptor plane and in the path of light rays that create the retinal image. The only part of the retina that is spared is the fovea, shown near the centre of this image. © Paul Parker/Science Photo Library

not change regardless of the scene viewed or the location of the eyes. Furthermore, even eye movements do not alter the shadow because the vessels are fixed in place within the retina and move together with the eyes. The constant location of this shadow on the photoreceptors in turn is responsible for the adaptation phenomenon described previously. In short, we do not see the shadow of our own retinal blood vessels due to the simple fact that they produce a constant and stabilized image (SideNote 13.30).

3. INVOLUNTARY EYE MOVEMENTS

Whereas fixational micromovements ensure that the eyes are in continuous motion while gazing at an object, a separate class of eye movements exist that play a seemingly contrary role, which is to preserve a stable image on the retina. The eye movements in this category are involuntary and occur in an automatic fashion when needed. In fact, we are constantly exposed to situations in which these oculomotor responses must be immediately triggered in order to maintain a stable line of sight, and hence the response is often referred to as *gaze-stabilizing* eye movements. Unlike fixational micromovements, the eye movements we describe in this section actually make the eyeballs move a considerable amount, and occasionally from one end to the other.

The vestibulo-ocular reflex

There are very few moments in our daily lives when we remain absolutely stationary. One of the conditions that gives rise to gaze-stabilizing eye movements concerns head movements. If our eyes were mere passive organs that were locked in their sockets, then they would constantly be at the mercy of self-movement and would have to tag along every time we rotated or tilted our head. The result would be visual mayhem because the retinal image would drift with any head movement in a similar fashion, giving rise to a false impression of the entire world moving along with it. In a moment, we will see just how such an impression can be artificially created.

The fact that the world appears stable despite continuous head movements can be attributed to an extremely fast and precise mechanism known as the **vestibulo-ocular reflex**, or VOR (Ebenholtz, 2001; Fetter, 2007). As the name suggests, this reflex is generated by the vestibular apparatus, which we came to know in the last chapter as a fluid-filled sensory organ located in the inner ear. The receptor cells in this organ register self-motion along the different rotational planes of the head and accordingly transmit a set of neural impulses. As Figure 13.22 shows, the vestibular apparatus transmits its neural output directly to the brain stem, which contains different sets of motor neurons that in turn control the oculomotor

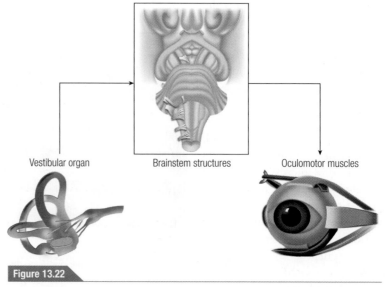

Vestibular organ   Brainstem structures   Oculomotor muscles

Figure 13.22

The vestibulo-ocular reflex is initiated by sensory neurons in the vestibular organ in response to head and body movements. The neural signals are transmitted to specific areas within the brain stem, from where motor signals are sent to the oculomotor muscles, resulting in compensatory eye movements that ensure retinal image stability.

muscles. Head movements, for example, produce fluid motion in the vestibular apparatus, causing a rapid set of signals to be generated and sent to the eyes to produce compensatory eye movements in the opposite direction (Ebenholtz, 2001).

An illustration of the VOR is shown by the sequence of images in Figure 13.23. In this example, the individual is rotating his head from left to right, though notice that gaze direction remains steady on the fixated object (the camera lens). The VOR is a fast, reflexive response that automatically occurs whenever we rotate our head. This fact can be easily demonstrated by viewing oneself in a mirror while turning the head from one side to the other. The interesting fact about the VOR is that it is generated entirely by the vestibular apparatus and does not depend upon visual input. This too can be easily demonstrated by having a friend rotate the head with eyes closed. The opposite rotation of the eyeballs is sometimes visible by way of minute undulations on the closed eyelid. The VOR also occurs for head movements along the other axes, such as up–down and even head tilt. In the latter case, there is a small rotary movement of both eyes in the opposite direction. All of these compensatory eye movements serve one purpose—to reduce or eliminate retinal image motion due to head movements and thereby prevent a false sense of environmental motion (Fetter, 2007; Palmer, 2002).

How would the world appear to us if we did not have a VOR? This is a difficult question to answer because we could never know what other neurological mechanisms would have arisen in its place. However, to give us some insight, a simple demonstration can be used to generate a false sense of motion in an otherwise stable world. Many children (and perhaps a few adults) find joy in spinning themselves around and then stopping suddenly because it yields a compelling illusion of the world rotating around them. A close look at a person who has just stopped spinning would show that the eyes themselves continue to rotate within the sockets. The eyes rotate as far as they can and then

make a sudden jump back to the centre before rotating again, a sequence that is referred to as a **nystagmus**. It turns out that after an individual has suddenly stopped spinning, the fluid in the vestibular apparatus continues to remain in motion for a brief period and therefore stimulates the oculomotor muscles. In effect, we create a VOR even though it is not required. This is simply due to the physics of fluid motion within the vestibular organ caused by the sudden deceleration. The continued movement of the eyes as a result, which is referred to as *rotational nystagmus*, generates the perception of a spinning world and offers a possible glimpse into what we might experience if the VOR never existed (SideNote 13.31).

Optokinetic nystagmus

Another type of gaze-stabilizing involuntary eye movement occurs when looking at a steadily moving display or when a large portion of a visual scene moves in one direction. One example of this common phenomenon is when we look out the window of a moving vehicle. We are usually gazing at a particular object outside the vehicle in this situation, such as a tree or animal, and therefore the eyes rotate in the direction of the moving scene in order to keep a stable retinal image of that object. As soon as they have reached their limit, the eyes snap back to the centre and pursue a different object within the moving scene. In other words, we have a nystagmus—a drifting eye movement in one direction followed by a fast return. Unlike the VOR, this nystagmus is driven entirely by visual stimulation, as can be easily demonstrated through its disappearance by closing the eyes. Consequently, this type of eye movement has been given the apt name **optokinetic nystagmus**, or OKN.

The OKN is a purely reflexive movement that spontaneously arises when viewing a large moving scene (Buttner & Kremmyda, 2007; Carpenter, 1988; Masseck & Hoffmann, 2009). The tendency for the eyes to follow the scene is so strong that it is impossible to abolish the OKN and maintain constant gaze. The biological circuitry for this function rests largely

SideNote 13.31

There are other situations in which stimulation of the vestibular fluids can generate a VOR-like eye movement. One way is to discharge ice-cold water into one ear (please do not try this unless it is part of a supervised laboratory exercise). The temperature difference sets up currents in the vestibular organ that in turn creates a vestibular-driven eye movement known as *caloric nystagmus*. A similar situation arises from excessive intake of alcohol (again, please do not try this). There are various effects on eye movements, known generally as *alcohol nystagmus*, that arise due to the effects of ethanol on the vestibular organ.

Figure 13.23

The VOR in action, as shown by head rotation from left to right (from the subject's perspective). The eyes rotate in the opposite direction so as to maintain gaze in the same direction and thereby minimize retinal image motion.

within the brain stem, where motor neurons discharge to produce an exactly matched oculomotor response. The OKN is seen in newborn babies and matures by the age of six months (Atkinson, 1984). The reflexive nature of this response and the fact that it requires visual input makes it ideally suited as a vision test in infants. As a result, gratings of different spatial frequency and contrast can be used to make an assessment of spatial vision for research purposes or in clinical situations if there is a suspected vision problem.

The primary function of the VOR and OKN is to maintain steady fixation on a target of interest. In the case of the VOR, the need to make corrective eye movements arises from head movements, whereas in the case of the OKN, it is due to a large-field movement of the visual scene. Although both types of eye movements serve the same purpose, the VOR is much faster and more precise than the visually driven OKN. This can be easily demonstrated by rotating the head while reading this text. On the other hand, if the book itself is moved back and forth at about the same speed, then the text becomes blurry to the point where it is not readable (SideNote 13.32).

Position constancy during involuntary eye movements

In both types of eye movements, we retain an accurate perception of object locations in the external world with respect to us, whether they are stationary or moving. This exact correspondence between the true world and our perception of it in the presence of eye movements requires constant comparison between the retinal image and the corollary discharge associated with eye movements, as discussed earlier and illustrated by way of Figure 13.20. The OKN provides an excellent example in this regard. The drifting visual scene induces an oculomotor response that effectively maintains a stable image of the scene on the retina. Thus, we should perceive a stationary external world in this case simply because there is no retinal motion, something that would not correspond to reality. However, the optokinetic drift of our eyes is registered by way of the corollary discharge. In effect, the neural mechanisms that generate visual perception take the movement of the eyes into account to make an inference of stimulus drift and in turn create a corresponding awareness, even though the retinal image does not provide this input.

4. VOLUNTARY EYE MOVEMENTS

Our visual experience is dominated by things that are either interesting or important to us. The appearance of a flying insect, for example, will often trigger an overt response to follow it as it buzzes around us. While driving, we generally scan the environment to obtain a sense of the relative positions of other cars and objects. In fact, our eyes are constantly in motion when we are attentive and engaged in seeking information from our visual world. The important departure here compared to the previous sections is that we voluntarily engage our eye movements in the process of selecting the objects that we wish to scrutinize, either by following them if they are moving or by intermittently directing our gaze to different stationary objects. The voluntary eye movements covered in this section are consequently referred to as *gaze-shifting* movements.

Smooth pursuit eye movements

One way in which we voluntarily shift our gaze is to track a moving object. A simple demonstration is to move the index finger back and forth in front of the eyes. The visual tracking of the finger is referred to as a **smooth pursuit** eye movement and is generated in a voluntary manner because we can just as easily ignore the finger and look off into the distance or at some other object. As a result, a set of higher-order mechanisms relating to selective attention are involved in choosing to undertake a smooth pursuit, with the purpose of tracking it exactly so as to keep its image stabilized on the fovea so that its fine detail can be visualized (Buttner & Kremmyda, 2007; Ebenholtz, 2001).

A smooth pursuit is therefore initiated by object movement combined with a voluntary desire to follow that movement. As the image deviates from the fovea, the retinal motion signal triggers a smooth pursuit that restores the image back on the fovea. Unlike the involuntary eye movements, the neural machinery for smooth pursuit involves many of the higher cortical modules where visual motion is processed (Ilg & Their, 2008; Mustari, Ono, & Das, 2009; Sharpe, 2008). If the target changes direction or speed, then the motion-sensing modules must transmit this information to the motor areas so that a necessary adjustment is made to the pursuit movement in order to keep pace with the object. Several subcortical areas, such as the superior colliculus, cerebellum, and brain stem, are recruited in fine tuning and executing the smooth pursuit motor signal (see Figure 13.19 on page 463).

The large number of diverse cortical and subcortical areas involved in smooth pursuit movements makes this circuitry especially vulnerable to certain disorders. There is now evidence to show that smooth pursuit deficits occur in certain psychotic conditions, schizophrenia, and autism, among others (Trillenberg et al., 2004). The deficit is usually manifested by an inability to maintain adequate tracking of the target or to pursue fast-moving objects. In some cases, the deficiency only becomes evident after a certain developmental period, such as in autism where the onset of the deficit occurs during adolescence.

Saccadic eye movements

It is impossible to generate a smooth pursuit movement in the absence of a moving target. Any attempt at smooth pursuit over a stationary object or scene would instead produce a set of jerky eye movements, which are known as **saccades** (Carpenter, 1988; Chalupa & Werner, 2004; Optican, 2005). Unlike smooth pursuit movements where the eyes' trajectory is defined by the nature of the stimulus, saccades are much more random in nature and arise either due to abrupt stimulus movement from one location to another or because we wish to shift our gaze to a different object of interest. Most saccades are small in amplitude, although it is possible to make a saccade that moves the eyes entirely from one side to the other (SideNote 13.33).

Saccades have been intensely studied by researchers because they represent an excellent example of ballistic eye movements that are undertaken to shift gaze to different objects of interest in the visual world (Catz & Their, 2007; Shiller & Tehovnik). The images in Figure 13.24 show the shifts in gaze direction that can be brought about by saccadic eye movements. We rarely fixate on a given point in a scene for prolonged periods and instead continually shift our eyes among different objects to create a mental map of our environment. Consequently, saccades are very much linked to goal-oriented gaze shifts and involve high-level cognitive mechanisms such as attention and object selection to choose the next saccadic target. In this regard, saccadic eye movements represent the first response in redirecting our gaze, which is often followed by head movements and their associated vestibulo-ocular reflex so that we become directionally oriented toward the new object of interest.

The voluntary gaze shifts that occur through saccades rarely follow a specific pattern. One exception is when reading a text, when we move our eyes from word to word by means of small saccades. Our saccadic system becomes much more exploratory if the cognitive demand shifts to surveying a scene. In such cases, we continually shift our eyes among different objects to create a mental map, often revisiting the more interesting objects where we hold our fixation for longer periods of time. An interesting example of such gaze-shifting strategy was discovered by Russian psychologist Alfred Yarbus in the 1950s and is shown in Figure 13.25 on page 470 (Yarbus, 1967). The right panel of this figure shows the profile of saccades that are undertaken while viewing the image in the left panel. We do not systematically survey the entire picture but instead devote more time upon specific facial parts, such as the eyes and mouth, which have been shown to be regions of particular importance in face recognition. Saccadic eye movements are therefore intrinsically linked to cognitive demands associated with object recognition and attention-driven target selection.

Saccadic suppression

An interesting question arises in terms of visual perception associated with saccadic eye movements—that is, why do we not see a blurred image in the midst of a saccade? After all, the image of the visual scene moves rapidly over the retina during a saccadic movement (SideNote 13.34). Our momentary blindness at

Figure 13.24

Saccadic eye movements result in gaze shifts so that the line of sight becomes oriented in a new direction and upon a different object. Unlike the VOR where head movements drive the oculomotor response, saccades are voluntary eye movements that are independent of head movements.

 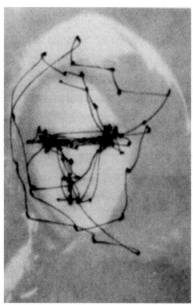

Figure 13.25

Gaze shifts continually take place through saccadic eye movements when viewing a scene. The visual system places greater emphasis on particular objects of interest, such as the eyes and mouth while viewing a facial image (right panel), rather than undertaking a systematic exploration of the entire image.

SideNote | **13.35**

A simple way to see the effect of saccadic suppression is to stand in front of a mirror and shift gaze back and forth from one eye to the other. The actual movements of the eyes cannot be made out during this process due to the phenomenon of saccadic suppression, which reduces visual sensitivity prior to and during the saccades.

this time has an intriguing explanation. It turns out that visual sensitivity during a saccade is actually reduced through neurological mechanisms, a phenomenon that has been referred to as **saccadic suppression**. Electrophysiological experiments in behaving monkeys have shown that the suppression effect begins prior to the onset of the saccade (Bremmer, Kubischik, Hoffmann, & Krekelberg, 2009; Ibbotson, Crowder, Cloherty, Prince, & Mustari, 2008). Neurons in area MT and surrounding cortical structures of the parietal lobe show reduced responsiveness around the time of a saccade, often starting well before the eye movement is initiated. The suppression effect is therefore not just due to changes in visual input but rather reflects an active neurological mechanism that is likely responsible for our failure to see retinal image blur in the midst of a saccade (SideNote 13.35).

Position constancy during voluntary eye movements

A similar dilemma arises for the visual system in terms of how it must dissociate true object motion from movement of the eyes to attain a true representation of reality. We encountered this situation before with involuntary eye movements and discovered that the visual brain resolves this problem by comparing retinal image motion with a motor copy (corollary discharge) of the oculomotor response (see Figure 13.20 on page 464). The visual system must undertake similar computations when it comes to voluntary eye movements, as illustrated by the following smooth pursuit example.

The back and forth movement of an object may trigger a tracking eye movement that matches the trajectory of the object's movement exactly. In this case, the moving object's image remains fixed on the fovea because object motion is exactly counterbalanced by the smooth pursuit movement. Although there is no retinal motion, the visual brain is aware that the eyes are moving in a systematic manner and the brain is able to use this information to infer object movement in the real world. Therefore, in this case, only the motor copy is responsible for generating the perceptual impression of object movement.

We may however choose not to track the object because we are uninterested in its movement and instead fixate on something stationary. In this case, the moving object creates a corresponding motion of its retinal image without any accompanying eye movements. Our perception of object movement in this case arises only from the sensory signals flowing out of the retina and is therefore visually generated without any corollary discharge.

D. Action and Perception

We end this chapter by discussing some key issues that relate to neurological processing in the parietal lobe. The objective is to provide an account of visual processing in the primate brain that complements our discussion on object perception in Chapter 10, concluding with a glimpse into a new way of thinking about brain mechanisms of vision.

1. THE DORSAL CORTICAL STREAM

The idea that the brain is composed of different anatomical and functional modules has a long and distinguished history, as discussed in Chapter 2. One of the significant advances made by modern neuroscience research was the discovery that the various cortical modules are linked together to create a system of interacting processors that are devoted to particular aspects of sensory or motor function. For the visual system, the idea emerged that the different modules are segregated along two processing channels—the so-called *dorsal* and *ventral streams*. We discussed the ventral stream in considerable detail in Chapter 10 where we came to know that it is composed of cortical areas that are primarily situated

within the temporal lobe of the brain. The dorsal stream, on the other hand, proceeds along the top part of the brain and encompasses various cortical areas that are situated in the parietal lobe, as shown in Figure 13.26 (Culham & Kanwisher, 2001).

The *what/where* dichotomy

A large body of research involving animals and humans had shown that lesions to temporal lobe areas produced significant impairment in visual pattern recognition, whereas lesions to parietal lobe areas caused deficits in associating the spatial relationships among objects. This body of knowledge laid the foundation for a highly influential theory that served as a unifying framework for visual information processing in the primate brain. American neuroscientists Leslie Ungerleider and Mortimer Miskin proposed a model in the 1980s in which the different demands on the visual system were mapped onto two cortical streams that diverge from the primary visual cortex (Mishkin, Ungerleider, & Mack, 1983; Ungerleider & Mishkin, 1982). They proposed that a division of labour exists in which the ventral stream is responsible for computing detailed information on the visual object itself, whereas the dorsal stream is

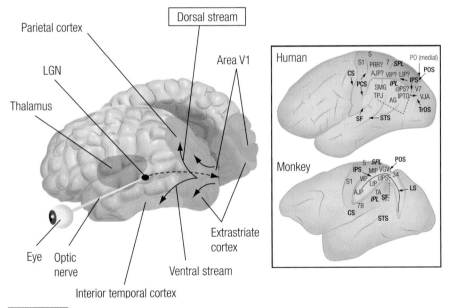

Figure 13.26

Cortical processing of vision is mediated by two pathways, the dorsal and ventral streams, starting at the primary visual cortex and proceeding through the parietal and temporal lobes, respectively. The parietal lobe areas are involved in processing visuomotor function and spatial vision. The different cortical areas associated with the dorsal stream are shown in the inset figure for the human and monkey brain. (Inset) Adapted from "Neuroimaging of Cognitive Functions in Human Parietal Cortex," by J. C. Culham and N. G. Kanwisher, 2001, *Current Opinion in Neurobiology, 11*, pp. 157–63.

concerned entirely with the object's location and spatial relationship to other objects.

The Ungerleider–Mishkin model soon became a cornerstone of modern visual neuroscience and stimulated a considerable amount of research in the anatomy, physiology, and computational biology of the two streams. The appeal of their model rested on the fact that it coalesced prevailing knowledge on the different parts of the brain, and particularly what happens when those parts are damaged, to arrive at a neat functional dichotomy. The simplicity of their scheme is perhaps best exemplified by the common names that became attached to the two streams. The ventral system came to be referred to as the *what* pathway—one that was specialized for object perception and culminating in its pinnacle property of face processing in the inferotemporal cortex. The dorsal stream, on the other hand, became known as the *where* pathway because of its primary function in computing the spatial relationships among objects (SideNote 13.36). An additional important facet of dorsal stream function relates to visuomotor processing for the coordination of voluntary eye movements and visual guidance of body movement.

Low-level input to cortical streams

The functional dichotomy in cortical visual processing was taken one step further by Margaret Livingstone and David Hubel at Harvard University (Livingstone & Hubel, 1988). They proposed that the two streams are actually cortical continuations of an anatomical and functional division that is seen as early as the retina. Recall from Chapter 9 that retinal ganglion cells can be broadly placed into two categories, which in turn separately project to the magnocellular (M) and parvocellular (P) divisions of the LGN. The M- and P-pathways also remain segregated within area V1 and to a certain extent, the ensuing visual areas such as V2, V3, etc.

Livingstone and Hubel proposed that the M- and P-channels retain their independence throughout the later cortical areas, to the point where the dorsal and ventral streams represent an anatomical and functional continuation of the M- and P-channels, respectively. Their model, which was based on a large set of observations on the characteristics of neurons belonging to the two pathways, tied in very nicely to the known properties of the higher cortical streams. For example, the functional

characteristics of P-neurons are ideally suited for the detailed analysis of colour, shape, and surface detail, which are exactly the features needed for the analysis of object properties carried out by the ventral stream. Similarly, the characteristics of M-neurons are ideally suited for computations on the spatiotemporal properties of the visual array, which is exactly the kind of operation carried out by the dorsal stream (SideNote 13.37).

The twin aspects of M/P and dorsal/ventral processing created an elegant model in which visual channels starting right from the retina remained segregated throughout the entire hierarchy of visual structures. It was argued that this separation permitted a division of labour by which the visual system allocated an independent set of cortical modules to separately process different aspects of vision and visually guided behaviour. The picture became somewhat complicated, however, when it was later shown that neither cortical stream receives an exclusive input from either the M- or the P-channel. Although the dorsal stream does receive a preferential M-input, the ventral stream receives a far more mixed input and therefore is not exclusively driven by the P-channel.

2. THE MILNER–GOODALE SCHEME

The fundamental idea that the dorsal and ventral streams mediate different aspects of visual perception was challenged a decade later in a way that would lead to a significant revision in our thinking of higher cortical function. David Milner and Melvyn Goodale argued in their highly influential book that the dorsal and ventral cortical streams should not be viewed solely in terms of visual perception (Milner & Goodale, 2006). Although they accept the anatomical separation of the two streams, Milner and Goodale claimed that the prior interpretation of the streams' function is flawed because it was based primarily on visual discrimination experiments that in turn relegated their roles to only perceptual processes. They do not dispute that the ventral system is primarily involved in object perception but instead take issue with the role of the dorsal stream being predominantly involved in spatial vision.

The *action/perception* dichotomy

The central argument offered by Milner and Goodale is that vision did not simply evolve to grant us with perception but instead arose as a sensory tool for interacting with the world around us. In fact, the emergence of vision as a sensory system was likely driven by the need to find food, avoid predators, and navigate around a complex environment. Thus, the requirement to act on the world represented a key driving force in the evolution of visual systems, and likely predated the emergence of brain structures that became concerned with object representation and perception. The twin demands of acting on the world and representing it, according to Milner and Goodale, therefore serve as the key differentiators for deducing dorsal *versus* ventral stream function. Whereas the Ungerleider–Mishkin model supposes that the dorsal stream is involved with a specific facet of visual perception (spatial vision), Milner and Goodale propose an entirely different role—the visual control of action.

The distinctive feature of the Milner–Goodale model is that it departs from the previous treatment of the dorsal stream as a processor of sensory input and instead recognizes its key role in terms of output characteristics. The execution of motor acts requires significant transformation and processing of the visual array to arrive at an appropriate goal-oriented action, such as manually grasping an object. The transformation of visual signals into motor acts in this case requires multiple coordinated events, from object fixation, spatial mapping of object location, analyzing the trajectory of movement, coding object shape, and finally visuomotor control in reaching for and grasping the object. These are precisely the roles attributed to the dorsal stream in the Milner–Goodale model.

A neural system dedicated to visuomotor control of action must have a core set of processing features, which are all found in dorsal stream structures. First, it must be able to represent visual space and encode target locations in an effective manner, a property that is known to be present in parietal lobe neurons. For example, neurons in area LIP of the monkey (see Figure 13.26) have been shown to transform object locations into a head-based frame of reference and therefore encode space in terms of external coordinates. Second, the system must be able to process visual motion for the coordination of action, such as oculomotor tracking or manually grasping a moving object. (We have discussed several cortical areas in this chapter, such as areas MT and MST, that are associated with the dorsal stream and that are dedicated to processing object motion.) And finally, the system must encode the structural properties of an object to ensure proper guidance of a motor act. In other words, the mere location and movement characteristics are insufficient and information on the size, shape, and orientation of an object are important requirements for skilled motor interaction. It is known that a visual representation of objects takes place in several parietal lobe structures, such as area AIP (see Figure 13.26), where neurons are responsive to the physical characteristics of an object (SideNote 13.38).

The Milner–Goodale model transformed our thinking of visual processing within the two cortical streams from one based on mere analysis of sensory input into a scheme that was based on the control of behaviour. They argued that it was only in the later stages of primate evolution that brain structures arose for the perceptual representation of the visual world, and that the original requirement for vision was to subserve motor function. The operations of the dorsal and ventral streams therefore reflect the purposes for which they originated—to mediate the visual control of goal-directed actions and to create perceptual representations of visual objects, respectively. In short, the visual brain evolved into segregated parallel cortical streams that separately mediate the twin functions of *action* and *perception*.

Mirror neurons

An interesting convergence of action and perception takes place in an area of the brain known as the ventral premotor cortex (area F5). Italian neuroscientist Giacomo Rizzolatti and his colleagues discovered a class of neurons in the monkey that is responsive to reaching and grasping movements (Rizzolatti & Sinigaglia, 2008; Iacoboni & Dapretto, 2006). This is not surprising because area F5 is known to be involved in motor function. What was astounding, however, was that a subclass of neurons in this area was additionally responsive when the animal merely observed another individual grasping the same object, as can be seen by the example in Figure 13.27 on page 474. These so-called **mirror neurons**, therefore, have the dual property of both visuomotor and perceptual function.

The existence of neurons with both motor and sensory properties has interesting

SideNote | **13.38**

It would be reasonable to suppose that dorsal stream structures receive information on object quality from the ventral stream, given its role in object perception. However, lesions to temporal lobe structures in monkeys do not produce deficits in skilled motor movements that require the processing of object structures. It is likely that parietal brain areas receive visual information on object shape and orientation from neural structures in the extrastriate cortex, such as areas V3 and V4.

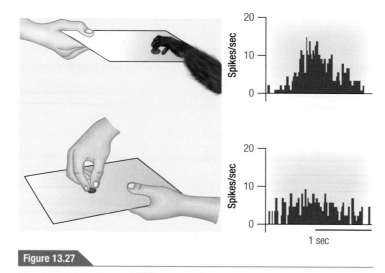

Figure 13.27

Mirror neurons in the monkey premotor cortex display both motor and perceptual properties. These neurons show strong firing during a motor act, such as reaching for and grasping an object (top panel). The same neurons also fire when the animal observes another individual undertaking the same task (bottom panel). Adapted from "The Mirror Neuron System and the Consequences of Its Dysfunction," by M. Iacoboni and M. Dapretto, 2006, *Nature Reviews Neuroscience, 7,* pp. 942–51.

consequences. To begin with, there must be convergence of information at this site from both the dorsal and ventral streams. The connection of this area with earlier sites in the dorsal stream provides a pathway for the arrival of visuomotor information. Furthermore, it is known that anatomical links exist among different modules in this circuit with the inferotemporal cortex, thereby providing a route for the integration of perceptual information. Thus, there is compelling evidence for anatomical integration of the two streams, which along with the physiological findings show that there is indeed a functional integration as well. What is less clear is the role played by these neurons. Rizzolatti and his colleagues have suggested that mirror neurons comprise a physiological mechanism for encoding an internal representation of action and therefore play an important global role in action recognition.

Summary

1. Motion is a *spatiotemporal event* that is defined by two parameters—speed and direction—which together define the velocity of an object. The nature of object motion can be depicted in a space-time diagram. The temporal aspects of visual processing, such as the ability to detect changes in stimulus sequence, play a key role in motion perception. The rate of change of a visual stimulus is referred to as *temporal frequency* and is specified in terms of cycles of change per second (hertz). Studies on the temporal resolution characteristics of the human visual system show that we are maximally sensitive to flicker rates around 10-15 Hz and that beyond 60 Hz (*critical flicker frequency*), we are unable to follow temporal changes.

2. The twin qualities required of a low-level motion detector are the ability to differentiate the direction and speed of a moving object. Motion detectors must be *directionally selective*—that is, display the ability to distinguish one direction of motion from all others. The *Reichardt detector* represents a simple model for encoding the direction and speed of object movement. This model is based on the convergence of two sensors upon a higher-level neuron, with one of the pathways containing an interneuron that imposes a time delay. Consequently, stimulus motion in one direction only will produce a coincidental arrival of signals from both pathways and thereby confer directional selectivity on the recipient neuron.

3. The earliest site in the visual pathway where directionally selective neurons have been found is area V1. These neurons display a vigorous response only when a light bar moves along the direction preferred by that neuron. Different neurons display different degrees of directional tuning preference. There is a broad range of directional preferences among area V1 neurons that cover all possible directions of movement. Layers 4B and 6 show the highest density of directionally selective neurons in area V1. Later cortical areas, notably areas MT and MST, appear to be almost exclusively dedicated to motion processing. Both *feed-forward* and *feedback* connections exist between these motion areas and earlier cortical sites, such as area V1, as well as other areas that together make up the dorsal visual stream.

4. Motion signals are important in vision for a variety of reasons. One use of motion signals occurs in support of perceptual organization. Motion signals are also important for helping to deduce the three-dimensional structure of objects (kinetic depth effect), providing guidance and stability during running or walking (optic flow), and judging the impact time of an approaching object (tau). Motion signals serve a crucial role in guiding our eye movements. And finally, motion signals help to determine the identity of complex objects, and even people.

5. Motion aftereffects arise from the adaptation of direction selective neurons tuned to the adapting direction, resulting in illusory motion of a stationary object in the opposite direction. The phenomenon of *interocular transfer* suggests that motion aftereffects arise at a level where neural output from both eyes is combined, such as in area V1. The phenomenon of *apparent motion* arises when a stimulus is presented at one location, turned off, and then presented at a different location shortly afterwards. The motion impression is so convincing that it cannot be distinguished from real motion. Apparent motion stimuli can activate the sensors of a Reichardt-type detector, causing a motion signal to be generated in the same way as if the stimulus actually moved between the two sensors in real time.

6. There are six oculomotor muscles that together are responsible for the precision and rapidity of eye movements. The neurobiological control of eye movements involves multiple cortical and subcortical structures. The cortical structures beyond area V1 include several areas in the parietal cortex (e.g., area LIP) and the frontal cortex (e.g., area FEF). The superior colliculus displays a major output to motor areas of the brain stem and through these areas controls the rapid orienting movements of the eyes. The brain stem also receives a direct projection from the frontal cortex and the cerebellum, which play a prominent role in guiding the tracking movements of the eyes.

7. Micromovements are involuntary eye movements of extremely small magnitude that constantly move the visual image over the retina. They help to counteract the problems associated with perfect retinal stabilization, such as image fading. Another type of involuntary eye movement is referred to as *gaze-stabilizing* and includes the vestibulo-ocular reflex (VOR) and optokinetic nystagmus (OKN). The VOR arises from head movements that stimulate the vestibular system, which in turn drives the eyes in the opposite direction to preserve retinal image stability. The OKN is also a reflexive movement that spontaneously arises when viewing a large moving scene.

8. Voluntary eye movements, also known as *gaze-shifting* movements, include smooth pursuit and saccades. Visually tracking an object (smooth pursuit) is undertaken to maintain fixation. As the image deviates from the fovea, the retinal motion signal triggers a corresponding smooth pursuit that restores the image back on the fovea. A number of diverse cortical and subcortical areas are involved in smooth pursuit movements, making this circuitry especially vulnerable to certain disorders, such as schizophrenia. Saccadic eye movements are undertaken to shift gaze to different objects of interest, such as when surveying a visual scene or when reading.

9. Processing dynamic visual information largely occurs in cortical areas that belong to the *dorsal stream*, which proceeds along the top part of the brain and encompasses various cortical areas that are situated in the parietal lobe. Ungerleider and Mishkin proposed a model suggesting that a division of labour exists in which the ventral stream is responsible for computing detailed information on the visual object itself, whereas the dorsal stream is concerned entirely with the object's location and spatial relationship to other objects. Milner and Goodale argued that the dorsal and ventral cortical streams should not be viewed solely in terms of visual perception, but rather in terms of an *action/perception* dichotomy. They proposed that the parietal lobe transforms visual signals into motor acts, rather than merely representing the spatial and dynamic relationships of objects in the visual sense. The dorsal and ventral streams, according to their model, mediate visual control of goal-directed actions and create perceptual representations of visual objects, respectively. In short, the visual brain evolved into segregated parallel cortical streams that separately mediate the twin functions of *action* and *perception*.

Key Terms

1. What is a space–time diagram, and what are some examples with regard to the different types of motion? How is *velocity* defined? What is the optimal temporal frequency of flicker detection? What is the *critical flicker fusion* frequency?

2. What is the difference between directional selectivity and orientation selectivity? How does a Reichardt detector function? What is the earliest site at which directional selectivity is found?

3. What is the distinctive feature of area MT? What is the difference between *feedforward* and *feedback* cortical connections? What are some examples of each?

4. Why is *correlated dot motion* advantageous for experiments on motion perception? What are the different uses of motion signals? What is the *kinetic depth effect*? How do motion signals help to guide locomotion?

5. How can the motion aftereffect be explained in physiological terms? What is apparent motion, and how is this phenomenon explained in terms of low-level motion detectors?

6. What is the difference between conjunctive and disjunctive eye movements? What are some of the cortical structures involved in generating eye movements? Why is the superior colliculus ideally suited for integrating multi-sensory signals?

7. What problem arises if a visual stimulus is perfectly stabilized on the retina? What types of eye movements help to prevent this problem, and why are they effective? What are the different types of involuntary eye movements?

8. How does a smooth pursuit eye movement differ from a saccade? What are the different roles of these two eye movements? Why is saccadic suppression necessary?

9. What are the different roles of the dorsal and ventral visual streams according to the Ungerleider-Mishkin model? What are the arguments offered by Milner and Goodale for the dorsal stream's role in the visual coordination of action? What are *mirror neurons*?

10. What is the *aperture problem*, and how is it resolved? What is the difference between first-order and second-order motion? What is the *correspondence problem*?

11. What is the role of the corollary discharge in eye movement function? How can it account for perceptual stability in both involuntary (e.g., OKN) and voluntary (e.g., smooth pursuit) eye movements?

- Carpenter, R. H. S. (1988). *Movements of the eyes* (2nd ed.). London, UK: Pion Ltd.

- Ebenholtz, S. M. (2001). *Oculomotor systems and perception.* Cambridge, UK: Cambridge University Press.

- Epstein, W., & Rogers, S. (1995). *Perception of space and motion.* San Diego, CA: Academic Press.

- Gibson, J. J. (1979). *The ecological approach to visual perception.* Boston, MA: Houghton Mifflin.

- Kolers, P. A. (1972). *Aspects of motion perception.* Oxford, UK: Pergamon Press.

- Milner, A. D., & Goodale, M. A. (2006). *The visual brain in action* (2nd ed.). New York, NY: Oxford University Press.

- Noë, A. (2005). *Action in perception.* Cambridge, MA: MIT Press.

- Rizzolatti, G., & Sinigaglia, C. (2008). *Mirrors in the brain.* Oxford, UK: Oxford University Press.

- Vaina, L. M., Beardsley, S. A., & Rushton, S. K. (2004). *Optic flow and beyond.* Dordrecht, The Netherlands: Kluwer Academic Publishers.

- Van Gompel, R. (2007). *Eye movements: A window on mind and brain.* Oxford, UK: Elsevier Science.

Glossary

Abney effect The shift in hue that occurs with changes in saturation.

absolute depth The actual distance between an external object and the perceiver.

absolute threshold The minimum physical intensity that is required for a stimulus to be detected. Also called *detection threshold*.

absorption spectrum The function relating light absorption by a particular material to wavelength.

accommodation A change in the surface curvatures of the lens, allowing it to assume different refractive powers depending on object distance.

accretion, deletion The appearance (accretion) or disappearance (deletion) of an object with respect to another when either one or the observer is moving.

achromatic channel The neurons and fibres that encode and transmit information related to the chromatic nature of a stimulus that results in the perception of brightness (emitted light source) or lightness (reflected light source).

acoustic cues The sound components that play an important role in speech perception.

action potential A regenerative process of NA^+ channel openings once threshold potential is reached, resulting in a large depolarizing event immediately followed by repolarization due to K^+ efflux. The resulting spike in membrane potential is called the *action potential*.

acuity The ability of the visual system to process image detail. Synonymous with *resolution*.

adaptation A brief period of reduced neuronal response that occurs after prolonged stimulation.

adaptation A reduction in the firing rates of neurons with continued application of a stimulus, which may in turn account for the reduced awareness of it with prolonged exposure.

adaptation The reduction in perceived intensity or sensitivity due to prior or ongoing background stimulation.

adaptation The reduction in perceived intensity that occurs with a continuously applied, non-varying tactile stimulus.

aerial perspective A pictorial cue derived from the haziness of distant objects caused by atmospheric light scattering. Also known as *atmospheric perspective*.

afferent fibre The peripheral and central branches of the DRG neuron that form a continuous cable, carrying somatosensory signals from the periphery to the spinal cord.

afferent signal A neural signal that is transmitted from the periphery toward the brain.

ageusia A total loss of taste sensation.

agnosia An inability to recognize or identify the structure and form of objects.

allocentric A frame of reference that specifies object locations independent of the viewer. Also known as *exocentric*.

amacrine cell A type of retinal neuron that may contribute to the surround response through the lateral connections among bipolar and ganglion cells.

amplitude The maximum pressure change of sound in one direction relative to the baseline. The greater the displacement of a vibrating body, the greater the amplitude of pressure change in the resulting sound wave.

analgesia The absence of the sense of pain.

anion, cation Anions are negatively charged ions, whereas cations are positively charged. Pronounced *an-eye-on* and *cat-eye-on*.

anosmia A loss of olfactory function that can be total (general anosmia) or specific to a particular odour (specific anosmia).

anterolateral system A fibre tract along the frontal (antero) and side (lateral) margins of the spinal cord that transmits touch signals present in Aδ and C fibres (i.e., warmth, cold, and pain).

aperture An opening, such as the hole in the iris (pupil), through which light may enter.

aperture condition A condition that restricts a visual scene to a small area, such as when viewing it through a tunnel or hole (aperture).

aperture problem An inability to distinguish the true movement direction of an edge or line when viewed through an aperture due to the fact that it will only be seen to move perpendicular to its axis.

aphasia An impaired ability to speak (Broca's aphasia) or understand language (Wernicke's aphasia).

apparent motion   An illusory motion that results when a stimulus is presented at one location, turned off, and then shown at a different location shortly afterwards.

aqueous humour   A watery liquid found in the compartment immediately behind the cornea.

area A1   The primary auditory cortex located in the temporal lobe of both cerebral hemispheres.

area FEF   *Frontal eye fields*—a cortical area in the frontal lobe that is involved in motor processing related to eye movements.

area LIP   *Lateral intraparietal area*—a cortical area in the parietal lobe that is involved in motor processing related to eye movements.

area MT   A cortical area first identified in monkeys in which the majority of neurons are directionally selective. The name *MT* is derived from its approximate anatomical location in the middle-temporal part of the brain.

area V1   The current and most commonly used scientific name for the primary visual cortex.

aromatherapy   The use of aromatic oils to enhance mood and, according to some claims, cure ailments from back pain to the discomforts of pregnancy.

articulation   The adjustments and movements of the vocal apparatus involved in producing a sound.

astigmatism   A lack of symmetry in the curvature of the cornea causing a blurred retinal image along the affected direction.

astrocyte   A type of glial cell that provides structural support to neurons, regulates the ionic balance in the fluid surrounding neurons, and helps form a tight seal around blood vessels.

audition   The sense of hearing with particular reference to the sensory aspects involved in that process. This is distinguished from the term *acoustics*, which refers only to the study of the physical characteristics of sound and sound waves.

auditory scene analysis (ASA) The process by which the auditory system segregates and analyzes incoming sounds from multiple sources to provide a perceptual representation of the entire auditory scene.

azimuth   The horizontal angular value of the direction of the sound source.

bandpass noise   A noise signal that contains a limited range of sound frequencies.

bandwidth   The range of frequencies contained in the noise signal (i.e., the difference between the highest and lowest frequency values).

bel, decibel   A measure of relative intensity given by the logarithm of the ratio of a measured sound intensity to that of a standard reference (log $[I_s/I_r]$). One decibel equals one-tenth of a bel. dB_{SPL}

Bell–Magendie law   The principle that the dorsal root of spinal nerves carries sensory signals into the spinal cord, whereas the ventral root carries motor signals out to the muscles.

Bezold–Brücke effect   A change to hue perception whereby increasing the intensity of wavelengths above 510 nm causes hues to shift more toward yellow and wavelengths below 510 nm to shift more toward blue.

binaural   Related to sound stimulation of both ears. Binaural neurons can be triggered by stimulation of both cochlea.

binaural masking level difference (BMLD)   The detection threshold improvement that accompanies the masking reduction of noise from binaural hearing.

binaural summation   The integration of sound signals from the two ears by the auditory nervous system.

binding problem   The problem of correctly assembling the elementary features at the pre-attentive stage into a coherent visual object.

binocular fusion   The process of integrating retinal images from the two eyes to create a single visual percept.

binocular rivalry   A phenomenon that occurs when different images are presented to each eye. Suppression of visual information from one eye on the other causes only one of the images to be perceived at any given time. Also known as *binocular suppression*.

binocular summation   The advantage in visual function that occurs though the additive input of signals from both eyes.

binocular vision   Vision with two eyes.

binocularity   Pertaining to both eyes. Binocular neurons are responsive to light stimulation through either eye.

biological motion perception The ability to recover complex object information from a sparse set of point-light sources.

bipolar cell A type of retinal neuron located in the inner nuclear layer that conducts signals between photoreceptors and ganglion cells.

bipolar neurons See **multipolar neurons, bipolar neurons**.

bistratified ganglion cell An anatomically distinct type of ganglion cell involved in processing chromatic information and whose receptive fields show B/Y and Y/B organization.

bleaching The process by which a non-functional form of rhodopsin is created after light absorption.

blindsight An ability to respond to visual stimuli in the absence of perceptual awareness or sight.

blob See **cytochrome oxidase blobs**.

Bloch's law The trade-off between threshold intensity (I) and stimulation time (T) such that the product of the two must reach a critical value (C) for light detection. Mathematically expressed as $I \times T = C$.

body reflection The reflection that occurs after light interacts with the molecules inside an object. The nature of the molecules is responsible for producing the wavelength content of the reflection and therefore the chromatic appearance of the object.

brightness, lightness The perceptual quality that correlates with the physical parameter of light intensity. *Brightness* is the term used when the light stimulus arises from an emitting source, whereas *lightness* is the term used when the stimulus arises from body reflection off an object.

broadband noise A noise signal that encompasses much of the audible frequency range.

Broca's aphasia A generalized loss of language production ability that follows from damage to Broca's area in the left frontal lobe.

calibration To establish a precise relationship between two different variables (e.g., the volume on a sound-producing device and the actual air pressure produced at the eardrum).

callus A hardened or thickened part of the skin that usually occurs from repetitive or excessive strain. A common site for calluses is the palm at the base of the fingers.

capsaicin The active ingredient in chili peppers, which causes the hot burning sensation.

categorical perception A perceptual pattern that is stable despite small changes in the acoustic signal (such as time)

until it comes to a point where it crosses a boundary and enters a new category.

cation See **anion, cation**.

central nervous system (CNS) The term given to the brain and spinal cord.

central pain Pain that occurs due to activation in the central pain pathways rather than nociceptive signals from peripheral sites.

centre–surround antagonism A common arrangement found in receptive fields where the neural response to light placed in the centre is opposite to that in the surround.

cerebral cortex A thin band of cells that covers the surface of the brain. Also known as *neocortex*.

cerebrum The largest part of the brain, consisting of the two cerebral hemispheres.

characteristic frequency The sound frequency at which the lowest sound intensity is required to produce a sufficient neural response in a single auditory fibre. This is the frequency at which the fibre is most sensitive.

chemogustometry The application of chemical solutions to the tongue to determine taste function.

chemotopic organization An organized representation of different taste primaries in the gustatory system.

chromatic channel The neurons and fibres that encode and transmit information related to the chromatic nature of a stimulus that results in the perception of hue.

chromaticity The quality of a colour.

cilia Small hair-like filaments that project from the terminal end of the sensory neuron's dendrites into the mucus layer. There can be anywhere from five to 30 cilia per dendrite.

ciliary muscle A thin muscle located around the peripheral rim of the lens whose contraction causes the lens to become more rounded, thereby increasing its refractive power.

circadian rhythms A set of cyclical biological functions based on the day–night light cycle.

co-articulation The effect of adjacent sound patterns on the production of a given phonetic segment.

co-articulation problem The difficulty in parsing speech due to overlapping speech segments that occur from the contextual relationship between adjacent phonetic segments.

cochlea A coiled, fluid-filled bony chamber within the temporal bone where sound energy is transduced into neural signals. Also referred to in broad terms as the *inner ear*.

cochlear implant A prosthetic device that partially restores hearing ability by converting sound into an electrical current that is used to directly stimulate the nerve fibres in the cochlea.

cochlear microphonic An alternating current generated by the movement of stereocilia belonging to the outer hair cells during acoustic stimulation of the organ of Corti.

cocktail party effect The ability to distinguish a signal, such as someone's speech, in the midst of background noise.

colour afterimage A transient visual impression with altered colours that appears on an empty field to which gaze has been shifted after prolonged viewing of a colourful stimulus.

colour circle A graphical scheme that portrays the spectral colours in a circular manner.

colour constancy The tendency for a colour to look the same under widely different viewing conditions.

colour contrast A phenomenon in which the colour of an object is affected by the colour of surrounding objects.

colour signal The wavelength content of light signals entering the eyes to produce colour perception. The colour signal depends on both the reflectance spectrum of the object and the emission spectrum of the light illuminating it.

colour space A spatial representation of colour according to perceptual similarity.

colour vision The ability to differentiate lights (or objects that reflect light) only on the basis of their spectral composition (i.e., wavelength content), even if the lights appear to be of equal subjective brightness.

colour-opponent neuron A neuron that shows an excitatory response to one colour and an inhibitory response to its opponent colour.

compass test Use of a standard compass—a two-pronged probe where the spatial separation between the points can be varied—to explore the minimum separation that is detectable as two separate points on the skin.

complementary colours Any pair of colours that lie at opposite ends of the colour circle, which when mixed together produce a neutral colour, such as white.

complex tone A sound made up of multiple frequency components that are equally spaced from one another (i.e., the fundamental and higher harmonics).

compression, rarefaction The alternating states of increased and decreased pressure, respectively, on a medium produced by a sound source.

computational load A neural processing requirement imposed by a particular sensory, motor, or behavioural function.

concave lens A lens with its surfaces bowed inward, causing light to diverge after passing through it.

concentration A measure of the amount of dissolved substance per unit volume of a solution.

conductive loss An impairment of sound transmission through the outer and middle ear components resulting in reduced transfer of sound energy to the cochlea.

conjunctive eye movements Simultaneous movement of both eyes in the same direction.

consonant A pleasant subjective impression created by certain superpositions of two or more musical tones.

consonant A speech sound made by constricting or closing the air path somewhere within the vocal tract.

contingent aftereffect An aftereffect that is dependent upon the combination of two different stimulus attributes.

contour The specific pattern of pitch changes as a function of time that forms a characteristic feature of each melody.

contralateral An anatomical structure on the opposite side of the body.

contrast sensitivity function (CSF) A general descriptor of spatial visual function. Shown by way of grating visibility, represented by the inverse of the contrast threshold value plotted for a range of spatial frequencies.

convergence An inward rotation of both eyes needed to shift gaze to a closer object.

convex lens A lens with its surfaces bowed outward, causing light to converge after passing through it.

cordotomy Surgical sectioning of a small segment of the spinal cord through which the anterolateral pathway traverses.

cornea The transparent front part of the eyeball that serves as the first refractive component.

corollary discharge A copy of a motor command that is sent to perceptual centres. Also known as *efference copy*.

corollary discharge When the motor centres of the brain produce a voluntary movement, a copy of the neural command to the muscles is made available to the perceptual centres of the brain so that it knows what limb movements have just been initiated. The term *efference copy* is also used.

correct rejection When no stimulus is present in a trial (noise trial) and the subject answers *NO*.

correlated dot motion A type of motion stimulus in which a certain proportion of dots move coherently in one direction, whereas the remainder move in random directions.

correspondence problem The challenge of finding a set of points in one image that can be correlated with the same set in a successively presented image.

correspondence problem The problem of identifying a set of points in one image with the same set in another image.

corresponding retinal images Retinal images that are formed at analogous points in the two eyes.

cranial nerves Sensory and motor nerves that emerge from the brain stem and proceed to various parts of the head, face, and neck.

criterion (β) A set-point or cut-off point that is internally established by the subject. On those trials where sensory magnitude exceeds ß, the subject will indicate that a detectable sensory event has occurred and will respond *YES*. If the sensory magnitude fails to reach ß, then the subject will respond *NO*.

criterion effects A pre-existing bias for a particular sensory quality that can affect recognition threshold measures. A discussion of this parameter was presented in Section C.4 of Chapter 1.

critical band The range of frequencies that can mask a tone of a particular frequency. The critical band provides an estimate of the functional bandwidth of an internal filter.

critical flicker fusion (CFF) A condition at which the temporal change in a stimulus is too rapid for flicker detection. The flickering stimulus becomes fused with the background and appears to be uniform.

cross-adaptation The reduction in perceived intensity or sensitivity to a compound due to the adaptation to a different one.

cross-correlation A measure of the similarity between two different inputs.

crossed disparity A disparity in the binocular retinal images whereby the temporal image is located farther away from the fovea than the nasal image. This situation arises when an object is situated closer than the horopter.

cross-fibre coding The notion that sensory neurons are triggered by a broad range of stimuli. In the gustatory system, this hypothesis asserts that taste neurons can be stimulated by multiple taste primaries.

cross-modality matching The use of stimuli from different domains (e.g., sound vs. light intensity) to make comparisons of the relative magnitudes that are produced in different sensory systems.

crystalline lens A convex, elastic structure situated within the eyeball that represents the second refractive element. Often referred to simply as the *lens*.

cycle The region spanning two adjacent identical points of a waveform.

cyclopean perception The perception of a unitary reality, such as the singleness of vision.

cytoarchitectonics The architecture of the cerebral cortex in terms of its cellular composition and distribution among different layers. Different regions of the cortex display distinctive cytoarchitectonic features.

cytochrome oxidase blobs A patch-like mosaic of discrete areas in the upper layers of area V1 that show more intense staining for the protein cytochrome oxidase than in neighbouring *interblob* areas.

d' (d–prime) The difference between the means of the noise and signal + noise distributions. According to SDT, d' can increase either by increasing the strength of the signal or by increasing the sensitivity of the detector.

dark adaptation Detection sensitivity to a light spot when measured in the dark at various times after photoreceptor bleaching.

dark current The inward flow of sodium ions through cGMP-gated sodium channels in the absence of light.

day vision Visual processing mechanism that operates under medium to intense light conditions.

deaf-mutism A loss of oral language ability due to profound deafness in early childhood.

decibel See **bel, decibel**.

deletion See **accretion, deletion**.

dendritic field The physical space covered by the dendrites of a single neuron over which it is able to collect signals from other neurons.

depolarization A positive shift in the membrane potential that is usually caused by the influx of Na^+ ions into the cell.

depth of field The range of object distances that produces a sharp image. The smaller the aperture, the greater the depth of field.

dermatome The area of skin innervated by the dorsal root of a single spinal nerve. The body representation of all dermatomes is called the *dermatomal map*.

deuteranopia   A form of dichromacy caused by a missing M cone photopigment.

dichotic stimulation   Binaural stimulation whereby the sound quality reaching each ear is different. The situation arises when the sound source is off the mid-sagittal axis, resulting in a greater path length to the farther ear.

dichromacy   A colour vision system that depends on the output of two independent detectors.

dichromatic   See **dichromacy**.

difference threshold   The minimum change in physical intensity that is required for a noticeable change in sensation. Difference thresholds are always determined at suprathreshold levels. Also called *discrimination threshold*.

diffraction   The bending of light around the edges of an object. This phenomenon can only be explained if light has wave-like motion rather than travelling merely as a stream of particles.

diffraction   The bending of waves around small obstacles.

diffusion   A fundamental law of physics in which molecules at high concentration in one compartment will migrate to a neighbouring one if the concentration there is lower.

diotic stimulation   Binaural stimulation whereby both ears receive the same quality of sound. The situation arises when the sound source is directly in front of or behind the head along the mid-sagittal axis, resulting in equal path lengths to both ears.

diplopia   Double vision.

directional selectivity   The preference of a neuron for a visual stimulus moving in a particular direction compared to all other possible directions.

directional selectivity   The preference of a neuron for a visual stimulus moving along a particular direction in comparison to all other possible directions.

directional tuning curve   A radial plot of neural response for stimulus movement in various directions.

discrimination scaling   The application of difference threshold measurements to estimate sensory magnitude functions. The theoretical foundation for this approach is based on the notion that JNDs represent a constant unit of sensory change, regardless of the actual operating level. Also known as *confusion scaling* (see SideNote 1.11).

disjunctive eye movements   Movement of the two eyes in opposite directions.

disparity selectivity   A property of binocular neurons showing enhanced firing when two retinal images are spatially positioned with respect to each in precise ways according to the optical definition of *zero*, *crossed*, or *uncrossed* disparity.

dissonant   An unpleasant subjective impression created by certain superpositions of two or more musical tones.

divergence   An outward rotation of both eyes needed to shift gaze to a more distant object.

dorsal column   A fibre tract along the dorsal margin of the spinal cord that transmits touch signals present in Aβ afferent fibres. These signals include both SA and FA types generated by steady and dynamic touch stimuli.

dorsal column nuclei   A pair of nuclei located on either side of the midline in the medulla (lower part of the brain stem). The dorsal column fibres terminate here and synapse onto neurons that project to the thalamus.

dorsal cortical stream   An interconnected network of anatomically and functionally distinct areas in the parietal lobe that process specific aspects of visual information.

dorsal root ganglion (DRG)   A collection of neurons located adjacent to the spinal cord. Fibres from these neurons reach the skin where they terminate either as free endings or in an encapsulated form. All somatosensory signals from the skin are captured and transmitted to the spinal cord by dorsal root ganglion neurons.

dorsal visual stream   A series of interconnected brain areas largely within the parietal lobe that together are responsible for processing spatiotemporal relationships and dynamic aspects of the visual signal, such as object movement.

double-opponent neurons   Neurons found in area V1 that are both spatially and chromatically opponent.

dual process theory   The idea that a two-stage mechanism exists in the visual system, combining both trichromatic and colour-opponent theories, for processing colour.

dual-theory of light   The theory that light is composed of particles known as *photons* that have wave-like motion when they travel.

dynamic range   The intensity range between the terminal and detection thresholds for a particular frequency. The dynamic range for all audible frequencies represents the auditory response region of suprathreshold hearing.

dysgeusia   A distortion of taste sensation.

eccentricity   Deviation from the centre.

efference copy   A copy of the motor command that is sent to various parts of the brain, including those engaged in perceptual function. Also known as *corollary discharge*.

egocentric   A frame of reference that specifies object locations relative to a viewer's current position.

Ekman's law   The amount of sensory change needed to produce a JND is not constant, as Fechner postulated, but rather a linear function of the initial or operating level of sensation. Ekman's law is the sensory counterpart of Weber's law.

elasticity   The property that enables an object to recover from distortion to its original shape.

electroencephalogram (EEG)   The record obtained by placing electrodes on the scalp and measuring the localized electrical activity in the underlying cortex.

electrogustometry   The application of electrical current to the tongue through an electrode to determine taste function.

electromagnetic radiation   The energy radiated in the form of a wave that results from the motion of an electric charge. The wave is characterized by a coincidental fluctuation in the intensity of an electric and a magnetic field as the wave propagates.

electromagnetic spectrum   The full range encompassing the shortest to the longest possible wavelength of electromagnetic radiation.

elevation   The vertical angular value of the direction of the sound source.

emission spectrum   A plot of intensity (or energy) of electromagnetic radiation emitted by a source, such as the Sun, as a function of wavelength.

emission spectrum   A plot of the energy content of a light source as a function of wavelength within the visible range. Also called *spectral diagram*.

Emmert's law   The perceived size of a constant retinal image is proportional to the perceived distance at which it is located.

emmetropia   An optically normal eye where the power of the cornea–lens combination is sufficient to refract incoming parallel light rays to produce an image on the retina.

endorphins   A family of morphine-like substances that are produced in the brain and bind to opiate receptors to produce analgesic function.

epithelial cells   Closely packed cells that fit together to form continuous sheets that are found on the surface of the body or in the lining of its cavities.

equal loudness contour   A function that shows the intensity values needed to match loudness among single tones within a range of frequencies. Also known as *Fletcher–Munson curves*.

equally tempered scale   The division of an octave into 12 equal intervals of log frequency.

esthesiometer   A set of calibrated fibres, each producing a different force when applied to the skin. The early sets used animal hair, whereas modern ones are developed from nylon fibres.

ether   An all-encompassing, massless fabric of space postulated in medieval times as the medium through which light transmission took place.

eustachian tube   A narrow tube that connects the middle ear and the nasopharynx (back of the throat). Its main purpose is to ventilate the middle ear chamber and equalize any pressure differences between it and the outside atmosphere.

event-related potentials (ERPs)   Electrical activity produced by sensory stimulation and picked up in an EEG.

external auditory canal   The narrow canal that transmits sound from the pinna to the eardrum.

extraocular muscles   The six muscles that insert into each eyeball and that are individually or collectively involved in its various movements.

extrastriate areas   Cortical areas that lie beyond the striate cortex (area V1). Many of these areas in the parietal and temporal lobes have been shown to process different aspects of visual function.

facial, glossopharyngeal, and vagus nerves   Cranial nerves VII, IX, and X, respectively. These nerves, especially VII and IX, carry gustatory signals to the brain.

false alarm   When no stimulus is present in a trial (noise trial) and the subject answers *YES*.

far point   The farthest point that can be seen clearly. For a normal eye, this point is optical infinity.

feature integration theory (FIT)   An influential theory of object perception based on the assembly of low-level features into a complex visual object.

Fechner's law   The logarithmic relationship between stimulus intensity and sensation magnitude proposed by Gustav Fechner in 1860.

feedback connection   An anatomical connection from a higher cortical area to a lower one.

feed-forward projection   An anatomical connection from a lower cortical area to a higher one.

hyposmia   A reduction in olfactory detection or recognition threshold.

ice-cube model   A 3-D model of area V1 where ocular dominance and orientation columns run perpendicular (90°) to each other.

ideal detector   A detector (animal or machine) that can always detect a signal when its intensity is above a certain defined level (threshold) and always fails to detect it when it is below that level.

image raster   The distribution of light in a point-wise manner across an area, such as the retina, a computer monitor, or television.

in vitro   See **in vivo, in vitro**.

in vivo, in vitro   In vivo studies take place within the living body of an animal, whereas in vitro studies take place outside.

increment threshold   The extra amount of light intensity needed to just distinguish a light spot from its background.

induced motion   A visual illusion in which a small stationary object appears to be moving when surrounded by a larger moving object or background.

inertia   The tendency of a body to maintain its state of motion, whether it is at rest (zero) or moving in a particular direction.

inferior temporal cortex (IT)   The cortical mass along the lower (posterior) segment of the temporal lobe where visual functions that make up the ventral stream are processed.

infrasonic   Sound frequencies below 20 Hz.

inner nuclear layer   The middle layer of neurons in the retina that process and transfer neural signals from photoreceptors to the ganglion cells.

insula   An area of the cerebral cortex in the frontal lobe that is located within the sylvian fissure. The insula and surrounding cortex together make up the primary gustatory cortex.

intensity   The amount of acoustic energy transmitted through a unit of area in a given time. Sound intensity is related to the square of sound pressure.

interaural intensity difference (IID)   A difference in sound intensity arriving at the two ears for dichotic sounds.

interaural time difference (ITD)   A difference in arrival time at the two ears for dichotic sounds.

internal capsule   A fibre tract containing axons from the thalamus and projecting to the somatosensory cortex.

International Phonetic Alphabet (IPA)   An internationally recognized set of symbols for designating the phonetic characteristics of all speech sounds.

interneurons   Neurons that process information within the central nervous system. Local interneurons process information within specific brain sites, whereas projection interneurons transmit information, often over large distances, to other brain sites in the same or opposite hemisphere.

interocular transfer   A phenomenon in which the effects of sensory adaptation through one eye can be experienced through the other eye, suggesting that the adaptation effects are being mediated in area V1 or beyond.

intramodal matching   Comparing different aspects of a stimulus within a particular sensory domain or modality (e.g., different wavelengths of light on brightness perception, different tone frequencies on loudness perception, taste sensations generated by sweet vs. sour substances, etc.).

inverse square law (sound)   Sound intensity is inversely proportional to the square of the distance. See chapter 5.

inverse square law (radiation)   The amount of radiation passing through a specific area is inversely proportional to the square of the distance. See chapter 8.

ipsilateral   An anatomical structure on the same side of the body.

iris   A pigmented curtain-like structure situated immediately in front of the lens.

isofrequency sheets   A single layer of neurons in the inferior colliculus that all display the same characteristic frequency.

isoluminance   A condition where the total light level is the same across a visual stimulus but the chromaticity varies.

isomerism   Difference in the spatial arrangement of atoms in an otherwise identical chemical compound.

just noticeable difference (JND)   A change in sensation (ΔS) that is sufficient to allow that mental event to be just detected. The JND, which is a psychological parameter and therefore cannot be experimentally determined, is the subjective counterpart of the difference threshold (ΔI), which is a physical parameter that can be experimentally derived.

kinesthesis   The sensation of the movement of the body, muscles, tendons, and joints.

kinetic depth   A depth cue that arises from the relative movements of different objects in the visual world.

kinetic depth effect (KDE)   The perception of a 3-D object generated from motion signals of a 2-D image.

labelled–line coding   The notion that sensory neurons are selective to only a specific type of stimulus. In the gustatory system, this hypothesis asserts that taste neurons are selective to only one of the taste primaries.

lateral inhibition   A fundamental property of the nervous system where a neuron is inhibited by sensory input into surrounding areas through a network of lateral connections.

lateralization   The idea that certain behavioural functions are dominated by one hemisphere.

lateralization   The specialization of certain sensory or cognitive functions within a particular cerebral hemisphere.

law of outward mobility   The greater the mobility of the body, the greater the spatial resolution. Although this is true for the upper extremities (e.g., arms, fingers), it does not necessarily hold true for other body parts.

L–cone   Cone photoreceptor type optimized for capturing long-wavelength light, with a peak absorbance at 560 nm.

lens aberrations   Optical factors in lens refraction that produce imperfect imaging, especially in the peripheral parts of the retina.

lesion studies   Surgical removal of a brain region in an animal followed by careful inspection of any behavioural deficits. An extension of this idea in humans is taken from behavioural studies following traumatic brain injury, surgical intervention, or pathology.

light ray   The straight-line path of a photon as it travels outward from the light source.

lightness   Perceptual impression of the amount of light reflected by an object surface.

lightness   See **brightness, lightness**.

lightness constancy   The similarity in the lightness perception of objects despite large changes in environmental illumination.

lightness contrast   Differences in lightness perception of an object or surface due to the intensity of the surround.

limbic system   A region of the brain concerned with motivation, emotion, and certain kinds of memory.

linear perspective   The projection of parallel lines in three-dimensions as a set of converging lines in a two-dimensional representation.

lobotomy   Surgical removal of brain tissue from one of the four cortical lobes, usually the frontal lobe.

log–log plot   A graph where both the x-axis and y-axis represent the logarithm of the respective data points.

longitudinal wave   A type of wave motion in which the direction of particle movement is parallel to the direction of wave propagation. In sound, for example, the back and forth movement of air particles occurs in the direction that the wave is travelling.

loudness   The magnitude of the perceived impression created by the sound of a particular physical intensity.

luminance   The amount of visible light coming into the eye from an emitted or reflected source.

Mach bands   An illusion of dark and light bands on either side of a boundary separating two bars of different light intensity.

magnitude estimation   A psychophysical scaling procedure developed by Stanley S. Stevens in which human subjects are required to make numerical estimates of the sensory magnitudes that are evoked by stimuli of different physical intensities.

magnocellular neurons   Neurons with large cell bodies (e.g., in layers 1 and 2 of the LGN).

masking   The process by which the detection threshold of a sound is elevated in the presence of other sounds.

McGurk effect   The influence of visual cues in combination with the acoustic signal in the perception of speech sounds.

M–cone   Cone photoreceptor type optimized for capturing middle-wavelength light, with a peak absorbance at 530 nm.

mechanoreceptors   Sensory receptors found in skin that transduce touch signals—such as pressure, vibration, heat, and cold—into neural signals that are transmitted to the brain.

medial lemniscus   A fibre tract containing axons from the dorsal column nuclei and projecting to the thalamus.

mel   A pitch scale in which a 1000 Hz tone has a value of 1000 mels.

melatonin   A hormone produced and secreted into the bloodstream by the pineal gland.

melody   A sequence of musical tones that forms a succession of pitches in musical time.

membrane potential   A voltage difference across the cell membrane that arises due to the separation of charges. The inside of the cell is negative compared to the outside.

metamer   A situation where two objects, surfaces, or light sources appear to be identical in colour even though the spectral content of the light coming from them is different.

metathetic Sensations that rely on a substitutive process such that changing some aspect of the stimulus alters the quality of the sensory impression.

Method of Adjustment A psychophysical method in which the subject directly adjusts stimulus intensity to produce a detectable sensation. The threshold is calculated from the means of several trials.

Method of Constant Stimuli A psychophysical method in which stimulus intensity values are randomly chosen from a preset range. The subject's responses over many trials are stored and later used to generate a response frequency for each intensity level.

method of fractionation A psychophysical scaling procedure where subjects are required to set the intensity of a stimulus so that its perceived magnitude is double that of a reference. The procedure can also be used to make intensity settings that evoke half the perceived magnitude.

Method of Limits A psychophysical method in which stimulus intensity is systematically increased or decreased by the experimenter until the subject gives a change in response.

method of magnitude estimation A psychophysical scaling procedure developed by S. S. Stevens in which human subjects are required to make numerical estimates of sensory magnitudes evoked by stimuli of different physical intensities.

microelectrode A thin, rigid metal wire that conducts current based on electrical changes taking place at its tip.

microneurography A technique developed in the 1960s that allowed nerve impulses to be recorded from sensory fibres in human skin.

microsaccade A jerky movement of the eyes of an extremely small magnitude that takes place while fixating on a stationary object.

microspectrophotometry The process of spectrophotometry applied on a miniature scale, allowing light absorption estimation at the single photoreceptor level.

microvilli The small folds in the membrane of receptor cells where tastant binding occurs.

midget ganglion cell A type of retinal ganglion cell that is characterized by its small physical size and found throughout the retina but especially concentrated in the fovea.

mid-line stereopsis Binocular depth perception for objects situated along the midline in front of or behind the horopter.

Mie scattering The absorption and re-emission of light, generally in the forward direction, by larger particles in a non-wavelength-dependent manner. Named after physicist Gustav Mie who described it in 1908.

minimal audibility curve A psychophysical function showing the relationship between absolute detection threshold and sound frequency.

minimum audible field (MAF) An open-field technique for obtaining detection thresholds by providing sound stimuli through a loudspeaker in front of the subject.

minimum audible pressure (MAP) A closed-ear method for obtaining detection thresholds whereby sound is provided through a set of earphones.

minute arc An angular measure. One minute arc equals 1/60 of a degree.

mirror neurons A class of neurons that fire when an animal grasps an object and also when it observes another individual doing the same task. These neurons display both motor and perceptual properties.

miss When a stimulus is present in a trial (signal + noise trial) and the subject answers *NO*.

modality One of the primary sensory forms such as vision, touch, etc.

modality segregation Functional organization within a sensory system where different aspects of sensation are separately processed.

monaural Related to sound stimulation of one ear alone. Monaural neurons can only be triggered by sound stimulation from the ear on that side.

mondegreen Accidentally mishearing a phrase so that it then acquires a new and different meaning.

monochromacy A visual system that receives all of its neural signals from a single type of light detector.

monochromatic See monochromacy.

monochromatic light A narrow spectrum light in which all of the energy is contained at a single wavelength.

monocular Pertaining to a single eye.

moon illusion The illusion of a very large moon when it rises just above the horizon, unlike its normal appearance at other locations in the sky.

motion adaptation Effects of the prolonged viewing of motion in one direction, leading to reduced responsiveness in neurons and associated sensory processes tuned to that direction.

motion aftereffect   A phenomenon that occurs following the prolonged viewing of a moving object, after which a stationary object is perceived to be moving in the opposite direction.

motion parallax   The apparent change in the direction of movement of objects at different depths caused by the changing line of sight of an observer.

motor map   Similar to the somatosensory map except that the motor map is an orderly representation of neurons that initiate voluntary muscular movements in specific parts of the body.

multi-dimensional scaling   A representation on a spatial map based on the similarity or dissimilarity of the sensory impression produced by metathetic stimuli.

multipolar neurons, bipolar neurons   Neurons in which multiple dendrites emerge from the cell body. Bipolar neurons have only a single dendritic process. Both types have only one axon.

multi-sensory integration   The simultaneous processing of sensory signals from multiple domains, such as visual, auditory, and tactile. Also referred to as *cross-modal integration*.

musical pitch   The pitch sensation induced by a complex tone generated by a musical instrument. The complex tone has a fundamental frequency component and a set of higher harmonics.

musical scale   A graduated sequence of musical tones, each producing a precise pitch sensation.

myelin   The insulating material formed by glial cells. These cells form the myelin sheath by wrapping their cell membranes around an axon several times.

myopia   A refractive condition of the eye in which the length of the eyeball is too long in comparison to its optical power.

nanometre   One billionth (10^{-9}) of a metre. A common unit used to express the wavelength of visible light.

near point   The closest distance at which an object can still be seen in focus, representing the point of maximum accommodation.

neurolinguistics   The study of the neurological basis of language function.

neuron doctrine   The principle that the nervous system is composed of a network of interconnected cellular elements, or neurons.

neurotransmitters   Specialized chemicals that are involved in the transmission of neural signals across the synapse.

neutral colour   A colour that is not found within the visible spectrum but which can blend in with all of the spectral colours. Colours such as white, grey, and black are neutral colours.

night vision   Visual processing mechanism that operates under low light conditions.

nociception   The generation of sensory signals at specialized receptors (nociceptors) and their subsequent processing by the nervous system to provide information about tissue damage.

nodal point   An imaginary point on the optic axis that represents the optical centre of the eye.

noise   **1** An aperiodic sound waveform composed of a broad range of frequencies with a random distribution of amplitudes. See chapter 5. **2** Background activity that is unrelated to the stimulus and which can interfere with its detection. See chapter 1.

nonspectral colour   A colour that does not appear in the visible spectrum and therefore cannot be generated by a single wavelength of light.

normal   An imaginary line running perpendicular to a boundary separating two media of different refractive indices.

nucleus (*nuclei*)   A collection of brain cells, generally residing below the cerebral cortex, within the central nervous system.

nucleus of the solitary tract (NST)   A collection of neurons located in the medulla of the brain stem. A subset of the neurons here serves to relay taste signals to the thalamus.

nyctalopia   The clinical term for *night blindness* caused by prolonged Vitamin A deficiency in one's diet.

Nyquist limit   The highest spatial frequency that a neural array can faithfully sample. Named in honour of American physicist Harry Nyquist.

nystagmus   A repetitive eye movement sequence composed of a drift to one side until the eyeballs reach their limit, followed by a rapid shift back to the centre.

object tracking   Eye movements that follow the motion trajectory of an external object precisely so that it remains fixated (i.e., its image remains on the fovea).

occlusion   One object blocking the sight of another. Also known as *interposition*.

octave   The interval encompassed by two tones that differ in pitch but sound alike. The fundamental frequency must be doubled to move up one octave. Widely considered to be the basic interval of musical pitch. The name derives from the time when only eight (octo) notes constituted an octave.

ocular   Pertaining to the eye.

ocular cue   Information that arises from the state or position of the eyeball.

ocular dominance   The weighting of eye input to a binocular neuron in area V1. Monocular neurons are dominated by inputs from only one eye, whereas binocular neurons can have various levels of dominance by each eye. Perfectly binocular neurons have equal eye (ocular) dominance.

ocular dominance columns   A vertically oriented collection of neurons spanning the entire thickness of area V1 that shows preference for light stimulation of a particular eye.

oculomotor   Pertaining to eye movements.

odotope   The molecular features of an odourant compound that are important for it to bind to a receptor and trigger a neural signal in olfactory sensory neurons.

odourant binding protein (OBP)   A protein found in the mucous layer just outside the olfactory epithelium. These proteins are believed to help shuttle hydrophobic odourants across the mucous layer.

odourants   Chemical stimuli in the air that generate signals in the olfactory epithelium and produce a sensation of smell.

OFF/ON ganglion cell   A type of retinal ganglion cell whose receptive field displays centre inhibitory (OFF) and surrounding excitatory (ON) sub-regions in response to light.

ogive   An S-shaped response function that is typically seen in psychophysical experiments where detection or discrimination performance is measured.

Ohm's law of hearing   The notion that the ear processes the spectral components of a complex sound wave after performing a type of Fourier analysis.

olfactometer   A mechanical device that precisely delivers controlled pulses of air containing a particular odourant.

olfactory epithelium   The olfactory sense organ located at the upper margins of the nasal cavity.

olfactory nerve   The unmyelinated axons from olfactory sensory neurons bundle together to form the olfactory nerve. These nerves represent the only route by which olfactory signals reach the next stage of processing in the olfactory bulb.

olfactory system   A chemosensory system that deals with the detection of airborne chemicals and which produces the perceptual impressions of smell.

oligodendrocyte   A type of glial cell found in the central nervous system that is responsible for producing the myelin sheath around axons.

olivocochlear neurons   Neurons in the superior olive that belong to the descending system and give rise to efferent fibres that project to the cochlea and innervate the hair cells.

ON/OFF ganglion cell   A type of retinal ganglion cell whose receptive field displays centre excitatory (ON) and surrounding inhibitory (OFF) sub-regions in response to light.

opponent colour theory   The idea that colour vision is mediated by opponent mechanisms whereby two colour pairs (red/green and blue/yellow) are not simultaneously processed and therefore cannot be jointly perceived.

opponent process   The notion that certain aspects of sensation are encoded and processed in an opposing manner whereby they cannot be simultaneously perceived.

optic axis   An imaginary line passing through the middle of the lens and connecting the midpoints of its refracting surfaces.

optic chiasm   A point at which the two optic nerves fuse together and at which a partial set of retinal fibres cross over to the opposite side.

optic disk   The point where nerve fibres from the retina come together and pierce through the eyeball to then project to the brain.

optic flow   The relative movement of different parts of a visual scene that occurs during self-motion.

optic tract   The nerve bundle beyond the optic chiasm containing retinal fibres from both eyes.

optical imaging   A technique that uses a sensitive camera to capture optical signals from the cortex in response to neural activity triggered by sensory stimulation.

optical infinity   A distance of 6 metres or more at which wave fronts flatten out (light rays become parallel).

optimal disparity   The disparity value that yields maximum firing in a binocular neuron.

optokinetic nystagmus (OKN)   A visually driven nystagmus generated by the movement of a large part of the visual field.

orbitofrontal cortex   A brain area located in the anterior portion of the frontal lobe. A part of this area has been called the secondary taste area and contains taste neurons that are influenced by high-level factors.

organ of Corti   The collection of cells and non-cellular structures that make up the receptor organ of hearing. It is located within the cochlear duct and rests upon the basilar membrane.

orientation columns   A vertically oriented collection of neurons in area V1 that shows preference for visual stimuli oriented along a particular axis.

orientation selectivity   The preference of a neuron for a visual stimulus of a particular orientation.

orientation tuning curve   The plot of neural response of an orientation-selective neuron as a function of stimulus orientation.

ossicles   Three of the smallest bones in the body that are connected and involved in sound transmission through the middle ear.

otitis media   An infection of the middle ear that is sometimes accompanied by the buildup of fluid. The resulting pressure on the eardrum can cause a sharp intense pain.

otosclerosis   Abnormal development and function of the ossicles.

ototoxic   Drugs or chemicals that cause damage to the auditory system.

palate   The roof of the mouth separating it from the nasal cavity. The hard palate is found toward the top front of the mouth where it has a bony reinforcement. The soft palate (velum) is at the top back of the mouth.

Panum's fusional area   A depth range encompassing the horopter within which objects appear fused and produce stereoscopic depth perception.

papilla   The small mounds of tissue found on the surface of the tongue. The term is derived from the Latin word for the nipple of the mammary gland.

paradigm   The model that scientists hold about a particular area of knowledge. Definition according to Thomas Kuhn in *The Structure of Scientific Revolutions*.

parallelism   The presence of multiple pathways within a given sensory system that transmit and process different features of a complex stimulus in a more or less independent manner.

parasol ganglion cell   A type of retinal ganglion cell that is characterized by its large physical size and dendritic field.

parvocellular neurons   Neurons with small cell bodies (e.g., in layers 3 to 6 of the LGN).

perfect pitch   The ability to accurately identify or reproduce an isolated musical tone by name. Also known as *absolute pitch*.

peripheral nervous system   The term given to the spinal nerves and associated neural structures that are physically outside of the central nervous system.

peripheral neuropathy   A rare neurological condition caused by degeneration of only the large myelinated sensory fibres of the peripheral nervous system. Limb and body movements are possible because the motor fibres remain unaffected.

perspective projection   A technique for representing depth relationships in three-dimensional space on a two-dimensional surface.

phantom pain   A lingering painful sensation that is attributed to a limb that has been amputated.

phase-locked response   Neural firing that has a precise timing relationship to the sound waveform, either linked to each compressive portion or spaced out every few cycles.

phenomenology   A mere descriptive account of phenomena without attempting to account for the underlying causes.

pheromone   A chemical substance emitted by specialized glands in many animals to attract mates, signal sexual receptivity, or affect the behaviour of other members of the same species.

phon   A unit of measurement to specify loudness across various frequencies. The number of phons of any tone is equal to the intensity value in dB_{SPL} of a 1000 Hz sound when they are judged to produce equal loudness sensation.

phoneme   An elemental speech sound, often considered by linguists to be the smallest unit that distinguishes one word element from another.

phonemic restoration effect   The correct perception of a phoneme in which a part of the acoustic signal is missing or replaced with another sound.

phonetic boundary   The VOT value that separates a voiced from a voiceless consonant sound.

photochromatic interval   The difference in sensitivity between scotopic and photopic vision at a particular wavelength.

photopic vision   Visual processes mediated by cone photoreceptors and taking place under relatively bright light conditions. Commonly referred to as *day vision*.

photoreceptor   A light-absorbing neuron that serves as the first element in the visual pathways. Photoreceptors convert the energy in light into a neural signal that is passed on to other neurons in the retina.

phototransduction   The process by which light energy is converted into neural signals by photoreceptor neurons.

phrenology The first complete theory of cerebral localization proposed by Gall in the late 18th century. Various mental faculties were believed to occupy discrete parts of the brain's surface, which in turn produced bumps or depressions on the skull.

physiological zero The null range on the temperature scale, about 30–36°C, where a discernible thermal percept does not occur. Changes in tissue temperature away from this zone produce sensations of warm or cool.

pigment epithelium A layer of pigmented cells lying adjacent to the photoreceptor array. These cells capture light that is not absorbed by the photoreceptors.

pinna A cartilaginous structure located on the side of the head. Its main function is to channel sound waves into the external auditory canal.

pitch **1** A perceptual quality that is most closely associated to vibrational frequency. Although this term is usually associated with hearing, pitch perception in the tactile domain has been extensively studied as well. See chapter 3. **2** The subjective impression of sound normally associated with frequency and characterized by a "high–low" descriptive scale. See chapter 6.

place theory The vibrational amplitude of the basilar membrane is not uniform, but rather, it is maximal at the point where its resonant frequency coincides with the frequency of the sound stimulus.

plane-polarized light A type of light in which the electric field is restricted to only one plane of oscillation. The magnetic field must therefore oscillate in a perpendicular plane.

point localization error A sequential test where a person must indicate the point on the body that was previously touched with a probe. The error between the two points is taken as a measure of tactile discrimination.

point source A very small light source from which light radiates outward in all directions.

point spread function Light distribution in a point image that is blurred due to physical factors.

polyphonic A signal composed of multiple musical tones that are sounded simultaneously.

pop-out phenomena The finding that certain elementary features are immediately perceptible regardless of the number of distracters that are present in its surround. Features that "pop-out" are believed to represent primitive tokens at the earliest (pre-attentive) stage of visual object processing.

position constancy The perception of object stability in the visual environment despite retinal image motion caused by eye movements.

postcentral gyrus The mound of cortex located between the central sulcus and the postcentral sulcus. A part of the primary somatosensory cortex (area 1) is located here.

postsynaptic See **presynaptic, postsynaptic**.

power function A class of mathematical relationships that takes the following general form: $y = k \cdot x^{exp}$ where k is a constant and ^{exp} can take on any value.

power law The relationship deduced by Stevens in which sensory magnitudes are related to stimulus intensity raised to some power (exponent).

precentral gyrus The mound of cortex located in front of the central sulcus where the primary motor cortex is found.

presbycusis Hearing loss that develops gradually with age.

presbyopia A gradual loss of lens elasticity with advancing age that leads to the loss of accommodative ability and hence blurred vision for near objects.

presynaptic, postsynaptic The neuron that carries action potentials toward a synapse is the presynaptic neuron, whereas the recipient of those signals is the postsynaptic neuron.

primary colour A colour that cannot be generated by mixing other colours. However, primary colours can themselves be mixed together to produce secondary colours.

primary olfactory cortex A general name given to the five brain areas that receive a direct projection from the olfactory bulb—anterior olfactory nucleus, olfactory tubercle, amygdala, piriform cortex, and entorhinal cortex.

primary somatosensory cortex (area S-I) The cortical area that serves as the starting point for somatosensory signal processing. It includes four anatomically distinct regions (areas 3a, 3b, 1, and 2) located along the wall of the central sulcus and on the postcentral gyrus.

principle of univariance The notion that cone photoreceptors do not convey any information about the wavelength of light in the retinal image but only how much light is absorbed at a given moment.

problem of the missing fundamental The perception of pitch associated with the fundamental frequency in a harmonic series when that component has been removed. Also known as the *case of the missing fundamental* and *residue pitch*.

PROP See **PTC, PROP**.

proprioception Perception of body position and movement arising from sensory signals generated by muscle contraction and joint movement.

proprioceptor Sensory receptors involved in proprioceptive signalling. The two most notable proprioceptors are the muscle spindle and Golgi tendon organ. In addition, there are receptors in the joints that signal a particular position.

prosopagnosia A disorder of high-level vision that specifically impairs face recognition ability.

protanopia A form of dichromacy caused by a missing L-cone photopigment.

prothetic Sensations that rely on an additive process where changing some aspect of the stimulus alters the magnitude of the sensory impression.

psycholinguistics The psychology of language. A discipline that is concerned with understanding the psychological processes underlying language use.

psychometric function The relationship between performance on a psychophysical task (e.g., proportion of times a stimulus is detected) and some feature of the stimulus (e.g., intensity).

psychophysical function The relationship between sensory thresholds and a particular dimension, feature, or parameter of the stimulus.

psychophysics The study of quantitative relationships between physical events and psychological experiences.

PTC, PROP PTC—phenylthiocarbamide; PROP—propylthiouracil.

pupil The hole in the iris through which light passes into the lens. The pupil diameter changes according to the light level.

pure tone A sound that can be represented by a single sinusoidal function of pressure change over time.

Purkinje shift The shift in peak wavelength of sensitivity between photopic (550 nm) and scotopic (500 nm) vision.

Purkinje tree A shadow of the retinal blood vessels, which have a branching tree-like structure. Originally described by Czech physiologist Jan Purkinje.

random-dot stereogram A stereogram made up of dots (or squares) that are randomly assigned one of two values (usually black or white) and containing no discernible shapes. Upon binocular fusion, a segment of the stimulus is perceived to be at a different depth from the background.

rarefaction See **compression/rarefaction**.

ratio scaling Direct estimations of sensory magnitudes produced by stimuli of different intensities. The technique is based on the theory that sensory magnitudes fall on a ratio scale and can therefore be directly measured by the perceiver.

raw primal sketch A collection of primitive features that are derived by applying an edge-detection algorithm to a visual image.

Rayleigh scattering The absorption and re-emission of short-wavelength light in random directions by very small particles (up to about 1/10 the wavelength of light). Named after Lord Rayleigh who described it in 1871.

reading glasses Small convex lens glasses that add a small amount of extra refractive power to make up for the lost accommodative ability in presbyopia.

receiver operating characteristic (ROC) A graphical plot of hits vs. false alarms that shows how these values change with respect to each other at all possible criterion levels. Pronounced *are-oh-see*.

receptive field 1 The area on a sensory surface that will influence the activity of a neuron, regardless of where it is located in the hierarchy of the nervous system. See chapter 2. 2 The region of the retina that affects the electrical state of a visual neuron such as a retinal ganglion cell. See chapter 3. 3 The area of skin that will generate an electrical response in a DRG neuron or its afferent fibre. The field size corresponds to the area of skin tissue that will sufficiently conduct physical energy to the mechanoreceptor to stimulate it. See chapter 3

receptor potential The result of the transduction process that creates a change in the membrane potential of receptor neurons.

recognition-by-components (RBC) The theory that visual objects are mentally assembled by various combinations of volumetric primitives.

referred pain The experience of pain at a site remote to where the pain signals are actually generated.

reflectance spectrum A plot of the amount of reflection (usually on a scale of 0–1) as a function of wavelength.

refraction The bending of light at a boundary separating two different media in which light travels at different speeds.

refractive index An indicator of the speed of light within a transparent object. The higher the refractive index of an object, the lower the light speed within it.

refractive power The refractive strength of a lens. The greater the refractive power, the more it is able to refract light.

Reichardt detector A simple neuronal circuit that creates the property of directional selectivity.

relative depth The distance between objects in the real world.

relative pitch The ability to accurately identify tonal intervals.

resonant frequency   The natural vibrational frequency of an object specified by its mass and stiffness.

response bias   The influence of factors unrelated to the sensory stimulus in the decision-making process that leads to judgments about that stimulus.

retina   A network of neurons lining the back of the eyeball that is involved in converting light energy into neural signals.

retinal disparity   The relative difference between the two retinal images of a given object.

retinal field   A portion of the retinal surface.

retinal ganglion cell (RGC)   The last set of neurons in the retina. The final output of the retina is sent to the visual brain through axons belonging to the RGCs.

retinal magnification   The size of a retinal image in comparison to the size of an object.

retinal stabilization   A perfectly stationary image on the retina, usually achieved by technological means to compensate for micromovements.

retinex theory   The notion that colour constancy requires both low-level (retina-based) and high-level (cortex-based) processing (retina + cortex = retinex).

retinotopic organization   An orderly arrangement of retinal space onto some other neural structure such as the LGN.

reverberation time   The time required for a reflected sound to be reduced by 60 dB after sound from the source is extinguished. The greater the total sound absorption in a room, the smaller its reverberation time.

rhodopsin   The light-absorbing photopigment found in all mammalian rod and cone photoreceptors.

rhythm   The perceived organization of a melodic sequence based on temporal grouping of musical tones.

Ricco's law   The trade-off between threshold intensity (I) and stimulation area (A) such that the product of the two must reach a critical value (C) for light detection. Mathematically expressed as $I \times A = C$.

saccade   Orienting movements of the eyes that allow gaze to be quickly shifted from one object to another, as in reading.

saccadic suppression   The reduction in visual sensitivity during a saccade, presumably explaining why retinal image blur is unnoticeable.

saturating power   The ability of a particular colour to evoke a sensation that can be distinguished from white.

saturation   The purity of a hue given by the amount of neutral colour (grey) that it contains.

scaling   A general psychophysical procedure to estimate the amount or magnitude of something related to perception or some other aspect of psychology.

schematic eye   A theoretical model of the eye that takes into account various optical parameters such as surface curvature, refractive index, etc.

Schwann cell   A type of glial cell found only in the peripheral nervous system that produces the myelin sheath in peripheral nerve fibres.

sclera   The tough outer membrane of the eye, commonly known as the *white* part at the front of the eyeball.

S-cone   Cone photoreceptor type optimized for capturing short-wavelength light, with a peak absorbance at 440 nm.

scotopic vision   Visual processes mediated by rod photoreceptors and taking place under very low light conditions. Commonly referred to as *night vision*.

second messenger   A specific chemical substance that is involved in the transduction cascade within cells.

second-order motion   Motion perception derived from the movement of objects that do not have a lightness (luminance) difference from their background. The moving borders can be defined by a variety of isoluminant cues.

segmentation problem   The difficulty in parsing speech due to the relative lack of acoustic boundaries between individual words in free-flowing speech.

semitone   The smallest interval of musical pitch. In the Western musical scale, a full octave encompasses 12 semitones.

sensorineural loss   An impairment in cochlear function or the neural elements of the inner ear resulting in loss or reduced auditory function.

sensory transducer theory   The notion that transformation (or transduction) of physical energy in the stimulus into biological (neural) signals is the basis of the power law. According to this theory, the power law exponent depends on the sensory mechanisms that are involved in this process.

signal   An event, action, or object that serves as a stimulus for detection or discrimination. The terms *signal* and *stimulus* are often used interchangeably.

signal detection theory (SDT)   A theory based on statistical concepts that takes into account detection and discrimination sensitivity as well as nonsensory factors that may affect the decision-making process.

simple harmonic motion   Back and forth repetitive movement through an equilibrium point where the maximum displacement on both sides is equal and the interval of each complete vibration is the same, as exemplified by the prongs of a tuning fork or pendulum.

sinusoidal function A smoothly varying back and forth change in some parameter that is described mathematically in terms of a sine wave. An object undergoing simple harmonic motion follows a sinusoidal function, as in the vibrational movement of a tuning fork's prongs.

size constancy The idea that objects retain constant (or near constant) perceived size regardless of their distance from the observer.

smooth pursuit A tracking eye movement that precisely follows a moving target with the objective of keeping its image on the fovea.

sodium–potassium pump A membrane-bound protein that ejects Na^+ ions from the cell and brings K^+ ions back in.

solmization The naming of each interval in a musical scale with a verbal sound, word, or syllable.

somatosensory The somatosensory system deals with all aspects of touch perception.

somatotopic map The orderly representation found in the somatosensory cortex where adjacent areas of the body surface are processed by adjacent areas of the cerebral cortex.

somatotopic representation Functional organization in the somatosensory system whereby neural processing occurs in an orderly manner, resulting in a spatial representation of the body within a neural structure.

sone A unit of loudness defined as the perceived magnitude of a 1000 Hz sound stimulus presented at 40 dB_{SPL}.

sound spectrograph An instrument that analyzes the distribution of sound frequencies over time.

spatial frequency The number of grating cycles per unit space. Usually specified as cycles per degree of visual angle subtended at the eye.

spatial resolution The ability to distinguish different physical stimuli that are separated in space. A system has high spatial resolution if it can detect objects that are closely spaced.

spatial sampling The process by which detection of individual stimulus points or entities occurs over space.

spatial summation Sensory summation in terms of area. The larger the area of the stimulated surface, the greater the magnitude of the sensory experience.

spatiotemporal A physical term that encompasses the twin qualities of space and time. Motion is an example of a spatiotemporal event.

spectral Pertaining to the wavelength of light or other types of electromagnetic radiation.

spectral sensitivity function The relative ability of the visual system to operate at different wavelengths along the visible spectrum.

spectrogram The graphical representation of sound frequency, intensity, and time that is produced by a sound spectrograph.

spectrophotometry The act of measuring light intensity at discrete points in the visible spectrum, often used to determine how much light is absorbed by a material at a particular wavelength.

specular reflection Light reflection at an object's surface.

spiral ganglion The collection of nerve cell bodies that follows the cochlear spiral. Nerve fibres arising from these neurons innervate hair cells of the cochlea.

spontaneous activity Action potentials that take place in a neuron in the absence of any externally driven stimulation.

spoonerism A speech error where words are transposed to create new, and often humorous, meanings.

staff A horizontal series of five lines, which along with the clef (bass and treble) is used to indicate the pitch of a musical note.

staircase procedure This is an example of an adaptive procedure in which the sequence of stimulus presentations is varied according to the subject's responses.

step function A response function that makes an abrupt transition from one level to another.

stereo-blindness The loss of stereoscopic depth perception due to poor vision or blindness in one eye.

stereocilia A set of filaments, or a hair bundle, that protrude from the upper surface of both inner and outer hair cells. The filaments are arranged in rows of varying length.

stereogram A pair of images in which the same components may be laterally displaced relative to each other.

stereopsis The perception of depth from binocular vision. Also known as *stereoscopic vision*.

stereoscope A device that allows independent viewing of separate images by each eye.

stimulus An object or event in the physical world that may be perceived through stimulation of one of the sensory systems.

striate cortex A common name for the primary visual cortex because of the striated appearance from a band of fibres in the middle layers.

structuralism   The psychological theory that mental experiences result from the assembly of elemental structural units that can be deduced through careful introspection.

structure-from-motion (SFM)   The use of moving 2-D images to reconstruct the 3-D shape of a rigid object. SFM and KDE are related concepts.

subcortical   The parts of the brain that reside below the cortex.

subcortical auditory structure   A collection of neurons that make up a defined anatomical unit residing below the cerebral cortex, usually in the brain stem or thalamus.

subglottal system   Structures located below the vocal folds (glottis), such as the windpipe (trachea), the lungs, and the various muscles that move air into and out of the lungs.

subthreshold   Physical intensity values that are below absolute threshold and therefore not detectable.

sulcus (*sulci*)   A narrow fissure that separates adjacent convolutions of the brain.

summation response   A type of binaural interaction where a neuron is excited by sound stimulation of both ears.

superior olive   An auditory nucleus located in the lower brain stem that codes for binaural sound differences.

superior temporal sulcus (STS)   A deep groove that spans the temporal lobe and includes several visual processing areas.

suppression response   A type of binaural interaction where a neuron is excited by one ear and inhibited by the other.

suprathreshold   Physical intensity values that are above absolute threshold and therefore generally detectable.

synapse   A physical gap at the junction between two neurons.

synaptic potential   A change in the membrane potential of the postsynaptic neuron that results from neurotransmitters binding to specialized receptors.

Tadoma   A method of tactile communication where the hands and fingers are placed on the lips and face of a person who is talking. The method is named after the first two deaf–blind children to whom it was taught, Tad Chapman and Oma Simpson.

tastants   Chemical stimuli derived from foods that are dissolved in saliva and which produce electrical signals in taste buds.

taste bud   A specialized pear-shaped sensory structure found primarily in the skin of the tongue. Taste buds contain the cells that are responsible for generating taste signals in response to chemicals dissolved in the saliva.

tau   Optic flow information of an approaching object that may signal time to collision. Mathematically, it is the ratio of retinal image size to the rate at which the image is expanding.

tectorial membrane   A gelatinous membrane that overlies the cellular elements of the organ of Corti. It is attached to the basilar membrane by way of the stereocilia on the outer hair cells.

tempo   The perceived speed of presentation of musical notes in a melodic sequence.

temporal contrast sensitivity function   The sensitivity profile of the visual system to different temporal frequencies. Often referred to as the *TSF* in vision literature.

temporal frequency   The rate at which a stimulus changes in some manner per unit time.

temporal resolution   The ability to distinguish physical stimuli that are applied at different moments in time. A system has high temporal resolution if it can detect objects that are alternated rapidly.

temporal summation   The integration of sound energy over time by the auditory system.

TENS   Transcutaneous electrical nerve stimulation.

terminal threshold   The sound pressure level that produces severe discomfort or pain thereby representing the upper intensity limit of auditory function.

texture gradient   A systematic change in the size and shape of objects whereby near objects produce coarse image texture and distant objects product fine image texture.

thermal   Pertaining to heat or the lack of it (cold) as determined by the temperature of an external object or source in relation to the body.

thermoreceptors   Free nerve endings in the skin that respond specifically to thermal stimulation (warmth or cold) and not to pressure or vibration.

timbre   (pronounced *tam-ber*) The characteristic quality of sound independent of pitch and loudness. Differences in timbre are produced by the number and relative strengths of the harmonic components in a complex tone.

time to collision (TTC)   The time required for an object to collide with an observer.

tinnitus   The annoying perception of sounds, often described as "ringing in the ears," when no such sounds are present in the external environment.

tip link   A very thin filament that connects two stereocilia. These fine fibres are believed to be connected to molecular gates at ionic pores.

tonal masking   The masking effect on a tone of a particular frequency by another single tone.

tone chroma   The relative positions of different intervals or divisions in an octave, usually represented in a circle.

tone height   The series of successive octave registers spanning the full musical pitch spectrum.

tonotopic map   A systematic representation of sound frequency in any physical or neural structure. The basilar membrane is the first site in the auditory system where tonotopy is apparent.

touch   Sensations produced by stimulation of receptors in the skin. Touch sensations include pressure, vibration, warmth, and cold as well as various blends of these attributes.

transduction   The transformation of energy contained in a physical stimulus into a biological signal by a sensory receptor neuron.

transmission spectrum   A plot of intensity (or energy) of electromagnetic radiation that is passed through a medium as a function of wavelength.

trichromatic theory   The idea that colour vision is mediated by three separate light-detection systems in the eye.

trigeminal chemoreception   Stimulation of free nerve endings belonging to the trigeminal nerve (cranial nerve V) by irritating chemicals. A more technical term for the common chemical sense.

tritanopia   A form of dichromacy caused by a missing S-cone photopigment.

tuning curve   A plot of the minimum sound intensity required to obtain a criterion neural response as a function of sound frequency.

tuning fork   A narrow, U-shaped metal bar that was invented by George Frideric Handel's trumpeter in the 18th century. This simple mechanical device produces a single tone whose sound characteristics are determined by the length of the prongs (or tines).

two-alternative forced choice (2AFC)   An experimental procedure where two presentations are made with only one of them containing the stimulus. The subject's task is to identify the presentation with the stimulus. Criterion effects are minimized in this procedure.

two-point limen   The minimal separation of two simultaneous indentations that can still be perceived as two separate points. The term *limen* is synonymous with *threshold*. The lower the threshold value, the greater the spatial resolution or acuity.

tympanic membrane   A tough membrane that closes off the external auditory canal in its innermost margin. Commonly called the *eardrum*, it vibrates in response to acoustic sound pressures.

ultrasonic   Sound frequencies above 20000 Hz.

umami   A Japanese word for a taste common to diverse foods such as fish, meats, cheese, and some vegetables. Corresponding words in English are *savoury*, *brothy*, and *meaty*.

uncrossed disparity   A disparity in the binocular retinal images whereby the nasal image is located farther away from the fovea than the temporal image. This situation arises when an object is situated farther than the horopter.

unpolarized light   The most common form of light where the electric field oscillates within all of the possible planes in space.

vagus nerve   See **facial, glossopharyngeal, and vagus nerves**.

value   A term used to refer to either the brightness or the lightness of light.

variation problem   The difficulty in parsing speech due to the variability of individual speech, which can be quite substantial due to different articulatory mannerisms and accents.

vection illusion   An illusion of self-movement generated by a large moving scene.

velocity   The rate and direction of an object's movement.

ventral cortical stream   An interconnected network of anatomically and functionally distinct areas in the temporal lobe that process specific aspects of visual information.

ventral posterior medial nucleus (VPMN)   A small nucleus in the thalamus that serves as the second relay for taste signals. Neurons here send their axons to the primary gustatory cortex.

vestibular apparatus   Fluid-filled chambers within the inner ear that are activated by rotational and linear movements of the head and body to provide information on self-motion.

vestibular system   A sensory organ that detects self-movement due to disturbances of fluid within a system of canals in the inner ear.

vestibulocochlear nerve   The nerve bundle that carries auditory signals out of the cochlea to higher centres of the nervous system.

vestibulo-ocular reflex (VOR)   An involuntary, reflexive eye movement in response to body and head movements that is generated by the vestibular apparatus and whose purpose is to maintain visual stability.

vibrotactile stimulation   A vibrating, tactile stimulus.

Vieth–Müller circle   A theoretical circle that passes through the fixation point and the nodal points of both eyes.

visible light   The segment of the electromagnetic spectrum in the wavelength range of 400 to 700 nm that produces sensory stimulation yielding the perceptual experience of vision.

visual cortex   A general term given to the collection of cortical areas that are involved in processing visual information.

visual egocentre   The visual point of reference for egocentric directional judgment.

visual field   The totality of space in the visual scene that is optically captured and processed by the visual system.

vitreous humour   A somewhat gelatinous liquid found in the compartment in front of the retina.

vocal folds   A firm structure found in the human larynx (Adam's apple) that is composed of two strips of ligaments and muscles. Also known as the *vocal cords*.

voiced, voiceless   Sounds in which the release of air is accompanied by vocal fold vibrations are called *voiced*, whereas those in which they are separated in time are called *voiceless*.

voiceless   See **voiced, voiceless**.

voice-onset time (VOT)   The time difference between the release of air and the onset of vocal fold vibration.

voiceprint   A spectrogram of a person's voice that was believed to be unique to that person.

vomeronasal organ (VNO)   A paired chemosensory organ located in the nasal cavities of many terrestrial species. Also known as Jacobson's organ, the VNO appears to be the primary sensory system for the detection of pheromones.

vowel   A speech sound made without blocking air passage through the mouth.

wagonwheel effect   The illusion of rotational motion in the opposite direction to true physical movement.

wave fronts   The representation of light propagation in space at a particular point in time through a series of expanding concentric circles.

wavelength   The physical distance between two identical points in a wave, thereby spanning a complete cycle.

Weber's fraction (k)   The proportion by which the difference threshold (ΔI) increases with intensity to produce a just noticeable difference in sensation. The Weber fraction is given by the following formula: $k = \Delta I / I$.

Weber's law   The difference threshold (ΔI) increases in a linear fashion with the intensity (I) at which the sensory discrimination is being made. The proportionate increase is given by the constant k in Weber's law.

Wernicke's aphasia   A generalized loss of language comprehension ability that follows from damage to Wernicke's area in the left temporal lobe.

white noise   A noise waveform that results from combining all frequencies within a certain range, each having the same amplitude.

References

Ackermann, H. (2008). Cerebellar contributions to speech production and speech perception: Psycholinguistic and neurobiological perspectives. *Trends in Neurosciences, 31,* 265–272.

Adelson, E. H., & Bergen, J. K. (1985). Spatiotemporal energy models for the perception of motion. *Journal of the Optical Society of America, 2,* 284–299.

Adelson, E. H., & Movshon, J. A. (1982). Phenomenal coherence of moving visual patterns. *Nature, 300,* 523–525.

Agnati, L. F., Genedani, S., Leo, G., Rivera, A., Guidolin, D., & Fuxe, K. (2007). One century of progress in neuroscience founded on Golgi and Cajal's outstanding experimental and theoretical contributions. *Brain Research Reviews, 55,* 167–189.

Aine, C. J. (1995). A conceptual overview and critique of functional neuro-imaging techniques in human: I. MRI/fMRI and PET. *Critical Reviews in Neurobiology, 9,* 229–309.

Albright, T. D. (1984). Direction and orientation selection of neurons in visual area MT of the macaque. *Journal of Neurophysiology, 52,* 1106–1130.

Albright, T. D., & Stoner, G. R. (2002). Contextual influences on visual processing. *Annual Review of Neuroscience, 25,* 339–379.

Algom, D., Ben-Aharon, B., & Cohen-Raz, L. (1989). Dichotic, diotic, and monaural summation of loudness: A comprehensive analysis of composition and psychophysical functions. *Perception and Psychophysics, 46,* 567–578.

Alonso, J. M., Yeh, C. I., Weng, C., & Stoelzel, C. (2006). Retinogeniculate connections: A balancing act between connection specificity and receptive field diversity. *Progress in Brain Research, 154,* 3–13.

Amesbury, E. C., & Schallhorn, S. C. (2003). Contrast sensitivity and limits of vision. *International Ophthalmology Clinics, 43,* 31–42.

Anderson, B. L., & Nakayama, K. (1994). Towards a general theory of stereopsis: Binocular matching, occluding contours and fusion. *Psychological Review, 101,* 414–445.

Anstis, S. M. (1974). A chart demonstrating variations in acuity with retinal position. *Vision Research, 14,* 589–592.

Ashmore, J. (2008). Cochlea router hair cell motility. *Physiological Reviews, 88,* 173–210.

Atkinson, J. (1984). Human visual development over the first 6 months of life: A review and a hypothesis. *Human Neurobiology, 3,* 61–74.

Averbeck, B. B., & Lee, D. (2004). Coding and transmission of information by neural ensembles. *Trends in Neurosciences, 27,* 225–230.

Backhaus, W. G. K., Kleigl, R., & Werner, J. S. (1998). *Color vision: Perspectives from different disciplines.* Berlin, Germany: de Gruyter.

Baird, J. C., & Noma, E. (1978). *Fundamentals of scaling and psychophysics.* Hoboken, NJ: Wiley.

Bamiou, D. E., Sisodiya, S., Musiek, F. E., & Luxon, L. M. (2007). The role of the interhemispheric pathway in hearing. *Brain Research Reviews, 56,* 170–182.

Barlow, H. B., Blakemore, C., & Pettigrew, J. O. (1967). The neural mechanism of binocular depth discrimination. *Journal of Physiology, 193,* 327–342.

Barten, P. G. J. (1999). *Contrast sensitivity of the human eye and its effects on image quality.* Bellingham, WA: SPIE Press.

Bartoshuk, L. M., Duffy, V. B, & Miller, I. J. (1994). PTC/PROP tasting: Anatomy, psychophysics, and sex effects. *Physiological Reviews, 56,* 1165–1171.

Batschauer, A. (2004). *Photoreceptors and light signaling.* London, UK: Royal Society of Chemistry.

Baxi, K. N., Dorries, K. M., & Eisthen, H. L. (2006). Is the vomeronasal system really specialized for detecting pheromones? *Trends in Neuroscience, 29,* 1–7.

Baylor, D. A., Lamb, T. D., & Yau, K. W. (1979). Response of retinal rods to single photons. *Journal of Physiology, London, 288,* 613–634.

Baylor, D. A., Nunn, B. J., & Schnapf, J. L. (1987). Spectral sensitivity of cones of the monkey (Macaca fascicularis). *Journal of Physiology, 390,* 145–160.

Bear, M. F., Connors, B., & Paradiso, M. (2006). *Neuroscience: Exploring the brain* (3rd ed.). New York, NY: Lippincott Williams & Wilkins.

Beauchamp, G. K., & Bartoshuk, L. (1997). *Tasting and smelling.* San Diego, CA: Academic Press.

Bell, A. (2004). Hearing: Traveling wave or resonance? *PLoS Biology, 2,* e337.

Bendor, D., & Wang, X. (2006). Cortical representations of pitch in monkeys and humans. *Current Opinion in Neurobiology, 16,* 391–399.

Bennett, A. G., & Rabbetts, R. B. (1989). *Clinical visual optics* (2nd ed.). Boston, MA: Butterworths.

Bennett, M., Dennett, D., Hacker, P., & Searle, J. (2007). *Neuroscience and philosophy: Brain, mind, and language.* New York, NY: Columbia University Press.

Bensmaia, S. J. (2008). Tactile intensity and population codes. *Behavioral Brain Research, 190,* 165–173.

Beranek, L. L. (2003). *Concert and opera houses: Music, acoustics, and architecture* (2nd ed.). New York, NY: Springer-Verlag.

Berg, R. E., & Stork, D. G. (2004). *Physics of sound* (3rd ed.). Upper Saddle River, NJ: Prentice Hall.

Berlin, B., & Kay, P. (1969). *Basic color terms: Their universality and evolution.* Berkeley, CA: University of California Press.

Biederman, I. (1987). Recognition-by-components: A theory of human image understanding. *Psychological Review, 94,* 115–147.

Blake, R. (2001). A primer on binocular rivalry, including current controversies. *Brain and Mind, 2,* 5–38.

Blomfield, S. A., & Dacheux, R. F. (2001). Rod vision: Pathways and processing in the mammalian retina. *Progress in Retinal Eye Research, 20,* 351–384.

Bloom, F. E. (1994). *Neuroscience: From the molecular to the cognitive.* Amsterdam, Netherlands: Elsevier.

Bolanowski, S. J. Jr., Gescheider, G. A., Verrillo, R. T., & Checkosky, C. M. (1988). Four channels mediate the mechanical aspects of touch. *Journal of the Acoustical Society of America, 84,* 1680–1694.

Bonhoeffer, T., & Grinvald, A. (1991). Iso-orientation domains in cat visual cortex are arranged in pinwheel-like patterns. *Nature, 353,* 429–431.

Boothe, R. G. (2002). *Perception of the visual environment.* New York, NY: Springer-Verlag.

Borg G., Diamant, H., Ström, L., & Zotterman, Y. (1967). The relation between neural and perceptual intensity: A comparative study on the neural and psychophysical response to taste stimuli. *Journal of Physiology, 192,* 13–20.

Borg, I., & Groenen, P. (1997). *Modern multidimensional scaling: Theory and applications.* New York, NY: Springer.

Borg, I., & Groenen, P. (2005). *Modern multidimensional scaling: Theory and applications.* New York, NY: Springer.

Boring, E. G. (1942). *Sensation and perception in the history of experimental psychology.* New York, NY: Appleton.

Boring, E. G. (1964). Size constancy in a picture. *American Journal of Psychology, 77,* 494–498.

Born, R. T., & Bradley, D. C. (2005). Structure and function of visual area MT. *Annual Review of Neuroscience, 28,* 157–189.

Boutet, I., & Chaudhuri, A. (2001). Multistability of overlapped face stimuli is dependent upon orientation. *Perception, 30,* 743–53.

Bowmaker, J. K. (1983). Trichromatic color vision: Why only three channels? *Trends in Neurosciences, 6,* 41–43.

Bowmaker, J. K. (1984). Microspectrophotometry of vertebrate photoreceptors: A brief review. *Vision Research, 24,* 1641–1650.

Bowmaker, J. K., & Dartnall, H. J. A. (1980). Visual pigments of rods and cones in a human retina. *Journal of Physiology, 298,* 501–511.

Boycott, B. B., & Dowling, J. (1969). Organization of the primate retina: Light microscopy. *Philosophical Transactions of the Royal Society B, 255,* 109–184.

Bradley, D. R., & Petry, H. M. (1977). Organizational determinants of subjective contour: The subjective Necker cube. *American Journal of Psychology, 90,* 253–262.

Bregman, A. S. (1994). *Auditory scene analysis: The perceptual organization of sound.* Cambridge, MA: MIT Press.

Bremmer, F., Kubischik, M., Hoffmann, K. P., & Krekelberg, B. (2009). Neural dynamics of saccadic suppression. *Journal of Neuroscience, 29,* 12374–12383.

Breslin, P. A. S. (2000). Human gustation. In T. E. Finger, W. L. Silver, & D. Restrepo (Eds.). *Neurobiology of taste and smell.* New York, NY: Wiley-Liss.

Bridge, H., & Clare, S. (2006). High-resolution MRI: In vivo histology? *Philosophical Transactions of the Royal Society of London B Biological Sciences, 361,* 137–146.

Brodmann, K., & Garey, L. J. (2005). *Brodmann's: Localisation in the cerebral cortex* (3rd ed.). New York, NY: Springer.

Brown, R. (1985). *Social odours in mammals.* Oxford, UK: Oxford University Press.

Bruce, C., Desimone, R., & Gross, C. (1981). Visual properties of neurons in a polysensory area in the superior temporal sulcus of the macaque. *Journal of Neurophysiology, 46,* 369–384.

Bruce, V., & Georgeson, M. S. (1996). *Visual perception: Physiology, psychology and ecology.* Hove, UK: Psychology Press.

Bruce, V., Green, P. R., & Georgeson, M. A. (2003). *Visual perception: Physiology, psychology and ecology* (4th ed.). Hove, UK: Psychology Press.

Buck, L. (2000). The molecular architecture of odor and pheromone sensing in mammals. *Cell, 100,* 611–618.

Buck, L., & Axel, R. (1991). A novel multigene family may encode odorant receptors: A molecular basis for odor recognition. *Cell, 65,* 175–187.

Bukach, C. M., Gauthier, I., & Tarr, M. J. (2006). Beyond faces and modularity: The power of an expertise framework. *Trends in Cognitive Science, 10,* 159–166.

Bullock, A. (2004). *The secret sales pitch: An overview of subliminal advertising.* San Jose, CA: Norwich Publishers.

Bundesen, C., & Habekost, T. (2008). *Principles of visual attention: Linking mind and brain.* Oxford, UK: Oxford University Press.

Burgess, N. (2008). Spatial cognition and the brain. *Annals of the New York Academy of Sciences, 1124,* 77–97.

Bushnell, M. C. et al. (1999). Pain perception: Is there a role for primary somatosensory cortex? *Proceedings of the National Academy of Sciences USA, 96,* 7705–7709.

Buttner, U., & Kremmyda, O. (2007). Smooth pursuit eye movements and optokinetic nystagmus. *Developments in Ophthalmology, 40,* 76–89.

Buttner-Ennever, J. A., Konakci, K. Z., & Blumer, R. (2006). Sensory control of extraocular muscles. *Progress in Brain Research, 151,* 81–93.

Byrne, A. (1997). *Readings on color, vol. 1: The philosophy of color.* Cambridge, MA: MIT Press.

Cabeza, R., Kingstone, A. (2006). *Handbook of functional neuroimaging of cognition* (2nd ed.). Cambridge, MA: MIT Press.

Cain, W. S. (1977). Differential sensitivity for smell: "Noise" at the nose. *Science, 195,* 796–798.

Cain, W. S. (1982). Odor identification by males and females: Predictions versus performance. *Chemical Senses, 7,* 129–142.

Caitlin, F. I. (1986). Noise-induced hearing loss. *American Journal of Otolaryngology, 7,* 141–149.

Calkins, D. J. (2001). Seeing with S cones. *Progress in Retinal Eye Research, 20,* 255–287.

Callaway, E. M. (2005). Structure and function of parallel pathways in the primate early visual system. *Journal of Physiology, 566,* 13–19.

Campbell, F. W., & Green, D. G. (1965). Monocular versus binocular visual acuity. *Nature, 208,* 191–192.

Campbell, F. W., & Green, D. G. (1965). Optical and retinal factors affecting visual resolution. *Journal of Physiology, London, 181,* 576–593.

Campbell, R. A., & King, A. J. (2004). Auditory neuroscience: A time for coincidence. *Current Biology, 14,* R866–888.

Carlile, S., Martin, R., & McAnally, K. (2005). Spectral information in sound localization. *International Review of Neurobiology, 70,* 399–434.

Carpenter, R. H. S. (1988). *Movements of the eyes* (2nd ed.). London, UK: Pion Ltd.

Catania, K. C., & Henry, E. C. (2006). Touching on somatosensory specialization in mammals. *Current Opinion in Neurobiology, 16,* 467–473.

Catz, N., & Their, P. (2007). Neural control of saccadic eye movements. *Developments in Ophthalmology, 40,* 52–75.

Cavanagh, P. (1992). Attention-based motion perception. *Science, 257,* 1563–1565.

Chalupa, L. M., & Werner, J. S. (2003). *The visual neurosciences* (Vols. 1 & 2). Cambridge, MA: MIT Press.

Chalupa, L. M., & Williams, R. W. (2008). *Eye, retina, and visual system of the mouse.* Cambridge, MA: MIT Press.

Chandrashekar, J., Hoon, M. A., Ryba, N. J., & Zuker, C. S. (2006). The receptors and cells for mammalian taste. *Nature, 444,* 288–294.

Chang, M. H., & Chiou, W. B. (2007). Psychophysical methods in study of consumers' perceived price change for food products. *Psychological Reports, 100,* 643–652.

Charman, N. (1991). *Visual optics and instrumentation.* Boca Raton, FL: CRC Press.

Chatterjee, S., & Callaway, E. M. (2002). S cone contributions to the magnocellular visual pathway in macaque monkey. *Neuron, 35,* 1135–1146.

Chaudhuri, A. (1990). Modulation of the motion aftereffect by selective attention. *Nature, 244,* 60–62.

Cherry, S. R., & Phelps, M. E. (1996). Imaging brain function with positron emission tomography. In A. W. Toga & J. C. Mazziotta (Eds.), *Brain mapping.* San Diego, CA: Academic Press.

Christman, S. (1997). *Cerebral asymmetries in sensory and perceptual processing.* Amsterdam, Netherlands: Elsevier.

Ciocca, V. (2008). The auditory organization of complex sounds. *Frontiers in Biosciences, 13,* 148–169.

Clahsen, H., & Felser, C. (2006). How native-like is non-native language processing. *Trends in Cognitive Science, 10,* 564–570.

Clark, G. M. (2006). The multiple-channel cochlear implant: The interface between sound and the central nervous system for hearing, speech, and language in deaf people—a personal perspective. *Philosophical Transactions of the Royal Society of London B Biological Sciences, 316*, 791–810.

Clarke, E. (1996). *An illustrated history of brain function*. San Francisco, CA: Norman Publishing.

Clayson, D. E. (1994). Marketing and psychophysics: Cornflakes and Stevens' power function. *Perceptual and Motor Skills, 78*, 593–594.

Cohen, Y. E., & Knudsen, E. I. (1999). Maps versus clusters: Different representations of auditory space in the midbrain and forebrain. *Trends in Neurosciences, 22*, 128–135.

Cohn, E. S. (1999). Hearing loss with aging: Presbycusis. *Clinical and Geriatric Medicine, 15*, 145–161.

Cole, J. (1995). *Pride and a daily marathon*. Cambridge, MA: MIT Press.

Collings, V. B. (1974). Human taste response as a function of locus of stimulation on the tongue and soft palate. *Perception and Psychophysics, 16*, 169–174.

Conway, B. R., & Livingstone, M. S. (2007). Perspectives on science and art. *Current Opinion in Neurobiology, 17*, 476–482.

Conway, B. R., & Tsao, D. Y. (2006). Color architecture in alert macaque cortex revealed by FMRI. *Cerebral Cortex, 16*, 1604–1613.

Conway, C. M., & Pisoni, D. B. (2008). Neurocognitive basis of implicit learning of sequential structure and its relation to language processing. *Annals of the New York Academy of Sciences, 1145*, 113–131.

Copeland, A. M., & Wenger, M. J. (2006). An investigation of perceptual and decisional influences on the perception of hierarchical forms. *Perception, 35*, 511–529.

Cornsweet, T. N. (1970). *Visual perception*. New York, NY: Academic Press.

Craig, J. C., & Rollman, G. B. (1999). Somesthesis. *Annual Review of Psychology, 50*, 305–331.

Crick, F., & Koch, C. (1998). Consciousness and neuroscience. *Cerebral Cortex, 8*, 97–107.

Culham, J. C., & Kanwisher, N. G. (2001). Neuroimaging of cognitive functions in human parietal cortex. *Current Opinion in Neurobiology, 11*, 157–163.

Cytowic, R. E. (1998). *The man who tasted shapes*. Cambridge, MA: MIT Press.

Dacey, D. M. (1993). The mosaic of midget ganglion cells in the human retina. *The Journal of Neuroscience, 13*, 5334–5355.

Dacey, D. M. (2000). Parallel pathways for spectral coding in primate retina. *Annual Review of Neuroscience, 23*, 743–775.

Dacey, D. M., & Packer, O. S. (2003). Colour coding in the primate retina: Diverse cell types and cone-specific circuitry. *Current Opinion in Neurobiology, 13*, 421–427.

Dalton, P. (2000). Psychophysical and behavioral characteristics of olfactory adaptation. *Chemical Senses, 25*, 487–492.

Damasio, H., Grabowski, T., Frank, R., Galaburda, A. M., & Damasio, A. R. (1994). The return of Phineas Gage: Clues about the brain from the skull of a famous patient. *Science, 264*, 1102–1105.

Darlington, C. L., & Smith, P. F. (2007). Drug treatments for tinnitus. *Progress in Brain Research, 166*, 249–262.

Davidoff, J., Davies, I. R. L., & Roberson, D. (1999). Is colour categorisation universal? New evidence from a stone-age culture. *Nature, 398*, 203–204.

Davson, H. (1962). *The eye: The visual process* (Vol. 2). New York, NY: Academic Press.

Davson, H. (1990). *Davson's physiology of the eye* (5th ed.). London, UK: Macmillan Academic and Professional Ltd.

Dayan, P., & Daw, N. D. (2008). Decision theory, reinforcement learning, and the brain. *Cognitive, Affective, and Behavioral Neuroscience, 8*, 429–453.

DeAngelis, G. C., Cumming, B. G., & Newsome, W. T. (1998). Cortical area MT and the perception of stereoscopic depth. *Nature, 394*, 677–680.

DeAngelis, G. C., Ohzawa, I., & Freeman, R. D. (1995). Neuronal mechanisms underlying stereopsis: How do simple cells in the visual cortex encode binocular disparity? *Perception, 24*, 3–31.

De Carlos, J. A., & Borrell, J. (2007). A historical reflection of the contributions of Cajal and Golgi to the foundations of neuroscience. *Brain Research Reviews, 55*, 8–16.

DeFelipe, J. (2006). Brain plasticity and mental processes: Cajal again. *Nature Reviews Neuroscience, 7*, 811–817.

Dehaene-Lambertz, G., & Gliga, T. (2004). Common neural basis for phoneme processing in infants and adults. *Journal of Cognitive Neuroscience, 16*, 1375–1387.

De Lange, D. Z. N. (1958). Research into the dynamic nature of the human fovea cortex systems with intermittent and modulated light. II. Phase shift in brightness and delay in color perception. *Journal of the Optical Society of America, 48*, 748–789.

Desmurget, M., & Grafton, S. (2003). Feedback or feedforward control: End of a dichotomy. In S. H. Johnson—Frey (Ed.), *Taking action: Cognitive neuroscience perspectives on intentional acts*. Cambridge, MA: MIT Press.

Deutsch, L. J., & Richards, A. M. (1979). *Elementary hearing science*. Baltimore, MD: University Park Press.

De Valois, R. L., & De Valois, K. K. (1975). Neural coding of color. In E. C. Carterette & M. P. Friedman (Eds), *Handbook of perception (Vol. 5)*. New York, NY: Academic Press.

De Valois, R. L., & De Valois, K. K. (1990). *Spatial vision*. New York, NY: Oxford University Press.

De Valois, R. L., & De Valois, K. K. (1993). A multi-stage color model. *Vision Research, 33*, 1053–65.

Dillon, H. (2000) *Hearing aids*. Turramurra, Australia: Boomerang Press.

Doherty, P., Brewer, W. J., Castle, D., & Pantelis, C. (2006). *Olfaction and the brain*. Cambridge, UK: Cambridge University Press.

Donaldson, D. I. (2004). Parsing brain activity with fMRI and mixed designs: What kind of a state is neuroimaging in? *Trends in Neurosciences, 27*, 442–444.

Doron, K. W., & Gazzaniga, M. S. (2008). Neuroimaging techniques offer new perspectives on callosal transfer and interhemispheric communication. *Cortex, 44*, 1023–1029.

Doty, R. L. (2003). *Handbook of olfaction and gustation* (2nd ed.). London, UK: Informa HealthCare.

Doty, R. L., & Kobal, G. (1995). Current trends in the measurement of olfactory function. In R. L. Doty (Ed.). *Handbook of olfaction and gustation*. New York, NY: Marcel Dekker.

Doty, R. L., Shaman, P., Applebaum, S. L., Gilberson, R., Siksorski, L., & Rosenberg, L. (1984). Smell identification ability: Changes with age. *Science, 226*, 1441–1443.

Dowling, J. E. (1979). Information processing by local circuits: The vertebrate retina as a model system. In F. O. Schmitt & F. G. Worden (Eds.). *The neurosciences: Fourth study program*. Cambridge, MA: MIT Press.

Dowling, J. E. (1987). *The retina: An approachable part of the brain*. Cambridge, MA: Harvard University Press.

Eadie, T. L., & Doyle, P. C. (2002). Direct magnitude estimation and interval scaling of pleasantness and severity in dysphonic and normal speakers. *Journal of the Acoustical Society of America, 112*, 3014–3021.

Eatock, R. A. (2000). Adaptation in hair cells. *Annual Review of Neuroscience, 23*, 285–314.

Ebenholtz, S. M. (2001). *Oculomotor systems and perception*. Cambridge, UK: Cambridge University Press.

Ebner, M. (2007). *Color constancy*. Chichester, UK: Wiley.

Ebrey, T., & Koutalos, Y. (2001). Vertebrate photoreceptors. *Progress in Retinal Eye Research, 20,* 49–94.

Egan, J. P. (1975). *Signal detection theory and ROC-analysis.* New York, NY: Academic Press.

Egan, J. P., & Hake, H. W. (1950). On the masking pattern of a single auditory stimulus. *Journal of the Acoustical Society of America, 22,* 622–630.

Eggermont, J. J. (2001). Between sound and perception: Reviewing the search for a neural code. *Hearing Research, 157,* 1–42.

Ehret, R. R. (1997). *The central auditory system.* New York, NY: Oxford University Press.

Ehret, G., & Romand, R. (1996). *The central auditory system.* New York, NY: Oxford University Press.

Ekman, G. (1962). Measurement of moral judgment: A comparison of scaling methods. *Perceptual and Motor Skills, 15,* 3–9.

Ekman, G., & Sjöbert, L. (1965). Scaling. *Annual Review of Psychology, 16,* 451–474.

Emanuel, D. C., & Letowski, T. (2007). *Hearing science.* Baltimore, MD: Lippincott Williams & Wilkins.

Engen, T. (1971). Psychophysics: I. Discrimination and detection. In J. W. Kling & L. A. Rig (Eds.), *Woodworth & Schlossberg's experimental psychology.* New York, NY: Holt, Rinehart & Winston.

Enns, J. T. (2004). *The thinking eye, the seeing brain: Explorations in visual cognition.* New York, NY: W. W. Norton & Co.

Epstein, M., & Florentine, M. (2006). Loudness of brief tones measured by magnitude estimation and loudness matching. *Journal of the Acoustical Society of America, 119,* 1943–1945.

Epstein, W., & Rogers, S. (1995). *Perception of space and motion.* San Diego, CA: Academic Press.

Erickson, D. (1990). Electronic earful: Cochlear implants sound better all the time. *Scientific American, 263,* 132–134.

Erkelens, C. J., & van Ee, R. (2002). The role of the cyclopean eye in vision: Sometimes inappropriate, always irrelevant. *Vision Research, 42,* 1157–1163.

Evans, E. F. (1992). Auditory processing of complex sounds: An overview. *Philosophical Transactions of the Royal Society of London B Biological Sciences, 336,* 295–306.

Everest, F. A. (2000). *Master handbook of acoustics* (4th ed.). New York, NY: McGraw–Hill.

Evilsizer, M. E. et al. (2002). Binaural detection with narrowband and wideband reproducible noise maskers: I. Results for humans. *Journal of the Acoustical Society of America, 111,* 336–345.

Fain, G. L., Matthews, H. R., & Cornwall, M. C. (1996). Dark adaptation in vertebrate photoreceptors. *Trends in Neurosciences, 19,* 502–507.

Fain, G. L., Matthews, H. R., Cornwall, M. C., & Koutalos, Y. (2001). Adaptation in vertebrate photoreceptors. *Physiological Reviews, 81,* 117–151.

Faller, C., & Merimaa, J. (2004). Source localization in complex listening situations: Selection of binaural cues based on interaural coherence. *Journal of the Acoustic Society of America, 116,* 3075–3089.

Falmagne, J. C. (2002). *Elements of psychophysical theory.* New York, NY: Oxford University Press.

Farah, M. J. (1990). *Visual agnosia: Disorders of object recognition and what they tell us about normal vision.* Cambridge, MA: MIT Press.

Farah, M. J. (2000). *The cognitive neuroscience of vision.* Malden, MA: Wiley-Blackwell.

Fay, R. R. (1988). Comparative psychoacoustics. *Hearing Research, 34,* 295–305.

Fechner, G. T. (1860/1966). *Elements of psychophysics.* H. E. Adler, D. H. Howes, E. G. Boring (Trans.). New York, NY: Holt, Rinehart and Winston.

Fechner, G. T., & Lowrie, W. (2008). *Religion of a scientist: Selections from Gustav Theodor Fechner.* Whitefish, MT: Kessinger Publishing.

Feddersen, W. E., Sandel, T. T., Teas, D. C., & Jeffress, L. A. (1957). Localization of high frequency tones. *Journal of the Acoustical Society of America, 29,* 988–991.

Fetter, M. (2007). Vestibulo-ocular reflex. *Developments in Ophthalmology, 40,* 35–51.

Fettiplace, R. (2006). Active hair bundle movements in auditory hair cells. *Journal of Physiology, 576,* 29–36.

Fettiplace, R., & Fuchs, P. A. (1999). Mechanisms of hair cell tuning. *Annual Review of Physiology, 61,* 809–834.

Field, G. D., & Chichilinisky, E. J. (2007). Information processing in the primate retina: Circuitry and coding. *Annual Review of Neuroscience, 30,* 1–30.

Field, G. D., Sampath, A. P., & Rieke, F. (2005). Retinal processing near absolute threshold: From behavior to mechanism. *Annual Review of Physiology, 67,* 491–514.

Fiesler, S. J., & Kisselev, O. G. (2007). *Signal transduction in the retina.* Boca Raton, FL: CRC Press.

Finger, S. (1994). *Origins of neuroscience: A history of explorations into brain function.* New York, NY: Oxford University Press.

Finger, T. E., Silver, W. L., & Restrepo, D. (2000). *Neurobiology of taste and smell.* New York, NY: Wiley-Liss.

Fletcher, H., & Munson, W. A. (1933). Loudness, its definition, measurement and calculation. *Journal of the Acoustical Society of America, 5,* 82–108.

Fletcher, N. H., & Rossing, T. D. (1991). *The physics of musical instruments.* New York, NY: Springer.

Flor, H., Nikolajsen, L., & Staehelin Jensen, T. (2006). Phantom limb pain: A case of maladaptive CNS plasticity? *Nature Reviews Neuroscience, 7,* 873–881.

Fox, C. J., Iaria, G., & Barton, J. J. (2008). Disconnection in prosopagnosia and face processing. *Cortex, 44,* 996–1009.

Frackowiak, R. S. J. (1997). *Human brain function.* San Diego, CA: Academic Press.

Freeman, M. H. (1990). *Optics* (10th ed.). Boston, MA: Butterworths.

Fregni, F., Freedman, S., & Pascual-Leone, A. (2007). Recent advances in the treatment of chronic pain with non-invasive brain stimulation techniques. *Lanced Neurology, 6,* 188–191.

Friston, K. (1998). Imaging neuroscience: Principles or maps? *Proceedings of the National Academy of Sciences USA, 95,* 796–802.

Friston, K. (2002). Beyond phrenology: What can neuroimaging tell us about distributed circuitry? *Annual Review of Neuroscience, 25,* 221–250.

Frith, C. (2007). *Making up the mind: How the brain creates our mental world.* Malden, MA: Wiley-Blackwell.

Fritz, J. B., Elhilali, M., David, S. V., & Shamma, S. A. (2007). Auditory attention: Focusing the searchlight on sound. *Current Opinion on Neurobiology, 17,* 437–455.

Fritzsch, B., Beisel, K. W., Pauley, S., & Soukup, G. (2007). Molecular evolution of the vertebrate mechanosensory cell and ear. *International Journal of Developmental Biology, 51,* 663–678.

Frye, R. E. et al. (2007). Linear coding of voice onset time. *Journal of Cognitive Neuroscience, 19,* 1476–1487.

Gage, J. (2000). *Color and meaning: Art, science, and symbolism.* Berkeley, CA: University of California Press.

Gattass, R., Nascimento-Silva, S., Soares, J. G., Lima, B., Jansen, A. K., Diogo, A. C., & Fiorani, M. (2005). Cortical visual areas in monkeys: Location, topography, connections, columns, plasticity and cortical dynamics. *Philosophical Transactions of the Royal Society of London B Biological Sciences, 360,* 709–731.

Gegenfurtner, K. R. (2000). *Color vision: From genes to perception.* Cambridge, UK: Cambridge University Press.

Gegenfurtner, K. R. (2003). Cortical mechanisms in colour vision. *Nature Reviews Neuroscience, 4,* 563–572.

Gegenfurtner, K. R., & Kiper, D. C. (2003). Color vision. *Annual Reviews of Neuroscience, 26,* 181–206.

Geisler, G. C. (1998). *From sound to synapse.* New York, NY: Oxford University Press.

Genders, R. (1972). *A history of scent.* London, UK: Hamish Hamilton.

Gescheider, G. A. (1984). *Psychophysics: Method, theory and application.* Hillsdale, NJ: Lawrence Erlbaum Associates.

Gescheider, G. A. (1988). Psychophysical scaling. *Annual Review of Psychology, 39,* 169–200.

Gescheider, G. A. (1997). *Psychophysics: The fundamentals.* Hillsdale, NJ: Lawrence Erlbaum.

Gibbons, B. (1986). The intimate sense of smell. *National Geographic, 170,* 324–361.

Gibson, J. J. (1950). *The perception of the visual world.* Westport, CT: Greenwood Press.

Gibson, J. J. (1962). Observations on active touch. *Psychological Review, 69,* 477–491.

Gibson, J. J. (1979). *The ecological approach to visual perception.* Boston, MA: Houghton Mifflin.

Gilmer, B. v. H. (1966). *Problems in cutaneous communication: From psychophysics to information processing.* New York, NY: American Foundation for the Blind.

Gleason, J. B., & Ratner, N. B. (1998). *Psycholinguistics.* Fort Worth, TX: Harcourt Brace.

Goodale, M. A., Kroliczak, G., & Westwood, D. A. (2005). Dual routes to action: Contributions of the dorsal and ventral streams to adaptive behavior. *Progress in Brain Research, 149,* 269–283.

Goodwin, A. W., & Wheat, H. E. (2004). Sensory signals in neural populations underlying tactile perception and manipulation. *Annual Review of Neuroscience, 27,* 53–77.

Gordon, C. (1978). *Active touch: The mechanism of recognition of objects by manipulation.* Oxford, UK: Pergamon Press.

Goss, D. A., & West, R. W. (2001). *Introduction to the optics of the eye.* Boston, MA: Butterworth-Heinemann.

Gracely, R. H., & Naliboff, B. D. (1996). Measurement of pain sensation. In L. Kruger (Ed.), *Pain and touch, handbook of perception and cognition* (2nd ed.). San Diego, CA: Academic Press.

Graham, C. H. (1965). *Vision and visual perception.* New York, NY: Wiley.

Granrud, C. E., & Yonal, A. (1984). Infants' perception of pictorially specified interposition. *Journal of Experimental Child Psychology, 37,* 500–511.

Green, B. G. (2004). Temperature perception and nociception. *Journal of Neurobiology, 61,* 13–29.

Green, D. M., & Swets, J. A. (1966). *Signal detection theory and psychophysics.* New York, NY: Wiley.

Green, D. M., & Swets, J. A. (1989). *Signal detection theory and psychophysics.* New York, NY: Peninsula Publishing.

Greenler, R. (1980). *Rainbows, halos, and glories.* Cambridge, UK: Cambridge University Press.

Greenspan, J. D., & Bolanowski, S. J. (1996). The psychophysics of tactile perception and its peripheral physiological basis. In L. Kruger (Ed.), *Pain and touch, handbook of perception and cognition* (2nd ed.). San Diego, CA: Academic Press.

Gregory, R. L. (1997). *Eye and brain.* Princeton, NJ: Princeton University Press.

Gregory, R. L. (2008). Emmert's law and the moon illusion. *Spatial Vision, 21,* 407–420.

Grill-Spector, K., Golarai, G., & Gabrieli, J. (2008). Developmental neuroimaging of the human ventral visual cortex. *Trends in Cognitive Science, 12,* 152–162.

Grodzinsky, Y., & Santi, A. (2008). The battle for Broca's region. *Trends in Cognitive Sciences, 12,* 474–480.

Gross, C. G. (1999). *Brain, vision, memory.* Cambridge, MA: MIT Press.

Gross, C. G., Rocha-Miranda, C. E., & Bender, D. B. (1972). Visual properties of cells in inferotemporal cortex of the macaque. *Journal of Neurophysiology, 35,* 96–111.

Grunwald, M. (2008). *Human haptic perception: Basics and applications.* Basel, Switzerland: Birkhäuser.

Guenther, R. (1990). *Modern optics.* New York, NY: Wiley.

Guido, W. (2008). Refinement of the retinogeniculate pathway. *Journal of Physiology, 586,* 4357–4362.

Guillery, R. W. (2007). Relating the neuron doctrine to the cell theory: Should contemporary knowledge change our view of the neuron doctrine? *Brain Research Reviews, 55,* 411–421.

Gulick, W. L., Gescheider, G. A., & Frisina, R. D. (1989). *Hearing: Physiological acoustics, neural coding, and psychoacoustics.* New York, NY: Oxford University Press.

Gur, M., & Snodderly, D. M. (2007). Directional selectivity in V1 of alert monkeys: Evidence for parallel pathways for motion processing. *The Journal of Physiology, 585,* 383–400.

Hall, Z. W. (1992). *Introduction to molecular neurobiology.* Sunderland, MA: Sinauer.

Hallett, P. E. (1969). The variations in visual threshold measurement. *Journal of Physiology, London, 202,* 403–419.

Halpern, B. P. (1983). Tasting and smelling as active, exploratory sensory processes. *American Journal of Otolaryngology, 4,* 246–249.

Halpern, B. P. (1997). Psychophysics of taste. In G. K. Beauchamp & L. M. Bartoshuk (Eds.). *Tasting and Smelling, Handbook of Perception and Cognition* (2nd ed.). San Diego, CA: Academic Press.

Hannon, E. E., & Trainor, L. J. (2007). Music acquisition: Effects of enculturation and formal training on development. *Trends in Cognitive Science, 11,* 466–472.

Hardcastle, V. G. (1999). *The myth of pain.* Cambridge, MA: MIT Press.

Hardin, C. L. (1997). *Color categories in thought and language.* Cambridge, UK: Cambridge University Press.

Harrington, A., & Rosario, V. (1992) Olfaction and the primitive: Nineteenth-century medical thinking on olfaction. In M. J. Serby & K. L. Chobor (Eds.), *Science of olfaction.* New York, NY: Springer-Verlag.

Harris, J. M., Nefs, H. T., & Grafton, C. E. (2008). Binocular vision and motion-in-depth. *Spatial Vision, 21,* 531–547.

Hart, W. M. Jr. (1987). The temporal responsiveness of vision. In R. A. Moses & W. M. Hart (Eds.), *Adler's physiology of the eye, clinical application.* St. Louis, MO: Mosby.

Hartmann, W. M. (1998). *Signal, sounds and sensation.* New York, NY: Springer.

Hawken, M. J., Parker, A. J., & Lund, J. S. (1988). Laminar organization and contrast sensitivity of direction-selective cells in the striate cortex of the old-world monkey. *Journal of Neuroscience, 8,* 3541–3548.

Hawkes, C. H., & Doty, R. (2009). *The neurology of olfaction.* Cambridge, UK: Cambridge University Press.

Hecht, E. (2001). *Optics* (4th ed.). Reading, MA: Addison Wesley.

Hecht, S., Schlaer, S., & Pirenne, M. H. (1942). Energy, quanta and vision. *Journal of the Optical Society of America, 38,* 196–208.

Heffner, R. S. (2004). Primate hearing from a mammalian perspective. *Anatomical Record, 281,* 1111–1122.

Heidelberger, M., & Klohr, C. (2004). *Nature from within: Gustav Theodor Fechner and his psychophysical worldview.* Pittsburgh, PA: University of Pittsburgh Press.

Heller, M. A., & Ballesteros, S. (2005). *Touch and blindness: Psychology and neuroscience.* Hillsdale, NJ: Lawrence Erlbaum.

Hennessy, J. J., & Romig, C. H. (1971). A review of the experiments using voiceprint identification. *Journal of Forensic Science, 16,* 183–198.

Herness, S. (2000). Coding in taste receptor cells: The early years of intracellular recordings. *Physiology and Behavior, 69,* 17–27.

Hershenson, M. (1989). *The moon illusion.* Hillsdale, NJ: Lawrence Erlbaum Associates.

Hilbert, D. R. (1992). What is color vision? *Philosophical Studies, 68,* 351–370.

Hollins, M., & Bensmaia, S. J. (2007). The coding of roughness. *Canadian Journal of Experimental Psychology, 61,* 184–195.

Hollins, M., Bensmaia, S. J., & Roy, E. A. (2002). Vibrotaction and texture perception. *Behavioral Brain Research, 135,* 51–56.

Hood, D. C., & Finkelstein, M. A. (1986). Sensitivity to light. In K. R. Boff, L. Kaufman & J. P. Thomas (Eds.), *Visual psychophysics: Its physiological basis.* New York, NY: Academic Press.

Howard, D. M. (2000). *Acoustics and psychoacoustics.* Oxford, UK: Focal Press.

Howard, I. P. (1982). *Human visual orientation.* New York, NY: Wiley.

Howard, I. P., & Rogers, B. J. (1995). *Binocular vision and stereopsis.* New York, NY: Oxford University Press.

Hubel, D. H. (1989). *Eye, brain and vision.* New York, NY: Scientific American Library.

Hubel, D. H. (1995). *Eye, brain, and vision.* New York, NY: Scientific American Library.

Hubel, D. H., & Wiesel, T. N. (1962). Receptive fields, binocular interaction and functional architecture in the cat's visual cortex. *Journal of Physiology (London), 160,* 106–154.

Hubel, D. H., & Wiesel, T. N. (1968). Receptive fields and functional architecture of monkey striate cortex. *Journal of Physiology (London), 195,* 215–243.

Hubel, D. H., & Wiesel, T. N. (1979). Brain mechanisms of vision. *Scientific American, 241,* 150–162.

Hubel, D. H, & Wiesel, T. N. (2004). *Brain and visual perception: The story of a 25-year collaboration.* New York, NY: Oxford University Press.

Huberman, A. D., Feller, M. B., & Chapman, B. (2008). Mechanisms underlying development of visual maps and receptive fields. *Annual Review of Neuroscience, 31,* 479–509.

Hudson, R. (1999). From molecule to mind: The role of experience in shaping olfactory function. *Journal of Comparative Physiology A, 185,* 295–304.

Hudspeth, A. J. (1997). How hearing happens. *Neuron, 19,* 947–950.

Hudspeth, A. J. (1999). Sensory transduction in the ear. In E. R. Kandel, J. H. Schwartz & T. M. Jessell (Eds.), *Principles of neural science* (4th ed.). Norwalk, CT: Appleton & Lange.

Hudspeth, A. J. (2008). Making an effort to listen: Mechanical amplification in the ear. *Neuron, 59,* 530–545.

Hummel, T. (2000). Assessment of intranasal trigeminal function. *International Journal of Psychophysiology, 36,* 147–155.

Humphrey, G. K., & Goodale, M. A. (1998). Probing unconscious visual processing with the McCollough effect. *Consciousness and Cognition, 1998,* 494–519.

Hurlbert, A. (1999). Is color constancy real? *Current Biology, 9,* R558–R561.

Hurlbert, A., & Wolf, K. (2004). Color contrast: A contributory mechanism to color constancy. *Progress in Brain Research, 144,* 147–160.

Hurvich, L. M. (1981). *Color vision.* Sunderland, MA: Sinauer Associates.

Hurvich, L. M., & Jameson, D. (1957). An opponent-process theory of color vision. *Psychological Reviews, 64,* 384–404.

Huttenbrink, K. B. (2003). Biomechanics of stapesplasty: A review. *Otolaryngology and Neurootology, 24,* 548–557.

Hwang, S. W., & Oh, U. (2007). Current concepts of nociception. *Current Opinion in Anaesthesiology, 20,* 427–434.

Hyakin, S., & Chen, Z. (2005). The cocktail party problem. *Neural Computation, 17,* 1875–1902.

Iacoboni, M., & Dapretto, M. (2006). The mirror neuron system and the consequences of its dysfunction. *Nature Reviews Neuroscience, 7,* 942–951.

Ibbotson, M. R., Crowder, N. A., Cloherty, S. L., Price, N. S. C., & Mustari, M. J. (2008). Saccadic modulation of neural responses: Possible roles in saccadic suppression, enhancement and time compression. *Journal of Neuroscience, 28,* 10952–10960.

Ilg, U. J., & Their, P. (2008). The neural basis of smooth pursuit eye movements in the rhesus monkey brain. *Brain & Cognition, 68,* 229–240.

Ings, S. (2008). *A natural history of seeing: The art and science of vision.* New York, NY: W. W. Norton.

Ittelson, W. H. (1951). Size as a cue to distance. *American Journal of Psychology, 64,* 54–67.

Iwamura, Y. (1998). Hierarchical somatosensory processing. *Current Opinion in Neurobiology, 8,* 522–528.

Jackendoff, R. (2003). *Foundations of language: Brain, meaning, grammar, evolution.* New York, NY: Oxford University Press.

Jackendoff, R., & Lerdahl, F. (2006). The capacity for music: What is it, and what's special about it? *Cognition, 100,* 33–72.

Jacobs, G. H. (1981). *Comparative color vision.* New York, NY: Academic Press.

Jacobs, G. H. (1993). The distribution and nature of color vision among the mammals. *Biological Reviews, 68,* 413–471.

Javel, E., & Mott, J. B. (1988). Physiological and psychophysical correlates of temporal processes in hearing. *Hearing Research, 34,* 275–294.

Jeffress, L. A. (1948). A place theory of sound localization. *Journal of Comparative Physiology and Psychology, 41,* 35–39.

Jenkin, M. R. M., & Harris, L. R. (2005). *Seeing spatial form.* New York, NY: Oxford University Press.

Jenkins, F. A., & White, H. E. (2001). *Fundamentals of optics* (4th ed.). New York, NY: McGraw-Hill.

Jesteadt, W. (1997). *Modeling sensorineural hearing loss.* Mahwah, NJ: Lawrence Erlbaum Associates.

Jesteadt, W., Wier, C. C., & Green, D. M. (1977). Intensity discrimination as a function of frequency and sensation level. *Journal of the Acoustical Society of America, 61,* 169–177.

Johansson, G. (1973). Visual perception of biological motion and a model for its analysis. *Perception and Psychophysics, 14,* 201–211.

Johansson, R. S., & Vallbo, A. B. (1983). Tactile sensory coding in the glabrous skin of the human hand. *Trends in Neurosciences, 6,* 27–32.

Johnson, E. O., Babis, G. C., Soultanis, K. C., & Soucacos, P. N. (2008). Functional neuroanatomy of proprioception. *Journal of Surgical Orthopaedic Advances, 17,* 159–164.

Johnson, K. O., Hsiao, S. S., & Yoshioka, T. (2002). Neural coding and the basic law of psychophysics. *Neuroscientist, 8,* 111–121.

Johnsrude, I. S., Giraud, A. L., & Frackowiak, R. S. (2002). Functional imaging of the auditory system: The use of positron emission tomography. *Audiology and Neurotology, 7,* 251–276.

Jordan, J. S., & Hunsinger, M. (2008). Learned patterns of action-effect anticipation contribute to the spatial displacement of continuously moving stimuli. *Journal of Experimental Psychology: Human Perception and Performance, 34,* 113–124.

Joris, P., & Yin, T. C. (2007). A matter of time: Internal delays in binaural processing. *Trends in Neuroscience, 30,* 70–78.

Julesz, B. (1971). *Foundations of cyclopean perception.* Chicago, IL: University of Chicago Press.

Kaas, J. H. (2005). The future of mapping sensory cortex in primates: Three of many remaining issues. *Philosophical Transactions of the Royal Society of London B Biological Sciences, 360,* 653–664.

Kaas, J. H. (2008). The evolution of the complex sensory and motor systems of the human brain. *Brain Research Bulletin, 75,* 384–390.

Kaas, J. H., & Lyon, D. C. (2007). Pulvinar contributions to the dorsal and ventral streams of visual processing in primates. *Brain Research Reviews, 55,* 285–296.

Kaas, J. H., Merzenich, M. M., & Killackey, H. P. (1983). The reorganization of somatosensory cortex following peripheral nerve damage in adult and developing mammals. *Annual Review of Neuroscience, 6*, 325–356.

Kaas, J. H., Nelson, R. J., Sur, M., Lin, C. S., & Merzenich, M. (1979). Multiple representations of the body within the primary somatosensory cortex of primates. *Science, 204*, 521–523.

Kaernbach, C., Schrger, E., Miler, H., & Muller, H. (2003). *Psychophysics beyond sensation: Laws and invariants of human cognition.* Hillsdale, NJ: Lawrence Erlbaum Associates.

Kaiser, P. K., & Boynton, R. M. (1996). *Human color vision* (2nd ed.). Washington, DC: Optical Society of America.

Kandel, E. R., Schwartz, J. H., & Jessell, T. M. (2000). *Principles of neural science* (4th ed.). New York, NY: McGraw-Hill.

Kanizsa, G. (1979). *Organization in vision: Essays on Gestalt perception.* New York, NY: Praeger.

Kanwisher, N., & Duncan, J. (2004). *Functional neuroimaging of visual cognition.* New York, NY: Oxford University Press.

Kanwisher, N., McDermott, J., & Chun, M. M. (1997). The fusiform face area: A module in human extrastriate cortex specialized for face perception. *Journal of Neuroscience, 17*, 4302–4311.

Kanwisher, N., & Yovel, G. (2006). The fusiform face area: A cortical region specialized for the perception of faces. *Philosophical Transactions of the Royal Society of London, B Biolocial Sciences, 361*, 2109–2128.

Kaplan, E., & Shapley, R. M. (1986). The primate retina contains two types of ganglion cells, with high and low contrast sensitivity. *Proceedings of the National Academy of Sciences USA, 83*, 2755–2757.

Keating, M. P. (2002). *Geometric, physical, and visual optics* (2nd ed.). Boston, MA: Butterworth-Heinemann.

Keller, H. (1903). *The story of my life.* New York, NY: Doubleday.

Kelly, D. H. (1974). Spatio-temporal frequency characteristics of color-vision mechanisms. *Journal of the Optical Society of America, 64*, 983–990.

Kenshalo, D. R. (1978). Biophysics and psychophysics of feeling. In E. C. Carterette & M. P. Friedman (Eds.), *Handbook of perception, Vol. VIB: Feeling and hurting* (pp. 29–74). New York, NY: Academic Press.

Kerr, N. L., & Tindale, R. S. (2004). Group performance and decision making. *Annual Review of Psychology, 55*, 623–655.

Keverne, E. B. (1999). The vomeronasal organ. *Science, 286*, 716–720.

Keysers, C., Xiao, D. K., Földiák. P., & Perrett, D. I. (2001). The speed of sight. *Journal of Cognitive Neuroscience, 13*, 90–101.

Kingdom, F. A. (2008). Perceiving light versus material. *Vision Research*, 2090–2105.

King-Smith, P. E. (2005). Threshold nonlinearities and signal detection theory. *Perception, 34*, 941–946.

Kinsbourne, M. (1978). *Asymmetrical function of the brain.* Cambridge, UK: Cambridge University Press.

Kitchen, C. K. (2007). *Fact and fiction of healthy vision: Eye care for adults and children.* New York, NY: Praeger.

Kleene, S. J. (2008). The electrochemical basis of odor transduction in vertebrate olfactory cilia. *Chemical Senses, 33*, 839–859.

Knig, R., Hall, P., Scheich, H., Budinger, E., & Konig, R. (2005). *Auditory cortex: Synthesis of human and animal research.* Hillsdale, NJ: Lawrence Erlbaum.

Knutsen, P. M., & Ahissar, E. (2009). Orthogonal coding of object location. *Trends in Neurosciences, 32*, 101–109.

Kochendoerfer, G. G., Lin, S. W., Sakmar, T. P., & Mathies, R. A. (1999). How color visual pigments are tuned. *Trends in Biochemical Sciences, 24*, 300–305.

Kohl, J. V. (1995). *The scent of eros: Mysteries of odor in human sexuality.* Lincoln, NE: Authors Choice Press.

Köhler, W. (1969). *The task of Gestalt psychology.* Princeton, NJ: Princeton University Press.

Kolb, H., Ripps, H., & Wu, S. (2003). *Concepts and challenges in retinal biology.* Amsterdam, Netherlands: Elsevier.

Kolers, P. A. (1972). *Aspects of motion perception.* Oxford, UK: Pergamon Press.

Konishi, M. (2003). Coding of auditory space. *Annual Review of Neuroscience, 26*, 31–55.

Kosik, K. S. (2003). Beyond phrenology, at last. *Nature Reviews Neuroscience, 4*, 234–239.

Kral, A., & Eggermont, J. J. (2007). What's to lose and what's to learn: Development under auditory deprivation, cochlear implants and the limits of cortical plasticity. *Brain Research Reviews, 56*, 259–269.

Krauzlis, R. J. (2005). The control of voluntary eye movements: New perspectives. *The Neuroscientist, 11*, 124–137.

Krueger, L. E. (1989). Reconciling Fechner and Stevens: Toward a unified psychophysical law. *Behavioral and Brain Sciences, 12*, 251–320.

Kruger, E. (1996). *Pain and touch, handbook of perception and cognition* (2nd ed.). San Diego, CA: Academic Press.

Kruger L., & Otis T. S. (2007). Whither withered Golgi? A retrospective evaluation of reticularist and synaptic constructs. *Brain Research Bulletin, 72*, 201–207.

Kryter, K. D. (1996). *Handbook of hearing and the effects of noise.* San Diego, CA: Academic Press.

Kuehni, R. G., & Schwarz, A. (2008). *Color ordered: A survey of color systems from antiquity to the present.* New York, NY: Oxford University Press.

Kuffler, S. W. (1953). Discharge patterns and functional organization of mammalian retina. *Journal of Neurophysiology, 16*, 37–68.

Kuriki, I., Ashida, H., Murakami, I., & Kitaoka, A. (2008). Functional brain imaging of the "Rotating Snakes" illusion. *Journal of Vision, 8*, 64, 64a. Retrieved from http://journalofvision.org/8/6/64/, doi:10.1167/8.6.64.

Kung, C. (2005). A possible unifying principle for mechanosensation. *Nature, 436*, 647–654.

Lacey, S., Campbell, C., & Sathian, K. (2007). Vision and touch: Multiple or multisensory representation of objects? *Perception, 36*, 1513–1521.

Lackner, J. R., & DiZio, P. (2005). Vestibular, proprioceptive, and haptic contributions to spatial orientation. *Annual Review of Psychology, 56*, 115–147.

Ladefoged, P. (2001). *Vowels and consonants: An introduction to the sounds of languages.* Malden, MA: Blackwell.

Ladefoged, P., & Maddieson, I. (1996). *The sounds of the world's languages.* Malden, MA: Blackwell.

LaGallienne, R. (1928). *The romance of perfume.* New York, NY: Richard Hudnut.

Lamming, D. (1991). Contrast sensitivity. In J. Cronly-Dillon (Ed.) *Vision and visual dysfunction* (Vol. 5). London, UK: Macmillan Press.

Land, E. H. (1977). The retinex theory of color vision. *Scientific American, 237*, 108–128.

Land, M. F. (1999). Motion and vision: Why animals move their eyes. *Journal of Comparative Physiology A, 185*, 341–352.

Large, E. W., & Tretakis, A. E. (2005). Tonality and nonlinear resonance. *Annals of the New York Academy of Sciences, 1060*, 53–56.

Lash, J. P. (1980). *Helen and teacher: The story of Helen Keller and Anne Sullivan Macy.* New York, NY: Delacorte.

Laszig, R., & Aschendorff, A. (1999). Cochlear implants and electrical brainstem stimulation in sensorineural hearing loss. *Current Opinion in Neurology, 12*, 41–44.

Laties, A., & Zrenner, E. (2002). Viagra (sildenafil citrate) and ophthalmology. *Progress in Retinal Eye Research, 21*, 485–506.

Lautenbacher, S., & Fillingim, R. B. (2004). *Pathophysiology of pain perception.* New York, NY: Plenum.

Laurent, G. (1999). A systems perspective on early olfactory coding. *Science, 286,* 723–728.

Lederman, S. J., & Klatzky, R. L. (1987). Hand movements: A window into haptic object recognition. *Cognitive Psychology, 19,* 342–368.

Lederman, S. J., & Klatzky, R. L. (1990). Haptic classification of common objects: Knowledge-driven exploration. *Cognitive Psychology, 22,* 421–459.

Lederman, S. J., & Klatzky, R. L. (2004). Haptic identification of common objects: Effects of constraining the manual exploration process. *Perception and Psychophysics, 66,* 618–628.

Lee, B. B. (2008). Neural models and physiological reality. *Visual Neuroscience, 25,* 231–241.

Lee, D. N. (1976). A theory of visual control of braking based on information about time-to-collision. *Perception, 5,* 437–459.

Lee, D. N. (1980). The optic flow field: The foundation of vision. *Philosophical Transactions of the Royal Society of London B, 290,* 169–179.

Lee, H. C. (2009). *Introduction to color imaging science.* Cambridge, UK: Cambridge University Press.

Lee, M. W., McPhee, R. W., & Stringer, M. D. (2008). An evidence-based approach to human dermatomes. *Clinical Anatomy, 21,* 363–373.

Legéndy, C. (2009). *Circuits in the brain.* New York, NY: Springer.

Le Grand, Y. (1980). *Physiological optics.* Berlin, Germany: Springer-Verlag.

Lennie, P. (1998). Single units and visual cortical organization. *Perception, 27,* 889–935.

Lerdahl, F., & Jackendoff, R. (1983). *A generative theory of tonal music.* Cambridge, MA: MIT Press.

LeVay, S., & Voigt, T. (1988). Ocular dominance and disparity coding in cat visual cortex. *Visual Neuroscience, 1,* 395–414.

Levine, M. W., & McAnany, J. J. (2008). The effects of curvature on the grid illusions. *Perception, 37,* 171–184.

Levitan, I. B., & Kaczmarek, L. K. (1997). *The neuron: Cell and molecular biology.* New York, NY: Oxford University Press.

Levitin, D. J., & Rogers, S. E. (2005). Absolute pitch: Perception, coding, and controversies. *Trends in Cognitive Science, 9,* 26–33.

Liberman, A. M., Cooper, F. S., Shankweiler, D. P., & Studdert-Kennedy, M. (1967). Perception of the speech code. *Psychological Review, 74,* 451–461.

Livingstone, M. S. (2002). *Vision and art: The biology of seeing.* New York, NY: Harry N. Abrams.

Livingstone, M. S., & Conway, B. R. (2004). Was Rembrandt stereoblind? *New England Journal of Medicine, 351,* 1264–1265.

Livingstone, M. S., & Hubel, D. (1988). Segregation of form, color, movement, and depth: Anatomy, physiology, and perception. *Science, 240,* 740–749.

Lodge, M. (1981). *Magnitude Scaling: Quantitative Measurement of Opinions.* Beverly Hills, CA: Sage Publications.

Logothetis, N. K. (1998). Single units and conscious vision. *Philosophical Transactions of the Royal Society of London B, 353,* 1801–1818.

Logothetis, N. K., & Schall, J. D. (1989). Neuronal correlates of subjective visual perception. *Science, 245,* 761–763.

Logvinenko, A. D. (2005). Does luminance contrast determine lightness? *Spatial Vision, 18,* 337–345.

Long, M., Levy, M., & Stern, R. (2006). *Architectural acoustics.* Burlington, MA: Elsevier.

Loomis, J. M. (1981). Tactile pattern perception. *Perception, 10,* 5–27.

Lopez-Munoz, F., Boya, J., & Alamo, C. (2006). Neuron theory, the cornerstone of neuroscience, on the centenary of the Nobel Prize award to Santiago Ramon y Cajal. *Brain Research Bulletin, 70,* 391–405.

Lotto, R. B., & Purves, D. (2002). The empirical basis of color perception. *Consciousness and Cognition, 11,* 609–629.

Loui, P., Wu, E. H., Wessel, D. L., & Knight, R. T. (2009). A generalized mechanism for perception of pitch patterns. *Journal of Neuroscience, 29,* 454–459.

Loula, F., Prasad, S., Harber, K., & Shiffrar, M. (2005). Recognizing people from their movements. *Journal of Experimental Psychology: Human Perception & Performance, 31,* 210–220.

Lu, Z. L., & Dosher, B. A. (2008). Characterizing observers using external noise and observer models: Assessing internal representations with external noise. *Psychological Review, 115,* 44–82.

Lu, Z. L., & Sperling, G. (1996). Second-order illusions: Mach bands, Chevreul, and Craik-O'Brien-Cornsweet. *Vision Research, 36,* 559–572.

Luce, R. D. (1990). "On the possible psychophysical laws" revisited: Remarks on cross-modality matching. *Psychological Review, 97,* 66–77.

Luce, R. D. (1993). *Sound and hearing.* Hillsdale, NJ: Lawrence Erlbaum.

Luck, S. J. (2005). *An introduction to the event-related potential technique.* Cambridge, MA: MIT Press.

Lumpkin, E. A., & Caterina, M. J. (2007). Mechanisms of sensory transduction in the skin. *Nature, 445,* 858–865.

Lund, J. S. (1973). Organization of neurons in the visual cortex, area 17, of the monkey (Macaca mulatta). *Journal of Comparative Neurology, 147,* 455–96.

Luo, L., & Flanagan, J. G. (2007). Development of continuous and discrete neural maps. *Neuron, 56,* 284–300.

Lynch, D. K., & Livingston, W. (2001). *Color and light in nature.* Cambridge, UK: Cambridge University Press.

Lynn, B., & Perl, E. R. (1996). Afferent mechanisms of pain. In L. Kruger (Ed.), *Pain and touch, handbook of perception and cognition* (2nd ed.). San Diego, CA: Academic Press.

Lythgoe, J. N. (1979). *The ecology of vision.* Oxford, UK: Clarendon Press.

Macmillan, M. (2002). *An odd kind of fame: Stories of Phineas Gage.* Cambridge, MA: MIT Press.

Macmillan, N. A., & Creelman, C. D. (2004). *Detection theory: A user's guide.* Hillsdale, NJ: Lawrence Erlbaum Associates.

MacLeish, P. R., Shepherd, G. M., Kinnamon, S. C., & Santos-Sacchi, J. (1999). Sensory transduction. In M. J. Zigmond, F. E. Bloom, S. C. Landis, J. L. Roberts & L. R. Squire (Eds.), *Fundamental neuroscience.* San Diego, CA: Academic Press.

Malacara, D. (2002). *Color vision and colorimetry: Theory and applications.* Bellingham, WA: SPIE Publications.

Manley, G. A. (2000). Cochlear mechanisms from a phylogenetic viewpoint. *Proceedings of the National Academy of Sciences USA, 97,* 11736–11743.

Manning, S. A. (1979). *Classical psychophysics and scaling.* New York, NY: Krieger.

Manning, S. A., & Rosenstock, E. H. (1967). *Classical psychophysics and scaling.* New York, NY: McGraw-Hill.

Marieb, E., & Hoehn, K. (2006). *Human anatomy and physiology* (7th ed.). San Francisco, CA: Benjamin Cummings.

Marks, L. E. (1988). Magnitude estimation and sensory matching. *Perception & Psychophysics, 43,* 511–525.

Marks, L. E. (1974). *Sensory processes: The new psychophysics.* New York, NY: Academic Press.

Marr, D. (1982). *Vision: A computational investigation into the human representation and processing of visual information.* San Francisco, CA: W.H. Freeman.

Marr, D., & Hildreth, E. C. (1980). Theory of edge detection. *Proceedings of the Royal Society of London, B, 207,* 187–217.

Marr, D., & Poggio, T. (1979). A computational theory of human stereo vision. *Proceedings of the Royal Society of London B, 204,* 301–328.

Martin, K. A. (2002). Microcircuits in visual cortex. *Current Opinion in Neurobiology, 12,* 418–425.

Martin, R. C. (2003). Language processing: Functional organization and neuroanatomical basis. *Annual Review of Psychology, 54,* 55–89.

Martinez-Conde, S., Macknik, S., Troncoso, X., & Dyar T (2006) Microsaccades counteract visual fading during fixation. *Neuron, 49,* 297–305.

Masland, R. H. (2001). The fundamental plan of the retina. *Nature Neuroscience, 4,* 877–886.

Masseck, O. A., & Hoffmann, K. P. (2009). Comparative neurobiology of the optokinetic reflex. *Annals of the New York Academy of Sciences, 1164,* 430–439.

Masud, M. (2002). *Classical optics and its applications.* Cambridge, UK: Cambridge University Press.

Mather, G. (1996). Image blur as a pictorial depth cue. *Proceedings: Biological Sciences, 263,* 169–172.

Mather, G. (2006). *Foundations of perception.* Hove, UK: Psychology Press.

Mather, G., Verstraten, F., & Anstis, S. (1998). *The motion aftereffect: A modern perspective.* Cambridge, MA: MIT Press.

Mathews, M. V., & Pierce, J. R. (1980). Harmony and nonharmonic partials. *Journal of the Acoustical Society of America, 68,* 1252–1257.

Matthews, G. G. (1997). *Neurobiology: Molecules, cells, and systems.* Malden, MA: Blackwell.

Maurer, D., Mondloch, C. J., & Lewis, T. L. (2007). Effects of early visual deprivation on perceptual and cognitive development. *Progress in Brain Research, 164,* 87–104.

McAlpine, D. (2005). Creating a sense of auditory space. *Journal of Physiology, 566,* 21–28.

McAlpine, D., & Grothe, B. (2003). Sound localization and delay lines: Do mammals fit the model? *Trends in Neuroscience, 26,* 347–350.

McBurney, D. H. (1978). Psychological dimensions and perceptual analysis of taste. In E. C. Carterette & M. P. Friedman (Eds.), *Handbook of perception.* New York, NY: Academic Press.

McBurney, D. H., Collings, V. B., & Glanz, L. M. (1973). Temperature dependence of human taste responses. *Physiology and Behavior, 11,* 89–94.

McClintock, M. (1971). Menstrual synchrony and suppression. *Nature, 229,* 244–245.

McCollough, C. (1965). Color adaptation of edge-detectors in the human visual system. *Science, 149,* 1115–1116.

McCulloch, W. S., & Pitts, W. P. (1943). A logical calculus in the ideas immanent in nervous activity. *Bulletin of Mathematical Biophysics, 5,* 115–133.

McGrath, P. A., Gracely, R. H., Dubner, R., & Heft, M. W. (1983). Non-pain and pain sensations evoked by tooth pulp stimulation. *Pain, 15,* 377–388.

McMahon, S., & Koltzenburg, M. (2005). *Wall and Melzack's textbook of pain.* Philadelphia: Elsevier/Churchill Livingstone.

McNicol, D. (2004). *A primer of signal detection theory.* Hillsdale, NJ: Lawrence Erlbaum.

Meinel, A. B., & Meinel, M. (1983). *Sunsets, twilights, and evening skies.* Cambridge, UK: Cambridge University Press.

Melzack, R. (1975). The McGill pain questionnaire: Major properties and scoring methods. *Pain, 1,* 277–299.

Melzack, R. (1989). Phantom limbs, the self and the brain. The D. O. Hebb Memorial Lecture. *Canadian Psychology, 30,* 1–16.

Melzack, R., & Wall, P. D. (1965). Pain mechanisms: A new theory. *Science, 150,* 971–979.

Melzack, R., & Wall, P. D. (1996). *The challenge of pain.* Harmondsworth, UK: Penguin.

Merigan, W. H., Byrne, C. E., & Maunsell, J. H. (1991). Does primate motion perception depend on the magnocellular pathway? *Journal of Neuroscience, 11,* 3422–3429.

Merzenich, M. M., & Brugge, J. F. (1973). Representation of the cochlear partition on the superior temporal plane of the macaque monkey. *Brain Research, 50,* 275–296.

Meyer, L. B. (1956). *Emotion and meaning in music.* Chicago, IL: Chicago University Press.

Meyer-Arendt, J. R. (1998). *Introduction to classical and modern optics* (2nd ed.). Upper Saddle River, NJ: Prentice-Hall.

Michaels, D. D. (1985). *Visual optics and refraction: A clinical approach* (3rd ed.). St. Louis, MO: Mosby.

Micheyl, C. et al. (2007). The role of auditory cortex in the formation of auditory streams. *Hearing Research, 229,* 116–131.

Millar, S. (2008). *Space and sense.* New York, NY: Psychology Press.

Miller, I. J., Jr. (1995). Anatomy of the peripheral taste system. In R. L. Doty (Ed.). *Handbook of olfaction and gustation.* New York, NY: Marcel Dekker.

Milner, A. D., & Goodale, M. A. (1995). *The visual brain in action.* Oxford, UK: Oxford University Press.

Milner, A. D., & Goodale, M. A. (2006). *The visual brain in action* (2nd ed.). New York, NY: Oxford University Press.

Minnaert, M. G. J. (1993). *Light and color in the outdoors.* New York, NY: Springer-Verlag.

Mishkin, M., Ungerleider, L. G., & Mack, K. A. (1983). Object vision and spatial vision: Two cortical pathways. *Trends in Neurosciences, 6,* 414–417.

Moller, A. R. (2006). *Hearing: Anatomy, physiology, and disorders of the auditory system* (2nd ed.). San Diego, CA: Academic Press.

Mombaerts, P. (1999). Molecular biology of odorant receptors in vertebrates. *Annual Review of Neuroscience, 22,* 487–509.

Mombaerts, P. (2004). Genes and ligands for odorant, vomeronasal and taste receptors. *Nature Reviews Neuroscience, 5,* 263–278.

Monti-Bloch, L., Jennings-White, C., & Berliner, D. (1998). The human vomeronasal system. *Ann NY Acad Sci, 855,* 373–389.

Moore, B. C. J. (1997). *An introduction to the psychology of hearing* (3rd ed.). London, UK: Academic Press.

Moore, B. C. J. (2003). *An introduction to the psychology of hearing* (5th ed.). London, UK: Academic Press.

Moore, B. C. J (2008). Basic auditory processes involved in the analysis of speech sounds. *Philosophical Transactions of the Royal Society of London B Biological Sciences, 363,* 974–963.

Morgan, M. J. (2009). *Molyneux's question: Vision, touch and the philosophy of perception.* Cambridge, UK: Cambridge University Press.

Mori, K., Nagao, H., & Yoshihara, Y. (1999) The olfactory bulb: Coding and processing of odor molecule information. *Science, 286,* 711–715.

Morley, J. W. (1998). *Neural aspects in tactile sensation.* Amsterdam, Netherlands: Elsevier.

Morris, E. T. (1984). *Fragrance—The story of perfume from Cleopatra to Chanel.* New York, NY: Charles Scribner's Sons.

Morsella, E., Bargh, J. A., & Gollwitzer, P. M. (2008). *Oxford handbook of human action.* New York, NY: Oxford University Press.

Mountcastle, V. B. (1995). The parietal system and some higher brain functions. *Cerebral Cortex, 5,* 377–390.

Mountcastle, V. B. (1997). The columnar organization of the neocortex. *Brain, 120,* 701–722.

Mountcastle, V. B. (1998). *Perceptual neuroscience: The cerebral cortex.* Cambridge, MA: Harvard University Press.

Mouroulis, P., & Mcdonald, J. (1997). *Geometrical optics and optical design.* New York, NY: Oxford University Press.

Mozel, M. M., Smith, B., Smith, P., Sullivan, R., & Swender, P. (1969). Nasal chemoreception in flavor identification. *Archives of Otolaryngology, 90,* 367–373.

Mullen, K. T., & Kingdom, F. A. (2002). Differential distributions of red-green and blue-yellow cone opponency across the visual field. *Visual Neuroscience, 19,* 109–118.

Munhall, K. G., & Buchan, J. N. (2004). Something in the way she moves. *Trends in Cognitive Science, 8,* 51–53.

Musiek, F. E., & Baran, J. A. (2006). *The auditory system: Anatomy, physiology, and clinical correlates.* Boston, MA: Allyn & Bacon.

Mustari, M. J., Ono, S., & Das, V. E. (2009). Signal processing and distribution in cortical-brainstem pathways for smooth pursuit eye movements. *Annals of the New York Academy of Sciences, 1164,* 147–154.

Nafe, J. P., Wagoner, K. S. (1941). The nature of sensory adaptation. *Journal of General Psychology, 25,* 295–321.

Nassau, K. (2001). *The physics and chemistry of color* (2nd ed.). New York, NY: Wiley-Interscience.

Nassi, J. J., Lyon, D. C., & Callaway, E. M. (2006). The parvocellular LGN provides a robust disynaptic input to the visual motion area MT. *Neuron, 50,* 319–327.

Nayak, G. D., Ratnayaka, H. S., Goodyear, R. J., & Richardson, G. P. (2007). Development of the hair bundle and mechanotransduction. *International Journal of Developmental Biology, 51,* 597–608.

Neitz, J., Neitz, M., & Jacobs, G. H. (1993). More than three different cone pigments among people with normal color vision. *Vision Research, 33,* 117–22.

Nelson, G. M. (1998). Biology of taste buds and the clinical problem of taste loss. *Anatomical Record, 253,* 70–78.

Newell, F. W. (1996). *Ophthalmology: Principles and concepts.* St. Louis, MO: Mosby.

Newman, E. A. (2003). New roles for astrocytes: Regulation of synaptic transmission. *Trends in Neurosciences, 26,* 536–542.

Newsome, S. T., & Pare, E. B. (1988). A selective impairment of motion perception following lesions of the middle temporal visual area (MT). *Journal of Neuroscience, 8,* 2201–2211.

Nickle, B., & Robinson, P. R. (2007). The opsins of the vertebrate retina: Insights from structural, biochemical, and evolutionary studies. *Cellular and Molecular Life Sciences, 64,* 2917–2932.

Nilsson, D. E., Pelger, S. (1994). A pessimistic estimate of the time required for an eye to evolve. *Proceedings of the Royal Society London B, 256,* 53–58.

Nobili, R., Mammano, F., & Ashmore, J. (1998). How well do we understand the cochlea? *Trends in Neurosciences, 21,* 159–167.

Noë, A. (2005). *Action in perception.* Cambridge, MA: MIT Press.

North, A. C., & Hargreaves, D. J. (2008). *The social and applied psychology of music.* Oxford, UK: Oxford University Press.

Obstfeld, H. (1978). *Optics in vision: Foundations of visual optics and associated computations.* Boston, MA: Butterworths.

O'Connor, D. H., Fukui, M. M., Pinsk, M. A., & Kastner, S. (2002). Attention modulates responses in the human lateral geniculate nucleus. *Nature Neuroscience, 5,* 1203–1209.

Ogle, K. N. (1950). *Researches in binocular vision.* London, UK: Saunders.

O'Leary, D. D., Yates, P. A., & McLaughlin, T. (1999). Molecular development of sensory maps: Representing sights and smells in the brain. *Cell, 96,* 255–269.

Olson, H. F. (1967). *Music, physics, and engineering.* New York, NY: Dover.

Olzak, L. A., & Thomaas, J. P. (1985). Seeing spatial patterns. In K. Boff et al. (Eds.). *Handbook of perception and human performance.* New York, NY: Wiley.

Olzak, L. A., & Wickens, T. D. (1999). Paradigm shifts: New techniques to answer new questions. *Perception, 28,* 1509–1531.

Ooi, T. L., & He, Z. J. (1999). Binocular rivalry and visual awareness: The role of attention. *Perception, 28,* 551–574.

Op de Beeck, H. P., Haushofer, J., & Kanwisher, N. G. (2008). Interpreting fMRI data: Maps, modules and dimensions. *Nature Reviews Neuroscience, 9,* 123–135.

Optican, L. M. (2005). Sensorimotor transformation for visually guided saccades. *Annals of the New York Academy of Sciences, 1039,* 132–148.

Orban, G. A. (2008). Higher order visual processing in macaque extrastriate cortex. *Physiological Reviews, 88,* 59–89.

Orban, G. A., Janssen, P., & Vogels, R. (2006). Extracting 3D structure from disparity. *Trends in Neuroscience, 29,* 466–473.

Orban, G. A., van Essen, D., & Vanduffel, W. (2004). Comparative mapping of higher visual areas in monkeys and humans. *Trends in Cognitive Science, 8,* 315–324.

Osorio, D., & Vorobyev, M. (2008). A review of the evolution of animal colour vision and visual communication signals. *Vision Research, 48,* 2042–2051.

Østerberg, G. (1935). Topography of the layer of rods and cones in the human retina. *Acta Ophthalmologica, 6,* 1–103.

Oyster, C. W. (1999). *The human eye: Structure and function.* Sunderland, MA: Sinauer Associates.

Ozaki, I., & Hashimoto, I. (2007). Human tonotopic maps and their rapid task-related changes studied by magnetic source imaging. *Canadian Journal of Neurological Sciences, 34,* 146–153.

Palmer, S. E. (2002). *Vision science: Photons to phenomenology.* Cambridge, MA: MIT Press.

Paradiso, M. A. (2006). Lightness, filling-in, and the fundamental role of context in visual perception. *Progress in Brain Research, 155,* 109–123.

Parker, A. J., & Cumming, B. G. (2001). Cortical mechanisms of binocular stereoscopic vision. *Progress in Brain Research, 134,* 205–216.

Pasupathy, A. (2006). Neural basis of shape representation in the primate brain. *Progress in Brain Research, 154,* 293–313.

Patel, A. (2010). *Music, language, and the brain.* New York, NY: Oxford University Press.

Paterson, M. (2007). *The senses of touch: Haptics, affects and technologies.* Oxford, UK: Berg Publishers.

Paz, R., Wise, S. P., & Vaadia, E. (2004). Viewing and doing: Similar cortical mechanisms for perceptual and motor learning. *Trends in Neuroscience, 27,* 496–503.

Pedrotti, F. L., Pedrotti, L. S., & Pedrotti, L. S. (2006). *Introduction to optics* (3rd ed.). San Francisco, CA, and New York, NY: Benjamin Cummings.

Pelli, D. G., & Tillman, K. A. (2008). The uncrowded window of object recognition. *Nature Neuroscience, 11,* 1129–1135.

Penfield, W. (1958). *The excitable cortex in conscious man.* Liverpool, UK: Liverpool University Press.

Penfield, W., & Rasmussen, T. (1950). *The cerebral cortex of man: A clinical study of localization of function.* New York, NY: Macmillan.

Peretz, I. (2006). The nature of music from a biological perspective. *Cognition, 100,* 1–32.

Peretz, I., & Zatorre, R. J. (2005). Brain organization for music processing. *Annual Review of Psychology, 56,* 89–114.

Peters, A. (2007). Golgi, Cajal, and the fine structure of the nervous system. *Brain Research Reviews, 55,* 256–263.

Peterson, M. A., Gillam, B., & Sedgwick, H. A. (2007). *In the mind's eye: Julian Hochberg on the perception of pictures, films, and the world.* New York, NY: Oxford University Press.

Pettigrew, J. D. (2001). Searching for the switch: Neural bases for perceptual rivalry alternations. *Brain and Mind, 2,* 85–118.

Phan, K. L., Wager, T., Taylor, S. F., & Liberzon, I. (2002). Functional neuroanatomy of emotion: A meta-analysis of emotion activation studies in PET and fMRI. *Neuroimage, 16,* 331–348.

Phelps, M. E. (1991). PET: A biological imaging technique. *Neurochemistry Research, 16,* 929–940.

Phillips, D. P. (2008). A perceptual architecture for sound lateralization in man. *Hearing Research, 238,* 124–132.

Pickett, J. M. (1999). *The acoustics of speech communication: Speech perception, theory, and technology.* Boston, MA: Allyn & Bacon.

Pierce, J. R. (1966). Attaining consonance in arbitrary scales. *Journal of the Acoustical Society of America, 40,* 249.

Pierce, J. R. (1983). *The science of musical sound.* New York, NY: Freeman.

Pisoni, D., & Remez, R. (2007). *The handbook of speech perception*. Oxford, UK: Wiley-Blackwell.

Plack, C. J., Oxenham, A. J., Fay, R. R., & Popper, A. N. (2005). *Pitch: Neural coding and perception*. New York, NY: Springer-Verlag.

Plomp, R., Levelt, W. J., & Levelt, M. (1965). Tonal consonance and critical bandwidth. *Journal of the Acoustical Society of America, 38*, 548–560.

Poggio, G. F. (1995). Mechanisms of stereopsis in monkey visual cortex. *Cerebral Cortex, 3*, 193–204.

Poggio, G. F., & Fisher, B. (1977). Binocular interaction and depth sensitivity in the striate and prestriate cortex of behaving rhesus monkey. *Journal of Neurophysiology, 40*, 1392–1405.

Polyak, S. L. (1957). *The vertebrate visual system*. Chicago, IL: University of Chicago Press.

Porter, R. H. (1999). Olfaction and human kin recognition. *Genetica, 104*, 259–263.

Poulton, E. C. (1968). The new psychophysics: Six models for magnitude estimation. *Psychological Bulletin, 1*, 1–19.

Pouratian, N. et al. (2003). Shedding light on brain mapping: Advances in human optical imaging. *Trends in Neuroscience, 26*, 277–282.

Pressnitzer, D., Sayles, M., Micheyl, C., & Winter, I. M. (2008). Perceptual organization of sound begins in the auditory periphery. *Current Biology, 18*, 1124–1128.

Proske, U. (2006). Kinesthesia: The role of muscle receptors. *Muscle and Nerve, 34*, 545–558.

Purves, D. (2007). *Neuroscience* (4th ed.). Sunderland, MA: Sinauer Associates.

Purves, D., Wiliams, S.M., Nundy, S., & Lotto, R.B. (2004). Perceiving the intensity of light. *Psychological Reviews, 111*, 142–158.

Puce, A., Allison, T., Asgari, M., Gore, J. C., & McCarthy, G. (1996). Differential sensitivity of human visual cortex to faces, letterstrings, and textures: A functional magnetic resonance imaging study. *Journal of Neuroscience, 16*, 5205–5215.

Puel, J. L., & Guitton, M. J. (2007). Salicylate-induced tinnitus: Molecular mechanisms and modulation by anxiety. *Progress in Brain Research, 166*, 141–146.

Punch, J., Joseph, A., & Rakerd, B. (2004). Most comfortable and uncomfortable loudness levels: Six decades of research. *American Journal of Audiology, 13*, 144–157.

Raichle, M. E. (1998). Behind the scenes of functional brain imaging: A historical and physiological perspective. *Proceedings of the National Academy of Sciences USA, 95*, 765–772.

Rajah, M. N., & D'Esposito, M. (2005). Region-specific changes in prefrontal function with age: A review of PET and fMRI studies on working and episodic memory. *Brain, 128*, 1964–1983.

Ramachandran, V. S. (1988) Perceiving shape from shading. *Scientific American, 159*, 76–83.

Ramachandran, V. S. (1991). Form, motion, and binocular rivalry. *Science, 251*, 950–951.

Ramachandran, V. S. (2005). Plasticity and functional recover in neurology. *Clinical Medicine, 5*, 368–373.

Ramón Y Cajal, S. (1933). *Histology*. Baltimore, MD: William Wood & Co.

Raphael, L. J., Borden, G. J., & Harris, K. S. (2006). *Speech science primer: Physiology, acoustics, and perception of speech*. Philadelphia: Lippincott Williams & Wilkins.

Rasmussen, T., & Milner, B. (1977). The role of early left-brain injury in determining lateralization of cerebral speech functions. *Annals of the New York Academy of Science, 299*, 355–369.

Ratliff, F., & Riggs, L. A. (1950). Involuntary motions of the eye during monocular fixation. *Journal of Experimental Psychology, 40*, 687–709.

Ratliff, R. (1974). *Studies on excitation and inhibition in the retina*. New York, NY: Rockefeller University Press.

Rauschecker, J. P. (2002). Cortical map plasticity in animals and humans. *Progress in Brain Research, 138*, 73–88.

Rauschecker, J. P. (2005). Neural encoding and retrieval of sound sequences. *Annals of the New York Academy of Sciences, 1060*, 125–135.

Rauschecker, J. P., & Scott, S. K. (2009). Maps and streams in the auditory cortex: Nonhuman primates illuminate human speech processing. *Nature Neuroscience, 12*, 718–724.

Rauschecker, J. P., & Shannon, R. V. (2002). Sending sound to the brain. *Science, 295*, 1025–1029.

Rauschecker, J. P., Tian, B., Pons, T., & Mishkin, M. (1997). Serial and parallel processing in rhesus monkey auditory cortex. *Journal of Comparative Neurology, 382*, 89–103.

Read, H. L., Winer, J. A., & Schreiner, C. E. (2002). Functional architecture of auditory cortex. *Current Opinion in Neurobiology, 12*, 433–440.

Recanzone, G. H., & Sutter, M. L. (2008). The biological basis of audition. *Annual Review of Psychology, 59*, 119–142.

Rees, G., Kreiman, G., & Koch, C. (2002). Neural correlates of consciousness in humans. *Nature Reviews Neuroscience, 3*, 261–270.

Reichardt, W. (1969). *Processing of optical data by organisms and by machines*. New York, NY: Academic Press.

Reichardt, W. (1986). Processing of optical information by the visual system of the fly. *Vision Research, 26*, 113–126.

Richardson, R. D. (2007). *William James: In the maelstrom of American Modernism*. New York, NY: Mariner Books.

Richardson, G. P., Lukashkin, A. N., & Russell, I. J. (2008). The tectorial membrane: One slice of a complex cochlear sandwich. *Current Opinion in Otolaryngology, Head, and Neck Surgery, 16*, 458–464.

Riggs, L. A., Armington, J. C., & Ratliff, F. (1954). Motions of the retinal image during fixation. *Journal of the Optical Society of America, 44*, 315–321.

Rizzolatti, G., & Sinigaglia, C. (2008). *Mirrors in the brain*. Oxford, UK: Oxford University Press.

Roberts, W. M., & Rutherford, M. A. (2008). Linear and nonlinear processing in hair cells. *Journal of Experimental Biology, 211*, 1775–1780.

Robinson, D. W., & Dadson, R. S. (1956). A re-determination of the equal loudness relations for pure tones. *British Journal of Applied Physics, 7*, 166–181.

Robinson, F. R., & Fuchs, A. F. (2001). The role of the cerebellum in voluntary eye movements. *Annual Review of Neuroscience, 24*, 981–1004.

Rock, I. (1984). *Perception*. New York, NY: Scientific American Books.

Rodieck, R. W. (1998). *The first steps in seeing*. Sunderland, MA: Sinauer Associates.

Roe, A. W., Parker, A. J., Bort, R. T., & DeAngelis, G. C. (2007). Disparity channels in early vision. *Journal of Neuroscience, 27*, 11820–11831.

Roederer, J. G. (1995). *The physics and psychophysics of music: An introduction*. New York, NY: Springer-Verlag.

Rogers, B. J. (1993). Motion parallax and other dynamic cues for depth in humans. *Review of Oculomotor Research, 5*, 119–137.

Rogers, W. L., Bregman, A.S. (1993). An experimental evaluation of three theories of auditory stream segregation. *Perception and Psychophysics, 53*, 179–189.

Rollman, G. B. (1977). Signal detection theory measurement of pain: A review and critique. *Pain, 3*, 187–211.

Rolls, E. T. (1995). Central taste anatomy and neurophysiology. In R. L. Doty (Ed.), *Handbook of olfaction and gustation*. New York, NY: Marcel Dekker.

Rose, J. E., Brugge, J. F., Anderson, D. J., & Hind, J. E. (1968). Patterns of activity in single auditory nerve fibers of the squirrel monkey. In *Hearing Mechanisms in Vertebrates*. London, UK: Churchill Livingstone.

Rosenthal, O., & Phillips, R. H. (1997). *Coping with colorblindness*. New York, NY: Avery.

Rosenzweig, M. R., Leiman, A. L., & Breedlove, S. M. (1999). *Biological psychology*. Sunderland, MA: Sinauer Associates.

Ross, H., & Plug, C. (2002). *The mystery of the moon illusion*. New York, NY: Oxford University Press.

Rossing, T. D., & Fletcher, N. H. (2004). *Principles of vibration and sound* (2nd ed.). New York, NY: Springer-Verlag.

Rossing, T. D., Moore, R. F., & Wheeler, P. A. (2001). *The science of sound* (3rd ed.). Reading, MA: Addison–Wesley.

Rossion, B., & Gauthier, I. (2002). How does the brain process upright and inverted faces? *Behavioural and Cognitive Neuroscience Reviews, 1,* 63–75.

Rousselet, G. A., Thorpe, S. J., & Fabre-Thorpe, M. (2004). How parallel is visual processing in the ventral pathway? *Trends in Cognitive Sciences, 8,* 363–370.

Rowe, M. J. (2002). Synaptic transmission between single tactile and kinesthetic sensory nerve fibers and their central target neurons. *Behavioral Brain Research, 135,* 197–212.

Ruytjens, L. et al. (2006). Functional imaging of the central auditory system using PET. *Acta Otolaryngologica, 126,* 1236–1244.

Sacks, O. (1998). *The island of the colorblind*. New York, NY: Vintage Press.

Sacks, O. (2008). *Musicophilia: Tales of music and the brain*. New York, NY: Vintage.

Sadato, N. (2005). How the blind "see" Braille: Lessons from functional magnetic resonance imaging. *Neuroscientist, 11,* 577–582.

Sajjadi, H., & Paparella, M. M. (2008). Meniere's disease. *Lancet, 373,* 406–414.

Sakamoto, Y., Jones, M., & Love, B. C. (2008). Putting the psychology back into psychological models: Mechanistic versus rational approaches. *Memory and Cognition, 36,* 1057–1065.

Sakata, H., Tsutsui, K., & Taira, M. (2005). Toward an understanding of the neural processing for 3D shape perception. *Neuropsychologia, 43,* 151–161.

Savage, C. W. (1970). *The measurement of sensation: A critique of perceptual psychophysics*. Berkeley, CA: University of California Press.

Scheich, H. (1991). Auditory cortex: Comparative aspects of maps and plasticity. *Current Opinion in Neurobiology, 1,* 236–247.

Schepers, R. J., & Ringkamp, M. (2009). Thermoreceptors and thermosensitive afferents. *Neuroscience and Biobehavioral Reviews, 33,* 205–212.

Schieber, F. (1992). Aging and the senses. In J. E. Birren, R. Sloan, & G. Cohen (Eds.), *Handbook of mental health and aging*. San Diego, CA: Academic Press.

Schiffman, S. S. (1974). Physiochemical correlates of olfactory quality. *Science, 185,* 112–117.

Schiffman, S. S. (2000). Taste quality and neural coding: Implications from psychophysics and neurophysiology. *Physiology & Behavior, 69,* 147–159.

Schiffman, S. S., Reynolds, M.L., & Young, F. W. (1981). *Introduction to multidimensional scaling: Theory, methods, and applications*. New York, NY: Academic Press.

Schiller, P. H., & Carvey, C. E. (2005). The Hermann grid illusion revisited. *Perception, 2005,* 1375–1397.

Schiller, P. H., & Tehovnik, E. J. (2005). Neural mechanisms underlying target selection with saccadic eye movements. *Progress in Brain Research, 149,* 157–171.

Schmalhofer, F., & Perfetti, C. A. (2007). *Higher level language processes in the brain: Inference and comprehension processes*. Mahwah, NJ: Lawrence Erlbaum.

Schnapf, J. L., Kraft, T. W., & Baylor, D. A. (1987). Spectral sensitivity of human cone photoreceptors. *Nature, 325,* 439–441.

Schreiner, C. E., Read, H. L., & Sutter, M. L. (2000). Modular organization of frequency integration in primary auditory cortex. *Annual Review of Neuroscience, 23,* 501–529.

Schreiner, C. E., & Winer, J. A. (2007). Auditory cortex mapmaking: Principles, projections, and plasticity. *Neuron, 56,* 356–365.

Schwartz, S. H. (1999). *Visual perception* (2nd ed.). Norwalk, CT: Appleton and Lange.

Schwartz, S. H. (2002). *Geometrical and visual optics: A clinical introduction*. New York, NY: McGraw-Hill.

Schwartz, S. H. (2004). *Visual perception*. New York, NY: McGraw-Hill.

Schwiegerling, J. (2000). Theoretical limits to visual performance. *Survey of Ophthalmology, 45,* 139–146.

Scott, K. (2005). Taste recognition: Food for thought. *Neuron, 48,* 455–464.

Scott, T. R., & Plata-Salaman, C. R. (1999). Taste in the monkey cortex. *Physiology and Behavior, 67,* 489–511.

Seiden, A. M. (1997). *Taste and smell disorders*. New York, NY: Thieme.

Sekuler, R., & Blake, R. (2002). *Perception*. New York, NY: McGraw-Hill.

Sellin, T., & Wolfgang, M. E. (1978). *The measurement of delinquency*. Montclair, NJ: Patterson Smith.

Seltzer, B. & Pandya, D. N. (1991). Post-rolandic cortical projections of the superior temporal sulcus in the rhesus monkey. *Journal of Comparative Neurology, 312,* 625–640.

Serby, M. J., & Chobor, K. L. (1992). *Science of olfaction*. New York, NY: Springer-Verlag.

Shamma, S. (2008). Characterizing auditory receptive fields. *Neuron, 58,* 829–831.

Shapley, R., & Enroth-Cugell, C. (1984). Visual adaptation and retinal gain controls. In N. N. Osborne, G. J. Chader (Eds.), *Progress in retinal research*. Oxford, UK: Pergamon Press.

Shapley, R., & Hawken, M. (2002). Neural mechanisms for color perception in the primary visual cortex. *Current Opinion in Neurobiology, 12,* 426–432.

Shapley, R., Hawken, M., & Xing, D. (2007). The dynamics of visual responses in the primary visual cortex. *Progress in Brain Research, 165,* 21–32.

Sharpe, J. A. (2008). Neurophysiology and neuroanatomy of smooth pursuit: Lesion studies. *Brain & Cognition, 68,* 241–254.

Sharpe, L. T., & Stockman, A. (1999). Rod pathways: The importance of seeing nothing. *Trends in Neurosciences, 22,* 497–504.

Shepherd, G. M. (1991). *Foundations of the neuron doctrine*. New York, NY: Oxford University Press.

Shepherd, G. M. (1998). *The synaptic organization of the brain*. New York, NY: Oxford University Press.

Sherlock, L. P., & Formby, C. (2005). Estimates of loudness, loudness discomfort, and the auditory dynamic range: Normative estimates, comparison of procedures, and test-retest reliability. *Journal of the American Academy of Audiology, 16,* 85–100.

Sherman, R. (1997). *Phantom pain*. New York, NY: Plenum Press.

Sherman, S. M. (2005). Thalamic relays and cortical functioning. *Progress in Brain Research, 149,* 107–126.

Shevell, S. K., & Kingdom, F. A. (2008). Color in complex scenes. *Annual Review of Psychology, 59,* 143–166.

Siegel, A., & Sapru, H. N. (2007). *Essential Neuroscience*. Baltimore, MD: Lippincott Williams & Wilkins.

Siegel, S., & Allan, L. G. (1998). Learning and homeostasis: Drug addiction and the McCollough effect. *Psychological Bulletin, 24,* 230–239.

Silveira, L. C., Saito, C. A., Lee, B. B., Kremers, J., da Silva, F. H. L., Kilavik, B. E., . . . Perry, V. H. (2004). Morphology and physiology of primate M- and P-cells. *Progress in Brain Research, 144,* 21–46.

Sincich, L. C., & Horton, J. C. (2005). The circuitry of V1 and V2: Integration of color, form, and motion. *Annual Review of Neuroscience, 28,* 303–326.

Small, D. M., & Prescott, J. (2005). Odor/taste integration and the perception of flavor. *Experimental Brain Research, 166,* 345–357.

Smith, A. (2006). Speech motor development: Integrating muscles, movements, and linguistic units. *Journal of Communicative Disorders, 39,* 331–349.

Smith, C. U. M. (2000). *The biology of sensory systems.* New York, NY: Wiley.

Smith, D. V., John, S. J., & Boughter, J. D. (2000). Neuronal cell types and taste quality coding. *Physiology and Behavior, 69,* 77–85.

Smith, G., & Atchison, D. A. (1997). *The eye and visual optical instruments.* Cambridge, UK: Cambridge University Press.

Solomon, S. G., & Lennie, P. (2007). The machinery of color vision. *Nature Reviews Neuroscience, 8,* 276–286.

Sommer, M. A., & Wurtz, R. H. (2008). Brain circuits for the internal monitoring of movements. *Annual Review of Neuroscience, 31,* 317–338.

Soto-Faraco, S., & Deco, G. (2009). Multisensory contributions to the perception of vibrotactile events. *Behavioral Brain Research, 196,* 145–154.

Speaks, C. E. (1999). *Introduction to sound: Acoustics for the hearing and speech sciences.* San Diego, CA: Singular.

Spoendlin, H. (1974). Neuroanatomy of the cochlea. In E. Zwicker & E. Terhardt (Eds.), *Facts and Models in Hearing.* New York, NY: Springer-Verlag.

Springer, S. P., & Deutsch, G. (1998). *Left brain, right brain: Perspectives on cognitive neuroscience.* New York, NY: Freeman.

Spruston, N. (2008). Pyramidal neurons: Dendritic structure and synaptic integration. *Nature Reviews Neuroscience, 9,* 206–221.

Squire, L. R., Berg, D., Bloom, F., & du Lac, S. (2008). *Fundamental neuroscience* (3rd ed.) San Diego, CA: Academic Press.

Squire, L. R., Bloom, F. E., & Spitzer, N. C. (2008). *Fundamental neuroscience* (3rd ed.). New York, NY: Academic Press.

Squire, L. R., Roberts, J. L., Spitzer, N. C., & Zigmond, M. J. (2002). *Fundamental neuroscience* (2nd ed.). San Diego, CA: Academic Press.

Steeves, J. K., Gonzalez, E. G., & Steinbach, M. J. (2008). Vision with one eye: A review of visual function following unilateral enucleation. *Spatial Vision, 21,* 509–529.

Stein, B. E. (1998). Neural mechanisms for synthesizing sensory information and producing adaptive behaviors. *Experimental Brain Research, 123,* 124–135.

Stenfelt, S., & Goode, R. L. (2005). Bone-conducted sound: Physiological and clinical aspects. *Otolaryngology and Neurootology, 26,* 1245–1261.

Stevens, J. C. (1997). Detection of very complex taste mixtures: Generous integration across constituent compounds. *Physiology and Behavior, 62,* 1137–1143.

Stevens, J. C., & Traverzo, A. (1997). Detection of a target taste in a complex masker. *Chemical Senses, 22,* 529–534.

Stevens, S. S. (1957). On the psychophysical law. *Psychological Review, 64,* 153–181.

Stevens, S. S. (1960). Ratio scales, partition scales and confusion scales. In H. Gulliksen and S. Messick (Eds), *Psychological scaling: Theory and applications.* New York, NY: Wiley.

Stevens, S. S. (1962). The surprising simplicity of sensory metrics. *American Psychologist, 17,* 29–39.

Stevens, S. S. (1966). Matching functions between loudness and ten other continua. *Perception and Psychophysics, 1,* 5–8.

Stevens, S. S. (1986). *Psychophysic: Introduction to its perceptual, neural, and social prospects.* New Brunswick, NJ: Transaction Publishers.

Stevens, S. S., & Volkmann, J. (1940). The relation of pitch to frequency. *American Journal of Psychology, 53,* 329–353.

Stevens, S. S., Volkmann, J., & Newman, E. B. (1937). A scale for the measurement of the psychological magnitude of pitch. *Journal of the Acoustical Society of America, 8,* 185–190.

Stewart, L. (2008). Do musicians have different brains? *Clinical Medicine, 8,* 304–308.

Stewart, L., von Kriegstein, K., Warren, J. D., & Griffiths, T. D. (2006). Music and the brain: Disorders of musical listening. *Brain, 129,* 2533–2553.

Stockman, A., & Sharpe, L. T. (2006). Into the twilight zone: The complexities of mesopic vision and luminous efficiency. *Ophthalmic and Physiological Optics, 26,* 225–239.

Stoner, G. R., & Albright, T. D. (1992). Neural correlates of perceptual motion coherence. *Nature, 358,* 412–414.

Strausfeld, N. J., & Hildebrand, J. G. (1999). Olfactory systems: Common design, uncommon origins? *Current Opinion in Neurobiology, 9,* 634–639.

Sullivan, A. H. (1923). The perceptions of liquidity, semi-liquidity and solidity. *American Journal of Psychology, 34,* 531–541.

Suzuki, Y., & Takeshima, H. (2004). Equal-loudness-level contours for pure tones. *Journal of the Acoustical Society of America, 116,* 918–933.

Swets, J. A. (1996). *Signal detection theory and ROC analysis in psychology and diagnostics: Collected papers.* Hillsdale, NJ: Lawrence Erlbaum Associates.

Syka, J., & Merzenich, M. M. (2005). *Plasticity and signal representation in the auditory system.* New York, NY: Springer.

Tanaka, K. (2003). Columns for complex visual object features in the inferotemporal cortex: Clustering of cells with similar but slightly different stimulus selectivities. *Cerebral Cortex, 13,* 90–99.

Tatham, M., & Morton, K. (2006). *Speech production and perception.* New York, NY: Palgrave Macmillan.

Taylor, A. J., & Roberts, D. D. (2004). *Flavor perception.* London, UK: Wiley-Blackwell.

Teghtsoonian, R. (1971). On the exponents in Stevens' power law and the constant in Ekman's law. *Psychological Review, 78,* 71–80.

Tessier-Lavigne, M. (2000). Visual processing by the retina. In E. R. Kandel, J. G. Schwartz, & T. M. Jessell (Eds.), *Principles of Neural Science* (4th ed.). New York, NY: McGraw-Hill.

Thompson, E. (1995). *Colour vision: A study in cognitive science and the philosophy of perception.* London, UK: Routledge Press.

Thompson, W. F. (2009). *Music, thought, and feeling: Understanding the psychology of music.* New York, NY: Oxford University Press.

Thurstone, L. L. (1959). *The measurement of values.* Chicago, IL: University of Chicago Press.

Toga, A. W., & Mazziotta, J. C. (1996). *Brain mapping: The methods.* San Diego, CA: Academic Press.

Tong, F., Meng, M., & Blake, R. (2006). Neural bases of binocular rivalry. *Trends in Cognitive Sciences, 10,* 502–511.

Tong, F., Nakayama, K., Vaughan, J. T., & Kanwisher, N. (1998). Binocular rivalry and visual awareness in human extrastriate cortex. *Neuron, 21,* 753–759.

Tootell, R. B. H. et al. (1995). Visual motion aftereffect in human cortical area MT revealed by functional magnetic resonance imaging. *Nature, 375,* 139–141.

Tootell, R. B. H. et al. (1998). Functional analysis of primary visual cortex (V1) in humans. *Proceedings of the National Academy of Sciences USA, 95,* 811–817.

Torgerson, W. S. (1958). *Theory and methods of scaling.* London, UK: Wiley.

Tortora, G. J., & Derrickson, B. H. (2008). *Principles of anatomy and physiology.* Hoboken, NJ: Wiley.

Tovée, M. J. (1996). *An introduction to the visual system.* Cambridge, UK: Cambridge University Press.

Tramo, M. J., Cariani, P. A., Koh, C. K., Makris, N., & Braida, L. D. (2005). Neurophysiology and neuroanatomy of pitch perception: Auditory cortex. *Annals of the New York Academy of Sciences, 1060,* 148–174.

Tramo, M. J., Shah, G. D., & Braida, L. D. (2002). Functional role of auditory cortex in frequency processing and pitch perception. *Journal of Neurophysiology, 87,* 122–139.

Trebub, S. E. (2003). The developmental origins of musicality. *Nature Neuroscience, 6,* 669–673.

Trillenberg, P., Lencer, R., & Heide, W. (2004). Eye movements and psychiatric disease. *Current Opinion in Neurology, 17,* 43–47.

Trobe, J. D., & Leonello, T. K. (2001). *The neurology of vision.* New York, NY: Oxford University Press.

Trout, J. D. (2001). The biological basis of speech: What to infer from talking to the animals. *Psychological Review, 108,* 523–549.

Tsao, D.Y., & Livingstone, M. S. (2008). Mechanisms of face perception. *Annual Review of Neuroscience, 31,* 411–437.

Turin, L. (2002). A method for the calculation of odor character from molecular structure. *Journal of Theoretical Biology, 216,* 367–385.

Turkington, C. (2000). *Living with hearing loss: The sourcebook of deafness and hearing disorders.* New York, NY: Checkmark Books.

Tyler, C. W. (1975). Spatial organization of binocular disparity sensitivity. *Vision Research, 15,* 583–590.

Ungerleider, L. G., & Mishkin, M. (1982). Two cortical visual systems. In D. G. Ingle, M. A. Goodale & R. J. Q. Mansfield (Eds.), *Analysis of visual behavior.* Cambridge, MA: MIT Press.

Vaina, L. M. (1991). *From the retina to the neocortex: Selected papers of David Marr.* Boston, MA: Birkhauser.

Vaina, L. M., Beardsley, S. A., & Rushton, S. K. (2004). *Optic flow and beyond.* Dordrecht, The Netherlands: Kluwer Academic Publishers.

Valberg, A. (2005). *Light vision color.* Chichester, UK: Wiley.

Van de Grind, W. A., Erkelens, C. J., & Laan, A. C. (1995). Binocular correspondence and visual direction. *Perception, 24,* 215–235.

Van Essen, D., Anderson, C. H., & Felleman, D. J. (1992). Information processing in the primate visual system: An integrated systems perspective. *Science, 255,* 419–423.

Van Gompel, R. (2007). *Eye movements: A window on mind and brain.* Oxford, UK: Elsevier Science.

Van Lancker Sidtis, D. (2006). Does functional neuroimaging solve the questions of neurolinguistics? *Brain and Language, 98,* 276–290.

Van Santen, J. P., & Sperling, G. (1984). Temporal covariance model of human motion perception. *Journal of the Optical Society of America A, 1,* 451–473.

Van Toller, S., Dodd, G. H. (1988). *The psychology and biology of fragrance.* London, UK: Chapman & Hall Ltd.

Verrillo, R. T. (1968). A duplex mechanism of mechanoreception. In D. R. Kenshalo (Ed.), *The skin senses.* Springfield, IL: Charles C. Thomas.

Verrillo, R. T. (1993). *Sensory research: Multimodal perspectives.* Hillsdale, NJ: Lawrence Erlbaum Associates.

Vertosick, F. T. (2000). *Why we hurt: The natural history of pain.* New York, NY: Harcourt.

Viirre, E. (2007). Cognitive neuroscience in tinnitus research: A current review. *International Tinnitus Journal, 13,* 110–117.

Vogten, L. L. M. (1974). Pure tone masking: A new result from a new method. In E. Zwicker & E. Terhardt (Eds.), *Facts and models in hearing.* Berlin, Germany: Springer-Verlag.

Vollrath, M. A., Kwan, K. Y., & Corey, D. P. (2007). The micromachinery of mechanotransduction in hair cells. *Annual Review of Neuroscience, 30,* 339–365.

Von Goethe, J. W. (1970). *Theory of colors.* Cambridge, MA: MIT Press. (Original work published 1810).

Von Helmholtz, H. (1911/2000). *Treatise on physiological optics* (Vol. 2). J. P. C. Southall (Trans.). Sterling, VA: Thoemmes Press.

Vrij, A. (2000). *Detecting lies and deceit: The psychology of lying and the implications for professional practice.* Chichester, UK: Wiley.

Wade, N. J. (1987). On the late invention of the stereoscope. *Perception, 16,* 785–818.

Wade, N. J. (1996). Descriptions of visual phenomena from Aristotle to Wheatstone. *Perception, 25,* 1137–1175.

Wade, N. J. (1999). *A natural history of vision.* Cambridge, MA: MIT Press.

Wade, N. J., & Swanston, M. T. (2001). *Visual perception: An introduction* (2nd ed.). Philadelphia, PA: Taylor and Francis.

Wald, G. (1968). The molecular basis of visual excitation. *Nature, 219,* 800–807.

Waldman, G. (1983). *Introduction to light, the physics of light, vision and color.* Upper Saddle River, NJ: Prentice-Hall.

Waldman, G. (2002). *Introduction to light: The physics of light, vision, and color.* Mineola, NY: Dover Publications.

Wall, J. T., Xu, J., & Wang, X. (2002). Human brain plasticity: An emerging view of the multiple substrates and mechanisms that cause cortical changes and related sensory dysfunctions after injuries of sensory inputs from the body. *Brain Research Reviews, 39,* 181–215.

Wall, P. D. (2000). *Pain: The science of suffering.* New York, NY: Columbia University Press.

Wall, P. D., & Melzack, R. (1999). *Textbook of pain* (4th ed.). Philadelphia: Elsevier/ Churchill Livingstone.

Wallach, H., & O'Connell, D.N. (1953). The kinetic depth effect. *Journal of Experimental Psychology, 45,* 205–217.

Wallin, N. L., Merker, B., & Brown, S. (2000). *The origins of music.* Cambridge, MA: MIT Press.

Walsh, V., & Kulikowski, J. (1998). *Perceptual constancy.* Cambridge, UK: Cambridge University Press.

Wandell, B. A. (1995). *Foundations of vision.* Sunderland, MA: Sinauer Associates.

Wang, Y., & Frost, B. J. (1992). Time to collision is signaled by neurons in the nucleus rotundus of pigeons. *Nature, 356,* 236–238.

Wang, Z., Nudelman, A., & Storm, D. R. (2007). Are pheromones detected through the main olfactory epithelium? *Molecular Neurobiology, 35,* 317–323.

Wark, B., Lundstrom, B. N., & Fairhall, A. (2007). Sensory adaptation. *Current Opinion in Neurobiology, 17,* 423–429.

Warren, J. (2008). How does the brain process music? *Clinical Medicine, 8,* 32–36.

Warren, R. M. (1970). Perceptual restoration of missing speech sounds. *Science, 167,* 392–395.

Warren, R. M. (1999). *Auditory perception: A new analysis and synthesis.* New York, NY: Cambridge University Press.

Warren, R. M. (2008). *Auditory perception: An analysis and synthesis.* New York, NY: Cambridge University Press.

Warren, W. H. Jr., Morris, M. W., & Kalish, M. L. (1988). Perception of translational heading from optical flow. *Journal of Experimental Psychology: Human Perception and Performance, 14,* 646–660.

Wassle, H. (2004). Parallel processing in the mammalian retina. *Nature Reviews Neuroscience, 5,* 747–757.

Watanabe, M., & Rodieck, R. W. (1989). Parasol and midget ganglion cells of the primate retina. *Journal of Comparative Neurology, 289,* 434–454.

Watson, A. B., & Ahumada, A. J. (1985). Model of human visual-motion sensing. *Journal of the Optical Society of America, 2,* 322–341.

Watson, L. (2000). *Jacobson's organ and the remarkable nature of smell.* New York, NY: W.W. Norton.

Weber, E. H. (1996). *E.H. Weber on the tactile senses* (2nd ed.). Hove, UK: Experimental Psychology Society.

Webster, M. A., & Malkoc, G. (2000). Color-luminance relationships and the McCollough effect. *Perception and Psychophysics, 62,* 659–672.

Wegel, R. L., & Lane, C. E. (1924). The auditory masking of one pure tone by another and its probable relation to the dynamics of the inner ear. *Physical Review, 23,* 266–285.

Weinstein, S. (1968). Intensive and extensive aspects of tactile sensitivity as a function of body part, sex, and laterality. In D. R. Kenshalo (Ed.), *The skin senses.* Springfield, IL: Charles C. Thomas.

Weiskrantz, L., Warrington, E. K., Sanders, M. D., & Marshall, J. (1974). Visual capacity in the hemianopic field following a restricted cortical ablation. *Brain, 97,* 709–728.

Welchman, A. E., Deubelius, A., Conrad, V., Bülthoff, H. H., & Kourtze, Z. (2005). 3D shape perception from combined depth cues in human visual cortex. *Nature Neuroscience, 8,* 820–827.

Welford, W. T. (1990). *Optics* (3rd ed.). New York, NY: Oxford University Press.

Weng, S., Sun, W., & He, S. (2005). Identification of ON-OFF direction-selective ganglion cells in the mouse retina. *Journal of Physiology, 562,* 915–923.

Wensel, T. G. (2008). Signal transducing membrane complexes of photoreceptor outer segments. *Vision Research, 48,* 2052–2061.

Werker, J. F., & Byers-Heinlein, K. (2008). Bilingualism in infancy: First steps in perception and comprehension. *Trends in Cognitive Science, 12,* 144–151.

Westheimer, G. (2007). The ON-OFF dichotomy in visual processing: From receptors to perception. *Progress in Retinal Eye Research, 26,* 636–648.

Wheatstone, C. (1838). Contributions to the physiology of vision. Part the First. On some remarkable, and hitherto unobserved, phenomena of binocular vision. *Philosophical Transactions of the Royal Society of London, 128,* 371–394.

Wickens, T. D. (2001). *Elementary signal detection theory.* New York, NY: Oxford University Press.

Williamson, S. J., & Cummins, H. Z. (1983). *Light and color in nature and art.* New York, NY: Wiley.

Willis, W. D. Jr. (2007). The somatosensory system, with emphasis on structures important for pain. *Brain Research Reviews, 55,* 297–313.

Wilson, D. A., & Stevenson, R. J. (2003). The fundamental role of memory in olfactory perception. *Trends in Neuroscience, 26,* 243–247.

Wilson, D. A., & Stevenson, R. J. (2006). *Learning to smell: Olfactory perception from neurobiology to behavior.* Baltimore, MD: Johns Hopkins University Press.

Wilson, R. I., & Mainen, Z. F. (2006). Early events in olfactory processing. *Annual Review of Neuroscience, 29,* 163–201.

Winer, J. A., & Lee, C. C. (2007). The distributed auditory cortex. *Hearing Research, 229,* 3–13.

Winer, J. A., Miller, L. M., Lee, C. C., & Schreiner, C. E. (2005). Auditory thalamocortical transformation: Structure and function. *Trends in Neurosciences, 28,* 255–263.

Winkler, S., Garg, A. K., Mekayarajjananonth, T., Bakaeen, L. G., & Khan, E. (1999). Depressed taste and smell in geriatric patients. *Journal of the American Dental Association, 130,* 1759–1765.

Wise, P. M., Olsson, M. J., & Cain, W. S. (2000). Quantification of odor quality. *Chemical Senses, 25,* 429–443.

Witelson, S. F. (1976). Sex and the single hemisphere: Specialization of the right hemisphere for spatial processing. *Science, 193,* 425–427.

Witten, I. B., & Knudsen, E. I. (2005). Why seeing is believing: Merging auditory and visual worlds. *Neuron, 48,* 489–496.

Wittgenstein, L. (1977). *Remarks on color.* L. L. McAlister & M. Schättle (Trans.). Berkeley, CA: University of California Press.

Wolken, J. J. (1995). *Light detectors, photoreceptors, and imaging systems in nature.* New York, NY: Oxford University Press.

Woolsey, C. N., Erickson, T. C., & Gilson, W. E. (1979). Localization in somatic sensory and motor areas of human cerebral cortex as determined by direct recording of evoked potential and electrical stimulation. *Journal of Neurosurgery, 51,* 476–506.

Wurtz, R. H., Sommer, M. A., & Cavanaugh, J. (2005). Drivers from the deep: The contribution of collicular input to thalamocortical processing. *Progress in Brain Research, 149,* 207–225.

Wyszecki, G., & Stiles, W. S. (2000). *Color science: Concepts and methods, quantitative data and formulae.* New York, NY: Wiley–Interscience.

Wyttenbach, R. A., & Farris, H. E. (2004). Psychophysics in insect hearing. *Microscopy Research and Technique, 63,* 375–387.

Xu, F., Greer, C. A., & Shepherd, G. M. (2000). Odor maps in the olfactory bulb. *Journal of Comparative Neurology, 422,* 489–495.

Yantis, S. (2001). *Visual perception.* Philadelphia: Psychology Press.

Yarbus, A. (1967). *Eye movements and vision.* New York, NY: Plenum Press.

Yau, K. W. (1994). Phototransduction mechanisms in retinal rods and cones. *Investigative Ophthalmology & Visual Science, 35,* 9–32.

Yonelinas, A. P., Parks, & C. M. (2007). Receiver operating characteristics (ROCs) in recognition memory: a review. *Psychological Bulletin, 133,* 800–832.

Yost, W. A. (2000). *Fundamentals of hearing: An introduction.* San Diego, CA: Academic Press.

Yost, W. A. (2006). *Fundamentals of hearing: An introduction* (5th ed.). San Diego, CA: Academic Press.

Yost, W. A., Fay, R. R., & Popper, A. N. (2007). *Auditory perception of sound sources.* New York, NY: Springer.

Young, T. (1802). The Bakerian lecture: On the theory of light and colors. *Philosophical Transactions of the Royal Society of London, 92,* 12–48.

Zald, D. H., & Pardo, J. V. (2000). Functional neuroimaging of the olfactory system in humans. *International Journal of Psychophysiology,* 165–181.

Zangenehpour, S., & Chaudhuri, A. (2005). Patchy organization and asymmetric distribution of the neural correlates of face processing in monkey inferotemporal cortex. *Current Biology, 15,* 993–1005.

Zatorre, R. J. (2003). Absolute pitch: A model for understanding the influence of genes and development on neural and cognitive function. *Nature Neuroscience, 6,* 692–695.

Zatorre, R. J., Chen, J. L., & Penhune, V. B. (2007). When the brain plays music: Auditory-motor interactions in music perception and production. *Nature Reviews Neuroscience, 8,* 547–558.

Zatorre, R. J., & Gandour, J. T. (2008). Neural specializations for speech and pitch: Moving beyond the dichotomies. *Philosophical Transactions of the Royal Society of London B Biological Sciences, 363,* 1087–1104.

Zdravkovic, S., Economou, E., & Gilchrist, A. (2006). Lightness of an object under two illumination levels. *Perception, 35,* 1185–1201.

Zeki, S. (1974). Functional organization of a visual area in the posterior bank of the superior temporal sulcus of the rhesus monkey. *Journal of Physiology, 236,* 549–573.

Zeki, S. (1993). *A vision of the brain.* New York, NY: Wiley.

Zeki, S. (2008). The disunity of consciousness. *Progress in Brain Research, 168,* 11–18.

Zeki, S. (2009). *Splendors and miseries of the brain: Love, creativity, and the quest for human happiness.* Malden, MA: Wiley Blackwell.

Ziegler, J. C., & Goswami, U. (2006). Becoming literate in different languages: Similar problems, different solutions. *Developmental Science, 9,* 429–436.

Zigmond, M. J., Bloom, F. E., Landis, S. C., Roberts, J. L., & Squire, L. R. (1999). *Fundamental Neuroscience.* San Diego, CA: Academic Press.

Zola-Morgan, S. (1995). Localization of brain function: The legacy of Franz Joseph Gall (1758–1828). *Annual Review of Neuroscience, 18,* 359–383.

Zufall, F., & Leinders-Zufall, T. (2000). The cellular and molecular basis of odor adaptation. *Chemical Senses, 25,* 473–481.

Zwislocki, J. J. (1965). Analysis of some auditory characteristics. In R. D. Luce, R. R. Bush, E. Galanter (Eds.), *Handbook of mathematical psychology.* New York, NY: Wiley.

Credits

Grateful acknowledgement is made for permission to reproduce the following figures and tables:

Table 1.2: Stevens, SS (1957) On the psychophyiscal law. Psychology Review 64, 153–181. Reprinted with permission.

Figure 1.8: Adapted from Stevens (1966).

Table 3.3: From Weinstein, 1968.

Table 4.1: Miller 1995

Figure 4.9: Reprinted from Physiology & Behavior, 11/1, Donald H. McBurney, Virginia B. Collings, Lawrence M. Glanz, Temperature dependence of human taste responses, 1973, with permission from Elsevier.

Figure 4.10: Adapted from Collings (1974).

Figure 4.12: From "Taste Quality and Neural Coding: Implications from Psychophysics and Neurophysiology" by S.S. Schiffman, 2000, Physiology & Behavior, 69, pp. 147–59.

Figure 4.13: Courtesy of Carling Brewing Company, Denmark.

Figure 4.14: Source: Mozel et al. (1969).

Figure 4.23: From Sciene, "To Know with the nose: keys to odor" by W.S. Cain, 1979. Reprinted with permission from AAAS

Figure 5.1: Adapted from Gulick et al. (1989).

Figure 5.3: Adapted from Gulick et al. (1989).

Figure 5.15: Adapted from Gulick et al. (1989).

Figure 5.21: Adapted from Hudspeth (1999).

Figure 5.22: Adapted from Spoendlin (1974).

Figure 5.25: Adapted from Rose et al. (1968).

Figure 5.28: Adapted from Merzenich and Brugge (1973).

Figure 6.2: Adapted from Gulick et al. (1989).

Figure 6.3: Adapted from Zwislocki (1965).

Figure 6.4: Adapted from Jesteadt et al. (1977).

Figure 6.5: Adapted from Gulick et al. (1989).

Figure 6.6: "Hearing: Physiological Acoustics, Neural Coding, and Psychoacoustics" by Gulick et al (1989). By permission of Oxford University Press, Inc.

Figure 6.7: "Hearing: Physiological Acoustics, Neural Coding, and Psychoacoustics" by Gulick et al (1989). By permission of Oxford University Press, Inc.

Figure 6.8: "Hearing: Physiological Acoustics, Neural Coding, and Psychoacoustics" by Gulick et al (1989). By permission of Oxford University Press, Inc.

Figure 6.10: Adapted from Vogten (1974).

Figure 6.12: Adapted from Egan and Hake (1950).

Figure 6.15: Adapted from Gulick et al. (1989).

Figure 6.17: Adapted from Gulick et al. (1989).

Figure 6.19: "Hearing: Physiological Acoustics, Neural Coding, and Psychoacoustics" by Gulick et al (1989). By permission of Oxford University Press, Inc.

Figure 6.20: Pearson US, Source Deutsch (1979).

Figure 6.21: Adapted from Gulick et al. (1989).

Figure 6.22: Adapted from Feddersen et al. (1957).

Figure 6.23: Adapted from Gulick et al. (1989).

Figure 6.24: Adapted from Zigmond et al. (1999).

Figure 7.4: Adapted from Olson (1967)

Figure 7.5: Adapted from Pierce (1983).

Figure 7.6: Adapted from Roederer (1995).

Figure 7.10: Adapted from Warren (1999).

Figure 7.11: Ladefoged P, Maddieson I (1996) The sounds of the world's languages. Blackwell, Malden, MA. Fig. 2.15, p. 20

Table 7.3: Adapted from Ladefoged (2001) and Gleason & Ratner (1998).

Table 7.4: Adapted from Ladefoged (2001).

Figure 7.12: Adapted from Warren (1999).

Figure 7.16: Coren, Ward, Enns Sensation and Perception, 4e (Wiley, 1999) Fig. 12-6, p. 423

Figure 7.17: Adapted from Liberman et al. (1967).

Figure 7.18: Adapted from Gleason and Ratner (1998).

Figure 7.19: From KENT, *The Speech Sciences*, 1E. © 1998 Delmar Learning, a part of Cengage Learing, Inc. Reproduced by permission. www.cengage.com/permissions

Table 7.5: Source: Rasmussen and Milner (1977).

Figure 9.3: Adapted from Kandel et al. (2000).

Figure 9.4: Kandel, Eric, et al, Principles of Neural Science, 4/e © 2000, © the McGraw-Hill Companies, Inc.

Figure 9.5: Kandel, Eric, et al, Principles of Neural Science, 4/e © 2000, © the McGraw-Hill Companies, Inc.

Figure 9.6: Kandel, Eric, et al, Principles of Neural Science, 4/e © 2000, © the McGraw-Hill Companies, Inc.

Figure 9.16: Kandel, Eric, et al, Principles of Neural Science, 4/e © 2000, © the McGraw-Hill Companies, Inc.

Figure 9.17: Kandel, Eric, et al, Principles of Neural Science, 4/e © 2000, © the McGraw-Hill Companies, Inc.

Figure 9.19: Rodieck & Rodieck *The First Steps in Seeing,* © Sinauer Associates, 1998, p. 227.

Figure 10.2: Palmer, Stephen E., *Vision Science: Photons to Phenomenology,* © 1999 Massachusetts Institute of Technology, by permission of The MIT Press

Figure 10.3: Rodieck & Rodieck The First Steps in Seeing, © Sinauer Associates, 1998, p. 227.

Figure 10.23: Palmer, Stephen E., Vision Science: Photons to Phenomenology, © 1999 Massachusetts Institute of Technology, by permission of The MIT Press

Figure 10.25: Beiderman, I. (1972). Recognizing-by-components: A theory of human image understanding. Psychological Review, 94(2), 115–17

Figure 10.26: Palmer, Stephen E., Vision Science: Photons to Phenomenology, © 1999 Massachusetts Institute of Technology, by permission of The MIT Press

Figure 10.27: Bruce C, Desimone R, Gross C (1981) Visual properties of neurons in a polysensory area in the superior temporal sulcus of the macaque. Journal of Neurophysiology 46, 369–84.

Figure 10.28: Image courtesy of Nancy Kanwisher, MIT.

Figure 11.5: Adapted from Wandell (1995).

Figure 11.17a: Adapted from Baylor et al. (1987).

Figure 11.23: Adapted from Palmer (2002).

Figure 11.24: Adapted from Palmer (2002).

Figure 11.25: Adapted from De Valois & De Valois (1975).

Figure 11.30: "Spatial Vision (Oxford Psychology Series)" by De Valois, RL, De Valois KK (1990). By permission of Oxford University Press, Inc.

Figure 11.33: Adapted from Graham (1965).

Figure 12.1: "Binocular Vision and Stereopsis" by Howard, IP, Rogers, BJ (1995). By permission of Oxford Unviersty Press, Inc.

Figure 12.5: Palmer, Stephen E., Vision Science: Photons to Phenomenology, © 1999 Massachusetts Institute of Technology, by permission of The MIT Press

Figure 12.13: Palmer, Stephen E., Vision Science: Photons to Phenomenology, © 1999 Massachusetts Institute of Technology, by permission of The MIT Press

Figure 12.19: Adapted from Sekuler and Blake (2002).

Figure 12.31: NASA/JPL/NIMA

Figure 13.2: Adapted from Hart (1987).

Figure 13.4: Adapted from Hawken et al. (1988).

Figure 13.5: Adapted from Kandel et al. (2000).

Figure 13.6: Reprinted by permission from Macmillan Publishers Ltd., Nature Publishing Group, Letters to Nature, Roger B.H. Tootell, John B. Reppas, Anders M. Dale, Rodney B. Loko, Martin I. Sereno, Rafael Malach, Thomas J. Brady, & Bruce R. Rosen, Vol. 375, 139–141, May 11, 1995.

Figure 13.26: Inset figure adapted from Culham & Kanwisher (2001).

Figure 13.27: Adapted from Iacoboni and Dapretto (2006).

Name Index

Subject Index